KEY TO WORLD MAP PAGES

ASIA 26-27

32-33   34-35   30-31

40-41

42-43

36-37

38-39

PACIFIC OCEAN 64-65

INDIAN OCEAN

59

60-61   62-63

59

AUSTRALIA AND OCEANIA

PHILIP'S

WORLD ATLAS

CONSULTANTS

Philip's are grateful to the following people for acting as specialist geography consultants on 'The World in Focus' front section:

Professor D. Brunsden, Kings College, University of London, UK
Dr C. Clarke, Oxford University, UK
Dr I. S. Evans, Durham University, UK
Professor P. Haggett, University of Bristol, UK
Professor K. McLachlan, University of London, UK
Professor M. Monmonier, Syracuse University, New York, USA
Professor M-L. Hsu, University of Minnesota, Minnesota, USA
Professor M. J. Tooley, University of St Andrews, UK
Dr T. Unwin, Royal Holloway, University of London, UK

THE WORLD IN FOCUS
Cartography by Philip's

Picture Acknowledgements
Science Photo Library/NOAA page 14

Illustrations: Stefan Chabluk

WORLD CITIES
Cartography by Philip's

**Page 11, Dublin. Based on Ordnance Survey Ireland by permission of the Government Permit No. 7336.
© Government of Ireland**

Page 15, London. Based upon the Ordnance Survey Maps with the permission of the Controller of Her Majesty's Stationery Office. © Crown copyright 2001. All rights reserved. Licence No. 339817

Vector data: Courtesy of Gräfe and Unser Verlag GmbH, München, Germany
(city centre maps of Bangkok, Beijing, Cape Town, Jerusalem, Mexico City, Moscow, Singapore, Sydney, Tokyo and Washington D.C.)

All satellite images in this section courtesy of NPA Group Limited, Edenbridge, Kent (www.satmaps.com)

Published in Great Britain in 2001
by George Philip Limited,
a division of Octopus Publishing Group Limited,
2–4 Heron Quays, London E14 4JP

Copyright © 2001 George Philip Limited

Cartography by Philip's

ISBN 0–540–08069–1

A CIP catalogue record for this book is available from the British Library.

Printed in Hong Kong

Details of other Philip's titles and services can be found on our website at: www.philips-maps.co.uk

Philip's is proud to announce that its World Atlases are now published in association with The Royal Geographical Society (with The Institute of British Geographers).

The Society was founded in 1830 and given a Royal Charter in 1859 for 'the advancement of geographical science'. It holds historical collections of national and international importance, many of which relate to the Society's association with and support for scientific exploration and research from the 19th century onwards. It was pivotal in establishing geography as a teaching and research discipline in British universities close to the turn of the century, and has played a key role in geographical and environmental education ever since.

Today the Society is a leading world centre for geographical learning – supporting education, teaching, research and expeditions, and promoting public understanding of the subject.

The Society welcomes those interested in geography as members. For further information, please visit the website at: www.rgs.org

PHILIP'S

WORLD ATLAS

ELEVENTH EDITION

IN ASSOCIATION WITH
THE ROYAL GEOGRAPHICAL SOCIETY
WITH THE INSTITUTE OF BRITISH GEOGRAPHERS

Contents

 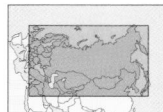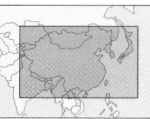

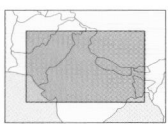
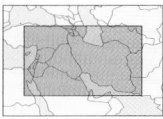

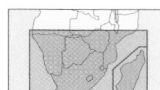

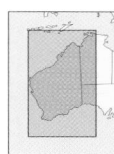
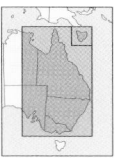

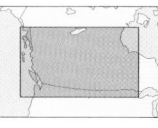

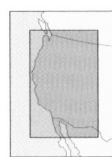
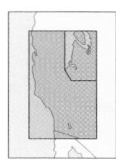
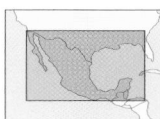

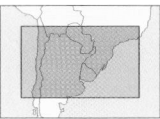

World Statistics: Countries

This alphabetical list includes all the countries and territories of the world. If a territory is not completely independent, the country it is associated with is named. The area figures give the total area of land, inland water and ice. The population figures are 2000 estimates. The annual income is the Gross National Product per capita in US dollars. The figures are the latest available, usually 1999 estimates.

Country/Territory	Area km² Thousands	Area miles² Thousands	Population Thousands	Capital	Annual Income US $
Afghanistan	652	252	26,511	Kabul	800
Albania	28.8	11.1	3,795	Tirana	870
Algeria	2,382	920	32,904	Algiers	1,550
American Samoa (US)	0.20	0.08	39	Pago Pago	2,600
Andorra	0.45	0.17	49	Andorra La Vella	18,000
Angola	1,247	481	13,295	Luanda	220
Anguilla (UK)	0.1	0.04	8	The Valley	6,800
Antigua & Barbuda	0.44	0.17	79	St John's	8,520
Argentina	2,767	1,068	36,238	Buenos Aires	7,600
Armenia	29.8	11.5	3,968	Yerevan	490
Aruba (Netherlands)	0.19	0.07	58	Oranjestad	22,000
Australia	7,687	2,968	18,855	Canberra	20,050
Austria	83.9	32.4	7,613	Vienna	25,970
Azerbaijan	86.6	33.4	8,324	Baku	550
Azores (Portugal)	2.2	0.87	238	Ponta Delgada	–
Bahamas	13.9	5.4	295	Nassau	20,100
Bahrain	0.68	0.26	683	Manama	7,640
Bangladesh	144	56	150,589	Dhaka	370
Barbados	0.43	0.17	265	Bridgetown	7,890
Belarus	207.6	80.1	10,697	Minsk	2,630
Belgium	30.5	11.8	9,832	Brussels	24,510
Belize	23	8.9	230	Belmopan	2,730
Benin	113	43	6,369	Porto-Novo	380
Bermuda (UK)	0.05	0.02	62	Hamilton	35,590
Bhutan	47	18.1	1,906	Thimphu	510
Bolivia	1,099	424	9,724	La Paz/Sucre	1,010
Bosnia-Herzegovina	51	20	4,601	Sarajevo	1,720
Botswana	582	225	1,822	Gaborone	3,240
Brazil	8,512	3,286	179,487	Brasília	4,420
Brunei	5.8	2.2	333	Bandar Seri Begawan	24,630
Bulgaria	111	43	9,071	Sofia	1,380
Burkina Faso	274	106	12,092	Ouagadougou	240
Burma (= Myanmar)	677	261	51,129	Rangoon	1,200
Burundi	27.8	10.7	7,358	Bujumbura	120
Cambodia	181	70	10,046	Phnom Penh	260
Cameroon	475	184	16,701	Yaoundé	580
Canada	9,976	3,852	28,488	Ottawa	19,320
Canary Is. (Spain)	7.3	2.8	1,494	Las Palmas/Santa Cruz	–
Cape Verde Is.	4	1.6	515	Praia	1,330
Cayman Is. (UK)	0.26	0.10	35	George Town	20,000
Central African Republic	623	241	4,074	Bangui	290
Chad	1,284	496	7,337	Ndjaména	200
Chile	757	292	15,272	Santiago	4,740
China	9,597	3,705	1,299,180	Beijing	780
Colombia	1,139	440	39,397	Bogotá	2,250
Comoros	2.2	0.86	670	Moroni	350
Congo	342	132	3,167	Brazzaville	670
Congo (Dem. Rep. of the)	2,345	905	49,190	Kinshasa	110
Cook Is. (NZ)	0.24	0.09	17	Avarua	900
Costa Rica	51.1	19.7	3,711	San José	2,740
Croatia	56.5	21.8	4,960	Zagreb	4,580
Cuba	111	43	11,504	Havana	1,560
Cyprus	9.3	3.6	762	Nicosia	11,960
Czech Republic	78.9	30.4	10,500	Prague	5,060
Denmark	43.1	16.6	5,153	Copenhagen	32,030
Djibouti	23.2	9	552	Djibouti	790
Dominica	0.75	0.29	87	Roseau	3,170
Dominican Republic	48.7	18.8	8,621	Santo Domingo	1,910
Ecuador	284	109	13,319	Quito	1,310
Egypt	1,001	387	64,210	Cairo	1,400
El Salvador	21	8.1	6,739	San Salvador	1,900
Equatorial Guinea	28.1	10.8	455	Malabo	1,170
Eritrea	94	36	4,523	Asmara	200
Estonia	44.7	17.3	1,647	Tallinn	3,480
Ethiopia	1,128	436	61,841	Addis Ababa	100
Faroe Is. (Denmark)	1.4	0.54	49	Tórshavn	16,000
Fiji	18.3	7.1	883	Suva	2,210
Finland	338	131	5,077	Helsinki	23,780
France	552	213	58,145	Paris	23,480
French Guiana (France)	90	34.7	130	Cayenne	6,000
French Polynesia (France)	4	1.5	268	Papeete	18,050
Gabon	268	103	1,612	Libreville	3,350
Gambia, The	11.3	4.4	1,119	Banjul	340
Georgia	69.7	26.9	5,777	Tbilisi	620
Germany	357	138	76,962	Berlin	25,350
Ghana	239	92	20,564	Accra	390
Gibraltar (UK)	0.007	0.003	32	Gibraltar Town	5,000
Greece	132	51	10,193	Athens	11,770
Greenland (Denmark)	2,176	840	60	Nuuk (Godthåb)	16,100
Grenada	0.34	0.13	83	St George's	3,450
Guadeloupe (France)	1.7	0.66	365	Basse-Terre	9,200
Guam (US)	0.55	0.21	128	Agana	19,000
Guatemala	109	42	12,222	Guatemala City	1,660
Guinea	246	95	7,830	Conakry	510
Guinea-Bissau	36.1	13.9	1,197	Bissau	160
Guyana	215	83	891	Georgetown	760
Haiti	27.8	10.7	8,003	Port-au-Prince	460
Honduras	112	43	6,846	Tegucigalpa	760
Hong Kong (China)	1.1	0.40	6,336	–	23,520
Hungary	93	35.9	10,531	Budapest	4,650
Iceland	103	40	274	Reykjavik	29,280
India	3,288	1,269	1,041,543	New Delhi	450
Indonesia	1,905	735	218,661	Jakarta	580
Iran	1,648	636	68,759	Tehran	1,760
Iraq	438	169	26,339	Baghdad	2,400
Ireland	70.3	27.1	4,086	Dublin	19,160
Israel	27	10.3	5,321	Jerusalem	17,450
Italy	301	116	57,195	Rome	19,710
Ivory Coast (Côte d'Ivoire)	322	125	17,600	Yamoussoukro	710
Jamaica	11	4.2	2,735	Kingston	2,330
Japan	378	146	128,470	Tokyo	32,230
Jordan	89.2	34.4	5,558	Amman	1,500
Kazakstan	2,717	1,049	19,006	Astana	1,230
Kenya	580	224	35,060	Nairobi	360
Kiribati	0.72	0.28	72	Tarawa	910
Korea, North	121	47	26,117	Pyŏngyang	1,000
Korea, South	99	38.2	46,403	Seoul	8,490
Kuwait	17.8	6.9	2,639	Kuwait City	22,700
Kyrgyzstan	198.5	76.6	5,403	Bishkek	300
Laos	237	91	5,463	Vientiane	280
Latvia	65	25	2,768	Riga	2,470
Lebanon	10.4	4	3,327	Beirut	3,700
Lesotho	30.4	11.7	2,370	Maseru	550
Liberia	111	43	3,575	Monrovia	1,000
Libya	1,760	679	6,500	Tripoli	6,700
Liechtenstein	0.16	0.06	28	Vaduz	50,000
Lithuania	65.2	25.2	3,935	Vilnius	2,620
Luxembourg	2.6	1	377	Luxembourg	44,640
Macau (China)	0.02	0.006	656	Macau	16,000
Macedonia (F.Y.R.O.M.)	25.7	9.9	2,157	Skopje	1,690
Madagascar	587	227	16,627	Antananarivo	250
Madeira (Portugal)	0.81	0.31	253	Funchal	–
Malawi	118	46	12,458	Lilongwe	190
Malaysia	330	127	21,983	Kuala Lumpur	3,400
Maldives	0.30	0.12	283	Malé	1,160
Mali	1,240	479	12,685	Bamako	240
Malta	0.32	0.12	366	Valletta	9,210
Marshall Is.	0.18	0.07	70	Dalap-Uliga-Darrit	1,560
Martinique (France)	1.1	0.42	362	Fort-de-France	10,700
Mauritania	1,030	412	2,702	Nouakchott	380
Mauritius	2.0	0.72	1,201	Port Louis	3,590
Mayotte (France)	0.37	0.14	141	Mamoundzou	1,430
Mexico	1,958	756	107,233	Mexico City	4,400
Micronesia, Fed. States of	0.70	0.27	110	Palikir	1,810
Moldova	33.7	13	4,707	Chişinău	370
Monaco	0.002	0.0001	30	Monaco	25,000
Mongolia	1,567	605	2,847	Ulan Bator	350
Montserrat (UK)	0.10	0.04	13	Plymouth	4,500
Morocco	447	172	31,559	Rabat	1,200
Mozambique	802	309	20,493	Maputo	230
Namibia	825	318	2,437	Windhoek	1,890
Nauru	0.02	0.008	10	Yaren District	10,000
Nepal	141	54	24,084	Katmandu	220
Netherlands	41.5	16	15,829	Amsterdam/The Hague	24,320
Netherlands Antilles (Neths)	0.99	0.38	203	Willemstad	11,500
New Caledonia (France)	18.6	7.2	195	Nouméa	11,400
New Zealand	269	104	3,662	Wellington	13,780
Nicaragua	130	50	5,261	Managua	430
Niger	1,267	489	10,752	Niamey	190
Nigeria	924	357	105,000	Abuja	310
Northern Mariana Is. (US)	0.48	0.18	50	Saipan	9,300
Norway	324	125	4,331	Oslo	32,880
Oman	212	82	2,176	Muscat	7,900
Pakistan	796	307	162,409	Islamabad	470
Palau	0.46	0.18	18	Koror	8,800
Panama	77.1	29.8	2,893	Panama City	3,070
Papua New Guinea	463	179	4,845	Port Moresby	800
Paraguay	407	157	5,538	Asunción	1,580
Peru	1,285	496	26,276	Lima	2,390
Philippines	300	116	77,473	Manila	1,020
Poland	313	121	40,366	Warsaw	3,960
Portugal	92.4	35.7	10,587	Lisbon	10,600
Puerto Rico (US)	9	3.5	3,836	San Juan	8,200
Qatar	11	4.2	499	Doha	17,100
Réunion (France)	2.5	0.97	692	Saint-Denis	4,800
Romania	238	92	24,000	Bucharest	1,520
Russia	17,075	6,592	155,096	Moscow	2,270
Rwanda	26.3	10.2	10,200	Kigali	250
St Kitts & Nevis	0.36	0.14	44	Basseterre	6,420
St Lucia	0.62	0.24	177	Castries	3,770
St Vincent & Grenadines	0.39	0.15	128	Kingstown	2,700
Samoa	2.8	1.1	171	Apia	1,060
San Marino	0.06	0.02	25	San Marino	20,000
São Tomé & Príncipe	0.96	0.37	151	São Tomé	270
Saudi Arabia	2,150	830	20,697	Riyadh	6,910
Senegal	197	76	8,716	Dakar	510
Seychelles	0.46	0.18	75	Victoria	6,540
Sierra Leone	71.7	27.7	5,437	Freetown	130
Singapore	0.62	0.24	3,000	Singapore	29,610
Slovak Republic	49	18.9	5,500	Bratislava	3,590
Slovenia	20.3	7.8	2,055	Ljubljana	9,890
Solomon Is.	28.9	11.2	429	Honiara	750
Somalia	638	246	9,736	Mogadishu	600
South Africa	1,220	471	43,666	C. Town/Pretoria/Bloem.	3,160
Spain	505	195	40,667	Madrid	14,000
Sri Lanka	65.6	25.3	19,416	Colombo	820
Sudan	2,506	967	33,625	Khartoum	330
Surinam	163	63	497	Paramaribo	1,660
Swaziland	17.4	6.7	1,121	Mbabane	1,360
Sweden	450	174	8,560	Stockholm	25,040
Switzerland	41.3	15.9	6,762	Bern	38,350
Syria	185	71	17,826	Damascus	970
Taiwan	36	13.9	22,000	Taipei	12,400
Tajikistan	143.1	55.2	7,041	Dushanbe	290
Tanzania	945	365	39,639	Dodoma	240
Thailand	513	198	63,670	Bangkok	1,960
Togo	56.8	21.9	4,861	Lomé	320
Tonga	0.75	0.29	92	Nuku'alofa	1,720
Trinidad & Tobago	5.1	2	1,484	Port of Spain	4,390
Tunisia	164	63	9,924	Tunis	2,100
Turkey	779	301	66,789	Ankara	2,900
Turkmenistan	488.1	188.5	4,585	Ashkhabad	660
Turks & Caicos Is. (UK)	0.43	0.17	12	Cockburn Town	5,000
Tuvalu	0.03	0.01	11	Fongafale	600
Uganda	236	91	26,958	Kampala	320
Ukraine	603.7	233.1	52,558	Kiev	750
United Arab Emirates	83.6	32.3	1,951	Abu Dhabi	17,870
United Kingdom	243.3	94	58,393	London	22,640
United States of America	9,373	3,619	266,096	Washington, DC	30,600
Uruguay	177	68	3,274	Montevideo	5,900
Uzbekistan	447.4	172.7	26,044	Tashkent	720
Vanuatu	12.2	4.7	206	Port-Vila	1,170
Venezuela	912	352	24,715	Caracas	3,670
Vietnam	332	127	82,427	Hanoi	370
Virgin Is. (UK)	0.15	0.06	15	Road Town	–
Virgin Is. (US)	0.34	0.13	135	Charlotte Amalie	12,500
Wallis & Futuna Is. (France)	0.20	0.08	26	Mata-Utu	–
Western Sahara	266	103	228	El Aaiún	300
Yemen	528	204	13,219	Sana	350
Yugoslavia	102.3	39.5	10,761	Belgrade	2,300
Zambia	753	291	12,267	Lusaka	320
Zimbabwe	391	151	13,123	Harare	520

World Statistics: Physical Dimensions

Each topic list is divided into continents and within a continent the items are listed in order of size. The bottom part of many of the lists is selective in order to give examples from as many different countries as possible. The order of the continents is the same as in the atlas, beginning with Europe and ending with South America. The figures are rounded as appropriate.

World, Continents, Oceans

	km^2	$miles^2$	%
The World	509,450,000	196,672,000	–
Land	149,450,000	57,688,000	29.3
Water	360,000,000	138,984,000	70.7
Asia	44,500,000	17,177,000	29.8
Africa	30,302,000	11,697,000	20.3
North America	24,241,000	9,357,000	16.2
South America	17,793,000	6,868,000	11.9
Antarctica	14,100,000	5,443,000	9.4
Europe	9,957,000	3,843,000	6.7
Australia & Oceania	8,557,000	3,303,000	5.7
Pacific Ocean	179,679,000	69,356,000	49.9
Atlantic Ocean	92,373,000	35,657,000	25.7
Indian Ocean	73,917,000	28,532,000	20.5
Arctic Ocean	14,090,000	5,439,000	3.9

Ocean Depths

Atlantic Ocean	m	ft
Puerto Rico (Milwaukee) Deep	9,220	30,249
Cayman Trench	7,680	25,197
Gulf of Mexico	5,203	17,070
Mediterranean Sea	5,121	16,801
Black Sea	2,211	7,254
North Sea	660	2,165

Indian Ocean	m	ft
Java Trench	7,450	24,442
Red Sea	2,635	8,454

Pacific Ocean	m	ft
Mariana Trench	11,022	36,161
Tonga Trench	10,882	35,702
Japan Trench	10,554	34,626
Kuril Trench	10,542	34,587

Arctic Ocean	m	ft
Molloy Deep	5,608	18,399

Mountains

Europe		m	ft
Elbrus	*Russia*	5,642	18,510
Mont Blanc	*France/Italy*	4,807	15,771
Monte Rosa	*Italy/Switzerland*	4,634	15,203
Dom	*Switzerland*	4,545	14,911
Liskamm	*Switzerland*	4,527	14,852
Weisshorn	*Switzerland*	4,505	14,780
Taschorn	*Switzerland*	4,490	14,730
Matterhorn/Cervino	*Italy/Switzerland*	4,478	14,691
Mont Maudit	*France/Italy*	4,465	14,649
Dent Blanche	*Switzerland*	4,356	14,291
Nadelhorn	*Switzerland*	4,327	14,196
Grandes Jorasses	*France/Italy*	4,208	13,806
Jungfrau	*Switzerland*	4,158	13,642
Grossglockner	*Austria*	3,797	12,457
Mulhacén	*Spain*	3,478	11,411
Zugspitze	*Germany*	2,962	9,718
Olympus	*Greece*	2,917	9,570
Triglav	*Slovenia*	2,863	9,393
Gerlachovka	*Slovak Republic*	2,655	8,711
Galdhöpiggen	*Norway*	2,468	8,100
Kebnekaise	*Sweden*	2,117	6,946
Ben Nevis	*UK*	1,343	4,406

Asia		m	ft
Everest	*China/Nepal*	8,850	29,035
K2 (Godwin Austen)	*China/Kashmir*	8,611	28,251
Kanchenjunga	*India/Nepal*	8,598	28,208
Lhotse	*China/Nepal*	8,516	27,939
Makalu	*China/Nepal*	8,481	27,824
Cho Oyu	*China/Nepal*	8,201	26,906
Dhaulagiri	*Nepal*	8,172	26,811
Manaslu	*Nepal*	8,156	26,758
Nanga Parbat	*Kashmir*	8,126	26,660
Annapurna	*Nepal*	8,078	26,502
Gasherbrum	*China/Kashmir*	8,068	26,469
Broad Peak	*China/Kashmir*	8,051	26,414
Xixabangma	*China*	8,012	26,286
Kangbachen	*India/Nepal*	7,902	25,925
Trivor	*Pakistan*	7,720	25,328
Pik Kommunizma	*Tajikistan*	7,495	24,590
Demavend	*Iran*	5,604	18,386
Ararat	*Turkey*	5,165	16,945
Gunong Kinabalu	*Malaysia (Borneo)*	4,101	13,455
Fuji-San	*Japan*	3,776	12,388

Africa		m	ft
Kilimanjaro	*Tanzania*	5,895	19,340
Mt Kenya	*Kenya*	5,199	17,057
Ruwenzori (Margherita)	*Ug./Congo (D.R.)*	5,109	16,762
Ras Dashan	*Ethiopia*	4,620	15,157
Meru	*Tanzania*	4,565	14,977
Karisimbi	*Rwanda/Congo (D.R.)*	4,507	14,787
Mt Elgon	*Kenya/Uganda*	4,321	14,176
Batu	*Ethiopia*	4,307	14,130
Toubkal	*Morocco*	4,165	13,665
Mt Cameroon	*Cameroon*	4,070	13,353

Oceania		m	ft
Puncak Jaya	*Indonesia*	5,029	16,499
Puncak Trikora	*Indonesia*	4,750	15,584
Puncak Mandala	*Indonesia*	4,702	15,427
Mt Wilhelm	*Papua New Guinea*	4,508	14,790
Mauna Kea	*USA (Hawaii)*	4,205	13,796
Mauna Loa	*USA (Hawaii)*	4,169	13,681
Mt Cook (Aoraki)	*New Zealand*	3,753	12,313
Mt Kosciuszko	*Australia*	2,237	7,339

North America		m	ft
Mt McKinley (Denali)	*USA (Alaska)*	6,194	20,321
Mt Logan	*Canada*	5,959	19,551
Citlaltepetl	*Mexico*	5,700	18,701
Mt St Elias	*USA/Canada*	5,489	18,008
Popocatepetl	*Mexico*	5,452	17,887
Mt Foraker	*USA (Alaska)*	5,304	17,401
Ixtaccihuatl	*Mexico*	5,286	17,342
Lucania	*Canada*	5,227	17,149
Mt Steele	*Canada*	5,073	16,644
Mt Bona	*USA (Alaska)*	5,005	16,420
Mt Whitney	*USA*	4,418	14,495
Tajumulco	*Guatemala*	4,220	13,845
Chirripó Grande	*Costa Rica*	3,837	12,589
Pico Duarte	*Dominican Rep.*	3,175	10,417

South America		m	ft
Aconcagua	*Argentina*	6,960	22,834
Bonete	*Argentina*	6,872	22,546
Ojos del Salado	*Argentina/Chile*	6,863	22,516
Pissis	*Argentina*	6,779	22,241
Mercedario	*Argentina/Chile*	6,770	22,211
Huascaran	*Peru*	6,768	22,204
Llullaillaco	*Argentina/Chile*	6,723	22,057
Nudo de Cachi	*Argentina*	6,720	22,047
Yerupaja	*Peru*	6,632	21,758
Sajama	*Bolivia*	6,542	21,463
Chimborazo	*Ecuador*	6,267	20,561
Pico Colon	*Colombia*	5,800	19,029
Pico Bolivar	*Venezuela*	5,007	16,427

Antarctica		m	ft
Vinson Massif		4,897	16,066
Mt Kirkpatrick		4,528	14,855

Rivers

Europe		km	miles
Volga	*Caspian Sea*	3,700	2,300
Danube	*Black Sea*	2,850	1,770
Ural	*Caspian Sea*	2,535	1,575
Dnepr (Dnipro)	*Black Sea*	2,285	1,420
Kama	*Volga*	2,030	1,260
Don	*Black Sea*	1,990	1,240
Petchora	*Arctic Ocean*	1,790	1,110
Oka	*Volga*	1,480	920
Dnister (Dniester)	*Black Sea*	1,400	870
Vyatka	*Kama*	1,370	850
Rhine	*North Sea*	1,320	820
N. Dvina	*Arctic Ocean*	1,290	800
Elbe	*North Sea*	1,145	710

Asia		km	miles
Yangtze	*Pacific Ocean*	6,380	3,960
Yenisey–Angara	*Arctic Ocean*	5,550	3,445
Huang He	*Pacific Ocean*	5,464	3,395
Ob–Irtysh	*Arctic Ocean*	5,410	3,360
Mekong	*Pacific Ocean*	4,500	2,795
Amur	*Pacific Ocean*	4,400	2,730
Lena	*Arctic Ocean*	4,400	2,730
Irtysh	*Ob*	4,250	2,640
Yenisey	*Arctic Ocean*	4,090	2,540
Ob	*Arctic Ocean*	3,680	2,285
Indus	*Indian Ocean*	3,100	1,925
Brahmaputra	*Indian Ocean*	2,900	1,800
Syrdarya	*Aral Sea*	2,860	1,775
Salween	*Indian Ocean*	2,800	1,740
Euphrates	*Indian Ocean*	2,700	1,675
Amudarya	*Aral Sea*	2,540	1,575

Africa		km	miles
Nile	*Mediterranean*	6,670	4,140
Congo	*Atlantic Ocean*	4,670	2,900
Niger	*Atlantic Ocean*	4,180	2,595
Zambezi	*Indian Ocean*	3,540	2,200
Oubangi/Uele	*Congo (D.R.)*	2,250	1,400
Kasai	*Congo (D.R.)*	1,950	1,210
Shaballe	*Indian Ocean*	1,930	1,200
Orange	*Atlantic Ocean*	1,860	1,155
Cubango	*Okavango Swamps*	1,800	1,120
Limpopo	*Indian Ocean*	1,600	995
Senegal	*Atlantic Ocean*	1,600	995

Australia		km	miles
Murray–Darling	*Indian Ocean*	3,750	2,330
Darling	*Murray*	3,070	1,905
Murray	*Indian Ocean*	2,575	1,600
Murrumbidgee	*Murray*	1,690	1,050

North America		km	miles
Mississippi–Missouri	*Gulf of Mexico*	6,020	3,740
Mackenzie	*Arctic Ocean*	4,240	2,630
Mississippi	*Gulf of Mexico*	3,780	2,350
Missouri	*Mississippi*	3,780	2,350
Yukon	*Pacific Ocean*	3,185	1,980
Rio Grande	*Gulf of Mexico*	3,030	1,880
Arkansas	*Mississippi*	2,340	1,450
Colorado	*Pacific Ocean*	2,330	1,445
Red	*Mississippi*	2,040	1,270
Columbia	*Pacific Ocean*	1,950	1,210
Saskatchewan	*Lake Winnipeg*	1,940	1,205

South America		km	miles
Amazon	*Atlantic Ocean*	6,450	4,010
Paraná–Plate	*Atlantic Ocean*	4,500	2,800
Purus	*Amazon*	3,350	2,080
Madeira	*Amazon*	3,200	1,990
São Francisco	*Atlantic Ocean*	2,900	1,800
Paraná	*Plate*	2,800	1,740
Tocantins	*Atlantic Ocean*	2,750	1,710
Paraguay	*Paraná*	2,550	1,580
Orinoco	*Atlantic Ocean*	2,500	1,550
Pilcomayo	*Paraná*	2,500	1,550
Araguaia	*Tocantins*	2,250	1,400

Lakes

Europe		km^2	$miles^2$
Lake Ladoga	*Russia*	17,700	6,800
Lake Onega	*Russia*	9,700	3,700
Saimaa system	*Finland*	8,000	3,100
Vänern	*Sweden*	5,500	2,100

Asia		km^2	$miles^2$
Caspian Sea	*Asia*	371,800	143,550
Lake Baykal	*Russia*	30,500	11,780
Aral Sea	*Kazakstan/Uzbekistan*	28,687	11,086
Tonlé Sap	*Cambodia*	20,000	7,700
Lake Balqash	*Kazakstan*	18,500	7,100

Africa		km^2	$miles^2$
Lake Victoria	*East Africa*	68,000	26,000
Lake Tanganyika	*Central Africa*	33,000	13,000
Lake Malawi/Nyasa	*East Africa*	29,600	11,430
Lake Chad	*Central Africa*	25,000	9,700
Lake Turkana	*Ethiopia/Kenya*	8,500	3,300
Lake Volta	*Ghana*	8,500	3,300

Australia		km^2	$miles^2$
Lake Eyre	*Australia*	8,900	3,400
Lake Torrens	*Australia*	5,800	2,200
Lake Gairdner	*Australia*	4,800	1,900

North America		km^2	$miles^2$
Lake Superior	*Canada/USA*	82,350	31,800
Lake Huron	*Canada/USA*	59,600	23,010
Lake Michigan	*USA*	58,000	22,400
Great Bear Lake	*Canada*	31,800	12,280
Great Slave Lake	*Canada*	28,500	11,000
Lake Erie	*Canada/USA*	25,700	9,900
Lake Winnipeg	*Canada*	24,400	9,400
Lake Ontario	*Canada/USA*	19,500	7,500
Lake Nicaragua	*Nicaragua*	8,200	3,200

South America		km^2	$miles^2$
Lake Titicaca	*Bolivia/Peru*	8,300	3,200
Lake Poopo	*Bolivia*	2,800	1,100

Islands

Europe		km^2	$miles^2$
Great Britain	*UK*	229,880	88,700
Iceland	*Atlantic Ocean*	103,000	39,800
Ireland	*Ireland/UK*	84,400	32,600
Novaya Zemlya (N.)	*Russia*	48,200	18,600
Sicily	*Italy*	25,500	9,800
Corsica	*France*	8,700	3,400

Asia		km^2	$miles^2$
Borneo	*Southeast Asia*	744,360	287,400
Sumatra	*Indonesia*	473,600	182,860
Honshu	*Japan*	230,500	88,980
Sulawesi (Celebes)	*Indonesia*	189,000	73,000
Java	*Indonesia*	126,700	48,900
Luzon	*Philippines*	104,700	40,400
Hokkaido	*Japan*	78,400	30,300

Africa		km^2	$miles^2$
Madagascar	*Indian Ocean*	587,040	226,660
Socotra	*Indian Ocean*	3,600	1,400
Réunion	*Indian Ocean*	2,500	965

Oceania		km^2	$miles^2$
New Guinea	*Indonesia/Papua NG*	821,030	317,000
New Zealand (S.)	*Pacific Ocean*	150,500	58,100
New Zealand (N.)	*Pacific Ocean*	114,700	44,300
Tasmania	*Australia*	67,800	26,200
Hawaii	*Pacific Ocean*	10,450	4,000

North America		km^2	$miles^2$
Greenland	*Atlantic Ocean*	2,175,600	839,800
Baffin Is.	*Canada*	508,000	196,100
Victoria Is.	*Canada*	212,200	81,900
Ellesmere Is.	*Canada*	212,000	81,800
Cuba	*Caribbean Sea*	110,860	42,800
Hispaniola	*Dominican Rep./Haiti*	76,200	29,400
Jamaica	*Caribbean Sea*	11,400	4,400
Puerto Rico	*Atlantic Ocean*	8,900	3,400

South America		km^2	$miles^2$
Tierra del Fuego	*Argentina/Chile*	47,000	18,100
Falkland Is. (E.)	*Atlantic Ocean*	6,800	2,600

Philip's World Maps

The reference maps which form the main body of this atlas have been prepared in accordance with the highest standards of international cartography to provide an accurate and detailed representation of the Earth. The scales and projections used have been carefully chosen to give balanced coverage of the world, while emphasizing the most densely populated and economically significant regions. A hallmark of Philip's mapping is the use of hill shading and relief colouring to create a graphic impression of landforms: this makes the maps exceptionally easy to read. However, knowledge of the key features employed in the construction and presentation of the maps will enable the reader to derive the fullest benefit from the atlas.

Map sequence

The atlas covers the Earth continent by continent: first Europe; then its land neighbour Asia (mapped north before south, in a clockwise sequence), then Africa, Australia and Oceania, North America and South America. This is the classic arrangement adopted by most cartographers since the 16th century. For each continent, there are maps at a variety of scales. First, physical relief and political maps of the whole continent; then a series of larger-scale maps of the regions within the continent, each followed, where required, by still larger-scale maps of the most important or densely populated areas. The governing principle is that by turning the pages of the atlas, the reader moves steadily from north to south through each continent, with each map overlapping its neighbours. A key map showing this sequence, and the area covered by each map, can be found on the endpapers of the atlas.

Map presentation

With very few exceptions (e.g. for the Arctic and Antarctica), the maps are drawn with north at the top, regardless of whether they are presented upright or sideways on the page. In the borders will be found the map title; a locator diagram showing the area covered and the page numbers for maps of adjacent areas; the scale; the projection used; the degrees of latitude and longitude; and the letters and figures used in the index for locating place names and geographical features. Physical relief maps also have a height reference panel identifying the colours used for each layer of contouring.

Map symbols

Each map contains a vast amount of detail which can only be conveyed clearly and accurately by the use of symbols. Points and circles of varying sizes locate and identify the relative importance of towns and cities; different styles of type are employed for administrative, geographical and regional place names. A variety of pictorial symbols denote features such as glaciers and marshes, as well

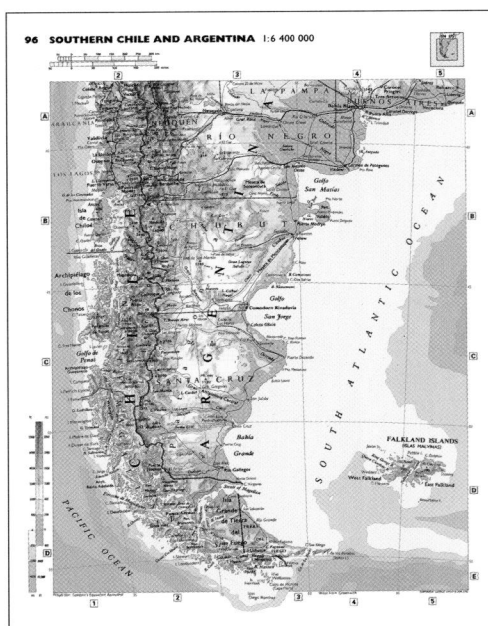

as man-made structures including roads, railways, airports and canals. International borders are shown by red lines. Where neighbouring countries are in dispute, for example in the Middle East, the maps show the *de facto* boundary between nations, regardless of the legal or historical situation. The symbols are explained on the first page of the World Maps section of the atlas.

Map scales

The scale of each map is given in the numerical form known as the 'representative fraction'. The first figure is always one, signifying one unit of distance on the map; the second figure, usually in millions, is the number by which the map unit must be multiplied to give the equivalent distance on the Earth's surface. Calculations can easily be made in centimetres and kilometres, by dividing the Earth units figure by 100 000 (i.e. deleting the last five 0s). Thus 1:1 000 000 means 1 cm = 10 km. The calculation for inches and miles is more laborious, but 1 000 000 divided by 63 360 (the number of inches in a mile) shows that the ratio 1:1 000 000 means approximately 1 inch = 16 miles. The table below provides distance equivalents for scales down to 1:50 000 000.

LARGE SCALE		
1:1 000 000	1 cm = 10 km	1 inch = 16 miles
1:2 500 000	1 cm = 25 km	1 inch = 39.5 miles
1:5 000 000	1 cm = 50 km	1 inch = 79 miles
1:6 000 000	1 cm = 60 km	1 inch = 95 miles
1:8 000 000	1 cm = 80 km	1 inch = 126 miles
1:10 000 000	1 cm = 100 km	1 inch = 158 miles
1:15 000 000	1 cm = 150 km	1 inch = 237 miles
1:20 000 000	1 cm = 200 km	1 inch = 316 miles
1:50 000 000	1 cm = 500 km	1 inch = 790 miles
SMALL SCALE		

Measuring distances

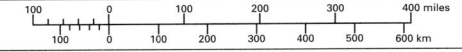

Although each map is accompanied by a scale bar, distances cannot always be measured with confidence because of the distortions involved in portraying the curved surface of the Earth on a flat page. As a general rule, the larger the map scale (i.e. the lower the number of Earth units in the representative fraction), the more accurate and reliable will be the distance measured. On small-scale maps such as those of the world and of entire continents, measurement may only be accurate along the 'standard parallels', or central axes, and should not be attempted without considering the map projection.

Latitude and longitude

Accurate positioning of individual points on the Earth's surface is made possible by reference to the geometrical system of latitude and longitude. Latitude *parallels* are drawn west-east around the Earth and numbered by degrees north and south of the Equator, which is designated 0° of latitude. Longitude *meridians* are drawn north–south and numbered by degrees east and west of the *prime meridian*, 0° of longitude, which passes through Greenwich in England. By referring to these co-ordinates and their subdivisions of minutes (¹/₆₀th of a degree) and seconds (¹/₆₀th of a minute), any place on Earth can be located to within a few hundred metres. Latitude and longitude are indicated by blue lines on the maps; they are straight or curved according to the projection employed. Reference to these lines is the easiest way of determining the relative positions of places on different maps, and for plotting compass directions.

Name forms

For ease of reference, both English and local name forms appear in the atlas. Oceans, seas and countries are shown in English throughout the atlas; country names may be abbreviated to their commonly accepted form (e.g. Germany, not The Federal Republic of Germany). Conventional English forms are also used for place names on the smaller-scale maps of the continents. However, local name forms are used on all large-scale and regional maps, with the English form given in brackets only for important cities – the large-scale map of Russia and Central Asia thus shows Moskva (Moscow). For countries which do not use a Roman script, place names have been transcribed according to the systems adopted by the British and US Geographic Names Authorities. For China, the Pin Yin system has been used, with some more widely known forms appearing in brackets, as with Beijing (Peking). Both English and local names appear in the index, the English form being cross-referenced to the local form.

THE WORLD IN FOCUS

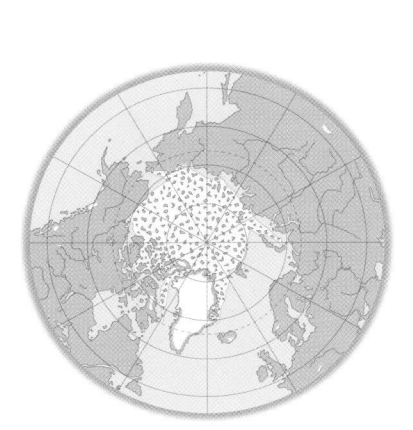

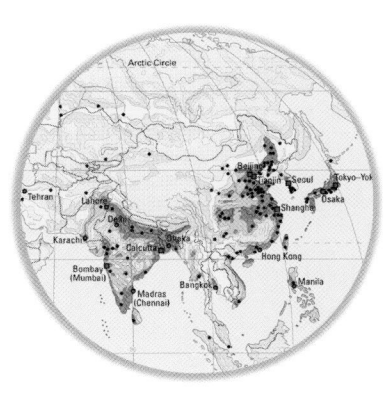

Planet Earth

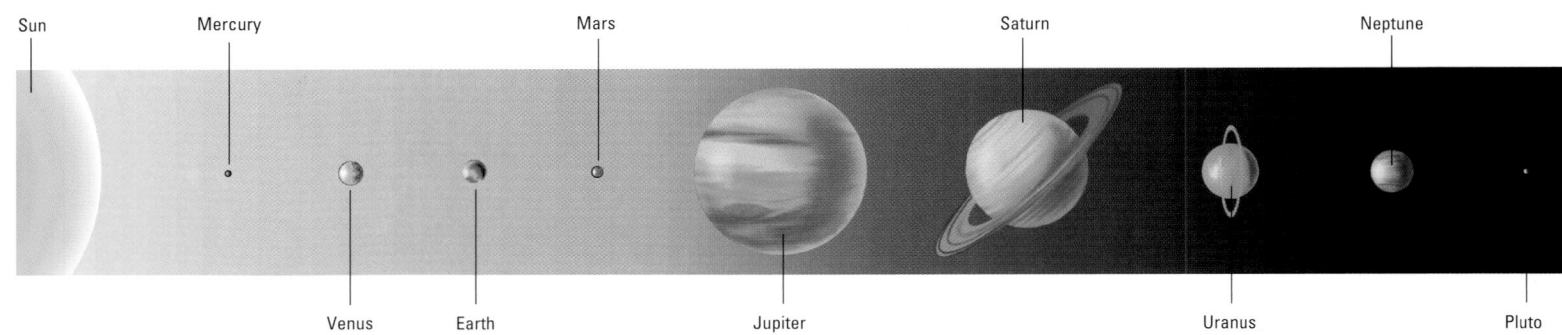

Sun   Mercury   Mars   Saturn   Neptune
Venus   Earth   Jupiter   Uranus   Pluto

The Solar System

A minute part of one of the billions of galaxies (collections of stars) that comprises the Universe, the Solar System lies some 27,000 light-years from the centre of our own galaxy, the 'Milky Way'. Thought to be about 4,600 million years old, it consists of a central sun with nine planets and their moons revolving around it, attracted by its gravitational pull. The planets orbit the Sun in the same direction – anti-clockwise when viewed from the Northern Heavens – and almost in the same plane. Their orbital paths, however, vary enormously.

The Sun's diameter is 109 times that of Earth, and the temperature at its core – caused by continuous thermonuclear fusions of hydrogen into helium – is estimated to be 15 million degrees Celsius. It is the Solar System's only source of light and heat.

Profile of the Planets

	Mean distance from Sun (million km)	Mass (Earth = 1)	Period of orbit (Earth years)	Period of rotation (Earth days)	Equatorial diameter (km)	Number of known satellites
Mercury	57.9	0.055	0.24 years	58.67	4,878	0
Venus	108.2	0.815	0.62 years	243.00	12,104	0
Earth	149.6	1.0	1.00 years	1.00	12,756	1
Mars	227.9	0.107	1.88 years	1.03	6,787	2
Jupiter	778.3	317.8	11.86 years	0.41	142,800	28
Saturn	1,427	95.2	29.46 years	0.43	120,000	30
Uranus	2,871	14.5	84.01 years	0.75	51,118	21
Neptune	4,497	17.1	164.80 years	0.80	49,528	8
Pluto	5,914	0.002	248.50 years	6.39	2,320	1

All planetary orbits are elliptical in form, but only Pluto and Mercury follow paths that deviate noticeably from a circular one. Near perihelion – its closest approach to the Sun – Pluto actually passes inside the orbit of Neptune, an event that last occurred in 1983. Pluto did not regain its station as outermost planet until February 1999.

The Seasons

Seasons occur because the Earth's axis is tilted at a constant angle of 23½°. When the northern hemisphere is tilted to a maximum extent towards the Sun, on 21 June, the Sun is overhead at the Tropic of Cancer (latitude 23½° North). This is midsummer, or the summer solstice, in the northern hemisphere.

On 22 or 23 September, the Sun is overhead at the Equator, and day and night are of equal length throughout the world. This is the autumn equinox in the northern hemisphere. On 21 or 22 December, the Sun is overhead at the Tropic of Capricorn (23½° South), the winter solstice in the northern hemisphere. The overhead Sun then tracks north until, on 21 March, it is overhead at the Equator. This is the spring (vernal) equinox in the northern hemisphere.

In the southern hemisphere, the seasons are the reverse of those in the north.

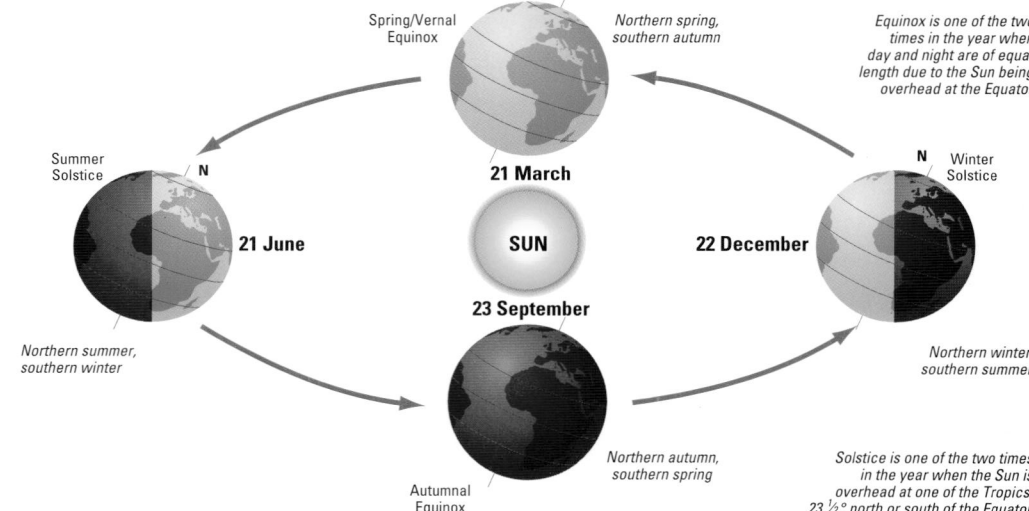

Spring/Vernal Equinox   Northern spring, southern autumn   Equinox is one of the two times in the year when day and night are of equal length due to the Sun being overhead at the Equator

Summer Solstice   N   21 March   N   Winter Solstice

21 June   SUN   22 December

23 September

Northern summer, southern winter   Northern winter, southern summer

Northern autumn, southern spring   Solstice is one of the two times in the year when the Sun is overhead at one of the Tropics, 23½° north or south of the Equator

Autumnal Equinox

Day and Night

The Sun appears to rise in the east, reach its highest point at noon, and then set in the west, to be followed by night. In reality, it is not the Sun that is moving but the Earth rotating from west to east. The moment when the Sun's upper limb first appears above the horizon is termed sunrise; the moment when the Sun's upper limb disappears below the horizon is sunset.

At the summer solstice in the northern hemisphere (21 June), the Arctic has total daylight and the Antarctic total darkness. The opposite occurs at the winter solstice (21 or 22 December). At the Equator, the length of day and night are almost equal all year.

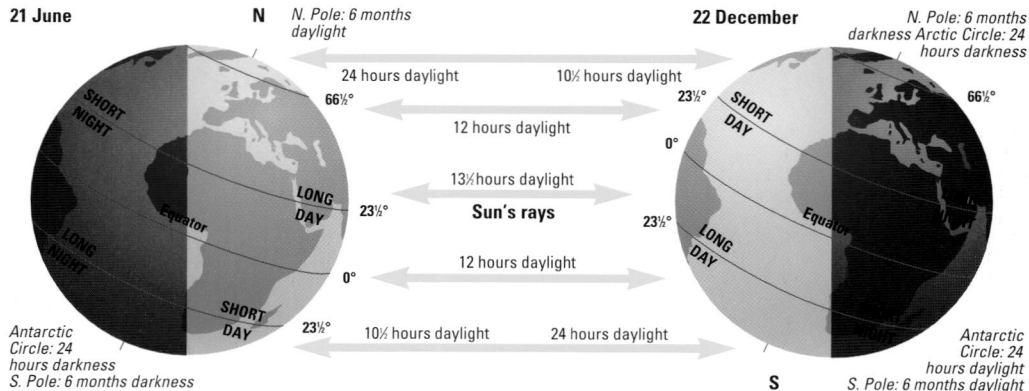

21 June   N   N. Pole: 6 months daylight   22 December   N. Pole: 6 months darkness Arctic Circle: 24 hours darkness

24 hours daylight   10½ hours daylight   66½°   23½°   66½°

SHORT NIGHT   0°   SHORT DAY

12 hours daylight

13½ hours daylight

LONG DAY   23½°   Sun's rays   23½°   LONG DAY

LONG NIGHT   0°

12 hours daylight

SHORT DAY   23½°   10½ hours daylight   24 hours daylight   Equator

Antarctic Circle: 24 hours darkness   S. Pole: 6 months darkness   S   Antarctic Circle: 24 hours daylight   S. Pole: 6 months daylight

Time

Year: The time taken by the Earth to revolve around the Sun, or 365.24 days.

Leap Year: A calendar year of 366 days, 29 February being the additional day. It offsets the difference between the calendar and the solar year.

Month: The approximate time taken by the Moon to revolve around the Earth. The 12 months of the year in fact vary from 28 (29 in a Leap Year) to 31 days.

Week: An artificial period of 7 days, not based on astronomical time.

Day: The time taken by the Earth to complete one rotation on its axis.

Hour: 24 hours make one day. Usually the day is divided into hours AM (ante meridiem or before noon) and PM (post meridiem or after noon), although most timetables now use the 24-hour system, from midnight to midnight.

Sunrise

Spring Equinox   Autumnal Equinox

Latitude: 60°N, 40°N, 20°N, 0°(Equator), 20°S, 40°S, 60°S

Hours AM: 9, 8, 7, 6, 5, 4, 3, 2

Months of the year: J F M A M J J A S O N D

Sunset

Spring Equinox   Autumnal Equinox

Latitude: 60°S, 40°S, 20°S, 0°(Equator), 20°N, 40°N, 60°N

Hours PM: 21, 20, 19, 18, 17, 16, 15, 14

Months of the year: J F M A M J J A S O N D

The Moon

The Moon rotates more slowly than the Earth, making one complete turn on its axis in just over 27 days. Since this corresponds to its period of revolution around the Earth, the Moon always presents the same hemisphere or face to us, and we never see 'the dark side'. The interval between one full Moon and the next (and between new Moons) is about 29½ days – a lunar month. The apparent changes in the shape of the Moon are caused by its changing position in relation to the Earth; like the planets, it produces no light of its own and shines only by reflecting the rays of the Sun.

Phases of the Moon

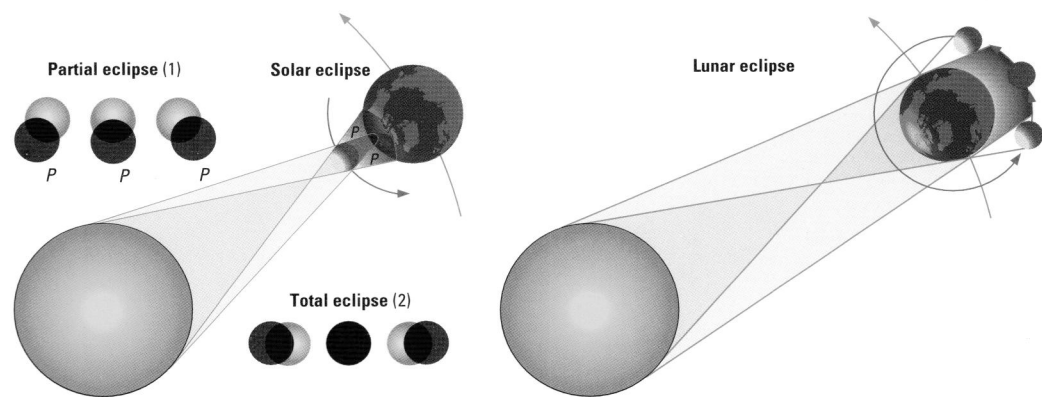

Distance from Earth: 356,410 km – 406,685 km; Mean diameter: 3,475.1 km; Mass: approx. 1/81 that of Earth; Surface gravity: one-sixth of Earth's; Daily range of temperature at lunar equator: 200°C; Average orbital speed: 3,683 km/h

New Moon | Crescent | First quarter | Gibbous | Full Moon | Gibbous | Last quarter | Crescent | New Moon

Eclipses

When the Moon passes between the Sun and the Earth it causes a partial eclipse of the Sun (1) if the Earth passes through the Moon's outer shadow (P), or a total eclipse (2) if the inner cone shadow crosses the Earth's surface. In a lunar eclipse, the Earth's shadow crosses the Moon and, again, provides either a partial or total eclipse.

Eclipses of the Sun and the Moon do not occur every month because of the 5° difference between the plane of the Moon's orbit and the plane in which the Earth moves. In the 1990s only 14 lunar eclipses were possible, for example, seven partial and seven total; each was visible only from certain, and variable, parts of the world. The same period witnessed 13 solar eclipses – six partial (or annular) and seven total.

Partial eclipse (1)   P   P   P

Solar eclipse   P P P

Total eclipse (2)

Lunar eclipse

Tides

The daily rise and fall of the ocean's tides are the result of the gravitational pull of the Moon and that of the Sun, though the effect of the latter is only 46.6% as strong as that of the Moon. This effect is greatest on the hemisphere facing the Moon and causes a tidal 'bulge'. When the Sun, Earth and Moon are in line, tide-raising forces are at a maximum and Spring tides occur: high tide reaches the highest values, and low tide falls to low levels. When lunar and solar forces are least coincidental with the Sun and Moon at an angle (near the Moon's first and third quarters), Neap tides occur, which have a small tidal range.

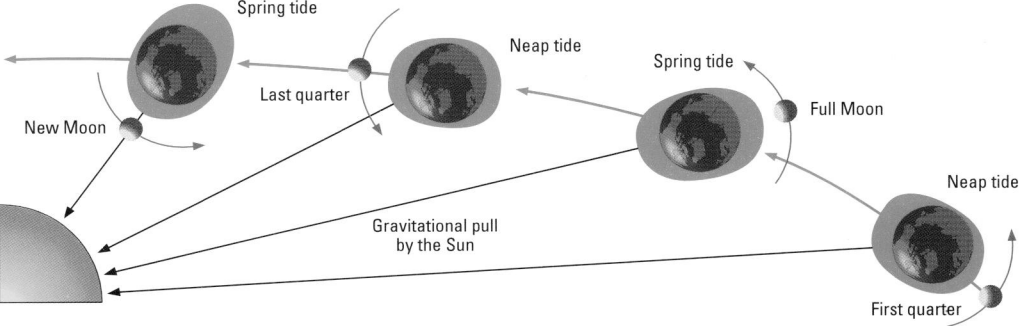

Spring tide

Neap tide

Spring tide

New Moon

Last quarter

Full Moon

Neap tide

Gravitational pull by the Sun

First quarter

Restless Earth

The Earth's Structure

Upper mantle (c. 370 km)

Crust (average 5–50 km)

Transitional zone (600 km)

Outer core (2,100 km)

Lower mantle (1,700 km)

Inner core (1,350 km)

Continental Drift

About 200 million years ago the original Pangaea landmass began to split into two continental groups, which further separated over time to produce the present-day configuration.

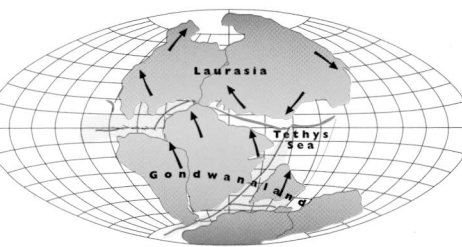

180 million years ago

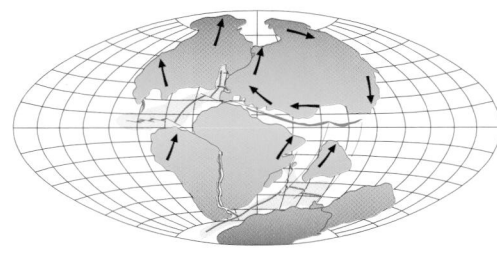

135 million years ago

Trench

Rift

New ocean floor

Zones of slippage

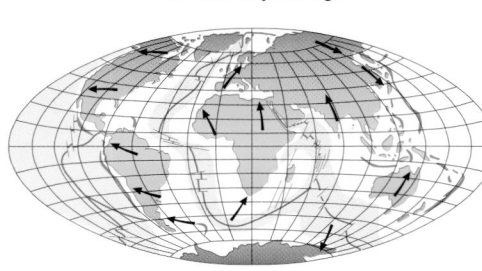

Present day

Notable Earthquakes Since 1900

Year	Location	Richter Scale	Deaths
1906	San Francisco, USA	8.3	503
1906	Valparaiso, Chile	8.6	22,000
1908	Messina, Italy	7.5	83,000
1915	Avezzano, Italy	7.5	30,000
1920	Gansu (Kansu), China	8.6	180,000
1923	Yokohama, Japan	8.3	143,000
1927	Nan Shan, China	8.3	200,000
1932	Gansu (Kansu), China	7.6	70,000
1933	Sanriku, Japan	8.9	2,990
1934	Bihar, India/Nepal	8.4	10,700
1935	Quetta, India (now Pakistan)	7.5	60,000
1939	Chillan, Chile	8.3	28,000
1939	Erzincan, Turkey	7.9	30,000
1960	Agadir, Morocco	5.8	12,000
1962	Khorasan, Iran	7.1	12,230
1968	N.E. Iran	7.4	12,000
1970	N. Peru	7.7	66,794
1972	Managua, Nicaragua	6.2	5,000
1974	N. Pakistan	6.3	5,200
1976	Guatemala	7.5	22,778
1976	Tangshan, China	8.2	255,000
1978	Tabas, Iran	7.7	25,000
1980	El Asnam, Algeria	7.3	20,000
1980	S. Italy	7.2	4,800
1985	Mexico City, Mexico	8.1	4,200
1988	N.W. Armenia	6.8	55,000
1990	N. Iran	7.7	36,000
1993	Maharashtra, India	6.4	30,000
1994	Los Angeles, USA	6.6	51
1995	Kobe, Japan	7.2	5,000
1995	Sakhalin Is., Russia	7.5	2,000
1997	N.E. Iran	7.1	2,500
1998	Takhar, Afghanistan	6.1	4,200
1998	Rostaq, Afghanistan	7.0	5,000
1999	Izmit, Turkey	7.4	15,000
1999	Taipei, Taiwan	7.6	1,700
2001	Gujarat, India	7.7	18,600

Earthquakes

Earthquake magnitude is usually rated according to either the Richter or the Modified Mercalli scale, both devised by seismologists in the 1930s. The Richter scale measures absolute earthquake power with mathematical precision: each step upwards represents a tenfold increase in shockwave amplitude. Theoretically, there is no upper limit, but the largest earthquakes measured have been rated at between 8.8 and 8.9. The 12–point Mercalli scale, based on observed effects, is often more meaningful, ranging from I (earthquakes noticed only by seismographs) to XII (total destruction); intermediate points include V (people awakened at night; unstable objects overturned), VII (collapse of ordinary buildings; chimneys and monuments fall) and IX (conspicuous cracks in ground; serious damage to reservoirs).

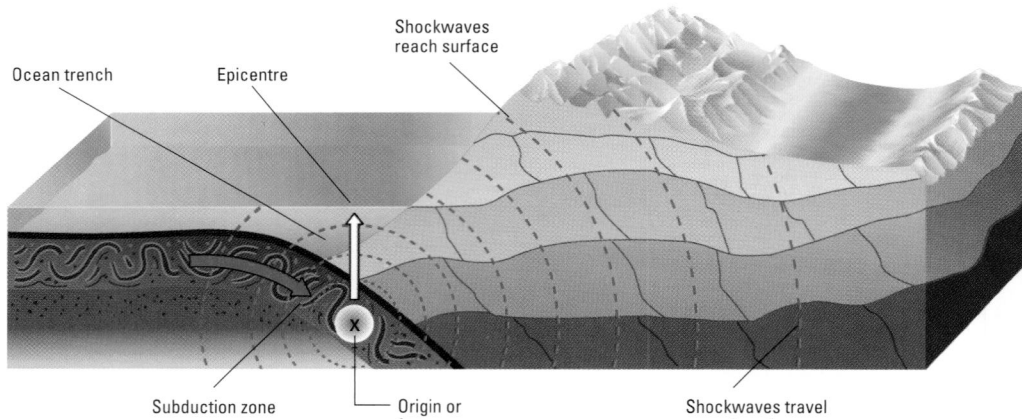

Ocean trench

Epicentre

Shockwaves reach surface

Subduction zone

Origin or focus

Shockwaves travel away from focus

Structure and Earthquakes

Mobile land areas

Submarine zones of mobile land areas

Stable land platforms

Submarine extensions of stable land platforms

Mid-oceanic volcanic ridges

Oceanic platforms

1976○   Principal earthquakes and dates

Earthquakes are a series of rapid vibrations originating from the slipping or faulting of parts of the Earth's crust when stresses within build up to breaking point. They usually happen at depths varying from 8 km to 30 km. Severe earthquakes cause extensive damage when they take place in populated areas, destroying structures and severing communications. Most initial loss of life occurs due to secondary causes such as falling masonry, fires and flooding.

Projection: Interrupted Mollweide

Plate Tectonics

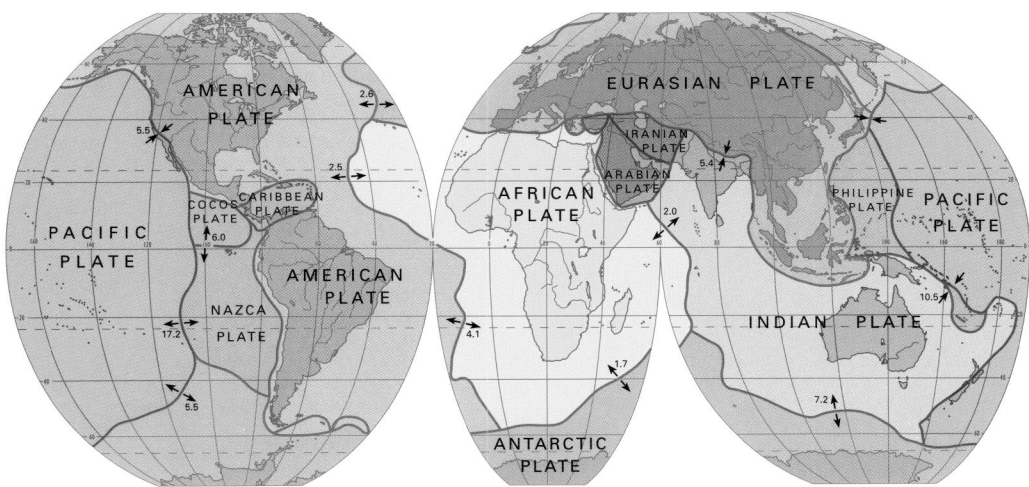

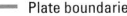

The drifting of the continents is a feature that is unique to Planet Earth. The complementary, almost jigsaw-puzzle fit of the coastlines on each side of the Atlantic Ocean inspired Alfred Wegener's theory of continental drift in 1915. The theory suggested that the ancient super-continent, which Wegener named Pangaea, incorporated all of the Earth's landmasses and gradually split up to form today's continents.

The original debate about continental drift was a prelude to a more radical idea: plate tectonics. The basic theory is that the Earth's crust is made up of a series of rigid plates which float on a soft layer of the mantle and are moved about by continental convection currents within the Earth's interior. These plates diverge and converge along margins marked by seismic activity. Plates diverge from mid-ocean ridges where molten lava pushes upwards and forces the plates apart at rates of up to 40 mm [1.6 in] a year.

The three diagrams, left, give some examples of plate boundaries from around the world. Diagram (a) shows sea-floor spreading at the Mid-Atlantic Ridge as the American and African plates slowly diverge. The same thing is happening in (b) where sea-floor spreading at the Mid-Indian Ocean Ridge is forcing the Indian plate to collide into the Eurasian plate. In (c) oceanic crust (sima) is being subducted beneath lighter continental crust (sial).

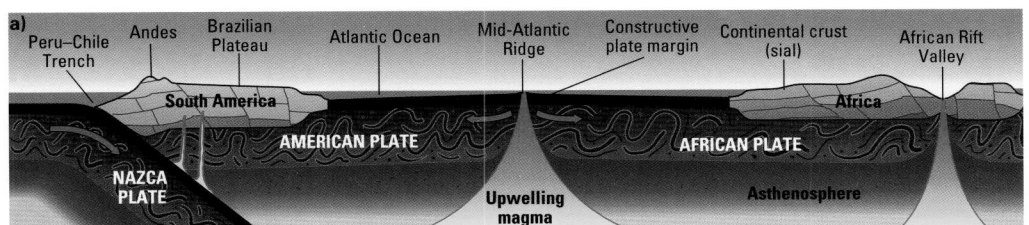

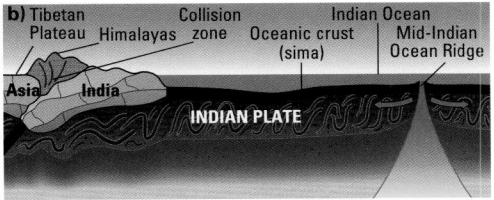

Volcanoes

Volcanoes occur when hot liquefied rock beneath the Earth's crust is pushed up by pressure to the surface as molten lava. Some volcanoes erupt in an explosive way, throwing out rocks and ash, whilst others are effusive and lava flows out of the vent. There are volcanoes which are both, such as Mount Fuji. An accumulation of lava and cinders creates cones of variable size and shape. As a result of many eruptions over centuries, Mount Etna in Sicily has a circumference of more than 120 km [75 miles].

Climatologists believe that volcanic ash, if ejected high into the atmosphere, can influence temperature and weather for several years afterwards. The 1991 eruption of Mount Pinatubo in the Philippines ejected more than 20 million tonnes of dust and ash 32 km [20 miles] into the atmosphere and is believed to have accelerated ozone depletion over a large part of the globe.

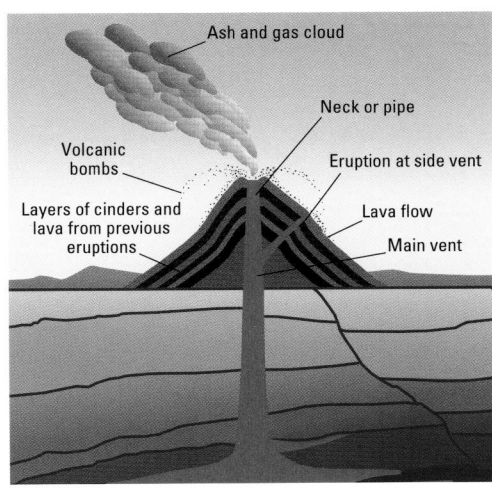

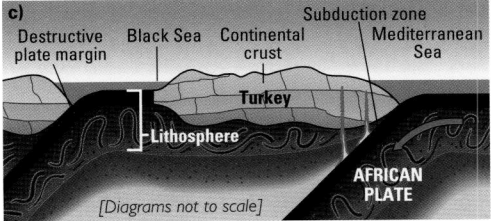

[Diagrams not to scale]

Distribution of Volcanoes

Volcanoes today may be the subject of considerable scientific study but they remain both dramatic and unpredictable: in 1991 Mount Pinatubo, 100 km [62 miles] north of the Philippines capital Manila, suddenly burst into life after lying dormant for more than six centuries. Most of the world's active volcanoes occur in a belt around the Pacific Ocean, on the edge of the Pacific plate, called the 'ring of fire'. Indonesia has the greatest concentration with 90 volcanoes, 12 of which are active. The most famous, Krakatoa, erupted in 1883 with such force that the resulting tidal wave killed 36,000 people and tremors were felt as far away as Australia.

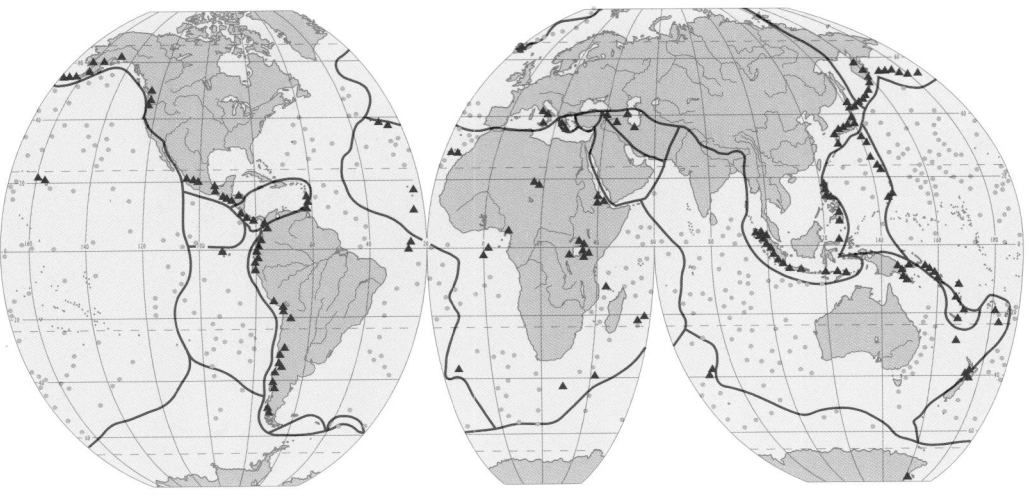

  ● Submarine volcanoes

  ▲ Land volcanoes active since 1700

  — Boundaries of tectonic plates

Landforms

The Rock Cycle

James Hutton first proposed the rock cycle in the late 1700s after he observed the slow but steady effects of erosion.

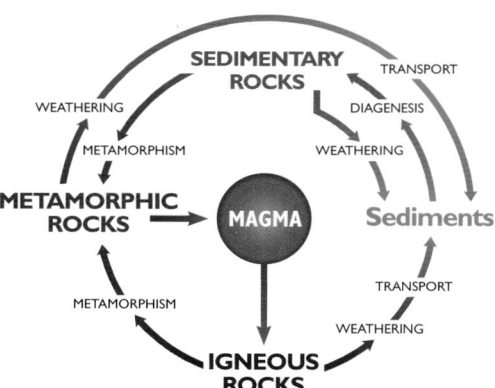

Above and below the surface of the oceans, the features of the Earth's crust are constantly changing. The phenomenal forces generated by convection currents in the molten core of our planet carry the vast segments or 'plates' of the crust across the globe in an endless cycle of creation and destruction. A continent may travel little more than 25 mm [1 in] per year, yet in the vast span of geological time this process throws up giant mountain ranges and creates new land.

Destruction of the landscape, however, begins as soon as it is formed. Wind, water, ice and sea, the main agents of erosion, mount a constant assault that even the most resistant rocks cannot withstand. Mountain peaks may dwindle by as little as a few millimetres each year, but if they are not uplifted by further movements of the crust they will eventually be reduced to rubble and transported away.

Water is the most powerful agent of erosion – it has been estimated that 100 billion tonnes of sediment are washed into the oceans every year. Three

Asian rivers account for 20% of this total, the Huang He, in China, and the Brahmaputra and Ganges in Bangladesh.

Rivers and glaciers, like the sea itself, generate much of their effect through abrasion – pounding the land with the debris they carry with them. But as well as destroying they also create new landforms, many of them spectacular: vast deltas like those of the Mississippi and the Nile, or the deep fjords cut by glaciers in British Columbia, Norway and New Zealand.

Geologists once considered that landscapes evolved from 'young', newly uplifted mountainous areas, through a 'mature' hilly stage, to an 'old age' stage when the land was reduced to an almost flat plain, or peneplain. This theory, called the 'cycle of erosion', fell into disuse when it became evident that so many factors, including the effects of plate tectonics and climatic change, constantly interrupt the cycle, which takes no account of the highly complex interactions that shape the surface of our planet.

Mountain Building

Mountains are formed when pressures on the Earth's crust caused by continental drift become so intense that the surface buckles or cracks. This happens where oceanic crust is subducted by continental crust or, more dramatically, where two tectonic plates collide: the Rockies, Andes, Alps, Urals and Himalayas resulted from such impacts. These are all known as fold mountains because they were formed by the compression of the rocks, forcing the surface to bend and fold like a crumpled rug. The Himalayas are formed from the folded former sediments of the Tethys Sea which was trapped in the collision zone between the Indian and Eurasian plates.

The other main mountain-building process occurs when the crust fractures to create faults, allowing rock to be forced upwards in large blocks; or when the pressure of magma within the crust forces the surface to bulge into a dome, or erupts to form a volcano. Large mountain ranges may reveal a combination of those features; the Alps, for example, have been compressed so violently that the folds are fragmented by numerous faults and intrusions of molten igneous rock.

Over millions of years, even the greatest mountain ranges can be reduced by the agents of erosion (most notably rivers) to a low rugged landscape known as a peneplain.

Types of faults: Faults occur where the crust is being stretched or compressed so violently that the rock strata break in a horizontal or vertical movement. They are classified by the direction in which the blocks of rock have moved. A normal fault results when a vertical movement causes the surface to break apart; compression causes a reverse fault. Horizontal movement causes shearing, known as a strike-slip fault. When the rock breaks in two places, the central block may be pushed up in a horst fault, or sink (creating a rift valley) in a graben fault.

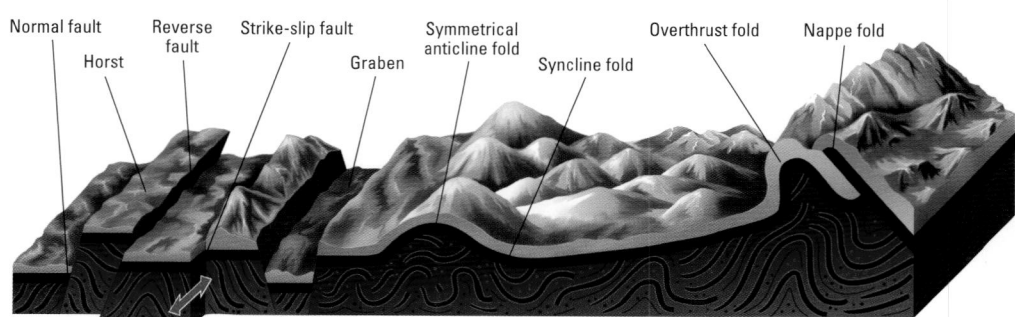

Types of fold: Folds occur when rock strata are squeezed and compressed. They are common therefore at destructive plate margins and where plates have collided, forcing the rocks to buckle into mountain ranges. Geographers give different names to the degrees of fold that result from continuing pressure on the rock. A simple fold may be symmetric, with even slopes on either side, but as the pressure builds up, one slope becomes steeper and the fold becomes asymmetric. Later, the ridge or 'anticline' at the top of the fold may slide over the lower ground or 'syncline' to form a recumbent fold. Eventually, the rock strata may break under the pressure to form an overthrust and finally a nappe fold.

Continental Glaciation

Ice sheets were at their greatest extent about 200,000 years ago. The maximum advance of the last Ice Age was about 18,000 years ago, when ice covered virtually all of Canada and reached as far south as the Bristol Channel in Britain.

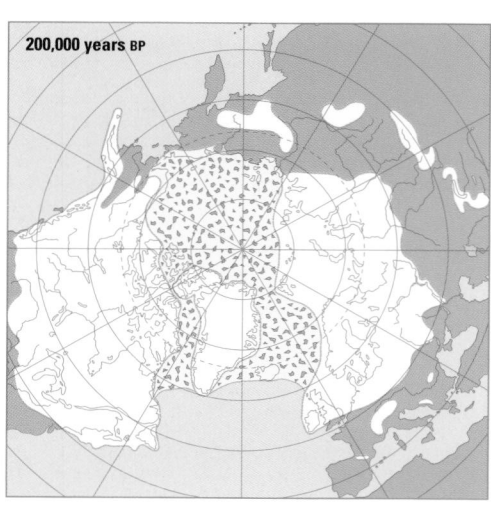

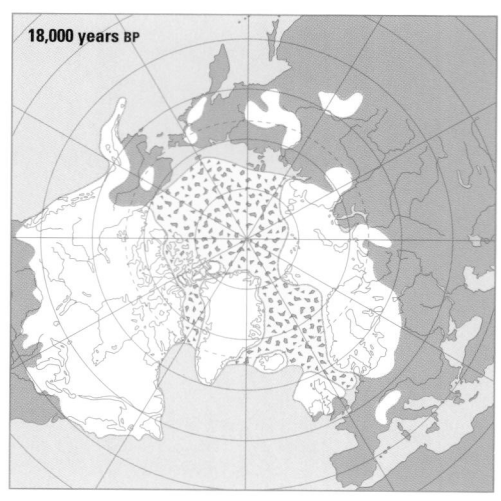

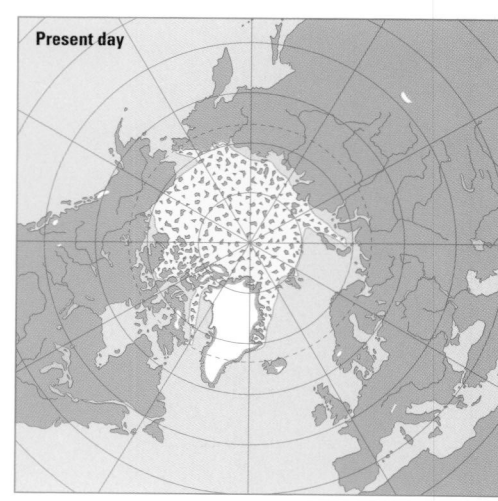

Natural Landforms

A stylized diagram to show a selection of landforms found in the mid-latitudes.

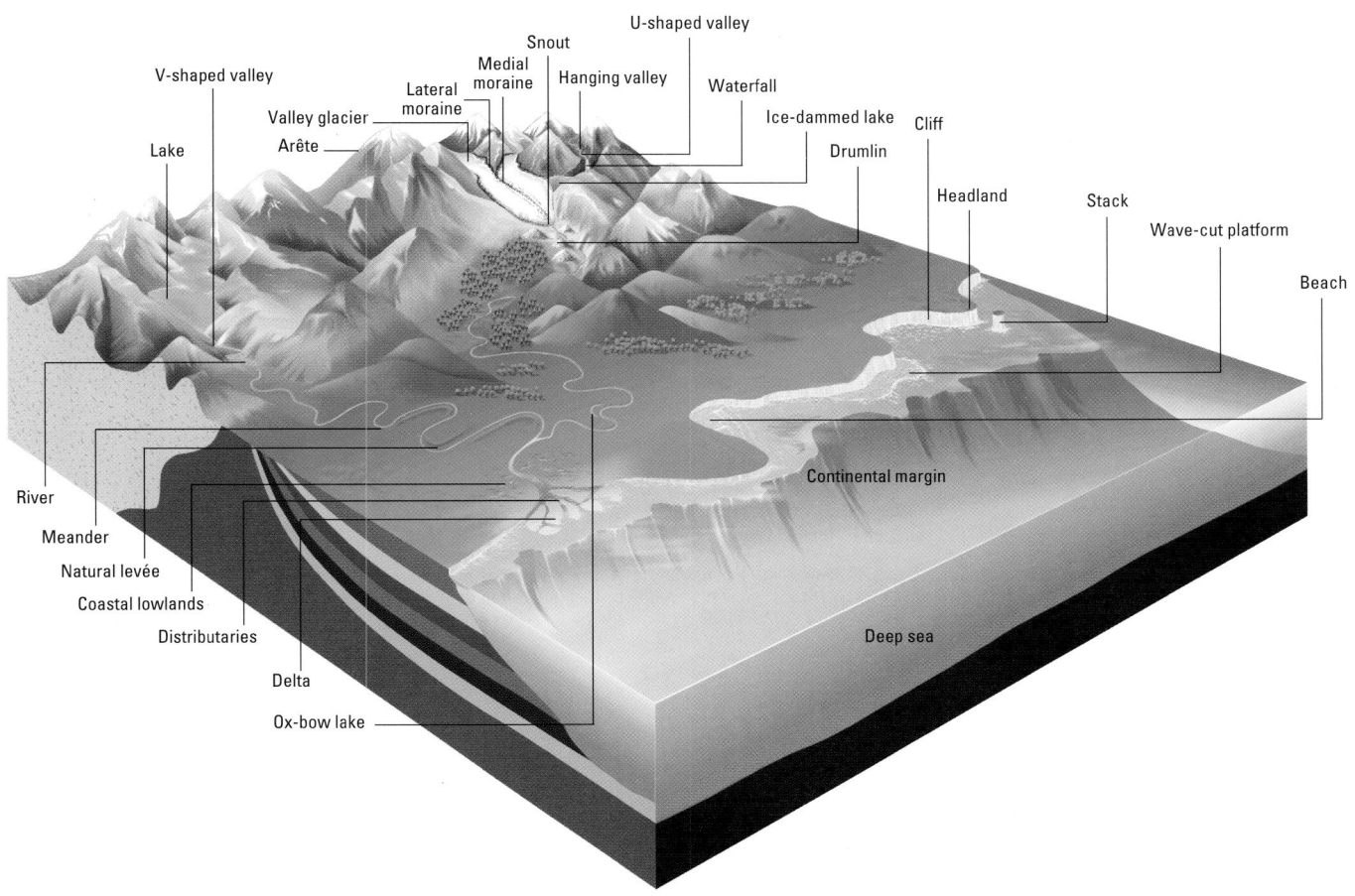

Desert Landscapes

The popular image that deserts are all huge expanses of sand is wrong. Despite harsh conditions, deserts contain some of the most varied and interesting landscapes in the world. They are also one of the most extensive environments – the hot and cold deserts together cover almost 40% of the Earth's surface.

The three types of hot desert are known by their Arabic names: sand desert, called *erg*, covers only about one-fifth of the world's desert; the rest is divided between *hammada* (areas of bare rock) and *reg* (broad plains covered by loose gravel or pebbles).

In areas of *erg*, such as the Namib Desert, the shape of the dunes reflects the character of local winds. Where winds are constant in direction, crescent-shaped *barchan* dunes form. In areas of bare rock, wind-blown sand is a major agent of erosion. The erosion is mainly confined to within 2 m [6.5 ft] of the surface, producing characteristic, mushroom-shaped rocks.

Erg

Hammada

Reg

Surface Processes

Catastrophic changes to natural landforms are periodically caused by such phenomena as avalanches, landslides and volcanic eruptions, but most of the processes that shape the Earth's surface operate extremely slowly in human terms. One estimate, based on a study in the United States, suggested that 1 m [3 ft] of land was removed from the entire surface of the country, on average, every 29,500 years. However, the time-scale varies from 1,300 years to 154,200 years depending on the terrain and climate.

In hot, dry climates, mechanical weathering, a result of rapid temperature changes, causes the outer layers of rock to peel away, while in cold mountainous regions, boulders are prised apart when water freezes in cracks in rocks. Chemical weathering, at its greatest in warm, humid regions, is responsible for hollowing out limestone caves and decomposing granites.

The erosion of soil and rock is greatest on sloping land and the steeper the slope, the greater the tendency for mass wasting – the movement of soil and rock downhill under the influence of gravity. The mechanisms of mass wasting (ranging from very slow to very rapid) vary with the type of material, but the presence of water as a lubricant is usually an important factor.

Running water is the world's leading agent of erosion and transportation. The energy of a river depends on several factors, including its velocity and volume, and its erosive power is at its peak when it is in full flood. Sea waves also exert tremendous erosive power during storms when they hurl pebbles against the shore, undercutting cliffs and hollowing out caves.

Glacier ice forms in mountain hollows and spills out to form valley glaciers, which transport rocks shattered by frost action. As glaciers move, rocks embedded into the ice erode steep-sided, U-shaped valleys. Evidence of glaciation in mountain regions includes cirques, knife-edged ridges, or arêtes, and pyramidal peaks.

Oceans

The Great Oceans

Relative sizes of the world's oceans

■	Pacific
■	Atlantic
■	Indian
■	Arctic

Pie chart: 49%, 4%, 21%, 26%

In a strict geographical sense there are only three true oceans – the Atlantic, Indian and Pacific. The legendary 'Seven Seas' would require these to be divided at the Equator and the addition of the Arctic Ocean – which accounts for less than 4% of the total sea area. The International Hydrographic Bureau does not recognize the Antarctic Ocean (even less the 'Southern Ocean') as a separate entity.

The Earth is a watery planet: more than 70% of its surface – over 360,000,000 sq km [140,000,000 sq miles] – is covered by the oceans and seas. The mighty Pacific alone accounts for nearly 36% of the total, and 49% of the sea area. Gravity holds in around 1,400 million cu. km [320 million cu. miles] of water, of which over 97% is saline.

The vast underwater world starts in the shallows of the seaside and plunges to depths of more than 11,000 m [36,000 ft]. The continental shelf, part of the landmass, drops gently to around 200 m [650 ft]; here the seabed falls away suddenly at an angle of 3° to 6° – the continental slope. The third stage, called the continental rise, is more gradual with gradients varying from 1 in 100 to 1 in 700. At an average depth of 5,000 m [16,500 ft] there begins the aptly-named abyssal plain – massive submarine depths where sunlight fails to penetrate and few creatures can survive.

From these plains rise volcanoes which, taken from base to top, rival and even surpass the tallest continental mountains in height. Mount Kea, on Hawaii, reaches a total of 10,203 m [33,400 ft], some 1,355 m [4,500 ft] more than Mount Everest, though scarcely 40% is visible above sea level.

In addition, there are underwater mountain chains up to 1,000 km [600 miles] across, whose peaks sometimes appear above sea level as islands such as Iceland and Tristan da Cunha.

The Ocean Depths

Average and maximum depths of the world's great oceans, in metres

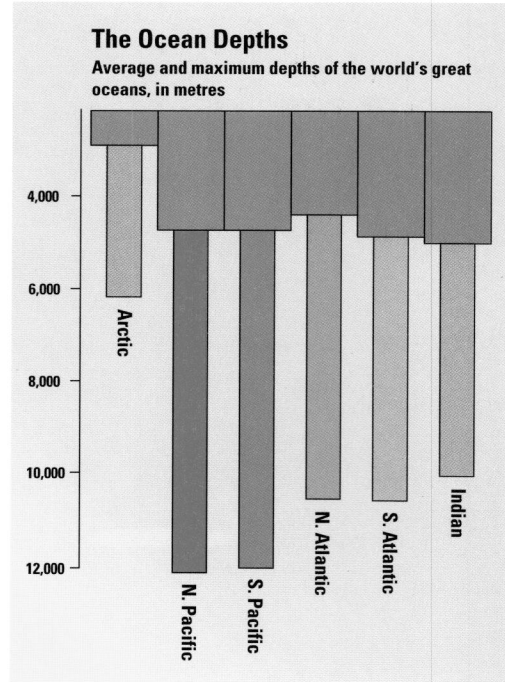

Ocean Currents

January temperatures and ocean currents

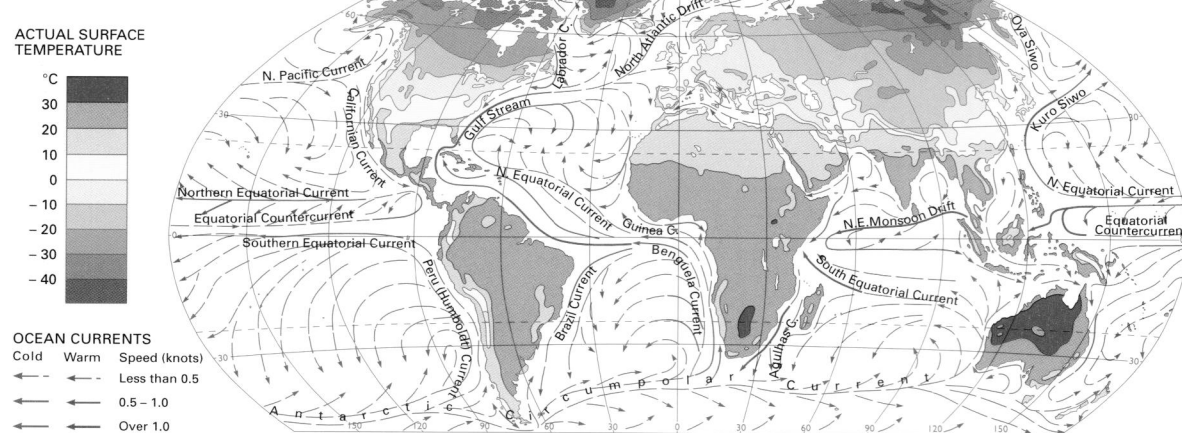

ACTUAL SURFACE TEMPERATURE

°C
30
20
10
0
– 10
– 20
– 30
– 40

OCEAN CURRENTS
Cold | Warm | Speed (knots)
←– – | ←– | Less than 0.5
←— | ←— | 0.5 – 1.0
←— | ←— | Over 1.0

July temperatures and ocean currents

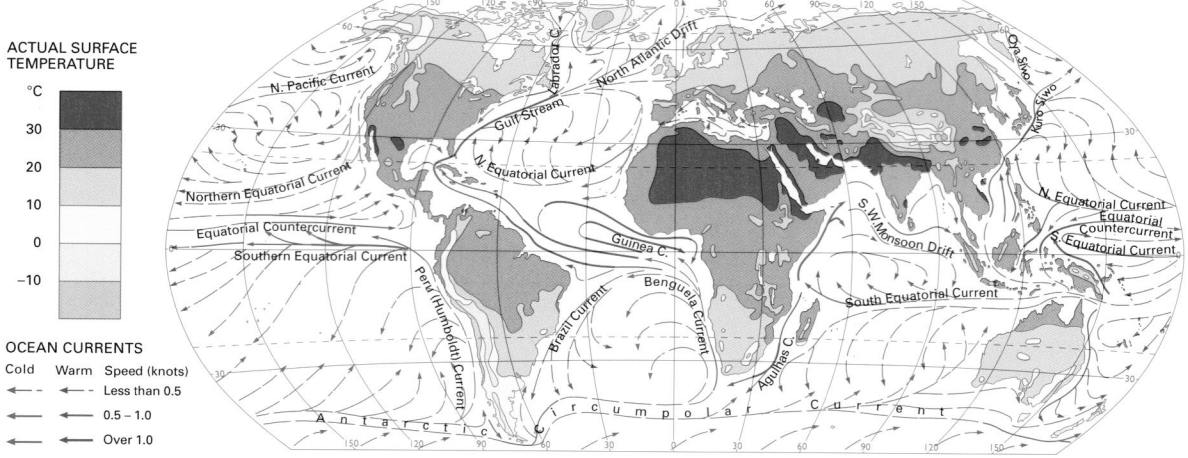

ACTUAL SURFACE TEMPERATURE

°C
30
20
10
0
–10

OCEAN CURRENTS
Cold | Warm | Speed (knots)
←– – | ←– | Less than 0.5
←— | ←— | 0.5 – 1.0
←— | ←— | Over 1.0

Moving immense quantities of energy as well as billions of tonnes of water every hour, the ocean currents are a vital part of the great heat engine that drives the Earth's climate. They themselves are produced by a twofold mechanism. At the surface, winds push huge masses of water before them; in the deep ocean, below an abrupt temperature gradient that separates the churning surface waters from the still depths, density variations cause slow vertical movements.

The pattern of circulation of the great surface currents is determined by the displacement known as the Coriolis effect. As the Earth turns beneath a moving object – whether it is a tennis ball or a vast mass of water – it appears to be deflected to one side. The deflection is most obvious near the Equator, where the Earth's surface is spinning eastwards at 1,700 km/h [1,050 mph]; currents moving polewards are curved clockwise in the northern hemisphere and anti-clockwise in the southern.

The result is a system of spinning circles known as gyres. The Coriolis effect piles up water on the left of each gyre, creating a narrow, fast-moving stream that is matched by a slower, broader returning current on the right. North and south of the Equator, the fastest currents are located in the west and in the east respectively. In each case, warm water moves from the Equator and cold water returns to it. Cold currents often bring an upwelling of nutrients with them, supporting the world's most economically important fisheries.

Depending on the prevailing winds, some currents on or near the Equator may reverse their direction in the course of the year – a seasonal variation on which Asian monsoon rains depend, and whose occasional failure can bring disaster to millions.

World Fishing Areas

Main commercial fishing areas (numbered FAO regions)

Catch by top marine fishing areas, thousand tonnes (1997)

1. Pacific, NW	[61]	26,785	28.7%
2. Pacific, SE	[87]	15,717	16.8%
3. Atlantic, NE	[27]	12,721	13.6%
4. Pacific, WC	[71]	9,753	10.5%
5. Indian, W	[51]	4,461	4.8%
6. Indian, E	[57]	4,228	4.5%
7. Atlantic, EC	[34]	3,873	4.2%
8. Pacific, NE	[67]	3,042	3.3%

 Principal fishing areas

Leading fishing nations

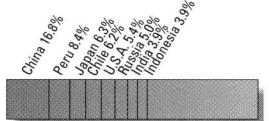
China 16.8% Peru 8.4% Japan 6.3% Chile 6.2% U.S.A. 5.4% Russia 5.0% India 3.5% Indonesia 3.9%

World total catch (1997): 93,329,200 tonnes
(Marine catch 91.7% Inland catch 8.3%)

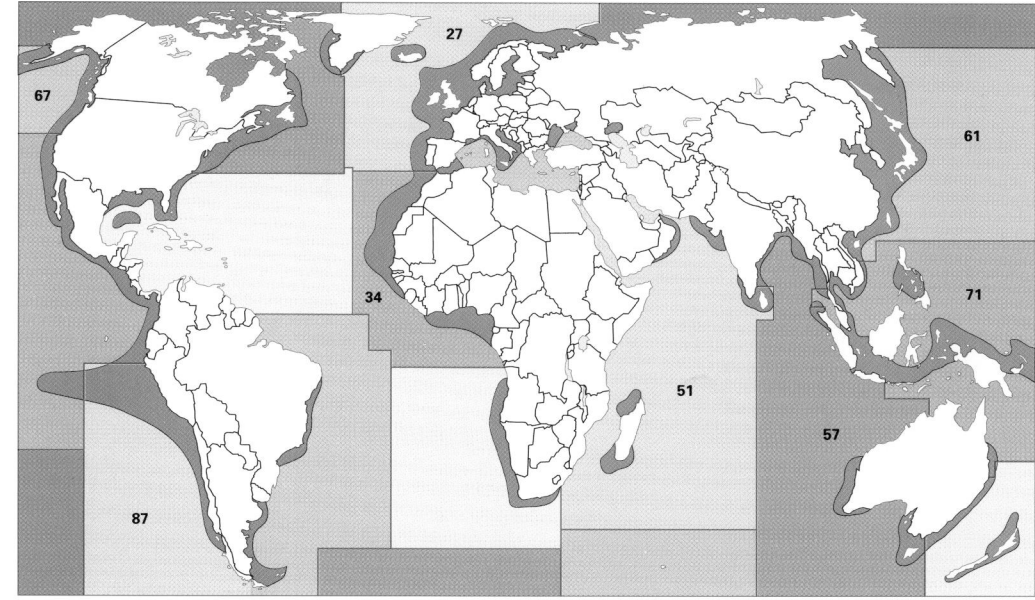

Marine Pollution

Sources of marine oil pollution (latest available year)

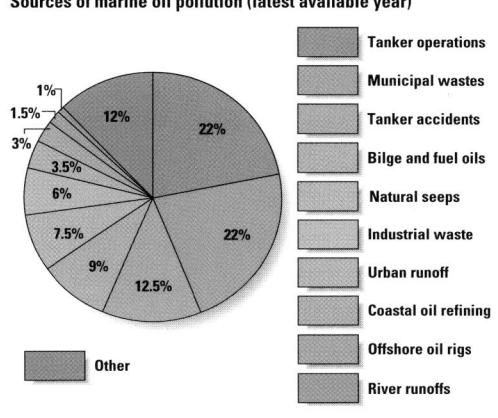

1% · 1.5% · 3% · 3.5% · 6% · 7.5% · 9% · 12.5% · 12% · 22% · 22%

- Tanker operations
- Municipal wastes
- Tanker accidents
- Bilge and fuel oils
- Natural seeps
- Industrial waste
- Urban runoff
- Coastal oil refining
- Offshore oil rigs
- River runoffs
- Other

Oil Spills

Major oil spills from tankers and combined carriers

Year	Vessel	Location	Spill (barrels)**	Cause
1979	Atlantic Empress	West Indies	1,890,000	collision
1983	Castillo De Bellver	South Africa	1,760,000	fire
1978	Amoco Cadiz	France	1,628,000	grounding
1991	Haven	Italy	1,029,000	explosion
1988	Odyssey	Canada	1,000,000	fire
1967	Torrey Canyon	UK	909,000	grounding
1972	Sea Star	Gulf of Oman	902,250	collision
1977	Hawaiian Patriot	Hawaiian Is.	742,500	fire
1979	Independenta	Turkey	696,350	collision
1993	Braer	UK	625,000	grounding
1996	Sea Empress	UK	515,000	grounding

Other sources of major oil spills

1983	Nowruz oilfield	The Gulf	4,250,000[†]	war
1979	Ixtoc 1 oilwell	Gulf of Mexico	4,200,000	blow-out
1991	Kuwait	The Gulf	2,500,000[†]	war

** 1 barrel = 0.136 tonnes/159 lit./35 Imperial gal./42 US gal.   [†] estimated

River Pollution

Sources of river pollution, USA (latest available year)

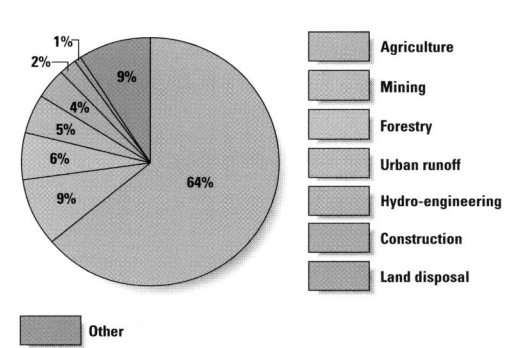

1% · 2% · 4% · 5% · 6% · 9% · 9% · 64%

- Agriculture
- Mining
- Forestry
- Urban runoff
- Hydro-engineering
- Construction
- Land disposal
- Other

Water Pollution

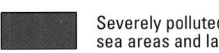

- Severely polluted sea areas and lakes
- Polluted sea areas and lakes
- Areas of frequent oil pollution by shipping
- ▶ Major oil tanker spills
- ▲ Major oil rig blow-outs
- ▼ Offshore dumpsites for industrial and municipal waste
- — Severely polluted rivers and estuaries

The most notorious tanker spillage of the 1980s occurred when the *Exxon Valdez* ran aground in Prince William Sound, Alaska, in 1989, spilling 267,000 barrels of crude oil close to shore in a sensitive ecological area. This rates as the world's 28th worst spill in terms of volume.

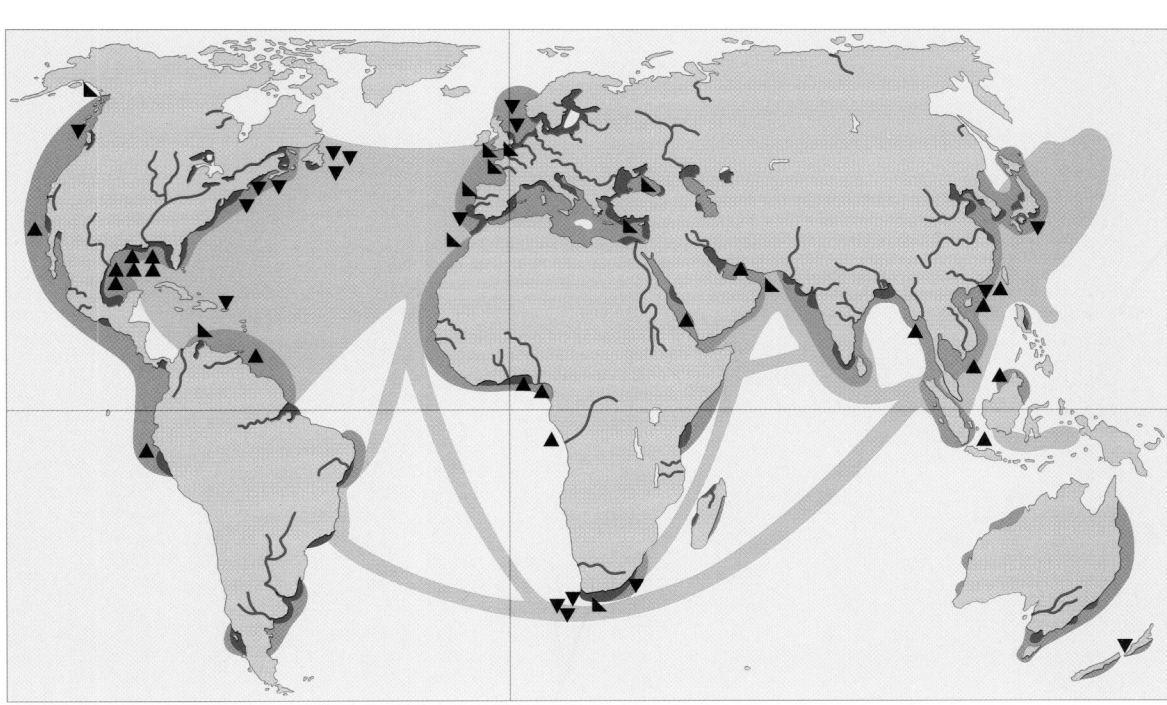

Climate

Climatic Regions

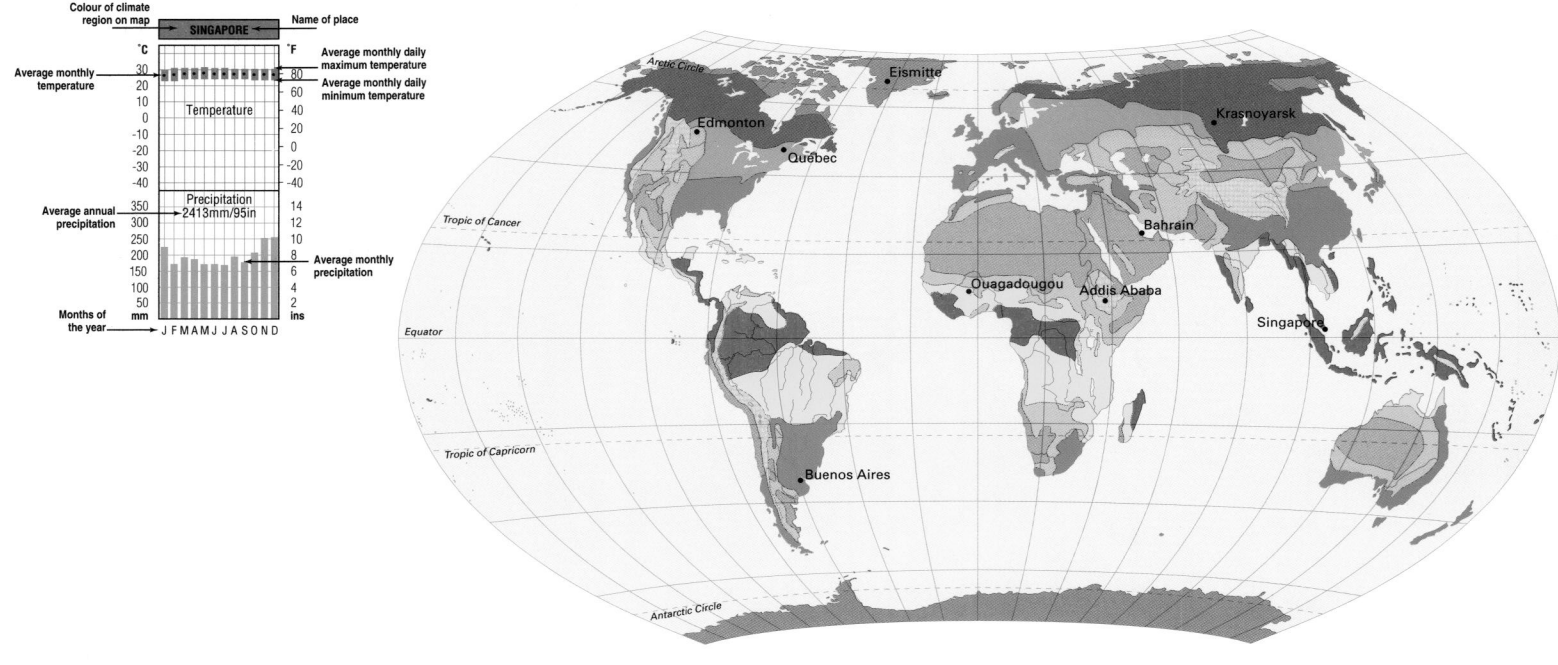

- Tropical climate (hot with rain all year)
- Desert climate (hot and very dry)
- Savanna climate (hot with dry season)
- Steppe climate (warm and dry)
- Mild climate (warm and wet)
- Continental climate (wet with cold winter)
- Subarctic climate (very cold winter)
- Polar climate (very cold and dry)
- Mountainous climate (altitude affects climate)

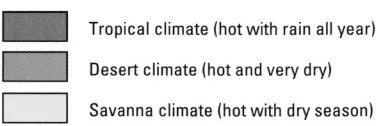
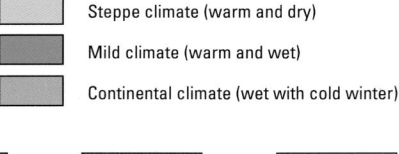
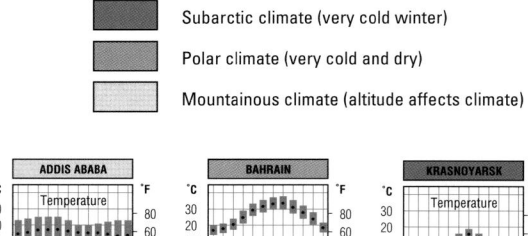
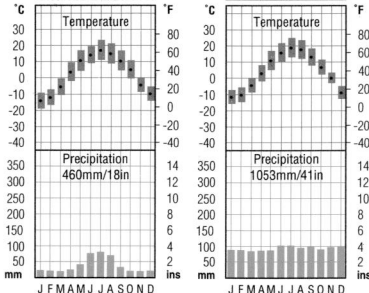
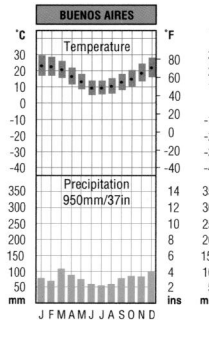
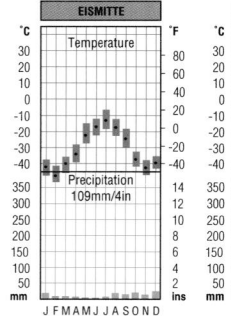
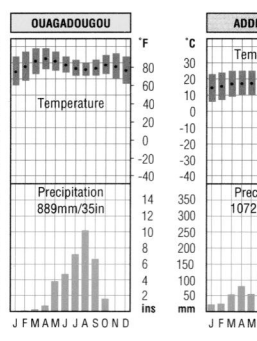
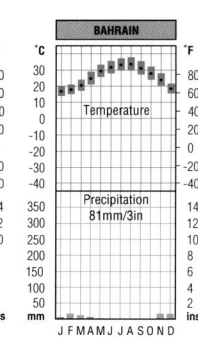
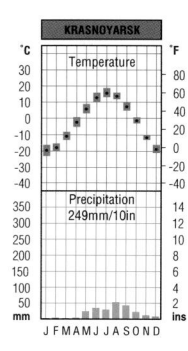

Climate Records

Temperature

Highest recorded shade temperature: Al Aziziyah, Libya, 58°C [136.4°F], 13 September 1922.

Highest mean annual temperature: Dallol, Ethiopia, 34.4°C [94°F], 1960–66.

Longest heatwave: Marble Bar, W. Australia, 162 days over 38°C [100°F], 23 October 1923 to 7 April 1924.

Lowest recorded temperature (outside poles): Verkhoyansk, Siberia, –68°C [–90°F], 6 February 1933.

Lowest mean annual temperature: Plateau Station, Antarctica, –56.6°C [–72.0°F]

Pressure

Longest drought: Calama, N. Chile, no recorded rainfall in 400 years to 1971.

Wettest place (12 months): Cherrapunji, Meghalaya, N. E. India, 26,470 mm [1,040 in], August 1860 to August 1861. Cherrapunji also holds the record for the most rainfall in one month: 2,930 mm [115 in], July 1861.

Wettest place (average): Mawsynram, India, mean annual rainfall 11,873 mm [467.4 in].

Wettest place (24 hours): Cilaos, Réunion, Indian Ocean, 1,870 mm [73.6 in], 15–16 March 1952.

Heaviest hailstones: Gopalganj, Bangladesh, up to 1.02 kg [2.25 lb], 14 April 1986 (killed 92 people).

Heaviest snowfall (continuous): Bessans, Savoie, France, 1,730 mm [68 in] in 19 hours, 5–6 April 1969.

Heaviest snowfall (season/year): Paradise Ranger Station, Mt Rainier, Washington, USA, 31,102 mm [1,224.5 in], 19 February 1971 to 18 February 1972.

Pressure and winds

Highest barometric pressure: Agata, Siberia (at 262 m [862 ft] altitude), 1,083.8 mb, 31 December 1968.

Lowest barometric pressure: Typhoon Tip, Guam, Pacific Ocean, 870 mb, 12 October 1979.

Highest recorded wind speed: Mt Washington, New Hampshire, USA, 371 km/h [231 mph], 12 April 1934. This is three times as strong as hurricane force on the Beaufort Scale.

Windiest place: Commonwealth Bay, Antarctica, where gales frequently reach over 320 km/h [200 mph].

Climate

Climate is weather in the long term: the seasonal pattern of hot and cold, wet and dry, averaged over time (usually 30 years). At the simplest level, it is caused by the uneven heating of the Earth. Surplus heat at the Equator passes towards the poles, levelling out the energy differential. Its passage is marked by a ceaseless churning of the atmosphere and the oceans, further agitated by the Earth's diurnal spin and the motion it imparts to moving air and water. The heat's means of transport – by winds and ocean currents, by the continual evaporation and recondensation of water molecules – is the weather itself. There are four basic types of climate, each of which can be further subdivided: tropical, desert (dry), temperate and polar.

Composition of Dry Air

Nitrogen	78.09%	Sulphur dioxide	trace
Oxygen	20.95%	Nitrogen oxide	trace
Argon	0.93%	Methane	trace
Water vapour	0.2–4.0%	Dust	trace
Carbon dioxide	0.03%	Helium	trace
Ozone	0.00006%	Neon	trace

El Niño

In a normal year, south-easterly trade winds drive surface waters westwards off the coast of South America, drawing cold, nutrient-rich water up from below. In an El Niño year (which occurs every 2–7 years), warm water from the west Pacific suppresses up-welling in the east, depriving the region of nutrients. The water is warmed by as much as 7°C [12°F], disturbing the tropical atmospheric circulation. During an intense El Niño, the south-east trade winds change direction and become equatorial westerlies, resulting in climatic extremes in many regions of the world, such as drought in parts of Australia and India, and heavy rainfall in south-eastern USA. An intense El Niño occurred in 1997–8, with resultant freak weather conditions across the entire Pacific region.

Normal year

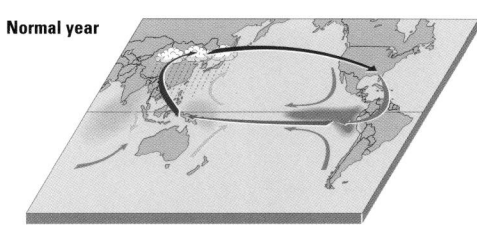

El Niño event

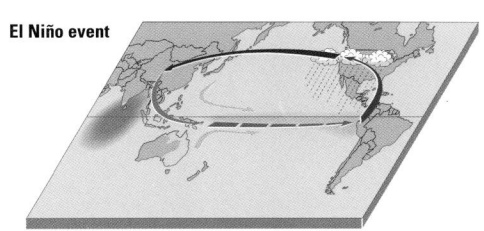

Beaufort Wind Scale

Named after the 19th-century British naval officer who devised it, the Beaufort Scale assesses wind speed according to its effects. It was originally designed as an aid for sailors, but has since been adapted for use on the land.

Scale	Wind speed km/h	mph	Effect
0	0–1	0–1	**Calm** Smoke rises vertically
1	1–5	1–3	**Light air** Wind direction shown only by smoke drift
2	6–11	4–7	**Light breeze** Wind felt on face; leaves rustle; vanes moved by wind
3	12–19	8–12	**Gentle breeze** Leaves and small twigs in constant motion; wind extends small flag
4	20–28	13–18	**Moderate** Raises dust and loose paper; small branches move
5	29–38	19–24	**Fresh** Small trees in leaf sway; wavelets on inland waters
6	39–49	25–31	**Strong** Large branches move; difficult to use umbrellas
7	50–61	32–38	**Near gale** Whole trees in motion; difficult to walk against wind
8	62–74	39–46	**Gale** Twigs break from trees; walking very difficult
9	75–88	47–54	**Strong gale** Slight structural damage
10	89–102	55–63	**Storm** Trees uprooted; serious structural damage
11	103–117	64–72	**Violent storm** Widespread damage
12	118+	73+	**Hurricane**

Conversions

°C = (°F − 32) × 5/9; °F = (°C × 9/5) + 32; 0°C = 32°F
1 in = 25.4 mm; 1 mm = 0.0394 in; 100 mm = 3.94 in

Temperature

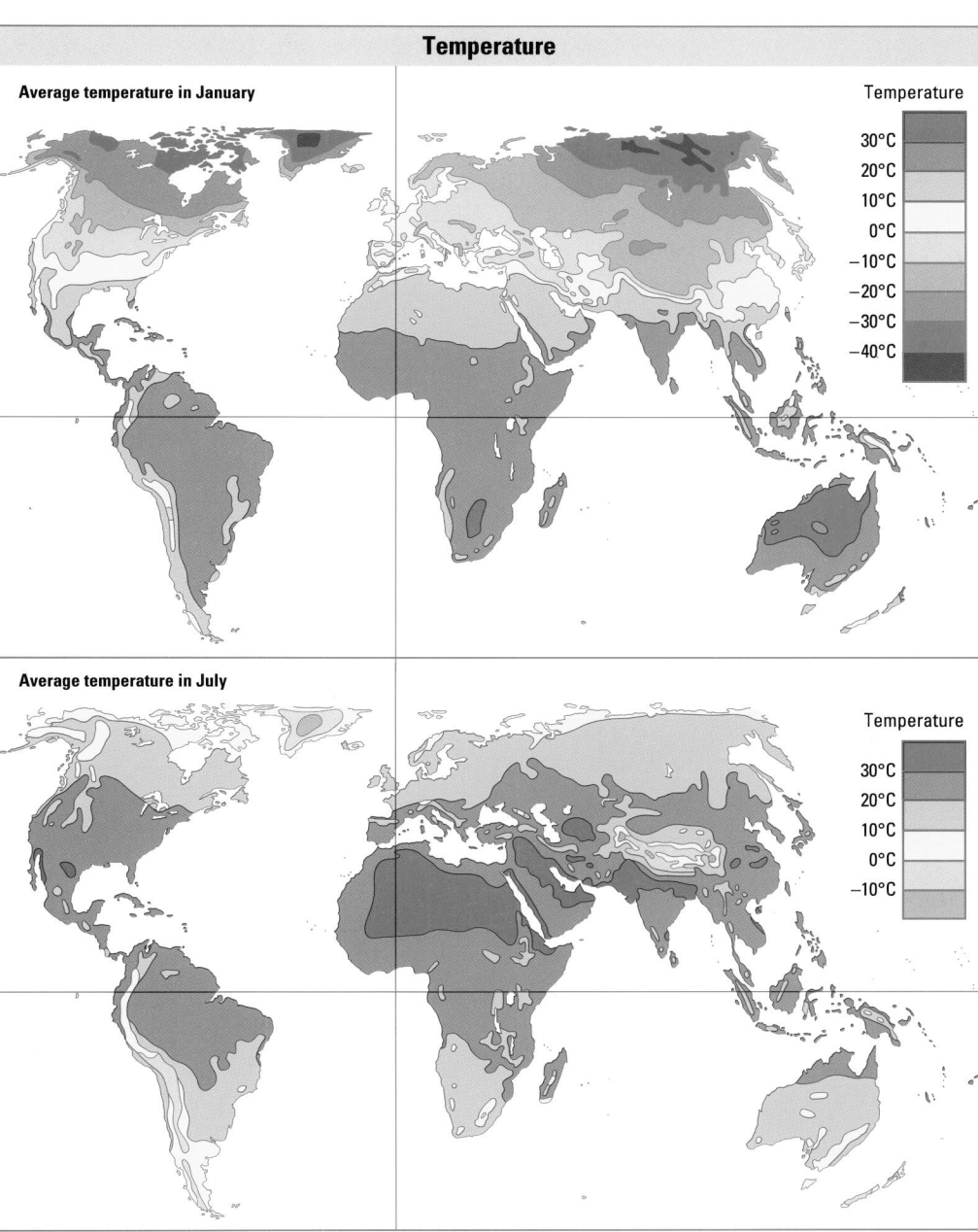

Average temperature in January

Temperature
30°C
20°C
10°C
0°C
−10°C
−20°C
−30°C
−40°C

Average temperature in July

Temperature
30°C
20°C
10°C
0°C
−10°C

Precipitation

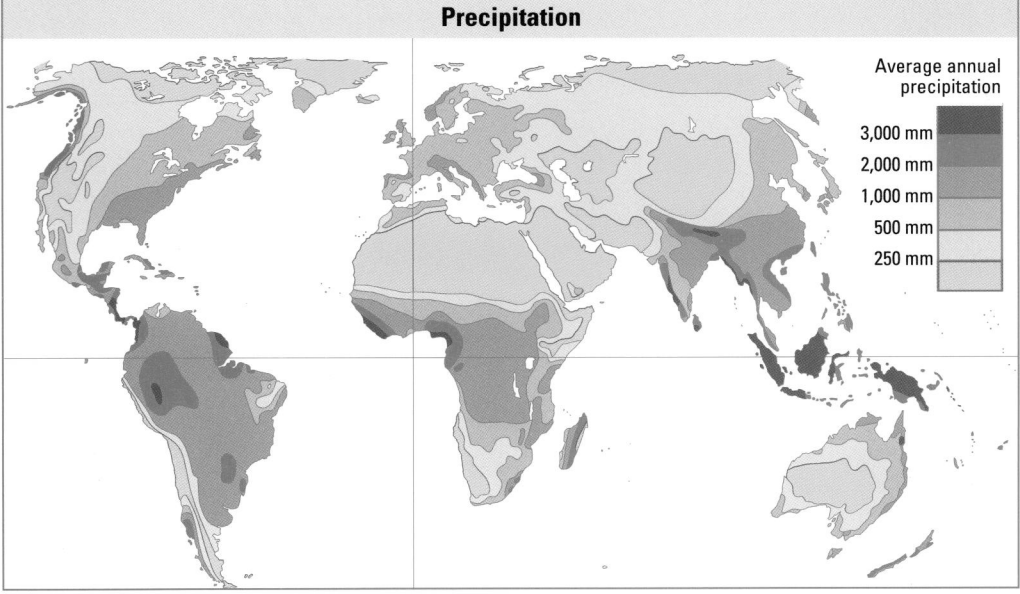

Average annual precipitation
3,000 mm
2,000 mm
1,000 mm
500 mm
250 mm

Water and Vegetation

The Hydrological Cycle

The world's water balance is regulated by the constant recycling of water between the oceans, atmosphere and land. The movement of water between these three reservoirs is known as the hydrological cycle. The oceans play a vital role in the hydrological cycle: 74% of the total precipitation falls over the oceans and 84% of the total evaporation comes from the oceans.

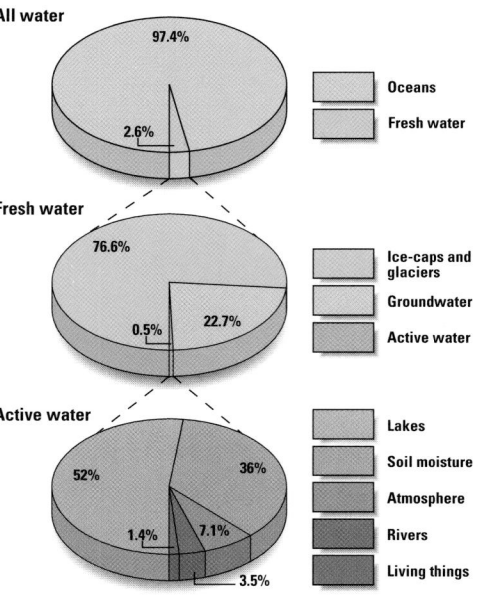

Water Distribution

The distribution of planetary water, by percentage. Oceans and ice-caps together account for more than 99% of the total; the breakdown of the remainder is estimated.

All water
- 97.4% — Oceans
- 2.6% — Fresh water

Fresh water
- 76.6% — Ice-caps and glaciers
- 22.7% — Groundwater
- 0.5% — Active water

Active water
- 52% — Lakes
- 36% — Soil moisture
- 7.1% — Atmosphere
- 3.5% — Rivers
- 1.4% — Living things

Water Utilization

Domestic   Industrial   Agriculture

The percentage breakdown of water usage by sector, selected countries (1996)

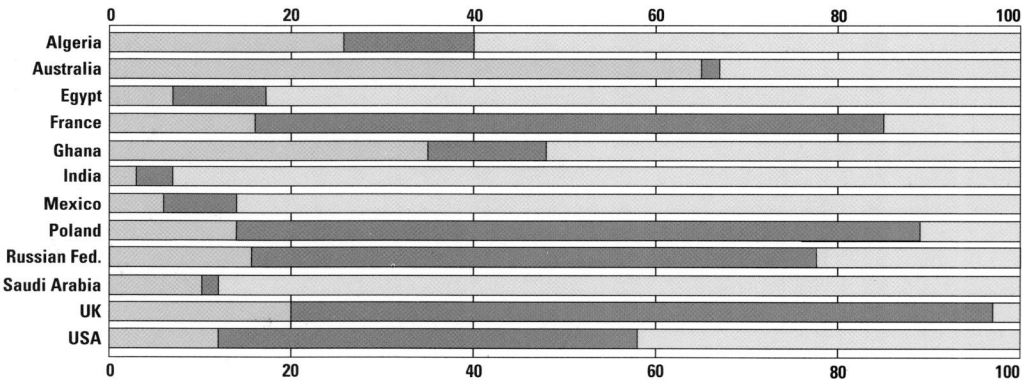

Countries listed: Algeria, Australia, Egypt, France, Ghana, India, Mexico, Poland, Russian Fed., Saudi Arabia, UK, USA

Scale: 0, 20, 40, 60, 80, 100

Water Usage

Almost all the world's water is 3,000 million years old, and all of it cycles endlessly through the hydrosphere, though at different rates. Water vapour circulates over days, even hours, deep ocean water circulates over millennia, and ice-cap water remains solid for millions of years.

Fresh water is essential to all terrestrial life. Humans cannot survive more than a few days without it, and even the hardiest desert plants and animals could not exist without some water. Agriculture requires huge quantities of fresh water: without large-scale irrigation most of the world's people would starve. In the USA, agriculture uses 42% and industry 45% of all water withdrawals.

The United States is one of the heaviest users of water in the world. According to the latest figures the average American uses 380 litres a day and the average household uses 415,000 litres a year. This is two to four times more than in Western Europe.

Water Supply

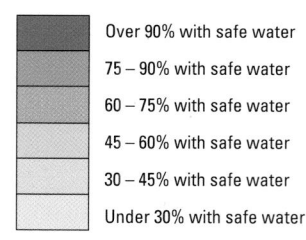

Percentage of total population with access to safe drinking water (1995)

- Over 90% with safe water
- 75 – 90% with safe water
- 60 – 75% with safe water
- 45 – 60% with safe water
- 30 – 45% with safe water
- Under 30% with safe water

- △ Under 80 litres per person per day domestic water consumption
- ▲ Over 320 litres per person per day domestic water consumption

NB: 80 litres of water a day is considered necessary for a reasonable quality of life.

Least well-provided countries

Paraguay	8%	Central Afr. Rep	18%
Afghanistan	10%	Bhutan	21%
Cambodia	13%	Congo (D. Rep.)	25%

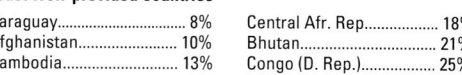

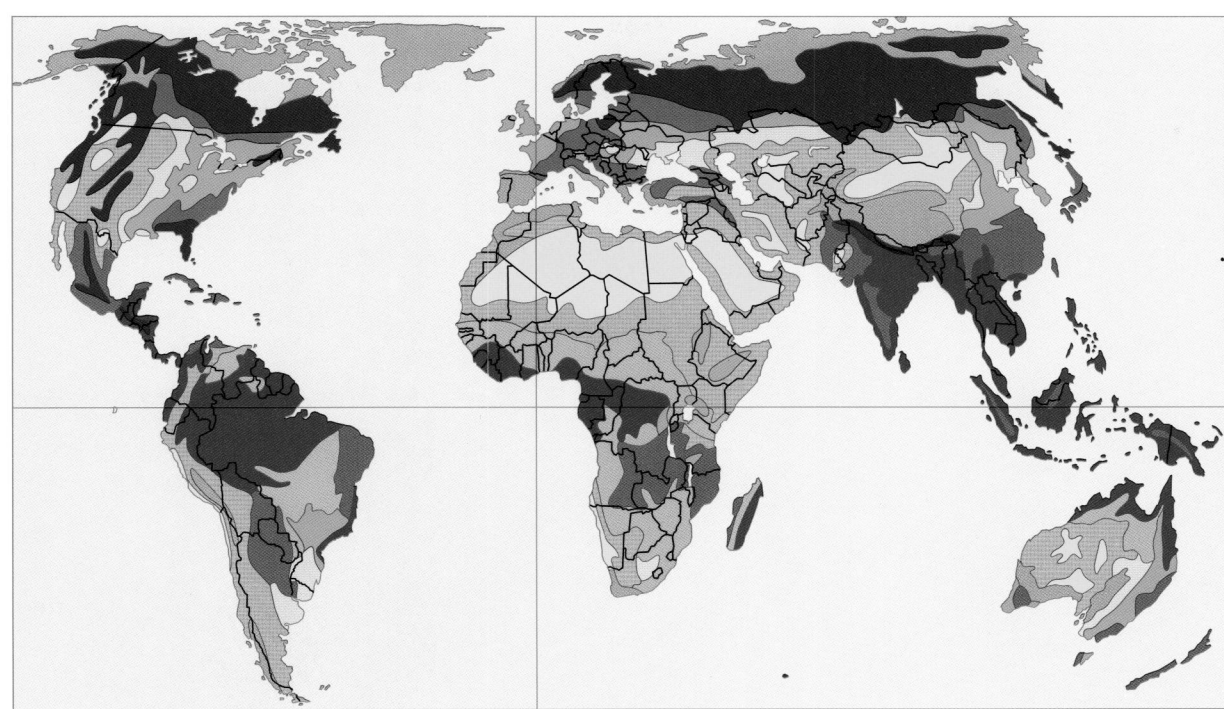

Natural Vegetation

Regional variation in vegetation

- Tundra and mountain vegetation
- Needleleaf evergreen forest
- Mixed needleleaf evergreen & broadleaf deciduous trees
- Broadleaf deciduous woodland
- Mid-latitude grassland
- Evergreen broadleaf and deciduous trees & shrubs
- Semi-desert scrub
- Desert
- Tropical grassland (savanna)
- Tropical broadleaf rainforest and monsoon forest
- Subtropical broadleaf and needleleaf forest

The map shows the natural 'climax vegetation' of regions, as dictated by climate and topography. In most cases, however, agricultural activity has drastically altered the vegetation pattern. Western Europe, for example, lost most of its broadleaf forest many centuries ago, while irrigation has turned some natural semi-desert into productive land.

Land Use by Continent

- Forest
- Permanent pasture and rough grazing
- Permanent crops and plantations
- Arable
- Non-productive

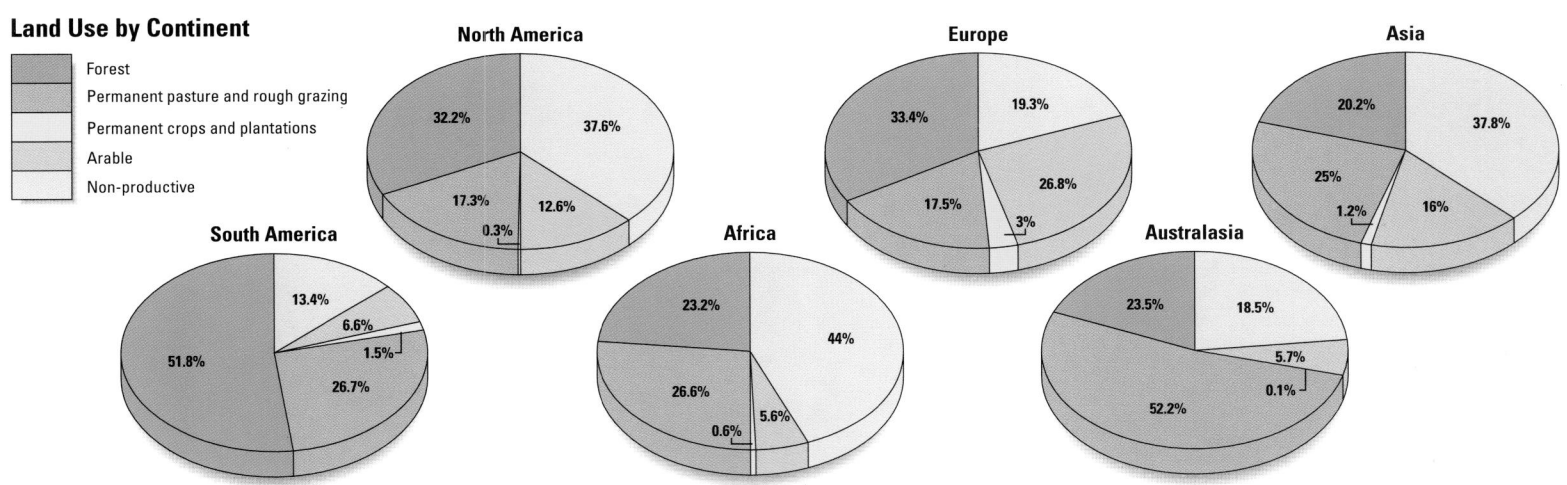

North America: 37.6%, 12.6%, 0.3%, 17.3%, 32.2%

Europe: 19.3%, 26.8%, 3%, 17.5%, 33.4%

Asia: 37.8%, 16%, 1.2%, 25%, 20.2%

South America: 13.4%, 6.6%, 1.5%, 26.7%, 51.8%

Africa: 44%, 5.6%, 0.6%, 26.6%, 23.2%

Australasia: 18.5%, 5.7%, 0.1%, 52.2%, 23.5%

Forestry: Production

	Forest and woodland (million hectares)	Annual production (1996, million cubic metres)	
		Fuelwood and charcoal	Industrial roundwood*
World	**3,987.9**	**1,864.8**	**1,489.5**
S. America	829.3	193.0	129.9
N. & C. America	709.8	155.4	600.4
Africa	684.6	519.9	67.9
Asia	131.8	905.2	280.2
Europe	157.3	82.4	369.7
Australasia	157.2	8.7	41.5

Paper and Board

Top producers (1996)**		Top exporters (1996)**	
USA	85,173	Canada	13,393
China	30,253	USA	9,113
Japan	30,014	Finland	8,529
Canada	18,414	Sweden	7,483
Germany	14,733	Germany	6,319

* roundwood is timber as it is felled
** in thousand tonnes

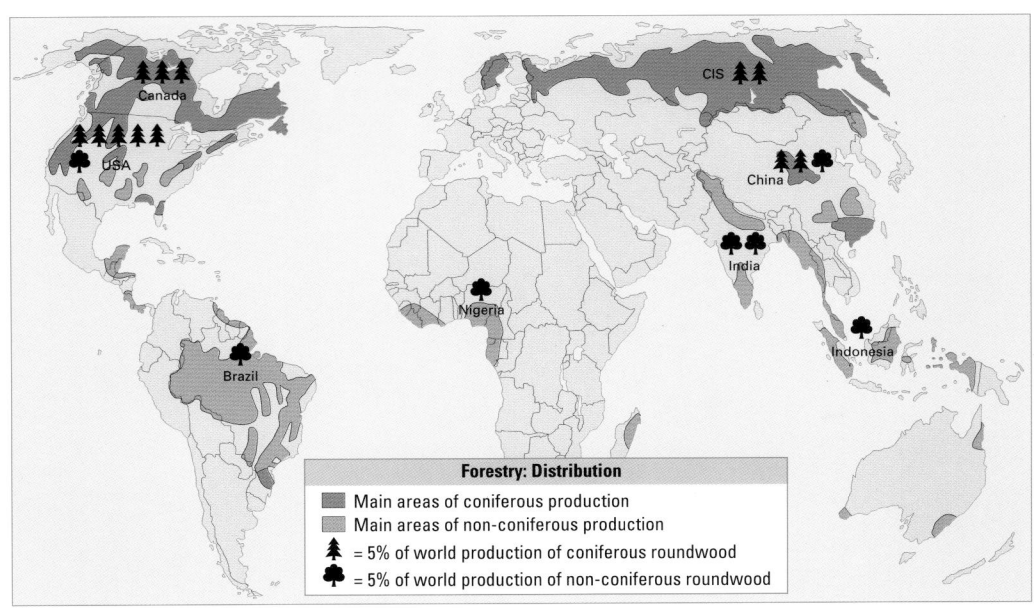

Forestry: Distribution

- Main areas of coniferous production
- Main areas of non-coniferous production
- 🌲 = 5% of world production of coniferous roundwood
- 🌳 = 5% of world production of non-coniferous roundwood

Environment

Humans have always had a dramatic effect on their environment, at least since the development of agriculture almost 10,000 years ago. Generally, the Earth has accepted human interference without obvious ill effects: the complex systems that regulate the global environment have been able to absorb substantial damage while maintaining a stable and comfortable home for the planet's trillions of lifeforms. But advancing human technology and the rapidly-expanding populations it supports are now threatening to overwhelm the Earth's ability to compensate.

Industrial wastes, acid rainfall, desertification and large-scale deforestation all combine to create environmental change at a rate far faster than the great slow cycles of planetary evolution can accommodate. As a result of overcultivation, overgrazing and overcutting of groundcover for firewood, desertification is affecting as much as 60% of the world's croplands. In addition, with fire and chain-saws, humans are destroying more forest in a day than their ancestors could have done in a century, upsetting the balance between plant and animal, carbon dioxide and oxygen, on which all life ultimately depends.

The fossil fuels that power industrial civilization have pumped enough carbon dioxide and other so-called greenhouse gases into the atmosphere to make climatic change a near-certainty. As a result of the combination of these factors, the Earth's average temperature has risen by approximately 0.5°C [1°F] since the beginning of the 20th century, and it is still rising.

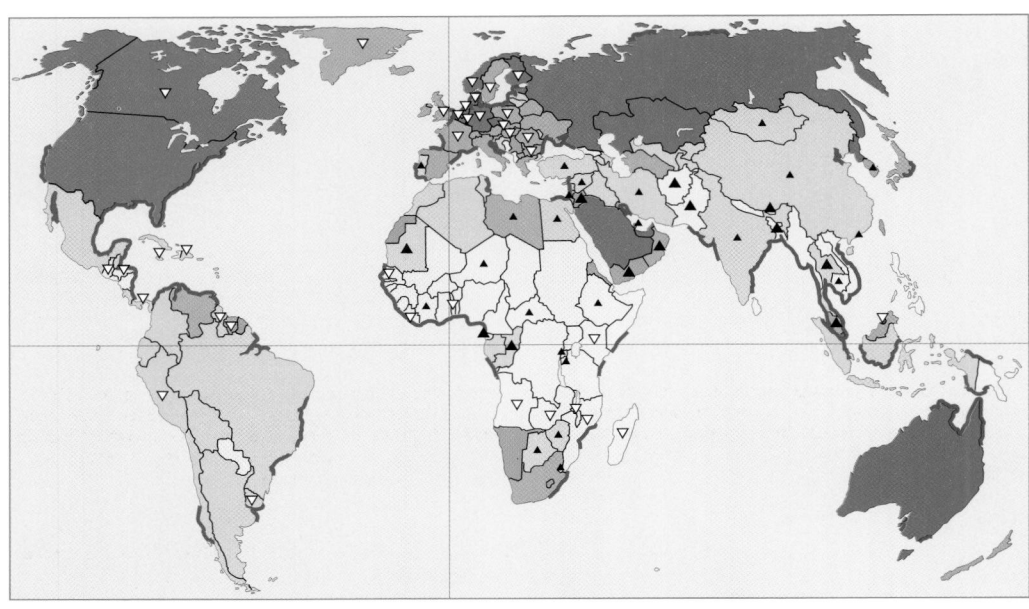

Global Warming

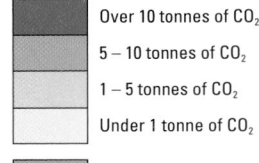

Carbon dioxide emissions in tonnes per person per year (1996)

- Over 10 tonnes of CO_2
- 5 – 10 tonnes of CO_2
- 1 – 5 tonnes of CO_2
- Under 1 tonne of CO_2
- No data available

Changes in CO_2 emissions 1980–90

- ▲ Over 100% increase in emissions
- ▲ 50–100% increase in emissions
- ▽ Reduction in emissions
- ▬ Coastal areas in danger of flooding from rising sea levels caused by global warming

High atmospheric concentrations of heat-absorbing gases, appear to be causing a rise in average temperatures worldwide – up to 1.5°C [3°F] by the year 2020, according to some estimates. Global warming is likely to bring about a rise in sea levels that may flood some of the world's densely populated coastal areas.

Greenhouse Power

Relative contributions to the Greenhouse Effect by the major heat-absorbing gases in the atmosphere.

The chart combines greenhouse potency and volume. Carbon dioxide has a greenhouse potential of only 1, but its concentration of 350 parts per million makes it predominate. CFC 12, with 25,000 times the absorption capacity of CO_2, is present only as 0.00044 ppm.

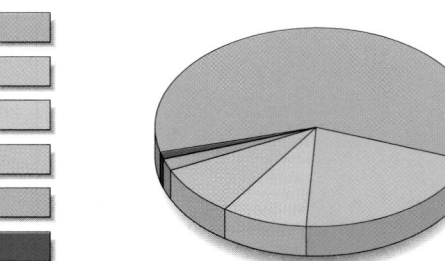

Ozone Layer

The ozone 'hole' over the northern hemisphere on 12 March 1995.

The colours represent Dobson Units (DU). The ozone 'hole' is seen as the dark blue and purple patch in the centre, where ozone values are around 120 DU or lower. Normal levels are around 280 DU. The ozone 'hole' over Antarctica is much larger.

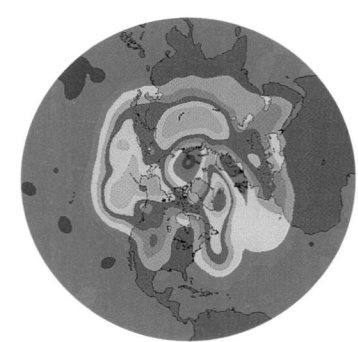

Carbon Dioxide

Cumulative carbon emissions, million tonnes of carbon (1950–96)

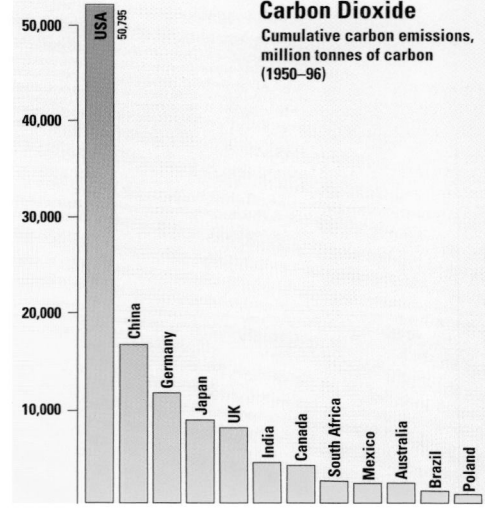

The Greenhouse Effect

Carbon dioxide is increased by burning fossil fuels and cutting forests

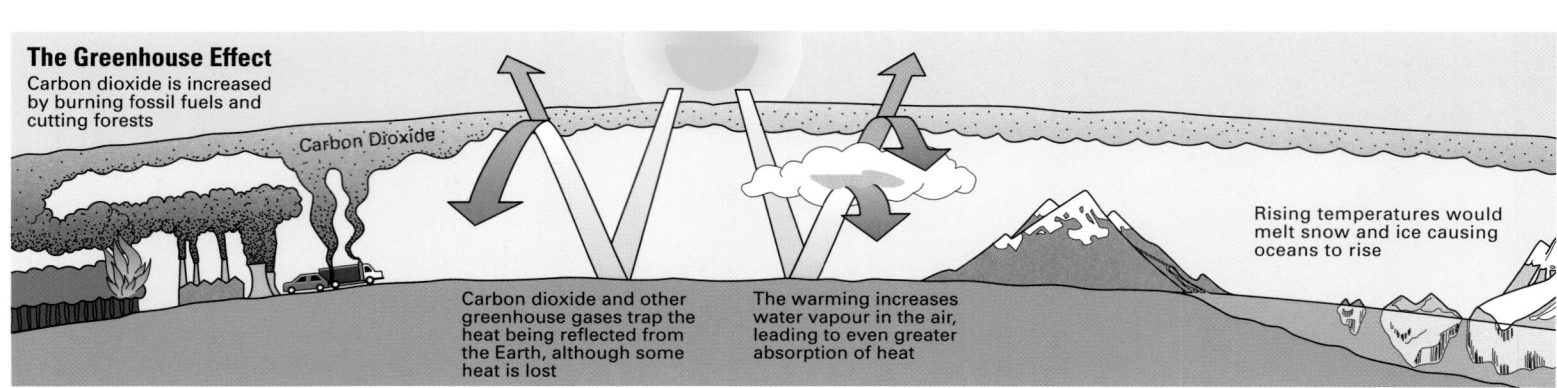

Carbon Dioxide

Carbon dioxide and other greenhouse gases trap the heat being reflected from the Earth, although some heat is lost

The warming increases water vapour in the air, leading to even greater absorption of heat

Rising temperatures would melt snow and ice causing oceans to rise

Desertification

- Existing deserts
- Areas with a high risk of desertification
- Areas with a moderate risk of desertification
- Former areas of rainforest
- Existing rainforest

Forest Clearance

Thousands of hectares of forest cleared annually, tropical countries surveyed 1981–85 and 1987–90. Loss as a percentage of remaining stocks is shown in figures on each column.

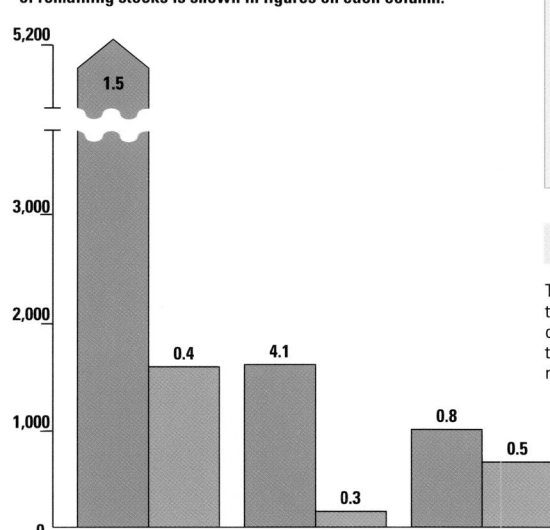

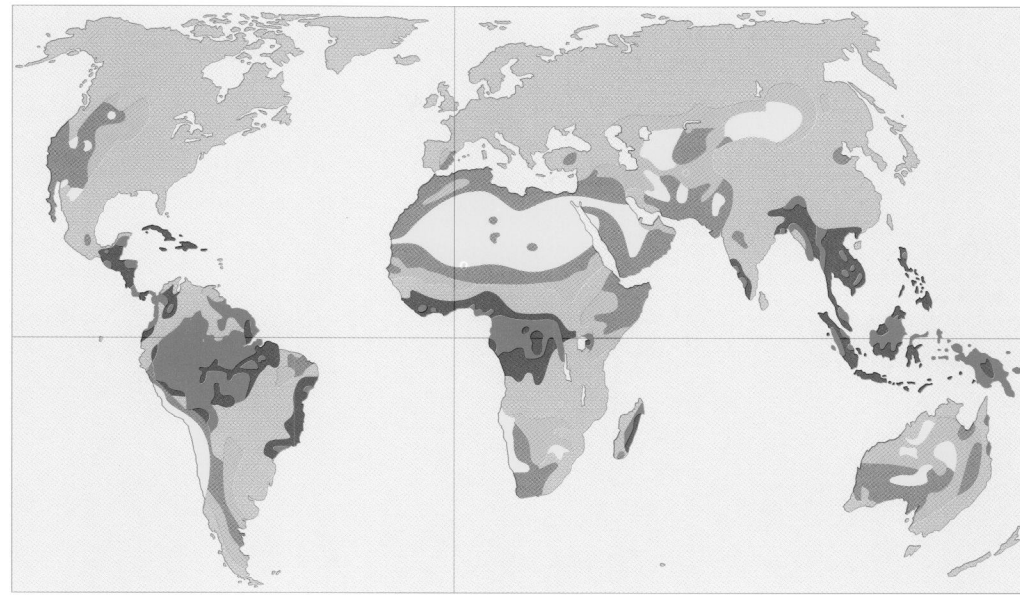

Deforestation

The Earth's remaining forests are under attack from three directions: expanding agriculture, logging, and growing consumption of fuelwood, often in combination. Sometimes deforestation is the direct result of government policy, as in the efforts made to resettle the urban poor in some parts of Brazil; just as often,

it comes about despite state attempts at conservation. Loggers, licensed or unlicensed, blaze a trail into virgin forest, often destroying twice as many trees as they harvest. Landless farmers follow, burning away most of what remains to plant their crops, completing the destruction.

1987–90   1981–85

Ozone Depletion

The ozone layer, 25–30 km [15–18 miles] above sea level, acts as a barrier to most of the Sun's harmful ultra-violet radiation, protecting us from the ionizing radiation that can cause skin cancer and cataracts. In recent years, however, two holes in the ozone layer have been observed during winter: one over the Arctic and the other, the size of the USA, over Antarctica. By 1996, ozone had been reduced to around a half of its 1970 amount. The ozone (O_3) is broken down by chlorine released into the atmosphere as CFCs (chlorofluorocarbons) – chemicals used in refrigerators, packaging and aerosols.

Air Pollution

Sulphur dioxide is the main pollutant associated with industrial cities. According to the World Health Organization, at least 600 million people live in urban areas where sulphur dioxide concentrations regularly reach damaging levels. One of the world's most dangerously polluted urban areas is Mexico City, due to a combination of its enclosed valley location, 3 million cars and 60,000 factories. In May 1998, this lethal cocktail was added to by nearby forest fires and the resultant air pollution led to over 20% of the population (3 million people) complaining of respiratory problems.

Acid Rain

Killing trees, poisoning lakes and rivers and eating away buildings, acid rain is mostly produced by sulphur dioxide emissions from industry and volcanic eruptions. By the mid 1990s, acid rain had sterilized 4,000 or more of Sweden's lakes and left 45% of Switzerland's alpine conifers dead or dying, while the monuments of Greece were dissolving in Athens' smog. Prevailing wind patterns mean that the acids often fall many hundred kilometres from where the original pollutants were discharged. In parts of Europe acid deposition has slightly decreased, following reductions in emissions, but not by enough.

World Pollution

Acid rain and sources of acidic emissions (latest available year)

Acid rain is caused by high levels of sulphur and nitrogen in the atmosphere. They combine with water vapour and oxygen to form acids (H_2SO_4 and HNO_3) which fall as precipitation.

- Regions where sulphur and nitrogen oxides are released in high concentrations, mainly from fossil fuel combustion
- 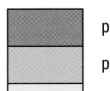 Major cities with high levels of air pollution (including nitrogen and sulphur emissions)

Areas of heavy acid deposition

pH numbers indicate acidity, decreasing from a neutral 7. Normal rain, slightly acid from dissolved carbon dioxide, never exceeds a pH of 5.6.

- pH less than 4.0 (most acidic)
- pH 4.0 to 4.5
- pH 4.5 to 5.0
- Areas where acid rain is a potential problem

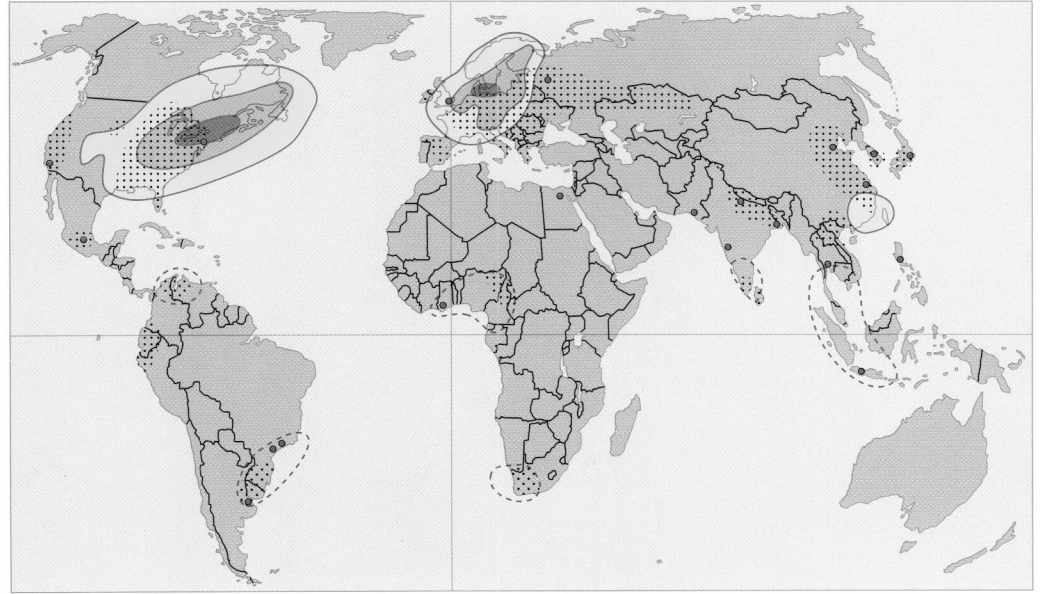

Population

Demographic Profiles

Developed nations such as the UK have populations evenly spread across the age groups and, usually, a growing proportion of elderly people. The great majority of the people in developing nations, however, are in the younger age groups, about to enter their most fertile years. In time, these population profiles should resemble the world profile (even Kenya has made recent progress with reducing its birth rate), but the transition will come about only after a few more generations of rapid population growth.

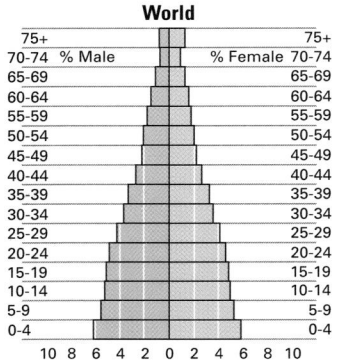

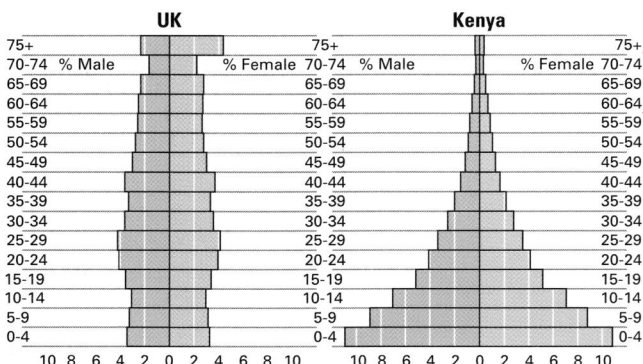

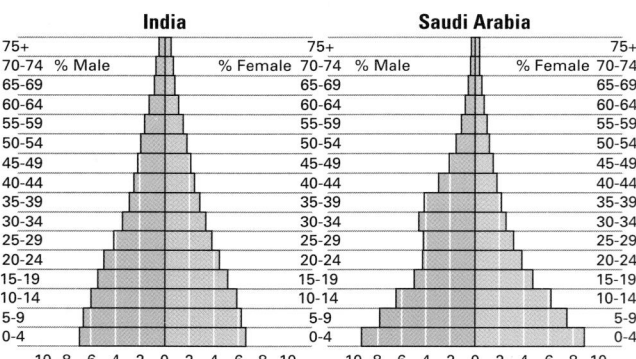

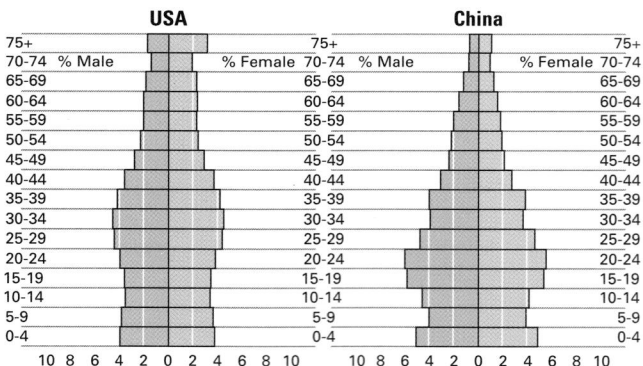

Most Populous Nations [in millions (2000 estimates)]

1.	China	1,299	9.	Japan	128	17. Egypt	64
2.	India	1,041	10.	Mexico	107	18. Thailand	63
3.	USA	266	11.	Nigeria	105	19. Ethiopia	61
4.	Indonesia	218	12.	Vietnam	82	20. France	58
5.	Brazil	179	13.	Philippines	77	21. UK	58
6.	Pakistan	162	14.	Germany	76	22. Italy	57
7.	Russia	155	15.	Iran	68	23. Ukraine	52
8.	Bangladesh	150	16.	Turkey	66	24. Burma (Myanmar)	51

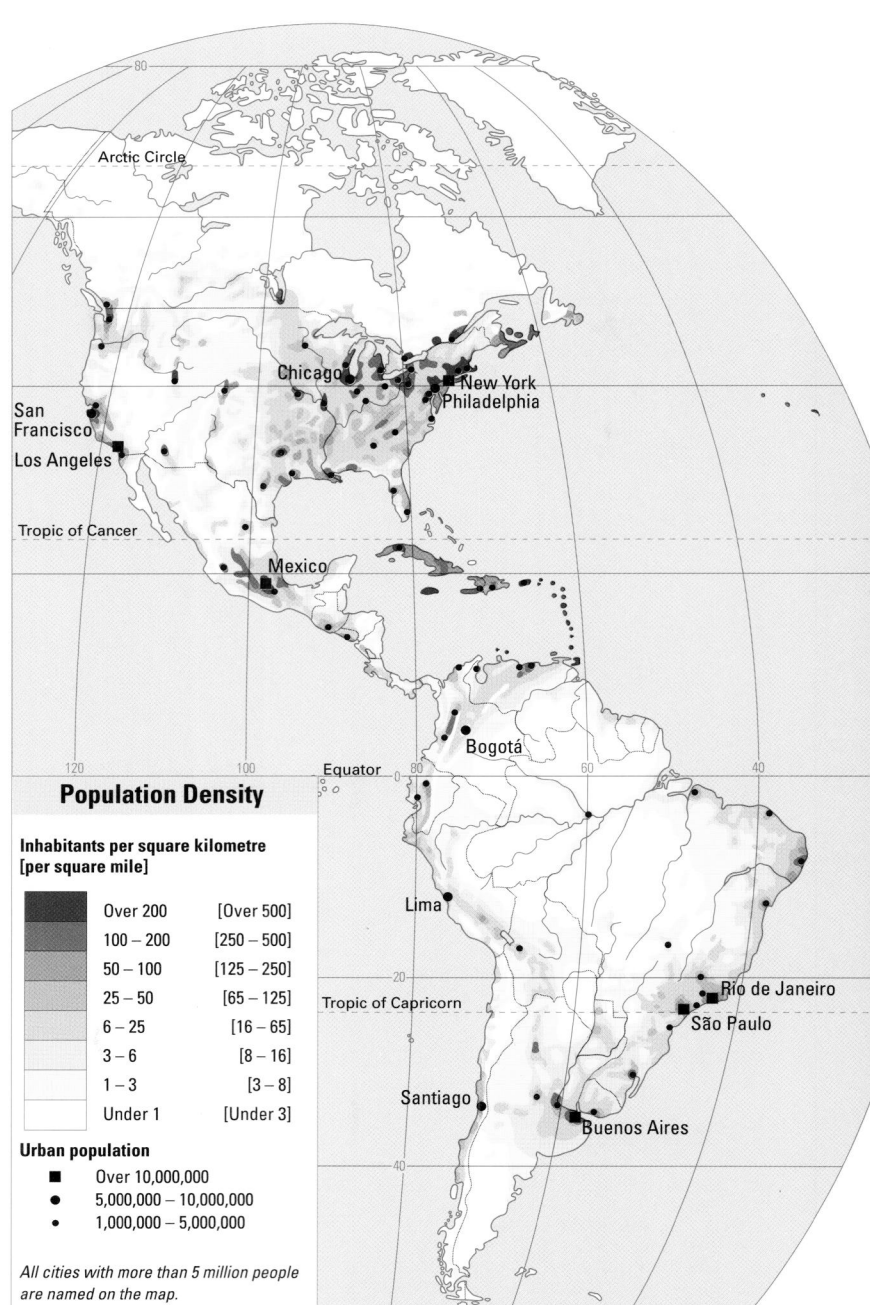

Population Density

Inhabitants per square kilometre [per square mile]

	Over 200	[Over 500]
	100 – 200	[250 – 500]
	50 – 100	[125 – 250]
	25 – 50	[65 – 125]
	6 – 25	[16 – 65]
	3 – 6	[8 – 16]
	1 – 3	[3 – 8]
	Under 1	[Under 3]

Urban population

■ Over 10,000,000

● 5,000,000 – 10,000,000

• 1,000,000 – 5,000,000

All cities with more than 5 million people are named on the map.

Continental Comparisons

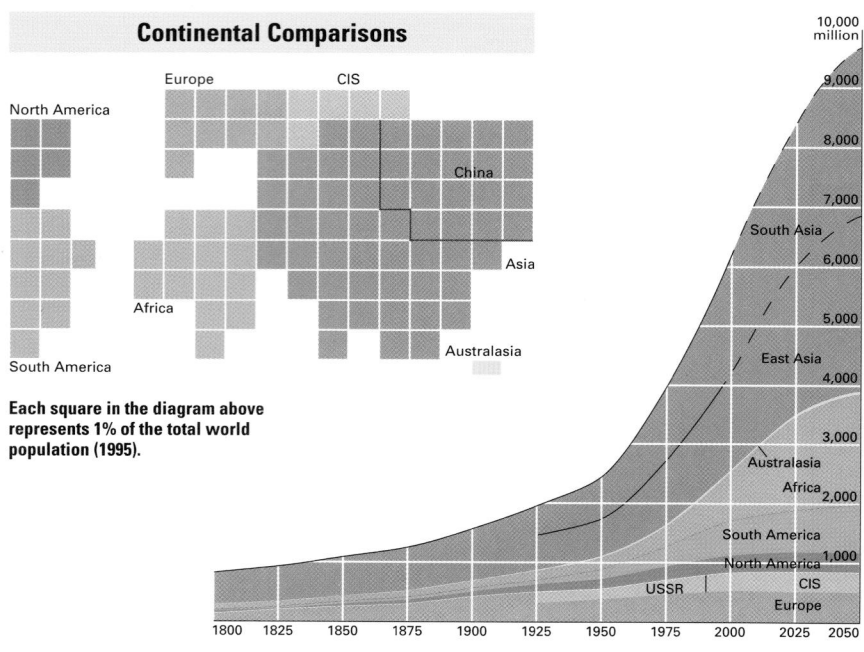

Each square in the diagram above represents 1% of the total world population (1995).

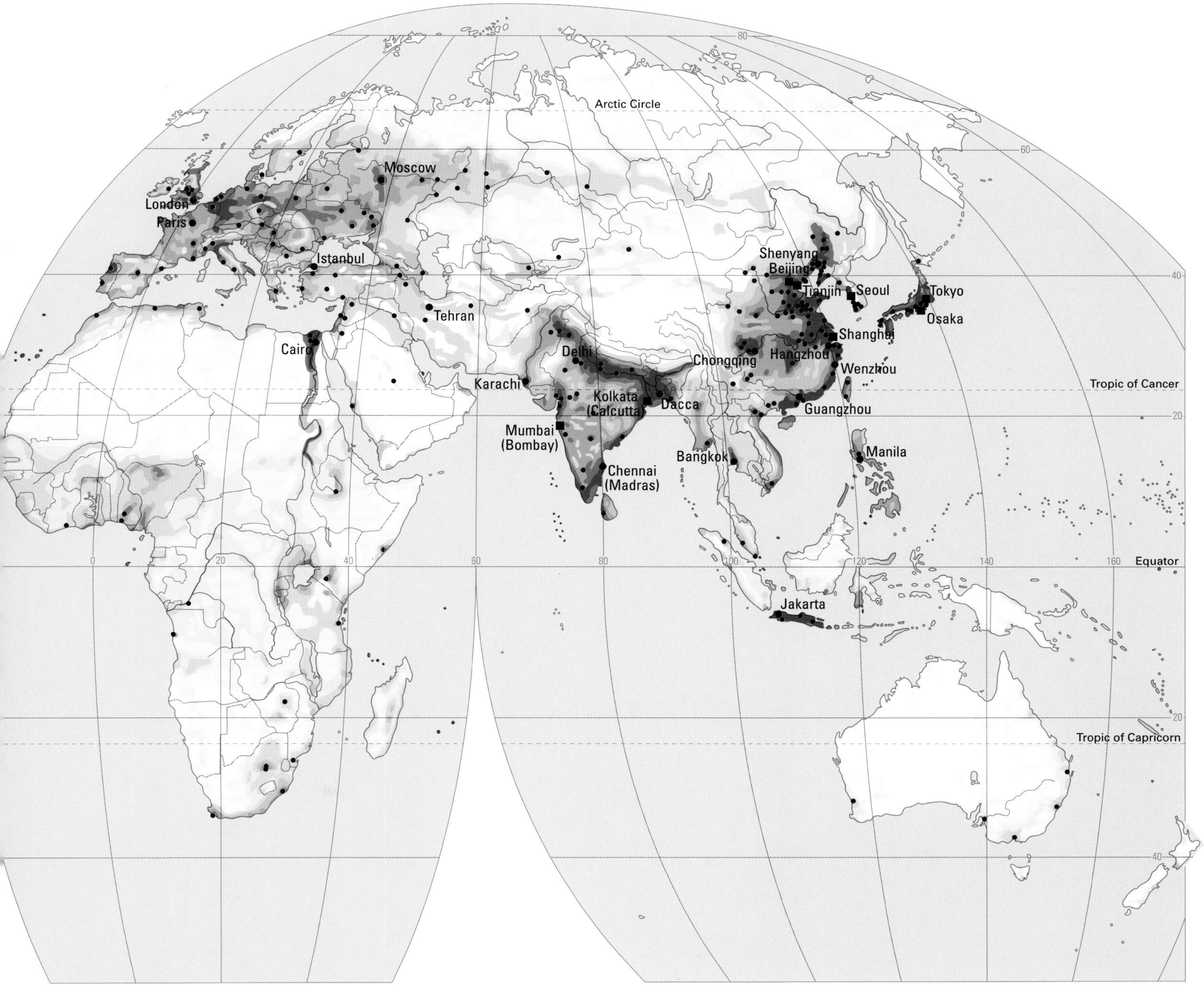

Arctic Circle

Moscow

London
Paris

Istanbul

Tehran

Cairo

Karachi

Delhi

Kolkata
(Calcutta)

Mumbai
(Bombay)

Chennai
(Madras)

Dacca

Bangkok

Shenyang
Beijing
Tianjin   Seoul   Tokyo
                              Osaka
Shanghai
Chongqing   Hangzhou
                 Wenzhou
                 Guangzhou   Manila

Jakarta

80

60

40

20

Tropic of Cancer

20

0   20   40   60   80   100   120   140   160   Equator

20

Tropic of Capricorn

40

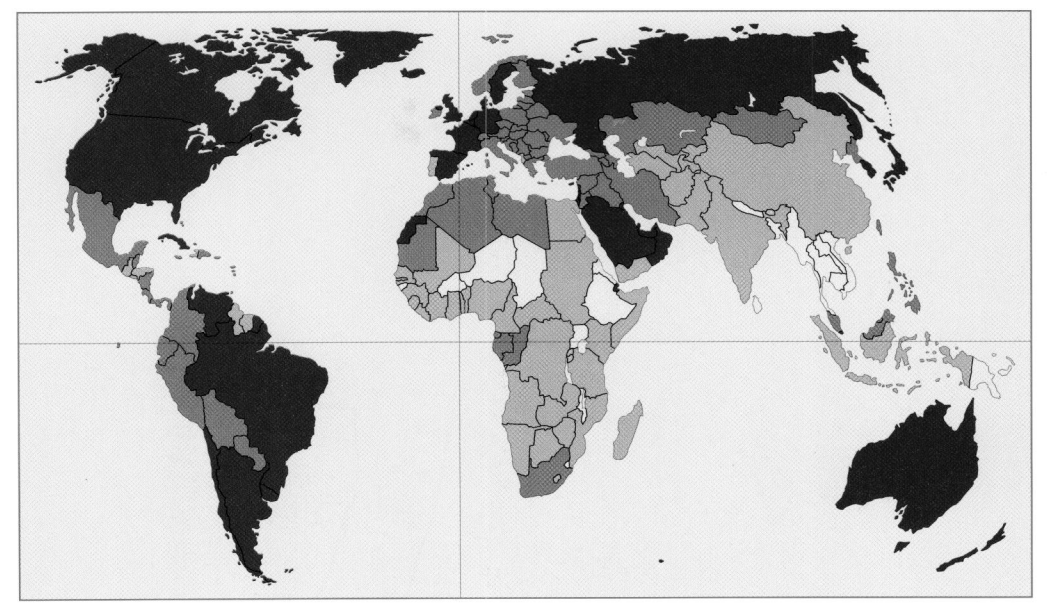

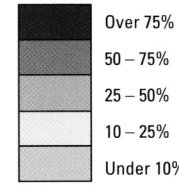

Urban Population

Percentage of total population living in towns and cities (1997)

⬛	Over 75%
◼	50 – 75%
▧	25 – 50%
☐	10 – 25%
▦	Under 10%

Most urbanized		**Least urbanized**	
Singapore	100%	Rwanda	6%
Belgium	97%	Bhutan	8%
Israel	91%	Burundi	8%
Uruguay	91%	Nepal	11%
Netherlands	89%	Swaziland	12%
[UK 89%]			

The Human Family

Predominant Languages

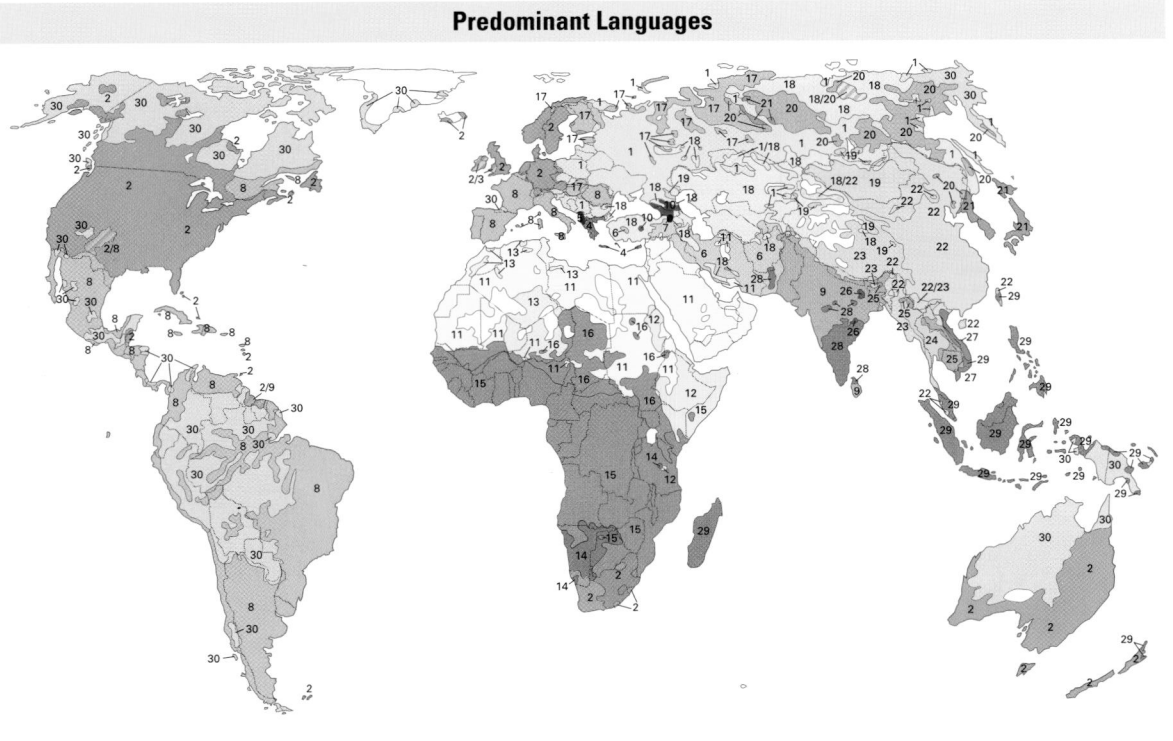

Languages of the World

Language can be classified by ancestry and structure. For example, the Romance and Germanic groups are both derived from an Indo-European language believed to have been spoken 5,000 years ago.

First-language speakers, 1999 (in millions)
Mandarin Chinese 885, Spanish 332, English 322, Bengali 189, Hindi 182, Portuguese 170, Russian 170, Japanese 125, German 98, Wu Chinese 77, Javanese 76, Korean 75, French 72, Vietnamese 68, Yue Chinese 66, Marathi 65, Tamil 63, Turkish 59, Urdu 58.

Official languages (% of total population)
English 27%, Chinese 19%, Hindi 13.5%, Spanish 5.4%, Russian 5.2%, French 4.2%, Arabic 3.3%, Portuguese 3%, Malay 3%, Bengali 2.9%, Japanese 2.3%.

INDO-EUROPEAN FAMILY

1	Balto-Slavic group (incl. Russian, Ukrainian)
2	Germanic group (incl. English, German)
3	Celtic group
4	Greek
5	Albanian
6	Iranian group
7	Armenian
8	Romance group (incl. Spanish, Portuguese, French, Italian)
9	Indo-Aryan group (incl. Hindi, Bengali, Urdu, Punjabi, Marathi)
10	CAUCASIAN FAMILY

AFRO-ASIATIC FAMILY

11	Semitic group (incl. Arabic)
12	Kushitic group
13	Berber group
14	KHOISAN FAMILY
15	NIGER-CONGO FAMILY
16	NILO-SAHARAN FAMILY
17	URALIC FAMILY

ALTAIC FAMILY

18	Turkic group
19	Mongolian group
20	Tungus-Manchu group
21	Japanese and Korean

SINO-TIBETAN FAMILY

22	Sinitic (Chinese) languages
23	Tibetic-Burmic languages
24	TAI FAMILY

AUSTRO-ASIATIC FAMILY

25	Mon-Khmer group
26	Munda group
27	Vietnamese
28	DRAVIDIAN FAMILY (incl. Telugu, Tamil)
29	AUSTRONESIAN FAMILY (incl. Malay-Indonesian)
30	OTHER LANGUAGES

Predominant Religions

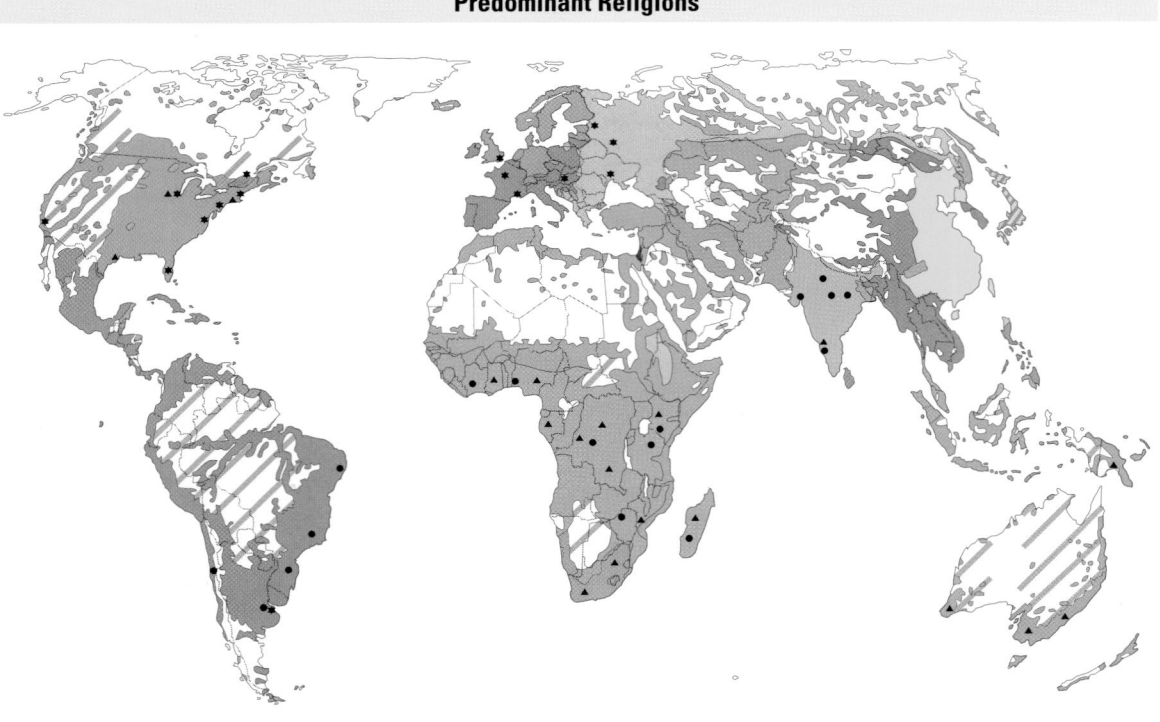

Religious Adherents

Religious adherents in millions (1998)

Christianity	1,980	Buddhist	360
Roman Catholic	1,300	Chinese Trad.	225
Orthodox	240	Indigenous	190
African sects	110	Sikh	23
Pentecostal	105	Yoruba	20
Others	225	Juche	19
Islam	1,300	Spiritism	14
Sunni	940	Judaism	14
Shiite	120	Baha'i	6
Others	240	Jainism	4
Hindu	900	Shinto	4
Secular	850		

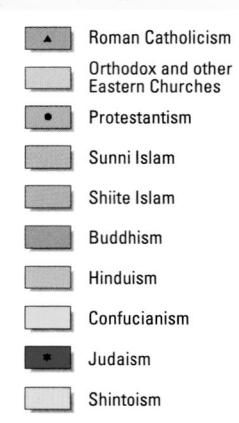

▲	Roman Catholicism
	Orthodox and other Eastern Churches
●	Protestantism
	Sunni Islam
	Shiite Islam
	Buddhism
	Hinduism
	Confucianism
✶	Judaism
	Shintoism
	Tribal Religions

United Nations

Created in 1945 to promote peace and co-operation and based in New York, the United Nations is the world's largest international organization, with 185 members and an annual budget of US $2.6 billion (1996–97). Each member of the General Assembly has one vote, while the permanent members of the 15-nation Security Council – USA, Russia, China, UK and France – hold a veto. The Secretariat is the UN's principal administrative arm. The 54 members of the Economic and Social Council are responsible for economic, social, cultural, educational, health and related matters. The UN has 16 specialized agencies – based in Canada, France, Switzerland and Italy, as well as the USA – which help members in fields such as education (UNESCO), agriculture (FAO), medicine (WHO) and finance (IFC). By the end of 1994, all the original 11 trust territories of the Trusteeship Council had become independent.

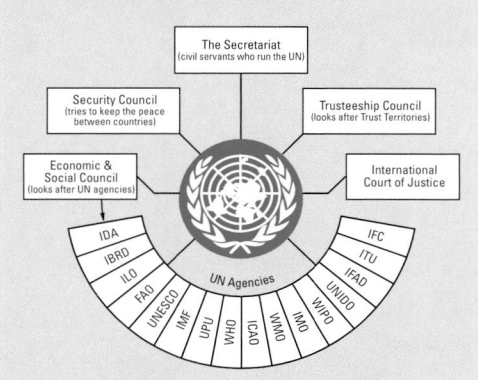

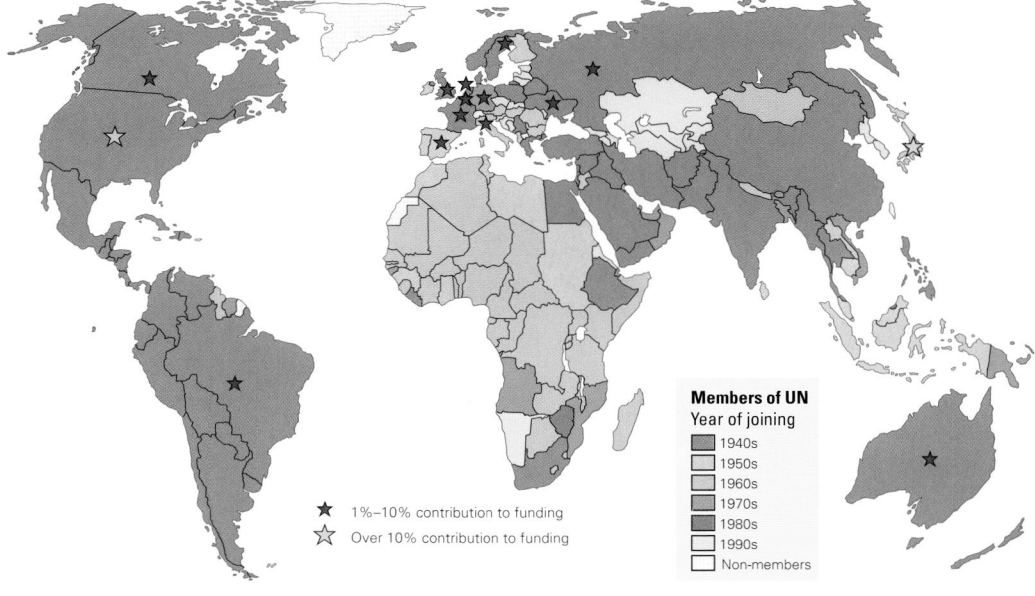

Members of UN
Year of joining
- 1940s
- 1950s
- 1960s
- 1970s
- 1980s
- 1990s
- Non-members

★ 1%–10% contribution to funding
☆ Over 10% contribution to funding

MEMBERSHIP OF THE UN In 1945 there were 51 members; by 2000 membership had increased to 188 following the admission of Kiribati, Nauru and Tonga. There are 4 independent states which are not members of the UN – Switzerland, Taiwan, Tuvalu and the Vatican City. All the successor states of the former USSR had joined by the end of 1992. The official languages of the UN are Chinese, English, French, Russian, Spanish and Arabic.

FUNDING The UN budget for 1996–97 was US $2.6 billion. Contributions are assessed by the members' ability to pay, with the maximum 25% of the total, the minimum 0.01%. Contributions for 1996 were: USA 25.0%, Japan 15.4%, Germany 9.0%, France 6.4%, UK 5.3%, Italy 5.2%, Russia 4.5%, Canada 3.1%, Spain 2.4%, Brazil 1.6%, Netherlands 1.6%, Australia 1.5%, Sweden 1.2%, Ukraine 1.1%, Belgium 1.0%.

International Organizations

EU European Union (evolved from the European Community in 1993). The 15 members – Austria, Belgium, Denmark, Finland, France, Germany, Greece, Ireland, Italy, Luxembourg, Netherlands, Portugal, Spain, Sweden and the UK – aim to integrate economies, co-ordinate social developments and bring about political union. These members of what is now the world's biggest market share agricultural and industrial policies and tariffs on trade. The original body, the European Coal and Steel Community (ECSC), was created in 1951 following the signing of the Treaty of Paris.

EFTA European Free Trade Association (formed in 1960). Portugal left the original 'Seven' in 1989 to join what was then the EC, followed by Austria, Finland and Sweden in 1995. Only 4 members remain: Norway, Iceland, Switzerland and Liechtenstein.

ACP African-Caribbean-Pacific (formed in 1963). Members have economic ties with the EU.

NATO North Atlantic Treaty Organization (formed in 1949). It continues after 1991 despite the winding up of the Warsaw Pact. The Czech Republic, Hungary and Poland were the latest members to join in 1999.

OAS Organization of American States (formed in 1948). It aims to promote social and economic co-operation between developed countries of North America and developing nations of Latin America.

ASEAN Association of South-east Asian Nations (formed in 1967). Cambodia joined in 1999.

OAU Organization of African Unity (formed in 1963). Its 53 members represent over 94% of Africa's population. Arabic, French, Portuguese and English are recognized as working languages.

LAIA Latin American Integration Association (1980). Its aim is to promote freer regional trade.

OECD Organization for Economic Co-operation and Development (formed in 1961). It comprises the 29 major Western free-market economies. Poland, Hungary and South Korea joined in 1996. 'G8' is its 'inner group' comprising Canada, France, Germany, Italy, Japan, Russia, the UK and the USA.

COMMONWEALTH The Commonwealth of Nations evolved from the British Empire; it comprises 16 Queen's realms, 32 republics and 5 indigenous monarchies, giving a total of 53.

OPEC Organization of Petroleum Exporting Countries (formed in 1960). It controls about three-quarters of the world's oil supply. Gabon left the organization in 1996.

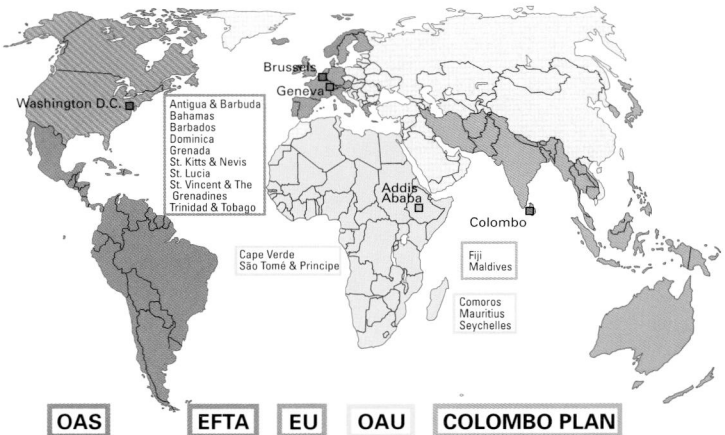

ARAB LEAGUE (formed in 1945). The League's aim is to promote economic, social, political and military co-operation. There are 21 member nations.

COLOMBO PLAN (formed in 1951). Its 26 members aim to promote economic and social development in Asia and the Pacific.

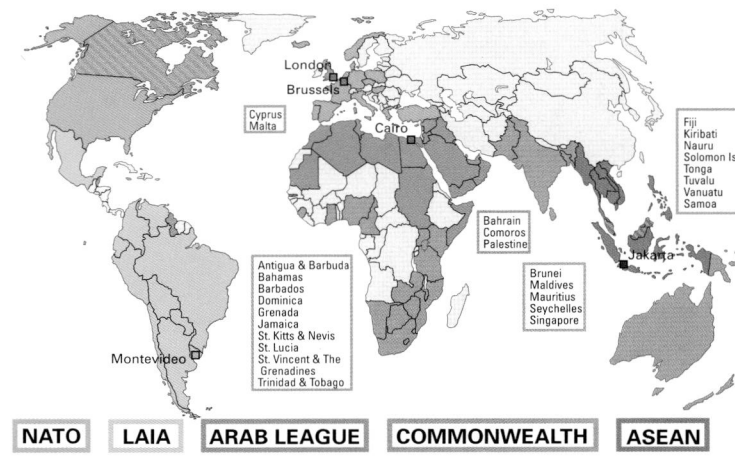

Wealth

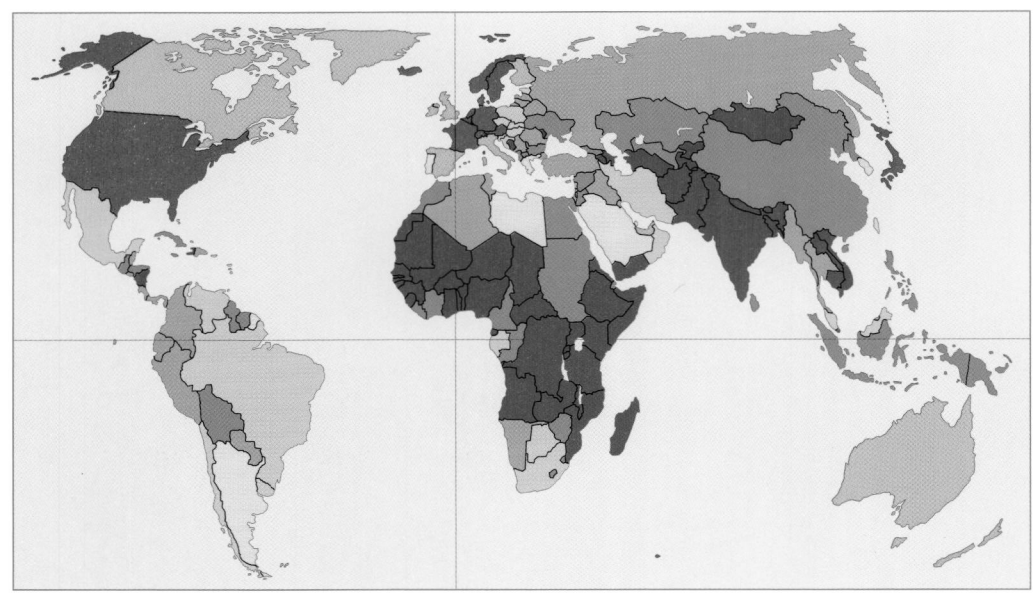
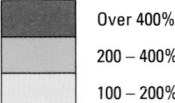
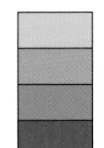

Levels of Income

Gross National Product per capita: the value of total production divided by the population (1997)

- Over 400% of world average
- 200 – 400% of world average
- 100 – 200% of world average

[World average wealth per person US $6,316]

- 50 – 100% of world average
- 25 – 50% of world average
- 10 – 25% of world average
- Under 10% of world average

GNP per capita growth rate (%), selected countries, 1985–94

Thailand	8.2	Brazil	–0.4
Chile	6.9	Zimbabwe	–0.6
Japan	3.2	USA	–1.3
Germany	1.9	UK	–1.4
Australia	1.2	Armenia	–12.9

Wealth Creation

The Gross National Product (GNP) of the world's largest economies, US $ million (1998)

1. USA	7,922,651	23. Saudi Arabia	186,000
2. Japan	4,089,910	24. Denmark	176,374
3. Germany	2,122,673	25. Hong Kong	158,286
4. Italy	1,666,178	26. Norway	152,082
5. France	1,466,014	27. Poland	150,798
6. UK	1,263,777	28. Indonesia	138,501
7. China	928,950	29. Thailand	134,433
8. Botswana	758,043	30. Finland	124,293
9. Canada	612,332	31. Greece	122,880
10. Spain	553,690	32. South Africa	119,001
11. India	421,259	33. Iran	109,645
12. Netherlands	388,682	34. Portugal	106,376
13. Mexico	380,917	35. Colombia	106,090
14. Australia	380,625	36. Israel	95,179
15. South Korea	369,890	37. Singapore	95,095
16. Russia	337,914	38. Venezuela	81,347
17. Argentina	324,084	39. Malaysia	79,848
18. Switzerland	284,808	40. Egypt	79,208
19. Belgium	259,045	41. Philippines	78,896
20. Sweden	226,861	42. Chile	71,294
21. Austria	217,163	43. Ireland	67,491
22. Turkey	200,505	44. Pakistan	63,159

The Wealth Gap

The world's richest and poorest countries, by Gross National Product per capita in US $ (1999 estimates)

1. Liechtenstein	50,000	1. Ethiopia	100
2. Luxembourg	44,640	2. Congo (D. Rep.)	110
3. Switzerland	38,350	3. Burundi	120
4. Bermuda	35,590	4. Sierra Leone	130
5. Norway	32,880	5. Guinea-Bissau	160
6. Japan	32,230	6. Niger	190
7. Denmark	32,030	7. Malawi	190
8. USA	30,600	8. Eritrea	200
9. Singapore	29,610	9. Chad	200
10. Iceland	29,280	10. Nepal	220
11. Austria	25,970	11. Angola	220
12. Germany	25,350	12. Mozambique	230
13. Sweden	25,040	13. Tanzania	240
14. Monaco	25,000	14. Burkina Faso	240
15. Belgium	24,510	15. Mali	240
16. Brunei	24,630	16. Rwanda	250
17. Netherlands	24,320	17. Madagascar	250
18. Finland	23,780	18. Cambodia	260
19. Hong Kong	23,520	19. São Tomé & Principe	270
20. France	23,480	20. Laos	280

GNP per capita is calculated by dividing a country's Gross National Product by its total population.

Continental Shares

Shares of population and of wealth (GNP) by continent

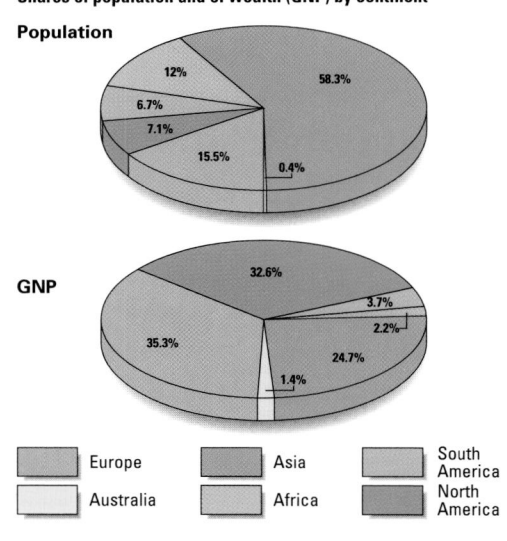

Population

GNP

- Europe
- Australia
- Asia
- Africa
- South America
- North America

Inflation

Average annual rate of inflation (1998–99)

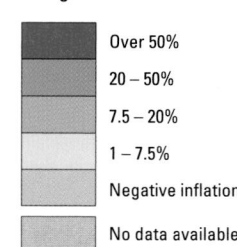

- Over 50%
- 20 – 50%
- 7.5 – 20%
- 1 – 7.5%
- Negative inflation
- No data available

Highest average inflation		Lowest average inflation	
Belarus	295%	Azerbaijan	–6.8%
Angola	270%	Nauru	–3.6%
Surinam	170%	Argentina	–2.0%
Laos	140%	China	–1.3%
Iraq	135%	Saudi Arabia	–1.2%

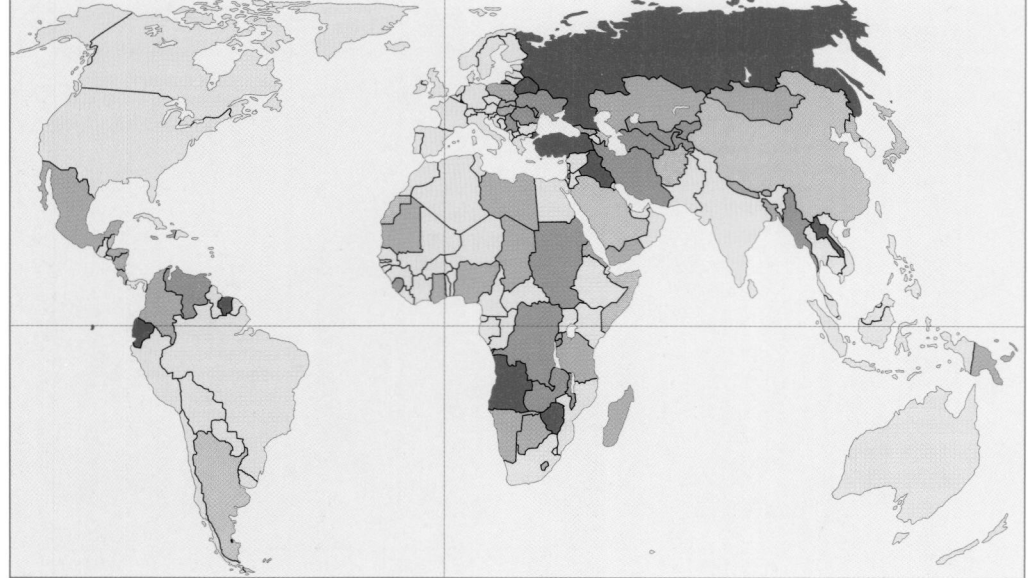

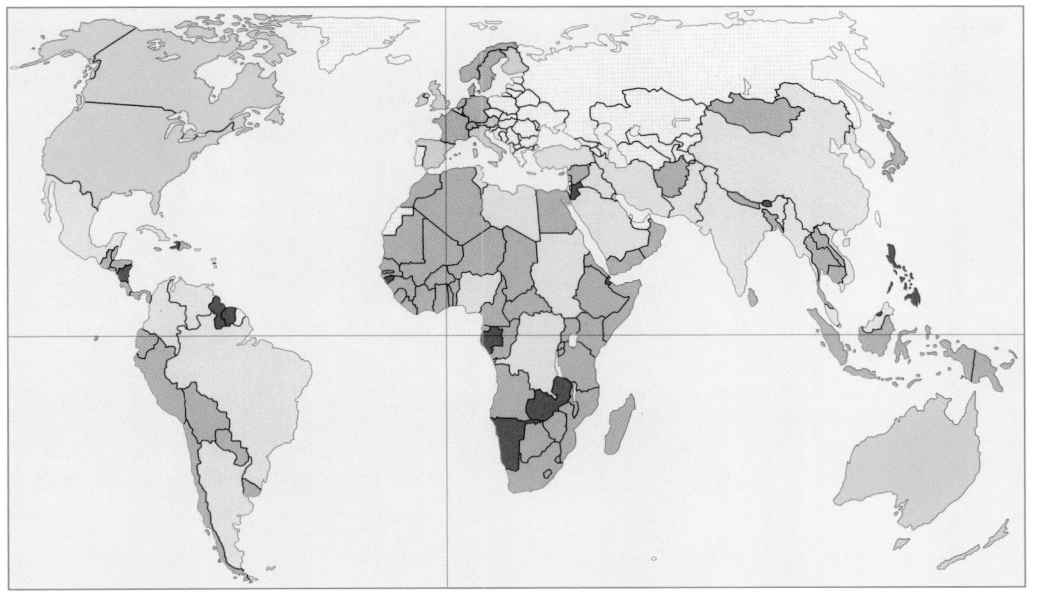

Aid provided or received, divided by the total population, in US $ (1995)

Over $100 per person
$10 – $100 per person
$0 – $10 per person — Providers
No aid given or received
$0 – $10 per person — Receivers
$10 – $100 per person
Over $100 per person

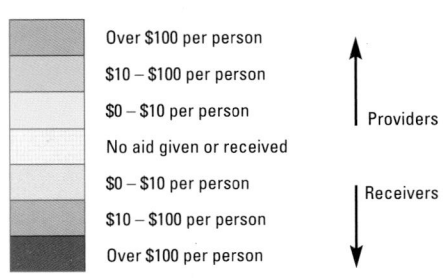

Top 5 providers per capita (1994)		Top 5 receivers per capita (1994)	
France	$279	São Tomé & P.	$378
Denmark	$260	Cape Verde	$314
Norway	$247	Djibouti	$235
Sweden	$201	Surinam	$198
Germany	$166	Mauritania	$153

Debt and Aid

International debtors and the aid they receive (1996)

Although aid grants make a vital contribution to many of the world's poorer countries, they are usually dwarfed by the burden of debt that the developing economies are expected to repay. In 1992, they had to pay US $160,000 million in debt service charges alone – more than two and a half times the amount of Official Development Assistance (ODA) the developing countries were receiving, and US $60,000 million more than total private flows of aid in the same year. In 1990, the debts of Mozambique, one of the world's poorest countries, were estimated to be 75 times its entire earnings from exports.

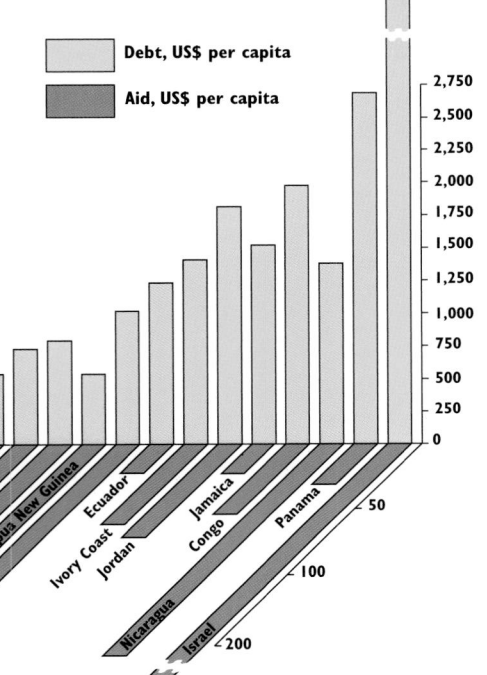

Debt, US$ per capita
Aid, US$ per capita

$5,014

$391

Distribution of Spending

Percentage share of household spending, selected countries

Food
Clothing
Energy & Housing
Medicine & Education
Transport
Other

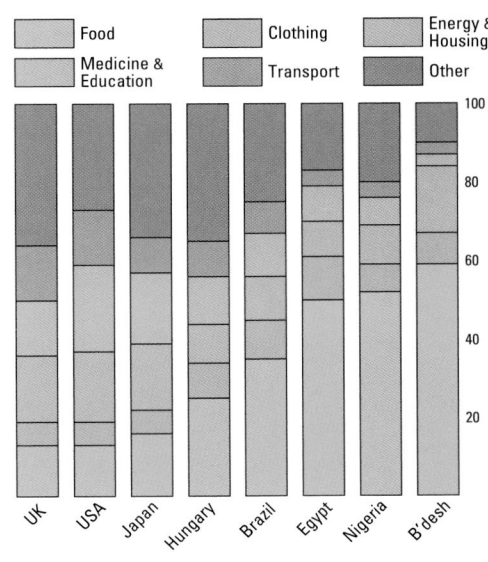

UK USA Japan Hungary Brazil Egypt Nigeria B'desh

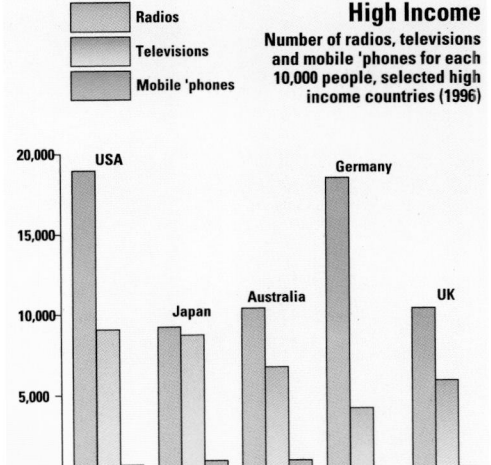

High Income

Radios
Televisions
Mobile 'phones

Number of radios, televisions and mobile 'phones for each 10,000 people, selected high income countries (1996)

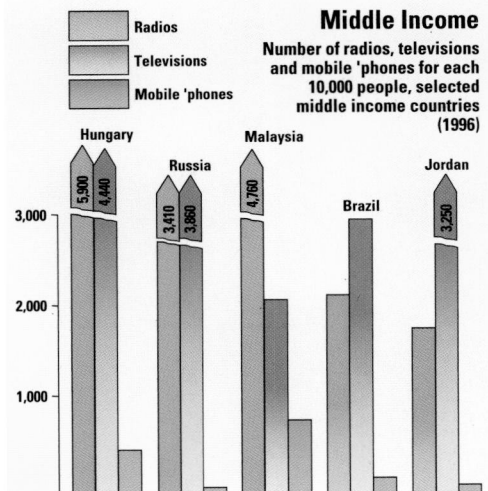

Middle Income

Radios
Televisions
Mobile 'phones

Number of radios, televisions and mobile 'phones for each 10,000 people, selected middle income countries (1996)

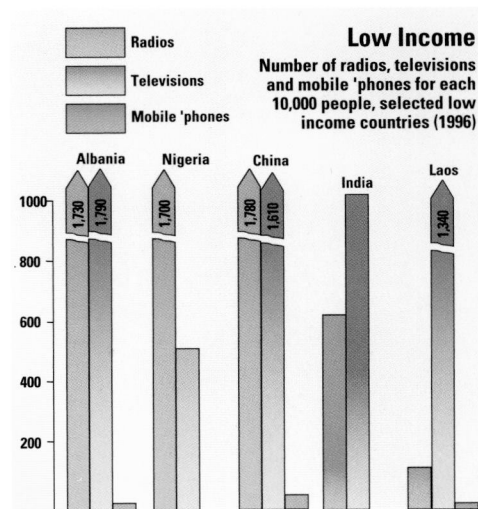

Low Income

Radios
Televisions
Mobile 'phones

Number of radios, televisions and mobile 'phones for each 10,000 people, selected low income countries (1996)

Quality of Life

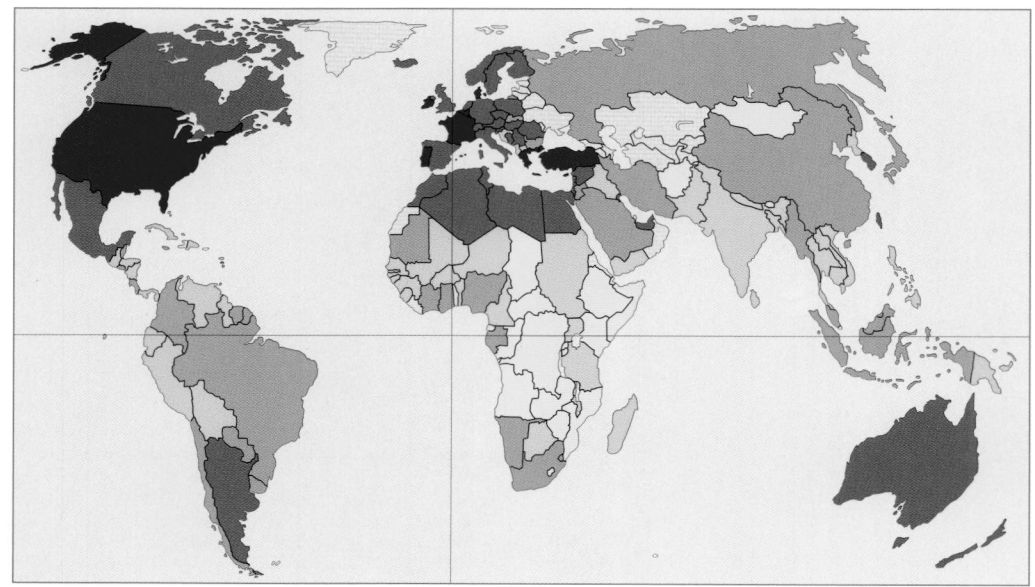

Daily Food Consumption

Average daily food intake in calories per person (1995)

- Over 3,500 calories per person
- 3,000 – 3,500 calories per person
- 2,500 – 3,000 calories per person
- 2,000 – 2,500 calories per person
- Under 2,000 calories per person
- No available data

Top 5 countries		Bottom 5 countries	
Cyprus	3,708 cal.	Congo (D.Rep.)	1,879 cal.
Denmark	3,704 cal.	Djibouti	1,831 cal.
Portugal	3,639 cal.	Togo	1,754 cal.
Ireland	3,638 cal.	Burundi	1,749 cal.
USA	3,603 cal.	Mozambique	1,678 cal.

[UK 3,149 calories]

Hospital Capacity

Hospital beds available for each 1,000 people (1996)

Highest capacity		Lowest capacity	
Switzerland	20.8	Benin	0.2
Japan	16.2	Nepal	0.2
Tajikistan	16.0	Afghanistan	0.3
Norway	13.5	Bangladesh	0.3
Belarus	12.4	Ethiopia	0.3
Kazakstan	12.2	Mali	0.4
Moldova	12.2	Burkina Faso	0.5
Ukraine	12.2	Niger	0.5
Latvia	11.9	Guinea	0.6
Russia	11.8	India	0.6

[UK 4.9] [USA 4.2]

Although the ratio of people to hospital beds gives a good approximation of a country's health provision, it is not an absolute indicator. Raw numbers may mask inefficiency and other weaknesses: the high availability of beds in Kazakstan, for example, has not prevented infant mortality rates over three times as high as in the United Kingdom and the United States.

Life Expectancy

Years of life expectancy at birth, selected countries (1997)

The chart shows combined data for both sexes. On average, women live longer than men worldwide, even in developing countries with high maternal mortality rates. Overall, life expectancy is steadily rising, though the difference between rich and poor nations remains dramatic.

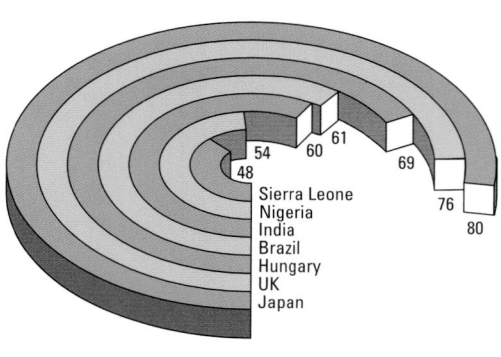

Sierra Leone 48
Nigeria 54
India 60
Brazil 61
Hungary 69
UK 76
Japan 80

Causes of Death

Causes of death for selected countries by % (1992–94)

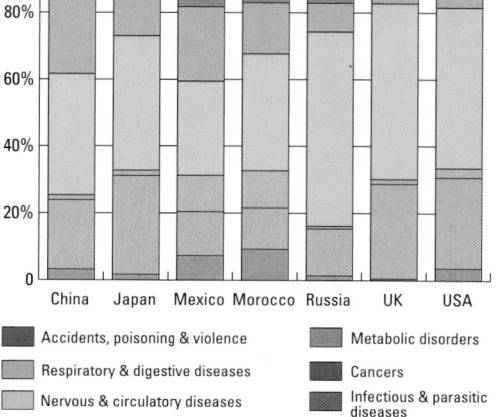

China   Japan   Mexico   Morocco   Russia   UK   USA

- Accidents, poisoning & violence
- Respiratory & digestive diseases
- Nervous & circulatory diseases
- Metabolic disorders
- Cancers
- Infectious & parasitic diseases

Child Mortality

Number of babies who will die under the age of one, per 1,000 births (average 1990–95)

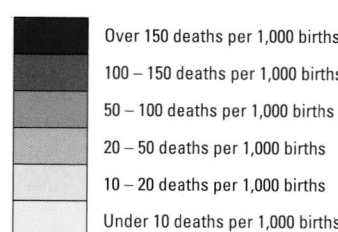

- Over 150 deaths per 1,000 births
- 100 – 150 deaths per 1,000 births
- 50 – 100 deaths per 1,000 births
- 20 – 50 deaths per 1,000 births
- 10 – 20 deaths per 1,000 births
- Under 10 deaths per 1,000 births

Highest child mortality		Lowest child mortality	
Afghanistan	162	Hong Kong	6
Mali	159	Denmark	6
Sierra Leone	143	Japan	5
Guinea-Bissau	140	Iceland	5
Malawi	138	Finland	5

[UK 8 deaths]

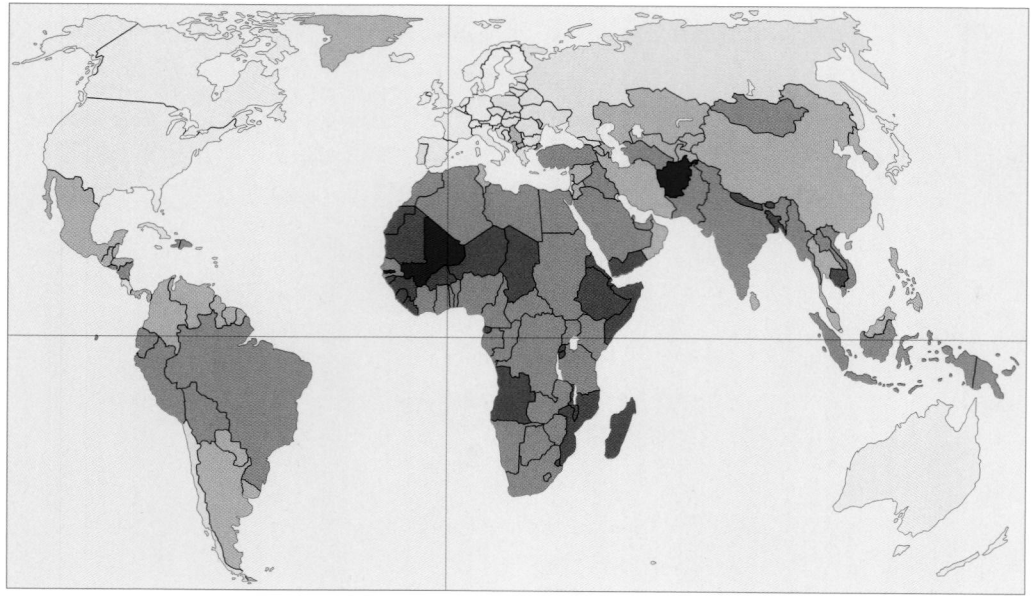

Illiteracy

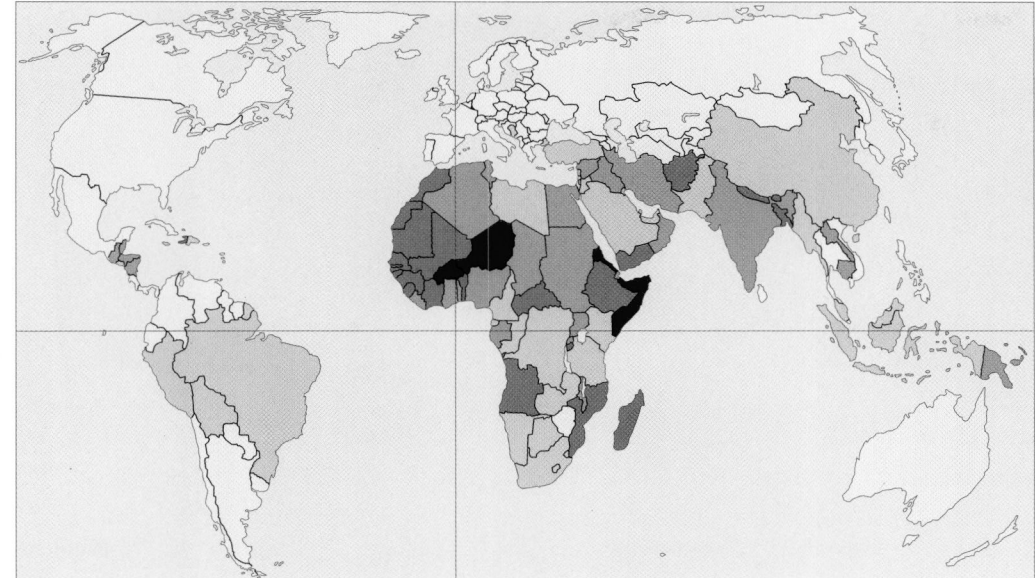

Percentage of the total population unable to read or write (1996)

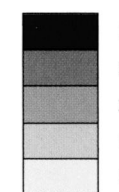

- Over 75% of population illiterate
- 50 – 75% of population illiterate
- 25 – 50% of population illiterate
- 10 – 25% of population illiterate
- Under 10% of population illiterate

Educational expenditure per person (latest available year)

Top 5 countries		Bottom 5 countries	
Sweden	$997	Chad	$2
Qatar	$989	Bangladesh	$3
Canada	$983	Ethiopia	$3
Norway	$971	Nepal	$4
Switzerland	$796	Somalia	$4

[UK $447]

Fertility and Education

Fertility rates compared with female education, selected countries (1992–95)

Percentage of females aged 12–17 in secondary education

Fertility rate: average number of children borne per woman

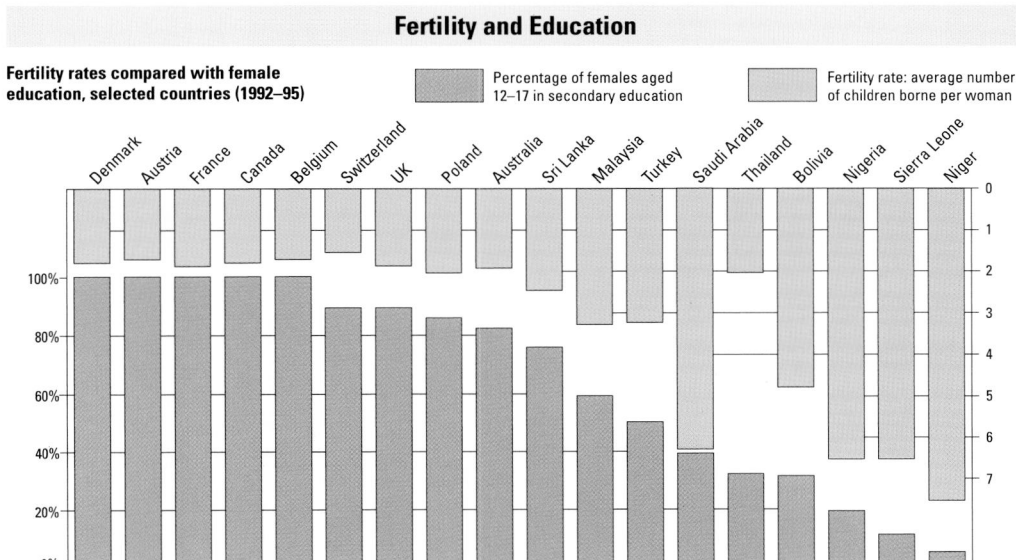

Living Standards

At first sight, most international contrasts in living standards are swamped by differences in wealth. The rich not only have more money, they have more of everything, including years of life. Those with only a little money are obliged to spend most of it on food and clothing, the basic maintenance costs of their existence; air travel and tourism are unlikely to feature on their expenditure lists. However, poverty and wealth are both relative: slum dwellers living on social security payments in an affluent industrial country have far more resources at their disposal than an average African peasant, but feel their own poverty nonetheless. A middle-class Indian lawyer cannot command a fraction of the earnings of a counterpart living in New York, London or Rome; nevertheless, he rightly sees himself as prosperous.

The rich not only live longer, on average, than the poor, they also die from different causes. Infectious and parasitic diseases, all but eliminated in the developed world, remain a scourge in the developing nations. On the other hand, more than two-thirds of the populations of OECD nations eventually succumb to cancer or circulatory disease.

Women in the Workforce

Women in paid employment as a percentage of the total workforce (1997)

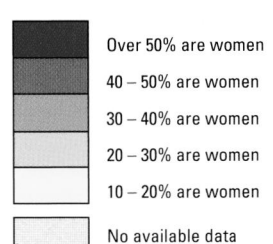

- Over 50% are women
- 40 – 50% are women
- 30 – 40% are women
- 20 – 30% are women
- 10 – 20% are women
- No available data

Most women in the workforce		Fewest women in the workforce	
Rwanda	56%	Oman	14%
Cambodia	53%	Saudi Arabia	13%
Ghana	51%	UAE	13%
Ukraine	50%	Qatar	13%
Vietnam	49%	Pakistan	13%

[USA 45%] [UK 44%]

Energy

Production

[Each square represents 1% of world energy production]

North America   Europe   CIS

Middle East

Japan

Africa   Asia

South America   Australasia

Consumption

[Each square represents 1% of world energy consumption]

North America   Europe   CIS

Middle East

Africa   Asia

Japan

South America   Australasia

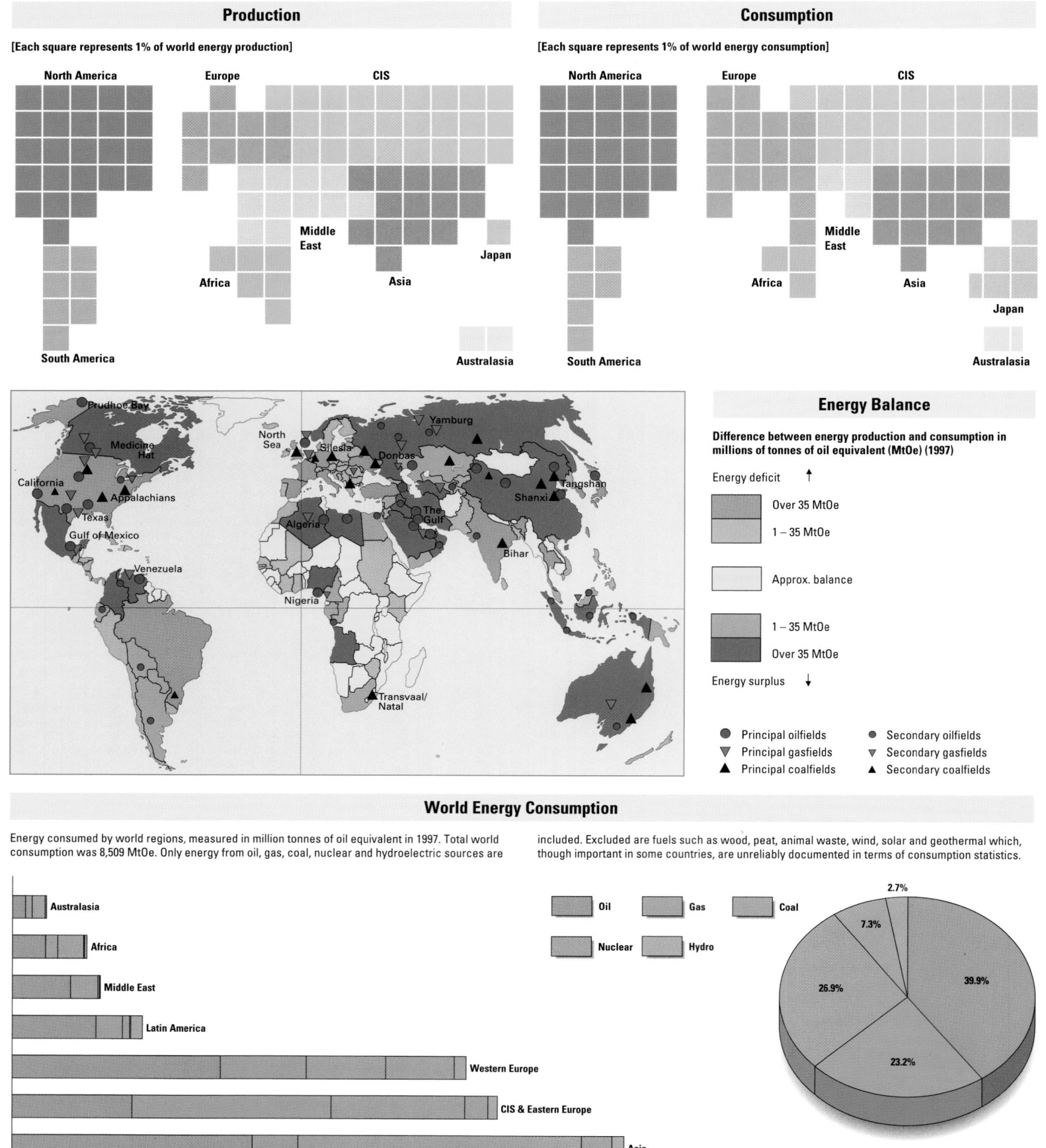

Prudhoe Bay
Medicine Hat
California
Appalachians
Texas
Gulf of Mexico
Venezuela
North Sea
Yamburg
Silesia
Donbas
Algeria
The Gulf
Shanxi
Tangshan
Bihar
Nigeria
Transvaal/Natal

Energy Balance

Difference between energy production and consumption in millions of tonnes of oil equivalent (MtOe) (1997)

Energy deficit ↑

Over 35 MtOe

1 – 35 MtOe

Approx. balance

1 – 35 MtOe

Over 35 MtOe

Energy surplus ↓

● Principal oilfields   ● Secondary oilfields
▽ Principal gasfields   ▽ Secondary gasfields
▲ Principal coalfields   ▲ Secondary coalfields

World Energy Consumption

Energy consumed by world regions, measured in million tonnes of oil equivalent in 1997. Total world consumption was 8,509 MtOe. Only energy from oil, gas, coal, nuclear and hydroelectric sources are included. Excluded are fuels such as wood, peat, animal waste, wind, solar and geothermal which, though important in some countries, are unreliably documented in terms of consumption statistics.

Australasia
Africa
Middle East
Latin America
Western Europe
CIS & Eastern Europe
Asia
North America

5   10   15   20   25

Oil   Gas   Coal
Nuclear   Hydro

2.7%
7.3%
39.9%
26.9%
23.2%

Energy

Energy is used to keep us warm or cool, fuel our industries and our transport systems, and even feed us; high-intensity agriculture, with its use of fertilizers, pesticides and machinery, is heavily energy-dependent. Although we live in a high-energy society, there are vast discrepancies between rich and poor; for example, a North American consumes 13 times as much energy as a Chinese person. But even developing nations have more power at their disposal than was imaginable a century ago.

The distribution of energy supplies, most importantly fossil fuels (coal, oil and natural gas), is very uneven. In addition, the diagrams and map opposite show that the largest producers of energy are not necessarily the largest consumers. The movement of energy supplies around the world is therefore an important component of international trade. In 1995, total world movements in oil amounted to 1,815 million tonnes.

As the finite reserves of fossil fuels are depleted, renewable energy sources, such as solar, hydro-thermal, wind, tidal and biomass, will become increasingly important around the world.

Nuclear Power

Percentage of nuclear in total domestic electricity generation, leading nations (1998)

1.	France	77%
2.	Sweden	47%
3.	Ukraine	44%
4.	Korea, South	38%
5.	Japan	32%
6.	Germany	29%
7.	UK	28%
8.	USA	19%
9.	Canada	13%
10.	Russia	13%

Although the 1980s were a bad time for the nuclear power industry (major projects ran over budget, and fears of long-term environmental damage were heavily reinforced by the 1986 disaster at Chernobyl), the industry picked up in the early 1990s. However, whilst the number of reactors is still increasing, orders for new plants have shrunk. This is partly due to the increasingly difficult task of disposing of nuclear waste.

Hydroelectricity

Percentage of hydroelectricity in total domestic electricity generation, leading nations (1998)

1.	Norway	99.4%
2.	Brazil	90.6%
3.	Canada	59.1%
4.	Sweden	47.0%
5.	Russia	19.3%
6.	China	17.4%
7.	India	16.8%
8.	France	12.9%
9.	Japan	9.8%
10.	USA	8.4%

Countries heavily reliant on hydroelectricity are usually small and non-industrial: a high proportion of hydroelectric power more often reflects a modest energy budget than vast hydroelectric resources. The USA, for instance, produces only 8.4% of power requirements from hydroelectricity; yet that 8.4% amounts to more than three times the hydropower generated by all of Africa.

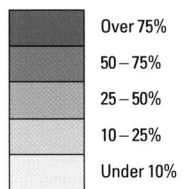

Fuel Exports

Fuels as a percentage of total value of exports (1996)

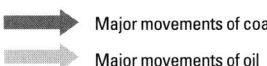

- Over 75%
- 50 – 75%
- 25 – 50%
- 10 – 25%
- Under 10%

Direction of Trade

- Major movements of coal
- Major movements of oil

Conversion Rates

1 barrel = 0.136 tonnes or 159 litres or 35 Imperial gallons or 42 US gallons

1 tonne = 7.33 barrels or 1,185 litres or 256 Imperial gallons or 261 US gallons

1 tonne oil = 1.5 tonnes hard coal or 3.0 tonnes lignite or 12,000 kWh

1 Imperial gallon = 1.201 US gallons or 4.546 litres or 277.4 cubic inches

Measurements
For historical reasons, oil is traded in 'barrels'. The weight and volume equivalents (shown right) are all based on average-density 'Arabian light' crude oil.

The energy equivalents given for a tonne of oil are also somewhat imprecise: oil and coal of different qualities will have varying energy contents, a fact usually reflected in their price on world markets.

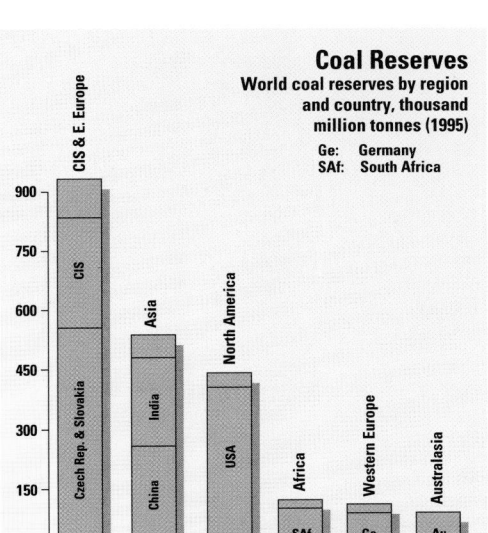

Coal Reserves
World coal reserves by region and country, thousand million tonnes (1995)

Ge: Germany
SAf: South Africa

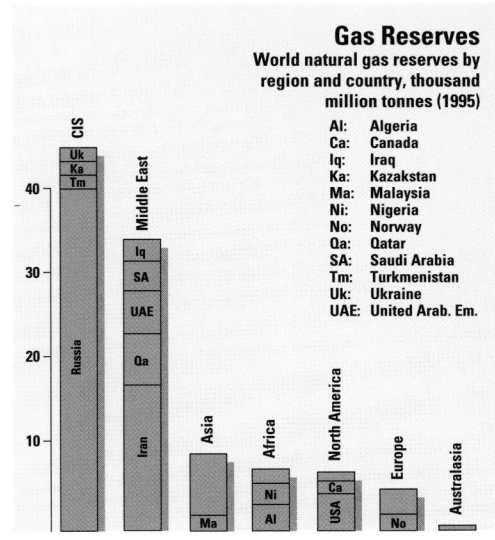

Gas Reserves
World natural gas reserves by region and country, thousand million tonnes (1995)

Al: Algeria
Ca: Canada
Iq: Iraq
Ka: Kazakstan
Ma: Malaysia
Ni: Nigeria
No: Norway
Qa: Qatar
SA: Saudi Arabia
Tm: Turkmenistan
Uk: Ukraine
UAE: United Arab. Em.

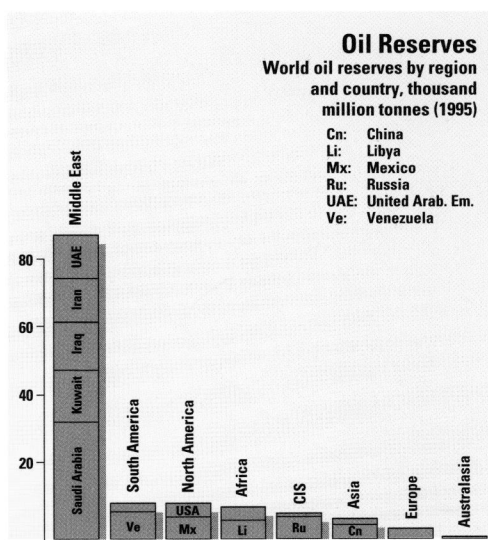

Oil Reserves
World oil reserves by region and country, thousand million tonnes (1995)

Cn: China
Li: Libya
Mx: Mexico
Ru: Russia
UAE: United Arab. Em.
Ve: Venezuela

Production

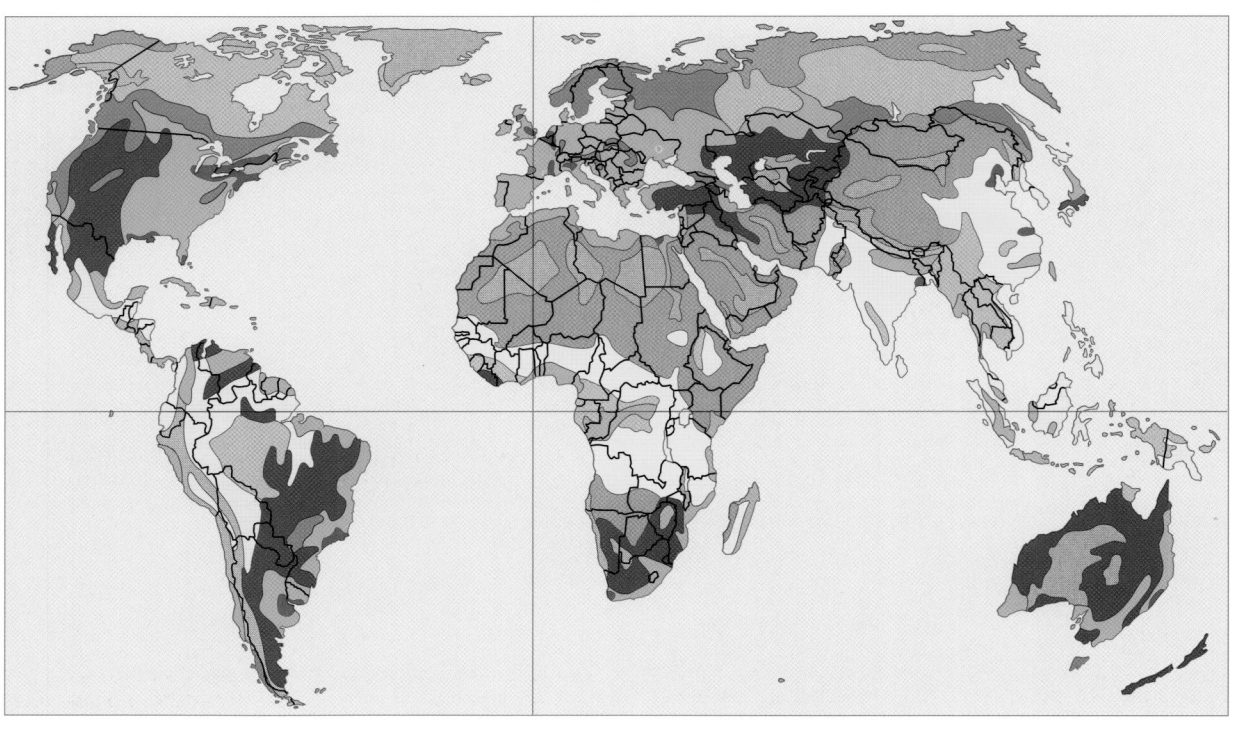

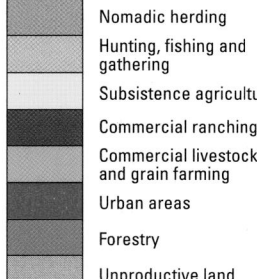

Agriculture

Predominant type of farming or land use.

- Nomadic herding
- Hunting, fishing and gathering
- Subsistence agriculture
- Commercial ranching
- Commercial livestock and grain farming
- Urban areas
- Forestry
- Unproductive land

The development of agriculture has transformed human existence more than any other. The whole business of farming is constantly developing: due mainly to the new varieties of rice and wheat, world grain production has increased by over 70% since 1965. New machinery and modern agricultural techniques enable relatively few farmers to produce enough food for the world's 6 billion or so people.

Staple Crops

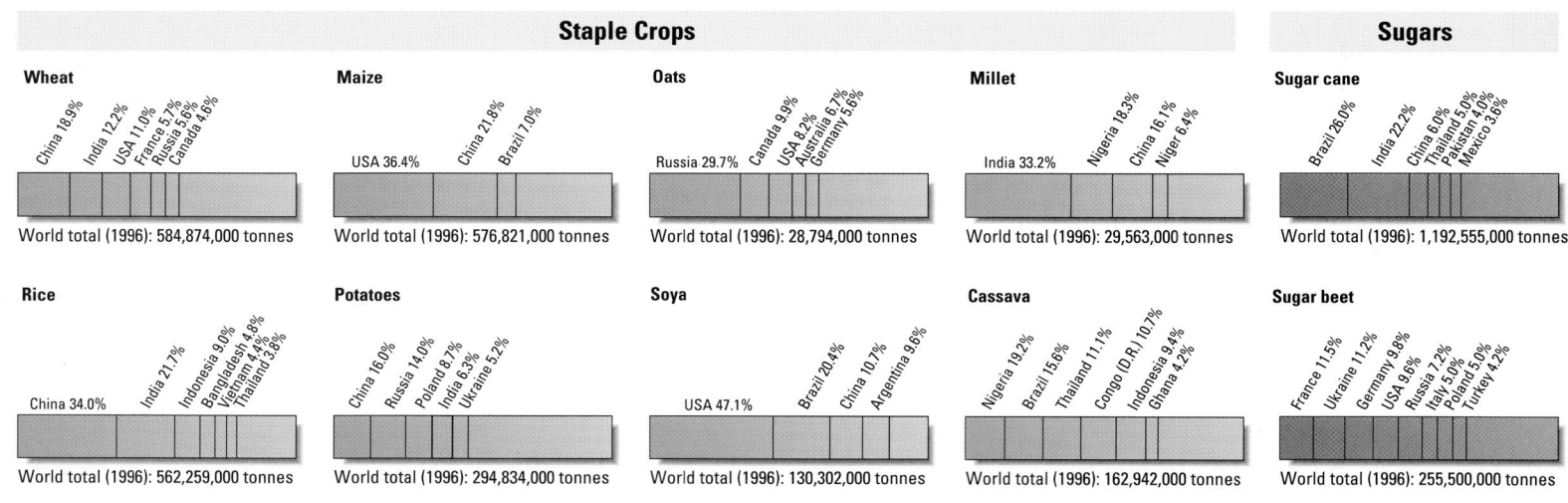

Wheat

China 18.9%
India 12.2%
USA 11.0%
France 5.7%
Russia 5.5%
Canada 4.6%

World total (1996): 584,874,000 tonnes

Maize

USA 36.4%
China 21.8%
Brazil 7.0%

World total (1996): 576,821,000 tonnes

Oats

Russia 29.7%
Canada 9.9%
USA 8.2%
Australia 6.7%
Germany 5.6%

World total (1996): 28,794,000 tonnes

Millet

India 33.2%
Nigeria 18.3%
China 16.1%
Niger 6.4%

World total (1996): 29,563,000 tonnes

Rice

China 34.0%
India 21.7%
Indonesia 9.0%
Bangladesh 4.8%
Vietnam 4.4%
Thailand 3.8%

World total (1996): 562,259,000 tonnes

Potatoes

China 16.0%
Russia 14.0%
Poland 8.7%
India 6.3%
Ukraine 5.2%

World total (1996): 294,834,000 tonnes

Soya

USA 47.1%
Brazil 20.4%
China 10.7%
Argentina 9.6%

World total (1996): 130,302,000 tonnes

Cassava

Nigeria 19.2%
Brazil 15.6%
Thailand 11.1%
Congo (D.R.) 10.7%
Indonesia 9.4%
Ghana 4.2%

World total (1996): 162,942,000 tonnes

Sugars

Sugar cane

Brazil 26.0%
India 22.2%
China 6.0%
Thailand 5.0%
Pakistan 4.0%
Mexico 3.6%

World total (1996): 1,192,555,000 tonnes

Sugar beet

France 11.5%
Ukraine 11.2%
Germany 9.8%
USA 9.0%
Russia 7.2%
Italy 5.0%
Poland 5.0%
Turkey 4.2%

World total (1996): 255,500,000 tonnes

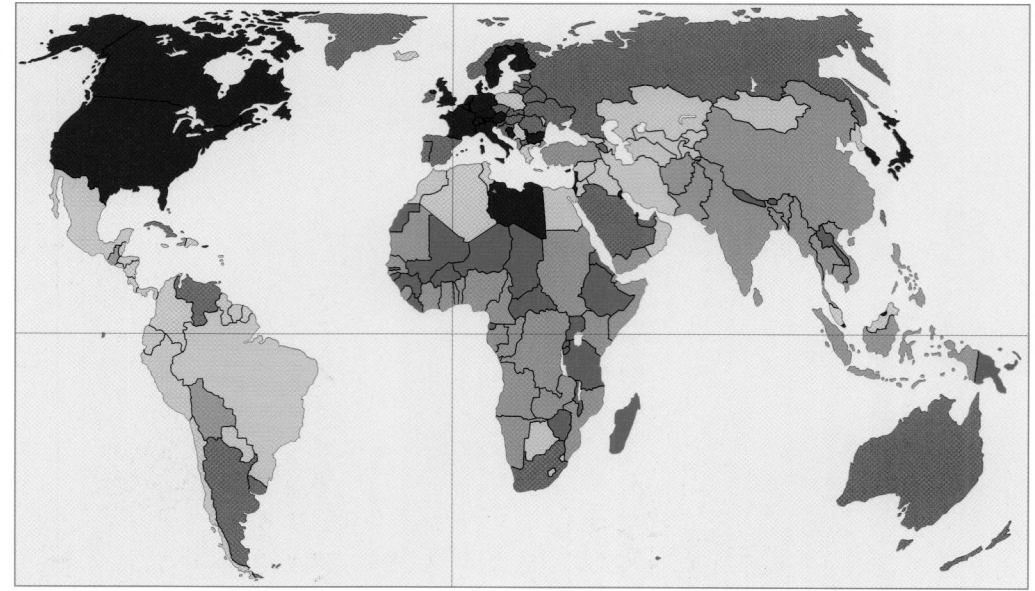

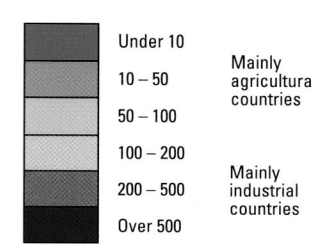

Employment

The number of workers employed in manufacturing for every 100 workers engaged in agriculture (1997)

- Under 10
- 10 – 50   Mainly agricultural countries
- 50 – 100
- 100 – 200
- 200 – 500   Mainly industrial countries
- Over 500

Selected countries (latest available year)

Singapore	8,860	Germany	800
Hong Kong	3,532	Kuwait	767
UK	1,270	Bahrain	660
Belgium	820	USA	657
Yugoslavia	809	Israel	633

CARTOGRAPHY BY PHILIP'S. COPYRIGHT GEORGE PHILIP LTD

*Figures for aluminium are for refined metal; all other figures refer to ore production.

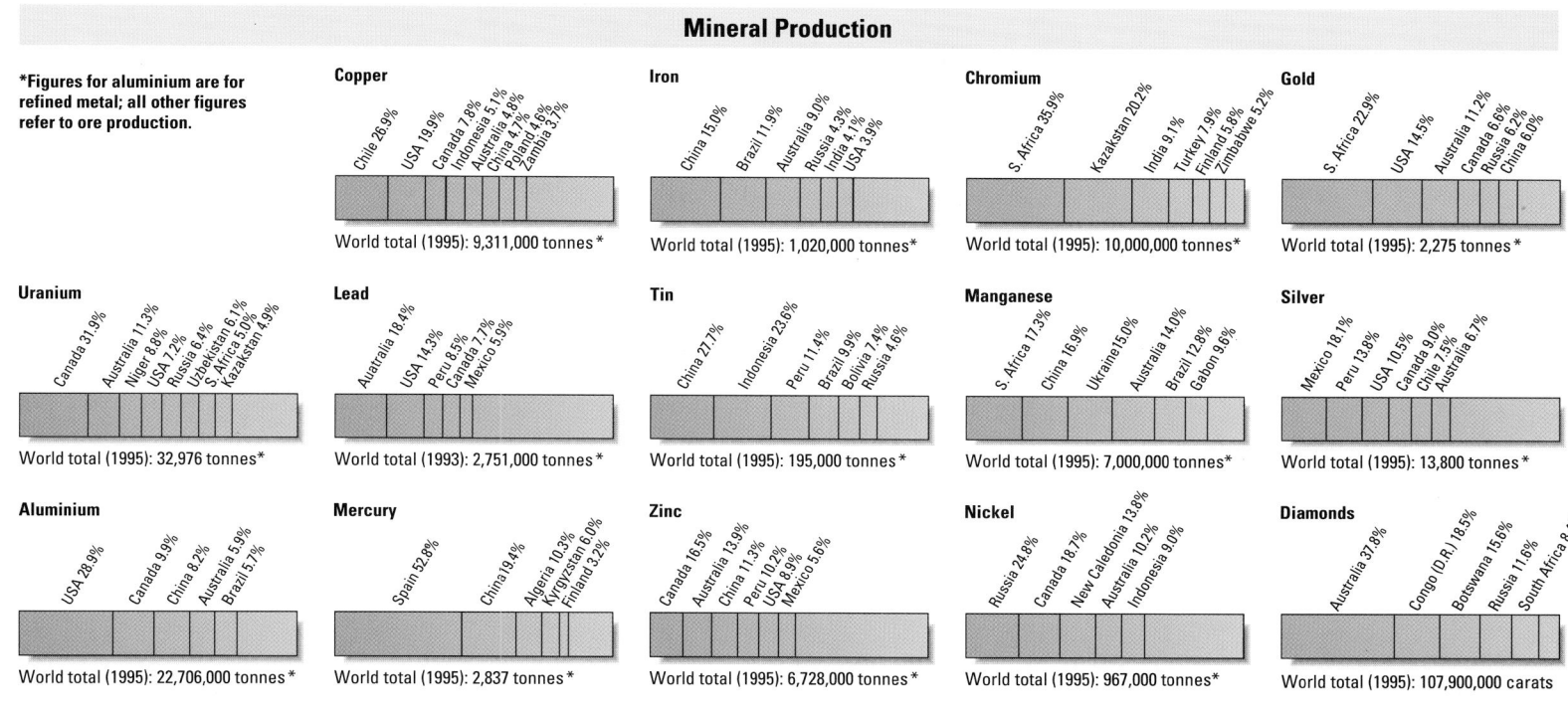

Copper
Chile 26.9% | USA 19.9% | Canada 7.8% | Indonesia 5.1% | Australia 4.8% | China 4.7% | Poland 4.6% | Zambia 3.7%
World total (1995): 9,311,000 tonnes *

Iron
China 15.0% | Brazil 11.9% | Australia 9.0% | Russia 4.3% | India 4.1% | USA 3.5%
World total (1995): 1,020,000 tonnes*

Chromium
S. Africa 35.9% | Kazakstan 20.2% | India 9.1% | Turkey 7.9% | Finland 5.8% | Zimbabwe 5.2%
World total (1995): 10,000,000 tonnes*

Gold
S. Africa 22.9% | USA 14.5% | Australia 11.2% | Canada 6.6% | Russia 6.2% | China 6.0%
World total (1995): 2,275 tonnes *

Uranium
Canada 31.9% | Australia 11.3% | Niger 8.8% | USA 7.2% | Russia 6.4% | Uzbekistan 6.1% | S. Africa 5.0% | Kazakstan 4.9%
World total (1995): 32,976 tonnes*

Lead
Australia 18.4% | USA 14.3% | Peru 8.5% | Canada 7.7% | Mexico 5.9%
World total (1993): 2,751,000 tonnes *

Tin
China 27.7% | Indonesia 23.6% | Peru 11.4% | Brazil 9.9% | Bolivia 7.4% | Russia 4.6%
World total (1995): 195,000 tonnes *

Manganese
S. Africa 17.3% | China 16.9% | Ukraine 15.0% | Australia 14.0% | Brazil 12.8% | Gabon 9.6%
World total (1995): 7,000,000 tonnes*

Silver
Mexico 18.1% | Peru 13.8% | USA 10.5% | Canada 9.0% | Chile 7.5% | Australia 6.7%
World total (1995): 13,800 tonnes *

Aluminium
USA 28.9% | Canada 9.9% | China 8.2% | Australia 5.9% | Brazil 5.7%
World total (1995): 22,706,000 tonnes *

Mercury
Spain 52.8% | China 19.4% | Algeria 10.3% | Kyrgyzstan 6.0% | Finland 3.2%
World total (1995): 2,837 tonnes *

Zinc
Canada 16.5% | Australia 13.9% | China 11.3% | Peru 10.2% | USA 8.9% | Mexico 5.6%
World total (1995): 6,728,000 tonnes *

Nickel
Russia 24.8% | Canada 18.7% | New Caledonia 13.8% | Australia 10.2% | Indonesia 9.0%
World total (1995): 967,000 tonnes*

Diamonds
Australia 37.8% | Congo (D.R.) 18.5% | Botswana 15.6% | Russia 11.6% | South Africa 8.4%
World total (1995): 107,900,000 carats

Mineral Distribution

The map shows the richest sources of the most important minerals. Major mineral locations are named.

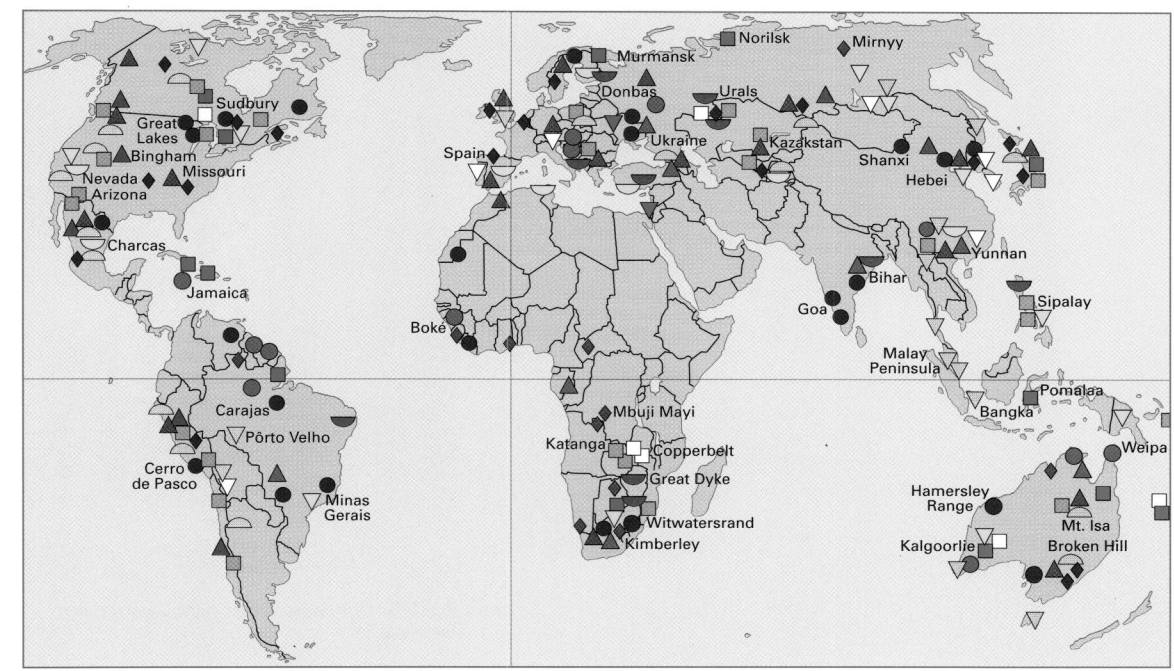

▽ Gold
◠ Silver
◆ Diamonds
▽ Tungsten
● Iron Ore
■ Nickel
◡ Chrome
▲ Manganese
□ Cobalt
▲ Molybdenum
▪ Copper
▲ Lead
● Bauxite
▽ Tin
◆ Zinc
◡ Mercury

The map does not show undersea deposits, most of which are considered inaccessible.

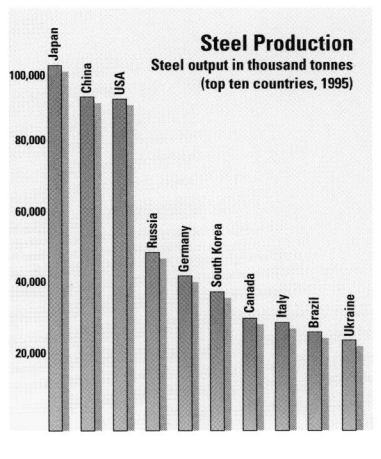

Steel Production
Steel output in thousand tonnes (top ten countries, 1995)

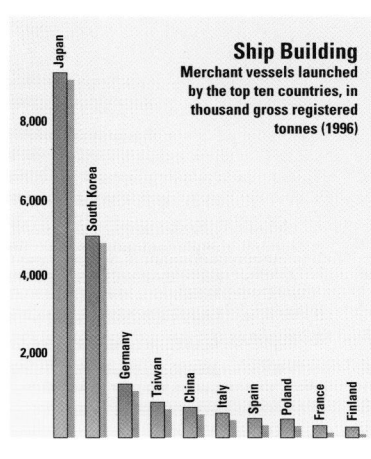

Ship Building
Merchant vessels launched by the top ten countries, in thousand gross registered tonnes (1996)

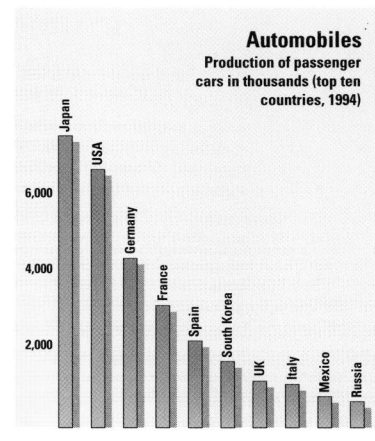

Automobiles
Production of passenger cars in thousands (top ten countries, 1994)

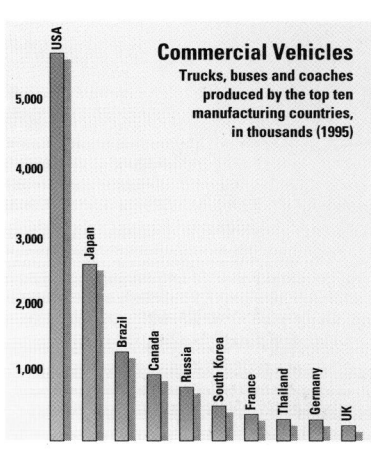

Commercial Vehicles
Trucks, buses and coaches produced by the top ten manufacturing countries, in thousands (1995)

CARTOGRAPHY BY PHILIP'S. COPYRIGHT GEORGE PHILIP LTD

27

Trade

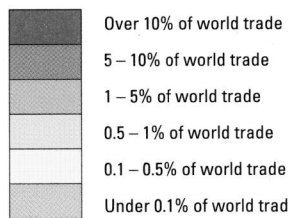

Share of World Trade

Percentage share of total world exports by value (1999)

- Over 10% of world trade
- 5 – 10% of world trade
- 1 – 5% of world trade
- 0.5 – 1% of world trade
- 0.1 – 0.5% of world trade
- Under 0.1% of world trade

International trade is dominated by a handful of powerful maritime nations. The members of 'G8', the inner circle of OECD (see page 19), and the top seven countries listed in the diagram below, account for more than half the total. The majority of nations – including all but four in Africa – contribute less than one quarter of 1% to the worldwide total of exports; the EU countries account for 40%, the Pacific Rim nations over 35%.

The Main Trading Nations

The imports and exports of the top ten trading nations as a percentage of world trade (1994). Each country's trade in manufactured goods is shown in dark blue.

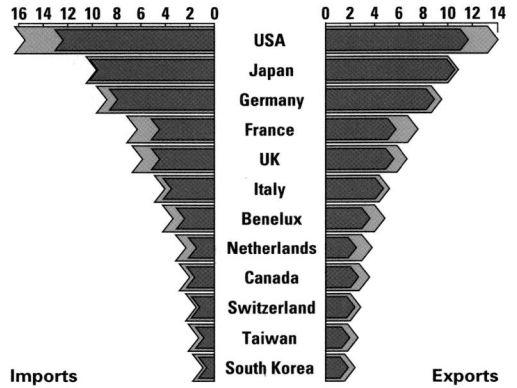

Patterns of Trade

Thriving international trade is the outward sign of a healthy world economy, the obvious indicator that some countries have goods to sell and others the means to buy them. Global exports expanded to an estimated US $3.92 trillion in 1994, an increase due partly to economic recovery in industrial nations but also to export-led growth strategies in many developing nations and lowered regional trade barriers. International trade remains dominated, however, by the rich, industrialized countries of the Organization for Economic Development: between them, OECD members account for almost 75% of world imports and exports in most years. However, continued rapid economic growth in some developing countries is altering global trade patterns. The 'tiger economies' of South-east Asia are particularly vibrant, averaging more than 8% growth between 1992 and 1994. The size of the largest trading economies means that imports and exports usually represent only a small percentage of their total wealth. In export-concious Japan, for example, trade in goods and services amounts to less than 18% of GDP. In poorer countries, trade – often in a single commodity – may amount to 50% of GDP.

Traded Products

Top ten manufactures traded, by value in billions of US $ (latest available year)

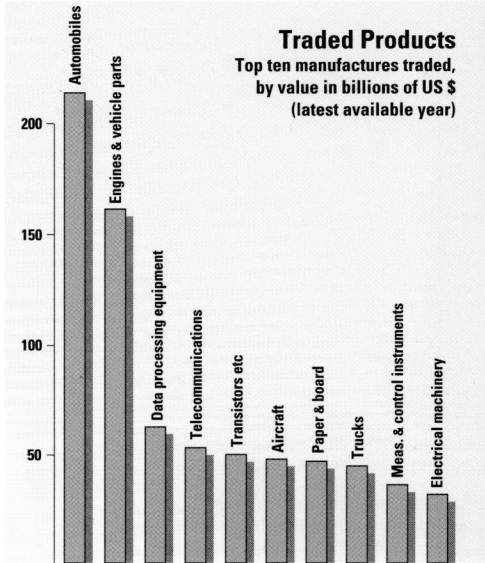

Balance of Trade

Value of exports in proportion to the value of imports (1995)

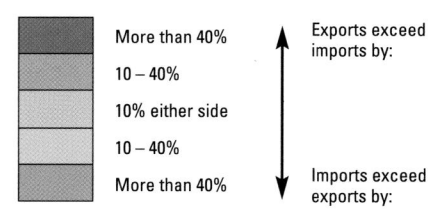

- More than 40%   ↑ Exports exceed imports by:
- 10 – 40%
- 10% either side
- 10 – 40%
- More than 40%   ↓ Imports exceed exports by:

The total world trade balance should amount to zero, since exports must equal imports on a global scale. In practice, at least $100 billion in exports go unrecorded, leaving the world with an apparent deficit and many countries in a better position than public accounting reveals. However, a favourable trade balance is not necessarily a sign of prosperity: many poorer countries must maintain a high surplus in order to service debts, and do so by restricting imports below the levels needed to sustain successful economies.

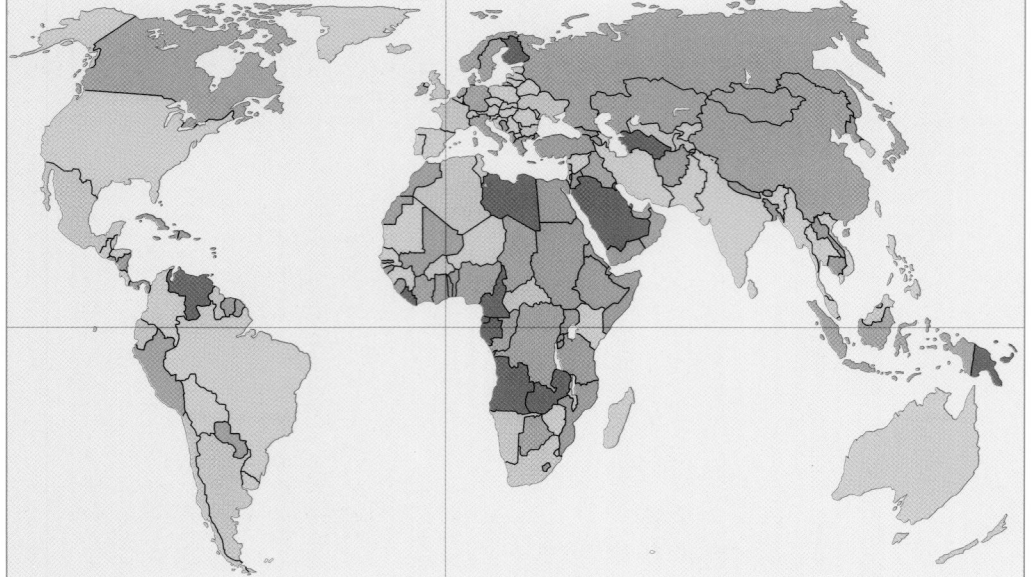

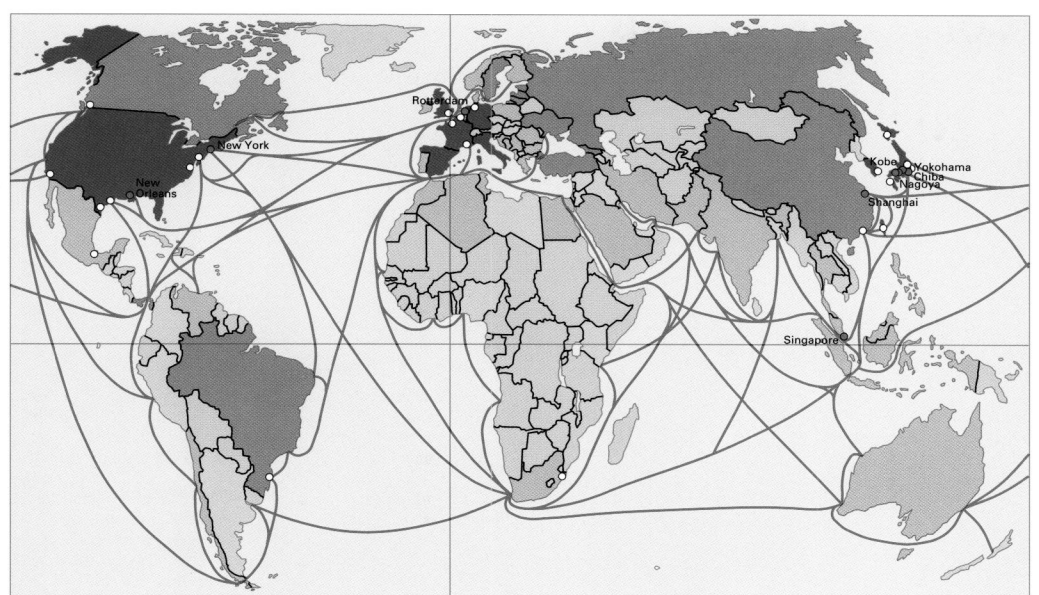

Seaborne Freight

Freight unloaded in millions of tonnes (latest available year)

- Over 100
- 50 – 100
- 10 – 50
- 5 – 10
- Under 5
- Landlocked countries

Major seaports

- ● Over 100 million tonnes per year
- ○ 50–100 million tonnes per year
- —— Major shipping routes

Cargoes

Type of seaborne freight

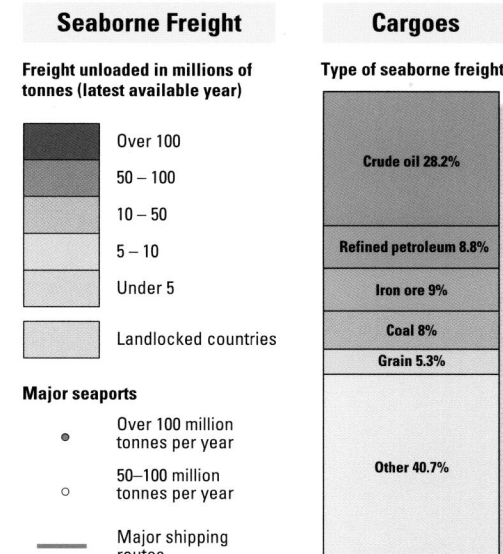

- Crude oil 28.2%
- Refined petroleum 8.8%
- Iron ore 9%
- Coal 8%
- Grain 5.3%
- Other 40.7%

Merchant Fleets

Merchant fleets in thousand gross tonnage (1996). A large number of vessels are registered in Liberia and Panama but they are not part of the national fleet.

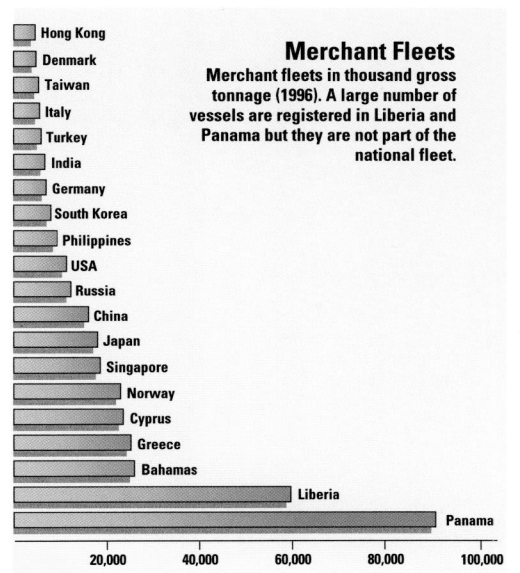

The Great Ports

Total Cargo Traffic (1995) '000 tonnes

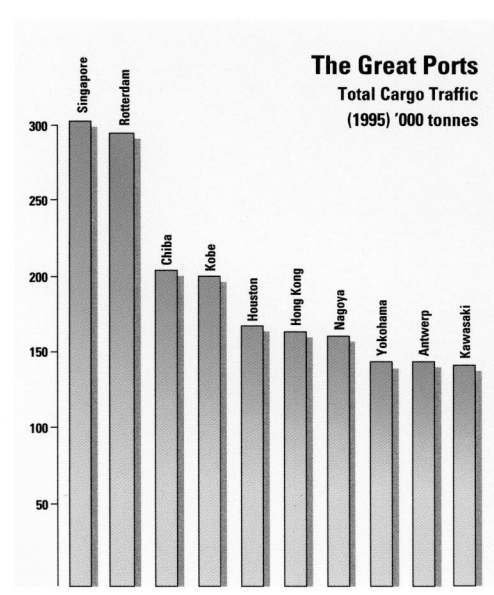

World Shipping

World merchant fleet by type of vessel and deadweight tonnage (latest available year)

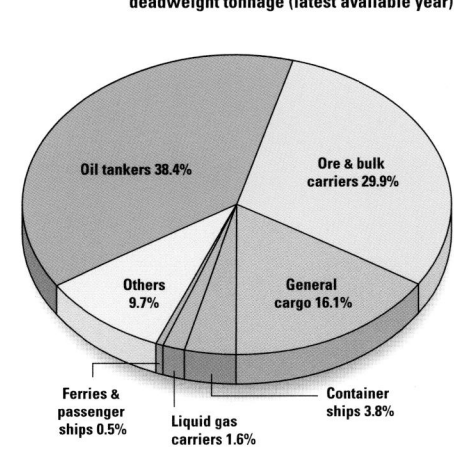

- Oil tankers 38.4%
- Ore & bulk carriers 29.9%
- General cargo 16.1%
- Others 9.7%
- Container ships 3.8%
- Liquid gas carriers 1.6%
- Ferries & passenger ships 0.5%

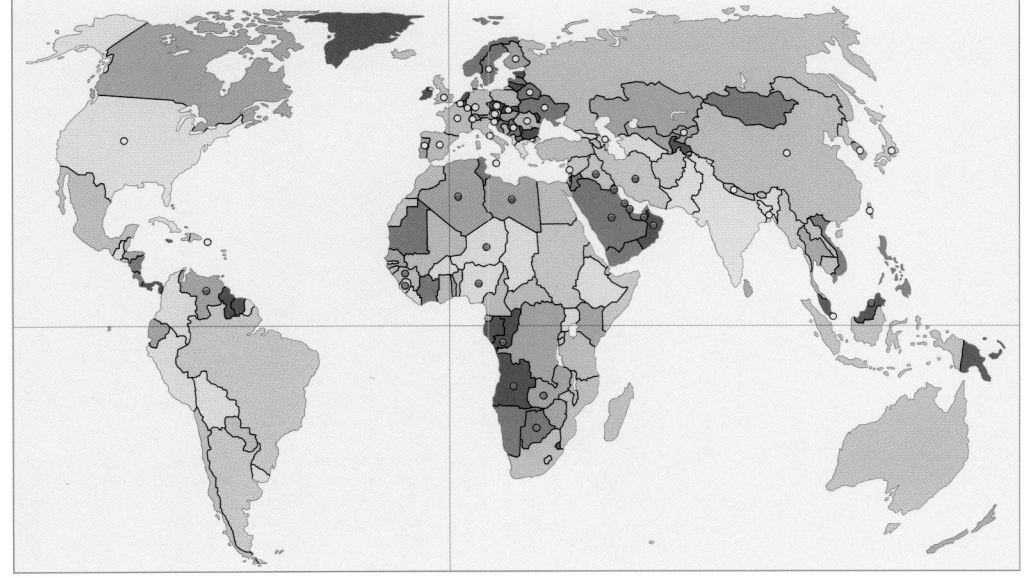

Dependence on Trade

Value of exports as a percentage of Gross Domestic Product (1997)

- Over 50% GDP from exports
- 40 – 50% GDP from exports
- 30 – 40% GDP from exports
- 20 – 30% GDP from exports
- 10 – 20% GDP from exports
- Under 10% GDP from exports

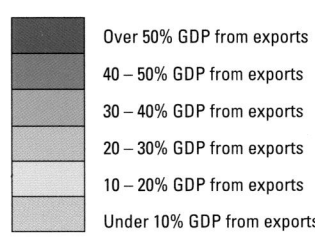

- ○ Most dependent on industrial exports (over 75% of total exports)
- ● Most dependent on fuel exports (over 75% of total exports)
- ● Most dependent on mineral and metal exports (over 75% of total exports)

Travel and Tourism

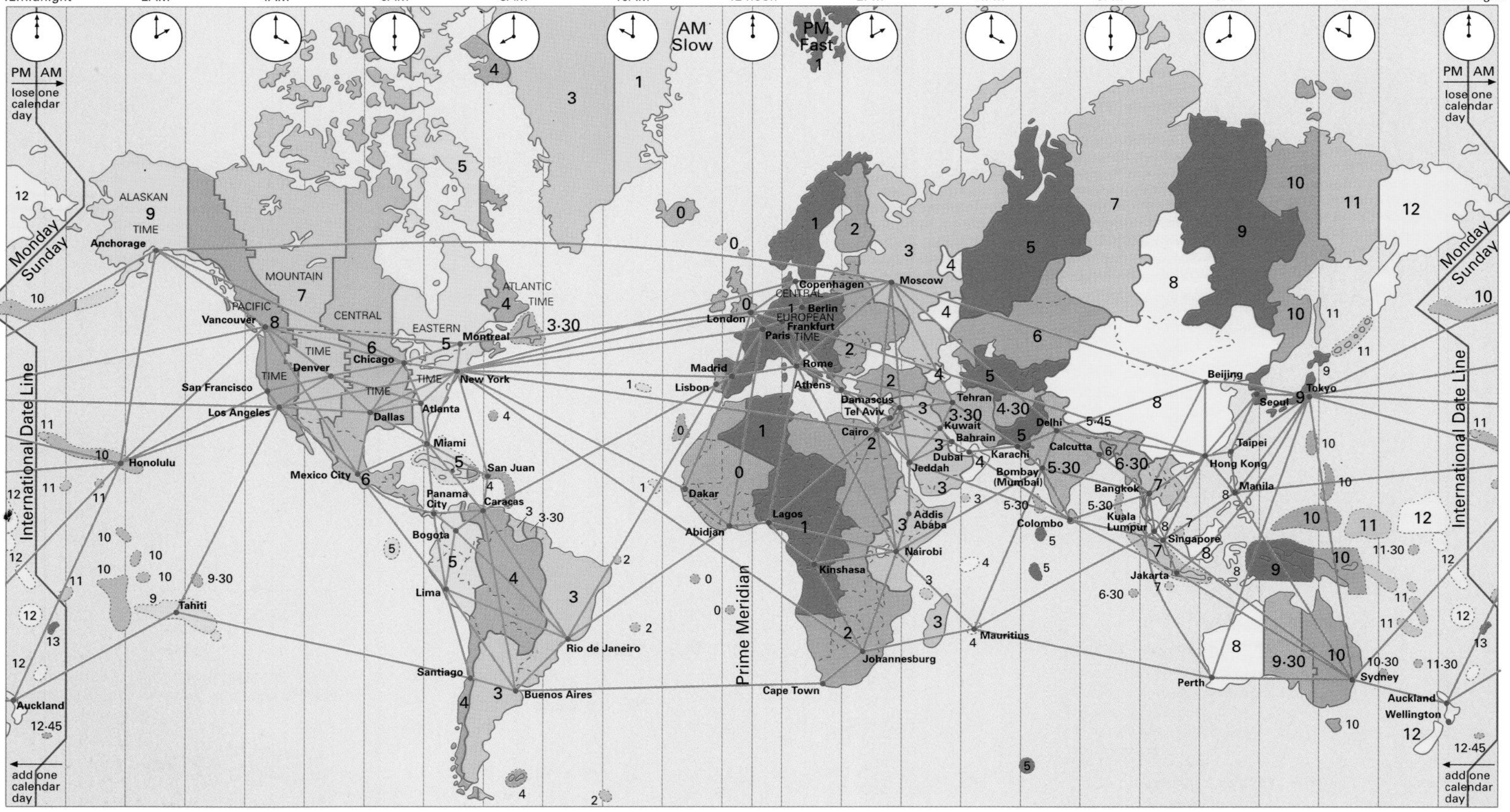

Time zone clock row across top: 12midnight, 2AM, 4AM, 6AM, 8AM, 10AM, 12 noon, 2PM, 4PM, 6PM, 8PM, 10PM, 12midnight

AM Slow / PM Fast

PM AM — lose one calendar day

Time Zones

- Zones using GMT
- Zones slow of GMT
- International boundaries
- 10 — Hours slow or fast of GMT
- Zones fast of GMT
- Half-hour zones
- Time zone boundaries
- International Date Line
- Selected air routes

Certain time zones are affected by the incidence of 'summer time' in countries where it is adopted.

Actual Solar Time, when it is noon at Greenwich, is shown along the top of the map.

The world is divided into 24 time zones, each centred on meridians at 15° intervals, which is the longitudinal distance the sun travels every hour. The meridian running through Greenwich, London, passes through the middle of the first zone.

Rail and Road: The Leading Nations

Total rail network ('000 km) (1995)	Passenger km per head per year	Total road network ('000 km)	Vehicle km per head per year	Number of vehicles per km of roads
1. USA 235.7	Japan 2,017	USA 6,277.9	USA.............12,505	Hong Kong 284
2. Russia 87.4	Belarus..............1,880	India 2,962.5	Luxembourg 7,989	Taiwan 211
3. India 62.7	Russia..............1,826	Brazil 1,824.4	Kuwait 7,251	Singapore.........152
4. China 54.6	Switzerland 1,769	Japan 1,130.9	France 7,142	Kuwait 140
5. Germany.........41.7	Ukraine.............1,456	China 1,041.1	Sweden 6,991	Brunei 96
6. Australia 35.8	Austria 1,168	Russia 884.0	Germany 6,806	Italy 91
7. Argentina 34.2	France 1,011	Canada 849.4	Denmark 6,764	Israel 87
8. France............31.9	Netherlands 994	France 811.6	Austria 6,518	Thailand 73
9. Mexico...........26.5	Latvia 918	Australia 810.3	Netherlands 5,984	Ukraine 73
10. South Africa....26.3	Denmark 884	Germany 636.3	UK 5,738	UK 67
11. Poland...........24.9	Slovak Rep. 862	Romania 461.9	Canada 5,493	Netherlands 66
12. Ukraine 22.6	Romania 851	Turkey 388.1	Italy 4,852	Germany 62

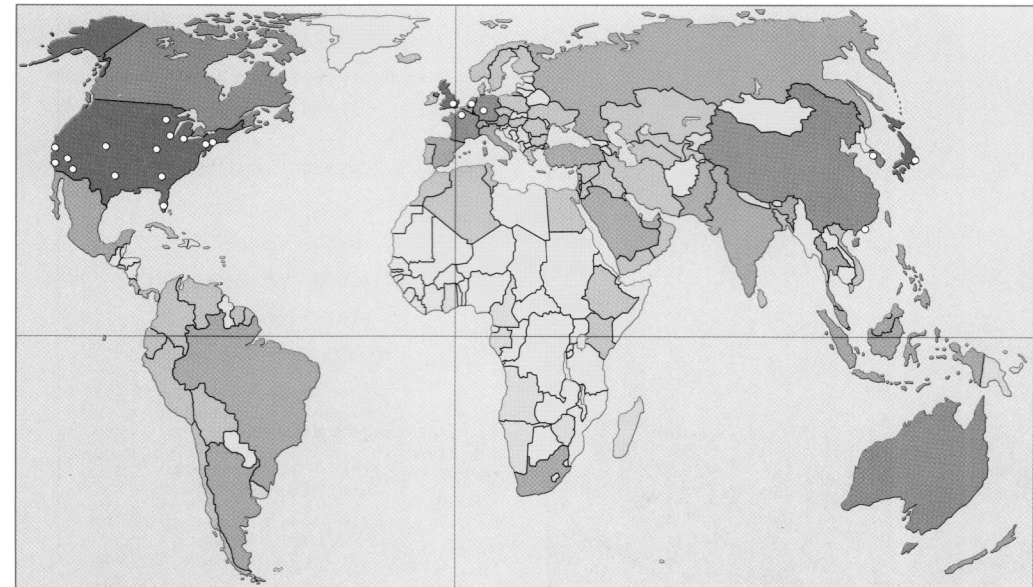

Air Travel

Passenger kilometres flown (the number of passengers – international and domestic – multiplied by the distance flown by each passenger from the airport of origin) (1997)

- Over 100,000 million
- 50,000 – 100,000 million
- 10,000 – 50,000 million
- 1,000 – 10,000 million
- 500 – 1,000 million
- Under 500 million

○ Major airports (handling over 25 million passengers in 2000)

World's busiest airports (total passengers)	World's busiest airports (international passengers)
1. Atlanta (Hartsfield)	1. London (Heathrow)
2. Chicago (O'Hare)	2. Tokyo (Haneda)
3. Los Angeles (Intern'l)	3. Frankfurt (International)
4. London (Heathrow)	4. Paris (De Gaulle)
5. Dallas (Dallas/Ft Worth)	5. Amsterdam (Schipol)

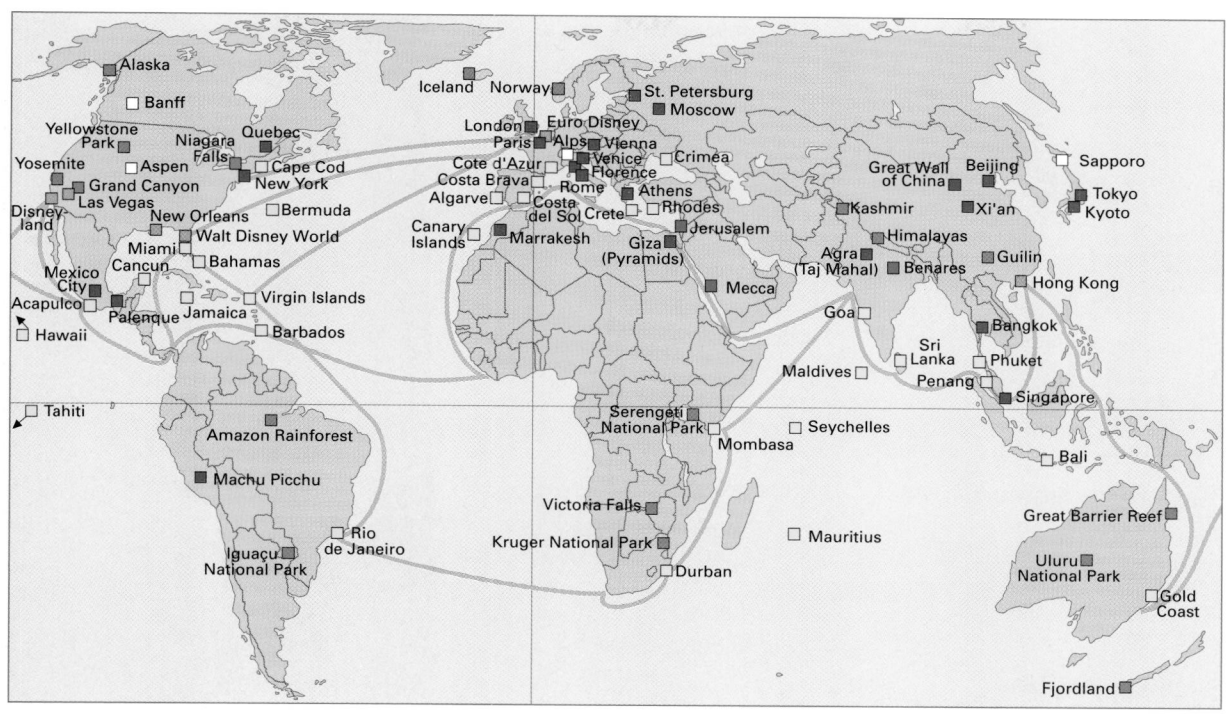

Destinations

- ■ Cultural and historical centres
- □ Coastal resorts
- □ Ski resorts
- ■ Centres of entertainment
- ■ Places of pilgrimage
- ▨ Places of great natural beauty
- ── Popular holiday cruise routes

Visitors to the USA

Overseas travellers to the USA, thousands (1997 estimates)

1.	Canada	13,900
2.	Mexico	12,370
3.	Japan	4,640
4.	UK	3,350
5.	Germany	1,990
6.	France	1,030
7.	Taiwan	885
8.	Venezuela	860
9.	South Korea	800
10.	Brazil	785

In 1996, the USA earned the most from tourism, with receipts of more than US $75 billion.

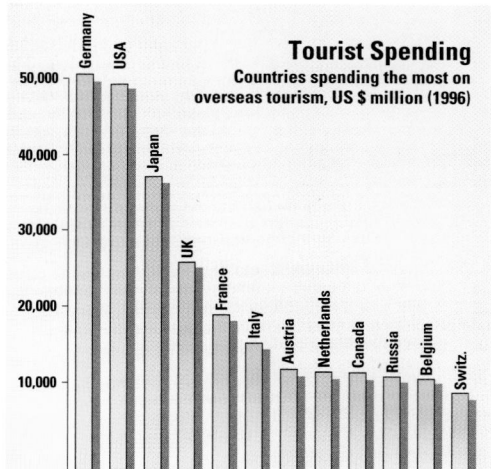

Tourist Spending
Countries spending the most on overseas tourism, US $ million (1996)

Importance of Tourism

		Arrivals from abroad (1996)	% of world total (1996)
1.	France	66,800,000	10.2%
2.	USA	49,038,000	7.5%
3.	Spain	43,403,000	6.6%
4.	Italy	34,087,000	5.2%
5.	UK	25,960,000	3.9%
6.	China	23,770,000	3.6%
7.	Poland	19,514,000	3.0%
8.	Mexico	18,667,000	2.9%
9.	Canada	17,610,000	2.7%
10.	Czech Republic	17,400,000	2.7%
11.	Hungary	17,248,000	2.6%
12.	Austria	16,642,000	2.5%

In 1996, there was a 4.6% rise, to 593 million, in the total number of people travelling abroad. Small economies in attractive areas are often completely dominated by tourism: in some West Indian islands, for example, tourist spending provides over 90% of total income.

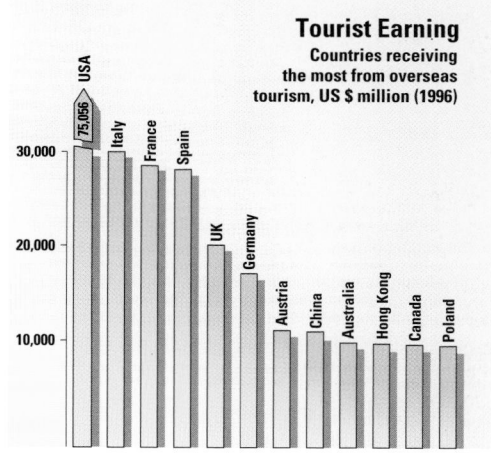

Tourist Earning
Countries receiving the most from overseas tourism, US $ million (1996)

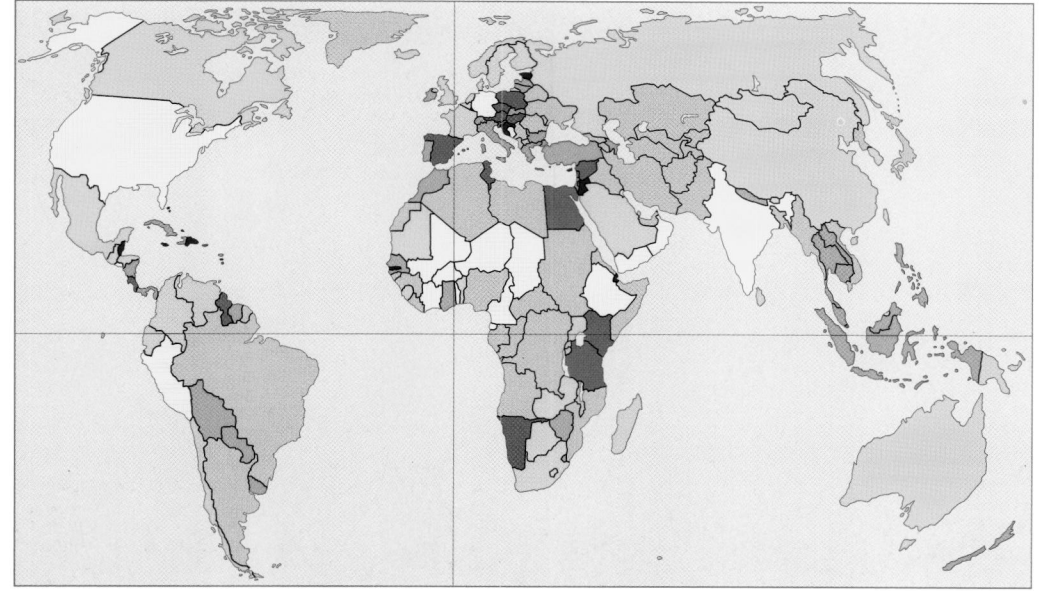

Tourism

Tourism receipts as a percentage of Gross National Product (1996)

- Over 10% of GNP from tourism
- 5 – 10% of GNP from tourism
- 2.5 – 5% of GNP from tourism
- 1 – 2.5% of GNP from tourism
- 0.5 – 1% of GNP from tourism
- Under 0.5% of GNP from tourism

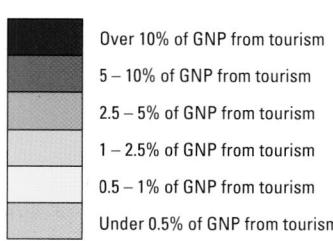

Countries spending the most on promoting tourism, millions of US $ (1996)		Countries with largest tourism receipts, millions of US $ (1996)	
Germany	51	USA	75
USA	49	Italy	30
Japan	37	France	28
UK	25	Spain	27
France	18	UK	21

The World In Focus: Index

WORLD CITIES

CITY MAPS

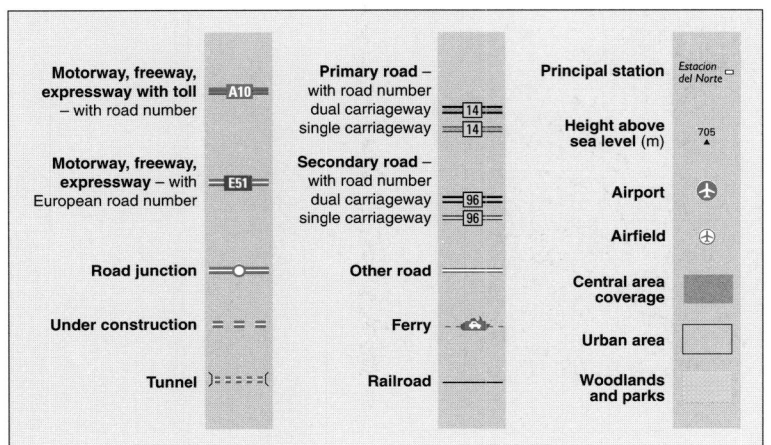

CENTRAL AREA MAPS

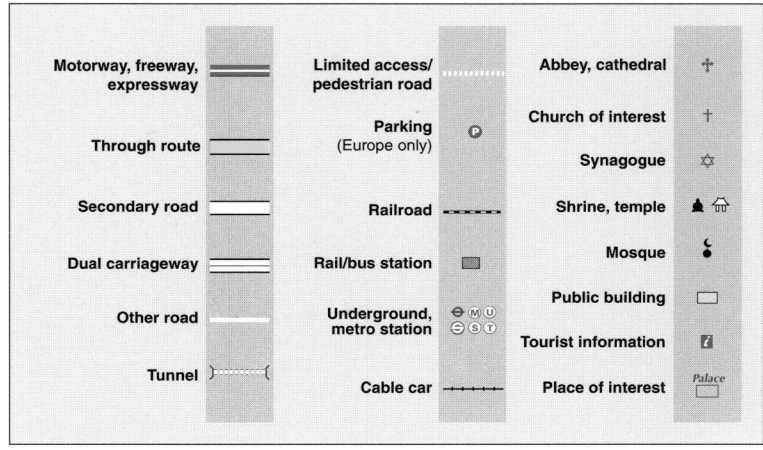

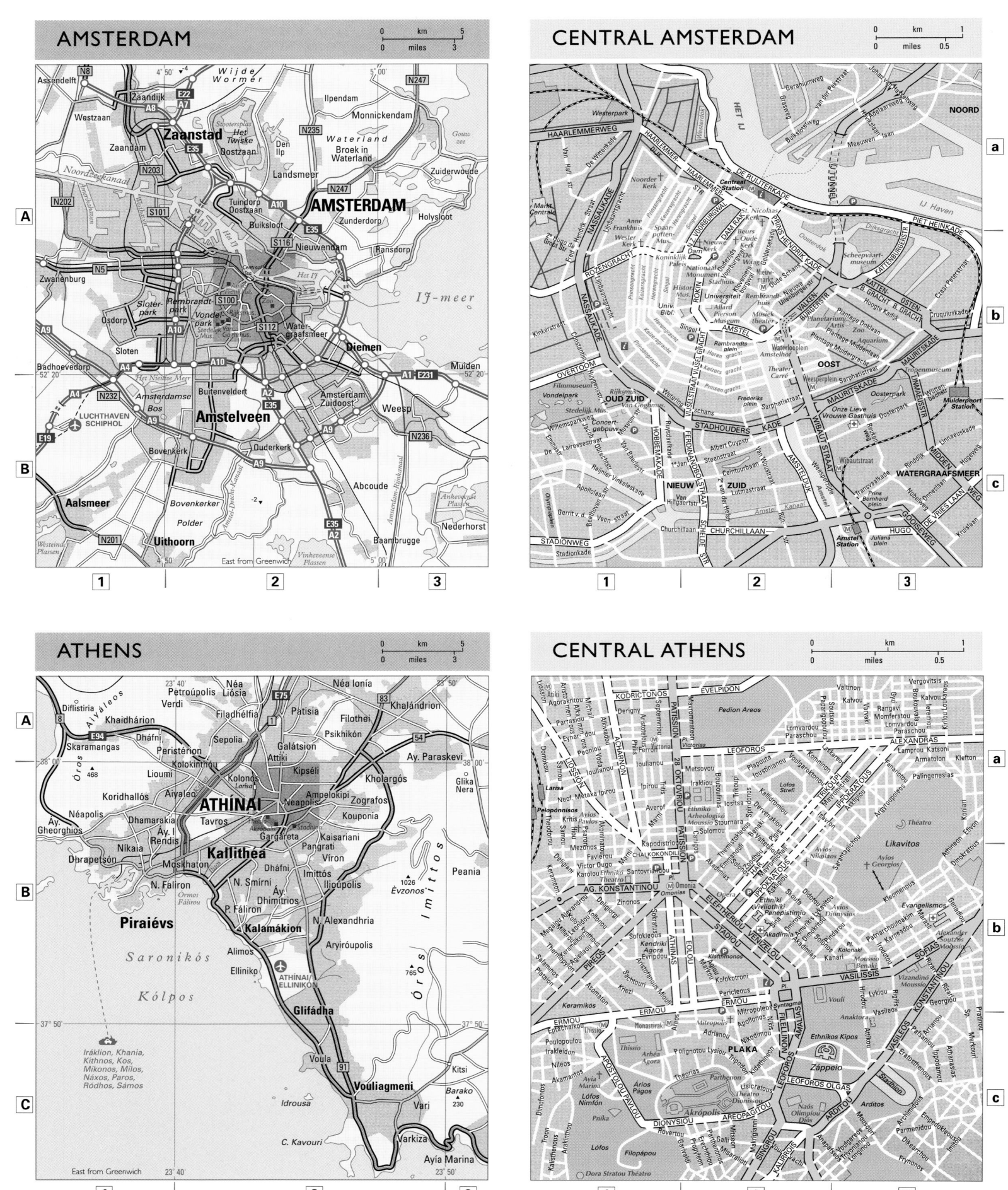

ATLANTA

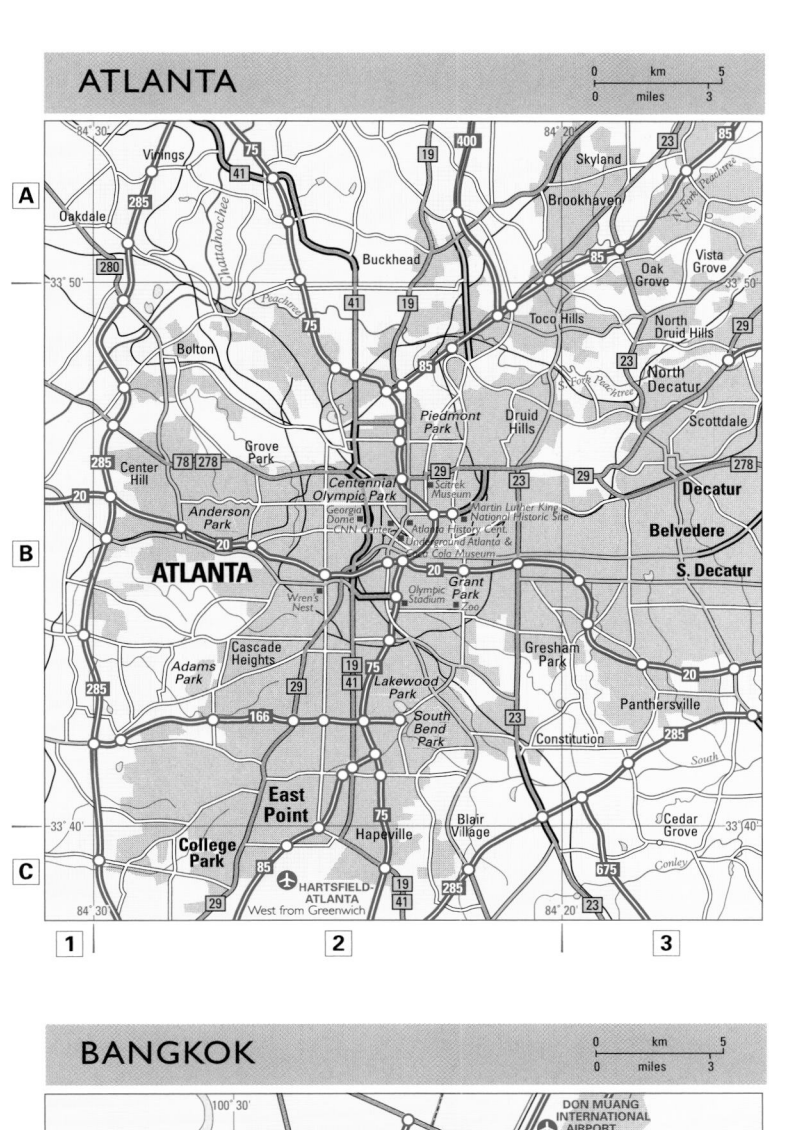

BAGHDAD

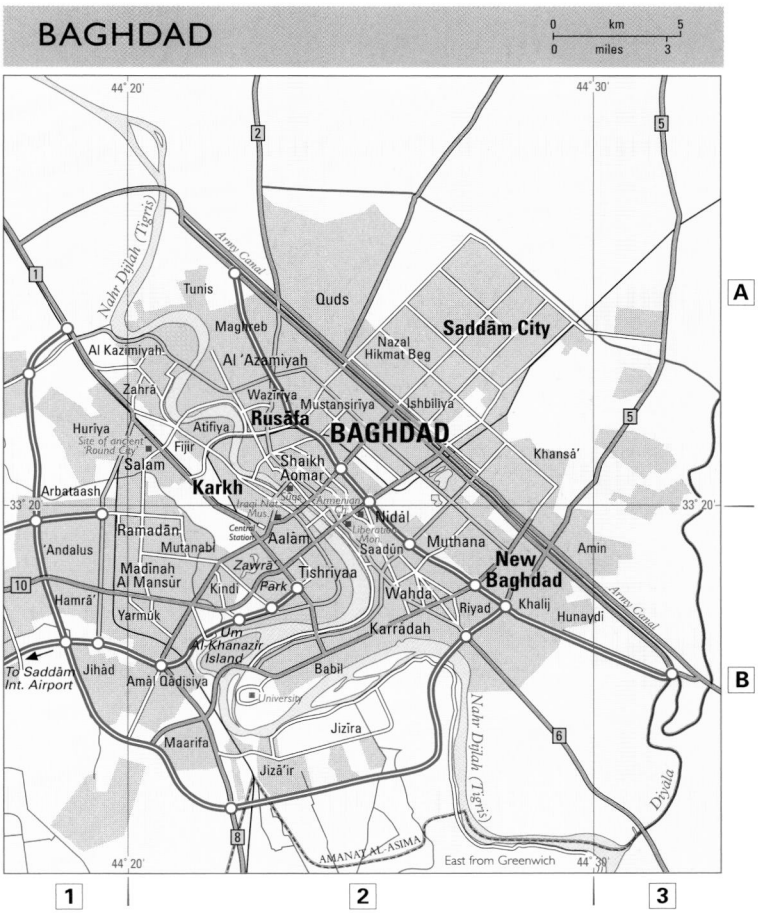

BANGKOK

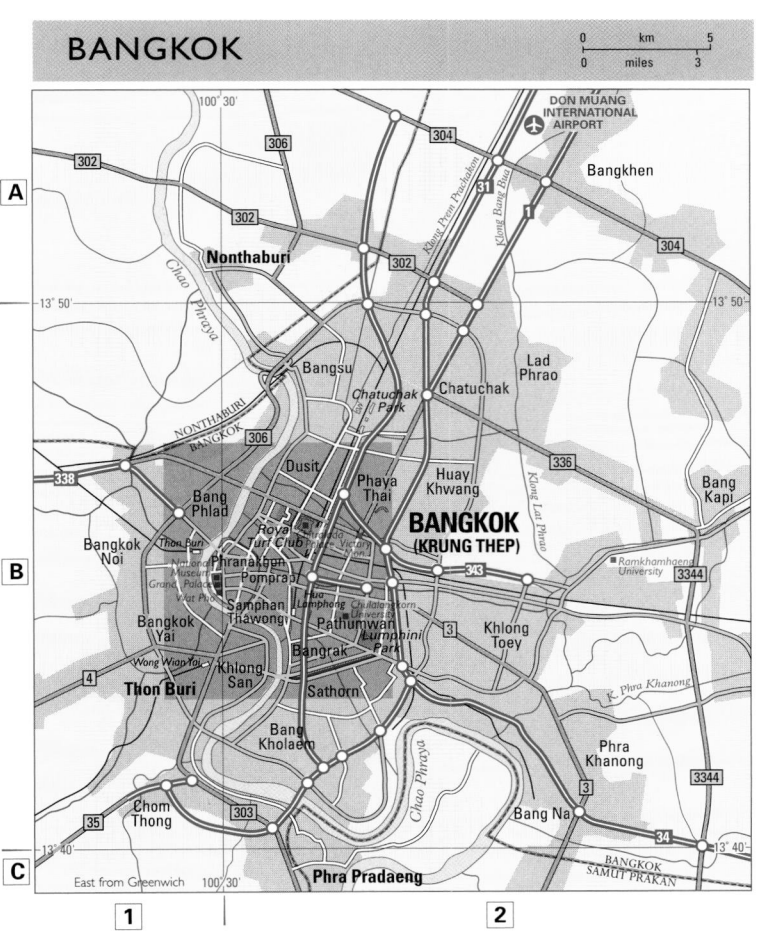

CENTRAL BANGKOK

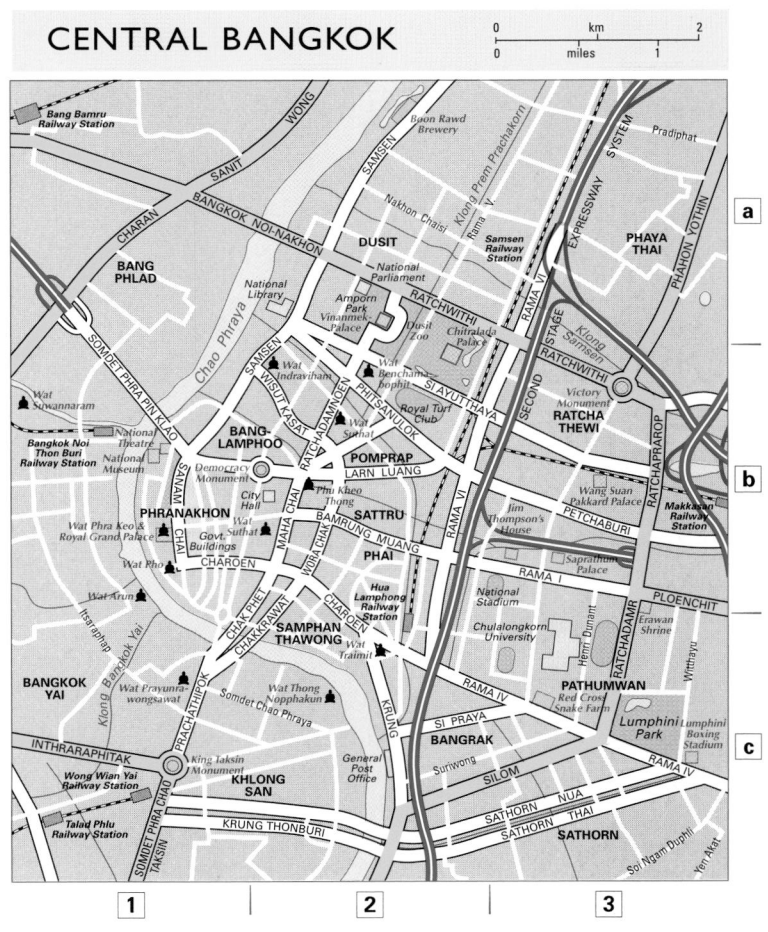

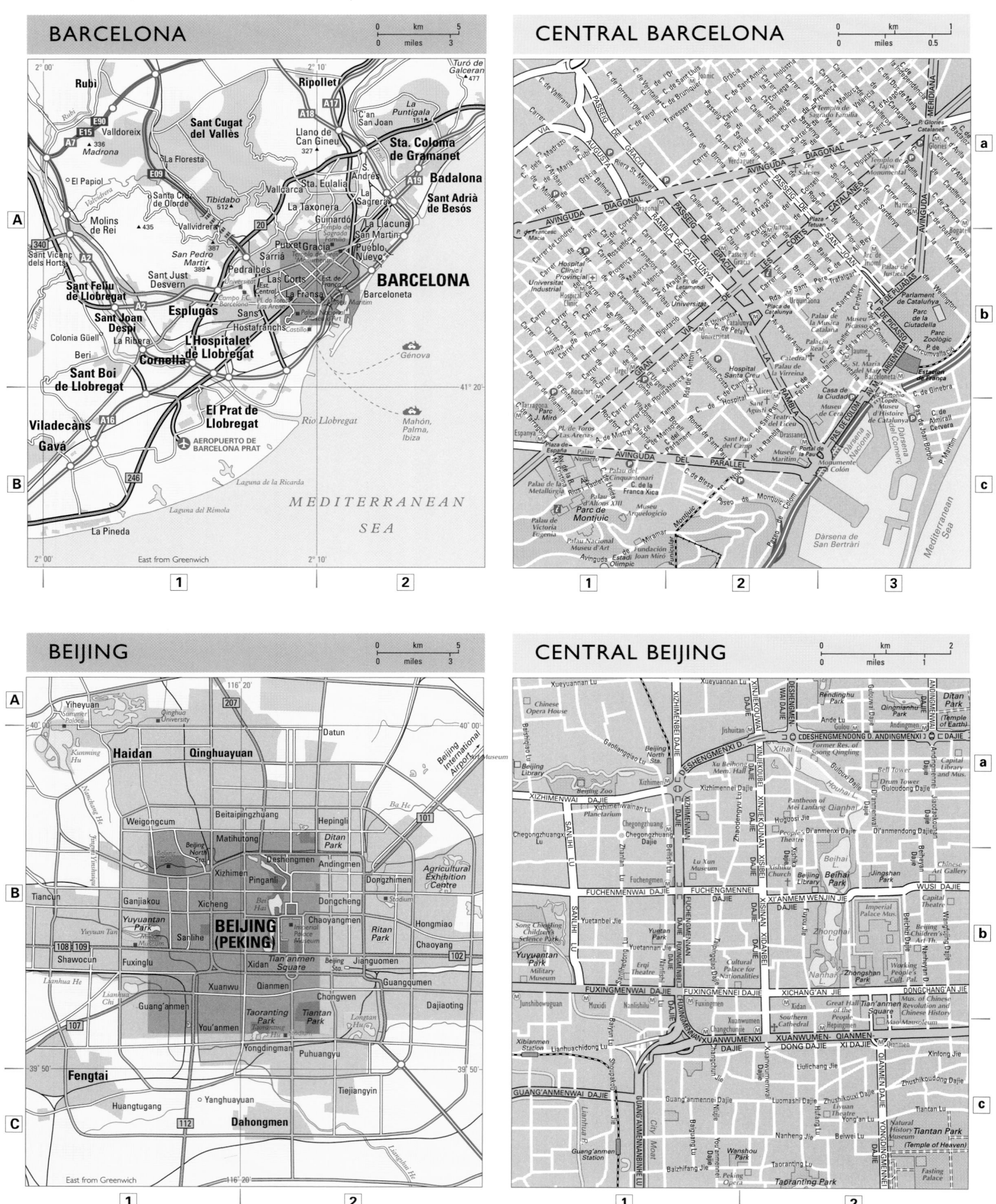

BERLIN

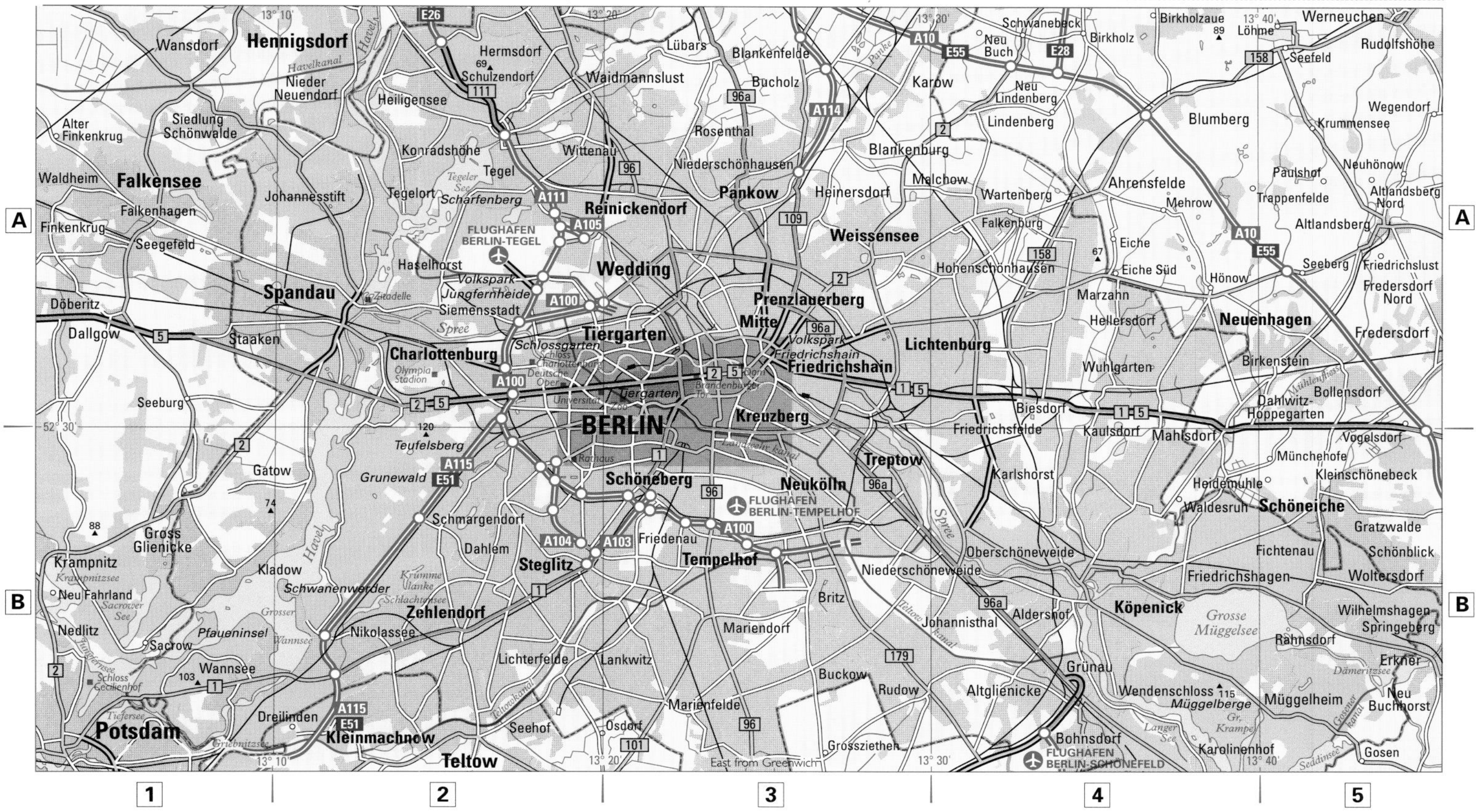

0 km 5
0 miles 3

Wansdorf · Hennigsdorf · Hermsdorf · Schulzendorf · Lübars · Blankenfelde · Schwanebeck · Birkholzaue · Werneuchen · Rudolfshöhe

Alter Finkenkrug · Nieder Neuendorf · Heiligensee · Waidmannslust · Bucholz · Neu Buch · Karow · Neu Lindenberg · Birkholz · Seefeld

Waldheim · **Falkensee** · Falkenhagen · Johannesstift · Tegelort · Tegel · Rosenthal · Niederschönhausen · Lindenberg · Blumberg · Krummensee

Finkenkrug · Seegefeld · Konrädshöhe · **Reinickendorf** · **Weissensee** · Hohenschönhausen · Wegendorf · Neuhönow

Spandau · Haselhorst · **Wedding** · **Prenzlauerberg** · Falkenburg · Eiche · Eiche Süd · Hönow · Seeberg · Friedrichslust

Döberitz · Staaken · Siemensstadt · **Charlottenburg** · **Tiergarten** · **Mitte** · Marzahn · Hellersdorf · Fredersdorf Nord

Dallgow · **BERLIN** · **Friedrichshain** · **Lichtenburg** · Wuhlgarten · Dahlwitz-Hoppegarten · Neuenhagen · Fredersdorf

Gatow · Teufelsberg · Grunewald · **Schöneberg** · **Kreuzberg** · Friedrichsfelde · Biesdorf · Kaulsdorf · Mahlsdorf · Vogelsdorf

Seeburg · Schmargendorf · Dahlem · **Neukölln** · **Treptow** · Karlshorst · Münchehofe · Kleinschönebeck

Zehlendorf · Steglitz · Tempelhof · Oberschöneweide · Heidemühle · Schöneiche · Gratzwalde

Krampnitz · Gross Glienicke · Kladow · Lichterfelde · Lankwitz · Britz · Niederschöneweide · Fichtenau · Schönblick

Nedlitz · Neu Fahrland · Nikolassee · Mariendorf · Johannisthal · Aldershof · Köpenick · Grosse Müggelsee · Friedrichshagen · Woltersdorf · Rahnsdorf · Wilhelmshagen-Springeberg · Erkner

Sacrow · Wannsee · Buckow · Rudow · Altglienicke · Grünau · Müggelberge · Müggelheim · Neu Buchhorst

Potsdam · Dreilinden · Schwanenwerder · Marienfelde · Seehof · Osdorf · Grossziethen · Bohnsdorf · Karolinenhof · Gosen

Kleinmachnow · **Teltow** · East from Greenwich · **FLUGHAFEN BERLIN-SCHÖNEFELD**

CENTRAL BERLIN

0 km 1
0 miles 0.5

CHARLOTTENBURG · **TIERGARTEN** · **MITTE** · **WILMERSDORF** · **KREUZBERG**

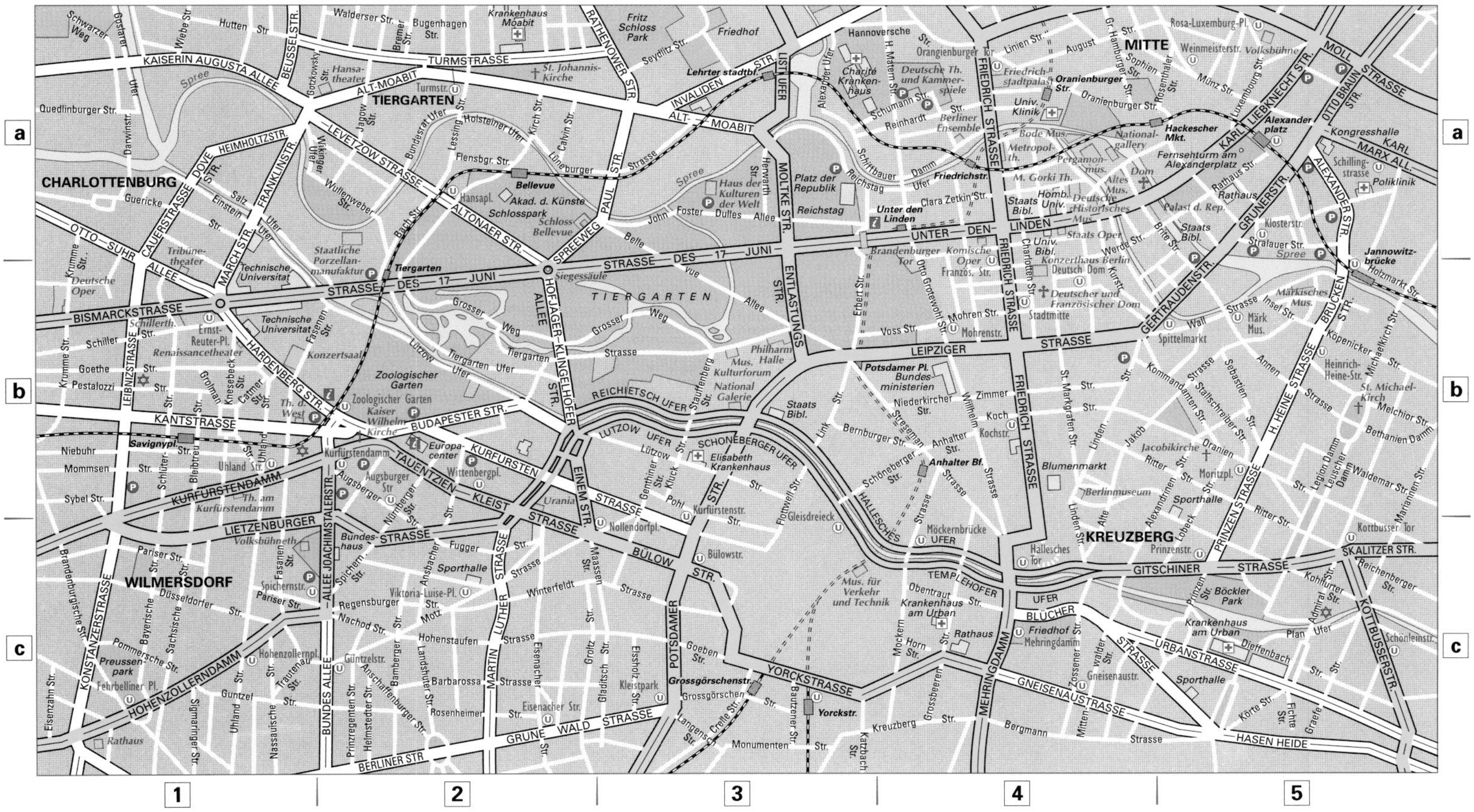

COPYRIGHT GEORGE PHILIP LTD

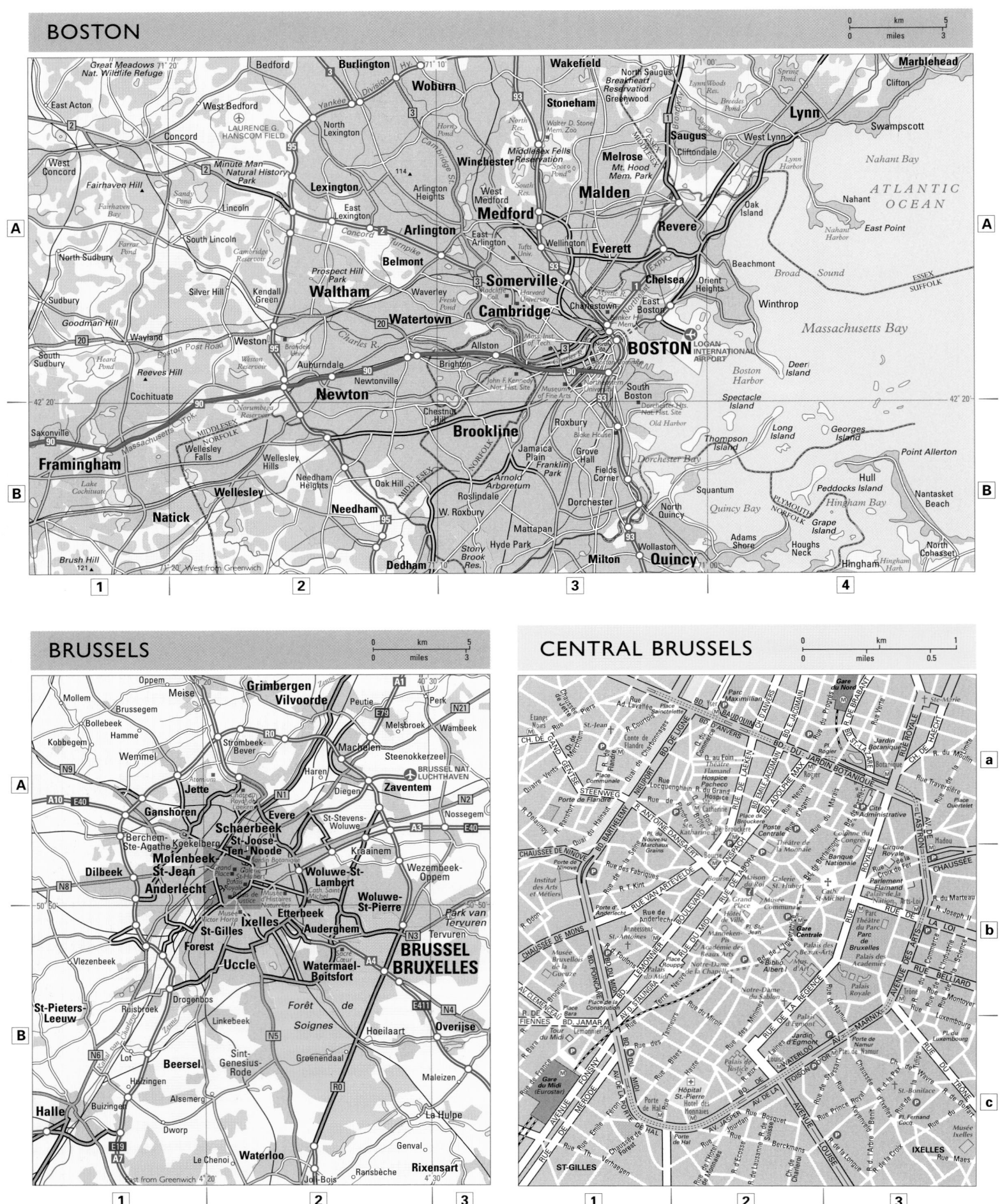

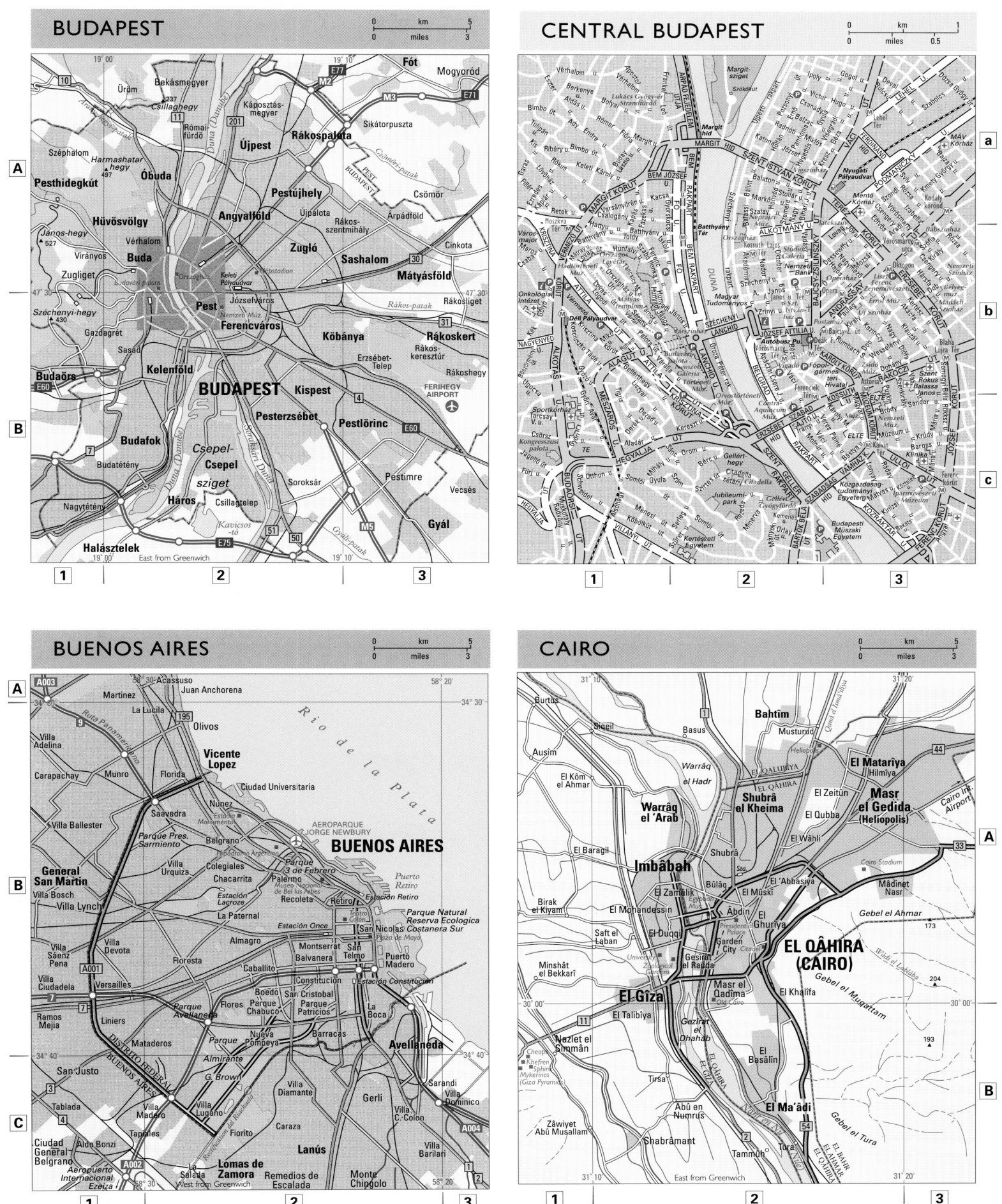

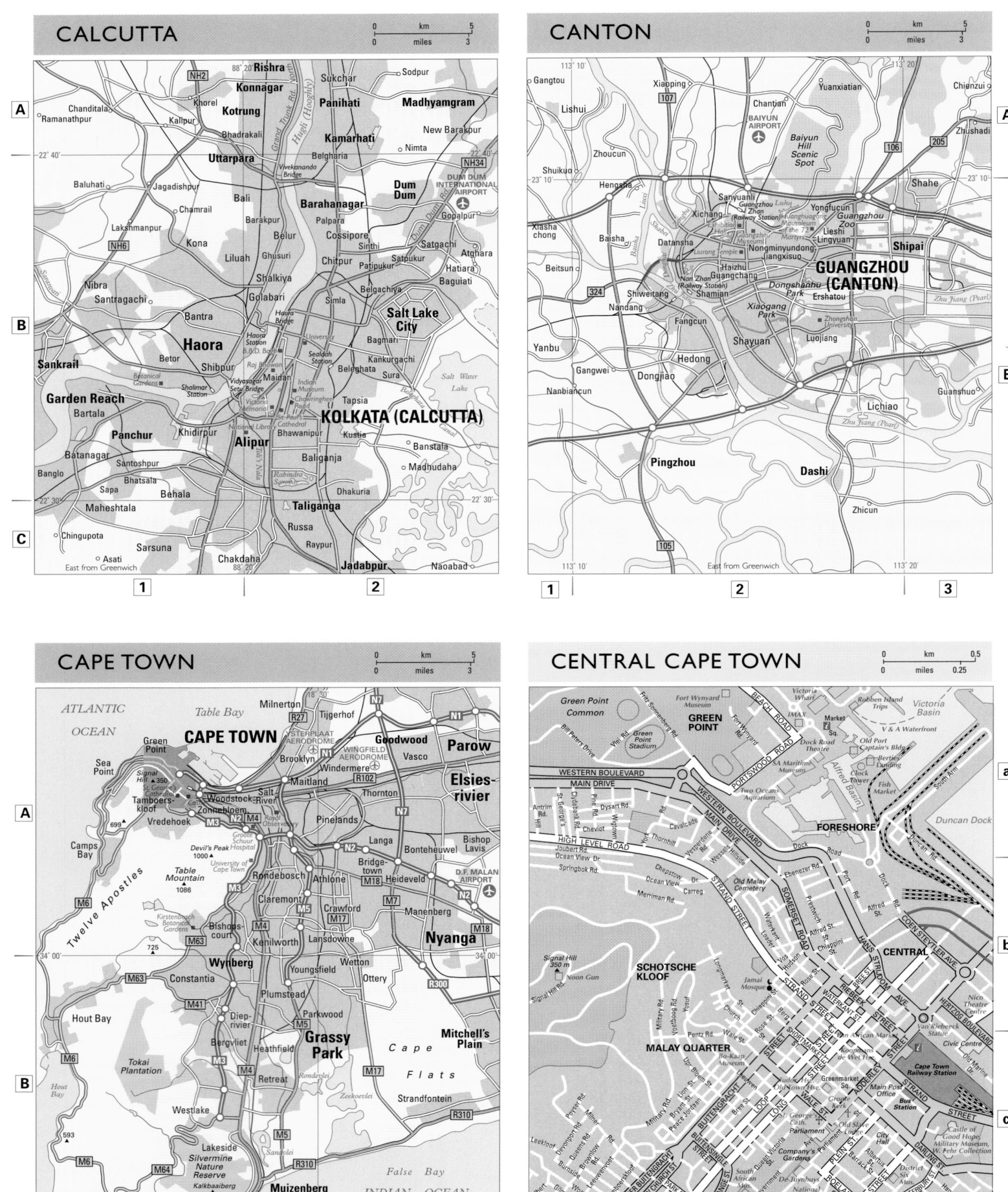

CALCUTTA

km 5 / miles 3

Chanditala, Ramanathpur, Rishra, Konnagar, Khorel, Kalipur, Kotrung, Bhadrakali, Panihati, Sukchar, Sodpur, Madhyamgram, NH2, New Barakpur, Kamarhati, Uttarpara, Belgharia, Nimta, Baluhati, Jagadishpur, Vivekananda Bridge, Dum Dum, DUM DUM INTERNATIONAL AIRPORT, NH34, Bali, Chamrail, Barahanagar, Palpara, Gopalpur, Lakshmanpur, Barakpur, Belur, Cossipore, NH6, Kona, Liluah, Ghusuri, Sinthi, Satgachi, Atghara, Nibra, Chitpur, Patipukur, Hatiara, Baguiati, Santragachi, Shalkiya, Simla, Bantra, Golabari, Belgachiya, Salt Lake City, Haora, Betor, Shibpur, Haora Station, Bagmari, Kankurgachi, Sura, Beleghata, Botanical Gardens, B.B.D. Bagh, Sealdah Station, Sankrail, University, Shalimar Station, Raj Bhawan, Vidyasagar Setu Bridge, Maidan, Indian Museum, Garden Reach, Bartala, Chavvringhee Road, Victoria Memorial, St. Paul's Cathedral, National Library, Tapsia, KOLKATA (CALCUTTA), Panchur, Khidirpur, Alipur, Bhawanipur, Kustia, Banstala, Batanagar, Santoshpur, Baliganja, Banglo, Bhatsala, Sapa, Behala, Madhudaha, Maheshtala, Taliganga, Chingupota, Russa, Asati, Sarsuna, Rayapur, Chakdaha, Jadabpur, Naoabad

East from Greenwich 88°20'

CANTON

km 5 / miles 3

Gangtou, Xiaoping, Yuanxiatian, Chienzui, Lishui, 107, Chantian, BAIYUN AIRPORT, Baiyun Hill Scenic Spot, Zhushadi, 106, 205, Shuikou, Zhoucun, 324, Sanyuanli, Guangzhou Zhan, Guangzhou Railway Station, Shahe, Hengsha, Xichang, Mausoleum of the 72 Martyrs, Yongfucun, Guangzhou Zoo, Lieshi, Lingyuan, Xiasha chong, Baisha, Luhu, Guangxiao, Haizhu, Nongminyundong, Jiangxisuo, Shipai, Beitsun, Luirong Temple, Nan Zhan (Railway Station), Guangchang, Shamian, Dongshanhu Park, Ershatou, Yanbu, Shiweitang, Nandang, Fangcun, Xiaogang Park, Luojiang, Zhongshan University, GUANGZHOU (CANTON), Zhu Jiang (Pearl), Shayuan, Hedong, Gangwei, Dongjiao, Guanshuo, Nanbiancun, Lichiao, Zhu Jiang (Pearl), Pingzhou, Dashi, 105, Zhicun

East from Greenwich 113°10' — 113°20'

CAPE TOWN

km 5 / miles 3

ATLANTIC OCEAN, Milnerton, Table Bay, Tijgerhof, N7, N1, Green Point, CAPE TOWN, YSTERPLAAT AERODROME, R27, Goodwood, Parow, Sea Point, Signal Hill 350, Brooklyn, Windermere, Vasco, Maitland, R102, Elsies-rivier, St George's Cathedral, Tamboerskloof, Castle, Woodstock, Salt River, Zonnebloem, Thornton, Vredehoek, M3, N2, M4, Pinelands, N7, Camps Bay, Devil's Peak 1000, Groote Schuur Hospital, Langa, Bishop Lavis, Observatory, University of Cape Town, Bridge-town, Bonteheuwel, Heideveld, D.F. MALAN AIRPORT, N2, Table Mountain 1086, Rondebosch, Athlone, M18, Twelve Apostles, Claremont, Crawford, M7, Manenberg, M5, Kirstenbosch Botanical Gardens, Bishop's court, M4, M17, M18, Kenilworth, Lansdowne, Nyanga, 725, Wynberg, Youngsfield, Wetton, Ottery, R300, Constantia, Plumstead, Parkwood, M41, Diep-rivier, M5, M63, Hout Bay, Bergvliet, Heathfield, Grassy Park, Mitchell's Plain, M6, Tokai Plantation, M3, M4, Retreat, Cape Flats, Hout Bay, 593, Westlake, Ronbevlei, Zeekoevlei, Strandfontein, R310, Lakeside, M5, Silvermine Nature Reserve, M64, R310, Kalkbaaiberg 516, Muizenberg, False Bay, INDIAN OCEAN, M6

East from Greenwich 18°30'

CENTRAL CAPE TOWN

km 0.5 / miles 0.25

Green Point Common, Fort Wynyard Museum, Victoria Basin, IMAX, Robben Island Trips, Victoria Basin, GREEN POINT, Market Sq., Green Point Stadium, Dock Road Theatre, Old Port Captain's Bldg, V & A Waterfront, WESTERN BOULEVARD, MAIN DRIVE, Two Oceans Aquarium, SA Maritime Museum, Clock Tower, Bertie's Landing, Fish Market, HIGH LEVEL ROAD, FORESHORE, Duncan Dock, Signal Hill 350 m, Noon Gun, Old Malay Cemetery, SCHOTSCHE KLOOF, CENTRAL, Jamai Mosque, MALAY QUARTER, Bo-Kaap Museum, Greenmarket, Van Riebeck Statue, Nico Theatre Centre, Civic Centre, Cape Town Railway Station, Parliament, Main Post Office, Bus Station, South African Museum, Company's Gardens, Old Slave Lodge, City Hall, Castle of Good Hope, Military Museum, W. Fehr Collection, Houses of Parliament, District Six Mus., De Tuynhuys, National Art Gallery, CANTERBURY STREET

CHICAGO

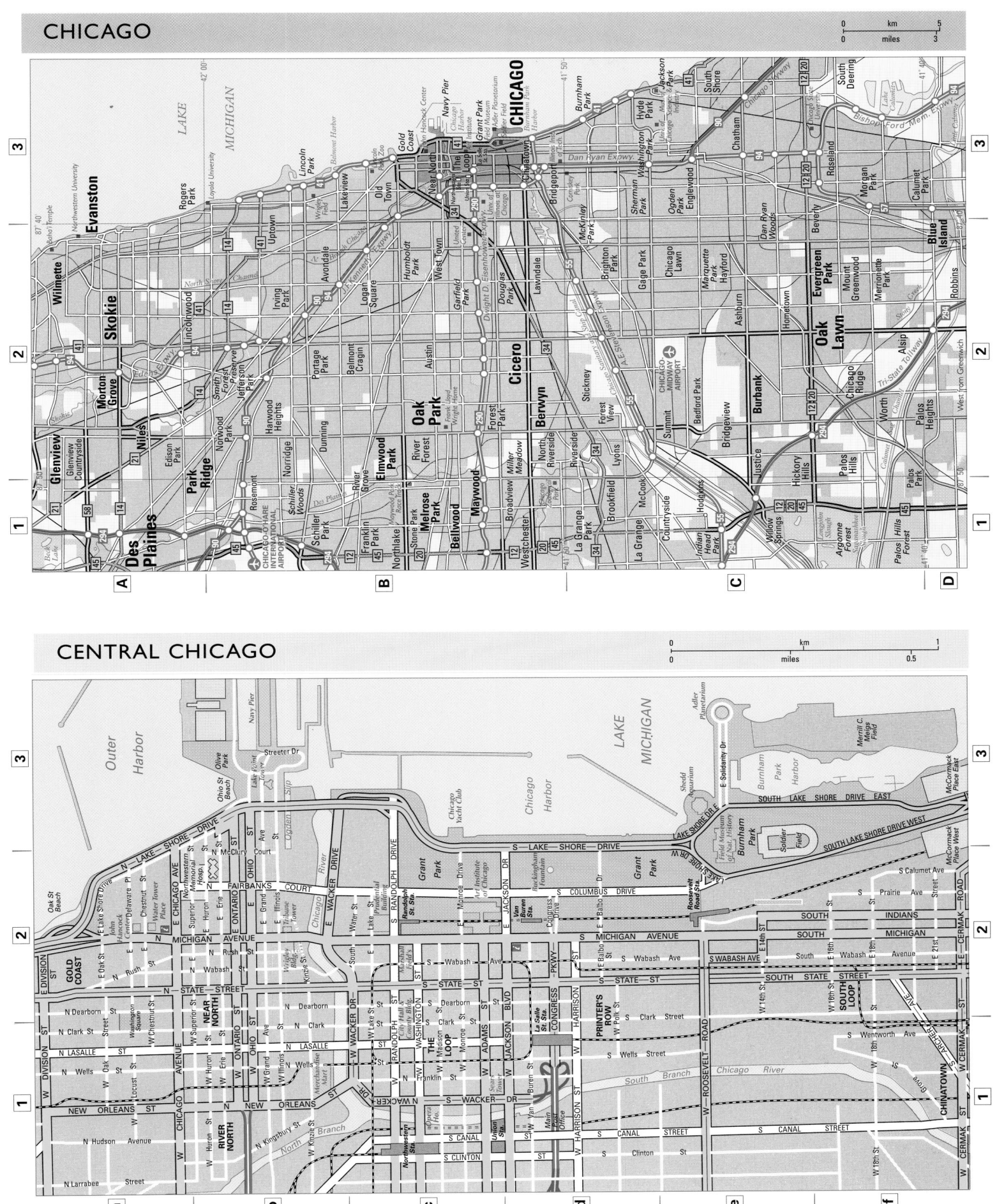

CENTRAL CHICAGO

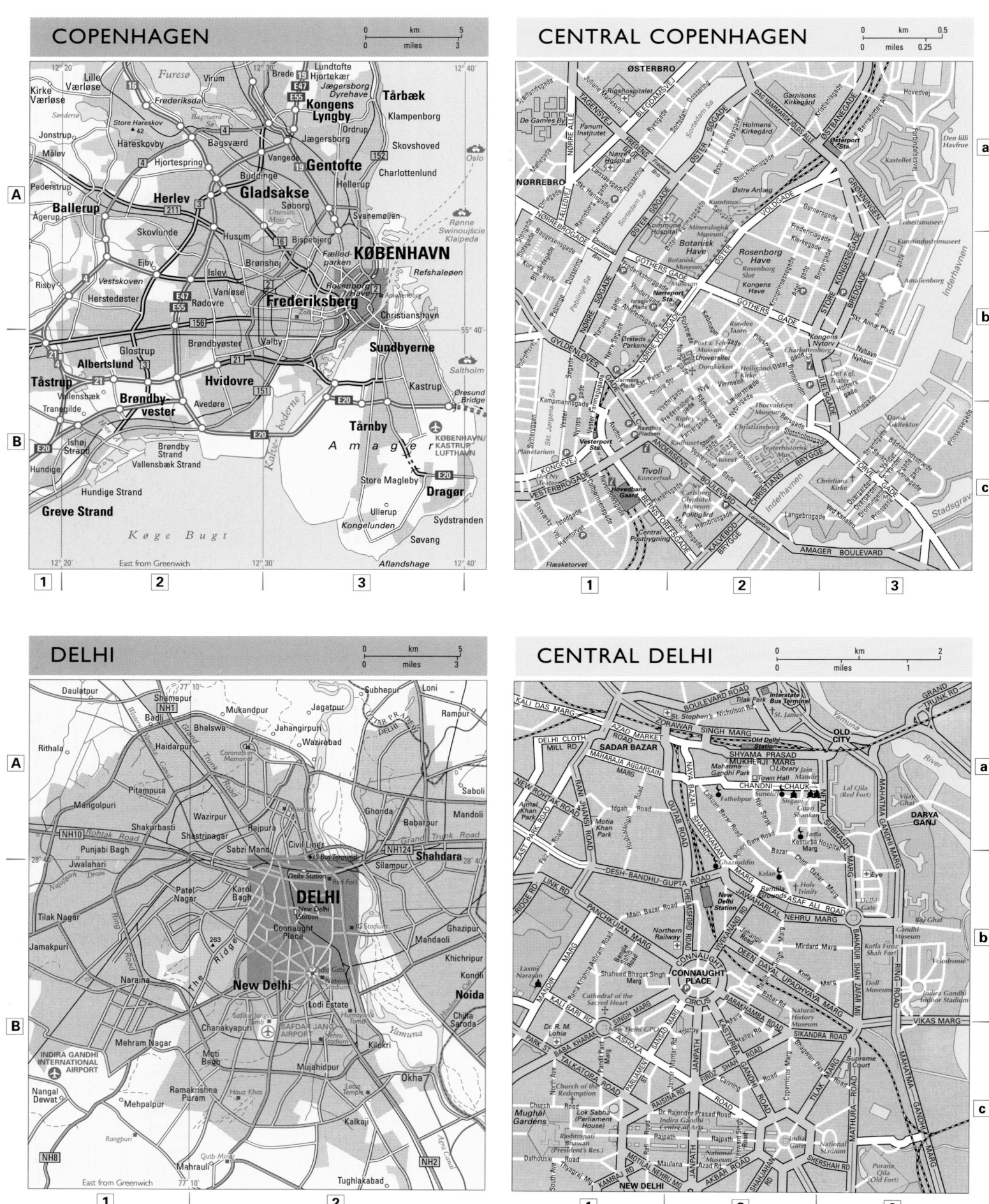

COPENHAGEN

km 0 — 5
miles 0 — 3

CENTRAL COPENHAGEN

km 0 — 0.5
miles 0 — 0.25

DELHI

km 0 — 5
miles 0 — 3

CENTRAL DELHI

km 0 — 2
miles 0 — 1

DUBLIN

CENTRAL DUBLIN

EDINBURGH

CENTRAL EDINBURGH

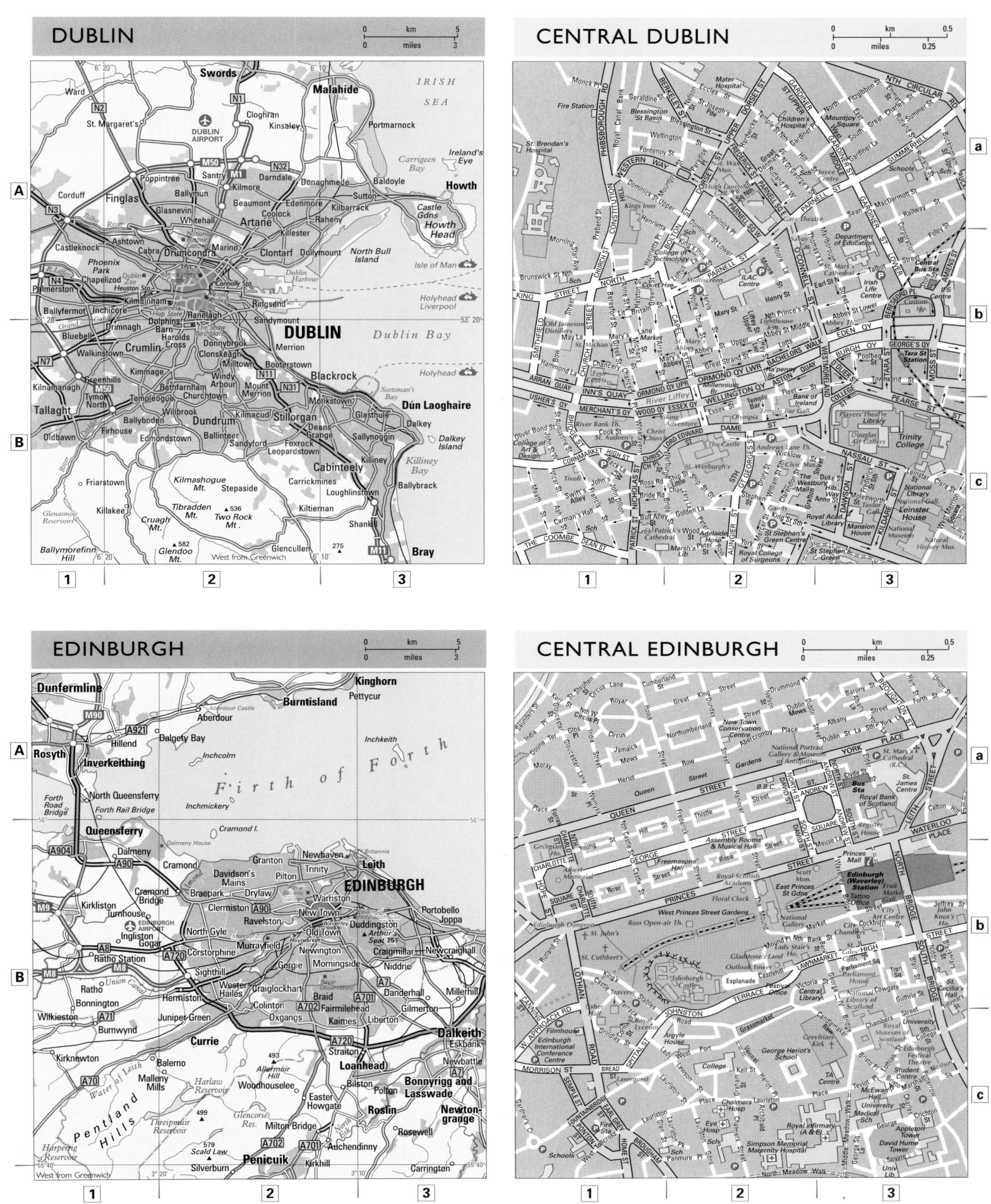

HELSINKI

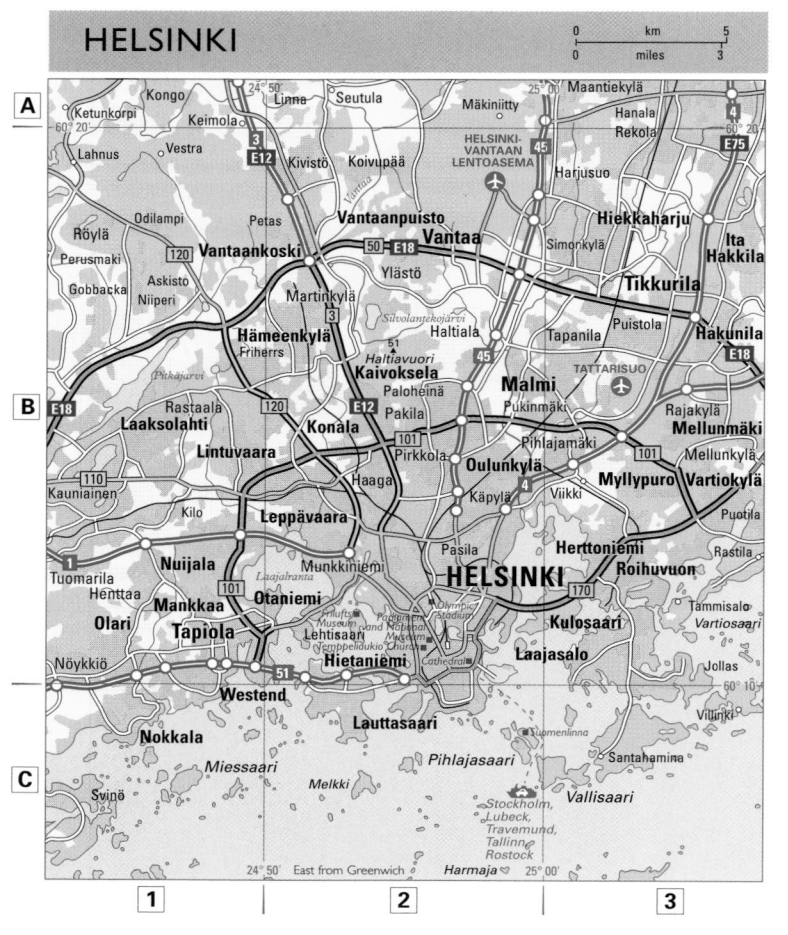

ISTANBUL

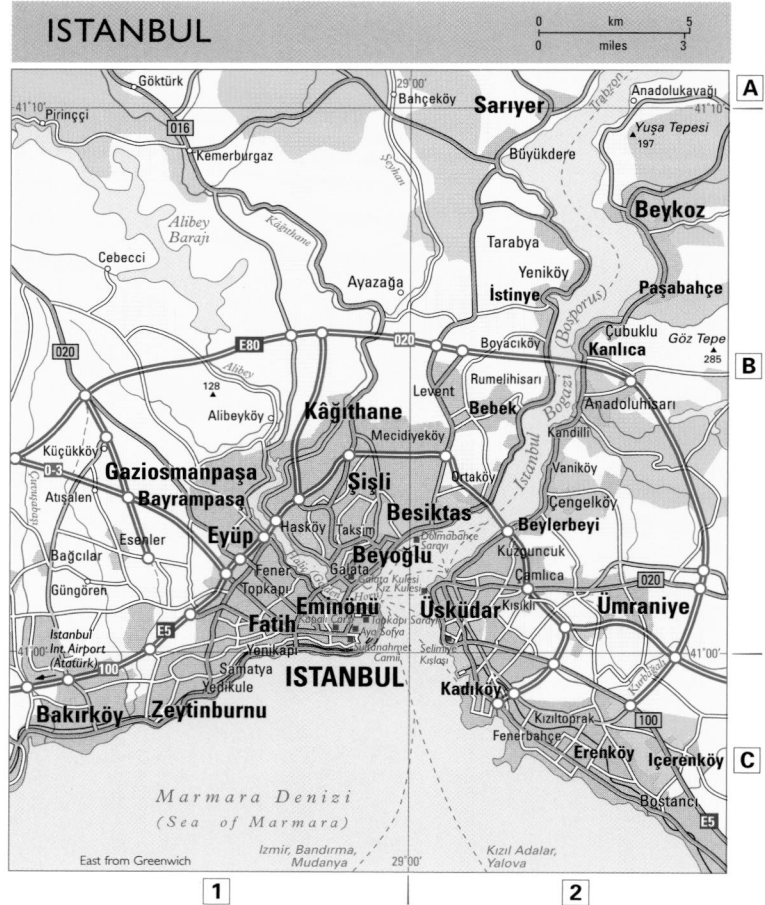

HONG KONG

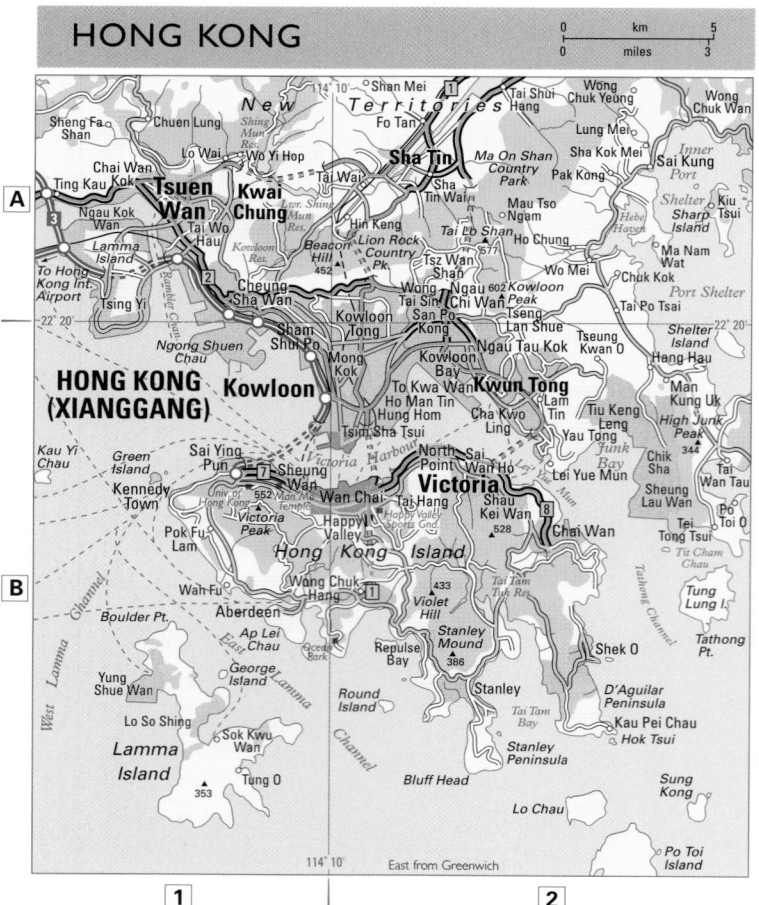

CENTRAL HONG KONG

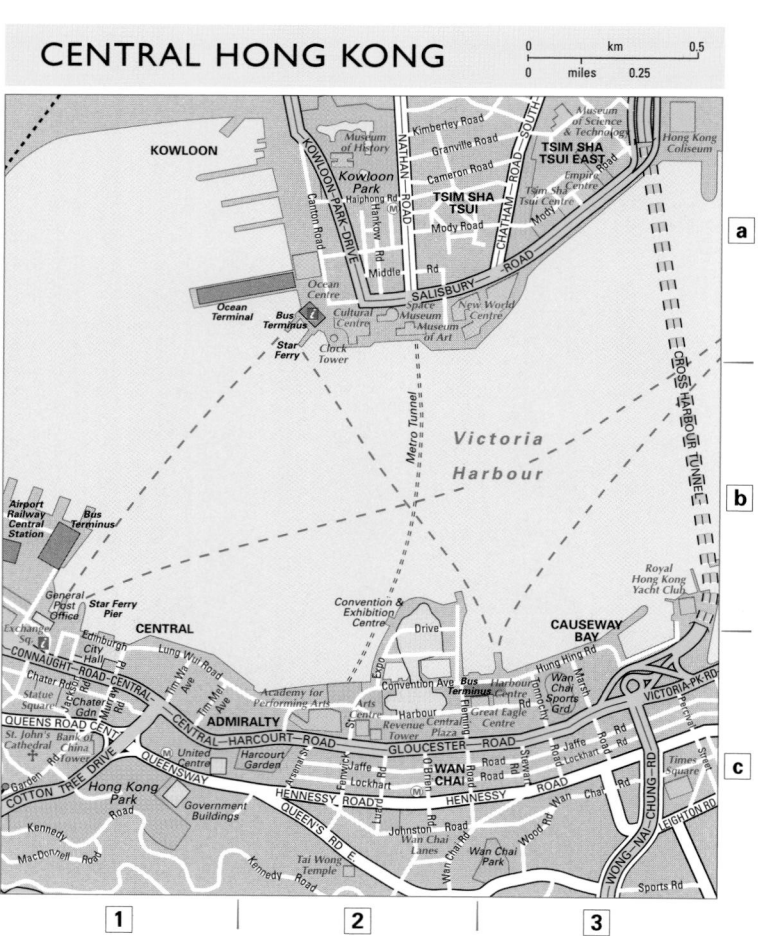

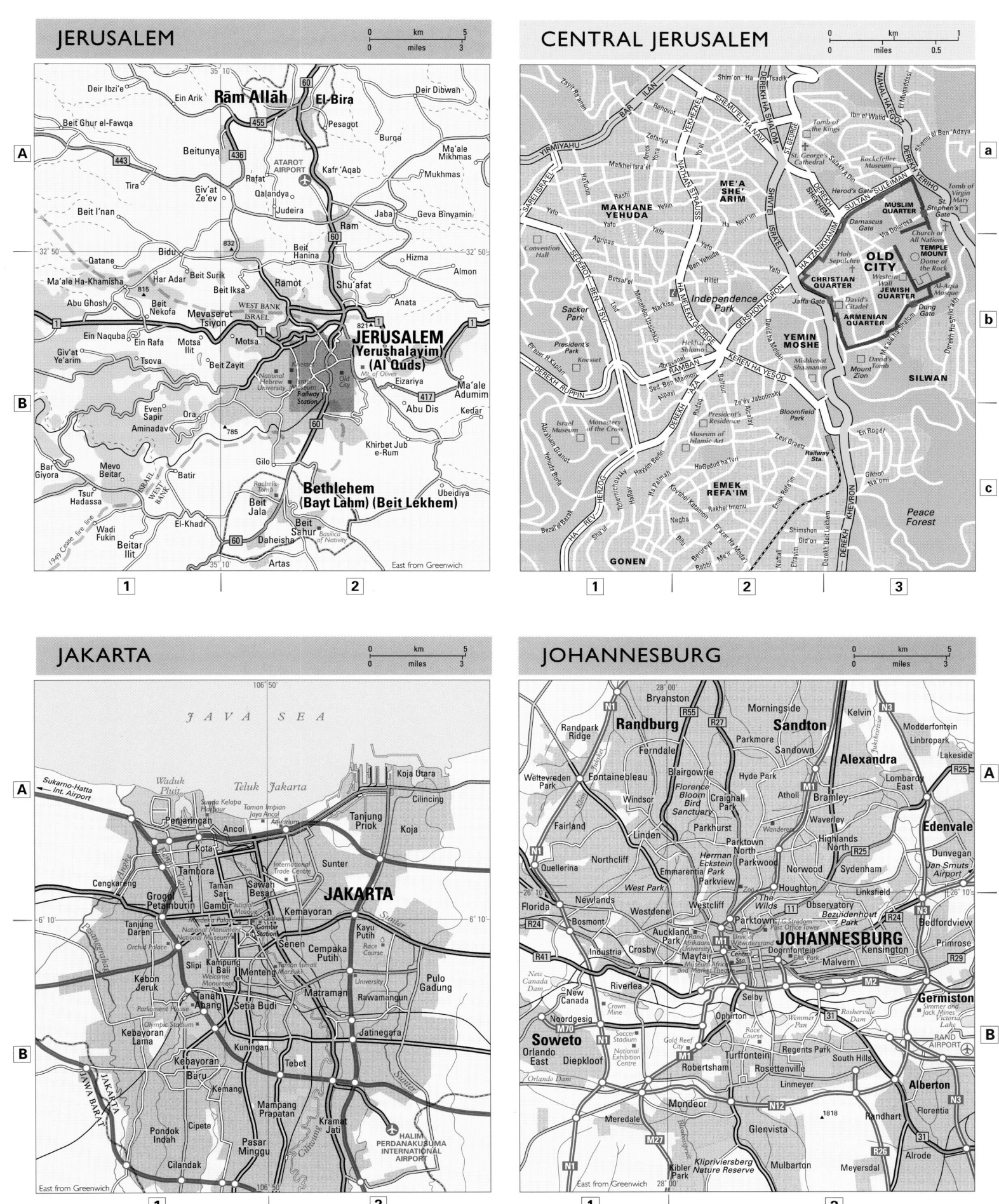

JERUSALEM

Ram Allāh · El-Bira · Deir Ibzi'e · Ein Arik · Deir Dibwan · Pesagot · Burqa · Beit Ghur el-Fawqa · Beitunya · Giv'at Ze'ev · Kafr 'Aqab · Ma'ale Mikhmas · Mukhmas · Tira · Rafat · Qalandya · Judeira · Jaba · Geva Binyamin · Beit I'nan · Ram · Qatane · Bidu · Har Adar · Beit Surik · Beit Iksa · Ramot · Shu'afat · Beit Hanina · Hizma · Almon · Ma'ale Ha-Khamisha · Abu Ghosh · Beit Nekofa · Mevaseret Tsiyon · WEST BANK ISRAEL · Anata · Ein Naquba · Ein Rafa · Motsa Ilit · Motsa · JERUSALEM (Yerushalayim) (Al Quds) · Giv'at Ye'arim · Tsova · Beit Zayit · Eizariya · Ma'ale Adumim · Even Sapir · Ora · Mt. of Olives · Abu Dis · Kedar · Aminadav · Old City · Bar Giyora · Mevo Beitar · Batir · Khirbet Jub e-Rum · Tsur Hadassa · Rachel's Tomb · Gilo · Bethlehem (Bayt Lahm) (Beit Lekhem) · Ubeidiya · Wadi Fukin · Beit Jala · El-Khadr · Beit Sahur · Basilica of Nativity · Daheisha · Artas · Beitar Ilit · 1949 cease fire line · ISRAEL WEST BANK · National Hebrew University · Israel Museum · Knesset · Railway Station

ATAROT AIRPORT

CENTRAL JERUSALEM

MAKHANE YEHUDA · ME'A SHE' ARIM · MUSLIM QUARTER · Tomb of the Kings · St. George's Cathedral · Rockefeller Museum · Herod's Gate · Tomb of Virgin Mary · St. Stephen's Gate · Damascus Gate · Via Dolorosa · Church of All Nations · Convention Hall · Holy Sepulchre · OLD CITY · TEMPLE MOUNT · Dome of the Rock · Independence Park · CHRISTIAN QUARTER · Western Wall · Al-Aqsa Mosque · Sacker Park · JEWISH QUARTER · Jaffa Gate · David's Citadel · ARMENIAN QUARTER · Dung Gate · President's Park · YEMIN MOSHE · Knesset · Mishkenot Sha'ananim · David's Tomb · Mount Zion · SILWAN · Israel Museum · Monastery of the Cross · President's Residence · Bloomfield Park · Museum of Islamic Art · En Rogel · Zevi Graetz · Railway Sta. · Gikhon Na'omi · EMEK REFA'IM · Peace Forest · GONEN

JAKARTA

JAVA SEA · Teluk Jakarta · Waduk Pluit · Koja Utara · Sukarno-Hatta Int. Airport · Sunda Kelapa Harbour · Taman Impian Jaya Ancol · Cilincing · Penjaringan · Ancol · Aquarium · Tanjung Priok · Kota · Koja · International Trade Centre · Sunter · Cengkareng · Tambora · Taman Sari · Sawah Besar · JAKARTA · Grogol Petamburan · Gambir · Istiqlal Mosque · Kemayoran · Tanjung Duren · Cathedral · Kayu Putih · Orchid Palace · National Monument · Gambir Station · Race Course · Slipi · Kampung I Bali · Welcome Monument · Senen · Cempaka Putih · Kebon Jeruk · Menteng · Taman Ismail Marzuki · Pulo Gadung · Parliament House · University · Tanah Abang · Setia Budi · Matraman · Rawamangun · Olympic Stadium · Kebayoran Lama · Kuningan · Jatinegara · Kebayoran Baru · Tebet · Kemang · Pondok Indah · Cipete · Mampang Prapatan · Kramat Jati · JAWA BARAT · Pasar Minggu · Cilandak · HALIM PERDANAKUSUMA INTERNATIONAL AIRPORT

JOHANNESBURG

Bryanston · Morningside · Kelvin · Randburg · Sandton · Modderfontein · Randpark Ridge · Parkmore · Sandown · Linbropark · Welverdiend Park · Ferndale · Fontainebleau · Blairgowrie · Hyde Park · Alexandra · Lakeside · Windsor · Florence Bloom Bird Sanctuary · Craighall Park · Atholl · Bramley · Lombardy East · Fairland · Linden · Parkhurst · Wanderers · Waverley · Highlands North · Edenvale · Northcliff · Parktown North · Norwood · Sydenham · Dunvegan · Jan Smuts Airport · Quellerina · Emmarentia Park · Parkwood · Houghton · Linksfield · West Park · Parkview · Zoo · Florida · Newlands · Westdene · Westcliff · The Wilds · Observatory · Bezuidenhout Park · Bedfordview · Bosmont · Strijdom Post Office Tower · Parktown · Primrose · Auckland Park · Rand Afrikaans University · Crosby · Univ. of Witwatersrand · Doornfontein · Kensington · JOHANNESBURG · Museum Africa and Market Theatre · Central Sta. · Mayfair · Malvern · Riverlea · Selby · Germiston · New Canada Dam · Crown Mine · Ophirton · Wemmer Pan · Rosherville Dam · Simmer and Jack Mines · Victoria Lake · Noordgesig · Soccer Stadium · Rock Course · RAND AIRPORT · Soweto · Gold Reef City · Turffonton · Regents Park · South Hills · Orlando East · Diepkloof · M1 · National Exhibition Centre · Robertsham · Rosettenville · Linmeyer · Alberton · Orlando Dam · Mondeor · Glenvista · Randhart · Florentia · Meredale · Kibler Park · Klipriviersberg Nature Reserve · Mulbarton · Meyersdal · Alrode

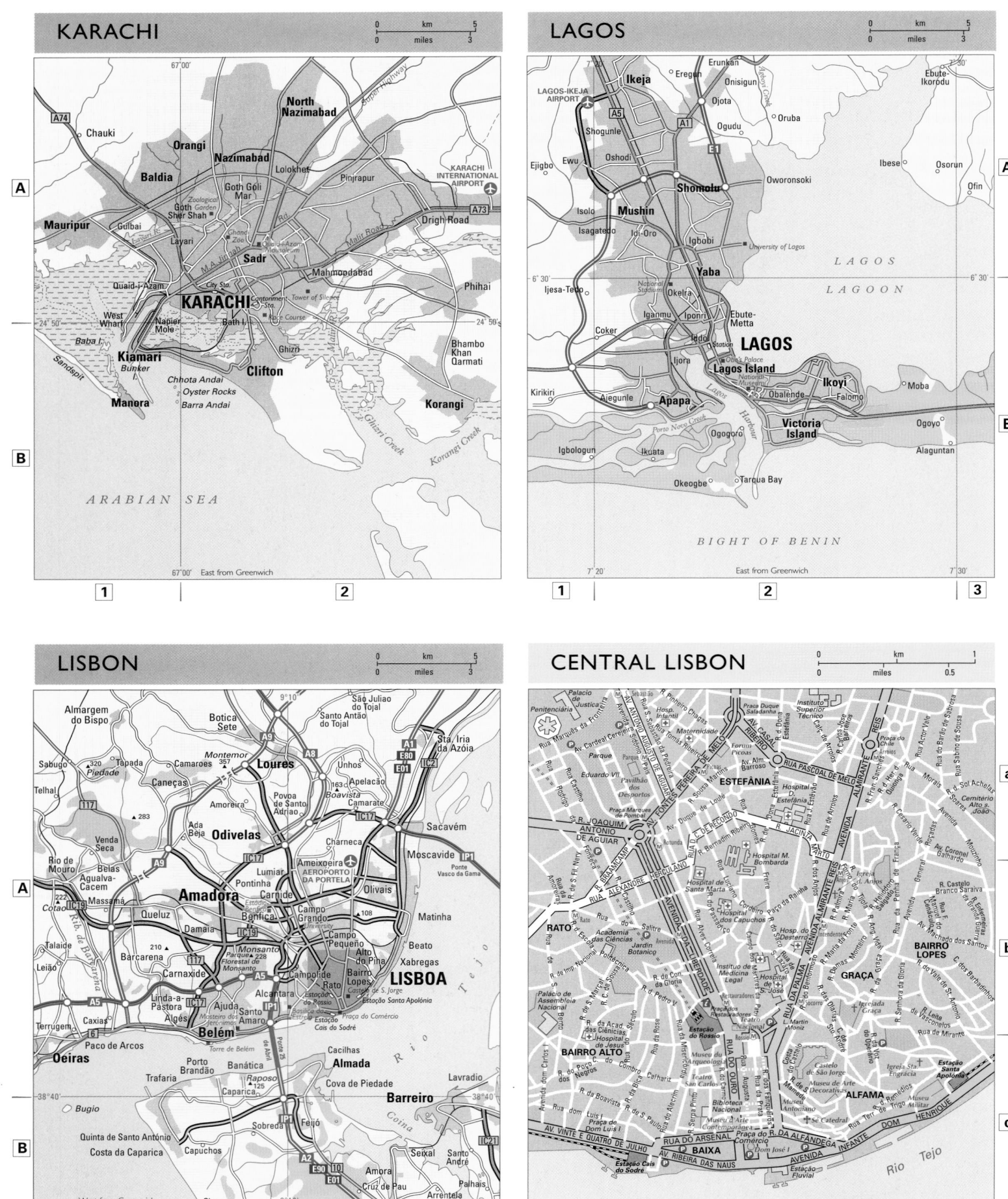

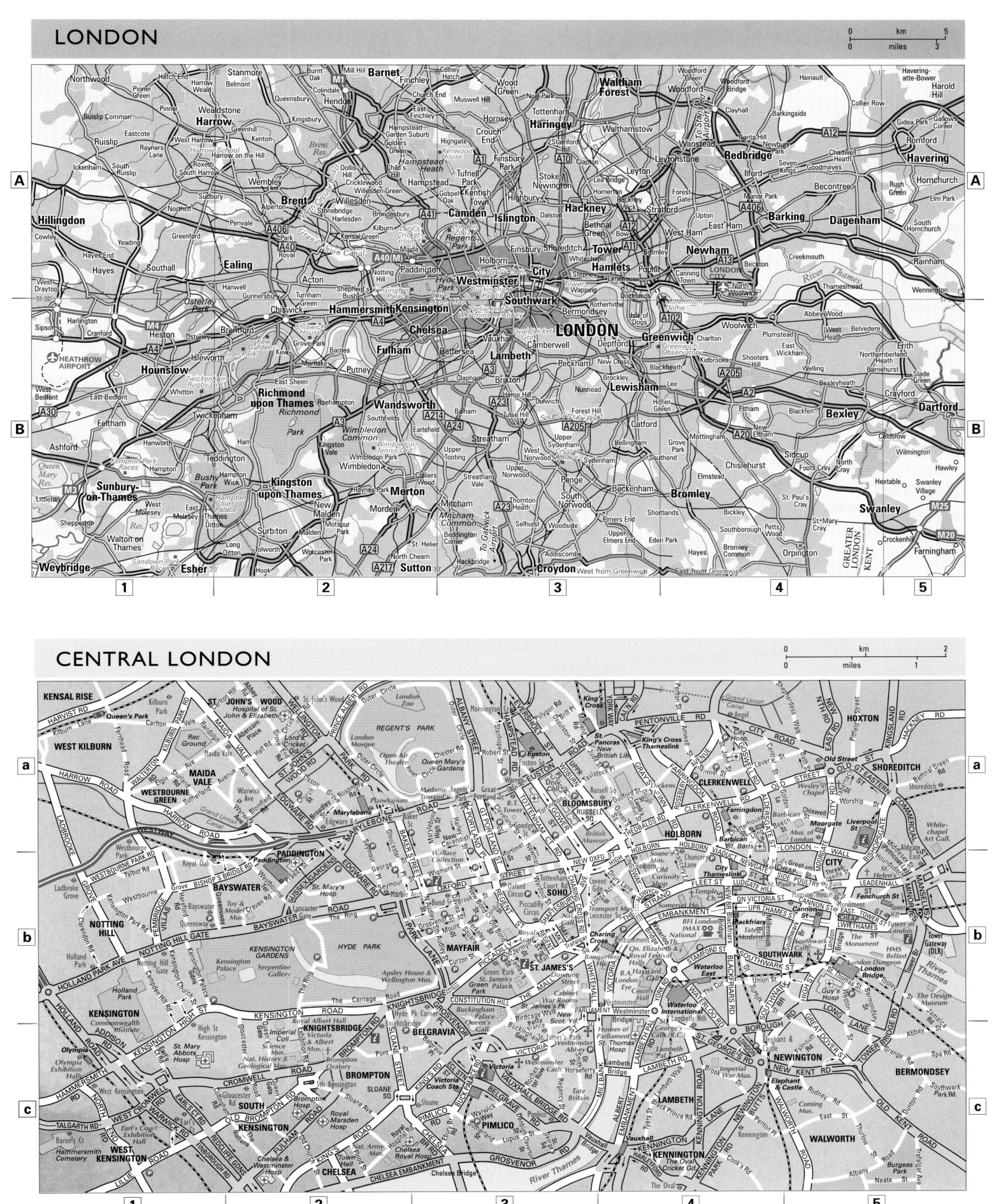

LONDON

CENTRAL LONDON

LOS ANGELES

LIMA

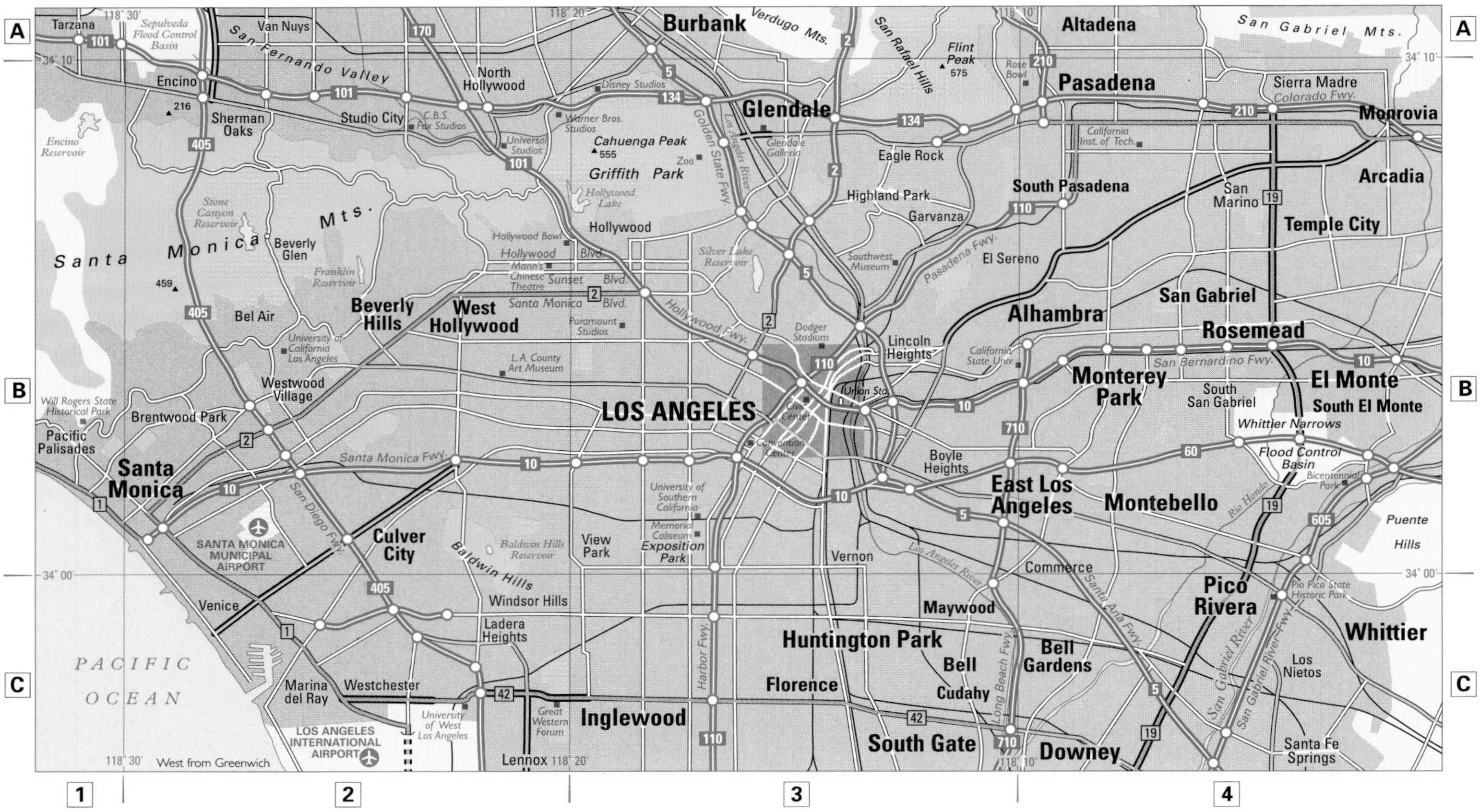

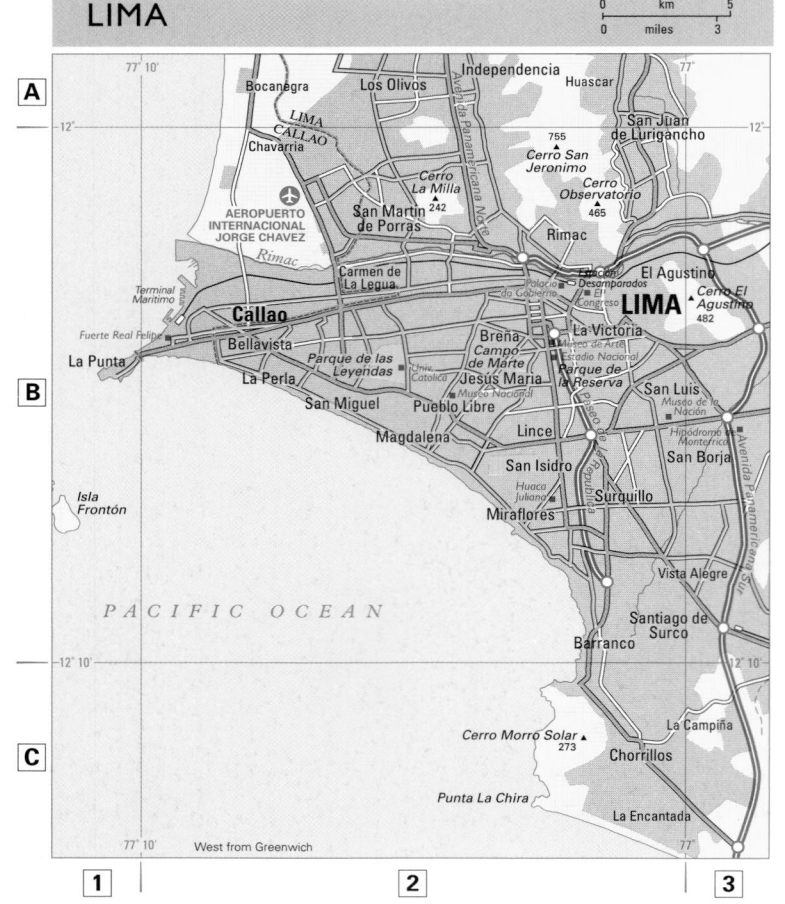

CENTRAL LOS ANGELES

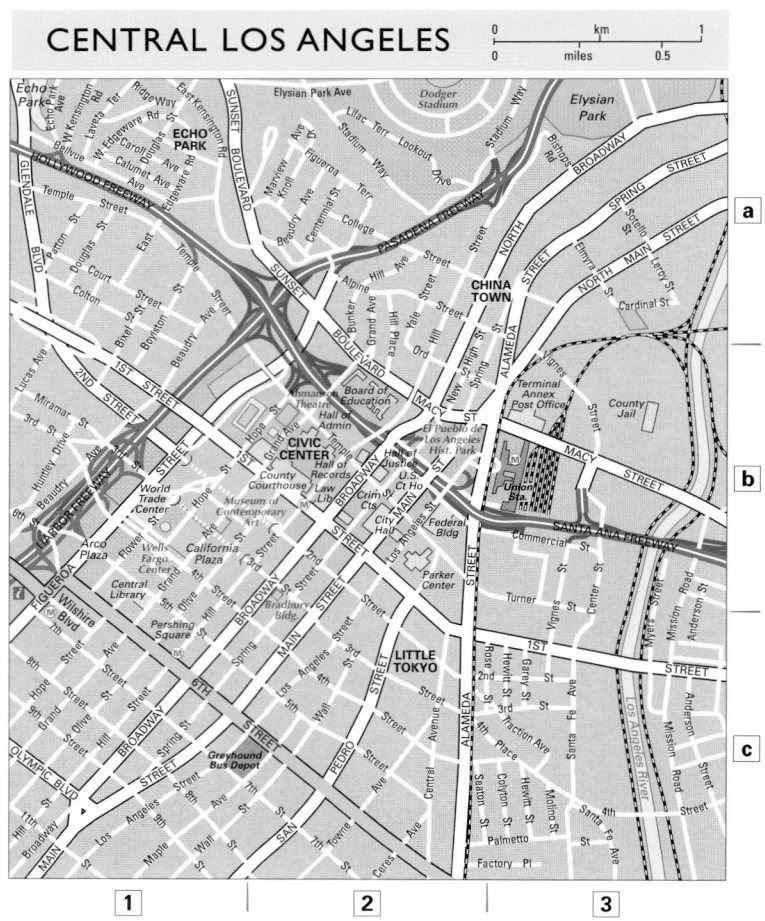

COPYRIGHT GEORGE PHILIP LTD

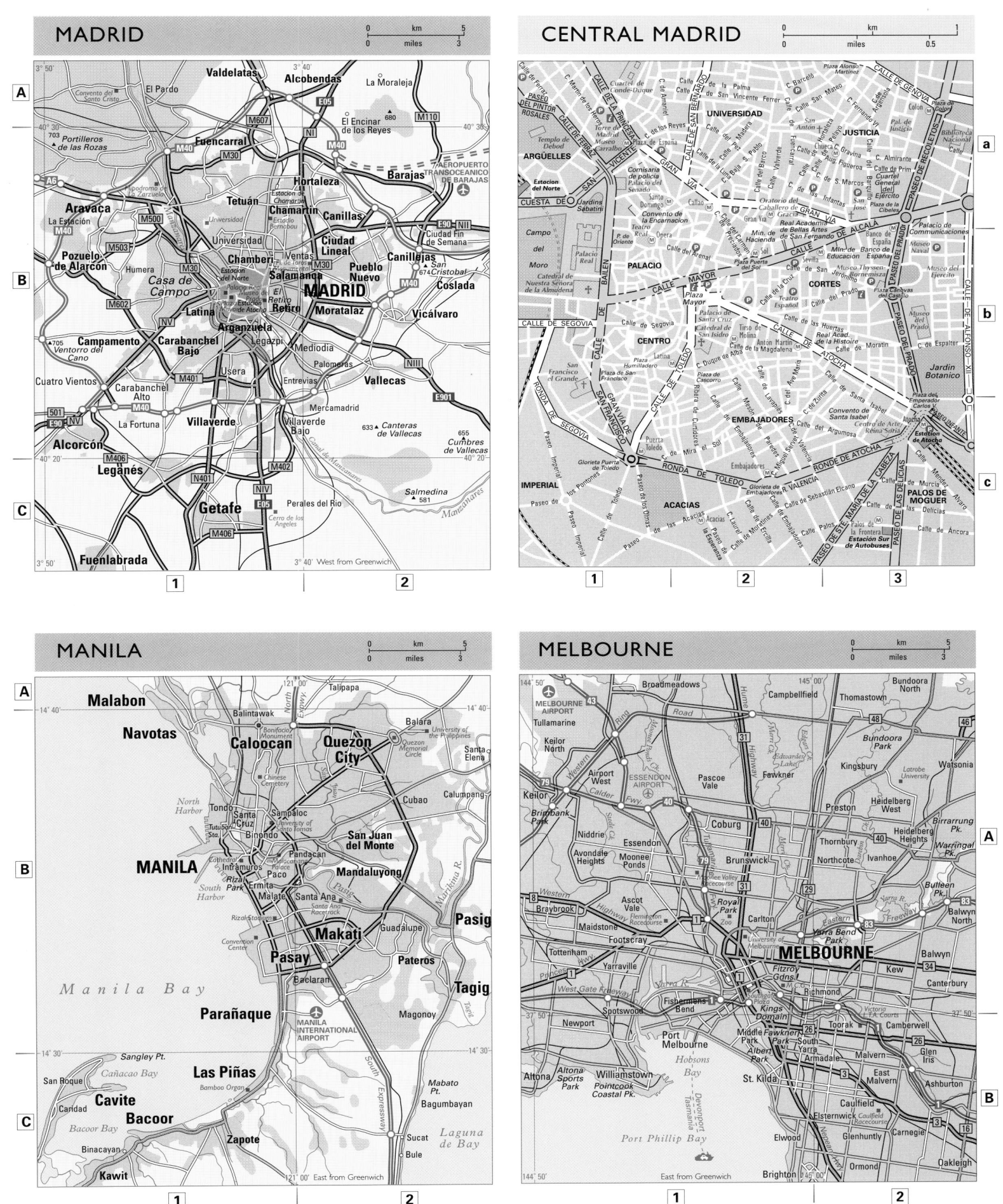

MADRID

0 — km — 5
0 — miles — 3

Valdelatas
Alcobendas
La Moraleja
Convento del Santo Cristo
El Pardo
3° 50'
3° 40'
E05
M607
La Moraleja
El Encinar de los Reyes
N1
M110
40° 30'
703
Portilleros de las Rozas
M40
M30
Fuencarral
Barajas
AEROPUERTO TRANSOCEANICO DE BARAJAS
A6
Hipódromo de la Zarzuela
M40
Hortaleza
Estación de Chamartín
Canillas
Aravaca
La Estación
M500
Tetuán
Chamartín
Estadio Bernabéu
Canillejas
Universidad
Chamberí
Ciudad Lineal
San Cristobal
Pozuelo de Alarcón
M503
Humera
M30
Ventas
M30
Pueblo Nuevo
Canillejas
Casa de Campo
Salamanca
MADRID
M40
Coslada
M602
Palacio Real
El Retiro
Moratalaz
Vicálvaro
705
Ventorro del Cano
NV
Latina
Arganzuela
Legazpi
Mediodía
Campamento
Carabanchel Bajo
Palomeras
NIII
Cuatro Vientos
Carabanchel Alto
Usera
Entrevías
Vallecas
M401
501
E90
NV
Villaverde
Mercamadrid
E901
La Fortuna
Villaverde Bajo
633 Canteras de Vallecas
Alcorcón
M406
40° 20'
Leganés
M402
N401
NIV
Salmedina
581
Getafe
E05
Perales del Río
M406
Cerro de los Ángeles
Fuenlabrada
3° 50'
3° 40' West from Greenwich

1 **2**

CENTRAL MADRID

0 — km — 1
0 — miles — 0.5

UNIVERSIDAD
JUSTICIA
ARGÜELLES
GRAN VÍA
PALACIO
CORTES
CENTRO
Plaza Mayor
EMBAJADORES
IMPERIAL
ACACIAS
PALOS DE MOGUER
Jardín Botánico
Estación de Atocha

1 **2** **3**

MANILA

0 — km — 5
0 — miles — 3

Malabon
Talipapa
121° 00'
14° 40'
Navotas
Balintawak
Balara
University of the Philippines
Caloocan
Quezon City
Santa Elena
North Harbor
Chinese Cemetery
Cubao
Calumpang
Tondo
Santa Cruz
Sampaloc
University of Santo Tomas
Binondo
Pandacan
San Juan del Monte
MANILA
Intramuros
Paco
Mandaluyong
Marikina R.
South Harbor
Rizal Park
Ermita
Pasig
Malate
Santa Ana
Pasig
Rizal Stadium
Santa Ana Racetrack
Makati
Guadalupe
Pateros
Pasay
Pateros
Tagig
Convention Center
Magonoy
Parañaque
MANILA INTERNATIONAL AIRPORT
Mabato Pt.
Bagumbayan
14° 30'
Sangley Pt.
Las Piñas
Bamboo Organ
Cañacao Bay
San Roque
Laguna de Bay
Caridad
Cavite
Bacoor
Zapote
Sucat
Bule
Bacoor Bay
Binacayan
Kawit
121° 00' East from Greenwich

Manila Bay

1 **2**

MELBOURNE

0 — km — 5
0 — miles — 3

144° 50'
Broadmeadows
145° 00'
Bundoora North
MELBOURNE AIRPORT
43
Campbellfield
Thomastown
Tullamarine
48
Bundoora Park
46
Keilor North
31
Fawkner
Kingsbury
Watsonia
Airport West
ESSENDON AIRPORT
Pascoe Vale
Latrobe University
Keilor
79
40
Coburg
40
Preston
Heidelberg West
Brimbank Park
Niddrie
Essendon
Brunswick
40
Thornbury
Heidelberg Heights
Birrarrung Pk.
Avondale Heights
Moonee Ponds
78
Northcote
Ivanhoe
Warringal Pk.
Maribyrnong River Valley Racecourse
31
29
Bulleen Pk.
Ascot Vale
Royal Park & Zoo
Carlton
83
Western Highway
Braybrook
Yarra R.
Eastern Freeway
Balwyn North
Maidstone
University of Melbourne
Yarra Bend Park
83
Footscray
MELBOURNE
Balwyn
Tottenham
Fitzroy Gdns.
Kew
Canterbury
Yarraville
West Gate Freeway
Richmond
34
Spotswood
Fishermens Bend
Kings Domain
Victoria Park Courts
37° 50'
Newport
Southgate Plaza
M.C.G.
Toorak
Camberwell
Port Melbourne
Middle Park
Fawkner Park
South Yarra
26
Malvern
Glen Iris
Albert Park
Armadale
26
Hobsons Bay
St. Kilda
East Malvern
Ashburton
Altona
Williamstown
3
Altona Sports Park
Pointcook Coastal Pk.
Caulfield
Caulfield Racecourse
Elsternwick
Glenhuntly
Carnegie
16
Devonport Tasmania
Elwood
3
Port Phillip Bay
Brighton
Ormond
Oakleigh
144° 50'
East from Greenwich
145° 00'
37° 50'

A **B**

1 **2**

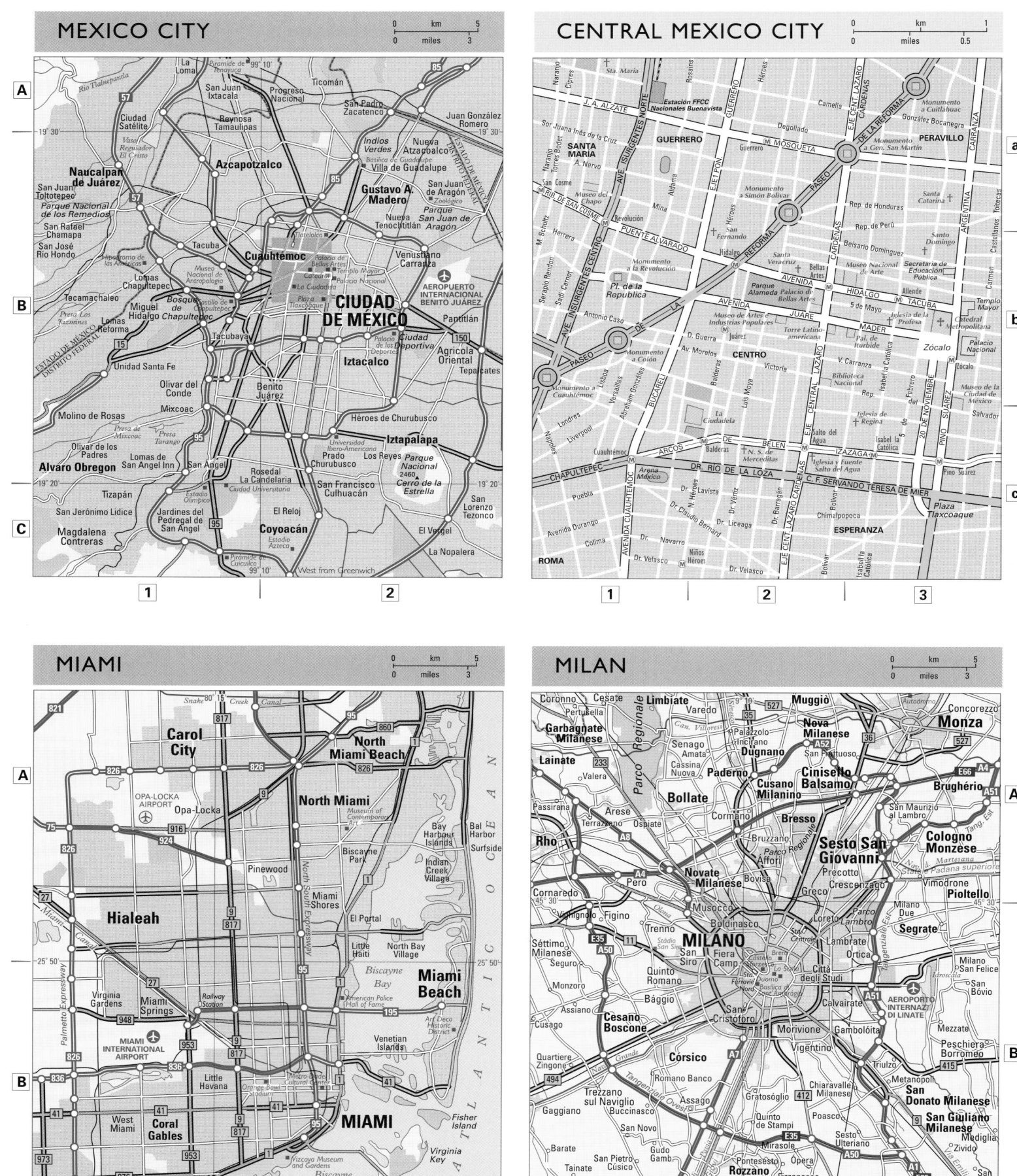

MEXICO CITY

km 5
miles 3

Rio Tlalnepantla
La Loma
Pirámide de Tenayuca
99° 10'
85
San Juan Ixtacala
Ticomán
Progreso Nacional
Ciudad Satélite
57
Reynosa Tamaulipas
San Pedro Zacatenco
Juan González Romero
19° 30'
Vaso Regulador El Cristo
Indios Verdes
Nueva Villa de Guadalupe
Basílica de Guadalupe
79° 30'
Naucalpan de Juárez
Azcapotzalco
85
San Rafael Chamapa
57
San Juan de Aragón
Gustavo A. Madero
Parque San Juan de Aragón
San José Río Hondo
Parque Nacional de los Remedios
Tacuba
Nueva Tenochtitlán
Nueva Atzacoalco
Hipódromo de las Américas
Cuauhtémoc
Palacio de Bellas Artes
Templo Mayor
Palacio Nacional
Venustiano Carranza
Zoológico
Lomas Chapultepec
Museo Nacional de Antropología
La Ciudadela
Plaza Tlatelolco
AEROPUERTO INTERNACIONAL BENITO JUÁREZ
Tecamachaleo
Bosque de Chapultepec
CIUDAD DE MÉXICO
Paptiltán
Miguel Hidalgo
Castillo de Chapultepec
150
Presa Los Fresnos
Lomas Reforma
Tacubaya
Ciudad Deportiva
Palac. de los Deportes
15
Agrícola Oriental
ESTADO DE MÉXICO
Unidad Santa Fe
Iztacalco
Tepalcates
DISTRITO FEDERAL
Olivar del Conde
Benito Juárez
Molino de Rosas
Mixcoac
Héroes de Churubusco
Presa de Mixcoac
95
Universidad Ibero-Americana
Iztapalapa
Olivar de los Padres
Presa Tarango
Lomas de San Angel Inn
San Angel
Prado Churubusco
Los Reyes
Parque Nacional 2460 Cerro de la Estrella
Álvaro Obregon
Rosedal La Candelaria
San Francisco Culhuacán
19° 20'
Tizapán
Ciudad Universitaria
19° 20'
San Lorenzo Tezonco
San Jerónimo Lídice
Estadio Olímpico
Jardines del Pedregal de San Angel
95
El Reloj
El Vergel
Magdalena Contreras
Estadio Azteca
Coyoacán
La Nopalera
Pirámide de Cuicuilco
99° 10'
West from Greenwich
99° 10'

A B C | 1 2

CENTRAL MEXICO CITY

km 1
miles 0.5

Naranjo
Cipres
Sta. María
Rosains
Héroes
Monumento a Cuitláhuac
J. A. ALZATE
Estación FFCC Nacionales Buenavista
GUERRERO
M. MOSQUETA
González Bocanegra
PERAVILLO
Sor Juana Inés de la Cruz
SANTA MARÍA
Guerrero
Monumento a Gen. San Martín
CARRANZA
Naranjo
A. Nervo
Monumento a Simón Bolívar
Santa Catarina
ARGENTINA
San Cosme
Rep. de Honduras
Castellanos
Toltecas
M. RIO DE SAN COSME
Museo del Chapo
Revolución
Mina
Rep. de Perú
Santo Domingo
M. Schultz
PUENTE ALVARADO
Heroes
San Fernando
Belisario Domínguez
Carmen
Herrera
Hidalgo
Santa Veracruz
Museo Nacional de Arte
Secretaría de Educación Pública
Monumento a la Revolución
Bellas Artes
5 de Mayo
Allende
Templo Mayor
Antonio Caso
Pl. de la República
Parque Alameda Palacio de Bellas Artes
HIDALGO
TACUBA
Catedral Metropolitana
Museo de Artes e Industrias Populares
D. Guerra
MADER
Iglesia de la Profesa
Monumento a Colón
Torre Latinoamericana
Pal. de Iturbide
Zócalo
Palacio Nacional
CENTRO
Av. Morelos
Victoria
V. Carranza
Zócalo
Biblioteca Nacional
Isabel la Católica
Museo de la Ciudad de México
La Ciudadela
Rep. del Salvador
Iglesia de Regina
20 DE NOVIEMBRE
PINO SUÁREZ
ARCOS
DE
BELÉN
N. S. de Mercedes
Isabel la Católica
Balderas
Iglesia y Fuente Salto del Agua
IZAZAGA
CHAPULTEPEC
Arena México
DR. RÍO DE LA LOZA
C. F. SERVANDO TERESA DE MIER
Plaza Tlaxcoaque
Puebla
Dr. Lavista
Dr. Vertiz
Dr. Barragán
Chimalpopoca
Avenida Durango
Dr. Claudio Bernard
Dr. Liceaga
ESPERANZA
Colima
Dr. Navarro
Niños Héroes
Bolívar
Isabel la Católica
ROMA
Dr. Velasco
Dr. Velasco

a b c | 1 2 3

MIAMI

km 5
miles 3

821
Snake Creek Canal
817
15
95
860
1
Carol City
826
North Miami Beach
826
826
1
OPA-LOCKA AIRPORT
Opa-Locka
North Miami
75
916
Museum of Contemporary Art
826
924
Biscayne Park
Bay Harbour Islands
Bal Harbor
Pinewood
Indian Creek Village
Surfside
27
North South Expressway
Miami Shores
1
Hialeah
817
El Portal
Little Haiti
North Bay Village
25° 50'
Biscayne Bay
25° 50'
Virginia Gardens
95
Miami Beach
948
Miami Springs
Railway Station
American Police (Hall of Fame)
195
27
MIAMI INTERNATIONAL AIRPORT
953
9
Art Deco Historic District
826
836
817
Venetian Islands
41
Little Havana
Metro-Dade Cultural Center
41
41
41
Orange Bowl Stadium
West Miami
973
41
Coral Gables
817
95
MIAMI
Fisher Island
976
953
9
Vizcaya Museum and Gardens
South Miami
Biscayne Bay
Seaquarium
Virginia Key
80° 15'
Barnacle State Historic Site
West from Greenwich
Key Biscayne

A T L A N T I C   O C E A N

A B | 1 2

MILAN

km 5
miles 3

Coronno
Cesate
Limbiate
Varedo
527
Muggiò
Autodromo
Concorezzo
Pertusella
Garbagnate Milanese
35
Nova Milanese
Monza
Lainate
Senago
Amata
Palazzolo
Cinisello
527
36
Valera
233
Cassina Nuova
Paderno
Cusano Milanino
Balsamo
E66 A4
Bollate
Brughério
A51
Passirana
Arese
Ospiate
Cormano
Bresso
San Maurizio al Lambro
Rho
Terrazzano
Bruzzano
Sesto San Giovanni
Cologno Monzese
A8
Novate Milanese
Parco Regionale
Precotto
Vimodrone
Cornaredo
Pero
Affori
Crescenzago
Pioltello
45° 30'
Bovisa
Greco
Milano Due
45° 30'
Vignolo
Figino
Olona
Musocco
Loreto
Segrate
Séttimo Milanese
E35
11
Trenno
Stádio
MILANO
Lambrate
Ortica
Milano San Felice
Seguro
San Siro
Fiera Camp.
Brera
Città degli Studi
Monzoro
Quinto Romano
Duomo
Basilica di Sant'Ambrogio
San Bóvio
Bággio
A50
AEROPORTO INTERNAZ. DI LINATE
Assiano
Calvairate
A51
Cúsago
San Cristóforo
Morivione
Gambolóita
Mezzate
Quartiere Zingone
Vigentino
Peschiera Borroméo
494
Córsico
A7
Triulzo
415
Trezzano sul Naviglio
Romano Banco
Chiaravalle Milanese
Metanopoli
San Donato Milanese
Gaggiano
Buccinasco
Gratosóglio
412
Quinto de' Stampi
Poasco
Sesto Ulteriano
San Giuliano Milanese
San Novo
E35
9
Medíglia
Barate
San Pietro Cúsico
Gudo Gamb
Mirasole
A50
Zívido
Zibido San Giacomo
Rozzano
Ponteséstro
Pizzonasco
Ópera
A1
San Brera
Noviglio
Tolcinasco
E35
Mezzano
Mairano
9° 10' East from Greenwich
Lócate di Triulzi
Zúnico

A B | 1 2

MOSCOW

MONTRÉAL

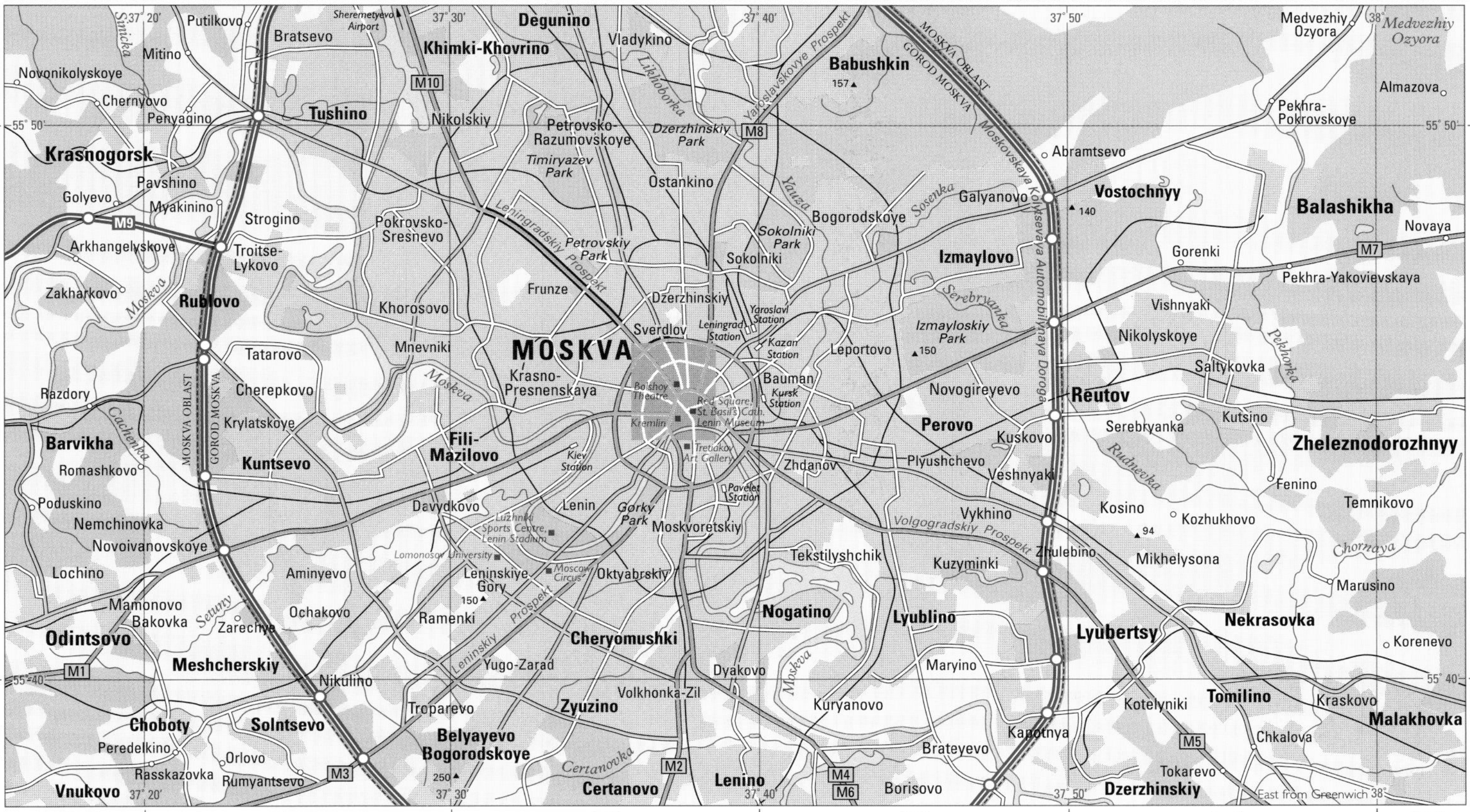

CENTRAL MOSCOW

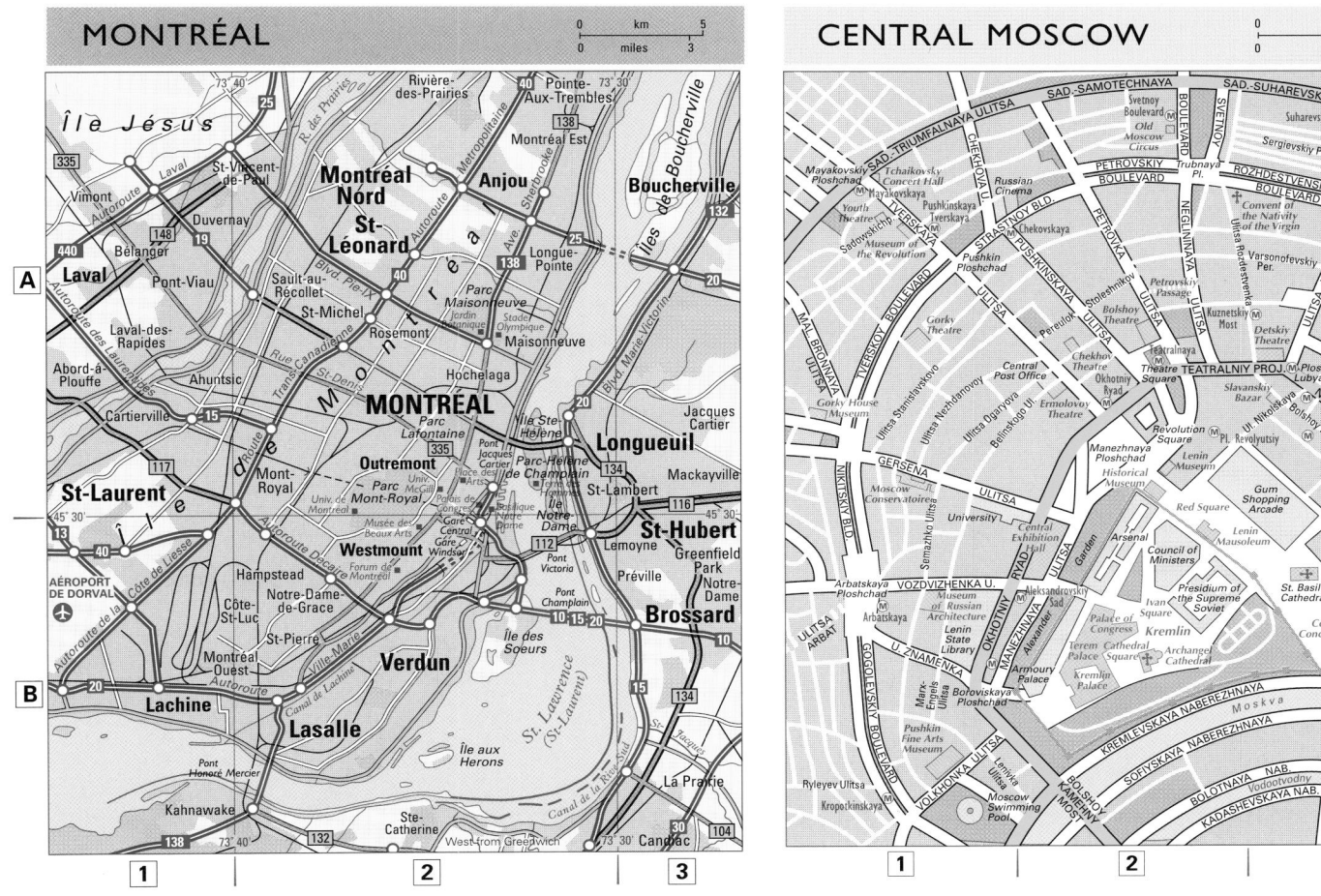

MUMBAI

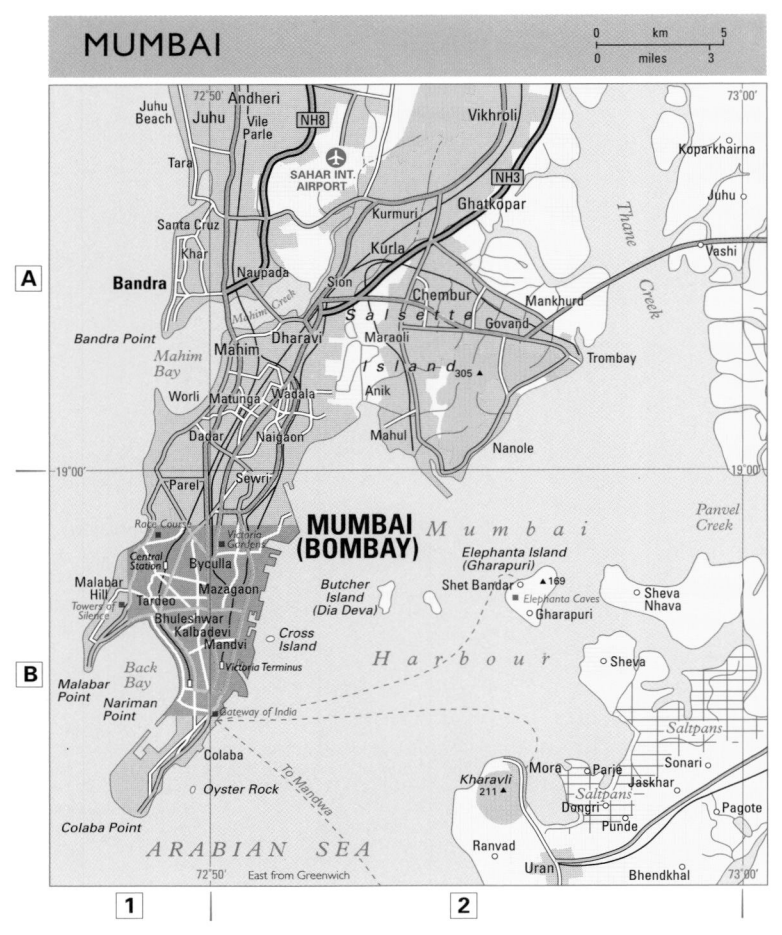

CENTRAL MUMBAI

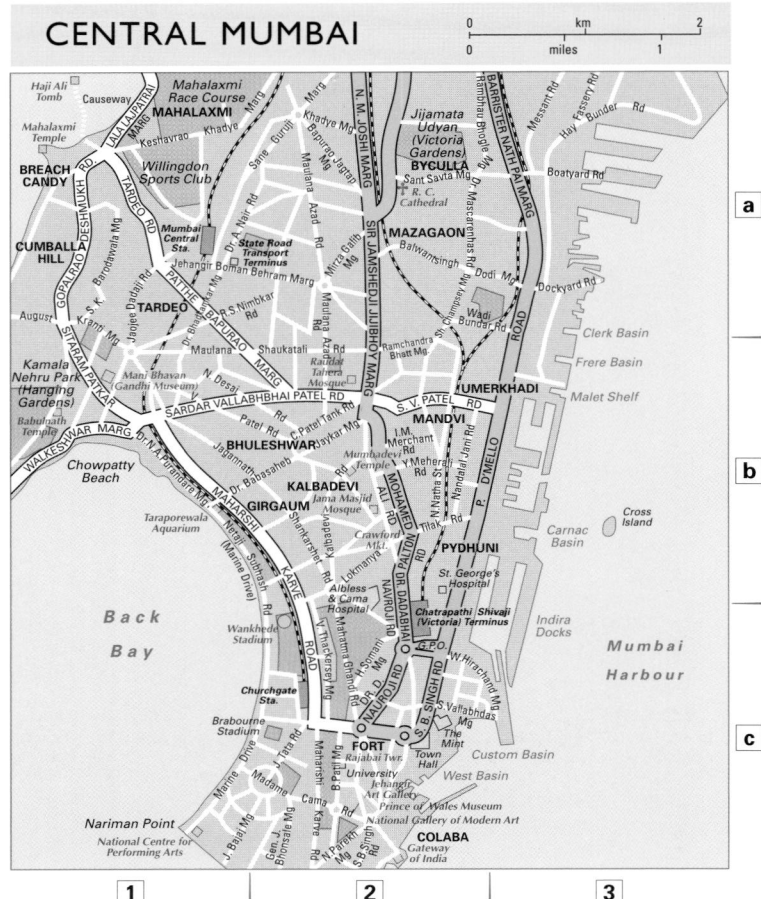

MUNICH

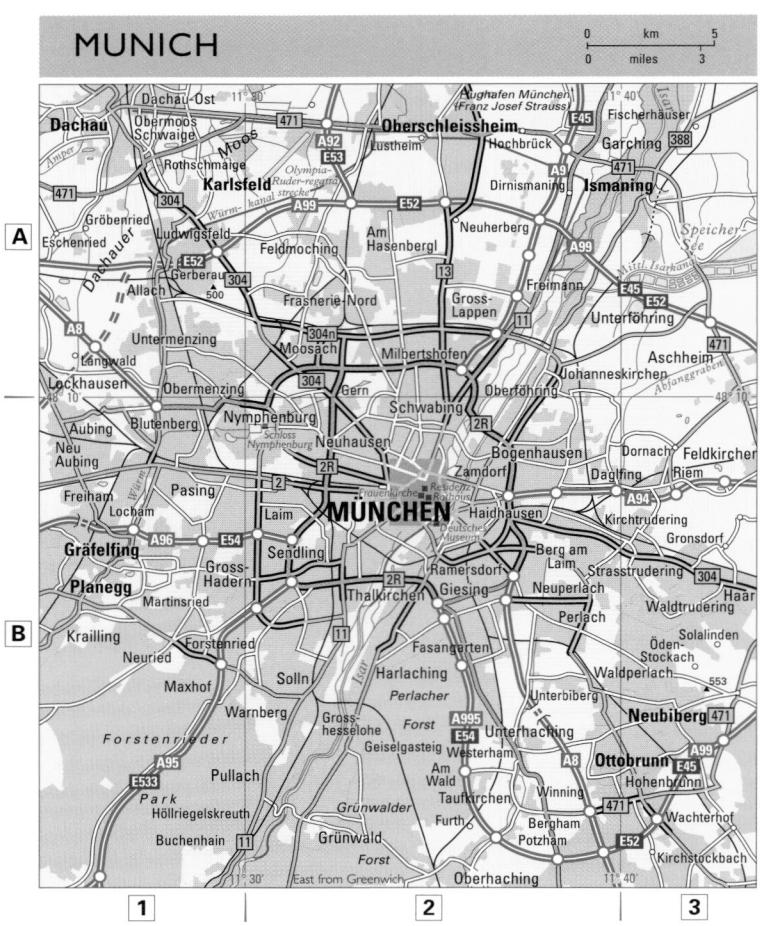

CENTRAL MUNICH

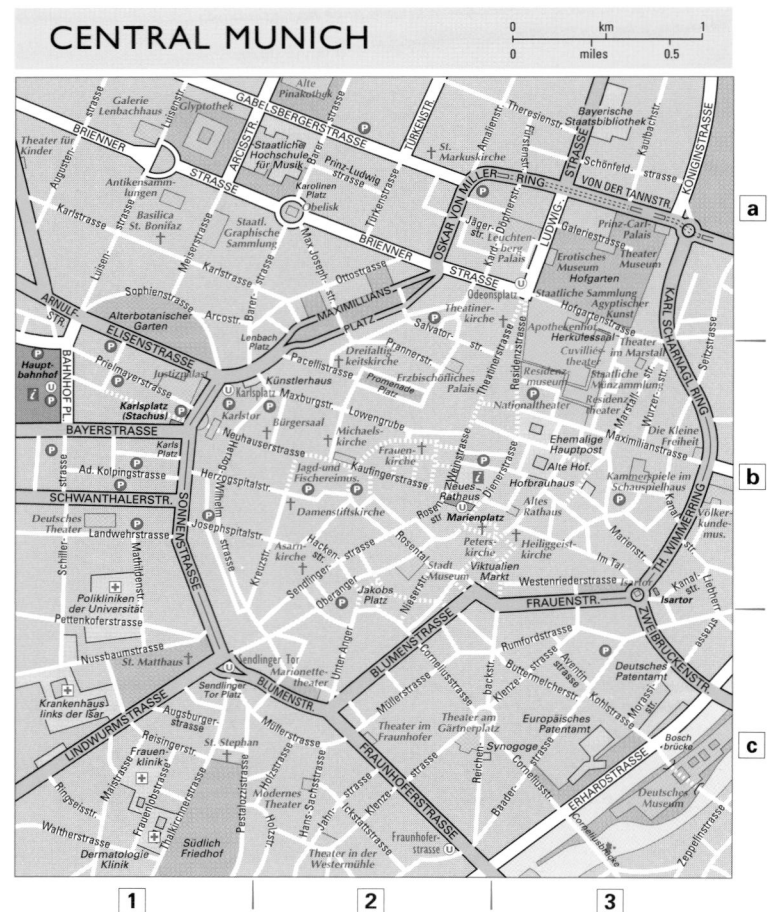

NEW YORK

0 km 5
0 miles 3

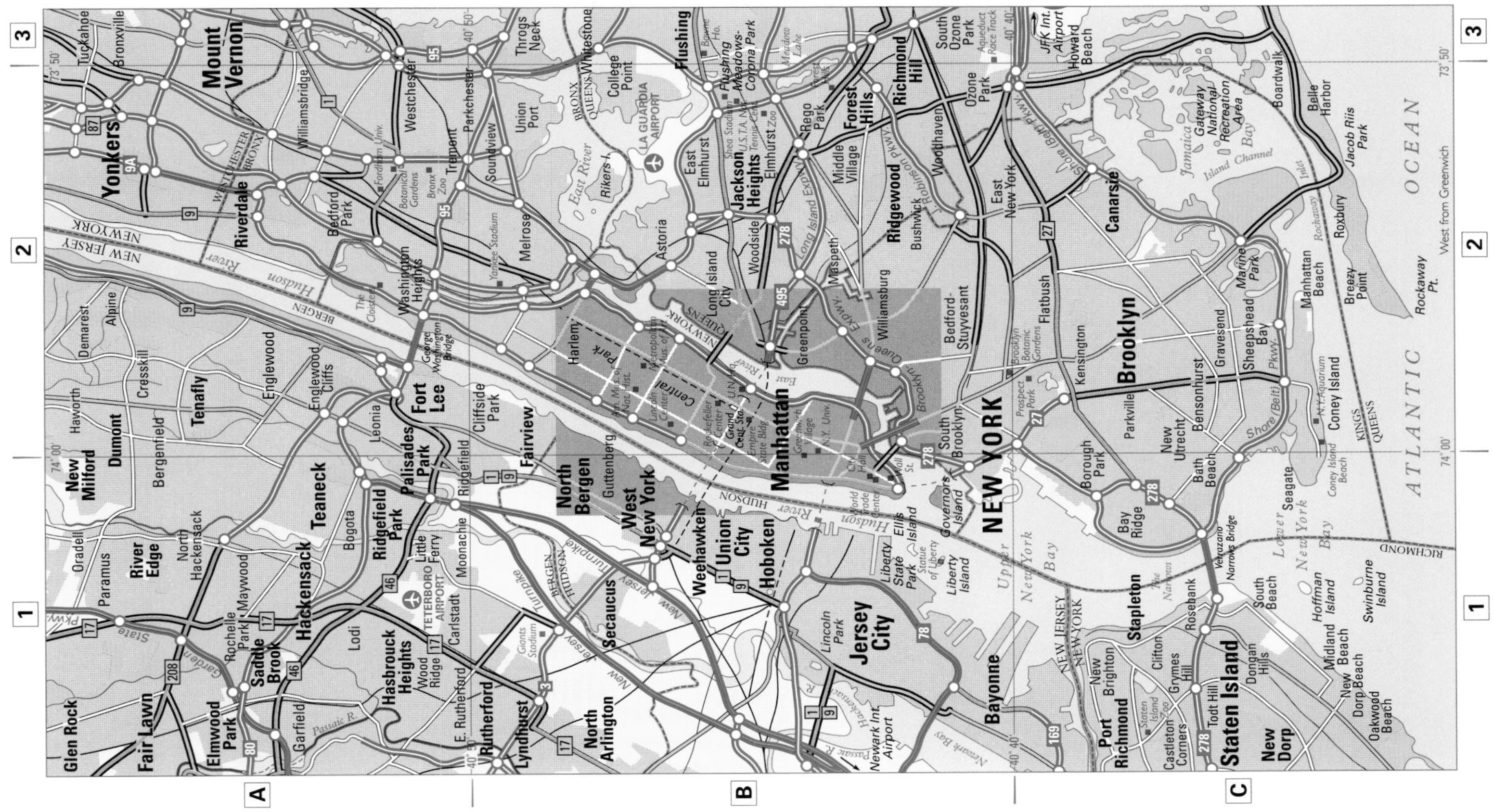

ATLANTIC OCEAN

Yonkers · Mount Vernon · Bronxville · Tuckahoe · Riverdale · Westchester · Scarsdale · Throgs Neck · Whitestone · Flushing · College Point · Richmond Hill · South Ozone Park · JFK Int. Airport · Howard Beach

Englewood · Tenafly · Fort Lee · Washington Heights · Harlem · Astoria · Jackson Heights · Forest Hills · Ozone Park · Rego Park · Ridgewood · Bushwick · East New York · Canarsie · Rockaway Pt. · Belle Harbor

New Milford · Dumont · Teaneck · Hackensack · Ridgefield Park · Palisades Park · Fairview · North Bergen · West New York · Weehawken · Union City · Hoboken · Manhattan · NEW YORK · Brooklyn · Flatbush · Sheepshead Bay · Coney Island

Glen Rock · Fair Lawn · Elmwood Park · Saddle Brook · Hasbrouck Heights · Rutherford · Lyndhurst · North Arlington · Secaucus · Jersey City · Bayonne · Port Richmond · Staten Island · New Dorp · Stapleton

ATLANTIC OCEAN

CENTRAL NEW YORK

0 km 2
0 miles 1

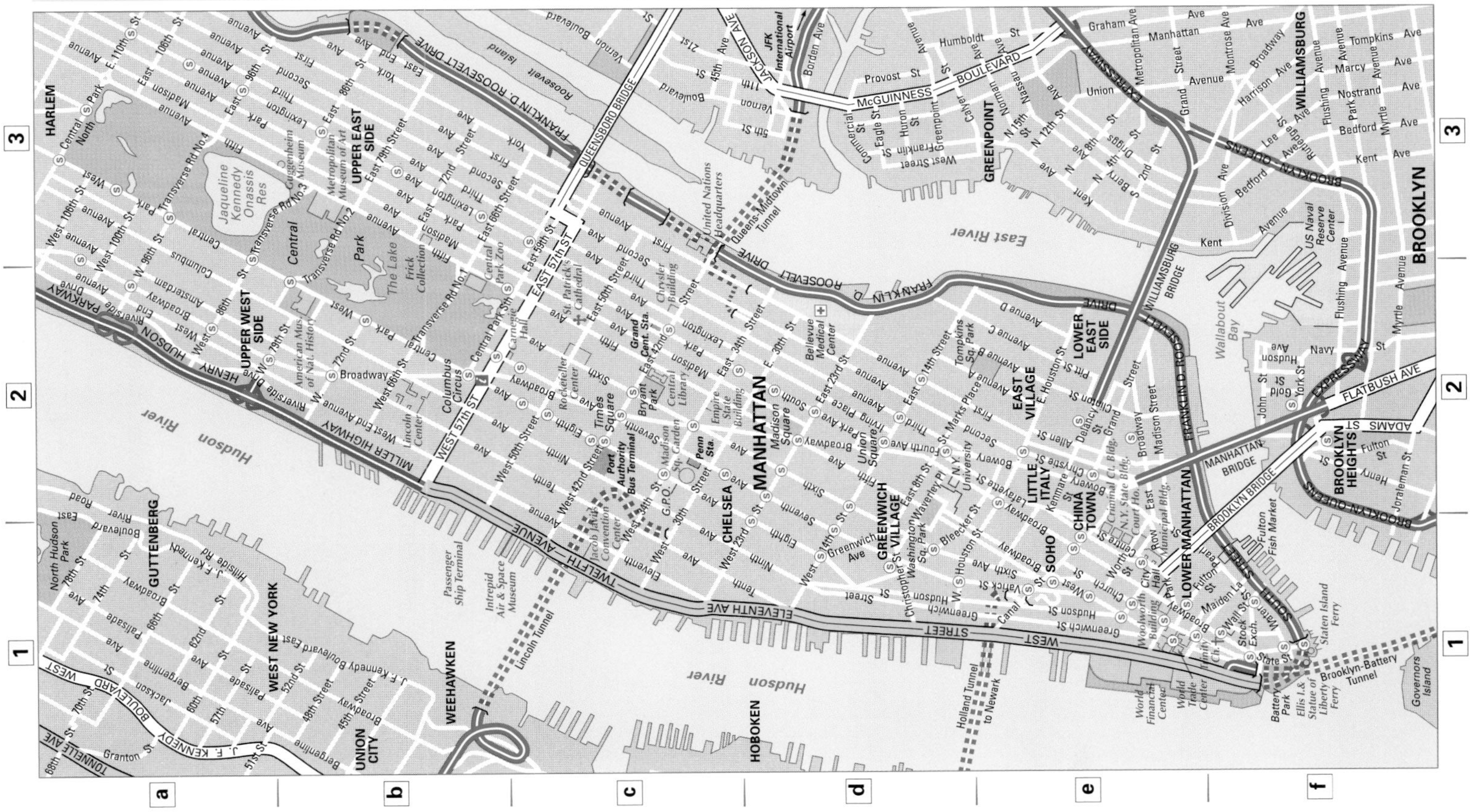

HARLEM · UPPER WEST SIDE · UPPER EAST SIDE · Central Park · The Lake · Jacqueline Kennedy Onassis Res. · Metropolitan Museum of Art · Guggenheim Museum · Frick Collection

Hudson River · East River · HENRY HUDSON PARKWAY · MILLER HIGHWAY · FRANKLIN D. ROOSEVELT DRIVE · Roosevelt Island · United Nations Headquarters · QUEENSBORO BRIDGE

Columbus Circle · Lincoln Center · Times Square · Rockefeller Center · Bryant Park · Port Authority Bus Terminal · Penn Sta. · Grand Central Sta. · Empire State Building · Chrysler Building · Madison Square · Bellevue Medical Center

CHELSEA · GREENWICH VILLAGE · EAST VILLAGE · LOWER EAST SIDE · MANHATTAN · Union Square · Washington Square · LITTLE ITALY · SOHO · CHINA TOWN · LOWER MANHATTAN · World Trade Center · Battery Park

GREENPOINT · WILLIAMSBURG · BROOKLYN · BROOKLYN HEIGHTS · WILLIAMSBURG BRIDGE · MANHATTAN BRIDGE · BROOKLYN BRIDGE · FLATBUSH AVE · Wallabout Bay · US Naval Reserve Center

WEEHAWKEN · UNION CITY · HOBOKEN · WEST NEW YORK · GUTTENBERG · Hudson River · Lincoln Tunnel · Holland Tunnel · Brooklyn-Battery Tunnel · Governors Island · Staten Island Ferry

OSAKA

0 km 5
0 miles 3

135° 10' 135° 20' 135° 30'

509
Funasaka
Takarazuka
Karato
Arima
462
722
Rokkō-Zan
932
598
Tanigami
Yamada
Iwazono
Hirota
Rokkō Tunnel
Kwansei Gakuin University
Mukō
Itami
OSAKA INTERNATIONAL AIRPORT
Toyonaka
Senriyama
Yamada
Settsu
Hirakata
Kori
1
Chūgoku-Jidōsha Expressway
Meishin Kōsoku Expressway
Suita
Neyagawa

A

428
Obu-tōge
365
Maya-Zan
699
Kōbe University
Okamoto
Nishinomiya
173
Higashiyodogawa
Kadoma
Shijonawate
170
A

Nada
403
Ashiya
43
Naruo
2
Amagasaki
Jūsō
Asahi
1
Moriguchi
Fukiai
Higashihada
Ōyodo
Miyakojima
Jōtō
Daitō
Ikuta
21
Rokkō Island
Nishiyodogawa
Yodo
Fukushima
Higashi Minami
Ōsaka Castle
Higashinari
Kōnoike
Ishikiri
KŌBE
Konohana
Aji
Nishi
Ikuno
Higashiōsaka
34° 40'
Nagata
Kōbe Harbour
Port Island
Minato
Naniwa
Tennōji
Zoo
Shitennō Temple
ŌSAKA
34° 40'

B
Suma
Ōsaka Aquarium
Suntory Museum
Osaka Harbour
Taishō
Liberty Park
Osaka Museum
Abeno
Nishinari
Kyūhōji
Kizuri
Yamamoto
Tainaka
25
Onchi
B

Higashisumiyoshi
Sumiyoshi Shrine
Sumiyoshi
Yao
Ikeuchi
YAO AIRPORT
Kashiwara
Sakai Harbour
Kizu
Yamato
26
Matsubara
Fujidera

Osaka Bay

Sakai
East from Greenwich

1 | **2** | **3** | **4**

OSLO

0 km 5
0 miles 3

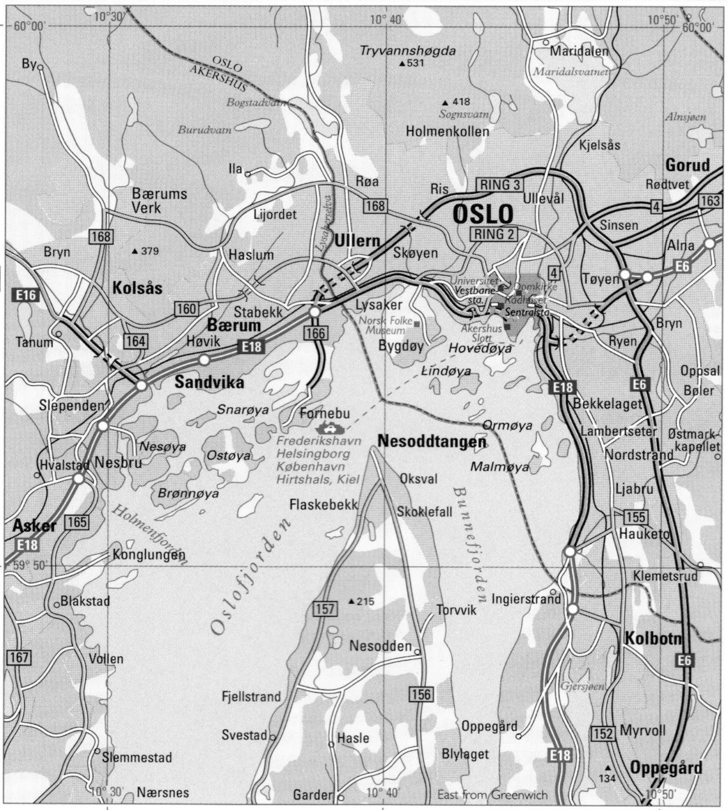

60°00' 10°30' 10°40' 10°50' 60°00'

By
OSLO AKERSHUS
Tryvannshøgda
531
Maridalen
Maridalsvatnet
Bogstadvatn
Burudvatn
418
Holmenkollen
Alnsjøen
Ila
Kjelsås
Gorud
A
Bærums Verk
Røa
Ris
RING 3
Ullevål
Rødtvet
163
Bryn
168
379
168
OSLO RING 2
Sinsen
Alna
E6
Kolsås
Haslum
Ullern
Skøyen
4
Tøyen
160
Stabekk
Lysaker
Bryn
Tahum
164
Bærum
166
Norsk Folke-Museum
Akershus Slott
Sentrum
Oppsal
Bøler
E18
Høvik
Bygdøy
Hovedøya
Ryen
E6
Sandvika
Snarøya
Forrnebu
Lindøya
Bekkelaget
E18
Slependen
Nesøya
Ostøya
Ormøya
Lambertseter
Nordstrand
Østmark-kapellet
155
Hvalstad
Nesbru
Brønnøya
Malmøya
Ljabru
Hauketo
Frederikshavn Helsingborg København Hirtshals, Kiel
Nesoddtangen
Asker
E18
Konglungen
Oksval
Flaskebekk
Skoklefall
Klemetsrud
165
59° 50'
Blåstad
Vollen
Nesodden
157
215
Torvvik
Ingierstrand
Kolbotn
167
Fjellstrand
Bunnefjorden
Gjersjøen
E6
B
Holmenfjorden
Oslofjorden
156
Oppegård
152
Myrvoll
Svestad
Hasle
Blylaget
E18
134
Slemmestad
Garder
Oppegård
Nærsnes
10° 30' 10° 40' 10° 50'
East from Greenwich

1 | **2** | **3** | **4**

CENTRAL OSLO

0 km 0.5
0 miles 0.25

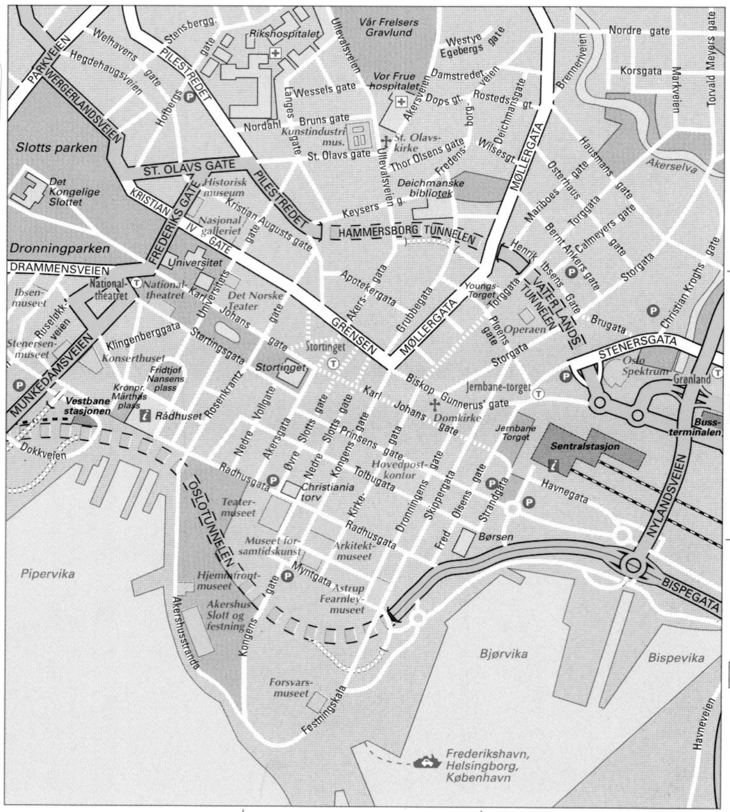

Wethaven's gate
Stensberg
Rikshospitalet
Vår Frelsers Gravlund
Westye Egebergs gate
Nordre gate
Korsgata
Markveien
Torvald Meyers gate
Hegdehaugsveien
Pilestredet
Vor Frue hospitalet
Damstredet
Brenneriveien
PARKVEIEN
Wessels gate
Nordahl
Kunstindustri mus.
St. Olavs kirke
St. Olavs gate
Thor Olsens gate
Fredens
Deichmanske
Mauhaus gate
Akerselva
a
Slotts parken
ST. OLAVS GATE
Historisk museum
PILESTREDET
Deichmanske bibliotek
Osterhaus gate
KRISTIAN IV S GATE
Det Kongelige Slott
Kr. Augusts gate
Keysers
HAMMERSBORG TUNNELEN
MØLLERGATA
Storgata
Henrik
FREDERIKS GATE
Universitet
Nasjonal galleriet
GRENSEN
Brent Anker gate
Calmeyers gate
Torggata
Dronningparken
DRAMMENSVEIEN
National theatret
Aperbergata
Grubbegata
Youngs Torget
MØLLERGATA
Operaen
Christian krohgs gate
STENERSGATA
Ibsen museet
Det Norske Teater
Klingenberggata
Stortinget
Storgata
Brugata
VATERLANDS TUNNELEN
P
Oslo Spektrum
Rosenkrantz
Karl Johans gate
Jernbane-torget
MUNKEDAMSVEIEN
Stenersen-museet
Konserthuset
Kronpr.
Bislet
P
b
Vestbane stasjonen
Fridtjof Nansens plass
T
Domkirke
BUSS-terminalen
Vestbane stasjonen
Kr. Augusts
Rådhuset
Nedre
Prinsens gate
Tollbugata
Sentralstasjon
Christiania torv
Dokkveien
Rådhusgata
Kongens gate
Hovedpost-kontor
Jernbane Torget
NYLANDSVEIEN
Dronningens
Havnegata
Teater-plass
OSLOTUNNELEN
Skippergata
Strandgata
Fred.
Børsen
Arkitekt museet
Rådhusgata
Strandgata
Myntgata
Åstrup
Pipervika
Hjemme-fronts-museet
Museet for samtidskunst
Akershus Slott og festning
Fearnley museet
Akershusstranda
Bjørvika
Festningen
c
Forsvars-museet
Bjørvika
BISPEGATA
Bispevika
Frederikshavn, Helsingborg, København
Hammerveien

1 | **2** | **3**

PARIS

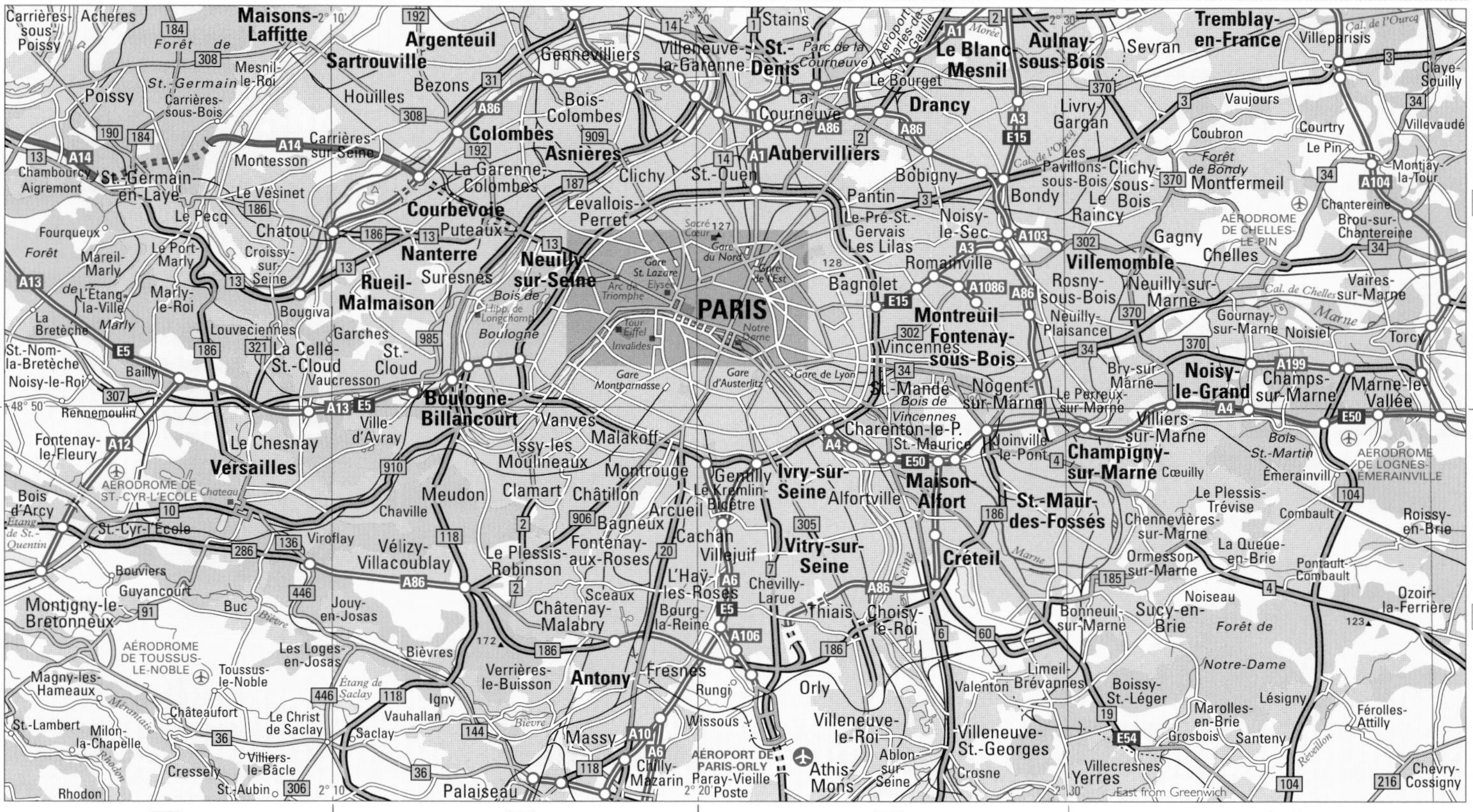

CENTRAL PARIS

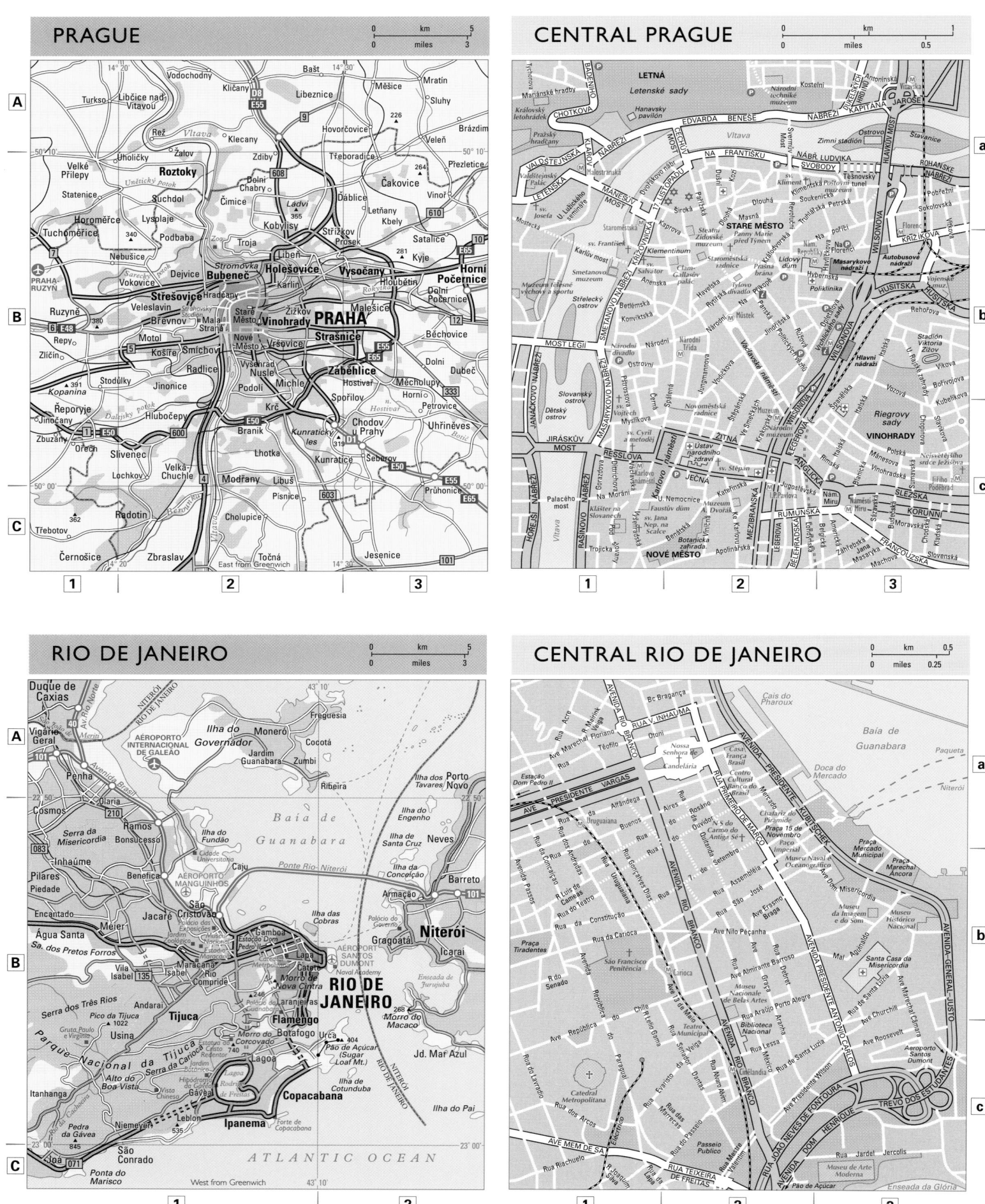

ROME

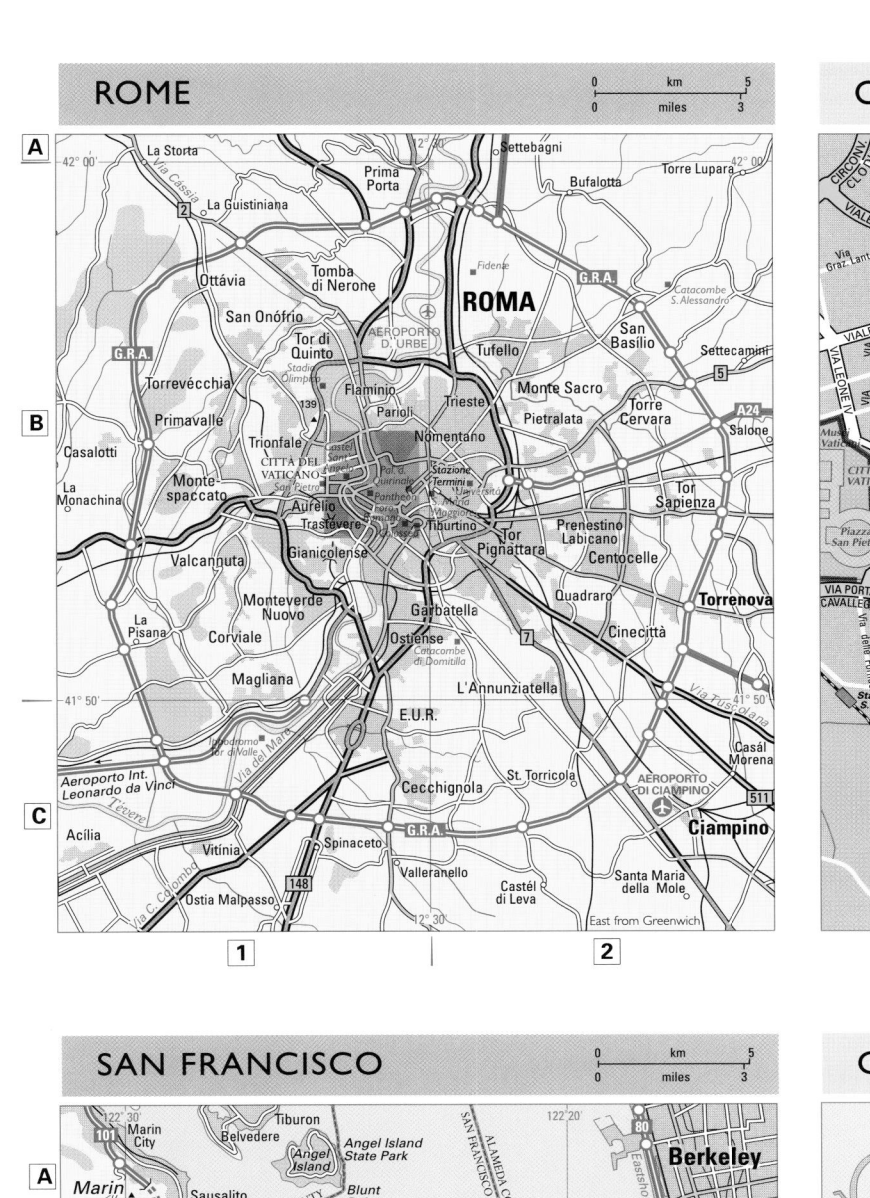

CENTRAL ROME

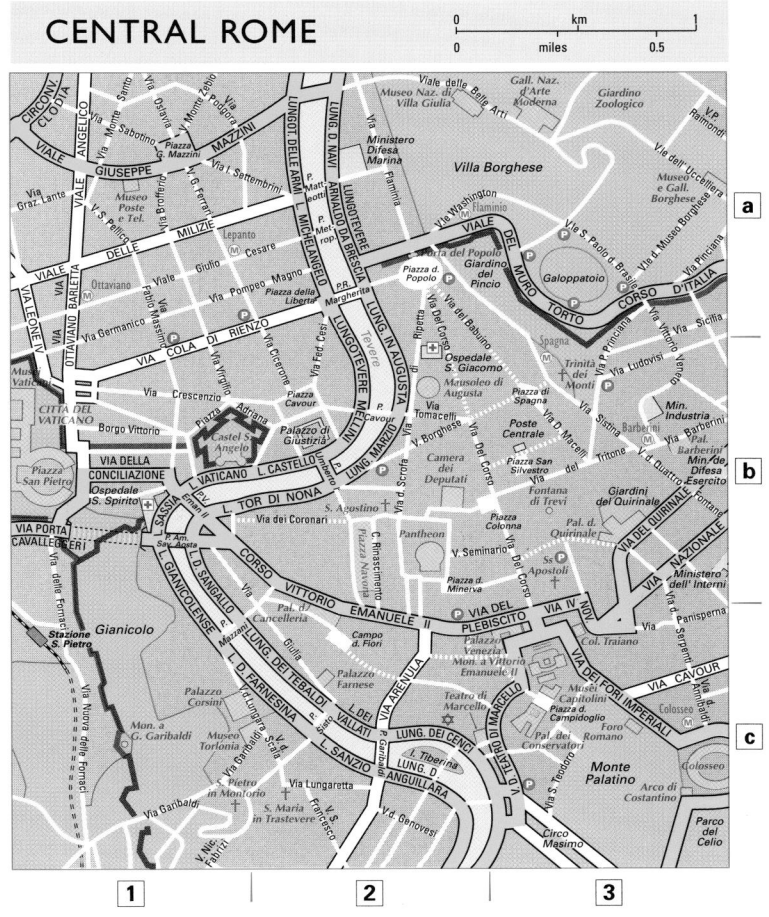

SAN FRANCISCO

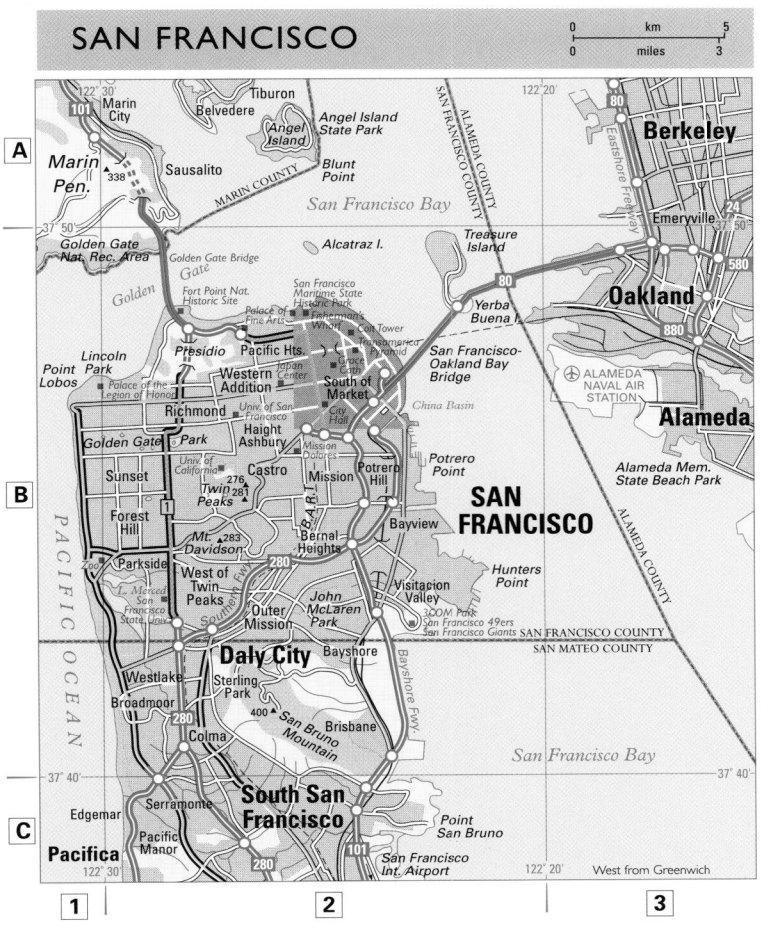

CENTRAL SAN FRANCISCO

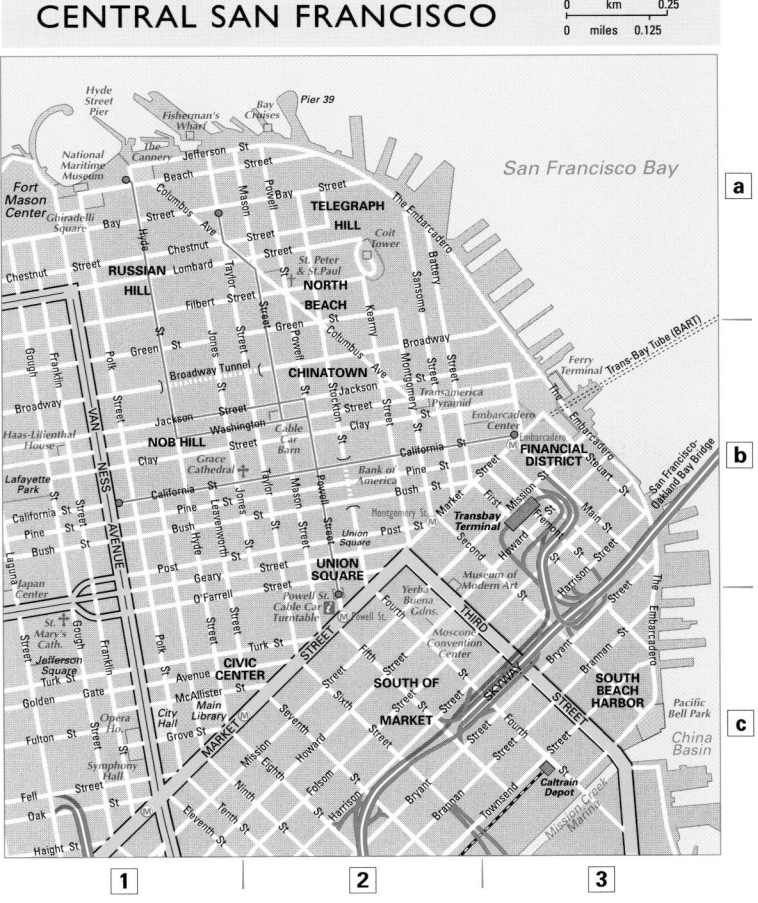

COPYRIGHT GEORGE PHILIP LTD

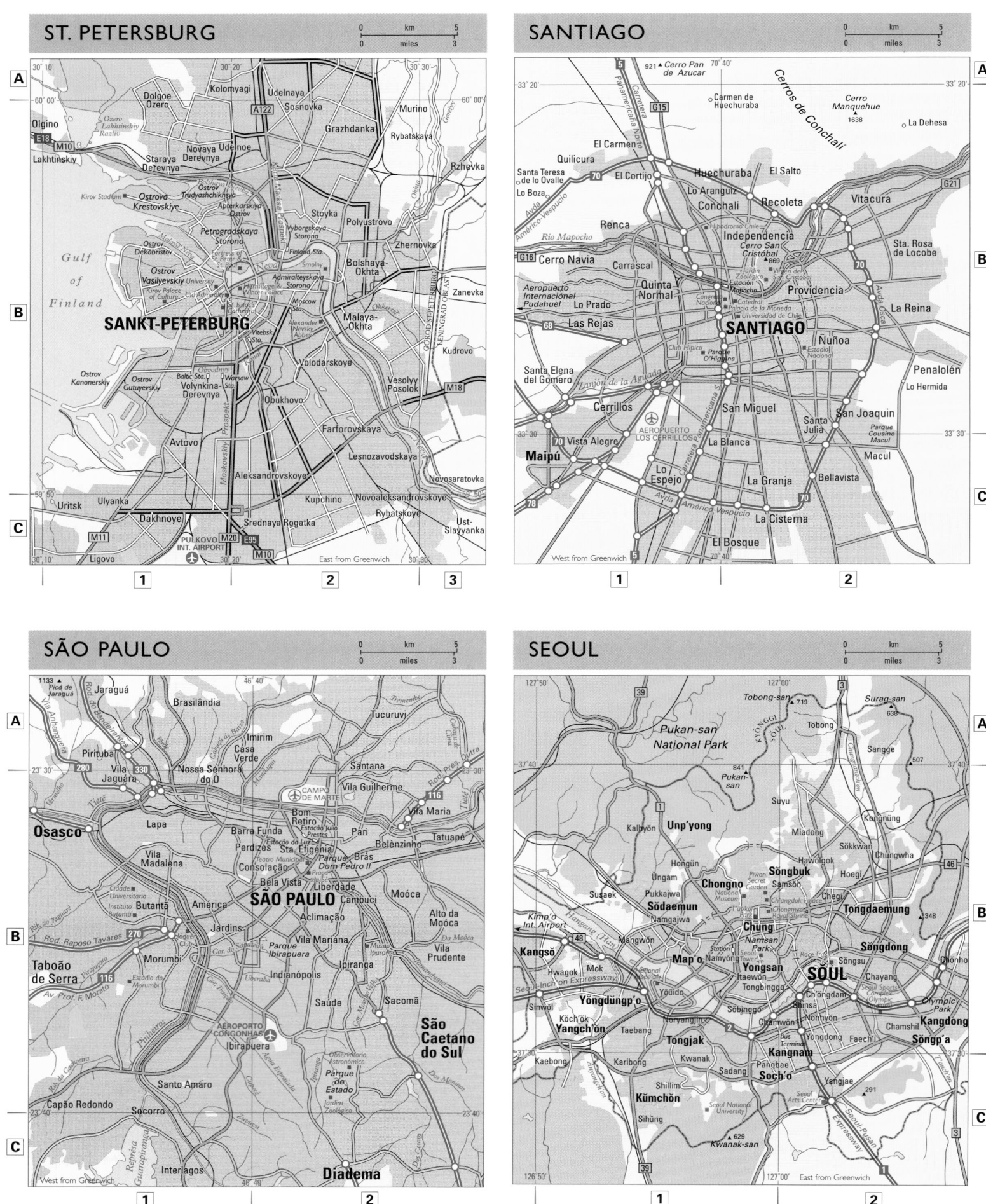

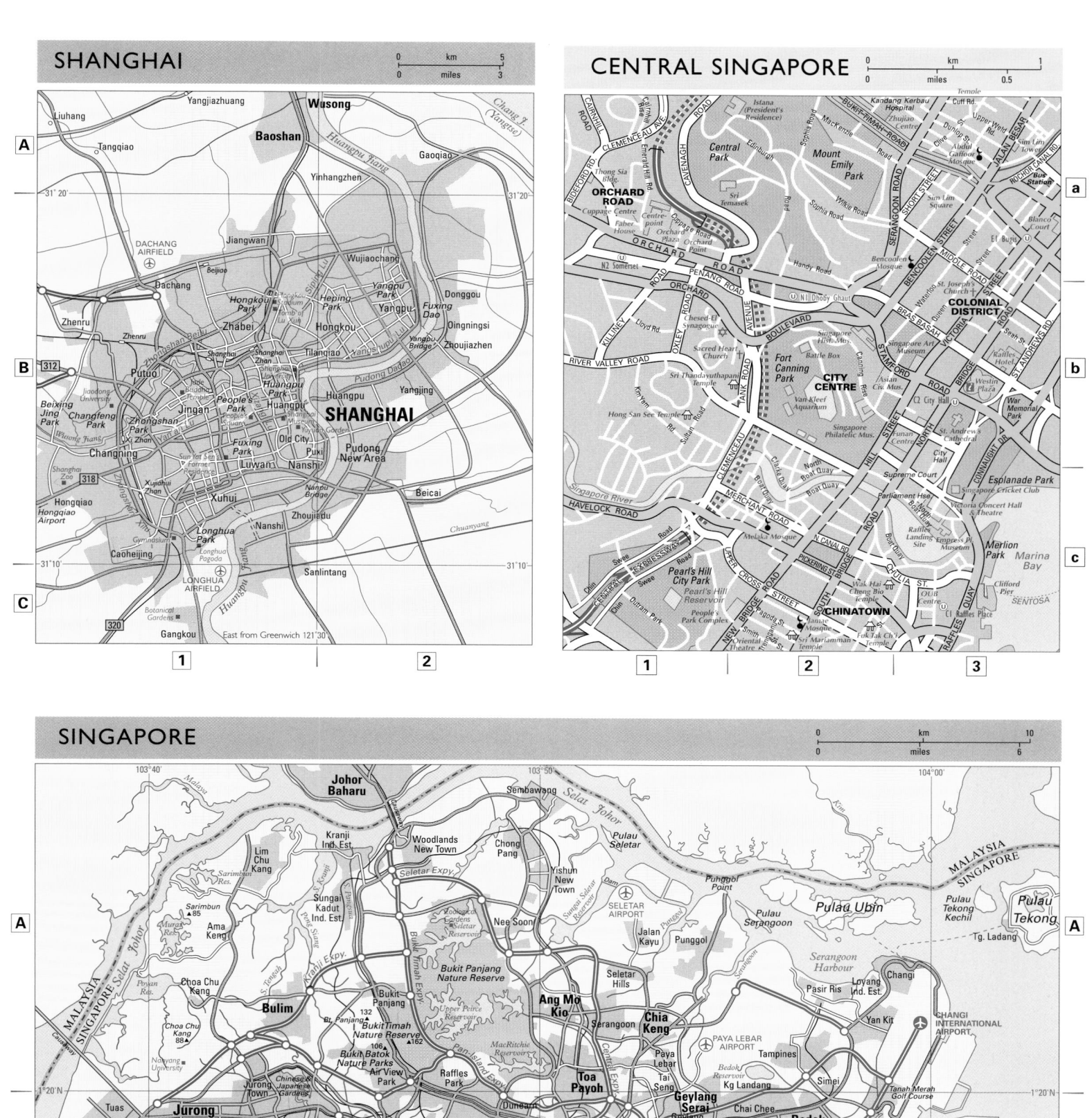

STOCKHOLM

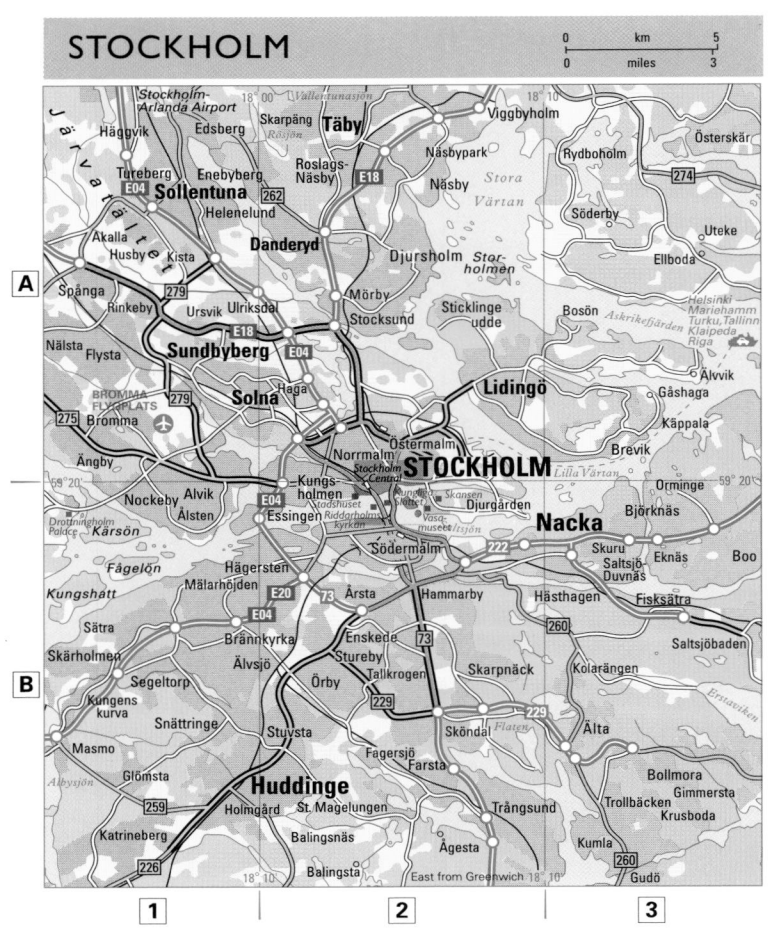

CENTRAL STOCKHOLM

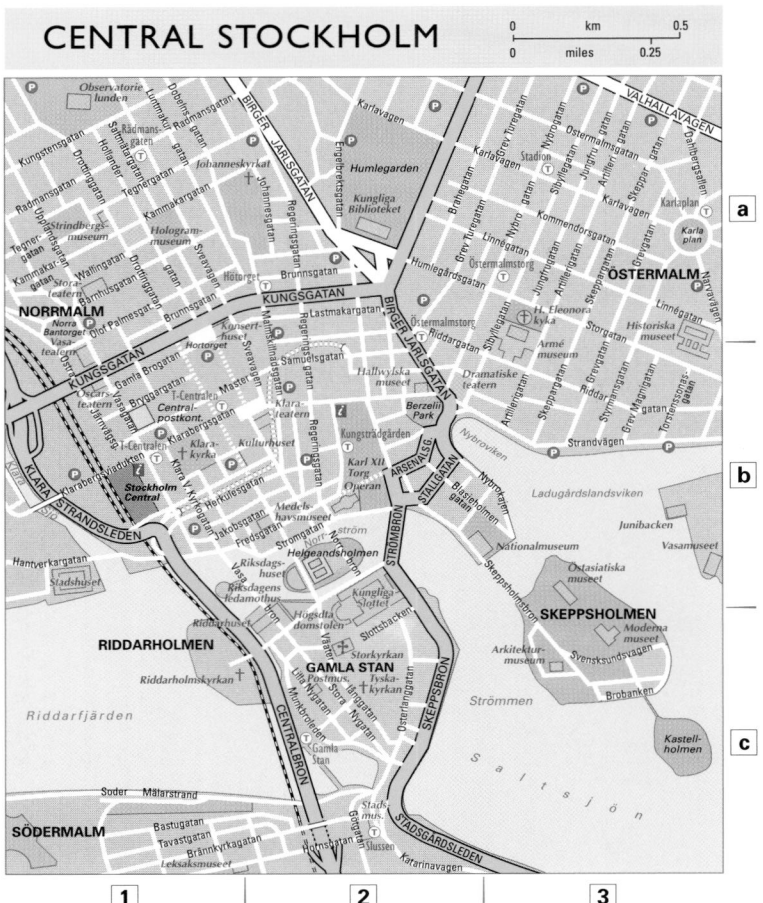

SYDNEY

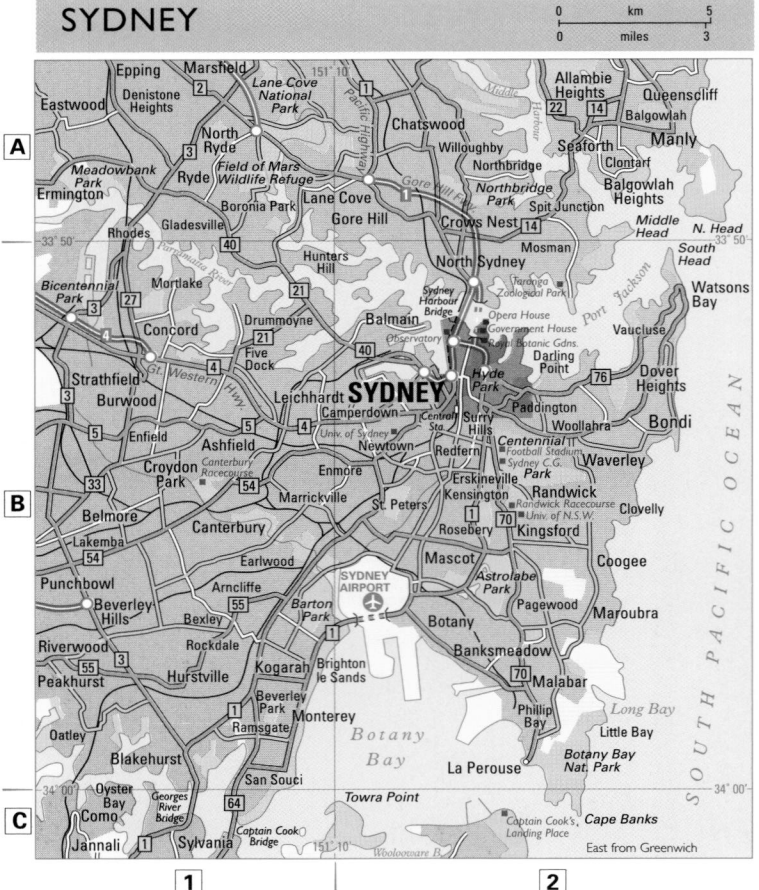

CENTRAL SYDNEY

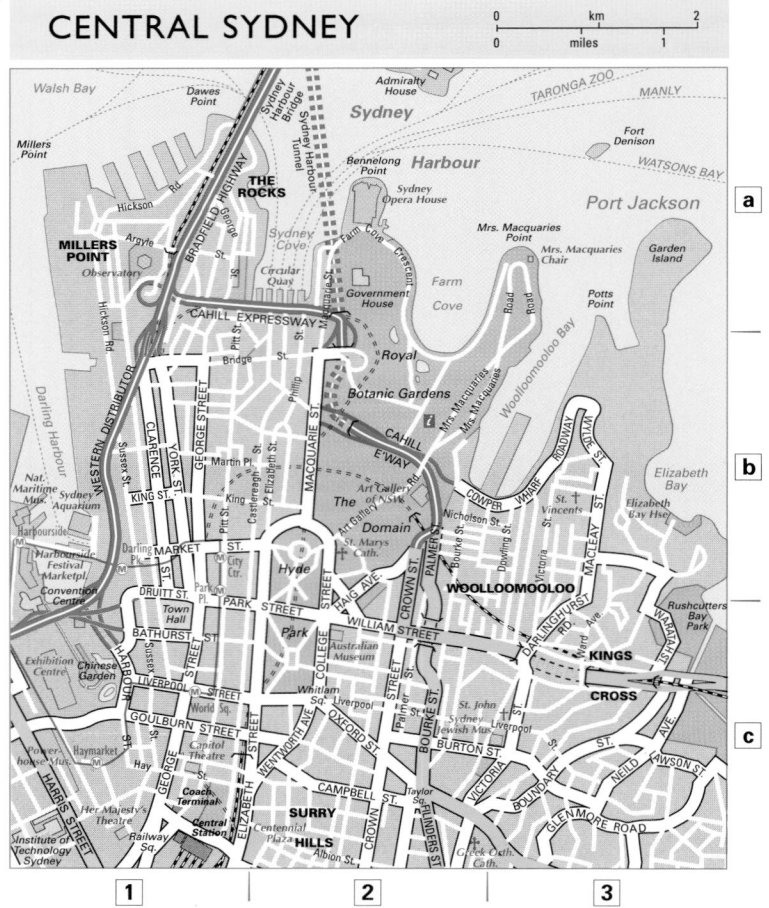

TOKYO

0 km 5
0 miles 3

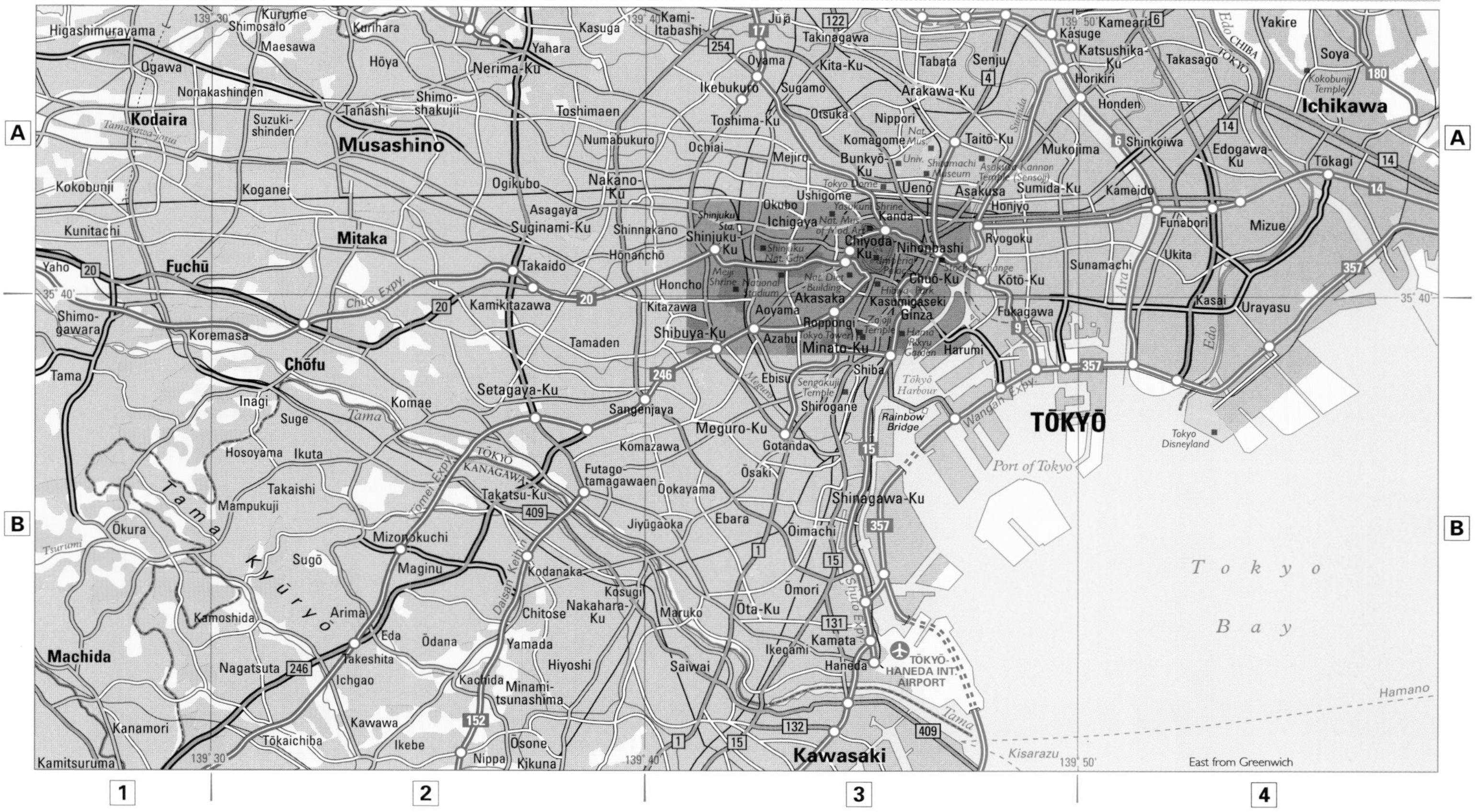

Higashimurayama · Kurume · Shimosato · Kurihara · Kasuga · Kami-Itabashi · Jūjō · Takinegawa · Kasuga · Kameari · Yakire · Soya
Ogawa · Shimosato · Maesawa · Nonakashinden · Yahara · Oyama · Kita-Ku · Tabata · Senju · Katsushika-Ku · Takasago · Kokubunji
Kodaira · Hōya · Nerima-Ku · Nakano · Ikebukuro · Sugamo · Otsuka · Arakawa-Ku · Horikiri · Honden · Ichikawa
Kokubunji · Koganei · Ogikubo · Toshimaen · Toshima-Ku · Nippori · Taitō-Ku · Mukojima · Kameido · Edogawa-Ku · Tōkagi
Musashino · Tanashi · Suzuki-shinden · Numabukuro · Ochiai · Mejiro · Bunkyō-Ku · Ueno · Asakusa · Sumida-Ku · Funabori · Mizue
Mitaka · Asagaya · Suginami-Ku · Shinnakano · Okubo · Ushigome · Ichigaya · Kanda · Honjyo · Ryogoku · Sunamachi · Urayasu
Fuchū · Takaido · Honancho · Shinjuku · Chiyoda-Ku · Nihonbashi · Kōtō-Ku · Kasai
Yaho · Kamikitazawa · Kitazawa · Akasaka · Chūō-Ku · Ginza · Fukagawa · Harumi
Shimogawara · Koremasa · Tamaden · Shibuya-Ku · Aoyama · Roppongi · Kasumigaseki · **TŌKYŌ**
Chōfu · Inagi · Setagaya-Ku · Sangenjaya · Ebisu · Shiba · Rainbow Bridge · Tokyo Disneyland
Tama · Suge · Komae · Meguro-Ku · Shirogane · Port of Tokyo
Hosoyama · Ikuta · Komazawa · Futago-tamagawaen · Gotanda · Ōsaki
Takaishi · Ōokayama · Shinagawa-Ku · Oimachi
Mampukuji · Jiyūgaoka · Ebara · Ōmori
Mizonokuchi · Maginu · Kodanaka · Nakahara-Ku · Kamata · Ikegami · Haneda · **TOKYO HANEDA INT'L AIRPORT**
Sugō · Arima · Kusugi · Yamada · Maruko · Ōta-Ku
Kamoshida · Eda · Ōdana · Chitose · Minami-tsunashima · Saiwai
Nagatsuta · Takeshita · Ichigao · Kachida · Hiyoshi · Kamata · **Kawasaki**
Kanamori · Kawawa · Ikebe · Ōsone · Kikuna · Kisarazu · Hamano
Kamitsuruma · Tōkaichiba · Nippa · *Tokyo Bay*
Machida

East from Greenwich

CENTRAL TOKYO

0 km 1
0 miles 0.5

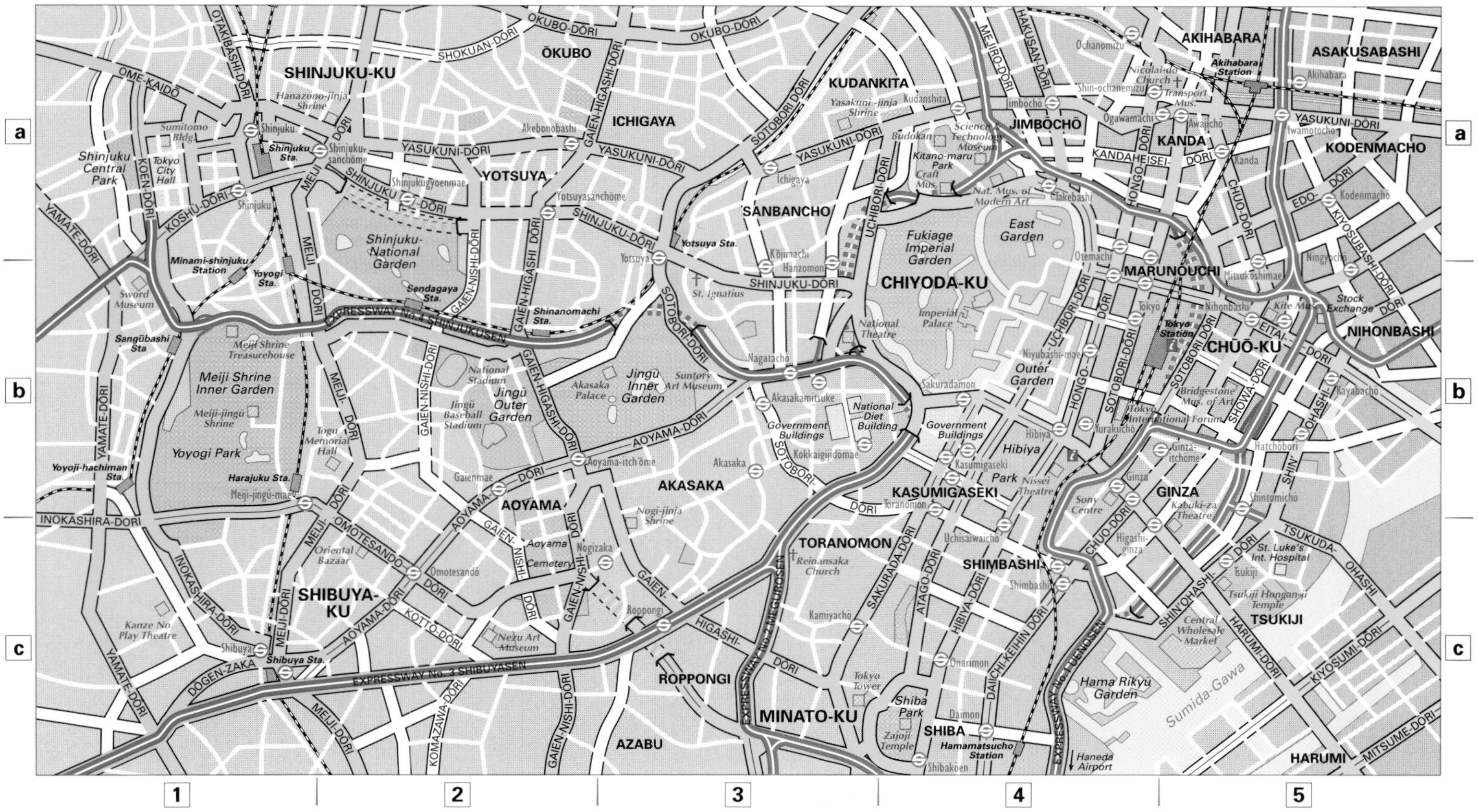

SHINJUKU-KU · ŌKUBO · KUDANKITA · AKIHABARA · ASAKUSABASHI
ICHIGAYA · JIMBOCHŌ · KANDA · KODENMACHO
YOTSUYA · SANBANCHO · MARUNOUCHI · NIHONBASHI
Meiji Shrine Inner Garden · Yoyogi Park · CHIYODA-KU · CHŪŌ-KU
AOYAMA · AKASAKA · Imperial Palace · GINZA
SHIBUYA-KU · TORANOMON · KASUMIGASEKI · SHIMBASHI · TSUKIJI
ROPPONGI · Hama Rikyu Garden
MINATO-KU · AZABU · SHIBA · HARUMI
Tokyo Tower · Shiba Park · Zojoji Temple · Hamamatsucho Station · Haneda Airport

COPYRIGHT GEORGE PHILIP LTD

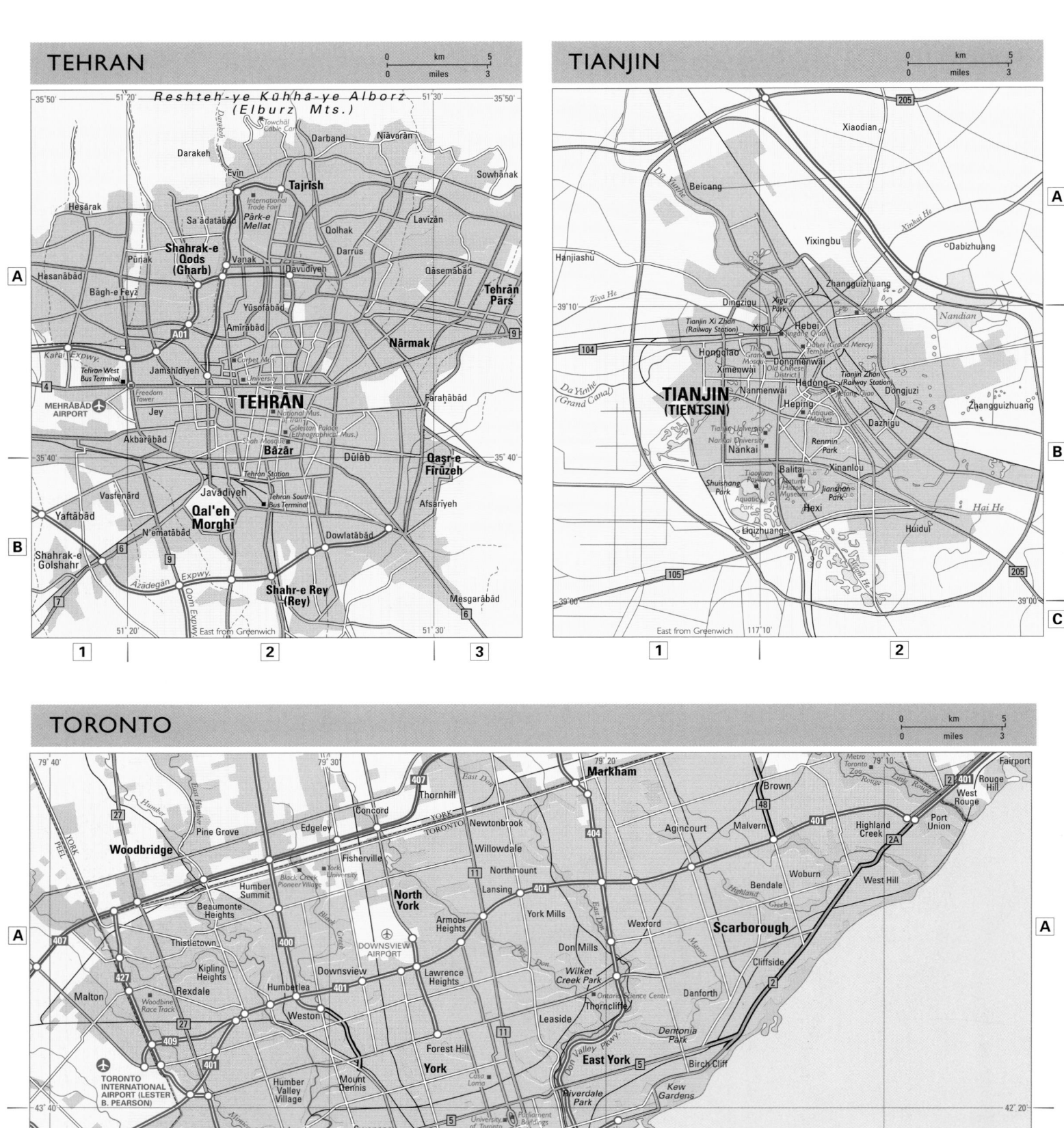

TEHRAN

km 0 — 5
miles 0 — 3

Reshteh-ye Kūhhā-ye Alborz
(Elburz Mts.)

Towchāl Cable Car
Darband · Nīāvarān
Darakeh
Evin · Sowhānak
Darakeh
Tajrīsh
International Trade Fair · Saʻādatābād · Pārk-e Mellat
Hesārak · Qolhak
Shahrak-e Qods (Gharb) · Lavīzān
Hasanābād · Vanak · Dāvūdīyeh · Darrūs
Pūnak · Qāsemābād
Bāgh-e Feyz · Yūsofābād · Tehrān Pārs
Amīrābād
Karaj Expwy. · A01 · Nārmak
Tehran West Bus Terminal · Jamshīdīyeh · Carpet Mu.
Freedom Tower · University · 9
MEHRĀBĀD AIRPORT · Jey · TEHRĀN · National Mus. of Iran · Farahābād
Akbarābād · Golestān Palace · Ethnographical Mus.
Shah Mosque · Dūlāb · Qaṣr-e Fīrūzeh
Bāzār
Tehran Station
Vāsfenārd · Javādīyeh · Afsarīyeh
Yaftābād · Qalʻeh Morghī · Tehran South Bus Terminal
N'ematābād · Dowlatābād
Shahrak-e Golshahr
Āzādegān · Shahr-e Rey (Rey) · Mesgarābād
Qom Expwy. · East from Greenwich

TIANJIN

km 0 — 5
miles 0 — 3

205
Xiaodian
Da Yunhe · Beicang · Xinhai He
Yixingbu · Dabizhuang
Hanjiashū · Zhangguizhuang
Ziya He · Dingzigu · Xigu Park · Hebei · Nandian
Tianjin Xi Zhan (Railway Station) · Xigu · Stadium
104 · Hongqiao · The Grand Mosque
Da Yunhe (Grand Canal) · Ximenwai · Old Chinese District · Tianjin Zhan (Railway Station)
Nanmenwai · Hedong · Dongjuzi · Zhangguizhuang
TIANJIN (TIENTSIN) · Heping · Antique Market · Dazhigu
Tianjin University · Renmin Park · Xinanlou
Nankai · Balitai · Natural History Museum · Hai He
Shuishang Park · Tiaoyuan Pavilion · Jianshan Park · Huidui
Aquatic Park · Hexi
Liuzhuang
105 · 205
East from Greenwich 117°10'

TORONTO

km 0 — 5
miles 0 — 3

Metro Toronto Zoo · Fairport
407 · Thornhill · Markham · Brown · Rouge · Little Rouge · 2 401 · Rouge Hill
Concord · Edgeley · YORK · Newtonbrook · 48 · West Rouge
Woodbridge · Pine Grove · Agincourt · Malvern · 401 · Highland Creek · Port Union
404 · Willowdale · 2A
Fisherville · York University · Northmount · Woburn · West Hill
Humber Summit · Black Creek Pioneer Village · North York · Lansing · Bendale
Beaumonte Heights · Armour Heights · York Mills · Wexford · Scarborough
Thistletown · 400 · DOWNSVIEW AIRPORT · Don Mills · Highland Creek
427 · Kipling Heights · Downsview · Lawrence Heights · Wilket Creek Park · Cliffside
Rexdale · Humberlea · 401 · Ontario Science Centre · 2
Malton · Danforth
Woodbine Race Track · 27 · Weston · Thorncliffe · Denlonia Park
409 · 11 · Leaside · Birch Cliff
TORONTO INTERNATIONAL AIRPORT (LESTER B. PEARSON) · 401 · Forest Hill · East York · 5 · Kew Gardens
Humber Valley Village · Mount Dennis · YORK · Casa Loma · Riverdale Park
Hanlon · Lambton Mills · Swansea · University of Toronto · Parliament Buildings · City Hall
Etobicoke · Kingsway · High Park · CN Tower & SkyDome · Old Fort York · Union Sta. · Gardiner Expwy. · TORONTO
Islington · Humber Bay · Parkdale · TORONTO CITY CENTRE AIRPORT · Toronto Harbour
427 · Markland Wood · Ontario Place · Island Park
Burnhamthorpe · Summerville · Humber Bay · Toronto Islands · Gibraltar Point · LAKE ONTARIO
Mimico
New Toronto · 2
Cooksville · Mississauga · Long Branch · West from Greenwich

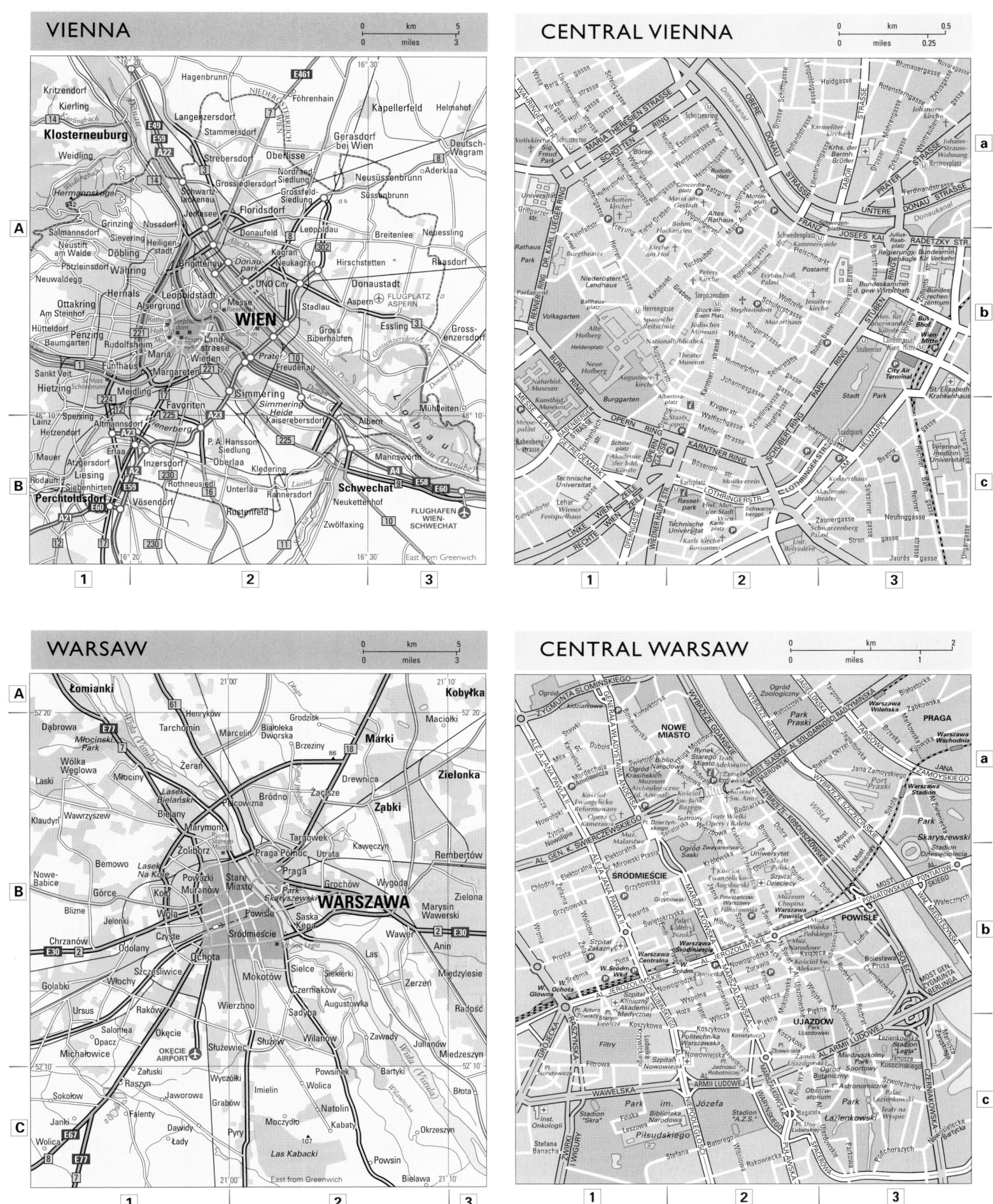

WASHINGTON

0 km 5
0 miles 3

CENTRAL WASHINGTON

0 km 1
0 miles 0.5

WELLINGTON

0 km 5
0 miles 3

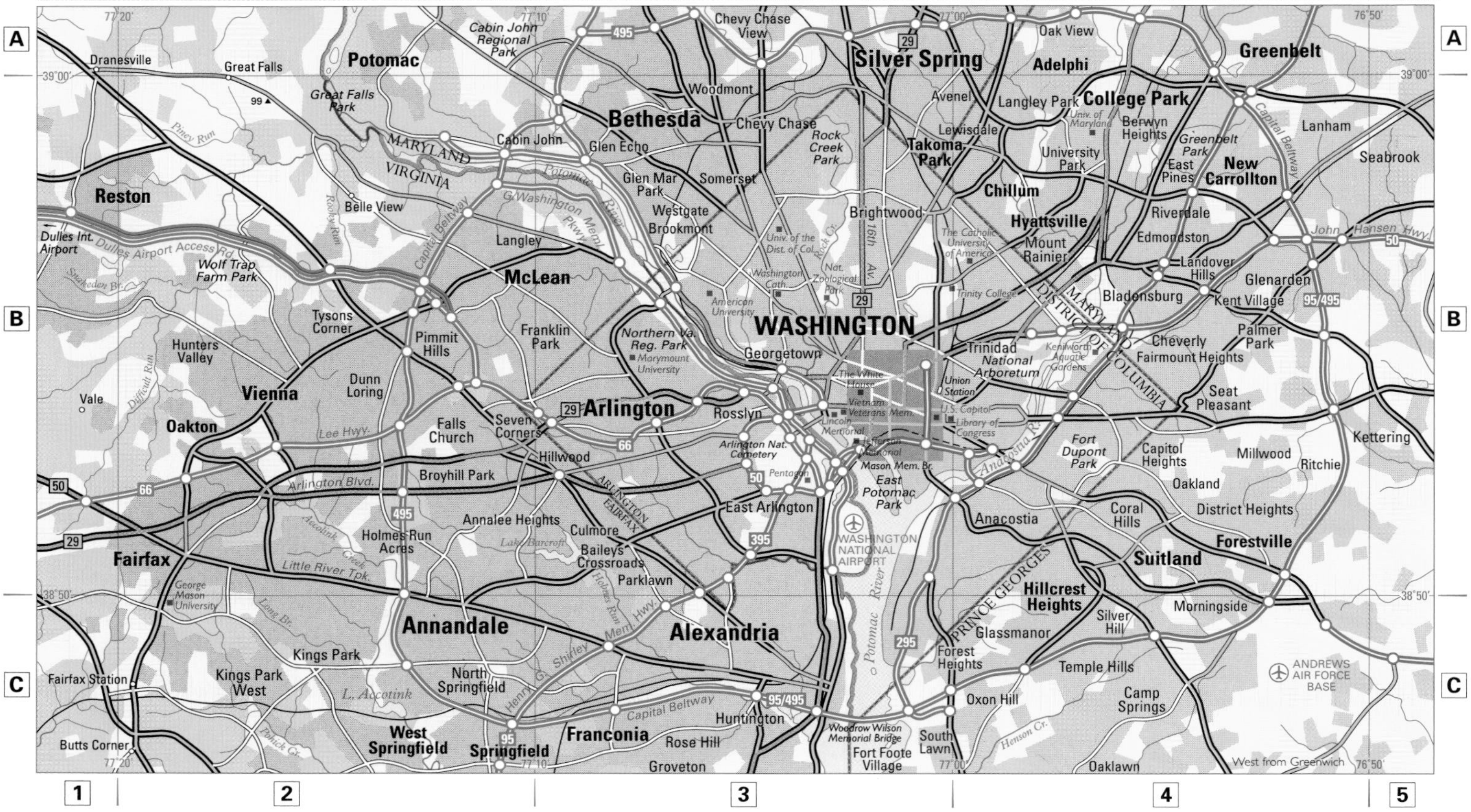

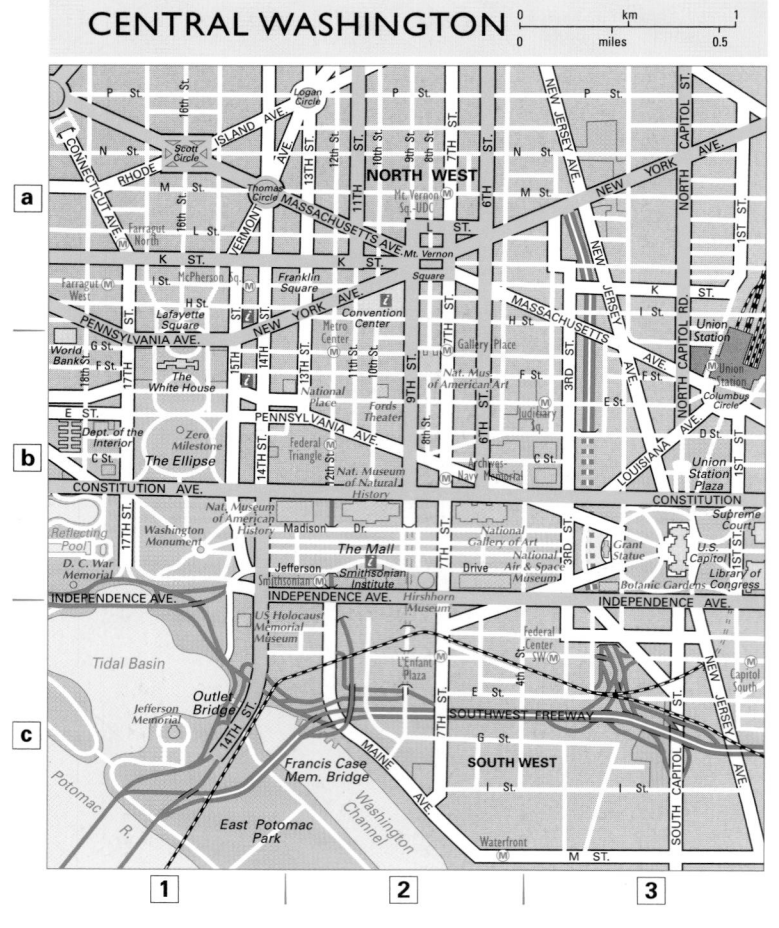

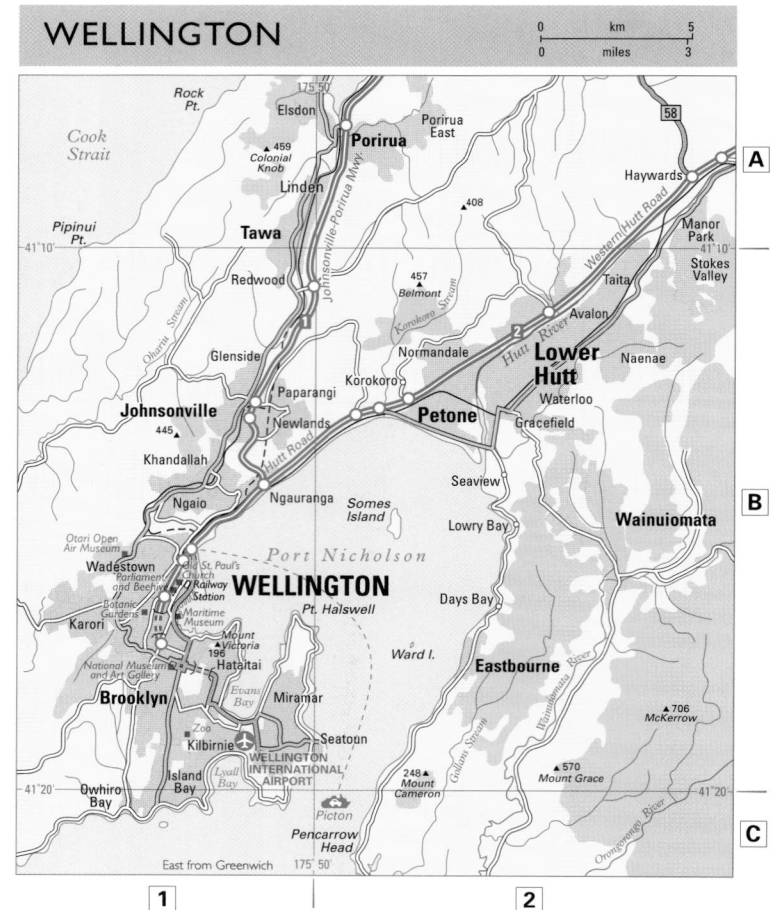

INDEX TO CITY MAPS

The index contains the names of all the principal places and features shown on the City Maps. Each name is followed by an additional entry in italics giving the name of the City Map within which it is located.

The number in bold type which follows each name refers to the number of the City Map page where that feature or place will be found.

The letter and figure which are immediately after the page number give the grid square on the map within which the feature or place is situated. The letter represents the latitude and the figure the longitude. Upper case letters refer to the City Maps, lower case letters to the Central Area Maps. The full geographic reference is provided in the border of the City Maps.

The location given is the centre of the city, suburb or feature and is not necessarily the name. Rivers, canals and roads are indexed to their name. Rivers carry the symbol → after their name.

An explanation of the alphabetical order rules and a list of the abbreviations used are to be found at the beginning of the World Map Index.

A

Aalām, *Baghdad* **3** B2
Aalsmeer, *Amsterdam* **2** B1
Abbey Wood, *London* **15** B4
Abcoude, *Amsterdam* **2** B2
Âbdin, *Cairo* **7** A2
Abeno, *Osaka* **22** B4
Aberdeen, *Hong Kong* **12** B2
Aberdour, *Edinburgh* **11** A2
Aberdour Castle, *Edinburgh* **11** A2
Abfanggraben →, *Munich* **20** A3
Ablon-sur-Seine, *Paris* **23** B3
Abord-à-Plouffe, *Montreal* **19** A1
Abramtsevo, *Moscow* **19** B4
Abu Dis, *Jerusalem* **13** B2
Abû en Numrus, *Cairo* **7** B2
Abu Ghosh, *Jerusalem* **13** B1
Acacias, *Madrid* **17** c2
Acassuso, *Buenos Aires* **7** A1
Accotink Cr. →, *Washington* **32** B2
Acheres, *Paris* **23** A1
Acilia, *Rome* **25** C1
Aclimação, *São Paulo* **26** B2
Acton, *London* **15** A2
Açúcar, Pão de, *Rio de Janeiro* **24** B2
Ada Beja, *Lisbon* **14** A1
Adams Park, *Atlanta* **3** B2
Adams Shore, *Boston* **6** B4
Addiscombe, *London* **15** B3
Adelphi, *Washington* **32** A4
Aderklaa, *Vienna* **31** A3
Admiralteyskaya Storona, *St. Petersburg* **26** B2
Áffori, *Milan* **18** A2
Aflandshage, *Copenhagen* **10** B3
Afsarīyeh, *Tehran* **30** B2
Agboyi Cr. →, *Lagos* **14** A2
Ågerup, *Copenhagen* **10** A1
Ågesta, *Stockholm* **28** B2
Agincourt, *Toronto* **30** A3
Agora, Arhéa, *Athens* **2** c1
Agra Canal, *Delhi* **10** B2
Agricola Oriental, *Mexico City* **18** B2
Agua Espraiada →, *São Paulo* **26** B2
Agualva-Cacem, *Lisbon* **14** A1
Agustino, Cerro El, *Lima* **16** B2
Ahrensfelde, *Berlin* **5** A4
Ahuntsic, *Montreal* **19** A1
Ai →, *Osaka* **22** A4
Aigremont, *Paris* **23** A1
Air View Park, *Singapore* **27** A2
Airport West, *Melbourne* **17** A1
Aiyaleo, *Athens* **2** B2
Aiyáleos, Óros, *Athens* **2** B1
Ajegunle, *Lagos* **14** B2
Aji, *Osaka* **22** A3
Ajuda, *Lisbon* **14** A1
Akalla, *Stockholm* **28** A1
Akasaka, *Tokyo* **29** b3
Akbarābād, *Tehran* **30** A2
Akershus Slott, *Oslo* **22** A3
Akihabara, *Tokyo* **29** a5
Akrópolis, *Athens* **2** c2
Al 'Azamiyah, *Baghdad* **3** A2
Al Quds = Jerusalem, *Jerusalem* **13** B2
Alaguntan, *Lagos* **14** B2
Alameda, *San Francisco* **25** B3
Alameda, Parque, *Mexico City* **18** b2
Alameda Memorial State Beach Park, *San Francisco* **25** B3
Albern, *Vienna* **31** B2
Albert Park, *Melbourne* **17** B1
Alberton, *Johannesburg* **13** B2
Albertslund, *Copenhagen* **10** B2
Albysjön, *Stockholm* **28** B1
Alcantara, *Lisbon* **14** A1
Alcatraz I., *San Francisco* **25** B2
Alcobendas, *Madrid* **17** A2
Alcorcón, *Madrid* **17** B1
Aldershof, *Berlin* **5** B4
Aldo Bonzi, *Buenos Aires* **7** C1
Aleksandrovskoye, *St. Petersburg* **26** B2
Alexander Nevsky Abbey, *St. Petersburg* **26** B2
Alexander Soutzos Moussío, *Athens* **2** b3
Alexandra, *Johannesburg* **13** A2
Alexandra, *Singapore* **27** B2
Alexandria, *Washington* **32** C3
Alfama, *Lisbon* **14** c3
Alfortville, *Paris* **23** B3
Algés, *Lisbon* **14** A1
Alhambra, *Los Angeles* **16** B4
Alibey →, *Istanbul* **12** B1
Alibey Barajı, *Istanbul* **12** B1
Alibeyköy, *Istanbul* **12** B1
Alimos, *Athens* **2** B2
Alipur, *Calcutta* **8** B1
Allach, *Munich* **20** A1
Allambie Heights, *Sydney* **28** A2
Allard Pierson Museum, *Amsterdam* **2** b2
Allermuir Hill, *Edinburgh* **11** B2
Allerton, Pt., *Boston* **6** B4
Allston, *Boston* **6** A3
Almada, *Lisbon* **14** A2
Almagro, *Buenos Aires* **7** B2
Almargem do Bispo, *Lisbon* **14** A1
Almazovo, *Moscow* **19** A6
Almirante G. Brown, Parque, *Buenos Aires* **7** C2
Almon, *Jerusalem* **13** B2
Almond →, *Edinburgh* **11** B2
Alnabru, *Oslo* **22** A4
Alnsjøen, *Oslo* **22** A4
Alperton, *London* **15** A2
Alpine, *New York* **21** A2
Alrode, *Johannesburg* **13** B2
Alsemerg, *Brussels* **6** B1
Alsergrund, *Vienna* **31** A2
Alsip, *Chicago* **9** C2
Ålsten, *Stockholm* **28** B1
Älta, *Stockholm* **28** B3
Altadena, *Los Angeles* **16** A4
Alte-Donau →, *Vienna* **31** A2
Alte Hofburg, *Vienna* **31** b1
Alter Finkenkrug, *Berlin* **5** A1
Altes Rathaus, *Munich* **20** b3
Altglienicke, *Berlin* **5** B4
Altlandsberg, *Berlin* **5** A5
Altlandsberg Nord, *Berlin* **5** A5
Altmannsdorf, *Vienna* **31** B1
Alto da Moóca, *São Paulo* **26** B2
Alto do Pina, *Lisbon* **14** A2
Altona, *Melbourne* **17** B1
Alvaro Obregon, *Mexico City* **18** B1
Alvik, *Stockholm* **28** B1
Älvsjo, *Stockholm* **28** B2
Älvvik, *Stockholm* **28** A3
Am Hasenbergl, *Munich* **20** A2
Am Steinhof, *Vienna* **31** A1
Am Wald, *Munich* **20** B2
Ama Keng, *Singapore* **27** A2
Amadora, *Lisbon* **14** A1
Amagasaki, *Osaka* **22** A3
Amager, *Copenhagen* **10** B3
Amāl Qādisiya, *Baghdad* **3** B2
Amalienborg, *Copenhagen* **10** b3
Amata, *Milan* **18** A1
Ameixoeira, *Lisbon* **14** A2
América, *São Paulo* **26** B1
Amin, *Baghdad* **3** B2
Aminadov, *Jerusalem* **13** B1
Aminyevo, *Moscow* **19** B2
Amīrābād, *Tehran* **30** A2
Amora, *Lisbon* **14** B2
Amoreira, *Lisbon* **14** A1
Ampelokipi, *Athens* **2** B2
Amper →, *Munich* **20** A1
Amstel, *Amsterdam* **2** b2
Amstel →, *Amsterdam* **2** c2
Amstel-Drecht-Kanaal, *Amsterdam* **2** B2
Amstel Station, *Amsterdam* **2** c3
Amstelhof, *Amsterdam* **2** b2
Amstelveen, *Amsterdam* **2** B2
Amsterdam, *Amsterdam* **2** A2
Amsterdam-Rijnkanaal, *Amsterdam* **2** B3
Amsterdam Zoo, *Amsterdam* **2** b3
Amsterdam Zuidoost, *Amsterdam* **2** B2
Amsterdamse Bos, *Amsterdam* **2** B1
Anacostia, *Washington* **32** B4
Anadoluhisarı, *Istanbul* **12** B2
Anadolukavağı, *Istanbul* **12** A2
Anata, *Jerusalem* **13** B2
Ancol, *Jakarta* **13** A1
'Andalus, *Baghdad* **3** B1
Andarai, *Rio de Janeiro* **24** B1
Anderlecht, *Brussels* **6** A1
Anderson Park, *Atlanta* **3** B2
Andingmen, *Beijing* **4** B2
Andrews Air Force Base, *Washington* **32** C4
Ang Mo Kio, *Singapore* **27** A3
Ängby, *Stockholm* **28** A1
Angel I., *San Francisco* **25** A2
Angel Island State Park, *San Francisco* **25** A2
Angke, Kali →, *Jakarta* **13** A1
Angyalföld, *Budapest* **7** A2
Anik, *Mumbai* **20** A2
Anin, *Warsaw* **31** B2
Anjou, *Montreal* **19** A2
Annalee Heights, *Washington* **32** B2
Annandale, *Washington* **32** C2
Anne Frankhuis, *Amsterdam* **2** a1
Antony, *Paris* **23** B2
Anyangch'on, *Seoul* **26** C1
Aoyama, *Tokyo* **29** b2
Ap Lei Chau, *Hong Kong* **12** B1
Apapa, *Lagos* **14** B2
Apelacão, *Lisbon* **14** A2
Apterkarskiy Ostrov, *St. Petersburg* **26** B2
Ar Kazimiyah, *Baghdad* **3** B1
Ara →, *Tokyo* **29** A4
Arakawa-Ku, *Tokyo* **29** A3
Arany-hegyi-patak →, *Budapest* **7** A2
Aravaca, *Madrid* **17** B1
Arbataash, *Baghdad* **3** A1
Arc de Triomphe, *Paris* **23** a2
Arcadia, *Los Angeles* **16** B4
Arceuil, *Paris* **23** B2
Arco Plaza, *Los Angeles* **16** b1
Arese, *Milan* **18** A1
Arganzuela, *Madrid* **17** B1
Argenteuil, *Paris* **23** A2
Argonne Forest, *Chicago* **9** C1
Argüelles, *Madrid* **17** a1
Arima, *Osaka* **22** A2
Arima, *Tokyo* **29** B2
Ários Págos, *Athens* **2** c1
Arkhangelyskoye, *Moscow* **19** B1
Arlington, *Boston* **6** A2
Arlington, *Washington* **32** B3
Arlington Heights, *Boston* **6** A2
Arlington Nat. Cemetery, *Washington* **32** B3
Armação, *Rio de Janeiro* **24** B2
Armadale, *Melbourne* **17** B2
Armenian Quarter, *Jerusalem* **13** b3
Armour Heights, *Toronto* **30** A2
Arncliffe, *Sydney* **28** B1
Arnold Arboretum, *Boston* **6** B3
Árpádföld, *Budapest* **7** A3
Arrentela, *Lisbon* **14** B2
Årsta, *Stockholm* **28** B2
Art Institute, *Chicago* **9** c2
Artane, *Dublin* **11** A2
Artas, *Jerusalem* **13** B2
Arthur's Seat, *Edinburgh* **11** B3
Aryiróupolis, *Athens* **2** B2
Asagaya, *Tokyo* **29** A2
Asahi, *Osaka* **22** A4
Asakusa, *Tokyo* **29** A3
Asakusabashi, *Tokyo* **29** a5
Asati, *Calcutta* **8** C1
Aschheim, *Munich* **20** A3
Ascot Vale, *Melbourne* **17** A1
Ashburn, *Chicago* **9** C2
Ashburton, *Melbourne* **17** B2
Ashfield, *Sydney* **28** B1
Ashford, *London* **15** B1
Ashiya, *Osaka* **22** A2
Ashiya →, *Osaka* **22** A2
Ashtown, *Dublin* **11** A2
Askisto, *Helsinki* **12** B1
Askrikefjärden, *Stockholm* **28** A3
Asnières, *Paris* **23** A2
Aspern, *Vienna* **31** A2
Aspern, Flugplatz, *Vienna* **31** A3
Assago, *Milan* **18** B1
Assemblée Nationale, *Paris* **23** b3
Assendelft, *Amsterdam* **2** A1
Assiano, *Milan* **18** B1
Astoria, *New York* **21** B2
Astrolabe Park, *Sydney* **28** B2
Atarot Airport, *Jerusalem* **13** A2
Atghara, *Calcutta* **8** B2
Athens = Athínai, *Athens* **2** B2
Athínai, *Athens* **2** B2
Athinai-Ellinikón Airport, *Athens* **2** B2
Athis-Mons, *Paris* **23** B3
Athlone, *Cape Town* **8** A2
Atholl, *Johannesburg* **13** A2
Atīfīya, *Baghdad* **3** A2
Atişalen, *Istanbul* **12** B1
Atlanta, *Atlanta* **3** B2
Atlanta History Center, *Atlanta* **3** B2
Atomium, *Brussels* **6** A2
Attiki, *Athens* **2** A2
Atzgersdorf, *Vienna* **31** B1
Aubervilliers, *Paris* **23** A3
Aubing, *Munich* **20** B1
Auburndale, *Boston* **6** A2
Aucherdinny, *Edinburgh* **11** B2
Auckland Park, *Johannesburg* **13** B2
Auderghem, *Brussels* **6** B2
Augusta, Mausoleo di, *Rome* **25** b2
Augustówka, *Warsaw* **31** B2
Aulnay-sous-Bois, *Paris* **23** A3
Aurelio, *Rome* **25** B1
Ausîm, *Cairo* **7** A1
Austerlitz, Gare d', *Paris* **23** A3
Austin, *Chicago* **9** B2
Avalon, *Wellington* **32** B2
Avedøre, *Copenhagen* **10** B2
Avellaneda, *Buenos Aires* **7** C2
Avenel, *Washington* **32** B4
Avondale, *Chicago* **9** B2
Avondale Heights, *Melbourne* **17** A1
Avtovo, *St. Petersburg* **26** B1
Ayazağa, *Istanbul* **12** B1
Ayer Chawan, P., *Singapore* **27** B2
Ayer Merbau, P., *Singapore* **27** B2
Ayía Marina, *Athens* **2** C3
Ayía Paraskevi, *Athens* **2** A2
Áyios Dhimitrios, *Athens* **2** B2
Áyios Ioánnis Rendis, *Athens* **2** B1
Azabu, *Tokyo* **29** c3
Azcapotzalco, *Mexico City* **18** B1
Azteca, Estadia, *Mexico City* **18** C2
Azucar, Cerro Pan de, *Santiago* **26** A1

B

Baambrugge, *Amsterdam* **2** B2
Baba I., *Karachi* **14** B1
Babarpur, *Delhi* **10** A2
Babushkin, *Moscow* **19** A4
Back B., *Mumbai* **20** B1
Baclaran, *Manila* **17** B2
Bacoor, *Manila* **17** C1
Bacoor B., *Manila* **17** C1
Badalona, *Barcelona* **4** A2
Badhoevedorp, *Amsterdam* **2** A1
Badli, *Delhi* **10** A1
Bærum, *Oslo* **22** A2
Bağcılar, *Istanbul* **12** B1
Bággio, *Milan* **18** B1
Bāgh-e-Feyz, *Tehran* **30** A1
Baghdād, *Baghdad* **3** A2
Bagmari, *Calcutta* **8** B2
Bagneux, *Paris* **23** B2
Bagnolet, *Paris* **23** A3
Bagsværd, *Copenhagen* **10** A2
Bagsværd Sø, *Copenhagen* **10** A2
Baguiati, *Calcutta* **8** B2
Bagumbayan, *Manila* **17** C2
Bahçeköy, *Istanbul* **12** A1
Bahtîm, *Cairo* **7** A2
Baileys Crossroads, *Washington* **32** B3
Bailly, *Paris* **23** A1
Bairro Alto, *Lisbon* **14** c1
Bairro Lopes, *Lisbon* **14** b3
Baisha, *Canton* **8** B2
Baisha →, *Canton* **8** B2
Baixa, *Lisbon* **14** c2
Baiyun Airport, *Canton* **8** A2
Baiyun Hill Scenic Spot, *Canton* **8** B2
Bakırköy, *Istanbul* **12** C1
Bakovka, *Moscow* **19** B2
Bal Harbor, *Miami* **18** A2
Balara, *Manila* **17** B2
Balashikha, *Moscow* **19** B5
Baldia, *Karachi* **14** A1
Baldoyle, *Dublin* **11** A3
Baldwin Hills, *Los Angeles* **16** B2
Baldwin Hills Res., *Los Angeles* **16** B2
Balgowlah, *Sydney* **28** A2
Balgowlah Heights, *Sydney* **28** A2
Balham, *London* **15** B3
Bali, *Calcutta* **8** B1
Baliganja, *Calcutta* **8** B2
Balingsnäs, *Stockholm* **28** B2
Balingsta, *Stockholm* **28** B2
Balintawak, *Manila* **17** B1
Balitai, *Tianjin* **30** B2
Ballerup, *Copenhagen* **10** A2
Ballinteer, *Dublin* **11** B2
Ballyboden, *Dublin* **11** B2
Ballybrack, *Dublin* **11** B3
Ballyfermot, *Dublin* **11** A1
Ballymorefinn Hill, *Dublin* **11** B1
Ballymun, *Dublin* **11** A2
Balmain, *Sydney* **28** B2
Baluhati, *Calcutta* **8** B1
Balvanera, *Buenos Aires* **7** B2
Balwyn, *Melbourne* **17** A2
Balwyn North, *Melbourne* **17** A2
Banática, *Lisbon* **14** A1
Banco do Brasil, Centro Cultural, *Rio de Janeiro* **24** a2
Bandra, *Mumbai* **20** A1
Bandra Pt., *Mumbai* **20** A1
Bang Kapi, *Bangkok* **3** B2
Bang Kholaem, *Bangkok* **3** A2
Bang Na, *Bangkok* **3** B2
Bang Phlad, *Bangkok* **3** a1
Bangkhen, *Bangkok* **3** A2
Bangkok = Krung Thep, *Bangkok* **3** B2
Bangkok Noi, *Bangkok* **3** B1
Bangkok Yai, *Bangkok* **3** B1
Banglamphoo, *Bangkok* **3** b2
Banglo, *Calcutta* **8** B1
Bangrak, *Bangkok* **3** B2
Bangsu, *Bangkok* **3** B2
Bank, *London* **15** b5
Bank of America, *San Francisco* **25** b2
Bank of China Tower, *Hong Kong* **12** c1
Banks, C., *Sydney* **28** C2
Banksmeadow, *Sydney* **28** B2
Banstala, *Calcutta* **8** B2
Bantra, *Calcutta* **8** B1
Baoshan, *Shanghai* **27** A1
Bar Giyora, *Jerusalem* **13** B1
Barahanagar, *Calcutta* **8** B2
Barajas, *Madrid* **17** B2
Barajas, Aeropuerto Transoceanico de, *Madrid* **17** B2
Barakpur, *Calcutta* **8** A2
Barberini, Palazzo, *Rome* **25** b3
Barbican, *London* **15** a4
Barcarena, *Lisbon* **14** A1
Barcarena, Rib. de →, *Lisbon* **14** A1
Barcelona, *Barcelona* **4** A2
Barcelona-Prat, Aeropuerta de, *Barcelona* **4** B1
Barceloneta, *Barcelona* **4** A2
Barking, *London* **15** A4
Barkingside, *London* **15** A4
Barnes, *London* **15** B2
Barnet, *London* **15** A2
Barra Andai, *Karachi* **14** B2
Barra Funda, *São Paulo* **26** B2
Barracas, *Buenos Aires* **7** B2
Barranco, *Lima* **16** B2
Barreiro, *Lisbon* **14** B2
Barreto, *Rio de Janeiro* **24** B2
Bartala, *Calcutta* **8** B1
Barton Park, *Sydney* **28** B1
Bartyki, *Warsaw* **31** C2
Barvikha, *Moscow* **19** B1
Bastille, Place de la, *Paris* **23** c5
Basus, *Cairo* **7** A2
Batanagar, *Calcutta* **8** B1
Bath Beach, *New York* **21** C1
Bath I., *Karachi* **14** B2
Batir, *Jerusalem* **13** B1
Batok, Bukit, *Singapore* **27** A2
Battersea, *London* **15** B3
Battery Park, *New York* **21** f1
Bauman, *Moscow* **19** B4
Baumgarten, *Vienna* **31** A1
Bay Harbour Islands, *Miami* **18** A2
Bay Ridge, *New York* **21** C1
Bayonne, *New York* **21** B1
Bayshore, *San Francisco* **25** B3
Bayswater, *London* **15** b2
Bayt Lahm = Bethlehem, *Jerusalem* **13** B2
Bayview, *San Francisco* **25** B2
Bāzār, *Tehran* **30** A2
Beachmont, *Boston* **6** A4
Beacon Hill, *Hong Kong* **12** A2
Beato, *Lisbon* **14** A2
Beaumont, *Dublin* **11** A2
Beaumonte Heights, *Toronto* **30** A1
Bebek, *Istanbul* **12** B2
Běchovice, *Prague* **24** B3
Beck L., *Chicago* **9** A1
Beckenham, *London* **15** B3
Beckton, *London* **15** A4
Becontree, *London* **15** A4
Beddington Corner, *London* **15** B3
Bedford, *Boston* **6** A2
Bedford Park, *Chicago* **9** C2
Bedford Park, *New York* **21** A2
Bedford Stuyvesant, *New York* **21** B2
Bedford View, *Johannesburg* **13** B2
Bedok, *Singapore* **27** B3
Bedok, Res., *Singapore* **27** A3
Beersel, *Brussels* **6** B1
Behala, *Calcutta* **8** B1
Bei Hai, *Beijing* **4** B2
Beicai, *Shanghai* **27** B2
Beicang, *Tianjin* **30** A1
Beihai Park, *Beijing* **4** b2
Beijing, *Beijing* **4** B1
Beit Ghur el-Fawqa, *Jerusalem* **13** A1
Beit Hanina, *Jerusalem* **13** B2
Beit Iksa, *Jerusalem* **13** B2
Beit I'nan, *Jerusalem* **13** A1
Beit Jala, *Jerusalem* **13** B2
Beit Lekhem = Bethlehem, *Jerusalem* **13** B2
Beit Nekofa, *Jerusalem* **13** B1
Beit Sahur, *Jerusalem* **13** B2
Beit Surik, *Jerusalem* **13** B1
Beit Zayit, *Jerusalem* **13** B1
Beitaipingzhuan, *Beijing* **4** B1
Beitar Ilit, *Jerusalem* **13** B1
Beitsun, *Canton* **8** B2
Beitunya, *Jerusalem* **13** A2
Beixing Jing Park, *Shanghai* **27** B1
Békásmegyer, *Budapest* **7** A2
Bekkelaget, *Oslo* **22** A3
Bel Air, *Los Angeles* **16** B2
Bela Vista, *São Paulo* **26** B2
Bélanger, *Montreal* **19** A1
Belas, *Lisbon* **14** A1
Belas Artes, Museu Nacionale de, *Rio de Janeiro* **24** b2
Beleghata, *Calcutta* **8** B2
Belém, *Lisbon* **14** A1
Belém, Torre de, *Lisbon* **14** A1
Belènzinho, *São Paulo* **26** B2
Belgachiya, *Calcutta* **8** B2
Belgharia, *Calcutta* **8** B2
Belgrano, *Buenos Aires* **7** B2
Belgravia, *London* **15** c3
Bell, *Los Angeles* **16** C3
Bell Gardens, *Los Angeles* **16** C4
Bell Tower, *Beijing* **4** a2
Bellavista, *Lima* **16** B2
Bellavista, *Santiago* **26** C2
Belle Harbor, *New York* **21** C2
Belle View, *Washington* **32** B2
Bellevue, Schloss, *Berlin* **5** a2
Bellingham, *London* **15** B3
Bellwood, *Chicago* **9** B1
Belmont, *Boston* **6** A2
Belmont, *London* **15** A2
Belmont, *Wellington* **32** B2
Belmont Harbor, *Chicago* **9** B3
Belmore, *Sydney* **28** B1
Belur, *Calcutta* **8** B2
Belvedere, *Atlanta* **3** B3
Belvedere, *London* **15** B4
Belvedere, *San Francisco* **25** A2
Belyayevo Bogorodskoye, *Moscow* **19** C3
Bemowo, *Warsaw* **31** B1
Benaki, Moussío, *Athens* **2** b3
Bendale, *Toronto* **30** A3
Bendkhal, *Mumbai* **20** B2
Benefica, *Rio de Janeiro* **24** B1
Benfica, *Lisbon* **14** A1
Benito Juárez, *Mexico City* **18** B2
Benito Juárez, Aeropuerto Int., *Mexico City* **18** B2
Bensonhurst, *New York* **21** C2
Berchem-Sainte-Agathe, *Brussels* **6** A1
Berg am Laim, *Munich* **20** B2
Bergenfield, *New York* **21** A2
Bergham, *Munich* **20** B2
Bergvliet, *Cape Town* **8** B1
Beri, *Barcelona* **4** A1
Berkeley, *San Francisco* **25** A3
Berlin, *Berlin* **5** A3
Bermondsey, *London* **15** B3
Bernabeu, Estadio, *Madrid* **17** B1
Bernal Heights, *San Francisco* **25** B2
Berwyn, *Chicago* **9** B2
Berwyn Heights, *Washington* **32** B4
Besiktas, *Istanbul* **12** B2
Besós →, *Barcelona* **4** A2
Bethesda, *Washington* **32** B3
Bethlehem, *Jerusalem* **13** B2
Bethnal Green, *London* **15** A3
Betor, *Calcutta* **8** B1
Beurs, *Amsterdam* **2** b2
Beverley Hills, *Sydney* **28** B1
Beverley Park, *Sydney* **28** B1
Beverly, *Chicago* **9** C3
Beverly Glen, *Los Angeles* **16** B2
Beverly Hills, *Los Angeles* **16** B2
Bexley, *London* **15** B4
Bexley, *Sydney* **28** B1
Bexleyheath, *London* **15** B4
Beykoz, *Istanbul* **12** B2
Beylerbeyi, *Istanbul* **12** B2
Beyoğlu, *Istanbul* **12** B1
Bezons, *Paris* **23** A2
Bezuidenhout Park, *Johannesburg* **13** B2
Bhadrakali, *Calcutta* **8** A2
Bhalswa, *Delhi* **10** A2
Bhambo Khan Qarmati, *Karachi* **14** B2
Bhatsala, *Calcutta* **8** B1
Bhawanipur, *Calcutta* **8** B2
Bhuleshwar, *Mumbai* **20** b2
Białołeka Dworska, *Warsaw* **31** B2
Biblioteca Nacional, *Rio de Janeiro* **24** c2
Bicentennial Park, *Sydney* **28** B1
Bickley, *London* **15** B4
Bidu, *Jerusalem* **13** B1
Bielany, *Warsaw* **31** B1
Bielawa, *Warsaw* **31** C2
Biesdorf, *Berlin* **5** A4
Bièvre →, *Paris* **23** B1
Bièvres, *Paris* **23** B2
Bilston, *Edinburgh* **11** B2
Binacayan, *Manila* **17** C1
Binondo, *Manila* **17** B1
Birak el Kiyam, *Cairo* **7** A1
Birch Cliff, *Toronto* **30** A3
Birkenstein, *Berlin* **5** A5
Birkholz, *Berlin* **5** A4
Birkholzaue, *Berlin* **5** A4
Birrarrung Park, *Melbourne* **17** A2
Biscayne Bay, *Miami* **18** B2
Biscayne Park, *Miami* **18** A2
Bishop Lavis, *Cape Town* **8** A2
Bishopscourt, *Cape Town* **8** A1
Bispebjerg, *Copenhagen* **10** A3
Biwon Secret Garden, *Seoul* **26** B1
Björknas, *Stockholm* **28** B3
Black Cr. →, *Toronto* **30** A2
Blackfen, *London* **15** B4
Blackheath, *London* **15** B4
Blackrock, *Dublin* **11** B2
Bladensburg, *Washington* **32** B4
Blair Village, *Atlanta* **3** C2
Blairgowrie, *Johannesburg* **13** A2
Blakehurst, *Sydney* **28** B1
Blakstad, *Oslo* **22** B1
Blankenburg, *Berlin* **5** A3
Blankenfelde, *Berlin* **5** A3
Blizne, *Warsaw* **31** B1
Bloomsbury, *London* **15** a3
Błota, *Warsaw* **31** C3
Blue Island, *Chicago* **9** C2
Bluebell, *Dublin* **11** B1
Bluff Hd., *Hong Kong* **12** B2
Blumberg, *Berlin* **5** A4
Blunt Pt., *San Francisco* **25** A2
Blutenberg, *Munich* **20** B1
Blylaget, *Oslo* **22** B3
Bo-Kaap Museum, *Cape Town* **8** c2
Boa Vista, Alto do, *Rio de Janeiro* **24** B1
Boardwalk, *New York* **21** C3
Boavista, *Lisbon* **14** A2
Bobigny, *Paris* **23** A3
Bocanegra, *Lima* **16** A2
Boedo, *Buenos Aires* **7** B2
Bogenhausen, *Munich* **20** B2
Bogorodskoye, *Moscow* **19** B4
Bogota, *New York* **21** A1
Bogstadvatnet, *Oslo* **22** A2
Bohnsdorf, *Berlin* **5** B4
Bois-Colombes, *Paris* **23** A2
Bois-d'Arcy, *Paris* **23** B1
Boissy-St.-Léger, *Paris* **23** B4
Boldinasco, *Milan* **18** B1
Bøler, *Oslo* **22** A4
Bollate, *Milan* **18** A1
Bollebeek, *Brussels* **6** A1
Bollensdorf, *Berlin* **5** A5
Bollmora, *Stockholm* **28** B3
Bolshaya-Okhta, *St. Petersburg* **26** B2
Bolton, *Atlanta* **3** B2
Bom Retiro, *São Paulo* **26** B2
Bombay = Mumbai, *Mumbai* **20** B2
Bondi, *Sydney* **28** B2
Bondy, *Paris* **23** A3
Bondy, Forêt de, *Paris* **23** A4
Bonifacio Monument, *Manila* **17** B1
Bonneuil-sur-Marne, *Paris* **23** B4
Bonnington, *Edinburgh* **11** B1
Bonnyrig and Lasswade, *Edinburgh* **11** B3
Bonsucesso, *Rio de Janeiro* **24** B1
Bonteheuwel, *Cape Town* **8** A2
Boo, *Stockholm* **28** A3
Booterstown, *Dublin* **11** B2
Borisovo, *Moscow* **19** C4
Borle, *Mumbai* **20** A2
Boronia Park, *Sydney* **28** A1
Borough Park, *New York* **21** C2
Bosmont, *Johannesburg* **13** B1
Bosön, *Stockholm* **28** A3
Bosporus = Istanbul Boğazi, *Istanbul* **12** B2
Bostancı, *Istanbul* **12** C2
Boston Harbor, *Boston* **6** A4
Botafogo, *Rio de Janeiro* **24** B1
Botanisk Have, *Copenhagen* **10** b2
Botany, *Sydney* **28** B2
Botany B., *Sydney* **28** B2
Botany Bay Nat. Park, *Sydney* **28** B2
Botič →, *Prague* **24** B3
Botica Sete, *Lisbon* **14** A1
Boucherville, *Montreal* **19** A3
Boucherville, Îs. de, *Montreal* **19** A3
Bougival, *Paris* **23** A1
Boulder Pt., *Hong Kong* **12** B1
Boulogne, Bois de, *Paris* **23** A2
Boulogne-Billancourt, *Paris* **23** A2
Bourg-la-Reine, *Paris* **23** B2
Bouviers, *Paris* **23** B1
Bovenkerk, *Amsterdam* **2** B2
Bovenkerker Polder, *Amsterdam* **2** B2
Bovisa, *Milan* **18** A2
Bow, *London* **15** A3
Bowery, *New York* **21** e2
Boyacıköy, *Istanbul* **12** B2
Boyle Heights, *Los Angeles* **16** B3
Bradbury Building, *Los Angeles* **16** b2
Braepark, *Edinburgh* **11** B2
Braid, *Edinburgh* **11** B2
Bramley, *Johannesburg* **13** A2
Brandenburger Tor, *Berlin* **5** A3
Brani, P., *Singapore* **27** B3
Branik, *Prague* **24** B2
Brännkyrka, *Stockholm* **28** B2
Brás, *São Paulo* **26** B2
Brasilândia, *São Paulo* **26** A1
Brateyevo, *Moscow* **19** C4
Bratsevo, *Moscow* **19** A2
Bray, *Dublin* **11** B3
Braybrook, *Melbourne* **17** A1
Brázdim, *Prague* **24** A3
Breach Candy, *Mumbai* **20** a1
Breakheart Reservation, *Boston* **6** A3
Brede, *Copenhagen* **10** A3
Breeds Pond, *Boston* **6** A4
Breezy Point, *New York* **21** C2
Breitenlee, *Vienna* **31** A3
Breña, *Lima* **16** B2
Brent, *London* **15** A2
Brent Res., *London* **15** A2
Brentford, *London* **15** B2
Brentwood Park, *Los Angeles* **16** B2
Brera, *Milan* **18** B2
Bresso, *Milan* **18** A2
Brevik, *Stockholm* **28** A3
Břevnov, *Prague* **24** B2
Bridgeport, *Chicago* **9** B3
Bridgetown, *Cape Town* **8** A2
Bridgeview, *Chicago* **9** C2
Brighton, *Boston* **6** A3
Brighton, *Melbourne* **17** B1
Brighton le Sands, *Sydney* **28** B1
Brighton Park, *Chicago* **9** C2
Brightwood, *Washington* **32** B3
Brigittenau, *Vienna* **31** A2
Brimbank Park, *Melbourne* **17** A1
Brisbane, *San Francisco* **25** B2
British Museum, *London* **15** a3
Britz, *Berlin* **5** B3
Brixton, *London* **15** B3
Broad Sd., *Boston* **6** A4
Broadmeadows, *Melbourne* **17** A1
Broadmoor, *San Francisco* **25** B2
Broadview, *Chicago* **9** B1
Broadway, *New York* **21** e1
Brockley, *London* **15** B3
Bródno, *Warsaw* **31** B2
Bródnowski, Kanal, *Warsaw* **31** B2
Broek in Waterland, *Amsterdam* **2** A2
Bromley, *London* **15** B4
Bromley Common, *London* **15** B4
Bromma, *Stockholm* **28** A1
Bromma flygplats, *Stockholm* **28** A1
Brompton, *London* **15** c2
Brøndby Strand, *Copenhagen* **10** B2
Brøndbyøster, *Copenhagen* **10** B2
Brøndbyvester, *Copenhagen* **10** B2
Brondesbury, *London* **15** A2
Brønnøya, *Oslo* **22** A2
Brønshøj, *Copenhagen* **10** A2

RAFFLES PARK

Monte Palatino, *Rome* 25 c3
Montebello, *Los Angeles* 16 B4
Montemor, *Lisbon* 14 A1
Monterey Park, *Los Angeles* 16 B4
Montespaccato, *Rome* 25 B1
Montesson, *Paris* 23 A1
Monteverde Nuovo, *Rome* 25 B1
Montfermeil, *Paris* 23 A4
Montigny-le-Bretonneux, *Paris* 23 B1
Montjay-la-Tour, *Paris* 23 A4
Montjuic, Parc de, *Barcelona* 4 c1
Montparnasse, Gare, *Paris* 23 A2
Montréal, *Montreal* 19 A2
Montréal, Î. de, *Montreal* 19 A2
Montréal, Univ. de, *Montreal* 19 B2
Montréal Est, *Montreal* 19 A2
Montréal Nord, *Montreal* 19 A2
Montréal Ouest, *Montreal* 19 B1
Montreuil, *Paris* 23 A3
Montrouge, *Paris* 23 B2
Montserrat, *Buenos Aires* 7 B2
Monza, *Milan* 18 A2
Monzoro, *Milan* 18 B1
Moóca, *São Paulo* 26 B2
Moonachie, *New York* 21 B1
Moonee Ponds, *Melbourne* 17 A1
Moonee Valley Racecourse, *Melbourne* 17 A1
Moosach, *Munich* 20 A2
Mora, *Mumbai* 20 B2
Moratalaz, *Madrid* 17 B2
Mörby, *Stockholm* 28 A2
Morden, *London* 15 B2
Morée ✈, *Paris* 23 A3
Morgan Park, *Chicago* 9 C3
Moriguchi, *Osaka* 22 A4
Morivione, *Milan* 18 B2
Morningside, *Edinburgh* 11 B2
Morningside, *Johannesburg* 13 A2
Morningside, *Washington* 32 C4
Morro Solar, Cerro, *Lima* 16 C2
Mortlake, *London* 15 B2
Mortlake, *Sydney* 28 B1
Morton Grove, *Chicago* 9 A2
Morumbi, *São Paulo* 26 B1
Moscavide, *Lisbon* 14 A2
Moscow = Moskva, *Moscow* 19 B3
Moskhaton, *Athens* 2 B2
Moskva, *Moscow* 19 B3
Moskva ✈, *Moscow* 19 B2
Moskvoretskiy, *Moscow* 19 B3
Mosman, *Sydney* 28 A2
Móstoles, *Madrid* 17 C1
Moti Bagh, *Delhi* 10 B2
Motol, *Prague* 24 B1
Motsa, *Jerusalem* 13 B2
Motsa Ilit, *Jerusalem* 13 B1
Motspur Park, *London* 15 B2
Mottingham, *London* 15 B4
Moulin Rouge, *Paris* 23 a3
Mount Dennis, *Toronto* 30 A2
Mount Greenwood, *Chicago* 9 C2
Mount Hood Memorial Park, *Boston* 6 A3
Mount Merrion, *Dublin* 11 B2
Mount Rainier, *Washington* 32 B4
Mount Vernon, *New York* 21 A3
Mount Vernon Square, *Washington* 32 a2
Mount Zion, *Jerusalem* 13 b3
Mozarthaus, *Vienna* 31 b2
Müggelberge, *Berlin* 5 B5
Müggelheim, *Berlin* 5 B5
Muggiò, *Milan* 18 A2
Mughal Gardens, *Delhi* 1 c1
Mühleiten, *Vienna* 31 A3
Mühlenfliess ✈, *Berlin* 5 A5
Muiden, *Amsterdam* 2 A3
Muiderpoort Station, *Amsterdam* 2 b3
Muizenberg, *Cape Town* 8 B1
Mujahidpur, *Delhi* 10 B2
Mukandpur, *Delhi* 10 A2
Mukhmas, *Jerusalem* 13 A2
Muko ✈, *Osaka* 22 A3
Mukojima, *Tokyo* 29 A3
Mulbarton, *Johannesburg* 13 B2
Mumbai, *Mumbai* 20 B2
Mumbai Harbour, *Mumbai* 20 B2
Münchehofe, *Berlin* 5 B5
München, *Munich* 20 B2
Munich = München, *Munich* 20 B2
Munkkiniemi, *Helsinki* 12 B2
Munro, *Buenos Aires* 7 B1
Murai Res., *Singapore* 27 A2
Muranów, *Warsaw* 31 B1
Murino, *St. Petersburg* 26 B2
Murrayfield, *Edinburgh* 11 B2
Musashino, *Tokyo* 29 A2
Museu Nacional, *Rio de Janeiro* 24 B1
Mushin, *Lagos* 14 A2
Musiektheater, *Amsterdam* 2 b2
Muslim Quarter, *Jerusalem* 13 a3
Musocco, *Milan* 18 B1
Mustansiriya, *Baghdad* 3 A2
Musturud, *Cairo* 7 A2
Muswell Hill, *London* 15 A3
Mutanabi, *Baghdad* 3 B2
Muthana, *Baghdad* 3 B2
Myakinino, *Moscow* 19 B2
Mykerinos, *Cairo* 7 B1
Myllypuro, *Helsinki* 12 B3

N

Nacka, *Stockholm* 28 B3
Nada, *Osaka* 22 A2
Naenae, *Wellington* 32 B2
Nærsnes, *Oslo* 22 B1
Nagata, *Osaka* 22 B1
Nagatsuta, *Tokyo* 29 B2
Nagytétény, *Budapest* 7 B1
Nahant, *Boston* 6 A4
Nahant B., *Boston* 6 A4
Nahant Harbor, *Boston* 6 A4
Nahr Dijlah ✈, *Baghdad* 3 B2
Najafgarh Drain ✈, *Delhi* 10 B1
Nakahara-Ku, *Tokyo* 29 B2
Nakano-Ku, *Tokyo* 29 A2
Namgajwa, *Seoul* 26 B1
Namsan Park, *Seoul* 26 B1
Namyŏng, *Seoul* 26 B1
Nanbiancun, *Canton* 8 B2
Nanchang He ✈, *Beijing* 4 B1
Nandang, *Canton* 8 B2
Nandian, *Tianjin* 30 A2
Nangal Dewat, *Delhi* 10 B1
Naniwa, *Osaka* 22 B1
Nankai, *Tianjin* 30 B1
Nanmenwai, *Tianjin* 30 B2
Nanole, *Mumbai* 20 A2
Nanpu Bridge, *Shanghai* 27 B2
Nanshi, *Shanghai* 27 B1
Nantasket Beach, *Boston* 6 B4
Nanterre, *Paris* 23 A2
Naoabad, *Calcutta* 8 C2
Napier Mole, *Karachi* 14 B1
Naraina, *Delhi* 10 B1
Nariman Point, *Mumbai* 20 c1
Nariman Pt., *Mumbai* 20 B1
Nārmak, *Tehran* 30 A2
Naruo, *Osaka* 22 A3
Näsby, *Stockholm* 28 A2
Näsbypark, *Stockholm* 28 A2
Nathan Road, *Hong Kong* 12 a2
Natick, *Boston* 6 B2
National Maritime Museum, *San Francisco* 25 a1
National Museum, *Bangkok* 3 b1
Nationalmuseum, *Stockholm* 28 b2
Natolin, *Warsaw* 31 C2
Naturhistorischesmuseum, *Vienna* 31 b1
Naucalpan de Juárez, *Mexico City* 18 B1
Naupada, *Mumbai* 20 A2
Naviglio di Pavia, *Milan* 18 B1
Naviglio Grande, *Milan* 18 B1
Navona, Piazza, *Rome* 25 b2
Navotas, *Manila* 17 B1
Navy Pier, *Chicago* 9 b3
Nazal Hikmat Beg, *Baghdad* 3 A2
Nazimabad, *Karachi* 14 A2
Nazlet el Simmân, *Cairo* 7 B1
Néa Alexandhria, *Athens* 2 B2
Néa Faliron, *Athens* 2 B1
Néa Ionía, *Athens* 2 A2
Néa Liósia, *Athens* 2 A2
Néa Smírni, *Athens* 2 B2
Neapolis, *Athens* 2 B2
Near North, *Chicago* 9 b2
Nebušice, *Prague* 24 B1
Nederhorst, *Amsterdam* 2 B3
Nedlitz, *Berlin* 5 B1
Nee Soon, *Singapore* 27 A2
Needham Heights, *Boston* 6 B2
Nekrasovka, *Moscow* 19 B5
N'ematābād, *Tehran* 30 B2
Nemchinovka, *Moscow* 19 B1
Nemzeti Muz, *Budapest* 7 c3
Neponsit, *New York* 21 C2
Nerima-Ku, *Tokyo* 29 A3
Nesodden, *Oslo* 22 B3
Nesoddtangen, *Oslo* 22 A3
Nesøya, *Oslo* 22 A2
Neu Aubing, *Munich* 20 B1
Neu Buch, *Berlin* 5 A4
Neu Buchhorst, *Berlin* 5 B5
Neu Fahrland, *Berlin* 5 B1
Neu Lindenberg, *Berlin* 5 A4
Neubiberg, *Munich* 20 B3
Neue Hofburg, *Vienna* 31 b1
Neuenhagen, *Berlin* 5 A4
Neuessling, *Vienna* 31 A3
Neuhausen, *Munich* 20 B2
Neuherberg, *Munich* 20 A2
Neuhönow, *Berlin* 5 A5
Neuilly-Plaisance, *Paris* 23 A4
Neuilly-sur-Marne, *Paris* 23 A4
Neuilly-sur-Seine, *Paris* 23 A2
Neukagran, *Vienna* 31 A2
Neukettenhof, *Vienna* 31 B2
Neukölln, *Berlin* 5 B3
Neuperlach, *Munich* 20 B2
Neuried, *Munich* 20 B1
Neustift am Walde, *Vienna* 31 A1
Neusüssenbrunn, *Vienna* 31 A2
Neuwaldegg, *Vienna* 31 A1
Neva ✈, *St. Petersburg* 26 B2
Neves, *Rio de Janeiro* 24 B2
New Baghdād, *Baghdad* 3 B2
New Barakpur, *Calcutta* 8 A2
New Brighton, *New York* 21 C1
New Canada, *Johannesburg* 13 B1
New Canada Dam, *Johannesburg* 13 B1
New Carrollton, *Washington* 32 B4
New Cross, *London* 15 B3
New Delhi, *Delhi* 10 B2
New Dorp, *New York* 21 C1
New Dorp Beach, *New York* 21 C1
New Malden, *London* 15 B2
New Milford, *New York* 21 A1
New Territories, *Hong Kong* 12 A1
New Toronto, *Toronto* 30 B1
New Town, *Edinburgh* 11 B2
New Utrecht, *New York* 21 C2
Newark B., *New York* 21 B1
Newbattle, *Edinburgh* 11 B3
Newbury Park, *London* 15 A4
Newcraighall, *Edinburgh* 11 B3
Newham, *London* 15 A4
Newhaven, *Edinburgh* 11 B2
Newington, *Edinburgh* 11 B2
Newington, *London* 15 c5
Newlands, *Johannesburg* 13 B1
Newlands, *Wellington* 32 B1
Newport, *Melbourne* 17 B1
Newton, *Boston* 6 B2
Newtonbrook, *Toronto* 30 A2
Newtongrange, *Edinburgh* 11 B3
Newtonville, *Boston* 6 A2
Newtown, *Sydney* 28 B2
Neyagawa, *Osaka* 22 A4
Ngaio, *Wellington* 32 B1
Ngau Chi Wan, *Hong Kong* 12 A2
Ngau Tau Kok, *Hong Kong* 12 B2
Ngauranga, *Wellington* 32 B1
Ngong Shuen Chau, *Hong Kong* 12 B1
Ngua Kok Wan, *Hong Kong* 12 A1
Niāvarān, *Tehran* 30 A2
Nibra, *Calcutta* 8 B1
Nidāl, *Baghdad* 3 B2
Niddrie, *Edinburgh* 11 B3
Niddrie, *Melbourne* 17 A1
Nieder Neuendorf, *Berlin* 5 A2
Niederschöneweide, *Berlin* 5 B3
Niederschönhausen, *Berlin* 5 A3
Niemeyer, *Rio de Janeiro* 24 B1
Nieuw Zuid, *Amsterdam* 2 c2
Nieuwe Kerk, *Amsterdam* 2 b2
Nieuwendam, *Amsterdam* 2 A2
Nihonbashi, *Tokyo* 29 b5
Niipperi, *Helsinki* 12 A2
Nīkaia, *Athens* 2 B1
Nikolassee, *Berlin* 5 B2
Nikolskiy, *Moscow* 19 C2
Nikolskoye, *Moscow* 19 B5
Nikulino, *Moscow* 19 B2
Nil, Nahr en ✈, *Cairo* 7 B2
Nile = Nil, Nahr en ✈, *Cairo* 7 B2
Niles, *Chicago* 9 A2
Nimta, *Calcutta* 8 A2
Ningyuan, *Tianjin* 30 B2
Nippa, *Tokyo* 29 B2
Nippori, *Tokyo* 29 A3
Nishi, *Osaka* 22 A3
Nishinari, *Osaka* 22 B3
Nishiyodogawa, *Osaka* 22 A3
Niterói, *Rio de Janeiro* 24 B2
Nob Hill, *San Francisco* 25 b1
Nockeby, *Stockholm* 28 B1
Noel Park, *London* 15 A3
Nogatino, *Moscow* 19 B4
Nogent-sur-Marne, *Paris* 23 A3
Noida, *Delhi* 10 B2
Noiseau, *Paris* 23 B4
Noisiel, *Paris* 23 A4
Noisy-le-Grand, *Paris* 23 A4
Noisy-le-Roi, *Paris* 23 A1
Noisy-le-Sec, *Paris* 23 A3
Nokkala, *Helsinki* 12 C1
Nomentano, *Rome* 25 B2
Nonakashinden, *Tokyo* 29 A2
Nongminyundong Jiangxisuo, *Canton* 8 B2
Nonhyŏn, *Seoul* 26 B2
Nonthaburi, *Bangkok* 3 A1
Noon Gun, *Cape Town* 8 b1
Noorder Kerk, *Amsterdam* 2 a1
Noordgesig, *Johannesburg* 13 B1
Noordzeekanaal, *Amsterdam* 2 A1
Nord, Gare du, *Paris* 23 a4
Nordrand-Siedlung, *Vienna* 31 A2
Nordstrand, *Oslo* 22 A3
Normandale, *Wellington* 32 B2
Nørrebro, *Copenhagen* 10 a1
Norridge, *Chicago* 9 B2
Norrmalm, *Stockholm* 28 a1
North Arlington, *New York* 21 B1
North Bay Village, *Miami* 18 A2
North Bergen, *New York* 21 B1
North Branch Chicago River ✈, *Chicago* 9 B2
North Bull Island, *Dublin* 11 A3
North Cambridge, *Boston* 6 A3
North Cheam, *London* 15 B2
North Cohasset, *Boston* 6 B4
North Cray, *London* 15 B4
North Decatur, *Atlanta* 3 B3
North Druid Hills, *Atlanta* 3 B3
North Esk ✈, *Edinburgh* 11 B2
North Gyle, *Edinburgh* 11 B1
North Hackensack, *New York* 21 A1
North Harbor, *Manila* 17 B1
North Hd., *Sydney* 28 A2
North Hollywood, *Los Angeles* 16 B2
North Lexington, *Boston* 6 A2
North Miami, *Miami* 18 A2
North Miami Beach, *Miami* 18 A2
North Nazimabad, *Karachi* 14 A2
North Pt., *Hong Kong* 12 B2
North Queensferry, *Edinburgh* 11 A1
North Quincy, *Boston* 6 B3
North Res., *Boston* 6 A3
North Riverside, *Chicago* 9 B2
North Saugus, *Boston* 6 A3
North Shore Channel ✈, *Chicago* 9 B2
North Springfield, *Washington* 32 C2
North Sudbury, *Boston* 6 A1
North Sydney, *Sydney* 28 B2
North Woolwich, *London* 15 A4
North York, *Toronto* 30 A2
Northbridge, *Sydney* 28 A2
Northbridge Park, *Sydney* 28 A2
Northcliff, *Johannesburg* 13 A1
Northcote, *Melbourne* 17 A2
Northlake, *Chicago* 9 B1
Northmount, *Toronto* 30 A2
Northolt, *London* 15 A1
Northumberland Heath, *London* 15 B5
Northwood, *London* 15 A1
Norumbega Res., *Boston* 6 B2
Norwood, *Johannesburg* 13 A2
Norwood Park, *Chicago* 9 B2
Noryangjin, *Seoul* 26 B1
Nossa Senhora de Candelária, *Rio de Janeiro* 24 a2
Nossa Senhora do Ó, *São Paulo* 26 B1
Nossegem, *Brussels* 6 A3
Notre-Dame, *Montreal* 19 B3
Notre-Dame, *Paris* 23 c4
Notre-Dame, Bois, *Paris* 23 B4
Notre-Dame-de-Grace, *Montreal* 19 B2
Notting Hill, *London* 15 A2
Nova Milanese, *Milan* 18 A2
Novate Milanese, *Milan* 18 A1
Novaya Derevnya, *St. Petersburg* 26 A1
Nové Město, *Prague* 24 B2
Novoalekssandrovskoye, *St. Petersburg* 26 B2
Novogireyevo, *Moscow* 19 B4
Novoivanovskoye, *Moscow* 19 B1
Novonikolskoye, *Moscow* 19 A1
Novosaratovka, *St. Petersburg* 26 B3
Nowe-Babice, *Warsaw* 31 B1
Nöykkiö, *Helsinki* 12 B1
Nueva Atzacoalco, *Mexico City* 18 B2
Nueva Pompeya, *Buenos Aires* 7 C2
Nueva Tenochtitlán, *Mexico City* 18 B2
Nuijala, *Helsinki* 12 B1
Numabukuro, *Tokyo* 29 A2
Nunez, *Buenos Aires* 7 B2
Nunhead, *London* 15 B3
Ñuñoa, *Santiago* 26 B2
Nusle, *Prague* 24 B2
Nussdorf, *Vienna* 31 A2
Nyanga, *Cape Town* 8 A2
Nymphenburg, *Munich* 20 B2
Nymphenburg, Schloss, *Munich* 20 B2

O

Oak Grove, *Atlanta* 3 A3
Oak Island, *Boston* 6 A4
Oak Lawn, *Chicago* 9 C2
Oak Park, *Chicago* 9 B2
Oak View, *Washington* 32 A4
Oakdale, *Atlanta* 3 A2
Oakland, *San Francisco* 25 B3
Oakland, *Washington* 32 B4
Oaklawn, *Washington* 32 C4
Oakleigh, *Melbourne* 17 B2
Oakton, *Washington* 32 B2
Oakwood Beach, *New York* 21 C1
Oatley, *Sydney* 28 B1
Obalende, *Lagos* 14 B2
Oba's Palace, *Lagos* 14 B2
Oberföhring, *Munich* 20 B2
Oberhaching, *Munich* 20 B2
Oberlaa, *Vienna* 31 B2
Oberlisse, *Vienna* 31 A2
Obermenzing, *Munich* 20 A1
Obermoos Schwaige, *Munich* 20 A1
Oberschleissheim, *Munich* 20 A2
Oberschöneweide, *Berlin* 5 B4
Observatory, *Johannesburg* 13 B2
Observatory, *Sydney* 28 a1
Ōbu, *Osaka* 22 A1
Obu-tōge, *Osaka* 22 A1
Óbuda, *Budapest* 7 A2
Obukhovo, *St. Petersburg* 26 B2
Obvodnyy Kanal, *St. Petersburg* 26 B1
Ocean Park, *Hong Kong* 12 B2
Ochakovo, *Moscow* 19 B2
Ochota, *Warsaw* 31 B1
O'Connell Street, *Dublin* 11 b2
O'Higgins, Parque, *Santiago* 26 B2
Ōimachi, *Tokyo* 29 B3
Ojota, *Lagos* 14 A2
Okamoto, *Osaka* 22 A2
Okęcie, *Warsaw* 31 B1
Okęcie Airport, *Warsaw* 31 B1
Okelra, *Lagos* 14 B2
Okeogbe, *Lagos* 14 B2
Okha, *Delhi* 10 B2
Okhta ✈, *St. Petersburg* 26 B2
Okkervil ✈, *St. Petersburg* 26 B2
Okrzeszyn, *Warsaw* 31 C2
Oksval, *Oslo* 22 A3
Oktyabrskiy, *Moscow* 19 B3
Ōkubo, *Tokyo* 29 a2
Ōkura, *Tokyo* 29 B2
Olari, *Helsinki* 12 B1
Olaria, *Rio de Janeiro* 24 B1
Old Admiralty, *St. Petersburg* 26 B1
Old City, *Delhi* 1 a3
Old City, *Jerusalem* 13 B2
Old City, *Shanghai* 27 B1
Old Fort = Purana Qila, *Delhi* 1 c3
Old Harbor, *Boston* 6 B3
Old Town, *Chicago* 9 B3
Old Town, *Edinburgh* 11 B2
Oldbawn, *Dublin* 11 B1
Olgino, *St. Petersburg* 26 A1
Olimpico, Estadio, *Mexico City* 18 C1
Olivais, *Lisbon* 14 A2
Olivar de los Padres, *Mexico City* 18 B1
Olivar del Conde, *Mexico City* 18 B1
Olivos, *Buenos Aires* 7 B2
Olona ✈, *Milan* 18 B1
Olympia, *London* 15 c1
Olympic Stadium, *Helsinki* 12 B2
Olympique, Stade, *Montreal* 19 A2
Omonias, Pl., *Athens* 2 b1
Omori, *Tokyo* 29 B3
Onchi, *Osaka* 22 B4
Onchi ✈, *Osaka* 22 B4
Onisigun, *Lagos* 14 A2
Ōokayama, *Tokyo* 29 B3
Oosterpark, *Amsterdam* 2 b3
Oostzaan, *Amsterdam* 2 A2
Opa-Locka, *Miami* 18 A1
Opa-Locka Airport, *Miami* 18 A1
Opacz, *Warsaw* 31 B1
Opera House, *Sydney* 28 b2
Ophirton, *Johannesburg* 13 B2
Oppegård, *Oslo* 22 B3
Oppem, *Brussels* 6 A1
Oppsal, *Oslo* 22 A4
Ora, *Jerusalem* 13 B1
Oradell, *New York* 21 A1
Orange Bowl Stadium, *Miami* 18 B2
Orangi, *Karachi* 14 A2
Orchard Road, *Singapore* 27 A2
Ordrup, *Copenhagen* 10 A3
Orech, *Prague* 24 B1
Øresund, *Copenhagen* 10 A3
Orient Heights, *Boston* 6 A4
Orlando Dam, *Johannesburg* 13 B1
Orlando East, *Johannesburg* 13 B1
Orlovo, *Moscow* 19 C2
Orly, *Paris* 23 B3
Ormesson-sur-Marne, *Paris* 23 B4
Ormond, *Melbourne* 17 B2
Ormøya, *Oslo* 22 A3
Orpington, *London* 15 B4
Orsay, Musée d', *Paris* 23 b3
Országház, *Budapest* 7 b2
Országos Levétár, *Budapest* 7 b1
Ortaköy, *Istanbul* 12 B2
Ortica, *Milan* 18 B2
Oruba, *Lagos* 14 A2
Orvosötorteneti Múz., *Budapest* 7 c2
Osaka, *Osaka* 22 B4
Osaka B., *Osaka* 22 B2
Osaka Castle, *Osaka* 22 A4
Osaka Harbour, *Osaka* 22 B3
Osaka International Airport, *Osaka* 22 A3
Ōsaki, *Tokyo* 29 B3
Osasco, *São Paulo* 26 B1
Osdorf, *Berlin* 5 B3
Osdorp, *Amsterdam* 2 A1
Oshodi, *Lagos* 14 A2
Oslo, *Oslo* 22 A3
Oslofjorden, *Oslo* 22 B2
Ōsone, *Tokyo* 29 B2
Osorun, *Lagos* 14 A2
Ospiate, *Milan* 18 A1
Ostankino, *Moscow* 19 B3
Östasiatiskamuséet, *Stockholm* 28 b3
Österalm, *Stockholm* 28 a3
Østerbro, *Copenhagen* 10 a1
Osterley, *London* 15 B1
Osterley Park, *London* 15 B1
Östermalm, *Stockholm* 28 A2
Österskär, *Stockholm* 28 A3
Ostiense, *Rome* 25 B1
Østmarkkapellet, *Oslo* 22 A4
Ostøya, *Oslo* 22 A2
Østre Aker, *Oslo* 22 A3
Ōta-Ku, *Tokyo* 29 B3
Otaniemi, *Helsinki* 12 B1
Otari Open Air Museum, *Wellington* 32 B1
Otsuka, *Tokyo* 29 A3
Ottakring, *Vienna* 31 A1
Ottávia, *Rome* 25 B1
Ottery, *Cape Town* 8 B2
Ottobrunn, *Munich* 20 B3
Oud Zuid, *Amsterdam* 2 b1
Oude Kerk, *Amsterdam* 2 b2
Ouderkerk, *Amsterdam* 2 B2
Oulunkylä, *Helsinki* 12 B2
Ourcq, Canal de l', *Paris* 23 A3
Outer Mission, *San Francisco* 25 B2
Outremont, *Montreal* 19 A2
Overijse, *Brussels* 6 B3
Owhiro Bay, *Wellington* 32 C1
Oworonsoki, *Lagos* 14 A2
Oxford Street, *London* 15 b3
Oxgangs, *Edinburgh* 11 B2
Oxon Hill, *Washington* 32 C4
Oyodo, *Osaka* 22 A3
Oyster B., *Sydney* 28 C1
Oyster Rock, *Mumbai* 20 B1
Oyster Rocks, *Karachi* 14 B2
Ozoir-la-Ferrière, *Paris* 23 B4
Ozone Park, *New York* 21 B2

P

Pacific Heights, *San Francisco* 25 B2
Pacific Manor, *San Francisco* 25 C2
Pacific Palisades, *Los Angeles* 16 B1
Pacifica, *San Francisco* 25 C2
Paco, *Manila* 17 B1
Paco de Arcos, *Lisbon* 14 A1
Paco Imperial, *Rio de Janeiro* 24 a2
Paddington, *London* 15 b2
Paddington, *Sydney* 28 B2
Paderno, *Milan* 18 A1
Pagewood, *Sydney* 28 B2
Pagote, *Mumbai* 20 B2
Pai, I. do, *Rio de Janeiro* 24 C2
Pak Kong, *Hong Kong* 12 A2
Pakila, *Helsinki* 12 B2
Palacio de Bellas Artes, *Mexico City* 18 b2
Palacio de Communicaciones, *Madrid* 17 a3
Palacio Nacional, *Mexico City* 18 b3
Palacio Real, *Barcelona* 4 b3
Palacio Real, *Madrid* 17 b1
Palaión Fáliron, *Athens* 2 B1
Palais de Justice, *Brussels* 6 c2
Palais Royal, *Paris* 23 b4
Palais Royale, *Brussels* 6 b3
Palaiseau, *Paris* 23 B2
Palau Nacional Museu d'Art, *Barcelona* 4 c1
Palazzolo, *Milan* 18 A1
Palermo, *Buenos Aires* 7 B2
Palhais, *Lisbon* 14 B2
Palisades Park, *New York* 21 A1
Palmer Park, *Washington* 32 B4
Palmerston, *Dublin* 11 A1
Paloheinä, *Helsinki* 12 B2
Palomeras, *Madrid* 17 B2
Palos Heights, *Chicago* 9 D2
Palos Hills, *Chicago* 9 C2
Palos Hills Forest, *Chicago* 9 C1
Palos Park, *Chicago* 9 C1
Palpara, *Calcutta* 8 B2
Panchur, *Calcutta* 8 B1
Pandacan, *Manila* 17 B2
Pandan, Selat, *Singapore* 27 B2
Pandan Res., *Singapore* 27 B2
Panepistimio, *Athens* 2 b2
Pangbae, *Seoul* 26 C1
Pangrati, *Athens* 2 B2
Pangsua, Sungei ✈, *Singapore* 27 A2
Panihati, *Calcutta* 8 A2
Panjang, Bukit, *Singapore* 27 A2
Panje, *Mumbai* 20 B2
Panke ✈, *Berlin* 5 A3
Pankow, *Berlin* 5 A3
Panthéon, *Paris* 23 c4
Pantheon, *Rome* 25 b2
Pantin, *Paris* 23 A3
Pantitlán, *Mexico City* 18 B2
Panvel Cr. ✈, *Mumbai* 20 B2
Paparangi, *Wellington* 32 B1
Papiol, *Barcelona* 4 A1
Paramus, *New York* 21 A1
Paranaque, *Manila* 17 C1
Paray-Vieille-Poste, *Paris* 23 B3
Parco Regionale, *Milan* 18 A1
Parel, *Mumbai* 20 B1
Pari, *São Paulo* 26 B2
Parioli, *Rome* 25 B1
Paris, *Paris* 23 A3
Paris-Orly, Aéroport de, *Paris* 23 B3
Pārk-e Mellat, *Tehran* 30 A2
Park Ridge, *Chicago* 9 A1
Park Royal, *London* 15 A2
Parkchester, *New York* 21 A2
Parkdale, *Toronto* 30 B2
Parkhurst, *Johannesburg* 13 A2
Parklawn, *Washington* 32 B3
Parkmore, *Johannesburg* 13 A2
Parkside, *San Francisco* 25 B2
Parktown, *Johannesburg* 13 B2
Parktown North, *Johannesburg* 13 A2
Parkview, *Johannesburg* 13 A2
Parkville, *New York* 21 C2
Parkwood, *Cape Town* 8 B1
Parkwood, *Johannesburg* 13 A2
Parow, *Cape Town* 8 A2
Parque Chabuco, *Buenos Aires* 7 B2
Parque Patricios, *Buenos Aires* 7 B2
Parramatta ✈, *Sydney* 28 A1
Parthenon, *Athens* 2 c2
Paşabahçe, *Istanbul* 12 B2
Pasadena, *Los Angeles* 16 B4
Pasar Minggu, *Jakarta* 13 B1
Pasay, *Manila* 17 B1
Pascoe Vale, *Melbourne* 17 A1
Paseo de la Reforma, *Mexico City* 18 b2
Pasig, *Manila* 17 B2
Pasig ✈, *Manila* 17 B2
Pasila, *Helsinki* 12 B2
Pasing, *Munich* 20 B1
Pasir Panjang, *Singapore* 27 B2
Pasir Ris, *Singapore* 27 A3
Passaic ✈, *New York* 21 A1
Passirana, *Milan* 18 A1
Patel Nagar, *Delhi* 10 B1
Pateros, *Manila* 17 B2
Pathersville, *Atlanta* 3 B3
Pathumwan, *Bangkok* 3 B2
Patipukur, *Calcutta* 8 B2
Patisia, *Athens* 2 A2
Paulo E. Virginia, Gruta, *Rio de Janeiro* 24 B1
Paulshof, *Berlin* 5 A5
Pavshino, *Moscow* 19 B1
Paya Lebar, *Singapore* 27 A3
Peachtree ✈, *Atlanta* 3 B2
Peakhurst, *Sydney* 28 B1
Peania, *Athens* 2 B3
Peckham, *London* 15 B3
Peddocks I., *Boston* 6 B4
Pederstrup, *Copenhagen* 10 A2
Pedralbes, *Barcelona* 4 A1
Pedregal de San Angel, Jardines del, *Mexico City* 18 C1
Pekhorka ✈, *Moscow* 19 C6
Pekhra-Pokrovskoye, *Moscow* 19 A5
Pekhra-Yakovievskaya, *Moscow* 19 B5
Peking = Beijing, *Beijing* 4 B1
Pelcowizna, *Warsaw* 31 B2
Pelopónnisos Sta., *Athens* 2 a1
Penalolén, *Santiago* 26 B2
Pencarrow Hd., *Wellington* 32 C2
Peng Siang ✈, *Singapore* 27 A2
Penge, *London* 15 B3
Penha, *Rio de Janeiro* 24 A1
Penicuik, *Edinburgh* 11 B2
Penjaringan, *Jakarta* 13 A1
Penn Station, *New York* 21 c2
Pennsylvania Avenue, *Washington* 32 b1
Pentland Hills, *Edinburgh* 11 B1
Penyagino, *Moscow* 19 A2
Penzing, *Vienna* 31 A1
People's Park, *Shanghai* 27 B1
People's Square, *Shanghai* 27 B1
Perales del Rio, *Madrid* 17 C2
Peravillo, *Mexico City* 18 a3
Perchtoldsdorf, *Vienna* 31 B1
Perdizes, *São Paulo* 26 B2
Peredelkino, *Moscow* 19 C2
Pergamon Museum, *Berlin* 5 a4
Peristérion, *Athens* 2 A2
Perivale, *London* 15 A2
Perk, *Brussels* 6 A2
Perlach, *Munich* 20 B2
Perlacher Forst, *Munich* 20 B2
Pero, *Milan* 18 A1
Peropok, Bukit, *Singapore* 27 B2
Perovo, *Moscow* 19 B4
Pershing Square, *Los Angeles* 16 c1
Pertusella, *Milan* 18 A1
Pesagot, *Jerusalem* 13 A2
Pesanggrahag, Kali ✈, *Jakarta* 13 B1
Peschiera Borromeo, *Milan* 18 B2
Pesek, P., *Singapore* 27 B2
Pest, *Budapest* 7 B2
Pesterzsébet, *Budapest* 7 B2
Pesthidegkút, *Budapest* 7 A1
Pestimre, *Budapest* 7 B3
Pestlőrinc, *Budapest* 7 B3
Pestújhely, *Budapest* 7 A2
Petas, *Helsinki* 12 B2
Petone, *Wellington* 32 B2
Petrogradskaya Storona, *St. Petersburg* 26 B2
Petroúpolis, *Athens* 2 A2
Petrovice, *Prague* 24 B3
Petrovskiy Park, *Moscow* 19 B3
Petrovsko-Razumovskoye, *Moscow* 19 B3
Pettycur, *Edinburgh* 11 A2
Peutie, *Brussels* 6 A2
Pfaueninsel, *Berlin* 5 B1
Phaya Thai, *Bangkok* 3 B2
Phihai, *Karachi* 14 A2
Phillip B., *Sydney* 28 B2
Phoenix Park, *Dublin* 11 A2
Phra Khanong, *Bangkok* 3 B2
Phra Pradaeng, *Bangkok* 3 C2
Phranakhon, *Bangkok* 3 B1
Picasso, Museu, *Barcelona* 4 c2
Piccadilly, *London* 15 b3
Pico Rivera, *Los Angeles* 16 C4
Piedade, *Lisbon* 14 A1
Piedade, *Rio de Janeiro* 24 B1
Piedade, Cova da, *Lisbon* 14 A2
Piedmont Park, *Atlanta* 3 B2
Pietralata, *Rome* 25 B2
Pihlajamäki, *Helsinki* 12 B2
Pihlajasaari, *Helsinki* 12 C2
Pilares, *Rio de Janeiro* 24 B1
Pilton, *Edinburgh* 11 B2
Pimlico, *London* 15 c3
Pimmit Hills, *Washington* 32 B2
Pine Grove, *Toronto* 30 A1
Pinewood, *Miami* 18 A2
Piney Run ✈, *Washington* 32 B2
Pinganli, *Beijing* 4 B2
Pingzhou, *Canton* 8 B2
Pinheiros ✈, *São Paulo* 26 B1
Pinjrapur, *Karachi* 14 A2
Pinner, *London* 15 A1
Pinner Green, *London* 15 A1
Pioltello, *Milan* 18 A2
Pipinui Pt., *Wellington* 32 A1
Piraévs, *Athens* 2 B1
Pirajuçara ✈, *São Paulo* 26 B1
Pirinççi, *Istanbul* 12 B1
Pirituba, *São Paulo* 26 A1
Pirkkola, *Helsinki* 12 B2
Pisnice, *Prague* 24 C2
Pitampura, *Delhi* 10 A1
Pitkäjärvi, *Helsinki* 12 B1
Plumstead, *Cape Town* 8 B1
Plumstead, *London* 15 B4
Plyushchevo, *Moscow* 19 B4
Pnĭka, *Athens* 2 c1
Po Toi I., *Hong Kong* 12 B2
Po Toi O, *Hong Kong* 12 B2
Poasco, *Milan* 18 B2
Podbaba, *Prague* 24 B2
Podolí, *Prague* 24 B2
Podolkino, *Moscow* 19 B1
Pointe-Aux-Trembles, *Montreal* 19 A2
Poissy, *Paris* 23 A1
Pok Fu Lam, *Hong Kong* 12 B1
Pokrovsko-Sresnevo, *Moscow* 19 B2
Polton, *Edinburgh* 11 B3
Polyustrovo, *St. Petersburg* 26 B2
Pompidou, Centre, *Paris* 23 b4
Pomprap, *Bangkok* 3 B2
Pondok Indah, *Jakarta* 13 B1
Pont-Viau, *Montreal* 19 A1
Ponta do Marisco, *Rio de Janeiro* 24 C1
Pontault-Combault, *Paris* 23 B4
Pontinha, *Lisbon* 14 A1
Poplar, *London* 15 A3
Popolo, Porta del, *Rome* 25 a2
Poppintree, *Dublin* 11 A2
Porirua, *Wellington* 32 A2
Porirua East, *Wellington* 32 A2
Port I., *Osaka* 22 A2
Port Melbourne, *Melbourne* 17 B1
Port Nicholson, *Wellington* 32 B2
Port Philip Bay, *Melbourne* 17 B1
Port Richmond, *New York* 21 C1
Port Shelter, *Hong Kong* 12 A2
Port Union, *Toronto* 30 A4
Portage Park, *Chicago* 9 B2
Portal de la Pau, Pl., *Barcelona* 4 c2
Portela, Aeroporto da, *Lisbon* 14 A2
Portmarnock, *Dublin* 11 A3
Porto Brandão, *Lisbon* 14 A1
Porto Novo, *Rio de Janeiro* 24 A2
Porto Novo Cr. ✈, *Lagos* 14 B2
Portobello, *Edinburgh* 11 B3
Portrero, *San Francisco* 25 B3
Potomac, *Washington* 32 A2
Potomac ✈, *Washington* 32 B3
Potrero Pt., *San Francisco* 25 B2
Potsdam, *Berlin* 5 B1
Potsdamer Platz, *Berlin* 5 b3
Potzham, *Munich* 20 B2
Pötzleinsdorf, *Vienna* 31 A1
Povoa de Santo Adriao, *Lisbon* 14 A2
Powązki, *Warsaw* 31 B1
Powiśle, *Warsaw* 31 B2
Powsin, *Warsaw* 31 C2
Powsinek, *Warsaw* 31 C2
Poyan Res., *Singapore* 27 A2
Pozuelo de Alarcon, *Madrid* 17 B1
Prado, Museo del, *Madrid* 17 b3
Prado Churubusco, *Mexico City* 18 B2
Praga, *Warsaw* 31 B2
Prague = Praha, *Prague* 24 B2
Praha, *Prague* 24 B2
Praha-Ruzyně Airport, *Prague* 24 B1
Praires, R. des ✈, *Montreal* 19 A2
Prater, *Vienna* 31 A2
Precotto, *Milan* 18 A2
Prenestino Labicano, *Rome* 25 B2
Prenzlauerberg, *Berlin* 5 A3
Preston, *Melbourne* 17 A1
Pretos Forros, Sa. dos, *Rio de Janeiro* 24 B1
Préville, *Montreal* 19 B3
Přezletice, *Prague* 24 B3
Prima Porta, *Rome* 25 B1
Primavalle, *Rome* 25 B1
Primrose, *Johannesburg* 13 B2
Princes Street, *Edinburgh* 11 b2
Printer's Row, *Chicago* 9 d2
Progreso Nacional, *Mexico City* 18 A2
Prosek, *Prague* 24 B3
Prospect Hill Park, *Boston* 6 A2
Providencia, *Santiago* 26 B2
Prudential Building, *Chicago* 9 c2
Průhonice, *Prague* 24 C3
Psikhikón, *Athens* 2 A2
Pudong New Area, *Shanghai* 27 B2
Pueblo Libre, *Lima* 16 B2
Pueblo Nuevo, *Barcelona* 4 A2
Pueblo Nuevo, *Madrid* 17 B2
Puerta del Sol, Plaza, *Madrid* 17 b2
Puerto Madero, *Buenos Aires* 7 B2
Puerto Retiro, *Buenos Aires* 7 B2
Puhuangyu, *Beijing* 4 B2
Puistola, *Helsinki* 12 B3
Pukan-san, *Seoul* 26 B1
Pukinmäki, *Helsinki* 12 B2
Pukkajwa, *Seoul* 26 B1
Pulkovo Int. Airport, *St. Petersburg* 26 C1
Pullach, *Munich* 20 B1
Pulo Gadung, *Jakarta* 13 B2
Pūnak, *Tehran* 30 A2
Punchbowl, *Sydney* 28 B1
Punde, *Mumbai* 20 B2
Punggol, *Singapore* 27 A3
Punggol, Sungei ✈, *Singapore* 27 A3
Punggol Pt., *Singapore* 27 A3
Punjabi Bagh, *Delhi* 10 A1
Puotila, *Helsinki* 12 B3
Purana Qila, *Delhi* 1 c3
Puteaux, *Paris* 23 A2
Putilkovo, *Moscow* 19 A2
Putney, *London* 15 B2
Putuo, *Shanghai* 27 B1
Putxet, *Barcelona* 4 A1
Puxi, *Shanghai* 27 B1
Pydhuni, *Mumbai* 20 b2
Pyramids, *Cairo* 7 B1
Pyry, *Warsaw* 31 C1

Q

Qalandya, *Jerusalem* 13 A2
Qal'eh Morghī, *Tehran* 30 B2
Qanā el Ismā'iliya, *Cairo* 7 A2
Qāsemābād, *Tehran* 30 A3
Qasr-e Firūzeh, *Tehran* 30 B3
Qatane, *Jerusalem* 13 B1
Qianmen, *Beijing* 4 B2
Qinghuayuan, *Beijing* 4 B1
Qingningsi, *Shanghai* 27 B2
Qolhak, *Tehran* 30 A2
Quadraro, *Rome* 25 B2
Quaid-i-Azam, *Karachi* 14 A1
Quartiere Zingone, *Milan* 18 B1
Quds, *Baghdad* 3 A2
Queen Mary Res., *London* 15 B1
Queen Street, *Edinburgh* 11 a1
Queensbury, *London* 15 A2
Queenscliffe, *Sydney* 28 A2
Queensferry, *Edinburgh* 11 B1
Queenstown, *Singapore* 27 B2
Quellerina, *Johannesburg* 13 A1
Queluz, *Lisbon* 14 A1
Quezon City, *Manila* 17 B2
Quezon Memorial Circle, *Manila* 17 B2
Quilicura, *Santiago* 26 B1
Quincy, *Boston* 6 B3
Quincy B., *Boston* 6 B4
Quinta Normal, *Santiago* 26 B1
Quinto de Stampi, *Milan* 18 B2
Quinto Romano, *Milan* 18 B1
Quirinale, *Rome* 25 b1
Quirinale, Palazzo dei, *Rome* 25 b3

R

Raasdorf, *Vienna* 31 A3
Rådhuset, *Oslo* 22 A3
Radlice, *Prague* 24 B2
Radość, *Warsaw* 31 B3
Radotín, *Prague* 24 C2
Rafat, *Jerusalem* 13 A2
Raffles Hotel, *Singapore* 27 b3
Raffles Park, *Singapore* 27 B2

S

T

ZYUZINO

Tacuba, *Mexico City* 18 B1
Tacubaya, *Mexico City* 18 B1
Taebang, *Seoul* 26 B1
Tagig, *Manila* 17 B2
Tagig →, *Manila* 17 B2
Tai Hang, *Hong Kong* 12 B2
Tai Lo Shan, *Hong Kong* 12 A2
Tai Po Tsai, *Hong Kong* 12 A2
Tai Seng, *Singapore* 27 A3
Tai Shui Hang, *Hong Kong* 12 A2
Tai Tam B., *Hong Kong* 12 B2
Tai Tam Tuk Res., *Hong Kong* 12 B2
Tai Wai, *Hong Kong* 12 A1
Tai Wan Tau, *Hong Kong* 12 B2
Tai Wo Hau, *Hong Kong* 12 A1
Tainaka, *Osaka* 22 B4
Taishō, *Osaka* 22 B3
Taita, *Wellington* 32 B2
Tajrīsh, *Tehran* 30 A2
Takaido, *Tokyo* 29 A2
Takaishi, *Tokyo* 29 B2
Takarazuka, *Osaka* 22 A2
Takasago, *Tokyo* 29 A4
Takatsu-Ku, *Tokyo* 29 B2
Takeshita, *Tokyo* 29 B2
Takinegawa, *Tokyo* 29 A3
Takoma Park, *Washington* 32 B3
Taksim, *Istanbul* 12 B1
Talaide, *Lisbon* 14 A1
Taliganga, *Calcutta* 8 B2
Talipapa, *Manila* 17 A2
Tallaght, *Dublin* 11 B1
Tallkrogen, *Stockholm* 28 B2
Tama, *Tokyo* 29 B1
Tama →, *Tokyo* 29 B2
Tama Kyūryō, *Tokyo* 29 B2
Tamaden, *Tokyo* 29 B2
Tamagawa-josui →, *Tokyo* 29 A1
Taman Sari, *Jakarta* 13 A1
Tamanduateí →, *São Paulo* 26 B2
Tamboerskloof, *Cape Town* 8 A1
Tambora, *Jakarta* 13 A1
Tammisalo, *Helsinki* 12 B3
Tammûh, *Cairo* 7 B2
Tampines, *Singapore* 27 A3
Tanah Abang, *Jakarta* 13 B1
Tanigami, *Osaka* 22 A2
Tanjung Duren, *Jakarta* 13 B1
Tanjung Priok, *Jakarta* 13 A2
Tanum, *Oslo* 22 A1
Taoranting Park, *Beijing* 4 c2
Tapada, *Lisbon* 14 A1
Tapanila, *Helsinki* 12 B3
Tapiales, *Buenos Aires* 7 C1
Tapiola, *Helsinki* 12 B1
Tapsia, *Calcutta* 8 B2
Tara, *Mumbai* 20 A1
Tarabya, *Istanbul* 12 B2
Tarango, Presa, *Mexico City* 18 B1
Tårbæk, *Copenhagen* 10 A3
Tarchomin, *Warsaw* 31 B1
Tardeo, *Mumbai* 20 B1
Targówek, *Warsaw* 31 B2
Tårnby, *Copenhagen* 10 B3
Tarqua Bay, *Lagos* 14 B2
Tåstrup, *Copenhagen* 10 B1
Tatarovo, *Moscow* 19 B2
Tathong Channel, *Hong Kong* 12 B2
Tathong Pt., *Hong Kong* 12 B2
Tatuapé, *São Paulo* 26 B2
Taufkirchen, *Munich* 20 B2
Tavares, I. dos, *Rio de Janeiro* 24 A2
Távros, *Athens* 2 B2
Tawa, *Wellington* 32 A1
Teaneck, *New York* 21 A1
Teatro Municipal, *Rio de Janeiro* 24 c2
Tebet, *Jakarta* 13 B2
Tecamachaleo, *Mexico City* 18 B1
Teddington, *London* 15 B1
Tegel, *Berlin* 5 A2
Tegel, Flughafen, *Berlin* 5 A2
Tegeler See, *Berlin* 5 A2
Tegelort, *Berlin* 5 A2
Tehrān, *Tehran* 30 A2
Tehrān Pārs, *Tehran* 30 A3
Tei Tong Tsui, *Hong Kong* 12 B2
Tejo, Rio →, *Lisbon* 14 A2
Tekstilyshchik, *Moscow* 19 B4
Telegraph hill, *San Francisco* 25 a2
Telhal, *Lisbon* 14 A1
Telok Blangah, *Singapore* 27 B2
Teltow, *Berlin* 5 B2
Teltow kanal, *Berlin* 5 B3
Temnikovo, *Moscow* 19 B6
Tempelhof, *Berlin* 5 B3
Tempelhof, Flughafen, *Berlin* 5 B3
Temple City, *Los Angeles* 16 B4
Temple Hills Park, *Washington* 32 C4
Temple Mount, *Jerusalem* 13 b3
Templeogue, *Dublin* 11 B2
Templo Mayor, *Mexico City* 18 b3
Tenafly, *New York* 21 A2
Tenayuca, Piramide de, *Mexico City* 18 A1
Tengah →, *Singapore* 27 A2
Tennoji, *Osaka* 22 B4
Tepalcates, *Mexico City* 18 B2
Terrazzano, *Milan* 18 A1
Terrugem, *Lisbon* 14 A1
Tervuren, *Brussels* 6 B3
Tervuren, Park van, *Brussels* 6 B3
Tetuán, *Madrid* 17 B1
Teufelsberg, *Berlin* 5 B2
Tévere →, *Rome* 25 B1
Thalkirchen, *Munich* 20 B2
Thames →, *London* 15 A4
Thames Ditton, *London* 15 B1
Thamesmead, *London* 15 A4
Thana Cr. →, *Mumbai* 20 A2
The Loop, *Chicago* 9 B3
The Ridge, *Delhi* 10 B2
The Wilds, *Johannesburg* 13 B2
Theater Carré, *Amsterdam* 2 b2
Théatro Dionissou, *Athens* 2 c2
Thiais, *Paris* 23 B3
Thissío, *Athens* 2 c1
Thistletown, *Toronto* 30 A1
Thomastown, *Melbourne* 17 A2
Thompson I., *Boston* 6 B4
Thon Buri, *Bangkok* 3 B1
Thornbury, *Melbourne* 17 A2
Thorncliffe, *Toronto* 30 A2
Thornhill, *Toronto* 30 A2
Thornton, *Cape Town* 8 A2
Thornton Heath, *London* 15 B3
Threipmuir Res., *Edinburgh* 11 B2
Throgs Neck, *New York* 21 B3
Thyssen Bornemisza, Museo, *Madrid* 17 b3
Tian'anmen Square, *Beijing* 4 B2
Tiancun, *Beijing* 4 B1
Tianjin, *Tianjin* 30 B1
Tiantan Park, *Beijing* 4 c2
Tibidabo, *Barcelona* 4 A1
Tibradden Mt., *Dublin* 11 B2
Tiburon, *San Francisco* 25 A2
Tiburtino, *Rome* 25 B2
Ticomán, *Mexico City* 18 A2
Tiefersee, *Berlin* 5 B1
Tiejiangyin, *Beijing* 4 C2
Tientsin = Tianjin, *Tianjin* 30 B1
Tiergarten, *Berlin* 5 A3
Tietê →, *São Paulo* 26 B2
Tigerhof, *Cape Town* 8 A2
Tigris = Nahr Dijlah →, *Baghdad* 3 B2
Tijuca, *Rio de Janeiro* 24 B1
Tijuca, Parque Nacional da, *Rio de Janeiro* 24 B1
Tijuca, Pico da, *Rio de Janeiro* 24 B1
Tikkurila, *Helsinki* 12 B3
Tilak Nagar, *Delhi* 10 B1
Tilanqiao, *Shanghai* 27 B1
Timah, Bukit, *Singapore* 27 A2
Times Square, *New York* 21 c2
Timiryazev Park, *Moscow* 19 B3
Ting Kau, *Hong Kong* 12 A1
Tira, *Jerusalem* 13 A1
Tirsa, *Cairo* 7 B2
Tishrīyaa, *Baghdad* 3 B2
Tiu Keng Leng, *Hong Kong* 12 B2
Tivoli, *Copenhagen* 10 a3
Tizapán, *Mexico City* 18 C1
Tlalnepantla →, *Mexico City* 18 A1
To Kwai Wan, *Hong Kong* 12 B2
Toa Payoh, *Singapore* 27 A3
Tobong, *Seoul* 26 B2
Tobong-san, *Seoul* 26 A2
Točná, *Prague* 24 C2
Toco Hills, *Atlanta* 3 B2
Todt Hill, *New York* 21 C1
Tōkagi, *Tokyo* 29 A4
Tokai Plantation, *Cape Town* 8 B1
Tōkaichiba, *Tokyo* 29 B2
Tokarevo, *Moscow* 19 C5
Tōkyō, *Tokyo* 29 B3
Tokyo B., *Tokyo* 29 B4
Tokyo-Haneda Int. Airport, *Tokyo* 29 B3
Tokyo Harbour, *Tokyo* 29 B3
Tolka R. →, *Dublin* 11 A1
Tolworth, *London* 15 B2
Tomb of Lu Xun, *Shanghai* 27 B1
Tomb of the Kings, *Jerusalem* 13 a2
Tomba di Nerone, *Rome* 25 B1
Tomilino, *Moscow* 19 C5
Tondo, *Manila* 17 B1
Tongbinggo, *Seoul* 26 B1
Tongjak, *Seoul* 26 B1
Tongmaemung, *Seoul* 26 B2
Tongqiao, *Shanghai* 27 A1
Toorak, *Melbourne* 17 B2
Topkapı, *Istanbul* 12 B1
Tor di Quinto, *Rome* 25 B1
Tor Pignattara, *Rome* 25 B2
Tor Sapienza, *Rome* 25 B2
Toranomon, *Tokyo* 29 c3
Torcy, *Paris* 23 A4
Toronto, *Toronto* 30 B3
Toronto, Univ. of, *Toronto* 30 B2
Toronto Harbour, *Toronto* 30 B2
Toronto I., *Toronto* 30 B2
Toronto Int. Airport, *Toronto* 30 A1
Toros Las Arenas, Pl. de, *Barcelona* 4 c1
Toros Monumental, Templo de, *Barcelona* 4 a3
Torre Latino-americana, *Mexico City* 18 b2
Torre Lupara, *Rome* 25 B2
Torre Nova, *Rome* 25 B2
Torrellas →, *Barcelona* 4 A1
Torrevécchia, *Rome* 25 B1
Toshima-Ku, *Tokyo* 29 A3
Toshimaen, *Tokyo* 29 A2
Tottenham, *London* 15 A3
Tottenham, *Melbourne* 17 A1
Tour Eiffel, *Paris* 23 c2
Toussus-le-Noble, *Paris* 23 B1
Toussus-le-Noble, Aérodrome de, *Paris* 23 B1
Tower Bridge, *London* 15 b5
Tower Hamlets, *London* 15 A3
Tower of London, *London* 15 A3
Towra Pt., *Sydney* 28 C2
Tøyen, *Oslo* 22 A3
Toyonaka, *Osaka* 22 A3
Trafalgar Square, *London* 15 b3
Trafaria, *Lisbon* 14 A1
Traição, Cor. →, *São Paulo* 26 B2
Tranegilde, *Copenhagen* 10 B2
Trångsund, *Stockholm* 28 B2
Transamerica Pyramid, *San Francisco* 25 b2
Transbay Terminal, *San Francisco* 25 b3
Trappenfelde, *Berlin* 5 A4
Trastévere, *Rome* 25 B1
Treasure I., *San Francisco* 25 B2
Třeboradice, *Prague* 24 B3
Třebotov, *Prague* 24 C1
Tremblay-en-France, *Paris* 23 A4
Tremembe →, *São Paulo* 26 A2
Tremont, *New York* 21 A2
Trenno, *Milan* 18 B1
Treptow, *Berlin* 5 B3
Trés Rios, Sa. dos, *Rio de Janeiro* 24 B1
Trevi, Fontana di, *Rome* 25 b3
Trezzano sul Navíglio, *Milan* 18 B1
Tribune Tower, *Chicago* 9 b2
Trieste, *Rome* 25 B2
Trinidad, *Washington* 32 B4
Trinity, *Edinburgh* 11 B2
Trinity College, *Dublin* 11 c3
Trionfale, *Rome* 25 B1
Triulzo, *Milan* 18 B2
Trocadero, *Paris* 23 b1
Troitse-Lykovo, *Moscow* 19 B2
Troja, *Prague* 24 B2
Trollbäcken, *Stockholm* 28 B3
Trombay, *Mumbai* 20 A2
Troparevo, *Moscow* 19 C2
Tropenmuseum, *Amsterdam* 2 b3
Trudyashchikhsya, Ostrov, *St. Petersburg* 26 B1
Tryvasshøgda, *Oslo* 22 A3
Tseng Lan Shue, *Hong Kong* 12 A2
Tsim Sha Tsui, *Hong Kong* 12 a2
Tsing Yi, *Hong Kong* 12 A1
Tsova, *Jerusalem* 13 B1
Tsuen Wan, *Hong Kong* 12 A1
Tsukiji, *Tokyo* 29 c5
Tsur Hadassa, *Jerusalem* 13 B1
Tsurumi →, *Tokyo* 29 B3
Tsz Wan Shan, *Hong Kong* 12 A2
Tuas, *Singapore* 27 B1
Tuchoměřice, *Prague* 24 B1
Tuckahoe, *New York* 21 A3
Tucuruvi, *São Paulo* 26 A2
Tufello, *Rome* 25 B2
Tufnell Park, *London* 15 A3
Tughlakabad, *Delhi* 10 B2
Tuileries, Jardin des, *Paris* 23 b3
Tuindorp Oostzaan, *Amsterdam* 2 A2
Tullamarine, *Melbourne* 17 A1
Tulse Hill, *London* 15 B3
Tung Lung I., *Hong Kong* 12 B2
Tung O, *Hong Kong* 12 B1
Tunis, *Baghdad* 3 A2
Tuomarila, *Helsinki* 12 B1
Tureberg, *Stockholm* 28 A1
Turffontein, *Johannesburg* 13 B2
Turkso, *Prague* 24 A1
Turnham Green, *London* 15 B2
Turnhouse, *Edinburgh* 11 B1
Tuscolana, Via, *Rome* 25 B2
Tushino, *Moscow* 19 A2
Twelve Apostles, *Cape Town* 8 A1
Twickenham, *London* 15 B1
Twickenham Rugby Ground, *London* 15 B1
Twin Peaks, *San Francisco* 25 B2
Two Rock Mt., *Dublin* 11 B2
Tymon North, *Dublin* 11 B1
Tysons Corner, *Washington* 32 B2

U

U.S. Capitol, *Washington* 32 b3
Ubeidiya, *Jerusalem* 13 B2
Uberaba →, *São Paulo* 26 B2
Ubin, P., *Singapore* 27 A3
Uccle, *Brussels* 6 B2
Udelnaya, *St. Petersburg* 26 A2
Udelnoe, *St. Petersburg* 26 B1
Udlding, *Munich* 20 A1
Ueno, *Tokyo* 29 A3
Úholičky, *Prague* 24 B1
Uhříněves, *Prague* 24 B3
Uithoorn, *Amsterdam* 2 B1
Újpalota, *Budapest* 7 A2
Újpest, *Budapest* 7 A2
Ukita, *Tokyo* 29 A4
Ullerup, *Copenhagen* 10 B3
Ullevål, *Oslo* 22 A3
Ulriksdal, *Stockholm* 28 A1
Ulyanka, *St. Petersburg* 26 B1
Um Al-Khanazir Island, *Baghdad* 3 B2
Umeda, *Osaka* 22 A3
Umerkhadi, *Mumbai* 20 b2
Ümraniye, *Istanbul* 12 B2
Underground Atlanta, *Atlanta* 3 B2
Unětický potok →, *Prague* 24 B2
Ŭngam, *Seoul* 26 B1
Unhos, *Lisbon* 14 A2
Unidad Santa Fe, *Mexico City* 18 B1
Union City, *New York* 21 B1
Union Port, *New York* 21 B2
Union Square, *New York* 21 d2
Union Square, *San Francisco* 25 b2
Union Station, *Washington* 32 b3
United Nations H.Q., *New York* 21 c3
Universidad, *Madrid* 17 B1
Universidad de Chile, *Santiago* 26 B2
University Park, *Washington* 32 B4
Unp'yong, *Seoul* 26 B1
Unter den Linden, *Berlin* 5 a4
Unterbiberg, *Munich* 20 B2
Unterföhring, *Munich* 20 A3
Unterhaching, *Munich* 20 B2
Unterlaa, *Vienna* 31 B2
Untermenzing, *Munich* 20 A1
Upper East Side, *New York* 21 b3
Upper Elmers End, *London* 15 B3
Upper New York B., *New York* 21 C1
Upper Norwood, *London* 15 B3
Upper Peirce Res., *Singapore* 27 A2
Upper Sydenham, *London* 15 B3
Upper Tooting, *London* 15 B3
Upper West Side, *New York* 21 a2
Upton, *London* 15 A4
Uptown, *Chicago* 9 B2
Uran, *Mumbai* 20 B2
Urayasu, *Tokyo* 29 B4
Urbe, Aeroporto d', *Rome* 25 B2
Urca, *Rio de Janeiro* 24 B2
Uritsk, *St. Petersburg* 26 C1
Üröm, *Budapest* 7 A2
Ursus, *Warsaw* 31 B1
Ursvik, *Stockholm* 28 A1
Usera, *Madrid* 17 B1
Ushigome, *Tokyo* 29 A3
Usina, *Rio de Janeiro* 24 B1
Üsküdar, *Istanbul* 12 B2
Ust-Slavyanka, *St. Petersburg* 26 C3
Uteke, *Stockholm* 28 A3
Utrata, *Warsaw* 31 B2
Uttarpara, *Calcutta* 8 B1
Utterslev Mose, *Copenhagen* 10 A2

V

Vadaul, *Mumbai* 20 A2
Vaires-sur-Marne, *Paris* 23 A4
Valby, *Copenhagen* 10 B2
Valcannuta, *Rome* 25 B1
Valdelatas, *Madrid* 17 A1
Vale, *Washington* 32 B1
Valenton, *Paris* 23 B3
Valera, *Milan* 18 A1
Vallcarca, *Barcelona* 4 A1
Valldoreix, *Barcelona* 4 A1
Vallecas, *Madrid* 17 B2
Vallensbæk, *Copenhagen* 10 B2
Vallensbæk Strand, *Copenhagen* 10 B2
Vallentunasjön, *Stockholm* 28 A2
Valleranello, *Rome* 25 C1
Vallisaari, *Helsinki* 12 C3
Vallvidrera, *Barcelona* 4 A1
Valvidrera →, *Barcelona* 4 A1
Van Goghmuseum, *Amsterdam* 2 c1
Vanak, *Tehran* 30 A2
Vangede, *Copenhagen* 10 A3
Vaniköy, *Istanbul* 12 B2
Vanløse, *Copenhagen* 10 A2
Vantaa, *Helsinki* 12 B2
Vantaa →, *Helsinki* 12 B2
Vantaankoski, *Helsinki* 12 B2
Vantaanpuisto, *Helsinki* 12 B2
Vanves, *Paris* 23 B2
Varedo, *Milan* 18 A1
Varkiza, *Athens* 2 C2
Varszínház, *Budapest* 7 b2
Vartiokylä, *Helsinki* 12 B3
Vartiosaari, *Helsinki* 12 B3
Vasamuseet, *Stockholm* 28 b3
Vasco, *Cape Town* 8 A2
Vasfanārd, *Tehran* 30 B2
Vashi, *Mumbai* 20 A2
Vasilyevskiy, Ostrov, *St. Petersburg* 26 B1
Vaso Regulador El Cristo, *Mexico City* 18 B1
Vaucluse, *Sydney* 28 B2
Vaucresson, *Paris* 23 A1
Vauhallan, *Paris* 23 B2
Vaujours, *Paris* 23 A4
Vauxhall, *London* 15 c4
Vecsés, *Budapest* 7 B3
Veleň, *Prague* 24 A3
Veleslavin, *Prague* 24 B2
Vélizy-Villacoublay, *Paris* 23 B2
Velka-Chuchle, *Prague* 24 B2
Velké Přilepy, *Prague* 24 B1
Venda Seca, *Lisbon* 14 A1
Venetian Islands, *Miami* 18 B2
Venezia, Palazzo, *Rome* 25 c2
Venice, *Los Angeles* 16 C2
Ventas, *Madrid* 17 B1
Ventorro del Cano, *Madrid* 17 B1
Venustiano Carranza, *Mexico City* 18 B2
Verde →, *São Paulo* 26 A1
Verdi, *Athens* 2 A2
Verdun, *Montreal* 19 B2
Vérhalom, *Budapest* 7 A2
Vermelho →, *São Paulo* 26 B1
Vernon, *Los Angeles* 16 B3
Verrières-le-Buisson, *Paris* 23 B2
Versailles, *Buenos Aires* 7 B1
Versailles, *Paris* 23 B1
Veshnyaki, *Moscow* 19 B4
Vesolyy Posolok, *St. Petersburg* 26 B2
Vestra, *Helsinki* 12 B1
Vestskoven, *Copenhagen* 10 A2
Vicálvaro, *Madrid* 17 B2
Vicente Lopez, *Buenos Aires* 7 B2
Victoria, *Hong Kong* 12 B2
Victoria, *London* 15 c3
Victoria, Mt., *Wellington* 32 B1
Victoria, Pont, *Montreal* 19 B2
Victoria and Albert Waterfront, *Cape Town* 8 a1
Victoria Gardens, *Mumbai* 20 B2
Victoria Harbour, *Hong Kong* 12 B1
Victoria Island, *Lagos* 14 B2
Victoria L., *Johannesburg* 13 B2
Victoria Lawn Tennis Courts, *Melbourne* 17 B2
Victoria Park, *Singapore* 27 B2
Victoria Peak, *Hong Kong* 12 B1
Victoria Wharf, *Cape Town* 8 a2
Vienna = Wien, *Vienna* 31 A2
Vienna, *Washington* 32 B2
View Park, *Los Angeles* 16 B3
Vigário Geral, *Rio de Janeiro* 24 A1
Vigentino, *Milan* 18 B2
Viggbyholm, *Stockholm* 28 A2
Vighignolo, *Milan* 18 B1
Viikki, *Helsinki* 12 B3
Vikhroli, *Mumbai* 20 A2
Vila Guilherme, *São Paulo* 26 B2
Vila Isabel, *Rio de Janeiro* 24 B1
Vila Jaguára, *São Paulo* 26 B1
Vila Madalena, *São Paulo* 26 B1
Vila Maria, *São Paulo* 26 B2
Vila Mariana, *São Paulo* 26 B2
Vila Prudente, *São Paulo* 26 B2
Viladecans, *Barcelona* 4 B1
Vile Parle, *Mumbai* 20 A2
Villa Adelina, *Buenos Aires* 7 B1
Villa Ballester, *Buenos Aires* 7 B1
Villa Barilari, *Buenos Aires* 7 C2
Villa Borghese, *Rome* 25 a3
Villa Bosch, *Buenos Aires* 7 B1
Villa C. Colon, *Buenos Aires* 7 C2
Villa Ciudadela, *Buenos Aires* 7 B1
Villa de Guadalupe, *Mexico City* 18 B2
Villa Devoto, *Buenos Aires* 7 B1
Villa Diamante, *Buenos Aires* 7 C2
Villa Dominico, *Buenos Aires* 7 C3
Villa Lugano, *Buenos Aires* 7 C2
Villa Lynch, *Buenos Aires* 7 B1
Villa Madero, *Buenos Aires* 7 C1
Villa Sáenz Pena, *Buenos Aires* 7 B1
Villa Urquiza, *Buenos Aires* 7 B2
Villaverde, *Madrid* 17 B1
Villaverde Bajo, *Madrid* 17 B1
Ville-d'Avray, *Paris* 23 B2
Villecresnes, *Paris* 23 B4
Villejuif, *Paris* 23 B3
Villemomble, *Paris* 23 A4
Villeneuve-la-Garenne, *Paris* 23 A2
Villeneuve-le-Roi, *Paris* 23 B3
Villeneuve-St.-Georges, *Paris* 23 B3
Villeparisis, *Paris* 23 A4
Villevaudé, *Paris* 23 A4
Villiers-le-Bâcle, *Paris* 23 B1
Villiers-sur-Marne, *Paris* 23 B4
Villinki, *Helsinki* 12 C3
Villoresi, Canale, *Milan* 18 A1
Vilvoorde, *Brussels* 6 A2
Vimodrone, *Milan* 18 A2
Vimont, *Montreal* 19 A1
Vinanmek Palace, *Bangkok* 3 a2
Vincennes, *Paris* 23 A3
Vincennes, Bois de, *Paris* 23 B3
Vinings, *Atlanta* 3 A2
Vinohrady, *Prague* 24 c3
Vinoř, *Prague* 24 B3
Violet Hill, *Hong Kong* 12 B2
Virányos, *Budapest* 7 A1
Virgen del San Cristóbal, *Santiago* 26 B2
Virginia Gardens, *Miami* 18 B1
Virginia Key, *Miami* 18 B2
Viroflay, *Paris* 23 B2
Víron, *Athens* 2 B2
Virum, *Copenhagen* 10 A2
Vishnyaki, *Moscow* 19 B5
Visitacion Valley, *San Francisco* 25 B2
Vista Alegre, *Lima* 16 B3
Vista Alegre, *Santiago* 26 C1
Vista Grove, *Atlanta* 3 A3
Vitacura, *Santiago* 26 B2
Vitinia, *Rome* 25 C1
Vitry-sur-Seine, *Paris* 23 B3
Vizandinó, Moussío, *Athens* 2 b3
Vladykino, *Moscow* 19 A3
Vlezenbeek, *Brussels* 6 B1
Vltava →, *Prague* 24 A2
Vnukovo, *Moscow* 19 C1
Vokovice, *Prague* 24 B2
Volgelsdorf, *Berlin* 5 B5
Volkhonka-Zil, *Moscow* 19 C3
Vollen, *Oslo* 22 B1
Volodarskoye, *St. Petersburg* 26 B2
Volynkina-Derevnya, *St. Petersburg* 26 B1
Vondelpark, *Amsterdam* 2 A2
Vösendorf, *Vienna* 31 B2
Vostochnyy, *Moscow* 19 B5
Voula, *Athens* 2 C2
Vouliagmeni, *Athens* 2 C2
Vredehoek, *Cape Town* 8 A1
Vršovice, *Prague* 24 B2
Vyborgskaya Storona, *St. Petersburg* 26 B2
Vykhino, *Moscow* 19 B4
Vyšehrad, *Prague* 24 B2

W

Wachterhof, *Munich* 20 B3
Wadala, *Mumbai* 20 A2
Wadestown, *Wellington* 32 B1
Wadi Fukin, *Jerusalem* 13 B1
Wah Fu, *Hong Kong* 12 B1
Wahda, *Baghdad* 3 B2
Währing, *Vienna* 31 A2
Waidmannslust, *Berlin* 5 A3
Wainuiomata, *Wellington* 32 B2
Wainuiomata R. →, *Wellington* 32 B2
Wakefield, *Boston* 6 A3
Waldesruh, *Berlin* 5 B4
Waldperlach, *Munich* 20 B3
Waldtrudering, *Munich* 20 B3
Walkinstown, *Dublin* 11 B1
Wall Street, *New York* 21 f1
Waltham, *Boston* 6 A2
Waltham Forest, *London* 15 A3
Walthamstow, *London* 15 A3
Walton on Thames, *London* 15 B1
Wambeek, *Brussels* 6 A3
Wan Chai, *Hong Kong* 12 B2
Wan Chai Lanes, *Hong Kong* 12 c2
Wandsworth, *London* 15 B2
Wankhede Stadium, *Mumbai* 20 c2
Wannsee, *Berlin* 5 B1
Wansdorf, *Berlin* 5 A1
Wanstead, *London* 15 A4
Wapping, *London* 15 A3
Ward, *Dublin* 11 A1
Ward I., *Wellington* 32 B2
Warnberg, *Munich* 20 B2
Warrâq el 'Arab, *Cairo* 7 A2
Warrâq el Hadr, *Cairo* 7 A2
Warringen Park, *Melbourne* 17 A2
Warriston, *Edinburgh* 11 B2
Warsaw = Warszawa, *Warsaw* 31 B2
Warszawa, *Warsaw* 31 B2
Wartenberg, *Berlin* 5 A4
Washington, *Washington* 32 B3
Washington Heights, *New York* 21 A2
Washington Monument, *Washington* 32 b1
Washington Nat. Airport, *Washington* 32 B3
Washington Park, *Chicago* 9 C3
Wat Arun, *Bangkok* 3 b1
Wat Pho, *Bangkok* 3 b1
Wat Phra Keo, *Bangkok* 3 b1
Wat Traimit, *Bangkok* 3 c2
Water of Leith, *Edinburgh* 11 B1
Water Tower Place, *Chicago* 9 a2
Watergraafsmeer, *Amsterdam* 2 A2
Waterland, *Amsterdam* 2 A2
Waterloo, *Brussels* 6 B2
Waterloo, *Wellington* 32 B2
Waterloo International, *London* 15 b4
Watermael-Boitsfort, *Brussels* 6 B2
Watertown, *Boston* 6 A2
Watsonia, *Melbourne* 17 A2
Waverley, *Boston* 6 A2
Waverley, *Johannesburg* 13 A2
Waverley, *Sydney* 28 B2
Waverley Station, *Edinburgh* 11 b3
Wawer, *Warsaw* 31 B2
Wawrzyszew, *Warsaw* 31 B1
Wayland, *Boston* 6 A1
Wazirabad, *Delhi* 10 A2
Wazīrīya, *Baghdad* 3 A2
Wazirpur, *Delhi* 10 A2
Wealdstone, *London* 15 A1
Wedding, *Berlin* 5 A3
Weehawken, *New York* 21 B1
Weesp, *Amsterdam* 2 B3
Weidling, *Vienna* 31 A1
Weidlingbach, *Vienna* 31 A1
Weigongcum, *Beijing* 4 B1
Weijin He →, *Tianjin* 30 B2
Weissensee, *Berlin* 5 A3
Wellesley, *Boston* 6 B2
Wellesley Falls, *Boston* 6 B2
Wellesley Hills, *Boston* 6 B2
Welling, *London* 15 B4
Wellington, *Boston* 6 A3
Wellington, *Wellington* 32 B1
Wells Fargo Center, *Los Angeles* 16 b1
Weltevreden Park, *Johannesburg* 13 A1
Wembley, *London* 15 A2
Wemmel, *Brussels* 6 A1
Wemmer Pan, *Johannesburg* 13 B2
Wenceslas Square, *Prague* 24 b2
Wendenschloss, *Berlin* 5 B4
Wenhuagong, *Tianjin* 30 B2
Wennington, *London* 15 A5
Werneuchen, *Berlin* 5 A5
West Bedford, *Boston* 6 A2
West Concord, *Boston* 6 A1
West Don →, *Toronto* 30 A2
West Drayton, *London* 15 A1
West Ham, *London* 15 A4
West Harrow, *London* 15 A1
West Heath, *London* 15 B4
West Hill, *Toronto* 30 A3
West Hollywood, *Los Angeles* 16 B2
West Kensington, *London* 15 c1
West Kilburn, *London* 15 a1
West Lamma Channel, *Hong Kong* 12 B1
West Lynn, *Boston* 6 A4
West Medford, *Boston* 6 A3
West Miami, *Miami* 18 B1
West Molesey, *London* 15 B1
West New York, *New York* 21 B1
West of Twin Peaks, *San Francisco* 25 B2
West Park, *Johannesburg* 13 A1
West Rouge, *Toronto* 30 A4
West Roxbury, *Boston* 6 B3
West Springfield, *Washington* 32 C2
West Town, *Chicago* 9 B2
West Wharf, *Karachi* 14 B1
Westbourne Green, *London* 15 a1
Westchester, *Chicago* 9 B1
Westchester, *Los Angeles* 16 C2
Westchester, *New York* 21 A2
Westcliff, *Johannesburg* 13 B2
Westdene, *Johannesburg* 13 B1
Westend, *Helsinki* 12 C1
Wester Hailes, *Edinburgh* 11 B2
Westerham, *Munich* 20 B2
Western Addition, *San Francisco* 25 B2
Western Wall, *Jerusalem* 13 b3
Westgate, *Washington* 32 B3
Westlake, *Cape Town* 8 B1
Westlake, *San Francisco* 25 B2
Westminster, *London* 15 A3
Westmount, *Montreal* 19 B2
Weston, *Boston* 6 A2
Weston, *Toronto* 30 A1
Weston Res., *Boston* 6 A2
Westwood Village, *Los Angeles* 16 B2
Westzaan, *Amsterdam* 2 A1
Wetton, *Cape Town* 8 B2
Wexford, *Toronto* 30 A3
Weybridge, *London* 15 B1
Wezembeek-Oppem, *Brussels* 6 A2
White House, The, *Washington* 32 b1
Whitechapel, *London* 15 A3
Whitehall, *Dublin* 11 A2
Whitehall, *London* 15 b3
Whittier, *Los Angeles* 16 C4
Whitton, *London* 15 B1
Wieden, *Vienna* 31 A2
Wien, *Vienna* 31 A2
Wien-Schwechat, Flughafen, *Vienna* 31 B3
Wienerberg, *Vienna* 31 B2
Wierzbno, *Warsaw* 31 B2
Wijde Wormer, *Amsterdam* 2 A2
Wilanów, *Warsaw* 31 B2
Wilanówka →, *Warsaw* 31 C2
Wilhelmshagen, *Berlin* 5 B5
Wilket Creek Park, *Toronto* 30 A2
Wilkieston, *Edinburgh* 11 B1
Willbrook, *Dublin* 11 B2
Willesden, *London* 15 A2
Willesden Green, *London* 15 A2
Williamsbridge, *New York* 21 A2
Williamsburg, *New York* 21 B2
Williamstown, *Melbourne* 17 B1
Willoughby, *Sydney* 28 A2
Willow Springs, *Chicago* 9 C1
Willowdale, *Toronto* 30 A2
Wilmersdorf, *Berlin* 5 c1
Wilmette, *Chicago* 9 A2
Wilmington, *London* 15 B5
Wilshire Boulevard, *Los Angeles* 16 c1
Wimbledon, *London* 15 B2
Wimbledon Common, *London* 15 B2
Wimbledon Park, *London* 15 B2
Wimbledon Tennis Ground, *London* 15 B2
Winchester, *Boston* 6 A3
Windermere, *Cape Town* 8 A2
Windsor, *Johannesburg* 13 A1
Windsor Hills, *Los Angeles* 16 C2
Windy Arbour, *Dublin* 11 B2
Winning, *Munich* 20 B2
Winthrop, *Boston* 6 A4
Wissous, *Paris* 23 B2
Wittenau, *Berlin* 5 A2
Witwatersrand, Univ. of, *Johannesburg* 13 B2
Włochy, *Warsaw* 31 B1
Wo Mei, *Hong Kong* 12 A2
Wo Yi Hop, *Hong Kong* 12 A1
Woburn, *Boston* 6 A3
Woburn, *Toronto* 30 A3
Woduk Pluit, *Jakarta* 13 A1
Wola, *Warsaw* 31 B1
Wolf Trap Farm Park, *Washington* 32 B2
Wolica, *Warsaw* 31 C2
Wolica, *Warsaw* 31 C1
Wólka Węglowa, *Warsaw* 31 B1
Wollaston, *Boston* 6 B3
Woltersdorf, *Berlin* 5 B5
Woluwe-Saint-Lambert, *Brussels* 6 A2
Woluwe-Saint-Pierre, *Brussels* 6 A2
Wong Chuk Hang, *Hong Kong* 12 B2
Wong Chuk Wan, *Hong Kong* 12 A2
Wong Chuk Yeung, *Hong Kong* 12 A2
Wong Tai Sin, *Hong Kong* 12 A2
Wood Green, *London* 15 A3
Wood Ridge, *New York* 21 A1
Woodbridge, *Toronto* 30 A1
Woodford, *London* 15 A4
Woodford Bridge, *London* 15 A4
Woodford Green, *London* 15 A4
Woodhaven, *New York* 21 B2
Woodhouselee, *Edinburgh* 11 B2
Woodlands New Town, *Singapore* 27 A2
Woodmont, *Washington* 32 B3
Woodside, *London* 15 B3
Woodside, *New York* 21 B2
Woodstock, *Cape Town* 8 A1
Woollahra, *Sydney* 28 B2
Woolloomooloo, *Sydney* 28 b2
Woolooware B., *Sydney* 28 C1
Woolwich, *London* 15 B4
Woolworth Building, *New York* 21 e1
World Trade Center, *New York* 21 B1
Worli, *Mumbai* 20 A1
Worth, *Chicago* 9 C2
Wren's Nest, *Atlanta* 3 B2
Wrigley Building, *Chicago* 9 b2
Wuhlgarten, *Berlin* 5 A4
Wujiaochang, *Shanghai* 27 B2
Würm →, *Munich* 20 B1
Würm-kanal, *Munich* 20 A1
Wusong, *Shanghai* 27 A1
Wyczółki, *Warsaw* 31 C1
Wygoda, *Warsaw* 31 B2
Wynberg, *Cape Town* 8 B1

X

Xabregas, *Lisbon* 14 A2
Xianggang = Hong Kong, *Hong Kong* 12 B1
Xiaodian, *Tianjin* 30 A2
Xiaogang Park, *Canton* 8 B2
Xiaoping, *Canton* 8 A2
Xiasha chong, *Canton* 8 B1
Xichang, *Canton* 8 B2
Xicheng, *Beijing* 4 B1
Xidan, *Beijing* 4 B2
Xigu Park, *Tianjin* 30 A2
Xigucun, *Tianjin* 30 A1
Ximenwai, *Tianjin* 30 B1
Xinanlou, *Tianjin* 30 B2
Xinkai He →, *Tianjin* 30 A2
Xizhimen, *Beijing* 4 B1
Xu Beihong Mem. Hall, *Beijing* 4 a1
Xuanwu, *Beijing* 4 B1
Xuhui, *Shanghai* 27 B1

Y

Yaba, *Lagos* 14 A2
Yaftābād, *Tehran* 30 B1
Yahara, *Tokyo* 29 A2
Yaho, *Tokyo* 29 A1
Yakire, *Tokyo* 29 A4
Yamada, *Osaka* 22 A4
Yamada, *Tokyo* 29 B2
Yamamoto, *Osaka* 22 B4
Yamato →, *Osaka* 22 B3
Yamuna →, *Delhi* 10 B2
Yan Kit, *Singapore* 27 A3
Yanbu, *Canton* 8 B1
Yangch'ŏn, *Seoul* 26 B1
Yanghuayuan, *Beijing* 4 C1
Yangjae, *Seoul* 26 C2
Yangjiazhuang, *Shanghai* 27 A1
Yangpu, *Shanghai* 27 B2
Yangpu Park, *Shanghai* 27 B2
Yao, *Osaka* 22 B4
Yao Airport, *Osaka* 22 B4
Yarmūk, *Baghdad* 3 B1
Yarra →, *Melbourne* 17 A1
Yarra Bend Park, *Melbourne* 17 A2
Yarraville, *Melbourne* 17 A1
Yau Tong, *Hong Kong* 12 B2
Yauza →, *Moscow* 19 A4
Yeading, *London* 15 A1
Yedikule, *Istanbul* 12 C1
Yemin Moshe, *Jerusalem* 13 b2
Yenikapı, *Istanbul* 12 B1
Yeniköy, *Istanbul* 12 B2
Yerba Buena Gardens, *San Francisco* 25 c2
Yerba Buena I., *San Francisco* 25 B2
Yerres, *Paris* 23 B4
Yerushalayim = Jerusalem, *Jerusalem* 13 B2
Yiheyuan, *Beijing* 4 A1
Yinhangzhen, *Shanghai* 27 A2
Yishun New Town, *Singapore* 27 A3
Yixingbu, *Tianjin* 30 A2
Ylästö, *Helsinki* 12 B2
Yodo →, *Osaka* 22 A4
Yongdingman, *Beijing* 4 B2
Yŏngdong, *Seoul* 26 B2
Yŏngdŭngp'o, *Seoul* 26 B1
Yongfucun, *Canton* 8 B2
Yongjing, *Shanghai* 27 B2
Yongsan, *Seoul* 26 B1
Yonkers, *New York* 21 A2
York, *Toronto* 30 A2
York Mills, *Toronto* 30 A2
Yotsuya, *Tokyo* 29 a2
You'anmen, *Beijing* 4 B1
Yŏŭido, *Seoul* 26 B1
Youndsfield, *Cape Town* 8 B1
Yuanxiatian, *Canton* 8 A2
Yugo-Zarad, *Moscow* 19 B3
Yung Shue Wan, *Hong Kong* 12 B1
Yūsofābād, *Tehran* 30 A2
Yuyuantan Park, *Beijing* 4 b2

Z

Zaandam, *Amsterdam* 2 A1
Zaandijk, *Amsterdam* 2 A1
Zaanstad, *Amsterdam* 2 A1
Záběhlice, *Prague* 24 B2
Ząbki, *Warsaw* 31 B2
Żacisze, *Warsaw* 31 B2
Zahrā, *Baghdad* 3 A1
Zakharkovo, *Moscow* 19 B1
Žalov, *Prague* 24 A2
Załuski, *Warsaw* 31 C1
Zamdorf, *Munich* 20 B2
Zamek Królewski, *Warsaw* 31 a2
Zamek Ujazdowski, *Warsaw* 31 c3
Zanevka, *St. Petersburg* 26 B3
Zapote, *Manila* 17 C1
Záppeio, *Athens* 2 c2
Zarechye, *Moscow* 19 B2
Zaventem, *Brussels* 6 A2
Zawady, *Warsaw* 31 B2
Zâwiyet Abû Musallam, *Cairo* 7 B1
Zawrā' Park, *Baghdad* 3 B2
Zbraslav, *Prague* 24 C2
Zbuzany, *Prague* 24 B1
Zdiby, *Prague* 24 B2
Zeekoevlei, *Cape Town* 8 B2
Zehlendorf, *Berlin* 5 B2
Zenne →, *Brussels* 6 B1
Żerań, *Warsaw* 31 B1
Zerzeń, *Warsaw* 31 B2
Zeytinburnu, *Istanbul* 12 C1
Zhabei, *Shanghai* 27 B1
Zhangguizhuang, *Tianjin* 30 B2
Zhdanov, *Moscow* 19 B4
Zheleznodorozhnyy, *Moscow* 19 B6
Zhenru, *Shanghai* 27 B1
Zhernovka, *St. Petersburg* 26 B2
Zhicun, *Canton* 8 B2
Zhongshan Park, *Beijing* 4 b2
Zhongshan Park, *Shanghai* 27 B1
Zhoucun, *Canton* 8 A2
Zhoujiadu, *Shanghai* 27 B1
Zhoujiazhen, *Shanghai* 27 B2
Zhu Jiang →, *Canton* 8 B3
Zhulebino, *Moscow* 19 B5
Zhushadi, *Canton* 8 A3
Zielona, *Warsaw* 31 B3
Zielonka, *Warsaw* 31 B2
Ziya He →, *Tianjin* 30 A1
Žižkov, *Prague* 24 B2
Zličin, *Prague* 24 B1
Zócalo, *Mexico City* 18 b3
Zografos, *Athens* 2 B2
Żoliborz, *Warsaw* 31 B1
Zonnenbloem, *Cape Town* 8 A1
Zoo, *Beijing* 4 a1
Zugliget, *Budapest* 7 B1
Zugló, *Budapest* 7 A2
Zuiderwoude, *Amsterdam* 2 A3
Zumbi, *Rio de Janeiro* 24 A1
Zunderdorp, *Amsterdam* 2 A2
Zuvuvu →, *São Paulo* 26 C1
Zwanenburg, *Amsterdam* 2 A1
Zwölfaxing, *Vienna* 31 B2
Zyuzino, *Moscow* 19 C3

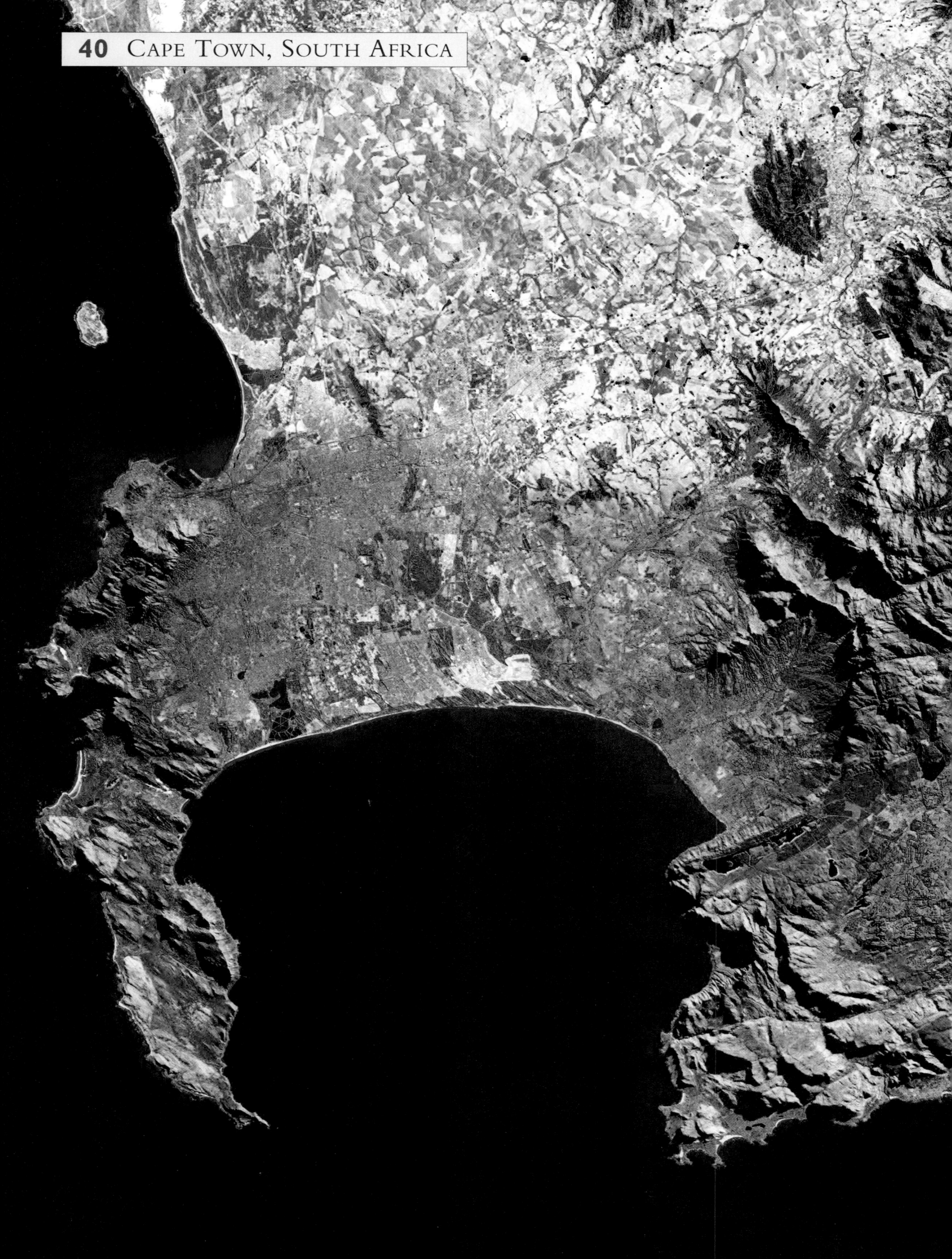

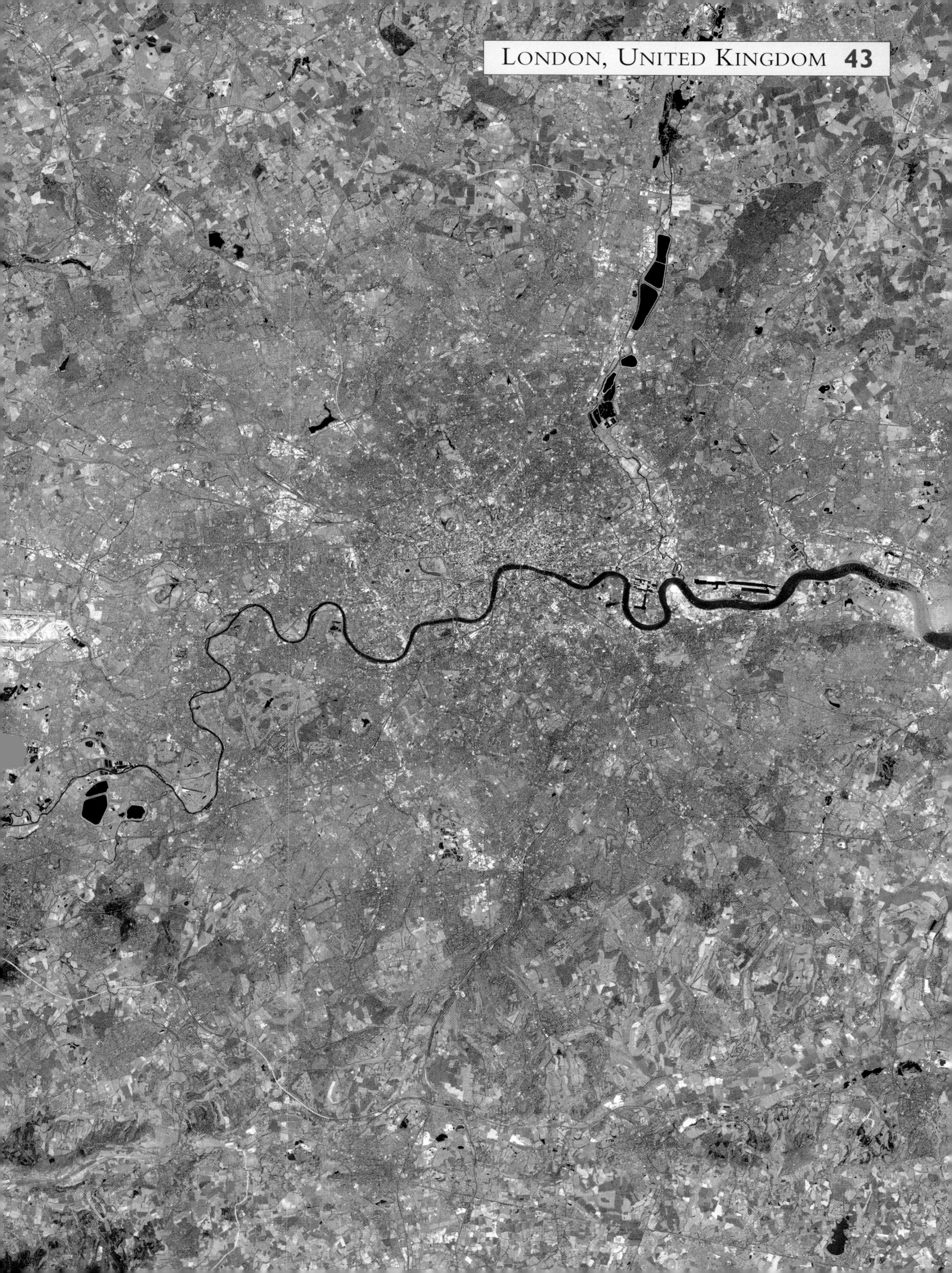

WORLD
MAPS

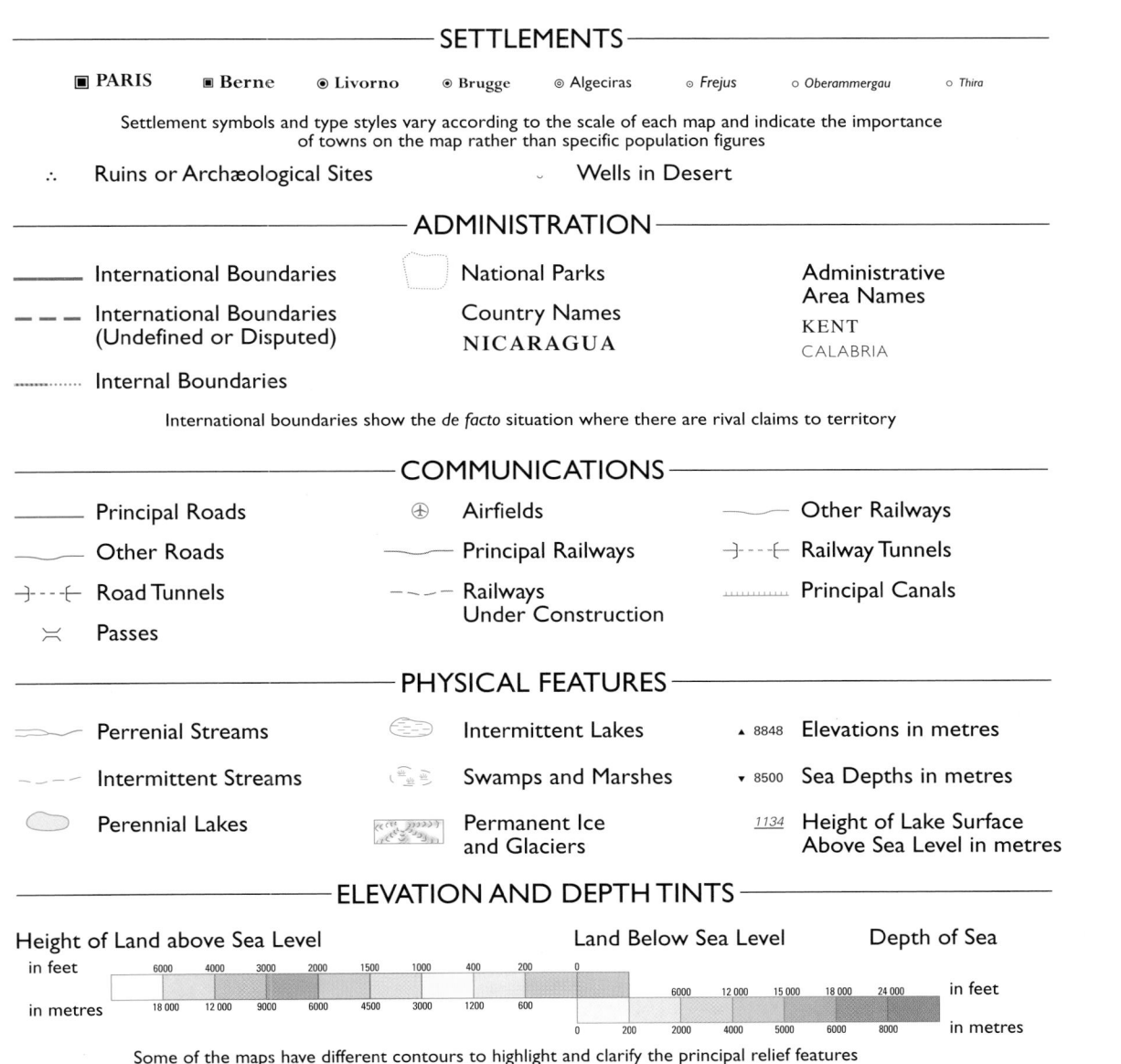

SETTLEMENTS

■ PARIS   ■ Berne   ◉ Livorno   ◉ Brugge   ◎ Algeciras   ○ Frejus   ○ Oberammergau   ○ Thira

Settlement symbols and type styles vary according to the scale of each map and indicate the importance
of towns on the map rather than specific population figures

∴ Ruins or Archæological Sites   ⌣ Wells in Desert

ADMINISTRATION

——— International Boundaries

– – – International Boundaries
(Undefined or Disputed)

·········· Internal Boundaries

National Parks

Country Names
NICARAGUA

Administrative
Area Names

KENT
CALABRIA

International boundaries show the *de facto* situation where there are rival claims to territory

COMMUNICATIONS

——— Principal Roads

——— Other Roads

+–··–+ Road Tunnels

⌣ Passes

⊕ Airfields

——— Principal Railways

– – – Railways
Under Construction

——— Other Railways

+–··–+ Railway Tunnels

·········· Principal Canals

PHYSICAL FEATURES

Perrenial Streams

Intermittent Streams

Perennial Lakes

Intermittent Lakes

Swamps and Marshes

Permanent Ice
and Glaciers

▲ 8848 Elevations in metres

▼ 8500 Sea Depths in metres

1134 Height of Lake Surface
Above Sea Level in metres

ELEVATION AND DEPTH TINTS

Height of Land above Sea Level   Land Below Sea Level   Depth of Sea

in feet   6000   4000   3000   2000   1500   1000   400   200   0   6000   12 000   15 000   18 000   24 000   in feet

in metres   18 000   12 000   9000   6000   4500   3000   1200   600   0   200   2000   4000   5000   6000   8000   in metres

Some of the maps have different contours to highlight and clarify the principal relief features

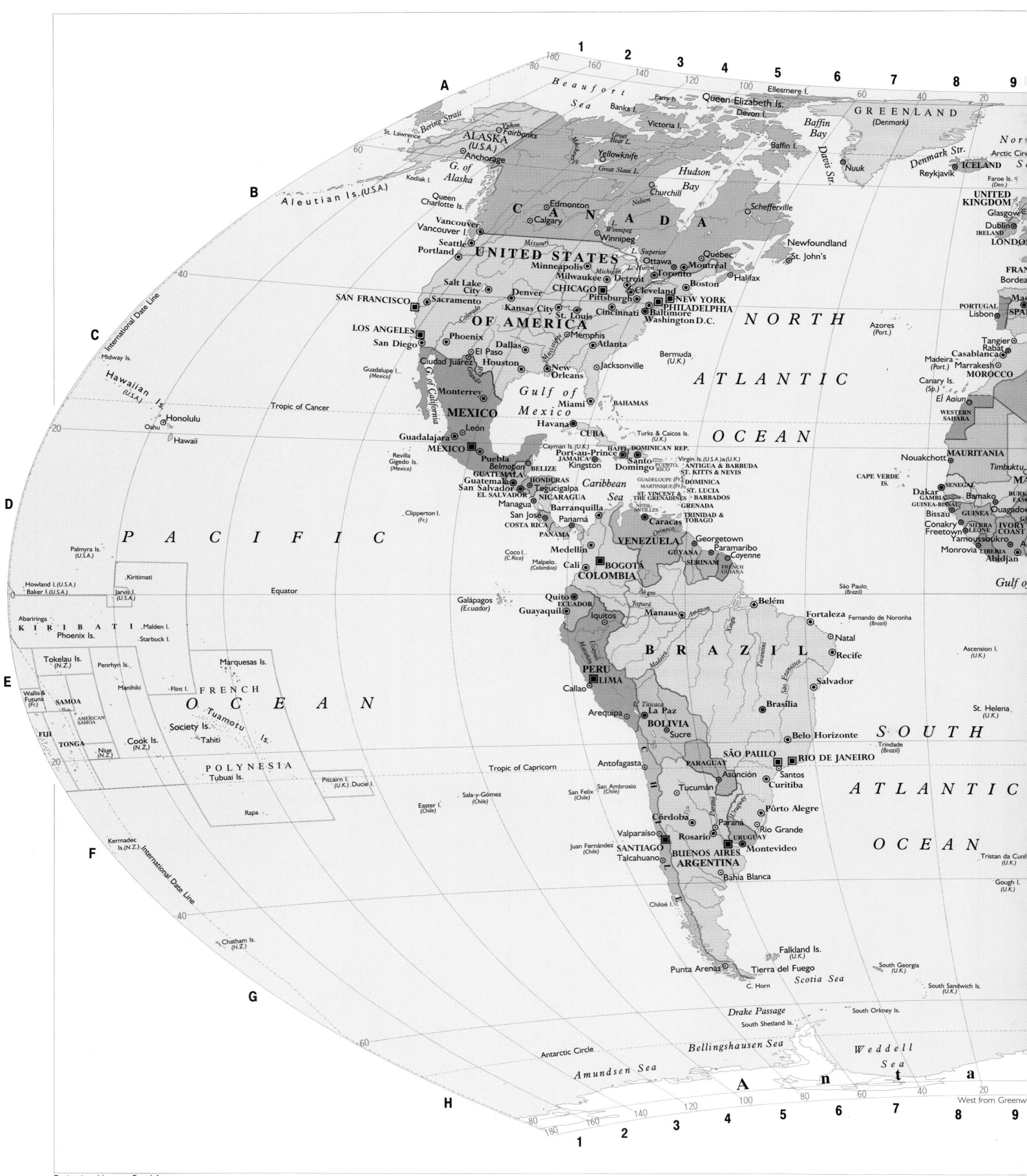

Projection: *Hammer Equal Area*

ARCTIC OCEAN

10 11 12 13 14 15 16 17 18

R 20 40 60 80 100 120 140 160 180 80

Barents Novaya Kara Severnaya Laptev Sea East Siberian Sea Wrangel New Siberian Is. **A**
Sea Zemlya Sea Zemlya Sea I.

Murmansk Norilsk Verkhoyansk Arctic Circle

Arkhangelsk Salekhard R U S S I A Yakutsk Okhotsk Magadan Bering **B**
NORWAY SWEDEN FINLAND Helsinki Yenisey Lena Sea of Sea
Oslo ST.PETERSBURG Perm Yekaterinburg Tomsk Krasnoyarsk L. Baikal Okhotsk Petropavlovsk- International
Stockholm EST. Volga Kazan Chelyabinsk Omsk Novosibirsk Irkutsk Ulan Ude Sakhalin Kamchatskiy Date Line
Copenhagen LATVIA MOSCOW Samara Astana Barnaul Komsomolsk
LITH. Saratov Qaraghandy Ulan Bator Harbin Khabarovsk
Berlin Minsk BELARUS Volgograd KAZAKSTAN MONGOLIA Changchun Vladivostok Kuril Sapporo
Brussels Prague Warsaw Odessa Astrakhan L. Balkhash Amur SHENYANG NORTH JAPAN TŌKYŌ
UKRAINE Aral Almaty Bishkek Ürümqi BEIJING TIANJIN KOREA Pyongyang SEOUL
Budapest Bucharest Sea UZBEKISTAN KYRGYZSTAN CHINA Lanzhou Taiyuan SOUTH Dalian Ōsaka **C**
ROMANIA Black GEORGIA Baku Samarkand Tashkent Xi'an Nanjing KOREA Kitakyūshū
Belgrade Sea Tbilisi TURKMENISTAN TAJIKISTAN T I B E T Chengdu Wuhan SHANGHAI PACIFIC
BULGARIA Yerevan AZER. Ashkhabad Lhasa CHONGQING East China
Istanbul Ankara ARM. Tabriz Mashhad Kābul Islamabad Katmandu Sea OCEAN
Athens TURKEY İzmir TEHRAN Esfahān AFGHANISTAN Lahore NEPAL BHU. Kunming Guangzhou Ryukyus
CYPRUS SYRIA Baghdad DELHI Fuzhou Taipei Bonin Is.
Crete Damascus IRAQ IRAN PAKISTAN New Delhi Kanpur Hanoi HONG KONG (Japan) Volcano Is. Marcus I. Tropic of Cancer
Mediterranean Beirut Shīrāz BANGLA- MYANMAR TAIWAN (Japan) (Japan)
Jerusalem ISR. Ammān KUWAIT DESH INDIA KOLKATA BURMA South Wake I.
Sea JORDAN BAHRAIN Abu Dhabi Ahmadabad (Calcutta) DACCA China (U.S.A.) **D**
Alexandria Riyadh QATAR KARACHI Nagpur Rangoon Sea NORTHERN
CAIRO U.A.E. Mumbai Bay of Bengal MARIANAS 20
LIBYA Aswân SAUDI Mecca Muscat OMAN (Bombay) Hyderabad THAILAND VIET- MANILA (U.S.A.)
EGYPT ARABIA Arabian Hainan NAM PHILIPPINES GUAM
Red Sea BANGKOK (U.S.A.) MARSHALL IS.
NIGER CHAD Omdurmân Sana Bangalore CHENNAI CAMBODIA Yap
Khartoum YEMEN (Madras) Andaman Is. Phnom Ho Chi Minh FEDERATED STATES
NIGERIA Ndjamena ERITREA Aden G. of Aden Socotra (India) Penh City PALAU Truk Pohnpei
Kano DJIBOUTI (Yemen) Lakshadweep Is. Nicobar Is. C a r o l i n e I s.
Abuja SUDAN (India) (India) OF MICRONESIA
Ibadan Addis Ababa SRI LANKA MALAYSIA
Lagos CENTRAL ETHIOPIA MALDIVES Medan SABAH Gilbert Is.
CAMEROON Douala AFRICAN SOMALI Colombo Kuala Lumpur BRUNEI
EQUATORIAL Yaoundé REP. REP. PEN. MALAYSIA NAURU KIRIBATI
GUINEA GABON Bangui Mogadishu SINGAPORE Borneo **E**
SÃO Libreville Zaïre UGANDA Equator I N D I A N Sumatra Palembang Banjarmasin IRIAN
TOMÉ CONGO Kisangani KENYA Ujung Pandang JAYA New
& PRÍNCIPE DEM.REP.OF THE Kigali RWANDA Nairobi O C E A N JAKARTA INDONESIA PAPUA Ireland
Brazzaville CONGO BURUNDI Victoria SEYCHELLES Chagos Arch. Bandung Surabaya NEW New
CABINDA Kinshasa Bujumbura Dodoma Mombasa Amirante (U.K.) Java EAST GUINEA Britain
(Angola) Kananga Zanzibar Is. Diego Garcia TIMOR Port SOLOMON
Luanda TANZANIA Dar es Salaam Aldabra Is. Timor Arafura Sea Moresby IS.
L. Tanganyika COMOROS Cocos Is. Darwin C. York Santa Cruz TUVALU
ANGOLA Mayotte (Austral.) Christmas I. Is.
Lubumbashi Malawi (Fr.) (Austral.) NEW
Benguela ZAMBIA Lilongwe MADAGASCAR Cargados Carajos Cairns CALEDONIA
Lusaka MALAWI Rodriguez AUSTRALIA (Fr.) VANUATU
NAMIBIA Harare Antananarivo MAURITIUS Tropic of Capricorn Port Hedland Townsville FIJI
ZIMBABWE MOZAMBIQUE RÉUNION Alice Springs Suva
Windhoek Bulawayo (Fr.) Rockhampton 20
BOTSWANA Geraldton Brisbane
Gaborone Pretoria Kalgoorlie- Lord Howe I.
Johannesburg Boulder Newcastle (Austral.) **F**
SOUTH Maputo SWAZILAND Perth Adelaide Sydney Norfolk I.
AFRICA LESOTHO Durban Fremantle Great Canberra (Austral.)
Cape Town Port Elizabeth Amsterdam I. Australian Darling Melbourne Tasman Auckland
C. of Good Hope (Fr.) St.Paul (Fr.) Bight NEW North I.
  Tasmania Sea ZEALAND
  Prince Edward Is. Crozet Is. Hobart Christchurch Wellington
  (S.Africa) (Fr.) South I. 40
  Kerguelen Stewart I. Dunedin
  (Fr.) Bounty Is. (N.Z.)
S O U T H E R N O C E A N Antipodes Is.
  McDonald Is. Heard I. Campbell I. Auckland I. (N.Z.)
  (Austral.) (Austral.) Macquarie I. (N.Z.) **G**
  (Austral.)
Antarctic Circle

c t i c a 60

10 11 12 13 14 15 16 17 18 Ross Sea **H**
20 40 60 80 100 120 140 160 180 80

from Greenwich

100 0   200   400   600   800   1000 1200 1400 km
100 0   200   400   600   800   1000 miles

PACIFIC OCEAN

JAPAN

Aleutian Islands
(U.S.A.)

Dutch Harbor
Unimak I.

▼ 7822

Near Is.
(U.S.A.)

D

Bering Sea

Komandorskiye
Ostrova

Mys Lopatka

Kurilskiye Ostrova
(Russia)

La Perouse Str.

Hokkaidō

Petropavlovsk-
Kamchatskiy

Gora Klyuchevskaya
4750

Poluostrov Kamchatka

Sea of
Okhotsk

Sakhalin
(Russia)

Sakhalinskiy Zaliv

Vanino

Bristol
Bay

Kodiak I.

Pribilof Is.
(U.S.A.)

▼ 42

St. Matthew
(U.S.A.)

Nunivak

St. Lawrence I.
(U.S.A.)

International Date Line

Mys Olyutorski

Ostrov
Karaginskiy

Penzhino

Penzhinskaya G.

Gizhiginskaya Guba

Tauiskaya
Guba

Nikolayevsk

Ulbanskiy
Zaliv

Udskaya
Guba

Amur

Khabarovsk

G. of Alaska

Seward
Prince
William Sd.
Cordova

Anchorage

Mt. McKinley
6194

Nome

Bering Str.

Mys
Dezhneva

Anadyrskiy
Zaliv

Anadyr

C

Chukotskoye
Nagorye

S

Odonan

Kolymskoye Nagorye

Okhotsk

Stanovoy Khrebet

Khabarovsk

Prince Rupert

Mt. St. Elias
5489

Skagway Mt. Logan
5959

Fairbanks

Cook Inlet

C. Prince of Wales

Kotzebue Sd.

Pt. Hope

C. Lisburne

B

Proliv Longa

Nizhne Kolymsk

Kolyma

Srednekolymsk

Indigirka

Zashiversk

Verkhoyansk

Yana

Aldan

Yakutsk

Lena

Zhigansk

Olekma

14

Whitehorse

ALASKA
(U.S.A.)

Yukon

Noatak

Chukchi
Sea

Ostrov
Vrangelya
(Russia)

▼ 46

Russkoye
Ustie

Kazachye

Bulun

Olenek

Vilyuy

120

Rocky Mountains

Dawson

Stewart

Pelly

Fort Yukon

Porcupine

Koyukuk

Prudhoe Bay
Pt. Halkett
Herschel I.
Harrison Bay

Fort McPherson

Pt. Barrow

Chaunskaya G.

Novosibirskiye
Ostrova

O. Bennetta
(Russia)

Lyakhovskiye
Ostrova

Tiksi

Anabar

13

Liard

Fort
Simpson

NORTH

Fort
Vermilion

Peace

Athabasca

Mackenzie

Great Bear
Lake

Fort
Good Hope

Tulita

Mackenzie
Bay

C. Bathurst

Beaufort Sea

3767
▼

Canada
Basin

ARCTIC

Mendeleyev Ridge

A

3327
▼

OCEAN

O. Kotelnyy

**Laptev
Sea**

Ostrova Petra

Nordvik

Lena

Olenek

Kotuy

Khatanga

Anabar

Kheta

Ozero Taymyr

Vilyuy

Nizhnyaya Tunguska

Podkamennaya Tunguska

Gory Putorana

12

2

Great Slave
Lake

Yellowknife

Coppermine

Kugluktuk

Coronation G.

Dolphin & Union Sd.

Banks I.

C. Prince Alfred

Prince
Albert
Pen.

C. Kellett

McClure Str.

Viscount
Melville
Sd.

Melville I.

3700
▼

Alpha
Cordillera

3546
▼

4007
▼

Makarov Basin

Lomonosov Ridge

Nansen Basin

4100
▼

3849
▼

Severnaya
Zemlya

O. Oktyabrskoy
Revolyutsii

**Poluostrov
Taymyr**

Norilsk

Dudinka

Igarka

Yenisey

Pyasina

100

Athabasca
Lake

AMERICA

Victoria
Island

King
William I.

Prince of
Wales I.

M'Clintock
Chan.

Bathurst I.

North
Magnetic Pole
1995

Parry Is.

Borden I.

Ellef Ringnes I.

Sverdrup Is.

Nansen Basin

2104
▼

NORTH
POLE

4484
▼

Fram Basin

Nansen Cordillera

O. Uedineniya

O. Vise

O. Ushakova

Ozero Taymyr

Golchikha

3

**Hudson
Bay**

Chesterfield
Inlet

Boothia
Pen.

Somerset

Gulf of
Boothia

Prince Regent Inlet

Devon I.

Axel
Heiberg I.

Ellesmere I.
(Canada)

3700
▼

4418
▼

3741
▼

C. Columbia

**Lincoln
Sea**

Alert

Eureka

Kong Morris Jesup

**McKinley
Sea**

Nordkapp

A

180

Zemlya
Frantsa
Iosifa
(Russia)

O. Graham Bell

Z. Vilcheka

Z. Aleksandry

O. Belyy

Urengoy

Taz

12

Southampton I.

Coats I.

Mansel I.

Foxe
Chan.

Foxe
Basin

Prince
Charles I.

Melville
Pen.

Bylot I.

Lancaster Sd.

Baffin I.

Nettilling L.

2399
▼

Smith Sund

Kane
Basin

Robeson Chan.

Qaanaaq

Uummannaq

K. York

Knud
Rasmussen
Land

Peary
Land

Independence Fjord

Kong Frederik
VIII.s Land

Nordaustlandet

**Kara
Sea**

Novaya

Baydaratskaya
Guba

Khabarovo

Novyy Port

Nadym

Poluostrov
Yamal

Ob

11

80

C. Wolstenholme

Hudson Str.

C. Dyer

Iqaluit

Cumberland Sd.

Upernavik

Uummannaq

Qeqertarsuaq

Ungava
Bay

Zemlya

B

Nordkapp

Svalbard
(Norway)

Vestspitsbergen

Longyearbyen

Edgeøya

2571
▼

**Barents
Sea**

O. Kolguyev

Vorkuta

Salekhard

Surgut

Berezovo

Tobolsk

1894
▼
Narodnaya

Uralskie Gory

4

12 000

6000

4500

3000

1200

600

Labrador

Resolution I.

C. Chidley

Hamilton Inlet

Davis Str.

Qeqertarsuaq

Paamiut

Nuuk

Kong Frederik
IX.s Land

GREENLAND

(Denmark)

KALAALLIT NUNAAT

Kong
Christian X.s Land

Kejsser Franz Joseph Fd.

Kong Oscar Fjord

Ittoqqortoormiit

Kap Brewster

**Greenland
Sea**

Jan Mayen
(Norway)

Bjørnøya

Nordkapp

Vardø

Hammerfest

Tromsø

Mys
Kanin
Nos

Pechora

Mezen

Narodnaya

YEKATERINBURG

PERM

UFA

11

4000
1500

500 1500

2000 6000

3000 9000

4000 12 000

5000 15 000

Qaqortoq

Alluitsup Paa

Kap Farvel
(Nunap Isua)

Mt.
Forel
3360

Kong
Frederik VI.s Kyst

Kong
Christian IX.s Land

Gunnbjørn
Fjeld
3700
▼

Tasiilaq

Denmark Str.

Iceland
Plateau

**Norwegian
Sea**

Arctic Circle

Lofoten

Murmansk

Kolskiy
Poluostrov

Beloye

Arkhangelsk

Onega

Sev. Dvina

Onezhskoye
Ozero

Volga

Kotlas

SAMARA

10

1000 3000

2000 6000

3000 9000

4000 12 000

5000 15 000

Breiðafjörður

Horn

Reykjavik

ICELAND

Orcæfajökull
2119
▼

Fontur

3800
▼

C

Bergen

Trondheim

Oslo

STOCKHOLM

Gulf of
Bothnia

Helsinki

G. of Finland

Tallinn

FINLAND

Ladozhskoye
Ozero

ST. PETERBURG

Chudskoye
Ozero

MOSKVA

Saratov

VOLGOGRAD

Føroyar
(Den.)

Shetland Is.
(U.K.)

4755
▼

Rockall
(U.K.)

Hebrides
(U.K.)

Orkney Is.
(U.K.)

Mid-Atlantic Ridge

**North
Sea**

Skagerrak

KØBENHAVN

EST.

LAT.

Riga

LITH.

Vilnius

Kaliningrad

Baltic Sea

ROSTOV

5

**ATLANTIC
OCEAN**

SCOTLAND

Edinburgh

**UNITED
KINGDOM**

Belfast

IRELAND

Dublin

WALES

ENGLAND

C. Clear

D

LONDON

AMSTERDAM

NETH.

HAMBURG

BERLIN

GERMANY

Elbe

PRAHA

DENMARK

POLAND

WARSZAWA

Wisła

BELARUS

UKRAINE

KYYIV

ODESA

Black Sea

**Maximum extent of
sea ice**

Summer extent of sea ice

**Ice caps and permanent
ice shelf**

Projection : Zenithal Equidistant

West from Greenwich 0 East from Greenwich

COPYRIGHT GEORGE PHILIP LTD

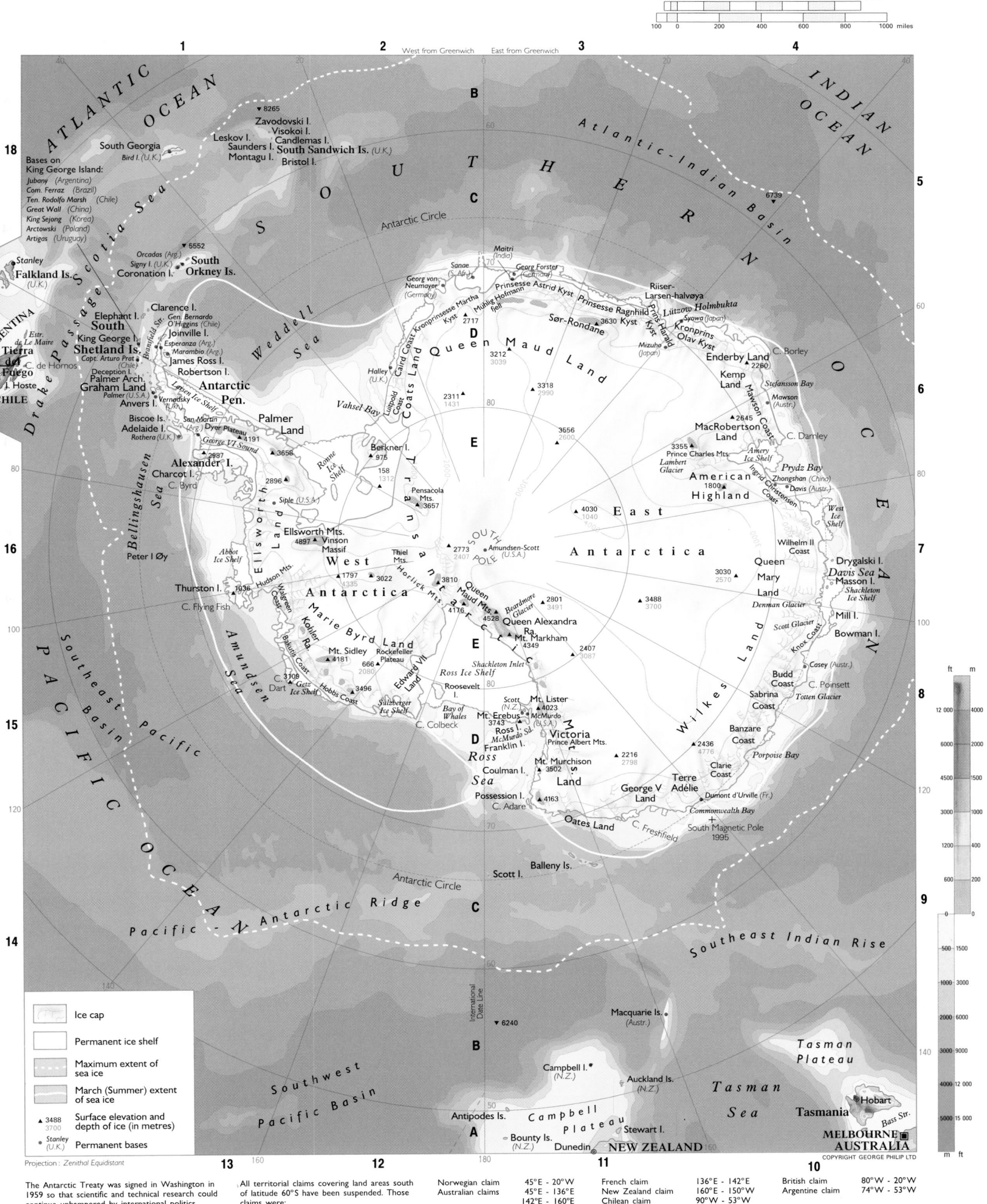

100 0   200   400   600   800 1000 1200 1400 km
100 0   200   400   600   800   1000 miles

The map shows:

ATLANTIC OCEAN

INDIAN OCEAN

South Georgia
Bird I. *(U.K.)*
Bases on King George Island:
Jubany *(Argentina)*
Com. Ferraz *(Brazil)*
Ten. Rodolfo Marsh *(Chile)*
Great Wall *(China)*
King Sejong *(Korea)*
Arctowski *(Poland)*
Artigas *(Uruguay)*

▼8265
Zavodovski I.
Visokoi I.
Leskov I.
Saunders I.   Candlemas I.
Montagu I.   **South Sandwich Is.** *(U.K.)*
Bristol I.

West from Greenwich   East from Greenwich

B

Atlantic-Indian Basin

C

Antarctic Circle

6739

SOUTHERN

Stanley
Falkland Is.
(U.K.)

Scotia Sea

Orcadas *(Arg.)* ▼5552
Signy I. *(U.K.)*   **South**
Coronation I.   **Orkney Is.**

Maitri *(India)*
Sanae *(S. Afr.)*
Georg Forster *(Germany)*
Georg von Neumayer *(Germany)*

Riiser-Larsen-halvøya

Prinsesse Astrid Kyst   Prinsesse Ragnhild
Kronprinsesse Martha Kyst   Mühlig Hofmann fjell   Kyst
▲2717   3630

Lützow Holmbukta
Syowa *(Japan)*
Kronprins Olav Kyst
Mizuho *(Japan)*

ARGENTINA

Drake Passage

Weddell Sea

Clarence I.
Elephant I.
South   Gen. Bernardo
King George I.   O'Higgins *(Chile)*
Joinville I.
Esperanza *(Arg.)*
Marambio *(Arg.)*
James Ross I.
Robertson I.

Halley *(U.K.)*

Caird Coast

Queen Maud Land
3212   3039
3318   2990

▲3556   2600

Enderby Land   C. Borley
Kemp   2260
Land   Stefansson Bay
Mawson *(Austr.)*
2645
MacRobertson   C. Darnley
Land
Prince Charles Mts.   3355
Lambert   Amery   Prydz Bay
Glacier   Ice Shelf   Zhongshan *(China)*
Davis *(Austr.)*

D

South Shetland Is.

Tierra del Fuego
C. de Hornos
I. Hoste
CHILE

Capt. Arturo Prat *(Chile)*
Deception I.
Palmer Arch.
Graham Land   Palmer *(U.S.A.)*
Anvers I.   Vernadsky *(U.K.)*

Vahsel Bay

2311   1431

6

Biscoe Is.
Adelaide I.   San Martin *(Arg.)*
Rothera *(U.K.)*   Dyer Plateau

Palmer Land

George VI Sound
4191

Berkner I.
975
158   1312

Pensacola Mts.
3657

East
Antarctica

4030
1040

American Highland
1800

Wilhelm II Coast

Queen Mary Land

West Ice Shelf

E

80

Bellingshausen Sea

Alexander I.
Charcot I.   C. Byrd
2987   2896

Ronne Ice Shelf

Larsen Ice Shelf

3030
2570

3488
3700

Drygalski I.
Davis Sea
Masson I.
Shackleton Ice Shelf

7

16

Peter I Øy

3658

Ellsworth Mts.
4897 ▲Vinson Massif

Thiel Mts.

South Pole
Amundsen-Scott *(U.S.A.)*
2773   2407

Mill I.
Bowman I.

100

Thurston I.   1036
C. Flying Fish

Hudson Mts.
1797   3022
4335

Horlick Mts.

3810
4176

Queen Maud Mts.
4528   Beardmore   2801
Glacier   3491
Queen Alexandra Ra.
Mt. Markham   2407
4349   3087

Budd Coast
Casey *(Austr.)*
Knox Coast
Sabrina
Coast   Totten Glacier

8

West Antarctica

Marie Byrd Land
Kohler Ra.

Mt. Sidley   Rockefeller
4181   666   Plateau
2080

Banzare Coast
2436
4776

15

Amundsen Sea

Bakutis Coast

C. Dart   3108
Getz Ice Shelf   3496
Hobbs Coast   Sulzberger Ice Shelf

Shackleton Inlet
Ross Ice Shelf
Roosevelt I.

80

Wilkes Land

Clarie Coast
2216
2798

George V Land   Terre Adélie
Dumont d'Urville *(Fr.)*

PACIFIC OCEAN

Edward VII Land

Bay of Whales
C. Colbeck

Scott *(N.Z.)*   Mt. Lister
4023
McMurdo *(U.S.A.)*
Ross I.   3743
McMurdo Sd.

Mt. Erebus

Victoria
Prince Albert Mts.

Porpoise Bay

Commonwealth Bay
South Magnetic Pole
1995

120

Southeast Pacific Basin

Ross Sea

Franklin I.
Coulman I.

Mt. Murchison   **Land**
3502
Possession I.
C. Adare   4163

Oates Land   C. Freshfield

Scott I.   Balleny Is.

Antarctic Circle

9

14

Pacific-Antarctic Ridge

Southeast Indian Rise

International Date Line

6240

Macquarie Is.
(Austr.)

Tasman Plateau

Southwest Pacific Basin

B

Campbell I. *(N.Z.)*   Auckland Is. *(N.Z.)*   *Tasman Sea*

Hobart
Tasmania

140

Antipodes Is.   *Campbell*
Plateau
Bounty Is. *(N.Z.)*   Stewart I.
Dunedin   **NEW ZEALAND**

A

MELBOURNE
AUSTRALIA
COPYRIGHT GEORGE PHILIP LTD

Legend:

	Ice cap
	Permanent ice shelf
	Maximum extent of sea ice
	March (Summer) extent of sea ice
▲3488 / 3700	Surface elevation and depth of ice (in metres)
• Stanley *(U.K.)*	Permanent bases

Projection : Zenithal Equidistant

Elevation scale:
ft / m
12 000 / 4000
6000 / 2000
4500 / 1500
3000 / 1000
1200 / 400
600 / 200
0 / 0
500 / 1500
1000 / 3000
2000 / 6000
3000 / 9000
4000 / 12 000
5000 / 15 000
m / ft

Norwegian claim	45°E - 20°W
Australian claims	45°E - 136°E
	142°E - 160°E
French claim	136°E - 142°E
New Zealand claim	160°E - 150°W
Chilean claim	90°W - 53°W
British claim	80°W - 20°W
Argentine claim	74°W - 53°W

SCANDINAVIA 1:5 000 000

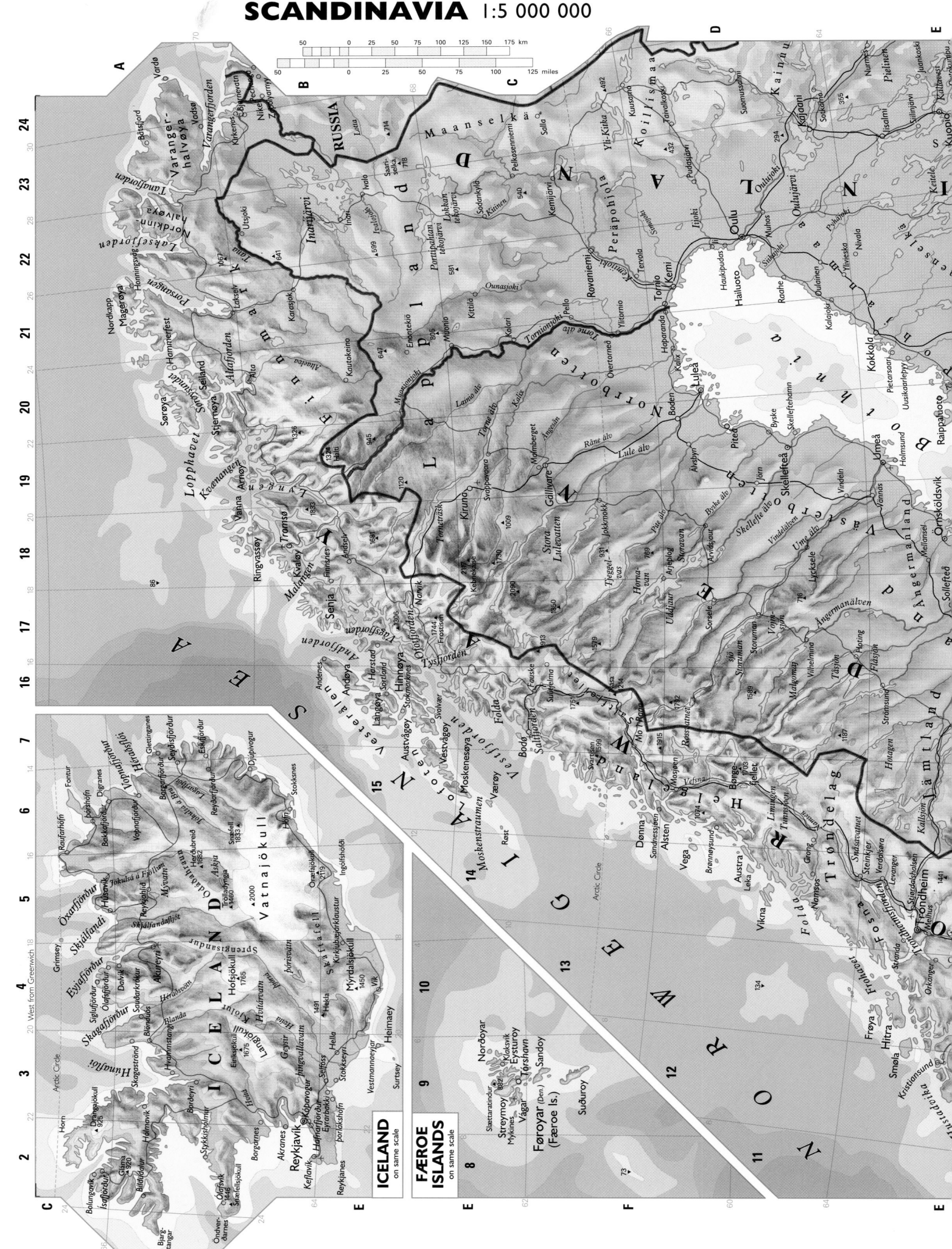

ICELAND
on same scale

FÆROE
ISLANDS
on same scale

Projection: Conical with two standard parallels

East from Greenwich

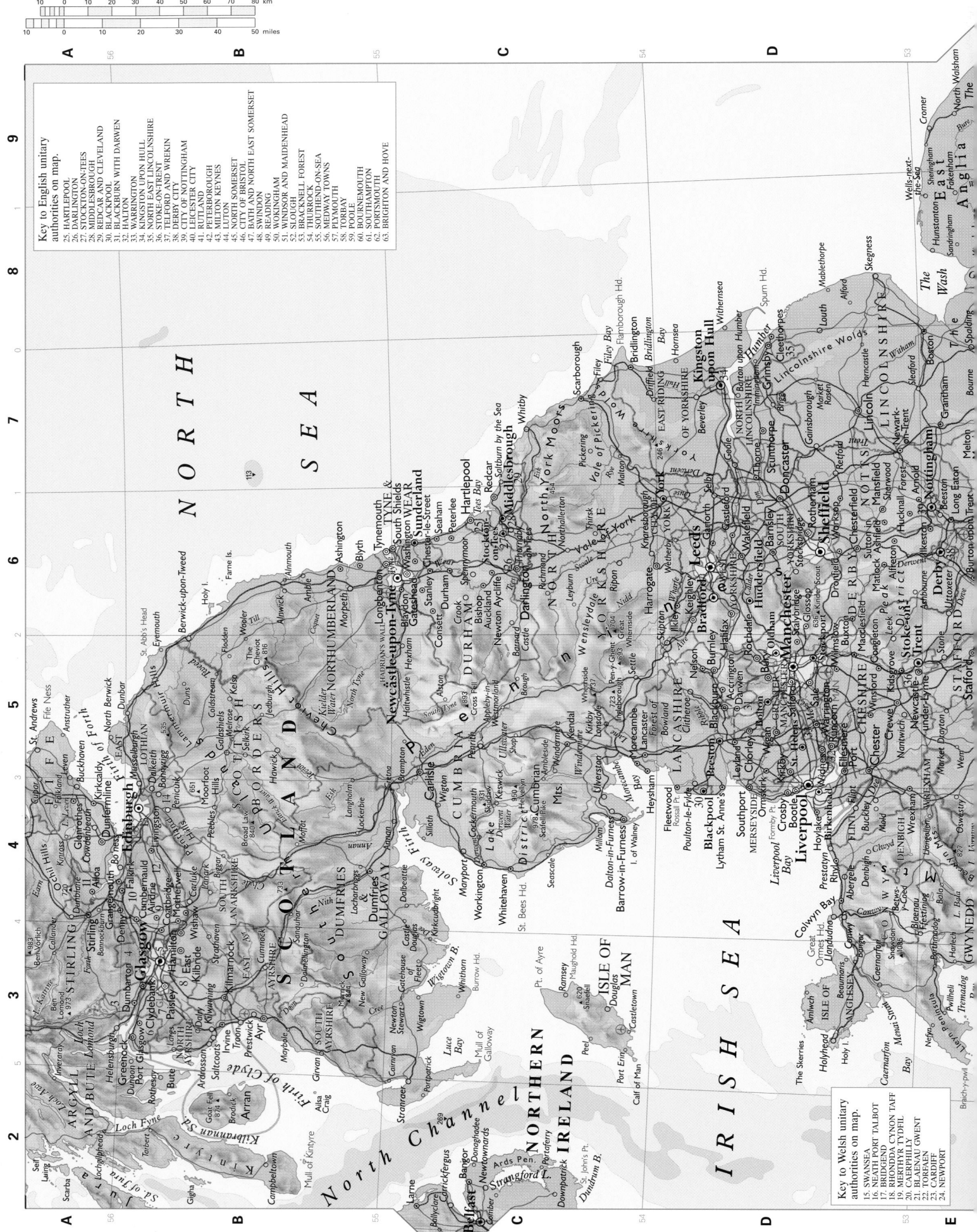

Key to English unitary authorities on map.

25. HARTLEPOOL
26. DARLINGTON
27. STOCKTON-ON-TEES
28. MIDDLESBROUGH
29. REDCAR AND CLEVELAND
30. BLACKPOOL
31. BLACKBURN WITH DARWEN
32. HALTON
33. WARRINGTON
34. KINGSTON UPON HULL
35. NORTH EAST LINCOLNSHIRE
36. STOKE-ON-TRENT
37. TELFORD AND WREKIN
38. DERBY CITY
39. CITY OF NOTTINGHAM
40. LEICESTER CITY
41. RUTLAND
42. PETERBOROUGH
43. MILTON KEYNES
44. LUTON
45. NORTH SOMERSET
46. CITY OF BRISTOL
47. BATH AND NORTH EAST SOMERSET
48. SWINDON
49. READING
50. WOKINGHAM
51. WINDSOR AND MAIDENHEAD
52. SLOUGH
53. BRACKNELL FOREST
54. THURROCK
55. SOUTHEND-ON-SEA
56. MEDWAY TOWNS
57. PLYMOUTH
58. TORBAY
59. POOLE
60. BOURNEMOUTH
61. SOUTHAMPTON
62. PORTSMOUTH
63. BRIGHTON AND HOVE

Key to Welsh unitary authorities on map.

15. SWANSEA
16. NEATH PORT TALBOT
17. BRIDGEND
18. RHONDDA CYNON TAFF
19. MERTHYR TYDFIL
20. CAERPHILLY
21. BLAENAU GWENT
22. TORFAEN
23. CARDIFF
24. NEWPORT

ENGLAND

WALES

FRANCE

NORMANDIE

HAUTE-NORMANDIE

SEINE-MARITIME

PAYS DE CAUX

CALVADOS

MANCHE

Cotentin

ENGLISH CHANNEL

Bristol Channel

Cardigan Bay

Carmarthen Bay

Lyme Bay

Strait of Dover

Baie de la Seine

Baie de la Somme

London

Birmingham

Bristol

Brighton Hove

Portsmouth

Southampton

Bournemouth

Plymouth

Cardiff

Exeter

Swansea

Newport

Le Havre

Rouen

Cherbourg

Caen

Dieppe

Calais

Boulogne-sur-Mer

Évreux

Lisieux

Bayeux

POWYS

CEREDIGION

PEMBROKESHIRE

CARMARTHENSHIRE

GLAMORGAN

VALE OF GLAMORGAN

SHROPSHIRE

HEREFORD

GLOUCS

WILTSHIRE

DORSET

SOMERSET

DEVON

CORNWALL

HANTS

WEST SUSSEX

EAST SUSSEX

SURREY

KENT

ESSEX

SUFFOLK

NORFOLK

CAMBRIDGE

NORTHAMPTON

BEDFORD

HERTS

BUCKS

BERKSHIRE

OXON

WARWICK

WORCESTER

LEICESTER

RUTLAND

Dartmoor

Exmoor

Mendip Hills

Salisbury Plain

Marlborough Downs

Cotswold Hills

South Downs

North Downs

The Weald

New Forest

Isle of Wight

Channel Islands (U.K.)

Jersey — St. Helier

Guernsey — St. Peter Port

Alderney

Sark

Herm

St. Catherine's Pt.

Needles

Selsey Bill

Beachy Head

Dungeness

North Foreland

South Foreland

Portland Bill

Start Pt.

Lizard Pt.

Land's End

Hartland Pt.

St. David's Hd.

Orford Ness

Lundy

Lowestoft

Yarmouth

Ipswich

Felixstowe

Harwich

Clacton-on-Sea

Walton-on-the-Naze

Colchester

Chelmsford

Southend-on-Sea

Thames Estuary

Whitstable

Margate

Ramsgate

Deal

Dover

Folkestone

New Romney

Hastings

Eastbourne

Canterbury

Maidstone

Rochester

Chatham

Gravesend

Gillingham

Sheerness

Isle of Sheppey

Sittingbourne

Ashford

Tenterden

Tunbridge Wells

Tonbridge

Sevenoaks

Bromley

Croydon

Epsom

Leatherhead

Guildford

Woking

Horsham

Crawley

Haywards Heath

East Grinstead

Lewes

Newhaven

Seaford

Worthing

Littlehampton

Bognor Regis

Chichester

Havant

Fareham

Gosport

Ryde

Newport

Cowes

Ventnor

Christchurch

Swanage

Weymouth

Dorchester

Bridport

Yeovil

Chard

Taunton

Bridgwater

Weston-super-Mare

Clevedon

Bath

Trowbridge

Chippenham

Swindon

Cirencester

Gloucester

Cheltenham

Stroud

Tewkesbury

Evesham

Worcester

Kidderminster

Stourbridge

Dudley

Wolverhampton

Walsall

Sutton Coldfield

Solihull

Coventry

Rugby

Nuneaton

Tamworth

Telford

Shrewsbury

Hereford

Ross-on-Wye

Monmouth

Abergavenny

Ebbw Vale

Merthyr Tydfil

Aberdare

Pontypool

Caerphilly

Barry

Penarth

Bridgend

Port Talbot

Neath

Llanelli

Carmarthen

Tenby

Pembroke

Milford Haven

Haverfordwest

Cardigan

New Quay

Aberystwyth

Aberaeron

Welshpool

Newtown

Machynlleth

Llandrindod Wells

Builth Wells

Brecon

Brecon Beacons

Black Mountains

Hay-on-Wye

Leominster

Ludlow

Oxford

Banbury

Bicester

Aylesbury

High Wycombe

Reading

Newbury

Basingstoke

Andover

Winchester

Salisbury

Romsey

Petersfield

Alton

Farnham

Aldershot

Bracknell

Maidenhead

Windsor

Slough

Staines

Watford

St. Albans

Hemel Hempstead

Luton

Dunstable

Bedford

Milton Keynes

Bletchley

Buckingham

Northampton

Wellingborough

Kettering

Corby

Market Harborough

Peterborough

March

Wisbech

Ely

Cambridge

Huntingdon

St. Neots

Royston

Saffron Walden

Bishop's Stortford

Harlow

Hertford

Hitchin

Stevenage

Welwyn Garden City

Hatfield

Enfield

Newmarket

Bury St. Edmunds

Sudbury

Stowmarket

Haverhill

Thetford

Diss

Downham Market

King's Lynn

Southwold

Aldeburgh

Woodbridge

Saxmundham

Beccles

Bungay

Halesworth

Great Yarmouth

Projection: Lambert's Conformal Conic

Isles of Scilly
On same scale

Tresco — St. Mary's — Isles of Scilly

St. Ives

Penzance

Newlyn

Camborne

Hayle

Redruth

Truro

Falmouth

Helston

Newquay

Bodmin

St. Austell

Launceston

Bude

Bideford

Barnstaple

Ilfracombe

Minehead

Tiverton

Torquay

Paignton

Dartmouth

Newton Abbot

Teignmouth

Dawlish

Sidmouth

Exmouth

Kingsbridge

Tavistock

Bodmin Moor

West from Greenwich

East from Greenwich

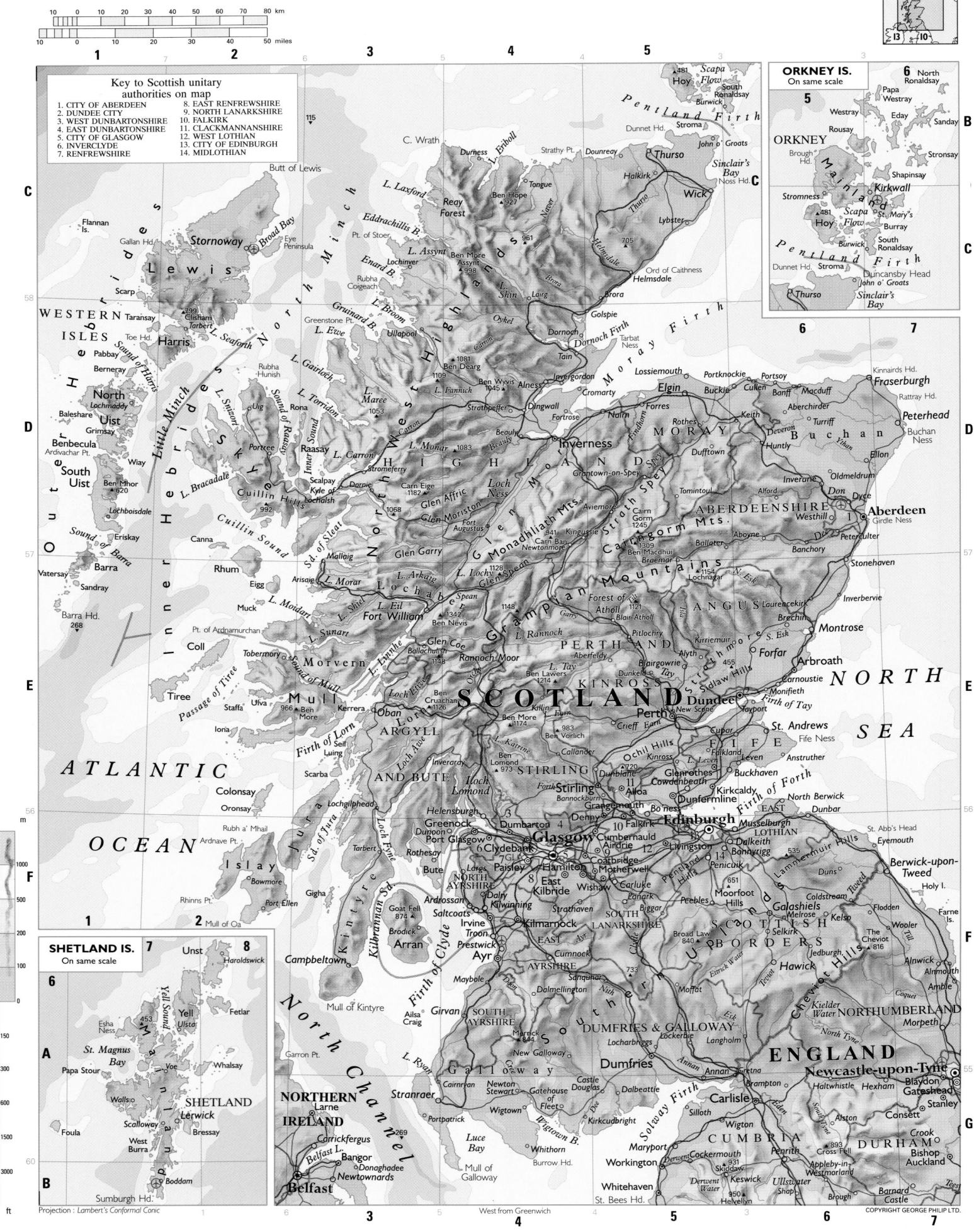

Key to Scottish unitary authorities on map
1. CITY OF ABERDEEN
2. DUNDEE CITY
3. WEST DUNBARTONSHIRE
4. EAST DUNBARTONSHIRE
5. CITY OF GLASGOW
6. INVERCLYDE
7. RENFREWSHIRE
8. EAST RENFREWSHIRE
9. NORTH LANARKSHIRE
10. FALKIRK
11. CLACKMANNANSHIRE
12. WEST LOTHIAN
13. CITY OF EDINBURGH
14. MIDLOTHIAN

ORKNEY IS.
On same scale

SHETLAND IS.
On same scale

Projection : Lambert's Conformal Conic

West from Greenwich

COPYRIGHT GEORGE PHILIP LTD.

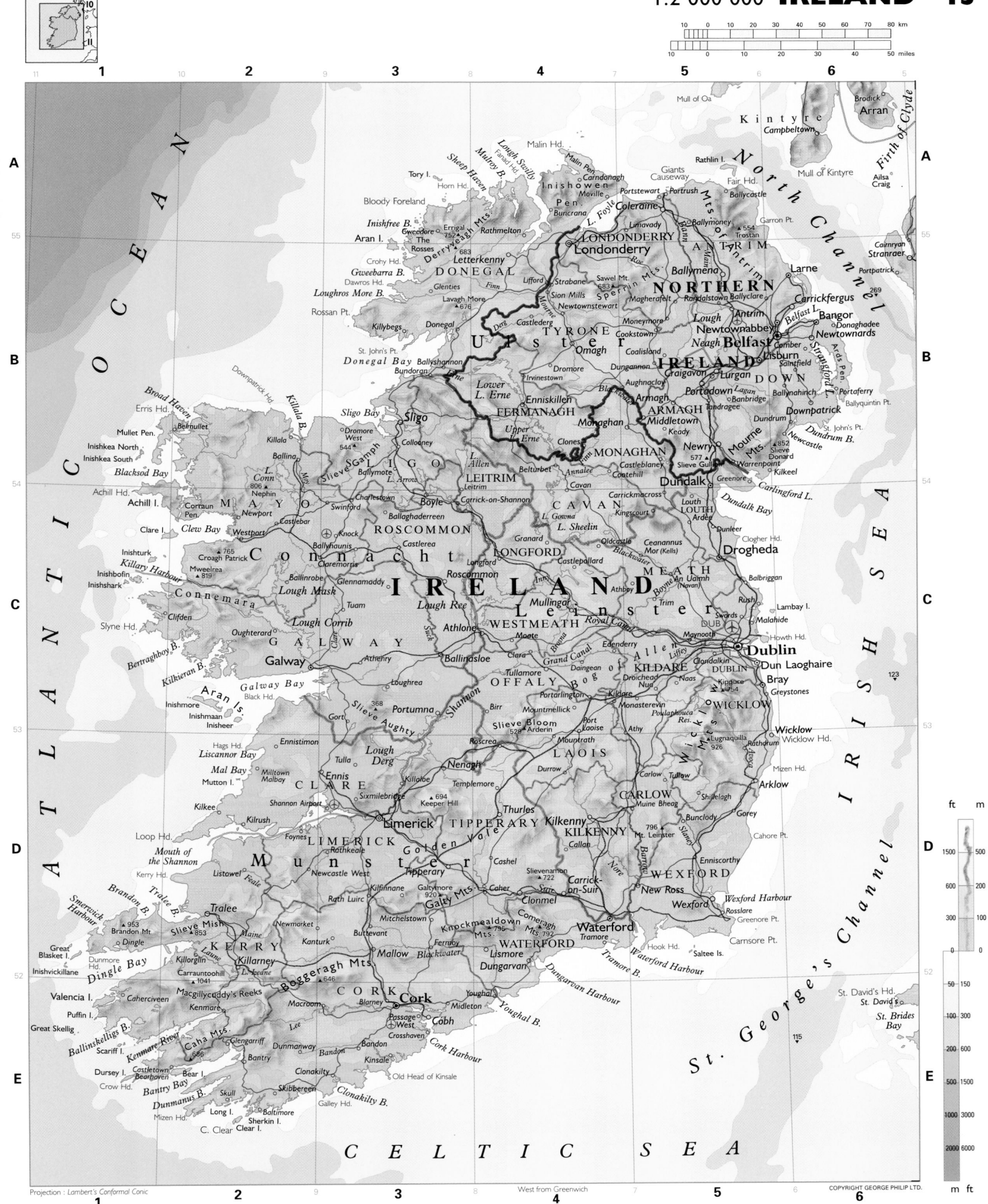

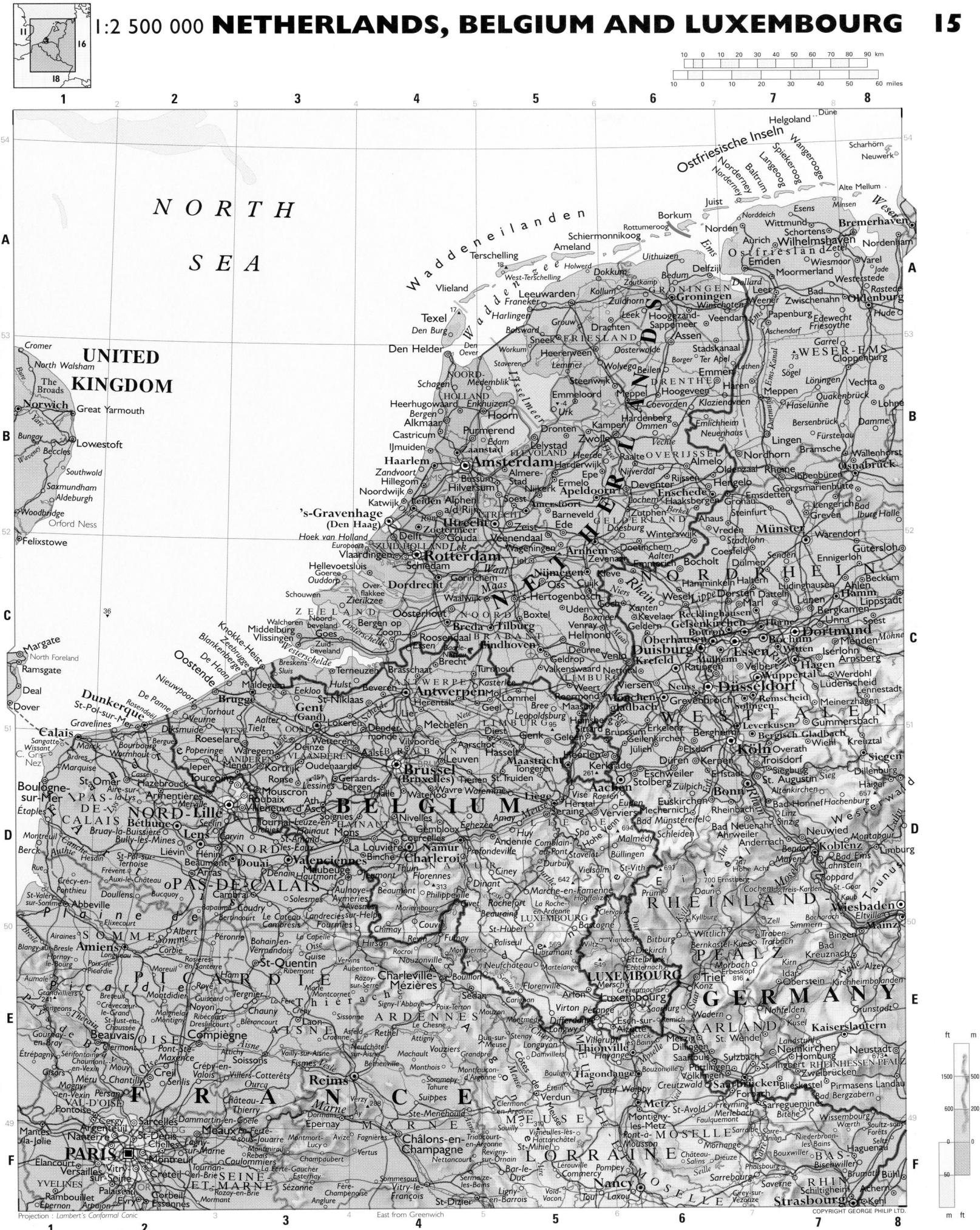

COPYRIGHT GEORGE PHILIP LTD.

Projection : Lambert's Conformal Conic

East from Greenwich

Underlined towns give their name to the
administrative area in which they stand.

9
24
25
18
20
21

9
10
11
12
13
14
15
16
B
C
D
E
F
G
East from Greenwich
LITHUANIA
BELARUS
POLAND
UKRAINE
MOLDOVA
SLOVAK REP.
HUNGARY
ROMANIA
YUGOSLAVIA
BOSNIA-HERZEGOVINA
BULGARIA
Zatoka Gdańska
Kaliningrad (Russia)
Vilnius
MINSK
WARSZAWA (Warsaw)
KYYIV (Kiev)
BUDAPEST
BUCUREȘTI (Bucharest)
BEOGRAD (Belgrade)
Chișinău
Bratislava
Sarajevo
Gdańsk
Gdynia
Elbląg
Olsztyn
Bydgoszcz
Toruń
Białystok
Hrodna
Baranavichy
Babruysk
Homyel
Mahilyow
Pinsk
Brest
Mazyr
Łódź
Lublin
Radom
Kielce
Częstochowa
Katowice
Kraków
Wrocław
Rzeszów
Lviv (Lvov)
Lutsk
Rivne
Kovel
Zhytomyr
Ternopil
Khmelnytskyy
Vinnytsya
Ivano-Frankivsk
Chernivtsi
Uzhhorod
Košice
Prešov
Miskolc
Debrecen
Nyíregyháza
Szeged
Oradea
Cluj-Napoca
Satu Mare
Baia Mare
Suceava
Iași
Bacău
Brașov
Sibiu
Timișoara
Arad
Craiova
Ploiești
Galați
Brăila
Constanța
Tulcea
Ruse
Varna
Novi Sad
Osijek
Pécs
Győr
Carpathian Mts.
Vysochyna
Transilvania
Carpații Meridionali
Pripet Marshes
Wisła
Dunaj
Dunărea (Danube)
Dnister
Prut
Siret

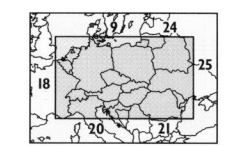

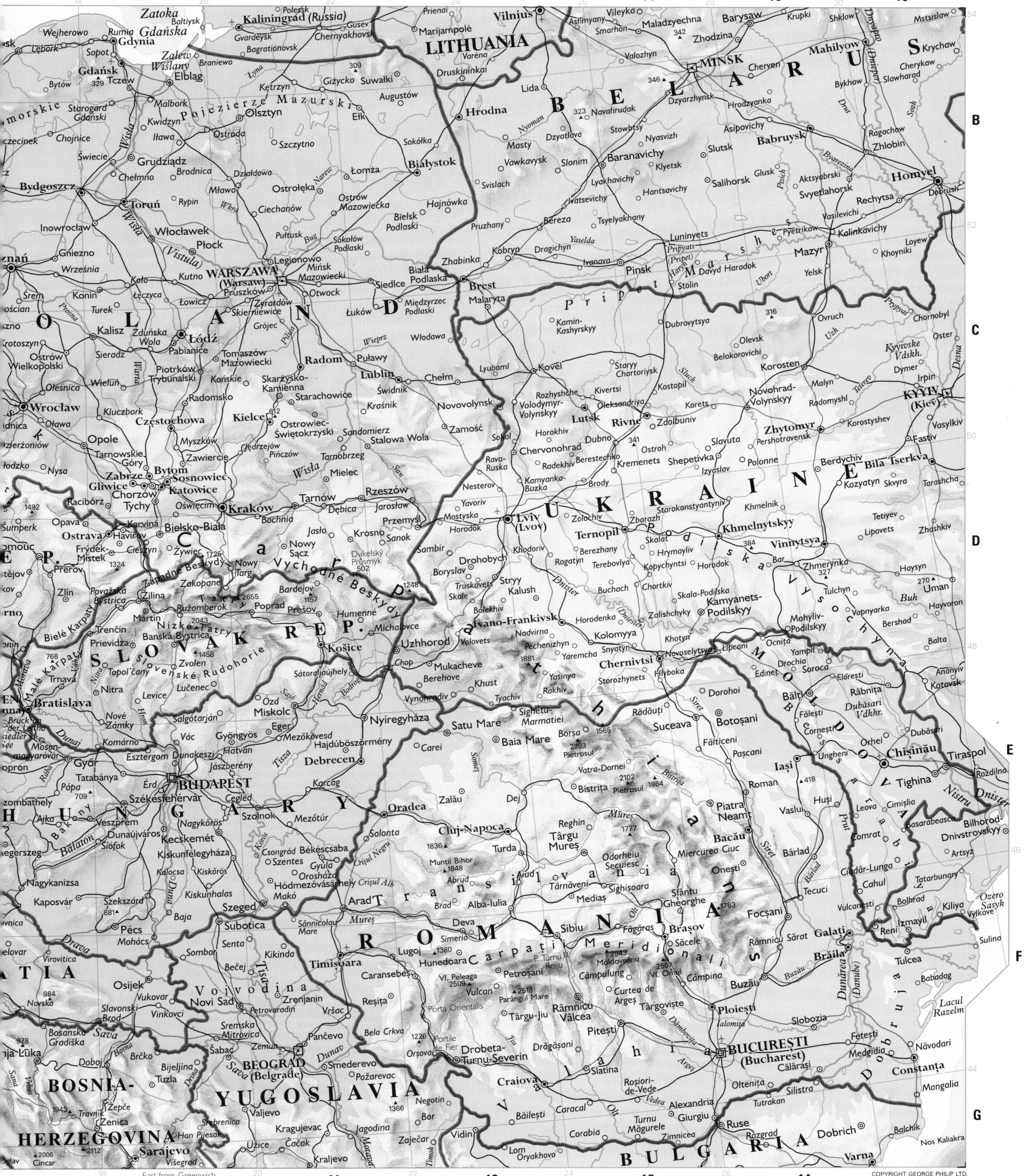

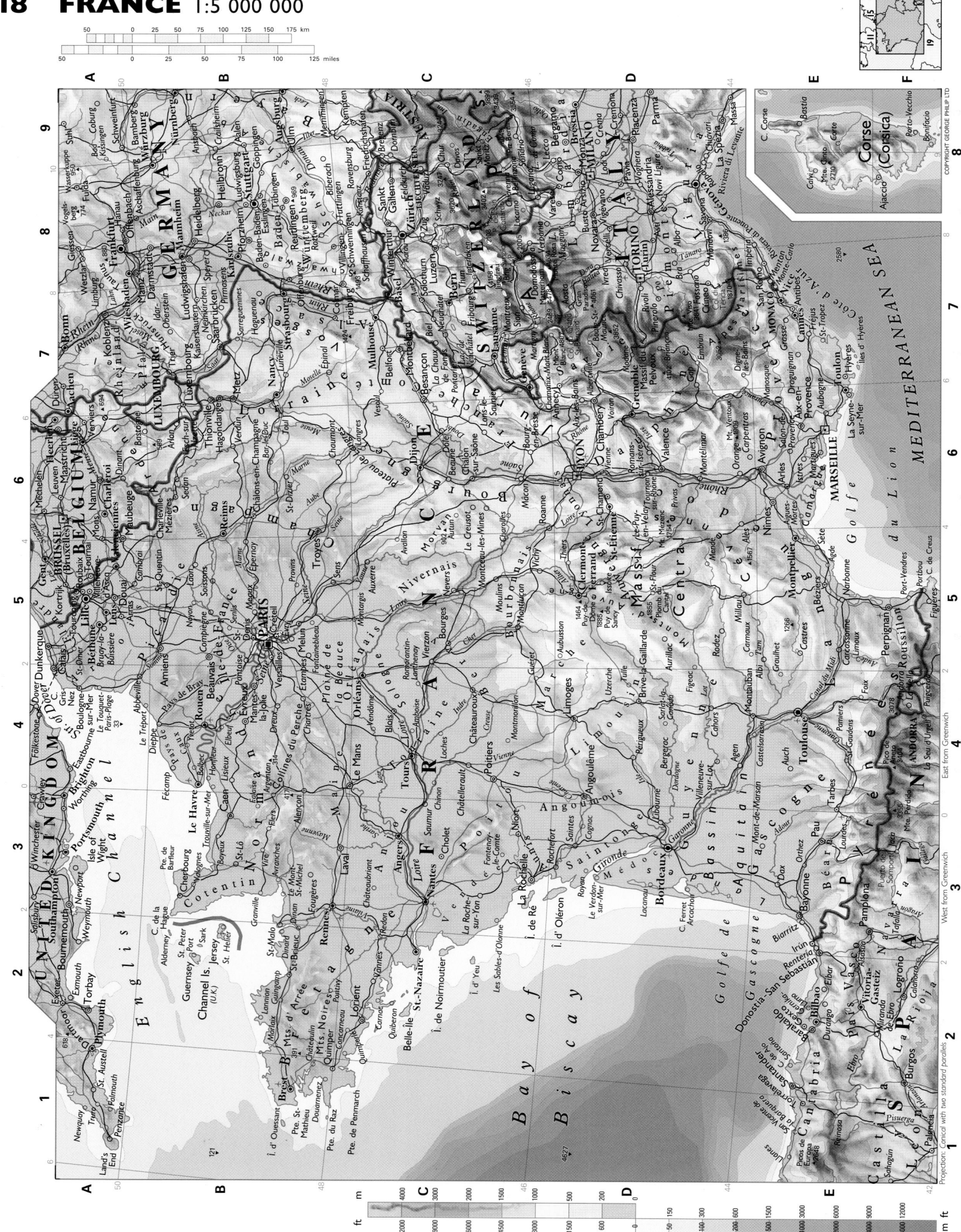

18 FRANCE 1:5 000 000

Projection: Conical with two standard parallels

COPYRIGHT GEORGE PHILIP LTD

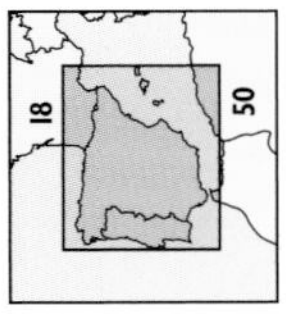

50 0 25 50 75 100 125 150 175 km
50 0 25 50 75 100 125 miles

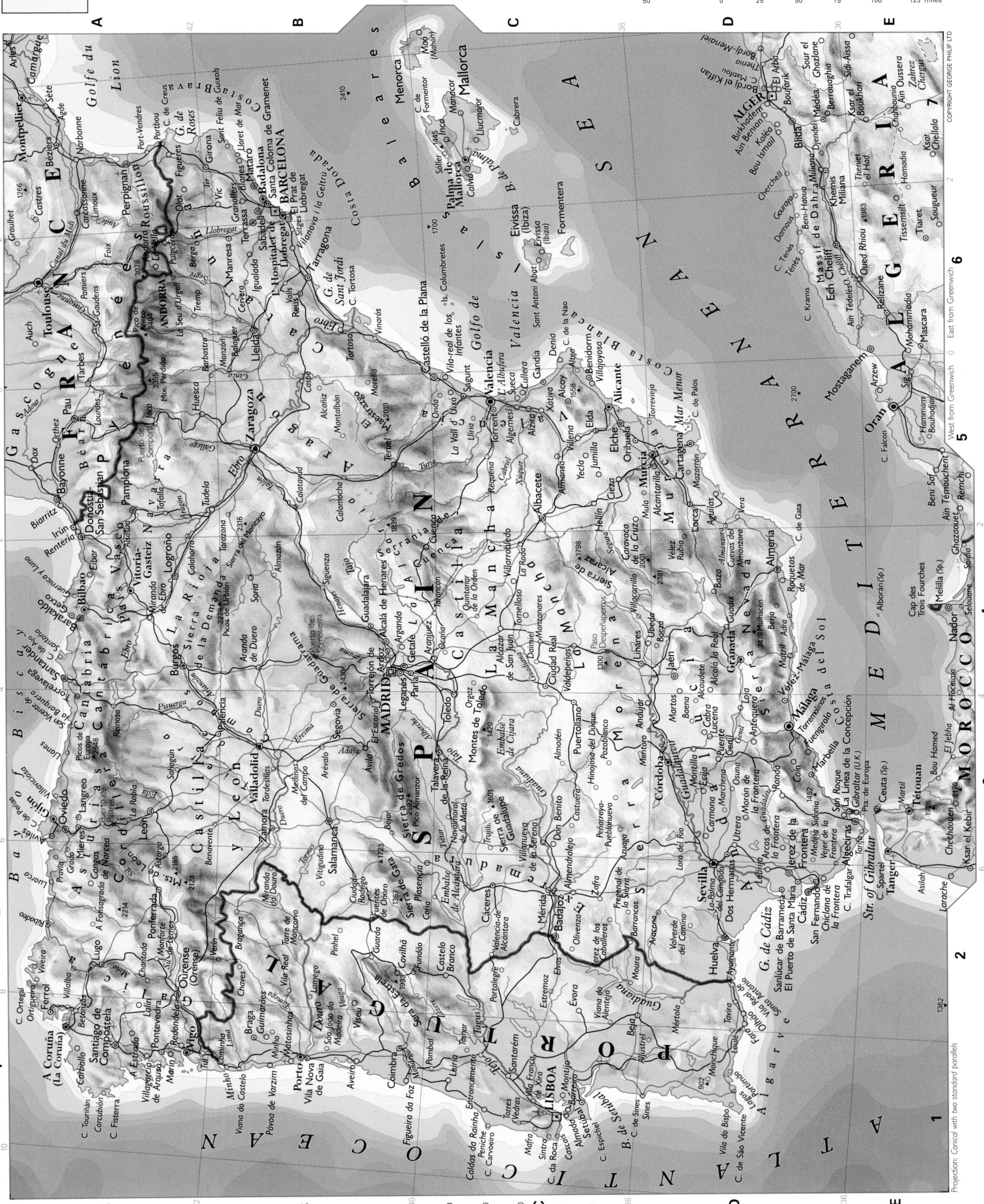

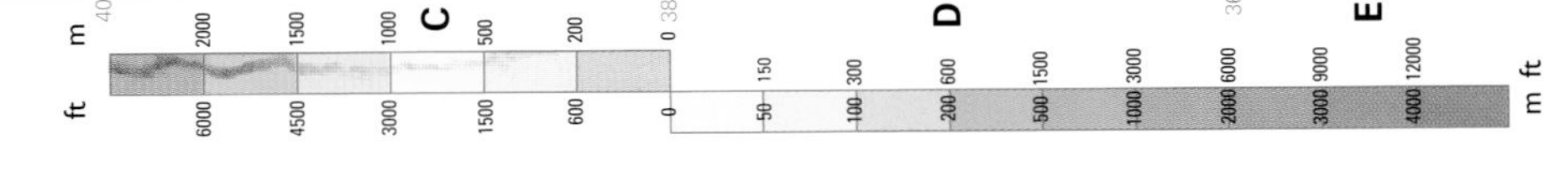

Projection: Conical with two standard parallels

West from Greenwich 0 East from Greenwich

FRANCE

SPAIN

PORTUGAL

MOROCCO

ALGERIA

MEDITERRANEAN SEA

Balearic Islands

ATLANTIC OCEAN

Golfe du Lion

Bay of Biscay

Pyrenees

ANDORRA

Mallorca

Menorca

Eivissa (Ibiza)

Formentera

Cabrera

G. de Cádiz

Golfo de Valencia

Costa Brava

Costa Dorada

Costa del Sol

Costa Blanca

Madrid

Barcelona

Valencia

Sevilla

Zaragoza

Bilbao

Málaga

Murcia

Alicante

Lisboa

Porto

Oran

Str. of Gibraltar

Gibraltar (U.K.)

Ceuta (Sp.)

Melilla (Sp.)

ft m
6000 2000
4500 1500
3000 1000
1500 500
  0 200
 0
-50 -150
-100 -300
-200 -600
-500 -1000
-1000 -2000
-2000 -6000
-3000 -9000
-4000 -12000
m ft

Projection: Conical with two standard parallels

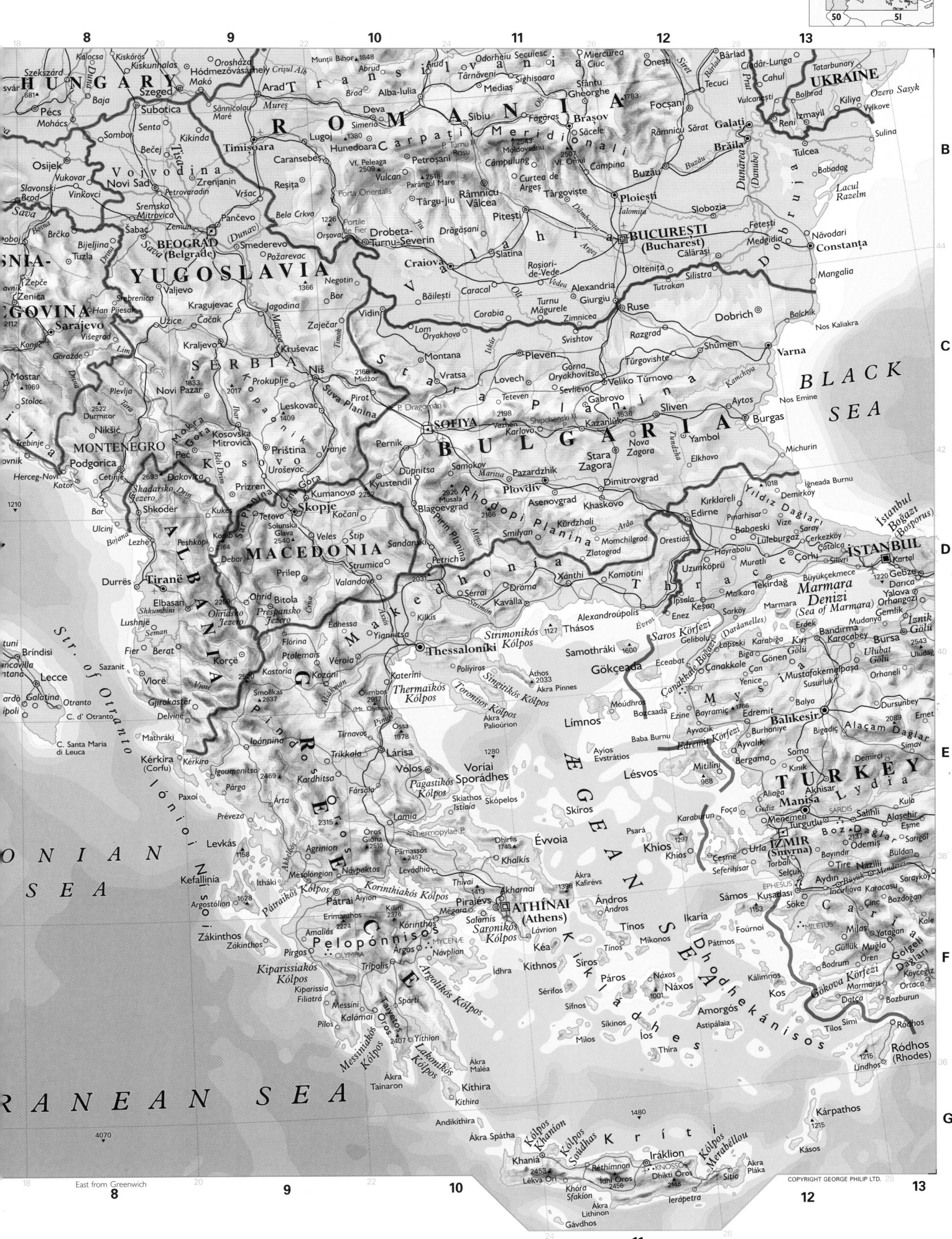

HUNGARY

ROMANIA

UKRAINE

YUGOSLAVIA

SERBIA

BULGARIA

BLACK SEA

MACEDONIA

ALBANIA

GREECE

TURKEY

AEGEAN SEA

IONIAN SEA

MEDITERRANEAN SEA

MONTENEGRO

Péloponnísos

Kríti

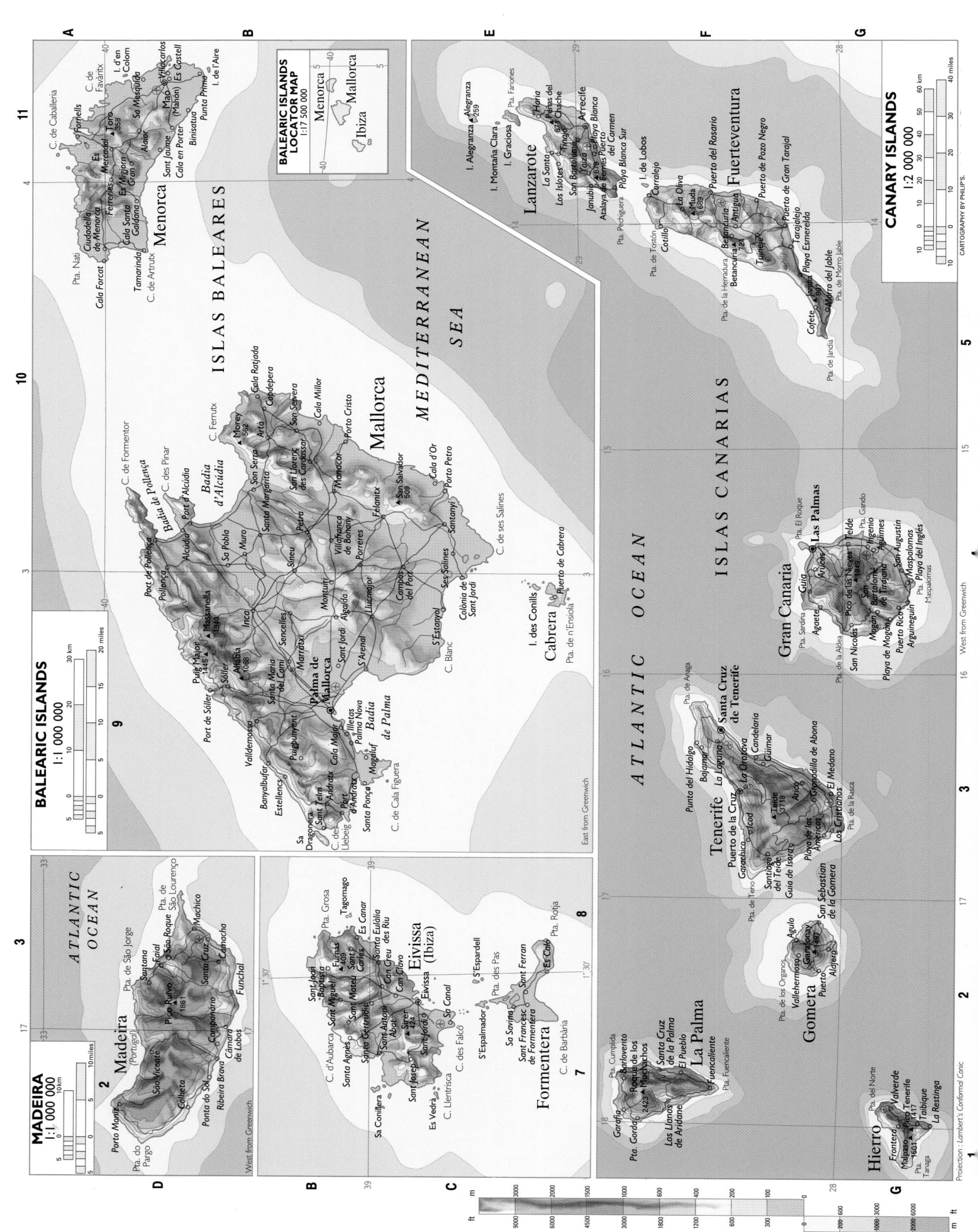

BALEARIC ISLANDS LOCATOR MAP
1:7 500 000

Menorca

Mallorca

Ibiza

CANARY ISLANDS
1:2 000 000

CARTOGRAPHY BY PHILIP'S.

ISLAS BALEARES

Menorca

C. de Caballería
Fornells
Es Mercadal
Ferreríes
Ciudadella de Menorca
Cala Santa Galdana
Pta. Nati
Tamarinda
C. de Artrutx
I. d'en Colom
Mao (Mahón)
Villacarlos
Es Castell
Punta Prima
Binisafúa
I. de l'Aire
Toro 358
Sa Mesquida
Alaior
Sant Jaume
Cala en Porter (Mahón)

Mallorca

C. de Formentor
Pta. de Pollença
C. des Pinar
Port de Pollença
Pollença
C. de Artrutx
Badia de Alcúdia
Port d'Alcúdia
Alcúdia
Badia d'Alcúdia
C. Ferrutx
Cala Ratjada
Capdepera
Artà
Morey 562
Son Serra
Son Servera
Cala Millor
Son Carrió
San Lorenç des Cardassar
Porto Cristo
Manacor
Santa Margarita
Muro
Sa Pobla
Inca
Petra
Sineu
Villafranca de Bonany
Porreres
Felanitx
San Salvador 509
Cala d'Or
Porto Petro
Puig Major 1445
Massanella 1340
Alfabia 1068
Sóller
Port de Sóller
Santa Maria del Camí
Marràtxi
Sencelles
Algaida
Montuiri
Santanyí
Cala Figuera
C. de ses Salines
Campos del Port
Ses Salines
Colonia de Sant Jordi
I. des Conills
Valldemossa
Banyalbufar
Estellencs
Andratx
Sant Telm
Sa Dragonera
C. de Cala Figuera
Port d'Andratx
Santa Ponça
Magaluf
Palma Nova
Cala Major
Illetes
Palma de Mallorca
S'Arenal
Llucmajor
S'Estanyol
S'Estanyol
S'Algar
Badia de Palma
Puigpunyent
Llebeig
Pta. de Cala Figuera
Marratxí
Sant Jordi
C. Blanc

Cabrera
Puerto de Cabrera
I. des Conills
Pta. de n'Ensiola

MEDITERRANEAN SEA

MADEIRA
1:1 000 000

Madeira (Portugal)

ATLANTIC OCEAN

Porto Moniz
Pta. do Pargo
Ponta do Sol
Ribeira Brava
Colheta
Câmara de Lobos
Pico Ruivo 1861
Campanário
São Vicente
Seixal
Santana
Faial
São Roque
São Jorge
Pta. de São Lourenço
Machico
Caniçal
Pta. de São Lourenço
Santa Cruz
Caniço
Funchal

Eivissa (Ibiza)

Pta. Grosa
Tagomago
Es Canar
Santa Eulàlia des Riu
Pta. d'Aubarca
Sant Joan Baptista
Sant Miquel
Portinatx
Santa Agnès
Sant Mateu
Sant Antoni
Sant Rafel
Sant Gertrudis
Sant Josep
Abad
Sant Jordi
Sant Francesc de Formentera
Eivissa
Can Clavo
Can Canar
Santa Eulària
Sant Carles
Es Cubells
Sa Talaia 409
Ses Salines
Sa Caleta
S'Espardell
S'Espalmador
Es Caló
Sant Ferran
Pta. des Pas
C. des Falcó
Sa Savina
Sa Conillera
Sa Vedra
C. Llentrisca
C. de Barbària

Formentera

ATLANTIC OCEAN

ISLAS CANARIAS

Lanzarote

I. Alegranza
Alegranza 289
I. Montaña Clara
I. Graciosa
Pta. Fariones
La Santa
Los Islotes
San Bartolomé
Haría
Peñas del Chache
Arrecife
Pta. de la Hermita
Betancuria
Tinajo
Yaiza
Janubio
Pta. Pechiguera
Playa Blanca
I. de Lobos

Fuerteventura

Corralejo
La Oliva
Tindaya
Puerto del Rosario
Betancuria
Antigua 679
La Muda 689
Puerto de Gran Tarajal
Tuineje
Tarajalejo
Jandía
Playa Esmerelda
Cofete
Morro del Jable
Pta. de Morro Jable
Pta. de Jandía
Pta. de la Herradura
Pta. de Tostón

Gran Canaria

Pta. El Roque
Las Palmas
Guía
Gáldar
Telde
Arúcas
Ingenio
San Agustín
Pico de las Nieves 1949
San Bartolomé de Tirajana
Mogán
Maspalomas
Puerto Rico
Arguineguín
Playa del Inglés
Maspalomas
Pta. Sardina
Agaete
San Nicolás
San Nicolás de la Aldea
Playa de Mogán

Tenerife

Pta. de Anaga
Pta. del Hidalgo
Bajamar
La Laguna
Santa Cruz de Tenerife
Puerto de la Cruz
La Orotava
Icod
Garachico
Candelaria
Güimar
Santiago del Teide
Teide 3718
Arico
Granadilla de Abona
El Médano
Guía de Isora
Playa de las Américas
Los Cristianos
Pta. de Teno
Pta. de la Rasca

Gomera

Pta. de los Organos
Vallehermoso
Agulo
Hermigua
San Sebastián de la Gomera
Garajonay 1487
Alojera
Puerto

La Palma

Pta. Cumplida
Barlovento
Roque de los Muchachos 2423
Santa Cruz de la Palma
Gorafía
Pta. Gorda
Los Llanos de Aridane
El Pueblo
Fuencaliente
Fuencaliente

Hierro

Pta. del Norte
Frontera
Valverde
Malpaso 1501
Pico Tenerife 1417
Taibique
Tanaga
La Restinga

BALEARIC ISLANDS
1:1 000 000

CANARY ISLANDS
1:2 000 000

Projection: Lambert's Conformal Conic

ft / m scale bars

West from Greenwich
East from Greenwich

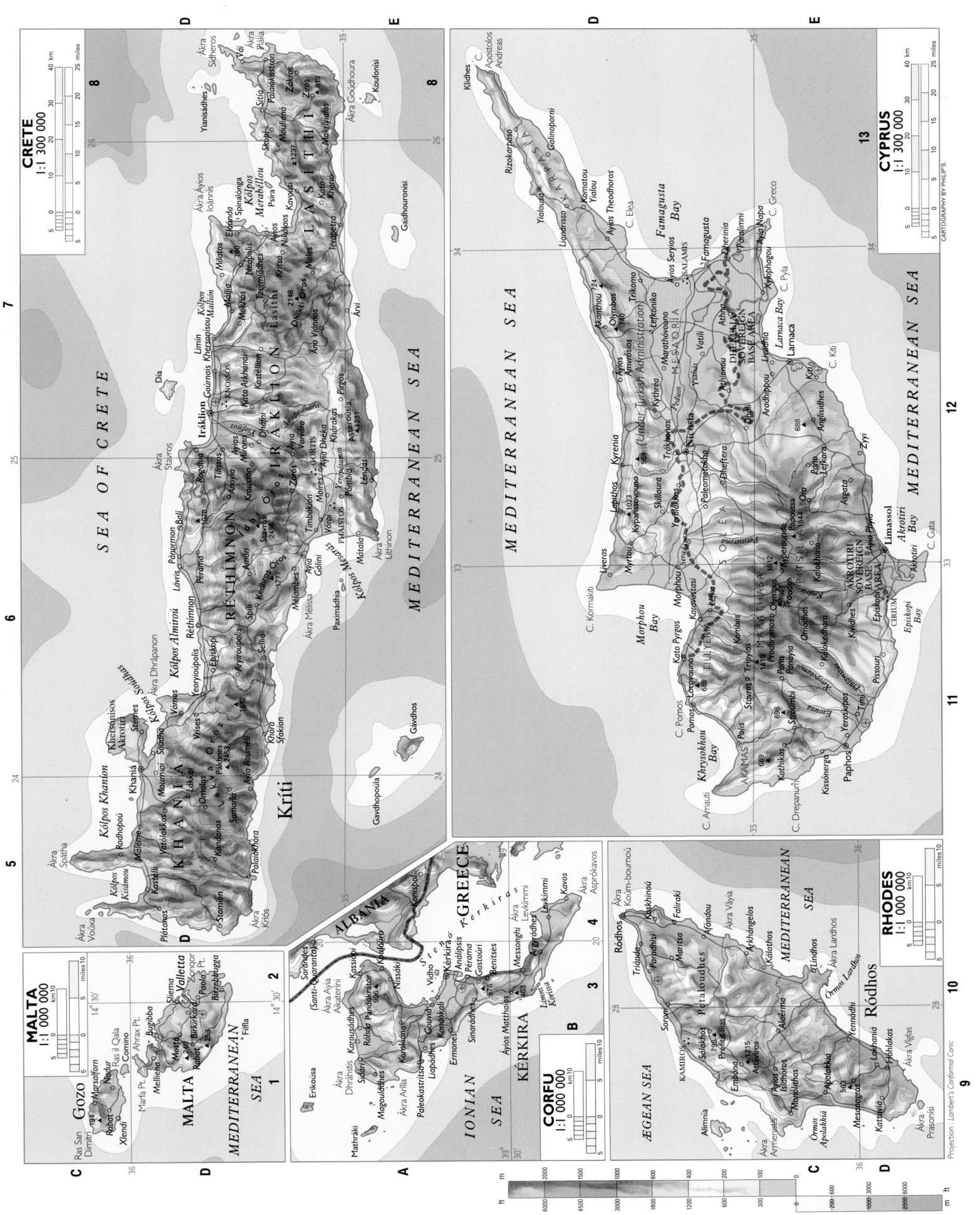

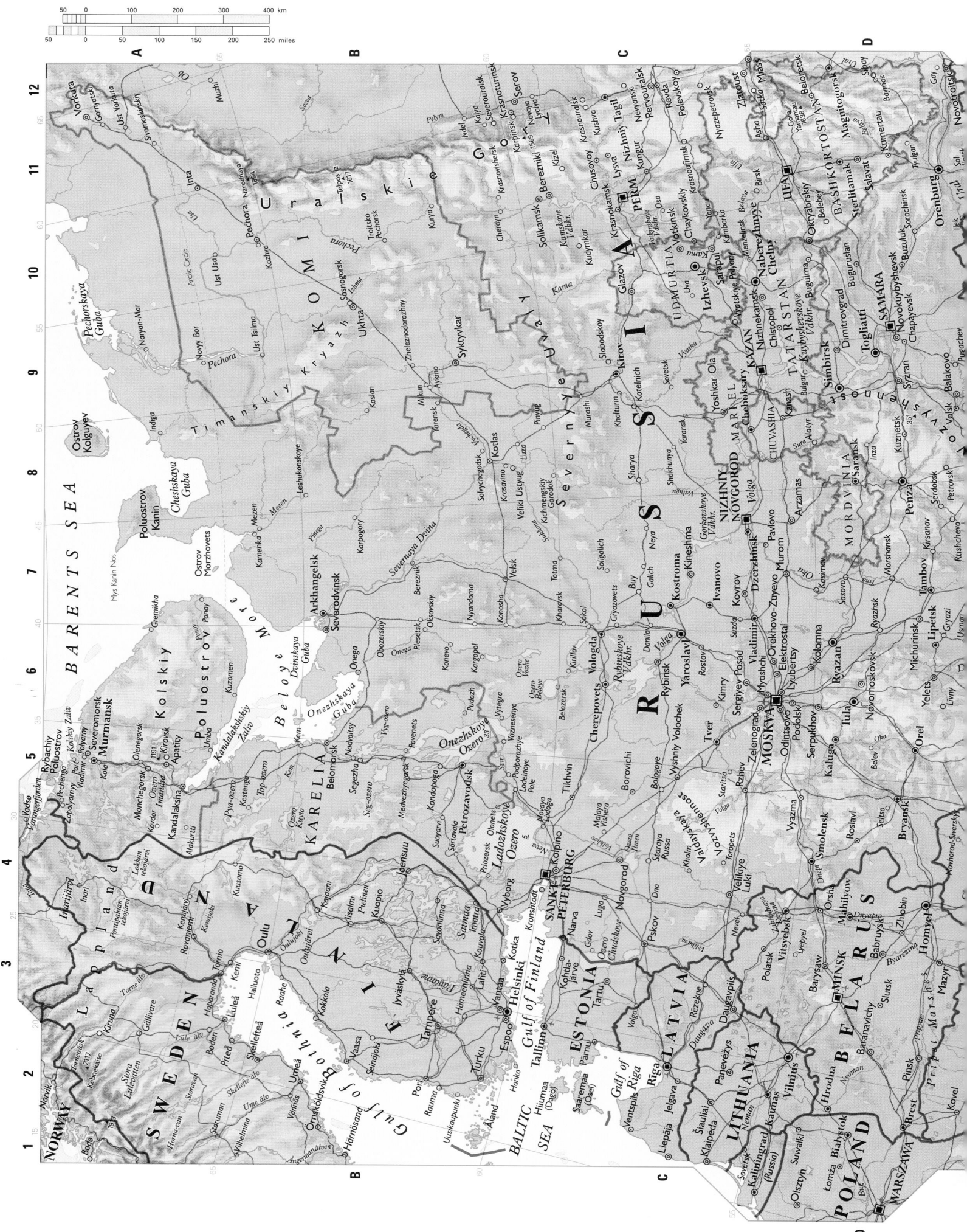

UKRAINE
KAZAKSTAN
MOLDOVA
ROMANIA
BULGARIA
TURKEY
GEORGIA
ARMENIA
AZERBAIJAN
SYRIA
IRAQ
IRAN
LEBANON
CYPRUS
TURKMENISTAN
KALMYKIA
CRIMEA
DAGESTAN
CHECHENIA
BLACK SEA
CASPIAN SEA
MEDITERRANEAN SEA
Sea of Azov
Kirgiziya Steppe
Caspian Depression
Carpathians
Caucasus Mountains
Kuzey Anadolu Dağları
Toros Dağları
Anadolu
Kurdistan
Kühhā-ye Zāgros
Reshteh-ye Kūhhā-ye Alborz
Bādiyat ash Shām
Dasht-e Kavīr
KYYIV
KHARKIV
DNIPROPETROVSK
DONETSK
ODESA
ROSTOV
VOLGOGRAD
BUCUREȘTI
İSTANBUL
ANKARA
TBILISI
YEREVAN
BAKI
TEHRĀN
HALAB
DIMASHQ
BAYRŪT
Projection: Conical with two standard parallels
East from Greenwich
E
F
G
H
4
5
6
7
8
9
ft
m
12 000
9000
6000
4500
3000
1500
600
0
200
500
1000
2000
4000
3000
2000
1500
1000
500
200
0
600
1500
3000
6000
m
ft
COPYRIGHT GEORGE PHILIP LTD.

26
17
44

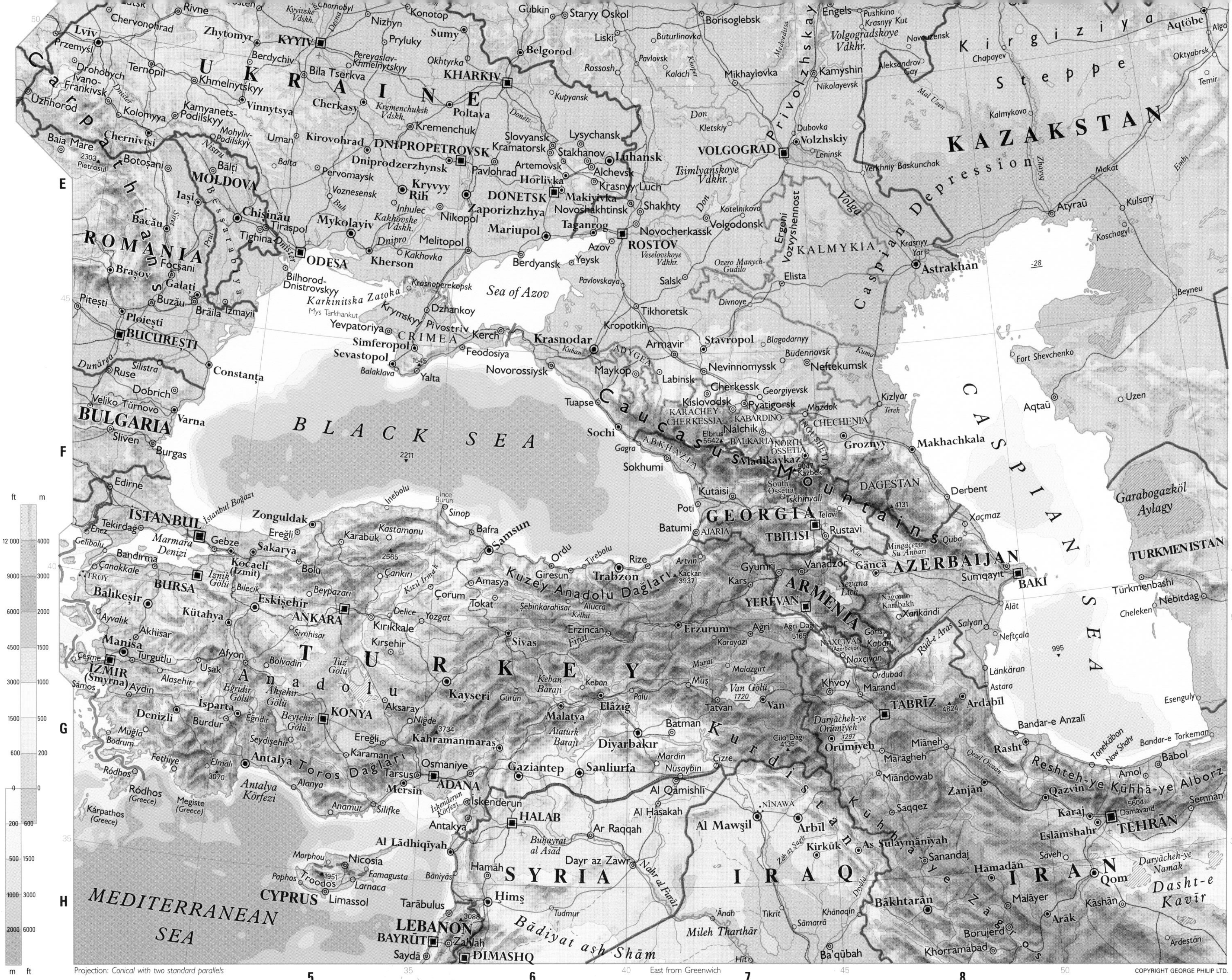

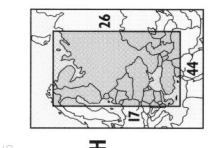

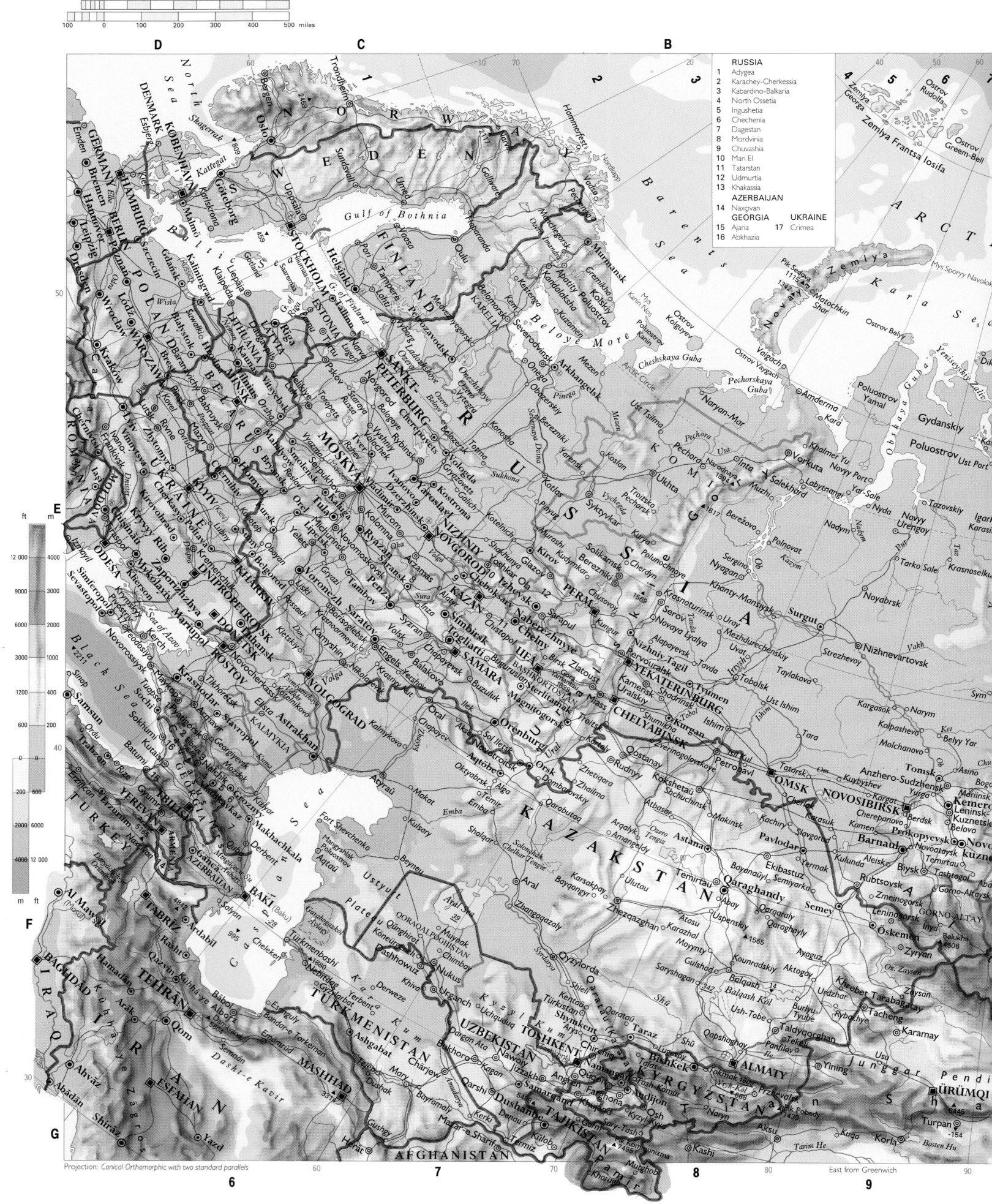

Projection: Conical Orthomorphic with two standard parallels

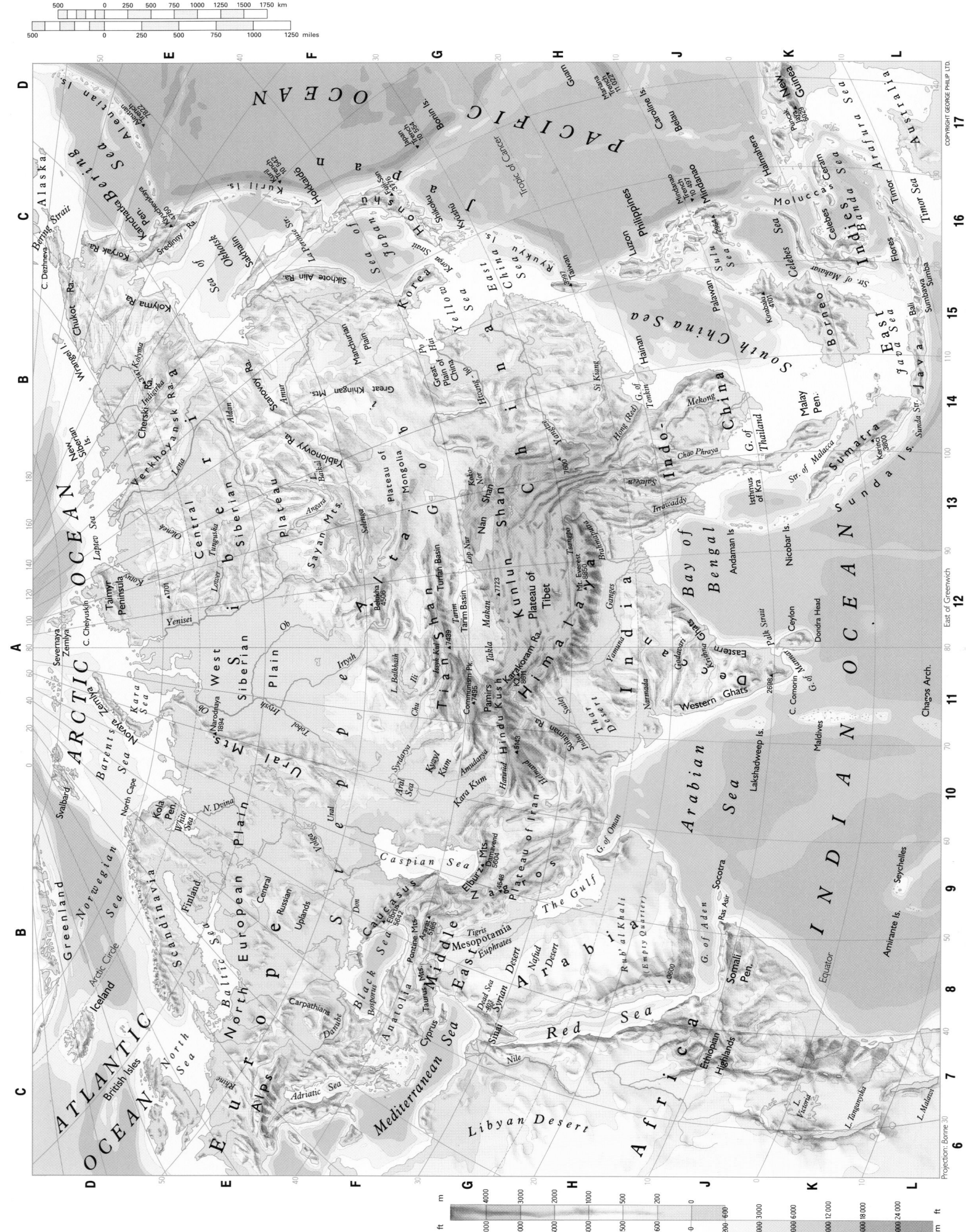

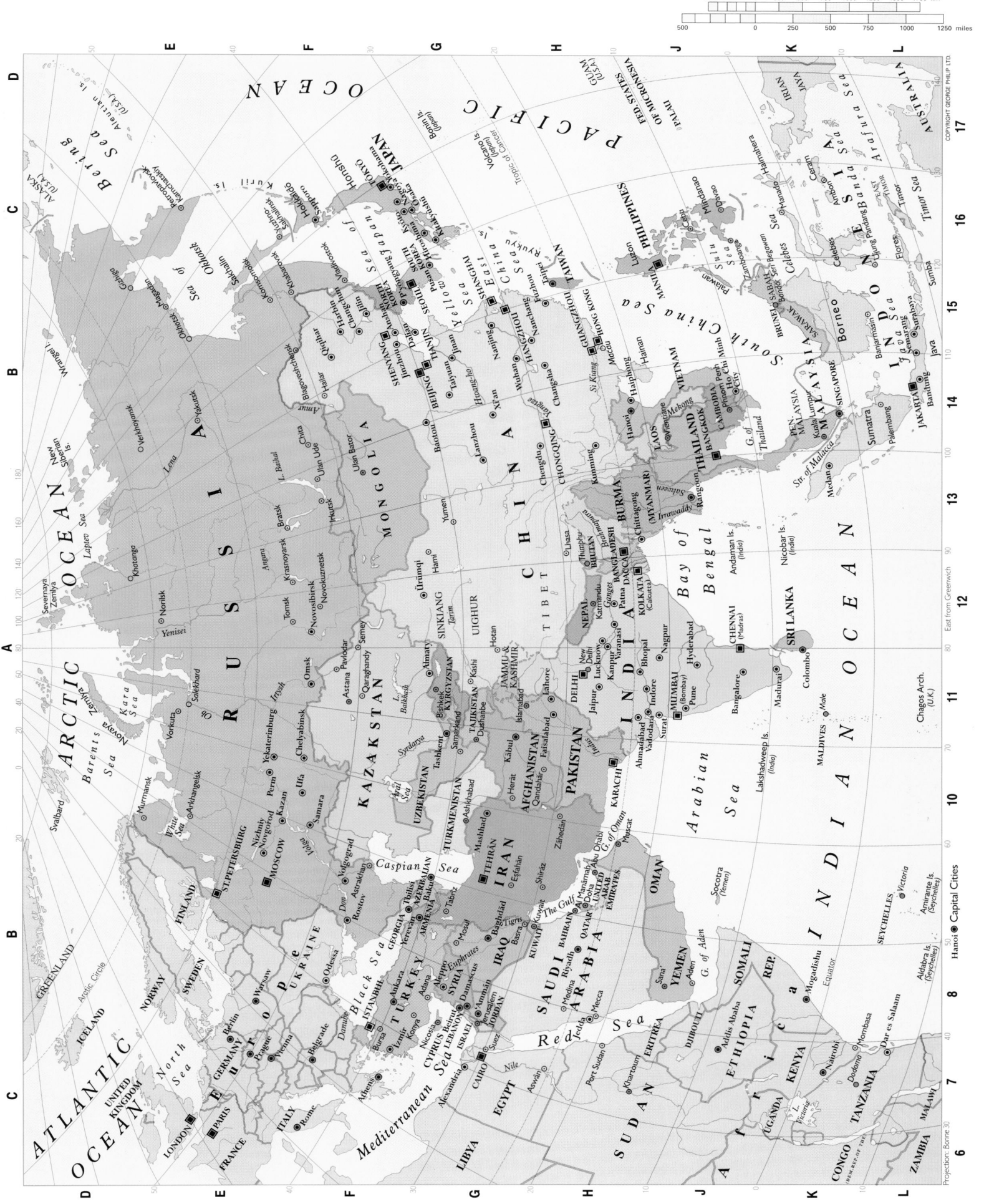

JAPAN 1:5 000 000

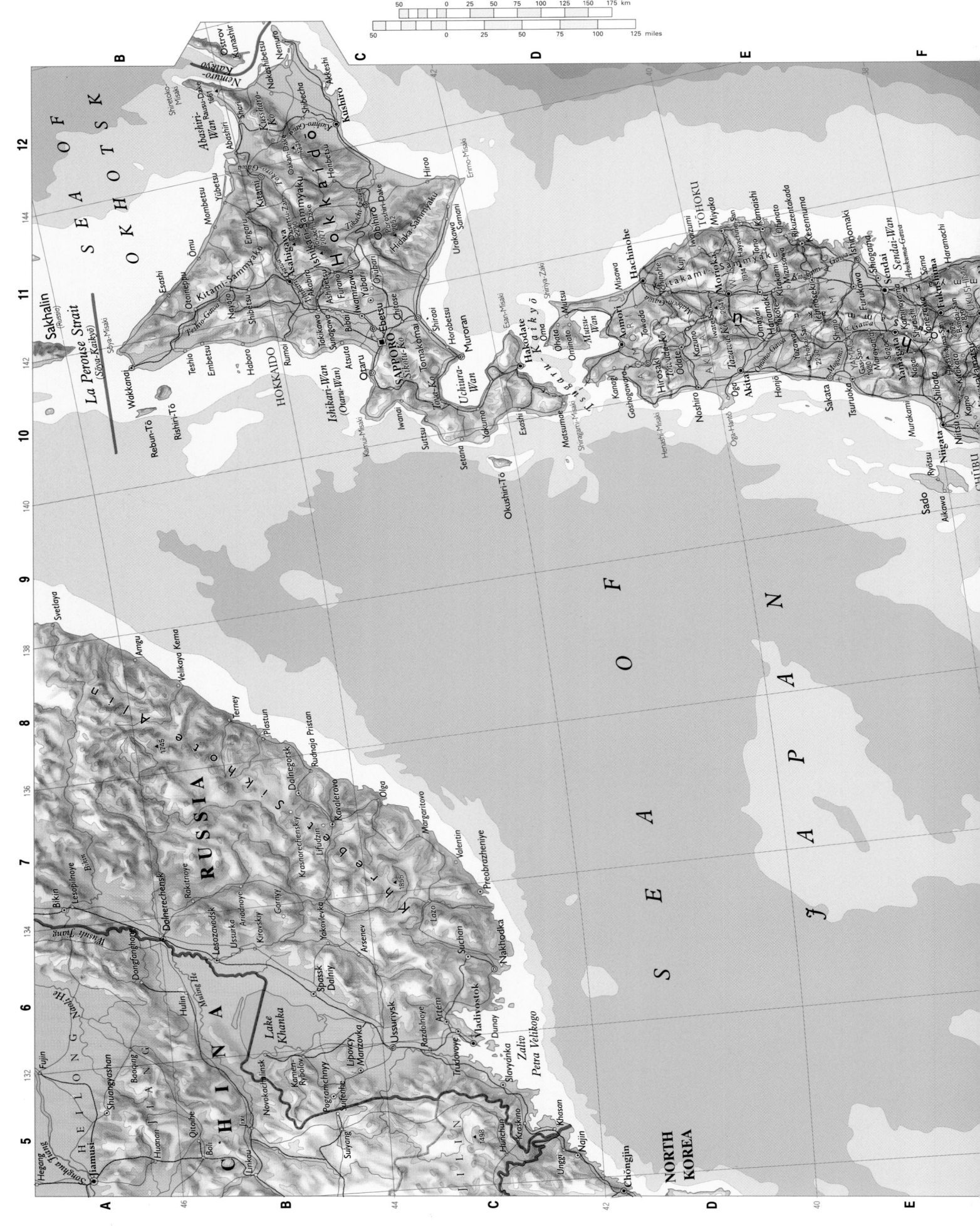

50   0   25   50   75   100   125   150   175 km

50   0   25   50   75   100   125 miles

SEA OF OKHOTSK

Sakhalin

La Perouse Strait
(Sōya-Kaikyō)

HOKKAIDO

SAPPORO

Hakodate

TŌHOKU

HONSHU

SEA OF JAPAN

RUSSIA

Sikhote

CHINA

Lake Khanka

Vladivostok

NORTH KOREA

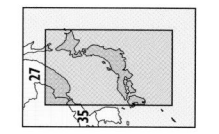

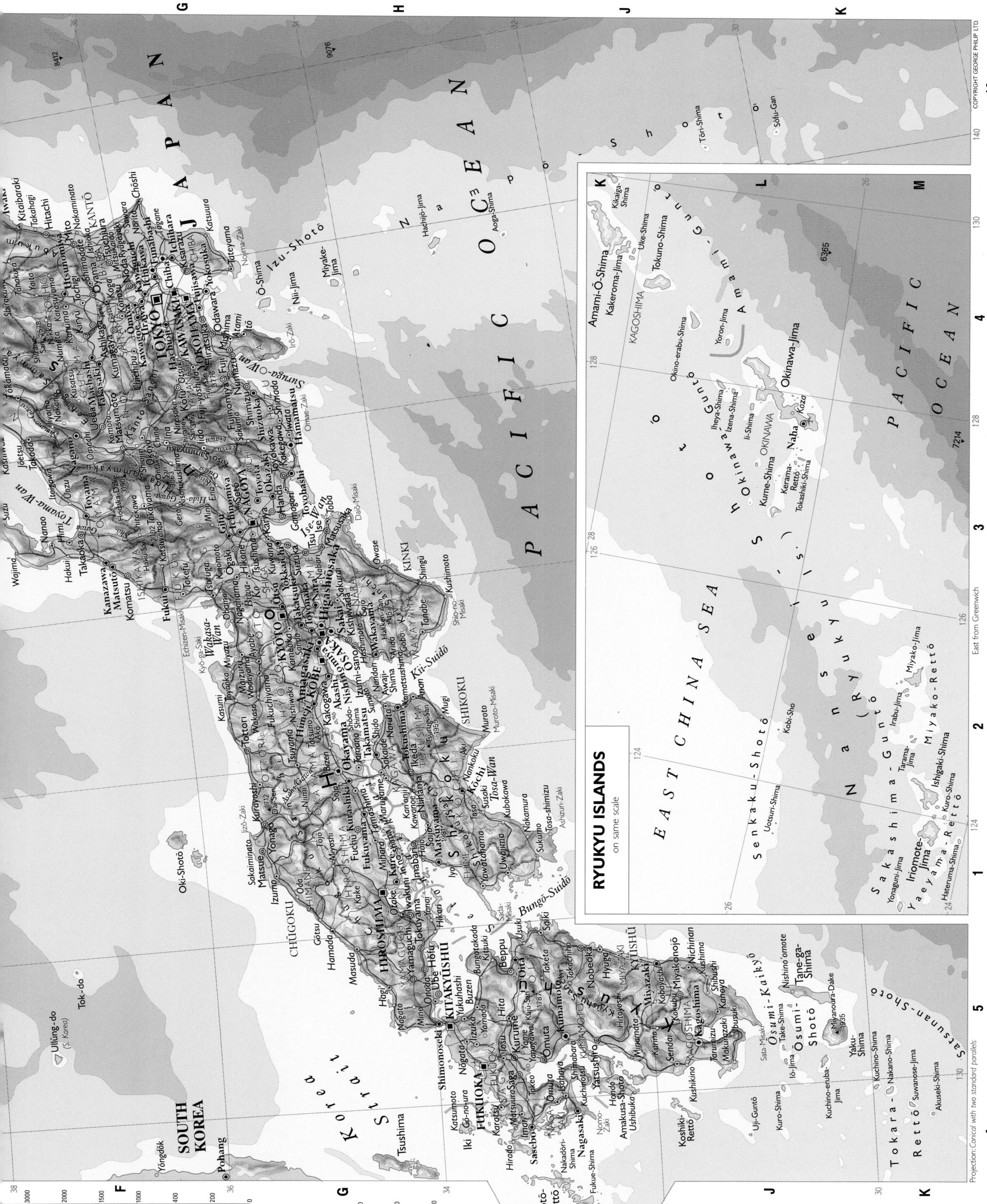

RYUKYU ISLANDS
on same scale

SOUTH KOREA

J A P A N

P A C I F I C   O C E A N

E A S T   C H I N A   S E A

PACIFIC OCEAN

K o r e a   S t r a i t

Korea Strait

TOKYO
YOKOHAMA
KAWASAKI
CHIBA
NAGOYA
KYOTO
OSAKA
KOBE
HIROSHIMA
FUKUOKA
KITAKYUSHU
KAGOSHIMA

KANTO
KINKI
CHUBU
CHUGOKU
SHIKOKU
KYUSHU

Izu-Shotō
Oki-Shotō
Tsushima
Yaku-Shima
Tane-ga-Shima
Ōsumi-Shotō
Tokara-Rettō
Satsunan-Shotō
Goto-Rettō
Amakusa-Shotō

Amami-Ō-Shima
Okinawa-Jima
Naha
OKINAWA
KAGOSHIMA
Nansei-Shotō (Ryukyu Is.)
Sakishima-Guntō
Yaeyama-Rettō
Miyako-Rettō
Ishigaki-Shima
Iriomote-Jima
Yonaguni-Shima
Senkaku-Shotō

Tōyama-Wan
Wakasa-Wan
Ise-Wan
Suruga-Wan
Tosa-Wan
Bungo-Suidō
Kii-Suidō
Ōsumi-Kaikyō

Ullŭng-do (S. Korea)
Tok-do (S. Korea)
Pohang
Yŏngdŏk

6365
7214
9042
9076

130
128
126
124
140
36
38
34
32
30
26
28

East from Greenwich

Projection: Conical with two standard parallels

ft
m
24 000
18 000
12 000
6000
4000
2000
1000
600
200
0
9000
6000
4500
3000
2000
1500
1200
600
300
0

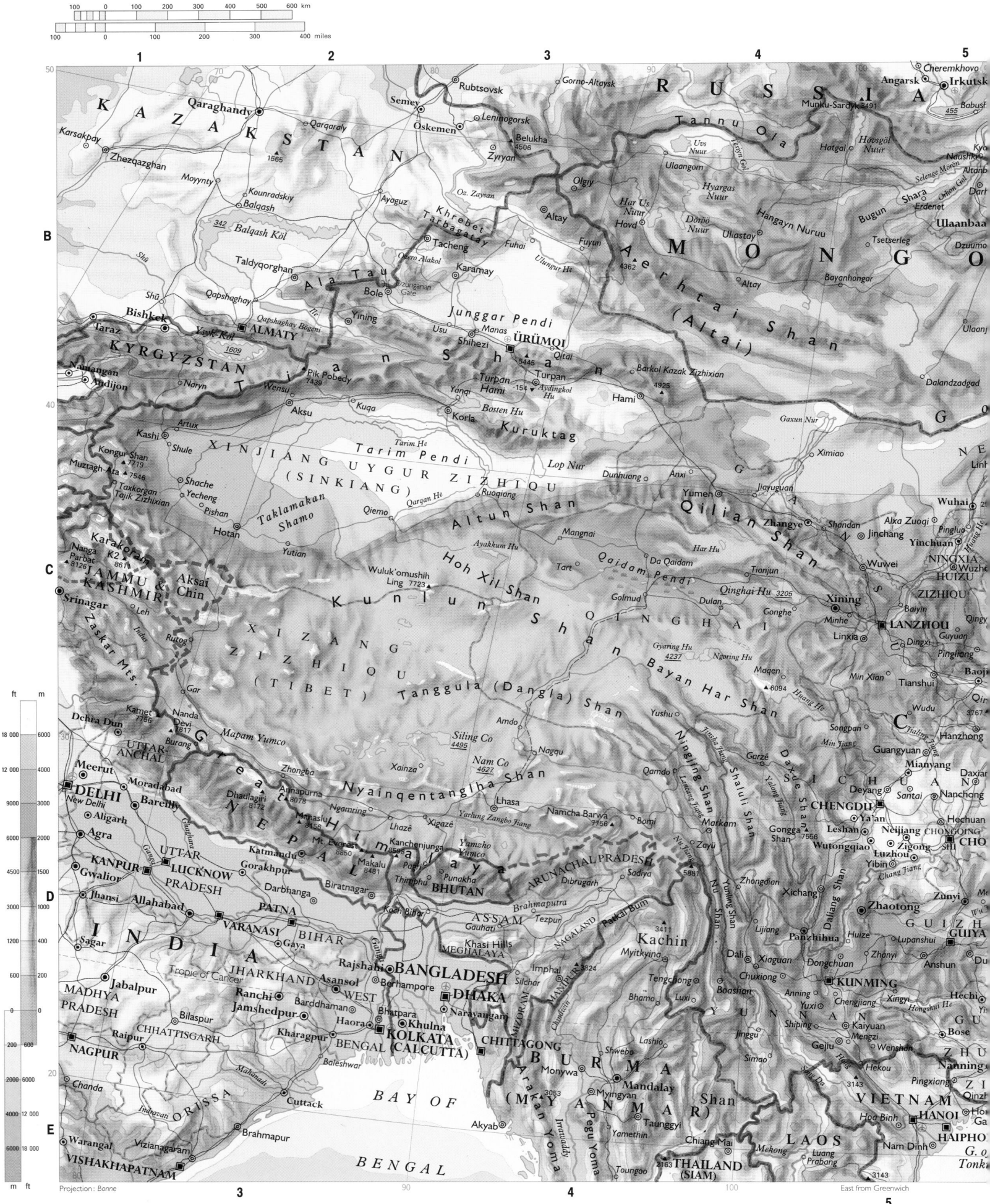

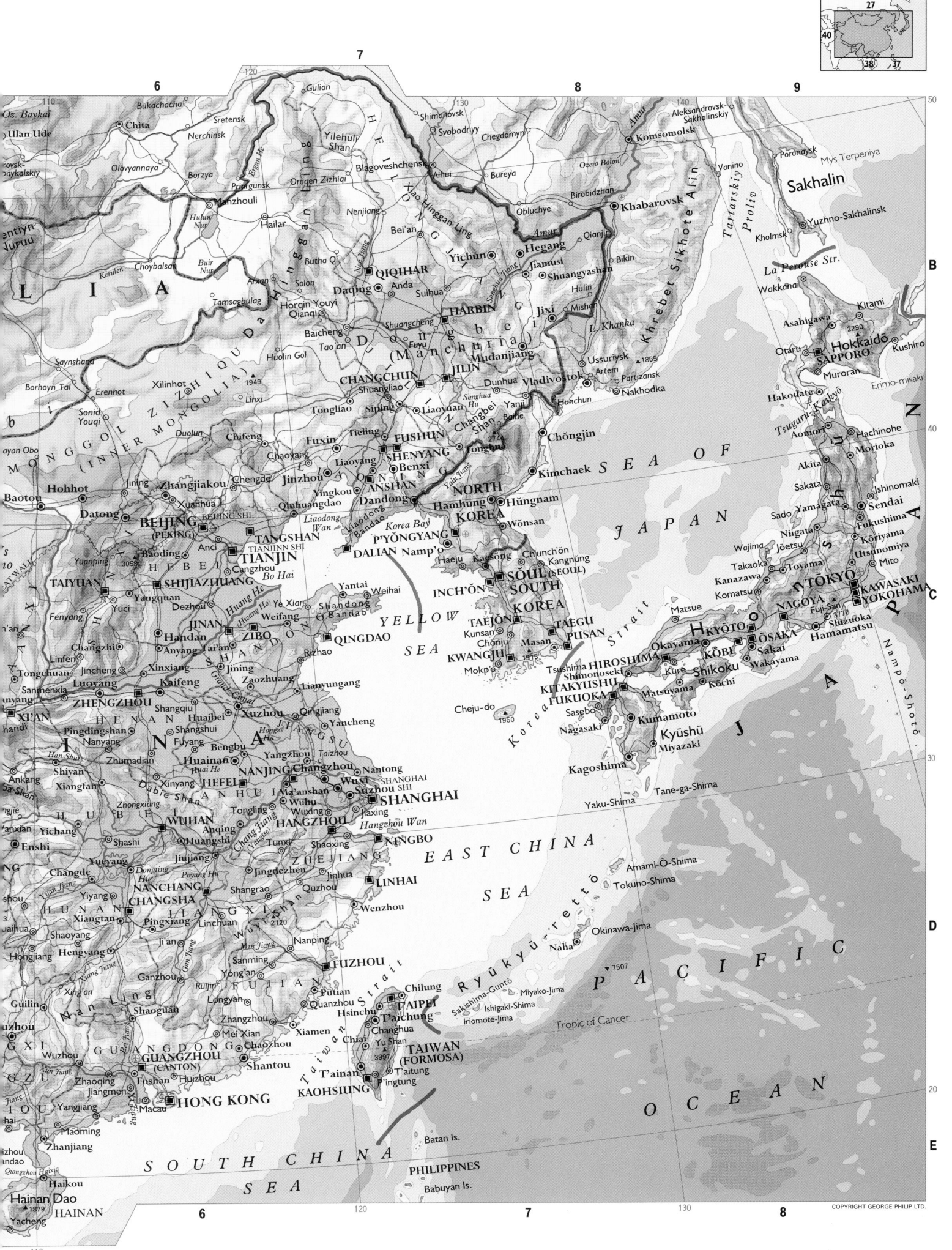

Oz. Baykal
Ulan Ude
rovskorbaykalskiy
entiyn
Juruu
LIA
Chita
Bukachacha
Sretensk
Nerchinsk
Olovyannaya
Borzya
Priargunsk
Manzhouli
Hailar
Choybalsan
Buir Nur
Kerulen
Hulun Nur
Tamsagbulag
Solon
Arxan
Nenjiang
Butha Qi
Horqin Youyi Qianqi
Baicheng
Tao'an
Fuyu
Huolin Gol
Linxi
Duolun
Chifeng
Chaoyang
Jinzhou
Chengde
Zhangjiakou
Jining
Xuanhua
Yingkou
Qinhuangdao
Tangshan
TIANJIN SHI
TIANJIN
Cangzhou
Bo Hai
Gulian
Shimanovsk
Svobodnyy
Chegdomyn
Aihui
Bureya
Blagoveshchensk
Obluchye
Birobidzhan
Khabarovsk
Komsomolsk
Ozero Bolon
Amur
Aleksandrovsk-Sakhalinskiy
Poronaysk
Mys Terpeniya
Sakhalin
Vanino
Tartarskiy Proliv
Kholmsk
Yuzhno-Sakhalinsk
La Perouse Str.
Wakkanai
Kitami
Asahigawa
Hokkaido
SAPPORO
Otaru
Muroran
Kushiro
Erimo-misaki
Hakodate
Tsugaru-Kaikyō
Aomori
Hachinohe
Morioka
Akita
Ishinomaki
Sendai
Fukushima
Kōriyama
Utsunomiya
Mito
TŌKYŌ
KAWASAKI
YOKOHAMA
NAGOYA
Shizuoka
Hamamatsu
Fuji-San 3776
KYŌTO
ŌSAKA
KŌBE
Sakai
Wakayama
Shikoku
Kōchi

YELLOW SEA

SEA OF JAPAN

EAST CHINA SEA

PACIFIC OCEAN

SOUTH CHINA SEA

HONG KONG
Macau
GUANGZHOU (CANTON)
HAINAN
Hainan Dao

COPYRIGHT GEORGE PHILIP LTD.

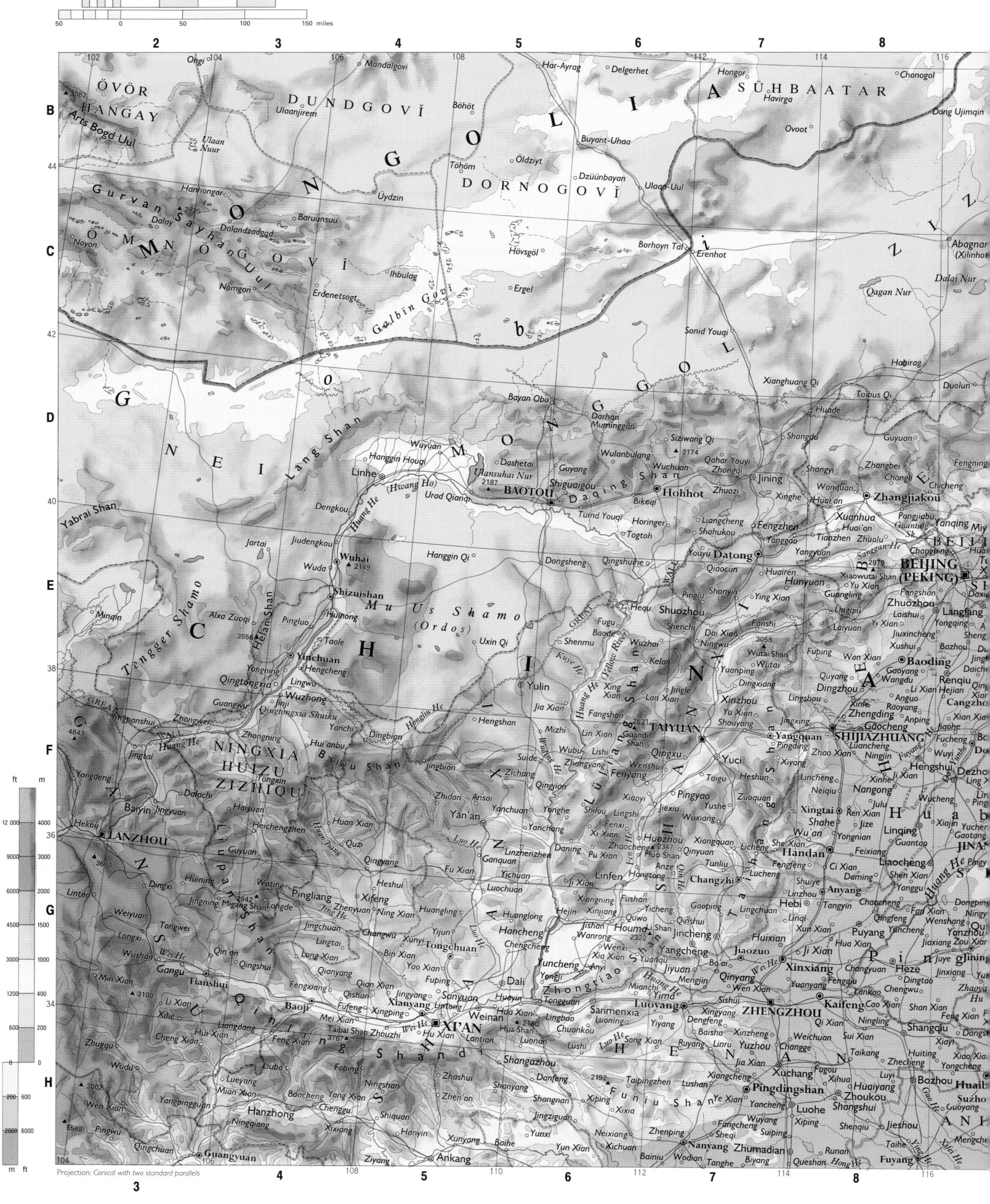

27
31
32
33

HARBIN
Bin Xian
Acheng
Shuangcheng
Horqin Youyi Qianqi
(Ulanhot)
Baicheng
Da'an
Zhenlai
Taonan
Hulingol
Tuquan
Anguang
Qian'an
Fuyu
Changchunling
Beitaolaizhao
Sanchahe
Wuchang
Lalin
Shangzhi
Yimianpo
Hengdaohezi
Mudanjiang
Linkou
Jixi
Muling
Hailin
Ning'an
Suiyang
Suifenhe
Dongning
Ussuriysk
Razdolnoye
Artem
Vladivostok
Nong'an
Dehui
Jiutai
Shulan
Jarud Qi
Zhanyu
Changling
CHANGCHUN
JILIN
Jiaohe
Dunhua
Tongliao
Shuangliao
Siping
Gongzhuling
Liaoyuan
Dongfeng
Meihekou
Huadian
Panshi
Yanji
Tumen
Hunchun
Longjing
Helong
Wangqing
Mingyuegue
Slavyanka
Posyet
Kraskino
Chifeng
Fuxin
Tieling
Kaiyuan
Faku
Tiefa
Xinmin
SHENYANG
FUSHUN
Beipiao
Chaoyang
Jinzhou
Panjin
Liaoyang
Benxi
ANSHAN
Haicheng
Yingkou
Dashiqiao
Huludao
Xingcheng
Suizhong
Fengcheng
Dandong
Sinŭiju
Wafangdian
Pulandian
Jin Xian
Lüshun
DALIAN
Qinhuangdao
Changli
TIANJIN
Tanggu
Hangu
Bo Hai
Korea Bay
Liaodong Wan
Liaodong Bandao
Changbai Shan
Paektu-san
Hyesan
Kanggye
Manp'o
Chongjin
Kimch'aek
(Songjin)
Hamhung
Hŭngnam
Sinp'o
NORTH KOREA
P'YŎNGYANG
Namp'o
Sariwŏn
Haeju
Kaesŏng
Wŏnsan
Tongjosŏn Man
SEA OF JAPAN
SOUL
INCH'ŎN
Suwŏn
Ch'unch'ŏn
Kangnŭng
Samch'ŏk
Ullŭng-do
SOUTH KOREA
Ch'ŏngju
TAEJŎN
Chŏnju
Kunsan
TAEGU
P'ohang
Ulsan
PUSAN
Masan
Chinju
KWANGJU
Mokp'o
Yŏsu
Cheju-do
Cheju
Halla-san
Sŏgwipo
Korea Strait
Tsushima
Izuhara
JAPAN
Sasebo
Nagasaki
Fukue-Shima
Yantai
Weihai
Penglai
Longkou
Laizhou Wan
Shandong Bandao
Weifang
ZIBO
Jimo
QINGDAO
Jiaozhou
Rizhao
Linyi
Lianyungang
Xuzhou
Huaiyin
Huai'an
Yancheng
HUANG HAI
(Yellow Sea)
Miaodao Qundao
East from Greenwich
COPYRIGHT GEORGE PHILIP LTD.

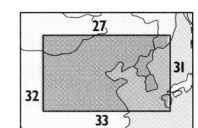

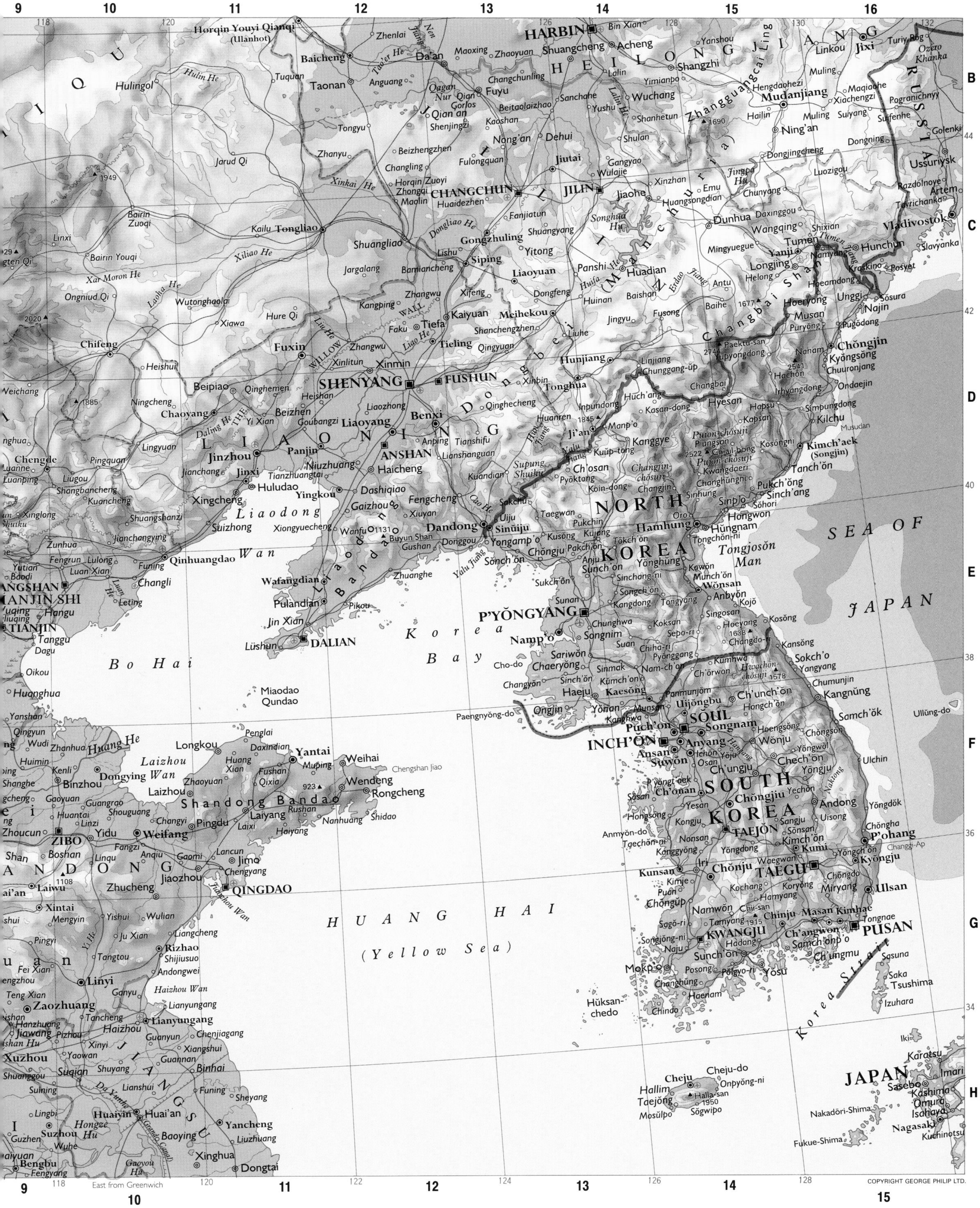

100 0 100 200 300 400 500 km
100 0 50 100 150 200 250 300 350 miles

BURMA
(MYANMAR)

Insein
Ma-ubin
RANGOON
(YANGON)
Thaton
Moulmein
Pyapon
G. of
Martaban
Kyaikkami
2080
Ye
Natkyizin
Tavoy
Moscos
Islands
2075
Mali Kyun
Kadan
Kyun
Mergui
Taninthari
Lenya
Myeik
Lambi Kyun
Letsok-
aw Kyun
Maliwun
Kyunzu
Bokpyin

THAILAND
Thoen
Uttaradit
Sawankhalok
Loei
Mae Sot
Tak
Phitsanulok
Phetchabun
Nong Khai
Udon Thani
Nakhon
Phanom
Khon Kaen
Nakhon
Sawan
Chaiyaphum
Roi Et
Ubon
Ratchathani
Nakhon
Ratchasima
Buriram
Sisaket
Phra Nakhon
Si Ayutthaya
Saraburi
Samut
Songkhram
BANGKOK
Samut Prakan
Chon Buri
Pattaya
Phet Buri
Sattahip
Rayong
Hua Hin
Chanthaburi
Trat
Ko Chang
Ko Kut
Bang Saphan
Prachuap
Khiri Khan
Chumphon
Kho Khot Kra
Ranong
Ko Phangan
Ko Samui
Surat Thani
Phangnga
1835
Nakhon Si Thammarat
Pak Phanang
Phuket
Thung Song
Phatthalung
Thale Luang
Trang
Kantang
Songkhla
Tarutao
Satun
Hat Yai
Yala
Narathiwat
Langkawi
Alor Setar
Pattani
Tumpat
Kota Baharu
Pasir Mas
Perhentian
Redang

LAOS
Vientiane
(Chanchan)
Muang
Khammouan
Savannakhet
Khemmarat
Pakxe
Attapu
Champasak
Stoeng Treng

Ba Don
Dong Hoi
Quang Tri
Hue
Da Nang
Hoi An
VIETNAM
Quang Ngai
Bong Son
Binh Dinh
Qui Nhon
Song Cau
Buon Me Thuot
2405
Nha Trang
Cam Ranh
Phan Rang
Mui Dinh
Phan Thiet
Vung Tau

Kon Tum
Plei Ku
A Yun Pa
Da Lat
Bien Hoa
THANH PHO HO CHI MINH

105
1701
2598
Mui Nay

CAMBODIA
Aranyaprathet
Siemreab
Batdambang
1813
Pouthisat
Kompong
Thom
Chhnang
Kompong
Cham
Kracheh
Senmonorom
Phnom Penh
(Phnum Penh)
Krong
Koh Kong
Kampong Saom
Takev
Kampot
Prey Veng
Svay Rieng
Kampong Cham

Phnom Dangrek
Khu Khan
Cheom Ksan
Kulen
461
Sisophon
Tonle Sap

Long
Xuyen
My Tho
Can Tho
Soc Trang
Bac Lieu
Ca Mau
Con Son
Mui Ca Mau
Rach Gia
Sa Dec
Dao Phu Quoc

Gulf
of
Thailand
Chaak Kampong Saom
Hon Chong
Phumi
Kaoh Kong

Coc
Chau O

SOUTH
CHINA
SEA

Paracel Is.
4424
Nanshan I.
Loaita I.
Itu Aba I.
Sin Cowe I.
Spratly Is.
Amboyna Cay
Spratly I.

ANDAMAN
SEA

Zadetkyi Kyan

Strait of Malacca

We
Sabang
Banda Aceh
Sigli
Meureudu
Bireuen
Idi
Lhokseumawe
A C E H
Peureulak
Langsa
Takengon
Kualasimpang
G. Leuser
3381
Pangkalanbrandan
Meulaboh
Calang
Ujung Raja
Belawan
Tapaktuan
Binjai
MEDAN
Tebingtinggi
Kabanjahe
Pematangsiantar
Prapat
Sinabang
Danau Toba
Simeulue
Tarutung
U T A R A
Kepulauan
Banyak
Sibolga
Rantauprapat
Lahewa
Gunungsitoli
Musala
Padangsidempuan
Nias
Telukdalem
Natal
Pini
Lubuksikaping
Kepulauan Batu
Tanahmasa
Tanahbala
Bukittinggi
B A R A T
Padangpanjang
Sawahlunto
Payakumbuh
Siberut
Sabulubbek
Padang
Solok
Sipura
Painan
Muarabungo
3805
Kerinci
Pulau
Pagai Utara
Sungaipenuh
Pulau
Pagai
Selatan
Bangko
Mukomuko
Muaratembesi
JAMBI
Jambi
Muaratebo

Lhokkruet

PENINSULAR
MALAYSIA
Butterworth
George Town
Sungai Petani
Pinang
Kuala
Taiping
Ipoh
Kuala Kubu
Baharu
Teluk
Intan
Kampar
Kuala Lipis
Gunong Tahan
2190
Temerloh
Kota Kinabalu
Seremban
KUALA LUMPUR
Kelang
Pelabuhan Kelang
Port Dickson
Melaka
Segamat
Muar
Batu Pahat
Keluang
Mersing
Johor Baharu
SINGAPORE
Bintan
Tanjungpinang

Kuantan
Kemaman
Dungun
Tenggol
Pulau
Tioman

Kuala Terengganu

MALAYSIA

Kepulauan
Natuna
Besar
Matak
Binjai
Natuna
Besar
Telukbutun
Laut

Siantan
Kepulauan
Anambas
Midai
Subi
Kepulauan
Natuna Selatan
Serasan

BRUNEI
Tutong
Kuala Belait
Seria
Miri
Niah
Bandar Seri Begawan
Pulau Labuan
Labuan

Kota Belud
Gunong
Kinabalu
4101
Kota Kinabalu
Beaufort
Papar
Ranau
Tenom

SABAH
Melalap
Lawas
Limbang
2438

Kudat
Langkon
Mt. Mantali
Bugs
Balabac
Balabac St.
C. Buliluyan

SARAWAK
Mukah
Oya
Bintulu
Bintangor
Sibu
Kanowit
Sarikei
Kapit
Saratok
Betung
Bau
Kuching
Lundu
Tanjung Datu
Niut
1701
Bandar Sri Aman
Ngabang

Pegunungan
2988
Longnawan
Tanjungredeb
Longiram
1758
G. Saran
2278
Putussibau
Semitau
Sintang
Nangapinoh
Muarajuloi
Sanggau
B A R A T
Sekadau
Serian

K A L I M A N T A N
T I M U R
Tanjungselor
Tarakan
Sangkulirang
Tanjungredeb
Muarakaman
Samarinda
Balikpapan

Tanjung
Puting

K A L I M A N T A N
T E N G A H
Nangatayap
Sukadana
Ketapang
Pangkalanbuun
Sampit
Kumai
Semuda
Palangkaraya
Kualakapuas
Muaratewe
Purukcahu
Tenggarong
Kualakurun
Kualapembuang
Buntok

Kendawangan

K A L I M A N T A N
S E L A T A N
Amuntai
Barabai
Kandangan
Martapura
BANJARMASIN
Pelaihari
Pagatan
Kotabaru
Sebuku
Karambu
Pulau Laut

I N D O N E S I A

Pekanbaru
Bangkinang
Siaksriindrapura
R I A U
Rengat
Dumai
Bengkalis
Rupat
Bagansiapiapi
Tanjungbalai

Kepulauan
Riau
Lingga
Singkep
Kepulauan
Lingga
Pulau
Berhala

Selat Berhala

Tanjungpandan
Belitung
Manggar
Toboali
Bangka
Pangkalpinang
Sungailiat
Mempawah
Singkawang
Sambas
Kepulauan
Tambelan
Kepulauan
Badas

Pontianak

Selat Karimata
Kepulauan
Karimata

Belinyu
Muntok
Dendang
Tanjungpandan

Sungaigerong
PALEMBANG
Sekayu
Lubuklinggau
Curup
Tebingtinggi
Muaraenim
Lahat
S E L A T A N
Perabumulih
Sarolangun
Bengkulu
Dempo
3159
BENGKULU
Baturaja
Menggala
Kotabumi
Manna
Martapura

Tg. Lumut

Tanjungkarang
Telukbetung
LAMPUNG
Kotaagung
Kalianda
Merak
Serang
Selat Sunda
Panaitan
Rakata
(Krakatau)
JAKARTA
Bogor
Sukabumi
BANDUNG
Tasikmalaya
Cilacap

Enggano
6073

Teluk Pelabuhan
Ratu

INDIAN
OCEAN

Java Trench
6650

Greater   *Sunda*   *Islands*

Java   *SEA*

Kepulauan
Seribu
Kepulauan
Karimunjawa
Bawean
Kepulauan
Sangkapura
Kepulauan
Masalembo
Kepulauan
Laut Kecil
Kepulauan
Masalim

Plered
Purwakarta
Jatibarang
Cirebon
Brebes
Tegal
Pemalang
Pekalongan
Kendal
SEMARANG
Tuban
Bojonegoro
Gresik
Bangkalan
Madura
Sampang
SURABAYA
Magelang
Slamet
3428
T E N G A H
Kebumen
Yogyakarta
Lawu
3265
Madiun
Kediri
Probolinggo
Pasuruan
Jember
Singaraja
Garut
Surakarta
2563
Blitar
3670
Malang
Semeru
Banyuwangi
BALI
Agung
Rinjani
3142
Lombok
T I M U R
Tulungagung
Deupasar
3726
Mataram
Praya
Taliwang
Sumb

NUSA TENGGARA
BARAT

J a v a
Lesser

ft   m
12 000   4000
9000   3000
6000   2000
4500   1500
3000   1000
1200   400
600   200
0   0
200   600
2000   6000
4000   12 000
6000   18 000
8000   24 000
m   ft

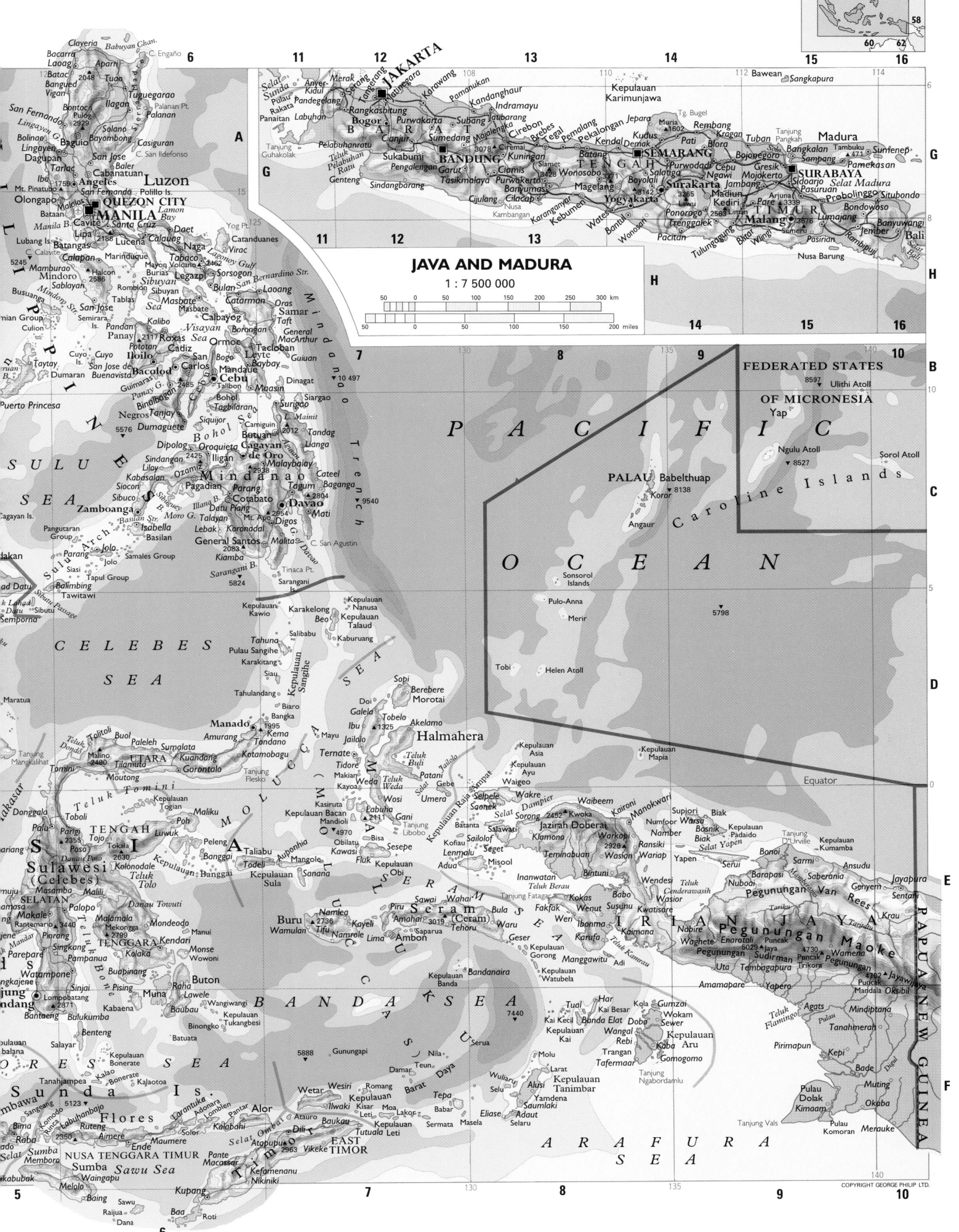

JAVA AND MADURA

1 : 7 500 000

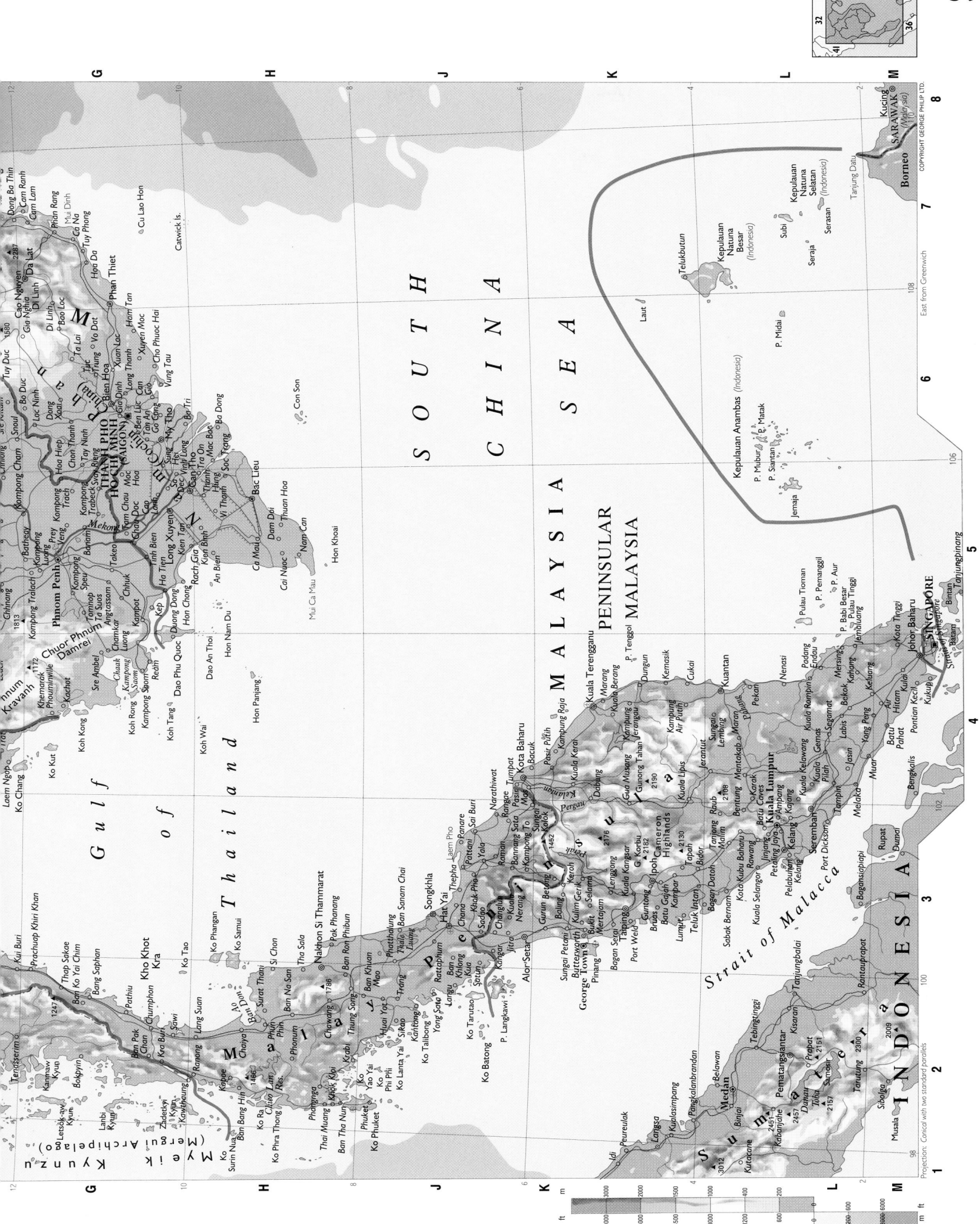

SOUTH CHINA SEA

Gulf of Thailand

Gulf

of

Thailand

MALAYSIA

PENINSULAR MALAYSIA

Strait of Malacca

INDONESIA

Sumatera

Borneo

SARAWAK (Malaysia)

Kucing

Kepulauan Natuna Selatan (Indonesia)

Kepulauan Natuna Besar (Indonesia)

Kepulauan Anambas (Indonesia)

SINGAPORE

Kuala Lumpur

George Town

East from Greenwich

Projection: Conic with two standard parallels

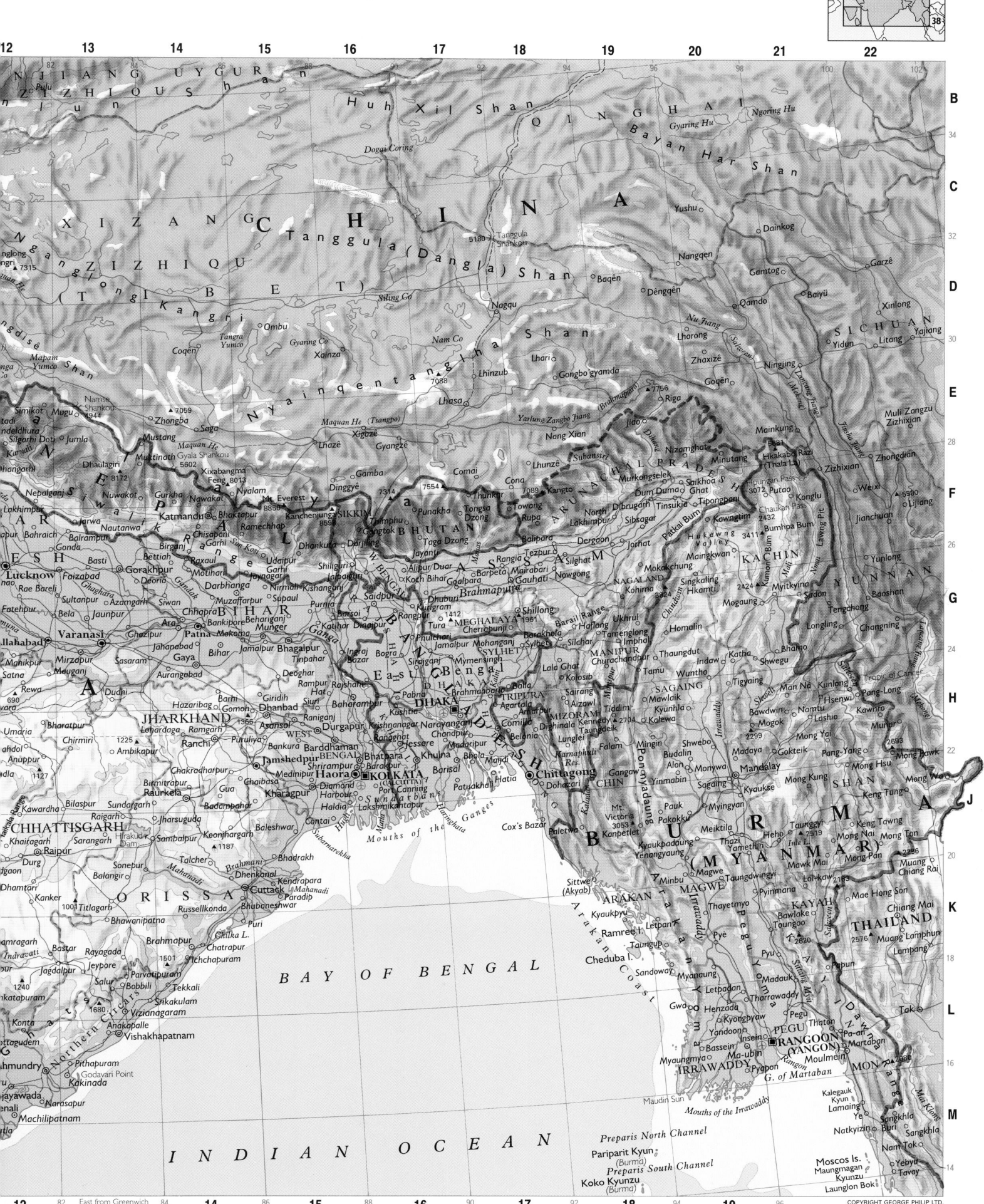

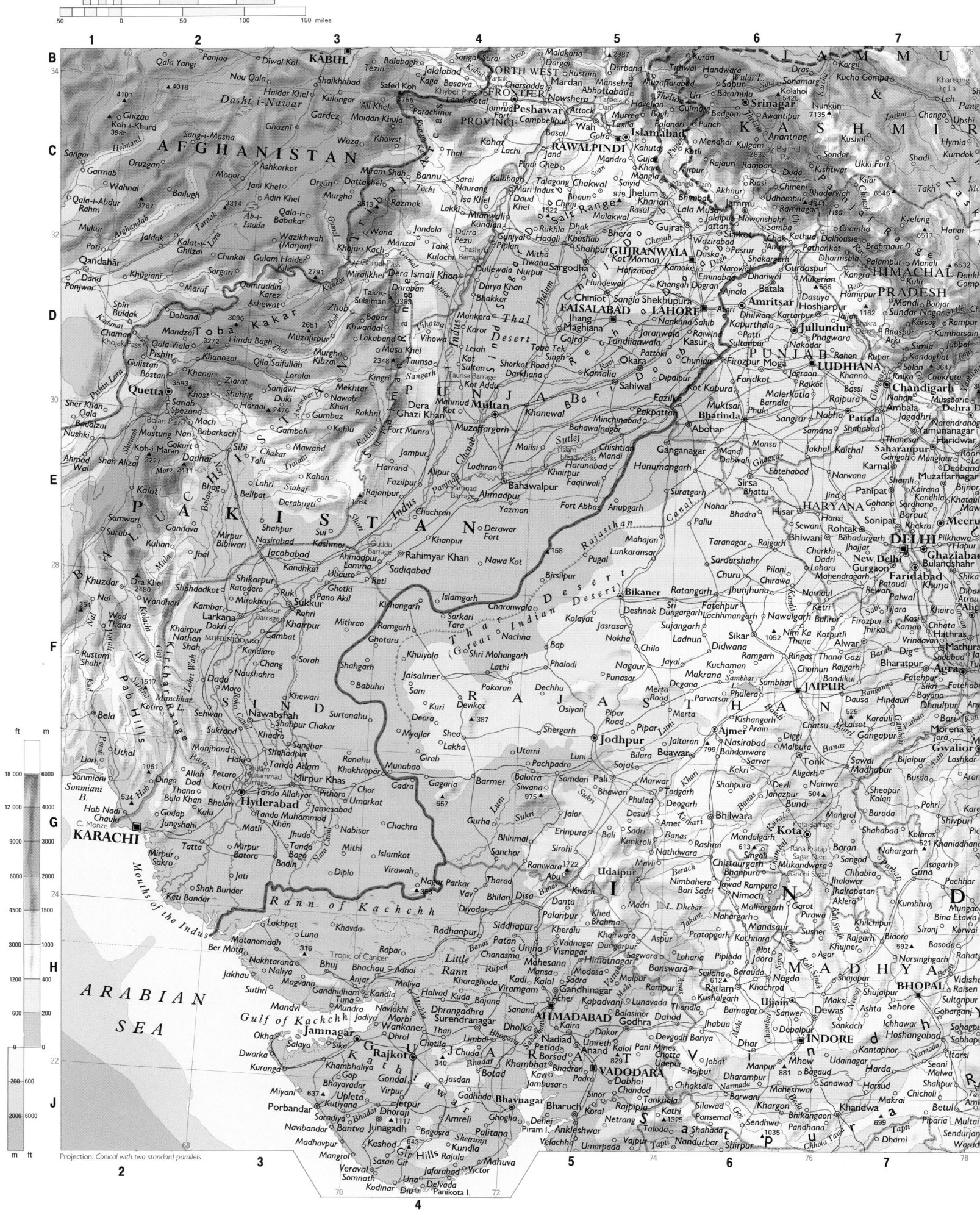

32
40
41
40

JAMMU AND KASHMIR
On same scale as Main Map
CHINA
Karakoram Range
Kunlun Shan
Aksai Chin
Northern Areas
NORTH WEST FRONTIER
PUNJAB
JAMMU & KASHMIR
Zaskar Mountains
Ladakh Range
HIMACHAL PRADESH
Srinagar
Islamabad
RAWALPINDI
AFGHANISTAN
CHINA
Gangdisê Shan
Nganglong Kangri
XIZANG ZIZHIQU (TIBET)
UTTARANCHAL
NEPAL
Himalaya
Mt. Everest
Katmandu
SIKKIM
BHUTAN
Thimphu
ASSAM
UTTAR PRADESH
LUCKNOW
KANPUR
Allahabad
VARANASI
BIHAR
PATNA
JHARKHAND
Ranchi
Dhanbad
MADHYA PRADESH
Jabalpur
CHHATTISGARH
WEST BENGAL
KOLKATA
BANGLADESH
DHAKA
Khulna
Mouths of the Ganges
The Sandheads
East from Greenwich
COPYRIGHT GEORGE PHILIP LTD.

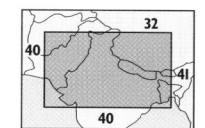

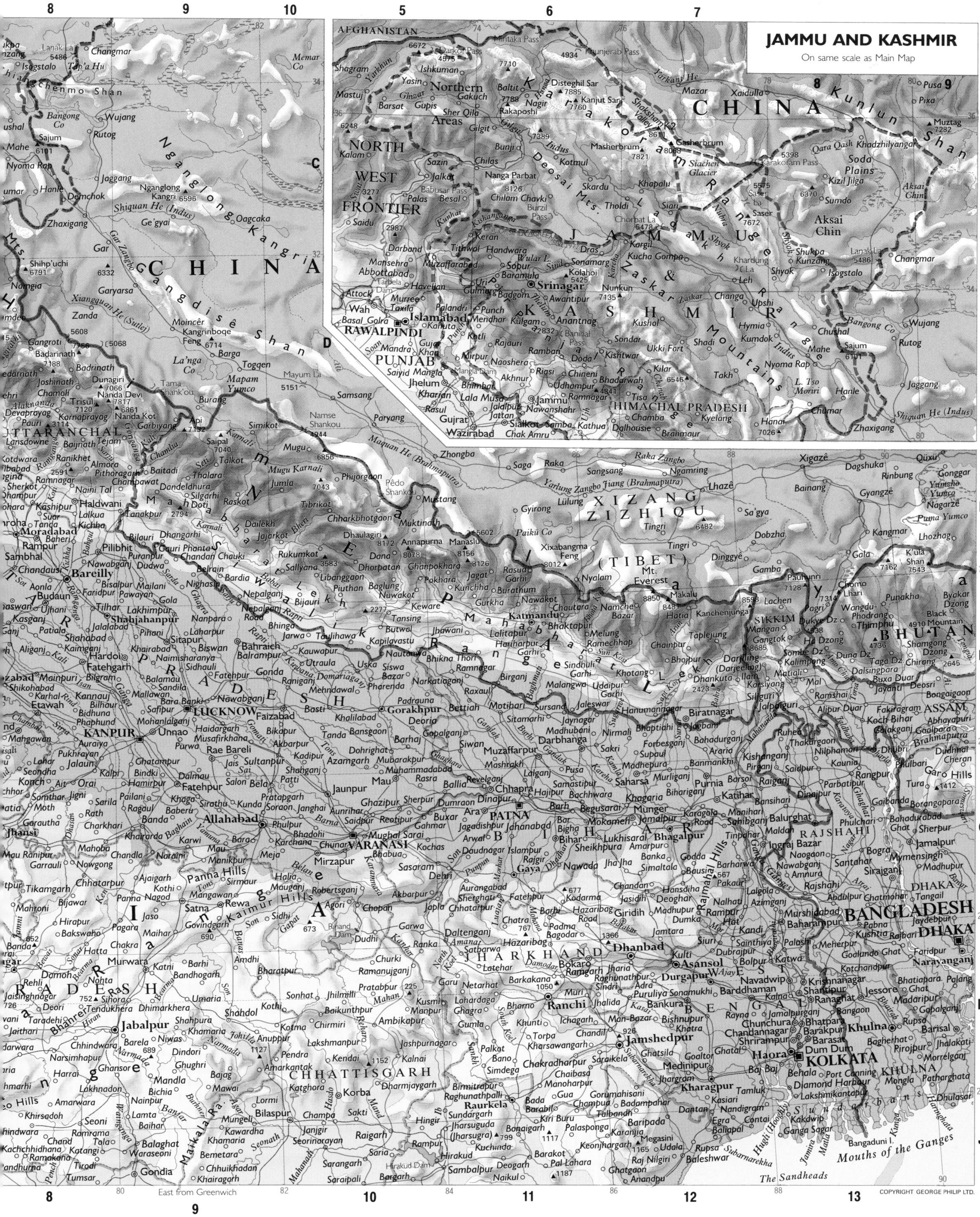

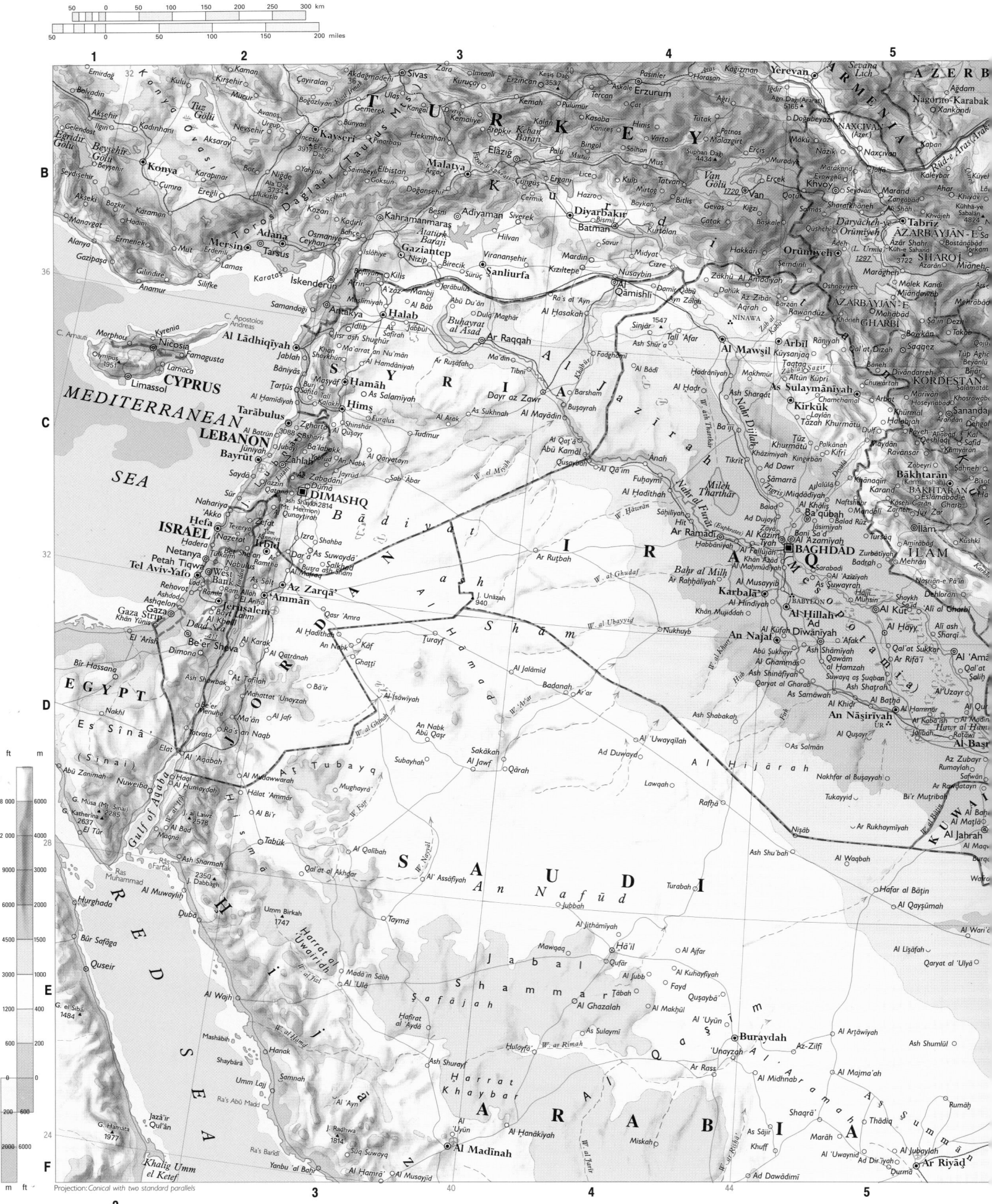

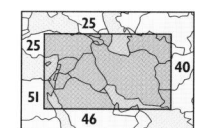

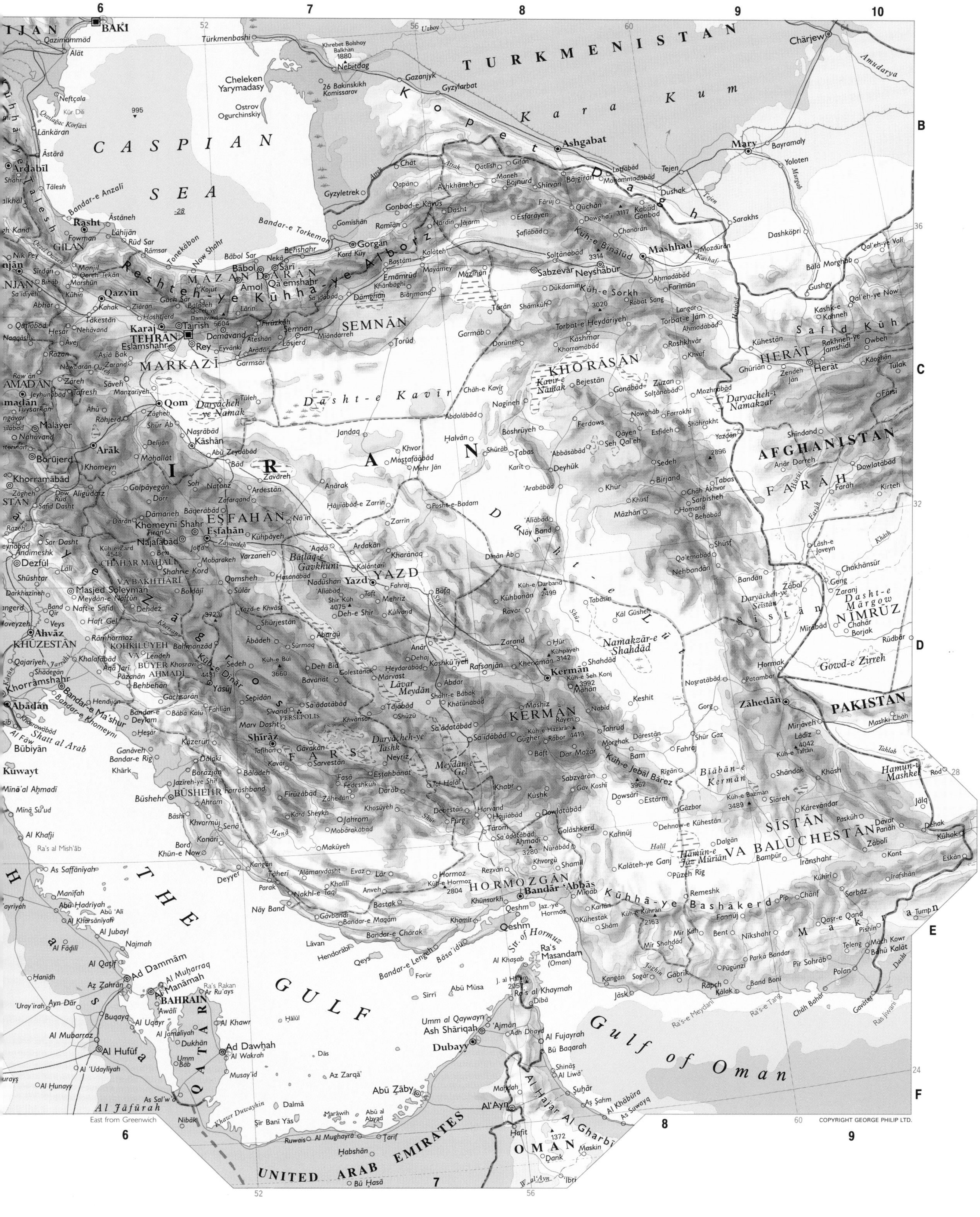

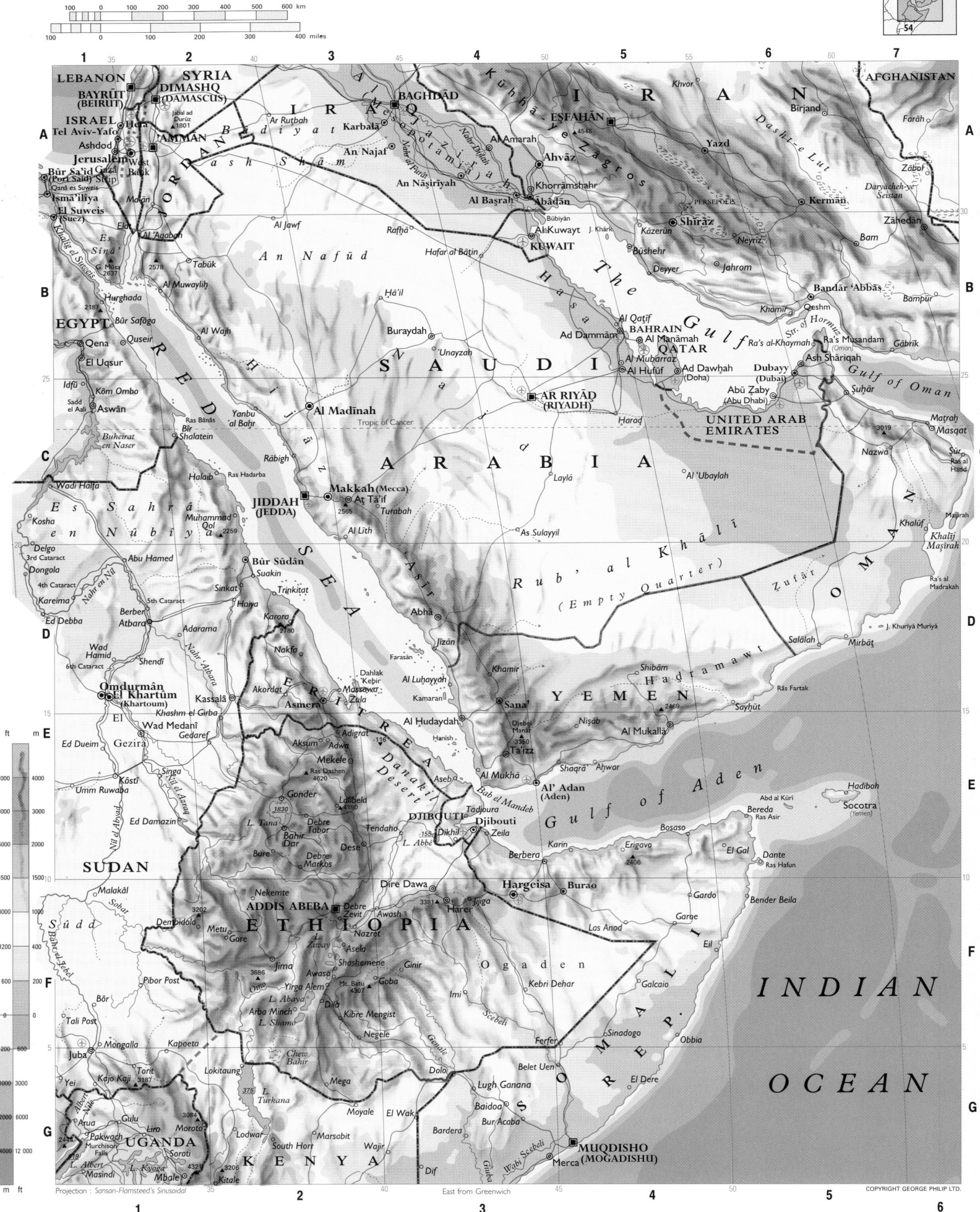

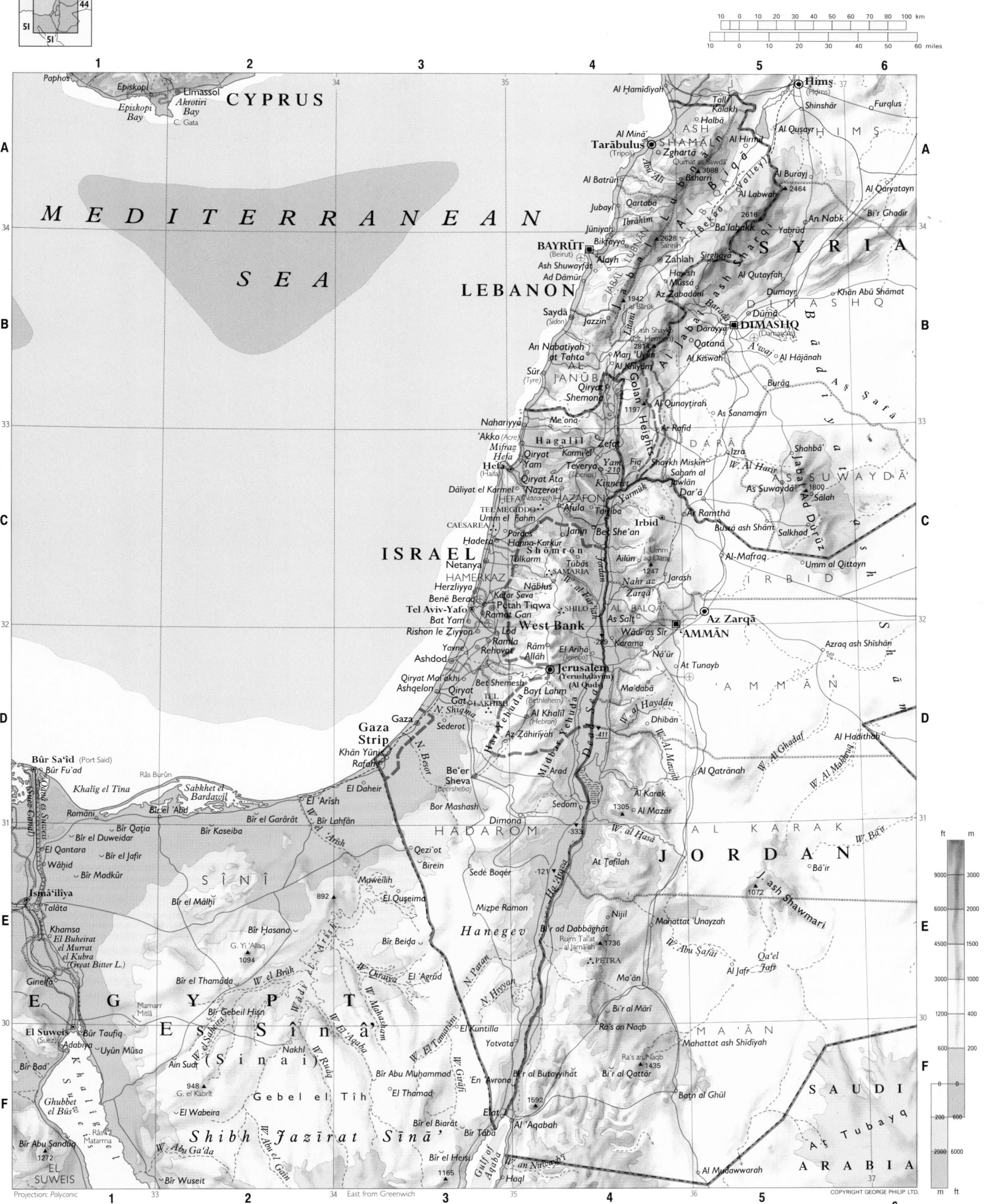

- - - 1974 Cease Fire Lines

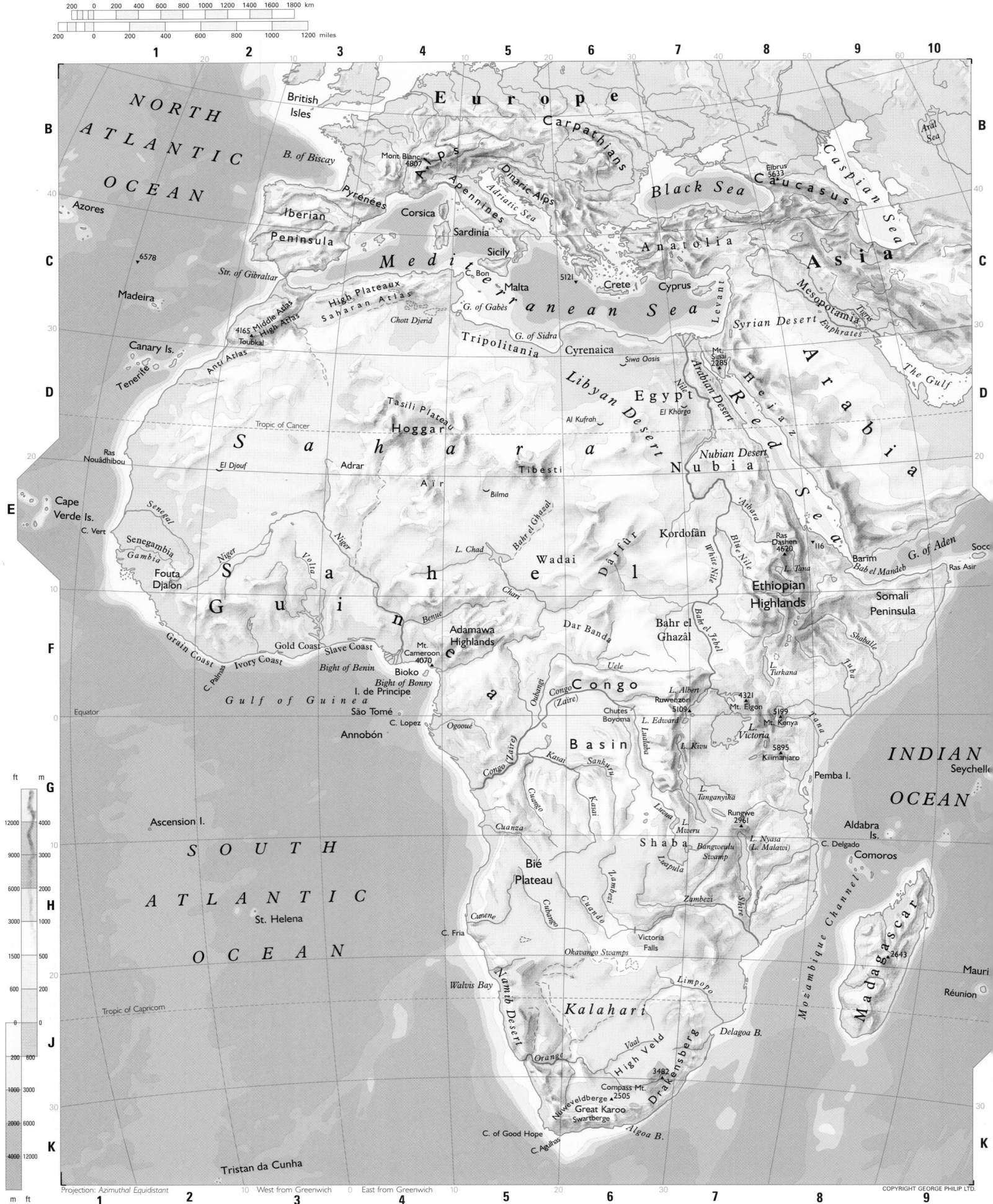

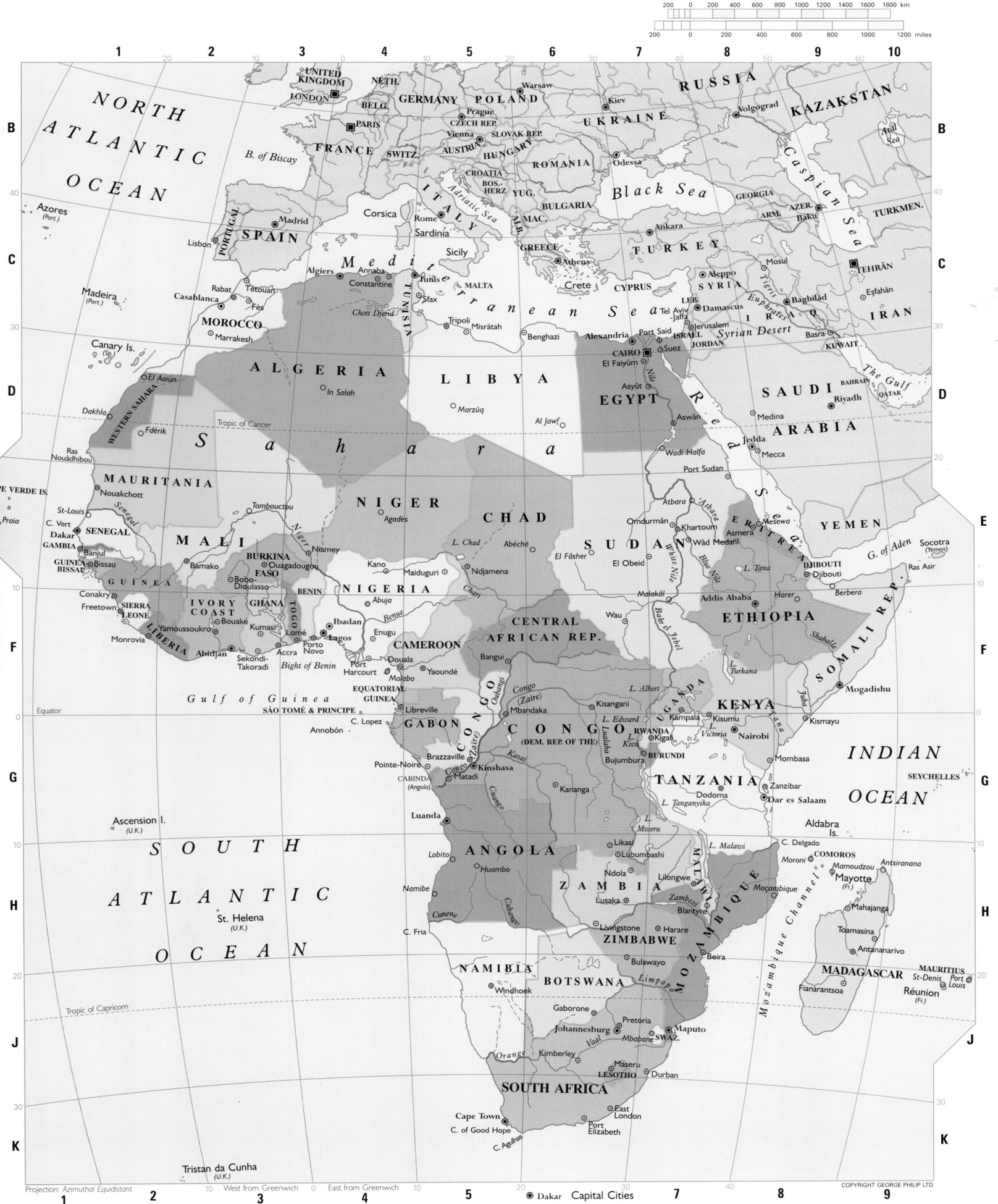

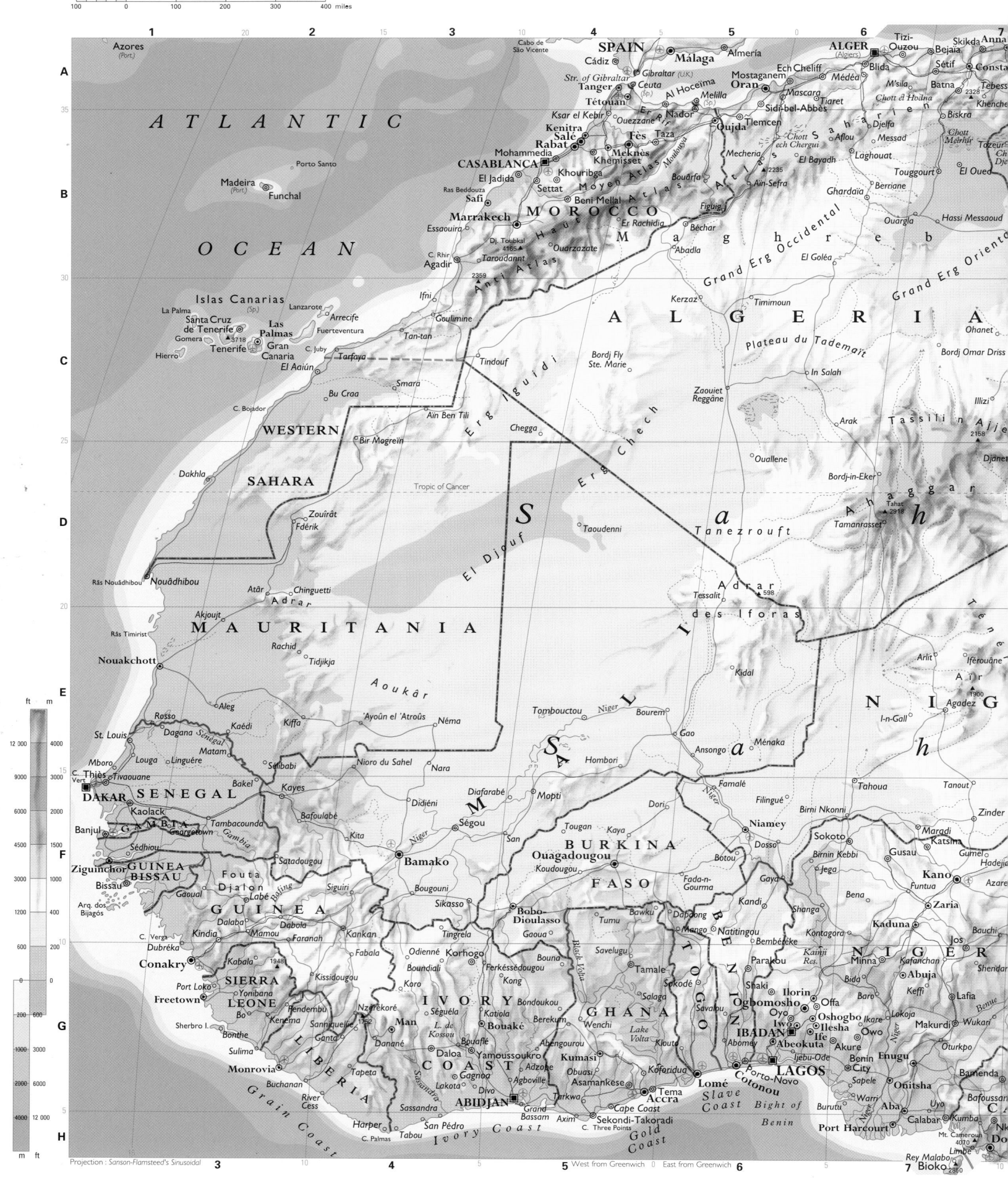

Projection: Sanson-Flamsteed's Sinusoidal

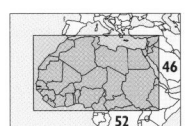

MEDITERRANEAN SEA

GREECE

TURKEY

Bizerte
Ariana
CARTHAGE
TUNIS
Béja
Nabeul
Sousse
Kairouan
Mahdia
Sfax
Golfe de Gabès
Gabès
Île de Djerba
Médenine
Zarzis
Dehibat
Ghudāmis
Daraj

Sicilia

MALTA
Valletta

Antalya
Ródhos
Kríti

Al Lādhiqiyah
Nicosia
CYPRUS

ADANA
Antakya
HALAB

SYRIA

IRAQ

Nahr al Furāt

Ar Rutbah

Tarābulus
Ḩimṣ

LEBANON
BAYRŪT
(Beirut)

DIMASHQ
(Damascus)

Bādiyat
ash Shām

Zāwiyat al Baydā
Darnah

Banghāzī
Al Marj
Tubruq
Bardīyah
Salūm
EL ISKANDARĪYA
(Alexandria)

El Mahalla el Kubra
Damanhūr
Dumyāt
Bûr Sa'îd

El Mansûra
Ismā'îlîya
Tanta
Zagazig
EL QAHIRA
(Cairo)
Qanâ es Suweis

Tel Aviv-Yafo
ISRAEL
Ashdod
Jerusalem
West Bank

Ḩefa
AMMAN

JORDAN

Jabal ad Durūz

Ma'ān

Zuwārah
Tarābulus (Tripoli)
Al Khums
Az Zāwiyah
Misrātah
Gharyān 968
Mizdah

Tripolitania
Surt
Khalīj Surt
Suluq
Ajdābiyā

Cyrenaica

Marsá Matrûh
El Alamein

EL GÎZA
Helwân
El Faiyûm
Beni Suef
Maghâgha
El Minya
Mallawi
Manfalût
Asyût
Tahta
Sohâg
Girga

EL QAHIRA
El Suweis
El Suweis

Es Sînâ'
G. Mûsa 2637

Al 'Aqabah
Elat

Tabûk 2578

SAUDI
ARABIA

Al Muwayliḥ

Al Jaghbūb
Munkhafed el Qattâra -133

Sîwa

Sahrâ'

EGYPT

Es Sahrâ
Esh Sharqîya

Hurghada
2187
Bûr Safâga
Quseir

Al Wajh

Hūn
Brach

Idehan-awbārī
LIBYA
▲1200
Sabhah

Lîbîya

Qasr Farâfra
Mût
Qena
THEBES KARNAK
El Uqsur
Idfû
Kom Ombo
Sadd el Aali
Aswân

El Wâhât el-Dakhla
El Khârga
El Wâhât el-Khârga

Girga
Sohâg

Quseir

Ras Bānās
Bîr Shalatein

Yanbu al Baḩr

Marzûq
Awbārī

Fezzan
Ghat

Waw al Kabir
Al Qatrūn
Sahrâ' Rebiana
Al Jawf
Al Kufrah

1082

ABU SIMBEL
Wâdi Halfa

J. Uweinat 1893

El Wâhât el Selîma

Buḩairat en Naser

Halaib
Ras Hadarba

Rābigh

Ḩijāz

RED SEA

Toummo
Madama
Chirfa
Fachi
Bilma

Bardai
Aozou
Pic Toussidé 3265
Tarso Emissi ▲3150

Tibesti
Zouar
Emi Koussi ▲3415

Aozou Strip

Ma'tan as Sarra

Es Sahrâ en Nûbîya

Kosha
Delgo
Dongola
Abu Hamed
3rd Cataract

Muhammad Qol ▲2259

Bûr Sûdân
Suakin
Sinkat
Trinkitât

Karora ▲2780
Nakfa

ERITREA

Grand Erg du Bilma

ER

Borkou
Faya-Largeau
Erg du Djourab
Ounianga Sérir
Dépression du Mourdi
Fada
Ennedi ▲1310
Zagaoua
Oum Chalouba

CHAD

Kareima
Ed Debba
4th Cataract
Berber
Atbara
5th Cataract
6th Cataract
Wad Hamid
Shendî

Adarama

Haiya

Akordat

Bilma

Zigey
Mao
Lac Tchad
Bosso
Bol
Moussoro
Ati
Massakory
Bahr el Ghazal

Abéché
Oum Hadjer
Biltine

Al Junaynah
Kutum
1954

Darfûr
Jebel Mara 3088
Zalingei
El Fâsher
Nyâlâ

Malha
Sodiri
Umm Keddada
En Nahud
Abū Zabad
El Odaiya

Kordofân

El Obeid
Umm Ruwaba
Er Rahad

SUDAN

Omdurmân
El Khartûm
(Khartoum)

El Gezira

Kassalâ

Khashm el Girba
Gedaref

Wâd Medanî
Ed Dueim
Kôstî
Singa

Nîl el Azraq

Gonder
▲1830
L. Tana
Bahir Dar
Bure
Debre Markos
Nekemte

Nguigmi
Gashua
Nguru
Geidam
Maiduguri
Potiskum
Bajoga
Kumo

Ndjamena
Kousseri
Bama
Maroua
Biu
Mubi
Guider

Bokoro
Massenya
Mongo
Bongor
Abou-Deia
Am Timan

Goz Beida

Birao
Songo

1325

Kâdugli

Sa'îd Bundas

Bahr el Arab
Raga
Ghazâl
Gogrial
Wâw
Tonj

Bahr el Ghazal
Malakâl
Sobat
Bahr el Jebel
Rumbêk

3202
ETHIOPIA
Dempidolo
Metu
Gore
▲3686
Jima

Yola
Garoua
Pala
Moundou
Laï
Koumra
Doba
Sarh
Ndélé

1276

CENTRAL AFRICAN REPUBLIC

Kaga Bandoro
Bossangoa
Bouar
Bozoum
Sibut
Bambari
Ippy
Bakouma
Obo

El Istiwâ'îya
Bôr
Amâdi
Tali Post
Toinya
Pibor Post

▲3187
Kapoeta
Lokitaung
L. Turkana

L. Abaya
Arba Minch
L. Shamo
Chew Bahir

Yaoundé
Bertoua
Abong-Mbang
Nanga-Eboko
Yoko
Foumban
Bétaré Oya
Berbérati
Carnot
Bossembélé
Bangui
Zongo
Mbaïki
Libenge
Bosobolo
Mobayi
Bondo
Uele
Ango
Dungu
Faradje
Yei
Juba
Torit
Kajo Kaji
Mongalla

Massif de Adamaoua
Gashaka
Banyo
Ngaoundéré
Paoua
Yalinga

MEROON

375

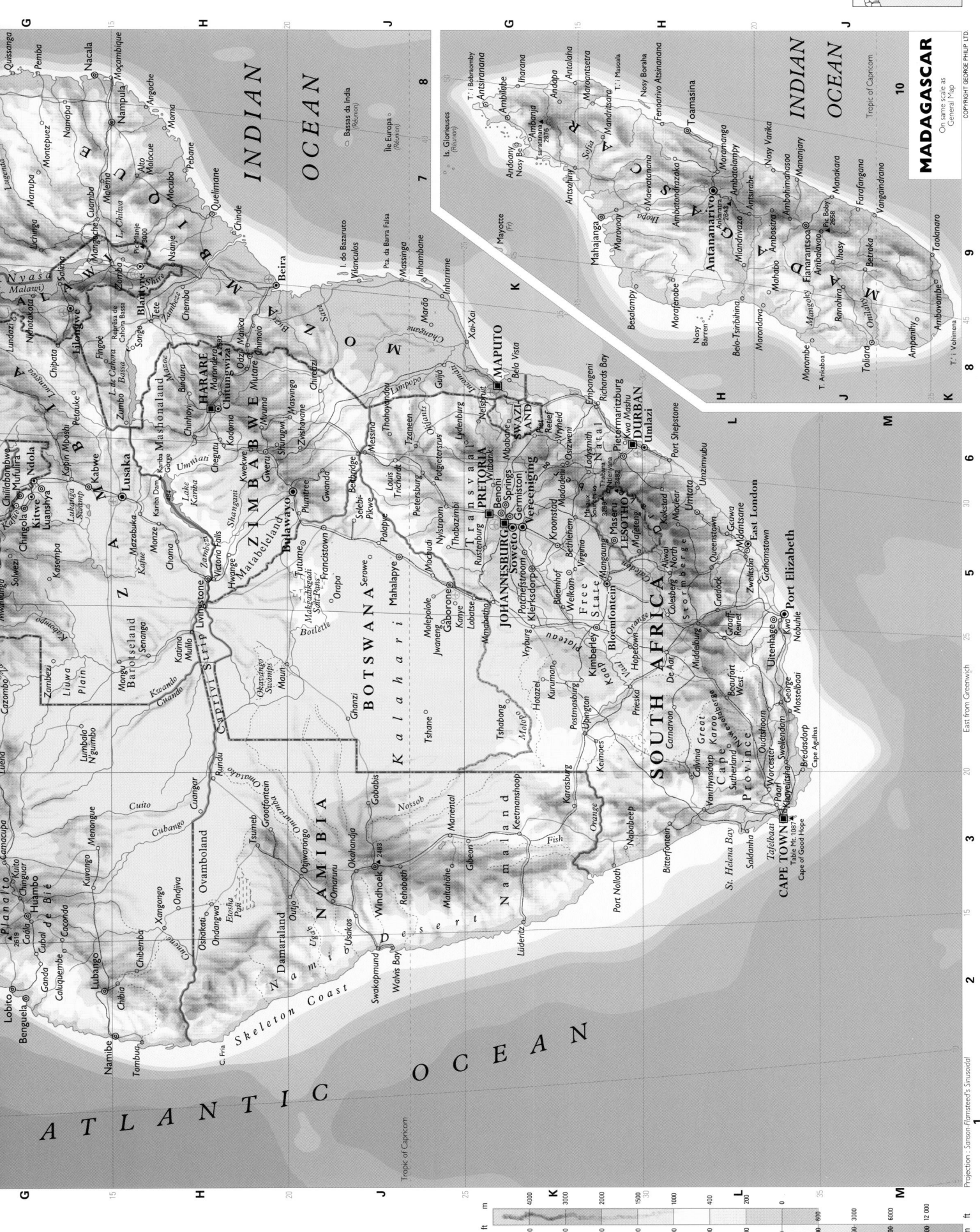

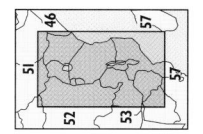

55

E   F   G

INDIAN

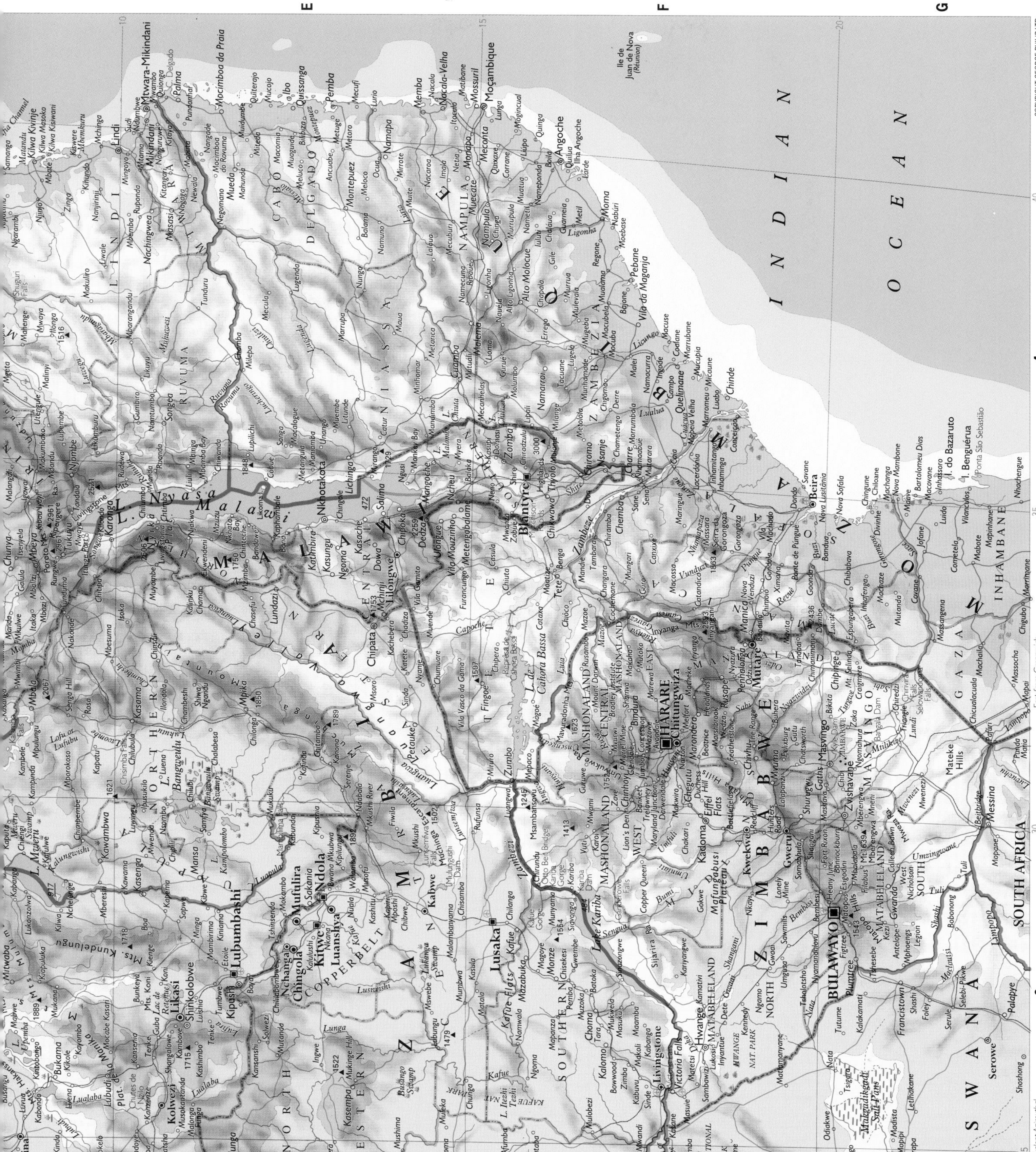

OCEAN

Ile de Juan de Nova (Réunion)

LINDI

CABO DELGADO

NIASSA

NAMPULA

ZAMBEZIA

L. Nyasa (L. Malawi)

MALAWI

Lilongwe

Blantyre

Zomba

Beira

MOÇAMBIQUE

ZAMBIA

Lusaka

Ndola

Kitwe

Luanshya

Mufulira

Chingola

Lubumbashi

Likasi

Kolwezi

COPPERBELT

NORTHERN

WESTERN

ZIMBABWE

HARARE

Chitungwiza

Mutare

Gweru

Kwekwe

Kadoma

BULAWAYO

MASHONALAND

MATABELELAND

MANICALAND

MASVINGO

MIDLANDS

Victoria Falls

Livingstone

Lake Kariba

Zambezi

BOTSWANA

Serowe

Shoshong

NAMIBIA

Caprivi Strip

ANGOLA

SOUTH AFRICA

Messina

Beitbridge

Limpopo

Mwanza-Mikindani

Lindi

Pemba

Nacala-Velha

Angoche

Quelimane

Tete

Chipata

Nata

Makgadikgadi Salt Pans

Projection: Lambert's Equivalent Azimuthal

East from Greenwich

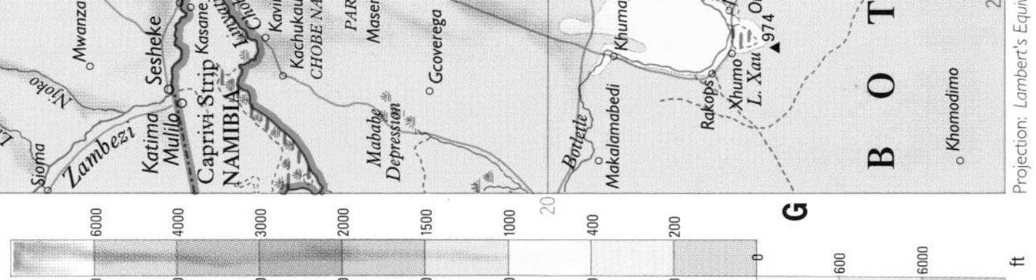

m   ft
6000   18 000
4000   12 000
3000   9000
2000   6000
1500   4500
1200   3000
600   1200
200   600
0   0
200   600
2000   6000
m   ft

1   2   3   4   5

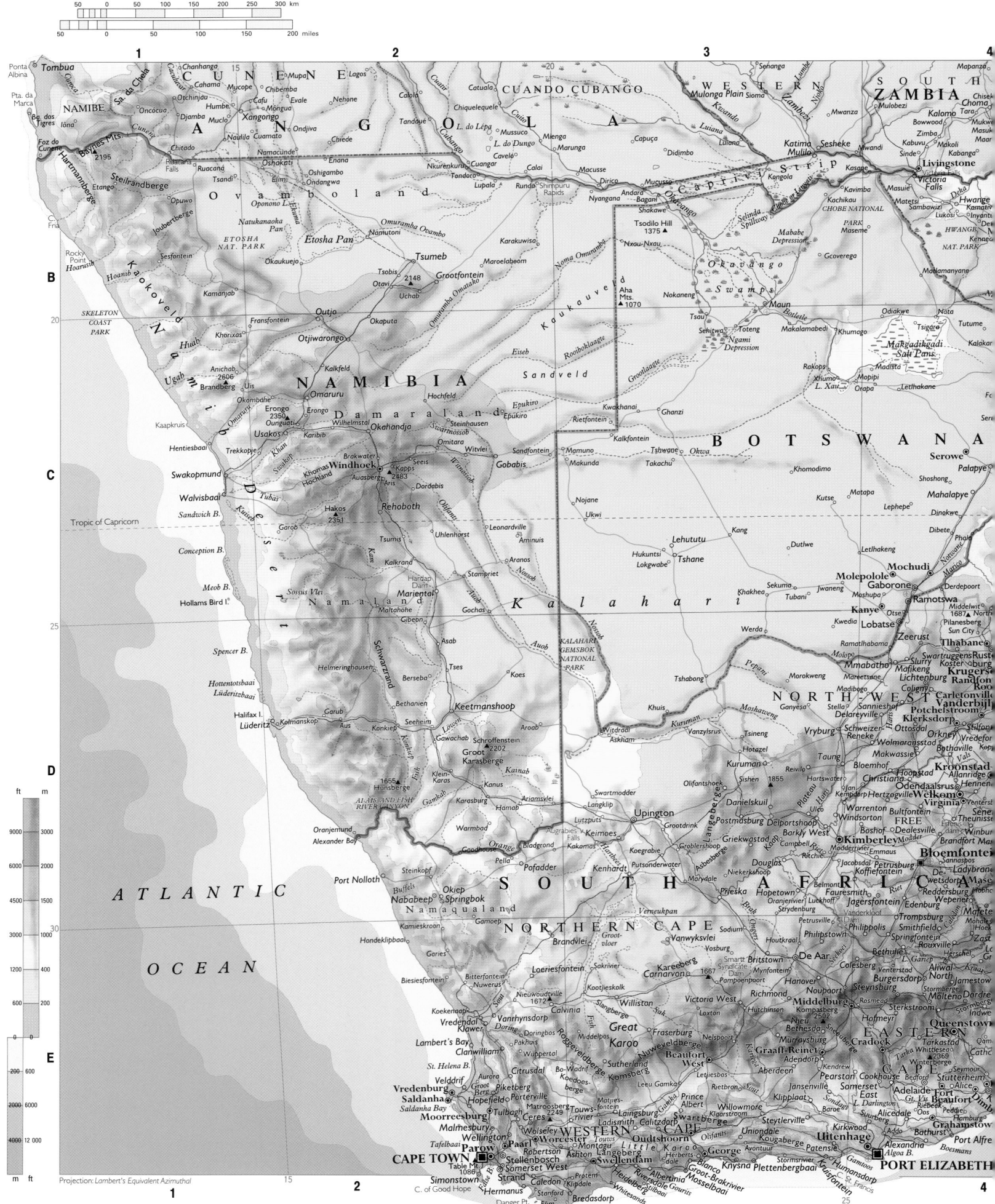

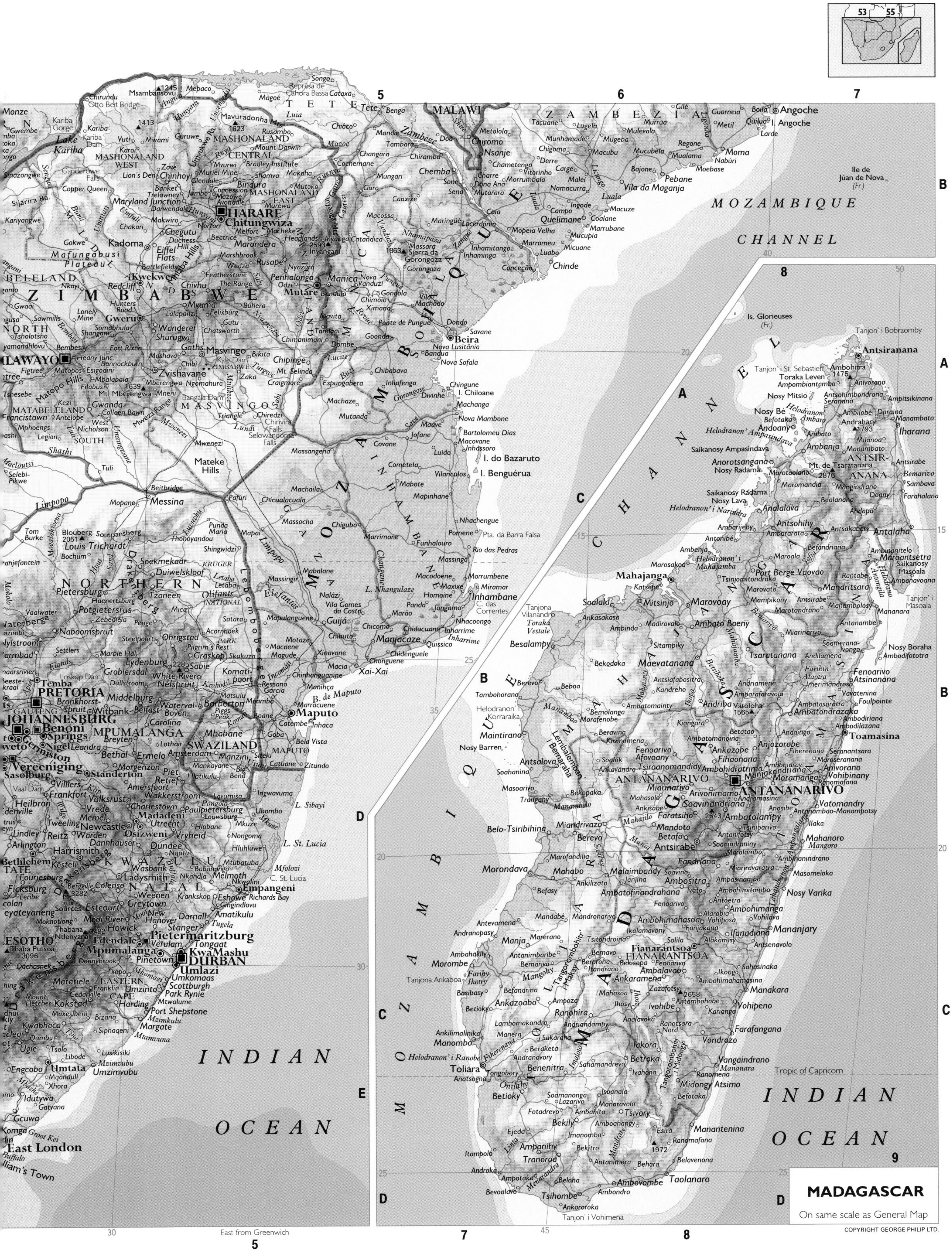

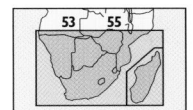

MOZAMBIQUE CHANNEL

ZIMBABWE

MOZAMBIQUE

MALAWI

ZAMBEZIA

TETE

MANICA

MASHONALAND

MASVINGO

MATABELELAND

NORTHERN

GAUTENG

MPUMALANGA

SWAZILAND

KWAZULU / NATAL

EASTERN CAPE

MADAGASCAR

ANTSIRANANA

MAHAJANGA

TOAMASINA

ANTANANARIVO

FIANARANTSOA

TOLIARA

INDIAN OCEAN

HARARE
Chitungwiza
BULAWAYO
Gweru
Kadoma
PRETORIA
JOHANNESBURG
Maputo
Beira
Quelimane
Mahajanga
Antananarivo
Antsirabe
Fianarantsoa
Toliara
Toamasina
Antsiranana
DURBAN
Pietermaritzburg
East London
Tropic of Capricorn
East from Greenwich

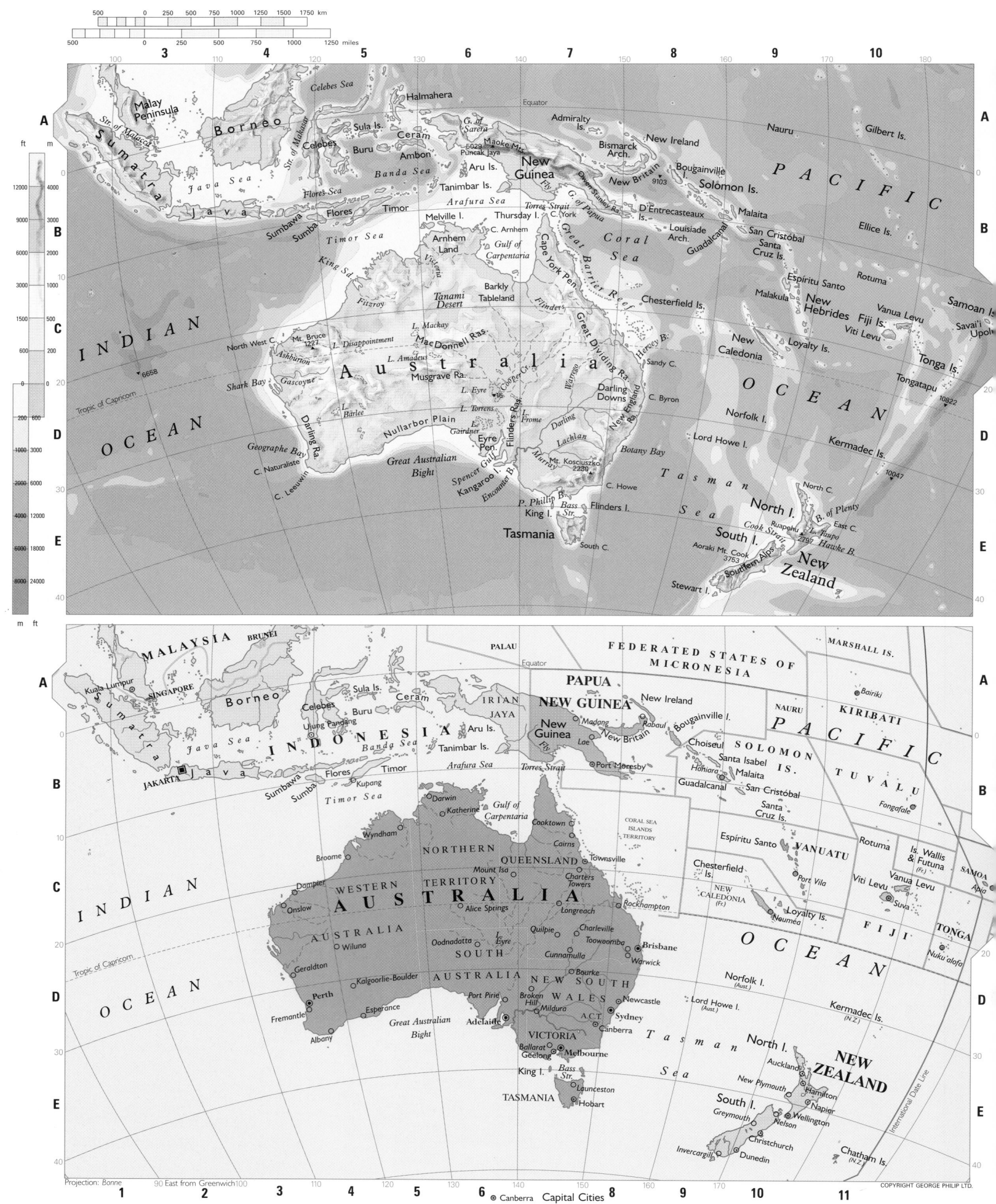

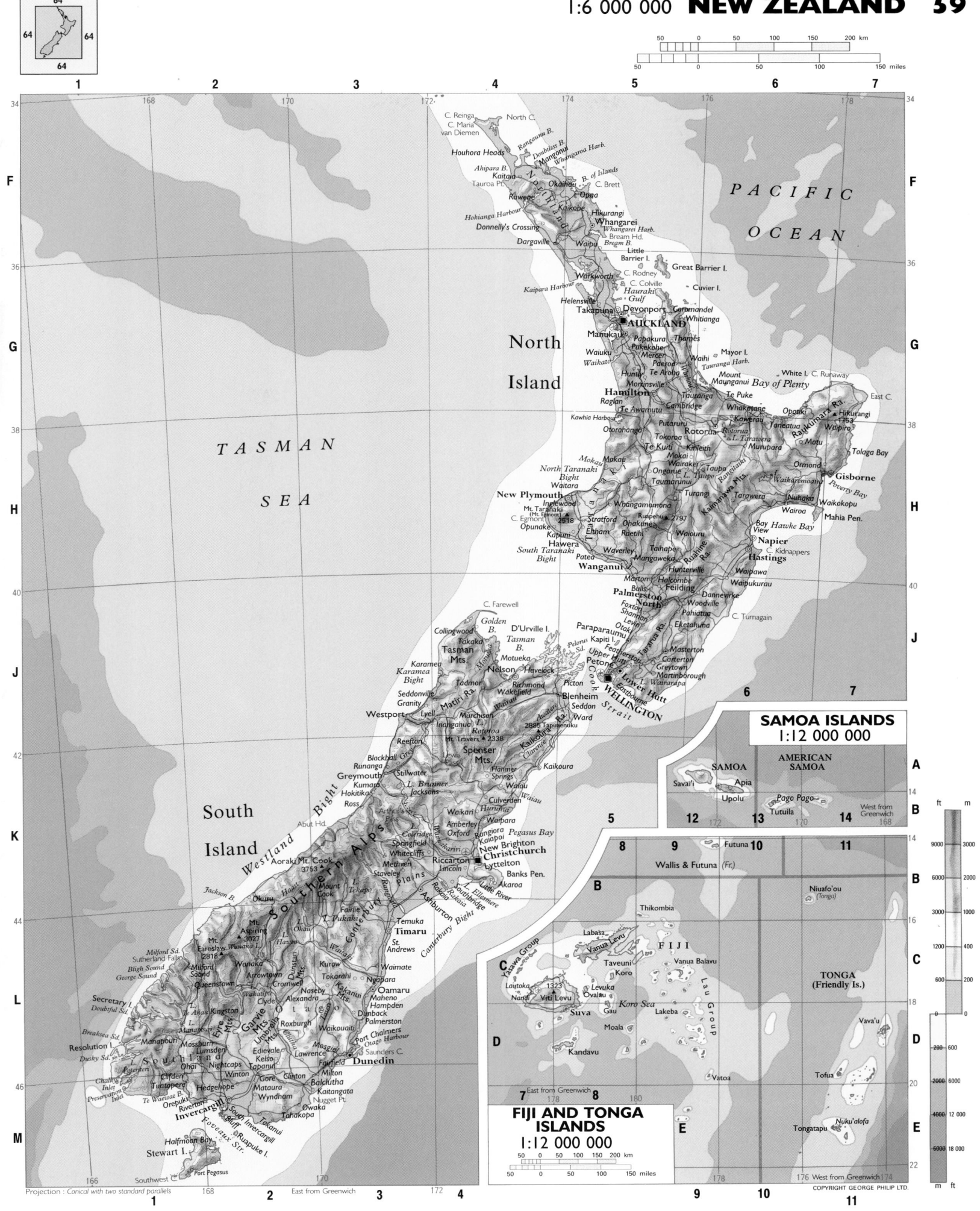

50   0   50   100   150   200 km
50   0   50   100   150 miles

F

PACIFIC

OCEAN

C. Reinga
C. Maria
van Diemen
North C.
Rangaunu B.
Houhora Heads
Doubtless B.
Mangonui
Whangaroa Harb.
Ahipara B.
Kaitaia
Tauroa Pt.
Okahu
C. Brett
Rawene
Kaikohe
B. of Islands
Opua
Hokianga Harbour
Hikurangi
Donnelly's Crossing
Whangarei
Whangarei Harb.
Dargaville
Bream Hd.
Waipu
Bream B.

Little
Barrier I.

North
C. Rodney
Great Barrier I.
Warkworth
C. Colville
Kaipara Harbour
Cuvier I.
Helensville
Coromandel
Takapuna
Devonport
Whitianga
AUCKLAND
Manukau
Papakura
Thames
North
Waiuku
Pukekohe
Mercer
Waihi
Mayor I.
Island
Waikato
Paeroa
Mount
Huntly
Te Aroha
Maunganui
Bay of Plenty
Morrinsville
Tauranga
White I.
C. Runaway
Hamilton
Te Puke
East C.
Raglan
Cambridge
Whakatane
Kawerau
Te Awamutu
Putaruru
Rotorua
Opotiki
Kawhia Harbour
Tokoroa
Rotorua
Taneatua
Raukumara Ra.
Hikurangi
1753
Otorohanga
Te Kuiti
Kinleith
L. Tarawera
Murupara
Wilpiro
Mokau
Mokau
Te Kuiti
Wairakei
Taupo
Motu
Tolaga Bay
North Taranaki
Ongarue
L. Taupo
Bight
Waitara
Taumarunui
Ormond
New Plymouth
Inglewood
Turangi
Waikaremoana
Gisborne
Whangamomona
Ruapehu
Poverty Bay
Mt. Taranaki
Stratford
2797
Kaimanawa Mts.
(Mt. Egmont)
Ohakune
Nuhaka
C. Egmont
2518
Eltham
Raetihi
Waikokopu
Opunake
Kapuni
Waiouru
Mahia Pen.
Hawera
Taihape
Bay
Hawke Bay
South Taranaki
Waverley
Mangaweka
View
Bight
Patea
Rangiwaea Ra.
Napier
Wanganui
Marton
Hunterville
C. Kidnappers
Halcombe
Hastings
Bulls
Feilding
Waipawa
Palmerston
Woodville
Waipukurau
Foxton
North
Dannevirke
Shannon
Pahiatua
Levin
Eketahuna

TASMAN

SEA

C. Farewell
Golden
B.
D'Urville I.
Paraparaumu
Collingwood
Takaka
Tasman
Kapiti I.
Tararua Ra.
C. Turnagain
Tasman
B.
Mts.
Motueka
Upper Hutt
Masterton
Karamea
Pelorus Sd.
Fethe...
Carterton
Karamea
Nelson
Greytown
Bight
Maitai Ra.
Havelock
Petone
Martinborough
Richmond
WELLINGTON
Wairarapa
Seddonville
Wakefield
Picton
Lower Hutt
Granity
Lyell
Blenheim
Cook Strait
Westport
Murchison
Rotoroa
Seddon
Inangahua J.
Ward

South
Reefton
Mt. Travers ▲ 2338
2885 Tapuaenuku
Blackball
Spenser
Kaikoura
Runanga
Grey
Mts.
Greymouth
Stillwater
Lewis
Hanmer
Clarence
Island
Kumara
Pass
Springs
Kaikoura
Hokitika
L. Brunner
Ross
Jacksons
Waiau
Arthur's
Culverden
Pass
Hurunui
Waikari
Waiau
Amberley
Abut Hd.
Oxford
Rangiora
Pegasus Bay
Kaiapoi
Coldridge
New Brighton
Springfield
Christchurch
Whitecliffs
Riccarton
Lyttelton
Aoraki Mt. Cook
Lincoln
Banks Pen.
3753
Methven
L. Ellesmere
Little River
Staveley
Akaroa
Jackson B.
Okuru
Mount
Ashburton
Fairlie
Cook
Bight
L. Tekapo
Temuka
Timaru
Mt. Aspiring ▲ 3027
St.
Milford Sd.
Mt.
Andrews
Sutherland Falls
Earnslaw
Ohau
Bligh Sound
2818
Milford
Waimate
George Sound
Wanaka
Kurow
Ngapara
Queenstown
Arrowtown
Oamaru
Secretary I.
Cromwell
Maheno
Doubtful Sd.
Naseby
Hampden
Clyde
Dunback
Alexandra
Palmerston
Breaksea Sd.
Roxburgh
Waikouaiti
Resolution I.
Kingston
Port Chalmers
Dusky Sd.
Otago Harbour
Saunders C.
Mossburn
Lawrence
Dunedin
Manapouri
Fairfield
Te Anau
Lumsden
Milton
Secretary I.
Mosgiel
Clinton
Balclutha
Nightcaps
Gore
Kaitangata
Cliffen
Tuatapere
Hedgehope
Mataura
Nugget Pt.
Te Waewae B.
Orepuki
Winton
Wyndham
Owaka
Preservation
Riverton
Tokanui
Inlet
Invercargill
Tahakopa
Bluff
South Invercargill
Foveaux Str.
Ruapuke I.
Halfmoon Bay
Stewart I.
Southwest C.
Port Pegasus

SAMOA ISLANDS
1:12 000 000

AMERICAN
SAMOA
SAMOA
Savai'i
Apia
Upolu
Pago Pago
Tutuila
West from
Greenwich

Futuna
Wallis & Futuna (Fr.)
Niuafo'ou
(Tonga)
Thikombia
Labasa
Vanua Levu
Yasawa Group
Vanua Balavu
Taveuni
Koro
FIJI
Lautoka
1323
Levuka
Nandi
Viti Levu
Ovalau
Koro Sea
Lau Group
TONGA
Suva
Gau
Lakeba
(Friendly Is.)
Vava'u
Moala
Kandavu
Vatoa
Tofua
Tongatapu
Nuku'alofa

FIJI AND TONGA
ISLANDS
1:12 000 000
50   0   50   100   150   200 km
50   0   50   100   150 miles
East from Greenwich   West from Greenwich

ft   m
9000   3000
6000   2000
3000   1000
1200   400
600   200
0   0
200   600
2000   6000
4000   12 000
6000   18 000
m   ft

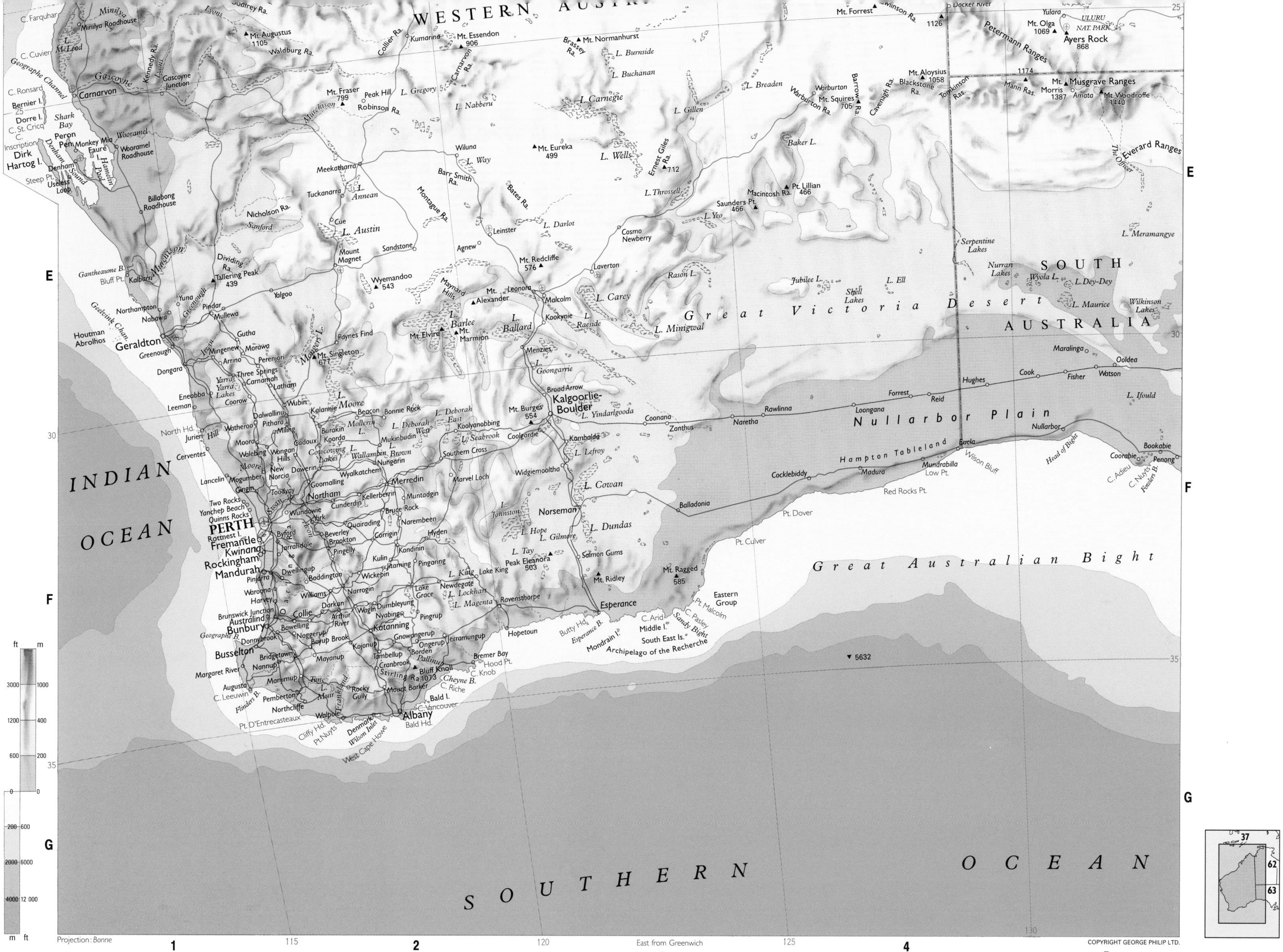

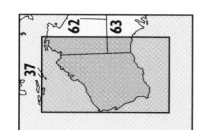

Projection: Bonne

East from Greenwich

COPYRIGHT GEORGE PHILIP LTD.

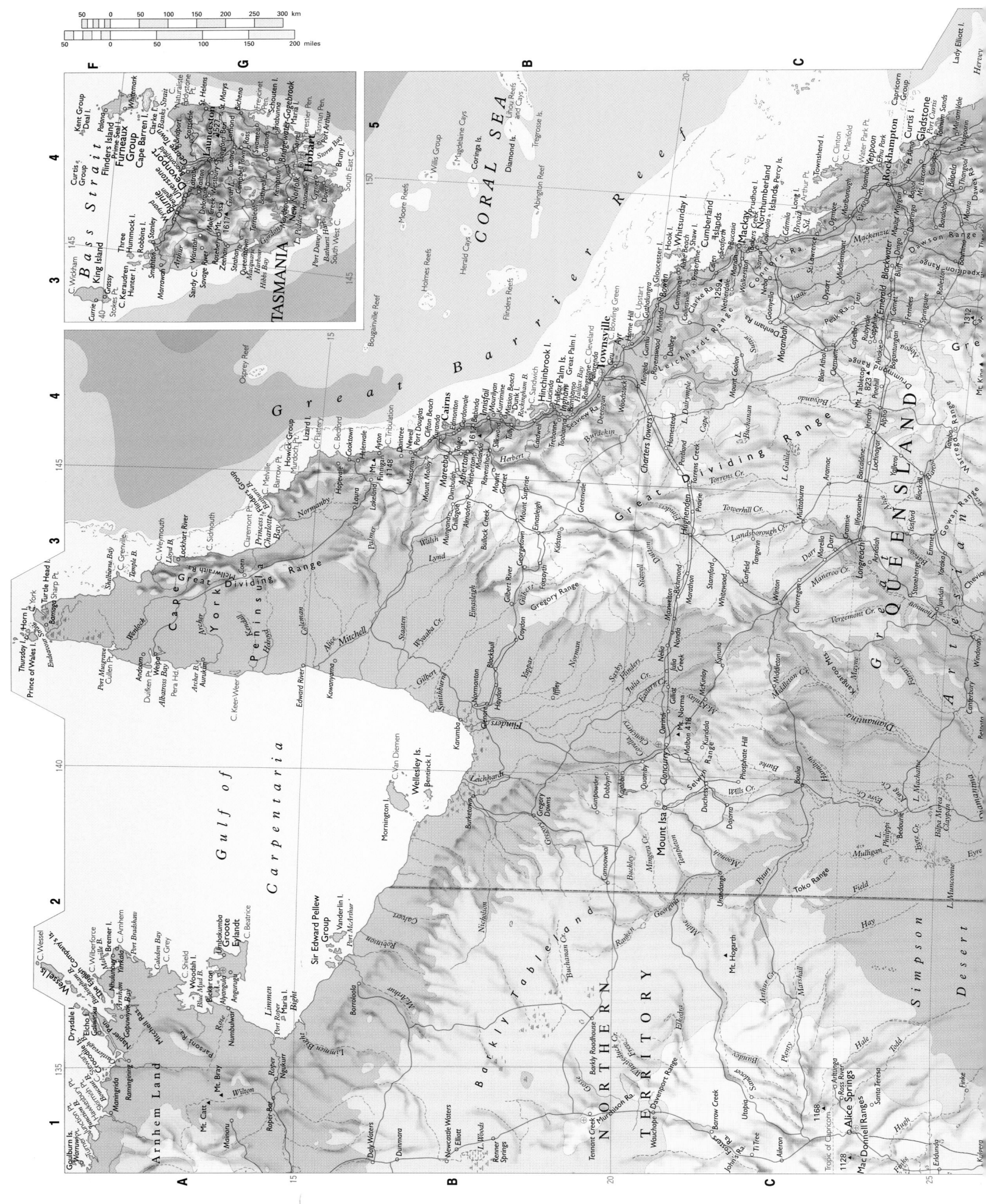

T A S M A N   S E A

NEW SOUTH WALES

SOUTH AUSTRALIA

V I C T O R I A

SOUTHERN   OCEAN

BRISBANE

SYDNEY

CANBERRA
(COMMONWEALTH TERRITORY)

ADELAIDE

MELBOURNE

Gold Coast

Newcastle

Wollongong

Darling Downs

Great Dividing Range

Flinders Ranges

Lake Eyre (North)

Lake Eyre (South)

Lake Torrens

Lake Gairdner

Lake Frome

Spencer Gulf

Kangaroo I.

Eyre Peninsula

Gulf St. Vincent

Flinders Island

Furneaux Group

Cape Barren I.

King Island

Bass Strait

Mount Gambier

Murray Bridge

Gippsland

Geelong

Ballarat

Bendigo

Broken Hill

Dubbo

Tamworth

Armidale

Coffs Harbour

Port Macquarie

Toowoomba

Mildura

Warrnambool

Projection Bonne

East from Greenwich

m   ft
1500   4500
1000   3000
400   1200
200   600
0   0
200   600
2000   6000
4000   12 000
ft   m

 Equatorial Scale 1:54 000 000

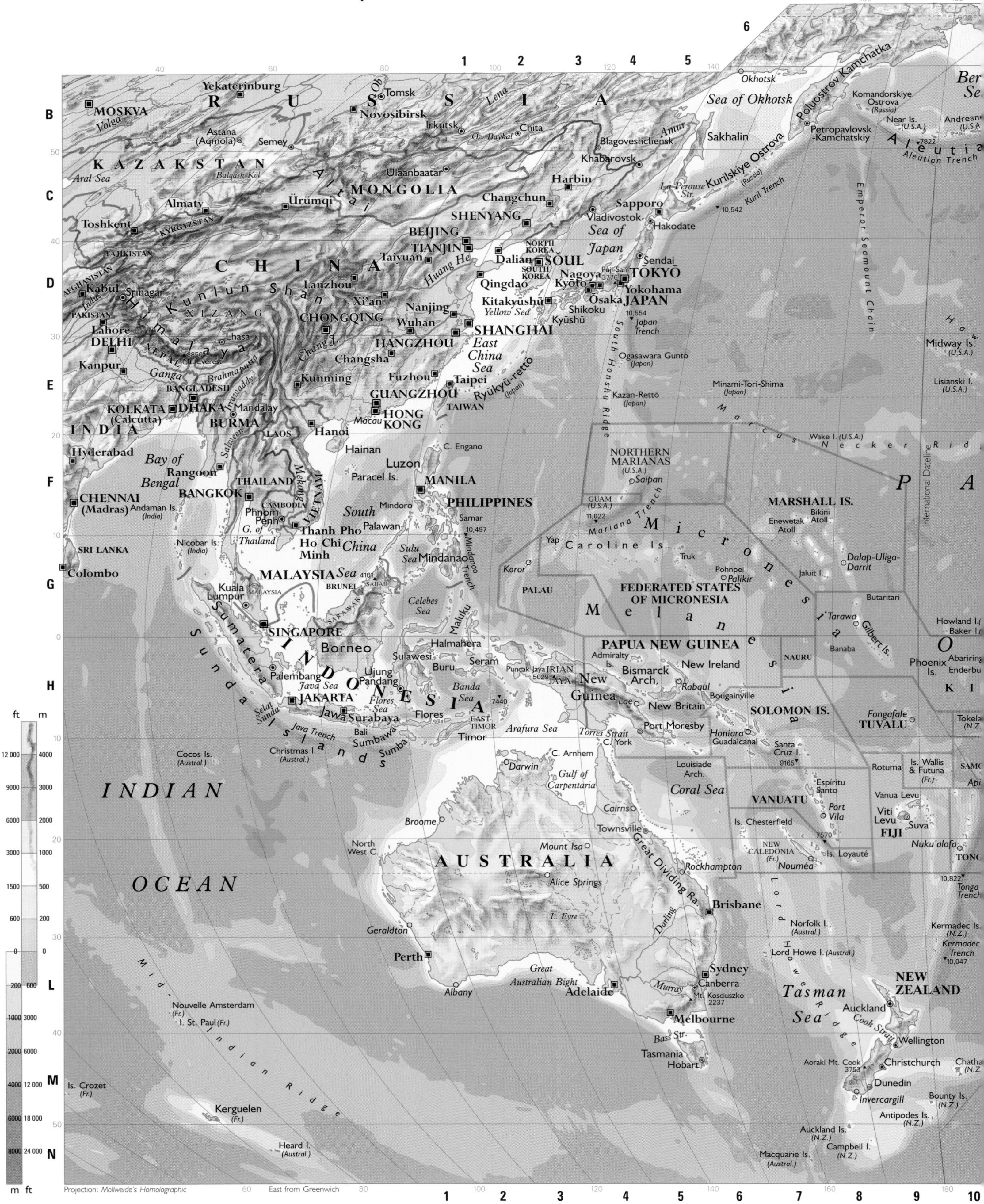
RUSSIA
MOSKVA
Volga
Yekaterinburg
Tomsk
Ob
Novosibirsk
Irkutsk
Oz. Baykal
Chita
Lena
Astana (Aqmola)
Semey
KAZAKSTAN
Balqash Kol
Aral Sea
Altai
Ulaanbaatar
MONGOLIA
Almaty
Ürümqi
KYRGYZSTAN
Toshkent
TAJIKISTAN
AFGHANISTAN
Kabul
Srinagar
PAKISTAN
Indus
Lahore
DELHI
Kanpur
Ganga
Himalaya
NEPAL
8850 Mt. Everest
Lhasa
XIZANG
Kunlun Shan
CHINA
Lanzhou
Xi'an
Taiyuan
Huang He
CHONGQING
Chang Jiang
Changsha
Kunming
Brahmaputra
BANGLADESH
DHAKA
KOLKATA (Calcutta)
INDIA
Mandalay
BURMA
Irrawaddy
Salween
LAOS
Hanoi
Hyderabad
Bay of Bengal
Rangoon
THAILAND
BANGKOK
Mekong
CAMBODIA
Phnom Penh
VIETNAM
Thanh Pho Ho Chi Minh
G. of Thailand
CHENNAI (Madras)
Andaman Is. (India)
Nicobar Is. (India)
SRI LANKA
Colombo
Blagoveshchensk
Amur
Khabarovsk
Harbin
Changchun
SHENYANG
BEIJING
TIANJIN
Dalian
NORTH KOREA
SÖUL
SOUTH KOREA
Qingdao
Yellow Sea
Nanjing
Wuhan
SHANGHAI
HANGZHOU
East China Sea
Fuzhou
Taipei
TAIWAN
GUANGZHOU
HONG KONG
Macau
Hainan
Ryūkyū-rettō (Japan)
Vladivostok
Sea of Japan
Sapporo
Hakodate
Sendai
TOKYO
Yokohama
Fuji-San 3776
Nagoya
Kyōto
Ōsaka
JAPAN
Kitakyūshū
Shikoku
Kyūshū
10,554 Japan Trench
South Honshu Ridge
Ogasawara Gunto (Japan)
Kazan-Rettō (Japan)
Okhotsk
Sea of Okhotsk
Sakhalin
La Perouse Str.
Kurilskiye Ostrova (Russia)
Kuril Trench
10,542
Poluostrov Kamchatka
Petropavlovsk-Kamchatskiy
Komandorskiye Ostrova (Russia)
Near Is. (U.S.A.)
Andreanof (U.S.A.)
Bering Sea
7822
Aleutian Trench
Aleutia
Emperor Seamount Chain
Midway Is. (U.S.A.)
Lisianski I. (U.S.A.)
Minami-Tori-Shima (Japan)
Marcus
Wake I. (U.S.A.)
Necker Ridge
International Dateline
PA
C. Engano
Luzon
Paracel Is.
MANILA
PHILIPPINES
Mindoro
Samar
10,497
South China Sea
Palawan
Sulu Sea
Mindanao
Mindanao Trench
NORTHERN MARIANAS (U.S.A.)
Saipan
GUAM (U.S.A.)
11,022
Mariana Trench
Micronesia
Yap
Caroline Is.
Koror
PALAU
Truk
Pohnpei
Palikir
FEDERATED STATES OF MICRONESIA
MARSHALL IS.
Bikini Atoll
Enewetak Atoll
Dalap-Uliga-Darrit
Jaluit I.
Butaritari
Tarawa
Gilbert Is.
Banaba
NAURU
Howland I.
Baker I.
O
Phoenix Is.
Abariring
Enderbury
KI
MALAYSIA
Kuala Lumpur
PEN. MALAYSIA
BRUNEI
SABAH
SARAWAK
4101
Celebes Sea
SINGAPORE
Borneo
Sumatera
INDONESIA
Palembang
Java Sea
JAKARTA
Jawa
Surabaya
Ujung Pandang
Sulawesi
Flores Sea
Flores
Bali
Sumbawa
Sumba
Selat Sunda
Java Trench
Sunda Islands
Halmahera
Maluku
Buru
Seram
Banda Sea
7440
EAST TIMOR
Timor
Puncak Jaya 5029
IRIAN JAYA
New Guinea
PAPUA NEW GUINEA
Admiralty Is.
Bismarck Arch.
New Ireland
Rabaul
New Britain
Lae
Port Moresby
Bougainville
SOLOMON IS.
Honiara
Guadalcanal
Melanesia
Santa Cruz I.
9165
Torres Strait
C. York
Arafura Sea
Christmas I. (Austral.)
Cocos Is. (Austral.)
INDIAN OCEAN
C. Arnhem
Darwin
Gulf of Carpentaria
Louisiade Arch.
Coral Sea
VANUATU
Espíritu Santo
Port Vila
Is. Chesterfield
7570
NEW CALEDONIA (Fr.)
Nouméa
Is. Loyauté
Fongafale
TUVALU
Tokelau (N.Z.)
Rotuma
Is. Wallis & Futuna (Fr.)
SAMOA
Apia
Vanua Levu
Viti Levu
Suva
FIJI
Nuku'alofa
TONGA
10,822
Tonga Trench
Cairns
Townsville
Broome
North West C.
Mount Isa
AUSTRALIA
Alice Springs
Great Dividing Ra.
Rockhampton
Brisbane
L. Eyre
Darling
Geraldton
Perth
Great Australian Bight
Albany
Adelaide
Murray
Sydney
Canberra
Mt. Kosciuszko 2237
Melbourne
Bass Str.
Tasmania
Hobart
Lord Howe Rise
Norfolk I. (Austral.)
Lord Howe I. (Austral.)
Tasman Sea
Kermadec Is. (N.Z.)
Kermadec Trench
10,047
NEW ZEALAND
Auckland
Cook Strait
Wellington
Aoraki Mt. Cook 3753
Christchurch
Chatham (N.Z.)
Dunedin
Invercargill
Bounty Is. (N.Z.)
Antipodes Is. (N.Z.)
Auckland Is. (N.Z.)
Campbell I. (N.Z.)
Macquarie Is. (Austral.)
Nouvelle Amsterdam (Fr.)
I. St. Paul (Fr.)
Mid-Indian Ridge
Is. Crozet (Fr.)
Kerguelen (Fr.)
Heard I. (Austral.)
ft m
12 000 4000
9000 3000
6000 2000
3000 1000
1500 500
600 200
0 0
200 600
1000 3000
2000 6000
4000 12 000
6000 18 000
8000 24 000
m ft
B C D E F G H L M N
1 2 3 4 5 6 7 8 9 10
Projection: Mollweide's Homolographic
East from Greenwich

11 12 13 14 15 16 17 18 19 20

Arctic Circle

ALASKA
(U.S.A.)
Anchorage
5959

Bristol Bay
Gulf of Alaska
Juneau

Is. (U.S.A.)

Prince of Wales I.
(U.S.A.) Prince Rupert
Queen Charlotte Is.
(Canada)

R O C K Y

C A N A D A

N O R T H

Edmonton

L. Winnipeg

Newfoundland

Vancouver
Vancouver I.
Victoria
Seattle
Portland

Calgary
Regina
Winnipeg

L. Superior

St. Lawrence

Québec
Montréal
Ottawa
Toronto
Detroit
Buffalo
Boston
St. John's

50

Boise

L. Huron
L. Michigan
L. Ontario
L. Erie

C

C. Mendocino

Salt Lake
City
Denver

Minneapolis
Missouri

CHICAGO
Pittsburgh
Kansas City
St. Louis
Cincinnati

Pittsburgh
NEW YORK CITY
PHILADELPHIA
Baltimore
Washington D.C.

A T L A N T I C

40

6741

Sacramento
SAN FRANCISCO
4418

UNITED STATES

Oklahoma City
Memphis
Atlanta

C. Hatteras

D

LOS ANGELES
San Diego

Phoenix

Colorado

Dallas
Houston

Mississippi

Jacksonville

Bermuda
(U.K.)

30

Ciudad
Juárez

Guadalupe
(Mex.)

M
E
X

San Antonio
New
Orleans

Sargasso Sea

OCEAN

E

Tropic of Cancer

Honolulu
Oahu
4205
HAWAIIAN IS.
(U.S.A.)
Hawaii

C. San Lucas

Baja California

Golfo de California

I
C
O

Monterrey

Gulf of Mexico
Miami

La Habana
Canal de Yucatán

Florida Str.
C U B A

BAHAMAS

West Indies

9200

Johnston I.
(U.S.A.)

C I F I C

Is. Revilla Gigedo
(Mex.)

Guadalajara
5700
MEXICO
Puebla
Acapulco

Mérida

7680

HAITI
JAMAICA
Kingston

DOMINICAN REP.

HAITI

PUERTO
RICO
(U.S.A.)

Leeward
Is.

20

BELIZE

Caribbean Sea

BARBADOS

F

Palmyra Is.
(U.S.A.)

I. Clipperton
(Fr.)

GUATEMALA
Guatemala
San Salvador
EL SALVADOR

HONDURAS

NICARAGUA

Managua

Barranquilla
San José

Windward Is.

Maracaibo

North West Christmas Ridge

Teraina
Tabuaeran
Kiritimati

COSTA
RICA

Colón Panamá

Caracas

Orinoco

Medellín

VENEZUELA

10

G

O
I

Jarvis I.
(U.S.A.)

E   A   N

Equator

Galápagos
(Ecuador)

I. del Coco
(Costa Rica)

I. de Malpelo
(Colombia)

Cali

Bogotá

COLOMBIA

Quito
ECUADOR

0

B A T I

Malden I.
Starbuck I.

Guayaquil

Iquitos

Amazonas

BRAZIL

H

Tongareva
Pukapuka
Manihiki

Caroline I.
Vostok I.
Flint I.

Is. Marquises

C. Paliñas

Trujillo

10

SAMOA
(U.S.A.)

Suwarrow Is.

Is. de la
Société

Is. Tuamotu

6369

PERU

LIMA
Cuzco

6950
Nevada Ancohuma

niue
Cook Is.
(N.Z.)

Rarotonga

Austral/seamount Chain

Papeete
Tahiti

Muriñoa

FRENCH POLYNESIA

Is. Tubuai

Tuamotu Ridge

East Pacific Ridge

Ducie I.

Pitcairn I.
(U.K.)

Rapa

Arequipa
6866
Perú-
Arica

L. Titicaca

La Paz
BOLIVIA

J

Iquique
Chile

20

Tropic of Capricorn

Antofagasta

PARAGUAY

Asunción

K

Sala-y-Gómez
(Chile)

I. de Pascua
(Chile)

San Félix
(Chile)

San Ambrosio
(Chile)

8050
Trench

San Miguel
de Tucumán

Pôrto
Alegre

30

Arch. de
Juan Fernández
(Chile)

Valparaíso

Concepción

Córdoba
Aconcagua
6960
Rosario

SANTIAGO

BUENOS
AIRES

Río de la Plata

URUGUAY
Montevideo

ARGENTINA

L

40

Chile Rise

SOUTH

M

Pacific-Antarctic Ridge

Patagonian Cordillera

ATLANTIC

6212 OCEAN

50

Punta Arenas

Est. de Magallanes
Tierra del Fuego

C. de Hornos

Falkland Is.
(U.K.)

South Georgia
(U.K.)

N

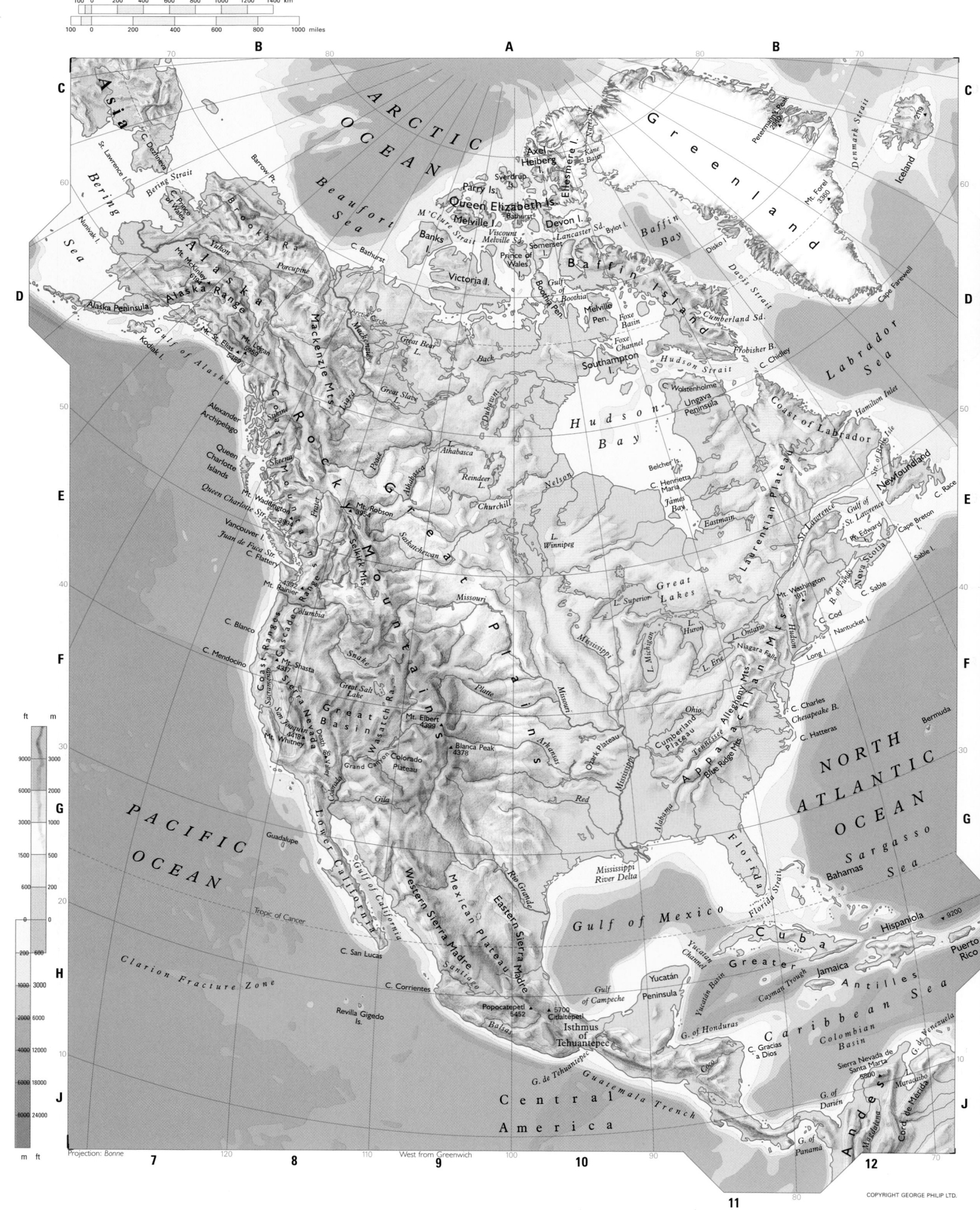

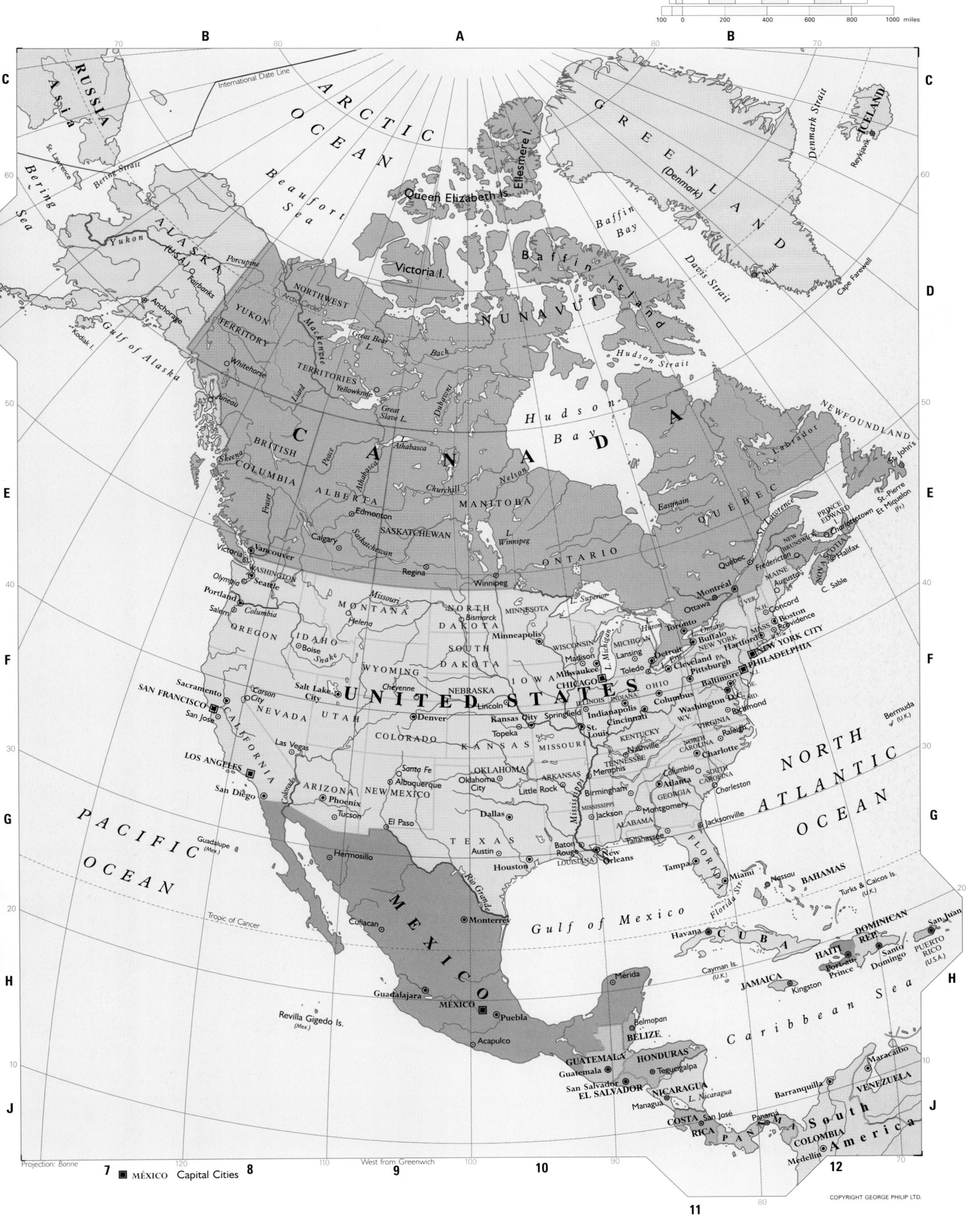

100 0 200 400 600 800 1000 1200 1400 km
100 0   200   400   600   800   1000 miles

B   A   B

C   RUSSIA   ARCTIC   GREENLAND   ICELAND   C
    Asia
    St. Lawrence I.   OCEAN   (Denmark)   Reykjavik
    Bering Strait
    Bering Sea   Beaufort Sea   Queen Elizabeth Is. Ellesmere I.
                    ALASKA   Baffin
                    (U.S.A.)   Porcupine   Bay
    Yukon   Victoria I.   Baffin Island Davis Strait   Nuuk   D
D   Gulf of Alaska Fairbanks   NORTHWEST   Denmark Strait   Cape Farewell
    Kodiak I. Anchorage YUKON   Arctic Circle   NUNAVUT
                TERRITORY   Mackenzie Great Bear L.
                Whitehorse TERRITORIES Back
                          Yellowknife Dubawnt   Hudson Strait
                Juneau   Liard Great Slave L.
E   BRITISH   Peace Athabasca   Churchill   Hudson   NEWFOUNDLAND E
            COLUMBIA Skeena Athabasca   MANITOBA   Bay   Labrador   St. John's
            Fraser ALBERTA Edmonton SASKATCHEWAN   Eastmain QUÉBEC   St. Pierre
    Victoria Vancouver Calgary Saskatchewan   L. Winnipeg   PRINCE Et Miquelon (Fr.)
    Seattle WASHINGTON Regina   ONTARIO   Québec NEW EDWARD Charlottetown
F   Olympia Portland Winnipeg   L. Superior Ottawa Montréal BRUNSWICK NOVA Halifax F
    Salem Columbia MONTANA NORTH MINNESOTA   Toronto   MAINE SCOTIA C. Sable
    OREGON Helena DAKOTA Bismarck WISCONSIN MICHIGAN L. Ontario Augusta N.H. Concord
    Boise IDAHO SOUTH   Minneapolis   Madison Milwaukee L. Huron Buffalo NEW YORK MASS Boston
    Snake WYOMING DAKOTA   IOWA CHICAGO Lansing Detroit Cleveland PA Hartford Providence
    Sacramento Salt Lake Cheyenne NEBRASKA Toledo OHIO Pittsburgh NEW YORK CITY PHILADELPHIA
    Carson City City UNITED STATES Lincoln ILLINOIS INDIANA Columbus Washington D.C. Richmond
    SAN FRANCISCO NEVADA UTAH Denver Kansas City St. Indianapolis Cincinnati W.V. VIRGINIA MD.
    San Jose CALIFORNIA COLORADO Topeka Louis KENTUCKY Nashville NORTH Raleigh Bermuda
    Las Vegas KANSAS MISSOURI Memphis TENNESSEE CAROLINA Charlotte (U.K.)
G   LOS ANGELES ARIZONA NEW MEXICO Santa Fe OKLAHOMA Little Rock ARKANSAS Birmingham Columbia SOUTH Charleston NORTH G
    San Diego Phoenix Albuquerque Oklahoma City Dallas ALABAMA Atlanta CAROLINA ATLANTIC
    Tucson El Paso TEXAS Jackson MISSISSIPPI Montgomery GEORGIA Jacksonville OCEAN
    PACIFIC Guadalupe Austin Houston Baton LOUISIANA New Tallahassee FLORIDA
    OCEAN (Mex.) Rio Grande Rouge Orleans Tampa Miami Nassau BAHAMAS
H   Hermosillo Monterrey Gulf of Mexico Florida Str.   Turks & Caicos Is. H
    Tropic of Cancer   Havana CUBA   (U.K.) DOMINICAN San Juan
    Culiacan MEXICO   Cayman Is.   HAITI REP. PUERTO
    Guadalajara Monterrey   (U.K.) JAMAICA Port-au- Santo RICO
    Revilla Gigedo Is. MÉXICO Puebla   Kingston Prince Domingo (U.S.A.)
    (Mex.)   Mérida   Caribbean Sea
    Acapulco Belmopan BELIZE
J   GUATEMALA HONDURAS   Maracaibo J
    Guatemala Tegucigalpa Barranquilla VENEZUELA
    San Salvador NICARAGUA L. Nicaragua
    EL SALVADOR Managua COSTA San José Panamá PANAMA South America
    RICA   COLOMBIA Medellín

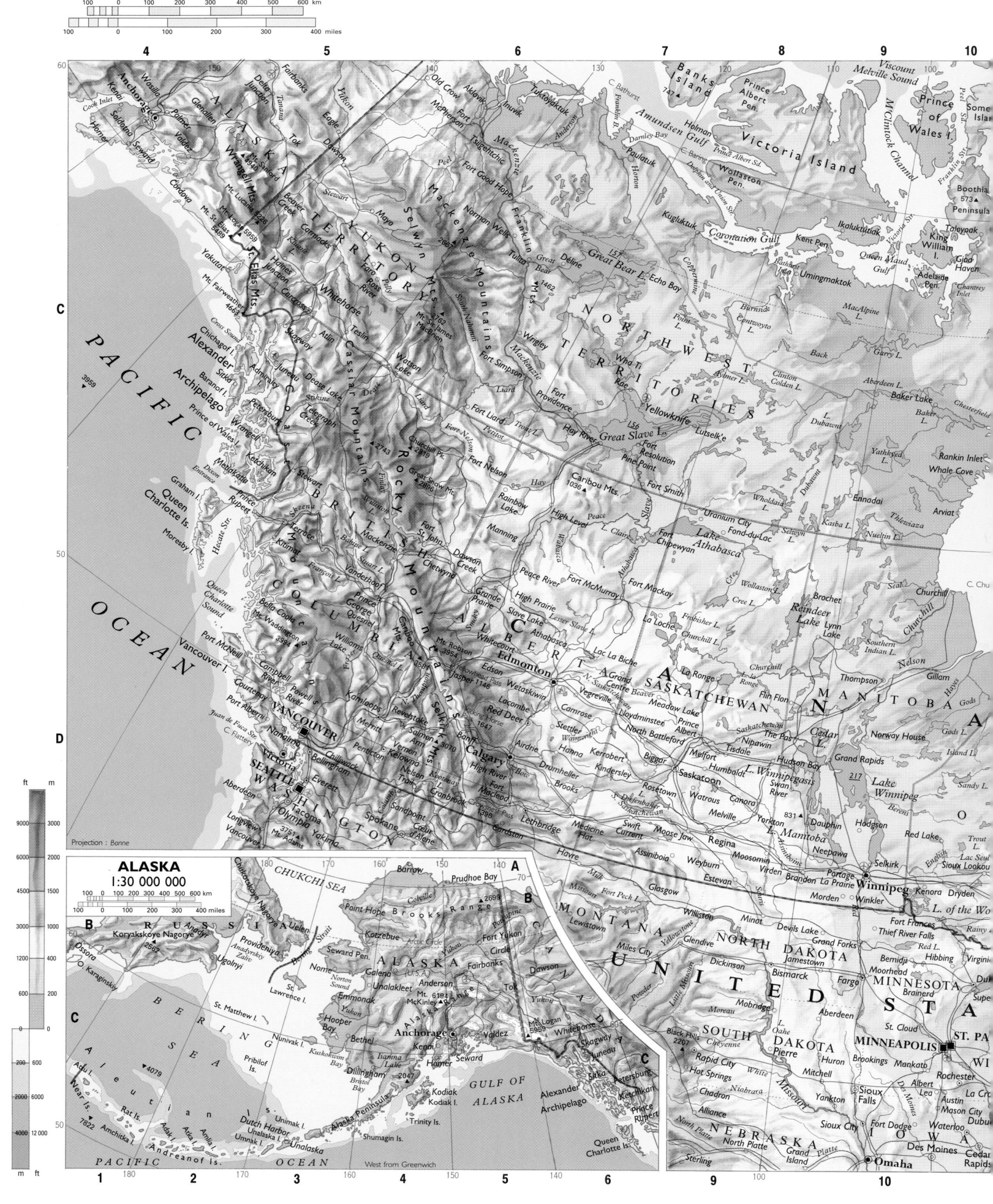

ALASKA
1:30 000 000

74
75

11
12
13
14
15
16
B
C
D
E
Devon I.
Lancaster Sound
Bylot I.
Arctic Bay
Nanisivik
Borden Pen.
Pond Inlet
Brodeur Peninsula
Baffin Bay
2136
C. Adair
Clyde River
C. Raper
Baffin Island
Home B.
Fury and Hecla Str.
Igloolik
Simpson Pen.
Pelly Bay
Committee B.
Melville Peninsula
Sanirajak
Prince Charles I.
Air Force I.
Foxe Basin
Nettilling L.
Rae Isthmus
Repulse Bay
NUNAVUT
C. Dorchester
Wager B.
Roes Welcome Sd.
Foxe Channel
Amadjuak L.
Foxe Pen.
Cape Dorset
Iqaluit
Hall Peninsula
Meta Incognita Peninsula
Kimmirut
Frobisher Bay
Resolution I.
Southampton I.
Salliq
Bell Pen.
Salisbury I.
Nottingham I.
Hudson Strait
Coats I.
Mansel I.
Ivujivik
Salluit
Kangiqsujuaq
Quaqtaq
Akpatok I.
C. Chidley
Kangirsuk
Ungava Bay
Péninsule d'Ungava
Puvirnituq
L. Payne
Arnaud
Feuilles
Kuujjuaq
Koksoak
Baleine
George
Kangiqsualujjuaq
Hebron
1652
Nain
Hudson Bay
Ottawa Is.
257
Inukjuak
L. Minto
Mélèzes
Caniapiscau
Sleeper Is.
King George Is.
Baker's Dozen Is.
Sanikiluaq
Belcher Is.
L. à l'Eau Claire
Grande Baleine
Kuujjuarapik
L. Bienville
Schefferville
C. Henrietta Maria
Pte. Louis XIV
Peawanuck
Winisk
Severn
James Bay
Akimiski I.
Chisasibi
Kanaaupscow
La Grande
Rés. de Caniapiscau
Wemindji
Eastmain
Big Trout L.
Attawapiskat
Fort Albany
Albany
Charlton I.
Waskaganish
Rupert
Moosonee
Nottaway
Harricana
L. Mistassini
Chibougamau
L. Albanel
Péribonca
St. Joseph
Nakina
Kenogami
Missinaibi
Matagami
L. Matagami
Hearst
Nipigon
L. Nipigon
Geraldton
Kapuskasing
Cochrane
Abitibi L.
Amos
Rés. Gouin
Marathon
Oba
Timmins
Kirkland Lake
Rouyn-Noranda
Val-d'Or
Thunder Bay
Lake Superior
Chapleau
Wawa
New Liskeard
Rés. Cabonga
Mont-Laurier
Houghton
Sault Ste. Marie
Elliot Lake
Sudbury
Ironwood
Marquette
L. Nipissing
North Bay
Pembroke
Outaouais
Manistique
Manitoulin I.
Parry Sound
Georgian Bay
Huntsville
Escanaba
Menominee
Petoskey
Traverse City
Lake Huron
Owen Sound
Barrie
Peterborough
Wausau
Green Bay
Cadillac
Oshawa
TORONTO
Kitchener
Hamilton
L. Ontario
Appleton
Sheboygan
Lake Michigan
MICHIGAN
Saginaw
Grand Rapids
Flint
London
Sarnia
MILWAUKEE
Lansing
Racine
Kenosha
CHICAGO
DETROIT
Windsor
L. Erie
Gary
South Bend
Toledo
CLEVELAND
INDIANA
OHIO
ILLINOIS
Niagara Falls
BUFFALO
Rochester
Syracuse
Erie
Jamestown
Elmira
Binghamton
Scranton
PENNSYLVANIA
Newark
Allentown
Trenton
N.J.
NEW YORK
Kingston
Belleville
Ottawa
Hull
MONTRÉAL
Cornwall
Granby
Burlington
L. Champlain
VERMONT
Montpelier
Sherbrooke
St-Hyacinthe
Joliette
Trois-Rivières
Shawinigan
La Tuque
Québec
Lévis
Thetford Mines
1190
Roberval
Jonquière
Dolbeau
L. St-Jean
Chicoutimi
Baie Comeau
St. Lawrence
Manicouagan
Rés. Manicouagan
Gagnon
Moisie
1135
Fermont
Labrador City
L. Ashuanipi
Petitsikapau L.
Esker
Churchill Falls
Churchill
Smallwood Res.
North West River
Happy Valley-Goose Bay
Labrador
NEWFOUNDLAND
Hopedale
C. Harrison
Rigolet
Cartwright
Port Hope Simpson
Belle Isle
C. Bauld
St. Anthony
Str. of Belle Isle
St-Augustin
Natashquan
Romaine
Havre-St-Pierre
Sept-Îles
Port-Cartier
Î. d'Anticosti
Gulf of St. Lawrence
QUÉBEC
CANADA
Matane
Gaspé
Pén. de Gaspé
Rimouski
Rivière-du-Loup
Campbellton
Bathurst
Edmundston
Miramichi
Grand Falls
NEW BRUNSWICK
Woodstock
Fredericton
Moncton
Saint John
B. of Fundy
Digby
Yarmouth
C. Sable
Bridgewater
Liverpool
NOVA SCOTIA
Halifax
Dartmouth
Truro
Kentville
Amherst
New Glasgow
Antigonish
Port Hawkesbury
Sydney
Glace Bay
Cape Breton I.
North C.
PR. EDWARD I.
Summerside
Charlottetown
Northumberland Str.
Îs. de la Madeleine
Cabot Str.
C. Ray
Channel-Port aux Basques
Stephenville
Corner Brook
Deer Lake
814
Baie Verte
Grand Falls
Gander
Lewisporte
Notre Dame B.
Bonavista
Trinity B.
Carbonear
St. John's
Placentia
Placentia B.
Marystown
C. Race
Newfoundland
ST.-PIERRE et MIQUELON (Fr.)
Sable I. (Nova Scotia)
MAINE
Bangor
Augusta
Lewiston
Portland
NEW HAMPSHIRE
Concord
Manchester
MASS.
BOSTON
C. Cod
Providence
R.I.
Springfield
HARTFORD
CONN.
Albany
New Haven
Bridgeport
NEW YORK
6309
ATLANTIC OCEAN
Labrador Sea
3809
Davis Strait
Nunavik
Uummannaq
Qeqertarsuaq
Ilulissat
Qasigiannguit
Qeqertarsuup Tunua
Kangerlussuaq
Sisimiut
Maniitsoq
Nuuk
2850
Kong Frederik VI's Kyst
GREENLAND (KALAALLIT NUNAAT) (Denmark)
Tasiilaq
Qeqertarsuatsiaat
Paamiut
Arsuk
Qaqortoq
Nanortalik
Alluitsup Paa
Uummannarsuaq
Qikiqtarjuaq
C. Dyer
Cumberland Peninsula
2591
Pangnirtung
Hoare B.
Mercy C.
Cumberland Sd.
183
177
174
175
West from Greenwich
80
70
60
50
40
30

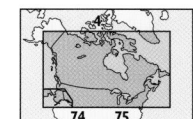

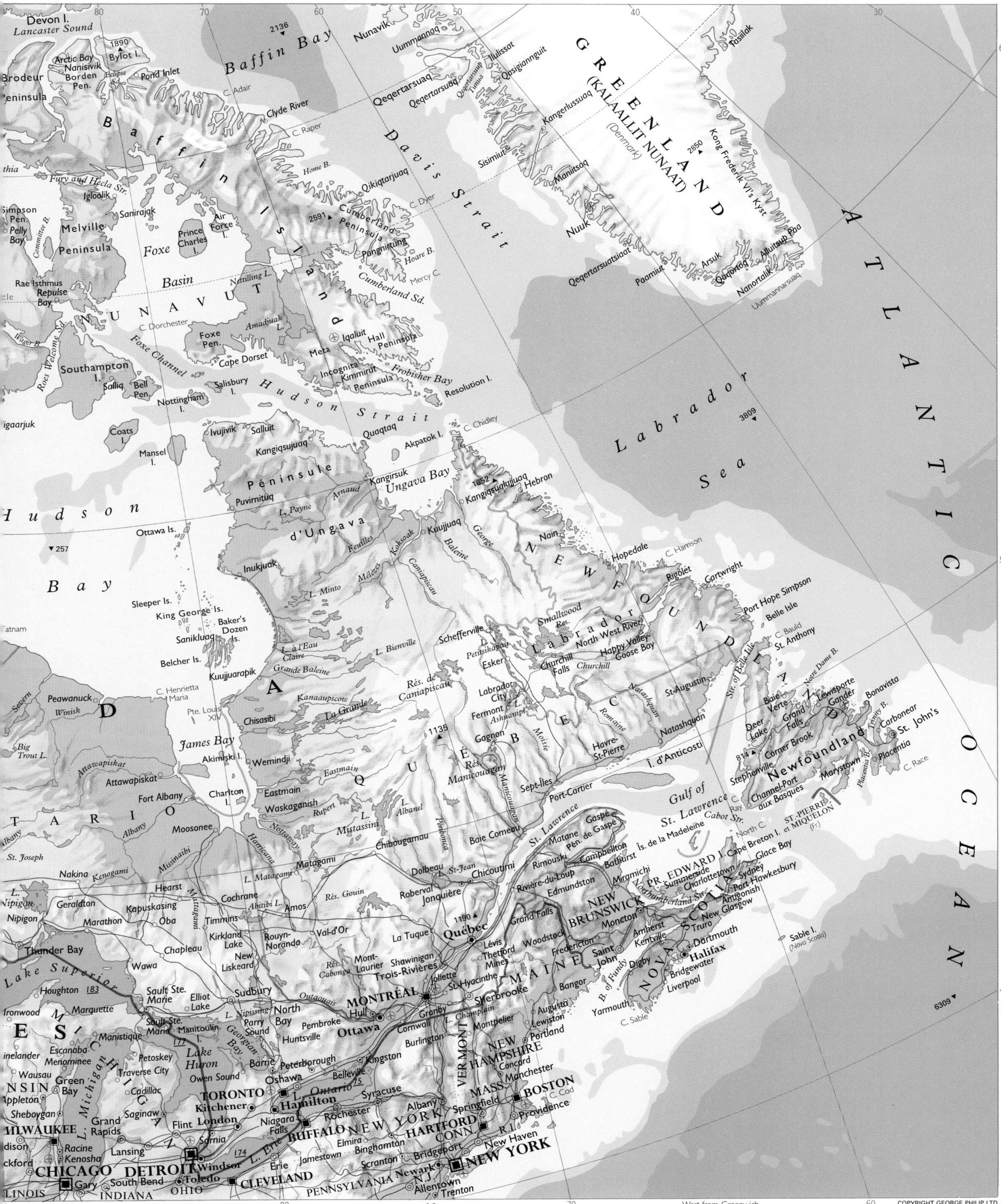

Projection: Lambert's Equivalent Azimuthal

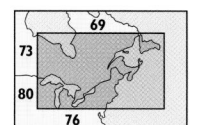

West from Greenwich

COPYRIGHT GEORGE PHILIP LTD.

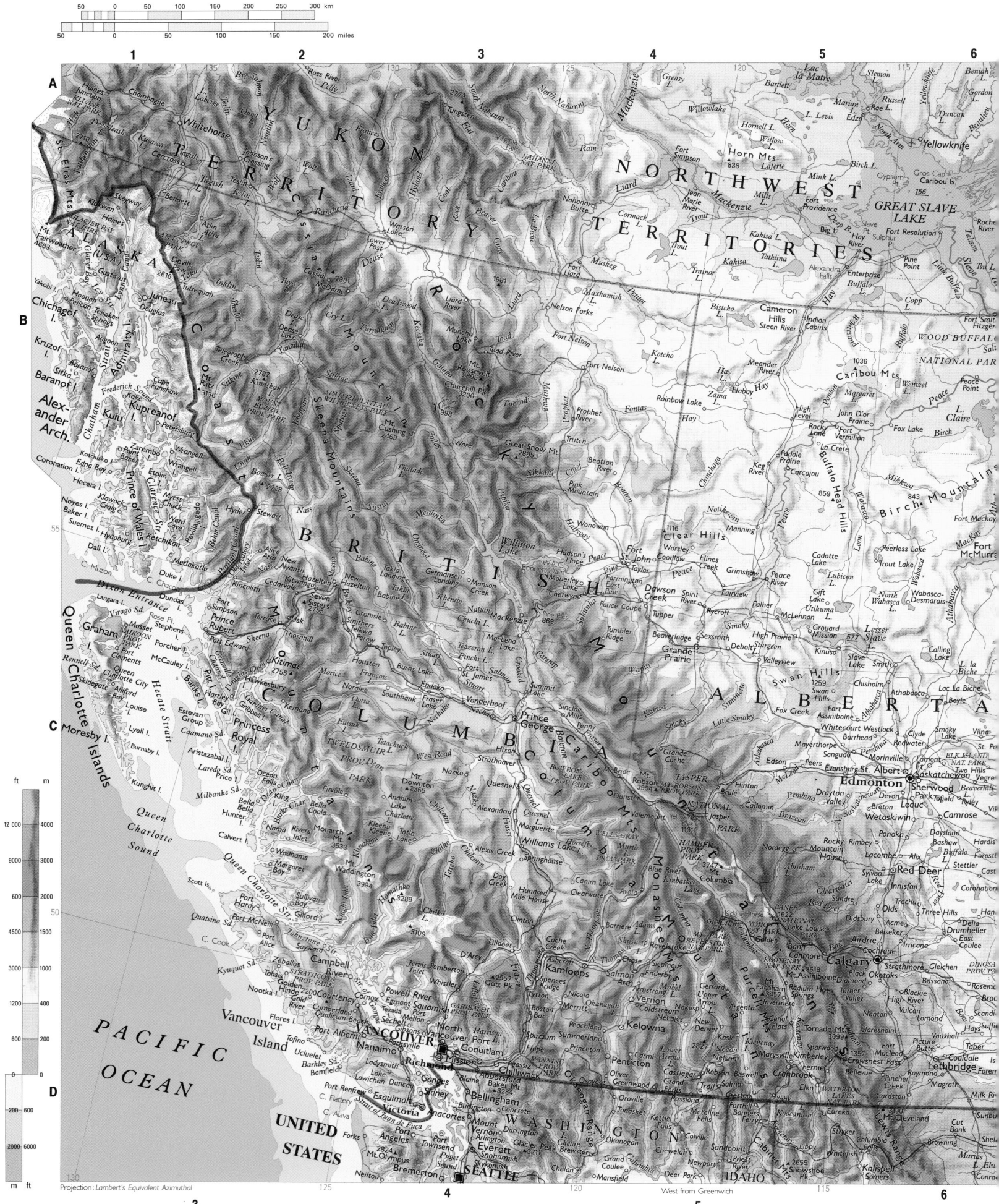

68
70
82
80

NUNAVUT
HUDSON BAY
MANITOBA
SASKATCHEWAN
ONTARIO
NORTH DAKOTA
MINNESOTA
MONTANA
LAKE WINNIPEG
Lake Winnipegosis
Lake Manitoba
Lake Athabasca
Reindeer Lake
Wollaston L.
Cedar Lake
Lake of the Woods
Winnipeg
Regina
Saskatoon
Prince Albert
Moose Jaw
Brandon
Churchill
Thompson
The Pas
Flin Flon
Yorkton
Swift Current
North Battleford
Lloydminster
Kenora
Dryden
Duluth
Grand Forks
Minot
Williston
Havre
Cypress Hills
Lac la Ronge
Lac Seul
Nelson
Churchill
Hayes
Severn
Saskatchewan
Assiniboine
Qu'Appelle
Souris
Red
Missouri
C. Churchill
C. Tatnam
Arviat
Whale Cove
Dawson Inlet
Fort Chipewyan
Uranium City
Lynn Lake
Gillam
Norway House
Steinbach
Estevan
Weyburn
Dauphin
Portage la Prairie
Fort Frances
International Falls
COPYRIGHT GEORGE PHILIP LTD.

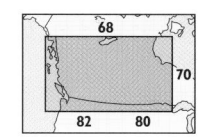

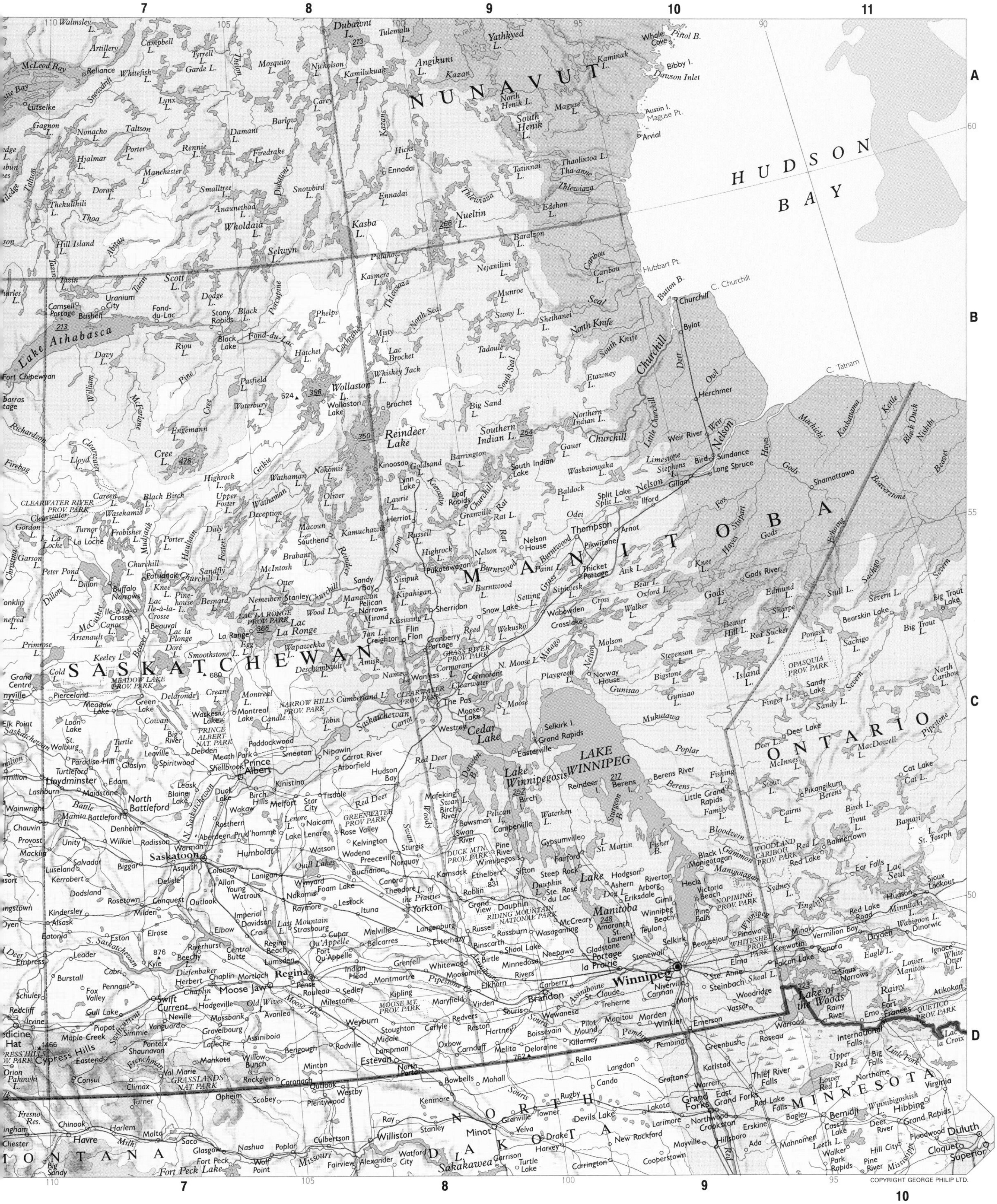

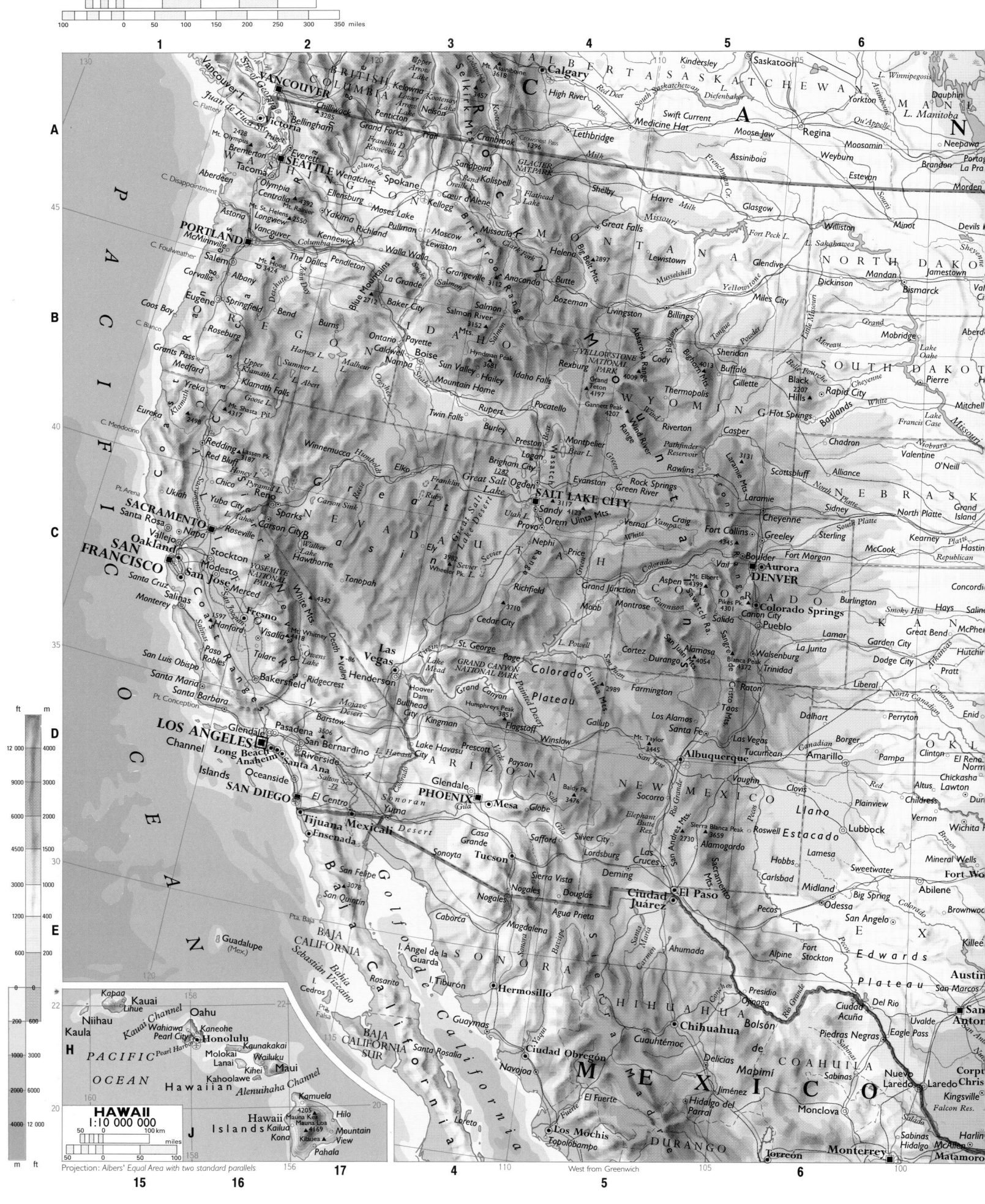

Projection: Albers' Equal Area with two standard parallels

68
69
86
87

8
9
10
11
12
13
A
B
C
D
E
F
Lake Winnipeg
Winnipeg
Lake of the Woods
Lake Superior
Lake Michigan
Lake Huron
Lake Erie
Lake Ontario
Lake Nipigon
Thunder Bay
Sault Ste. Marie
Sudbury
North Bay
Ottawa
MONTRÉAL
Québec
Trois-Rivières
Sherbrooke
Chicoutimi
Jonquière
Rimouski
Edmundston
Saint John
Calais
Bangor
Augusta
Portland
MAINE
VERMONT
NEW HAMPSHIRE
BOSTON
Providence
HARTFORD
NEW YORK
PHILADELPHIA
BALTIMORE
WASHINGTON D.C.
Richmond
Norfolk
Virginia Beach
TORONTO
Hamilton
BUFFALO
Rochester
Syracuse
Albany
PITTSBURGH
CLEVELAND
DETROIT
Toledo
COLUMBUS
CINCINNATI
INDIANAPOLIS
Louisville
Lexington
CHICAGO
MILWAUKEE
MINNEAPOLIS
ST. PAUL
Duluth
Des Moines
Omaha
KANSAS CITY
ST. LOUIS
Springfield
Memphis
Nashville
Knoxville
Chattanooga
CHARLOTTE
Raleigh
Greensboro
Columbia
Charleston
Savannah
ATLANTA
Birmingham
Montgomery
Mobile
Jackson
NEW ORLEANS
Baton Rouge
Shreveport
Little Rock
DALLAS
HOUSTON
Galveston
Tulsa
Jacksonville
Tallahassee
Orlando
TAMPA
MIAMI
Key West
BAHAMAS
Nassau
Grand Bahama I.
Eleuthera I.
Andros I.
GULF OF MEXICO
ATLANTIC OCEAN
MINNESOTA
WISCONSIN
MICHIGAN
IOWA
ILLINOIS
INDIANA
OHIO
KENTUCKY
TENNESSEE
MISSOURI
ARKANSAS
MISSISSIPPI
ALABAMA
GEORGIA
FLORIDA
LOUISIANA
NORTH CAROLINA
SOUTH CAROLINA
VIRGINIA
WEST VIRGINIA
PENNSYLVANIA
NEW YORK
Midwest
Appalachian Mts.
Ozark Plateau
Straits of Florida
95
90
85
80
45
40
35
30
25
8
9
10
11
12

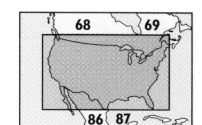

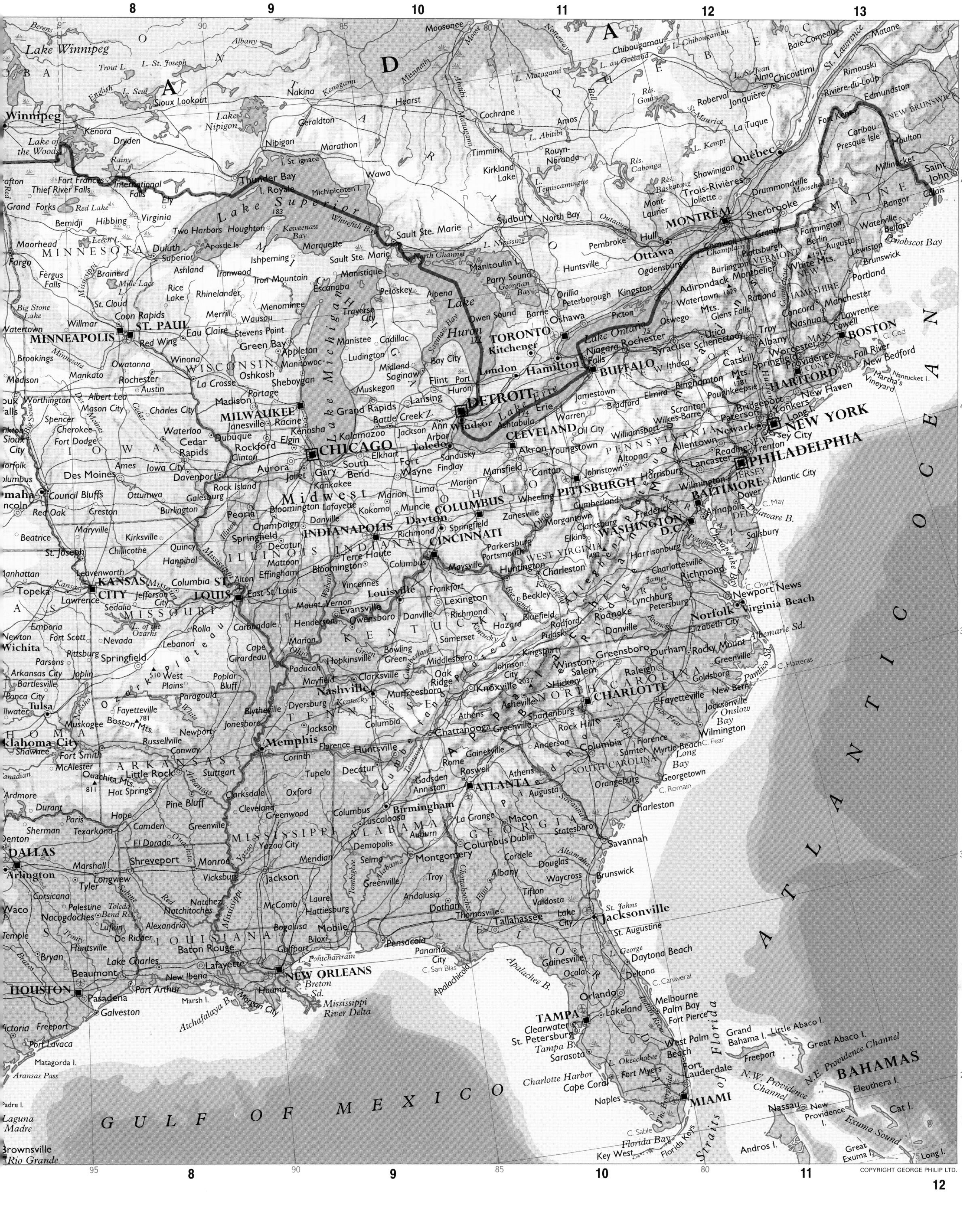

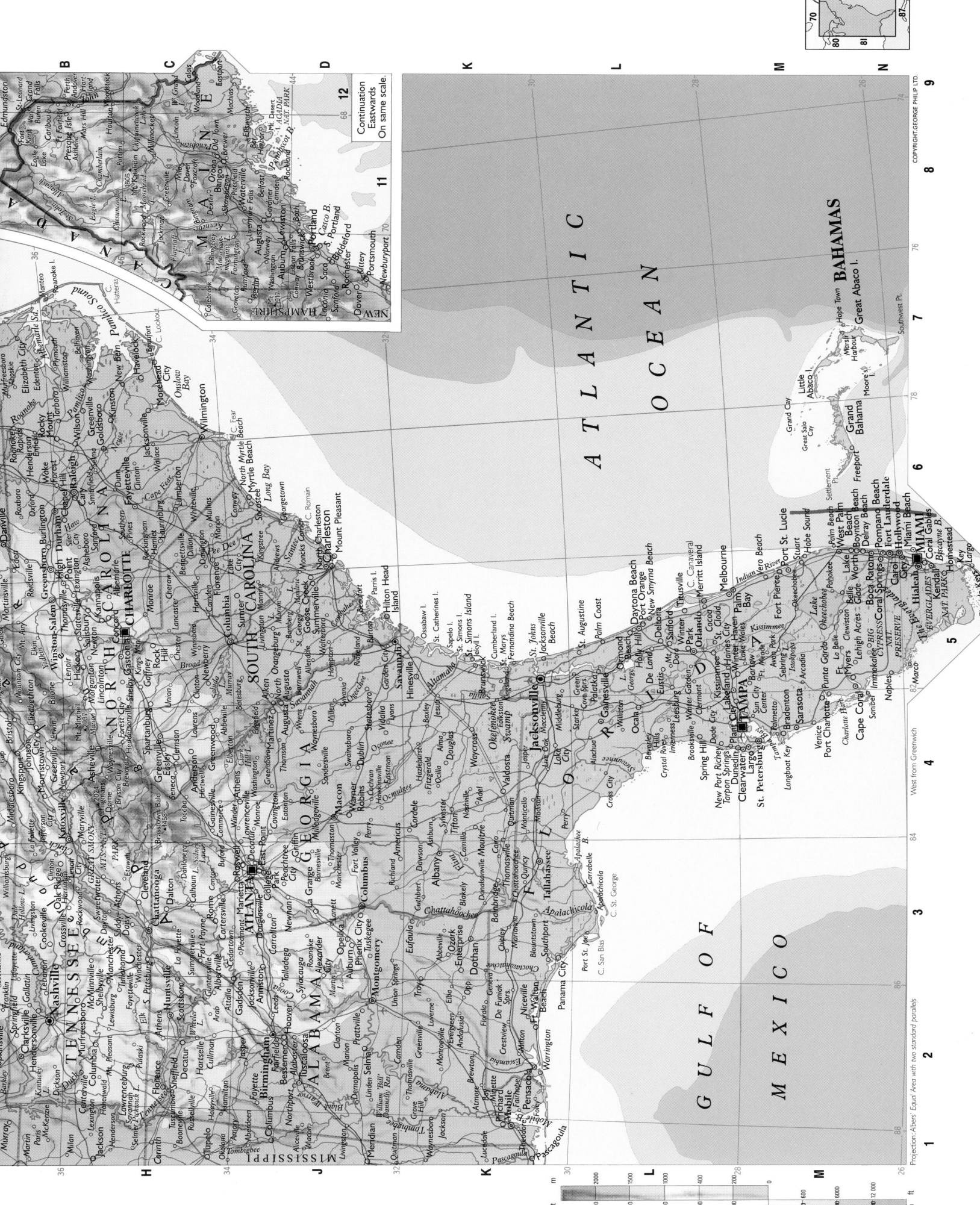

77

Continuation Eastwards
On same scale.

A T L A N T I C

O C E A N

BAHAMAS

G U L F   O F

M E X I C O

TENNESSEE

NORTH CAROLINA

SOUTH CAROLINA

GEORGIA

ALABAMA

F L O R I D A

MISSISSIPPI

MAINE

NEW HAMPSHIRE

CANADA

CHARLOTTE

ATLANTA

TAMPA

MIAMI

Projection: Albers' Equal Area with two standard parallels

COPYRIGHT GEORGE PHILIP LTD.

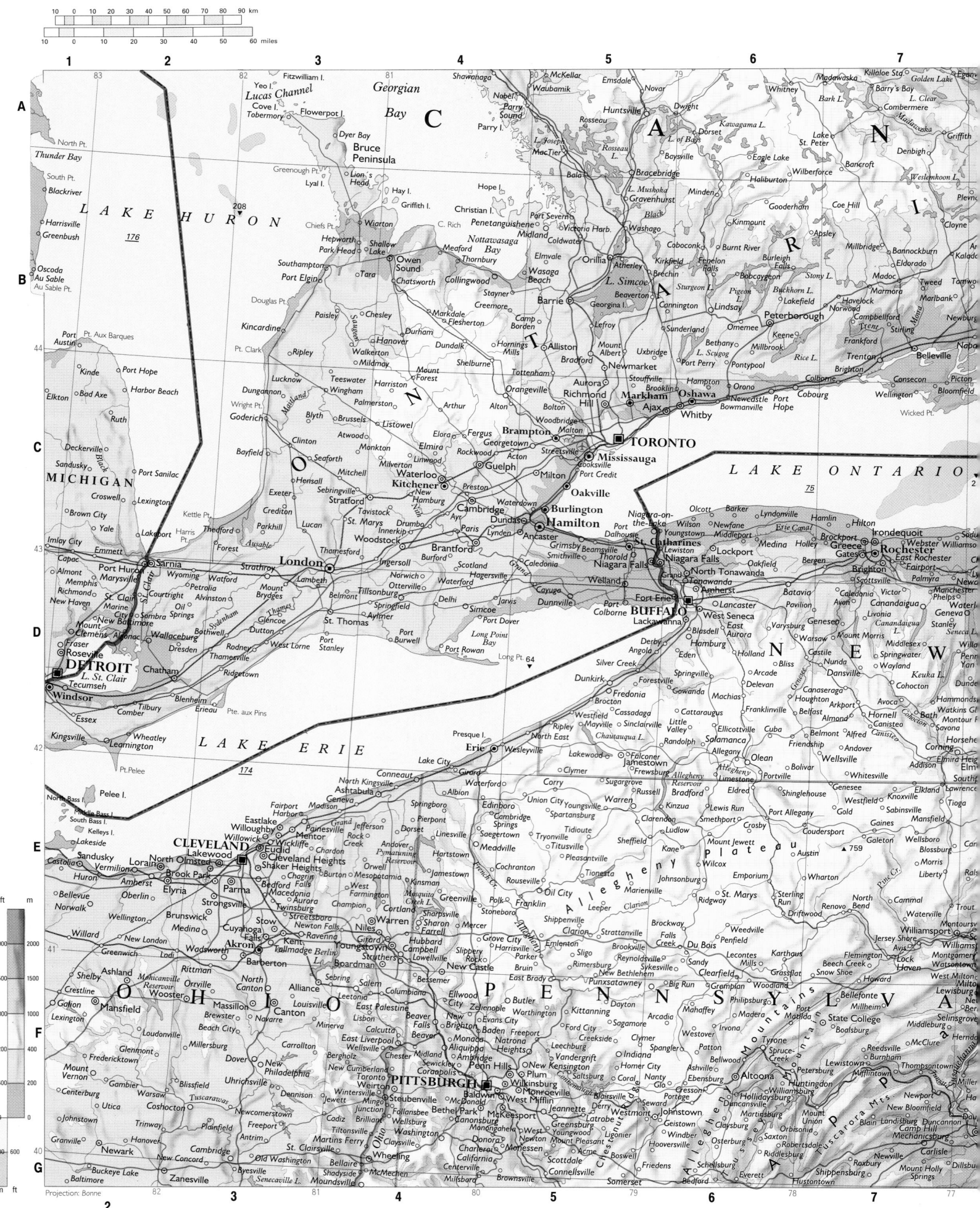

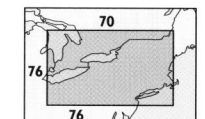

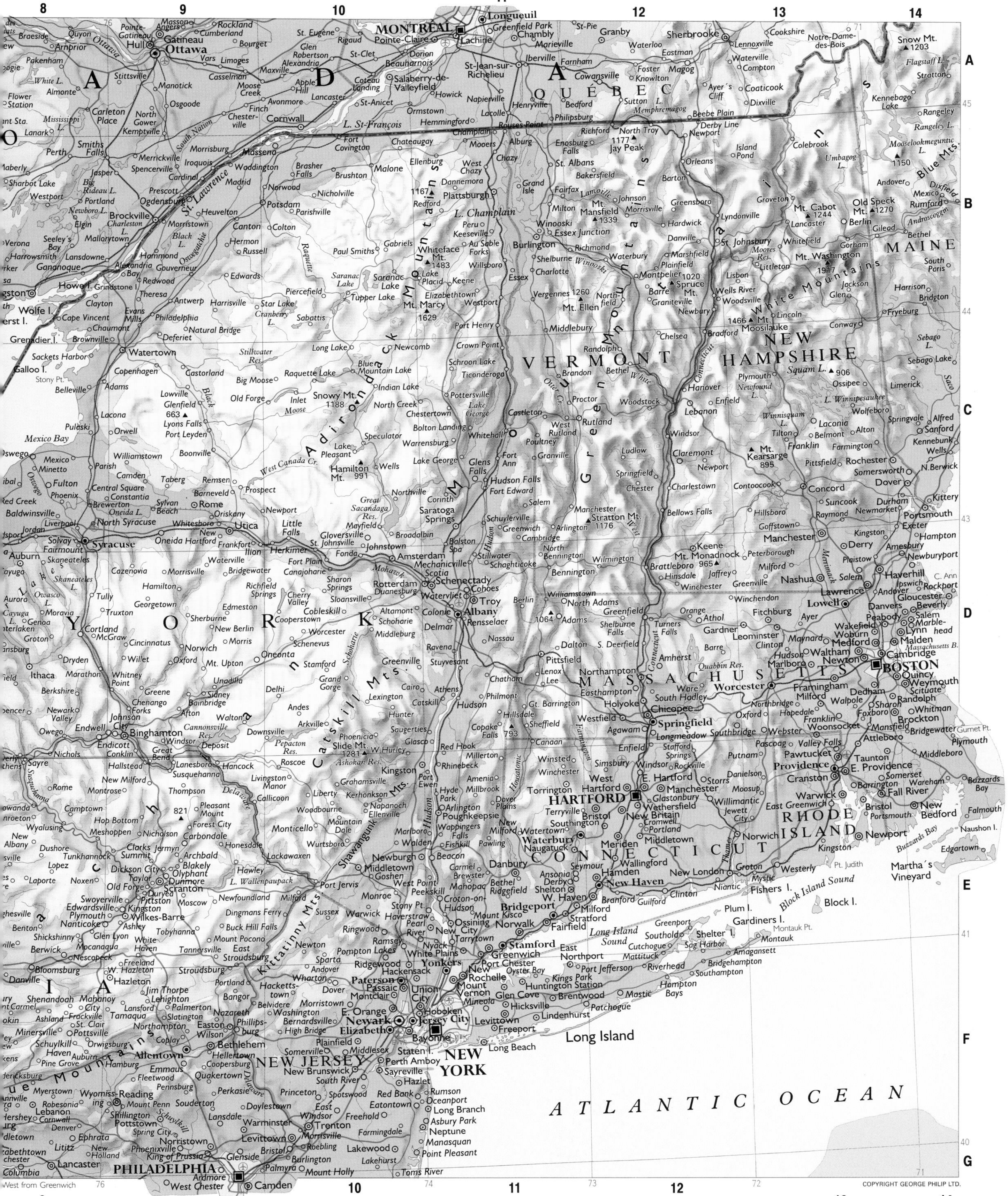

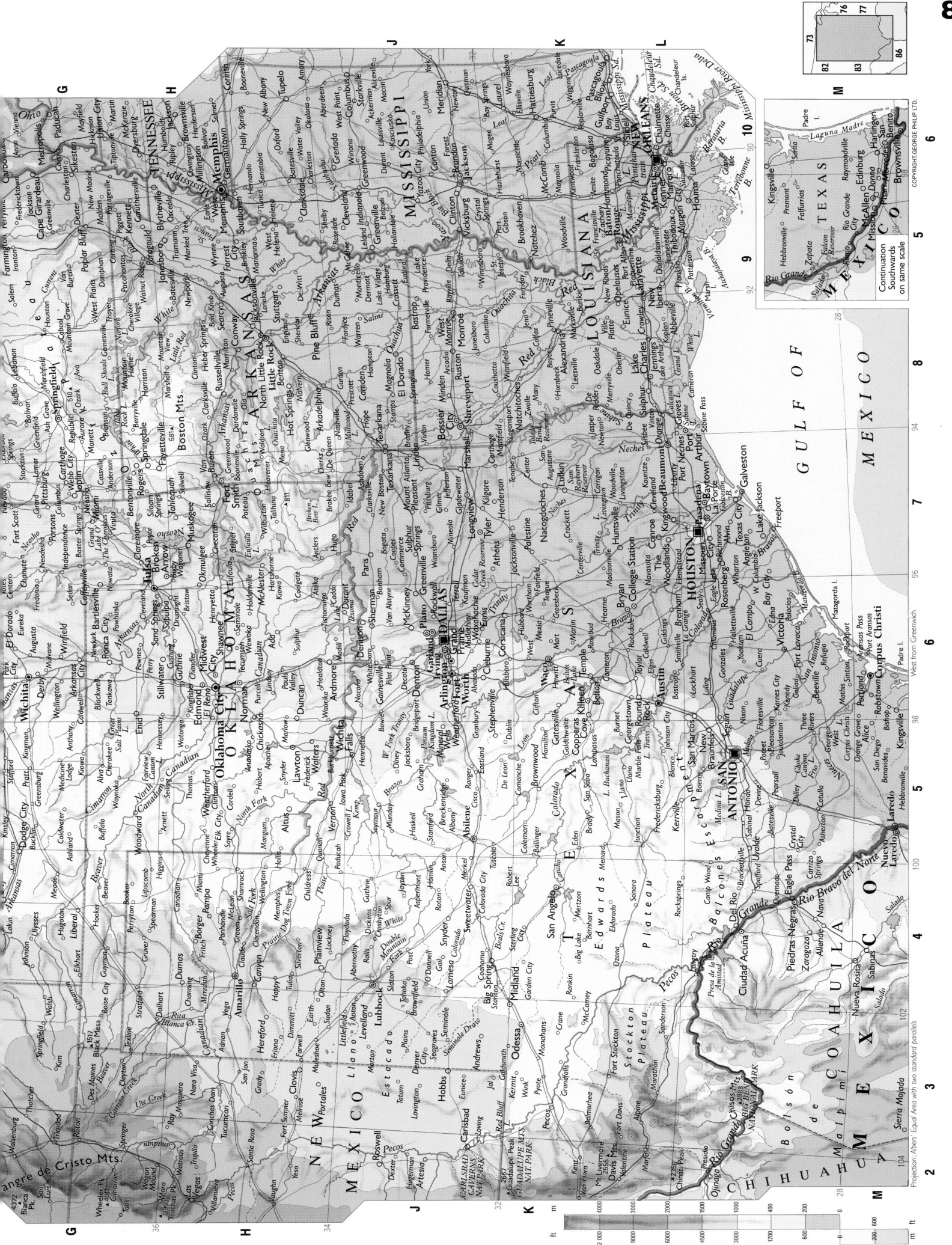

81

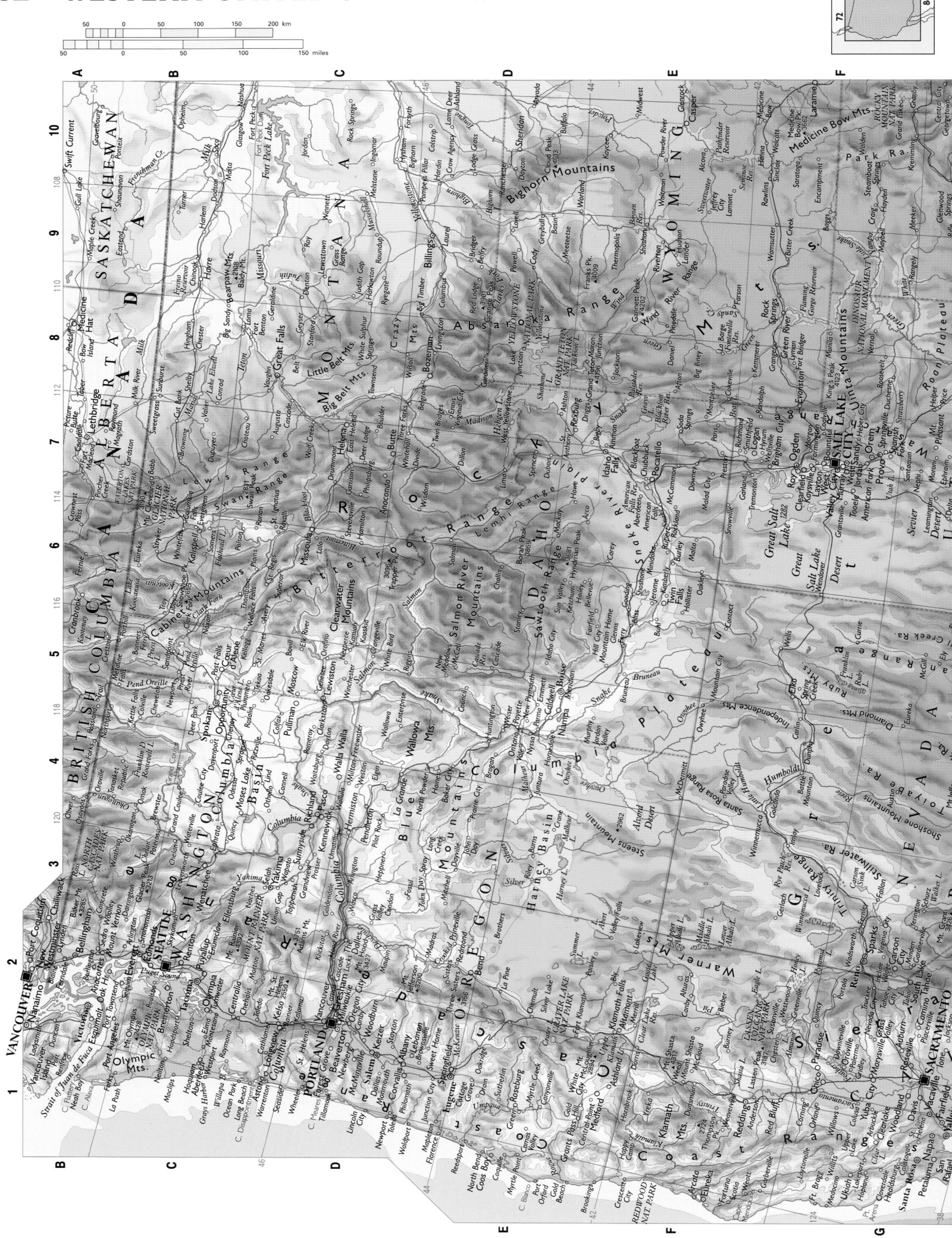

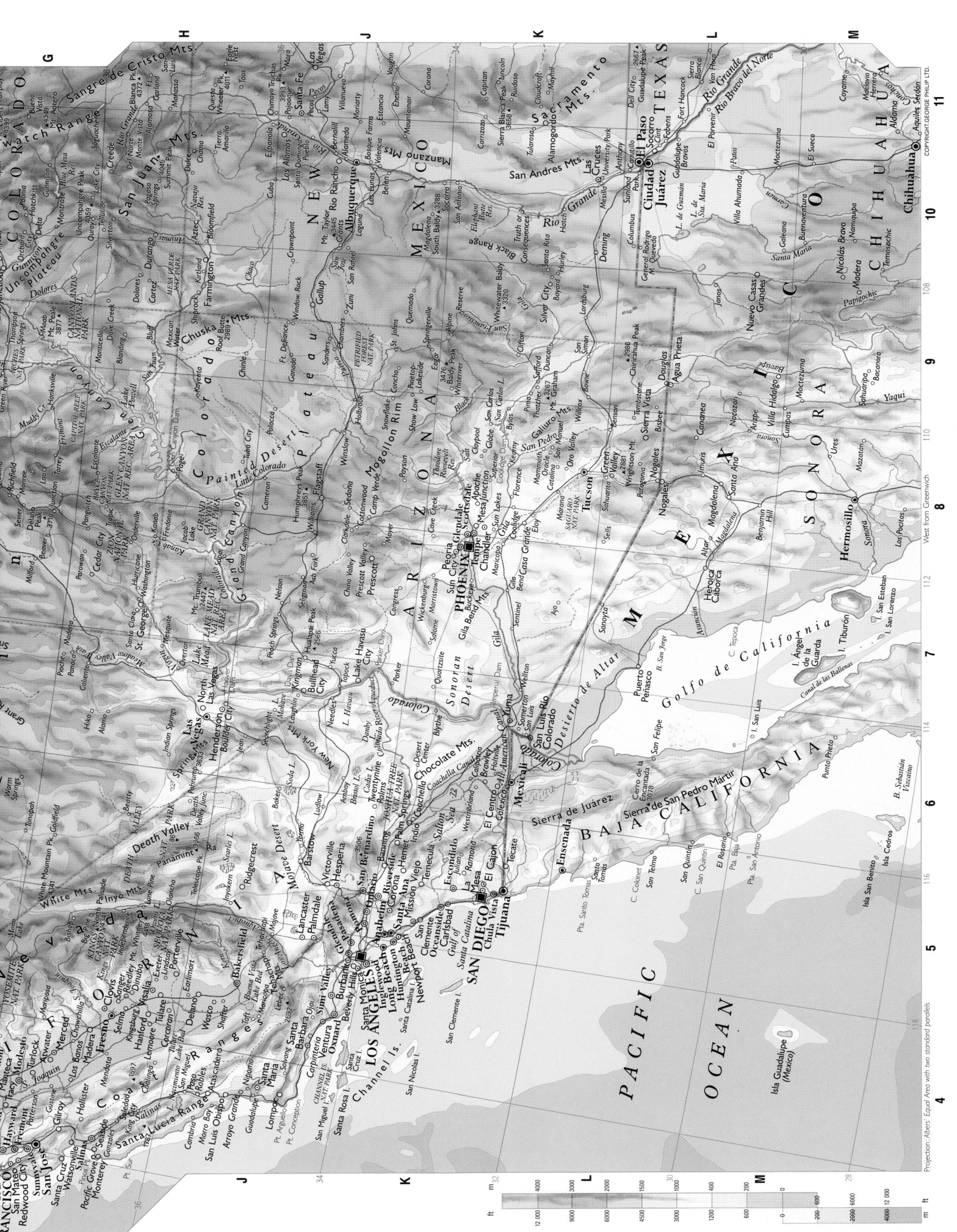

Projection: Albers' Equal Area with two standard parallels

WESTERN WASHINGTON
REGION
On same scale

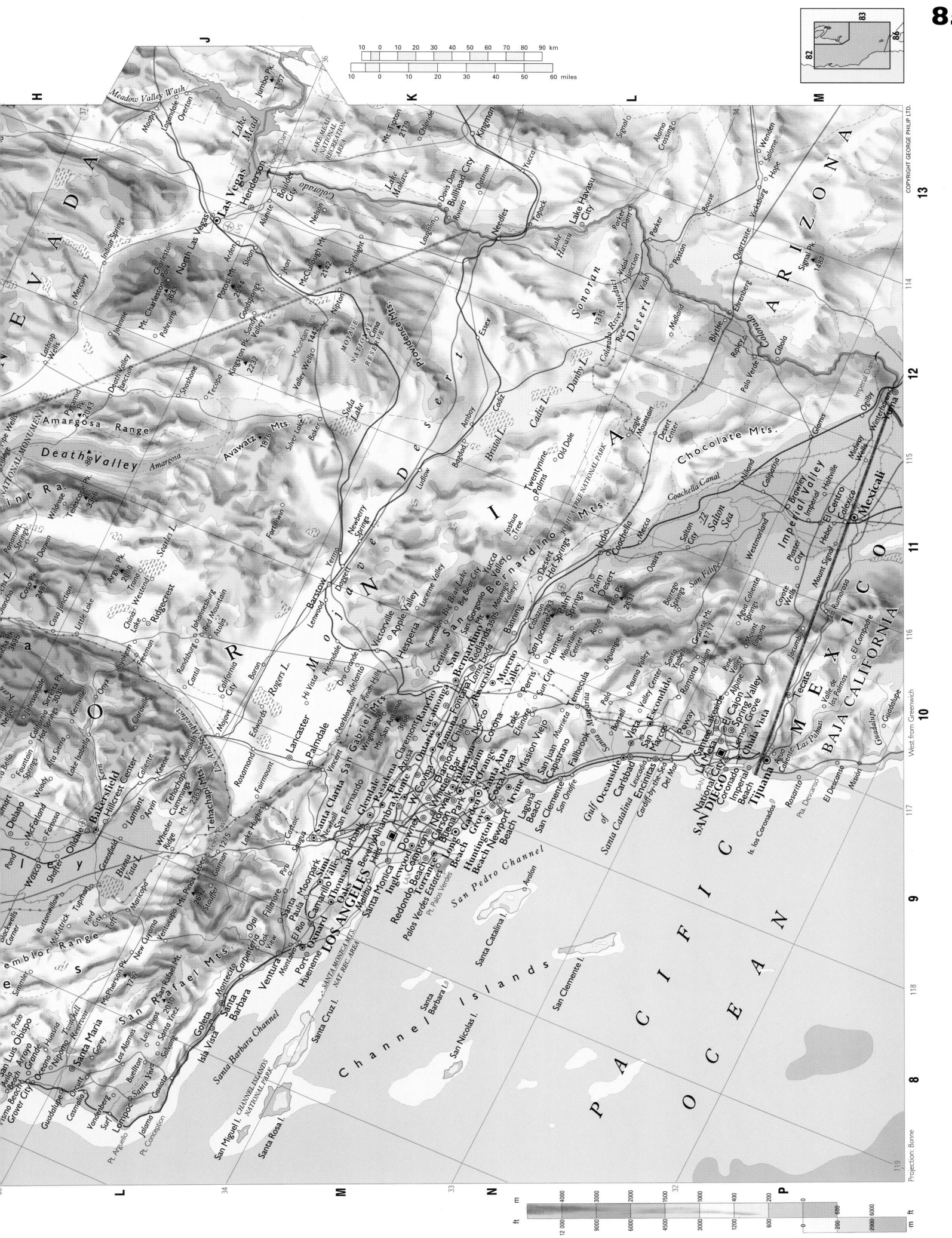

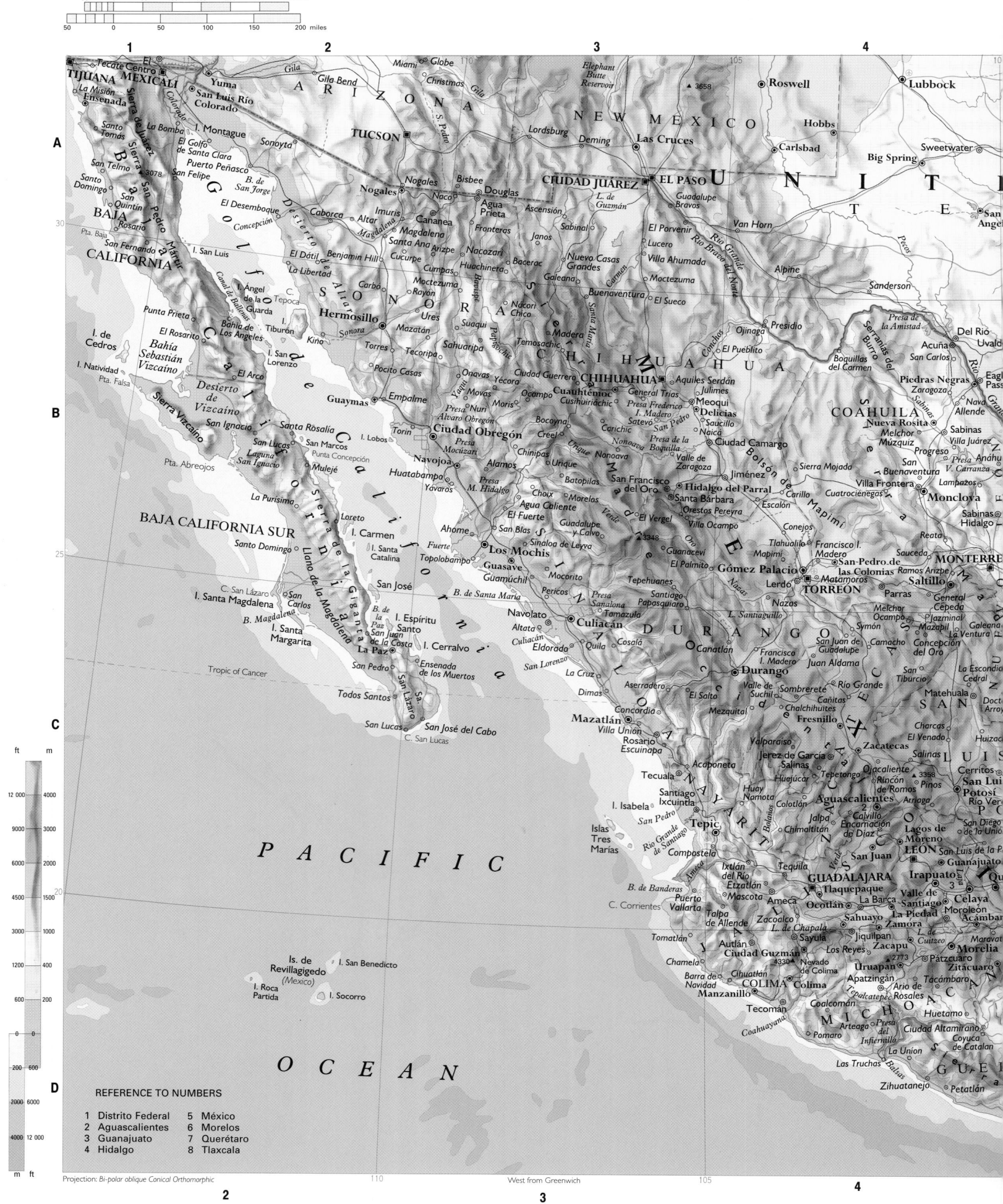

REFERENCE TO NUMBERS

1 Distrito Federal   5 México
2 Aguascalientes   6 Morelos
3 Guanajuato   7 Querétaro
4 Hidalgo   8 Tlaxcala

Projection: Bi-polar oblique Conical Orthomorphic

West from Greenwich

74
75
88

5
6
7
8
A
B
C
D
E
GULF OF MEXICO
Golfo de Campeche
Golfo de Tehuantepec
Golfo de Honduras
Canal de Yucatán
Tropic of Cancer
UNITED STATES
TEXAS
ARKANSAS
LOUISIANA
MISSISSIPPI
ALABAMA
GEORGIA
FLORIDA
MEXICO
TAMAULIPAS
VERACRUZ
PUEBLA
OAXACA
CHIAPAS
TABASCO
CAMPECHE
YUCATÁN
QUINTANA ROO
GUATEMALA
BELIZE
HONDURAS
CUBA
Wichita Falls
Denison
Sherman
Paris
Hope
Camden
Texarkana
El Dorado
Greenville
Tuscaloosa
Opelika
Columbus
Denton
Greenville
FORT WORTH
DALLAS
Marshall
Monroe
Vicksburg
Jackson
Meridian
Selma
Montgomery
Phenix City
McRae
Americus
Cordele
Albany
Tifton
Waycross
Ranger
Longview
Tyler
Shreveport
Tallulah
Laurel
Troy
Cleburne
Hillsboro
Corsicana
Palestine
Nacogdoches
Natchez
Hattiesburg
Dothan
Valdosta
Brownwood
Waco
Lufkin
Jewett
Alexandria
McComb
Flomaton
Chattahoochee
Tallahassee
Temple
Huntsville
Bryan
Baton Rouge
Hammond
Bogalusa
Biloxi
Gulfport
MOBILE
Pensacola
Panama City
Lake City
Apalachee Bay
Austin
Navasota
Beaumont
Lake Charles
Lafayette
NEW ORLEANS
L. Pontchartrain
Breton Sd.
Mobile Bay
C. San Blas
Suwannee
HOUSTON
Port Arthur
Atchafalaya Bay
Terrebonne Bay
Mississippi River Delta
Rosenberg
Galveston
SAN ANTONIO
Victoria
Clearwater
Dilley
Alice
Corpus Christi
Laredo
Kingsville
Nuevo Laredo
Zapata
Laguna Madre
Camargo
McAllen
Harlingen
Brownsville
Reynosa
Matamoros
Valle Hermoso
Santa Teresa
Montemorelos
Mendez
Laguna Madre
San Fernando
Linares
Villagrán
Hidalgo
Santander Jiménez
La Pesca
Soto la Marina
Ciudad Victoria
Sierra de Tamaulipas
Llera
Aldama
Pta. Jerez
Ciudad Mante
Altamira
Ciudad Madero
Tampico
Ciudad Cárdenas de Valles
Pánuco
Ozuluama
L. de Tamiahua
C. Rojo
Tempoal
Tantoyuca
Tamazunchale
Tuxpan
Poza Rica
Papantla
Huauchinango
Nautla
Misantla
Pachuca
Tulancingo
Teziutlán
Jalapa Enriquez
MÉXICO
Apizaco
Coatepec
Veracruz
PUEBLA
Córdoba
Orizaba
Alvarado
Tlacotalpan
San Andrés Tuxtla
Tehuacán
Cosamaloapan
Coatzacoalcos
Minatitlán
Cárdenas
Villahermosa
Frontera
Ciudad del Carmen
L. de Términos
Champotón
Chenkán
Campeche
Tenabo
Hopelchén
Bolonchenticul
Tekax
Ticul
Peto
Maxcanú
Mérida
Progreso
Motul
Temax
Izamal
Tizimín
Espita
Valladolid
Sotuta
Dzilam de Bravo
Rio Lagartos
El Cuyo
C. Catoche
Cancún
Puerto Juárez
Puerto Morelos
Cozumel
Isla Cozumel
I. Desterrada
I. Pérez (Mexico)
Pta. Yalkubul
Vigía Chico
B. de la Ascensión
B. del Espíritu Santo
Felipe Carrillo Puerto
Bacalar
Chetumal
B. de Chetumal
Banco Chinchorro
Ambergris Cay
Corozal
Orange Walk
Belize City
Belmopan
Dangriga
Turneffe Is.
Matamoros
Concepción
Palizada
Balancán
Tenosique
Uaxactún
Flores
L. Petén Itzá
La Libertad
San Ignacio
Benque Viejo
Maya Mts.
Monkey River
San Antonio
Punta Gorda
Puerto Barrios
Livingston
San Luis
Is. de la Bahía
Roatán
Puerto Castilla
Trujillo
Tela
Oaxaca
Tlacolula
Tehuantepec
Juchitán
Salina Cruz
Arriaga
Tonalá
Pijijiapan
Mapastepec
Huixtla
Tapachula
Tuxtla Gutiérrez
San Cristóbal de las Casas
Comitán
La Independencia
Ocosingo
Acapulco
Chilpancingo
Iguala
Ometepec
Pinotepa Nacional
Jamiltepec
Puerto Escondido
Puerto Ángel
Pochutla
Miahuatlán
Ejutla
Ocotlán
Punta Maldonado
GUATEMALA
Cobán
Huehuetenango
Quetzaltenango
San Marcos
Totonicapán
Sololá
Antigua
Jalapa
Chiquimula
Zacapa
L. de Izabal
HONDURAS
San Pedro Sula
El Progreso
Tegucigalpa
Comayagua
Santa Rosa de Copán
La Esperanza
Juticalpa
Catacamas
Olanchito
Yoro
La Esperanza
Guane
La Fe
C. San Antonio
C. Corrientes
30
25
20
15
95
90
85

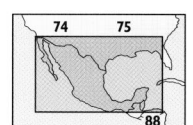

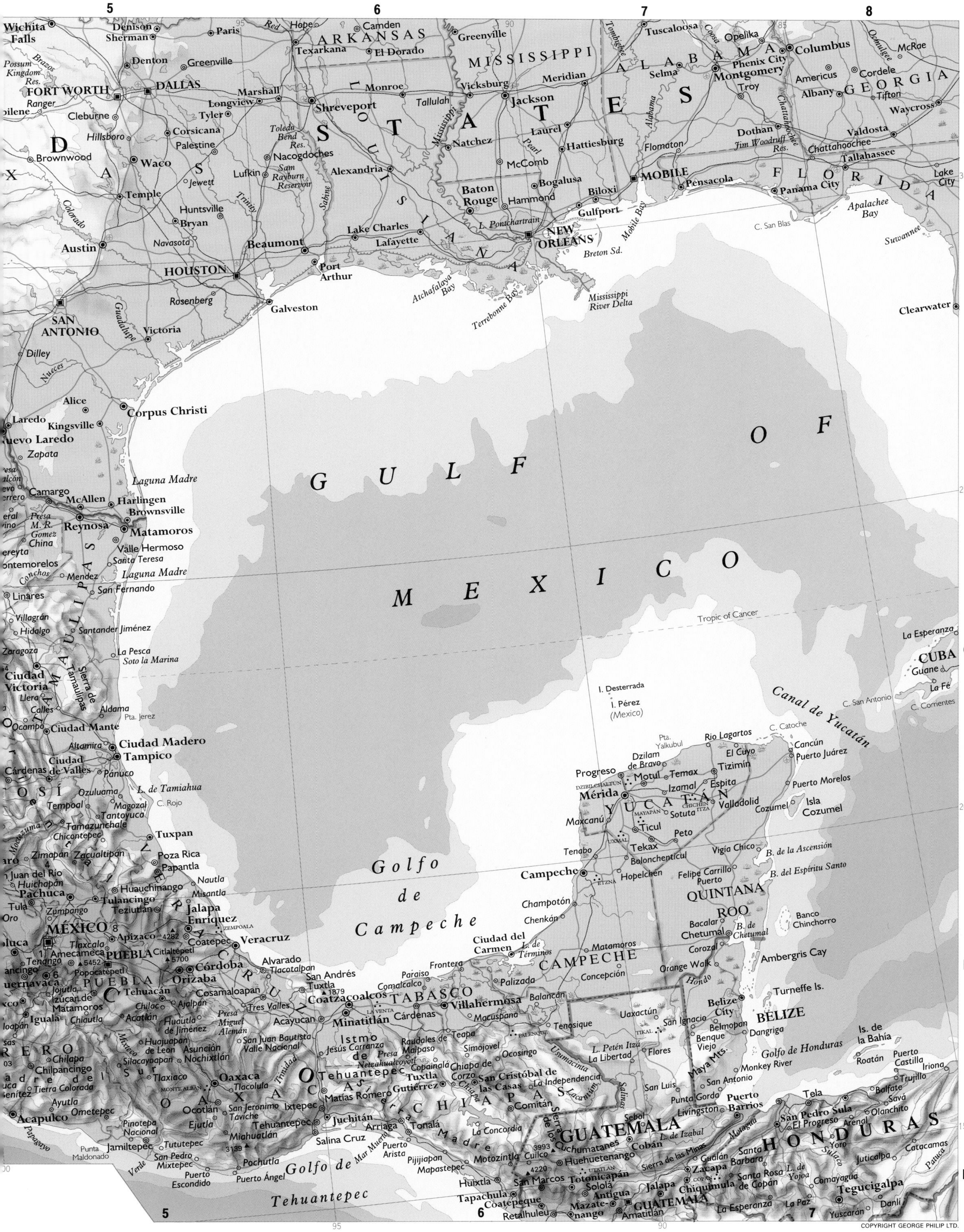

1:8 000 000

GULF OF MEXICO

PACIFIC OCEAN

CARIBBEAN

U.S.A.

MEXICO

YUCATÁN

QUINTANA ROO

CAMPECHE

GUATEMALA

BELIZE

HONDURAS

EL SALVADOR

NICARAGUA

COSTA RICA

PANAMÁ

CUBA

JAMAICA

BAHAMAS

Cayman Islands (U.K.)

Swan Islands (U.S.A. & Honduras)

Cayos Miskitos (Nicaragua)

I. de San Andrés (Colombia)

I. de Providencia (Colombia)

Cayos Roncador (U.S.A. & Colombia)

Cayos de Albuquerque (Colombia)

Is. del Maíz (Nicaragua. U.S.A.)

MIAMI

Fort Myers · Naples · Fort Lauderdale · West Palm Beach · Boca Raton

Key West · Dry Tortugas (U.S.A.) · Florida Keys

LA HABANA (Havana) · MARIANAO · Matanzas · Cárdenas · Cienfuegos · Santa Clara · Camagüey · HOLGUÍN · Bayamo · Manzanillo · SANTIAGO DE CUBA

Pinar del Río · Guane

Montego Bay · KINGSTON · Spanish Town · May Pen · Mandeville

Mérida · Progreso · Motul · Valladolid · Cancún · Puerto Juárez · Cozumel · Isla Cozumel

Campeche · Champotón · Ciudad del Carmen

Chetumal · Corozal · Orange Walk · Belize City · Belmopan · Dangriga

Flores · Tikal · Cobán

GUATEMALA · Quetzaltenango · Escuintla

San Salvador · Santa Ana · San Miguel · Sonsonate

San Pedro Sula · La Ceiba · Tela · El Progreso · Comayagua · Tegucigalpa · Juticalpa · Catacamas · Puerto Cortés · Trujillo

Roatán · Is. de la Bahía

Puerto Cabezas · Puerto Cabo Gracias a Dios · Bluefields · El Bluff

MANAGUA · León · Chinandega · Corinto · Granada · Masaya · Matagalpa · Estelí · Jinotega · Rama

Lago de Nicaragua · L. de Managua · I. de Ometepe

Liberia · Puntarenas · Alajuela · SAN JOSÉ · Cartago · Limón

PANAMÁ · Colón · David · Panama Canal · Golfo de Panamá · Golfo del Darién · Archipiélago de San Blas · Arch. de las Perlas

Golfo de Honduras · Golfo de Fonseca

Canal de Yucatán

Straits of Florida

Sierra Maestra

Projection: Conical with two standard parallels

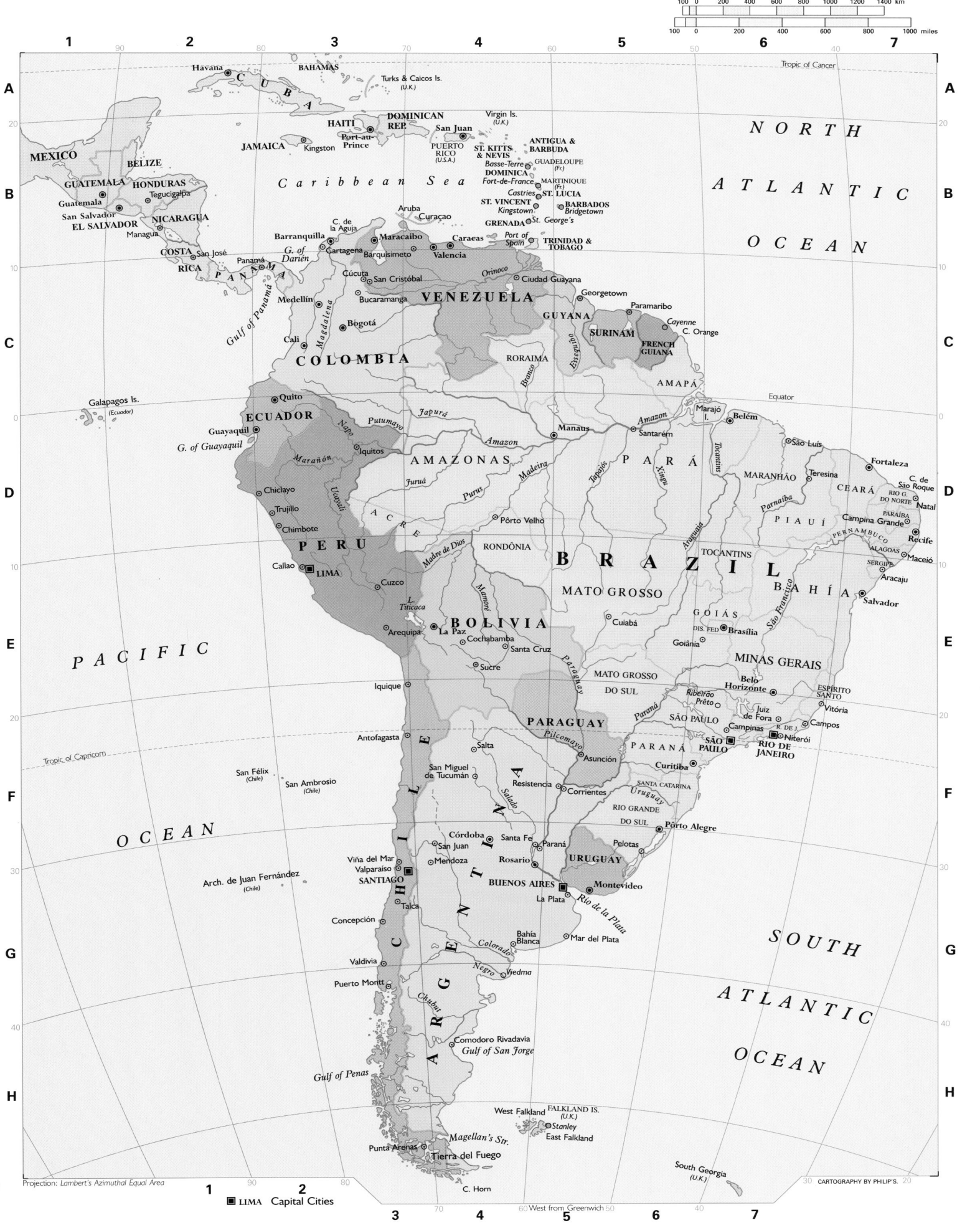

■ LIMA Capital Cities

Projection: Lambert's Azimuthal Equal Area

CARTOGRAPHY BY PHILIP'S

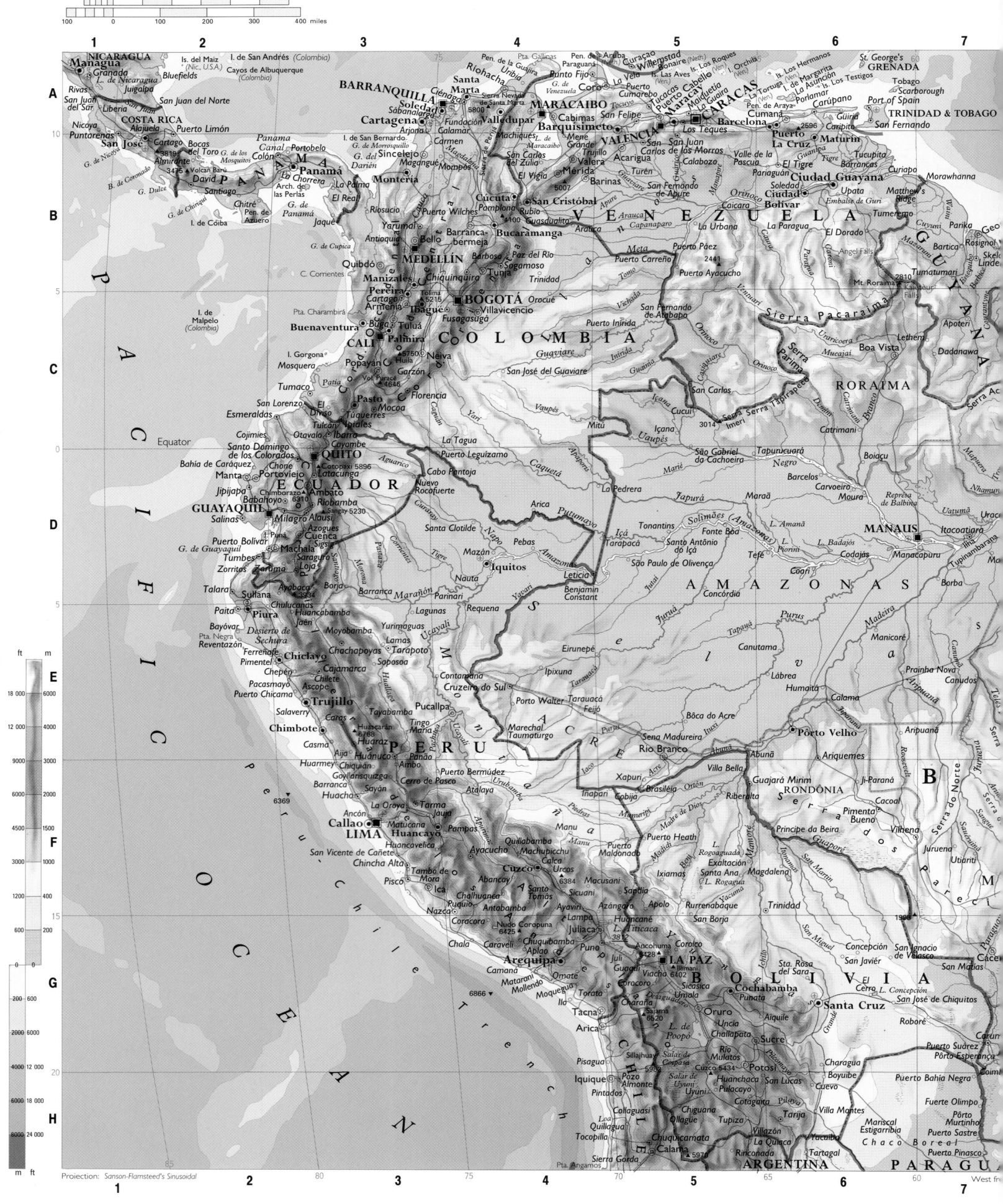

87
88
89
94
95

8
9
10
11
12
13
A
B
C
D
E
F
G
H
55
50
45
40
35
30
10
5
0
5
10
15
20
A T L A N T I C
O C E A N
Equator
São Paulo (Braz.)
Rocas
Fernando de Noronha (Braz.)
Trindade (Braz.)
6059
Paramaribo
Nieuw Amsterdam
Nickerie
Totness
Moengo
St.-Laurent
Iracoubo
Sinnamary
Kourou
Cayenne
Kwakoegron
Albina
Approuague
C. Orange
St. Georges
Oiapoque
Kaw
FRENCH GUIANA
RINAM
Camopi
Serra Tumucumaque
Amapá
I. de Maracá
AMAPÁ
Araguari
Merirumã
Serra do Navio
Macapá
I. Caviana
I. Mexiana
C. Maguarinho
Mazagão
Afuá
Chaves
Soure
Salinópolis
Curuçá
Vigia
Bragança
I. Grande de Gurupá
I. de Marajó
BELÉM
Almeirim
Gurupá
Breves
Castanhal
Viseu
Cururupu
Óbidos
Monte Alegre
Prainha
Pôrto de Móz
Curralinho
Abaetetuba
Turiaçu
Alenquer
Amazonas (Amazon)
Cametá
Juruti
Santarém
Belterra
Aveiro
Brasília Legal
Altamira
Baião
Tucuruí
Represa de Tucuruí
Itaituba
Iriri
P A R Á
B. de São Marcos
São Luís
Alcântara
Barreirinhas
Tutóia
Luís Correia
Camocim
Granja
Itapipoca
Caucaia
FORTALEZA
Cascavel
Pinheiro
Rosário
Itapecuru-Mirim
Viana
Parnaíba
Santa Inês
Brejo
Piracuruca
Sobral
Maranguape
Bacabal
Coroatá
Codó
Piripiri
Ipu
Baturité
Aracati
Russas
Quixadá
Areia Branca
Macau
Ceará Mirim
C. de São Roque
Açailândia
Pedreiras
Caxias
Campo Maior
Oiticica
Crateús
Teresina
MARANHÃO
Marabá
Tocantins
São João do Araguaia
Imperatriz
Barra do Corda
Grajaú
Carajás
Serra dos Carajás
Tocantinópolis
Pôrto Franco
Estreito
Carolina
Colinas
Amarante
Valença do Piauí
Senador Pompeu
Iguatu
CEARÁ
Mossoró
RIO GRANDE DO NORTE
Natal
Caraúbas
Caicó
Currais Novos
Canguaretama
Mamanguape
Alagoa Grande
Cabedelo
João Pessoa
Floriano
Oeiras
Picos
Crato
Cajàzeiras
Sousa
Patos
PARAÍBA
Campina Grande
Olinda
RECIFE
Jaboatão
Vitória de Santo Antão
Loreto
Nova Iorque
Uruçuí
PIAUÍ
Ouricuri
Chapada do Araripe
Juàzeiro do Norte
Araguaína
Riachão
Conceição do Araguaia
Araguacema
Paulistana
Salgueiro
Pesqueira
Caruaru
PERNAMBUCO
Garanhuns
Palmares
Petrolândia
Palmeira dos Índios
Rio Largo
Maceió
Arapiraca
ALAGOAS
Penedo
Petrolina
Juàzeiro
Paulo Afonso
São Francisco
Pedro Afonso
São João do Piauí
Santa Filomena
Caracol
Novo Remanso
Sa. Dois Irmãos
Nova Casa Nova
Represa de Sobradinho
Senhor-do-Bonfim
Propriá
SERGIPE
Capela
Aracaju
São Cristóvão
Estância
Serra do Cachimbo
Serra do Estrondo
Chapada das Mangabeiras
Serra da Tabatinga
Palmas
Parnaguá
Pôrto Nacional
Barra
Xique-Xique
Jacobina
TOCANTINS
Queimadas
Serrinha
Feira de Santana
Alagoinhas
Santo Amaro
Cachoeira
SALVADOR
Santa Isabel do Morro
Gurupi
Peixe
Taguatinga
Barreiras
Ibotirama
Itaberaba
Mundo Novo
Castro Alves
Nazaré
B. de Todos os Santos
Valença
Jequié
Serra Formosa
Serra do Roncador
Paranã
Campos Belos
São Domingos
Santa Maria da Vitória
Bom Jesus da Lapa
Serra do Sincorá
Contas
BAHIA
R A Z I L
O GROSSO
Planalto do Mato Grosso
Uruaçu
Niquelândia
1678
Posse
Carinhanha
Caetité
Brumado
Ubaitaba
Itabuna
Ilhéus
Vitória da Conquista
Condeúba
Aruanã
Monte Azul
Canavieiras
DIST. FED.
Formosa
BRASÍLIA
Taguatinga
Januária
São Francisco
Janaúba
Pedra Azul
Belmonte
Pôrto Seguro
Santo Antônio
Barra do Garças
Goiás
Anápolis
Luziânia
Rondonópolis
Goiânia
Montes Claros
Salinas
Jequitinhonha
Araçuaí
Itamaraju
Prado
Caravelas
Nanuque
Mucuri
GOIÁS
Alto Araguaia
Vianópolis
Morrinhos
Paracatu
Pirapora
Teófilo Otoni
MATO GROSSO DO SUL
Jataí
Rio Verde
Ipameri
Catalão
Patos de Minas
Diamantina
Governador Valadares
Coxim
Quirinópolis
Itumbiara
Araguari
Corinto
1340
Nova Venécia
Conceição da Barra
São Mateus
Linhares
MINAS GERAIS
Uberlândia
Patrocínio
Ituiutaba
Prata
Araxá
Ibiá
Curvelo
Sete Lagoas
Ipatinga
Itabira
Colatina
Campo Grande
Paranaíba
Santa Fé do Sul
Uberaba
Frutal
BELO HORIZONTE
Sabará
Caratinga
Cariacica
Vitória
Vila Velha
Miranda
Água Clara
São José do Rio Prêto
Ponte Nova
ESPÍRITO SANTO
2890
Aquidauana
Ribas do Rio Pardo
Três Lagoas
Rio Prêto
Igarapava
Franca
Divinópolis
Passos
Conselheiro Lafaiete
Ouro Prêto
Ubá
Cachoeiro de Itapemirim
Araçatuba
Andradina
Ribeirão Prêto
Itaperuna
Panorama
Penápolis
Catanduva
Lins
Guaxupé
São João del Rei
Barbacena
Juiz de Fora
Campos
Dourados
Presidente Epitácio
SÃO PAULO
Araraquara
Poços de Caldas
Marília
São Carlos
São Lourenço
Três Rios
Nova Friburgo
Presidente Prudente
Bauru
Jaú
Moji-Mirim
2787
Petrópolis
Ponta Porã
Assis
Piracicaba
Limeira
Volta Redonda
RIO DE JANEIRO
Botucatu
Campinas
Niterói
Cabo Frio
Pedro Juan Caballero
RIO DE JANEIRO
nwich
8
9
10
11
12
13

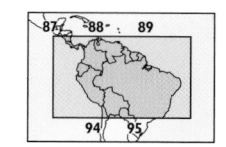

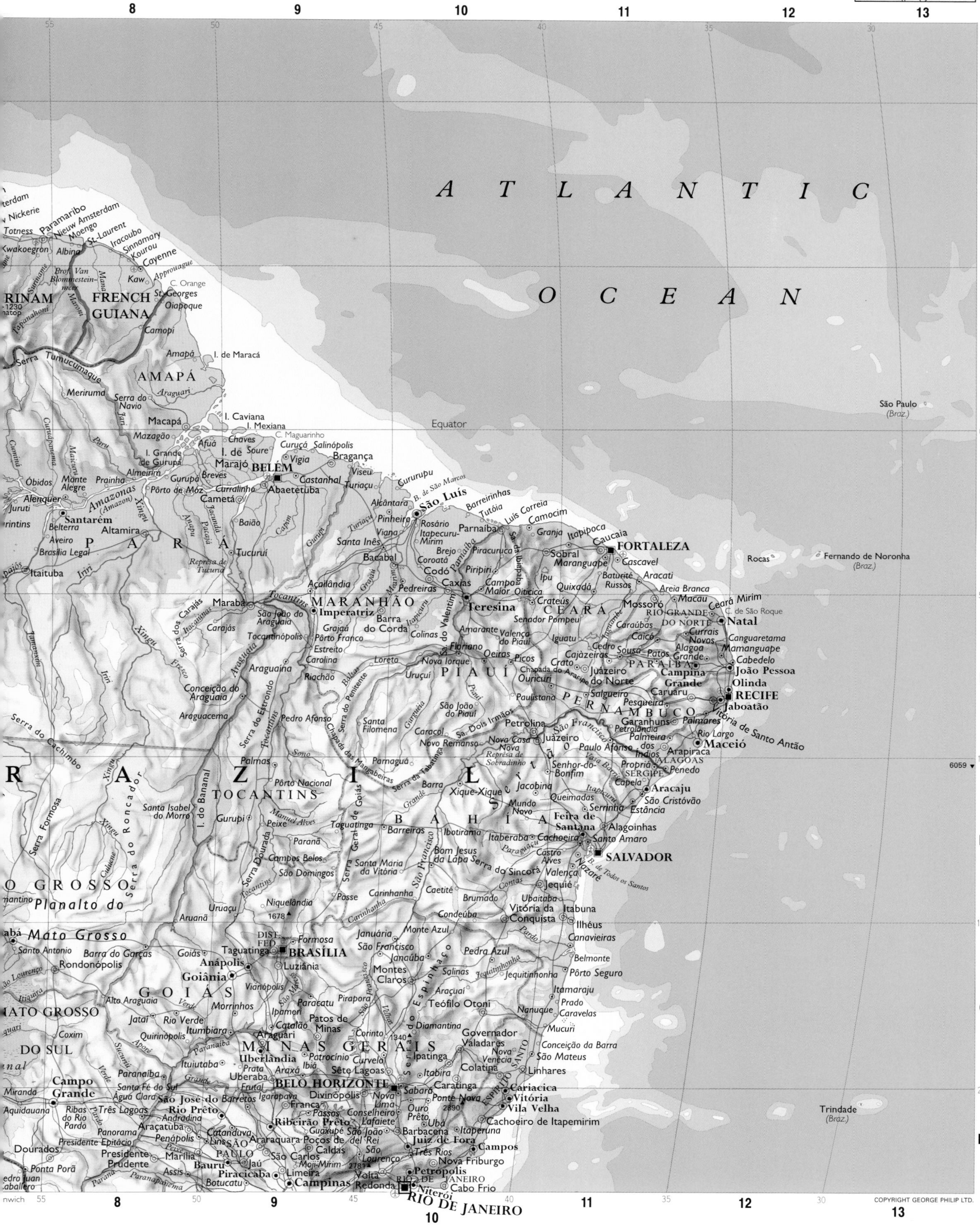

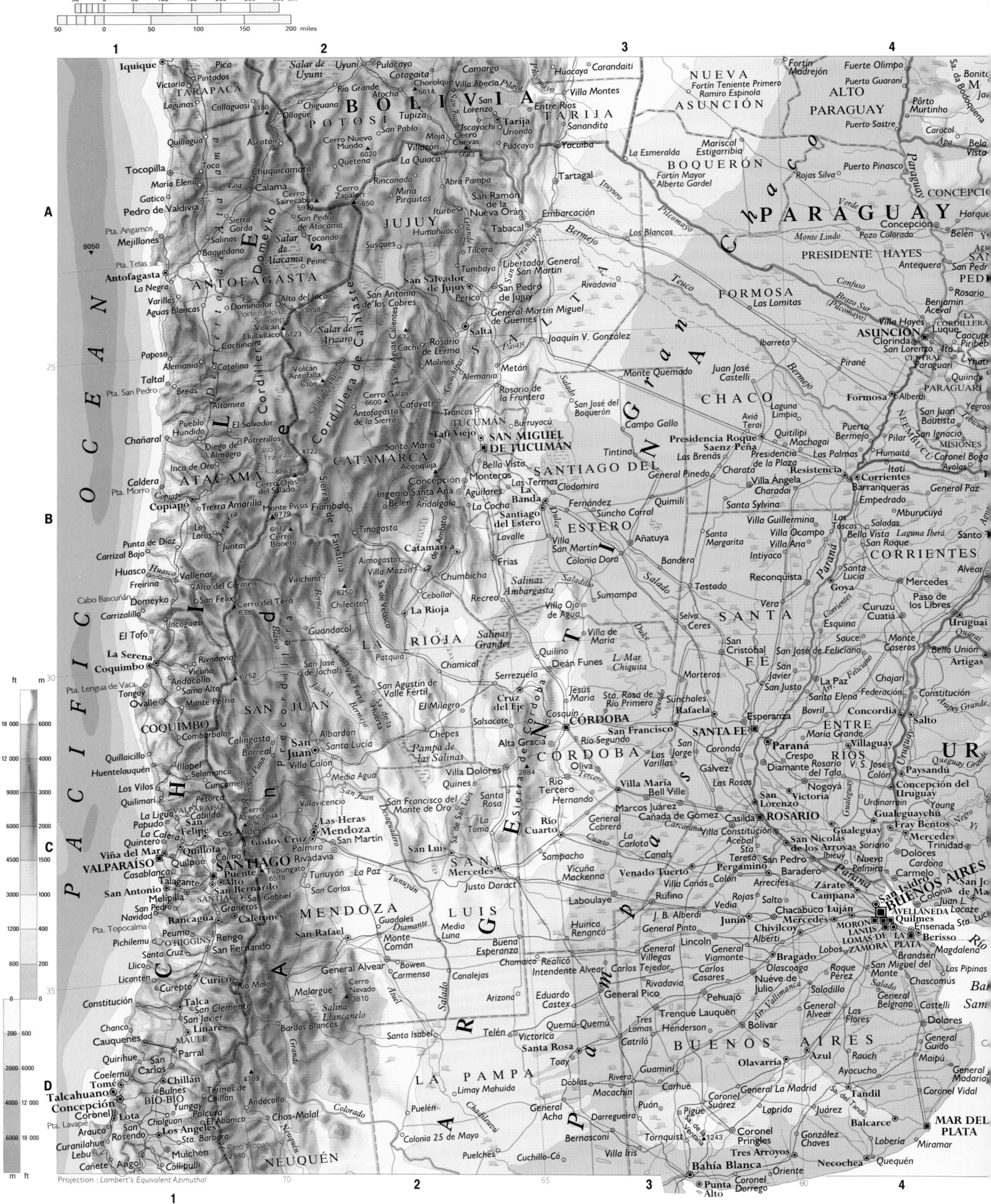

92 93 96

5 6 7

BELO HORIZONTE
Nova Lima
Itabirito

Vitória
Itaquari
Vila Velha
Guarapari

Sidrolândia
Nioaque
T O G R O S S O
uía Lopes
Capitán
e Laguna
Maracaju
Nova Alvorada
do Sul
Xavantina
Três Lagoas
Mirassol
Andradina
Mirandópolis
Panorama
Olímpia
São José
do Rio Prêto
Batatais
Passos
Oliveira
Conselheiro
Lafaiete
Congonhas
Ouro
Prêto
Ponte Nova
Carangola
Muriaé
Pico da
Bandeira
2880
Castelo
Cachoeiro
de Itapemirim

Dourados
D O S U L
Rio
Brilhante
Nova
Andradina
Adamantina
Santo
Anastácio
Lins
Penápolis
Aracatuba
Birigui
Catanduva
Novo
Horizonte
Jaboticabal
Ribeirão
Prêto
Guaxupé
São Sebastião
do Paraíso
Mocóca
Casa
Branca
Represa de
Furnas
Campo Belo
Barbacena
Cataguases
Ubá
Itaperuna
Cambuci
Guarus

Ponta Porã
Dourados
Pedro Juan Caballero
Pôrto São José
Presidente
Epitácio
Euclides da
Cunha Paulista
Presidente
Prudente
Martinópolis
S Ã O
Tupã
Marília
Paraguaçu
Paulista
Bauru
Jaú
Garça
Bariri
Araraquara
São
Carlos
São João
da Boa Vista
Araras
Alfenas
Poços de
Caldas
Varginha
Pouso
Alegre
Três
Corações
Lavras
São João
del Rei
Santos
Dumont
Juiz de Fora
Leopoldina
Além Paraíba
Paraíba do Sul
Macaé
RIO DE JANEIRO
Cabo de
São Tomé
CAMPOS

Amambaí
Ivinhema
Rosana
Rancharia
P A U L O
Pirajuí
Garça
Jaú
Rio Claro
Piracicaba
Limeira
Ouro Fino
Pinhal
Itajubá
2787
Volta
Redonda
Barra do Piraí
Barra
Mansa
Nova Friburgo

Centenário do Sul
Paranapanema
Assis
Cambará
Ourinhos
Botucatu
CAMPINAS
Americana
Mogi-Mirim
Guaratinguetá
Bragança
Paulista
Serra
Cruzeiro
Petrópolis
DUQUE DE CAXIAS
SÃO GONÇALO

Navirai
Paranavaí
Nova
Esperança
Rolândia
Cornélio
Procópio
Jacarèzinho
Avaré
Itu
Jundiaí
São José
do C.
Taubate
Jacarei
NOVA IGUAÇU
NITERÓI

Umuarama
Londrina
Maringá
Cianorte
Apucarana
Joaquim
Távora
Itapeva
Itu
SÃO PAULO
São Bernardo
do Campo
SANTO ANDRÉ
Moji das Cruzes
Ilha Grande
Bahia da Ilha Grande
RIO DE JANEIRO

CANINDEYÚ
Caruguatý
anislao
Represa de
Itaipú
Goio-Erê
Campo
Mourão
Ibaiti
Itapetininga
São Vicente
SANTOS
Guarujá
Angra dos
Reis
Pta. de Juatinga
Cabo Frio
La. de Araruama
Tropic of Capricorn

hú
Hernandarias
nel Oviedo
ALTO
Cascavel
Medianeira
Pitanga
Castro
Itararé
Paranapiacaba
Itanhaém
Ilha de São Sebastião
Pta. de Boi

Abai
Ciudad
del Este
Irala
rica
PARANÁ
B R A Z I L
Prudentópolis
Guarapuava
Ponta
Grossa
Tibagi
Jaguariaíva
Apiaí
Juquiá
Iguape

apá
APA
Eldorado
Foz do Iguaçu
Cat. del
Iguaçu
Francisco
Beltrão
Laranjeiras
do Sul
Irati
Palmeira
CURITIBA
Antonina
Paranaguá
Matinhos
Guaratuba
1889
Registro
Ilha Comprida

TAPUÁ
Pedro
Parana
Bernardo
de Irigoyen
Chopim
União da
Vitória
Lapa
São Mateus
do Sul
Rio Negro
Joinville
Ilha do Cardoso

mera Corpus
MISIONES
eral Artigas
Uruguai
Pato Branco
Clevelândia
Palmas
Pôrto União
Mafra
São Francisco do Sul

Pedro
Juan
San
Javier
São Miguel
do Oeste
Xanxerê
1340
Caçador
Santa Cecília
Itajaí

Encarnación
Obera
Monteagudo
Chapecó
Joaçaba
SANTA CATARINA
Blumenau
Brusque

Candelaria
Leandro N. Alem
Santa Rosa
Frederico
Westphalen
Enerchim
Palmeira
das Missões
Campos
Novos
Curitibanos
Rio do Sul
São José
Ilha de Santa Catarina
Florianópolis

Apóstoles
Santo Ângelo
Ijuí
Carazinho
Passo
Fundo
Lajes
São
Joaquim
1808

São Luís
Gonzaga
Cruz Alta
Coxilha
Grande
Guaporé
Vacaria
Tubarão
Laguna
Cabo Santa Marta Grande

ão Borja
Sa. do Espinho
Santiago
RIO GRANDE
Bento Gonçalves
Caxias do Sul
Criciúma
Araranguá

Ibicuí
Santa Maria
Santa Cruz
do Sul
Montenegro
Novo Hamburgo
Taquara
Torres

Alegrete
sário do Sul
D O S U L
Cachoeira do Sul
Rio Pardo
Canoas
São
Leopoldo
Osório

Coxilha
Santana do
Livramento
São
Gabriel
Caçapava
do Sul
Sa.
Encantadas
Viamão
PÔRTO ALEGRE

Rivera
Santana
Dom Pedrito
Camaquã
Tapes
Camaquã

UAY
Tacuarembó
Bagé
Pinheiro
Machado
Sa. do Canguçu
Canguçu
Pelotas
São Lourenço
do Sul
Mostardas
Lagoa
dos Patos

A T L A N T I C

Fraile
Muerto
San Gregorio
Blanquillo
Cerro
Chato
Melo
Rio
Branco
Jaguarão
Lagoa Mirim
São José
do Norte
Rio Grande

adí
José Batlle
y Ordóñez
Sarandí del Yí
Vergara
Treinta y Tres
Lagoa Mangueira

rida
Tala
elones
Minas
Piedras
Pando
Rocha
San Carlos
Maldonado
Aigua
Lascano
Santa Vitória do Palmar
Chuy
Castillos

O C E A N

ONTEVIDEO
Plata
bón

Antonio

5304

55 West from Greenwich 50 45 40 COPYRIGHT GEORGE PHILIP LTD

A
B
C
D

25
30
35

5 6 7

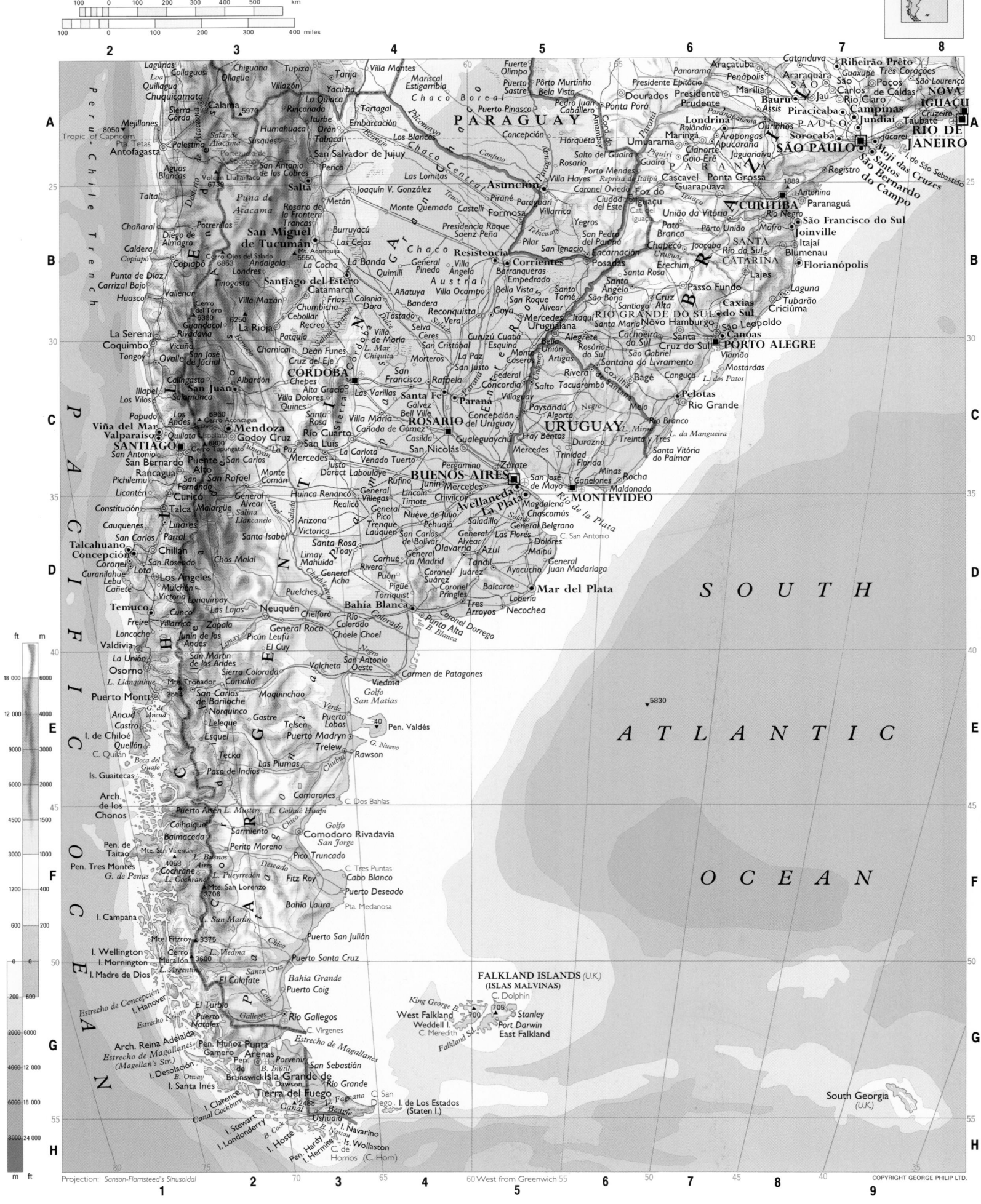

Projection: Sanson-Flamsteed's Sinusoidal

INDEX

The index contains the names of all the principal places and features shown on the World Maps. Each name is followed by an additional entry in italics giving the country or region within which it is located. The alphabetical order of names composed of two or more words is governed primarily by the first word and then by the second. This is an example of the rule:

Mīr Kūh, *Iran*	**45 E8**	26 22N	58 55 E
Mīr Shahdād, *Iran*	**45 E8**	26 15N	58 29 E
Mira, *Italy*	**20 B5**	45 26N	12 8 E
Mira por vos Cay, *Bahamas*	**89 B5**	22 9N	74 30 W
Miraj, *India*	**40 L9**	16 50N	74 45 E

Physical features composed of a proper name (Erie) and a description (Lake) are positioned alphabetically by the proper name. The description is positioned after the proper name and is usually abbreviated:

Erie, L., *N. Amer.*	**78 D4**	42 15N	81 0W

Where a description forms part of a settlement or administrative name however, it is always written in full and put in its true alphabetic position:

Mount Morris, *U.S.A.*	**78 D7**	42 44N	77 52 W

Names beginning with M' and Mc are indexed as if they were spelled Mac. Names beginning St. are alphabetised under Saint, but Sankt, Sint, Sant', Santa and San are all spelt in full and are alphabetised accordingly. If the same place name occurs two or more times in the index and all are in the same country, each is followed by the name of the administrative subdivision in which it is located. The names are placed in the alphabetical order of the subdivisions. For example:

Jackson, *Ky., U.S.A.*	**76 G4**	37 33N	83 23 W
Jackson, *Mich., U.S.A.*	**76 D3**	42 15N	84 24 W
Jackson, *Minn., U.S.A.*	**80 D7**	43 37N	95 1 W

The number in bold type which follows each name in the index refers to the number of the map page where that feature or place will be found. This is usually the largest scale at which the place or feature appears.

The letter and figure which are in bold type immediately after the page number give the grid square on the map page, within which the feature is situated. The letter represents the latitude and the figure the longitude.

In some cases the feature itself may fall within the specified square, while the name is outside. This is usually the case only with features which are larger than a grid square.

For a more precise location the geographical coordinates which follow the letter/figure references give the latitude and the longitude of each place. The first set of figures represent the latitude which is the distance north or south of the Equator measured as an angle at the centre of the earth. The Equator is latitude 0°, the North Pole is 90°N, and the South Pole 90°S.

The second set of figures represent the longitude, which is the distance East or West of the prime meridian, which runs through Greenwich, England. Longitude is also measured as an angle at the centre of the earth and is given East or West of the prime meridian, from 0° to 180° in either direction.

The unit of measurement for latitude and longitude is the degree, which is subdivided into 60 minutes. Each index entry states the position of a place in degrees and minutes, a space being left between the degrees and the minutes.

The latitude is followed by N(orth) or S(outh) and the longitude by E(ast) or W(est).

Rivers are indexed to their mouths or confluences, and carry the symbol ➜ after their names. A solid square ■ follows the name of a country, while an open square □ refers to a first order administrative area.

Abbreviations used in the index

A.C.T. – Australian Capital Territory
Afghan. – Afghanistan
Ala. – Alabama
Alta. – Alberta
Amer. – America(n)
Arch. – Archipelago
Ariz. – Arizona
Ark. – Arkansas
Atl. Oc. – Atlantic Ocean
B. – Baie, Bahía, Bay, Bucht, Bugt
B.C. – British Columbia
Bangla. – Bangladesh
Barr. – Barrage
Bos.-H. – Bosnia-Herzegovina
C. – Cabo, Cap, Cape, Coast
C.A.R. – Central African Republic
C. Prov. – Cape Province
Calif. – California
Cent. – Central
Chan. – Channel
Colo. – Colorado
Conn. – Connecticut
Cord. – Cordillera
Cr. – Creek
Czech. – Czech Republic
D.C. – District of Columbia
Del. – Delaware
Dep. – Dependency
Des. – Desert
Dist. – District
Dj. – Djebel
Domin. – Dominica
Dom. Rep. – Dominican Republic
E. – East

E. Salv. – El Salvador
Eq. Guin. – Equatorial Guinea
Fla. – Florida
Falk. Is. – Falkland Is.
G. – Golfe, Golfo, Gulf, Guba, Gebel
Ga. – Georgia
Gt. – Great, Greater
Guinea-Biss. – Guinea-Bissau
H.K. – Hong Kong
H.P. – Himachal Pradesh
Hants. – Hampshire
Harb. – Harbor, Harbour
Hd. – Head
Hts. – Heights
I.(s). – Île, Ilha, Insel, Isla, Island, Isle
Ill. – Illinois
Ind. – Indiana
Ind. Oc. – Indian Ocean
Ivory C. – Ivory Coast
J. – Jabal, Jebel, Jazira
Junc. – Junction
K. – Kap, Kapp
Kans. – Kansas
Kep. – Kepulauan
Ky. – Kentucky
L. – Lac, Lacul, Lago, Lagoa, Lake, Limni, Loch, Lough
La. – Louisiana
Liech. – Liechtenstein
Lux. – Luxembourg
Mad. P. – Madhya Pradesh
Madag. – Madagascar
Man. – Manitoba
Mass. – Massachusetts

Md. – Maryland
Me. – Maine
Medit. S. – Mediterranean Sea
Mich. – Michigan
Minn. – Minnesota
Miss. – Mississippi
Mo. – Missouri
Mont. – Montana
Mozam. – Mozambique
Mt.(e) – Mont, Monte, Monti, Montaña, Mountain
N. – Nord, Norte, North, Northern, Nouveau
N.B. – New Brunswick
N.C. – North Carolina
N. Cal. – New Caledonia
N. Dak. – North Dakota
N.H. – New Hampshire
N.I. – North Island
N.J. – New Jersey
N. Mex. – New Mexico
N.S. – Nova Scotia
N.S.W. – New South Wales
N.W.T. – North West Territory
N.Y. – New York
N.Z. – New Zealand
Nebr. – Nebraska
Neths. – Netherlands
Nev. – Nevada
Nfld. – Newfoundland
Nic. – Nicaragua
O. – Oued, Ouadi
Occ. – Occidentale
Okla. – Oklahoma
Ont. – Ontario
Or. – Orientale

Oreg. – Oregon
Os. – Ostrov
Oz. – Ozero
P. – Pass, Passo, Pasul, Pulau
P.E.I. – Prince Edward Island
Pa. – Pennsylvania
Pac. Oc. – Pacific Ocean
Papua N.G. – Papua New Guinea
Pass. – Passage
Pen. – Peninsula, Péninsule
Phil. – Philippines
Pk. – Park, Peak
Plat. – Plateau
Prov. – Province, Provincial
Pt. – Point
Pta. – Ponta, Punta
Pte. – Pointe
Qué. – Québec
Queens. – Queensland
R. – Rio, River
R.I. – Rhode Island
Ra.(s). – Range(s)
Raj. – Rajasthan
Reg. – Region
Rep. – Republic
Res. – Reserve, Reservoir
S. – San, South, Sea
Si. Arabia – Saudi Arabia
S.C. – South Carolina
S. Dak. – South Dakota
S.I. – South Island
S. Leone – Sierra Leone
Sa. – Serra, Sierra
Sask. – Saskatchewan
Scot. – Scotland
Sd. – Sound

Sev. – Severnaya
Sib. – Siberia
Sprs. – Springs
St. – Saint
Sta. – Santa, Station
Ste. – Sainte
Sto. – Santo
Str. – Strait, Stretto
Switz. – Switzerland
Tas. – Tasmania
Tenn. – Tennessee
Tex. – Texas
Tg. – Tanjung
Trin. & Tob. – Trinidad & Tobago
U.A.E. – United Arab Emirates
U.K. – United Kingdom
U.S.A. – United States of America
Ut. P. – Uttar Pradesh
Va. – Virginia
Vdkhr. – Vodokhranilishche
Vf. – Vîrful
Vic. – Victoria
Vol. – Volcano
Vt. – Vermont
W. – Wadi, West
W. Va. – West Virginia
Wash. – Washington
Wis. – Wisconsin
Wlkp. – Wielkopolski
Wyo. – Wyoming
Yorks. – Yorkshire
Yug. – Yugoslavia

A Coruña

A

A Coruña, *Spain* **19 A1** 43 20N 8 25W
A Estrada, *Spain* **19 A1** 42 43N 8 27W
A Fonsagrada, *Spain* **19 A2** 43 8N 7 4W
Aachen, *Germany* **16 C4** 50 45N 6 6 E
Aalborg = Ålborg, *Denmark* **9 H13** 57 2N 9 54 E
Aalen, *Germany* **16 D6** 48 51N 10 6 E
Aalst, *Belgium* **15 D4** 50 56N 4 2 E
Aalten, *Neths.* **15 C6** 51 56N 6 35 E
Aalter, *Belgium* **15 C3** 51 5N 3 28 E
Äänekoski, *Finland* **9 E21** 62 36N 25 44 E
Aarau, *Switz.* **18 C8** 47 23N 8 4 E
Aare →, *Switz.* **18 C8** 47 33N 8 14 E
Aarhus = Århus, *Denmark* **9 H14** 56 8N 10 11 E
Aarschot, *Belgium* **15 D4** 50 59N 4 49 E
Aba, *Dem. Rep. of the Congo* **54 B3** 3 58N 30 17 E
Aba, *Nigeria* **50 G7** 5 10N 7 19 E
Ābādān, *Iran* **45 D6** 30 22N 48 20 E
Ābādeh, *Iran* **45 D7** 31 8N 52 40 E
Abadla, *Algeria* **50 B5** 31 2N 2 45W
Abaetetuba, *Brazil* **93 D9** 1 40S 48 50W
Abagnar Qi, *China* **34 C9** 43 52N 116 2 E
Abai, *Paraguay* **95 B4** 25 58S 55 54W
Abakan, *Russia* **27 D10** 53 40N 91 10 E
Abancay, *Peru* **92 F4** 13 35S 72 55W
Abariringa, *Kiribati* **64 H10** 2 50S 171 40W
Abarqū, *Iran* **45 D7** 31 10N 53 20 E
Abashiri, *Japan* **30 B12** 44 0N 144 15 E
Abashiri-Wan, *Japan* **30 C12** 44 0N 144 30 E
Ābay = Nîl el Azraq →, *Sudan* **51 E12** 15 38N 32 31 E
Abay, *Kazakstan* **26 E8** 49 38N 72 53 E
Abaya, L., *Ethiopia* **46 F2** 6 30N 37 50 E
Abaza, *Russia* **26 D9** 52 39N 90 6 E
'Abbāsābād, *Iran* **45 C8** 33 34N 58 23 E
Abbay = Nîl el Azraq →, *Sudan* **51 E12** 15 38N 32 31 E
Abbaye, Pt., *U.S.A.* **76 B1** 46 58N 88 8W
Abbé, L., *Ethiopia* **46 E3** 11 8N 41 47 E
Abbeville, *France* **18 A4** 50 6N 1 49 E
Abbeville, *Ala., U.S.A.* **77 K3** 31 34N 85 15W
Abbeville, *La., U.S.A.* **81 L8** 29 58N 92 8W
Abbeville, *S.C., U.S.A.* **77 H4** 34 11N 82 23W
Abbot Ice Shelf, *Antarctica* **5 D16** 73 0S 92 0W
Abbottabad, *Pakistan* **42 B5** 34 10N 73 15 E
Abd al Kūrī, *Ind. Oc.* **46 E5** 12 5N 52 20 E
Ābdar, *Iran* **45 D7** 30 16N 55 19 E
'Abdolābād, *Iran* **45 C8** 34 12N 56 30 E
Abdulpur, *Bangla.* **43 G13** 24 15N 88 59 E
Abéché, *Chad* **51 F10** 13 50N 20 35 E
Abengourou, *Ivory C.* **50 G5** 6 42N 3 27W
Åbenrå, *Denmark* **9 J13** 55 3N 9 25 E
Abeokuta, *Nigeria* **50 G6** 7 3N 3 19 E
Aber, *Uganda* **54 B3** 2 12N 32 25 E
Aberaeron, *U.K.* **11 E3** 52 15N 4 15W
Aberayron = Aberaeron, *U.K.* **11 E3** 52 15N 4 15W
Aberchirder, *U.K.* **12 D6** 57 34N 2 37W
Abercorn = Mbala, *Zambia* **55 D3** 8 46S 31 24 E
Abercorn, *Australia* **63 D5** 25 12S 151 5 E
Aberdare, *U.K.* **11 F4** 51 43N 3 27W
Aberdare Ra., *Kenya* **54 C4** 0 15S 36 50 E
Aberdeen, *Canada* **73 C7** 52 20N 106 8W
Aberdeen, *S. Africa* **56 E3** 32 28S 24 2 E
Aberdeen, *U.K.* **12 D6** 57 9N 2 5W
Aberdeen, *Ala., U.S.A.* **77 J1** 33 49N 88 33W
Aberdeen, *Idaho, U.S.A.* **82 E7** 42 57N 112 50W
Aberdeen, *Md., U.S.A.* **76 F7** 39 31N 76 10W
Aberdeen, *S. Dak., U.S.A.* **80 C5** 45 28N 98 29W
Aberdeen, *Wash., U.S.A.* **84 D3** 46 59N 123 50W
Aberdeen, City of □, *U.K.* **12 D6** 57 10N 2 10W
Aberdeenshire □, *U.K.* **12 D6** 57 17N 2 36W
Aberdovey = Aberdyfi, *U.K.* **11 E3** 52 33N 4 3W
Aberdyfi, *U.K.* **11 E3** 52 33N 4 3W
Aberfeldy, *U.K.* **12 E5** 56 37N 3 51W
Abergavenny, *U.K.* **11 F4** 51 49N 3 1W
Abergele, *U.K.* **10 D4** 53 17N 3 35W
Abernathy, *U.S.A.* **81 J4** 33 50N 101 51W
Abert, L., *U.S.A.* **82 E3** 42 38N 120 14W
Aberystwyth, *U.K.* **11 E3** 52 25N 4 5W
Abhā, *Si. Arabia* **46 D3** 18 0N 42 34 E
Abhar, *Iran* **45 B6** 36 9N 49 13 E
Abhayapuri, *India* **43 F14** 26 24N 90 38 E
Abidjan, *Ivory C.* **50 G5** 5 26N 3 58W
Abilene, *Kans., U.S.A.* **80 F6** 38 55N 97 13W
Abilene, *Tex., U.S.A.* **81 J5** 32 28N 99 43W
Abingdon, *U.K.* **11 F6** 51 40N 1 17W
Abingdon, *U.S.A.* **77 G5** 36 43N 81 59W
Abington Reef, *Australia* **62 B4** 18 0S 149 35 E
Abitau →, *Canada* **73 B7** 59 53N 109 3W
Abitibi →, *Canada* **70 B3** 51 3N 80 55W
Abitibi, L., *Canada* **70 C4** 48 40N 79 40W
Abkhaz Republic = Abkhazia □, *Georgia* **25 F7** 43 12N 41 5 E
Abkhazia □, *Georgia* **25 F7** 43 12N 41 5 E
Abminga, *Australia* **63 D1** 26 8S 134 51 E
Åbo = Turku, *Finland* **9 F20** 60 30N 22 19 E
Abohar, *India* **42 D6** 30 10N 74 10 E
Abomey, *Benin* **50 G6** 7 10N 2 5 E
Abong-Mbang, *Cameroon* **52 D2** 4 0N 13 8 E
Abou-Deïa, *Chad* **51 F9** 11 20N 19 20 E
Aboyne, *U.K.* **12 D6** 57 4N 2 47W
Abra Pampa, *Argentina* **94 A2** 22 43S 65 42W
Abraham L., *Canada* **72 C5** 52 15N 116 35W
Abreojos, Pta., *Mexico* **86 B2** 26 50N 113 40W
Abrud, *Romania* **17 E12** 46 19N 23 5 E
Absaroka Range, *U.S.A.* **82 D9** 44 45N 109 50W
Abu, *India* **42 G5** 24 41N 72 50 E
Abū al Abyad, *U.A.E.* **45 E7** 24 11N 53 50 E
Abū al Khaşīb, *Iraq* **45 D6** 30 25N 48 0 E
Abū 'Alī, *Si. Arabia* **45 E6** 27 20N 49 27 E
Abū 'Alī →, *Lebanon* **47 A4** 34 25N 35 50 E
Abu Dhabi = Abū Ẓāby, *U.A.E.* **46 C5** 24 28N 54 22 E
Abū Du'ān, *Syria* **44 B3** 36 25N 38 15 E
Abu el Gairi, W. →, *Egypt* **47 F2** 29 35N 33 30 E
Abu Ga'da, W. →, *Egypt* **47 F1** 29 15N 32 53 E
Abū Ḩadrīyah, *Si. Arabia* **45 E6** 27 20N 48 58 E
Abu Hamed, *Sudan* **51 E12** 19 32N 33 13 E
Abū Kamāl, *Syria* **44 C4** 34 30N 41 0 E
Abū Madd, Ra's, *Si. Arabia* **44 E3** 24 50N 37 7 E
Abū Mūsā, *U.A.E.* **45 E7** 25 52N 55 3 E
Abū Qaşr, *Si. Arabia* **44 D3** 30 21N 38 34 E
Abu Şafāt, W. →, *Jordan* **47 E5** 30 24N 36 7 E
Abu Simbel, *Egypt* **51 D12** 22 18N 31 40 E
Abū Şukhayr, *Iraq* **44 D5** 31 54N 44 30 E
Abu Zabad, *Sudan* **51 F11** 12 25N 29 10 E
Abū Ẓāby, *U.A.E.* **46 C5** 24 28N 54 22 E
Abū Zeydābād, *Iran* **45 C6** 33 54N 51 45 E
Abuja, *Nigeria* **50 G7** 9 16N 7 2 E
Abukuma-Gawa →, *Japan* **30 E10** 38 6N 140 52 E
Abukuma-Sammyaku, *Japan* **30 F10** 37 30N 140 45 E
Abunã, *Brazil* **92 E5** 9 40S 65 20W
Abunã →, *Brazil* **92 E5** 9 41S 65 20W
Aburo, *Dem. Rep. of the Congo* **54 B3** 2 4N 30 53 E
Abut Hd., *N.Z.* **59 K3** 43 7S 170 15 E
Acadia National Park, *U.S.A.* **77 C11** 44 20N 68 13W
Açailândia, *Brazil* **93 D9** 4 57S 47 0W
Acajutla, *El Salv.* **88 D2** 13 36N 89 50W
Acámbaro, *Mexico* **86 D4** 20 0N 100 40W
Acaponeta, *Mexico* **86 C3** 22 30N 105 20W
Acapulco, *Mexico* **87 D5** 16 51N 99 56W
Acarai, Serra, *Brazil* **92 C7** 1 50N 57 50W
Acarigua, *Venezuela* **92 B5** 9 33N 69 12W
Acatlán, *Mexico* **87 D5** 18 10N 98 3W
Acayucan, *Mexico* **87 D6** 17 59N 94 58W
Accomac, *U.S.A.* **76 G8** 37 43N 75 40W
Accra, *Ghana* **50 G5** 5 35N 0 6W
Accrington, *U.K.* **10 D5** 53 45N 2 22W
Acebal, *Argentina* **94 C3** 33 20S 60 50W
Aceh □, *Indonesia* **36 D1** 4 15N 97 30 E
Achalpur, *India* **40 J10** 21 22N 77 32 E
Acheng, *China* **35 B14** 45 30N 126 58 E
Acher, *India* **42 H5** 23 10N 72 32 E
Achill Hd., *Ireland* **13 C1** 53 58N 10 15W
Achill I., *Ireland* **13 C1** 53 58N 10 1W
Achinsk, *Russia* **27 D10** 56 20N 90 20 E
Acireale, *Italy* **20 F6** 37 37N 15 10 E
Ackerman, *U.S.A.* **81 J10** 33 19N 89 11W
Acklins I., *Bahamas* **89 B5** 22 30N 74 0W
Acme, *Canada* **72 C6** 51 33N 113 30W
Acme, *U.S.A.* **78 F5** 40 8N 79 26W
Aconcagua, Cerro, *Argentina* **94 C2** 32 39S 70 0W
Aconquija, Mt., *Argentina* **94 B2** 27 0S 66 0W
Açores, Is. dos = Azores, *Atl. Oc.* **50 A1** 38 44N 29 0W
Acornhoek, *S. Africa* **57 C5** 24 37S 31 2 E
Acraman, L., *Australia* **63 E2** 32 2S 135 23 E
Acre = 'Akko, *Israel* **47 C4** 32 55N 35 4 E
Acre □, *Brazil* **92 E4** 9 1S 71 0W
Acre →, *Brazil* **92 E5** 8 45S 67 22W
Acton, *Canada* **78 C4** 43 38N 80 3W
Acuña, *Mexico* **86 B4** 29 18N 100 55W
Ad Dammām, *Si. Arabia* **45 E6** 26 20N 50 5 E
Ad Dāmūr, *Lebanon* **47 B4** 33 44N 35 27 E
Ad Dawādimī, *Si. Arabia* **44 E5** 24 35N 44 15 E
Ad Dawḩah, *Qatar* **46 B5** 25 15N 51 35 E
Ad Dawr, *Iraq* **44 C4** 34 27N 43 47 E
Ad Dir'īyah, *Si. Arabia* **44 E5** 24 44N 46 35 E
Ad Dīwānīyah, *Iraq* **44 D5** 32 0N 45 0 E
Ad Dujayl, *Iraq* **44 C5** 33 51N 44 14 E
Ad Duwayd, *Si. Arabia* **44 D4** 30 15N 42 17 E
Ada, *Minn., U.S.A.* **80 B6** 47 18N 96 31W
Ada, *Okla., U.S.A.* **81 H6** 34 46N 96 41W
Adabiya, *Egypt* **47 F1** 29 53N 32 28 E
Adair, C., *Canada* **69 A12** 71 31N 71 24W
Adaja →, *Spain* **19 B3** 41 32N 4 52W
Adak I., *U.S.A.* **68 C2** 51 45N 176 45W
Adamaoua, Massif de l', *Cameroon* **51 G7** 7 20N 12 20 E
Adamawa Highlands = Adamaoua, Massif de l', *Cameroon* **51 G7** 7 20N 12 20 E
Adamello, Mte., *Italy* **18 C9** 46 9N 10 30 E
Adams, *Mass., U.S.A.* **79 D11** 42 38N 73 7W
Adams, *N.Y., U.S.A.* **79 C8** 43 49N 76 1W
Adams, *Wis., U.S.A.* **80 D10** 43 57N 89 49W
Adam's Bridge, *Sri Lanka* **40 Q11** 9 15N 79 40 E
Adams L., *Canada* **72 C5** 51 10N 119 40W
Adams Mt., *U.S.A.* **84 D5** 46 12N 121 30W
Adam's Peak, *Sri Lanka* **40 R12** 6 48N 80 30 E
Adana, *Turkey* **25 G6** 37 0N 35 16 E
Adapazarı = Sakarya, *Turkey* **25 F5** 40 48N 30 25 E
Adarama, *Sudan* **51 E12** 17 10N 34 52 E
Adare, C., *Antarctica* **5 D11** 71 0S 171 0 E
Adaut, *Indonesia* **37 F8** 8 8S 131 7 E
Adavale, *Australia* **63 D3** 25 52S 144 32 E
Adda →, *Italy* **18 D8** 45 8N 9 53 E
Addis Ababa = Addis Abeba, *Ethiopia* **46 F2** 9 2N 38 42 E
Addis Abeba, *Ethiopia* **46 F2** 9 2N 38 42 E
Addison, *U.S.A.* **78 D7** 42 1N 77 14W
Addo, *S. Africa* **56 E4** 33 32S 25 45 E
Ādeh, *Iran* **44 B5** 37 42N 45 11 E
Adel, *U.S.A.* **77 K4** 31 8N 83 25W
Adelaide, *Bahamas* **88 A4** 25 4N 77 31W
Adelaide, *S. Africa* **56 E4** 32 42S 26 20 E
Adelaide I., *Antarctica* **5 C17** 67 15S 68 30W
Adelaide Pen., *Canada* **68 B10** 68 15N 97 30W
Adelaide River, *Australia* **60 B5** 13 15S 131 7 E
Adelanto, *U.S.A.* **85 L9** 34 35N 117 22W
Adele I., *Australia* **60 C3** 15 32S 123 9 E
Adélie, Terre, *Antarctica* **5 C10** 68 0S 140 0 E
Adélie Land = Adélie, Terre, *Antarctica* **5 C10** 68 0S 140 0 E
Aden = Al 'Adan, *Yemen* **46 E4** 12 45N 45 0 E
Aden, G. of, *Asia* **46 E4** 12 30N 47 30 E
Adendorp, *S. Africa* **56 E3** 32 15S 24 30 E
Adh Dhayd, *U.A.E.* **45 E7** 25 17N 55 53 E
Adhoi, *India* **42 H4** 23 26N 70 32 E
Adi, *Indonesia* **37 E8** 4 15S 133 30 E
Adieu, C., *Australia* **61 F5** 32 0S 132 10 E
Adieu Pt., *Australia* **60 C3** 15 14S 124 35 E
Adige →, *Italy* **20 B5** 45 9N 12 20 E
Adigrat, *Ethiopia* **46 E2** 14 20N 39 26 E
Adilabad, *India* **40 K11** 19 33N 78 20 E
Adirondack Mts., *U.S.A.* **79 C10** 44 0N 74 0W
Adjumani, *Uganda* **54 B3** 3 20N 31 50 E
Adlavik Is., *Canada* **71 A8** 55 0N 58 40W
Admiralty G., *Australia* **60 B4** 14 20S 125 55 E
Admiralty I., *U.S.A.* **72 B2** 57 30N 134 30W
Admiralty Is., *Papua N. G.* **64 H6** 2 0S 147 0 E
Adonara, *Indonesia* **37 F6** 8 15S 123 5 E
Adoni, *India* **40 M10** 15 33N 77 18 E
Adour →, *France* **18 E3** 43 32N 1 32W
Adra, *India* **43 H12** 23 30N 86 42 E
Adra, *Spain* **19 D4** 36 43N 3 3W
Adrano, *Italy* **20 F6** 37 40N 14 50 E
Adrar, *Mauritania* **50 D3** 20 30N 7 30 E
Adrar des Iforas, *Algeria* **50 C5** 27 51N 0 11 E
Adrian, *Mich., U.S.A.* **76 E3** 41 54N 84 2W
Adrian, *Tex., U.S.A.* **81 H3** 35 16N 102 40W
Adriatic Sea, *Medit. S.* **20 C6** 43 0N 16 0 E
Adua, *Indonesia* **37 E7** 1 45S 129 50 E
Adwa, *Ethiopia* **46 E2** 14 15N 38 52 E
Adygea □, *Russia* **25 F7** 45 0N 40 0 E
Adzhar Republic = Ajaria □, *Georgia* **25 F7** 41 30N 42 0 E
Adzopé, *Ivory C.* **50 G5** 6 7N 3 49W
Ægean Sea, *Medit. S.* **21 E11** 38 30N 25 0 E
Aerhtai Shan, *Mongolia* **32 B4** 46 40N 92 45 E
'Afak, *Iraq* **44 C5** 32 4N 45 15 E
Afándou, *Greece* **23 C10** 36 18N 28 12 E
Afghanistan ■, *Asia* **40 C4** 33 0N 65 0 E
Aflou, *Algeria* **50 B6** 34 7N 2 3 E
Africa **48 E6** 10 0N 20 0 E
'Afrīn, *Syria* **44 B3** 36 32N 36 50 E
Afton, *N.Y., U.S.A.* **79 D9** 42 14N 75 32W
Afton, *Wyo., U.S.A.* **82 E8** 42 44N 110 56W
Afuá, *Brazil* **93 D8** 0 15S 50 20W
'Afula, *Israel* **47 C4** 32 37N 35 17 E
Afyon, *Turkey* **25 G5** 38 45N 30 33 E
Afyonkarahisar = Afyon, *Turkey* **25 G5** 38 45N 30 33 E
Agadès = Agadez, *Niger* **50 E7** 16 58N 7 59 E
Agadez, *Niger* **50 E7** 16 58N 7 59 E
Agadir, *Morocco* **50 B4** 30 28N 9 55W
Agaete, *Canary Is.* **22 F4** 28 6N 15 43W
Agar, *India* **42 H7** 23 40N 76 2 E
Agartala, *India* **41 H17** 23 50N 91 23 E
Agassiz, *Canada* **72 D4** 49 14N 121 46W
Agats, *Indonesia* **37 F9** 5 33S 138 0 E
Agawam, *U.S.A.* **79 D12** 42 5N 72 37W
Agboville, *Ivory C.* **50 G5** 5 55N 4 15W
Ağdam, *Azerbaijan* **44 B5** 40 0N 46 58 E
Agde, *France* **18 E5** 43 19N 3 28 E
Agen, *France* **18 D4** 44 12N 0 38 E
Āgh Kand, *Iran* **45 B6** 37 15N 48 4 E
Aginskoye, *Russia* **27 D12** 51 6N 114 32 E
Agnew, *Australia* **61 E3** 28 1S 120 31 E
Agori, *India* **43 G10** 24 33N 82 57 E
Agra, *India* **42 F7** 27 17N 77 58 E
Ağri, *Turkey* **25 G7** 39 44N 43 3 E
Agri →, *Italy* **20 D7** 40 13N 16 44 E
Ağrı Dağı, *Turkey* **25 G7** 39 50N 44 15 E
Ağri Karakose = Ağri, *Turkey* **25 G7** 39 44N 43 3 E
Agrigento, *Italy* **20 F5** 37 19N 13 34 E
Agrínion, *Greece* **21 E9** 38 37N 21 27 E
Agua Caliente, *Baja Calif., Mexico* **85 N10** 32 29N 116 59W
Agua Caliente, *Sinaloa, Mexico* **86 B3** 26 30N 108 20W
Agua Caliente Springs, *U.S.A.* **85 N10** 32 56N 116 19W
Água Clara, *Brazil* **93 H8** 20 25S 52 45W
Agua Hechicero, *Mexico* **85 N10** 32 26N 116 14W
Agua Prieta, *Mexico* **86 A3** 31 20N 109 32W
Aguadilla, *Puerto Rico* **89 C6** 18 26N 67 10W
Aguadulce, *Panama* **88 E3** 8 15N 80 32W
Aguanga, *U.S.A.* **85 M10** 33 27N 116 51W
Aguanish, *Canada* **71 B7** 50 14N 62 2W
Aguanus →, *Canada* **71 B7** 50 13N 62 5W
Aguapey →, *Argentina* **94 B4** 29 7S 56 36W
Aguaray Guazú →, *Paraguay* **94 A4** 24 47S 57 19W
Aguarico →, *Ecuador* **92 D3** 0 59S 75 11W
Aguas Blancas, *Chile* **94 A2** 24 15S 69 55W
Aguas Calientes, Sierra de, *Argentina* **94 B2** 25 26S 66 40W
Aguascalientes, *Mexico* **86 C4** 21 53N 102 12W
Aguascalientes □, *Mexico* **86 C4** 22 0N 102 20W
Aguilares, *Argentina* **94 B2** 27 26S 65 35W
Aguilas, *Spain* **19 D5** 37 23N 1 35W
Agüimes, *Canary Is.* **22 G4** 27 58N 15 27W
Aguja, C. de la, *Colombia* **90 B3** 11 18N 74 12W
Agulhas, C., *S. Africa* **56 E3** 34 52S 20 0 E
Agulo, *Canary Is.* **22 F2** 28 11N 17 12W
Agung, *Indonesia* **36 F5** 8 20S 115 28 E
Agur, *Uganda* **54 B3** 2 28N 32 55 E
Agusan →, *Phil.* **37 C7** 9 0N 125 30 E
Aha Mts., *Botswana* **56 B3** 19 45S 21 0 E
Ahaggar, *Algeria* **50 D7** 23 0N 6 30 E
Ahar, *Iran* **44 B5** 38 35N 47 0 E
Ahipara B., *N.Z.* **59 F4** 35 5S 173 5 E
Ahiri, *India* **40 K12** 19 30N 80 0 E
Ahmad Wal, *Pakistan* **42 E1** 29 18N 65 58 E
Ahmadabad, *India* **42 H5** 23 0N 72 40 E
Aḩmadābād, *Khorāsān, Iran* **45 C9** 35 3N 60 50 E
Aḩmadābād, *Khorāsān, Iran* **45 C8** 35 49N 59 42 E
Aḩmadī, *Iran* **45 E8** 27 56N 56 42 E
Ahmadnagar, *India* **40 K9** 19 7N 74 46 E
Ahmadpur, *Pakistan* **42 E4** 29 12N 71 10 E
Ahmadpur Lamma, *Pakistan* **42 E4** 28 19N 70 3 E
Ahmedabad = Ahmadabad, *India* **42 H5** 23 0N 72 40 E
Ahmednagar = Ahmadnagar, *India* **40 K9** 19 7N 74 46 E
Ahome, *Mexico* **86 B3** 25 55N 109 11W
Ahoskie, *U.S.A.* **77 G7** 36 17N 76 59W
Ahram, *Iran* **45 D6** 28 52N 51 16 E
Ahrax Pt., *Malta* **23 D1** 35 59N 14 22 E
Āhū, *Iran* **45 C6** 34 33N 50 2 E
Ahuachapán, *El Salv.* **88 D2** 13 54N 89 52W
Ahvāz, *Iran* **45 D6** 31 20N 48 40 E
Ahvenanmaa = Åland, *Finland* **9 F19** 60 15N 20 0 E
Aḩwar, *Yemen* **46 E4** 13 30N 46 40 E
Ai →, *India* **43 F14** 26 26N 90 44 E
Ai-Ais, *Namibia* **56 D2** 27 54S 17 59 E
Aichi □, *Japan* **31 G8** 35 0N 137 15 E
Aigua, *Uruguay* **95 C5** 34 13S 54 46W
Aigues-Mortes, *France* **18 E6** 43 35N 4 12 E
Aihui, *China* **33 A7** 50 10N 127 30 E
Aija, *Peru* **92 E3** 9 50S 77 45W
Aikawa, *Japan* **30 E9** 38 2N 138 15 E
Aiken, *U.S.A.* **77 J5** 33 34N 81 43W
Aileron, *Australia* **62 C1** 22 39S 133 20 E
Aillik, *Canada* **71 A8** 55 11N 59 18W
Ailsa Craig, *U.K.* **12 F3** 55 15N 5 6W
'Ailūn, *Jordan* **47 C4** 32 18N 35 47 E
Aim, *Russia* **27 D14** 59 0N 133 55 E
Aimere, *Indonesia* **37 F6** 8 45S 121 3 E
Aimogasta, *Argentina* **94 B2** 28 33S 66 50W
Aïn Ben Tili, *Mauritania* **50 C4** 25 59N 9 27W
Aïn Sefra, *Algeria* **50 B5** 32 47N 0 37W
Ain Sudr, *Egypt* **47 F2** 29 50N 33 6 E
Ainaži, *Latvia* **9 H21** 57 50N 24 24 E
Ainsworth, *U.S.A.* **80 D5** 42 33N 99 52W
Aiquile, *Bolivia* **92 G5** 18 10S 65 10W
Aïr, *Niger* **50 E7** 18 30N 8 0 E
Air Force I., *Canada* **69 B12** 67 58N 74 5W
Air Hitam, *Malaysia* **39 M4** 1 55N 103 11 E
Airdrie, *Canada* **72 C6** 51 18N 114 2W
Airdrie, *U.K.* **12 F5** 55 52N 3 57W
Aire →, *U.K.* **10 D7** 53 43N 0 55W
Aire, I. de l', *Spain* **22 B11** 39 48N 4 16 E
Airlie Beach, *Australia* **62 C4** 20 16S 148 43 E
Aisne →, *France* **18 B5** 49 26N 2 50 E
Ait, *India* **43 G8** 25 54N 79 14 E
Aitkin, *U.S.A.* **80 B8** 46 32N 93 42W
Aiud, *Romania* **17 E12** 46 19N 23 44 E
Aix-en-Provence, *France* **18 E6** 43 32N 5 27 E
Aix-la-Chapelle = Aachen, *Germany* **16 C4** 50 45N 6 6 E
Aix-les-Bains, *France* **18 D6** 45 41N 5 53 E
Aíyion, *Greece* **21 E10** 38 15N 22 5 E
Aizawl, *India* **41 H18** 23 40N 92 44 E
Aizkraukle, *Latvia* **9 H21** 56 36N 25 11 E
Aizpute, *Latvia* **9 H19** 56 43N 21 40 E
Aizuwakamatsu, *Japan* **30 F9** 37 30N 139 56 E
Ajaccio, *France* **18 F8** 41 55N 8 40 E
Ajaigarh, *India* **43 G9** 24 52N 80 16 E
Ajalpan, *Mexico* **87 D5** 18 22N 97 15W
Ajanta Ra., *India* **40 J9** 20 28N 75 50 E
Ajari Rep. = Ajaria □, *Georgia* **25 F7** 41 30N 42 0 E
Ajaria □, *Georgia* **25 F7** 41 30N 42 0 E
Ajax, *Canada* **78 C5** 43 50N 79 1W
Ajdābiyā, *Libya* **51 B10** 30 54N 20 4 E
Ajka, *Hungary* **17 E9** 47 4N 17 31 E
'Ajmān, *U.A.E.* **45 E7** 25 25N 55 30 E
Ajmer, *India* **42 F6** 26 28N 74 37 E
Ajnala, *India* **42 D6** 31 50N 74 48 E
Ajo, *U.S.A.* **83 K7** 32 22N 112 52W
Ajo, C. de, *Spain* **19 A4** 43 31N 3 35W
Akabira, *Japan* **30 C11** 43 33N 142 5 E
Akamas □, *Cyprus* **23 D11** 35 3N 32 18 E
Akanthou, *Cyprus* **23 D12** 35 22N 33 45 E
Akaroa, *N.Z.* **59 K4** 43 49S 172 59 E
Akashi, *Japan* **31 G7** 34 45N 134 58 E
Akbarpur, *Bihar, India* **43 G10** 24 39N 83 58 E
Akbarpur, *Ut. P., India* **43 F10** 26 25N 82 32 E
Akelamo, *Indonesia* **37 D7** 1 35N 129 40 E
Aketi, *Dem. Rep. of the Congo* **52 D4** 2 38N 23 47 E
Akharnaí, *Greece* **21 E10** 38 5N 23 44 E
Akhelóös →, *Greece* **21 E9** 38 19N 21 7 E
Akhisar, *Turkey* **21 E12** 38 56N 27 48 E
Akhnur, *India* **43 C6** 32 52N 74 45 E
Akhtyrka = Okhtyrka, *Ukraine* **25 D5** 50 25N 35 0 E
Aki, *Japan* **31 H6** 33 30N 133 54 E
Akimiski I., *Canada* **70 B3** 52 50N 81 30W
Akita, *Japan* **30 E10** 39 45N 140 7 E
Akita □, *Japan* **30 E10** 39 40N 140 30 E
Akjoujt, *Mauritania* **50 E3** 19 45N 14 15W
Akkeshi, *Japan* **30 C12** 43 2N 144 51 E
'Akko, *Israel* **47 C4** 32 55N 35 4 E
Aklavik, *Canada* **68 B6** 68 12N 135 0W
Aklera, *India* **42 G7** 24 26N 76 32 E
Akmolinsk = Astana, *Kazakstan* **26 D8** 51 10N 71 30 E
Akō, *Japan* **31 G7** 34 45N 134 24 E
Akola, *India* **40 J10** 20 42N 77 2 E
Akordat, *Eritrea* **46 D2** 15 30N 37 40 E
Akpatok I., *Canada* **69 B13** 60 25N 68 8W
Åkrahamn, *Norway* **9 G11** 59 15N 5 10 E
Akranes, *Iceland* **8 D2** 64 19N 22 5W
Akron, *Colo., U.S.A.* **80 E3** 40 10N 103 13W
Akron, *Ohio, U.S.A.* **78 E3** 41 5N 81 31W
Akrotiri, *Cyprus* **23 E11** 34 36N 32 57 E
Akrotiri Bay, *Cyprus* **23 E12** 34 35N 33 10 E
Aksai Chin, *India* **43 B8** 35 15N 79 55 E
Aksaray, *Turkey* **25 G5** 38 25N 34 2 E
Aksay, *Kazakstan* **25 D9** 51 11N 53 0 E
Akşehir, *Turkey* **44 B1** 38 18N 31 30 E
Akşehir Gölü, *Turkey* **25 G5** 38 30N 31 25 E
Aksu, *China* **32 B3** 41 5N 80 10 E
Aksum, *Ethiopia* **46 E2** 14 5N 38 40 E
Aktogay, *Kazakstan* **26 E8** 46 57N 79 40 E
Aktsyabrski, *Belarus* **17 B15** 52 38N 28 53 E
Aktyubinsk = Aqtöbe, *Kazakstan* **25 D10** 50 17N 57 10 E
Akure, *Nigeria* **50 G7** 7 15N 5 5 E
Akureyri, *Iceland* **8 D4** 65 40N 18 6W
Akuseki-Shima, *Japan* **31 K4** 29 27N 129 37 E
Akyab = Sittwe, *Burma* **41 J18** 20 18N 92 45 E
Al 'Adan, *Yemen* **46 E4** 12 45N 45 0 E
Al Aḩsā = Hasa □, *Si. Arabia* **45 E6** 25 50N 49 0 E
Al Ajfar, *Si. Arabia* **44 E4** 27 26N 43 0 E
Al Amādīyah, *Iraq* **44 B4** 37 5N 43 30 E
Al 'Amārah, *Iraq* **44 D5** 31 55N 47 15 E
Al 'Aqabah, *Jordan* **47 F4** 29 31N 35 0 E
Al Arak, *Syria* **44 C3** 34 38N 38 35 E
Al 'Aramah, *Si. Arabia* **44 E5** 25 30N 46 0 E
Al Arţāwīyah, *Si. Arabia* **44 E5** 26 31N 45 20 E
Al 'Āşimah = 'Ammān □, *Jordan* **47 D5** 31 40N 36 30 E
Al 'Assāfīyah, *Si. Arabia* **44 D3** 28 17N 38 59 E
Al 'Ayn, *Oman* **45 E7** 24 15N 55 45 E
Al 'Ayn, *Si. Arabia* **44 E3** 25 4N 38 6 E
Al 'Aẓamīyah, *Iraq* **44 C5** 33 22N 44 22 E
Al 'Azīzīyah, *Iraq* **44 C5** 32 54N 45 4 E
Al Bāb, *Syria* **44 B3** 36 23N 37 29 E
Al Bad', *Si. Arabia* **44 D2** 28 28N 35 1 E
Al Bādī, *Iraq* **44 C4** 35 56N 41 32 E
Al Baḩrah, *Kuwait* **44 D5** 29 40N 47 52 E
Al Baḩral Mayyit = Dead Sea, *Asia* **47 D4** 31 30N 35 30 E
Al Balqā' □, *Jordan* **47 C4** 32 5N 35 45 E
Al Bārūk, J., *Lebanon* **47 B4** 33 39N 35 40 E
Al Başrah, *Iraq* **44 D5** 30 30N 47 50 E
Al Baţḩā, *Iraq* **44 D5** 31 6N 45 53 E
Al Batrūn, *Lebanon* **47 A4** 34 15N 35 40 E
Al Bayḑā, *Libya* **51 B10** 32 50N 21 44 E
Al Biqā, *Lebanon* **47 A5** 34 10N 36 10 E

Amalner

Al Bi'r, *Si. Arabia* **44 D3** 28 51N 36 16 E
Al Burayj, *Syria* **47 A5** 34 15N 36 46 E
Al Faḑilī, *Si. Arabia* **45 E6** 26 58N 49 10 E
Al Fallūjah, *Iraq* **44 C4** 33 20N 43 55 E
Al Fāw, *Iraq* **45 D6** 30 0N 48 30 E
Al Fujayrah, *U.A.E.* **45 E8** 25 7N 56 18 E
Al Ghadaf, W. →, *Jordan* **47 D5** 31 26N 36 43 E
Al Ghammās, *Iraq* **44 D5** 31 45N 44 37 E
Al Ghazālah, *Si. Arabia* **44 E4** 26 48N 41 19 E
Al Ḩadīthah, *Iraq* **44 C4** 34 0N 41 13 E
Al Ḩadīthah, *Si. Arabia* **47 D6** 31 28N 37 8 E
Al Ḩaḑr, *Iraq* **44 C4** 35 35N 42 44 E
Al Hājānah, *Syria* **47 B5** 33 20N 36 33 E
Al Hajar al Gharbī, *Oman* **45 E8** 24 10N 56 15 E
Al Hāmad, *Si. Arabia* **44 D3** 31 30N 39 30 E
Al Hamdānīyah, *Syria* **44 C3** 35 25N 36 50 E
Al Ḩamīdīyah, *Syria* **47 A4** 34 42N 35 57 E
Al Ḩammār, *Iraq* **44 D5** 30 57N 46 51 E
Al Ḩamrā', *Si. Arabia* **44 E3** 24 2N 38 55 E
Al Ḩanākīyah, *Si. Arabia* **44 E4** 24 51N 40 31 E
Al Harīr, W. →, *Syria* **47 C4** 32 44N 35 59 E
Al Ḩasā, W. →, *Jordan* **47 D4** 31 4N 35 29 E
Al Ḩasakah, *Syria* **44 B4** 36 35N 40 45 E
Al Haydān, W. →, *Jordan* **47 D4** 31 29N 35 34 E
Al Ḩayy, *Iraq* **44 C5** 32 5N 46 5 E
Al Ḩijarah, *Asia* **44 D4** 30 0N 44 0 E
Al Ḩillah, *Iraq* **44 C5** 32 30N 44 25 E
Al Ḩillah, *Si. Arabia* **46 B4** 23 35N 46 50 E
Al Hindīyah, *Iraq* **44 C5** 32 30N 44 10 E
Al Hirmil, *Lebanon* **47 A5** 34 26N 36 24 E
Al Hoceïma, *Morocco* **50 A5** 35 8N 3 58W
Al Ḩudaydah, *Yemen* **46 E3** 14 50N 43 0 E
Al Hufūf, *Si. Arabia* **46 B4** 25 25N 49 45 E
Al Ḩumayḑah, *Si. Arabia* **44 D2** 29 14N 34 56 E
Al Ḩunayy, *Si. Arabia* **45 E6** 25 58N 48 45 E
Al Īsāwīyah, *Si. Arabia* **44 D3** 30 43N 37 59 E
Al Jafr, *Jordan* **47 E5** 30 18N 36 14 E
Al Jāfūrah, *Si. Arabia* **45 E7** 25 0N 50 15 E
Al Jaghbūb, *Libya* **51 C10** 29 42N 24 38 E
Al Jahrah, *Kuwait* **44 D5** 29 25N 47 40 E
Al Jalāmīd, *Si. Arabia* **44 D3** 31 20N 40 6 E
Al Jamalīyah, *Qatar* **45 E6** 25 37N 51 5 E
Al Janūb □, *Lebanon* **47 B4** 33 20N 35 20 E
Al Jawf, *Libya* **51 D10** 24 10N 23 24 E
Al Jawf, *Si. Arabia* **44 D3** 29 55N 39 40 E
Al Jazirah, *Iraq* **44 C5** 33 30N 44 0 E
Al Jithāmīyah, *Si. Arabia* **44 E4** 27 41N 41 43 E
Al Jubayl, *Si. Arabia* **45 E6** 27 0N 49 50 E
Al Jubaylah, *Si. Arabia* **44 E5** 24 55N 46 25 E
Al Jubb, *Si. Arabia* **44 E4** 27 11N 42 17 E
Al Junaynah, *Sudan* **51 F10** 13 27N 22 45 E
Al Kabā'ish, *Iraq* **44 D5** 30 58N 47 0 E
Al Karak, *Jordan* **47 D4** 31 11N 35 42 E
Al Karak □, *Jordan* **47 E5** 31 0N 36 0 E
Al Kāzim Tyah, *Iraq* **44 C5** 33 22N 44 12 E
Al Khābūra, *Oman* **45 F8** 23 57N 57 5 E
Al Khafji, *Si. Arabia* **45 E6** 28 24N 48 29 E
Al Khalīl, *West Bank* **47 D4** 31 32N 35 6 E
Al Khāliş, *Iraq* **44 C5** 33 49N 44 32 E
Al Kharsānīyah, *Si. Arabia* **45 E6** 27 13N 49 18 E
Al Khaşab, *Oman* **45 E8** 26 14N 56 15 E
Al Khawr, *Qatar* **45 E6** 25 41N 51 30 E
Al Khiḑr, *Iraq* **44 D5** 31 12N 45 33 E
Al Khiyām, *Lebanon* **47 B4** 33 20N 35 36 E
Al Kiswah, *Syria* **47 B5** 33 23N 36 14 E
Al Kūfah, *Iraq* **44 C5** 32 2N 44 24 E
Al Kufrah, *Libya* **51 D10** 24 17N 23 15 E
Al Kuhayfīyah, *Si. Arabia* **44 E4** 27 12N 43 3 E
Al Kūt, *Iraq* **44 C5** 32 30N 46 0 E
Al Kuwayt, *Kuwait* **46 B4** 29 30N 48 0 E
Al Labwah, *Lebanon* **47 A5** 34 11N 36 20 E
Al Lādhiqīyah, *Syria* **44 C2** 35 30N 35 45 E
Al Līth, *Si. Arabia* **46 C3** 20 9N 40 15 E
Al Liwā', *Oman* **45 E8** 24 31N 56 36 E
Al Luḩayyah, *Yemen* **46 D3** 15 45N 42 40 E
Al Madīnah, *Iraq* **44 D5** 30 57N 47 16 E
Al Madīnah, *Si. Arabia* **46 C2** 24 35N 39 52 E
Al Mafraq, *Jordan* **47 C5** 32 17N 36 14 E
Al Maḩmūdīyah, *Iraq* **44 C5** 33 3N 44 21 E
Al Majma'ah, *Si. Arabia* **44 E5** 25 57N 45 22 E
Al Makhruq, W. →, *Jordan* **47 D6** 31 28N 37 0 E
Al Makḩūl, *Si. Arabia* **44 E4** 26 37N 42 39 E
Al Manāmah, *Bahrain* **46 B5** 26 10N 50 30 E
Al Maqwa', *Kuwait* **44 D5** 29 10N 47 59 E
Al Marj, *Libya* **51 B10** 32 25N 20 30 E
Al Maţlā, *Kuwait* **44 D5** 29 24N 47 40 E
Al Mawjib, W. →, *Jordan* **47 D4** 31 28N 35 36 E
Al Mawşil, *Iraq* **44 B4** 36 15N 43 5 E
Al Mayādin, *Syria* **44 C4** 35 1N 40 27 E
Al Mazār, *Jordan* **47 D4** 31 4N 35 41 E
Al Midhnab, *Si. Arabia* **44 E5** 25 50N 44 18 E
Al Minā', *Lebanon* **47 A4** 34 24N 35 49 E
Al Miqdādīyah, *Iraq* **44 C5** 34 0N 45 0 E
Al Mubarraz, *Si. Arabia* **45 E6** 25 30N 49 40 E
Al Mudawwarah, *Jordan* **47 F5** 29 19N 36 0 E
Al Mughayrā', *U.A.E.* **45 E7** 24 5N 53 32 E
Al Muḩarraq, *Bahrain* **45 E6** 26 15N 50 40 E
Al Mukallā, *Yemen* **46 E4** 14 33N 49 2 E
Al Mukhā, *Yemen* **46 E3** 13 18N 43 15 E
Al Musayjīd, *Si. Arabia* **44 E3** 24 5N 39 5 E
Al Musayyib, *Iraq* **44 C5** 32 49N 44 20 E
Al Muwayliḩ, *Si. Arabia* **44 E2** 27 40N 35 30 E
Al Qā'im, *Iraq* **44 C4** 34 21N 41 7 E
Al Qalībah, *Si. Arabia* **44 D3** 28 24N 37 42 E
Al Qāmishlī, *Syria* **44 B4** 37 2N 41 14 E
Al Qaryatayn, *Syria* **47 A6** 34 12N 37 13 E
Al Qaşīm, *Si. Arabia* **44 E4** 26 0N 43 0 E
Al Qaţ'ā, *Syria* **44 C4** 34 40N 40 48 E
Al Qaţīf, *Si. Arabia* **45 E6** 26 35N 50 0 E
Al Qatrānah, *Jordan* **47 D5** 31 12N 36 6 E
Al Qaţrūn, *Libya* **51 D9** 24 56N 15 3 E
Al Qayşūmah, *Si. Arabia* **44 D5** 28 20N 46 7 E
Al Quds = Jerusalem, *Israel* **47 D4** 31 47N 35 10 E
Al Qunayţirah, *Syria* **47 C4** 32 55N 35 45 E
Al Qurnah, *Iraq* **44 D5** 31 1N 47 25 E
Al Quşayr, *Iraq* **44 D5** 30 39N 45 50 E
Al Quşayr, *Syria* **47 A5** 34 31N 36 34 E
Al Qutayfah, *Syria* **47 B5** 33 44N 36 36 E
Al 'Ubaylah, *Si. Arabia* **46 C5** 21 59N 50 57 E
Al 'Uḑaylīyah, *Si. Arabia* **45 E6** 25 8N 49 18 E
Al 'Ulā, *Si. Arabia* **44 E3** 26 35N 38 0 E
Al 'Uqayr, *Si. Arabia* **45 E6** 25 40N 50 15 E
Al 'Uwaynid, *Si. Arabia* **44 E5** 24 50N 46 0 E
Al 'Uwayqīlah, *Si. Arabia* **44 D4** 30 30N 42 10 E
Al 'Uyūn, *Ḩijāz, Si. Arabia* **44 E3** 24 33N 39 35 E
Al 'Uyūn, *Najd, Si. Arabia* **44 E4** 26 30N 43 50 E
Al 'Uzayr, *Iraq* **44 D5** 31 19N 47 25 E
Al Wajh, *Si. Arabia* **44 E3** 26 10N 36 30 E
Al Wakrah, *Qatar* **45 E6** 25 10N 51 40 E
Al Waqbah, *Si. Arabia* **44 D5** 28 48N 45 33 E
Al Wari'āh, *Si. Arabia* **44 E5** 27 51N 47 25 E
Ala Dağ, *Turkey* **44 B2** 37 44N 35 9 E
Ala Tau Shankou = Dzungarian Gates, *Asia* **32 B3** 45 0N 82 0 E
Alabama □, *U.S.A.* **77 J2** 33 0N 87 0W
Alabama →, *U.S.A.* **77 K2** 31 8N 87 57W
Alabaster, *U.S.A.* **77 J2** 33 15N 86 49W
Alaçam Dağları, *Turkey* **21 E13** 39 18N 28 49 E
Alachua, *U.S.A.* **77 L4** 29 47N 82 30W
Alaérma, *Greece* **23 C9** 36 9N 27 57 E
Alagoa Grande, *Brazil* **93 E11** 7 3S 35 35W
Alagoas □, *Brazil* **93 E11** 9 0S 36 0W
Alagoinhas, *Brazil* **93 F11** 12 7S 38 20W
Alaior, *Spain* **22 B11** 39 57N 4 8 E
Alajero, *Canary Is.* **22 F2** 28 3N 17 13W
Alajuela, *Costa Rica* **88 D3** 10 2N 84 8W
Alakamisy, *Madag.* **57 C8** 21 19S 47 14 E
Alaknanda →, *India* **43 D8** 30 8N 78 36 E
Alakurtti, *Russia* **24 A5** 67 0N 30 30 E
Alamarvdasht, *Iran* **45 E7** 27 37N 52 59 E
Alameda, *Calif., U.S.A.* **84 H4** 37 46N 122 15W
Alameda, *N. Mex., U.S.A.* **83 J10** 35 11N 106 37W
Alamo, *U.S.A.* **85 J11** 37 22N 115 10W
Alamo Crossing, *U.S.A.* **85 L13** 34 16N 113 33W
Alamogordo, *U.S.A.* **83 K11** 32 54N 105 57W
Alamos, *Mexico* **86 B3** 27 0N 109 0W
Alamosa, *U.S.A.* **83 H11** 37 28N 105 52W
Åland, *Finland* **9 F19** 60 15N 20 0 E
Ålands hav, *Sweden* **9 F18** 60 0N 19 30 E
Alania = North Ossetia □, *Russia* **25 F7** 43 30N 44 30 E
Alanya, *Turkey* **25 G5** 36 38N 32 0 E
Alaotra, Farihin', *Madag.* **57 B8** 17 30S 48 30 E
Alapayevsk, *Russia* **26 D7** 57 52N 61 42 E
Alappuzha = Alleppey, *India* **40 Q10** 9 30N 76 28 E
Alarobia-Vohiposa, *Madag.* **57 C8** 20 59S 47 9 E
Alaşehir, *Turkey* **21 E13** 38 23N 28 30 E
Alaska □, *U.S.A.* **68 B5** 64 0N 154 0W
Alaska, G. of, *Pac. Oc.* **68 C5** 58 0N 145 0W
Alaska Peninsula, *U.S.A.* **68 C4** 56 0N 159 0W
Alaska Range, *U.S.A.* **68 B4** 62 50N 151 0W
Älät, *Azerbaijan* **25 G8** 39 58N 49 25 E
Alatyr, *Russia* **24 D8** 54 55N 46 35 E
Alausi, *Ecuador* **92 D3** 2 0S 78 50W
Alava, C., *U.S.A.* **82 B1** 48 10N 124 44W
Alavus, *Finland* **9 E20** 62 35N 23 36 E
'Alayh, *Lebanon* **47 B4** 33 46N 35 33 E
Alba, *Italy* **18 D8** 44 42N 8 2 E
Alba-Iulia, *Romania* **17 E12** 46 8N 23 39 E
Albacete, *Spain* **19 C5** 39 0N 1 50W
Albanel, L., *Canada* **70 B5** 50 55N 73 12W
Albania ■, *Europe* **21 D9** 41 0N 20 0 E
Albany, *Australia* **61 G2** 35 1S 117 58 E
Albany, *Ga., U.S.A.* **77 K3** 31 35N 84 10W
Albany, *N.Y., U.S.A.* **79 D11** 42 39N 73 45W
Albany, *Oreg., U.S.A.* **82 D2** 44 38N 123 6W
Albany, *Tex., U.S.A.* **81 J5** 32 44N 99 18W
Albany →, *Canada* **70 B3** 52 17N 81 31W
Albardón, *Argentina* **94 C2** 31 20S 68 30W
Albatross B., *Australia* **62 A3** 12 45S 141 30 E
Albemarle, *U.S.A.* **77 H5** 35 21N 80 11W
Albemarle Sd., *U.S.A.* **77 H7** 36 5N 76 0W
Alberche →, *Spain* **19 C3** 39 58N 4 46W
Alberdi, *Paraguay* **94 B4** 26 14S 58 20W
Albert, L., *Africa* **54 B3** 1 30N 31 0 E
Albert Edward Ra., *Australia* **60 C4** 18 17S 127 57 E
Albert Lea, *U.S.A.* **80 D8** 43 39N 93 22W
Albert Nile →, *Uganda* **54 B3** 3 36N 32 2 E
Albert Town, *Bahamas* **89 B5** 22 37N 74 33W
Alberta □, *Canada* **72 C6** 54 40N 115 0W
Alberti, *Argentina* **94 D3** 35 1S 60 16W
Albertinia, *S. Africa* **56 E3** 34 11S 21 34 E
Alberton, *Canada* **71 C7** 46 50N 64 0W
Albertville = Kalemie, *Dem. Rep. of the Congo* **54 D2** 5 55S 29 9 E
Albertville, *France* **18 D7** 45 40N 6 22 E
Albertville, *U.S.A.* **77 H2** 34 16N 86 13W
Albi, *France* **18 E5** 43 56N 2 9 E
Albia, *U.S.A.* **80 E8** 41 2N 92 48W
Albina, *Surinam* **93 B8** 5 37N 54 15W
Albina, Ponta, *Angola* **56 B1** 15 52S 11 44 E
Albion, *Mich., U.S.A.* **76 D3** 42 15N 84 45W
Albion, *Nebr., U.S.A.* **80 E6** 41 42N 98 0W
Albion, *Pa., U.S.A.* **78 E4** 41 53N 80 22W
Alborán, *Medit. S.* **19 E4** 35 57N 3 0W
Ålborg, *Denmark* **9 H13** 57 2N 9 54 E
Alborz, Reshteh-ye Kūhhā-ye, *Iran* **45 C7** 36 0N 52 0 E
Albuquerque, *U.S.A.* **83 J10** 35 5N 106 39W
Albuquerque, Cayos de, *Caribbean* **88 D3** 12 10N 81 50W
Alburg, *U.S.A.* **79 B11** 44 59N 73 18W
Alcalá de Henares, *Spain* **19 B4** 40 28N 3 22W
Alcalá la Real, *Spain* **19 D4** 37 27N 3 57W
Álcamo, *Italy* **20 F5** 37 59N 12 55 E
Alcañiz, *Spain* **19 B5** 41 2N 0 8W
Alcântara, *Brazil* **93 D10** 2 20S 44 30W
Alcántara, Embalse de, *Spain* **19 C2** 39 44N 6 50W
Alcantarilla, *Spain* **19 D5** 37 59N 1 12W
Alcaraz, Sierra de, *Spain* **19 C4** 38 40N 2 20W
Alcaudete, *Spain* **19 D3** 37 35N 4 5W
Alcázar de San Juan, *Spain* **19 C4** 39 24N 3 12W
Alchevsk, *Ukraine* **25 E6** 48 30N 38 45 E
Alcira = Alzira, *Spain* **19 C5** 39 9N 0 30W
Alcova, *U.S.A.* **82 E10** 42 34N 106 43W
Alcoy, *Spain* **19 C5** 38 43N 0 30W
Alcúdia, *Spain* **22 B10** 39 51N 3 7 E
Alcúdia, B. d', *Spain* **22 B10** 39 47N 3 15 E
Aldabra Is., *Seychelles* **49 G8** 9 22S 46 28 E
Aldama, *Mexico* **87 C5** 23 0N 98 4W
Aldan, *Russia* **27 D13** 58 40N 125 30 E
Aldan →, *Russia* **27 C13** 63 28N 129 35 E
Aldea, Pta. de la, *Canary Is.* **22 G4** 28 0N 15 50W
Aldeburgh, *U.K.* **11 E9** 52 10N 1 37 E
Alder Pk., *U.S.A.* **84 K5** 35 53N 121 22W
Alderney, *U.K.* **11 H5** 49 42N 2 11W
Aldershot, *U.K.* **11 F7** 51 15N 0 44W
Aledo, *U.S.A.* **80 E9** 41 12N 90 45W
Aleg, *Mauritania* **50 E3** 17 3N 13 55W
Alegranza, *Canary Is.* **22 E6** 29 23N 13 32W
Alegranza, I., *Canary Is.* **22 E6** 29 23N 13 32W
Alegre, *Brazil* **95 A7** 20 50S 41 30W
Alegrete, *Brazil* **95 B4** 29 40S 56 0W
Aleisk, *Russia* **26 D9** 52 40N 83 0 E
Aleksandriya = Oleksandriya, *Ukraine* **17 C14** 50 37N 26 19 E
Aleksandrov Gay, *Russia* **25 D8** 50 9N 48 34 E
Aleksandrovsk-Sakhalinskiy, *Russia* **27 D15** 50 50N 142 20 E
Além Paraíba, *Brazil* **95 A7** 21 52S 42 41W
Alemania, *Argentina* **94 B2** 25 40S 65 30W
Alemania, *Chile* **94 B2** 25 10S 69 55W
Alençon, *France* **18 B4** 48 27N 0 4 E
Alenquer, *Brazil* **93 D8** 1 56S 54 46W
Alenuihaha Channel, *U.S.A.* **74 H17** 20 30N 156 0W
Aleppo = Ḩalab, *Syria* **44 B3** 36 10N 37 15 E
Alès, *France* **18 D6** 44 9N 4 5 E
Alessándria, *Italy* **18 D8** 44 54N 8 37 E
Ålesund, *Norway* **9 E12** 62 28N 6 12 E
Aleutian Is., *Pac. Oc.* **68 C2** 52 0N 175 0W
Aleutian Trench, *Pac. Oc.* **64 C10** 48 0N 180 0 E
Alexander, *U.S.A.* **80 B3** 47 51N 103 39W
Alexander, Mt., *Australia* **61 E3** 28 58S 120 16 E
Alexander Arch., *U.S.A.* **68 C6** 56 0N 136 0W
Alexander Bay, *S. Africa* **56 D2** 28 40S 16 30 E
Alexander City, *U.S.A.* **77 J3** 32 56N 85 58W
Alexander I., *Antarctica* **5 C17** 69 0S 70 0W
Alexandra, *N.Z.* **59 L2** 45 14S 169 25 E
Alexandra Falls, *Canada* **72 A5** 60 29N 116 18W
Alexandria = El Iskandarîya, *Egypt* **51 B11** 31 13N 29 58 E
Alexandria, *B.C., Canada* **72 C4** 52 35N 122 27W
Alexandria, *Ont., Canada* **79 A10** 45 19N 74 38W
Alexandria, *Romania* **17 G13** 43 57N 25 24 E
Alexandria, *S. Africa* **56 E4** 33 38S 26 28 E
Alexandria, *U.K.* **12 F4** 55 59N 4 35W
Alexandria, *La., U.S.A.* **81 K8** 31 18N 92 27W
Alexandria, *Minn., U.S.A.* **80 C7** 45 53N 95 22W
Alexandria, *S. Dak., U.S.A.* **80 D6** 43 39N 97 47W
Alexandria, *Va., U.S.A.* **76 F7** 38 48N 77 3W
Alexandria Bay, *U.S.A.* **79 B9** 44 20N 75 55W
Alexandroúpolis, *Greece* **21 D11** 40 50N 25 54 E
Alexis →, *Canada* **71 B8** 52 33N 56 8W
Alexis Creek, *Canada* **72 C4** 52 10N 123 20W
Alfabia, *Spain* **22 B9** 39 44N 2 44 E
Alfenas, *Brazil* **95 A6** 21 20S 46 10W
Alford, *Aberds., U.K.* **12 D6** 57 14N 2 41W
Alford, *Lincs., U.K.* **10 D8** 53 15N 0 10 E
Alfred, *Maine, U.S.A.* **79 C14** 43 29N 70 43W
Alfred, *N.Y., U.S.A.* **78 D7** 42 16N 77 48W
Alfreton, *U.K.* **10 D6** 53 6N 1 24W
Alga, *Kazakstan* **25 E10** 49 53N 57 20 E
Algaida, *Spain* **22 B9** 39 33N 2 53 E
Ålgård, *Norway* **9 G11** 58 46N 5 53 E
Algarve, *Portugal* **19 D1** 36 58N 8 20W
Algeciras, *Spain* **19 D3** 36 9N 5 28W
Algemesí, *Spain* **19 C5** 39 11N 0 27W
Alger, *Algeria* **50 A6** 36 42N 3 8 E
Algeria ■, *Africa* **50 C6** 28 30N 2 0 E
Alghero, *Italy* **20 D3** 40 33N 8 19 E
Algiers = Alger, *Algeria* **50 A6** 36 42N 3 8 E
Algoa B., *S. Africa* **56 E4** 33 50S 25 45 E
Algoma, *U.S.A.* **76 C2** 44 36N 87 26W
Algona, *U.S.A.* **80 D7** 43 4N 94 14W
Algonac, *U.S.A.* **78 D2** 42 37N 82 32W
Algonquin Prov. Park, *Canada* **70 C4** 45 50N 78 30W
Algorta, *Uruguay* **96 C5** 32 25S 57 23W
Alhambra, *U.S.A.* **85 L8** 34 8N 118 6W
Alhucemas = Al Hoceïma, *Morocco* **50 A5** 35 8N 3 58W
'Alī al Gharbī, *Iraq* **44 C5** 32 30N 46 45 E
'Alī ash Sharqī, *Iraq* **44 C5** 32 7N 46 44 E
'Alī Khēl, *Afghan.* **42 C3** 33 57N 69 43 E
Alī Shāh, *Iran* **44 B5** 38 9N 45 50 E
'Alīābād, *Khorāsān, Iran* **45 C8** 32 30N 57 30 E
'Alīābād, *Kordestān, Iran* **44 C5** 35 4N 46 58 E
'Alīābād, *Yazd, Iran* **45 D7** 31 41N 53 49 E
Aliağa, *Turkey* **21 E12** 38 47N 26 59 E
Aliákmon →, *Greece* **21 D10** 40 30N 22 36 E
Alicante, *Spain* **19 C5** 38 23N 0 30W
Alice, *S. Africa* **56 E4** 32 48S 26 55 E
Alice, *U.S.A.* **81 M5** 27 45N 98 5W
Alice →, *Queens., Australia* **62 C3** 24 2S 144 50 E
Alice →, *Queens., Australia* **62 B3** 15 35S 142 20 E
Alice Arm, *Canada* **72 B3** 55 29N 129 31W
Alice Springs, *Australia* **62 C1** 23 40S 133 50 E
Alicedale, *S. Africa* **56 E4** 33 15S 26 4 E
Aliceville, *U.S.A.* **77 J1** 33 8N 88 9W
Aliganj, *India* **43 F8** 27 30N 79 10 E
Aligarh, *Raj., India* **42 G7** 25 55N 76 15 E
Aligarh, *Ut. P., India* **42 F8** 27 55N 78 10 E
Alīgūdarz, *Iran* **45 C6** 33 25N 49 45 E
Alimnía, *Greece* **23 C9** 36 16N 27 43 E
Alingsås, *Sweden* **9 H15** 57 56N 12 31 E
Alipur, *Pakistan* **42 E4** 29 25N 70 55 E
Alipur Duar, *India* **41 F16** 26 30N 89 35 E
Aliquippa, *U.S.A.* **78 F4** 40 37N 80 15W
Alitus = Alytus, *Lithuania* **9 J21** 54 24N 24 3 E
Aliwal North, *S. Africa* **56 E4** 30 45S 26 45 E
Alix, *Canada* **72 C6** 52 24N 113 11W
Aljustrel, *Portugal* **19 D1** 37 55N 8 10W
Alkmaar, *Neths.* **15 B4** 52 37N 4 45 E
All American Canal, *U.S.A.* **83 K6** 32 45N 115 15W
Allagash →, *U.S.A.* **77 B11** 47 5N 69 3W
Allah Dad, *Pakistan* **42 G2** 25 38N 67 34 E
Allahabad, *India* **43 G9** 25 25N 81 58 E
Allan, *Canada* **73 C7** 51 53N 106 4W
Allanridge, *S. Africa* **56 D4** 27 45S 26 40 E
Allegany, *U.S.A.* **78 D6** 42 6N 78 30W
Allegheny →, *U.S.A.* **78 F5** 40 27N 80 1W
Allegheny Mts., *U.S.A.* **76 G6** 38 15N 80 10W
Allegheny Reservoir, *U.S.A.* **78 E6** 41 50N 79 0W
Allen, Bog of, *Ireland* **13 C5** 53 15N 7 0W
Allen, L., *Ireland* **13 B3** 54 8N 8 4W
Allendale, *U.S.A.* **77 J5** 33 1N 81 18W
Allende, *Mexico* **86 B4** 28 20N 100 50W
Allentown, *U.S.A.* **79 F9** 40 37N 75 29W
Alleppey, *India* **40 Q10** 9 30N 76 28 E
Aller →, *Germany* **16 B5** 52 56N 9 12 E
Alliance, *Nebr., U.S.A.* **80 D3** 42 6N 102 52W
Alliance, *Ohio, U.S.A.* **78 F3** 40 55N 81 6W
Allier →, *France* **18 C5** 46 57N 3 4 E
Alliford Bay, *Canada* **72 C2** 53 12N 131 58W
Alliston, *Canada* **78 B5** 44 9N 79 52W
Alloa, *U.K.* **12 E5** 56 7N 3 47W
Allora, *Australia* **63 D5** 28 2S 152 0 E
Alluitsup Paa, *Greenland* **4 C5** 60 30N 45 35W
Alma, *Canada* **71 C5** 48 35N 71 40W
Alma, *Ga., U.S.A.* **77 K4** 31 33N 82 28W
Alma, *Kans., U.S.A.* **80 F6** 39 1N 96 17W
Alma, *Mich., U.S.A.* **76 D3** 43 23N 84 39W
Alma, *Nebr., U.S.A.* **80 E5** 40 6N 99 22W
Alma Ata = Almaty, *Kazakstan* **26 E8** 43 15N 76 57 E
Almada, *Portugal* **19 C1** 38 40N 9 9W
Almaden, *Australia* **62 B3** 17 22S 144 40 E
Almadén, *Spain* **19 C3** 38 49N 4 52W
Almanor, L., *U.S.A.* **82 F3** 40 14N 121 9W
Almansa, *Spain* **19 C5** 38 51N 1 5W
Almanzor, Pico, *Spain* **19 B3** 40 15N 5 18W
Almanzora →, *Spain* **19 D5** 37 14N 1 46W
Almaty, *Kazakstan* **26 E8** 43 15N 76 57 E
Almazán, *Spain* **19 B4** 41 30N 2 30W
Almeirim, *Brazil* **93 D8** 1 30S 52 34W
Almelo, *Neths.* **15 B6** 52 22N 6 42 E
Almendralejo, *Spain* **19 C2** 38 41N 6 26W
Almere-Stad, *Neths.* **15 B5** 52 20N 5 15 E
Almería, *Spain* **19 D4** 36 52N 2 27W
Almirante, *Panama* **88 E3** 9 10N 82 30W
Almiroú, Kólpos, *Greece* **23 D6** 35 23N 24 20 E
Almond, *U.S.A.* **78 D7** 42 19N 77 44W
Almont, *U.S.A.* **78 D1** 42 55N 83 3W
Almonte, *Canada* **79 A8** 45 14N 76 12W
Almora, *India* **43 E8** 29 38N 79 40 E
Alness, *U.K.* **12 D4** 57 41N 4 16W
Alnmouth, *U.K.* **10 B6** 55 24N 1 37W
Alnwick, *U.K.* **10 B6** 55 24N 1 42W
Aloi, *Uganda* **54 B3** 2 16N 33 10 E
Alon, *Burma* **41 H19** 22 12N 95 5 E
Alor, *Indonesia* **37 F6** 8 15S 124 30 E
Alor Setar, *Malaysia* **39 J3** 6 7N 100 22 E
Alot, *India* **42 H6** 23 56N 75 40 E
Aloysius, Mt., *Australia* **61 E4** 26 0S 128 38 E
Alpaugh, *U.S.A.* **84 K7** 35 53N 119 29W
Alpena, *U.S.A.* **76 C4** 45 4N 83 27W
Alpha, *Australia* **62 C4** 23 39S 146 37 E
Alphen aan den Rijn, *Neths.* **15 B4** 52 7N 4 40 E
Alpine, *Ariz., U.S.A.* **83 K9** 33 51N 109 9W
Alpine, *Calif., U.S.A.* **85 N10** 32 50N 116 46W
Alpine, *Tex., U.S.A.* **81 K3** 30 22N 103 40W
Alps, *Europe* **18 C8** 46 30N 9 30 E
Alsace, *France* **18 B7** 48 15N 7 25 E
Alsask, *Canada* **73 C7** 51 21N 109 59W
Alsasua, *Spain* **19 A4** 42 54N 2 10W
Alsek →, *U.S.A.* **72 B1** 59 10N 138 12W
Alsten, *Norway* **8 D15** 65 58N 12 40 E
Alston, *U.K.* **10 C5** 54 49N 2 25W
Alta, *Norway* **8 B20** 69 57N 23 10 E
Alta Gracia, *Argentina* **94 C3** 31 40S 64 30W
Alta Sierra, *U.S.A.* **85 K8** 35 42N 118 33W
Altaelva →, *Norway* **8 B20** 69 54N 23 17 E
Altafjorden, *Norway* **8 A20** 70 5N 23 5 E
Altai = Aerhtai Shan, *Mongolia* **32 B4** 46 40N 92 45 E
Altamaha →, *U.S.A.* **77 K5** 31 20N 81 20W
Altamira, *Brazil* **93 D8** 3 12S 52 10W
Altamira, *Chile* **94 B2** 25 47S 69 51W
Altamira, *Mexico* **87 C5** 22 24N 97 55W
Altamont, *U.S.A.* **79 D10** 42 43N 74 3W
Altamura, *Italy* **20 D7** 40 49N 16 33 E
Altanbulag, *Mongolia* **32 A5** 50 16N 106 30 E
Altar, *Mexico* **86 A2** 30 40N 111 50W
Altar, Desierto de, *Mexico* **86 B2** 30 10N 112 0W
Altata, *Mexico* **86 C3** 24 30N 108 0W
Altavista, *U.S.A.* **76 G6** 37 6N 79 17W
Altay, *China* **32 B3** 47 48N 88 10 E
Altea, *Spain* **19 C5** 38 38N 0 2W
Altiplano = Bolivian Plateau, *S. Amer.* **90 E4** 20 0S 67 30W
Alto Araguaia, *Brazil* **93 G8** 17 15S 53 20W
Alto Cuchumatanes = Cuchumatanes, Sierra de los, *Guatemala* **88 C1** 15 35N 91 25W
Alto del Carmen, *Chile* **94 B1** 28 46S 70 30W
Alto del Inca, *Chile* **94 A2** 24 10S 68 10W
Alto Ligonha, *Mozam.* **55 F4** 15 30S 38 11 E
Alto Molocue, *Mozam.* **55 F4** 15 50S 37 35 E
Alto Paraguay □, *Paraguay* **94 A4** 21 0S 58 30W
Alto Paraná □, *Paraguay* **95 B5** 25 30S 54 50W
Alton, *Canada* **78 C4** 43 54N 80 5W
Alton, *U.K.* **11 F7** 51 9N 0 59W
Alton, *Ill., U.S.A.* **80 F9** 38 53N 90 11W
Alton, *N.H., U.S.A.* **79 C13** 43 27N 71 13W
Altoona, *U.S.A.* **78 F6** 40 31N 78 24W
Altūn Kūprī, *Iraq* **44 C5** 35 45N 44 9 E
Altun Shan, *China* **32 C3** 38 30N 88 0 E
Alturas, *U.S.A.* **82 F3** 41 29N 120 32W
Altus, *U.S.A.* **81 H5** 34 38N 99 20W
Alucra, *Turkey* **25 F6** 40 22N 38 47 E
Alūksne, *Latvia* **9 H22** 57 24N 27 3 E
Alunite, *U.S.A.* **85 K12** 35 59N 114 55W
Alusi, *Indonesia* **37 F8** 7 35S 131 40 E
Alva, *U.S.A.* **81 G5** 36 48N 98 40W
Alvarado, *Mexico* **87 D5** 18 40N 95 50W
Alvarado, *U.S.A.* **81 J6** 32 24N 97 13W
Alvaro Obregón, Presa, *Mexico* **86 B3** 27 55N 109 52W
Alvear, *Argentina* **94 B4** 29 5S 56 30W
Alvesta, *Sweden* **9 H16** 56 54N 14 35 E
Alvin, *U.S.A.* **81 L7** 29 26N 95 15W
Alvinston, *Canada* **78 D3** 42 49N 81 52W
Älvkarleby, *Sweden* **9 F17** 60 34N 17 26 E
Alvord Desert, *U.S.A.* **82 E4** 42 30N 118 25W
Älvsbyn, *Sweden* **8 D19** 65 40N 21 0 E
Alwar, *India* **42 F7** 27 38N 76 34 E
Alxa Zuoqi, *China* **34 E3** 38 50N 105 40 E
Alyangula, *Australia* **62 A2** 13 55S 136 30 E
Alyata = Älät, *Azerbaijan* **25 G8** 39 58N 49 25 E
Alyth, *U.K.* **12 E5** 56 38N 3 13W
Alytus, *Lithuania* **9 J21** 54 24N 24 3 E
Alzada, *U.S.A.* **80 C2** 45 2N 104 25W
Alzira, *Spain* **19 C5** 39 9N 0 30W
Am Timan, *Chad* **51 F10** 11 0N 20 10 E
Amadeus, L., *Australia* **61 D5** 24 54S 131 0 E
Amadi, *Dem. Rep. of the Congo* **54 B2** 3 40N 26 40 E
Amâdi, *Sudan* **51 G12** 5 29N 30 25 E
Amadjuak L., *Canada* **69 B12** 65 0N 71 8W
Amagansett, *U.S.A.* **79 F12** 40 59N 72 9W
Amagasaki, *Japan* **31 G7** 34 42N 135 20 E
Amahai, *Indonesia* **37 E7** 3 20S 128 55 E
Amakusa-Shotō, *Japan* **31 H5** 32 15N 130 10 E
Åmål, *Sweden* **9 G15** 59 3N 12 42 E
Amaliás, *Greece* **21 F9** 37 47N 21 22 E
Amalner, *India* **40 J9** 21 5N 75 5 E

Amamapare

Amamapare, Indonesia 37 E9 4 53S 136 38 E
Amambaí, Brazil 95 A4 23 5S 55 13W
Amambaí →, Brazil 95 A5 23 22S 53 56W
Amambay □, Paraguay 95 A4 23 0S 56 0W
Amambay, Cordillera de, S. Amer. 95 A4 23 0S 55 45W
Amami-Guntō, Japan 31 L4 27 16N 129 21 E
Amami-Ō-Shima, Japan 31 L4 28 0N 129 0 E
Amaná, L., Brazil 92 D6 2 35S 64 40W
Amanat →, India 43 G11 24 7N 84 4 E
Amanda Park, U.S.A. 84 C3 47 28N 123 55W
Amangeldy, Kazakstan 26 D7 50 10N 65 10 E
Amapá, Brazil 93 C8 2 5N 50 50W
Amapá □, Brazil 93 C8 1 40N 52 0W
Amarante, Brazil 93 E10 6 14S 42 50W
Amaranth, Canada 73 C9 50 36N 98 43W
Amargosa →, U.S.A. 85 J10 36 14N 116 51W
Amargosa Range, U.S.A. 85 J10 36 20N 116 45W
Amári, Greece 23 D6 35 13N 24 40 E
Amarillo, U.S.A. 81 H4 35 13N 101 50W
Amarkantak, India 43 H9 22 40N 81 45 E
Amaro, Mte., Italy 20 C6 42 5N 14 5 E
Amarpur, India 43 G12 25 5N 87 0 E
Amarwara, India 43 H8 22 18N 79 10 E
Amasya □, Turkey 25 F6 40 40N 35 50 E
Amata, Australia 61 E5 26 9S 131 9 E
Amatikulu, S. Africa 57 D5 29 3S 31 33 E
Amatitlán, Guatemala 88 D1 14 29N 90 38W
Amay, Belgium 15 D5 50 33N 5 19 E
Amazon = Amazonas →, S. Amer. 93 D9 0 5S 50 0W
Amazonas □, Brazil 92 E6 5 0S 65 0W
Amazonas →, S. Amer. 93 D9 0 5S 50 0W
Ambah, India 42 F8 26 43N 78 13 E
Ambahakily, Madag. 57 C7 21 36S 43 41 E
Ambahita, Madag. 57 C8 24 1S 45 16 E
Ambala, India 42 D7 30 23N 76 56 E
Ambalavao, Madag. 57 C8 21 50S 46 56 E
Ambanja, Madag. 57 A8 13 40S 48 27 E
Ambararata, Madag. 57 B8 15 3S 48 33 E
Ambarchik, Russia 27 C17 69 40N 162 20 E
Ambarijeby, Madag. 57 A8 14 56S 47 41 E
Ambaro, Helodranon', Madag. 57 A8 13 23S 48 38 E
Ambato, Ecuador 92 D3 1 5S 78 42W
Ambato, Madag. 57 A8 13 24S 48 29 E
Ambato, Sierra de, Argentina 94 B2 28 25S 66 10W
Ambato Boeny, Madag. 57 B8 16 28S 46 43 E
Ambatofinandrahana, Madag. 57 C8 20 33S 46 48 E
Ambatolampy, Madag. 57 B8 19 20S 47 35 E
Ambatomainty, Madag. 57 B8 17 41S 45 40 E
Ambatomanoina, Madag. 57 B8 18 18S 47 37 E
Ambatondrazaka, Madag. 57 B8 17 55S 48 28 E
Ambatosoratra, Madag. 57 B8 17 37S 48 31 E
Ambenja, Madag. 57 B8 15 17S 46 58 E
Amberg, Germany 16 D6 49 26N 11 52 E
Ambergris Cay, Belize 87 D7 18 0N 88 0W
Amberley, N.Z. 59 K4 43 9S 172 44 E
Ambikapur, India 43 H10 23 15N 83 15 E
Ambilobé, Madag. 57 A8 13 10S 49 3 E
Ambinanindrano, Madag. 57 C8 20 5S 48 23 E
Ambinanitelo, Madag. 57 B8 15 21S 49 35 E
Ambinda, Madag. 57 B8 16 25S 45 52 E
Amble, U.K. 10 B6 55 20N 1 36W
Ambleside, U.K. 10 C5 54 26N 2 58W
Ambo, Peru 92 F3 10 5S 76 10W
Amboahangy, Madag. 57 C8 24 15S 46 22 E
Ambodifototra, Madag. 57 B8 16 59S 49 52 E
Ambodilazana, Madag. 57 B8 18 6S 49 10 E
Ambodiriana, Madag. 57 B8 17 55S 49 18 E
Ambohidratrimo, Madag. 57 B8 18 50S 47 26 E
Ambohidray, Madag. 57 B8 18 36S 48 18 E
Ambohimahamasina, Madag. 57 C8 21 56S 47 11 E
Ambohimahasoa, Madag. 57 C8 21 7S 47 13 E
Ambohimanga, Madag. 57 C8 20 52S 47 36 E
Ambohimitombo, Madag. 57 C8 20 43S 47 26 E
Ambohitra, Madag. 57 A8 12 30S 49 10 E
Amboise, France 18 C4 47 24N 1 2 E
Ambon, Indonesia 37 E7 3 43S 128 12 E
Ambondro, Madag. 57 D8 25 13S 45 44 E
Amboseli, L., Kenya 54 C4 2 40S 37 10 E
Ambositra, Madag. 57 C8 20 31S 47 25 E
Ambovombe, Madag. 57 D8 25 11S 46 5 E
Amboy, U.S.A. 85 L11 34 33N 115 45W
Amboyna Cay, S. China Sea 36 C4 7 50N 112 50 E
Ambridge, U.S.A. 78 F4 40 36N 80 14W
Ambriz, Angola 52 F2 7 48S 13 8 E
Amchitka I., U.S.A. 68 C1 51 32N 179 0 E
Amderma, Russia 26 C7 69 45N 61 30 E
Amdhi, India 43 H9 23 51N 81 27 E
Ameca, Mexico 86 C4 20 30N 104 0W
Ameca →, Mexico 86 C3 20 40N 105 15W
Amecameca, Mexico 87 D5 19 7N 98 46W
Ameland, Neths. 15 A5 53 27N 5 45 E
Amenia, U.S.A. 79 E11 41 51N 73 33W
American Falls, U.S.A. 82 E7 42 47N 112 51W
American Falls Reservoir, U.S.A. 82 E7 42 47N 112 52W
American Fork, U.S.A. 82 F8 40 23N 111 48W
American Highland, Antarctica 5 D6 73 0S 75 0 E
American Samoa ■, Pac. Oc. 59 B13 14 20S 170 40W
Americana, Brazil 95 A6 22 45S 47 20W
Americus, U.S.A. 77 K3 32 4N 84 14W
Amersfoort, Neths. 15 B5 52 9N 5 23 E
Amersfoort, S. Africa 57 D4 26 59S 29 53 E
Amery Ice Shelf, Antarctica 5 C6 69 30S 72 0 E
Ames, U.S.A. 80 E8 42 2N 93 37W
Amesbury, U.S.A. 79 D14 42 51N 70 56W
Amet, India 42 G5 25 18N 73 56 E
Amga, Russia 27 C14 60 50N 132 0 E
Amga →, Russia 27 C14 62 38N 134 32 E
Amgu, Russia 27 E14 45 45N 137 15 E
Amgun →, Russia 27 D14 52 56N 139 38 E
Amherst, Canada 71 C7 45 48N 64 8W
Amherst, Mass., U.S.A. 79 D12 42 23N 72 31W
Amherst, N.Y., U.S.A. 78 D6 42 59N 78 48W
Amherst, Ohio, U.S.A. 78 E2 41 24N 82 14W
Amherst I., Canada 79 B8 44 8N 76 43W
Amherstburg, Canada 70 D3 42 6N 83 6W
Amiata, Mte., Italy 20 C4 42 53N 11 37 E
Amidon, U.S.A. 80 B3 46 29N 103 19W
Amiens, France 18 B5 49 54N 2 16 E
Aminuis, Namibia 56 C2 23 43S 19 21 E
Amīrābād, Iran 44 C5 33 20N 46 16 E
Amirante Is., Seychelles 28 K9 6 0S 53 0 E
Amisk L., Canada 73 C8 54 35N 102 15W
Amistad, Presa de la, Mexico 86 B4 29 24N 101 0W
Amite, U.S.A. 81 K9 30 44N 90 30W
Amla, India 42 J8 21 56N 78 7 E
Amlia I., U.S.A. 68 C2 52 4N 173 30W
Amlwch, U.K. 10 D3 53 24N 4 20W
'Ammān, Jordan 47 D4 31 57N 35 52 E
'Ammān □, Jordan 47 D5 31 40N 36 30 E
Ammanford, U.K. 11 F4 51 48N 3 59W
Ammassalik = Tasiilaq, Greenland 4 C6 65 40N 37 20W
Ammon, U.S.A. 82 E8 43 28N 111 58W
Amnat Charoen, Thailand 38 E5 15 51N 104 38 E
Amnura, Bangla. 43 G13 24 37N 88 25 E
Āmol, Iran 45 B7 36 23N 52 20 E
Amorgós, Greece 21 F11 36 50N 25 57 E
Amory, U.S.A. 77 J1 33 59N 88 29W
Amos, Canada 70 C4 48 35N 78 5W
Åmot, Norway 9 G13 59 57N 9 54 E
Amoy = Xiamen, China 33 D6 24 25N 118 4 E
Ampanavoana, Madag. 57 B9 15 41S 50 22 E
Ampang, Malaysia 39 L3 3 8N 101 45 E
Ampangalana, Lakandranon', Madag. 57 C8 22 48S 47 50 E
Ampanihy, Madag. 57 C7 24 40S 44 45 E
Amparafaravola, Madag. 57 B8 17 35S 48 13 E
Ampasinambo, Madag. 57 C8 20 31S 48 0 E
Ampasindava, Helodranon', Madag. 57 A8 13 40S 48 15 E
Ampasindava, Saikanosy, Madag. 57 A8 13 42S 47 55 E
Ampenan, Indonesia 36 F5 8 35S 116 13 E
Amper →, Germany 16 D6 48 29N 11 55 E
Ampitsikinana, Réunion 57 A8 12 57S 49 49 E
Ampombiantambo, Madag. 57 A8 12 42S 48 57 E
Ampotaka, Madag. 57 D7 25 3S 44 41 E
Ampoza, Madag. 57 C7 22 20S 44 44 E
Amqui, Canada 71 C6 48 28N 67 27W
Amravati, India 40 J10 20 55N 77 45 E
Amreli, India 42 J4 21 35N 71 17 E
Amritsar, India 42 D6 31 35N 74 57 E
Amroha, India 43 E8 28 53N 78 30 E
Amsterdam, Neths. 15 B4 52 23N 4 54 E
Amsterdam, U.S.A. 79 D10 42 56N 74 11W
Amsterdam, I. = Nouvelle-Amsterdam, I., Ind. Oc. 3 F13 38 30S 77 30 E
Amstetten, Austria 16 D8 48 7N 14 51 E
Amudarya →, Uzbekistan 26 E6 43 58N 59 34 E
Amundsen Gulf, Canada 68 A7 71 0N 124 0W
Amundsen Sea, Antarctica 5 D15 72 0S 115 0W
Amuntai, Indonesia 36 E5 2 28S 115 25 E
Amur →, Russia 27 D15 52 56N 141 10 E
Amurang, Indonesia 37 D6 1 5N 124 40 E
Amursk, Russia 27 D14 50 14N 136 54 E
Amyderya = Amudarya →, Uzbekistan 26 E6 43 58N 59 34 E
An Bien, Vietnam 39 H5 9 45N 105 0 E
An Hoa, Vietnam 38 E7 15 40N 108 5 E
An Nabatīyah at Tahta, Lebanon 47 B4 33 23N 35 27 E
An Nabk, Si. Arabia 44 D3 31 20N 37 20 E
An Nabk, Syria 47 A5 34 2N 36 44 E
An Nafūd, Si. Arabia 44 D4 28 15N 41 0 E
An Najaf, Iraq 44 C5 32 3N 44 15 E
An Nāşirīyah, Iraq 44 D5 31 0N 46 15 E
An Nhon, Vietnam 38 F7 13 55N 109 7 E
An Nu'ayrīyah, Si. Arabia 45 E6 27 30N 48 30 E
An Nuwayb'ī, W. →, Si. Arabia 47 F3 29 18N 34 57 E
An Thoi, Dao, Vietnam 39 H4 9 58N 104 0 E
An Uaimh, Ireland 13 C5 53 39N 6 41W
Anabar →, Russia 27 B12 73 8N 113 36 E
'Anabtā, West Bank 47 C4 32 19N 35 7 E
Anaconda, U.S.A. 82 C7 46 8N 112 57W
Anacortes, U.S.A. 84 B4 48 30N 122 37W
Anadarko, U.S.A. 81 H5 35 4N 98 15W
Anadolu, Turkey 25 G5 39 0N 30 0 E
Anadyr, Russia 27 C18 64 35N 177 20 E
Anadyr →, Russia 27 C18 64 55N 176 5 E
Anadyrskiy Zaliv, Russia 27 C19 64 0N 180 0 E
Anaga, Pta. de, Canary Is. 22 F3 28 34N 16 9W
'Ānah, Iraq 44 C4 34 25N 42 0 E
Anaheim, U.S.A. 85 M9 33 50N 117 55W
Anahim Lake, Canada 72 C3 52 28N 125 18W
Anáhuac, Mexico 86 B4 27 14N 100 9W
Anakapalle, India 41 L13 17 42N 83 6 E
Anakie, Australia 62 C4 23 32S 147 45 E
Analalava, Madag. 57 A8 14 35S 48 0 E
Analavoka, Madag. 57 C8 22 23S 46 30 E
Análipsis, Greece 23 A3 39 36N 19 55 E
Anambar →, Pakistan 42 D3 30 15N 68 50 E
Anambas, Kepulauan, Indonesia 39 L6 3 20N 106 30 E
Anambas Is. = Anambas, Kepulauan, Indonesia 39 L6 3 20N 106 30 E
Anamosa, U.S.A. 80 D9 42 7N 91 17W
Anamur, Turkey 25 G5 36 8N 32 58 E
Anan, Japan 31 H7 33 54N 134 40 E
Anand, India 42 H5 22 32N 72 59 E
Anantnag, India 43 C6 33 45N 75 10 E
Ananyiv, Ukraine 17 E15 47 44N 29 58 E
Anapodháris →, Greece 23 E7 34 59N 25 20 E
Anápolis, Brazil 93 G9 16 15S 48 50W
Anapu →, Brazil 93 D8 1 53S 50 53W
Anār, Iran 45 D7 30 55N 55 13 E
Anārak, Iran 45 C7 33 25N 53 40 E
Anas →, India 42 H5 23 26N 74 0 E
Anatolia = Anadolu, Turkey 25 G5 39 0N 30 0 E
Anatsogno, Madag. 57 C7 23 33S 43 46 E
Añatuya, Argentina 94 B3 28 20S 62 50W
Anaunethad L., Canada 73 A8 60 55N 104 25W
Anbyŏn, N. Korea 35 E14 39 1N 127 35 E
Ancaster, Canada 78 C5 43 13N 79 59W
Anchor Bay, U.S.A. 84 G3 38 48N 123 34W
Anchorage, U.S.A. 68 B5 61 13N 149 54W
Anci, China 34 E9 39 20N 116 40 E
Ancohuma, Nevada, Bolivia 92 G5 16 0S 68 50W
Ancón, Peru 92 F3 11 50S 77 10W
Ancona, Italy 20 C5 43 38N 13 30 E
Ancud, Chile 96 E2 42 0S 73 50W
Ancud, G. de, Chile 96 E2 42 0S 73 0W
Anda, China 33 B7 46 24N 125 19 E
Andacollo, Argentina 94 D1 37 10S 70 42W
Andacollo, Chile 94 C1 30 14S 71 6W
Andaingo, Madag. 57 B8 18 12S 48 17 E
Andalgalá, Argentina 94 B2 27 40S 66 30W
Åndalsnes, Norway 9 E12 62 35N 7 43 E
Andalucía □, Spain 19 D3 37 35N 5 0W
Andalusia = Andalucía □, Spain 19 D3 37 35N 5 0W
Andalusia, U.S.A. 77 K2 31 18N 86 29W
Andaman Is., Ind. Oc. 29 H13 12 30N 92 30 E
Andaman Sea, Ind. Oc. 36 B1 13 0N 96 0 E
Andamooka Opal Fields, Australia 63 E2 30 27S 137 9 E
Andapa, Madag. 57 A8 14 39S 49 39 E
Andara, Namibia 56 B3 18 2S 21 9 E
Andenes, Norway 8 B17 69 19N 16 18 E
Andenne, Belgium 15 D5 50 28N 5 5 E
Anderson, Alaska, U.S.A. 68 B5 64 25N 149 15W
Anderson, Calif., U.S.A. 82 F2 40 27N 122 18W
Anderson, Ind., U.S.A. 76 E3 40 10N 85 41W
Anderson, Mo., U.S.A. 81 G7 36 39N 94 27W
Anderson, S.C., U.S.A. 77 H4 34 31N 82 39W
Anderson →, Canada 68 B7 69 42N 129 0W
Andes, U.S.A. 79 D10 42 12N 74 47W
Andes, Cord. de los, S. Amer. 92 H5 20 0S 68 0W
Andfjorden, Norway 8 B17 69 10N 16 20 E
Andhra Pradesh □, India 40 L11 18 0N 79 0 E
Andijon, Uzbekistan 26 E8 41 10N 72 15 E
Andikíthira, Greece 21 G10 35 52N 23 15 E
Andilamena, Madag. 57 B8 17 1S 48 35 E
Andīmeshk, Iran 45 C6 32 27N 48 21 E
Andizhan = Andijon, Uzbekistan 26 E8 41 10N 72 15 E
Andoany, Madag. 57 A8 13 25S 48 16 E
Andong, S. Korea 35 F15 36 40N 128 43 E
Andongwei, China 35 G10 35 6N 119 20 E
Andoom, Australia 62 A3 12 25S 141 53 E
Andorra ■, Europe 18 E4 42 30N 1 30 E
Andorra La Vella, Andorra 18 E4 42 31N 1 32 E
Andover, U.K. 11 F6 51 12N 1 29W
Andover, Maine, U.S.A. 79 B14 44 38N 70 45W
Andover, Mass., U.S.A. 79 D13 42 40N 71 8W
Andover, N.J., U.S.A. 79 F10 40 59N 74 45W
Andover, N.Y., U.S.A. 78 D7 42 10N 77 48W
Andover, Ohio, U.S.A. 78 E4 41 36N 80 34W
Andøya, Norway 8 B16 69 10N 15 50 E
Andradina, Brazil 93 H8 20 54S 51 23W
Andrahary, Mt., Madag. 57 A8 13 37S 49 17 E
Andramasina, Madag. 57 B8 19 11S 47 35 E
Andranopasy, Madag. 57 C7 21 17S 43 44 E
Andranovory, Madag. 57 C7 23 8S 44 10 E
Andratx, Spain 22 B9 39 39N 2 25 E
Andreanof Is., U.S.A. 68 C2 51 30N 176 0W
Andrews, S.C., U.S.A. 77 J6 33 27N 79 34W
Andrews, Tex., U.S.A. 81 J3 32 19N 102 33W
Ándria, Italy 20 D7 41 13N 16 17 E
Andriamena, Madag. 57 B8 17 26S 47 30 E
Andriandampy, Madag. 57 C8 22 45S 45 41 E
Andriba, Madag. 57 B8 17 30S 46 58 E
Androka, Madag. 57 C7 24 58S 44 2 E
Andropov = Rybinsk, Russia 24 C6 58 5N 38 50 E
Ándros, Greece 21 F11 37 50N 24 57 E
Andros I., Bahamas 88 B4 24 30N 78 0W
Andros Town, Bahamas 88 B4 24 43N 77 47W
Androscoggin →, U.S.A. 79 C14 43 58N 70 0W
Andselv, Norway 8 B18 69 4N 18 34 E
Andújar, Spain 19 C3 38 3N 4 5W
Andulo, Angola 52 G3 11 25S 16 45 E
Anegada I., U.S. Virgin Is. 89 C7 18 45N 64 20W
Anegada Passage, W. Indies 89 C7 18 15N 63 45W
Aneto, Pico de, Spain 19 A6 42 37N 0 40 E
Ang Thong, Thailand 38 E3 14 35N 100 31 E
Angamos, Punta, Chile 94 A1 23 1S 70 32W
Angara →, Russia 27 D10 58 5N 94 20 E
Angarsk, Russia 27 D11 52 30N 104 0 E
Angas Hills, Australia 60 D4 23 0S 127 50 E
Angaur I., Pac. Oc. 37 C8 6 54N 134 9 E
Ånge, Sweden 9 E16 62 31N 15 35 E
Ángel, Salto = Angel Falls, Venezuela 92 B6 5 57N 62 30W
Ángel de la Guarda, I., Mexico 86 B2 29 30N 113 30W
Angel Falls, Venezuela 92 B6 5 57N 62 30W
Angeles, Phil. 37 A6 15 9N 120 33 E
Ängelholm, Sweden 9 H15 56 15N 12 58 E
Angels Camp, U.S.A. 84 G6 38 4N 120 32W
Ångermanälven →, Sweden 8 E17 62 40N 18 0 E
Ångermanland, Sweden 8 E18 63 36N 17 45 E
Angers, Canada 79 A9 45 31N 75 29W
Angers, France 18 C3 47 30N 0 35W
Ängesån →, Sweden 8 C20 66 16N 22 47 E
Angikuni L., Canada 73 A9 62 0N 100 0W
Angkor, Cambodia 38 F4 13 22N 103 50 E
Anglesey, Isle of □, U.K. 10 D3 53 16N 4 18W
Angleton, U.S.A. 81 L7 29 10N 95 26W
Anglisidhes, Cyprus 23 E12 34 51N 33 27 E
Angmagssalik = Tasiilaq, Greenland 4 C6 65 40N 37 20W
Ango, Dem. Rep. of the Congo 54 B2 4 10N 26 5 E
Angoche, Mozam. 55 F4 16 8S 39 55 E
Angoche, I., Mozam. 55 F4 16 20S 39 50 E
Angol, Chile 94 D1 37 56S 72 45W
Angola, Ind., U.S.A. 76 E3 41 38N 85 0W
Angola, N.Y., U.S.A. 78 D5 42 38N 79 2W
Angola ■, Africa 53 G3 12 0S 18 0 E
Angoulême, France 18 D4 45 39N 0 10 E
Angoumois, France 18 D3 45 50N 0 25 E
Angra dos Reis, Brazil 95 A7 23 0S 44 10W
Angren, Uzbekistan 26 E8 41 1N 70 12 E
Angtassom, Cambodia 39 G5 11 1N 104 41 E
Angu, Dem. Rep. of the Congo 54 B1 3 23N 24 30 E
Anguang, China 35 B12 45 15N 123 45 E
Anguilla ■, W. Indies 89 C7 18 14N 63 5W
Anguo, China 34 E8 38 28N 115 15 E
Angurugu, Australia 62 A2 14 0S 136 25 E
Angus □, U.K. 12 E6 56 46N 2 56W
Angwa →, Zimbabwe 57 B5 16 0S 30 23 E
Anhanduí →, Brazil 95 A5 21 46S 52 9W
Anholt, Denmark 9 H14 56 42N 11 33 E
Anhui □, China 33 C6 32 0N 117 0 E
Anhwei = Anhui □, China 33 C6 32 0N 117 0 E
Anichab, Namibia 56 C1 21 0S 14 46 E
Animas →, U.S.A. 83 H9 36 43N 108 13W
Anivorano, Madag. 57 B8 18 44S 48 58 E
Anjalankoski, Finland 9 F22 60 45N 26 51 E
Anjar, India 42 H4 23 6N 70 10 E
Anjou, France 18 C3 47 20N 0 15W
Anjozorobe, Madag. 57 B8 18 22S 47 52 E
Anju, N. Korea 35 E13 39 36N 125 40 E
Ankaboa, Tanjona, Madag. 57 C7 21 58S 43 20 E
Ankang, China 34 H5 32 40N 109 1 E
Ankara, Turkey 25 G5 39 57N 32 54 E
Ankaramena, Madag. 57 C8 21 57S 46 39 E
Ankaratra, Madag. 53 H9 19 25S 47 12 E
Ankasakasa, Madag. 57 B7 16 21S 44 52 E
Ankavandra, Madag. 57 B8 18 46S 45 18 E
Ankazoabo, Madag. 57 C7 22 18S 44 31 E
Ankazobe, Madag. 57 B8 18 20S 47 10 E
Ankeny, U.S.A. 80 E8 41 44N 93 36W
Ankilimalinika, Madag. 57 C7 22 58S 43 45 E
Ankilizato, Madag. 57 C8 20 25S 45 1 E
Ankisabe, Madag. 57 B8 19 17S 46 29 E
Ankoro, Dem. Rep. of the Congo 54 D2 6 45S 26 55 E
Ankororoka, Madag. 57 D8 25 30S 45 11 E
Anmyŏn-do, S. Korea 35 F14 36 25N 126 25 E
Ann, C., U.S.A. 79 D14 42 38N 70 35W
Ann Arbor, U.S.A. 76 D4 42 17N 83 45W
Anna, U.S.A. 81 G10 37 28N 89 15W
Annaba, Algeria 50 A7 36 50N 7 46 E
Annalee →, Ireland 13 B4 54 2N 7 24W
Annam, Vietnam 38 E7 16 0N 108 0 E
Annamitique, Chaîne, Asia 38 D6 17 0N 106 0 E
Annan, U.K. 12 G5 54 59N 3 16W
Annan →, U.K. 12 G5 54 58N 3 16W
Annapolis, U.S.A. 76 F7 38 59N 76 30W
Annapolis Royal, Canada 71 D6 44 44N 65 32W
Annapurna, Nepal 43 E10 28 34N 83 50 E
Annean, L., Australia 61 E2 26 54S 118 14 E
Annecy, France 18 D7 45 55N 6 8 E
Anning, China 32 D5 24 55N 102 26 E
Anniston, U.S.A. 77 J3 33 39N 85 50W
Annobón, Atl. Oc. 49 G4 1 25S 5 36 E
Annotto Bay, Jamaica 88 C4 18 17N 76 45W
Annville, U.S.A. 79 F8 40 20N 76 31W
Áno Viánnos, Greece 23 D7 35 2N 25 21 E
Anorotsangana, Madag. 57 A8 13 56S 47 55 E
Anosibe, Madag. 57 B8 19 26S 48 13 E
Anóyia, Greece 23 D6 35 16N 24 52 E
Anping, Hebei, China 34 E8 38 15N 115 30 E
Anping, Liaoning, China 35 D12 41 5N 123 30 E
Anqing, China 33 C6 30 30N 117 3 E
Anqiu, China 35 F10 36 25N 119 10 E
Ansai, China 34 F5 36 50N 109 20 E
Ansbach, Germany 16 D6 49 28N 10 34 E
Anshan, China 35 D12 41 5N 122 58 E
Anshun, China 32 D5 26 18N 105 57 E
Ansley, U.S.A. 80 E5 41 18N 99 23W
Anson, U.S.A. 81 J5 32 45N 99 54W
Anson B., Australia 60 B5 13 20S 130 6 E
Ansongo, Mali 50 E6 15 25N 0 35 E
Ansonia, U.S.A. 79 E11 41 21N 73 5W
Anstruther, U.K. 12 E6 56 14N 2 41W
Ansudu, Indonesia 37 E9 2 11S 139 22 E
Antabamba, Peru 92 F4 14 40S 73 0W
Antakya, Turkey 25 G6 36 14N 36 10 E
Antalaha, Madag. 57 A9 14 57S 50 20 E
Antalya, Turkey 25 G5 36 52N 30 45 E
Antalya Körfezi, Turkey 25 G5 36 15N 31 30 E
Antambohobe, Madag. 57 C8 22 20S 46 47 E
Antanambao-Manampotsy, Madag. 57 B8 19 29S 48 34 E
Antanambe, Madag. 57 B8 16 26S 49 52 E
Antananarivo, Madag. 57 B8 18 55S 47 31 E
Antananarivo □, Madag. 57 B8 19 0S 47 0 E
Antanifotsy, Madag. 57 B8 19 39S 47 19 E
Antanimbaribe, Madag. 57 C7 21 30S 44 48 E
Antanimora, Madag. 57 C8 24 49S 45 40 E
Antarctic Pen., Antarctica 5 C18 67 0S 60 0W
Antarctica 5 E3 90 0S 0 0W
Antelope, Zimbabwe 55 G2 21 2S 28 31 E
Antequera, Paraguay 94 A4 24 8S 57 7W
Antequera, Spain 19 D3 37 5N 4 33W
Antero, Mt., U.S.A. 83 G10 38 41N 106 15W
Antevamena, Madag. 57 C7 21 2S 44 8 E
Anthony, Kans., U.S.A. 81 G5 37 9N 98 2W
Anthony, N. Mex., U.S.A. 83 K10 32 0N 106 36W
Anti Atlas, Morocco 50 C4 30 0N 8 30W
Anti-Lebanon = Ash Sharqi, Al Jabal, Lebanon 47 B5 33 40N 36 10 E
Antibes, France 18 E7 43 34N 7 6 E
Anticosti, Î. d', Canada 71 C7 49 30N 63 0W
Antigo, U.S.A. 80 C10 45 9N 89 9W
Antigonish, Canada 71 C7 45 38N 61 58W
Antigua, Canary Is. 22 F5 28 24N 14 1W
Antigua, W. Indies 89 C7 17 0N 61 50W
Antigua & Barbuda ■, W. Indies 89 C7 17 20N 61 48W
Antigua Guatemala, Guatemala 88 D1 14 34N 90 41W
Antilla, Cuba 88 B4 20 40N 75 50W
Antilles = West Indies, Cent. Amer. 89 D7 15 0N 65 0W
Antioch, U.S.A. 84 G5 38 1N 121 48W
Antioquia, Colombia 92 B3 6 40N 75 55W
Antipodes Is., Pac. Oc. 64 M9 49 45S 178 40 E
Antlers, U.S.A. 81 H7 34 14N 95 37W
Antoetra, Madag. 57 C8 20 46S 47 20 E
Antofagasta, Chile 94 A1 23 50S 70 30W
Antofagasta □, Chile 94 A2 24 0S 69 0W
Antofagasta de la Sierra, Argentina 94 B2 26 5S 67 20W
Antofalla, Argentina 94 B2 25 30S 68 5W
Antofalla, Salar de, Argentina 94 B2 25 40S 67 45W
Anton, U.S.A. 81 J3 33 49N 102 10W
Antongila, Helodrano, Madag. 57 B8 15 30S 49 50 E
Antonibé, Madag. 57 B8 15 7S 47 24 E
Antonibé, Presqu'île d', Madag. 57 A8 14 55S 47 20 E
Antonina, Brazil 95 B6 25 26S 48 42W
Antrim, U.K. 13 B5 54 43N 6 14W
Antrim, U.S.A. 78 F3 40 7N 81 21W
Antrim □, U.K. 13 B5 54 56N 6 25W
Antrim, Mts. of, U.K. 13 A5 55 3N 6 14W
Antrim Plateau, Australia 60 C4 18 8S 128 20 E
Antsakabary, Madag. 57 B8 15 3S 48 56 E
Antsalova, Madag. 57 B7 18 40S 44 37 E

Ashland

Antsenavolo, *Madag.* **57 C8** 21 24S 48 3 E
Antsiafabositra, *Madag.* **57 B8** 17 18S 46 57 E
Antsirabe, *Antananarivo, Madag.* **57 B8** 19 55S 47 2 E
Antsirabe, *Antsiranana, Madag.* **57 A8** 14 0S 49 59 E
Antsirabe, *Mahajanga, Madag.* **57 B8** 15 57S 48 58 E
Antsiranana, *Madag.* **57 A8** 12 25S 49 20 E
Antsiranana □, *Madag.* **57 A8** 12 16S 49 17 E
Antsohihy, *Madag.* **57 A8** 14 50S 47 59 E
Antsohimbondrona Seranana, *Madag.* **57 A8** 13 7S 48 48 E
Antu, *China* **35 C15** 42 30N 128 20 E
Antwerp = Antwerpen, *Belgium* **15 C4** 51 13N 4 25 E
Antwerp, *U.S.A.* **79 B9** 44 12N 75 37W
Antwerpen, *Belgium* **15 C4** 51 13N 4 25 E
Antwerpen □, *Belgium* **15 C4** 51 15N 4 40 E
Anupgarh, *India* **42 E5** 29 10N 73 10 E
Anuppur, *India* **43 H9** 23 6N 81 41 E
Anuradhapura, *Sri Lanka* **40 Q12** 8 22N 80 28 E
Anveh, *Iran* **45 E7** 27 23N 54 11 E
Anvers = Antwerpen, *Belgium* **15 C4** 51 13N 4 25 E
Anvers I., *Antarctica* **5 C17** 64 30S 63 40W
Anxi, *China* **32 B4** 40 30N 95 43 E
Anxious B., *Australia* **63 E1** 33 24S 134 45 E
Anyang, *China* **34 F8** 36 5N 114 21 E
Anyer-Kidul, *Indonesia* **37 G11** 6 4S 105 53 E
Anyi, *China* **34 G6** 35 2N 111 2 E
Anza, *U.S.A.* **85 M10** 33 35N 116 39W
Anze, *China* **34 F7** 36 10N 112 12 E
Anzhero-Sudzhensk, *Russia* **26 D9** 56 10N 86 0 E
Ánzio, *Italy* **20 D5** 41 27N 12 37 E
Aoga-Shima, *Japan* **31 H9** 32 28N 139 46 E
Aomen = Macau □, *China* **33 D6** 22 16N 113 35 E
Aomori, *Japan* **30 D10** 40 45N 140 45 E
Aomori □, *Japan* **30 D10** 40 45N 140 40 E
Aonla, *India* **43 E8** 28 16N 79 11 E
Aoraki Mount Cook, *N.Z.* **59 K3** 43 36S 170 9 E
Aosta, *Italy* **18 D7** 45 45N 7 20 E
Aoukâr, *Mauritania* **50 E4** 17 40N 10 0W
Apa →, *S. Amer.* **94 A4** 22 6S 58 2W
Apache, *U.S.A.* **81 H5** 34 54N 98 22W
Apache Junction, *U.S.A.* **83 K8** 33 25N 111 33W
Apalachee B., *U.S.A.* **77 L4** 30 0N 84 0W
Apalachicola, *U.S.A.* **77 L3** 29 43N 84 59W
Apalachicola →, *U.S.A.* **77 L3** 29 43N 84 58W
Apaporis →, *Colombia* **92 D5** 1 23S 69 25W
Aparri, *Phil.* **37 A6** 18 22N 121 38 E
Apatity, *Russia* **24 A5** 67 34N 33 22 E
Apatzingán, *Mexico* **86 D4** 19 0N 102 20W
Apeldoorn, *Neths.* **15 B5** 52 13N 5 57 E
Apennines = Appennini, *Italy* **20 B4** 44 0N 10 0 E
Apia, *Samoa* **59 A13** 13 50S 171 50W
Apiacás, Serra dos, *Brazil* **92 E7** 9 50S 57 0W
Apies →, *S. Africa* **57 D4** 25 15S 28 8 E
Apizaco, *Mexico* **87 D5** 19 26N 98 9W
Aplao, *Peru* **92 G4** 16 0S 72 40W
Apo, Mt., *Phil.* **37 C7** 6 53N 125 14 E
Apolakkiá, *Greece* **23 C9** 36 5N 27 48 E
Apolakkiá, Órmos, *Greece* **23 C9** 36 5N 27 45 E
Apolo, *Bolivia* **92 F5** 14 30S 68 30W
Aporé →, *Brazil* **93 G8** 19 27S 50 57W
Apostle Is., *U.S.A.* **80 B9** 47 0N 90 40W
Apóstoles, *Argentina* **95 B4** 28 0S 56 0W
Apostolos Andreas, C., *Cyprus* **23 D13** 35 42N 34 35 E
Apoteri, *Guyana* **92 C7** 4 2N 58 32W
Appalachian Mts., *U.S.A.* **76 G6** 38 0N 80 0W
Appennini, *Italy* **20 B4** 44 0N 10 0 E
Apple Hill, *Canada* **79 A10** 45 13N 74 46W
Apple Valley, *U.S.A.* **85 L9** 34 32N 117 14W
Appleby-in-Westmorland, *U.K.* **10 C5** 54 35N 2 29W
Appleton, *U.S.A.* **76 C1** 44 16N 88 25W
Approuague →, *Fr. Guiana* **93 C8** 4 30N 51 57W
Aprília, *Italy* **20 D5** 41 36N 12 39 E
Apsley, *Canada* **78 B6** 44 45N 78 6W
Apucarana, *Brazil* **95 A5** 23 55S 51 33W
Apure →, *Venezuela* **92 B5** 7 37N 66 25W
Apurimac →, *Peru* **92 F4** 12 17S 73 56W
Āqā Jarī, *Iran* **45 D6** 30 42N 49 50 E
Aqaba = Al 'Aqabah, *Jordan* **47 F4** 29 31N 35 0 E
Aqaba, G. of, *Red Sea* **44 D2** 28 15N 33 20 E
'Aqabah, Khalīj al = Aqaba, G. of, *Red Sea* **44 D2** 28 15N 33 20 E
'Aqdā, *Iran* **45 C7** 32 26N 53 37 E
Aqmola = Astana, *Kazakstan* **26 D8** 51 10N 71 30 E
'Aqrah, *Iraq* **44 B4** 36 46N 43 45 E
Aqtaū, *Kazakstan* **26 E6** 43 39N 51 12 E
Aqtöbe, *Kazakstan* **25 D10** 50 17N 57 10 E
Aquidauana, *Brazil* **93 H7** 20 30S 55 50W
Aquiles Serdán, *Mexico* **86 B3** 28 37N 105 54W
Aquin, *Haiti* **89 C5** 18 16N 73 24W
Aquitain, Bassin, *France* **18 D3** 44 0N 0 30W
Aqviligjuaq = Pelly Bay, *Canada* **69 B11** 68 38N 89 50W
Ar Rachidiya = Er Rachidia, *Morocco* **50 B5** 31 58N 4 20W
Ar Rafīd, *Syria* **47 C4** 32 57N 35 52 E
Ar Raḥḥālīyah, *Iraq* **44 C4** 32 44N 43 23 E
Ar Ramādī, *Iraq* **44 C4** 33 25N 43 20 E
Ar Ramthā, *Jordan* **47 C5** 32 34N 36 0 E
Ar Raqqah, *Syria* **44 C3** 35 59N 39 8 E
Ar Rass, *Si. Arabia* **44 E4** 25 50N 43 40 E
Ar Rifā'ī, *Iraq* **44 D5** 31 50N 46 10 E
Ar Riyāḍ, *Si. Arabia* **46 C4** 24 41N 46 42 E
Ar Ru'ays, *Qatar* **45 E6** 26 8N 51 12 E
Ar Rukhaymīyah, *Iraq* **44 D5** 29 22N 45 38 E
Ar Ruṣāfah, *Syria* **44 C3** 35 45N 38 49 E
Ar Ruṭbah, *Iraq* **44 C4** 33 0N 40 15 E
Ara, *India* **43 G11** 25 35N 84 32 E
Arab, *U.S.A.* **77 H2** 34 19N 86 30W
'Arab, Bahr el →, *Sudan* **51 G11** 9 0N 29 30 E
Arab, Shatt al →, *Asia* **45 D6** 30 0N 48 31 E
'Arabābād, *Iran* **45 C8** 33 2N 57 41 E
Arabia, *Asia* **28 G8** 25 0N 45 0 E
Arabian Desert = Es Sahrâ' Esh Sharqîya, *Egypt* **51 C12** 27 30N 32 30 E
Arabian Gulf = Gulf, The, *Asia* **45 E6** 27 0N 50 0 E
Arabian Sea, *Ind. Oc.* **29 H10** 16 0N 65 0 E
Aracaju, *Brazil* **93 F11** 10 55S 37 4W
Aracati, *Brazil* **93 D11** 4 30S 37 44W
Araçatuba, *Brazil* **95 A5** 21 10S 50 30W
Aracena, *Spain* **19 D2** 37 53N 6 38W
Araçuai, *Brazil* **93 G10** 16 52S 42 4W
'Arad, *Israel* **47 D4** 31 15N 35 12 E
Arad, *Romania* **17 E11** 46 10N 21 20 E
Arādān, *Iran* **45 C7** 35 21N 52 30 E
Aradhippou, *Cyprus* **23 E12** 34 57N 33 36 E
Arafura Sea, *E. Indies* **28 K17** 9 0S 135 0 E
Aragón □, *Spain* **19 B5** 41 25N 0 40W
Aragón →, *Spain* **19 A5** 42 13N 1 44W
Araguacema, *Brazil* **93 E9** 8 50S 49 20W
Araguaia →, *Brazil* **93 E9** 5 21S 48 41W
Araguaína, *Brazil* **93 E9** 7 12S 48 12W
Araguari, *Brazil* **93 G9** 18 38S 48 11W
Araguari →, *Brazil* **93 C9** 1 15N 49 55W
Arain, *India* **42 F6** 26 27N 75 2 E
Arak, *Algeria* **50 C6** 25 20N 3 45 E
Arāk, *Iran* **45 C6** 34 0N 49 40 E
Arakan Coast, *Burma* **41 K19** 19 0N 94 0 E
Arakan Yoma, *Burma* **41 K19** 20 0N 94 40 E
Araks = Aras, Rūd-e →, *Asia* **44 B5** 40 5N 48 29 E
Aral, *Kazakstan* **26 E7** 46 41N 61 45 E
Aral Sea, *Asia* **26 E7** 44 30N 60 0 E
Aral Tengizi = Aral Sea, *Asia* **26 E7** 44 30N 60 0 E
Aralsk = Aral, *Kazakstan* **26 E7** 46 41N 61 45 E
Aralskoye More = Aral Sea, *Asia* **26 E7** 44 30N 60 0 E
Aramac, *Australia* **62 C4** 22 58S 145 14 E
Aran I., *Ireland* **13 A3** 55 0N 8 30W
Aran Is., *Ireland* **13 C2** 53 6N 9 38W
Aranda de Duero, *Spain* **19 B4** 41 39N 3 42W
Arandān, *Iran* **44 C5** 35 23N 46 55 E
Aranjuez, *Spain* **19 B4** 40 1N 3 40W
Aranos, *Namibia* **56 C2** 24 9S 19 7 E
Aransas Pass, *U.S.A.* **81 M6** 27 55N 97 9W
Aranyaprathet, *Thailand* **38 F4** 13 41N 102 30 E
Arapahoe, *U.S.A.* **80 E5** 40 18N 99 54W
Arapey Grande →, *Uruguay* **94 C4** 30 55S 57 49W
Arapgir, *Turkey* **44 B3** 39 5N 38 30 E
Arapiraca, *Brazil* **93 E11** 9 45S 36 39W
Arapongas, *Brazil* **95 A5** 23 29S 51 28W
Ar'ar, *Si. Arabia* **44 D4** 30 59N 41 2 E
Araranguá, *Brazil* **95 B6** 29 0S 49 30W
Araraquara, *Brazil* **93 H9** 21 50S 48 0W
Ararás, Serra das, *Brazil* **95 B5** 25 0S 53 10W
Ararat, Mt. = Ağrı Dağı, *Turkey* **25 G7** 39 50N 44 15 E
Araria, *India* **43 F12** 26 9N 87 33 E
Araripe, Chapada do, *Brazil* **93 E11** 7 20S 40 0W
Araruama, L. de, *Brazil* **95 A7** 22 53S 42 12W
Aras, Rūd-e →, *Asia* **44 B5** 40 5N 48 29 E
Arauca, *Colombia* **92 B4** 7 0N 70 40W
Arauca →, *Venezuela* **92 B5** 7 24N 66 35W
Arauco, *Chile* **94 D1** 37 16S 73 25W
Araxá, *Brazil* **93 G9** 19 35S 46 55W
Araya, Pen. de, *Venezuela* **92 A6** 10 40N 64 0W
Arba Minch, *Ethiopia* **46 F2** 6 0N 37 30 E
Arbat, *Iraq* **44 C5** 35 25N 45 35 E
Árbatax, *Italy* **20 E3** 39 56N 9 42 E
Arbīl, *Iraq* **44 B5** 36 15N 44 5 E
Arborfield, *Canada* **73 C8** 53 6N 103 39W
Arborg, *Canada* **73 C9** 50 54N 97 13W
Arbroath, *U.K.* **12 E6** 56 34N 2 35W
Arbuckle, *U.S.A.* **84 F4** 39 1N 122 3W
Arcachon, *France* **18 D3** 44 40N 1 10W
Arcade, *Calif., U.S.A.* **85 L8** 34 2N 118 15W
Arcade, *N.Y., U.S.A.* **78 D6** 42 32N 78 25W
Arcadia, *Fla., U.S.A.* **77 M5** 27 13N 81 52W
Arcadia, *La., U.S.A.* **81 J8** 32 33N 92 55W
Arcadia, *Pa., U.S.A.* **78 F6** 40 47N 78 51W
Arcata, *U.S.A.* **82 F1** 40 52N 124 5W
Archangel = Arkhangelsk, *Russia* **24 B7** 64 38N 40 36 E
Archbald, *U.S.A.* **79 E9** 41 30N 75 32W
Archer →, *Australia* **62 A3** 13 28S 141 41 E
Archer B., *Australia* **62 A3** 13 20S 141 30 E
Archers Post, *Kenya* **54 B4** 0 35N 37 35 E
Arches National Park, *U.S.A.* **83 G9** 38 45N 109 25W
Arckaringa Cr. →, *Australia* **63 D2** 28 10S 135 22 E
Arco, *U.S.A.* **82 E7** 43 38N 113 18W
Arcos de la Frontera, *Spain* **19 D3** 36 45N 5 49W
Arcot, *India* **40 N11** 12 53N 79 20 E
Arctic Bay, *Canada* **69 A11** 73 1N 85 7W
Arctic Ocean, *Arctic* **4 B18** 78 0N 160 0W
Arctic Red River = Tsiigehtchic, *Canada* **68 B6** 67 15N 134 0W
Arda →, *Bulgaria* **21 D12** 41 40N 26 30 E
Ardabīl, *Iran* **45 B6** 38 15N 48 18 E
Ardakān = Sepīdān, *Iran* **45 D7** 30 20N 52 5 E
Ardakān, *Iran* **45 C7** 32 19N 53 59 E
Ardee, *Ireland* **13 C5** 53 52N 6 33W
Arden, *Canada* **78 B8** 44 43N 76 56W
Arden, *Calif., U.S.A.* **84 G5** 38 36N 121 33W
Arden, *Nev., U.S.A.* **85 J11** 36 1N 115 14W
Ardenne, *Belgium* **16 D3** 49 50N 5 5 E
Ardennes = Ardenne, *Belgium* **16 D3** 49 50N 5 5 E
Arderin, *Ireland* **13 C4** 53 2N 7 39W
Ardestān, *Iran* **45 C7** 33 20N 52 25 E
Ardivachar Pt., *U.K.* **12 D1** 57 23N 7 26W
Ardmore, *Okla., U.S.A.* **81 H6** 34 10N 97 8W
Ardmore, *Pa., U.S.A.* **79 G9** 39 58N 75 18W
Ardnamurchan, Pt. of, *U.K.* **12 E2** 56 43N 6 14W
Ardnave Pt., *U.K.* **12 F2** 55 53N 6 20W
Ardrossan, *U.K.* **12 F4** 55 39N 4 49W
Ards Pen., *U.K.* **13 B6** 54 33N 5 34W
Arecibo, *Puerto Rico* **89 C6** 18 29N 66 43W
Areia Branca, *Brazil* **93 E11** 5 0S 37 0W
Arena, Pt., *U.S.A.* **84 G3** 38 57N 123 44W
Arenal, *Honduras* **88 C2** 15 21N 86 50W
Arendal, *Norway* **9 G13** 58 28N 8 46 E
Arequipa, *Peru* **92 G4** 16 20S 71 30W
Arévalo, *Spain* **19 B3** 41 3N 4 43W
Arezzo, *Italy* **20 C4** 43 25N 11 53 E
Arga, *Turkey* **44 B3** 38 21N 37 59 E
Arganda, *Spain* **19 B4** 40 19N 3 26W
Argenta, *Canada* **72 C5** 50 11N 116 56W
Argentan, *France* **18 B3** 48 45N 0 1W
Argentário, Mte., *Italy* **20 C4** 42 24N 11 9 E
Argentia, *Canada* **71 C9** 47 18N 53 58W
Argentina ■, *S. Amer.* **96 D3** 35 0S 66 0W
Argentina Is., *Antarctica* **5 C17** 66 0S 64 0W
Argentino, L., *Argentina* **96 G2** 50 10S 73 0W
Argeş →, *Romania* **17 F14** 44 5N 26 38 E
Arghandab →, *Afghan.* **42 D1** 31 30N 64 15 E
Argolikós Kólpos, *Greece* **21 F10** 37 20N 22 52 E
Árgos, *Greece* **21 F10** 37 40N 22 43 E
Argostólion, *Greece* **21 E9** 38 12N 20 33 E
Arguello, Pt., *U.S.A.* **85 L6** 34 35N 120 39W
Arguineguín, *Canary Is.* **22 G4** 27 46N 15 41W
Argun →, *Russia* **27 D13** 53 20N 121 28 E
Argus Pk., *U.S.A.* **85 K9** 35 52N 117 26W
Argyle, L., *Australia* **60 C4** 16 20S 128 40 E
Argyll & Bute □, *U.K.* **12 E3** 56 13N 5 28W
Århus, *Denmark* **9 H14** 56 8N 10 11 E
Ariadnoye, *Russia* **30 B7** 45 8N 134 25 E
Ariamsvlei, *Namibia* **56 D2** 28 9S 19 51 E
Arica, *Chile* **92 G4** 18 32S 70 20W
Arica, *Colombia* **92 D4** 2 0S 71 50W
Arico, *Canary Is.* **22 F3** 28 9N 16 29W
Arid, C., *Australia* **61 F3** 34 1S 123 10 E
Arida, *Japan* **31 G7** 34 5N 135 8 E
Arílla, Ákra, *Greece* **23 A3** 39 43N 19 39 E
Arima, *Trin. & Tob.* **89 D7** 10 38N 61 17W
Arinos →, *Brazil* **92 F7** 10 25S 58 20W
Ario de Rosales, *Mexico* **86 D4** 19 12N 102 0W
Aripuanã, *Brazil* **92 E6** 9 25S 60 30W
Aripuanã →, *Brazil* **92 E6** 5 7S 60 25W
Ariquemes, *Brazil* **92 E6** 9 55S 63 6W
Arisaig, *U.K.* **12 E3** 56 55N 5 51W
Aristazabal I., *Canada* **72 C3** 52 40N 129 10W
Arivonimamo, *Madag.* **57 B8** 19 1S 47 11 E
Arizaro, Salar de, *Argentina* **94 A2** 24 40S 67 50W
Arizona, *Argentina* **94 D2** 35 45S 65 25W
Arizona □, *U.S.A.* **83 J8** 34 0N 112 0W
Arizpe, *Mexico* **86 A2** 30 20N 110 11W
Arjeplog, *Sweden* **8 D18** 66 3N 18 2 E
Arjona, *Colombia* **92 A3** 10 14N 75 22W
Arjuna, *Indonesia* **37 G15** 7 49S 112 34 E
Arka, *Russia* **27 C15** 60 15N 142 0 E
Arkadelphia, *U.S.A.* **81 H8** 34 7N 93 4W
Arkaig, L., *U.K.* **12 E3** 56 59N 5 10W
Arkalyk = Arqalyk, *Kazakstan* **26 D7** 50 13N 66 50 E
Arkansas □, *U.S.A.* **81 H8** 35 0N 92 30W
Arkansas →, *U.S.A.* **81 J9** 33 47N 91 4W
Arkansas City, *U.S.A.* **81 G6** 37 4N 97 2W
Arkaroola, *Australia* **63 E2** 30 20S 139 22 E
Arkhángelos, *Greece* **23 C10** 36 13N 28 7 E
Arkhangelsk, *Russia* **24 B7** 64 38N 40 36 E
Arki, *India* **42 D7** 31 9N 76 58 E
Arklow, *Ireland* **13 D5** 52 48N 6 10W
Arkport, *U.S.A.* **78 D7** 42 24N 77 42W
Arkticheskiy, Mys, *Russia* **27 A10** 81 10N 95 0 E
Arkville, *U.S.A.* **79 D10** 42 9N 74 37W
Arlanzón →, *Spain* **19 A3** 42 3N 4 17W
Arlbergpass, *Austria* **16 E6** 47 9N 10 12 E
Arles, *France* **18 E6** 43 41N 4 40 E
Arlington, *S. Africa* **57 D4** 28 1S 27 53 E
Arlington, *N.Y., U.S.A.* **79 E11** 41 42N 73 54W
Arlington, *Oreg., U.S.A.* **82 D3** 45 43N 120 12W
Arlington, *S. Dak., U.S.A.* **80 C6** 44 22N 97 8W
Arlington, *Tex., U.S.A.* **81 J6** 32 44N 97 7W
Arlington, *Va., U.S.A.* **76 F7** 38 53N 77 7W
Arlington, *Vt., U.S.A.* **79 C11** 43 5N 73 9W
Arlington, *Wash., U.S.A.* **84 B4** 48 12N 122 8W
Arlington Heights, *U.S.A.* **76 D2** 42 5N 87 59W
Arlit, *Niger* **50 E7** 19 0N 7 38 E
Arlon, *Belgium* **15 E5** 49 42N 5 49 E
Arltunga, *Australia* **62 C1** 23 26S 134 41 E
Armagh, *U.K.* **13 B5** 54 21N 6 39W
Armagh □, *U.K.* **13 B5** 54 18N 6 37W
Armavir, *Russia* **25 E7** 45 2N 41 7 E
Armenia, *Colombia* **92 C3** 4 35N 75 45W
Armenia ■, *Asia* **25 F7** 40 20N 45 0 E
Armenistís, Ákra, *Greece* **23 C9** 36 8N 27 42 E
Armour, *U.S.A.* **80 D5** 43 19N 98 21W
Armstrong, *B.C., Canada* **72 C5** 50 25N 119 10W
Armstrong, *Ont., Canada* **70 B2** 50 18N 89 4W
Arnarfjörður, *Iceland* **8 D2** 65 48N 23 40W
Arnaud →, *Canada* **69 B12** 60 0N 70 0W
Arnauti, C., *Cyprus* **23 D11** 35 6N 32 17 E
Arnett, *U.S.A.* **81 G5** 36 8N 99 46W
Arnhem, *Neths.* **15 C5** 51 58N 5 55 E
Arnhem, C., *Australia* **62 A2** 12 20S 137 30 E
Arnhem B., *Australia* **62 A2** 12 20S 136 10 E
Arnhem Land, *Australia* **62 A1** 13 10S 134 30 E
Arno →, *Italy* **20 C4** 43 41N 10 17 E
Arnold, *U.K.* **10 D6** 53 1N 1 7W
Arnold, *U.S.A.* **84 G6** 38 15N 120 20W
Arnot, *Canada* **73 B9** 55 56N 96 41W
Arnøy, *Norway* **8 A19** 70 9N 20 40 E
Arnprior, *Canada* **79 A8** 45 26N 76 21W
Arnsberg, *Germany* **16 C5** 51 24N 8 5 E
Aroab, *Namibia* **56 D2** 26 41S 19 39 E
Aron, *India* **42 G6** 25 57N 77 56 E
Arqalyk, *Kazakstan* **26 D7** 50 13N 66 50 E
Arrah = Ara, *India* **43 G11** 25 35N 84 32 E
Arran, *U.K.* **12 F3** 55 34N 5 12W
Arras, *France* **18 A5** 50 17N 2 46 E
Arrecife, *Canary Is.* **22 F6** 28 57N 13 37W
Arrecifes, *Argentina* **94 C3** 34 6S 60 9W
Arrée, Mts. d', *France* **18 B2** 48 26N 3 55W
Arriaga, *Chiapas, Mexico* **87 D6** 16 15N 93 52W
Arriaga, *San Luis Potosí, Mexico* **86 C4** 21 55N 101 23W
Arrilalah, *Australia* **62 C3** 23 43S 143 54 E
Arrino, *Australia* **61 E2** 29 30S 115 40 E
Arrow, L., *Ireland* **13 B3** 54 3N 8 19W
Arrowhead, L., *U.S.A.* **85 L9** 34 16N 117 10W
Arrowtown, *N.Z.* **59 L2** 44 57S 168 50 E
Arroyo Grande, *U.S.A.* **85 K6** 35 7N 120 35W
Ars, *Iran* **44 B5** 37 9N 47 46 E
Arsenault L., *Canada* **73 B7** 55 6N 108 32W
Arsenev, *Russia* **30 B6** 44 10N 133 15 E
Árta, *Greece* **21 E9** 39 8N 21 2 E
Artà, *Spain* **22 B10** 39 41N 3 21 E
Arteaga, *Mexico* **86 D4** 18 50N 102 20W
Artem, *Russia* **30 C6** 43 22N 132 13 E
Artemovsk, *Russia* **27 D10** 54 45N 93 35 E
Artemovsk, *Ukraine* **25 E6** 48 35N 38 0 E
Artesia = Mosomane, *Botswana* **56 C4** 24 2S 26 19 E
Artesia, *U.S.A.* **81 J2** 32 51N 104 24W
Arthur, *Canada* **78 C4** 43 50N 80 32W
Arthur →, *Australia* **62 G3** 41 2S 144 40 E
Arthur Cr. →, *Australia* **62 C2** 22 30S 136 25 E
Arthur Pt., *Australia* **62 C5** 22 7S 150 3 E
Arthur River, *Australia* **61 F2** 33 20S 117 2 E
Arthur's Pass, *N.Z.* **59 K3** 42 54S 171 35 E
Arthur's Town, *Bahamas* **89 B4** 24 38N 75 42W
Artigas, *Uruguay* **94 C4** 30 20S 56 30W
Artillery L., *Canada* **73 A7** 63 9N 107 52W
Artois, *France* **18 A5** 50 20N 2 30 E
Artrutx, C. de, *Spain* **22 B10** 39 55N 3 49 E
Artsyz, *Ukraine* **17 E15** 46 4N 29 26 E
Artvin, *Turkey* **25 F7** 41 14N 41 44 E
Aru, Kepulauan, *Indonesia* **37 F8** 6 0S 134 30 E
Aru Is. = Aru, Kepulauan, *Indonesia* **37 F8** 6 0S 134 30 E
Arua, *Uganda* **54 B3** 3 1N 30 58 E
Aruanã, *Brazil* **93 F8** 14 54S 51 10W
Aruba ■, *W. Indies* **89 D6** 12 30N 70 0W
Arucas, *Canary Is.* **22 F4** 28 7N 15 32W
Arun →, *Nepal* **43 F12** 26 55N 87 10 E
Arun →, *U.K.* **11 G7** 50 49N 0 33W
Arunachal Pradesh □, *India* **41 F19** 28 0N 95 0 E
Arusha, *Tanzania* **54 C4** 3 20S 36 40 E
Arusha □, *Tanzania* **54 C4** 4 0S 36 30 E
Arusha Chini, *Tanzania* **54 C4** 3 32S 37 20 E
Aruwimi →, *Dem. Rep. of the Congo* **54 B1** 1 13N 23 36 E
Arvada, *Colo., U.S.A.* **80 F2** 39 48N 105 5W
Arvada, *Wyo., U.S.A.* **82 D10** 44 39N 106 8W
Árvi, *Greece* **23 E7** 34 59N 25 28 E
Arviat, *Canada* **73 A10** 61 6N 93 59W
Arvidsjaur, *Sweden* **8 D18** 65 35N 19 10 E
Arvika, *Sweden* **9 G15** 59 40N 12 36 E
Arvin, *U.S.A.* **85 K8** 35 12N 118 50W
Arwal, *India* **43 G11** 25 15N 84 41 E
Arxan, *China* **33 B6** 47 11N 119 57 E
Aryirádhes, *Greece* **23 B3** 39 27N 19 58 E
Aryiroúpolis, *Greece* **23 D6** 35 17N 24 20 E
Arys, *Kazakstan* **26 E7** 42 26N 68 48 E
Arzamas, *Russia* **24 C7** 55 27N 43 55 E
Aş Şafā, *Syria* **47 B6** 33 10N 37 0 E
As Saffānīyah, *Si. Arabia* **45 E6** 27 55N 48 50 E
As Safīrah, *Syria* **44 B3** 36 5N 37 21 E
Aş Şahm, *Oman* **45 E8** 24 10N 56 53 E
As Sājir, *Si. Arabia* **44 E5** 25 11N 44 36 E
As Salamīyah, *Syria* **44 C3** 35 1N 37 2 E
As Salmān, *Iraq* **44 D5** 30 30N 44 32 E
As Salṭ, *Jordan* **47 C4** 32 2N 35 43 E
As Sal'w'a, *Qatar* **45 E6** 24 23N 50 50 E
As Samāwah, *Iraq* **44 D5** 31 15N 45 15 E
As Sanamayn, *Syria* **47 B5** 33 3N 36 10 E
As Sohar = Şuḥār, *Oman* **46 C6** 24 20N 56 40 E
As Sukhnah, *Syria* **44 C3** 34 52N 38 52 E
As Sulaymānīyah, *Iraq* **44 C5** 35 35N 45 29 E
As Sulaymī, *Si. Arabia* **44 E4** 26 17N 41 21 E
As Sulayyil, *Si. Arabia* **46 C4** 20 27N 45 34 E
As Summān, *Si. Arabia* **44 E5** 25 0N 47 0 E
As Suwaydā', *Syria* **47 C5** 32 40N 36 30 E
As Suwaydā' □, *Syria* **47 C5** 32 45N 36 45 E
As Suwayq, *Oman* **45 F8** 23 51N 57 26 E
As Şuwayrah, *Iraq* **44 C5** 32 55N 45 0 E
Asab, *Namibia* **56 D2** 25 30S 18 0 E
Asad, Buḥayrat al, *Syria* **44 C3** 36 0N 38 15 E
Asahi-Gawa →, *Japan* **31 G6** 34 36N 133 58 E
Asahigawa, *Japan* **30 C11** 43 46N 142 22 E
Asamankese, *Ghana* **50 G5** 5 50N 0 40W
Asan →, *India* **43 F8** 26 37N 78 24 E
Asansol, *India* **43 H12** 23 40N 87 1 E
Asbesberge, *S. Africa* **56 D3** 29 0S 23 0 E
Asbestos, *Canada* **71 C5** 45 47N 71 58W
Asbury Park, *U.S.A.* **79 F10** 40 13N 74 1W
Ascensión, *Mexico* **86 A3** 31 6N 107 59W
Ascensión, B. de la, *Mexico* **87 D7** 19 50N 87 20W
Ascension I., *Atl. Oc.* **49 G2** 8 0S 14 15W
Aschaffenburg, *Germany* **16 D5** 49 58N 9 6 E
Aschersleben, *Germany* **16 C6** 51 45N 11 29 E
Áscoli Piceno, *Italy* **20 C5** 42 51N 13 34 E
Ascope, *Peru* **92 E3** 7 46S 79 8W
Ascotán, *Chile* **94 A2** 21 45S 68 17W
Aseb, *Eritrea* **46 E3** 13 0N 42 40 E
Asela, *Ethiopia* **46 F2** 8 0N 39 0 E
Asenovgrad, *Bulgaria* **21 C11** 42 1N 24 51 E
Aserradero, *Mexico* **86 C3** 23 40N 105 43W
Asgata, *Cyprus* **23 E12** 34 46N 33 15 E
Ash Fork, *U.S.A.* **83 J7** 35 13N 112 29W
Ash Grove, *U.S.A.* **81 G8** 37 19N 93 35W
Ash Shabakah, *Iraq* **44 D4** 30 49N 43 39 E
Ash Shamāl □, *Lebanon* **47 A5** 34 25N 36 0 E
Ash Shāmīyah, *Iraq* **44 D5** 31 55N 44 35 E
Ash Shāriqah, *U.A.E.* **46 B6** 25 23N 55 26 E
Ash Sharmah, *Si. Arabia* **44 D2** 28 1N 35 16 E
Ash Sharqāt, *Iraq* **44 C4** 35 27N 43 16 E
Ash Sharqi, Al Jabal, *Lebanon* **47 B5** 33 40N 36 10 E
Ash Shaṭrah, *Iraq* **44 D5** 31 30N 46 10 E
Ash Shawbak, *Jordan* **44 D2** 30 32N 35 34 E
Ash Shawmari, J., *Jordan* **47 E5** 30 35N 36 35 E
Ash Shināfīyah, *Iraq* **44 D5** 31 35N 44 39 E
Ash Shu'bah, *Si. Arabia* **44 D5** 28 54N 44 44 E
Ash Shumlūl, *Si. Arabia* **44 E5** 26 31N 47 20 E
Ash Shūr'a, *Iraq* **44 C4** 35 58N 43 13 E
Ash Shurayf, *Si. Arabia* **44 E3** 25 43N 39 14 E
Ash Shuwayfāt, *Lebanon* **47 B4** 33 45N 35 30 E
Asha, *Russia* **24 D10** 55 0N 57 16 E
Ashau, *Vietnam* **38 D6** 16 6N 107 22 E
Ashbourne, *U.K.* **10 D6** 53 2N 1 43W
Ashburn, *U.S.A.* **77 K4** 31 43N 83 39W
Ashburton, *N.Z.* **59 K3** 43 53S 171 48 E
Ashburton →, *Australia* **60 D1** 21 40S 114 56 E
Ashcroft, *Canada* **72 C4** 50 40N 121 20W
Ashdod, *Israel* **47 D3** 31 49N 34 35 E
Ashdown, *U.S.A.* **81 J7** 33 40N 94 8W
Asheboro, *U.S.A.* **77 H6** 35 43N 79 49W
Ashern, *Canada* **73 C9** 51 11N 98 21W
Asherton, *U.S.A.* **81 L5** 28 27N 99 46W
Asheville, *U.S.A.* **77 H4** 35 36N 82 33W
Ashewat, *Pakistan* **42 D3** 31 22N 68 32 E
Asheweig →, *Canada* **70 B2** 54 17N 87 12W
Ashford, *Australia* **63 D5** 29 15S 151 3 E
Ashford, *U.K.* **11 F8** 51 8N 0 53 E
Ashgabat, *Turkmenistan* **26 F6** 38 0N 57 50 E
Ashibetsu, *Japan* **30 C11** 43 31N 142 11 E
Ashikaga, *Japan* **31 F9** 36 28N 139 29 E
Ashington, *U.K.* **10 B6** 55 11N 1 33W
Ashizuri-Zaki, *Japan* **31 H6** 32 44N 133 0 E
Ashkarkot, *Afghan.* **42 C2** 33 3N 67 58 E
Ashkhabad = Ashgabat, *Turkmenistan* **26 F6** 38 0N 57 50 E
Āshkhāneh, *Iran* **45 B8** 37 26N 56 55 E
Ashland, *Kans., U.S.A.* **81 G5** 37 11N 99 46W

Ashland

Ashland, Ky., U.S.A. **76 F4** 38 28N 82 38W
Ashland, Mont., U.S.A. **82 D10** 45 36N 106 16W
Ashland, Ohio, U.S.A. **78 F2** 40 52N 82 19W
Ashland, Oreg., U.S.A. **82 E2** 42 12N 122 43W
Ashland, Pa., U.S.A. **79 F8** 40 45N 76 22W
Ashland, Va., U.S.A. **76 G7** 37 46N 77 29W
Ashland, Wis., U.S.A. **80 B9** 46 35N 90 53W
Ashley, N. Dak., U.S.A. **80 B5** 46 2N 99 22W
Ashley, Pa., U.S.A. **79 E9** 41 12N 75 55W
Ashmore Reef, Australia **60 B3** 12 14S 123 5 E
Ashmyany, Belarus **9 J21** 54 26N 25 52 E
Ashokan Reservoir, U.S.A. **79 E10** 41 56N 74 13W
Ashqelon, Israel **47 D3** 31 42N 34 35 E
Ashta, India **42 H7** 23 1N 76 43 E
Ashtabula, U.S.A. **78 E4** 41 52N 80 47W
Ashton, S. Africa **56 E3** 33 50S 20 5 E
Ashton, U.S.A. **82 D8** 44 4N 111 27W
Ashuanipi, L., Canada **71 B6** 52 45N 66 15W
Ashville, U.S.A. **78 F6** 40 34N 78 33W
Asia **28 E11** 45 0N 75 0 E
Asia, Kepulauan, Indonesia **37 D8** 1 0N 131 13 E
Āsīā Bak, Iran **45 C6** 35 19N 50 30 E
Asifabad, India **40 K11** 19 20N 79 24 E
Asinara, Italy **20 D3** 41 4N 8 16 E
Asinara, G. dell', Italy **20 D3** 41 0N 8 30 E
Asino, Russia **26 D9** 57 0N 86 0 E
Asipovichy, Belarus **17 B15** 53 19N 28 33 E
'Asīr □, Si. Arabia **46 D3** 18 40N 42 30 E
Asir, Ras, Somali Rep. **46 E5** 11 55N 51 10 E
Askersund, Sweden **9 G16** 58 53N 14 55 E
Askham, S. Africa **56 D3** 26 59S 20 47 E
Askim, Norway **9 G14** 59 35N 11 10 E
Askja, Iceland **8 D5** 65 3N 16 48W
Askøy, Norway **9 F11** 60 29N 5 10 E
Asmara = Asmera, Eritrea **46 D2** 15 19N 38 55 E
Asmera, Eritrea **46 D2** 15 19N 38 55 E
Åsnen, Sweden **9 H16** 56 37N 14 45 E
Aspen, U.S.A. **83 G10** 39 11N 106 49W
Aspermont, U.S.A. **81 J4** 33 8N 100 14W
Aspiring, Mt., N.Z. **59 L2** 44 23S 168 46 E
Asprókavos, Ákra, Greece **23 B4** 39 21N 20 6 E
Aspur, India **42 H6** 23 58N 74 7 E
Asquith, Canada **73 C7** 52 8N 107 13W
Assam □, India **41 G18** 26 0N 93 0 E
Asse, Belgium **15 D4** 50 24N 4 10 E
Assen, Neths. **15 A6** 53 0N 6 35 E
Assiniboia, Canada **73 D7** 49 40N 105 59W
Assiniboine →, Canada **73 D9** 49 53N 97 8W
Assiniboine, Mt., Canada **72 C5** 50 52N 115 39W
Assis, Brazil **95 A5** 22 40S 50 20W
Assisi, Italy **20 C5** 43 4N 12 37 E
Assynt, L., U.K. **12 C3** 58 10N 5 3W
Astana, Kazakstan **26 D8** 51 10N 71 30 E
Āstāneh, Iran **45 B6** 37 17N 49 59 E
Astara, Azerbaijan **25 G8** 38 30N 48 50 E
Asteroúsia, Greece **23 E7** 34 59N 25 3 E
Asti, Italy **18 D8** 44 54N 8 12 E
Astipálaia, Greece **21 F12** 36 32N 26 22 E
Astorga, Spain **19 A2** 42 29N 6 8W
Astoria, U.S.A. **84 D3** 46 11N 123 50W
Astrakhan, Russia **25 E8** 46 25N 48 5 E
Asturias □, Spain **19 A3** 43 15N 6 0W
Asunción, Paraguay **94 B4** 25 10S 57 30W
Asunción Nochixtlán, Mexico **87 D5** 17 28N 97 14W
Aswa →, Uganda **54 B3** 3 43N 31 55 E
Aswân, Egypt **51 D12** 24 4N 32 57 E
Aswân High Dam = Sadd el Aali, Egypt **51 D12** 23 54N 32 54 E
Asyût, Egypt **51 C12** 27 11N 31 4 E
At Ṭafīlah, Jordan **47 E4** 30 45N 35 30 E
Aṭ Ṭā'if, Si. Arabia **46 C3** 21 5N 40 27 E
Aṭ Ṭirāq, Si. Arabia **44 E5** 27 19N 44 33 E
Aṭ Ṭubayq, Si. Arabia **44 D3** 29 30N 37 0 E
Atacama □, Chile **94 B2** 27 30S 70 0W
Atacama, Desierto de, Chile **94 A2** 24 0S 69 20W
Atacama, Salar de, Chile **94 A2** 23 30S 68 20W
Atalaya, Peru **92 F4** 10 45S 73 50W
Atalaya de Femes, Canary Is. **22 F6** 28 56N 13 47W
Atami, Japan **31 G9** 35 5N 139 4 E
Atapupu, Indonesia **37 F6** 9 0S 124 51 E
Atâr, Mauritania **50 D3** 20 30N 13 5W
Atari, Pakistan **42 D6** 30 56N 74 2 E
Atascadero, U.S.A. **84 K6** 35 29N 120 40W
Atasu, Kazakstan **26 E8** 48 30N 71 0 E
Atatürk Barajı, Turkey **25 G6** 37 28N 38 30 E
Atauro, Indonesia **37 F7** 8 10S 125 30 E
'Atbara, Sudan **51 E12** 17 42N 33 59 E
'Atbara, Nahr →, Sudan **51 E12** 17 40N 33 56 E
Atbasar, Kazakstan **26 D7** 51 48N 68 20 E
Atchafalaya B., U.S.A. **81 L9** 29 25N 91 25W
Atchison, U.S.A. **80 F7** 39 34N 95 7W
Āteshān, Iran **45 C7** 35 35N 52 37 E
Ath, Belgium **15 D3** 50 38N 3 47 E
Athabasca, Canada **72 C6** 54 45N 113 20W
Athabasca →, Canada **73 B6** 58 40N 110 50W
Athabasca, L., Canada **73 B7** 59 15N 109 15W
Athboy, Ireland **13 C5** 53 37N 6 56W
Athenry, Ireland **13 C3** 53 18N 8 44W
Athens = Athínai, Greece **21 F10** 37 58N 23 46 E
Athens, Ala., U.S.A. **77 H2** 34 48N 86 58W
Athens, Ga., U.S.A. **77 J4** 33 57N 83 23W
Athens, N.Y., U.S.A. **79 D11** 42 16N 73 49W
Athens, Ohio, U.S.A. **76 F4** 39 20N 82 6W
Athens, Pa., U.S.A. **79 E8** 41 57N 76 31W
Athens, Tenn., U.S.A. **77 H3** 35 27N 84 36W
Athens, Tex., U.S.A. **81 J7** 32 12N 95 51W
Atherley, Canada **78 B5** 44 37N 79 20W
Atherton, Australia **62 B4** 17 17S 145 30 E
Athienou, Cyprus **23 D12** 35 3N 33 32 E
Athínai, Greece **21 F10** 37 58N 23 46 E
Athlone, Ireland **13 C4** 53 25N 7 56W
Athna, Cyprus **23 D12** 35 3N 33 47 E
Athol, U.S.A. **79 D12** 42 36N 72 14W
Atholl, Forest of, U.K. **12 E5** 56 51N 3 50W
Atholville, Canada **71 C6** 47 59N 66 43W
Áthos, Greece **21 D11** 40 9N 24 22 E
Athy, Ireland **13 C5** 53 0N 7 0W
Ati, Chad **51 F9** 13 13N 18 20 E
Atiak, Uganda **54 B3** 3 12N 32 2 E
Atik L., Canada **73 B9** 55 15N 96 0W
Atikameg →, Canada **70 B3** 52 30N 82 46W
Atikokan, Canada **70 C1** 48 45N 91 37W
Atikonak L., Canada **71 B7** 52 40N 64 32W
Atka, Russia **27 C16** 60 50N 151 48 E
Atka I., U.S.A. **68 C2** 52 7N 174 30W
Atkinson, U.S.A. **80 D5** 42 32N 98 59W
Atlanta, Ga., U.S.A. **77 J3** 33 45N 84 23W
Atlanta, Tex., U.S.A. **81 J7** 33 7N 94 10W
Atlantic, U.S.A. **80 E7** 41 24N 95 1W
Atlantic City, U.S.A. **76 F8** 39 21N 74 27W
Atlantic Ocean **2 E9** 0 0 20 0W
Atlas Mts. = Haut Atlas, Morocco **50 B4** 32 30N 5 0W
Atlin, Canada **72 B2** 59 31N 133 41W
Atlin, L., Canada **72 B2** 59 26N 133 45W
Atlin Prov. Park, Canada **72 B2** 59 10N 134 30W
Atmore, U.S.A. **77 K2** 31 2N 87 29W
Atoka, U.S.A. **81 H6** 34 23N 96 8W
Atolia, U.S.A. **85 K9** 35 19N 117 37W
Atrai →, Bangla. **43 G13** 24 7N 89 22 E
Atrak = Atrek →, Turkmenistan **45 B8** 37 35N 53 58 E
Atrauli, India **42 E8** 28 2N 78 20 E
Atrek →, Turkmenistan **45 B8** 37 35N 53 58 E
Atsuta, Japan **30 C10** 43 24N 141 26 E
Attalla, U.S.A. **77 H2** 34 1N 86 6W
Attapu, Laos **38 E6** 14 48N 106 50 E
Attáviros, Greece **23 C9** 36 12N 27 50 E
Attawapiskat, Canada **70 B3** 52 56N 82 24W
Attawapiskat →, Canada **70 B3** 52 57N 82 18W
Attawapiskat L., Canada **70 B2** 52 18N 87 54W
Attica, Ind., U.S.A. **76 E2** 40 18N 87 15W
Attica, Ohio, U.S.A. **78 E2** 41 4N 82 53W
Attikamagen L., Canada **71 B6** 55 0N 66 30W
Attleboro, U.S.A. **79 E13** 41 57N 71 17W
Attock, Pakistan **42 C5** 33 52N 72 20 E
Attopeu = Attapu, Laos **38 E6** 14 48N 106 50 E
Attu I., U.S.A. **68 C1** 52 55N 172 55 E
Attur, India **40 P11** 11 35N 78 30 E
Atuel →, Argentina **94 D2** 36 17S 66 50W
Åtvidaberg, Sweden **9 G17** 58 12N 16 0 E
Atwater, U.S.A. **84 H6** 37 21N 120 37W
Atwood, Canada **78 C3** 43 40N 81 1W
Atwood, U.S.A. **80 F4** 39 48N 101 3W
Atyraū, Kazakstan **25 E9** 47 5N 52 0 E
Au Sable, U.S.A. **78 B1** 44 25N 83 20W
Au Sable →, U.S.A. **76 C4** 44 25N 83 20W
Au Sable Forks, U.S.A. **79 B11** 44 27N 73 41W
Au Sable Pt., U.S.A. **78 B1** 44 20N 83 20W
Aubagne, France **18 E6** 43 17N 5 37 E
Aubarca, C. d', Spain **22 B7** 39 4N 1 22 E
Aube →, France **18 B5** 48 34N 3 43 E
Auberry, U.S.A. **84 H7** 37 7N 119 29W
Auburn, Ala., U.S.A. **77 J3** 32 36N 85 29W
Auburn, Calif., U.S.A. **84 G5** 38 54N 121 4W
Auburn, Ind., U.S.A. **76 E3** 41 22N 85 4W
Auburn, Maine, U.S.A. **77 C10** 44 6N 70 14W
Auburn, N.Y., U.S.A. **79 D8** 42 56N 76 34W
Auburn, Nebr., U.S.A. **80 E7** 40 23N 95 51W
Auburn, Pa., U.S.A. **79 F8** 40 36N 76 6W
Auburn, Wash., U.S.A. **84 C4** 47 18N 122 14W
Auburn Ra., Australia **63 D5** 25 15S 150 30 E
Auburndale, U.S.A. **77 L5** 28 4N 81 48W
Aubusson, France **18 D5** 45 57N 2 11 E
Auch, France **18 E4** 43 39N 0 36 E
Auckland, N.Z. **59 G5** 36 52S 174 46 E
Auckland Is., Pac. Oc. **64 N8** 50 40S 166 5 E
Aude →, France **18 E5** 43 13N 3 14 E
Auden, Canada **70 B2** 50 14N 87 53W
Audubon, U.S.A. **80 E7** 41 43N 94 56W
Augathella, Australia **63 D4** 25 48S 146 35 E
Aughnacloy, U.K. **13 B5** 54 25N 6 59W
Augrabies Falls, S. Africa **56 D3** 28 35S 20 20 E
Augsburg, Germany **16 D6** 48 25N 10 52 E
Augusta, Australia **61 F2** 34 19S 115 9 E
Augusta, Italy **20 F6** 37 13N 15 13 E
Augusta, Ark., U.S.A. **81 H9** 35 17N 91 22W
Augusta, Ga., U.S.A. **77 J5** 33 28N 81 58W
Augusta, Kans., U.S.A. **81 G6** 37 41N 96 59W
Augusta, Maine, U.S.A. **69 D13** 44 19N 69 47W
Augusta, Mont., U.S.A. **82 C7** 47 30N 112 24W
Augustów, Poland **17 B12** 53 51N 23 0 E
Augustus, Mt., Australia **61 D2** 24 20S 116 50 E
Augustus I., Australia **60 C3** 15 20S 124 30 E
Aukum, U.S.A. **84 G6** 38 34N 120 43W
Auld, L., Australia **60 D3** 22 25S 123 50 E
Ault, U.S.A. **80 E2** 40 35N 104 44W
Aunis, France **18 C3** 46 5N 0 50W
Auponhia, Indonesia **37 E7** 1 58S 125 27 E
Aur, Pulau, Malaysia **39 L5** 2 35N 104 10 E
Auraiya, India **43 F8** 26 28N 79 33 E
Aurangabad, Bihar, India **43 G11** 24 45N 84 18 E
Aurangabad, Maharashtra, India **40 K9** 19 50N 75 23 E
Aurich, Germany **16 B4** 53 28N 7 28 E
Aurillac, France **18 D5** 44 55N 2 26 E
Aurora, Canada **78 C5** 44 0N 79 28W
Aurora, S. Africa **56 E2** 32 40S 18 29 E
Aurora, Colo., U.S.A. **80 F2** 39 44N 104 52W
Aurora, Ill., U.S.A. **76 E1** 41 45N 88 19W
Aurora, Mo., U.S.A. **81 G8** 36 58N 93 43W
Aurora, N.Y., U.S.A. **79 D8** 42 45N 76 42W
Aurora, Nebr., U.S.A. **80 E6** 40 52N 98 0W
Aurora, Ohio, U.S.A. **78 E3** 41 21N 81 20W
Aurukun, Australia **62 A3** 13 20S 141 45 E
Aus, Namibia **56 D2** 26 35S 16 12 E
Ausable →, Canada **78 C3** 43 19N 81 46W
Auschwitz = Oświęcim, Poland **17 C10** 50 2N 19 11 E
Austin, Minn., U.S.A. **80 D8** 43 40N 92 58W
Austin, Nev., U.S.A. **82 G5** 39 30N 117 4W
Austin, Pa., U.S.A. **78 E6** 41 38N 78 6W
Austin, Tex., U.S.A. **81 K6** 30 17N 97 45W
Austin, L., Australia **61 E2** 27 40S 118 0 E
Austin I., Canada **73 A10** 61 10N 94 0W
Austra, Norway **8 D14** 65 8N 11 55 E
Austral Is. = Tubuai Is., Pac. Oc. **65 K13** 25 0S 150 0W
Austral Seamount Chain, Pac. Oc. **65 K13** 24 0S 150 0W
Australia ■, Oceania **64 K5** 23 0S 135 0 E
Australind, Australia **61 F2** 33 17S 115 42 E
Austria ■, Europe **16 E8** 47 0N 14 0 E
Austvågøy, Norway **8 B16** 68 20N 14 40 E
Autlán, Mexico **86 D4** 19 40N 104 30W
Autun, France **18 C6** 46 58N 4 17 E
Auvergne, France **18 D5** 45 20N 3 15 E
Auvergne, Mts. d', France **18 D5** 45 20N 2 55 E
Auxerre, France **18 C5** 47 48N 3 32 E
Ava, U.S.A. **81 G8** 36 57N 92 40W
Avallon, France **18 C5** 47 30N 3 53 E
Avalon, U.S.A. **85 M8** 33 21N 118 20W
Avalon Pen., Canada **71 C9** 47 30N 53 20W
Avanos, Turkey **44 B2** 38 43N 34 51 E
Avaré, Brazil **95 A6** 23 4S 48 58W
Avawatz Mts., U.S.A. **85 K10** 35 40N 116 30W
Aveiro, Brazil **93 D7** 3 10S 55 5W
Aveiro, Portugal **19 B1** 40 37N 8 38W
Āvej, Iran **45 C6** 35 40N 49 15 E
Avellaneda, Argentina **94 C4** 34 50S 58 10W
Avellino, Italy **20 D6** 40 54N 14 47 E
Avenal, U.S.A. **84 K6** 36 0N 120 8W
Aversa, Italy **20 D6** 40 58N 14 12 E
Avery, U.S.A. **82 C6** 47 15N 115 49W
Aves, Is. las, Venezuela **89 D6** 12 0N 67 30W
Avesta, Sweden **9 F17** 60 9N 16 10 E
Avezzano, Italy **20 C5** 42 2N 13 25 E
Aviá Terai, Argentina **94 B3** 26 45S 60 50W
Aviemore, U.K. **12 D5** 57 12N 3 50W
Avignon, France **18 E6** 43 57N 4 50 E
Ávila, Spain **19 B3** 40 39N 4 43W
Avila Beach, U.S.A. **85 K6** 35 11N 120 44W
Avilés, Spain **19 A3** 43 35N 5 57W
Avis, U.S.A. **78 E7** 41 11N 77 19W
Avoca, U.S.A. **78 D7** 42 25N 77 25W
Avoca →, Ireland **13 D5** 52 48N 6 10W
Avola, Canada **72 C5** 51 45N 119 19W
Avola, Italy **20 F6** 36 56N 15 7 E
Avon, U.S.A. **78 D7** 42 55N 77 45W
Avon →, Australia **61 F2** 31 40S 116 7 E
Avon →, Bristol, U.K. **11 F5** 51 29N 2 41W
Avon →, Dorset, U.K. **11 G6** 50 44N 1 46W
Avon →, Warks., U.K. **11 E5** 52 0N 2 8W
Avon Park, U.S.A. **77 M5** 27 36N 81 31W
Avondale, Zimbabwe **55 F3** 17 43S 30 58 E
Avonlea, Canada **73 D8** 50 0N 105 0W
Avonmore, Canada **79 A10** 45 10N 74 58W
Avranches, France **18 B3** 48 40N 1 20W
A'waj →, Syria **47 B5** 33 23N 36 20 E
Awaji-Shima, Japan **31 G7** 34 30N 134 50 E
'Awālī, Bahrain **45 E6** 26 0N 50 30 E
Awantipur, India **43 C6** 33 55N 75 3 E
Awasa, Ethiopia **46 F2** 7 2N 38 28 E
Awash, Ethiopia **46 F3** 9 1N 40 10 E
Awatere →, N.Z. **59 J5** 41 37S 174 10 E
Awbārī, Libya **51 C8** 26 46N 12 57 E
Awe, L., U.K. **12 E3** 56 17N 5 16W
Awjilah, Libya **51 C10** 29 8N 21 7 E
Axe →, U.K. **11 F5** 50 42N 3 4W
Axel Heiberg I., Canada **4 B3** 80 0N 90 0W
Axim, Ghana **50 H5** 4 51N 2 15W
Axiós →, Greece **21 D10** 40 57N 22 35 E
Axminster, U.K. **11 G4** 50 46N 3 0W
Ayabaca, Peru **92 D3** 4 40S 79 53W
Ayabe, Japan **31 G7** 35 20N 135 20 E
Ayacucho, Argentina **94 D4** 37 5S 58 20W
Ayacucho, Peru **92 F4** 13 0S 74 0W
Ayaguz, Kazakstan **26 E9** 48 10N 80 10 E
Ayamonte, Spain **19 D2** 37 12N 7 24W
Ayan, Russia **27 D14** 56 30N 138 16 E
Ayaviri, Peru **92 F4** 14 50S 70 35W
Aydın, Turkey **21 F12** 37 51N 27 51 E
Aydin □, Turkey **25 G4** 37 50N 28 0 E
Ayer, U.S.A. **79 D13** 42 34N 71 35W
Ayer's Cliff, Canada **79 A12** 45 10N 72 3W
Ayers Rock, Australia **61 E5** 25 23S 131 5 E
Ayia Aikateríni, Ákra, Greece **23 A3** 39 50N 19 50 E
Ayia Dhéka, Greece **23 D6** 35 3N 24 58 E
Ayia Gálini, Greece **23 D6** 35 6N 24 41 E
Áyia Napa, Cyprus **23 E13** 34 59N 34 0 E
Áyia Phyla, Cyprus **23 E12** 34 43N 33 1 E
Ayia Varvára, Greece **23 D7** 35 8N 25 1 E
Áyios Amvrósios, Cyprus **23 D12** 35 20N 33 35 E
Áyios Evstrátios, Greece **21 E11** 39 34N 24 58 E
Áyios Ioánnis, Ákra, Greece **23 D7** 35 20N 25 40 E
Áyios Isidhoros, Greece **23 C9** 36 9N 27 51 E
Áyios Matthaíos, Greece **23 B3** 39 30N 19 47 E
Áyios Nikólaos, Greece **23 D7** 35 11N 25 41 E
Áyios Seryios, Cyprus **23 D12** 35 12N 33 53 E
Áyios Theodhoros, Cyprus **23 D13** 35 22N 34 1 E
Aykino, Russia **24 B8** 62 15N 49 56 E
Aylesbury, U.K. **11 F7** 51 49N 0 49W
Aylmer, Canada **78 D4** 42 46N 80 59W
Aylmer, L., Canada **68 B8** 64 0N 110 8W
'Ayn, Wādī al, Oman **45 F7** 22 15N 55 28 E
Ayn Dār, Si. Arabia **45 E7** 25 55N 49 10 E
Ayn Zālah, Iraq **44 B4** 36 45N 42 35 E
Ayolas, Paraguay **94 B4** 27 10S 56 59W
Ayon, Ostrov, Russia **27 C17** 69 50N 169 0 E
'Ayoûn el 'Atroûs, Mauritania **50 E4** 16 38N 9 37W
Ayr, Australia **62 B4** 19 35S 147 25 E
Ayr, Canada **78 C4** 43 17N 80 27W
Ayr, U.K. **12 F4** 55 28N 4 38W
Ayr →, U.K. **12 F4** 55 28N 4 38W
Ayre, Pt. of, U.K. **10 C3** 54 25N 4 21W
Ayton, Australia **62 B4** 15 56S 145 22 E
Aytos, Bulgaria **21 C12** 42 42N 27 16 E
Ayu, Kepulauan, Indonesia **37 D8** 0 35N 131 5 E
Ayutla, Guatemala **88 D1** 14 40N 92 10W
Ayutla, Mexico **87 D5** 16 58N 99 17W
Ayvacık, Turkey **21 E12** 39 36N 26 24 E
Ayvalık, Turkey **21 E12** 39 20N 26 46 E
Az Zabadānī, Syria **47 B5** 33 43N 36 5 E
Az Ẓāhirīyah, West Bank **47 D3** 31 25N 34 58 E
Az Ẓahrān, Si. Arabia **45 E6** 26 10N 50 7 E
Az Zarqā, Jordan **47 C5** 32 5N 36 4 E
Az Zarqā', U.A.E. **45 E7** 24 53N 53 4 E
Az Zībār, Iraq **44 B5** 36 52N 44 4 E
Az Zilfī, Si. Arabia **44 E5** 26 12N 44 52 E
Az Zubayr, Iraq **44 D5** 30 26N 47 40 E
Azamgarh, India **43 F10** 26 5N 83 13 E
Azangaro, Peru **92 F4** 14 55S 70 13W
Āzār Shahr, Iran **44 B5** 37 45N 45 59 E
Azarān, Iran **44 B5** 37 25N 47 16 E
Azärbayjan = Azerbaijan ■, Asia **25 F8** 40 20N 48 0 E
Āzarbāyjān-e Gharbī □, Iran **44 B5** 37 0N 44 30 E
Āzarbāyjān-e Sharqī □, Iran **44 B5** 37 20N 47 0 E
Azare, Nigeria **50 F8** 11 55N 10 10 E
A'zāz, Syria **44 B3** 36 36N 37 4 E
Azbine = Aïr, Niger **50 E7** 18 30N 8 0 E
Azerbaijan ■, Asia **25 F8** 40 20N 48 0 E
Azerbaijchan = Azerbaijan ■, Asia **25 F8** 40 20N 48 0 E
Azimganj, India **43 G13** 24 14N 88 16 E
Azogues, Ecuador **92 D3** 2 35S 78 0W
Azores, Atl. Oc. **50 A1** 38 44N 29 0W
Azov, Russia **25 E6** 47 3N 39 25 E
Azov, Sea of, Europe **25 E6** 46 0N 36 30 E
Azovskoye More = Azov, Sea of, Europe **25 E6** 46 0N 36 30 E
Azraq ash Shīshān, Jordan **47 D5** 31 50N 36 49 E
Aztec, U.S.A. **83 H10** 36 49N 107 59W
Azúa de Compostela, Dom. Rep. **89 C5** 18 25N 70 44W
Azuaga, Spain **19 C3** 38 16N 5 39W
Azuero, Pen. de, Panama **88 E3** 7 30N 80 30W
Azul, Argentina **94 D4** 36 42S 59 43W
Azusa, U.S.A. **85 L9** 34 8N 117 52W

B

Ba Don, Vietnam **38 D6** 17 45N 106 26 E
Ba Dong, Vietnam **39 H6** 9 40N 106 33 E
Ba Ngoi = Cam Lam, Vietnam **39 G7** 11 54N 109 10 E
Ba Tri, Vietnam **39 G6** 10 2N 106 36 E
Ba Xian = Bazhou, China **34 E9** 39 8N 116 22 E
Baa, Indonesia **37 F6** 10 50S 123 0 E
Baarle-Nassau, Belgium **15 C4** 51 27N 4 56 E
Bab el Mandeb, Red Sea **46 E3** 12 35N 43 25 E
Bābā, Koh-i-, Afghan. **40 B5** 34 30N 67 0 E
Baba Burnu, Turkey **21 E12** 39 29N 26 2 E
Bābā Kalū, Iran **45 D6** 30 7N 50 49 E
Babadag, Romania **17 F15** 44 53N 28 44 E
Babadayhan, Turkmenistan **26 F7** 37 42N 60 23 E
Babaeski, Turkey **21 D12** 41 26N 27 6 E
Babahoyo, Ecuador **92 D3** 1 40S 79 30W
Babai = Sarju →, India **43 F9** 27 21N 81 23 E
Babar, Indonesia **37 F7** 8 0S 129 30 E
Babar, Pakistan **42 D3** 31 7N 69 32 E
Babarkach, Pakistan **42 E2** 29 45N 68 0 E
Babb, U.S.A. **82 B7** 48 51N 113 27W
Babelthuap, Pac. Oc. **37 C8** 7 30N 134 30 E
Baberu, India **43 G9** 25 33N 80 43 E
Babi Besar, Pulau, Malaysia **39 L4** 2 25N 103 59 E
Babinda, Australia **62 B4** 17 20S 145 56 E
Babine, Canada **72 B3** 55 22N 126 37W
Babine →, Canada **72 B3** 55 45N 127 44W
Babine L., Canada **72 C3** 54 48N 126 0W
Babo, Indonesia **37 E8** 2 30S 133 30 E
Bābol, Iran **45 B7** 36 40N 52 50 E
Bābol Sar, Iran **45 B7** 36 45N 52 45 E
Babruysk, Belarus **17 B15** 53 10N 29 15 E
Babuhri, India **42 F3** 26 49N 69 43 E
Babusar Pass, Pakistan **43 B5** 35 12N 73 59 E
Babuyan Chan., Phil. **37 A6** 18 40N 121 30 E
Babylon, Iraq **44 C5** 32 34N 44 22 E
Bac Can, Vietnam **38 A5** 22 8N 105 49 E
Bac Giang, Vietnam **38 B6** 21 16N 106 11 E
Bac Lieu, Vietnam **39 H5** 9 17N 105 43 E
Bac Ninh, Vietnam **38 B6** 21 13N 106 4 E
Bac Phan, Vietnam **38 B5** 22 0N 105 0 E
Bac Quang, Vietnam **38 A5** 22 30N 104 48 E
Bacabal, Brazil **93 D10** 4 15S 44 45W
Bacalar, Mexico **87 D7** 18 50N 87 27W
Bacan, Kepulauan, Indonesia **37 E7** 0 35S 127 30 E
Bacarra, Phil. **37 A6** 18 15N 120 37 E
Bacău, Romania **17 E14** 46 35N 26 55 E
Bacerac, Mexico **86 A3** 30 18N 108 50W
Bach Long Vi, Dao, Vietnam **38 B6** 20 10N 107 40 E
Bachelina, Russia **26 D7** 57 45N 67 20 E
Bachhwara, India **43 G11** 25 35N 85 54 E
Back →, Canada **68 B9** 65 10N 104 0W
Bacolod, Phil. **37 B6** 10 40N 122 57 E
Bacuk, Malaysia **39 J4** 6 4N 102 25 E
Bād, Iran **45 C7** 33 41N 52 1 E
Bad →, U.S.A. **80 C4** 44 21N 100 22W
Bad Axe, U.S.A. **78 C2** 43 48N 83 0W
Bad Ischl, Austria **16 E7** 47 44N 13 38 E
Bad Kissingen, Germany **16 C6** 50 11N 10 4 E
Bad Lands, U.S.A. **80 D3** 43 40N 102 10W
Bada Barabil, India **43 H11** 22 7N 85 24 E
Badagara, India **40 P9** 11 35N 75 40 E
Badajós, L., Brazil **92 D6** 3 15S 62 50W
Badajoz, Spain **19 C2** 38 50N 6 59W
Badalona, Spain **19 B7** 41 26N 2 15 E
Badalzai, Afghan. **42 E1** 29 50N 65 35 E
Badampahar, India **41 H15** 22 10N 86 10 E
Badanah, Si. Arabia **44 D4** 30 58N 41 30 E
Badarinath, India **43 D8** 30 45N 79 30 E
Badas, Kepulauan, Indonesia **36 D3** 0 45N 107 5 E
Baddo →, Pakistan **40 F4** 28 0N 64 20 E
Bade, Indonesia **37 F9** 7 10S 139 35 E
Baden, Austria **16 D9** 48 1N 16 13 E
Baden, U.S.A. **78 F4** 40 38N 80 14W
Baden-Baden, Germany **16 D5** 48 44N 8 13 E
Baden-Württemberg □, Germany **16 D5** 48 20N 8 40 E
Badgastein, Austria **16 E7** 47 7N 13 9 E
Badger, Canada **71 C8** 49 0N 56 4W
Badger, U.S.A. **84 J7** 36 38N 119 1W
Bādghīsāt □, Afghan. **40 B3** 35 0N 63 0 E
Badgom, India **43 B6** 34 1N 74 45 E
Badin, Pakistan **42 G3** 24 38N 68 54 E
Badlands National Park, U.S.A. **80 D3** 43 38N 102 56W
Badrah, Iraq **44 C5** 33 6N 45 58 E
Badrinath, India **43 D8** 30 44N 79 29 E
Badulla, Sri Lanka **40 R12** 7 1N 81 7 E
Baena, Spain **19 D3** 37 37N 4 20W
Baeza, Spain **19 D4** 37 57N 3 25W
Baffin B., Canada **69 A13** 72 0N 64 0W
Baffin I., Canada **69 B12** 68 0N 75 0W
Bafing →, Mali **50 F3** 13 49N 10 50W
Bafliyūn, Syria **44 B3** 36 37N 36 59 E
Bafoulabé, Mali **50 F3** 13 50N 10 55W
Bāfq, Iran **45 D7** 31 40N 55 25 E
Bafra, Turkey **25 F6** 41 34N 35 54 E
Bāft, Iran **45 D8** 29 15N 56 38 E
Bafwasende, Dem. Rep. of the Congo **54 B2** 1 3N 27 5 E
Bagamoyo, Tanzania **54 D4** 6 28S 38 55 E
Bagan Datoh, Malaysia **39 L3** 3 59N 100 47 E
Bagan Serai, Malaysia **39 K3** 5 1N 100 32 E
Baganga, Phil. **37 C7** 7 34N 126 33 E
Bagani, Namibia **56 B3** 18 7S 21 41 E
Bagansiapiapi, Indonesia **36 D2** 2 12N 100 50 E
Bagasra, India **42 J4** 21 30N 71 0 E

Baranof

Bagaud, India **42 H6** 22 19N 75 53 E
Bagdad, U.S.A. **85 L11** 34 35N 115 53W
Bagdarin, Russia **27 D12** 54 26N 113 36 E
Bagé, Brazil **95 C5** 31 20S 54 15W
Bagenalstown = Muine Bheag, Ireland **13 D5** 52 42N 6 58W
Baggs, U.S.A. **82 F10** 41 2N 107 39W
Bagh, Pakistan **43 C5** 33 59N 73 45 E
Baghain →, India **43 G9** 25 32N 81 1 E
Baghdād, Iraq **44 C5** 33 20N 44 30 E
Bagheria, Italy **20 E5** 38 5N 13 30 E
Baghlān, Afghan. **40 A6** 36 12N 69 0 E
Bagley, U.S.A. **80 B7** 47 32N 95 24W
Bago = Pegu, Burma **41 L20** 17 20N 96 29 E
Bagodar, India **43 G11** 24 5N 85 52 E
Bagrationovsk, Russia **9 J19** 54 23N 20 39 E
Baguio, Phil. **37 A6** 16 26N 120 34 E
Bah, India **43 F8** 26 53N 78 36 E
Bahadurganj, India **43 F12** 26 16N 87 49 E
Bahadurgarh, India **42 E7** 28 40N 76 57 E
Bahama, Canal Viejo de, W. Indies **88 B4** 22 10N 77 30W
Bahamas ■, N. Amer. **89 B5** 24 0N 75 0W
Baharampur, India **43 G13** 24 2N 88 27 E
Bahawalnagar, Pakistan **42 E5** 30 0N 73 15 E
Bahawalpur, Pakistan **42 E4** 29 24N 71 40 E
Baheri, India **43 E8** 28 45N 79 34 E
Bahgul →, India **43 F8** 27 45N 79 36 E
Bahi, Tanzania **54 D4** 5 58S 35 21 E
Bahi Swamp, Tanzania **54 D4** 6 10S 35 0 E
Bahía = Salvador, Brazil **93 F11** 13 0S 38 30W
Bahía □, Brazil **93 F10** 12 0S 42 0W
Bahía, Is. de la, Honduras **88 C2** 16 45N 86 15W
Bahía Blanca, Argentina **94 D3** 38 35S 62 13W
Bahía de Caráquez, Ecuador **92 D2** 0 40S 80 27W
Bahía Honda, Cuba **88 B3** 22 54N 83 10W
Bahía Laura, Argentina **96 F3** 48 10S 66 30W
Bahía Negra, Paraguay **92 H7** 20 5S 58 5W
Bahir Dar, Ethiopia **46 E2** 11 37N 37 10 E
Bahmanzād, Iran **45 D6** 31 15N 51 47 E
Bahr el Ghazâl □, Sudan **51 G11** 7 0N 28 0 E
Bahraich, India **43 F9** 27 38N 81 37 E
Bahrain ■, Asia **46 B5** 26 0N 50 35 E
Bahror, India **42 F7** 27 51N 76 20 E
Bāhū Kalāt, Iran **45 E9** 25 43N 61 25 E
Bai Bung, Mui = Ca Mau, Mui, Vietnam **39 H5** 8 38N 104 44 E
Bai Duc, Vietnam **38 C5** 18 3N 105 49 E
Bai Thuong, Vietnam **38 C5** 19 54N 105 23 E
Baia Mare, Romania **17 E12** 47 40N 23 35 E
Baião, Brazil **93 D9** 2 40S 49 40W
Baïbokoum, Chad **51 G9** 7 46N 15 43 E
Baicheng, China **35 B12** 45 38N 122 42 E
Baidoa, Somali Rep. **46 G3** 3 8N 43 30 E
Baie Comeau, Canada **71 C6** 49 12N 68 10W
Baie-St-Paul, Canada **71 C5** 47 28N 70 32W
Baie Trinité, Canada **71 C6** 49 25N 67 20W
Baie Verte, Canada **71 C8** 49 55N 56 12W
Baihar, India **43 H9** 22 6N 80 33 E
Baihe, China **34 H6** 32 50N 110 5 E
Ba'ījī, Iraq **44 C4** 35 0N 43 30 E
Baijnath, India **43 E8** 29 55N 79 37 E
Baikal, L. = Baykal, Oz., Russia **27 D11** 53 0N 108 0 E
Baikunthpur, India **43 H10** 23 15N 82 33 E
Baile Atha Cliath = Dublin, Ireland **13 C5** 53 21N 6 15W
Băileşti, Romania **17 F12** 44 1N 23 20 E
Bainbridge, Ga., U.S.A. **77 K3** 30 55N 84 35W
Bainbridge, N.Y., U.S.A. **79 D9** 42 18N 75 29W
Baing, Indonesia **37 F6** 10 14S 120 34 E
Bainiu, China **34 H7** 32 50N 112 15 E
Bā'ir, Jordan **47 E5** 30 45N 36 55 E
Bairin Youqi, China **35 C10** 43 30N 118 35 E
Bairin Zuoqi, China **35 C10** 43 58N 119 15 E
Baisha, China **34 G7** 34 20N 112 32 E
Baitadi, Nepal **43 E9** 29 35N 80 25 E
Baiyin, China **34 F3** 36 45N 104 14 E
Baiyu Shan, China **34 F4** 37 15N 107 30 E
Baj Baj, India **43 H13** 22 30N 88 5 E
Baja, Hungary **17 E10** 46 12N 18 59 E
Baja, Pta., Mexico **86 B1** 29 50N 116 0W
Baja California, Mexico **86 A1** 31 10N 115 12W
Baja California □, Mexico **86 B2** 30 0N 115 0W
Baja California Sur □, Mexico **86 B2** 25 50N 111 50W
Bajag, India **43 H9** 22 40N 81 21 E
Bajamar, Canary Is. **22 F3** 28 33N 16 20W
Bajana, India **42 H4** 23 7N 71 49 E
Bājgīrān, Iran **45 B8** 37 36N 58 24 E
Bajimba, Mt., Australia **63 D5** 29 17S 152 6 E
Bajo Nuevo, Caribbean **88 C4** 15 40N 78 50W
Bajoga, Nigeria **51 F8** 10 57N 11 20 E
Bajool, Australia **62 C5** 23 40S 150 35 E
Bakel, Senegal **50 F3** 14 56N 12 20W
Baker, Calif., U.S.A. **85 K10** 35 16N 116 4W
Baker, Mont., U.S.A. **80 B2** 46 22N 104 17W
Baker, L., Canada **68 B10** 64 0N 96 0W
Baker City, U.S.A. **82 D5** 44 47N 117 50W
Baker I., Pac. Oc. **64 G10** 0 10N 176 35W
Baker I., U.S.A. **72 B2** 55 20N 133 40W
Baker L., Australia **61 E4** 26 54S 126 5 E
Baker Lake, Canada **68 B10** 64 20N 96 3W
Baker Mt., U.S.A. **82 B3** 48 50N 121 49W
Bakers Creek, Australia **62 C4** 21 13S 149 7 E
Baker's Dozen Is., Canada **70 A4** 56 45N 78 45W
Bakersfield, Calif., U.S.A. **85 K8** 35 23N 119 1W
Bakersfield, Vt., U.S.A. **79 B12** 44 45N 72 48W
Bākhtarān, Iran **44 C5** 34 23N 47 0 E
Bākhtarān □, Iran **44 C5** 34 0N 46 30 E
Bakı, Azerbaijan **25 F8** 40 29N 49 56 E
Bakkafjörður, Iceland **8 C6** 66 2N 14 48W
Bakony, Hungary **17 E9** 47 10N 17 30 E
Bakony Forest = Bakony, Hungary **17 E9** 47 10N 17 30 E
Bakouma, C.A.R. **52 C4** 5 40N 22 56 E
Bakswaho, India **43 G8** 24 15N 79 18 E
Baku = Bakı, Azerbaijan **25 F8** 40 29N 49 56 E
Bakutis Coast, Antarctica **5 D15** 74 0S 120 0W
Baky = Bakı, Azerbaijan **25 F8** 40 29N 49 56 E
Bala, Canada **78 A5** 45 1N 79 37W
Bala, U.K. **10 E4** 52 54N 3 36W
Bala, L., U.K. **10 E4** 52 53N 3 37W
Balabac I., Phil. **36 C5** 8 0N 117 0 E
Balabac Str., E. Indies **36 C5** 7 53N 117 5 E
Balabagh, Afghan. **42 B4** 34 25N 70 12 E
Ba'labakk, Lebanon **47 B5** 34 0N 36 10 E
Balabalangan, Kepulauan, Indonesia **36 E5** 2 20S 117 30 E
Balad, Iraq **44 C5** 34 1N 44 9 E
Balad Rūz, Iraq **44 C5** 33 42N 45 5 E
Bālādeh, Fārs, Iran **45 D6** 29 17N 51 56 E
Bālādeh, Māzandaran, Iran **45 B6** 36 12N 51 48 E
Balaghat, India **40 J12** 21 49N 80 12 E
Balaghat Ra., India **40 K10** 18 50N 76 30 E
Balaguer, Spain **19 B6** 41 50N 0 50 E
Balaklava, Ukraine **25 F5** 44 30N 33 30 E
Balakovo, Russia **24 D8** 52 4N 47 55 E
Balamau, India **43 F9** 27 10N 80 21 E
Balancán, Mexico **87 D6** 17 48N 91 32W
Balashov, Russia **25 D7** 51 30N 43 10 E
Balasinor, India **42 H5** 22 57N 73 23 E
Balasore = Baleshwar, India **41 J15** 21 35N 87 3 E
Balaton, Hungary **17 E9** 46 50N 17 40 E
Balbina, Reprêsa de, Brazil **92 D7** 2 0S 59 30W
Balboa, Panama **88 E4** 8 57N 79 34W
Balbriggan, Ireland **13 C5** 53 37N 6 11W
Balcarce, Argentina **94 D4** 38 0S 58 10W
Balcarres, Canada **73 C8** 50 50N 103 35W
Balchik, Bulgaria **21 C13** 43 28N 28 11 E
Balclutha, N.Z. **59 M2** 46 15S 169 45 E
Balcones Escarpment, U.S.A. **81 L5** 29 30N 99 15W
Bald Hd., Australia **61 G2** 35 6S 118 1 E
Bald I., Australia **61 F2** 34 57S 118 27 E
Bald Knob, U.S.A. **81 H9** 35 19N 91 34W
Baldock L., Canada **73 B9** 56 33N 97 57W
Baldwin, Mich., U.S.A. **76 D3** 43 54N 85 51W
Baldwin, Pa., U.S.A. **78 F5** 40 23N 79 59W
Baldwinsville, U.S.A. **79 C8** 43 10N 76 20W
Baldy Mt., U.S.A. **82 B9** 48 9N 109 39W
Baldy Peak, U.S.A. **83 K9** 33 54N 109 34W
Baleares, Is., Spain **22 B10** 39 30N 3 0 E
Balearic Is. = Baleares, Is., Spain **22 B10** 39 30N 3 0 E
Baleine = Whale →, Canada **71 A6** 58 15N 67 40W
Baler, Phil. **37 A6** 15 46N 121 34 E
Baleshare, U.K. **12 D1** 57 31N 7 22W
Baleshwar, India **41 J15** 21 35N 87 3 E
Balfate, Honduras **88 C2** 15 48N 86 25W
Balí, Greece **23 D6** 35 25N 24 47 E
Bali, India **42 G5** 25 11N 73 17 E
Bali, Indonesia **36 F4** 8 20S 115 0 E
Bali □, Indonesia **36 F5** 8 20S 115 0 E
Bali, Selat, Indonesia **37 H16** 8 18S 114 25 E
Baliapal, India **43 J12** 21 40N 87 17 E
Balikeşir, Turkey **21 E12** 39 39N 27 53 E
Balikpapan, Indonesia **36 E5** 1 10S 116 55 E
Balimbing, Phil. **37 C5** 5 5N 119 58 E
Baling, Malaysia **39 K3** 5 41N 100 55 E
Balipara, India **41 F18** 26 50N 92 45 E
Balkan Mts. = Stara Planina, Bulgaria **21 C10** 43 15N 23 0 E
Balkhash = Balqash, Kazakstan **26 E8** 46 50N 74 50 E
Balkhash, Ozero = Balqash Köl, Kazakstan **26 E8** 46 0N 74 50 E
Balla, Bangla. **41 G17** 24 10N 91 35 E
Ballachulish, U.K. **12 E3** 56 41N 5 8W
Balladonia, Australia **61 F3** 32 27S 123 51 E
Ballaghaderreen, Ireland **13 C3** 53 55N 8 34W
Ballard, L., Australia **61 E3** 29 20S 120 40 E
Ballater, U.K. **12 D5** 57 3N 3 3W
Ballenas, Canal de, Mexico **86 B2** 29 10N 113 45W
Balleny Is., Antarctica **5 C11** 66 30S 163 0 E
Ballia, India **43 G11** 25 46N 84 12 E
Ballina, Australia **63 D5** 28 50S 153 31 E
Ballina, Ireland **13 B2** 54 7N 9 9W
Ballinasloe, Ireland **13 C3** 53 20N 8 13W
Ballinger, U.S.A. **81 K5** 31 45N 99 57W
Ballinrobe, Ireland **13 C2** 53 38N 9 13W
Ballinskelligs B., Ireland **13 E1** 51 48N 10 13W
Ballston Spa, U.S.A. **79 D11** 43 0N 73 51W
Ballycastle, U.K. **13 A5** 55 12N 6 15W
Ballyclare, U.K. **13 B5** 54 46N 6 0W
Ballyhaunis, Ireland **13 C3** 53 46N 8 46W
Ballymena, U.K. **13 B5** 54 52N 6 17W
Ballymoney, U.K. **13 A5** 55 5N 6 31W
Ballymote, Ireland **13 B3** 54 5N 8 31W
Ballynahinch, U.K. **13 B6** 54 24N 5 54W
Ballyquintin Pt., U.K. **13 B6** 54 20N 5 30W
Ballyshannon, Ireland **13 B3** 54 30N 8 11W
Balmaceda, Chile **96 F2** 46 0S 71 50W
Balmertown, Canada **73 C10** 51 4N 93 41W
Balmorhea, U.S.A. **81 K3** 30 59N 103 45W
Balonne →, Australia **63 D4** 28 47S 147 56 E
Balotra, India **42 G5** 25 50N 72 14 E
Balqash, Kazakstan **26 E8** 46 50N 74 50 E
Balqash Köl, Kazakstan **26 E8** 46 0N 74 50 E
Balrampur, India **43 F10** 27 30N 82 20 E
Balsas, Mexico **87 D5** 18 0N 99 40W
Balsas →, Brazil **93 E9** 7 15S 44 35W
Balsas →, Mexico **86 D4** 17 55N 102 10W
Balston Spa, U.S.A. **79 D11** 43 0N 73 52W
Balta, Ukraine **17 D15** 48 2N 29 45 E
Bălţi, Moldova **17 E14** 47 48N 27 58 E
Baltic Sea, Europe **9 H18** 57 0N 19 0 E
Baltimore, Ireland **13 E2** 51 29N 9 22W
Baltimore, Md., U.S.A. **76 F7** 39 17N 76 37W
Baltimore, Ohio, U.S.A. **78 G2** 39 51N 82 36W
Baltit, Pakistan **43 A6** 36 15N 74 40 E
Baltiysk, Russia **9 J18** 54 41N 19 58 E
Baluchistan □, Pakistan **40 F4** 27 30N 65 0 E
Balurghat, India **43 G13** 25 15N 88 44 E
Balvi, Latvia **9 H22** 57 8N 27 15 E
Balya, Turkey **21 E12** 39 44N 27 35 E
Bam, Iran **45 D8** 29 7N 58 14 E
Bama, Nigeria **51 F8** 11 33N 13 41 E
Bamaga, Australia **62 A3** 10 50S 142 25 E
Bamaji L., Canada **70 B1** 51 9N 91 25W
Bamako, Mali **50 F4** 12 34N 7 55W
Bambari, C.A.R. **52 C4** 5 40N 20 35 E
Bambaroo, Australia **62 B4** 18 50S 146 10 E
Bamberg, Germany **16 D6** 49 54N 10 54 E
Bamberg, U.S.A. **77 J5** 33 18N 81 2W
Bambili, Dem. Rep. of the Congo **54 B2** 3 40N 26 0 E
Bamfield, Canada **72 D3** 48 45N 125 10W
Bāmīān □, Afghan. **40 B5** 35 0N 67 0 E
Bamiancheng, China **35 C13** 43 15N 124 2 E
Bampūr, Iran **45 E9** 27 15N 60 21 E
Ban Ban, Laos **38 C4** 19 31N 103 30 E
Ban Bang Hin, Thailand **39 H2** 9 32N 98 35 E
Ban Chiang Klang, Thailand **38 C3** 19 25N 100 55 E
Ban Chik, Laos **38 D4** 17 15N 102 22 E
Ban Choho, Thailand **38 E4** 15 2N 102 9 E
Ban Dan Lan Hoi, Thailand **38 D2** 17 0N 99 35 E
Ban Don = Surat Thani, Thailand **39 H2** 9 6N 99 20 E
Ban Don, Vietnam **38 F6** 12 53N 107 48 E
Ban Don, Ao →, Thailand **39 H2** 9 20N 99 25 E
Ban Dong, Thailand **38 C3** 19 30N 100 59 E
Ban Hong, Thailand **38 C2** 18 18N 98 50 E
Ban Kaeng, Thailand **38 D3** 17 29N 100 7 E
Ban Kantang, Thailand **39 J2** 7 25N 99 31 E
Ban Keun, Laos **38 C4** 18 22N 102 35 E
Ban Khai, Thailand **38 F3** 12 46N 101 18 E
Ban Kheun, Laos **38 B3** 20 13N 101 7 E
Ban Khlong Kua, Thailand **39 J3** 6 57N 100 8 E
Ban Khuan Mao, Thailand **39 J2** 7 50N 99 37 E
Ban Ko Yai Chim, Thailand **39 G2** 11 17N 99 26 E
Ban Kok, Thailand **38 D4** 16 40N 103 40 E
Ban Laem, Thailand **38 F2** 13 13N 99 59 E
Ban Lao Ngam, Laos **38 E6** 15 28N 106 10 E
Ban Le Kathe, Thailand **38 E2** 15 49N 98 53 E
Ban Mae Chedi, Thailand **38 C2** 19 11N 99 31 E
Ban Mae Laeng, Thailand **38 B2** 20 1N 99 17 E
Ban Mae Sariang, Thailand **38 C1** 18 10N 97 56 E
Ban Mê Thuôt = Buon Ma Thuot, Vietnam **38 F7** 12 40N 108 3 E
Ban Mi, Thailand **38 E3** 15 3N 100 32 E
Ban Muong Mo, Laos **38 C4** 19 4N 103 58 E
Ban Na Mo, Laos **38 D5** 17 7N 105 40 E
Ban Na San, Thailand **39 H2** 8 53N 99 52 E
Ban Na Tong, Laos **38 B3** 20 56N 101 47 E
Ban Nam Bac, Laos **38 B4** 20 38N 102 20 E
Ban Nam Ma, Laos **38 A3** 22 2N 101 37 E
Ban Ngang, Laos **38 E6** 15 59N 106 11 E
Ban Nong Bok, Laos **38 D5** 17 5N 104 48 E
Ban Nong Boua, Laos **38 E6** 15 40N 106 33 E
Ban Nong Pling, Thailand **38 E3** 15 40N 100 10 E
Ban Pak Chan, Thailand **39 G2** 10 32N 98 51 E
Ban Phai, Thailand **38 D4** 16 4N 102 44 E
Ban Pong, Thailand **38 F2** 13 50N 99 55 E
Ban Ron Phibun, Thailand **39 H2** 8 9N 99 51 E
Ban Sanam Chai, Thailand **39 J3** 7 33N 100 25 E
Ban Sangkha, Thailand **38 E4** 14 37N 103 52 E
Ban Tak, Thailand **38 D2** 17 2N 99 4 E
Ban Tako, Thailand **38 E4** 14 5N 102 40 E
Ban Tha Dua, Thailand **38 D2** 17 59N 98 39 E
Ban Tha Li, Thailand **38 D3** 17 37N 101 25 E
Ban Tha Nun, Thailand **39 H2** 8 12N 98 18 E
Ban Thahine, Laos **38 E5** 14 12N 105 33 E
Ban Xien Kok, Laos **38 B3** 20 54N 100 39 E
Ban Yen Nhan, Vietnam **38 B6** 20 57N 106 2 E
Banaba, Kiribati **64 H8** 0 45S 169 50 E
Banalia, Dem. Rep. of the Congo **54 B2** 1 32N 25 5 E
Banam, Cambodia **39 G5** 11 20N 105 17 E
Bananal, I. do, Brazil **93 F8** 11 30S 50 30W
Banaras = Varanasi, India **43 G10** 25 22N 83 0 E
Banas →, Gujarat, India **42 H4** 23 45N 71 25 E
Banas →, Mad. P., India **43 G9** 24 15N 81 30 E
Bânâs, Ras, Egypt **51 D13** 23 57N 35 59 E
Banbridge, U.K. **13 B5** 54 22N 6 16W
Banbury, U.K. **11 E6** 52 4N 1 20W
Banchory, U.K. **12 D6** 57 3N 2 29W
Bancroft, Canada **78 A7** 45 3N 77 51W
Band Bonī, Iran **45 E8** 25 30N 59 33 E
Band Qīr, Iran **45 D6** 31 39N 48 53 E
Banda, Mad. P., India **43 G8** 24 3N 78 57 E
Banda, Ut. P., India **43 G9** 25 30N 80 26 E
Banda, Kepulauan, Indonesia **37 E7** 4 37S 129 50 E
Banda Aceh, Indonesia **36 C1** 5 35N 95 20 E
Banda Elat, Indonesia **37 F8** 5 40S 133 5 E
Banda Is. = Banda, Kepulauan, Indonesia **37 E7** 4 37S 129 50 E
Banda Sea, Indonesia **37 F7** 6 0S 130 0 E
Bandai-San, Japan **30 F10** 37 36N 140 4 E
Bandān, Iran **45 D9** 31 23N 60 44 E
Bandanaira, Indonesia **37 E7** 4 32S 129 54 E
Bandanwara, India **42 F6** 26 9N 74 38 E
Bandar = Machilipatnam, India **41 L12** 16 12N 81 8 E
Bandār 'Abbās, Iran **45 E8** 27 15N 56 15 E
Bandar-e Anzalī, Iran **45 B6** 37 30N 49 30 E
Bandar-e Bushehr = Būshehr, Iran **45 D6** 28 55N 50 55 E
Bandar-e Chārak, Iran **45 E7** 26 45N 54 20 E
Bandar-e Deylam, Iran **45 D6** 30 5N 50 10 E
Bandar-e Khomeynı, Iran **45 D6** 30 30N 49 5 E
Bandar-e Lengeh, Iran **45 E7** 26 35N 54 58 E
Bandar-e Maqām, Iran **45 E7** 26 56N 53 29 E
Bandar-e Ma'shur, Iran **45 D6** 30 35N 49 10 E
Bandar-e Rīg, Iran **45 D6** 29 29N 50 38 E
Bandar-e Torkeman, Iran **45 B7** 37 0N 54 10 E
Bandar Maharani = Muar, Malaysia **39 L4** 2 3N 102 34 E
Bandar Penggaram = Batu Pahat, Malaysia **39 M4** 1 50N 102 56 E
Bandar Seri Begawan, Brunei **36 C4** 4 52N 115 0 E
Bandar Sri Aman, Malaysia **36 D4** 1 15N 111 32 E
Bandawe, Malawi **55 E3** 11 58S 34 5 E
Bandeira, Pico da, Brazil **95 A7** 20 26S 41 47W
Bandera, Argentina **94 B3** 28 55S 62 20W
Banderas, B. de, Mexico **86 C3** 20 40N 105 30W
Bandhogarh, India **43 H9** 23 40N 81 2 E
Bandi →, India **42 F6** 26 12N 75 47 E
Bandikui, India **42 F7** 27 3N 76 34 E
Bandırma, Turkey **21 D13** 40 20N 28 0 E
Bandon, Ireland **13 E3** 51 44N 8 44W
Bandon →, Ireland **13 E3** 51 43N 8 37W
Bandula, Mozam. **55 F3** 19 0S 33 7 E
Bandundu, Dem. Rep. of the Congo **52 E3** 3 15S 17 22 E
Bandung, Indonesia **36 F3** 6 54S 107 36 E
Bāneh, Iran **44 C5** 35 59N 45 53 E
Banes, Cuba **89 B4** 21 0N 75 42W
Banff, Canada **72 C5** 51 10N 115 34W
Banff, U.K. **12 D6** 57 40N 2 33W
Banff Nat. Park, Canada **72 C5** 51 30N 116 15W
Bang Fai →, Laos **38 D5** 16 57N 104 45 E
Bang Hieng →, Laos **38 D5** 16 10N 105 10 E
Bang Krathum, Thailand **38 D3** 16 34N 100 18 E
Bang Lamung, Thailand **38 F3** 13 3N 100 56 E
Bang Mun Nak, Thailand **38 D3** 16 2N 100 23 E
Bang Pa In, Thailand **38 E3** 14 14N 100 35 E
Bang Rakam, Thailand **38 D3** 16 45N 100 7 E
Bang Saphan, Thailand **39 G2** 11 14N 99 28 E
Bangaduni I., India **43 J13** 21 34N 88 52 E
Bangala Dam, Zimbabwe **55 G3** 21 7S 31 25 E
Bangalore, India **40 N10** 12 59N 77 40 E
Banganga →, India **42 F6** 27 6N 77 25 E
Bangaon, India **43 H13** 23 0N 88 47 E
Bangassou, C.A.R. **52 D4** 4 55N 23 7 E
Banggai, Indonesia **37 E6** 1 34S 123 30 E
Banggai, Kepulauan, Indonesia **37 E6** 1 40S 123 30 E
Banggai Arch. = Banggai, Kepulauan, Indonesia **37 E6** 1 40S 123 30 E
Banggi, Malaysia **36 C5** 7 17N 117 12 E
Banghāzī, Libya **51 B10** 32 11N 20 3 E
Bangka, Sulawesi, Indonesia **37 D7** 1 50N 125 5 E
Bangka, Sumatera, Indonesia **36 E3** 2 0S 105 50 E
Bangka, Selat, Indonesia **36 E3** 2 30S 105 30 E
Bangkalan, Indonesia **37 G15** 7 2S 112 46 E
Bangkinang, Indonesia **36 D2** 0 18N 101 5 E
Bangko, Indonesia **36 E2** 2 5S 102 9 E
Bangkok, Thailand **38 F3** 13 45N 100 35 E
Bangladesh ■, Asia **41 H17** 24 0N 90 0 E
Bangong Co, India **43 B8** 35 50N 79 20 E
Bangor, Down, U.K. **13 B6** 54 40N 5 40W
Bangor, Gwynedd, U.K. **10 D3** 53 14N 4 8W
Bangor, Maine, U.S.A. **69 D13** 44 48N 68 46W
Bangor, Pa., U.S.A. **79 F9** 40 52N 75 13W
Bangued, Phil. **37 A6** 17 40N 120 37 E
Bangui, C.A.R. **52 D3** 4 23N 18 35 E
Banguru, Dem. Rep. of the Congo **54 B2** 0 30N 27 10 E
Bangweulu, L., Zambia **55 E3** 11 0S 30 0 E
Bangweulu Swamp, Zambia **55 E3** 11 20S 30 15 E
Bani, Dom. Rep. **89 C5** 18 16N 70 22W
Banī Sa'd, Iraq **44 C5** 33 34N 44 32 E
Banihal Pass, India **43 C6** 33 30N 75 12 E
Bāniyās, Syria **44 C3** 35 10N 36 0 E
Banja Luka, Bos.-H. **20 B7** 44 49N 17 11 E
Banjar, India **42 D7** 31 38N 77 21 E
Banjar →, India **43 H9** 22 36N 80 22 E
Banjarmasin, Indonesia **36 E4** 3 20S 114 35 E
Banjul, Gambia **50 F2** 13 28N 16 40W
Banka, India **43 G12** 24 53N 86 55 E
Banket, Zimbabwe **55 F3** 17 27S 30 19 E
Bankipore, India **41 G14** 25 35N 85 10 E
Banks I., B.C., Canada **72 C3** 53 20N 130 0W
Banks I., N.W.T., Canada **68 A7** 73 15N 121 30W
Banks Pen., N.Z. **59 K4** 43 45S 173 15 E
Banks Str., Australia **62 G4** 40 40S 148 10 E
Bankura, India **43 H12** 23 11N 87 18 E
Banmankhi, India **43 G12** 25 53N 87 11 E
Bann →, Arm., U.K. **13 B5** 54 30N 6 31W
Bann →, L'derry., U.K. **13 A5** 55 8N 6 41W
Bannang Sata, Thailand **39 J3** 6 16N 101 16 E
Banning, U.S.A. **85 M10** 33 56N 116 53W
Banningville = Bandundu, Dem. Rep. of the Congo **52 E3** 3 15S 17 22 E
Bannockburn, Canada **78 B7** 44 39N 77 33W
Bannockburn, U.K. **12 E5** 56 5N 3 55W
Bannockburn, Zimbabwe **55 G2** 20 17S 29 48 E
Bannu, Pakistan **40 C7** 33 0N 70 18 E
Bano, India **43 H11** 22 40N 84 55 E
Bansgaon, India **43 F10** 26 33N 83 21 E
Banská Bystrica, Slovak Rep. **17 D10** 48 46N 19 14 E
Banswara, India **42 H6** 23 32N 74 24 E
Bantaeng, Indonesia **37 F5** 5 32S 119 56 E
Bantry, Ireland **13 E2** 51 41N 9 27W
Bantry B., Ireland **13 E2** 51 37N 9 44W
Bantul, Indonesia **37 G14** 7 55S 110 19 E
Bantva, India **42 J4** 21 29N 70 12 E
Banyak, Kepulauan, Indonesia **36 D1** 2 10N 97 10 E
Banyalbufar, Spain **22 B9** 39 42N 2 31 E
Banyo, Cameroon **52 C2** 6 52N 11 45 E
Banyumas, Indonesia **37 G13** 7 32S 109 18 E
Banyuwangi, Indonesia **37 H16** 8 13S 114 21 E
Banzare Coast, Antarctica **5 C9** 68 0S 125 0 E
Banzyville = Mobayi, Dem. Rep. of the Congo **52 D4** 4 15N 21 8 E
Bao Ha, Vietnam **38 A5** 22 11N 104 21 E
Bao Lac, Vietnam **38 A5** 22 57N 105 40 E
Bao Loc, Vietnam **39 G6** 11 32N 107 48 E
Baocheng, China **34 H4** 33 12N 106 56 E
Baode, China **34 E6** 39 1N 111 5 E
Baodi, China **35 E9** 39 38N 117 20 E
Baoding, China **34 E8** 38 50N 115 28 E
Baoji, China **34 G4** 34 20N 107 5 E
Baoshan, China **32 D4** 25 10N 99 5 E
Baotou, China **34 D6** 40 32N 110 2 E
Baoying, China **35 H10** 33 17N 119 20 E
Bap, India **42 F5** 27 23N 72 18 E
Bapatla, India **41 M12** 15 55N 80 30 E
Bāqerābād, Iran **45 C6** 33 2N 51 58 E
Ba'qūbah, Iraq **44 C5** 33 45N 44 50 E
Baquedano, Chile **94 A2** 23 20S 69 52W
Bar, Montenegro, Yug. **21 C8** 42 8N 19 6 E
Bar, Ukraine **17 D14** 49 4N 27 40 E
Bar Bigha, India **43 G11** 25 21N 85 47 E
Bar Harbor, U.S.A. **77 C11** 44 23N 68 13W
Bar-le-Duc, France **18 B6** 48 47N 5 10 E
Bara, India **43 G9** 25 16N 81 43 E
Bara Banki, India **43 F9** 26 55N 81 12 E
Barabai, Indonesia **36 E5** 2 32S 115 34 E
Baraboo, U.S.A. **80 D10** 43 28N 89 45W
Baracoa, Cuba **89 B5** 20 20N 74 30W
Baradā →, Syria **47 B5** 33 33N 36 34 E
Baradero, Argentina **94 C4** 33 52S 59 29W
Baraga, U.S.A. **80 B10** 46 47N 88 30W
Barah →, India **42 F6** 27 42N 77 5 E
Barahona, Dom. Rep. **89 C5** 18 13N 71 7W
Barail Range, India **41 G18** 25 15N 93 20 E
Barakaldo, Spain **19 A4** 43 18N 2 59W
Barakar →, India **43 G12** 24 7N 86 14 E
Barakhola, India **41 G18** 25 0N 92 45 E
Barakot, India **43 J11** 21 33N 84 59 E
Barakpur, India **43 H13** 22 44N 88 30 E
Baralaba, Australia **62 C4** 24 13S 149 50 E
Baralzon L., Canada **73 B9** 60 0N 98 3W
Baramula, India **43 B6** 34 15N 74 20 E
Baran, India **42 G7** 25 9N 76 40 E
Baran →, Pakistan **42 G3** 25 13N 68 17 E
Baranavichy, Belarus **17 B14** 53 10N 26 0 E
Baranof, U.S.A. **72 B2** 57 5N 134 50W

Baranof I.

Baranof I., U.S.A. 68 C6 57 0N 135 0W
Barapasi, Indonesia 37 E9 2 15S 137 5 E
Barasat, India 43 H13 22 46N 88 31 E
Barat Daya, Kepulauan, Indonesia 37 F7 7 30S 128 0 E
Barataria B., U.S.A. 81 L10 29 20N 89 55W
Barauda, India 42 H6 23 33N 75 15 E
Baraut, India 42 E7 29 13N 77 7 E
Barbacena, Brazil 95 A7 21 15S 43 56W
Barbados ■, W. Indies 89 D8 13 10N 59 30W
Barbària, C. de, Spain 22 C7 38 39N 1 24 E
Barbastro, Spain 19 A6 42 2N 0 5 E
Barberton, S. Africa 57 D5 25 42S 31 2 E
Barberton, U.S.A. 78 E3 41 0N 81 39W
Barbosa, Colombia 92 B4 5 57N 73 37W
Barbourville, U.S.A. 77 G4 36 52N 83 53W
Barbuda, W. Indies 89 C7 17 30N 61 40W
Barcaldine, Australia 62 C4 23 43S 145 6 E
Barcellona Pozzo di Gotto, Italy 20 E6 38 9N 15 13 E
Barcelona, Spain 19 B7 41 21N 2 10 E
Barcelona, Venezuela 92 A6 10 10N 64 40W
Barcelos, Brazil 92 D6 1 0S 63 0W
Barcoo →, Australia 62 D3 25 30S 142 50 E
Bardaï, Chad 51 D9 21 25N 17 0 E
Bardas Blancas, Argentina 94 D2 35 49S 69 45W
Barddhaman, India 43 H12 23 14N 87 39 E
Bardejov, Slovak Rep. 17 D11 49 18N 21 15 E
Bardera, Somali Rep. 46 G3 2 20N 42 27 E
Bardīyah, Libya 51 B10 31 45N 25 5 E
Bardsey I., U.K. 10 E3 52 45N 4 47W
Bardstown, U.S.A. 76 G3 37 49N 85 28W
Bareilly, India 43 E8 28 22N 79 27 E
Barela, India 43 H9 23 6N 80 3 E
Barents Sea, Arctic 4 B9 73 0N 39 0 E
Barfleur, Pte. de, France 18 B3 49 42N 1 16W
Bargara, Australia 62 C5 24 50S 152 25 E
Barguzin, Russia 27 D11 53 37N 109 37 E
Barh, India 43 G11 25 29N 85 46 E
Barhaj, India 43 F10 26 18N 83 44 E
Barharwa, India 43 G12 24 52N 87 47 E
Barhi, India 43 G11 24 15N 85 25 E
Bari, India 42 F7 26 39N 77 39 E
Bari, Italy 20 D7 41 8N 16 51 E
Bari Doab, Pakistan 42 D5 30 20N 73 0 E
Bari Sadri, India 42 G6 24 28N 74 30 E
Barīdī, Ra's, Si. Arabia 44 E3 24 17N 37 31 E
Barīm, Yemen 48 E8 12 39N 43 25 E
Barinas, Venezuela 92 B4 8 36N 70 15W
Baring, C., Canada 68 B8 70 0N 117 30W
Baringo, Kenya 54 B4 0 47N 36 16 E
Baringo, L., Kenya 54 B4 0 47N 36 16 E
Barisal, Bangla. 41 H17 22 45N 90 20 E
Barisan, Bukit, Indonesia 36 E2 3 30S 102 15 E
Barito →, Indonesia 36 E4 4 0S 114 50 E
Bark L., Canada 78 A7 45 27N 77 51W
Barkakana, India 43 H11 23 37N 85 29 E
Barker, U.S.A. 78 C6 43 20N 78 33W
Barkley, L., U.S.A. 77 G2 37 1N 88 14W
Barkley Sound, Canada 72 D3 48 50N 125 10W
Barkly East, S. Africa 56 E4 30 58S 27 33 E
Barkly Roadhouse, Australia 62 B2 19 52S 135 50 E
Barkly Tableland, Australia 62 B2 17 50S 136 40 E
Barkly West, S. Africa 56 D3 28 5S 24 31 E
Barkol Kazak Zizhixian, China 32 B4 43 37N 93 2 E
Bârlad, Romania 17 E14 46 15N 27 38 E
Bârlad →, Romania 17 F14 45 38N 27 32 E
Barlee, L., Australia 61 E2 29 15S 119 30 E
Barlee, Mt., Australia 61 D4 24 38S 128 13 E
Barletta, Italy 20 D7 41 19N 16 17 E
Barlovento, Canary Is. 22 F2 28 48N 17 48W
Barlow L., Canada 73 A8 62 0N 103 0W
Barmer, India 42 G4 25 45N 71 20 E
Barmouth, U.K. 10 E3 52 44N 4 4W
Barna →, India 43 G10 25 21N 83 3 E
Barnagar, India 42 H6 23 7N 75 19 E
Barnala, India 42 D6 30 23N 75 33 E
Barnard Castle, U.K. 10 C6 54 33N 1 55W
Barnaul, Russia 26 D9 53 20N 83 40 E
Barnesville, U.S.A. 77 J3 33 3N 84 9W
Barnet □, U.K. 11 F7 51 38N 0 9W
Barneveld, Neths. 15 B5 52 7N 5 36 E
Barneveld, U.S.A. 79 C9 43 16N 75 14W
Barnhart, U.S.A. 81 K4 31 8N 101 10W
Barnsley, U.K. 10 D6 53 34N 1 27W
Barnstaple, U.K. 11 F3 51 5N 4 4W
Barnstaple Bay = Bideford Bay, U.K. 11 F3 51 5N 4 20W
Barnsville, U.S.A. 80 B6 46 43N 96 28W
Barnwell, U.S.A. 77 J5 33 15N 81 23W
Baro, Nigeria 50 G7 8 35N 6 18 E
Baroda = Vadodara, India 42 H5 22 20N 73 10 E
Baroda, India 42 G7 25 29N 76 35 E
Baroe, S. Africa 56 E3 33 13S 24 33 E
Baron Ra., Australia 60 D4 23 30S 127 45 E
Barotseland, Zambia 53 H4 15 0S 24 0 E
Barpeta, India 41 F17 26 20N 91 10 E
Barques, Pt. Aux, U.S.A. 78 B2 44 4N 82 58W
Barquísimeto, Venezuela 92 A5 10 4N 69 19W
Barr Smith Range, Australia 61 E3 27 4S 120 20 E
Barra, Brazil 93 F10 11 5S 43 10W
Barra, U.K. 12 E1 57 0N 7 29W
Barra, Sd. of, U.K. 12 D1 57 4N 7 25W
Barra de Navidad, Mexico 86 D4 19 12N 104 41W
Barra do Corda, Brazil 93 E9 5 30S 45 10W
Barra do Piraí, Brazil 95 A7 22 30S 43 50W
Barra Falsa, Pta. da, Mozam. 57 C6 22 58S 35 37 E
Barra Hd., U.K. 12 E1 56 47N 7 40W
Barra Mansa, Brazil 95 A7 22 35S 44 12W
Barrackpur = Barakpur, India 43 H13 22 44N 88 30 E
Barradale Roadhouse, Australia 60 D1 22 42S 114 58 E
Barraigh = Barra, U.K. 12 E1 57 0N 7 29W
Barranca, Lima, Peru 92 F3 10 45S 77 50W
Barranca, Loreto, Peru 92 D3 4 50S 76 50W
Barrancabermeja, Colombia 92 B4 7 0N 73 50W
Barrancas, Venezuela 92 B6 8 55N 62 5W
Barrancos, Portugal 19 C2 38 10N 6 58W
Barranqueras, Argentina 94 B4 27 30S 59 0W
Barranquilla, Colombia 92 A4 11 0N 74 50W
Barraute, Canada 70 C4 48 26N 77 38W
Barre, Mass., U.S.A. 79 D12 42 25N 72 6W
Barre, Vt., U.S.A. 79 B12 44 12N 72 30W
Barreal, Argentina 94 C2 31 33S 69 28W
Barreiras, Brazil 93 F10 12 8S 45 0W
Barreirinhas, Brazil 93 D10 2 30S 42 50W
Barreiro, Portugal 19 C1 38 40N 9 6W
Barren, Nosy, Madag. 57 B7 18 25S 43 40 E
Barretos, Brazil 93 H9 20 30S 48 35W
Barrhead, Canada 72 C6 54 10N 114 24W
Barrie, Canada 78 B5 44 24N 79 40W
Barrière, Canada 72 C4 51 12N 120 7W
Barrington, U.S.A. 79 E13 41 44N 71 18W
Barrington L., Canada 73 B8 56 55N 100 15W
Barringun, Australia 63 D4 29 1S 145 41 E
Barro do Garças, Brazil 93 G8 15 54S 52 16W
Barron, U.S.A. 80 C9 45 24N 91 51W
Barrow, U.S.A. 68 A4 71 18N 156 47W
Barrow →, Ireland 13 D5 52 25N 6 58W
Barrow, Pt., U.S.A. 66 B4 71 10N 156 20W
Barrow Creek, Australia 62 C1 21 30S 133 55 E
Barrow I., Australia 60 D2 20 45S 115 20 E
Barrow-in-Furness, U.K. 10 C4 54 7N 3 14W
Barrow Pt., Australia 62 A3 14 20S 144 40 E
Barrow Ra., Australia 61 E4 26 0S 127 40 E
Barrow Str., Canada 4 B3 74 20N 95 0W
Barry, U.K. 11 F4 51 24N 3 16W
Barry's Bay, Canada 78 A7 45 29N 77 41W
Barsat, Pakistan 43 A5 36 10N 72 45 E
Barsham, Syria 44 C4 35 21N 40 33 E
Barsi, India 40 K9 18 10N 75 50 E
Barsoi, India 41 G15 25 48N 87 57 E
Barstow, U.S.A. 85 L9 34 54N 117 1W
Barthélemy, Col, Vietnam 38 C5 19 26N 104 6 E
Bartica, Guyana 92 B7 6 25N 58 40W
Bartlesville, U.S.A. 81 G7 36 45N 95 59W
Bartlett, U.S.A. 84 J8 36 29N 118 2W
Bartlett, L., Canada 72 A5 63 5N 118 20W
Bartolomeu Dias, Mozam. 55 G4 21 10S 35 8 E
Barton, U.S.A. 79 B12 44 45N 72 11W
Barton upon Humber, U.K. 10 D7 53 41N 0 25W
Bartow, U.S.A. 77 M5 27 54N 81 50W
Barú, Volcan, Panama 88 E3 8 55N 82 35W
Barumba, Dem. Rep. of the Congo 54 B1 1 3N 23 37 E
Baruunsuu, Mongolia 34 C3 43 43N 105 35 E
Barwani, India 42 H6 22 2N 74 57 E
Barysaw, Belarus 17 A15 54 17N 28 28 E
Barzān, Iraq 44 B5 36 55N 44 3 E
Bāsa'idū, Iran 45 E7 26 35N 55 20 E
Basal, Pakistan 42 C5 33 33N 72 13 E
Basankusa, Dem. Rep. of the Congo 52 D3 1 5N 19 50 E
Basarabeasca, Moldova 17 E15 46 21N 28 58 E
Basawa, Afghan. 42 B4 34 15N 70 50 E
Bascuñán, C., Chile 94 B1 28 52S 71 35W
Basel, Switz. 18 C7 47 35N 7 35 E
Bashākerd, Kūhhā-ye, Iran 45 E8 26 42N 58 35 E
Bashaw, Canada 72 C6 52 35N 112 58W
Bāshī, Iran 45 D6 28 41N 51 4 E
Bashkir Republic = Bashkortostan □, Russia 24 D10 54 0N 57 0 E
Bashkortostan □, Russia 24 D10 54 0N 57 0 E
Basibasy, Madag. 57 C7 22 10S 43 40 E
Basilan I., Phil. 37 C6 6 35N 122 0 E
Basilan Str., Phil. 37 C6 6 50N 122 0 E
Basildon, U.K. 11 F8 51 34N 0 28 E
Basim = Washim, India 40 J10 20 3N 77 0 E
Basin, U.S.A. 82 D9 44 23N 108 2W
Basingstoke, U.K. 11 F6 51 15N 1 5W
Baskatong, Rés., Canada 70 C4 46 46N 75 50W
Basle = Basel, Switz. 18 C7 47 35N 7 35 E
Basoda, India 42 H7 23 52N 77 54 E
Basoka, Dem. Rep. of the Congo 54 B1 1 16N 23 40 E
Basque Provinces = País Vasco □, Spain 19 A4 42 50N 2 45W
Basra = Al Başrah, Iraq 44 D5 30 30N 47 50 E
Bass Str., Australia 62 F4 39 15S 146 30 E
Bassano, Canada 72 C6 50 48N 112 20W
Bassano del Grappa, Italy 20 B4 45 46N 11 44 E
Bassas da India, Ind. Oc. 53 J7 22 0S 39 0 E
Basse-Terre, Guadeloupe 89 C7 16 0N 61 44W
Bassein, Burma 41 L19 16 45N 94 30 E
Basseterre, St. Kitts & Nevis 89 C7 17 17N 62 43W
Bassett, U.S.A. 80 D5 42 35N 99 32W
Bassi, India 42 D7 30 44N 76 21 E
Bastak, Iran 45 E7 27 15N 54 25 E
Baştām, Iran 45 B7 36 29N 55 4 E
Bastar, India 41 K12 19 15N 81 40 E
Basti, India 43 F10 26 52N 82 55 E
Bastia, France 18 E8 42 40N 9 30 E
Bastogne, Belgium 15 D5 50 1N 5 43 E
Bastrop, La., U.S.A. 81 J9 32 47N 91 55W
Bastrop, Tex., U.S.A. 81 K6 30 7N 97 19W
Bat Yam, Israel 47 C3 32 2N 34 44 E
Bata, Eq. Guin. 52 D1 1 57N 9 50 E
Bataan □, Phil. 37 B6 14 40N 120 25 E
Batabanó, Cuba 88 B3 22 40N 82 20W
Batabanó, G. de, Cuba 88 B3 22 30N 82 30W
Batac, Phil. 37 A6 18 3N 120 34 E
Batagai, Russia 27 C14 67 38N 134 38 E
Batala, India 42 D6 31 48N 75 12 E
Batama, Dem. Rep. of the Congo 54 B2 0 58N 26 33 E
Batamay, Russia 27 C13 63 30N 129 15 E
Batang, Indonesia 37 G13 6 55S 109 45 E
Batangas, Phil. 37 B6 13 35N 121 10 E
Batanta, Indonesia 37 E8 0 55S 130 40 E
Batatais, Brazil 95 A6 20 54S 47 37W
Batavia, U.S.A. 78 D6 43 0N 78 11W
Batchelor, Australia 60 B5 13 4S 131 1 E
Batdambang, Cambodia 38 F4 13 7N 103 12 E
Bates Ra., Australia 61 E3 27 27S 121 5 E
Batesburg-Leesville, U.S.A. 77 J5 33 54N 81 33W
Batesville, Ark., U.S.A. 81 H9 35 46N 91 39W
Batesville, Miss., U.S.A. 81 H10 34 19N 89 57W
Batesville, Tex., U.S.A. 81 L5 28 58N 99 37W
Bath, Canada 79 B8 44 11N 76 47W
Bath, U.K. 11 F5 51 23N 2 22W
Bath, Maine, U.S.A. 77 D11 43 55N 69 49W
Bath, N.Y., U.S.A. 78 D7 42 20N 77 19W
Bath & North East Somerset □, U.K. 11 F5 51 21N 2 27W
Batheay, Cambodia 39 G5 11 59N 104 57 E
Bathurst = Banjul, Gambia 50 F2 13 28N 16 40W
Bathurst, Canada 71 C6 47 37N 65 43W
Bathurst, S. Africa 56 E4 33 30S 26 50 E
Bathurst, C., Canada 68 A7 70 34N 128 0W
Bathurst B., Australia 62 A3 14 16S 144 25 E
Bathurst Harb., Australia 62 G4 43 15S 146 10 E
Bathurst I., Australia 60 B5 11 30S 130 10 E
Bathurst I., Canada 4 B2 76 0N 100 30W
Bathurst Inlet, Canada 68 B9 66 50N 108 1W
Batman, Turkey 25 G7 37 55N 41 5 E
Baţn al Ghūl, Jordan 47 F4 29 36N 35 56 E
Batna, Algeria 50 A7 35 34N 6 15 E
Batoka, Zambia 55 F2 16 45S 27 15 E
Baton Rouge, U.S.A. 81 K9 30 27N 91 11W
Batong, Ko, Thailand 39 J2 6 32N 99 12 E
Batopilas, Mexico 86 B3 27 0N 107 45W
Batouri, Cameroon 52 D2 4 30N 14 25 E
Båtsfjord, Norway 8 A23 70 38N 29 39 E
Battambang = Batdambang, Cambodia 38 F4 13 7N 103 12 E
Batticaloa, Sri Lanka 40 R12 7 43N 81 45 E
Battipáglia, Italy 20 D6 40 37N 14 58 E
Battle, U.K. 11 G8 50 55N 0 30 E
Battle →, Canada 73 C7 52 43N 108 15W
Battle Creek, U.S.A. 76 D3 42 19N 85 11W
Battle Ground, U.S.A. 84 E4 45 47N 122 32W
Battle Harbour, Canada 71 B8 52 16N 55 35W
Battle Lake, U.S.A. 80 B7 46 17N 95 43W
Battle Mountain, U.S.A. 82 F5 40 38N 116 56W
Battlefields, Zimbabwe 55 F2 18 37S 29 47 E
Battleford, Canada 73 C7 52 45N 108 15W
Batu, Ethiopia 46 F2 6 55N 39 45 E
Batu, Kepulauan, Indonesia 36 E1 0 30S 98 25 E
Batu Caves, Malaysia 39 L3 3 15N 101 40 E
Batu Gajah, Malaysia 39 K3 4 28N 101 3 E
Batu Is. = Batu, Kepulauan, Indonesia 36 E1 0 30S 98 25 E
Batu Pahat, Malaysia 39 M4 1 50N 102 56 E
Batuata, Indonesia 37 F6 6 12S 122 42 E
Batumi, Georgia 25 F7 41 39N 41 44 E
Baturaja, Indonesia 36 E2 4 11S 104 15 E
Baturité, Brazil 93 D11 4 28S 38 45W
Bau, Malaysia 36 D4 1 25N 110 9 E
Baubau, Indonesia 37 F6 5 25S 122 38 E
Bauchi, Nigeria 50 F7 10 22N 9 48 E
Baudette, U.S.A. 80 A7 48 43N 94 36W
Bauer, C., Australia 63 E1 32 44S 134 4 E
Bauhinia, Australia 62 C4 24 35S 149 18 E
Baukau, E. Timor 37 F7 8 27S 126 27 E
Bauld, C., Canada 69 C14 51 38N 55 26W
Bauru, Brazil 95 A6 22 10S 49 0W
Bausi, India 43 G12 24 48N 87 1 E
Bauska, Latvia 9 H21 56 24N 24 15 E
Bautzen, Germany 16 C8 51 10N 14 26 E
Bavānāt, Iran 45 D7 30 28N 53 27 E
Bavaria = Bayern □, Germany 16 D6 48 50N 12 0 E
Bavispe →, Mexico 86 B3 29 30N 109 11W
Bawdwin, Burma 41 H20 23 5N 97 20 E
Bawean, Indonesia 36 F4 5 46S 112 35 E
Bawku, Ghana 50 F5 11 3N 0 19W
Bawlake, Burma 41 K20 19 11N 97 21 E
Baxley, U.S.A. 77 K4 31 47N 82 21W
Baxter, U.S.A. 80 B7 46 21N 94 17W
Baxter Springs, U.S.A. 81 G7 37 2N 94 44W
Bay City, Mich., U.S.A. 76 D4 43 36N 83 54W
Bay City, Tex., U.S.A. 81 L7 28 59N 95 58W
Bay Minette, U.S.A. 77 K2 30 53N 87 46W
Bay Roberts, Canada 71 C9 47 36N 53 16W
Bay St. Louis, U.S.A. 81 K10 30 19N 89 20W
Bay Springs, U.S.A. 81 K10 31 59N 89 17W
Bay View, N.Z. 59 H6 39 25S 176 50 E
Baya, Dem. Rep. of the Congo 55 E2 11 53S 27 25 E
Bayamo, Cuba 88 B4 20 20N 76 40W
Bayamón, Puerto Rico 89 C6 18 24N 66 10W
Bayan Har Shan, China 32 C4 34 0N 98 0 E
Bayan Hot = Alxa Zuoqi, China 34 E3 38 50N 105 40 E
Bayan Obo, China 34 D5 41 52N 109 59 E
Bayan-Ovoo = Erdenetsogt, Mongolia 34 C4 42 55N 106 5 E
Bayana, India 42 F7 26 55N 77 18 E
Bayanaūyl, Kazakstan 26 D8 50 45N 75 45 E
Bayandalay, Mongolia 34 C2 43 30N 103 29 E
Bayanhongor, Mongolia 32 B5 46 8N 102 43 E
Bayard, N. Mex., U.S.A. 83 K9 32 46N 108 8W
Bayard, Nebr., U.S.A. 80 E3 41 45N 103 20W
Baybay, Phil. 37 B6 10 40N 124 55 E
Bayern □, Germany 16 D6 48 50N 12 0 E
Bayeux, France 18 B3 49 17N 0 42W
Bayfield, Canada 78 C3 43 34N 81 42W
Bayfield, U.S.A. 80 B9 46 49N 90 49W
Bayındır, Turkey 21 E12 38 13N 27 39 E
Baykal, Oz., Russia 27 D11 53 0N 108 0 E
Baykan, Turkey 44 B4 38 7N 41 44 E
Baykonur = Bayqongyr, Kazakstan 26 E7 47 48N 65 50 E
Baymak, Russia 24 D10 52 36N 58 19 E
Baynes Mts., Namibia 56 B1 17 15S 13 0 E
Bayombong, Phil. 37 A6 16 30N 121 10 E
Bayonne, France 18 E3 43 30N 1 28W
Bayonne, U.S.A. 79 F10 40 40N 74 7W
Bayovar, Peru 92 E2 5 50S 81 0W
Bayqongyr, Kazakstan 26 E7 47 48N 65 50 E
Bayram-Ali = Bayramaly, Turkmenistan 26 F7 37 37N 62 10 E
Bayramaly, Turkmenistan 26 F7 37 37N 62 10 E
Bayramiç, Turkey 21 E12 39 48N 26 36 E
Bayreuth, Germany 16 D6 49 56N 11 35 E
Bayrūt, Lebanon 47 B4 33 53N 35 31 E
Bays, L. of, Canada 78 A5 45 15N 79 4W
Baysville, Canada 78 A5 45 9N 79 7W
Bayt Lahm, West Bank 47 D4 31 43N 35 12 E
Baytown, U.S.A. 81 L7 29 43N 94 59W
Baza, Spain 19 D4 37 30N 2 47W
Bazaruto, I. do, Mozam. 57 C6 21 40S 35 28 E
Bazhou, China 34 E9 39 8N 116 22 E
Bazmān, Kūh-e, Iran 45 D9 28 4N 60 1 E
Beach, U.S.A. 80 B3 46 58N 104 0W
Beach City, U.S.A. 78 F3 40 39N 81 35W
Beachy Hd., U.K. 11 G8 50 44N 0 15 E
Beacon, Australia 61 F2 30 26S 117 52 E
Beacon, U.S.A. 79 E11 41 30N 73 58W
Beaconsfield, Australia 62 G4 41 11S 146 48 E
Beagle, Canal, S. Amer. 96 H3 55 0S 68 30W
Beagle Bay, Australia 60 C3 16 58S 122 40 E
Bealanana, Madag. 57 A8 14 33S 48 44 E
Beals Cr. →, U.S.A. 81 J4 32 10N 100 51W
Beamsville, Canada 78 C5 43 12N 79 28W
Bear →, Calif., U.S.A. 84 G5 38 56N 121 36W
Bear →, Utah, U.S.A. 74 B4 41 30N 112 8W
Bear I., Ireland 13 E2 51 38N 9 50W
Bear L., Canada 73 B9 55 8N 96 0W
Bear L., U.S.A. 82 F8 41 59N 111 21W
Beardmore, Canada 70 C2 49 36N 87 57W
Beardmore Glacier, Antarctica 5 E11 84 30S 170 0 E
Beardstown, U.S.A. 80 F9 40 1N 90 26W
Bearma →, India 43 G8 24 20N 79 51 E
Béarn, France 18 E3 43 20N 0 30W
Bearpaw Mts., U.S.A. 82 B9 48 12N 109 30W
Bearskin Lake, Canada 70 B1 53 58N 91 2W
Beas →, India 42 D6 31 10N 74 59 E
Beata, C., Dom. Rep. 89 C5 17 40N 71 30W
Beata, I., Dom. Rep. 89 C5 17 34N 71 31W
Beatrice, U.S.A. 80 E6 40 16N 96 45W
Beatrice, Zimbabwe 55 F3 18 15S 30 55 E
Beatrice, C., Australia 62 A2 14 20S 136 55 E
Beatton →, Canada 72 B4 56 15N 120 45W
Beatton River, Canada 72 B4 57 26N 121 20W
Beatty, U.S.A. 84 J10 36 54N 116 46W
Beauce, Plaine de la, France 18 B4 48 10N 1 45 E
Beauceville, Canada 71 C5 46 13N 70 46W
Beaudesert, Australia 63 D5 27 59S 153 0 E
Beaufort, Malaysia 36 C5 5 30N 115 40 E
Beaufort, N.C., U.S.A. 77 H7 34 43N 76 40W
Beaufort, S.C., U.S.A. 77 J5 32 26N 80 40W
Beaufort Sea, Arctic 4 B1 72 0N 140 0W
Beaufort West, S. Africa 56 E3 32 18S 22 36 E
Beauharnois, Canada 79 A11 45 20N 73 52W
Beaulieu →, Canada 72 A6 62 3N 113 11W
Beauly, U.K. 12 D4 57 30N 4 28W
Beauly →, U.K. 12 D4 57 29N 4 27W
Beaumaris, U.K. 10 D3 53 16N 4 6W
Beaumont, Belgium 15 D4 50 15N 4 14 E
Beaumont, U.S.A. 81 K7 30 5N 94 6W
Beaune, France 18 C6 47 2N 4 50 E
Beaupré, Canada 71 C5 47 3N 70 54W
Beauraing, Belgium 15 D4 50 7N 4 57 E
Beauséjour, Canada 73 C9 50 5N 96 35W
Beauvais, France 18 B5 49 25N 2 8 E
Beauval, Canada 73 B7 55 9N 107 37W
Beaver, Okla., U.S.A. 81 G4 36 49N 100 31W
Beaver, Pa., U.S.A. 78 F4 40 42N 80 19W
Beaver, Utah, U.S.A. 83 G7 38 17N 112 38W
Beaver →, B.C., Canada 72 B4 59 52N 124 20W
Beaver →, Ont., Canada 70 A2 55 55N 87 48W
Beaver →, Sask., Canada 73 B7 55 26N 107 45W
Beaver →, U.S.A. 81 G5 36 35N 99 30W
Beaver City, U.S.A. 80 E5 40 8N 99 50W
Beaver Creek, Canada 68 B5 63 0N 141 0W
Beaver Dam, U.S.A. 80 D10 43 28N 88 50W
Beaver Falls, U.S.A. 78 F4 40 46N 80 20W
Beaver Hill L., Canada 73 C10 54 5N 94 50W
Beaver I., U.S.A. 76 C3 45 40N 85 33W
Beaverhill L., Canada 72 C6 53 27N 112 32W
Beaverlodge, Canada 72 B5 55 11N 119 29W
Beaverstone →, Canada 70 B2 54 59N 89 25W
Beaverton, Canada 78 B5 44 26N 79 9W
Beaverton, U.S.A. 84 E4 45 29N 122 48W
Beawar, India 42 F6 26 3N 74 18 E
Bebedouro, Brazil 95 A6 21 0S 48 25W
Beboa, Madag. 57 B7 17 22S 44 33 E
Beccles, U.K. 11 E9 52 27N 1 35 E
Bečej, Serbia, Yug. 21 B9 45 36N 20 3 E
Béchar, Algeria 50 B5 31 38N 2 18W
Beckley, U.S.A. 76 G5 37 47N 81 11W
Beddouza, Ras, Morocco 50 B4 32 33N 9 9W
Bedford, Canada 79 A12 45 7N 72 59W
Bedford, S. Africa 56 E4 32 40S 26 10 E
Bedford, U.K. 11 E7 52 8N 0 28W
Bedford, Ind., U.S.A. 76 F2 38 52N 86 29W
Bedford, Iowa, U.S.A. 80 E7 40 40N 94 44W
Bedford, Ohio, U.S.A. 78 E3 41 23N 81 32W
Bedford, Pa., U.S.A. 78 F6 40 1N 78 30W
Bedford, Va., U.S.A. 76 G6 37 20N 79 31W
Bedford, C., Australia 62 B4 15 14S 145 21 E
Bedfordshire □, U.K. 11 E7 52 4N 0 28W
Bedourie, Australia 62 C2 24 30S 139 30 E
Bedum, Neths. 15 A6 53 18N 6 36 E
Beebe Plain, Canada 79 A12 45 1N 72 9W
Beech Creek, U.S.A. 78 E7 41 5N 77 36W
Beenleigh, Australia 63 D5 27 43S 153 10 E
Be'er Menuḥa, Israel 44 D2 30 19N 35 8 E
Be'er Sheva, Israel 47 D3 31 15N 34 48 E
Beersheba = Be'er Sheva, Israel 47 D3 31 15N 34 48 E
Beestekraal, S. Africa 57 D4 25 23S 27 38 E
Beeston, U.K. 10 E6 52 56N 1 14W
Beeville, U.S.A. 81 L6 28 24N 97 45W
Befale, Dem. Rep. of the Congo 52 D4 0 25N 20 45 E
Befandriana, Mahajanga, Madag. 57 B8 15 16S 48 32 E
Befandriana, Toliara, Madag. 57 C7 21 55S 44 0 E
Befasy, Madag. 57 C7 20 33S 44 23 E
Befotaka, Antsiranana, Madag. 57 A8 13 15S 48 16 E
Befotaka, Fianarantsoa, Madag. 57 C8 23 49S 47 0 E
Begusarai, India 43 G12 25 24N 86 9 E
Behābād, Iran 45 C8 32 24N 59 47 E
Behala, India 43 H13 22 30N 88 20 E
Behara, Madag. 57 C8 24 55S 46 20 E
Behbehān, Iran 45 D6 30 30N 50 15 E
Behm Canal, U.S.A. 72 B2 55 10N 131 0W
Behshahr, Iran 45 B7 36 45N 53 35 E
Bei Jiang →, China 33 D6 23 2N 112 58 E
Bei'an, China 33 B7 48 10N 126 20 E
Beihai, China 33 D5 21 28N 109 6 E
Beijing, China 34 E9 39 55N 116 20 E
Beijing □, China 34 E9 39 55N 116 20 E
Beilen, Neths. 15 B6 52 52N 6 27 E
Beinn na Faoghla = Benbecula, U.K. 12 D1 57 26N 7 21W
Beipiao, China 35 D11 41 52N 120 32 E
Beira, Mozam. 55 F3 19 50S 34 52 E
Beirut = Bayrūt, Lebanon 47 B4 33 53N 35 31 E
Beiseker, Canada 72 C6 51 23N 113 32W
Beitaolaizhao, China 35 B13 44 58N 125 58 E
Beitbridge, Zimbabwe 55 G3 22 12S 30 0 E
Beizhen = Binzhou, China 35 F10 37 20N 118 2 E
Beizhen, China 35 D11 41 38N 121 54 E
Beizhengzhen, China 35 B12 44 31N 123 30 E
Beja, Portugal 19 C2 38 2N 7 53W
Béja, Tunisia 51 A7 36 43N 9 12 E
Bejaïa, Algeria 50 A7 36 42N 5 2 E

Big Bend

Béjar, *Spain* 19 B3 40 23N 5 46W
Bejestān, *Iran* 45 C8 34 30N 58 5 E
Békéscsaba, *Hungary* 17 E11 46 40N 21 5 E
Bekily, *Madag.* 57 C8 24 13S 45 19 E
Bekisopa, *Madag.* 57 C8 21 40S 45 54 E
Bekitro, *Madag.* 57 C8 24 33S 45 18 E
Bekodoka, *Madag.* 57 B8 16 58S 45 7 E
Bekok, *Malaysia* 39 L4 2 20N 103 7 E
Bekopaka, *Madag.* 57 B7 19 9S 44 48 E
Bela, *India* 43 G10 25 50N 82 0 E
Bela, *Pakistan* 42 F2 26 12N 66 20 E
Bela Crkva, *Serbia, Yug.* 21 B9 44 55N 21 27 E
Bela Vista, *Brazil* 94 A4 22 12S 56 20W
Bela Vista, *Mozam.* 57 D5 26 10S 32 44 E
Belan →, *India* 43 G9 24 2N 81 45 E
Belarus ■, *Europe* 17 B14 53 30N 27 0 E
Belau = Palau ■, *Pac. Oc.* 28 J17 7 30N 134 30 E
Belavenona, *Madag.* 57 C8 24 50S 47 4 E
Belawan, *Indonesia* 36 D1 3 33N 98 32 E
Belaya →, *Russia* 24 C9 54 40N 56 0 E
Belaya Tserkov = Bila Tserkva, *Ukraine* 17 D16 49 45N 30 10 E
Belcher Is., *Canada* 70 A3 56 15N 78 45W
Belden, *U.S.A.* 84 E5 40 2N 121 17W
Belebey, *Russia* 24 D9 54 7N 54 7 E
Belém, *Brazil* 93 D9 1 20S 48 30W
Belén, *Argentina* 94 B2 27 40S 67 5W
Belén, *Paraguay* 94 A4 23 30S 57 6W
Belen, *U.S.A.* 83 J10 34 40N 106 46W
Belet Uen, *Somali Rep.* 46 G4 4 30N 45 5 E
Belev, *Russia* 24 D6 53 50N 36 5 E
Belfair, *U.S.A.* 84 C4 47 27N 122 50W
Belfast, *S. Africa* 57 D5 25 42S 30 2 E
Belfast, *U.K.* 13 B6 54 37N 5 56W
Belfast, *Maine, U.S.A.* 77 C11 44 26N 69 1W
Belfast, *N.Y., U.S.A.* 78 D6 42 21N 78 7W
Belfast L., *U.K.* 13 B6 54 40N 5 50W
Belfield, *U.S.A.* 80 B3 46 53N 103 12W
Belfort, *France* 18 C7 47 38N 6 50 E
Belfry, *U.S.A.* 82 D9 45 9N 109 1W
Belgaum, *India* 40 M9 15 55N 74 35 E
Belgium ■, *Europe* 15 D4 50 30N 5 0 E
Belgorod, *Russia* 25 D6 50 35N 36 35 E
Belgorod-Dnestrovskiy = Bilhorod-Dnistrovskyy, *Ukraine* 25 E5 46 11N 30 23 E
Belgrade = Beograd, *Serbia, Yug.* 21 B9 44 50N 20 37 E
Belgrade, *U.S.A.* 82 D8 45 47N 111 11W
Belhaven, *U.S.A.* 77 H7 35 33N 76 37W
Beli Drim →, *Europe* 21 C9 42 6N 20 25 E
Belinyu, *Indonesia* 36 E3 1 35S 105 50 E
Beliton Is. = Belitung, *Indonesia* 36 E3 3 10S 107 50 E
Belitung, *Indonesia* 36 E3 3 10S 107 50 E
Belize ■, *Cent. Amer.* 87 D7 17 0N 88 30W
Belize City, *Belize* 87 D7 17 25N 88 0W
Belkovskiy, Ostrov, *Russia* 27 B14 75 32N 135 44 E
Bell →, *Canada* 70 C4 49 48N 77 38W
Bell I., *Canada* 71 B8 50 46N 55 35W
Bell-Irving →, *Canada* 72 B3 56 12N 129 5W
Bell Peninsula, *Canada* 69 B11 63 50N 82 0W
Bell Ville, *Argentina* 94 C3 32 40S 62 40W
Bella Bella, *Canada* 72 C3 52 10N 128 10W
Bella Coola, *Canada* 72 C3 52 25N 126 40W
Bella Unión, *Uruguay* 94 C4 30 15S 57 40W
Bella Vista, *Corrientes, Argentina* 94 B4 28 33S 59 0W
Bella Vista, *Tucuman, Argentina* 94 B2 27 10S 65 25W
Bellaire, *U.S.A.* 78 F4 40 1N 80 45W
Bellary, *India* 40 M10 15 10N 76 56 E
Bellata, *Australia* 63 D4 29 53S 149 46 E
Belle-Chasse, *U.S.A.* 81 L10 29 51N 89 59W
Belle Fourche, *U.S.A.* 80 C3 44 40N 103 51W
Belle Fourche →, *U.S.A.* 80 C3 44 26N 102 18W
Belle Glade, *U.S.A.* 77 M5 26 41N 80 40W
Belle-Île, *France* 18 C2 47 20N 3 10W
Belle Isle, *Canada* 71 B8 51 57N 55 25W
Belle Isle, Str. of, *Canada* 71 B8 51 30N 56 30W
Belle Plaine, *U.S.A.* 80 E8 41 54N 92 17W
Bellefontaine, *U.S.A.* 76 E4 40 22N 83 46W
Bellefonte, *U.S.A.* 78 F7 40 55N 77 47W
Belleoram, *Canada* 71 C8 47 31N 55 25W
Belleville, *Canada* 78 B7 44 10N 77 23W
Belleville, *Ill., U.S.A.* 80 F10 38 31N 89 59W
Belleville, *Kans., U.S.A.* 80 F6 39 50N 97 38W
Belleville, *N.Y., U.S.A.* 79 C8 43 46N 76 10W
Bellevue, *Canada* 72 D6 49 35N 114 22W
Bellevue, *Idaho, U.S.A.* 82 E6 43 28N 114 16W
Bellevue, *Nebr., U.S.A.* 80 E7 41 8N 95 53W
Bellevue, *Ohio, U.S.A.* 78 E2 41 17N 82 51W
Bellevue, *Wash., U.S.A.* 84 C4 47 37N 122 12W
Bellin = Kangirsuk, *Canada* 69 B13 60 0N 70 0W
Bellingham, *U.S.A.* 68 D7 48 46N 122 29W
Bellingshausen Sea, *Antarctica* 5 C17 66 0S 80 0W
Bellinzona, *Switz.* 18 C8 46 11N 9 1 E
Bello, *Colombia* 92 B3 6 20N 75 33W
Bellows Falls, *U.S.A.* 79 C12 43 8N 72 27W
Bellpat, *Pakistan* 42 E3 29 0N 68 5 E
Belluno, *Italy* 20 A5 46 9N 12 13 E
Bellwood, *U.S.A.* 78 F6 40 36N 78 20W
Belmont, *Canada* 78 D3 42 53N 81 5W
Belmont, *S. Africa* 56 D3 29 28S 24 22 E
Belmont, *U.S.A.* 78 D6 42 14N 78 2W
Belmonte, *Brazil* 93 G11 16 0S 39 0W
Belmopan, *Belize* 87 D7 17 18N 88 30W
Belmullet, *Ireland* 13 B2 54 14N 9 58W
Belo Horizonte, *Brazil* 93 G10 19 55S 43 56W
Belo-sur-Mer, *Madag.* 57 C7 20 42S 44 0 E
Belo-Tsiribihina, *Madag.* 57 B7 19 40S 44 30 E
Belogorsk, *Russia* 27 D13 51 0N 128 20 E
Beloha, *Madag.* 57 D8 25 10S 45 3 E
Beloit, *Kans., U.S.A.* 80 F5 39 28N 98 6W
Beloit, *Wis., U.S.A.* 80 D10 42 31N 89 2W
Belokorovichi, *Ukraine* 17 C15 51 7N 28 2 E
Belomorsk, *Russia* 24 B5 64 35N 34 54 E
Belonia, *India* 41 H17 23 15N 91 30 E
Beloretsk, *Russia* 24 D10 53 58N 58 24 E
Belorussia = Belarus ■, *Europe* 17 B14 53 30N 27 0 E
Belovo, *Russia* 26 D9 54 30N 86 0 E
Beloye, Ozero, *Russia* 24 B6 60 10N 37 35 E
Beloye More, *Russia* 24 A6 66 30N 38 0 E
Belozersk, *Russia* 24 B6 60 1N 37 45 E
Belpre, *U.S.A.* 76 F5 39 17N 81 34W
Belrain, *India* 43 E9 28 23N 80 55 E
Belt, *U.S.A.* 82 C8 47 23N 110 55W
Belterra, *Brazil* 93 D8 2 45S 55 0W
Belton, *U.S.A.* 81 K6 31 3N 97 28W
Belton L., *U.S.A.* 81 K6 31 8N 97 32W
Beltsy = Bălţi, *Moldova* 17 E14 47 48N 27 58 E
Belturbet, *Ireland* 13 B4 54 6N 7 26W
Belukha, *Russia* 26 E9 49 50N 86 50 E
Beluran, *Malaysia* 36 C5 5 48N 117 35 E
Belvidere, *Ill., U.S.A.* 80 D10 42 15N 88 50W
Belvidere, *N.J., U.S.A.* 79 F9 40 50N 75 5W
Belyando →, *Australia* 62 C4 21 38S 146 50 E
Belyy, Ostrov, *Russia* 26 B8 73 30N 71 0 E
Belyy Yar, *Russia* 26 D9 58 26N 84 39 E
Belzoni, *U.S.A.* 81 J9 33 11N 90 29W
Bemaraha, Lembalemban' i, *Madag.* 57 B7 18 40S 44 45 E
Bemarivo, *Madag.* 57 C7 21 45S 44 45 E
Bemarivo →, *Antsiranana, Madag.* 57 A9 14 9S 50 9 E
Bemarivo →, *Mahajanga, Madag.* 57 B8 15 27S 47 40 E
Bemavo, *Madag.* 57 C8 21 33S 45 25 E
Bembéréke, *Benin* 50 F6 10 11N 2 43 E
Bembesi, *Zimbabwe* 55 G2 20 0S 28 58 E
Bembesi →, *Zimbabwe* 55 F2 18 57S 27 47 E
Bemetara, *India* 43 J9 21 42N 81 32 E
Bemidji, *U.S.A.* 80 B7 47 28N 94 53W
Bemolanga, *Madag.* 57 B8 17 44S 45 6 E
Ben, *Iran* 45 C6 32 32N 50 45 E
Ben Cruachan, *U.K.* 12 E3 56 26N 5 8W
Ben Dearg, *U.K.* 12 D4 57 47N 4 56W
Ben Hope, *U.K.* 12 C4 58 25N 4 36W
Ben Lawers, *U.K.* 12 E4 56 32N 4 14W
Ben Lomond, *N.S.W., Australia* 63 E5 30 1S 151 43 E
Ben Lomond, *Tas., Australia* 62 G4 41 38S 147 42 E
Ben Lomond, *U.K.* 12 E4 56 11N 4 38W
Ben Luc, *Vietnam* 39 G6 10 39N 106 29 E
Ben Macdhui, *U.K.* 12 D5 57 4N 3 40W
Ben Mhor, *U.K.* 12 D1 57 15N 7 18W
Ben More, *Arg. & Bute, U.K.* 12 E2 56 26N 6 1W
Ben More, *Stirl., U.K.* 12 E4 56 23N 4 32W
Ben More Assynt, *U.K.* 12 C4 58 8N 4 52W
Ben Nevis, *U.K.* 12 E3 56 48N 5 1W
Ben Quang, *Vietnam* 38 D6 17 3N 106 55 E
Ben Vorlich, *U.K.* 12 E4 56 21N 4 14W
Ben Wyvis, *U.K.* 12 D4 57 40N 4 35W
Bena, *Nigeria* 50 F7 11 20N 5 50 E
Benares = Varanasi, *India* 43 G10 25 22N 83 0 E
Benavente, *Spain* 19 A3 42 2N 5 43W
Benavides, *U.S.A.* 81 M5 27 36N 98 25W
Benbecula, *U.K.* 12 D1 57 26N 7 21W
Bend, *U.S.A.* 82 D3 44 4N 121 19W
Bender Beila, *Somali Rep.* 46 F5 9 30N 50 48 E
Bendery = Tighina, *Moldova* 17 E15 46 50N 29 30 E
Benē Beraq, *Israel* 47 C3 32 6N 34 51 E
Benenitra, *Madag.* 57 C8 23 27S 45 5 E
Benevento, *Italy* 20 D6 41 8N 14 45 E
Benga, *Mozam.* 55 F3 16 11S 33 40 E
Bengal, Bay of, *Ind. Oc.* 41 M17 15 0N 90 0 E
Bengbu, *China* 35 H9 32 58N 117 20 E
Benghazi = Banghāzī, *Libya* 51 B10 32 11N 20 3 E
Bengkalis, *Indonesia* 36 D2 1 30N 102 10 E
Bengkulu, *Indonesia* 36 E2 3 50S 102 12 E
Bengkulu □, *Indonesia* 36 E2 3 48S 102 16 E
Bengough, *Canada* 73 D7 49 25N 105 10W
Benguela, *Angola* 53 G2 12 37S 13 25 E
Benguérua, I., *Mozam.* 57 C6 21 58S 35 28 E
Beni, *Dem. Rep. of the Congo* 54 B2 0 30N 29 27 E
Beni →, *Bolivia* 92 F5 10 23S 65 24W
Beni Mellal, *Morocco* 50 B4 32 21N 6 21W
Beni Suef, *Egypt* 51 C12 29 5N 31 6 E
Beniah L., *Canada* 72 A6 63 23N 112 17W
Benicia, *U.S.A.* 84 G4 38 3N 122 9W
Benidorm, *Spain* 19 C5 38 33N 0 9W
Benin ■, *Africa* 50 G6 10 0N 2 0 E
Benin, Bight of, *W. Afr.* 50 H6 5 0N 3 0 E
Benin City, *Nigeria* 50 G7 6 20N 5 31 E
Benitses, *Greece* 23 A3 39 32N 19 55 E
Benjamin Aceval, *Paraguay* 94 A4 24 58S 57 34W
Benjamin Constant, *Brazil* 92 D4 4 40S 70 15W
Benjamin Hill, *Mexico* 86 A2 30 10N 111 10W
Benkelman, *U.S.A.* 80 E4 40 3N 101 32W
Bennett, *Canada* 72 B2 59 56N 134 53W
Bennett, L., *Australia* 60 D5 22 50S 131 2 E
Bennetta, Ostrov, *Russia* 27 B15 76 21N 148 56 E
Bennettsville, *U.S.A.* 77 H6 34 37N 79 41W
Bennington, *N.H., U.S.A.* 79 D11 43 0N 71 55W
Bennington, *Vt., U.S.A.* 79 D11 42 53N 73 12W
Benoni, *S. Africa* 57 D4 26 11S 28 18 E
Benque Viejo, *Belize* 87 D7 17 5N 89 8W
Benson, *Ariz., U.S.A.* 83 L8 31 58N 110 18W
Benson, *Minn., U.S.A.* 80 C7 45 19N 95 36W
Bent, *Iran* 45 E8 26 20N 59 31 E
Benteng, *Indonesia* 37 F6 6 10S 120 30 E
Bentinck I., *Australia* 62 B2 17 3S 139 35 E
Bento Gonçalves, *Brazil* 95 B5 29 10S 51 31W
Benton, *Ark., U.S.A.* 81 H8 34 34N 92 35W
Benton, *Calif., U.S.A.* 84 H8 37 48N 118 32W
Benton, *Ill., U.S.A.* 80 G10 38 0N 88 55W
Benton, *Pa., U.S.A.* 79 E8 41 12N 76 23W
Benton Harbor, *U.S.A.* 76 D2 42 6N 86 27W
Bentonville, *U.S.A.* 81 G7 36 22N 94 13W
Bentung, *Malaysia* 39 L3 3 31N 101 55 E
Benue →, *Nigeria* 50 G7 7 48N 6 46 E
Benxi, *China* 35 D12 41 20N 123 48 E
Beo, *Indonesia* 37 D7 4 25N 126 50 E
Beograd, *Serbia, Yug.* 21 B9 44 50N 20 37 E
Beppu, *Japan* 31 H5 33 15N 131 30 E
Beqaa Valley = Al Biqā, *Lebanon* 47 A5 34 10N 36 10 E
Ber Mota, *India* 42 H3 23 27N 68 34 E
Berach →, *India* 42 G6 25 15N 75 2 E
Beraketa, *Madag.* 57 C7 23 7S 44 25 E
Berat, *Albania* 21 D8 40 43N 19 59 E
Berau, Teluk, *Indonesia* 37 E8 2 30S 132 30 E
Beravina, *Madag.* 57 B8 18 10S 45 14 E
Berber, *Sudan* 51 E12 18 0N 34 0 E
Berbera, *Somali Rep.* 46 E4 10 30N 45 2 E
Berbérati, *C.A.R.* 52 D3 4 15N 15 40 E
Berbice →, *Guyana* 92 B7 6 20N 57 32W
Berdichev = Berdychiv, *Ukraine* 17 D15 49 57N 28 30 E
Berdsk, *Russia* 26 D9 54 47N 83 2 E
Berdyansk, *Ukraine* 25 E6 46 45N 36 50 E
Berdychiv, *Ukraine* 17 D15 49 57N 28 30 E
Berea, *U.S.A.* 76 G3 37 34N 84 17W
Berebere, *Indonesia* 37 D7 2 25N 128 45 E
Bereda, *Somali Rep.* 46 E5 11 45N 51 0 E
Berehove, *Ukraine* 17 D12 48 15N 22 35 E
Berekum, *Ghana* 50 G5 7 29N 2 34W
Berens →, *Canada* 73 C9 52 25N 97 2W
Berens I., *Canada* 73 C9 52 18N 97 18W
Berens River, *Canada* 73 C9 52 25N 97 0W
Beresford, *U.S.A.* 80 D6 43 5N 96 47W
Berestechko, *Ukraine* 17 C13 50 22N 25 5 E
Berevo, *Mahajanga, Madag.* 57 B7 17 14S 44 17 E
Berevo, *Toliara, Madag.* 57 B7 19 44S 44 58 E
Bereza = Byaroza, *Belarus* 17 B13 52 31N 24 51 E
Berezhany, *Ukraine* 17 D13 49 26N 24 58 E
Berezina = Byarezina →, *Belarus* 17 B16 52 33N 30 14 E
Berezniki, *Russia* 24 B7 62 51N 42 40 E
Berezniki, *Russia* 24 C10 59 24N 56 46 E
Berezovo, *Russia* 26 C7 64 0N 65 0 E
Berga, *Spain* 19 A6 42 6N 1 48 E
Bergama, *Turkey* 21 E12 39 8N 27 11 E
Bérgamo, *Italy* 18 D8 45 41N 9 43 E
Bergen, *Neths.* 15 B4 52 40N 4 43 E
Bergen, *Norway* 9 F11 60 20N 5 20 E
Bergen, *U.S.A.* 78 C7 43 5N 77 57W
Bergen op Zoom, *Neths.* 15 C4 51 28N 4 18 E
Bergerac, *France* 18 D4 44 51N 0 30 E
Bergholz, *U.S.A.* 78 F4 40 31N 80 53W
Bergisch Gladbach, *Germany* 15 D7 50 59N 7 8 E
Bergville, *S. Africa* 57 D4 28 52S 29 18 E
Berhala, Selat, *Indonesia* 36 E2 1 0S 104 15 E
Berhampore = Baharampur, *India* 43 G13 24 2N 88 27 E
Berhampur = Brahmapur, *India* 41 K14 19 15N 84 54 E
Bering Sea, *Pac. Oc.* 68 C1 58 0N 171 0 E
Bering Strait, *Pac. Oc.* 68 B3 65 30N 169 0W
Beringovskiy, *Russia* 27 C18 63 3N 179 19 E
Berisso, *Argentina* 94 C4 34 56S 57 50W
Berja, *Spain* 19 D4 36 50N 2 56W
Berkeley, *U.S.A.* 84 H4 37 52N 122 16W
Berkner I., *Antarctica* 5 D18 79 30S 50 0W
Berkshire, *U.S.A.* 79 D8 42 19N 76 11W
Berkshire Downs, *U.K.* 11 F6 51 33N 1 29W
Berlin, *Germany* 16 B7 52 30N 13 25 E
Berlin, *Md., U.S.A.* 76 F8 38 20N 75 13W
Berlin, *N.H., U.S.A.* 79 B13 44 28N 71 11W
Berlin, *N.Y., U.S.A.* 79 D11 42 42N 73 23W
Berlin, *Wis., U.S.A.* 76 D1 43 58N 88 57W
Berlin L., *U.S.A.* 78 E4 41 3N 81 0W
Bermejo →, *Formosa, Argentina* 94 B4 26 51S 58 23W
Bermejo →, *San Juan, Argentina* 94 C2 32 30S 67 30W
Bermen, L., *Canada* 71 B6 53 35N 68 55W
Bermuda ■, *Atl. Oc.* 66 F13 32 45N 65 0W
Bern, *Switz.* 18 C7 46 57N 7 28 E
Bernalillo, *U.S.A.* 83 J10 35 18N 106 33W
Bernardo de Irigoyen, *Argentina* 95 B5 26 15S 53 40W
Bernardo O'Higgins □, *Chile* 94 C1 34 15S 70 45W
Bernardsville, *U.S.A.* 79 F10 40 43N 74 34W
Bernasconi, *Argentina* 94 D3 37 55S 63 44W
Bernburg, *Germany* 16 C6 51 47N 11 44 E
Berne = Bern, *Switz.* 18 C7 46 57N 7 28 E
Berneray, *U.K.* 12 D1 57 43N 7 11W
Bernier I., *Australia* 61 D1 24 50S 113 12 E
Bernina, Piz, *Switz.* 18 C8 46 20N 9 54 E
Beroroha, *Madag.* 57 C8 21 40S 45 10 E
Beroun, *Czech Rep.* 16 D8 49 57N 14 5 E
Berriane, *Algeria* 50 B6 32 50N 3 46 E
Berry, *France* 18 C5 46 50N 2 0 E
Berry Is., *Bahamas* 88 A4 25 40N 77 50W
Berryessa L., *U.S.A.* 84 G4 38 31N 122 6W
Berryville, *U.S.A.* 81 G8 36 22N 93 34W
Berseba, *Namibia* 56 D2 26 0S 17 46 E
Bershad, *Ukraine* 17 D15 48 22N 29 31 E
Berthold, *U.S.A.* 80 A4 48 19N 101 44W
Berthoud, *U.S.A.* 80 E2 40 19N 105 5W
Bertoua, *Cameroon* 52 D2 4 30N 13 45 E
Bertraghboy B., *Ireland* 13 C2 53 22N 9 54W
Berwick, *U.S.A.* 79 E8 41 3N 76 14W
Berwick-upon-Tweed, *U.K.* 10 B6 55 46N 2 0W
Berwyn Mts., *U.K.* 10 E4 52 54N 3 26W
Besal, *Pakistan* 43 B5 35 4N 73 56 E
Besalampy, *Madag.* 57 B7 16 43S 44 29 E
Besançon, *France* 18 C7 47 15N 6 2 E
Besar, *Indonesia* 36 E5 2 40S 116 0 E
Besnard L., *Canada* 73 B7 55 25N 106 0W
Besni, *Turkey* 44 B3 37 41N 37 52 E
Besor, N. →, *Egypt* 47 D3 31 28N 34 22 E
Bessarabiya, *Moldova* 17 E15 47 0N 28 10 E
Bessarabka = Basarabeasca, *Moldova* 17 E15 46 21N 28 58 E
Bessemer, *Ala., U.S.A.* 77 J2 33 24N 86 58W
Bessemer, *Mich., U.S.A.* 80 B9 46 29N 90 3W
Bessemer, *Pa., U.S.A.* 78 F4 40 59N 80 30W
Beswick, *Australia* 60 B5 14 34S 132 53 E
Bet She'an, *Israel* 47 C4 32 30N 35 30 E
Bet Shemesh, *Israel* 47 D4 31 44N 35 0 E
Betafo, *Madag.* 57 B8 19 50S 46 51 E
Betancuria, *Canary Is.* 22 F5 28 25N 14 3W
Betanzos, *Spain* 19 A1 43 15N 8 12W
Bétaré Oya, *Cameroon* 52 C2 5 40N 14 5 E
Betatao, *Madag.* 57 B8 18 11S 47 52 E
Bethal, *S. Africa* 57 D4 26 27S 29 28 E
Bethanien, *Namibia* 56 D2 26 31S 17 8 E
Bethany, *Canada* 78 B6 44 11N 78 34W
Bethany, *U.S.A.* 80 E7 40 16N 94 2W
Bethel, *Alaska, U.S.A.* 68 B3 60 48N 161 45W
Bethel, *Conn., U.S.A.* 79 E11 41 22N 73 25W
Bethel, *Maine, U.S.A.* 79 B14 44 25N 70 47W
Bethel, *Vt., U.S.A.* 79 C12 43 50N 72 38W
Bethel Park, *U.S.A.* 78 F4 40 20N 80 1W
Bethlehem = Bayt Lahm, *West Bank* 47 D4 31 43N 35 12 E
Bethlehem, *S. Africa* 57 D4 28 14S 28 18 E
Bethlehem, *U.S.A.* 79 F9 40 37N 75 23W
Bethulie, *S. Africa* 56 E4 30 30S 25 59 E
Béthune, *France* 18 A5 50 30N 2 38 E
Betioky, *Madag.* 57 C7 23 48S 44 20 E
Betong, *Thailand* 39 K3 5 45N 101 5 E
Betoota, *Australia* 62 D3 25 45S 140 42 E
Betroka, *Madag.* 57 C8 23 16S 46 0 E
Betsiamites, *Canada* 71 C6 48 56N 68 40W
Betsiamites →, *Canada* 71 C6 48 56N 68 38W
Betsiboka →, *Madag.* 57 B8 16 3S 46 36 E
Bettendorf, *U.S.A.* 80 E9 41 32N 90 30W
Bettiah, *India* 43 F11 26 48N 84 33 E
Betul, *India* 40 J10 21 58N 77 59 E
Betung, *Malaysia* 36 D4 1 24N 111 31 E
Betws-y-Coed, *U.K.* 10 D4 53 5N 3 48W
Beulah, *Mich., U.S.A.* 76 C2 44 38N 86 6W
Beulah, *N. Dak., U.S.A.* 80 B4 47 16N 101 47W
Beveren, *Belgium* 15 C4 51 12N 4 16 E
Beverley, *Australia* 61 F2 32 9S 116 56 E
Beverley, *U.K.* 10 D7 53 51N 0 26W
Beverley Hills, *U.S.A.* 77 L4 28 56N 82 28W
Beverly, *U.S.A.* 79 D14 42 33N 70 53W
Beverly Hills, *U.S.A.* 85 L8 34 4N 118 25W
Bevoalavo, *Madag.* 57 D7 25 13S 45 26 E
Bewas →, *India* 43 H8 23 59N 79 21 E
Bexhill, *U.K.* 11 G8 50 51N 0 29 E
Beyānlū, *Iran* 44 C5 36 0N 47 51 E
Beyneu, *Kazakstan* 25 E10 45 18N 55 9 E
Beypazarı, *Turkey* 25 F5 40 10N 31 56 E
Beyşehir Gölü, *Turkey* 25 G5 37 41N 31 33 E
Béziers, *France* 18 E5 43 20N 3 12 E
Bezwada = Vijayawada, *India* 41 L12 16 31N 80 39 E
Bhabua, *India* 43 G10 25 3N 83 37 E
Bhachau, *India* 40 H7 23 20N 70 16 E
Bhadar →, *Gujarat, India* 42 H5 22 17N 72 20 E
Bhadar →, *Gujarat, India* 42 J3 21 27N 69 47 E
Bhadarwah, *India* 43 C6 32 58N 75 46 E
Bhadohi, *India* 43 G10 25 25N 82 34 E
Bhadra, *India* 42 E6 29 8N 75 14 E
Bhadrakh, *India* 41 J15 21 10N 86 30 E
Bhadran, *India* 42 H5 22 19N 72 6 E
Bhadravati, *India* 40 N9 13 49N 75 40 E
Bhag, *Pakistan* 42 E2 29 2N 67 49 E
Bhagalpur, *India* 43 G12 25 10N 87 0 E
Bhagirathi →, *Ut. P., India* 43 D8 30 8N 78 35 E
Bhagirathi →, *W. Bengal, India* 43 H13 23 25N 88 23 E
Bhakkar, *Pakistan* 42 D4 31 40N 71 5 E
Bhakra Dam, *India* 42 D7 31 30N 76 45 E
Bhamo, *Burma* 41 G20 24 15N 97 15 E
Bhandara, *India* 40 J11 21 5N 79 42 E
Bhanpura, *India* 42 G6 24 31N 75 44 E
Bhanrer Ra., *India* 43 H8 23 40N 79 45 E
Bhaptiahi, *India* 43 F12 26 19N 86 44 E
Bharat = India ■, *Asia* 40 K11 20 0N 78 0 E
Bharatpur, *Mad. P., India* 43 H9 23 44N 81 46 E
Bharatpur, *Raj., India* 42 F7 27 15N 77 30 E
Bharno, *India* 43 H11 23 14N 84 53 E
Bhatinda, *India* 42 D6 30 15N 74 57 E
Bhatpara, *India* 43 H13 22 50N 88 25 E
Bhattu, *India* 42 E6 29 36N 75 19 E
Bhaun, *Pakistan* 42 C5 32 55N 72 40 E
Bhaunagar = Bhavnagar, *India* 40 J8 21 45N 72 10 E
Bhavnagar, *India* 40 J8 21 45N 72 10 E
Bhawari, *India* 42 G5 25 42N 73 4 E
Bhayavadar, *India* 42 J4 21 51N 70 15 E
Bhera, *Pakistan* 42 C5 32 29N 72 57 E
Bhikangaon, *India* 42 J6 21 52N 75 57 E
Bhilsa = Vidisha, *India* 42 H7 23 28N 77 53 E
Bhilwara, *India* 42 G6 25 25N 74 38 E
Bhima →, *India* 40 L10 16 25N 77 17 E
Bhimbar, *Pakistan* 43 C6 32 59N 74 3 E
Bhind, *India* 43 F8 26 30N 78 46 E
Bhinga, *India* 43 F9 27 43N 81 56 E
Bhinmal, *India* 42 G5 25 0N 72 15 E
Bhiwandi, *India* 40 K8 19 20N 73 0 E
Bhiwani, *India* 42 E7 28 50N 76 9 E
Bhogava →, *India* 42 H5 22 26N 72 20 E
Bhola, *Bangla.* 41 H17 22 45N 90 35 E
Bholari, *Pakistan* 42 G3 25 19N 68 13 E
Bhopal, *India* 42 H7 23 20N 77 30 E
Bhubaneshwar, *India* 41 J14 20 15N 85 50 E
Bhuj, *India* 42 H3 23 15N 69 49 E
Bhusaval, *India* 40 J9 21 3N 75 46 E
Bhutan ■, *Asia* 41 F17 27 25N 90 30 E
Biafra, B. of = Bonny, Bight of, *Africa* 52 D1 3 30N 9 20 E
Biak, *Indonesia* 37 E9 1 10S 136 6 E
Biała Podlaska, *Poland* 17 B12 52 4N 23 6 E
Białogard, *Poland* 16 A8 54 2N 15 58 E
Białystok, *Poland* 17 B12 53 10N 23 10 E
Biaora, *India* 42 H7 23 56N 76 56 E
Bīārjmand, *Iran* 45 B7 36 6N 55 53 E
Biaro, *Indonesia* 37 D7 2 5N 125 26 E
Biarritz, *France* 18 E3 43 29N 1 33W
Bibai, *Japan* 30 C10 43 19N 141 52 E
Bibby I., *Canada* 73 A10 61 55N 93 0W
Biberach, *Germany* 16 D5 48 5N 9 47 E
Bibungwa, *Dem. Rep. of the Congo* 54 C2 2 40S 28 15 E
Bic, *Canada* 71 C6 48 20N 68 41W
Bicester, *U.K.* 11 F6 51 54N 1 9W
Bicheno, *Australia* 62 G4 41 52S 148 18 E
Bichia, *India* 43 H9 22 27N 80 42 E
Bickerton I., *Australia* 62 A2 13 45S 136 10 E
Bida, *Nigeria* 50 G7 9 3N 5 58 E
Bidar, *India* 40 L10 17 55N 77 35 E
Biddeford, *U.S.A.* 77 D10 43 30N 70 28W
Bideford, *U.K.* 11 F3 51 1N 4 13W
Bideford Bay, *U.K.* 11 F3 51 5N 4 20W
Bidhuna, *India* 43 F8 26 49N 79 31 E
Bidor, *Malaysia* 39 K3 4 6N 101 15 E
Bié, Planalto de, *Angola* 53 G3 12 0S 16 0 E
Bieber, *U.S.A.* 82 F3 41 7N 121 8W
Biel, *Switz.* 18 C7 47 8N 7 14 E
Bielefeld, *Germany* 16 B5 52 1N 8 33 E
Biella, *Italy* 18 D8 45 34N 8 3 E
Bielsk Podlaski, *Poland* 17 B12 52 47N 23 12 E
Bielsko-Biała, *Poland* 17 D10 49 50N 19 2 E
Bien Hoa, *Vietnam* 39 G6 10 57N 106 49 E
Bienne = Biel, *Switz.* 18 C7 47 8N 7 14 E
Bienville, L., *Canada* 70 A5 55 5N 72 40W
Biesiesfontein, *S. Africa* 56 E2 30 57S 17 58 E
Big →, *Canada* 71 B8 54 50N 58 55W
Big B., *Canada* 71 A7 55 43N 60 35W
Big Bear City, *U.S.A.* 85 L10 34 16N 116 51W
Big Bear Lake, *U.S.A.* 85 L10 34 15N 116 56W
Big Belt Mts., *U.S.A.* 82 C8 46 30N 111 25W
Big Bend, *Swaziland* 57 D5 26 50S 31 58 E

Big Bend National Park

Big Bend National Park, *U.S.A.* **81 L3** 29 20N 103 5W
Big Black →, *U.S.A.* **81 K9** 32 3N 91 4W
Big Blue →, *U.S.A.* **80 F6** 39 35N 96 34W
Big Creek, *U.S.A.* **84 H7** 37 11N 119 14W
Big Cypress National Preserve, *U.S.A.* **77 M5** 26 0N 81 10W
Big Cypress Swamp, *U.S.A.* **77 M5** 26 12N 81 10W
Big Falls, *U.S.A.* **80 A8** 48 12N 93 48W
Big Fork →, *U.S.A.* **80 A8** 48 31N 93 43W
Big Horn Mts. = Bighorn Mts., *U.S.A.* **82 D10** 44 30N 107 30W
Big I., *Canada* **72 A5** 61 7N 116 45W
Big Lake, *U.S.A.* **81 K4** 31 12N 101 28W
Big Moose, *U.S.A.* **79 C10** 43 49N 74 58W
Big Muddy Cr. →, *U.S.A.* **80 A2** 48 8N 104 36W
Big Pine, *U.S.A.* **84 H8** 37 10N 118 17W
Big Piney, *U.S.A.* **82 E8** 42 32N 110 7W
Big Rapids, *U.S.A.* **76 D3** 43 42N 85 29W
Big Rideau L., *Canada* **79 B8** 44 40N 76 15W
Big River, *Canada* **73 C7** 53 50N 107 0W
Big Run, *U.S.A.* **78 F6** 40 57N 78 55W
Big Sable Pt., *U.S.A.* **76 C2** 44 3N 86 1W
Big Salmon →, *Canada* **72 A2** 61 52N 134 55W
Big Sand L., *Canada* **73 B9** 57 45N 99 45W
Big Sandy, *U.S.A.* **82 B8** 48 11N 110 7W
Big Sandy →, *U.S.A.* **76 F4** 38 25N 82 36W
Big Sandy Cr. →, *U.S.A.* **80 F3** 38 7N 102 29W
Big Sioux →, *U.S.A.* **80 D6** 42 29N 96 27W
Big Spring, *U.S.A.* **81 J4** 32 15N 101 28W
Big Stone City, *U.S.A.* **80 C6** 45 18N 96 28W
Big Stone Gap, *U.S.A.* **77 G4** 36 52N 82 47W
Big Stone L., *U.S.A.* **80 C6** 45 30N 96 35W
Big Sur, *U.S.A.* **84 J5** 36 15N 121 48W
Big Timber, *U.S.A.* **82 D9** 45 50N 109 57W
Big Trout L., *Canada* **70 B2** 53 40N 90 0W
Big Trout Lake, *Canada* **70 B2** 53 45N 90 0W
Biğa, *Turkey* **21 D12** 40 13N 27 14 E
Bigadiç, *Turkey* **21 E13** 39 22N 28 7 E
Biggar, *Canada* **73 C7** 52 4N 108 0W
Biggar, *U.K.* **12 F5** 55 38N 3 32W
Bigge I., *Australia* **60 B4** 14 35S 125 10 E
Biggenden, *Australia* **63 D5** 25 31S 152 4 E
Biggleswade, *U.K.* **11 E7** 52 5N 0 14W
Biggs, *U.S.A.* **84 F5** 39 25N 121 43W
Bighorn, *U.S.A.* **82 C10** 46 10N 107 27W
Bighorn →, *U.S.A.* **82 C10** 46 10N 107 28W
Bighorn L., *U.S.A.* **82 D9** 44 55N 108 15W
Bighorn Mts., *U.S.A.* **82 D10** 44 30N 107 30W
Bigstone L., *Canada* **73 C9** 53 42N 95 44W
Bigwa, *Tanzania* **54 D4** 7 10S 39 10 E
Bihać, *Bos.-H.* **16 F8** 44 49N 15 57 E
Bihar, *India* **43 G11** 25 5N 85 40 E
Bihar □, *India* **43 G12** 25 0N 86 0 E
Biharamulo, *Tanzania* **54 C3** 2 25S 31 25 E
Bihariganj, *India* **43 G12** 25 44N 86 59 E
Bihor, Munţii, *Romania* **17 E12** 46 29N 22 47 E
Bijagós, Arquipélago dos, *Guinea-Biss.* **50 F2** 11 15N 16 10W
Bijaipur, *India* **42 F7** 26 2N 77 20 E
Bijapur, *Karnataka, India* **40 L9** 16 50N 75 55 E
Bijapur, *Mad. P., India* **41 K12** 18 50N 80 50 E
Bījār, *Iran* **44 C5** 35 52N 47 35 E
Bijawar, *India* **43 G8** 24 38N 79 30 E
Bijeljina, *Bos.-H.* **21 B8** 44 46N 19 14 E
Bijnor, *India* **42 E8** 29 27N 78 11 E
Bikaner, *India* **42 E5** 28 2N 73 18 E
Bikapur, *India* **43 F10** 26 30N 82 7 E
Bikeqi, *China* **34 D6** 40 43N 111 20 E
Bikfayyā, *Lebanon* **47 B4** 33 55N 35 41 E
Bikin, *Russia* **27 E14** 46 50N 134 20 E
Bikin →, *Russia* **30 A7** 46 51N 134 2 E
Bikini Atoll, *Marshall Is.* **64 F8** 12 0N 167 30 E
Bikita, *Zimbabwe* **57 C5** 20 6S 31 41 E
Bila Tserkva, *Ukraine* **17 D16** 49 45N 30 10 E
Bilara, *India* **42 F5** 26 14N 73 53 E
Bilaspur, *Mad. P., India* **43 H10** 22 2N 82 15 E
Bilaspur, *Punjab, India* **42 D7** 31 19N 76 50 E
Bilauk Taungdan, *Thailand* **38 F2** 13 0N 99 0 E
Bilbao, *Spain* **19 A4** 43 16N 2 56W
Bilbo = Bilbao, *Spain* **19 A4** 43 16N 2 56W
Bíldudalur, *Iceland* **8 D2** 65 41N 23 36W
Bílé Karpaty, *Europe* **17 D9** 49 5N 18 0 E
Bilecik, *Turkey* **25 F5** 40 5N 30 5 E
Bilgram, *India* **43 F9** 27 11N 80 2 E
Bilhaur, *India* **43 F9** 26 51N 80 5 E
Bilhorod-Dnistrovskyy, *Ukraine* **25 E5** 46 11N 30 23 E
Bilibino, *Russia* **27 C17** 68 3N 166 20 E
Bilibiza, *Mozam.* **55 E5** 12 30S 40 20 E
Billabalong Roadhouse, *Australia* **61 E2** 27 25S 115 49 E
Billiluna, *Australia* **60 C4** 19 37S 127 41 E
Billings, *U.S.A.* **82 D9** 45 47N 108 30W
Billiton Is. = Belitung, *Indonesia* **36 E3** 3 10S 107 50 E
Bilma, *Niger* **51 E8** 18 50N 13 30 E
Biloela, *Australia* **62 C5** 24 24S 150 31 E
Biloxi, *U.S.A.* **81 K10** 30 24N 88 53W
Bilpa Morea Claypan, *Australia* **62 D3** 25 0S 140 0 E
Biltine, *Chad* **51 F10** 14 40N 20 50 E
Bima, *Indonesia* **37 F5** 8 22S 118 49 E
Bimini Is., *Bahamas* **88 A4** 25 42N 79 25W
Bin Xian, *Heilongjiang, China* **35 B14** 45 42N 127 32 E
Bin Xian, *Shaanxi, China* **34 G5** 35 2N 108 4 E
Bina-Etawah, *India* **42 G8** 24 13N 78 14 E
Bināb, *Iran* **45 B6** 36 35N 48 41 E
Binalbagan, *Phil.* **37 B6** 10 12N 122 50 E
Binālūd, Kūh-e, *Iran* **45 B8** 36 30N 58 30 E
Binatang = Bintangor, *Malaysia* **36 D4** 2 10N 111 40 E
Binche, *Belgium* **15 D4** 50 26N 4 10 E
Bindki, *India* **43 F9** 26 2N 80 36 E
Bindura, *Zimbabwe* **55 F3** 17 18S 31 18 E
Bingara, *Australia* **63 D5** 29 52S 150 36 E
Bingham, *U.S.A.* **77 C11** 45 3N 69 53W
Binghamton, *U.S.A.* **79 D9** 42 6N 75 55W
Bingöl, *Turkey* **44 B4** 38 53N 40 29 E
Binh Dinh = An Nhon, *Vietnam* **38 F7** 13 55N 109 7 E
Binh Khe, *Vietnam* **38 F7** 13 57N 108 51 E
Binh Son, *Vietnam* **38 E7** 15 20N 108 40 E
Binhai, *China* **35 G10** 34 2N 119 49 E
Binisatua, *Spain* **22 B11** 39 50N 4 11 E
Binjai, *Indonesia* **36 D3** 3 20N 98 30 E
Binongko, *Indonesia* **37 F6** 5 57S 124 2 E
Binscarth, *Canada* **73 C8** 50 37N 101 17W
Bintan, *Indonesia* **36 D2** 1 0N 104 0 E
Bintangor, *Malaysia* **36 D4** 2 10N 111 40 E
Bintulu, *Malaysia* **36 D4** 3 10N 113 0 E
Bintuni, *Indonesia* **37 E8** 2 7S 133 32 E
Binzert = Bizerte, *Tunisia* **51 A7** 37 15N 9 50 E
Binzhou, *China* **35 F10** 37 20N 118 2 E
Bío Bío □, *Chile* **94 D1** 37 35S 72 0W
Bioko, *Eq. Guin.* **52 D1** 3 30N 8 40 E
Bir, *India* **40 K9** 19 4N 75 46 E
Bîr Abu Muḥammad, *Egypt* **47 F3** 29 44N 34 14 E
Bi'r ad Dabbāghāt, *Jordan* **47 E4** 30 26N 35 32 E
Bi'r al Butayyihāt, *Jordan* **47 F4** 29 47N 35 20 E
Bi'r al Mārī, *Jordan* **47 E4** 30 4N 35 33 E
Bi'r al Qattār, *Jordan* **47 F4** 29 47N 35 32 E
Bir Atrun, *Sudan* **51 E11** 18 15N 26 40 E
Bîr Beida, *Egypt* **47 E3** 30 25N 34 29 E
Bîr el 'Abd, *Egypt* **47 D2** 31 2N 33 0 E
Bîr el Biarât, *Egypt* **47 F3** 29 30N 34 43 E
Bîr el Duweidar, *Egypt* **47 E1** 30 56N 32 32 E
Bîr el Garârât, *Egypt* **47 D2** 31 3N 33 34 E
Bîr el Heisi, *Egypt* **47 F3** 29 22N 34 36 E
Bîr el Jafir, *Egypt* **47 E1** 30 50N 32 41 E
Bîr el Mâlḥi, *Egypt* **47 E2** 30 38N 33 19 E
Bîr el Thamâda, *Egypt* **47 E2** 30 12N 33 27 E
Bîr Gebeil Ḥiṣn, *Egypt* **47 E2** 30 2N 33 18 E
Bi'r Ghadīr, *Syria* **47 A6** 34 6N 37 3 E
Bîr Ḥasana, *Egypt* **47 E2** 30 29N 33 46 E
Bîr Kaseiba, *Egypt* **47 E2** 31 0N 33 17 E
Bîr Lahfân, *Egypt* **47 E2** 31 0N 33 51 E
Bîr Madkûr, *Egypt* **47 E1** 30 44N 32 33 E
Bîr Mogreïn, *Mauritania* **50 C3** 25 10N 11 25W
Bi'r Muṭribah, *Kuwait* **44 D5** 29 54N 47 17 E
Bîr Qaṭia, *Egypt* **47 E1** 30 58N 32 45 E
Bîr Shalatein, *Egypt* **51 D13** 23 5N 35 25 E
Biratnagar, *Nepal* **43 F12** 26 27N 87 17 E
Birawa, *Dem. Rep. of the Congo* **54 C2** 2 20S 28 48 E
Birch →, *Canada* **72 B6** 58 28N 112 17W
Birch Hills, *Canada* **73 C7** 52 59N 105 25W
Birch I., *Canada* **73 C9** 52 26N 99 54W
Birch L., *N.W.T., Canada* **72 A5** 62 4N 116 33W
Birch L., *Ont., Canada* **70 B1** 51 23N 92 18W
Birch Mts., *Canada* **72 B6** 57 30N 113 10W
Birch River, *Canada* **73 C8** 52 24N 101 6W
Bird, *Canada* **73 B10** 56 30N 94 13W
Bird I. = Las Aves, Is., *W. Indies* **89 C7** 15 45N 63 55W
Birdsville, *Australia* **62 D2** 25 51S 139 20 E
Birdum Cr. →, *Australia* **60 C5** 15 14S 133 0 E
Birecik, *Turkey* **44 B3** 37 2N 38 0 E
Birein, *Israel* **47 E3** 30 50N 34 28 E
Bireuen, *Indonesia* **36 C1** 5 14N 96 39 E
Birigui, *Brazil* **95 A5** 21 18S 50 16W
Birjand, *Iran* **45 C8** 32 53N 59 13 E
Birkenhead, *U.K.* **10 D4** 53 23N 3 2W
Bîrlad = Bârlad, *Romania* **17 E14** 46 15N 27 38 E
Birmingham, *U.K.* **11 E6** 52 29N 1 52W
Birmingham, *U.S.A.* **77 J2** 33 31N 86 48W
Birmitrapur, *India* **41 H14** 22 24N 84 46 E
Birni Nkonni, *Niger* **50 F7** 13 55N 5 15 E
Birnin Kebbi, *Nigeria* **50 F6** 12 32N 4 12 E
Birobidzhan, *Russia* **27 E14** 48 50N 132 50 E
Birr, *Ireland* **13 C4** 53 6N 7 54W
Birrie →, *Australia* **63 D4** 29 43S 146 37 E
Birsilpur, *India* **42 E5** 28 11N 72 15 E
Birsk, *Russia* **24 C10** 55 25N 55 30 E
Birtle, *Canada* **73 C8** 50 30N 101 5W
Birur, *India* **40 N9** 13 30N 75 55 E
Biržai, *Lithuania* **9 H21** 56 11N 24 45 E
Birzebbugga, *Malta* **23 D2** 35 49N 14 32 E
Bisa, *Indonesia* **37 E7** 1 15S 127 28 E
Bisalpur, *India* **43 E8** 28 14N 79 48 E
Bisbee, *U.S.A.* **83 L9** 31 27N 109 55W
Biscay, B. of, *Atl. Oc.* **18 D1** 45 0N 2 0W
Biscayne B., *U.S.A.* **77 N5** 25 40N 80 12W
Biscoe Bay, *Antarctica* **5 D13** 77 0S 152 0W
Biscoe Is., *Antarctica* **5 C17** 66 0S 67 0W
Biscostasing, *Canada* **70 C3** 47 18N 82 9W
Bishkek, *Kyrgyzstan* **26 E8** 42 54N 74 46 E
Bishnupur, *India* **43 H12** 23 8N 87 20 E
Bisho, *S. Africa* **57 E4** 32 50S 27 23 E
Bishop, *Calif., U.S.A.* **84 H8** 37 22N 118 24W
Bishop, *Tex., U.S.A.* **81 M6** 27 35N 97 48W
Bishop Auckland, *U.K.* **10 C6** 54 39N 1 40W
Bishop's Falls, *Canada* **71 C8** 49 2N 55 30W
Bishop's Stortford, *U.K.* **11 F8** 51 52N 0 10 E
Bisina, L., *Uganda* **54 B3** 1 38N 33 56 E
Biskra, *Algeria* **50 B7** 34 50N 5 44 E
Bismarck, *U.S.A.* **80 B4** 46 48N 100 47W
Bismarck Arch., *Papua N. G.* **64 H7** 2 30S 150 0 E
Biso, *Uganda* **54 B3** 1 44N 31 26 E
Bison, *U.S.A.* **80 C3** 45 31N 102 28W
Bīsotūn, *Iran* **44 C5** 34 23N 47 26 E
Bissagos = Bijagós, Arquipélago dos, *Guinea-Biss.* **50 F2** 11 15N 16 10W
Bissau, *Guinea-Biss.* **50 F2** 11 45N 15 45W
Bistcho L., *Canada* **72 B5** 59 45N 118 50W
Bistriţa, *Romania* **17 E13** 47 9N 24 35 E
Bistriţa →, *Romania* **17 E14** 46 30N 26 57 E
Biswan, *India* **43 F9** 27 29N 81 2 E
Bitlis, *Turkey* **44 B4** 38 20N 42 3 E
Bitola, *Macedonia* **21 D9** 41 1N 21 20 E
Bitolj = Bitola, *Macedonia* **21 D9** 41 1N 21 20 E
Bitter Creek, *U.S.A.* **82 F9** 41 33N 108 33W
Bitterfontein, *S. Africa* **56 E2** 31 1S 18 32 E
Bitterroot →, *U.S.A.* **82 C6** 46 52N 114 7W
Bitterroot Range, *U.S.A.* **82 D6** 46 0N 114 20W
Bitterwater, *U.S.A.* **84 J6** 36 23N 121 0W
Biu, *Nigeria* **51 F8** 10 40N 12 3 E
Biwa-Ko, *Japan* **31 G8** 35 15N 136 10 E
Biwabik, *U.S.A.* **80 B8** 47 32N 92 21W
Bixby, *U.S.A.* **81 H7** 35 57N 95 53W
Biyang, *China* **34 H7** 32 38N 113 21 E
Biysk, *Russia* **26 D9** 52 40N 85 0 E
Bizana, *S. Africa* **57 E4** 30 50S 29 52 E
Bizen, *Japan* **31 G7** 34 43N 134 8 E
Bizerte, *Tunisia* **51 A7** 37 15N 9 50 E
Bjargtangar, *Iceland* **8 D1** 65 30N 24 30W
Bjelovar, *Croatia* **20 B7** 45 56N 16 49 E
Bjørnevatn, *Norway* **8 B23** 69 40N 30 0 E
Bjørnøya, *Arctic* **4 B8** 74 30N 19 0 E
Black = Da →, *Vietnam* **38 B5** 21 15N 105 20 E
Black →, *Canada* **78 B5** 44 42N 79 19W
Black →, *Ariz., U.S.A.* **83 K8** 33 44N 110 13W
Black →, *Ark., U.S.A.* **81 H9** 35 38N 91 20W
Black →, *Mich., U.S.A.* **78 D2** 42 59N 82 27W
Black →, *N.Y., U.S.A.* **79 C8** 43 59N 76 4W
Black →, *Wis., U.S.A.* **80 D9** 43 57N 91 22W
Black Bay Pen., *Canada* **70 C2** 48 38N 88 21W
Black Birch L., *Canada* **73 B7** 56 53N 107 45W
Black Diamond, *Canada* **72 C6** 50 45N 114 14W
Black Duck →, *Canada* **70 A2** 56 51N 89 2W
Black Forest = Schwarzwald, *Germany* **16 D5** 48 30N 8 20 E
Black Forest, *U.S.A.* **80 F2** 39 0N 104 43W
Black Hd., *Ireland* **13 C2** 53 9N 9 16W
Black Hills, *U.S.A.* **80 D3** 44 0N 103 45W
Black I., *Canada* **73 C9** 51 12N 96 30W
Black L., *Canada* **73 B7** 59 12N 105 15W
Black L., *Mich., U.S.A.* **76 C3** 45 28N 84 16W
Black L., *N.Y., U.S.A.* **79 B9** 44 31N 75 36W
Black Lake, *Canada* **73 B7** 59 11N 105 20W
Black Mesa, *U.S.A.* **81 G3** 36 58N 102 58W
Black Mt. = Mynydd Du, *U.K.* **11 F4** 51 52N 3 50W
Black Mts., *U.K.* **11 F4** 51 55N 3 7W
Black Range, *U.S.A.* **83 K10** 33 15N 107 50W
Black River, *Jamaica* **88 C4** 18 0N 77 50W
Black River Falls, *U.S.A.* **80 C9** 44 18N 90 51W
Black Sea, *Eurasia* **25 F6** 43 30N 35 0 E
Black Tickle, *Canada* **71 B8** 53 28N 55 45W
Black Volta →, *Africa* **50 G5** 8 41N 1 33W
Black Warrior →, *U.S.A.* **77 J2** 32 32N 87 51W
Blackall, *Australia* **62 C4** 24 25S 145 45 E
Blackball, *N.Z.* **59 K3** 42 22S 171 26 E
Blackbull, *Australia* **62 B3** 17 55S 141 45 E
Blackburn, *U.K.* **10 D5** 53 45N 2 29W
Blackburn with Darwen □, *U.K.* **10 D5** 53 45N 2 29W
Blackfoot, *U.S.A.* **82 E7** 43 11N 112 21W
Blackfoot →, *U.S.A.* **82 C7** 46 52N 113 53W
Blackfoot River Reservoir, *U.S.A.* **82 E8** 43 0N 111 43W
Blackpool, *U.K.* **10 D4** 53 49N 3 3W
Blackpool □, *U.K.* **10 D4** 53 49N 3 3W
Blackriver, *U.S.A.* **78 B1** 44 46N 83 17W
Blacks Harbour, *Canada* **71 C6** 45 3N 66 49W
Blacksburg, *U.S.A.* **76 G5** 37 14N 80 25W
Blacksod B., *Ireland* **13 B1** 54 6N 10 0W
Blackstone, *U.S.A.* **76 G7** 37 4N 78 0W
Blackstone Ra., *Australia* **61 E4** 26 0S 128 30 E
Blackwater, *Australia* **62 C4** 23 35S 148 53 E
Blackwater →, *Meath, Ireland* **13 C4** 53 39N 6 41W
Blackwater →, *Waterford, Ireland* **13 D4** 52 4N 7 52W
Blackwater →, *U.K.* **13 B5** 54 31N 6 35W
Blackwell, *U.S.A.* **81 G6** 36 48N 97 17W
Blackwells Corner, *U.S.A.* **85 K7** 35 37N 119 47W
Blaenau Ffestiniog, *U.K.* **10 E4** 53 0N 3 56W
Blaenau Gwent □, *U.K.* **11 F4** 51 48N 3 12W
Blagodarnoye = Blagodarnyy, *Russia* **25 E7** 45 7N 43 37 E
Blagodarnyy, *Russia* **25 E7** 45 7N 43 37 E
Blagoevgrad, *Bulgaria* **21 C10** 42 2N 23 5 E
Blagoveshchensk, *Russia* **27 D13** 50 20N 127 30 E
Blain, *U.S.A.* **78 F7** 40 20N 77 31W
Blaine, *Minn., U.S.A.* **80 C8** 45 10N 93 13W
Blaine, *Wash., U.S.A.* **84 B4** 48 59N 122 45W
Blaine Lake, *Canada* **73 C7** 52 51N 106 52W
Blair, *U.S.A.* **80 E6** 41 33N 96 8W
Blair Athol, *Australia* **62 C4** 22 42S 147 31 E
Blair Atholl, *U.K.* **12 E5** 56 46N 3 50W
Blairgowrie, *U.K.* **12 E5** 56 35N 3 21W
Blairsden, *U.S.A.* **84 F6** 39 47N 120 37W
Blairsville, *U.S.A.* **78 F5** 40 26N 79 16W
Blake Pt., *U.S.A.* **80 A10** 48 11N 88 25W
Blakely, *Ga., U.S.A.* **77 K3** 31 23N 84 56W
Blakely, *Pa., U.S.A.* **79 E9** 41 28N 75 37W
Blanc, C., *Spain* **22 B9** 39 21N 2 51 E
Blanc, Mont, *Alps* **18 D7** 45 48N 6 50 E
Blanc-Sablon, *Canada* **71 B8** 51 24N 57 12W
Blanca, B., *Argentina* **96 D4** 39 10S 61 30W
Blanca Peak, *U.S.A.* **83 H11** 37 35N 105 29W
Blanche, C., *Australia* **63 E1** 33 1S 134 9 E
Blanche, L., *S. Austral., Australia* **63 D2** 29 15S 139 40 E
Blanche, L., *W. Austral., Australia* **60 D3** 22 25S 123 17 E
Blanco, *S. Africa* **56 E3** 33 55S 22 23 E
Blanco, *U.S.A.* **81 K5** 30 6N 98 25W
Blanco →, *Argentina* **94 C2** 30 20S 68 42W
Blanco, C., *Costa Rica* **88 E2** 9 34N 85 8W
Blanco, C., *U.S.A.* **82 E1** 42 51N 124 34W
Blanda →, *Iceland* **8 D3** 65 37N 20 9W
Blandford Forum, *U.K.* **11 G5** 50 51N 2 9W
Blanding, *U.S.A.* **83 H9** 37 37N 109 29W
Blanes, *Spain* **19 B7** 41 40N 2 48 E
Blankenberge, *Belgium* **15 C3** 51 20N 3 9 E
Blanquilla, I., *Venezuela* **89 D7** 11 51N 64 37W
Blanquillo, *Uruguay* **95 C4** 32 53S 55 37W
Blantyre, *Malawi* **55 F4** 15 45S 35 0 E
Blarney, *Ireland* **13 E3** 51 56N 8 33W
Blasdell, *U.S.A.* **78 D6** 42 48N 78 50W
Blåvands Huk, *Denmark* **9 J13** 55 33N 8 4 E
Blaydon, *U.K.* **10 C6** 54 58N 1 42W
Blaze, Pt., *Australia* **60 B5** 12 56S 130 11 E
Blekinge, *Sweden* **9 H16** 56 25N 15 20 E
Blenheim, *Canada* **78 D3** 42 20N 82 0W
Blenheim, *N.Z.* **59 J4** 41 38S 173 57 E
Bletchley, *U.K.* **11 F7** 51 59N 0 44W
Blida, *Algeria* **50 A6** 36 30N 2 49 E
Bligh Sound, *N.Z.* **59 L1** 44 47S 167 32 E
Blind River, *Canada* **70 C3** 46 10N 82 58W
Bliss, *Idaho, U.S.A.* **82 E6** 42 56N 114 57W
Bliss, *N.Y., U.S.A.* **78 D6** 42 34N 78 15W
Blissfield, *U.S.A.* **78 F3** 40 24N 81 58W
Blitar, *Indonesia* **37 H15** 8 5S 112 11 E
Block I., *U.S.A.* **79 E13** 41 11N 71 35W
Block Island Sd., *U.S.A.* **79 E13** 41 15N 71 40W
Blodgett Iceberg Tongue, *Antarctica* **5 C9** 66 8S 130 35 E
Bloemfontein, *S. Africa* **56 D4** 29 6S 26 7 E
Bloemhof, *S. Africa* **56 D4** 27 38S 25 32 E
Blois, *France* **18 C4** 47 35N 1 20 E
Blönduós, *Iceland* **8 D3** 65 40N 20 12W
Bloodvein →, *Canada* **73 C9** 51 47N 96 43W
Bloody Foreland, *Ireland* **13 A3** 55 10N 8 17W
Bloomer, *U.S.A.* **80 C9** 45 6N 91 29W
Bloomfield, *Canada* **78 C7** 43 59N 77 14W
Bloomfield, *Iowa, U.S.A.* **80 E8** 40 45N 92 25W
Bloomfield, *N. Mex., U.S.A.* **83 H10** 36 43N 107 59W
Bloomfield, *Nebr., U.S.A.* **80 D6** 42 36N 97 39W
Bloomington, *Ill., U.S.A.* **80 E10** 40 28N 89 0W
Bloomington, *Ind., U.S.A.* **76 F2** 39 10N 86 32W
Bloomington, *Minn., U.S.A.* **80 C8** 44 50N 93 17W
Bloomsburg, *U.S.A.* **79 F8** 41 0N 76 27W
Blora, *Indonesia* **37 G14** 6 57S 111 25 E
Blossburg, *U.S.A.* **78 E7** 41 41N 77 4W
Blouberg, *S. Africa* **57 C4** 23 8S 28 59 E
Blountstown, *U.S.A.* **77 K3** 30 27N 85 3W
Blue Earth, *U.S.A.* **80 D8** 43 38N 94 6W
Blue Mesa Reservoir, *U.S.A.* **83 G10** 38 28N 107 20W
Blue Mountain Lake, *U.S.A.* **79 C10** 43 52N 74 30W
Blue Mts., *Maine, U.S.A.* **79 B14** 44 50N 70 35W
Blue Mts., *Oreg., U.S.A.* **82 D4** 45 15N 119 0W
Blue Mts., *Pa., U.S.A.* **79 F8** 40 30N 76 30W
Blue Mud B., *Australia* **62 A2** 13 30S 136 0 E
Blue Nile = Nîl el Azraq →, *Sudan* **51 E12** 15 38N 32 31 E
Blue Rapids, *U.S.A.* **80 F6** 39 41N 96 39W
Blue Ridge Mts., *U.S.A.* **77 G5** 36 30N 80 15W
Blue River, *Canada* **72 C5** 52 6N 119 18W
Bluefield, *U.S.A.* **76 G5** 37 15N 81 17W
Bluefields, *Nic.* **88 D3** 12 20N 83 50W
Bluff, *Australia* **62 C4** 23 35S 149 4 E
Bluff, *N.Z.* **59 M2** 46 37S 168 20 E
Bluff, *U.S.A.* **83 H9** 37 17N 109 33W
Bluff Knoll, *Australia* **61 F2** 34 24S 118 15 E
Bluff Pt., *Australia* **61 E1** 27 50S 114 5 E
Bluffton, *U.S.A.* **76 E3** 40 44N 85 11W
Blumenau, *Brazil* **95 B6** 27 0S 49 0W
Blunt, *U.S.A.* **80 C5** 44 31N 99 59W
Bly, *U.S.A.* **82 E3** 42 24N 121 3W
Blyth, *Canada* **78 C3** 43 44N 81 26W
Blyth, *U.K.* **10 B6** 55 8N 1 31W
Blythe, *U.S.A.* **85 M12** 33 37N 114 36W
Blytheville, *U.S.A.* **81 H10** 35 56N 89 55W
Bo, *S. Leone* **50 G3** 7 55N 11 50W
Bo Duc, *Vietnam* **39 G6** 11 58N 106 50 E
Bo Hai, *China* **35 E10** 39 0N 119 0 E
Bo Xian = Bozhou, *China* **34 H8** 33 55N 115 41 E
Boa Vista, *Brazil* **92 C6** 2 48N 60 30W
Boaco, *Nic.* **88 D2** 12 29N 85 35W
Bo'ai, *China* **34 G7** 35 10N 113 3 E
Boalsburg, *U.S.A.* **78 F7** 40 46N 77 47W
Boane, *Mozam.* **57 D5** 26 6S 32 19 E
Boardman, *U.S.A.* **78 E4** 41 2N 80 40W
Bobbili, *India* **41 K13** 18 35N 83 30 E
Bobcaygeon, *Canada* **78 B6** 44 33N 78 33W
Bobo-Dioulasso, *Burkina Faso* **50 F5** 11 8N 4 13W
Bóbr →, *Poland* **16 B8** 52 4N 15 4 E
Bobraomby, Tanjon' i, *Madag.* **57 A8** 12 40S 49 10 E
Bobruysk = Babruysk, *Belarus* **17 B15** 53 10N 29 15 E
Boby, Pic, *Madag.* **53 J9** 22 12S 46 55 E
Bôca do Acre, *Brazil* **92 E5** 8 50S 67 27W
Boca Raton, *U.S.A.* **77 M5** 26 21N 80 5W
Bocas del Toro, *Panama* **88 E3** 9 15N 82 20W
Bochnia, *Poland* **17 D11** 49 58N 20 27 E
Bochum, *Germany* **16 C4** 51 28N 7 13 E
Bocoyna, *Mexico* **86 B3** 27 52N 107 35W
Bodaybo, *Russia* **27 D12** 57 50N 114 0 E
Boddam, *U.K.* **12 B7** 59 56N 1 17W
Boddington, *Australia* **61 F2** 32 50S 116 30 E
Bodega Bay, *U.S.A.* **84 G3** 38 20N 123 3W
Boden, *Sweden* **8 D19** 65 50N 21 42 E
Bodensee, *Europe* **18 C8** 47 35N 9 25 E
Bodhan, *India* **40 K10** 18 40N 77 44 E
Bodmin, *U.K.* **11 G3** 50 28N 4 43W
Bodmin Moor, *U.K.* **11 G3** 50 33N 4 36W
Bodø, *Norway* **8 C16** 67 17N 14 24 E
Bodrog →, *Hungary* **17 D11** 48 11N 21 22 E
Bodrum, *Turkey* **21 F12** 37 3N 27 30 E
Boende, *Dem. Rep. of the Congo* **52 E4** 0 24S 21 12 E
Boerne, *U.S.A.* **81 L5** 29 47N 98 44W
Boesmans →, *S. Africa* **56 E4** 33 42S 26 39 E
Bogalusa, *U.S.A.* **81 K10** 30 47N 89 52W
Bogan →, *Australia* **63 D4** 29 59S 146 17 E
Bogantungan, *Australia* **62 C4** 23 41S 147 17 E
Bogata, *U.S.A.* **81 J7** 33 28N 95 13W
Boggabilla, *Australia* **63 D5** 28 36S 150 24 E
Boggeragh Mts., *Ireland* **13 D3** 52 2N 8 55W
Boglan = Solhan, *Turkey* **44 B4** 38 57N 41 3 E
Bognor Regis, *U.K.* **11 G7** 50 47N 0 40W
Bogo, *Phil.* **37 B6** 11 3N 124 0 E
Bogor, *Indonesia* **36 F3** 6 36S 106 48 E
Bogotá, *Colombia* **92 C4** 4 34N 74 0W
Bogotol, *Russia* **26 D9** 56 15N 89 50 E
Bogra, *Bangla.* **41 G16** 24 51N 89 22 E
Boguchany, *Russia* **27 D10** 58 40N 97 30 E
Bohemian Forest = Böhmerwald, *Germany* **16 D7** 49 8N 13 14 E
Böhmerwald, *Germany* **16 D7** 49 8N 13 14 E
Bohol □, *Phil.* **37 C6** 9 50N 124 10 E
Bohol Sea, *Phil.* **37 C6** 9 0N 124 0 E
Bohuslän, *Sweden* **9 G14** 58 25N 12 0 E
Boi, Pta. de, *Brazil* **95 A6** 23 55S 45 15W
Boiaçu, *Brazil* **92 D6** 0 27S 61 46W
Boileau, C., *Australia* **60 C3** 17 40S 122 7 E
Boise, *U.S.A.* **82 E5** 43 37N 116 13W
Boise City, *U.S.A.* **81 G3** 36 44N 102 31W
Boissevain, *Canada* **73 D8** 49 15N 100 5W
Bojador C., *W. Sahara* **50 C3** 26 0N 14 30W
Bojana →, *Albania* **21 D8** 41 52N 19 22 E
Bojnūrd, *Iran* **45 B8** 37 30N 57 20 E
Bojonegoro, *Indonesia* **37 G14** 7 11S 111 54 E
Bokaro, *India* **43 H11** 23 46N 85 55 E
Bokhara →, *Australia* **63 D4** 29 55S 146 42 E
Boknafjorden, *Norway* **9 G11** 59 14N 5 40 E
Bokoro, *Chad* **51 F9** 12 25N 17 14 E
Bokpyin, *Burma* **39 G2** 11 18N 98 42 E
Bolan →, *Pakistan* **42 E2** 28 38N 67 42 E
Bolan Pass, *Pakistan* **40 E5** 29 50N 67 20 E
Bolaños →, *Mexico* **86 C4** 21 14N 104 8W
Bolbec, *France* **18 B4** 49 30N 0 30 E
Boldājī, *Iran* **45 D6** 31 56N 51 3 E
Bole, *China* **32 B3** 45 11N 81 37 E
Bolekhiv, *Ukraine* **17 D12** 49 0N 23 57 E
Bolesławiec, *Poland* **16 C8** 51 17N 15 37 E
Bolgrad = Bolhrad, *Ukraine* **17 F15** 45 40N 28 32 E
Bolhrad, *Ukraine* **17 F15** 45 40N 28 32 E
Bolívar, *Argentina* **94 D3** 36 15S 60 53W

Bristol, City of

Bristol, City of □, *U.K.* **11 F5** 51 27N 2 36W
Bristol B., *U.S.A.* **68 C4** 58 0N 160 0W
Bristol Channel, *U.K.* **11 F3** 51 18N 4 30W
Bristol I., *Antarctica* **5 B1** 58 45S 28 0W
Bristol L., *U.S.A.* **83 J5** 34 23N 116 50W
Bristow, *U.S.A.* **81 H6** 35 50N 96 23W
Britain = Great Britain, *Europe* **6 E5** 54 0N 2 15W
British Columbia □, *Canada* **72 C3** 55 0N 125 15W
British Indian Ocean Terr. = Chagos Arch., *Ind. Oc.* **29 K11** 6 0S 72 0 E
British Isles, *Europe* **6 E5** 54 0N 4 0W
Brits, *S. Africa* **57 D4** 25 37S 27 48 E
Britstown, *S. Africa* **56 E3** 30 37S 23 30 E
Britt, *Canada* **70 C3** 45 46N 80 34W
Brittany = Bretagne, *France* **18 B2** 48 10N 3 0W
Britton, *U.S.A.* **80 C6** 45 48N 97 45W
Brive-la-Gaillarde, *France* **18 D4** 45 10N 1 32 E
Brixen = Bressanone, *Italy* **20 A4** 46 43N 11 39 E
Brixham, *U.K.* **11 G4** 50 23N 3 31W
Brno, *Czech Rep.* **17 D9** 49 10N 16 35 E
Broad →, *U.S.A.* **77 J5** 34 1N 81 4W
Broad Arrow, *Australia* **61 F3** 30 23S 121 15 E
Broad B., *U.K.* **12 C2** 58 14N 6 18W
Broad Haven, *Ireland* **13 B2** 54 20N 9 55W
Broad Law, *U.K.* **12 F5** 55 30N 3 21W
Broad Sd., *Australia* **62 C4** 22 0S 149 45 E
Broadalbin, *U.S.A.* **79 C10** 43 4N 74 12W
Broadback →, *Canada* **70 B4** 51 21N 78 52W
Broadhurst Ra., *Australia* **60 D3** 22 30S 122 30 E
Broads, The, *U.K.* **10 E9** 52 45N 1 30 E
Broadus, *U.S.A.* **80 C2** 45 27N 105 25W
Brochet, *Canada* **73 B8** 57 53N 101 40W
Brochet, L., *Canada* **73 B8** 58 36N 101 35W
Brocken, *Germany* **16 C6** 51 47N 10 37 E
Brockport, *U.S.A.* **78 C7** 43 13N 77 56W
Brockton, *U.S.A.* **79 D13** 42 5N 71 1W
Brockville, *Canada* **79 B9** 44 35N 75 41W
Brockway, *Mont., U.S.A.* **80 B2** 47 18N 105 45W
Brockway, *Pa., U.S.A.* **78 E6** 41 15N 78 47W
Brocton, *U.S.A.* **78 D5** 42 23N 79 26W
Brodeur Pen., *Canada* **69 A11** 72 30N 88 10W
Brodhead, Mt., *U.S.A.* **78 E7** 41 39N 77 47W
Brodick, *U.K.* **12 F3** 55 35N 5 9W
Brodnica, *Poland* **17 B10** 53 15N 19 25 E
Brody, *Ukraine* **17 C13** 50 5N 25 10 E
Brogan, *U.S.A.* **82 D5** 44 15N 117 31W
Broken Arrow, *U.S.A.* **81 G7** 36 3N 95 48W
Broken Bow, *Nebr., U.S.A.* **80 E5** 41 24N 99 38W
Broken Bow, *Okla., U.S.A.* **81 H7** 34 2N 94 44W
Broken Bow Lake, *U.S.A.* **81 H7** 34 9N 94 40W
Broken Hill = Kabwe, *Zambia* **55 E2** 14 30S 28 29 E
Bromley □, *U.K.* **11 F8** 51 24N 0 2 E
Bromsgrove, *U.K.* **11 E5** 52 21N 2 2W
Brønderslev, *Denmark* **9 H13** 57 16N 9 57 E
Bronkhorstspruit, *S. Africa* **57 D4** 25 46S 28 45 E
Brønnøysund, *Norway* **8 D15** 65 28N 12 14 E
Brook Park, *U.S.A.* **78 E4** 41 24N 81 51W
Brookhaven, *U.S.A.* **81 K9** 31 35N 90 26W
Brookings, *Oreg., U.S.A.* **82 E1** 42 3N 124 17W
Brookings, *S. Dak., U.S.A.* **80 C6** 44 19N 96 48W
Brooklin, *Canada* **78 C6** 43 55N 78 55W
Brooklyn Park, *U.S.A.* **80 C8** 45 6N 93 23W
Brooks, *Canada* **72 C6** 50 35N 111 55W
Brooks Range, *U.S.A.* **68 B5** 68 0N 152 0W
Brooksville, *U.S.A.* **77 L4** 28 33N 82 23W
Brookton, *Australia* **61 F2** 32 22S 117 0 E
Brookville, *U.S.A.* **78 E5** 41 10N 79 5W
Broom, L., *U.K.* **12 D3** 57 55N 5 15W
Broome, *Australia* **60 C3** 18 0S 122 15 E
Brora, *U.K.* **12 C5** 58 0N 3 52W
Brora →, *U.K.* **12 C5** 58 0N 3 51W
Brosna →, *Ireland* **13 C4** 53 14N 7 58W
Brothers, *U.S.A.* **82 E3** 43 49N 120 36W
Brough, *U.K.* **10 C5** 54 32N 2 18W
Brough Hd., *U.K.* **12 B5** 59 8N 3 20W
Broughton Island = Qikiqtarjuaq, *Canada* **69 B13** 67 33N 63 0W
Brown, L., *Australia* **61 F2** 31 5S 118 15 E
Brown, Pt., *Australia* **63 E1** 32 32S 133 50 E
Brown City, *U.S.A.* **78 C2** 43 13N 82 59W
Brown Willy, *U.K.* **11 G3** 50 35N 4 37W
Brownfield, *U.S.A.* **81 J3** 33 11N 102 17W
Browning, *U.S.A.* **82 B7** 48 34N 113 1W
Brownsville, *Oreg., U.S.A.* **82 D2** 44 24N 122 59W
Brownsville, *Pa., U.S.A.* **78 F5** 40 1N 79 53W
Brownsville, *Tenn., U.S.A.* **81 H10** 35 36N 89 16W
Brownsville, *Tex., U.S.A.* **81 N6** 25 54N 97 30W
Brownville, *U.S.A.* **79 C9** 44 0N 75 59W
Brownwood, *U.S.A.* **81 K5** 31 43N 98 59W
Browse I., *Australia* **60 B3** 14 7S 123 33 E
Bruas, *Malaysia* **39 K3** 4 30N 100 47 E
Bruay-la-Buissière, *France* **18 A5** 50 29N 2 33 E
Bruce, Mt., *Australia* **60 D2** 22 37S 118 8 E
Bruce Pen., *Canada* **78 B3** 45 0N 81 30W
Bruce Rock, *Australia* **61 F2** 31 52S 118 8 E
Bruck an der Leitha, *Austria* **17 D9** 48 1N 16 47 E
Bruck an der Mur, *Austria* **16 E8** 47 24N 15 16 E
Brue →, *U.K.* **11 F5** 51 13N 2 59W
Bruges = Brugge, *Belgium* **15 C3** 51 13N 3 13 E
Brugge, *Belgium* **15 C3** 51 13N 3 13 E
Bruin, *U.S.A.* **78 E5** 41 3N 79 43W
Brûlé, *Canada* **72 C5** 53 15N 117 58W
Brumado, *Brazil* **93 F10** 14 14S 41 40W
Brumunddal, *Norway* **9 F14** 60 53N 10 56 E
Bruneau, *U.S.A.* **82 E6** 42 53N 115 48W
Bruneau →, *U.S.A.* **82 E6** 42 56N 115 57W
Brunei = Bandar Seri Begawan, *Brunei* **36 C4** 4 52N 115 0 E
Brunei ■, *Asia* **36 D4** 4 50N 115 0 E
Brunner, L., *N.Z.* **59 K3** 42 37S 171 27 E
Brunssum, *Neths.* **15 D5** 50 57N 5 59 E
Brunswick = Braunschweig, *Germany* **16 B6** 52 15N 10 31 E
Brunswick, *Ga., U.S.A.* **77 K5** 31 10N 81 30W
Brunswick, *Maine, U.S.A.* **77 D11** 43 55N 69 58W
Brunswick, *Md., U.S.A.* **76 F7** 39 19N 77 38W
Brunswick, *Mo., U.S.A.* **80 F8** 39 26N 93 8W
Brunswick, *Ohio, U.S.A.* **78 E3** 41 14N 81 51W
Brunswick, Pen. de, *Chile* **96 G2** 53 30S 71 30W
Brunswick B., *Australia* **60 C3** 15 15S 124 50 E
Brunswick Junction, *Australia* **61 F2** 33 15S 115 50 E
Bruny I., *Australia* **62 G4** 43 20S 147 15 E
Brus Laguna, *Honduras* **88 C3** 15 47N 84 35W
Brush, *U.S.A.* **80 E3** 40 15N 103 37W
Brushton, *U.S.A.* **79 B10** 44 50N 74 31W
Brusque, *Brazil* **95 B6** 27 5S 49 0W
Brussel, *Belgium* **15 D4** 50 51N 4 21 E
Brussels = Brussel, *Belgium* **15 D4** 50 51N 4 21 E
Brussels, *Canada* **78 C3** 43 44N 81 15W
Bruxelles = Brussel, *Belgium* **15 D4** 50 51N 4 21 E
Bryan, *Ohio, U.S.A.* **76 E3** 41 28N 84 33W
Bryan, *Tex., U.S.A.* **81 K6** 30 40N 96 22W
Bryansk, *Russia* **24 D4** 53 13N 34 25 E
Bryce Canyon National Park, *U.S.A.* **83 H7** 37 30N 112 10W
Bryne, *Norway* **9 G11** 58 44N 5 38 E
Bryson City, *U.S.A.* **77 H4** 35 26N 83 27W
Bsharri, *Lebanon* **47 A5** 34 15N 36 0 E
Bū Baqarah, *U.A.E.* **45 E8** 25 35N 56 25 E
Bu Craa, *W. Sahara* **50 C3** 26 45N 12 50W
Bū Ḩasā, *U.A.E.* **45 F7** 23 30N 53 20 E
Bua Yai, *Thailand* **38 E4** 15 33N 102 26 E
Buapinang, *Indonesia* **37 E6** 4 40S 121 30 E
Bubanza, *Burundi* **54 C2** 3 6S 29 23 E
Būbiyān, *Kuwait* **46 B4** 29 45N 48 15 E
Bucaramanga, *Colombia* **92 B4** 7 0N 73 0W
Bucasia, *Australia* **62 C4** 21 2S 149 10 E
Buccaneer Arch., *Australia* **60 C3** 16 7S 123 20 E
Buchach, *Ukraine* **17 D13** 49 5N 25 25 E
Buchan, *U.K.* **12 D6** 57 32N 2 21W
Buchan Ness, *U.K.* **12 D7** 57 29N 1 46W
Buchanan, *Canada* **73 C8** 51 40N 102 45W
Buchanan, *Liberia* **50 G3** 5 57N 10 2W
Buchanan, L., *Queens., Australia* **62 C4** 21 35S 145 52 E
Buchanan, L., *W. Austral., Australia* **61 E3** 25 33S 123 2 E
Buchanan, L., *U.S.A.* **81 K5** 30 45N 98 25W
Buchanan Cr. →, *Australia* **62 B2** 19 13S 136 33 E
Buchans, *Canada* **71 C8** 48 50N 56 52W
Bucharest = Bucureşti, *Romania* **17 F14** 44 27N 26 10 E
Buchon, Pt., *U.S.A.* **84 K6** 35 15N 120 54W
Buck Hill Falls, *U.S.A.* **79 E9** 41 11N 75 16W
Buckeye, *U.S.A.* **83 K7** 33 22N 112 35W
Buckeye Lake, *U.S.A.* **78 G2** 39 55N 82 29W
Buckhannon, *U.S.A.* **76 F5** 39 0N 80 8W
Buckhaven, *U.K.* **12 E5** 56 11N 3 3W
Buckhorn L., *Canada* **78 B6** 44 29N 78 23W
Buckie, *U.K.* **12 D6** 57 41N 2 58W
Buckingham, *Canada* **70 C4** 45 37N 75 24W
Buckingham, *U.K.* **11 F7** 51 59N 0 57W
Buckingham B., *Australia* **62 A2** 12 10S 135 40 E
Buckinghamshire □, *U.K.* **11 F7** 51 53N 0 55W
Buckle Hd., *Australia* **60 B4** 14 26S 127 52 E
Buckley, *U.K.* **10 D4** 53 10N 3 5W
Buckley →, *Australia* **62 C2** 20 10S 138 49 E
Bucklin, *U.S.A.* **81 G5** 37 33N 99 38W
Bucks L., *U.S.A.* **84 F5** 39 54N 121 12W
Buctouche, *Canada* **71 C7** 46 30N 64 45W
Bucureşti, *Romania* **17 F14** 44 27N 26 10 E
Bucyrus, *U.S.A.* **76 E4** 40 48N 82 59W
Budalin, *Burma* **41 H19** 22 20N 95 10 E
Budapest, *Hungary* **17 E10** 47 29N 19 5 E
Budaun, *India* **43 E8** 28 5N 79 10 E
Budd Coast, *Antarctica* **5 C8** 68 0S 112 0 E
Bude, *U.K.* **11 G3** 50 49N 4 34W
Budennovsk, *Russia* **25 F7** 44 50N 44 10 E
Budge Budge = Baj Baj, *India* **43 H13** 22 30N 88 5 E
Budjala, *Dem. Rep. of the Congo* **52 D3** 2 50N 19 40 E
Buellton, *U.S.A.* **85 L6** 34 37N 120 12W
Buena Esperanza, *Argentina* **94 C2** 34 45S 65 15W
Buena Park, *U.S.A.* **85 M9** 33 52N 117 59W
Buena Vista, *Colo., U.S.A.* **83 G10** 38 51N 106 8W
Buena Vista, *Va., U.S.A.* **76 G6** 37 44N 79 21W
Buena Vista Lake Bed, *U.S.A.* **85 K7** 35 12N 119 18W
Buenaventura, *Colombia* **92 C3** 3 53N 77 4W
Buenaventura, *Mexico* **86 B3** 29 50N 107 30W
Buenos Aires, *Argentina* **94 C4** 34 30S 58 20W
Buenos Aires, *Costa Rica* **88 E3** 9 10N 83 20W
Buenos Aires □, *Argentina* **94 D4** 36 30S 60 0W
Buenos Aires, L., *Chile* **96 F2** 46 35S 72 30W
Buffalo, *Mo., U.S.A.* **81 G8** 37 39N 93 6W
Buffalo, *N.Y., U.S.A.* **78 D6** 42 53N 78 53W
Buffalo, *Okla., U.S.A.* **81 G5** 36 50N 99 38W
Buffalo, *S. Dak., U.S.A.* **80 C3** 45 35N 103 33W
Buffalo, *Wyo., U.S.A.* **82 D10** 44 21N 106 42W
Buffalo →, *Canada* **72 A5** 60 5N 115 5W
Buffalo →, *S. Africa* **57 D5** 28 43S 30 37 E
Buffalo Head Hills, *Canada* **72 B5** 57 25N 115 55W
Buffalo L., *Alta., Canada* **72 C6** 52 27N 112 54W
Buffalo L., *N.W.T., Canada* **72 A5** 60 12N 115 25W
Buffalo Narrows, *Canada* **73 B7** 55 51N 108 29W
Buffels →, *S. Africa* **56 D2** 29 36S 17 3 E
Buford, *U.S.A.* **77 H4** 34 10N 84 0W
Bug = Buh →, *Ukraine* **25 E5** 46 59N 31 58 E
Bug →, *Poland* **17 B11** 52 31N 21 5 E
Buga, *Colombia* **92 C3** 4 0N 76 15W
Buganda, *Uganda* **54 C3** 0 0 31 30 E
Buganga, *Uganda* **54 C3** 0 3S 32 0 E
Bugel, Tanjung, *Indonesia* **37 G14** 6 26S 111 3 E
Bugibba, *Malta* **23 D1** 35 57N 14 25 E
Bugsuk, *Phil.* **36 C5** 8 15N 117 15 E
Bugulma, *Russia* **24 D9** 54 33N 52 48 E
Bugun Shara, *Mongolia* **32 B5** 49 0N 104 0 E
Buguruslan, *Russia* **24 D9** 53 39N 52 26 E
Buh →, *Ukraine* **25 E5** 46 59N 31 58 E
Buhera, *Zimbabwe* **57 B5** 19 18S 31 29 E
Buhl, *U.S.A.* **82 E6** 42 36N 114 46W
Builth Wells, *U.K.* **11 E4** 52 9N 3 25W
Buir Nur, *Mongolia* **33 B6** 47 50N 117 42 E
Bujumbura, *Burundi* **54 C2** 3 16S 29 18 E
Bukachacha, *Russia* **27 D12** 52 55N 116 50 E
Bukama, *Dem. Rep. of the Congo* **55 D2** 9 10S 25 50 E
Bukavu, *Dem. Rep. of the Congo* **54 C2** 2 20S 28 52 E
Bukene, *Tanzania* **54 C3** 4 15S 32 48 E
Bukhara = Bukhoro, *Uzbekistan* **26 F7** 39 48N 64 25 E
Bukhoro, *Uzbekistan* **26 F7** 39 48N 64 25 E
Bukima, *Tanzania* **54 C3** 1 50S 33 25 E
Bukit Mertajam, *Malaysia* **39 K3** 5 22N 100 28 E
Bukittinggi, *Indonesia* **36 E2** 0 20S 100 20 E
Bukoba, *Tanzania* **54 C3** 1 20S 31 49 E
Bukuya, *Uganda* **54 B3** 0 40N 31 52 E
Būl, Kuh-e, *Iran* **45 D7** 30 48N 52 45 E
Bula, *Indonesia* **37 E8** 3 6S 130 30 E
Bulan, *Phil.* **37 B6** 12 40N 123 52 E
Bulandshahr, *India* **42 E7** 28 28N 77 51 E
Bulawayo, *Zimbabwe* **55 G2** 20 7S 28 32 E
Buldan, *Turkey* **21 E13** 38 2N 28 50 E
Bulgar, *Russia* **24 D8** 54 57N 49 4 E
Bulgaria ■, *Europe* **21 C11** 42 35N 25 30 E
Buli, Teluk, *Indonesia* **37 D7** 0 48N 128 25 E
Buliluyan, C., *Phil.* **36 C5** 8 20N 117 15 E
Bulkley →, *Canada* **72 B3** 55 15N 127 40W
Bull Shoals L., *U.S.A.* **81 G8** 36 22N 92 35W
Bullhead City, *U.S.A.* **85 K12** 35 8N 114 32W
Büllingen, *Belgium* **15 D6** 50 25N 6 16 E
Bullock Creek, *Australia* **62 B3** 17 43S 144 31 E
Bulloo →, *Australia* **63 D3** 28 43S 142 30 E
Bulloo L., *Australia* **63 D3** 28 43S 142 25 E
Bulls, *N.Z.* **59 J5** 40 10S 175 24 E
Bulnes, *Chile* **94 D1** 36 42S 72 19W
Bulsar = Valsad, *India* **40 J8** 20 40N 72 58 E
Bultfontein, *S. Africa* **56 D4** 28 18S 26 10 E
Bulukumba, *Indonesia* **37 F6** 5 33S 120 11 E
Bulun, *Russia* **27 B13** 70 37N 127 30 E
Bumba, *Dem. Rep. of the Congo* **52 D4** 2 13N 22 30 E
Bumbiri I., *Tanzania* **54 C3** 1 40S 31 55 E
Bumhpa Bum, *Burma* **41 F20** 26 51N 97 14 E
Bumi →, *Zimbabwe* **55 F2** 17 0S 28 20 E
Buna, *Kenya* **54 B4** 2 58N 39 30 E
Bunazi, *Tanzania* **54 C3** 1 3S 31 23 E
Bunbury, *Australia* **61 F2** 33 20S 115 35 E
Bunclody, *Ireland* **13 D5** 52 39N 6 40W
Buncrana, *Ireland* **13 A4** 55 8N 7 27W
Bundaberg, *Australia* **63 C5** 24 54S 152 22 E
Bundey →, *Australia* **62 C2** 21 46S 135 37 E
Bundi, *India* **42 G6** 25 30N 75 35 E
Bundoran, *Ireland* **13 B3** 54 28N 8 16W
Bung Kan, *Thailand* **38 C4** 18 23N 103 37 E
Bungay, *U.K.* **11 E9** 52 27N 1 28 E
Bungil Cr. →, *Australia* **63 D4** 27 5S 149 5 E
Bungo-Suidō, *Japan* **31 H6** 33 0N 132 15 E
Bungoma, *Kenya* **54 B3** 0 34N 34 34 E
Bungotakada, *Japan* **31 H5** 33 35N 131 25 E
Bungu, *Tanzania* **54 D4** 7 35S 39 0 E
Bunia, *Dem. Rep. of the Congo* **54 B3** 1 35N 30 20 E
Bunji, *Pakistan* **43 B6** 35 45N 74 40 E
Bunkie, *U.S.A.* **81 K8** 30 57N 92 11W
Bunnell, *U.S.A.* **77 L5** 29 28N 81 16W
Buntok, *Indonesia* **36 E4** 1 40S 114 58 E
Bunyu, *Indonesia* **36 D5** 3 35N 117 50 E
Buol, *Indonesia* **37 D6** 1 15N 121 32 E
Buon Brieng, *Vietnam* **38 F7** 13 9N 108 12 E
Buon Ma Thuot, *Vietnam* **38 F7** 12 40N 108 3 E
Buong Long, *Cambodia* **38 F6** 13 44N 106 59 E
Buorkhaya, Mys, *Russia* **27 B14** 71 50N 132 40 E
Buqayq, *Si. Arabia* **45 E6** 26 0N 49 45 E
Bur Acaba, *Somali Rep.* **46 G3** 3 12N 44 20 E
Bûr Safâga, *Egypt* **44 E2** 26 43N 33 57 E
Bûr Sa'îd, *Egypt* **51 B12** 31 16N 32 18 E
Bûr Sûdân, *Sudan* **51 E13** 19 32N 37 9 E
Bura, *Kenya* **54 C4** 1 4S 39 58 E
Burakin, *Australia* **61 F2** 30 31S 117 10 E
Burao, *Somali Rep.* **46 F4** 9 32N 45 32 E
Burāq, *Syria* **47 B5** 33 11N 36 29 E
Buraydah, *Si. Arabia* **44 E4** 26 20N 43 59 E
Burbank, *U.S.A.* **85 L8** 34 11N 118 19W
Burda, *India* **42 G6** 25 50N 77 35 E
Burdekin →, *Australia* **62 B4** 19 38S 147 25 E
Burdur, *Turkey* **25 G5** 37 45N 30 17 E
Burdwan = Barddhaman, *India* **43 H12** 23 14N 87 39 E
Bure, *Ethiopia* **46 E2** 10 40N 37 4 E
Bure →, *U.K.* **10 E9** 52 38N 1 43 E
Bureya →, *Russia* **27 E13** 49 27N 129 30 E
Burford, *Canada* **78 C4** 43 7N 80 27W
Burgas, *Bulgaria* **21 C12** 42 33N 27 29 E
Burgeo, *Canada* **71 C8** 47 37N 57 38W
Burgersdorp, *S. Africa* **56 E4** 31 0S 26 20 E
Burges, Mt., *Australia* **61 F3** 30 50S 121 5 E
Burgos, *Spain* **19 A4** 42 21N 3 41W
Burgsvik, *Sweden* **9 H18** 57 3N 18 19 E
Burgundy = Bourgogne, *France* **18 C6** 47 0N 4 50 E
Burhaniye, *Turkey* **21 E12** 39 30N 26 58 E
Burhanpur, *India* **40 J10** 21 18N 76 14 E
Burhi Gandak →, *India* **43 G12** 25 20N 86 37 E
Burhner →, *India* **43 H9** 22 43N 80 31 E
Burias I., *Phil.* **37 B6** 12 55N 123 5 E
Burica, Pta., *Costa Rica* **88 E3** 8 3N 82 51W
Burien, *U.S.A.* **84 C4** 47 28N 122 21W
Burigi, L., *Tanzania* **54 C3** 2 2S 31 22 E
Burin, *Canada* **71 C8** 47 1N 55 14W
Buriram, *Thailand* **38 E4** 15 0N 103 0 E
Burj Sāfitā, *Syria* **44 C3** 34 48N 36 7 E
Burkburnett, *U.S.A.* **81 H5** 34 6N 98 34W
Burke →, *Australia* **62 C2** 23 12S 139 33 E
Burke Chan., *Canada* **72 C3** 52 10N 127 30W
Burketown, *Australia* **62 B2** 17 45S 139 33 E
Burkina Faso ■, *Africa* **50 F5** 12 0N 1 0W
Burk's Falls, *Canada* **70 C4** 45 37N 79 24W
Burleigh Falls, *Canada* **78 B6** 44 33N 78 12W
Burley, *U.S.A.* **82 E7** 42 32N 113 48W
Burlingame, *U.S.A.* **84 H4** 37 35N 122 21W
Burlington, *Canada* **78 C5** 43 18N 79 45W
Burlington, *Colo., U.S.A.* **80 F3** 39 18N 102 16W
Burlington, *Iowa, U.S.A.* **80 E9** 40 49N 91 14W
Burlington, *Kans., U.S.A.* **80 F7** 38 12N 95 45W
Burlington, *N.C., U.S.A.* **77 G6** 36 6N 79 26W
Burlington, *N.J., U.S.A.* **79 F10** 40 4N 74 51W
Burlington, *Vt., U.S.A.* **79 B11** 44 29N 73 12W
Burlington, *Wash., U.S.A.* **84 B4** 48 28N 122 20W
Burlington, *Wis., U.S.A.* **76 D1** 42 41N 88 17W
Burlyu-Tyube, *Kazakstan* **26 E8** 46 30N 79 10 E
Burma ■, *Asia* **41 J20** 21 0N 96 30 E
Burnaby I., *Canada* **72 C2** 52 25N 131 19W
Burnet, *U.S.A.* **81 K5** 30 45N 98 14W
Burney, *U.S.A.* **82 F3** 40 53N 121 40W
Burnham, *U.S.A.* **78 F7** 40 38N 77 34W
Burnham-on-Sea, *U.K.* **11 F5** 51 14N 3 0W
Burnie, *Australia* **62 G4** 41 4S 145 56 E
Burnley, *U.K.* **10 D5** 53 47N 2 14W
Burns, *U.S.A.* **82 E4** 43 35N 119 3W
Burns Lake, *Canada* **72 C3** 54 20N 125 45W
Burnside →, *Canada* **68 B9** 66 51N 108 4W
Burnside, L., *Australia* **61 E3** 25 22S 123 0 E
Burnsville, *U.S.A.* **80 C8** 44 47N 93 17W
Burnt L., *Canada* **71 B7** 53 35N 64 4W
Burnt River, *Canada* **78 B6** 44 41N 78 42W
Burntwood →, *Canada* **73 B9** 56 8N 96 34W
Burntwood L., *Canada* **73 B8** 55 22N 100 26W
Burqān, *Kuwait* **44 D5** 29 0N 47 57 E
Burray, *U.K.* **12 C6** 58 51N 2 54W
Burren Junction, *Australia* **63 E4** 30 7S 148 59 E
Burro, Serranías del, *Mexico* **86 B4** 29 0N 102 0W
Burrow Hd., *U.K.* **12 G4** 54 41N 4 24W
Burruyacú, *Argentina* **94 B3** 26 30S 64 40W
Burry Port, *U.K.* **11 F3** 51 41N 4 15W
Bursa, *Turkey* **21 D13** 40 15N 29 5 E
Burstall, *Canada* **73 C7** 50 39N 109 54W
Burton, *Ohio, U.S.A.* **78 E3** 41 28N 81 8W
Burton, *S.C., U.S.A.* **77 J5** 32 25N 80 45W
Burton, L., *Canada* **70 B4** 54 45N 78 20W
Burton upon Trent, *U.K.* **10 E6** 52 48N 1 38W
Buru, *Indonesia* **37 E7** 3 30S 126 30 E
Burûn, Râs, *Egypt* **47 D2** 31 14N 33 7 E
Burundi ■, *Africa* **54 C3** 3 15S 30 0 E
Bururi, *Burundi* **54 C2** 3 57S 29 37 E
Burutu, *Nigeria* **50 G7** 5 20N 5 29 E
Burwell, *U.S.A.* **80 E5** 41 47N 99 8W
Burwick, *U.K.* **12 C5** 58 45N 2 58W
Bury, *U.K.* **10 D5** 53 35N 2 17W
Bury St. Edmunds, *U.K.* **11 E8** 52 15N 0 43 E
Buryatia □, *Russia* **27 D11** 53 0N 110 0 E
Busango Swamp, *Zambia* **55 E2** 14 15S 25 45 E
Buşayrah, *Syria* **44 C4** 35 9N 40 26 E
Būshehr, *Iran* **45 D6** 28 55N 50 55 E
Būshehr □, *Iran* **45 D6** 28 20N 51 45 E
Bushell, *Canada* **73 B7** 59 31N 108 45W
Bushenyi, *Uganda* **54 C3** 0 35S 30 10 E
Bushire = Būshehr, *Iran* **45 D6** 28 55N 50 55 E
Businga, *Dem. Rep. of the Congo* **52 D4** 3 16N 20 59 E
Buşra ash Shām, *Syria* **47 C5** 32 30N 36 25 E
Busselton, *Australia* **61 F2** 33 42S 115 15 E
Bussum, *Neths.* **15 B5** 52 16N 5 10 E
Busto Arsízio, *Italy* **18 D8** 45 37N 8 51 E
Busu-Djanoa, *Dem. Rep. of the Congo* **52 D4** 1 43N 21 23 E
Busuanga I., *Phil.* **37 B5** 12 10N 120 0 E
Buta, *Dem. Rep. of the Congo* **54 B1** 2 50N 24 53 E
Butare, *Rwanda* **54 C2** 2 31S 29 52 E
Butaritari, *Kiribati* **64 G9** 3 30N 174 0 E
Bute, *U.K.* **12 F3** 55 48N 5 2W
Bute Inlet, *Canada* **72 C4** 50 40N 124 53W
Butemba, *Uganda* **54 B3** 1 9N 31 37 E
Butembo, *Dem. Rep. of the Congo* **54 B2** 0 9N 29 18 E
Butha Qi, *China* **33 B7** 48 0N 122 32 E
Butiaba, *Uganda* **54 B3** 1 50N 31 20 E
Butler, *Mo., U.S.A.* **80 F7** 38 16N 94 20W
Butler, *Pa., U.S.A.* **78 F5** 40 52N 79 54W
Buton, *Indonesia* **37 E6** 5 0S 122 45 E
Butte, *Mont., U.S.A.* **82 C7** 46 0N 112 32W
Butte, *Nebr., U.S.A.* **80 D5** 42 58N 98 51W
Butte Creek →, *U.S.A.* **84 F5** 39 12N 121 56W
Butterworth = Gcuwa, *S. Africa* **57 E4** 32 20S 28 11 E
Butterworth, *Malaysia* **39 K3** 5 24N 100 23 E
Buttevant, *Ireland* **13 D3** 52 14N 8 40W
Buttfield, Mt., *Australia* **61 D4** 24 45S 128 9 E
Button B., *Canada* **73 B10** 58 45N 94 23W
Buttonwillow, *U.S.A.* **85 K7** 35 24N 119 28W
Butty Hd., *Australia* **61 F3** 33 54S 121 39 E
Butuan, *Phil.* **37 C7** 8 57N 125 33 E
Butung = Buton, *Indonesia* **37 E6** 5 0S 122 45 E
Buturlinovka, *Russia* **25 D7** 50 50N 40 35 E
Buxa Duar, *India* **43 F13** 27 45N 89 35 E
Buxar, *India* **43 G10** 25 34N 83 58 E
Buxtehude, *Germany* **16 B5** 53 28N 9 39 E
Buxton, *U.K.* **10 D6** 53 16N 1 54W
Buy, *Russia* **24 C7** 58 28N 41 28 E
Büyük Menderes →, *Turkey* **21 F12** 37 28N 27 11 E
Büyükçekmece, *Turkey* **21 D13** 41 2N 28 35 E
Buzău, *Romania* **17 F14** 45 10N 26 50 E
Buzău →, *Romania* **17 F14** 45 26N 27 44 E
Buzen, *Japan* **31 H5** 33 35N 131 5 E
Buzi →, *Mozam.* **55 F3** 19 50S 34 43 E
Buzuluk, *Russia* **24 D9** 52 48N 52 12 E
Buzzards B., *U.S.A.* **79 E14** 41 45N 70 37W
Buzzards Bay, *U.S.A.* **79 E14** 41 44N 70 37W
Bwana Mkubwe, *Dem. Rep. of the Congo* **55 E2** 13 8S 28 38 E
Byarezina →, *Belarus* **17 B16** 52 33N 30 14 E
Byaroza, *Belarus* **17 B13** 52 31N 24 51 E
Bydgoszcz, *Poland* **17 B9** 53 10N 18 0 E
Byelarus = Belarus ■, *Europe* **17 B14** 53 30N 27 0 E
Byelorussia = Belarus ■, *Europe* **17 B14** 53 30N 27 0 E
Byers, *U.S.A.* **80 F2** 39 43N 104 14W
Byesville, *U.S.A.* **78 G3** 39 58N 81 32W
Byford, *Australia* **61 F2** 32 15S 116 0 E
Bykhaw, *Belarus* **17 B16** 53 31N 30 14 E
Bykhov = Bykhaw, *Belarus* **17 B16** 53 31N 30 14 E
Bylas, *U.S.A.* **83 K8** 33 8N 110 7W
Bylot, *Canada* **73 B10** 58 25N 94 8W
Bylot I., *Canada* **69 A12** 73 13N 78 34W
Byrd, C., *Antarctica* **5 C17** 69 38S 76 7W
Byron Bay, *Australia* **63 D5** 28 43S 153 37 E
Byrranga, Gory, *Russia* **27 B11** 75 0N 100 0 E
Byrranga Mts. = Byrranga, Gory, *Russia* **27 B11** 75 0N 100 0 E
Byske, *Sweden* **8 D19** 64 57N 21 11 E
Byske älv →, *Sweden* **8 D19** 64 57N 21 13 E
Bytom, *Poland* **17 C10** 50 25N 18 54 E
Bytów, *Poland* **17 A9** 54 10N 17 30 E
Byumba, *Rwanda* **54 C3** 1 35S 30 4 E

C

Ca →, *Vietnam* **38 C5** 18 45N 105 45 E
Ca Mau, *Vietnam* **39 H5** 9 7N 105 8 E
Ca Mau, Mui, *Vietnam* **39 H5** 8 38N 104 44 E
Ca Na, *Vietnam* **39 G7** 11 20N 108 54 E
Caacupé, *Paraguay* **94 B4** 25 23S 57 5W
Caála, *Angola* **53 G3** 12 46S 15 30 E
Caamano Sd., *Canada* **72 C3** 52 55N 129 25W
Caazapá, *Paraguay* **94 B4** 26 8S 56 19W

Carbó

Caazapá □, Paraguay 95 B4 26 10S 56 0W
Cabanatuan, Phil. 37 A6 15 30N 120 58 E
Cabano, Canada 71 C6 47 40N 68 56W
Cabazon, U.S.A. 85 M10 33 55N 116 47W
Cabedelo, Brazil 93 E12 7 0S 34 50W
Cabildo, Chile 94 C1 32 30S 71 5W
Cabimas, Venezuela 92 A4 10 23N 71 25W
Cabinda, Angola 52 F2 5 33S 12 11 E
Cabinda □, Angola 52 F2 5 0S 12 30 E
Cabinet Mts., U.S.A. 82 C6 48 0N 115 30W
Cabo Blanco, Argentina 96 F3 47 15S 65 47W
Cabo Frio, Brazil 95 A7 22 51S 42 3W
Cabo Pantoja, Peru 92 D3 1 0S 75 10W
Cabonga, Réservoir, Canada 70 C4 47 20N 76 40W
Cabool, U.S.A. 81 G8 37 7N 92 6W
Caboolture, Australia 63 D5 27 5S 152 58 E
Cabora Bassa Dam = Cahora Bassa, Représa de, Mozam. 55 F3 15 20S 32 50 E
Caborca, Mexico 86 A2 30 40N 112 10W
Cabot, Mt., U.S.A. 79 B13 44 30N 71 25W
Cabot Hd., Canada 78 A3 45 14N 81 17W
Cabot Str., Canada 71 C8 47 15N 59 40W
Cabra, Spain 19 D3 37 30N 4 28W
Cabrera, Spain 22 B9 39 8N 2 57 E
Cabri, Canada 73 C7 50 35N 108 25W
Cabriel →, Spain 19 C5 39 14N 1 3W
Caçador, Brazil 95 B5 26 47S 51 0W
Čačak, Serbia, Yug. 21 C9 43 54N 20 20 E
Caçapava do Sul, Brazil 95 C5 30 30S 53 30W
Cáceres, Brazil 92 G7 16 5S 57 40W
Cáceres, Spain 19 C2 39 26N 6 23W
Cache Bay, Canada 70 C4 46 22N 80 0W
Cache Cr. →, U.S.A. 84 G5 38 42N 121 42W
Cache Creek, Canada 72 C4 50 48N 121 19W
Cachi, Argentina 94 B2 25 5S 66 10W
Cachimbo, Serra do, Brazil 93 E7 9 30S 55 30W
Cachinal de la Sierra, Chile 94 A2 24 58S 69 32W
Cachoeira, Brazil 93 F11 12 30S 39 0W
Cachoeira do Sul, Brazil 95 C5 30 3S 52 53W
Cachoeiro de Itapemirim, Brazil 95 A7 20 51S 41 7W
Cacoal, Brazil 92 F6 11 32S 61 18W
Cacólo, Angola 52 G3 10 9S 19 21 E
Caconda, Angola 53 G3 13 48S 15 8 E
Caddo, U.S.A. 81 H6 34 7N 96 16W
Cader Idris, U.K. 11 E4 52 42N 3 53W
Cadereyta, Mexico 86 B5 25 36N 100 0W
Cadibarrawirracanna, L., Australia 63 D2 28 52S 135 27 E
Cadillac, U.S.A. 76 C3 44 15N 85 24W
Cadiz, Phil. 37 B6 10 57N 123 15 E
Cádiz, Spain 19 D2 36 30N 6 20W
Cadiz, Calif., U.S.A. 85 L11 34 30N 115 28W
Cadiz, Ohio, U.S.A. 78 F4 40 22N 81 0W
Cádiz, G. de, Spain 19 D2 36 40N 7 0W
Cadiz L., U.S.A. 83 J6 34 18N 115 24W
Cadney Park, Australia 63 D1 27 55S 134 3 E
Cadomin, Canada 72 C5 53 2N 117 20W
Cadotte Lake, Canada 72 B5 56 26N 116 23W
Cadoux, Australia 61 F2 30 46S 117 7 E
Caen, France 18 B3 49 10N 0 22W
Caernarfon, U.K. 10 D3 53 8N 4 16W
Caernarfon B., U.K. 10 D3 53 4N 4 40W
Caernarvon = Caernarfon, U.K. 10 D3 53 8N 4 16W
Caerphilly, U.K. 11 F4 51 35N 3 13W
Caerphilly □, U.K. 11 F4 51 37N 3 12W
Caesarea, Israel 47 C3 32 30N 34 53 E
Caetité, Brazil 93 F10 13 50S 42 32W
Cafayate, Argentina 94 B2 26 2S 66 0W
Cafu, Angola 56 B2 16 30S 15 8 E
Cagayan de Oro, Phil. 37 C6 8 30N 124 40 E
Cagayan Is., Phil. 37 C5 9 40N 121 16 E
Cágliari, Italy 20 E3 39 13N 9 7 E
Cágliari, G. di, Italy 20 E3 39 8N 9 11 E
Caguán →, Colombia 92 D4 0 8S 74 18W
Caguas, Puerto Rico 89 C6 18 14N 66 2W
Caha Mts., Ireland 13 E2 51 45N 9 40W
Cahama, Angola 56 B1 16 17S 14 19 E
Caher, Ireland 13 D4 52 22N 7 56W
Caherciveen, Ireland 13 E1 51 56N 10 14W
Cahora Bassa, Représa de, Mozam. 55 F3 15 20S 32 50 E
Cahore Pt., Ireland 13 D5 52 33N 6 12W
Cahors, France 18 D4 44 27N 1 27 E
Cahul, Moldova 17 F15 45 50N 28 15 E
Cai Bau, Dao, Vietnam 38 B6 21 10N 107 27 E
Cai Nuoc, Vietnam 39 H5 8 56N 105 1 E
Caia, Mozam. 55 F4 17 51S 35 24 E
Caianda, Angola 55 E1 11 2S 23 31 E
Caibarién, Cuba 88 B4 22 30N 79 30W
Caicara, Venezuela 92 B5 7 38N 66 10W
Caicó, Brazil 93 E11 6 20S 37 0W
Caicos Is., Turks & Caicos 89 B5 21 40N 71 40W
Caicos Passage, W. Indies 89 B5 22 45N 72 45W
Caird Coast, Antarctica 5 D1 75 0S 25 0W
Cairn Gorm, U.K. 12 D5 57 7N 3 39W
Cairngorm Mts., U.K. 12 D5 57 6N 3 42W
Cairnryan, U.K. 12 G3 54 59N 5 1W
Cairns, Australia 62 B4 16 57S 145 45 E
Cairns L., Canada 73 C10 51 42N 94 30W
Cairo = El Qâhira, Egypt 51 B12 30 1N 31 14 E
Cairo, Ga., U.S.A. 77 K3 30 52N 84 13W
Cairo, Ill., U.S.A. 81 G10 37 0N 89 11W
Cairo, N.Y., U.S.A. 79 D11 42 18N 74 0W
Caithness, Ord of, U.K. 12 C5 58 8N 3 36W
Cajamarca, Peru 92 E3 7 5S 78 28W
Cajàzeiras, Brazil 93 E11 6 52S 38 30W
Cala d'Or, Spain 22 B10 39 23N 3 14 E
Cala en Porter, Spain 22 B11 39 52N 4 8 E
Cala Figuera, C. de, Spain 22 B9 39 27N 2 31 E
Cala Forcat, Spain 22 B10 40 0N 3 47 E
Cala Major, Spain 22 B9 39 33N 2 37 E
Cala Mezquida = Sa Mesquida, Spain 22 B11 39 55N 4 16 E
Cala Millor, Spain 22 B10 39 35N 3 22 E
Cala Ratjada, Spain 22 B10 39 43N 3 27 E
Cala Santa Galdana, Spain 22 B10 39 56N 3 58 E
Calabar, Nigeria 50 H7 4 57N 8 20 E
Calabogie, Canada 79 A8 45 18N 76 43W
Calabozo, Venezuela 92 B5 9 0N 67 28W
Calábria □, Italy 20 E7 39 0N 16 30 E
Calafate, Argentina 96 G2 50 19S 72 15W
Calahorra, Spain 19 A5 42 18N 1 59W
Calais, France 18 A4 50 57N 1 56 E
Calais, U.S.A. 77 C12 45 11N 67 17W
Calalaste, Cord. de, Argentina 94 B2 25 0S 67 0W
Calama, Brazil 92 E6 8 0S 62 50W
Calama, Chile 94 A2 22 30S 68 55W
Calamar, Colombia 92 A4 10 15N 74 55W
Calamian Group, Phil. 37 B5 11 50N 119 55 E
Calamocha, Spain 19 B5 40 50N 1 17W
Calang, Indonesia 36 D1 4 37N 95 37 E
Calapan, Phil. 37 B6 13 25N 121 7 E
Călăraşi, Romania 17 F14 44 12N 27 20 E
Calatayud, Spain 19 B5 41 20N 1 40W
Calauag, Phil. 37 B6 13 55N 122 15 E
Calavite, C., Phil. 37 B6 13 26N 120 20 E
Calbayog, Phil. 37 B6 12 4N 124 38 E
Calca, Peru 92 F4 13 22S 72 0W
Calcasieu L., U.S.A. 81 L8 29 55N 93 18W
Calcutta = Kolkata, India 43 H13 22 36N 88 24 E
Calcutta, U.S.A. 78 F4 40 40N 80 34W
Caldas da Rainha, Portugal 19 C1 39 24N 9 8W
Calder →, U.K. 10 D6 53 44N 1 22W
Caldera, Chile 94 B1 27 5S 70 55W
Caldwell, Idaho, U.S.A. 82 E5 43 40N 116 41W
Caldwell, Kans., U.S.A. 81 G6 37 2N 97 37W
Caldwell, Tex., U.S.A. 81 K6 30 32N 96 42W
Caledon, S. Africa 56 E2 34 14S 19 26 E
Caledon →, S. Africa 56 E4 30 31S 26 5 E
Caledon B., Australia 62 A2 12 45S 137 0 E
Caledonia, Canada 78 C5 43 7N 79 58W
Caledonia, U.S.A. 78 D7 42 58N 77 51W
Calemba, Angola 56 B2 16 0S 15 44 E
Calen, Australia 62 C4 20 56S 148 48 E
Caletones, Chile 94 C1 34 6S 70 27W
Calexico, U.S.A. 85 N11 32 40N 115 30W
Calf of Man, U.K. 10 C3 54 3N 4 48W
Calgary, Canada 72 C6 51 0N 114 10W
Calheta, Madeira 22 D2 32 44N 17 11W
Calhoun, U.S.A. 77 H3 34 30N 84 57W
Cali, Colombia 92 C3 3 25N 76 35W
Calicut, India 40 P9 11 15N 75 43 E
Caliente, U.S.A. 83 H6 37 37N 114 31W
California, Mo., U.S.A. 80 F8 38 38N 92 34W
California, Pa., U.S.A. 78 F5 40 4N 79 54W
California □, U.S.A. 84 H7 37 30N 119 30W
California, Baja, Mexico 86 A1 32 10N 115 12W
California, Baja, T.N. = Baja California □, Mexico 86 B2 30 0N 115 0W
California, Baja, T.S. = Baja California Sur □, Mexico 86 B2 25 50N 111 50W
California, G. de, Mexico 86 B2 27 0N 111 0W
California City, U.S.A. 85 K9 35 10N 117 55W
California Hot Springs, U.S.A. 85 K8 35 51N 118 41W
Calingasta, Argentina 94 C2 31 15S 69 30W
Calipatria, U.S.A. 85 M11 33 8N 115 31W
Calistoga, U.S.A. 84 G4 38 35N 122 35W
Calitzdorp, S. Africa 56 E3 33 33S 21 42 E
Callabonna, L., Australia 63 D3 29 40S 140 5 E
Callan, Ireland 13 D4 52 32N 7 24W
Callander, U.K. 12 E4 56 15N 4 13W
Callao, Peru 92 F3 12 0S 77 0W
Calles, Mexico 87 C5 23 2N 98 42W
Callicoon, U.S.A. 79 E9 41 46N 75 3W
Calling Lake, Canada 72 B6 55 15N 113 12W
Calliope, Australia 62 C5 24 0S 151 16 E
Calne, U.K. 11 F6 51 26N 2 0W
Calola, Angola 56 B2 16 25S 17 48 E
Caloundra, Australia 63 D5 26 45S 153 10 E
Calpella, U.S.A. 84 F3 39 14N 123 12W
Calpine, U.S.A. 84 F6 39 40N 120 27W
Calstock, Canada 70 C3 49 47N 84 9W
Caltagirone, Italy 20 F6 37 14N 14 31 E
Caltanissetta, Italy 20 F6 37 29N 14 4 E
Calulo, Angola 52 G2 10 1S 14 56 E
Calvert →, Australia 62 B2 16 17S 137 44 E
Calvert I., Canada 72 C3 51 30N 128 0W
Calvert Ra., Australia 60 D3 24 0S 122 30 E
Calvi, France 18 E8 42 34N 8 45 E
Calviá, Spain 19 C7 39 34N 2 31 E
Calvillo, Mexico 86 C4 21 51N 102 43W
Calvinia, S. Africa 56 E2 31 28S 19 45 E
Calwa, U.S.A. 84 J7 36 42N 119 46W
Cam →, U.K. 11 E8 52 21N 0 16 E
Cam Lam, Vietnam 39 G7 11 54N 109 10 E
Cam Pha, Vietnam 38 B6 21 7N 107 18 E
Cam Ranh, Vietnam 39 G7 11 54N 109 12 E
Cam Xuyen, Vietnam 38 C6 18 15N 106 0 E
Camabatela, Angola 52 F3 8 20S 15 26 E
Camacha, Madeira 22 D3 32 41N 16 49W
Camacho, Mexico 86 C4 24 25N 102 18W
Camacupa, Angola 53 G3 11 58S 17 22 E
Camagüey, Cuba 88 B4 21 20N 78 0W
Camaná, Peru 92 G4 16 30S 72 50W
Camanche Reservoir, U.S.A. 84 G6 38 14N 121 1W
Camaquã, Brazil 95 C5 30 51S 51 49W
Camaquã →, Brazil 95 C5 31 17S 51 47W
Câmara de Lobos, Madeira 22 D3 32 39N 16 59W
Camargo, Mexico 87 B5 26 19N 98 50W
Camargue, France 18 E6 43 34N 4 34 E
Camarillo, U.S.A. 85 L7 34 13N 119 2W
Camarón, C., Honduras 88 C2 16 0N 85 5W
Camarones, Argentina 96 E3 44 50S 65 40W
Camas, U.S.A. 84 E4 45 35N 122 24W
Camas Valley, U.S.A. 82 E2 43 2N 123 40W
Camballin, Australia 60 C3 17 59S 124 12 E
Cambará, Brazil 95 A5 23 2S 50 5W
Cambay = Khambhat, India 42 H5 22 23N 72 33 E
Cambay, G. of = Khambhat, G. of, India 40 J8 20 45N 72 30 E
Cambodia ■, Asia 38 F5 12 15N 105 0 E
Camborne, U.K. 11 G2 50 12N 5 19W
Cambrai, France 18 A5 50 11N 3 14 E
Cambria, U.S.A. 84 K5 35 34N 121 5W
Cambrian Mts., U.K. 11 E4 52 3N 3 57W
Cambridge, Canada 78 C4 43 23N 80 15W
Cambridge, Jamaica 88 C4 18 18N 77 54W
Cambridge, N.Z. 59 G5 37 54S 175 29 E
Cambridge, U.K. 11 E8 52 12N 0 8 E
Cambridge, Mass., U.S.A. 79 D13 42 22N 71 6W
Cambridge, Minn., U.S.A. 80 C8 45 34N 93 13W
Cambridge, N.Y., U.S.A. 79 C11 43 2N 73 22W
Cambridge, Nebr., U.S.A. 80 E4 40 17N 100 10W
Cambridge, Ohio, U.S.A. 78 F3 40 2N 81 35W
Cambridge Bay = Ikaluktutiak, Canada 68 B9 69 10N 105 0W
Cambridge G., Australia 60 B4 14 55S 128 15 E
Cambridge Springs, U.S.A. 78 E4 41 48N 80 4W
Cambridgeshire □, U.K. 11 E7 52 25N 0 7W
Cambuci, Brazil 95 A7 21 35S 41 55W
Cambundi-Catembo, Angola 52 G3 10 10S 17 35 E
Camden, Ala., U.S.A. 77 K2 31 59N 87 17W
Camden, Ark., U.S.A. 81 J8 33 35N 92 50W
Camden, Maine, U.S.A. 77 C11 44 13N 69 4W
Camden, N.J., U.S.A. 79 G9 39 56N 75 7W
Camden, N.Y., U.S.A. 79 C9 43 20N 75 45W
Camden, S.C., U.S.A. 77 H5 34 16N 80 36W
Camden Sd., Australia 60 C3 15 27S 124 25 E
Camdenton, U.S.A. 81 F8 38 1N 92 45W
Cameron, Ariz., U.S.A. 83 J8 35 53N 111 25W
Cameron, La., U.S.A. 81 L8 29 48N 93 20W
Cameron, Mo., U.S.A. 80 F7 39 44N 94 14W
Cameron, Tex., U.S.A. 81 K6 30 51N 96 59W
Cameron Highlands, Malaysia 39 K3 4 27N 101 22 E
Cameron Hills, Canada 72 B5 59 48N 118 0W
Cameroon ■, Africa 52 C2 6 0N 12 30 E
Cameroun, Mt., Cameroon 52 D1 4 13N 9 10 E
Cametá, Brazil 93 D9 2 12S 49 30W
Camiguin I., Phil. 37 C6 18 56N 121 55 E
Camilla, U.S.A. 77 K3 31 14N 84 12W
Caminha, Portugal 19 B1 41 50N 8 50W
Camino, U.S.A. 84 G6 38 44N 120 41W
Camira Creek, Australia 63 D5 29 15S 152 58 E
Cammal, U.S.A. 78 E7 41 24N 77 28W
Camocim, Brazil 93 D10 2 55S 40 50W
Camooweal, Australia 62 B2 19 56S 138 7 E
Camopi, Fr. Guiana 93 C8 3 12N 52 17W
Camp Borden, Canada 78 B5 44 18N 79 56W
Camp Hill, U.S.A. 78 F8 40 14N 76 55W
Camp Nelson, U.S.A. 85 J8 36 8N 118 39W
Camp Pendleton, U.S.A. 85 M9 33 16N 117 23W
Camp Verde, U.S.A. 83 J8 34 34N 111 51W
Camp Wood, U.S.A. 81 L5 29 40N 100 1W
Campana, Argentina 94 C4 34 10S 58 55W
Campana, I., Chile 96 F1 48 20S 75 20W
Campanário, Madeira 22 D2 32 39N 17 2W
Campánia □, Italy 20 D6 41 0N 14 30 E
Campbell, S. Africa 56 D3 28 48S 23 44 E
Campbell, Calif., U.S.A. 84 H5 37 17N 121 57W
Campbell, Ohio, U.S.A. 78 E4 41 5N 80 37W
Campbell I., Pac. Oc. 64 N8 52 30S 169 0 E
Campbell L., Canada 73 A7 63 14N 106 55W
Campbell River, Canada 72 C3 50 5N 125 20W
Campbell Town, Australia 62 G4 41 52S 147 30 E
Campbellford, Canada 78 B7 44 18N 77 48W
Campbellpur, Pakistan 42 C5 33 46N 72 26 E
Campbellsville, U.S.A. 76 G3 37 21N 85 20W
Campbellton, Canada 71 C6 47 57N 66 43W
Campbeltown, U.K. 12 F3 55 26N 5 36W
Campeche, Mexico 87 D6 19 50N 90 32W
Campeche □, Mexico 87 D6 19 50N 90 32W
Campeche, Golfo de, Mexico 87 D6 19 30N 93 0W
Camperville, Canada 73 C8 51 59N 100 9W
Câmpina, Romania 17 F13 45 10N 25 45 E
Campina Grande, Brazil 93 E11 7 20S 35 47W
Campinas, Brazil 95 A6 22 50S 47 0W
Campo Grande, Brazil 93 H8 20 25S 54 40W
Campo Maíor, Brazil 93 D10 4 50S 42 12W
Campo Mourão, Brazil 95 A5 24 3S 52 22W
Campobasso, Italy 20 D6 41 34N 14 39 E
Campos, Brazil 95 A7 21 50S 41 20W
Campos Belos, Brazil 93 F9 13 10S 47 3W
Campos del Puerto, Spain 22 B10 39 26N 3 1 E
Campos Novos, Brazil 95 B5 27 21S 51 50W
Camptonville, U.S.A. 84 F5 39 27N 121 3W
Camptown, U.S.A. 79 E8 41 44N 76 14W
Câmpulung, Romania 17 F13 45 17N 25 3 E
Camrose, Canada 72 C6 53 0N 112 50W
Camsell Portage, Canada 73 B7 59 37N 109 15W
Çan, Turkey 21 D12 40 2N 27 3 E
Can Clavo, Spain 22 C7 38 57N 1 27 E
Can Creu, Spain 22 C7 38 58N 1 28 E
Can Gio, Vietnam 39 G6 10 25N 106 58 E
Can Tho, Vietnam 39 G5 10 2N 105 46 E
Canaan, U.S.A. 79 D11 42 2N 73 20W
Canada ■, N. Amer. 68 C10 60 0N 100 0W
Cañada de Gómez, Argentina 94 C3 32 40S 61 30W
Canadian, U.S.A. 81 H4 35 55N 100 23W
Canadian →, U.S.A. 81 H7 35 28N 95 3W
Canajoharie, U.S.A. 79 D10 42 54N 74 35W
Çanakkale, Turkey 21 D12 40 8N 26 24 E
Çanakkale Boğazı, Turkey 21 D12 40 17N 26 32 E
Canal Flats, Canada 72 C5 50 10N 115 48W
Canalejas, Argentina 94 D2 35 15S 66 34W
Canals, Argentina 94 C3 33 35S 62 53W
Canandaigua, U.S.A. 78 D7 42 54N 77 17W
Canandaigua L., U.S.A. 78 D7 42 47N 77 19W
Cananea, Mexico 86 A2 31 0N 110 20W
Canarias, Is., Atl. Oc. 22 F4 28 30N 16 0W
Canarreos, Arch. de los, Cuba 88 B3 21 35N 81 40W
Canary Is. = Canarias, Is., Atl. Oc. 22 F4 28 30N 16 0W
Canaseraga, U.S.A. 78 D7 42 27N 77 45W
Canatlán, Mexico 86 C4 24 31N 104 47W
Canaveral, C., U.S.A. 77 L5 28 27N 80 32W
Canavieiras, Brazil 93 G11 15 39S 39 0W
Canby, Calif., U.S.A. 82 F3 41 27N 120 52W
Canby, Minn., U.S.A. 80 C6 44 43N 96 16W
Canby, Oreg., U.S.A. 84 E4 45 16N 122 42W
Cancún, Mexico 87 C7 21 8N 86 44W
Candelaria, Argentina 95 B4 27 29S 55 44W
Candelaria, Canary Is. 22 F3 28 22N 16 22W
Candia = Iráklion, Greece 23 D7 35 20N 25 12 E
Candle L., Canada 73 C7 53 50N 105 18W
Candlemas I., Antarctica 5 B1 57 3S 26 40W
Cando, U.S.A. 80 A5 48 32N 99 12W
Canea = Khaniá, Greece 23 D6 35 30N 24 4 E
Canelones, Uruguay 95 C4 34 32S 56 17W
Cañete, Chile 94 D1 37 50S 73 30W
Cañete, Peru 92 F3 13 8S 76 30W
Cangas de Narcea, Spain 19 A2 43 10N 6 32W
Canguaretama, Brazil 93 E11 6 20S 35 5W
Canguçu, Brazil 95 C5 31 22S 52 43W
Canguçu, Serra do, Brazil 95 C5 31 20S 52 40W
Cangzhou, China 34 E9 38 19N 116 52 E
Caniapiscau →, Canada 71 A6 56 40N 69 30W
Caniapiscau, Rés. de, Canada 71 B6 54 10N 69 55W
Canicattì, Italy 20 F5 37 21N 13 51 E
Canim Lake, Canada 72 C4 51 47N 120 54W
Canindeyu □, Paraguay 95 A5 24 10S 55 0W
Canisteo, U.S.A. 78 D7 42 16N 77 36W
Canisteo →, U.S.A. 78 D7 42 7N 77 8W
Cañitas, Mexico 86 C4 23 36N 102 43W
Çankırı, Turkey 25 F5 40 40N 33 37 E
Cankuzo, Burundi 54 C3 3 10S 30 31 E
Canmore, Canada 72 C5 51 7N 115 18W
Canna, U.K. 12 D2 57 3N 6 33W
Cannanore, India 40 P9 11 53N 75 27 E
Cannes, France 18 E7 43 32N 7 1 E
Canning Town = Port Canning, India 43 H13 22 23N 88 40 E
Cannington, Canada 78 B5 44 20N 79 2W
Cannock, U.K. 11 E5 52 41N 2 1W
Cannon Ball →, U.S.A. 80 B4 46 20N 100 38W
Cannondale Mt., Australia 62 D4 25 13S 148 57 E
Cannonsville Reservoir, U.S.A. 79 D9 42 4N 75 22W
Cannonvale, Australia 62 C4 20 17S 148 43 E
Canoas, Brazil 95 B5 29 56S 51 11W
Canoe L., Canada 73 B7 55 10N 108 15W
Canon City, U.S.A. 80 F2 38 27N 105 14W
Canora, Canada 73 C8 51 40N 102 30W
Canso, Canada 71 C7 45 20N 61 0W
Cantabria □, Spain 19 A4 43 10N 4 0W
Cantabrian Mts. = Cantábrica, Cordillera, Spain 19 A3 43 0N 5 10W
Cantábrica, Cordillera, Spain 19 A3 43 0N 5 10W
Cantal, Plomb du, France 18 D5 45 3N 2 45 E
Canterbury, Australia 62 D3 25 23S 141 53 E
Canterbury, U.K. 11 F9 51 16N 1 6 E
Canterbury Bight, N.Z. 59 L3 44 16S 171 55 E
Canterbury Plains, N.Z. 59 K3 43 55S 171 22 E
Cantil, U.S.A. 85 K9 35 18N 117 58W
Canton = Guangzhou, China 33 D6 23 5N 113 10 E
Canton, Ga., U.S.A. 77 H3 34 14N 84 29W
Canton, Ill., U.S.A. 80 E9 40 33N 90 2W
Canton, Miss., U.S.A. 81 J9 32 37N 90 2W
Canton, Mo., U.S.A. 80 E9 40 8N 91 32W
Canton, N.Y., U.S.A. 79 B9 44 36N 75 10W
Canton, Ohio, U.S.A. 78 F3 40 48N 81 23W
Canton, Pa., U.S.A. 78 E8 41 39N 76 51W
Canton, S. Dak., U.S.A. 80 D6 43 18N 96 35W
Canton L., U.S.A. 81 G5 36 6N 98 35W
Canudos, Brazil 92 E7 7 13S 58 5W
Canumã →, Brazil 92 D7 3 55S 59 10W
Canutama, Brazil 92 E6 6 30S 64 20W
Canutillo, U.S.A. 83 L10 31 55N 106 36W
Canvey, U.K. 11 F8 51 31N 0 37 E
Canyon, U.S.A. 81 H4 34 59N 101 55W
Canyonlands National Park, U.S.A. 83 G9 38 15N 110 0W
Canyonville, U.S.A. 82 E2 42 56N 123 17W
Cao Bang, Vietnam 38 A6 22 40N 106 15 E
Cao He →, China 35 D13 40 10N 124 32 E
Cao Lanh, Vietnam 39 G5 10 27N 105 38 E
Cao Xian, China 34 G8 34 50N 115 35 E
Cap-aux-Meules, Canada 71 C7 47 23N 61 52W
Cap-Chat, Canada 71 C6 49 6N 66 40W
Cap-de-la-Madeleine, Canada 70 C5 46 22N 72 31W
Cap-Haïtien, Haiti 89 C5 19 40N 72 20W
Capac, U.S.A. 78 C2 43 1N 82 56W
Capanaparo →, Venezuela 92 B5 7 1N 67 7W
Cape →, Australia 62 C4 20 59S 146 51 E
Cape Barren I., Australia 62 G4 40 25S 148 15 E
Cape Breton Highlands Nat. Park, Canada 71 C7 46 50N 60 40W
Cape Breton I., Canada 71 C7 46 0N 60 30W
Cape Charles, U.S.A. 76 G8 37 16N 76 1W
Cape Coast, Ghana 50 G5 5 5N 1 15W
Cape Coral, U.S.A. 77 M5 26 33N 81 57W
Cape Dorset, Canada 69 B12 64 14N 76 32W
Cape Fear →, U.S.A. 77 H6 33 53N 78 1W
Cape Girardeau, U.S.A. 81 G10 37 19N 89 32W
Cape May, U.S.A. 76 F8 38 56N 74 56W
Cape May Point, U.S.A. 76 F8 38 56N 74 58W
Cape Province, S. Africa 53 L3 32 0S 23 0 E
Cape Tormentine, Canada 71 C7 46 8N 63 47W
Cape Town, S. Africa 56 E2 33 55S 18 22 E
Cape Verde Is. ■, Atl. Oc. 49 E1 17 10N 25 20W
Cape Vincent, U.S.A. 79 B8 44 8N 76 20W
Cape York Peninsula, Australia 62 A3 12 0S 142 30 E
Capela, Brazil 93 F11 10 30S 37 0W
Capella, Australia 62 C4 23 2S 148 1 E
Capim →, Brazil 93 D9 1 40S 47 47W
Capitan, U.S.A. 83 K11 33 35N 105 35W
Capitol Reef National Park, U.S.A. 83 G8 38 15N 111 10W
Capitola, U.S.A. 84 J5 36 59N 121 57W
Capoche →, Mozam. 55 F3 15 35S 33 0 E
Capraia, Italy 18 E8 43 2N 9 50 E
Capreol, Canada 70 C3 46 43N 80 56W
Capri, Italy 20 D6 40 33N 14 14 E
Capricorn Group, Australia 62 C5 23 30S 151 55 E
Capricorn Ra., Australia 60 D2 23 20S 116 50 E
Caprivi Strip, Namibia 56 B3 18 0S 23 0 E
Caquetá →, Colombia 92 D5 1 15S 69 15W
Caracal, Romania 17 F13 44 8N 24 22 E
Caracas, Venezuela 92 A5 10 30N 66 55W
Caracol, Mato Grosso do Sul, Brazil 94 A4 22 18S 57 1W
Caracol, Piauí, Brazil 93 E10 9 15S 43 22W
Carajas, Brazil 93 E8 6 5S 50 23W
Carajás, Serra dos, Brazil 93 E8 6 0S 51 30W
Carangola, Brazil 95 A7 20 44S 42 5W
Caransebeş, Romania 17 F12 45 28N 22 18 E
Caraquet, Canada 71 C6 47 48N 64 57W
Caras, Peru 92 E3 9 3S 77 47W
Caratasca, L., Honduras 88 C3 15 20N 83 40W
Caratinga, Brazil 93 G10 19 50S 42 10W
Caraúbas, Brazil 93 E11 5 43S 37 33W
Caravaca = Caravaca de la Cruz, Spain 19 C5 38 8N 1 52W
Caravaca de la Cruz, Spain 19 C5 38 8N 1 52W
Caravelas, Brazil 93 G11 17 45S 39 15W
Caraveli, Peru 92 G4 15 45S 73 25W
Caràzinho, Brazil 95 B5 28 16S 52 46W
Carballo, Spain 19 A1 43 13N 8 41W
Carberry, Canada 73 D9 49 50N 99 25W
Carbó, Mexico 86 B2 29 42N 110 58W

Carbonara, C.

Carbonara, C., *Italy* **20 E3** 39 6N 9 31 E
Carbondale, *Colo., U.S.A.* **82 G10** 39 24N 107 13W
Carbondale, *Ill., U.S.A.* **81 G10** 37 44N 89 13W
Carbondale, *Pa., U.S.A.* **79 E9** 41 35N 75 30W
Carbonear, *Canada* **71 C9** 47 42N 53 13W
Carbónia, *Italy* **20 E3** 39 10N 8 30 E
Carcajou, *Canada* **72 B5** 57 47N 117 6W
Carcarana →, *Argentina* **94 C3** 32 27S 60 48W
Carcasse, C., *Haiti* **89 C5** 18 30N 74 28W
Carcassonne, *France* **18 E5** 43 13N 2 20 E
Carcross, *Canada* **72 A2** 60 13N 134 45W
Cardamon Hills, *India* **40 Q10** 9 30N 77 15 E
Cárdenas, *Cuba* **88 B3** 23 0N 81 30W
Cárdenas, *San Luis Potosí, Mexico* **87 C5** 22 0N 99 41W
Cárdenas, *Tabasco, Mexico* **87 D6** 17 59N 93 21W
Cardiff, *U.K.* **11 F4** 51 29N 3 10W
Cardiff □, *U.K.* **11 F4** 51 31N 3 12W
Cardiff-by-the-Sea, *U.S.A.* **85 M9** 33 1N 117 17W
Cardigan, *U.K.* **11 E3** 52 5N 4 40W
Cardigan B., *U.K.* **11 E3** 52 30N 4 30W
Cardinal, *Canada* **79 B9** 44 47N 75 23W
Cardona, *Uruguay* **94 C4** 33 53S 57 18W
Cardoso, Ilha do, *Brazil* **95 B5** 25 8S 47 58W
Cardston, *Canada* **72 D6** 49 15N 113 20W
Cardwell, *Australia* **62 B4** 18 14S 146 2 E
Careen L., *Canada* **73 B7** 57 0N 108 11W
Carei, *Romania* **17 E12** 47 40N 22 29 E
Careme = Ciremai, *Indonesia* **37 G13** 6 55S 108 27 E
Carey, *U.S.A.* **82 E7** 43 19N 113 57W
Carey, L., *Australia* **61 E3** 29 0S 122 15 E
Carey L., *Canada* **73 A8** 62 12N 102 55W
Carhué, *Argentina* **94 D3** 37 10S 62 50W
Caria, *Turkey* **21 F13** 37 20N 28 10 E
Cariacica, *Brazil* **93 H10** 20 16S 40 25W
Caribbean Sea, *W. Indies* **89 D5** 15 0N 75 0W
Cariboo Mts., *Canada* **72 C4** 53 0N 121 0W
Caribou, *U.S.A.* **77 B12** 46 52N 68 1W
Caribou →, *Man., Canada* **73 B10** 59 20N 94 44W
Caribou →, *N.W.T., Canada* **72 A3** 61 27N 125 45W
Caribou I., *Canada* **70 C2** 47 22N 85 49W
Caribou Is., *Canada* **72 A6** 61 55N 113 15W
Caribou L., *Man., Canada* **73 B9** 59 21N 96 10W
Caribou L., *Ont., Canada* **70 B2** 50 25N 89 5W
Caribou Mts., *Canada* **72 B5** 59 12N 115 40W
Carichic, *Mexico* **86 B3** 27 56N 107 3W
Carillo, *Mexico* **86 B4** 26 50N 103 55W
Carinhanha, *Brazil* **93 F10** 14 15S 44 46W
Carinhanha →, *Brazil* **93 F10** 14 20S 43 47W
Carinthia = Kärnten □, *Austria* **16 E8** 46 52N 13 30 E
Caripito, *Venezuela* **92 A6** 10 8N 63 6W
Carleton, Mt., *Canada* **71 C6** 47 23N 66 53W
Carleton Place, *Canada* **79 A8** 45 8N 76 9W
Carletonville, *S. Africa* **56 D4** 26 23S 27 22 E
Carlin, *U.S.A.* **82 F5** 40 43N 116 7W
Carlingford L., *U.K.* **13 B5** 54 3N 6 9W
Carlinville, *U.S.A.* **80 F10** 39 17N 89 53W
Carlisle, *U.K.* **10 C5** 54 54N 2 56W
Carlisle, *U.S.A.* **78 F7** 40 12N 77 12W
Carlos Casares, *Argentina* **94 D3** 35 32S 61 20W
Carlos Tejedor, *Argentina* **94 D3** 35 25S 62 25W
Carlow, *Ireland* **13 D5** 52 50N 6 56W
Carlow □, *Ireland* **13 D5** 52 43N 6 50W
Carlsbad, *Calif., U.S.A.* **85 M9** 33 10N 117 21W
Carlsbad, *N. Mex., U.S.A.* **81 J2** 32 25N 104 14W
Carlsbad Caverns National Park, *U.S.A.* **81 J2** 32 10N 104 35W
Carluke, *U.K.* **12 F5** 55 45N 3 50W
Carlyle, *Canada* **73 D8** 49 40N 102 20W
Carmacks, *Canada* **68 B6** 62 5N 136 16W
Carman, *Canada* **73 D9** 49 30N 98 0W
Carmarthen, *U.K.* **11 F3** 51 52N 4 19W
Carmarthen B., *U.K.* **11 F3** 51 40N 4 30W
Carmarthenshire □, *U.K.* **11 F3** 51 55N 4 13W
Carmaux, *France* **18 D5** 44 3N 2 10 E
Carmel, *U.S.A.* **79 E11** 41 26N 73 41W
Carmel-by-the-Sea, *U.S.A.* **84 J5** 36 33N 121 55W
Carmel Valley, *U.S.A.* **84 J5** 36 29N 121 43W
Carmelo, *Uruguay* **94 C4** 34 0S 58 20W
Carmen, *Colombia* **92 B3** 9 43N 75 8W
Carmen, *Paraguay* **95 B4** 27 13S 56 12W
Carmen →, *Mexico* **86 A3** 30 42N 106 29W
Carmen, I., *Mexico* **86 B2** 26 0N 111 20W
Carmen de Patagones, *Argentina* **96 E4** 40 50S 63 0W
Carmensa, *Argentina* **94 D2** 35 15S 67 40W
Carmi, *Canada* **72 D5** 49 36N 119 8W
Carmi, *U.S.A.* **76 F1** 38 5N 88 10W
Carmichael, *U.S.A.* **84 G5** 38 38N 121 19W
Carmila, *Australia* **62 C4** 21 55S 149 24 E
Carmona, *Costa Rica* **88 E2** 10 0N 85 15W
Carmona, *Spain* **19 D3** 37 28N 5 42W
Carn Ban, *U.K.* **12 D4** 57 7N 4 15W
Carn Eige, *U.K.* **12 D3** 57 17N 5 8W
Carnac, *France* **18 C2** 47 35N 3 6W
Carnamah, *Australia* **61 E2** 29 41S 115 53 E
Carnarvon, *Australia* **61 D1** 24 51S 113 42 E
Carnarvon, *S. Africa* **56 E3** 30 56S 22 8 E
Carnarvon Ra., *Queens., Australia* **62 D4** 25 15S 148 30 E
Carnarvon Ra., *W. Austral., Australia* **61 E3** 25 20S 120 45 E
Carnation, *U.S.A.* **84 C5** 47 39N 121 55W
Carndonagh, *Ireland* **13 A4** 55 16N 7 15W
Carnduff, *Canada* **73 D8** 49 10N 101 50W
Carnegie, *U.S.A.* **78 F4** 40 24N 80 5W
Carnegie, L., *Australia* **61 E3** 26 5S 122 30 E
Carnic Alps = Karnische Alpen, *Europe* **16 E7** 46 36N 13 0 E
Carniche Alpi = Karnische Alpen, *Europe* **16 E7** 46 36N 13 0 E
Carnot, *C.A.R.* **52 D3** 4 59N 15 56 E
Carnot, C., *Australia* **63 E2** 34 57S 135 38 E
Carnot B., *Australia* **60 C3** 17 20S 122 15 E
Carnoustie, *U.K.* **12 E6** 56 30N 2 42W
Carnsore Pt., *Ireland* **13 D5** 52 10N 6 22W
Caro, *U.S.A.* **76 D4** 43 29N 83 24W
Carol City, *U.S.A.* **77 N5** 25 56N 80 16W
Carolina, *Brazil* **93 E9** 7 10S 47 30W
Carolina, *Puerto Rico* **89 C6** 18 23N 65 58W
Carolina, *S. Africa* **57 D5** 26 5S 30 6 E
Caroline I., *Kiribati* **65 H12** 9 15S 150 3W
Caroline Is., *Micronesia* **28 J17** 8 0N 150 0 E
Caroni →, *Venezuela* **92 B6** 8 21N 62 43W
Caronie = Nébrodi, Monti, *Italy* **20 F6** 37 54N 14 35 E
Carpathians, *Europe* **17 D11** 49 30N 21 0 E
Carpaţii Meridionali, *Romania* **17 F13** 45 30N 25 0 E
Carpentaria, G. of, *Australia* **62 A2** 14 0S 139 0 E
Carpentras, *France* **18 D6** 44 3N 5 2 E
Carpi, *Italy* **20 B4** 44 47N 10 53 E
Carpinteria, *U.S.A.* **85 L7** 34 24N 119 31W
Carr Boyd Ra., *Australia* **60 C4** 16 15S 128 35 E
Carrabelle, *U.S.A.* **77 L3** 29 51N 84 40W
Carranza, Presa V., *Mexico* **86 B4** 27 20N 100 50W
Carrara, *Italy* **18 D9** 44 5N 10 6 E
Carrauntoohill, *Ireland* **13 D2** 52 0N 9 45W
Carrick-on-Shannon, *Ireland* **13 C3** 53 57N 8 5W
Carrick-on-Suir, *Ireland* **13 D4** 52 21N 7 24W
Carrickfergus, *U.K.* **13 B6** 54 43N 5 49W
Carrickmacross, *Ireland* **13 C5** 53 59N 6 43W
Carrington, *U.S.A.* **80 B5** 47 27N 99 8W
Carrizal Bajo, *Chile* **94 B1** 28 5S 71 20W
Carrizalillo, *Chile* **94 B1** 29 5S 71 30W
Carrizo Cr. →, *U.S.A.* **81 G3** 36 55N 103 55W
Carrizo Springs, *U.S.A.* **81 L5** 28 31N 99 52W
Carrizozo, *U.S.A.* **83 K11** 33 38N 105 53W
Carroll, *U.S.A.* **80 D7** 42 4N 94 52W
Carrollton, *Ga., U.S.A.* **77 J3** 33 35N 85 5W
Carrollton, *Ill., U.S.A.* **80 F9** 39 18N 90 24W
Carrollton, *Ky., U.S.A.* **76 F3** 38 41N 85 11W
Carrollton, *Mo., U.S.A.* **80 F8** 39 22N 93 30W
Carrollton, *Ohio, U.S.A.* **78 F3** 40 34N 81 5W
Carron →, *U.K.* **12 D4** 57 53N 4 22W
Carron, L., *U.K.* **12 D3** 57 22N 5 35W
Carrot →, *Canada* **73 C8** 53 50N 101 17W
Carrot River, *Canada* **73 C8** 53 17N 103 35W
Carruthers, *Canada* **73 C7** 52 52N 109 16W
Carson, *Calif., U.S.A.* **85 M8** 33 48N 118 17W
Carson, *N. Dak., U.S.A.* **80 B4** 46 25N 101 34W
Carson →, *U.S.A.* **84 F8** 39 45N 118 40W
Carson City, *U.S.A.* **84 F7** 39 10N 119 46W
Carson Sink, *U.S.A.* **82 G4** 39 50N 118 25W
Cartagena, *Colombia* **92 A3** 10 25N 75 33W
Cartagena, *Spain* **19 D5** 37 38N 0 59W
Cartago, *Colombia* **92 C3** 4 45N 75 55W
Cartago, *Costa Rica* **88 E3** 9 50N 83 55W
Cartersville, *U.S.A.* **77 H3** 34 10N 84 48W
Carterton, *N.Z.* **59 J5** 41 2S 175 31 E
Carthage, *Tunisia* **51 A8** 36 50N 10 21 E
Carthage, *Ill., U.S.A.* **80 E9** 40 25N 91 8W
Carthage, *Mo., U.S.A.* **81 G7** 37 11N 94 19W
Carthage, *N.Y., U.S.A.* **76 D8** 43 59N 75 37W
Carthage, *Tex., U.S.A.* **81 J7** 32 9N 94 20W
Cartier I., *Australia* **60 B3** 12 31S 123 29 E
Cartwright, *Canada* **71 B8** 53 41N 56 58W
Caruaru, *Brazil* **93 E11** 8 15S 35 55W
Carúpano, *Venezuela* **92 A6** 10 39N 63 15W
Caruthersville, *U.S.A.* **81 G10** 36 11N 89 39W
Carvoeiro, *Brazil* **92 D6** 1 30S 61 59W
Carvoeiro, C., *Portugal* **19 C1** 39 21N 9 24W
Cary, *U.S.A.* **77 H6** 35 47N 78 46W
Casa Grande, *U.S.A.* **83 K8** 32 53N 111 45W
Casablanca, *Chile* **94 C1** 33 20S 71 25W
Casablanca, *Morocco* **50 B4** 33 36N 7 36W
Cascade, *Idaho, U.S.A.* **82 D5** 44 31N 116 2W
Cascade, *Mont., U.S.A.* **82 C8** 47 16N 111 42W
Cascade Locks, *U.S.A.* **84 E5** 45 40N 121 54W
Cascade Ra., *U.S.A.* **84 D5** 47 0N 121 30W
Cascade Reservoir, *U.S.A.* **82 D5** 44 32N 116 3W
Cascais, *Portugal* **19 C1** 38 41N 9 25W
Cascavel, *Brazil* **95 A5** 24 57S 53 28W
Cáscina, *Italy* **20 C4** 43 41N 10 33 E
Casco B., *U.S.A.* **77 D10** 43 45N 70 0W
Caserta, *Italy* **20 D6** 41 4N 14 20 E
Cashel, *Ireland* **13 D4** 52 30N 7 53W
Casiguran, *Phil.* **37 A6** 16 22N 122 7 E
Casilda, *Argentina* **94 C3** 33 10S 61 10W
Casino, *Australia* **63 D5** 28 52S 153 3 E
Casiquiare →, *Venezuela* **92 C5** 2 1N 67 7W
Casma, *Peru* **92 E3** 9 30S 78 20W
Casmalia, *U.S.A.* **85 L6** 34 50N 120 32W
Caspe, *Spain* **19 B5** 41 14N 0 1W
Casper, *U.S.A.* **82 E10** 42 51N 106 19W
Caspian Depression, *Eurasia* **25 E8** 47 0N 48 0 E
Caspian Sea, *Eurasia* **25 F9** 43 0N 50 0 E
Cass Lake, *U.S.A.* **80 B7** 47 23N 94 37W
Cassadaga, *U.S.A.* **78 D5** 42 20N 79 19W
Casselman, *Canada* **79 A9** 45 19N 75 5W
Casselton, *U.S.A.* **80 B6** 46 54N 97 13W
Cassiar, *Canada* **72 B3** 59 16N 129 40W
Cassiar Mts., *Canada* **72 B2** 59 30N 130 30W
Cassino, *Italy* **20 D5** 41 30N 13 49 E
Cassville, *U.S.A.* **81 G8** 36 41N 93 52W
Castaic, *U.S.A.* **85 L8** 34 30N 118 38W
Castalia, *U.S.A.* **78 E2** 41 24N 82 49W
Castanhal, *Brazil* **93 D9** 1 18S 47 55W
Castellammare di Stábia, *Italy* **20 D6** 40 42N 14 29 E
Castelli, *Argentina* **94 D4** 36 7S 57 47W
Castelló de la Plana, *Spain* **19 C5** 39 58N 0 3W
Castelo, *Brazil* **95 A7** 20 33S 41 14W
Castelo Branco, *Portugal* **19 C2** 39 50N 7 31W
Castelsarrasin, *France* **18 E4** 44 2N 1 7 E
Castelvetrano, *Italy* **20 F5** 37 41N 12 47 E
Castile, *U.S.A.* **78 D6** 42 38N 78 3W
Castilla-La Mancha □, *Spain* **19 C4** 39 30N 3 30W
Castilla y Leon □, *Spain* **19 B3** 42 0N 5 0W
Castillos, *Uruguay* **95 C5** 34 12S 53 52W
Castle Dale, *U.S.A.* **82 G8** 39 13N 111 1W
Castle Douglas, *U.K.* **12 G5** 54 56N 3 56W
Castle Rock, *Colo., U.S.A.* **80 F2** 39 22N 104 51W
Castle Rock, *Wash., U.S.A.* **84 D4** 46 17N 122 54W
Castlebar, *Ireland* **13 C2** 53 52N 9 18W
Castleblaney, *Ireland* **13 B5** 54 7N 6 44W
Castlederg, *U.K.* **13 B4** 54 42N 7 35W
Castleford, *U.K.* **10 D6** 53 43N 1 21W
Castlegar, *Canada* **72 D5** 49 20N 117 40W
Castlepollard, *Ireland* **13 C4** 53 41N 7 19W
Castlerea, *Ireland* **13 C3** 53 46N 8 29W
Castlereagh →, *Australia* **63 E4** 30 12S 147 32 E
Castlereagh B., *Australia* **62 A2** 12 10S 135 10 E
Castleton, *U.S.A.* **79 C11** 43 37N 73 11W
Castletown, *U.K.* **10 C3** 54 5N 4 38W
Castletown Bearhaven, *Ireland* **13 E2** 51 39N 9 55W
Castor, *Canada* **72 C6** 52 15N 111 50W
Castor →, *Canada* **70 B4** 53 24N 78 58W
Castorland, *U.S.A.* **79 C9** 43 53N 75 31W
Castres, *France* **18 E5** 43 37N 2 13 E
Castricum, *Neths.* **15 B4** 52 33N 4 40 E
Castries, *St. Lucia* **89 D7** 14 2N 60 58W
Castro, *Brazil* **95 A6** 24 45S 50 0W
Castro, *Chile* **96 E2** 42 30S 73 50W
Castro Alves, *Brazil* **93 F11** 12 46S 39 33W
Castroville, *U.S.A.* **84 J5** 36 46N 121 45W
Castuera, *Spain* **19 C3** 38 43N 5 37W
Cat Ba, Dao, *Vietnam* **38 B6** 20 50N 107 0 E
Cat I., *Bahamas* **89 B4** 24 30N 75 30W
Cat L., *Canada* **70 B1** 51 40N 91 50W
Cat Lake, *Canada* **70 B1** 51 40N 91 50W
Catacamas, *Honduras* **88 D2** 14 54N 85 56W
Cataguases, *Brazil* **95 A7** 21 23S 42 39W
Catalão, *Brazil* **93 G9** 18 10S 47 57W
Çatalca, *Turkey* **21 D13** 41 8N 28 27 E
Catalina, *Canada* **71 C9** 48 31N 53 4W
Catalina, *Chile* **94 B2** 25 13S 69 43W
Catalina, *U.S.A.* **83 K8** 32 30N 110 50W
Catalonia = Cataluña □, *Spain* **19 B6** 41 40N 1 15 E
Cataluña □, *Spain* **19 B6** 41 40N 1 15 E
Catamarca, *Argentina* **94 B2** 28 30S 65 50W
Catamarca □, *Argentina* **94 B2** 27 0S 65 50W
Catanduanes □, *Phil.* **37 B6** 13 50N 124 20 E
Catanduva, *Brazil* **95 A6** 21 5S 48 58W
Catánia, *Italy* **20 F6** 37 30N 15 6 E
Catanzaro, *Italy* **20 E7** 38 54N 16 35 E
Catarman, *Phil.* **37 B6** 12 28N 124 35 E
Cateel, *Phil.* **37 C7** 7 47N 126 24 E
Catembe, *Mozam.* **57 D5** 26 0S 32 33 E
Caterham, *U.K.* **11 F7** 51 15N 0 4W
Cathcart, *S. Africa* **56 E4** 32 18S 27 10 E
Cathlamet, *U.S.A.* **84 D3** 46 12N 123 23W
Catlettsburg, *U.S.A.* **76 F4** 38 25N 82 36W
Catoche, C., *Mexico* **87 C7** 21 40N 87 8W
Catriló, *Argentina* **94 D3** 36 26S 63 24W
Catrimani, *Brazil* **92 C6** 0 27N 61 41W
Catrimani →, *Brazil* **92 C6** 0 28N 61 44W
Catskill, *U.S.A.* **79 D11** 42 14N 73 52W
Catskill Mts., *U.S.A.* **79 D10** 42 10N 74 25W
Catt, Mt., *Australia* **62 A1** 13 49S 134 23 E
Cattaraugus, *U.S.A.* **78 D6** 42 22N 78 52W
Catuala, *Angola* **56 B2** 16 25S 19 2 E
Catuane, *Mozam.* **57 D5** 26 48S 32 18 E
Catur, *Mozam.* **55 E4** 13 45S 35 30 E
Catwick Is., *Vietnam* **39 G7** 10 0N 109 0 E
Cauca →, *Colombia* **92 B4** 8 54N 74 28W
Caucaia, *Brazil* **93 D11** 3 40S 38 35W
Caucasus Mountains, *Eurasia* **25 F7** 42 50N 44 0 E
Caungula, *Angola* **52 F3** 8 26S 18 38 E
Cauquenes, *Chile* **94 D1** 36 0S 72 22W
Caura →, *Venezuela* **92 B6** 7 38N 64 53W
Cauresi →, *Mozam.* **55 F3** 17 8S 33 0 E
Causapscal, *Canada* **71 C6** 48 19N 67 12W
Cauvery →, *India* **40 P11** 11 9N 78 52 E
Caux, Pays de, *France* **18 B4** 49 38N 0 35 E
Cavalier, *U.S.A.* **80 A6** 48 48N 97 37W
Cavalleria, C. de, *Spain* **22 A11** 40 5N 4 5 E
Cavan, *Ireland* **13 B4** 54 0N 7 22W
Cavan □, *Ireland* **13 C4** 53 58N 7 10W
Cave Creek, *U.S.A.* **83 K7** 33 50N 111 57W
Cavenagh Ra., *Australia* **61 E4** 26 12S 127 55 E
Caviana, I., *Brazil* **93 C8** 0 10N 50 10W
Cavite, *Phil.* **37 B6** 14 29N 120 55 E
Cawnpore = Kanpur, *India* **43 F9** 26 28N 80 20 E
Caxias, *Brazil* **93 D10** 4 55S 43 20W
Caxias do Sul, *Brazil* **95 B5** 29 10S 51 10W
Cay Sal Bank, *Bahamas* **88 B4** 23 45N 80 0W
Cayambe, *Ecuador* **92 C3** 0 3N 78 8W
Cayenne, *Fr. Guiana* **93 B8** 5 5N 52 18W
Cayman Brac, *Cayman Is.* **88 C4** 19 43N 79 49W
Cayman Is. ■, *W. Indies* **88 C3** 19 40N 80 30W
Cayo Romano, *Cuba* **88 B4** 22 0N 78 0W
Cayuga, *Canada* **78 D5** 42 59N 79 50W
Cayuga, *U.S.A.* **79 D8** 42 54N 76 44W
Cayuga L., *U.S.A.* **79 D8** 42 41N 76 41W
Cazenovia, *U.S.A.* **79 D9** 42 56N 75 51W
Cazombo, *Angola* **53 G4** 11 54S 22 56 E
Ceanannus Mor, *Ireland* **13 C5** 53 44N 6 53W
Ceará = Fortaleza, *Brazil* **93 D11** 3 45S 38 35W
Ceará □, *Brazil* **93 E11** 5 0S 40 0W
Ceará Mirim, *Brazil* **93 E11** 5 38S 35 25W
Cebaco, I. de, *Panama* **88 E3** 7 33N 81 9W
Cebollar, *Argentina* **94 B2** 29 10S 66 35W
Cebu, *Phil.* **37 B6** 10 18N 123 54 E
Cecil Plains, *Australia* **63 D5** 27 30S 151 11 E
Cedar →, *U.S.A.* **80 E9** 41 17N 91 21W
Cedar City, *U.S.A.* **83 H7** 37 41N 113 4W
Cedar Creek Reservoir, *U.S.A.* **81 J6** 32 11N 96 4W
Cedar Falls, *Iowa, U.S.A.* **80 D8** 42 32N 92 27W
Cedar Falls, *Wash., U.S.A.* **84 C5** 47 25N 121 45W
Cedar Key, *U.S.A.* **77 L4** 29 8N 83 2W
Cedar L., *Canada* **73 C9** 53 10N 100 0W
Cedar Rapids, *U.S.A.* **80 E9** 41 59N 91 40W
Cedartown, *U.S.A.* **77 H3** 34 1N 85 15W
Cedarvale, *Canada* **72 B3** 55 1N 128 22W
Cedarville, *S. Africa* **57 E4** 30 23S 29 3 E
Cedral, *Mexico* **86 C4** 23 50N 100 42W
Cedro, *Brazil* **93 E11** 6 34S 39 3W
Cedros, I. de, *Mexico* **86 B1** 28 10N 115 20W
Ceduna, *Australia* **63 E1** 32 7S 133 46 E
Cefalù, *Italy* **20 E6** 38 2N 14 1 E
Cegléd, *Hungary* **17 E10** 47 11N 19 47 E
Celaya, *Mexico* **86 C4** 20 31N 100 37W
Celebes Sea, *Indonesia* **37 D6** 3 0N 123 0 E
Celina, *U.S.A.* **76 E3** 40 33N 84 35W
Celje, *Slovenia* **16 E8** 46 16N 15 18 E
Celle, *Germany* **16 B6** 52 37N 10 4 E
Cenderwasih, Teluk, *Indonesia* **37 E9** 3 0S 135 20 E
Center, *N. Dak., U.S.A.* **80 B4** 47 7N 101 18W
Center, *Tex., U.S.A.* **81 K7** 31 48N 94 11W
Centerburg, *U.S.A.* **78 F2** 40 18N 82 42W
Centerville, *Calif., U.S.A.* **84 J7** 36 44N 119 30W
Centerville, *Iowa, U.S.A.* **80 E8** 40 44N 92 52W
Centerville, *Pa., U.S.A.* **78 F5** 40 3N 79 59W
Centerville, *Tenn., U.S.A.* **77 H2** 35 47N 87 28W
Centerville, *Tex., U.S.A.* **81 K7** 31 16N 95 59W
Central □, *Kenya* **54 C4** 0 30S 37 30 E
Central □, *Malawi* **55 E3** 13 30S 33 30 E
Central □, *Zambia* **55 E2** 14 25S 28 50 E
Central, Cordillera, *Colombia* **92 C4** 5 0N 75 0W
Central, Cordillera, *Costa Rica* **88 D3** 10 10N 84 5W
Central, Cordillera, *Dom. Rep.* **89 C5** 19 15N 71 0W
Central African Rep. ■, *Africa* **52 C4** 7 0N 20 0 E
Central America, *America* **66 H11** 12 0N 85 0W
Central Butte, *Canada* **73 C7** 50 48N 106 31W
Central City, *Colo., U.S.A.* **82 G11** 39 48N 105 31W
Central City, *Ky., U.S.A.* **76 G2** 37 18N 87 7W
Central City, *Nebr., U.S.A.* **80 E6** 41 7N 98 0W
Central I., *Kenya* **54 B4** 3 30N 36 0 E
Central Makran Range, *Pakistan* **40 F4** 26 30N 64 15 E
Central Patricia, *Canada* **70 B1** 51 30N 90 9W
Central Point, *U.S.A.* **82 E2** 42 23N 122 55W
Central Russian Uplands, *Europe* **6 E13** 54 0N 36 0 E
Central Siberian Plateau, *Russia* **28 C14** 65 0N 105 0 E
Central Square, *U.S.A.* **79 C8** 43 17N 76 9W
Centralia, *Ill., U.S.A.* **80 F10** 38 32N 89 8W
Centralia, *Mo., U.S.A.* **80 F8** 39 13N 92 8W
Centralia, *Wash., U.S.A.* **84 D4** 46 43N 122 58W
Cephalonia = Kefallinía, *Greece* **21 E9** 38 20N 20 30 E
Cepu, *Indonesia* **37 G14** 7 9S 111 35 E
Ceram = Seram, *Indonesia* **37 E7** 3 10S 129 0 E
Ceram Sea = Seram Sea, *Indonesia* **37 E7** 2 30S 128 30 E
Ceredigion □, *U.K.* **11 E3** 52 16N 4 15W
Ceres, *Argentina* **94 B3** 29 55S 61 55W
Ceres, *S. Africa* **56 E2** 33 21S 19 18 E
Ceres, *U.S.A.* **84 H6** 37 35N 120 57W
Cerignola, *Italy* **20 D6** 41 17N 15 53 E
Cerigo = Kíthira, *Greece* **21 F10** 36 8N 23 0 E
Çerkezköy, *Turkey* **21 D12** 41 17N 28 0 E
Cerralvo, I., *Mexico* **86 C3** 24 20N 109 45W
Cerritos, *Mexico* **86 C4** 22 27N 100 20W
Cerro Chato, *Uruguay* **95 C4** 33 6S 55 8W
Cervantes, *Australia* **61 F2** 30 31S 115 3 E
Cervera, *Spain* **19 B6** 41 40N 1 16 E
Cesena, *Italy* **20 B5** 44 8N 12 15 E
Cēsis, *Latvia* **9 H21** 57 18N 25 15 E
České Budějovice, *Czech Rep.* **16 D8** 48 55N 14 25 E
Českomoravská Vrchovina, *Czech Rep.* **16 D8** 49 30N 15 40 E
Çeşme, *Turkey* **21 E12** 38 20N 26 23 E
Cetinje, *Montenegro, Yug.* **21 C8** 42 23N 18 59 E
Cetraro, *Italy* **20 E6** 39 31N 15 55 E
Ceuta, *N. Afr.* **19 E3** 35 52N 5 18W
Cévennes, *France* **18 D5** 44 10N 3 50 E
Ceyhan, *Turkey* **44 B2** 37 4N 35 47 E
Ceylon = Sri Lanka ■, *Asia* **40 R12** 7 30N 80 50 E
Cha-am, *Thailand* **38 F2** 12 48N 99 58 E
Cha Pa, *Vietnam* **38 A4** 22 20N 103 47 E
Chacabuco, *Argentina* **94 C3** 34 40S 60 27W
Chachapoyas, *Peru* **92 E3** 6 15S 77 50W
Chachoengsao, *Thailand* **38 F3** 13 42N 101 5 E
Chachran, *Pakistan* **40 E7** 28 55N 70 30 E
Chachro, *Pakistan* **42 G4** 25 5N 70 15 E
Chaco □, *Argentina* **94 B3** 26 30S 61 0W
Chaco □, *Paraguay* **94 B4** 26 0S 60 0W
Chaco →, *U.S.A.* **83 H9** 36 46N 108 39W
Chaco Austral, *S. Amer.* **96 B4** 27 0S 61 30W
Chaco Boreal, *S. Amer.* **92 H6** 22 0S 60 0W
Chaco Central, *S. Amer.* **96 A4** 24 0S 61 0W
Chacon, C., *U.S.A.* **72 C2** 54 42N 132 0W
Chad ■, *Africa* **51 F8** 15 0N 17 15 E
Chad, L. = Tchad, L., *Chad* **51 F8** 13 30N 14 30 E
Chadan, *Russia* **27 D10** 51 17N 91 35 E
Chadileuvú →, *Argentina* **94 D2** 37 46S 66 0W
Chadiza, *Zambia* **55 E3** 14 45S 32 27 E
Chadron, *U.S.A.* **80 D3** 42 50N 103 0W
Chadyr-Lunga = Ciadâr-Lunga, *Moldova* **17 E15** 46 3N 28 51 E
Chae Hom, *Thailand* **38 C2** 18 43N 99 35 E
Chaem →, *Thailand* **38 C2** 18 11N 98 38 E
Chaeryŏng, *N. Korea* **35 E13** 38 24N 125 36 E
Chagai Hills = Chāh Gay, *Afghan.* **40 E3** 29 30N 64 0 E
Chagda, *Russia* **27 D14** 58 45N 130 38 E
Chagos Arch., *Ind. Oc.* **29 K11** 6 0S 72 0 E
Chagrin Falls, *U.S.A.* **78 E3** 41 26N 81 24W
Chāh Ākhvor, *Iran* **45 C8** 32 41N 59 40 E
Chāh Bahar, *Iran* **45 E9** 25 20N 60 40 E
Chāh-e Kavīr, *Iran* **45 C8** 34 29N 56 52 E
Chāh Gay, *Afghan.* **40 E3** 29 30N 64 0 E
Chahar Burjak, *Afghan.* **40 D3** 30 15N 62 0 E
Chahār Mahāll va Bakhtīarī □, *Iran* **45 C6** 32 0N 49 0 E
Chaibasa, *India* **41 H14** 22 42N 85 49 E
Chainat, *Thailand* **38 E3** 15 11N 100 8 E
Chaiya, *Thailand* **39 H2** 9 23N 99 14 E
Chaj Doab, *Pakistan* **42 C5** 32 15N 73 0 E
Chajari, *Argentina* **94 C4** 30 42S 58 0W
Chak Amru, *Pakistan* **42 C6** 32 22N 75 11 E
Chakar →, *Pakistan* **42 E3** 29 29N 68 2 E
Chakari, *Zimbabwe* **57 B4** 18 5S 29 51 E
Chake Chake, *Tanzania* **54 D4** 5 15S 39 45 E
Chakhānsūr, *Afghan.* **40 D3** 31 10N 62 0 E
Chakonipau, L., *Canada* **71 A6** 56 18N 68 30W
Chakradharpur, *India* **43 H11** 22 45N 85 40 E
Chakrata, *India* **42 D7** 30 42N 77 51 E
Chakwal, *Pakistan* **42 C5** 32 56N 72 53 E
Chala, *Peru* **92 G4** 15 48S 74 20W
Chalchihuites, *Mexico* **86 C4** 23 29N 103 53W
Chalcis = Khalkís, *Greece* **21 E10** 38 27N 23 42 E
Chaleur B., *Canada* **71 C6** 47 55N 65 30W
Chalfant, *U.S.A.* **84 H8** 37 32N 118 21W
Chalhuanca, *Peru* **92 F4** 14 15S 73 15W
Chalisgaon, *India* **40 J9** 20 30N 75 10 E
Chalk River, *Canada* **70 C4** 46 1N 77 27W
Chalky Inlet, *N.Z.* **59 M1** 46 3S 166 31 E
Challapata, *Bolivia* **92 G5** 18 53S 66 50W
Challis, *U.S.A.* **82 D6** 44 30N 114 14W
Chalmette, *U.S.A.* **81 L10** 29 56N 89 58W
Chalon-sur-Saône, *France* **18 C6** 46 48N 4 50 E
Châlons-en-Champagne, *France* **18 B6** 48 58N 4 20 E
Chalyaphum, *Thailand* **38 E4** 15 48N 102 2 E
Cham, Cu Lao, *Vietnam* **38 E7** 15 57N 108 30 E
Chama, *U.S.A.* **83 H10** 36 54N 106 35W
Chamaicó, *Argentina* **94 D3** 35 3S 64 58W

Chimaltitán

Chaman, Pakistan 40 D5 30 58N 66 25 E
Chamba, India 42 C7 32 35N 76 10 E
Chamba, Tanzania 55 E4 11 37S 37 0 E
Chambal →, India 43 F8 26 29N 79 15 E
Chamberlain, U.S.A. 80 D5 43 49N 99 20W
Chamberlain →, Australia 60 C4 15 30S 127 54 E
Chamberlain L., U.S.A. 77 B11 46 14N 69 19W
Chambers, U.S.A. 83 J9 35 11N 109 26W
Chambersburg, U.S.A. 76 F7 39 56N 77 40W
Chambéry, France 18 D6 45 34N 5 55 E
Chambeshi →, Zambia 52 G6 11 53S 29 48 E
Chambly, Canada 79 A11 45 27N 73 17W
Chambord, Canada 71 C5 48 25N 72 6W
Chamchamal, Iraq 44 C5 35 32N 44 50 E
Chamela, Mexico 86 D3 19 32N 105 5W
Chamical, Argentina 94 C2 30 22S 66 27W
Chamkar Luong, Cambodia 39 G4 11 0N 103 45 E
Chamoli, India 43 D8 30 24N 79 21 E
Chamonix-Mont Blanc, France 18 D7 45 55N 6 51 E
Chamouchouane →, Canada 70 C5 48 37N 72 20W
Champa, India 43 H10 22 2N 82 43 E
Champagne, Canada 72 A1 60 49N 136 30W
Champagne, France 18 B6 48 40N 4 20 E
Champaign, U.S.A. 76 E1 40 7N 88 15W
Champassak, Laos 38 E5 14 53N 105 52 E
Champawat, India 43 E9 29 20N 80 6 E
Champdoré, L., Canada 71 A6 55 55N 65 49W
Champion, U.S.A. 78 E4 41 19N 80 51W
Champlain, U.S.A. 79 B11 44 59N 73 27W
Champlain, L., U.S.A. 79 B11 44 40N 73 20W
Champotón, Mexico 87 D6 19 20N 90 50W
Champua, India 43 H11 22 5N 85 40 E
Chana, Thailand 39 J3 6 55N 100 44 E
Chañaral, Chile 94 B1 26 23S 70 40W
Chanārān, Iran 45 B8 36 39N 59 6 E
Chanasma, India 42 H5 23 44N 72 5 E
Chanco, Chile 94 D1 35 44S 72 32W
Chand, India 43 J8 21 57N 79 7 E
Chandan, India 43 G12 24 38N 86 40 E
Chandan Chauki, India 43 E9 28 33N 80 47 E
Chandannagar, India 43 H13 22 52N 88 24 E
Chandausi, India 43 E8 28 27N 78 49 E
Chandeleur Is., U.S.A. 81 L10 29 55N 88 57W
Chandeleur Sd., U.S.A. 81 L10 29 55N 89 0W
Chandigarh, India 42 D7 30 43N 76 47 E
Chandil, India 43 H12 22 58N 86 3 E
Chandler, Australia 63 D1 27 0S 133 19 E
Chandler, Canada 71 C7 48 18N 64 46W
Chandler, Ariz., U.S.A. 83 K8 33 18N 111 50W
Chandler, Okla., U.S.A. 81 H6 35 42N 96 53W
Chandod, India 42 J5 21 59N 73 28 E
Chandpur, Bangla. 41 H17 23 8N 90 45 E
Chandrapur, India 40 K11 19 57N 79 25 E
Chānf, Iran 45 E9 26 38N 60 29 E
Chang, Pakistan 42 F3 26 59N 68 30 E
Chang, Ko, Thailand 39 F4 12 0N 102 23 E
Ch'ang Chiang = Chang Jiang →, China 33 C7 31 48N 121 10 E
Chang Jiang →, China 33 C7 31 48N 121 10 E
Changa, India 43 C7 33 53N 77 35 E
Changanacheri, India 40 Q10 9 25N 76 31 E
Changane →, Mozam. 57 C5 24 30S 33 30 E
Changbai, China 35 D15 41 25N 128 5 E
Changbai Shan, China 35 C15 42 20N 129 0 E
Changchiak'ou = Zhangjiakou, China 34 D8 40 48N 114 55 E
Ch'angchou = Changzhou, China 33 C6 31 47N 119 58 E
Changchun, China 35 C13 43 57N 125 17 E
Changchunling, China 35 B13 45 18N 125 27 E
Changde, China 33 D6 29 4N 111 35 E
Changdo-ri, N. Korea 35 E14 38 30N 127 40 E
Changhai = Shanghai, China 33 C7 31 15N 121 26 E
Changhua, Taiwan 33 D7 24 2N 120 30 E
Changhŭng, S. Korea 35 G14 34 41N 126 52 E
Changhŭngni, N. Korea 35 D15 40 24N 128 19 E
Changjiang, China 38 C7 19 20N 108 55 E
Changjin, N. Korea 35 D14 40 23N 127 15 E
Changjin-chŏsuji, N. Korea 35 D14 40 30N 127 15 E
Changli, China 35 E10 39 40N 119 13 E
Changling, China 35 B12 44 20N 123 58 E
Changlun, Malaysia 39 J3 6 25N 100 26 E
Changping, China 34 D9 40 14N 116 12 E
Changsha, China 33 D6 28 12N 113 0 E
Changwu, China 34 G4 35 10N 107 45 E
Changyi, China 35 F10 36 40N 119 30 E
Changyŏn, N. Korea 35 E13 38 15N 125 6 E
Changyuan, China 34 G8 35 15N 114 42 E
Changzhi, China 34 F7 36 10N 113 6 E
Changzhou, China 33 C6 31 47N 119 58 E
Chanhanga, Angola 56 B1 16 0S 14 8 E
Channapatna, India 40 N10 12 40N 77 15 E
Channel Is., U.K. 11 H5 49 19N 2 24W
Channel Is., U.S.A. 85 M7 33 40N 119 15W
Channel Islands National Park, U.S.A. 85 M8 33 30N 119 0W
Channel-Port aux Basques, Canada 71 C8 47 30N 59 9W
Channel Tunnel, Europe 11 F9 51 0N 1 30 E
Channing, U.S.A. 81 H3 35 41N 102 20W
Chantada, Spain 19 A2 42 36N 7 46W
Chanthaburi, Thailand 38 F4 12 38N 102 12 E
Chantrey Inlet, Canada 68 B10 67 48N 96 20W
Chanute, U.S.A. 81 G7 37 41N 95 27W
Chao Phraya →, Thailand 38 F3 13 32N 100 36 E
Chao Phraya Lowlands, Thailand 38 E3 15 30N 100 0 E
Chaocheng, China 34 F8 36 4N 115 37 E
Chaoyang, China 35 D11 41 35N 120 22 E
Chaozhou, China 33 D6 23 42N 116 32 E
Chapais, Canada 70 C5 49 47N 74 51W
Chapala, Mozam. 55 F4 15 50S 37 35 E
Chapala, L. de, Mexico 86 C4 20 10N 103 20W
Chapayev, Kazakstan 25 D9 50 25N 51 10 E
Chapayevsk, Russia 24 D8 53 0N 49 40 E
Chapecó, Brazil 95 B5 27 14S 52 41W
Chapel Hill, U.S.A. 77 H6 35 55N 79 4W
Chapleau, Canada 70 C3 47 50N 83 24W
Chaplin, Canada 73 C7 50 28N 106 40W
Chaplin L., Canada 73 C7 50 22N 106 36W
Chappell, U.S.A. 80 E3 41 6N 102 28W
Chapra = Chhapra, India 43 G11 25 48N 84 44 E
Chara, Russia 27 D12 56 54N 118 20 E
Charadai, Argentina 94 B4 27 35S 59 55W
Charagua, Bolivia 92 G6 19 45S 63 10W
Charambirá, Punta, Colombia 92 C3 4 16N 77 32W
Charaña, Bolivia 92 G5 17 30S 69 25W
Charanwala, India 42 F5 27 51N 72 10 E
Charata, Argentina 94 B3 27 13S 61 14W
Charcas, Mexico 86 C4 23 10N 101 20W
Chard, U.K. 11 G5 50 52N 2 58W
Chardon, U.S.A. 78 E3 41 35N 81 12W
Chardzhou = Chärjew, Turkmenistan 26 F7 39 6N 63 34 E
Charente →, France 18 D3 45 57N 1 5W
Chari →, Chad 51 F8 12 58N 14 31 E
Chārīkār, Afghan. 40 B6 35 0N 69 10 E
Chariton →, U.S.A. 80 F8 39 19N 92 58W
Chärjew, Turkmenistan 26 F7 39 6N 63 34 E
Charkhari, India 43 G8 25 24N 79 45 E
Charkhi Dadri, India 42 E7 28 37N 76 17 E
Charleroi, Belgium 15 D4 50 24N 4 27 E
Charleroi, U.S.A. 78 F5 40 9N 79 57W
Charles, C., U.S.A. 76 G8 37 7N 75 58W
Charles City, U.S.A. 80 D8 43 4N 92 41W
Charles L., Canada 73 B6 59 50N 110 33W
Charles Town, U.S.A. 76 F7 39 17N 77 52W
Charleston, Ill., U.S.A. 76 F1 39 30N 88 10W
Charleston, Miss., U.S.A. 81 H9 34 1N 90 4W
Charleston, Mo., U.S.A. 81 G10 36 55N 89 21W
Charleston, S.C., U.S.A. 77 J6 32 46N 79 56W
Charleston, W. Va., U.S.A. 76 F5 38 21N 81 38W
Charleston L., Canada 79 B9 44 32N 76 0W
Charleston Peak, U.S.A. 85 J11 36 16N 115 42W
Charlestown, Ireland 13 C3 53 58N 8 48W
Charlestown, S. Africa 57 D4 27 26S 29 53 E
Charlestown, Ind., U.S.A. 76 F3 38 27N 85 40W
Charlestown, N.H., U.S.A. 79 C12 43 14N 72 25W
Charleville = Rath Luirc, Ireland 13 D3 52 21N 8 40W
Charleville, Australia 63 D4 26 24S 146 15 E
Charleville-Mézières, France 18 B6 49 44N 4 40 E
Charlevoix, U.S.A. 76 C3 45 19N 85 16W
Charlotte, Mich., U.S.A. 76 D3 42 34N 84 50W
Charlotte, N.C., U.S.A. 77 H5 35 13N 80 51W
Charlotte, Vt., U.S.A. 79 B11 44 19N 73 14W
Charlotte Amalie, U.S. Virgin Is. 89 C7 18 21N 64 56W
Charlotte Harbor, U.S.A. 77 M4 26 50N 82 10W
Charlotte L., Canada 72 C3 52 12N 125 19W
Charlottesville, U.S.A. 76 F6 38 2N 78 30W
Charlottetown, Nfld., Canada 71 B8 52 46N 56 7W
Charlottetown, P.E.I., Canada 71 C7 46 14N 63 8W
Charlton, U.S.A. 80 E8 40 59N 93 20W
Charlton I., Canada 70 B4 52 0N 79 20W
Charny, Canada 71 C5 46 43N 71 15W
Charolles, France 18 C6 46 27N 4 16 E
Charre, Mozam. 55 F4 17 13S 35 10 E
Charsadda, Pakistan 42 B4 34 7N 71 45 E
Charters Towers, Australia 62 C4 20 5S 146 13 E
Chartres, France 18 B4 48 29N 1 30 E
Chascomús, Argentina 94 D4 35 30S 58 0W
Chasefu, Zambia 55 E3 11 55S 33 8 E
Chashma Barrage, Pakistan 42 C4 32 27N 71 20 E
Chāt, Iran 45 B7 37 59N 55 16 E
Châteaubriant, France 18 C3 47 43N 1 23W
Chateaugay, U.S.A. 79 B10 44 56N 74 5W
Châteauguay, L., Canada 71 A5 56 26N 70 3W
Châteaulin, France 18 B1 48 11N 4 8W
Châteauroux, France 18 C4 46 50N 1 40 E
Châtellerault, France 18 C4 46 50N 0 30 E
Chatham = Miramichi, Canada 71 C6 47 2N 65 28W
Chatham, Canada 78 D2 42 24N 82 11W
Chatham, U.K. 11 F8 51 22N 0 32 E
Chatham, U.S.A. 79 D11 42 21N 73 36W
Chatham Is., Pac. Oc. 64 M10 44 0S 176 40W
Chatmohar, Bangla. 43 G13 24 15N 89 15 E
Chatra, India 43 G11 24 12N 84 56 E
Chatrapur, India 41 K14 19 22N 85 2 E
Chats, L. des, Canada 79 A8 45 30N 76 20W
Chatsu, India 42 F6 26 36N 75 57 E
Chatsworth, Canada 78 B4 44 27N 80 54W
Chatsworth, Zimbabwe 55 F3 19 38S 31 13 E
Chattahoochee, U.S.A. 77 K3 30 42N 84 51W
Chattahoochee →, U.S.A. 77 K3 30 54N 84 57W
Chattanooga, U.S.A. 77 H3 35 3N 85 19W
Chatteris, U.K. 11 E8 52 28N 0 2 E
Chaturat, Thailand 38 E3 15 40N 101 51 E
Chau Doc, Vietnam 39 G5 10 42N 105 7 E
Chaukan Pass, Burma 41 F20 27 0N 97 15 E
Chaumont, France 18 B6 48 7N 5 8 E
Chaumont, U.S.A. 79 B8 44 4N 76 8W
Chautauqua L., U.S.A. 78 D5 42 10N 79 24W
Chauvin, Canada 73 C6 52 45N 110 10W
Chaves, Brazil 93 D9 0 15S 49 55W
Chaves, Portugal 19 B2 41 45N 7 32W
Chawang, Thailand 39 H2 8 25N 99 30 E
Chaykovskiy, Russia 24 C9 56 47N 54 9 E
Chazy, U.S.A. 79 B11 44 53N 73 26W
Cheb, Czech Rep. 16 C7 50 9N 12 28 E
Cheboksary, Russia 24 C8 56 8N 47 12 E
Cheboygan, U.S.A. 76 C3 45 39N 84 29W
Chech, Erg, Africa 50 D5 25 0N 2 15W
Chechenia □, Russia 25 F8 43 30N 45 29 E
Checheno-Ingush Republic = Chechenia □, Russia 25 F8 43 30N 45 29 E
Chechnya = Chechenia □, Russia 25 F8 43 30N 45 29 E
Chech'ŏn, S. Korea 35 F15 37 8N 128 12 E
Checotah, U.S.A. 81 H7 35 28N 95 31W
Chedabucto B., Canada 71 C7 45 25N 61 8W
Cheduba I., Burma 41 K18 18 45N 93 40 E
Cheepie, Australia 63 D4 26 33S 145 1 E
Chegdomyn, Russia 27 D14 51 7N 133 1 E
Chegga, Mauritania 50 C4 25 27N 5 40W
Chegutu, Zimbabwe 55 F3 18 10S 30 14 E
Chehalis, U.S.A. 84 D4 46 40N 122 58W
Chehalis →, U.S.A. 84 D3 46 57N 123 50W
Cheju do, S. Korea 35 H14 33 29N 126 34 E
Chekiang = Zhejiang □, China 33 D7 29 0N 120 0 E
Chela, Sa. da, Angola 56 B1 16 20S 13 20 E
Chelan, U.S.A. 82 C4 47 51N 120 1W
Chelan, L., U.S.A. 82 B3 48 11N 120 30W
Cheleken, Turkmenistan 25 G9 39 34N 53 16 E
Cheleken Yarymadasy, Turkmenistan 45 B7 39 30N 53 15 E
Chelforó, Argentina 96 D3 39 0S 66 33W
Chelkar = Shalqar, Kazakstan 26 E6 47 48N 59 39 E
Chelkar Tengiz, Solonchak, Kazakstan 26 E7 48 5N 63 7 E
Chełm, Poland 17 C12 51 8N 23 30 E
Chełmno, Poland 17 B10 53 20N 18 30 E
Chelmsford, U.K. 11 F8 51 44N 0 29 E
Chelsea, U.S.A. 79 C12 43 59N 72 27W
Cheltenham, U.K. 11 F5 51 54N 2 4W
Chelyabinsk, Russia 26 D7 55 10N 61 24 E
Chelyuskin, C., Russia 28 B14 77 30N 103 0 E
Chemainus, Canada 84 B3 48 55N 123 42W
Chemba, Mozam. 53 H6 17 9S 34 53 E
Chemnitz, Germany 16 C7 50 51N 12 54 E
Chemult, U.S.A. 82 E3 43 14N 121 47W
Chen, Gora, Russia 27 C15 65 16N 141 50 E
Chenab →, Pakistan 42 D4 30 23N 71 2 E
Chenango Forks, U.S.A. 79 D9 42 15N 75 51W
Cheney, U.S.A. 82 C5 47 30N 117 35W
Cheng Xian, China 34 H3 33 43N 105 42 E
Chengcheng, China 34 G5 35 8N 109 56 E
Chengchou = Zhengzhou, China 34 G7 34 45N 113 34 E
Chengde, China 35 D9 40 59N 117 58 E
Chengdu, China 32 C5 30 38N 104 2 E
Chenggu, China 34 H4 33 10N 107 21 E
Chengjiang, China 32 D5 24 39N 103 0 E
Ch'engmai, China 38 C7 19 50N 109 58 E
Ch'engtu = Chengdu, China 32 C5 30 38N 104 2 E
Chengwu, China 34 G8 34 58N 115 50 E
Chengyang, China 35 F11 36 18N 120 21 E
Chenjiagang, China 35 G10 34 23N 119 47 E
Chenkán, Mexico 87 D6 19 8N 90 58W
Chennai, India 40 N12 13 8N 80 19 E
Cheo Reo, Vietnam 36 B3 13 25N 108 28 E
Cheom Ksan, Cambodia 38 E5 14 13N 104 56 E
Chepén, Peru 92 E3 7 15S 79 23W
Chepes, Argentina 94 C2 31 20S 66 35W
Chepo, Panama 88 E4 9 10N 79 6W
Chepstow, U.K. 11 F5 51 38N 2 41W
Cheptulil, Mt., Kenya 54 B4 1 25N 35 35 E
Chequamegon B., U.S.A. 80 B9 46 40N 90 30W
Cher →, France 18 C4 47 21N 0 29 E
Cheraw, U.S.A. 77 H6 34 42N 79 53W
Cherbourg, France 18 B3 49 39N 1 40W
Cherdyn, Russia 24 B10 60 24N 56 29 E
Cheremkhovo, Russia 27 D11 53 8N 103 1 E
Cherepanovo, Russia 26 D9 54 15N 83 30 E
Cherepovets, Russia 24 C6 59 5N 37 55 E
Chergui, Chott ech, Algeria 50 B6 34 21N 0 25 E
Cherikov = Cherykaw, Belarus 17 B16 53 32N 31 20 E
Cherkasy, Ukraine 25 E5 49 27N 32 4 E
Cherkessk, Russia 25 F7 44 15N 42 5 E
Cherlak, Russia 26 D8 54 15N 74 55 E
Chernaya, Russia 27 B9 70 30N 89 10 E
Chernigov = Chernihiv, Ukraine 24 D5 51 28N 31 20 E
Chernihiv, Ukraine 24 D5 51 28N 31 20 E
Chernivtsi, Ukraine 17 D13 48 15N 25 52 E
Chernobyl = Chornobyl, Ukraine 17 C16 51 20N 30 15 E
Chernogorsk, Russia 27 D10 53 49N 91 18 E
Chernovtsy = Chernivtsi, Ukraine 17 D13 48 15N 25 52 E
Chernyakhovsk, Russia 9 J19 54 36N 21 48 E
Chernysheyskiy, Russia 27 C12 63 0N 112 30 E
Cherokee, Iowa, U.S.A. 80 D7 42 45N 95 33W
Cherokee, Okla., U.S.A. 81 G5 36 45N 98 21W
Cherokee Village, U.S.A. 81 G9 36 17N 91 30W
Cherokees, Grand Lake O' The, U.S.A. 81 G7 36 28N 95 2W
Cherrapunji, India 41 G17 25 17N 91 47 E
Cherry Valley, Calif., U.S.A. 85 M10 33 59N 116 57W
Cherry Valley, N.Y., U.S.A. 79 D10 42 48N 74 45W
Cherskiy, Russia 27 C17 68 45N 161 18 E
Cherskogo Khrebet, Russia 27 C15 65 0N 143 0 E
Cherven, Belarus 17 B15 53 45N 28 28 E
Chervonohrad, Ukraine 17 C13 50 25N 24 10 E
Cherwell →, U.K. 11 F6 51 44N 1 14W
Cherykaw, Belarus 17 B16 53 32N 31 20 E
Chesapeake, U.S.A. 76 G7 36 50N 76 17W
Chesapeake B., U.S.A. 76 G7 38 0N 76 10W
Cheshire □, U.K. 10 D5 53 14N 2 30W
Cheshskaya Guba, Russia 24 A8 67 20N 47 0 E
Cheshunt, U.K. 11 F7 51 43N 0 1W
Chesil Beach, U.K. 11 G5 50 37N 2 33W
Chesley, Canada 78 B3 44 17N 81 5W
Chester, U.K. 10 D5 53 12N 2 53W
Chester, Calif., U.S.A. 82 F3 40 19N 121 14W
Chester, Ill., U.S.A. 81 G10 37 55N 89 49W
Chester, Mont., U.S.A. 82 B8 48 31N 110 58W
Chester, Pa., U.S.A. 76 F8 39 51N 75 22W
Chester, S.C., U.S.A. 77 H5 34 43N 81 12W
Chester, Vt., U.S.A. 79 C12 43 16N 72 36W
Chester, W. Va., U.S.A. 78 F4 40 37N 80 34W
Chester-le-Street, U.K. 10 C6 54 51N 1 34W
Chesterfield, U.K. 10 D6 53 15N 1 25W
Chesterfield, Is., N. Cal. 64 J7 19 52S 158 15 E
Chesterfield Inlet, Canada 68 B10 63 30N 90 45W
Chesterton Ra., Australia 63 D4 25 30S 147 27 E
Chestertown, U.S.A. 79 C11 43 40N 73 48W
Chesterville, Canada 79 A9 45 6N 75 14W
Chestnut Ridge, U.S.A. 78 F5 40 20N 79 10W
Chesuncook L., U.S.A. 77 C11 46 0N 69 21W
Chéticamp, Canada 71 C7 46 37N 60 59W
Chetumal, Mexico 87 D7 18 30N 88 20W
Chetumal, B. de, Mexico 87 D7 18 40N 88 10W
Chetwynd, Canada 72 B4 55 45N 121 36W
Cheviot, The, U.K. 10 B5 55 29N 2 9W
Cheviot Hills, U.K. 10 B5 55 20N 2 30W
Cheviot Ra., Australia 62 D3 25 20S 143 45 E
Chew Bahir, Ethiopia 46 G2 4 40N 36 50 E
Chewelah, U.S.A. 82 B5 48 17N 117 43W
Cheyenne, Okla., U.S.A. 81 H5 35 37N 99 40W
Cheyenne, Wyo., U.S.A. 80 E2 41 8N 104 49W
Cheyenne →, U.S.A. 80 C4 44 41N 101 18W
Cheyenne Wells, U.S.A. 80 F3 38 49N 102 21W
Cheyne B., Australia 61 F2 34 35S 118 50 E
Chhabra, India 42 G7 24 40N 76 54 E
Chhaktala, India 42 H6 22 6N 74 11 E
Chhapra, India 43 G11 25 48N 84 44 E
Chhata, India 42 F7 27 42N 77 30 E
Chhatarpur, Bihar, India 43 G11 24 23N 84 11 E
Chhatarpur, Mad. P., India 43 G8 24 55N 79 35 E
Chhattisgarh □, India 43 J10 22 0N 82 0 E
Chhep, Cambodia 38 F5 13 45N 105 24 E
Chhindwara, Mad. P., India 43 H8 23 3N 79 29 E
Chhindwara, Mad. P., India 43 H8 22 2N 78 59 E
Chhlong, Cambodia 39 F5 12 15N 105 58 E
Chhota Tawa →, India 42 H7 22 14N 76 36 E
Chhoti Kali Sindh →, India 42 G6 24 2N 75 31 E
Chhuikhadan, India 43 J9 21 32N 80 59 E
Chhuk, Cambodia 39 G5 10 46N 104 28 E
Chi →, Thailand 38 E5 15 11N 104 43 E
Chiai, Taiwan 33 D7 23 29N 120 25 E
Chiamboni, Somali Rep. 52 E8 1 39S 41 35 E
Chiamussu = Jiamusi, China 33 B8 46 40N 130 26 E
Chiang Dao, Thailand 38 C2 19 22N 98 58 E
Chiang Kham, Thailand 38 C3 19 32N 100 18 E
Chiang Khan, Thailand 38 D3 17 52N 101 36 E
Chiang Khong, Thailand 38 B3 20 17N 100 24 E
Chiang Mai, Thailand 38 C2 18 47N 98 59 E
Chiang Rai, Thailand 38 C2 19 52N 99 50 E
Chiang Saen, Thailand 38 B3 20 16N 100 5 E
Chiapa →, Mexico 87 D6 16 42N 93 0W
Chiapa de Corzo, Mexico 87 D6 16 42N 93 0W
Chiapas □, Mexico 87 D6 17 0N 92 45W
Chiautla, Mexico 87 D5 18 18N 98 34W
Chiávari, Italy 18 D8 44 19N 9 19 E
Chiavenna, Italy 18 C8 46 19N 9 24 E
Chiba, Japan 31 G10 35 30N 140 7 E
Chiba □, Japan 31 G10 35 30N 140 20 E
Chibabava, Mozam. 57 C5 20 17S 33 35 E
Chibemba, Cunene, Angola 53 H2 15 48S 14 8 E
Chibemba, Huila, Angola 56 B2 16 20S 15 20 E
Chibi, Zimbabwe 57 C5 20 18S 30 25 E
Chibia, Angola 53 H2 15 10S 13 42 E
Chibougamau, Canada 70 C5 49 56N 74 24W
Chibougamau, L., Canada 70 C5 49 50N 74 20W
Chibuto, Mozam. 57 C5 24 40S 33 33 E
Chic-Chocs, Mts., Canada 71 C6 48 55N 66 0W
Chicacole = Srikakulam, India 41 K13 18 14N 83 58 E
Chicago, U.S.A. 76 E2 41 53N 87 38W
Chicago Heights, U.S.A. 76 E2 41 30N 87 38W
Chichagof I., U.S.A. 68 C6 57 30N 135 30W
Chichén-Itzá, Mexico 87 C7 20 40N 88 36W
Chicheng, China 34 D8 40 55N 115 55 E
Chichester, U.K. 11 G7 50 50N 0 47W
Chichester Ra., Australia 60 D2 22 12S 119 15 E
Chichibu, Japan 31 F9 35 59N 139 10 E
Ch'ich'ihaerh = Qiqihar, China 27 E13 47 26N 124 0 E
Chicholi, India 42 H8 22 1N 77 40 E
Chickasha, U.S.A. 81 H6 35 3N 97 58W
Chiclana de la Frontera, Spain 19 D2 36 26N 6 9W
Chiclayo, Peru 92 E3 6 42S 79 50W
Chico, U.S.A. 84 F5 39 44N 121 50W
Chico →, Chubut, Argentina 96 E3 44 0S 67 0W
Chico →, Santa Cruz, Argentina 96 G3 50 0S 68 30W
Chicomo, Mozam. 57 C5 24 31S 34 6 E
Chicontepec, Mexico 87 C5 20 58N 98 10W
Chicopee, U.S.A. 79 D12 42 9N 72 37W
Chicoutimi, Canada 71 C5 48 28N 71 5W
Chicualacuala, Mozam. 57 C5 22 6S 31 42 E
Chidambaram, India 40 P11 11 20N 79 45 E
Chidenguele, Mozam. 57 C5 24 55S 34 11 E
Chidley, C., Canada 69 B13 60 23N 64 26W
Chiducuane, Mozam. 57 C5 24 35S 34 25 E
Chiede, Angola 56 B2 17 15S 16 22 E
Chiefs Pt., Canada 78 B3 44 41N 81 18W
Chiem Hoa, Vietnam 38 A5 22 12N 105 17 E
Chiemsee, Germany 16 E7 47 53N 12 28 E
Chiengi, Zambia 55 D2 8 45S 29 10 E
Chiengmai = Chiang Mai, Thailand 38 C2 18 47N 98 59 E
Chiese →, Italy 18 D9 45 8N 10 25 E
Chieti, Italy 20 C6 42 21N 14 10 E
Chifeng, China 35 C10 42 18N 118 58 E
Chignecto B., Canada 71 C7 45 30N 64 40W
Chiguana, Bolivia 94 A2 21 0S 67 58W
Chigwell, U.K. 11 F8 51 37N 0 5 E
Chiha-ri, N. Korea 35 E14 38 40N 126 30 E
Chihli, G. of = Bo Hai, China 35 E10 39 0N 119 0 E
Chihuahua, Mexico 86 B3 28 40N 106 3W
Chihuahua □, Mexico 86 B3 28 40N 106 3W
Chiili = Shīeli, Kazakstan 26 E7 44 20N 66 15 E
Chik Bollapur, India 40 N10 13 25N 77 45 E
Chikmagalur, India 40 N9 13 15N 75 45 E
Chikwawa, Malawi 55 F3 16 2S 34 50 E
Chilac, Mexico 87 D5 18 20N 97 24W
Chilam Chavki, Pakistan 43 B6 35 5N 75 5 E
Chilanga, Zambia 55 F2 15 33S 28 16 E
Chilapa, Mexico 87 D5 17 40N 99 11W
Chilas, Pakistan 43 B6 35 25N 74 5 E
Chilaw, Sri Lanka 40 R11 7 30N 79 50 E
Chilcotin →, Canada 72 C4 51 44N 122 23W
Childers, Australia 63 D5 25 15S 152 17 E
Childress, U.S.A. 81 H4 34 25N 100 13W
Chile ■, S. Amer. 96 D2 35 0S 72 0W
Chile Rise, Pac. Oc. 65 L18 38 0S 92 0W
Chilecito, Argentina 94 B2 29 10S 67 30W
Chilete, Peru 92 E3 7 10S 78 50W
Chililabombwe, Zambia 55 E2 12 18S 27 43 E
Chilin = Jilin, China 35 C14 43 44N 126 30 E
Chilka L., India 41 K14 19 40N 85 25 E
Chilko →, Canada 72 C4 52 0N 123 40W
Chilko L., Canada 72 C4 51 20N 124 10W
Chillagoe, Australia 62 B3 17 7S 144 33 E
Chillán, Chile 94 D1 36 40S 72 10W
Chillicothe, Ill., U.S.A. 80 E10 40 55N 89 29W
Chillicothe, Mo., U.S.A. 80 F8 39 48N 93 33W
Chillicothe, Ohio, U.S.A. 76 F4 39 20N 82 59W
Chilliwack, Canada 72 D4 49 10N 121 54W
Chilo, India 42 F5 27 25N 73 32 E
Chiloane, I., Mozam. 57 C5 20 40S 34 55 E
Chiloé, I. de, Chile 96 E2 42 30S 73 50W
Chilpancingo, Mexico 87 D5 17 30N 99 30W
Chiltern Hills, U.K. 11 F7 51 40N 0 53W
Chilton, U.S.A. 76 C1 44 2N 88 10W
Chilubi, Zambia 55 E2 11 5S 29 58 E
Chilubula, Zambia 55 E3 10 14S 30 51 E
Chilumba, Malawi 55 E3 10 28S 34 12 E
Chilung, Taiwan 33 D7 25 3N 121 45 E
Chilwa, L., Malawi 55 F4 15 15S 35 40 E
Chimaltitán, Mexico 86 C4 21 46N 103 50W

Corrientes

Coaldale, *Canada* **72 D6** 49 45N 112 35W
Coalgate, *U.S.A.* **81 H6** 34 32N 96 13W
Coalinga, *U.S.A.* **84 J6** 36 9N 120 21W
Coalisland, *U.K.* **13 B5** 54 33N 6 42W
Coalville, *U.K.* **10 E6** 52 44N 1 23W
Coalville, *U.S.A.* **82 F8** 40 55N 111 24W
Coari, *Brazil* **92 D6** 4 8S 63 7W
Coast □, *Kenya* **54 C4** 2 40S 39 45 E
Coast Mts., *Canada* **72 C3** 55 0N 129 20W
Coast Ranges, *U.S.A.* **84 G4** 39 0N 123 0W
Coatbridge, *U.K.* **12 F4** 55 52N 4 6W
Coatepec, *Mexico* **87 D5** 19 27N 96 58W
Coatepeque, *Guatemala* **88 D1** 14 46N 91 55W
Coatesville, *U.S.A.* **76 F8** 39 59N 75 50W
Coaticook, *Canada* **79 A13** 45 10N 71 46W
Coats I., *Canada* **69 B11** 62 30N 83 0W
Coats Land, *Antarctica* **5 D1** 77 0S 25 0W
Coatzacoalcos, *Mexico* **87 D6** 18 7N 94 25W
Cobalt, *Canada* **70 C4** 47 25N 79 42W
Cobán, *Guatemala* **88 C1** 15 30N 90 21W
Cóbh, *Ireland* **13 E3** 51 51N 8 17W
Cobija, *Bolivia* **92 F5** 11 0S 68 50W
Cobleskill, *U.S.A.* **79 D10** 42 41N 74 29W
Coboconk, *Canada* **78 B6** 44 39N 78 48W
Cobourg, *Canada* **78 C6** 43 58N 78 10W
Cobourg Pen., *Australia* **60 B5** 11 20S 132 15 E
Cóbué, *Mozam.* **55 E3** 12 0S 34 58 E
Coburg, *Germany* **16 C6** 50 15N 10 58 E
Cocanada = Kakinada, *India* **41 L13** 16 57N 82 11 E
Cochabamba, *Bolivia* **92 G5** 17 26S 66 10W
Cochemane, *Mozam.* **55 F3** 17 0S 32 54 E
Cochin, *India* **40 Q10** 9 59N 76 22 E
Cochin China = Nam-Phan, *Vietnam* **39 G6** 10 30N 106 0 E
Cochran, *U.S.A.* **77 J4** 32 23N 83 21W
Cochrane, *Alta., Canada* **72 C6** 51 11N 114 30W
Cochrane, *Ont., Canada* **70 C3** 49 0N 81 0W
Cochrane, *Chile* **96 F2** 47 15S 72 33W
Cochrane →, *Canada* **73 B8** 59 0N 103 40W
Cochrane, L., *Chile* **96 F2** 47 10S 72 0W
Cochranton, *U.S.A.* **78 E4** 41 31N 80 3W
Cockburn, Canal, *Chile* **96 G2** 54 30S 72 0W
Cockburn I., *Canada* **70 C3** 45 55N 83 22W
Cockburn Ra., *Australia* **60 C4** 15 46S 128 0 E
Cockermouth, *U.K.* **10 C4** 54 40N 3 22W
Cocklebiddy, *Australia* **61 F4** 32 0S 126 3 E
Coco →, *Cent. Amer.* **88 D3** 15 0N 83 8W
Coco, I. del, *Pac. Oc.* **65 G19** 5 25N 87 55W
Cocoa, *U.S.A.* **77 L5** 28 21N 80 44W
Cocobeach, *Gabon* **52 D1** 0 59N 9 34 E
Cocos Is., *Ind. Oc.* **64 J1** 12 10S 96 55 E
Cod, C., *U.S.A.* **76 D10** 42 5N 70 10W
Codajás, *Brazil* **92 D6** 3 55S 62 0W
Codó, *Brazil* **93 D10** 4 30S 43 55W
Cody, *U.S.A.* **82 D9** 44 32N 109 3W
Coe Hill, *Canada* **78 B7** 44 52N 77 50W
Coelemu, *Chile* **94 D1** 36 30S 72 48W
Coen, *Australia* **62 A3** 13 52S 143 12 E
Cœur d'Alene, *U.S.A.* **82 C5** 47 45N 116 51W
Cœur d'Alene L., *U.S.A.* **82 C5** 47 32N 116 48W
Coevorden, *Neths.* **15 B6** 52 40N 6 44 E
Cofete, *Canary Is.* **22 F5** 28 6N 14 23W
Coffeyville, *U.S.A.* **81 G7** 37 2N 95 37W
Coffin B., *Australia* **63 E2** 34 38S 135 28 E
Coffin Bay, *Australia* **63 E2** 34 37S 135 29 E
Coffin Bay Peninsula, *Australia* **63 E2** 34 32S 135 15 E
Cognac, *France* **18 D3** 45 41N 0 20W
Cohocton, *U.S.A.* **78 D7** 42 30N 77 30W
Cohocton →, *U.S.A.* **78 D7** 42 9N 77 6W
Cohoes, *U.S.A.* **79 D11** 42 46N 73 42W
Coiba, I., *Panama* **88 E3** 7 30N 81 40W
Coig →, *Argentina* **96 G3** 51 0S 69 10W
Coigeach, Rubha, *U.K.* **12 C3** 58 6N 5 26W
Coihaique, *Chile* **96 F2** 45 30S 71 45W
Coimbatore, *India* **40 P10** 11 2N 76 59 E
Coimbra, *Brazil* **92 G7** 19 55S 57 48W
Coimbra, *Portugal* **19 B1** 40 15N 8 27W
Coín, *Spain* **19 D3** 36 40N 4 48W
Coipasa, Salar de, *Bolivia* **92 G5** 19 26S 68 9W
Cojimies, *Ecuador* **92 C3** 0 20N 80 0W
Cojutepequé, *El Salv.* **88 D2** 13 41N 88 54W
Cokeville, *U.S.A.* **82 E8** 42 5N 110 57W
Colatina, *Brazil* **93 G10** 19 32S 40 37W
Colbeck, C., *Antarctica* **5 D13** 77 6S 157 48W
Colborne, *Canada* **78 C7** 44 0N 77 53W
Colby, *U.S.A.* **80 F4** 39 24N 101 3W
Colchester, *U.K.* **11 F8** 51 54N 0 55 E
Cold L., *Canada* **73 C7** 54 33N 110 5W
Coldstream, *Canada* **72 C5** 50 13N 119 11W
Coldstream, *U.K.* **12 F6** 55 39N 2 15W
Coldwater, *Canada* **78 B5** 44 42N 79 40W
Coldwater, *Kans., U.S.A.* **81 G5** 37 16N 99 20W
Coldwater, *Mich., U.S.A.* **76 E3** 41 57N 85 0W
Colebrook, *U.S.A.* **79 B13** 44 54N 71 30W
Coleman, *U.S.A.* **81 K5** 31 50N 99 26W
Coleman →, *Australia* **62 B3** 15 6S 141 38 E
Colenso, *S. Africa* **57 D4** 28 44S 29 50 E
Coleraine, *U.K.* **13 A5** 55 8N 6 41W
Coleridge, L., *N.Z.* **59 K3** 43 17S 171 30 E
Colesberg, *S. Africa* **56 E4** 30 45S 25 5 E
Coleville, *U.S.A.* **84 G7** 38 34N 119 30W
Colfax, *Calif., U.S.A.* **84 F6** 39 6N 120 57W
Colfax, *La., U.S.A.* **81 K8** 31 31N 92 42W
Colfax, *Wash., U.S.A.* **82 C5** 46 53N 117 22W
Colhué Huapi, L., *Argentina* **96 F3** 45 30S 69 0W
Coligny, *S. Africa* **57 D4** 26 17S 26 15 E
Colima, *Mexico* **86 D4** 19 14N 103 43W
Colima □, *Mexico* **86 D4** 19 10N 103 40W
Colima, Nevado de, *Mexico* **86 D4** 19 35N 103 45W
Colina, *Chile* **94 C1** 33 13S 70 45W
Colinas, *Brazil* **93 E10** 6 0S 44 10W
Coll, *U.K.* **12 E2** 56 39N 6 34W
Collaguasi, *Chile* **94 A2** 21 5S 68 45W
Collarenebri, *Australia* **63 D4** 29 33S 148 34 E
Colleen Bawn, *Zimbabwe* **55 G2** 21 0S 29 12 E
College Park, *U.S.A.* **77 J3** 33 40N 84 27W
College Station, *U.S.A.* **81 K6** 30 37N 96 21W
Collie, *Australia* **61 F2** 33 22S 116 8 E
Collier B., *Australia* **60 C3** 16 10S 124 15 E
Collier Ra., *Australia* **61 D2** 24 45S 119 10 E
Collina, Passo di, *Italy* **20 B4** 44 2N 10 56 E
Collingwood, *Canada* **78 B4** 44 29N 80 13W
Collingwood, *N.Z.* **59 J4** 40 41S 172 40 E
Collins, *Canada* **70 B2** 50 17N 89 27W
Collinsville, *Australia* **62 C4** 20 30S 147 56 E
Collipulli, *Chile* **94 D1** 37 55S 72 30W
Collooney, *Ireland* **13 B3** 54 11N 8 29W
Colmar, *France* **18 B7** 48 5N 7 20 E
Cologne = Köln, *Germany* **16 C4** 50 56N 6 57 E
Colom, I. d'en, *Spain* **22 B11** 39 58N 4 16 E
Coloma, *U.S.A.* **84 G6** 38 48N 120 53W
Colomb-Béchar = Béchar, *Algeria* **50 B5** 31 38N 2 18W
Colombia ■, *S. Amer.* **92 C4** 3 45N 73 0W
Colombian Basin, *S. Amer.* **66 H12** 14 0N 76 0W
Colombo, *Sri Lanka* **40 R11** 6 56N 79 58 E
Colón, *Buenos Aires, Argentina* **94 C3** 33 53S 61 7W
Colón, *Entre Ríos, Argentina* **94 C4** 32 12S 58 10W
Colón, *Cuba* **88 B3** 22 42N 80 54W
Colón, *Panama* **88 E4** 9 20N 79 54W
Colonia de Sant Jordi, *Spain* **22 B9** 39 19N 2 59 E
Colonia del Sacramento, *Uruguay* **94 C4** 34 25S 57 50W
Colonia Dora, *Argentina* **94 B3** 28 34S 62 59W
Colonial Beach, *U.S.A.* **76 F7** 38 15N 76 58W
Colonie, *U.S.A.* **79 D11** 42 43N 73 50W
Colonsay, *Canada* **73 C7** 51 59N 105 52W
Colonsay, *U.K.* **12 E2** 56 5N 6 12W
Colorado □, *U.S.A.* **83 G10** 39 30N 105 30W
Colorado →, *Argentina* **96 D4** 39 50S 62 8W
Colorado →, *N. Amer.* **83 L6** 31 45N 114 40W
Colorado →, *U.S.A.* **81 L7** 28 36N 95 59W
Colorado City, *U.S.A.* **81 J4** 32 24N 100 52W
Colorado Plateau, *U.S.A.* **83 H8** 37 0N 111 0W
Colorado River Aqueduct, *U.S.A.* **85 L12** 34 17N 114 10W
Colorado Springs, *U.S.A.* **80 F2** 38 50N 104 49W
Colotlán, *Mexico* **86 C4** 22 6N 103 16W
Colstrip, *U.S.A.* **82 D10** 45 53N 106 38W
Colton, *U.S.A.* **79 B10** 44 33N 74 56W
Columbia, *Ky., U.S.A.* **76 G3** 37 6N 85 18W
Columbia, *La., U.S.A.* **81 J8** 32 6N 92 5W
Columbia, *Miss., U.S.A.* **81 K10** 31 15N 89 50W
Columbia, *Mo., U.S.A.* **80 F8** 38 57N 92 20W
Columbia, *Pa., U.S.A.* **79 F8** 40 2N 76 30W
Columbia, *S.C., U.S.A.* **77 J5** 34 0N 81 2W
Columbia, *Tenn., U.S.A.* **77 H2** 35 37N 87 2W
Columbia →, *N. Amer.* **84 D2** 46 15N 124 5W
Columbia, C., *Canada* **4 A4** 83 0N 70 0W
Columbia, District of □, *U.S.A.* **76 F7** 38 55N 77 0W
Columbia, Mt., *Canada* **72 C5** 52 8N 117 20W
Columbia Basin, *U.S.A.* **82 C4** 46 45N 119 5W
Columbia Falls, *U.S.A.* **82 B6** 48 23N 114 11W
Columbia Mts., *Canada* **72 C5** 52 0N 119 0W
Columbia Plateau, *U.S.A.* **82 D5** 44 0N 117 30W
Columbiana, *U.S.A.* **78 F4** 40 53N 80 42W
Columbretes, Is., *Spain* **19 C6** 39 50N 0 50 E
Columbus, *Ga., U.S.A.* **77 J3** 32 28N 84 59W
Columbus, *Ind., U.S.A.* **76 F3** 39 13N 85 55W
Columbus, *Kans., U.S.A.* **81 G7** 37 10N 94 50W
Columbus, *Miss., U.S.A.* **77 J1** 33 30N 88 25W
Columbus, *Mont., U.S.A.* **82 D9** 45 38N 109 15W
Columbus, *N. Mex., U.S.A.* **83 L10** 31 50N 107 38W
Columbus, *Nebr., U.S.A.* **80 E6** 41 26N 97 22W
Columbus, *Ohio, U.S.A.* **76 F4** 39 58N 83 0W
Columbus, *Tex., U.S.A.* **81 L6** 29 42N 96 33W
Colusa, *U.S.A.* **84 F4** 39 13N 122 1W
Colville, *U.S.A.* **82 B5** 48 33N 117 54W
Colville →, *U.S.A.* **68 A4** 70 25N 150 30W
Colville, C., *N.Z.* **59 G5** 36 29S 175 21 E
Colwood, *Canada* **84 B3** 48 26N 123 29W
Colwyn Bay, *U.K.* **10 D4** 53 18N 3 44W
Comácchio, *Italy* **20 B5** 44 42N 12 11 E
Comalcalco, *Mexico* **87 D6** 18 16N 93 13W
Comallo, *Argentina* **96 E2** 41 0S 70 5W
Comanche, *U.S.A.* **81 K5** 31 54N 98 36W
Comayagua, *Honduras* **88 D2** 14 25N 87 37W
Combahee →, *U.S.A.* **77 J5** 32 30N 80 31W
Combarbalá, *Chile* **94 C1** 31 11S 71 2W
Comber, *Canada* **78 D2** 42 14N 82 33W
Comber, *U.K.* **13 B6** 54 33N 5 45W
Combermere, *Canada* **78 A7** 45 22N 77 37W
Comblain-au-Pont, *Belgium* **15 D5** 50 29N 5 35 E
Comeragh Mts., *Ireland* **13 D4** 52 18N 7 34W
Comet, *Australia* **62 C4** 23 36S 148 38 E
Comilla, *Bangla.* **41 H17** 23 28N 91 10 E
Comino, *Malta* **23 C1** 36 2N 14 20 E
Comino, C., *Italy* **20 D3** 40 32N 9 49 E
Comitán, *Mexico* **87 D6** 16 18N 92 9W
Commerce, *Ga., U.S.A.* **77 H4** 34 12N 83 28W
Commerce, *Tex., U.S.A.* **81 J7** 33 15N 95 54W
Committee B., *Canada* **69 B11** 68 30N 86 30W
Commonwealth B., *Antarctica* **5 C10** 67 0S 144 0 E
Commoron Cr. →, *Australia* **63 D5** 28 22S 150 8 E
Communism Pk. = Kommunizma, Pik, *Tajikistan* **26 F8** 39 0N 72 2 E
Como, *Italy* **18 D8** 45 47N 9 5 E
Como, Lago di, *Italy* **18 D8** 46 0N 9 11 E
Comodoro Rivadavia, *Argentina* **96 F3** 45 50S 67 40W
Comorin, C., *India* **40 Q10** 8 3N 77 40 E
Comoro Is. = Comoros ■, *Ind. Oc.* **49 H8** 12 10S 44 15 E
Comoros ■, *Ind. Oc.* **49 H8** 12 10S 44 15 E
Comox, *Canada* **72 D4** 49 42N 124 55W
Compiègne, *France* **18 B5** 49 24N 2 50 E
Compostela, *Mexico* **86 C4** 21 15N 104 53W
Comprida, I., *Brazil* **95 A6** 24 50S 47 42W
Compton, *Canada* **79 A13** 45 14N 71 49W
Compton, *U.S.A.* **85 M8** 33 54N 118 13W
Comrat, *Moldova* **17 E15** 46 18N 28 40 E
Con Cuong, *Vietnam* **38 C5** 19 2N 104 54 E
Con Son, *Vietnam* **39 H6** 8 41N 106 37 E
Conakry, *Guinea* **50 G3** 9 29N 13 49W
Conara, *Australia* **62 G4** 41 50S 147 26 E
Concarneau, *France* **18 C2** 47 52N 3 56W
Conceição, *Mozam.* **55 F4** 18 47S 36 7 E
Conceição da Barra, *Brazil* **93 G11** 18 35S 39 45W
Conceição do Araguaia, *Brazil* **93 E9** 8 0S 49 2W
Concepción, *Argentina* **94 B2** 27 20S 65 35W
Concepción, *Bolivia* **92 G6** 16 15S 62 8W
Concepción, *Chile* **94 D1** 36 50S 73 0W
Concepción, *Mexico* **87 D6** 18 15N 90 5W
Concepción, *Paraguay* **94 A4** 23 22S 57 26W
Concepción □, *Chile* **94 D1** 37 0S 72 30W
Concepción →, *Mexico* **86 A2** 30 32N 113 2W
Concepción, Est. de, *Chile* **96 G2** 50 30S 74 55W
Concepción, L., *Bolivia* **92 G6** 17 20S 61 20W
Concepción, Punta, *Mexico* **86 B2** 26 55N 111 59W
Concepción del Oro, *Mexico* **86 C4** 24 40N 101 30W
Concepción del Uruguay, *Argentina* **94 C4** 32 35S 58 20W
Conception, Pt., *U.S.A.* **85 L6** 34 27N 120 28W
Conception B., *Canada* **71 C9** 47 45N 53 0W
Conception B., *Namibia* **56 C1** 23 55S 14 22 E
Conception I., *Bahamas* **89 B4** 23 52N 75 9W
Concession, *Zimbabwe* **55 F3** 17 27S 30 56 E
Conchas Dam, *U.S.A.* **81 H2** 35 22N 104 11W
Concho, *U.S.A.* **83 J9** 34 28N 109 36W
Concho →, *U.S.A.* **81 K5** 31 34N 99 43W
Conchos →, *Chihuahua, Mexico* **86 B4** 29 32N 105 0W
Conchos →, *Tamaulipas, Mexico* **87 B5** 25 9N 98 35W
Concord, *Calif., U.S.A.* **84 H4** 37 59N 122 2W
Concord, *N.C., U.S.A.* **77 H5** 35 25N 80 35W
Concord, *N.H., U.S.A.* **79 C13** 43 12N 71 32W
Concordia, *Argentina* **94 C4** 31 20S 58 2W
Concórdia, *Brazil* **92 D5** 4 36S 66 36W
Concordia, *Mexico* **86 C3** 23 18N 106 2W
Concordia, *U.S.A.* **80 F6** 39 34N 97 40W
Concrete, *U.S.A.* **82 B3** 48 32N 121 45W
Condamine, *Australia* **63 D5** 26 56S 150 9 E
Conde, *U.S.A.* **80 C5** 45 9N 98 6W
Condeúba, *Brazil* **93 F10** 14 52S 42 0W
Condon, *U.S.A.* **82 D3** 45 14N 120 11W
Conegliano, *Italy* **20 B5** 45 53N 12 18 E
Conejera, I. = Conills, I. des, *Spain* **22 B9** 39 11N 2 58 E
Conejos, *Mexico* **86 B4** 26 14N 103 53W
Confuso →, *Paraguay* **94 B4** 25 9S 57 34W
Congleton, *U.K.* **10 D5** 53 10N 2 13W
Congo (Kinshasa) = Congo, Dem. Rep. of the ■, *Africa* **52 E4** 3 0S 23 0 E
Congo ■, *Africa* **52 E3** 1 0S 16 0 E
Congo →, *Africa* **52 F2** 6 4S 12 24 E
Congo, Dem. Rep. of the ■, *Africa* **52 E4** 3 0S 23 0 E
Congo Basin, *Africa* **52 E4** 0 10S 24 30 E
Congonhas, *Brazil* **95 A7** 20 30S 43 52W
Congress, *U.S.A.* **83 J7** 34 9N 112 51W
Conills, I. des, *Spain* **22 B9** 39 11N 2 58 E
Coniston, *Canada* **70 C3** 46 29N 80 51W
Conjeeveram = Kanchipuram, *India* **40 N11** 12 52N 79 45 E
Conklin, *Canada* **73 B6** 55 38N 111 5W
Conklin, *U.S.A.* **79 D9** 42 2N 75 49W
Conn, L., *Ireland* **13 B2** 54 3N 9 15W
Connacht □, *Ireland* **13 C2** 53 43N 9 12W
Conneaut, *U.S.A.* **78 E4** 41 57N 80 34W
Connecticut □, *U.S.A.* **79 E12** 41 30N 72 45W
Connecticut →, *U.S.A.* **79 E12** 41 16N 72 20W
Connell, *U.S.A.* **82 C4** 46 40N 118 52W
Connellsville, *U.S.A.* **78 F5** 40 1N 79 35W
Connemara, *Ireland* **13 C2** 53 29N 9 45W
Connemaugh →, *U.S.A.* **78 F5** 40 28N 79 19W
Connersville, *U.S.A.* **76 F3** 39 39N 85 8W
Connors Ra., *Australia* **62 C4** 21 40S 149 10 E
Conquest, *Canada* **73 C7** 51 32N 107 14W
Conrad, *U.S.A.* **82 B8** 48 10N 111 57W
Conroe, *U.S.A.* **81 K7** 30 19N 95 27W
Consecon, *Canada* **78 C7** 44 0N 77 31W
Conselheiro Lafaiete, *Brazil* **95 A7** 20 40S 43 48W
Consett, *U.K.* **10 C6** 54 51N 1 50W
Consort, *Canada* **73 C6** 52 1N 110 46W
Constance = Konstanz, *Germany* **16 E5** 47 40N 9 10 E
Constance, L. = Bodensee, *Europe* **18 C8** 47 35N 9 25 E
Constanța, *Romania* **17 F15** 44 14N 28 38 E
Constantia, *U.S.A.* **79 C8** 43 15N 76 1W
Constantine, *Algeria* **50 A7** 36 25N 6 42 E
Constitución, *Chile* **94 D1** 35 20S 72 30W
Constitución, *Uruguay* **94 C4** 31 0S 57 50W
Consul, *Canada* **73 D7** 49 20N 109 30W
Contact, *U.S.A.* **82 F6** 41 46N 114 45W
Contai, *India* **43 J12** 21 54N 87 46 E
Contamana, *Peru* **92 E4** 7 19S 74 55W
Contas →, *Brazil* **93 F11** 14 17S 39 1W
Contoocook, *U.S.A.* **79 C13** 43 13N 71 45W
Contra Costa, *Mozam.* **57 D5** 25 9S 33 30 E
Contwoyto L., *Canada* **68 B8** 65 42N 110 50W
Conway = Conwy, *U.K.* **10 D4** 53 17N 3 50W
Conway = Conwy →, *U.K.* **10 D4** 53 17N 3 50W
Conway, *Ark., U.S.A.* **81 H8** 35 5N 92 26W
Conway, *N.H., U.S.A.* **79 C13** 43 59N 71 7W
Conway, *S.C., U.S.A.* **77 J6** 33 51N 79 3W
Conway, L., *Australia* **63 D2** 28 17S 135 35 E
Conwy, *U.K.* **10 D4** 53 17N 3 50W
Conwy □, *U.K.* **10 D4** 53 10N 3 44W
Conwy →, *U.K.* **10 D4** 53 17N 3 50W
Coober Pedy, *Australia* **63 D1** 29 1S 134 43 E
Cooch Behar = Koch Bihar, *India* **41 F16** 26 22N 89 29 E
Cooinda, *Australia* **60 B5** 13 15S 130 5 E
Cook, *Australia* **61 F5** 30 37S 130 25 E
Cook, *U.S.A.* **80 B8** 47 49N 92 39W
Cook, B., *Chile* **96 H3** 55 10S 70 0W
Cook, C., *Canada* **72 C3** 50 8N 127 55W
Cook, Mt. = Aoraki Mount Cook, *N.Z.* **59 K3** 43 36S 170 9 E
Cook Inlet, *U.S.A.* **68 C4** 60 0N 152 0W
Cook Is., *Pac. Oc.* **65 J12** 17 0S 160 0W
Cook Strait, *N.Z.* **59 J5** 41 15S 174 29 E
Cookeville, *U.S.A.* **77 G3** 36 10N 85 30W
Cookhouse, *S. Africa* **56 E4** 32 44S 25 47 E
Cookshire, *Canada* **79 A13** 45 25N 71 38W
Cookstown, *U.K.* **13 B5** 54 39N 6 45W
Cooksville, *Canada* **78 C5** 43 36N 79 35W
Cooktown, *Australia* **62 B4** 15 30S 145 16 E
Cooladdi, *Australia* **63 D4** 26 37S 145 23 E
Coolgardie, *Australia* **61 F3** 30 55S 121 8 E
Coolidge, *U.S.A.* **83 K8** 32 59N 111 31W
Coolidge Dam, *U.S.A.* **83 K8** 33 0N 110 20W
Coon Rapids, *U.S.A.* **80 C8** 45 9N 93 19W
Coonana, *Australia* **61 F3** 31 0S 123 0 E
Coondapoor, *India* **40 N9** 13 42N 74 40 E
Cooninie, L., *Australia* **63 D2** 26 4S 139 59 E
Cooper, *U.S.A.* **81 J7** 33 23N 95 42W
Cooper Cr. →, *Australia* **63 D2** 28 29S 137 46 E
Cooperstown, *N. Dak., U.S.A.* **80 B5** 47 27N 98 8W
Cooperstown, *N.Y., U.S.A.* **79 D10** 42 42N 74 56W
Coorabie, *Australia* **61 F5** 31 54S 132 18 E
Coorow, *Australia* **61 E2** 29 53S 116 2 E
Cooroy, *Australia* **63 D5** 26 22S 152 54 E
Coos Bay, *U.S.A.* **82 E1** 43 22N 124 13W
Coosa →, *U.S.A.* **77 J2** 32 30N 86 16W
Cootehill, *Ireland* **13 B4** 54 4N 7 5W
Copahue Paso, *Argentina* **94 D1** 37 49S 71 8W
Copainalá, *Mexico* **87 D6** 17 8N 93 11W
Copake Falls, *U.S.A.* **79 D11** 42 7N 73 31W
Copán, *Honduras* **88 D2** 14 50N 89 9W
Cope, *U.S.A.* **80 F3** 39 40N 102 51W
Copenhagen = København, *Denmark* **9 J15** 55 41N 12 34 E
Copenhagen, *U.S.A.* **79 C9** 43 54N 75 41W
Copiapó, *Chile* **94 B1** 27 30S 70 20W
Copiapó →, *Chile* **94 B1** 27 19S 70 56W
Coplay, *U.S.A.* **79 F9** 40 44N 75 29W
Copp L., *Canada* **72 A6** 60 14N 114 40W
Coppename →, *Surinam* **93 B7** 5 48N 55 55W
Copper Harbor, *U.S.A.* **76 B2** 47 28N 87 53W
Copper Queen, *Zimbabwe* **55 F2** 17 29S 29 18 E
Copperas Cove, *U.S.A.* **81 K6** 31 8N 97 54W
Copperbelt □, *Zambia* **55 E2** 13 15S 27 30 E
Coppermine = Kugluktuk, *Canada* **68 B8** 67 50N 115 5W
Coppermine →, *Canada* **68 B8** 67 49N 116 4W
Copperopolis, *U.S.A.* **84 H6** 37 58N 120 38W
Coquet →, *U.K.* **10 B6** 55 20N 1 32W
Coquille, *U.S.A.* **82 E1** 43 11N 124 11W
Coquimbo, *Chile* **94 C1** 30 0S 71 20W
Coquimbo □, *Chile* **94 C1** 31 0S 71 0W
Corabia, *Romania* **17 G13** 43 48N 24 30 E
Coracora, *Peru* **92 G4** 15 5S 73 45W
Coraki, *Australia* **63 D5** 28 59S 153 17 E
Coral, *U.S.A.* **78 F5** 40 29N 79 10W
Coral Gables, *U.S.A.* **77 N5** 25 45N 80 16W
Coral Harbour = Salliq, *Canada* **69 B11** 64 8N 83 10W
Coral Sea, *Pac. Oc.* **64 J7** 15 0S 150 0 E
Coral Springs, *U.S.A.* **77 M5** 26 16N 80 13W
Coraopolis, *U.S.A.* **78 F4** 40 31N 80 10W
Corato, *Italy* **20 D7** 41 9N 16 25 E
Corbin, *U.S.A.* **76 G3** 36 57N 84 6W
Corby, *U.K.* **11 E7** 52 30N 0 41W
Corcaigh = Cork, *Ireland* **13 E3** 51 54N 8 29W
Corcoran, *U.S.A.* **84 J7** 36 6N 119 33W
Corcubión, *Spain* **19 A1** 42 56N 9 12W
Cordele, *U.S.A.* **77 K4** 31 58N 83 47W
Cordell, *U.S.A.* **81 H5** 35 17N 98 59W
Córdoba, *Argentina* **94 C3** 31 20S 64 10W
Córdoba, *Mexico* **87 D5** 18 50N 97 0W
Córdoba, *Spain* **19 D3** 37 50N 4 50W
Córdoba □, *Argentina* **94 C3** 31 22S 64 15W
Córdoba, Sierra de, *Argentina* **94 C3** 31 10S 64 25W
Cordova, *U.S.A.* **68 B5** 60 33N 145 45W
Corella →, *Australia* **62 B3** 19 34S 140 47 E
Corfield, *Australia* **62 C3** 21 40S 143 21 E
Corfu = Kérkira, *Greece* **23 A3** 39 38N 19 50 E
Corfu, Str. of, *Greece* **23 A4** 39 34N 20 0 E
Coria, *Spain* **19 C2** 39 58N 6 33W
Corigliano Cálabro, *Italy* **20 E7** 39 36N 16 31 E
Coringa Is., *Australia* **62 B4** 16 58S 149 58 E
Corinth = Kórinthos, *Greece* **21 F10** 37 56N 22 55 E
Corinth, *Miss., U.S.A.* **77 H1** 34 56N 88 31W
Corinth, *N.Y., U.S.A.* **79 C11** 43 15N 73 49W
Corinth, G. of = Korinthiakós Kólpos, *Greece* **21 E10** 38 16N 22 30 E
Corinto, *Brazil* **93 G10** 18 20S 44 30W
Corinto, *Nic.* **88 D2** 12 30N 87 10W
Cork, *Ireland* **13 E3** 51 54N 8 29W
Cork □, *Ireland* **13 E3** 51 57N 8 40W
Cork Harbour, *Ireland* **13 E3** 51 47N 8 16W
Çorlu, *Turkey* **21 D12** 41 11N 27 49 E
Cormack L., *Canada* **72 A4** 60 56N 121 37W
Cormorant, *Canada* **73 C8** 54 14N 100 35W
Cormorant L., *Canada* **73 C8** 54 15N 100 50W
Corn Is. = Maiz, Is. del, *Nic.* **88 D3** 12 15N 83 4W
Cornélio Procópio, *Brazil* **95 A5** 23 7S 50 40W
Corner Brook, *Canada* **71 C8** 48 57N 57 58W
Cornești, *Moldova* **17 E15** 47 21N 28 1 E
Corning, *Ark., U.S.A.* **81 G9** 36 25N 90 35W
Corning, *Calif., U.S.A.* **82 G2** 39 56N 122 11W
Corning, *Iowa, U.S.A.* **80 E7** 40 59N 94 44W
Corning, *N.Y., U.S.A.* **78 D7** 42 9N 77 3W
Cornwall, *Canada* **79 A10** 45 2N 74 44W
Cornwall, *U.S.A.* **79 F8** 40 17N 76 25W
Cornwall □, *U.K.* **11 G3** 50 26N 4 40W
Coro, *Venezuela* **92 A5** 11 25N 69 41W
Coroatá, *Brazil* **93 D10** 4 8S 44 0W
Corocoro, *Bolivia* **92 G5** 17 15S 68 28W
Coroico, *Bolivia* **92 G5** 16 0S 67 50W
Coromandel, *N.Z.* **59 G5** 36 45S 175 31 E
Coromandel Coast, *India* **40 N12** 12 30N 81 0 E
Corona, *Calif., U.S.A.* **85 M9** 33 53N 117 34W
Corona, *N. Mex., U.S.A.* **83 J11** 34 15N 105 36W
Coronach, *Canada* **73 D7** 49 7N 105 31W
Coronado, *U.S.A.* **85 N9** 32 41N 117 11W
Coronado, B. de, *Costa Rica* **88 E3** 9 0N 83 40W
Coronados, Is. los, *U.S.A.* **85 N9** 32 25N 117 15W
Coronation, *Canada* **72 C6** 52 5N 111 27W
Coronation Gulf, *Canada* **68 B8** 68 25N 110 0W
Coronation I., *Antarctica* **5 C18** 60 45S 46 0W
Coronation Is., *Australia* **60 B3** 14 57S 124 55 E
Coronda, *Argentina* **94 C3** 31 58S 60 56W
Coronel, *Chile* **94 D1** 37 0S 73 10W
Coronel Bogado, *Paraguay* **94 B4** 27 11S 56 18W
Coronel Dorrego, *Argentina* **94 D3** 38 40S 61 10W
Coronel Oviedo, *Paraguay* **94 B4** 25 24S 56 30W
Coronel Pringles, *Argentina* **94 D3** 38 0S 61 30W
Coronel Suárez, *Argentina* **94 D3** 37 30S 61 52W
Coronel Vidal, *Argentina* **94 D4** 37 28S 57 45W
Coropuna, Nevado, *Peru* **92 G4** 15 30S 72 41W
Corozal, *Belize* **87 D7** 18 23N 88 23W
Corpus, *Argentina* **95 B4** 27 10S 55 30W
Corpus Christi, *U.S.A.* **81 M6** 27 47N 97 24W
Corpus Christi, L., *U.S.A.* **81 L6** 28 2N 97 52W
Corralejo, *Canary Is.* **22 F6** 28 43N 13 53W
Corraun Pen., *Ireland* **13 C2** 53 54N 9 54W
Correntes, C. das, *Mozam.* **57 C6** 24 6S 35 34 E
Corrib, L., *Ireland* **13 C2** 53 27N 9 16W
Corrientes, *Argentina* **94 B4** 27 30S 58 45W
Corrientes □, *Argentina* **94 B4** 28 0S 57 0W

Corrientes

Corrientes →, *Argentina* **94 C4** 30 42S 59 38W
Corrientes →, *Peru* **92 D4** 3 43S 74 35W
Corrientes, C., *Colombia* **92 B3** 5 30N 77 34W
Corrientes, C., *Cuba* **88 B3** 21 43N 84 30W
Corrientes, C., *Mexico* **86 C3** 20 25N 105 42W
Corrigan, *U.S.A.* **81 K7** 31 0N 94 52W
Corrigin, *Australia* **61 F2** 32 20S 117 53 E
Corry, *U.S.A.* **78 E5** 41 55N 79 39W
Corse, *France* **18 F8** 42 0N 9 0 E
Corse, C., *France* **18 E8** 43 1N 9 25 E
Corsica = Corse, *France* **18 F8** 42 0N 9 0 E
Corsicana, *U.S.A.* **81 J6** 32 6N 96 28W
Corte, *France* **18 E8** 42 19N 9 11 E
Cortez, *U.S.A.* **83 H9** 37 21N 108 35W
Cortland, *N.Y., U.S.A.* **79 D8** 42 36N 76 11W
Cortland, *Ohio, U.S.A.* **78 E4** 41 20N 80 44W
Çorum, *Turkey* **25 F5** 40 30N 34 57 E
Corumbá, *Brazil* **92 G7** 19 0S 57 30W
Corunna = A Coruña, *Spain* **19 A1** 43 20N 8 25W
Corvallis, *U.S.A.* **82 D2** 44 34N 123 16W
Corvette, L. de la, *Canada* **70 B5** 53 25N 74 3W
Corydon, *U.S.A.* **80 E8** 40 46N 93 19W
Cosalá, *Mexico* **86 C3** 24 28N 106 40W
Cosamaloapan, *Mexico* **87 D5** 18 23N 95 50W
Cosenza, *Italy* **20 E7** 39 18N 16 15 E
Coshocton, *U.S.A.* **78 F3** 40 16N 81 51W
Cosmo Newberry, *Australia* **61 E3** 28 0S 122 54 E
Coso Junction, *U.S.A.* **85 J9** 36 3N 117 57W
Coso Pk., *U.S.A.* **85 J9** 36 13N 117 44W
Cosquín, *Argentina* **94 C3** 31 15S 64 30W
Costa Blanca, *Spain* **19 C5** 38 25N 0 10W
Costa Brava, *Spain* **19 B7** 41 30N 3 0 E
Costa del Sol, *Spain* **19 D3** 36 30N 4 30W
Costa Dorada, *Spain* **19 B6** 41 12N 1 15 E
Costa Mesa, *U.S.A.* **85 M9** 33 38N 117 55W
Costa Rica ■, *Cent. Amer.* **88 E3** 10 0N 84 0W
Cosumnes →, *U.S.A.* **84 G5** 38 16N 121 26W
Cotabato, *Phil.* **37 C6** 7 14N 124 15 E
Cotagaita, *Bolivia* **94 A2** 20 45S 65 40W
Côte d'Azur, *France* **18 E7** 43 25N 7 10 E
Côte-d'Ivoire = Ivory Coast ■, *Africa* **50 G4** 7 30N 5 0W
Coteau des Prairies, *U.S.A.* **80 C6** 45 20N 97 50W
Coteau du Missouri, *U.S.A.* **80 B4** 47 0N 100 0W
Coteau Landing, *Canada* **79 A10** 45 15N 74 13W
Cotentin, *France* **18 B3** 49 15N 1 30W
Cotillo, *Canary Is.* **22 F5** 28 41N 14 1W
Cotonou, *Benin* **50 G6** 6 20N 2 25 E
Cotopaxi, *Ecuador* **92 D3** 0 40S 78 30W
Cotswold Hills, *U.K.* **11 F5** 51 42N 2 10W
Cottage Grove, *U.S.A.* **82 E2** 43 48N 123 3W
Cottbus, *Germany* **16 C8** 51 45N 14 20 E
Cottonwood, *U.S.A.* **83 J7** 34 45N 112 1W
Cotulla, *U.S.A.* **81 L5** 28 26N 99 14W
Coudersport, *U.S.A.* **78 E6** 41 46N 78 1W
Coulee City, *U.S.A.* **82 C4** 47 37N 119 17W
Coulman I., *Antarctica* **5 D11** 73 35S 170 0 E
Coulonge →, *Canada* **70 C4** 45 52N 76 46W
Coulterville, *U.S.A.* **84 H6** 37 43N 120 12W
Council, *U.S.A.* **82 D5** 44 44N 116 26W
Council Bluffs, *U.S.A.* **80 E7** 41 16N 95 52W
Council Grove, *U.S.A.* **80 F6** 38 40N 96 29W
Coupeville, *U.S.A.* **84 B4** 48 13N 122 41W
Courantyne →, *S. Amer.* **92 B7** 5 55N 57 5W
Courcelles, *Belgium* **15 D4** 50 28N 4 22 E
Courtenay, *Canada* **72 D4** 49 45N 125 0W
Courtland, *U.S.A.* **84 G5** 38 20N 121 34W
Courtrai = Kortrijk, *Belgium* **15 D3** 50 50N 3 17 E
Courtright, *Canada* **78 D2** 42 49N 82 28W
Coushatta, *U.S.A.* **81 J8** 32 1N 93 21W
Coutts Crossing, *Australia* **63 D5** 29 49S 152 55 E
Couvin, *Belgium* **15 D4** 50 3N 4 29 E
Cove I., *Canada* **78 A3** 45 17N 81 44W
Coventry, *U.K.* **11 E6** 52 25N 1 28W
Covilhã, *Portugal* **19 B2** 40 17N 7 31W
Covington, *Ga., U.S.A.* **77 J4** 33 36N 83 51W
Covington, *Ky., U.S.A.* **76 F3** 39 5N 84 31W
Covington, *Okla., U.S.A.* **81 G6** 36 18N 97 35W
Covington, *Tenn., U.S.A.* **81 H10** 35 34N 89 39W
Covington, *Va., U.S.A.* **76 G5** 37 47N 79 59W
Cowan, L., *Australia* **61 F3** 31 45S 121 45 E
Cowan L., *Canada* **73 C7** 54 0N 107 15W
Cowansville, *Canada* **79 A12** 45 14N 72 46W
Coward Springs, *Australia* **63 D2** 29 24S 136 49 E
Cowcowing Lakes, *Australia* **61 F2** 30 55S 117 20 E
Cowdenbeath, *U.K.* **12 E5** 56 7N 3 21W
Cowes, *U.K.* **11 G6** 50 45N 1 18W
Cowichan L., *Canada* **84 B2** 48 53N 124 17W
Cowlitz →, *U.S.A.* **84 D4** 46 6N 122 55W
Coxilha Grande, *Brazil* **95 B5** 28 18S 51 30W
Coxim, *Brazil* **93 G8** 18 30S 54 55W
Cox's Bazar, *Bangla.* **41 J17** 21 26N 91 59 E
Coyote Wells, *U.S.A.* **85 N11** 32 44N 115 58W
Coyuca de Benítez, *Mexico* **87 D4** 17 1N 100 8W
Coyuca de Catalan, *Mexico* **86 D4** 18 18N 100 41W
Cozad, *U.S.A.* **80 E5** 40 52N 99 59W
Cozumel, *Mexico* **87 C7** 20 31N 86 55W
Cozumel, Isla, *Mexico* **87 C7** 20 30N 86 40W
Cracow = Kraków, *Poland* **17 C10** 50 4N 19 57 E
Cracow, *Australia* **63 D5** 25 17S 150 17 E
Cradock, *Australia* **63 E2** 32 6S 138 31 E
Cradock, *S. Africa* **56 E4** 32 8S 25 36 E
Craig, *U.S.A.* **82 F10** 40 31N 107 33W
Craigavon, *U.K.* **13 B5** 54 27N 6 23W
Craigmore, *Zimbabwe* **55 G3** 20 28S 32 50 E
Craik, *Canada* **73 C7** 51 3N 105 49W
Crailsheim, *Germany* **16 D6** 49 8N 10 5 E
Craiova, *Romania* **17 F12** 44 21N 23 48 E
Cramsie, *Australia* **62 C3** 23 20S 144 15 E
Cranberry L., *U.S.A.* **79 B10** 44 11N 74 50W
Cranberry Portage, *Canada* **73 C8** 54 35N 101 23W
Cranbrook, *Australia* **61 F2** 34 18S 117 33 E
Cranbrook, *Canada* **72 D5** 49 30N 115 46W
Crandon, *U.S.A.* **80 C10** 45 34N 88 54W
Crane, *Oreg., U.S.A.* **82 E4** 43 25N 118 35W
Crane, *Tex., U.S.A.* **81 K3** 31 24N 102 21W
Cranston, *U.S.A.* **79 E13** 41 47N 71 26W
Crater L., *U.S.A.* **82 E2** 42 56N 122 6W
Crater Lake National Park, *U.S.A.* **82 E2** 42 55N 122 10W
Crateús, *Brazil* **93 E10** 5 10S 40 39W
Crato, *Brazil* **93 E11** 7 10S 39 25W
Craven, L., *Canada* **70 B4** 54 20N 76 56W
Crawford, *U.S.A.* **80 D3** 42 41N 103 25W
Crawfordsville, *U.S.A.* **76 E2** 40 2N 86 54W
Crawley, *U.K.* **11 F7** 51 7N 0 11W
Crazy Mts., *U.S.A.* **82 C8** 46 12N 110 20W
Crean L., *Canada* **73 C7** 54 5N 106 9W
Crediton, *Canada* **78 C3** 43 17N 81 33W
Cree →, *Canada* **73 B7** 58 57N 105 47W
Cree →, *U.K.* **12 G4** 54 55N 4 25W
Cree L., *Canada* **73 B7** 57 30N 106 30W
Creede, *U.S.A.* **83 H10** 37 51N 106 56W
Creekside, *U.S.A.* **78 F5** 40 40N 79 11W
Creel, *Mexico* **86 B3** 27 45N 107 38W
Creemore, *Canada* **78 B4** 44 19N 80 6W
Creighton, *Canada* **73 C8** 54 45N 101 54W
Creighton, *U.S.A.* **80 D6** 42 28N 97 54W
Crema, *Italy* **18 D8** 45 22N 9 41 E
Cremona, *Italy* **18 D9** 45 7N 10 2 E
Cres, *Croatia* **16 F8** 44 58N 14 25 E
Crescent City, *U.S.A.* **82 F1** 41 45N 124 12W
Crespo, *Argentina* **94 C3** 32 2S 60 19W
Cresson, *U.S.A.* **78 F6** 40 28N 78 36W
Crestline, *Calif., U.S.A.* **85 L9** 34 14N 117 18W
Crestline, *Ohio, U.S.A.* **78 F2** 40 47N 82 44W
Creston, *Canada* **72 D5** 49 10N 116 31W
Creston, *Calif., U.S.A.* **84 K6** 35 32N 120 33W
Creston, *Iowa, U.S.A.* **80 E7** 41 4N 94 22W
Crestview, *Calif., U.S.A.* **84 H8** 37 46N 118 58W
Crestview, *Fla., U.S.A.* **77 K2** 30 46N 86 34W
Crete = Kríti, *Greece* **23 D7** 35 15N 25 0 E
Crete, *U.S.A.* **80 E6** 40 38N 96 58W
Créteil, *France* **18 B5** 48 47N 2 28 E
Creus, C. de, *Spain* **19 A7** 42 20N 3 19 E
Creuse →, *France* **18 C4** 47 0N 0 34 E
Crewe, *U.K.* **10 D5** 53 6N 2 26W
Crewkerne, *U.K.* **11 G5** 50 53N 2 48W
Criciúma, *Brazil* **95 B6** 28 40S 49 23W
Crieff, *U.K.* **12 E5** 56 22N 3 50W
Crimea □, *Ukraine* **25 E5** 45 30N 33 10 E
Crimean Pen. = Krymskyy Pivostriv, *Ukraine* **25 F5** 45 0N 34 0 E
Crişul Alb →, *Romania* **17 E11** 46 42N 21 17 E
Crişul Negru →, *Romania* **17 E11** 46 42N 21 16 E
Crna →, *Macedonia* **21 D9** 41 33N 21 59 E
Crna Gora = Montenegro □, *Yugoslavia* **21 C8** 42 40N 19 20 E
Crna Gora, *Macedonia* **21 C9** 42 10N 21 30 E
Crna Reka = Crna →, *Macedonia* **21 D9** 41 33N 21 59 E
Croagh Patrick, *Ireland* **13 C2** 53 46N 9 40W
Croatia ■, *Europe* **16 F9** 45 20N 16 0 E
Crocker, Banjaran, *Malaysia* **36 C5** 5 40N 116 30 E
Crockett, *U.S.A.* **81 K7** 31 19N 95 27W
Crocodile = Krokodil →, *Mozam.* **57 D5** 25 14S 32 18 E
Crocodile Is., *Australia* **62 A1** 12 3S 134 58 E
Crohy Hd., *Ireland* **13 B3** 54 55N 8 26W
Croix, L. La, *Canada* **70 C1** 48 20N 92 15W
Croker, C., *Australia* **60 B5** 10 58S 132 35 E
Croker, C., *Canada* **78 B4** 44 58N 80 59W
Croker I., *Australia* **60 B5** 11 12S 132 32 E
Cromarty, *U.K.* **12 D4** 57 40N 4 2W
Cromer, *U.K.* **10 E9** 52 56N 1 17 E
Cromwell, *N.Z.* **59 L2** 45 3S 169 14 E
Cromwell, *U.S.A.* **79 E12** 41 36N 72 39W
Crook, *U.K.* **10 C6** 54 43N 1 45W
Crooked →, *Canada* **72 C4** 54 50N 122 54W
Crooked →, *U.S.A.* **82 D3** 44 32N 121 16W
Crooked I., *Bahamas* **89 B5** 22 50N 74 10W
Crooked Island Passage, *Bahamas* **89 B5** 23 0N 74 30W
Crookston, *Minn., U.S.A.* **80 B6** 47 47N 96 37W
Crookston, *Nebr., U.S.A.* **80 D4** 42 56N 100 45W
Crosby, *U.K.* **10 D4** 53 30N 3 3W
Crosby, *N. Dak., U.S.A.* **80 A3** 48 55N 103 18W
Crosby, *Pa., U.S.A.* **78 E6** 41 45N 78 23W
Crosbyton, *U.S.A.* **81 J4** 33 40N 101 14W
Cross City, *U.S.A.* **77 L4** 29 38N 83 7W
Cross Fell, *U.K.* **10 C5** 54 43N 2 28W
Cross L., *Canada* **73 C9** 54 45N 97 30W
Cross Lake, *Canada* **73 C9** 54 37N 97 47W
Cross Sound, *U.S.A.* **68 C6** 58 0N 135 0W
Crossett, *U.S.A.* **81 J9** 33 8N 91 58W
Crosshaven, *Ireland* **13 E3** 51 47N 8 17W
Crossville, *U.S.A.* **77 G3** 35 57N 85 2W
Croswell, *U.S.A.* **78 C2** 43 16N 82 37W
Croton-on-Hudson, *U.S.A.* **79 E11** 41 12N 73 55W
Crotone, *Italy* **20 E7** 39 5N 17 8 E
Crow →, *Canada* **72 B4** 59 41N 124 20W
Crow Agency, *U.S.A.* **82 D10** 45 36N 107 28W
Crow Hd., *Ireland* **13 E1** 51 35N 10 9W
Crowell, *U.S.A.* **81 J5** 33 59N 99 43W
Crowley, *U.S.A.* **81 K8** 30 13N 92 22W
Crowley, L., *U.S.A.* **84 H8** 37 35N 118 42W
Crown Point, *Ind., U.S.A.* **76 E2** 41 25N 87 22W
Crown Point, *N.Y., U.S.A.* **79 C11** 43 57N 73 26W
Crownpoint, *U.S.A.* **83 J9** 35 41N 108 9W
Crows Landing, *U.S.A.* **84 H5** 37 23N 121 6W
Crows Nest, *Australia* **63 D5** 27 16S 152 4 E
Crowsnest Pass, *Canada* **72 D6** 49 40N 114 40W
Croydon, *Australia* **62 B3** 18 13S 142 14 E
Croydon □, *U.K.* **11 F7** 51 22N 0 5W
Crozet, Is., *Ind. Oc.* **3 G12** 46 27S 52 0 E
Cruz, C., *Cuba* **88 C4** 19 50N 77 50W
Cruz Alta, *Brazil* **95 B5** 28 45S 53 40W
Cruz del Eje, *Argentina* **94 C3** 30 45S 64 50W
Cruzeiro, *Brazil* **95 A7** 22 33S 45 0W
Cruzeiro do Oeste, *Brazil* **95 A5** 23 46S 53 4W
Cruzeiro do Sul, *Brazil* **92 E4** 7 35S 72 35W
Cry L., *Canada* **72 B3** 58 45N 129 0W
Crystal Bay, *U.S.A.* **84 F7** 39 15N 120 0W
Crystal City, *U.S.A.* **81 L5** 28 41N 99 50W
Crystal Falls, *U.S.A.* **76 B1** 46 5N 88 20W
Crystal River, *U.S.A.* **77 L4** 28 54N 82 35W
Crystal Springs, *U.S.A.* **81 K9** 31 59N 90 21W
Csongrád, *Hungary* **17 E11** 46 43N 20 12 E
Cu Lao Hon, *Vietnam* **39 G7** 10 54N 108 18 E
Cua Rao, *Vietnam* **38 C5** 19 16N 104 27 E
Cuácua →, *Mozam.* **55 F4** 17 54S 37 0 E
Cuamato, *Angola* **56 B2** 17 2S 15 7 E
Cuamba, *Mozam.* **55 E4** 14 45S 36 22 E
Cuando →, *Angola* **53 H4** 17 30S 23 15 E
Cuando Cubango □, *Angola* **56 B3** 16 25S 20 0 E
Cuangar, *Angola* **56 B2** 17 36S 18 39 E
Cuango = Kwango →, *Dem. Rep. of the Congo* **52 E3** 3 14S 17 22 E
Cuanza →, *Angola* **52 F2** 9 21S 13 9 E
Cuarto →, *Argentina* **94 C3** 33 25S 63 2W
Cuatrociénegas, *Mexico* **86 B4** 26 59N 102 5W
Cuauhtémoc, *Mexico* **86 B3** 28 25N 106 52W
Cuba, *N. Mex., U.S.A.* **83 J10** 36 1N 107 4W
Cuba, *N.Y., U.S.A.* **78 D6** 42 13N 78 17W
Cuba ■, *W. Indies* **88 B4** 22 0N 79 0W
Cubango →, *Africa* **56 B3** 18 50S 22 25 E
Cuchumatanes, Sierra de los, *Guatemala* **88 C1** 15 35N 91 25W
Cuckfield, *U.K.* **11 F7** 51 1N 0 8W
Cucuí, *Brazil* **92 C5** 1 12N 66 50W
Cucurpe, *Mexico* **86 A2** 30 20N 110 43W
Cúcuta, *Colombia* **92 B4** 7 54N 72 31W
Cuddalore, *India* **40 P11** 11 46N 79 45 E
Cuddapah, *India* **40 M11** 14 30N 78 47 E
Cuddapan, L., *Australia* **62 D3** 25 45S 141 26 E
Cue, *Australia* **61 E2** 27 25S 117 54 E
Cuenca, *Ecuador* **92 D3** 2 50S 79 9W
Cuenca, *Spain* **19 B4** 40 5N 2 10W
Cuenca, Serranía de, *Spain* **19 C5** 39 55N 1 50W
Cuernavaca, *Mexico* **87 D5** 18 55N 99 15W
Cuero, *U.S.A.* **81 L6** 29 6N 97 17W
Cuevas del Almanzora, *Spain* **19 D5** 37 18N 1 58W
Cuevo, *Bolivia* **92 H6** 20 15S 63 30W
Cuiabá, *Brazil* **93 G7** 15 30S 56 0W
Cuiabá →, *Brazil* **93 G7** 17 5S 56 36W
Cuijk, *Neths.* **15 C5** 51 44N 5 50 E
Cuilco, *Guatemala* **88 C1** 15 24N 91 58W
Cuillin Hills, *U.K.* **12 D2** 57 13N 6 15W
Cuillin Sd., *U.K.* **12 D2** 57 4N 6 20W
Cuito →, *Angola* **56 B3** 18 1S 20 48 E
Cuitzeo, L. de, *Mexico* **86 D4** 19 55N 101 5W
Cukai, *Malaysia* **39 K4** 4 13N 103 25 E
Culbertson, *U.S.A.* **80 A2** 48 9N 104 31W
Culgoa →, *Australia* **63 D4** 29 56S 146 20 E
Culiacán, *Mexico* **86 C3** 24 50N 107 23W
Culiacán →, *Mexico* **86 C3** 24 30N 107 42W
Culion, *Phil.* **37 B6** 11 54N 119 58 E
Cullen, *U.K.* **12 D6** 57 42N 2 49W
Cullen Pt., *Australia* **62 A3** 11 57S 141 54 E
Cullera, *Spain* **19 C5** 39 9N 0 17W
Cullman, *U.S.A.* **77 H2** 34 11N 86 51W
Culpeper, *U.S.A.* **76 F7** 38 30N 78 0W
Culuene →, *Brazil* **93 F8** 12 56S 52 51W
Culver, Pt., *Australia* **61 F3** 32 54S 124 43 E
Culverden, *N.Z.* **59 K4** 42 47S 172 49 E
Cumaná, *Venezuela* **92 A6** 10 30N 64 5W
Cumberland, *B.C., Canada* **72 D4** 49 40N 125 0W
Cumberland, *Ont., Canada* **79 A9** 45 29N 75 24W
Cumberland, *U.S.A.* **76 F6** 39 39N 78 46W
Cumberland →, *U.S.A.* **77 G2** 36 15N 87 0W
Cumberland, L., *U.S.A.* **77 G3** 36 57N 84 55W
Cumberland I., *U.S.A.* **77 K5** 30 50N 81 25W
Cumberland Is., *Australia* **62 C4** 20 35S 149 10 E
Cumberland L., *Canada* **73 C8** 54 3N 102 18W
Cumberland Pen., *Canada* **69 B13** 67 0N 64 0W
Cumberland Plateau, *U.S.A.* **77 H3** 36 0N 85 0W
Cumberland Sd., *Canada* **69 B13** 65 30N 66 0W
Cumbernauld, *U.K.* **12 F5** 55 57N 3 58W
Cumborah, *Australia* **63 D4** 29 40S 147 45 E
Cumbria □, *U.K.* **10 C5** 54 42N 2 52W
Cumbrian Mts., *U.K.* **10 C5** 54 30N 3 0W
Cumbum, *India* **40 M11** 15 40N 79 10 E
Cuminá →, *Brazil* **93 D7** 1 30S 56 0W
Cummings Mt., *U.S.A.* **85 K8** 35 2N 118 34W
Cummins, *Australia* **63 E2** 34 16S 135 43 E
Cumnock, *U.K.* **12 F4** 55 28N 4 17W
Cumpas, *Mexico* **86 B3** 30 0N 109 48W
Cumplida, Pta., *Canary Is.* **22 F2** 28 50N 17 48W
Cunco, *Chile* **96 D2** 38 55S 72 2W
Cuncumén, *Chile* **94 C1** 31 53S 70 38W
Cunderdin, *Australia* **61 F2** 31 37S 117 12 E
Cunene →, *Angola* **56 B1** 17 20S 11 50 E
Cúneo, *Italy* **18 D7** 44 23N 7 32 E
Çüngüş, *Turkey* **44 B3** 38 13N 39 17 E
Cunillera, I. = Sa Conillera, *Spain* **22 C7** 38 59N 1 13 E
Cunnamulla, *Australia* **63 D4** 28 2S 145 38 E
Cupar, *Canada* **73 C8** 50 57N 104 10W
Cupar, *U.K.* **12 E5** 56 19N 3 1W
Cupica, G. de, *Colombia* **92 B3** 6 25N 77 30W
Curaçao, *Neth. Ant.* **89 D6** 12 10N 69 0W
Curanilahue, *Chile* **94 D1** 37 29S 73 28W
Curaray →, *Peru* **92 D4** 2 20S 74 5W
Curepto, *Chile* **94 D1** 35 8S 72 1W
Curiapo, *Venezuela* **92 B6** 8 33N 61 5W
Curicó, *Chile* **94 C1** 34 55S 71 20W
Curitiba, *Brazil* **95 B6** 25 20S 49 10W
Curitibanos, *Brazil* **95 B5** 27 18S 50 36W
Currais Novos, *Brazil* **93 E11** 6 13S 36 30W
Curralinho, *Brazil* **93 D9** 1 45S 49 46W
Currant, *U.S.A.* **82 G6** 38 51N 115 32W
Current →, *U.S.A.* **81 G9** 36 15N 90 55W
Currie, *Australia* **62 F3** 39 56S 143 53 E
Currie, *U.S.A.* **82 F6** 40 16N 114 45W
Curtea de Argeş, *Romania* **17 F13** 45 12N 24 42 E
Curtis, *U.S.A.* **80 E4** 40 38N 100 31W
Curtis Group, *Australia* **62 F4** 39 30S 146 37 E
Curtis I., *Australia* **62 C5** 23 35S 151 10 E
Curuápanema →, *Brazil* **93 D7** 2 25S 55 2W
Curuçá, *Brazil* **93 D9** 0 43S 47 50W
Curuguaty, *Paraguay* **95 A4** 24 31S 55 42W
Curup, *Indonesia* **36 E2** 4 26S 102 13 E
Cururupu, *Brazil* **93 D10** 1 50S 44 50W
Curuzú Cuatiá, *Argentina* **94 B4** 29 50S 58 5W
Curvelo, *Brazil* **93 G10** 18 45S 44 27W
Cushing, *U.S.A.* **81 H6** 35 59N 96 46W
Cushing, Mt., *Canada* **72 B3** 57 35N 126 57W
Cusihuiriáchic, *Mexico* **86 B3** 28 10N 106 50W
Custer, *U.S.A.* **80 D3** 43 46N 103 36W
Cut Bank, *U.S.A.* **82 B7** 48 38N 112 20W
Cutchogue, *U.S.A.* **79 E12** 41 1N 72 30W
Cuthbert, *U.S.A.* **77 K3** 31 46N 84 48W
Cutler, *U.S.A.* **84 J7** 36 31N 119 17W
Cuttaburra →, *Australia* **63 D3** 29 43S 144 22 E
Cuttack, *India* **41 J14** 20 25N 85 57 E
Cuvier, C., *Australia* **61 D1** 23 14S 113 22 E
Cuvier I., *N.Z.* **59 G5** 36 27S 175 50 E
Cuxhaven, *Germany* **16 B5** 53 51N 8 41 E
Cuyahoga Falls, *U.S.A.* **78 E3** 41 8N 81 29W
Cuyo, *Phil.* **37 B6** 10 50N 121 5 E
Cuyuni →, *Guyana* **92 B7** 6 23N 58 41W
Cuzco, *Bolivia* **92 H5** 20 0S 66 50W
Cuzco, *Peru* **92 F4** 13 32S 72 0W
Cwmbran, *U.K.* **11 F4** 51 39N 3 2W
Cyangugu, *Rwanda* **54 C2** 2 29S 28 54 E
Cyclades = Kikládhes, *Greece* **21 F11** 37 0N 24 30 E
Cygnet, *Australia* **62 G4** 43 8S 147 1 E
Cynthiana, *U.S.A.* **76 F3** 38 23N 84 18W
Cypress Hills, *Canada* **73 D7** 49 40N 109 30W
Cypress Hills Prov. Park, *Canada* **73 D7** 49 40N 109 30W
Cyprus ■, *Asia* **23 E12** 35 0N 33 0 E
Cyrenaica, *Libya* **51 C10** 27 0N 23 0 E
Czar, *Canada* **73 C6** 52 27N 110 50W
Czech Rep. ■, *Europe* **16 D8** 50 0N 15 0 E
Częstochowa, *Poland* **17 C10** 50 49N 19 7 E

D

Da →, *Vietnam* **38 B5** 21 15N 105 20 E
Da Hinggan Ling, *China* **33 B7** 48 0N 121 0 E
Da Lat, *Vietnam* **39 G7** 11 56N 108 25 E
Da Nang, *Vietnam* **38 D7** 16 4N 108 13 E
Da Qaidam, *China* **32 C4** 37 50N 95 15 E
Da Yunhe →, *China* **35 G11** 34 25N 120 5 E
Da'an, *China* **35 B13** 45 30N 124 7 E
Daba Shan, *China* **33 C5** 32 0N 109 0 E
Dabbagh, Jabal, *Si. Arabia* **44 E2** 27 52N 35 45 E
Dabhoi, *India* **42 H5** 22 10N 73 20 E
Dabo = Pasirkuning, *Indonesia* **36 E2** 0 30S 104 33 E
Dabola, *Guinea* **50 F3** 10 50N 11 5W
Dabung, *Malaysia* **39 K4** 5 23N 102 1 E
Dacca = Dhaka, *Bangla.* **43 H14** 23 43N 90 26 E
Dacca = Dhaka □, *Bangla.* **43 G14** 24 25N 90 25 E
Dachau, *Germany* **16 D6** 48 15N 11 26 E
Dadanawa, *Guyana* **92 C7** 2 50N 59 30W
Dade City, *U.S.A.* **77 L4** 28 22N 82 11W
Dadhar, *Pakistan* **42 E2** 29 28N 67 39 E
Dadra & Nagar Haveli □, *India* **40 J8** 20 5N 73 0 E
Dadri = Charkhi Dadri, *India* **42 E7** 28 37N 76 17 E
Dadu, *Pakistan* **42 F2** 26 45N 67 45 E
Daet, *Phil.* **37 B6** 14 2N 122 55 E
Dagana, *Senegal* **50 E2** 16 30N 15 35W
Dagestan □, *Russia* **25 F8** 42 30N 47 0 E
Daggett, *U.S.A.* **85 L10** 34 52N 116 52W
Daghestan Republic = Dagestan □, *Russia* **25 F8** 42 30N 47 0 E
Dağlıq Qarabağ = Nagorno-Karabakh, *Azerbaijan* **25 F8** 39 55N 46 45 E
Dagö = Hiiumaa, *Estonia* **9 G20** 58 50N 22 45 E
Dagu, *China* **35 E9** 38 59N 117 40 E
Dagupan, *Phil.* **37 A6** 16 3N 120 20 E
Daguragu, *Australia* **60 C5** 17 33S 130 30 E
Dahlak Kebir, *Eritrea* **46 D3** 15 50N 40 10 E
Dahlonega, *U.S.A.* **77 H4** 34 32N 83 59W
Dahod, *India* **42 H6** 22 50N 74 15 E
Dahomey = Benin ■, *Africa* **50 G6** 10 0N 2 0 E
Dahūk, *Iraq* **44 B3** 36 50N 43 1 E
Dai Hao, *Vietnam* **38 C6** 18 1N 106 25 E
Dai-Sen, *Japan* **31 G6** 35 22N 133 32 E
Dai Xian, *China* **34 E7** 39 4N 112 58 E
Daicheng, *China* **34 E9** 38 42N 116 38 E
Daingean, *Ireland* **13 C4** 53 18N 7 17W
Daintree, *Australia* **62 B4** 16 20S 145 20 E
Daiō-Misaki, *Japan* **31 G8** 34 15N 136 45 E
Daisetsu-Zan, *Japan* **30 C11** 43 30N 142 57 E
Dajarra, *Australia* **62 C2** 21 42S 139 30 E
Dak Dam, *Cambodia* **38 F6** 12 20N 107 21 E
Dak Nhe, *Vietnam* **38 E6** 15 28N 107 48 E
Dak Pek, *Vietnam* **38 E6** 15 4N 107 44 E
Dak Song, *Vietnam* **39 F6** 12 19N 107 35 E
Dak Sui, *Vietnam* **38 E6** 14 55N 107 43 E
Dakar, *Senegal* **50 F2** 14 34N 17 29W
Dakhla, *W. Sahara* **50 D2** 23 50N 15 53W
Dakhla, El Wâhât el-, *Egypt* **51 C11** 25 30N 28 50 E
Dakor, *India* **42 H5** 22 45N 73 11 E
Dakota City, *U.S.A.* **80 D6** 42 25N 96 25W
Đakovica, *Kosovo, Yug.* **21 C9** 42 22N 20 26 E
Dalachi, *China* **34 F3** 36 48N 105 0 E
Dalai Nur, *China* **34 C9** 43 20N 116 45 E
Dālakī, *Iran* **45 D6** 29 26N 51 17 E
Dalälven →, *Sweden* **9 F17** 60 12N 16 43 E
Dalaman →, *Turkey* **21 F13** 36 41N 28 43 E
Dalandzadgad, *Mongolia* **34 C3** 43 27N 104 30 E
Dalap-Uliga-Darrit, *Marshall Is.* **64 G9** 7 7N 171 24 E
Dalarna, *Sweden* **9 F16** 61 0N 14 0 E
Dālbandīn, *Pakistan* **40 E4** 29 0N 64 23 E
Dalbeattie, *U.K.* **12 G5** 54 56N 3 50W
Dalbeg, *Australia* **62 C4** 20 16S 147 18 E
Dalby, *Australia* **63 D5** 27 10S 151 17 E
Dale City, *U.S.A.* **76 F7** 38 38N 77 18W
Dale Hollow L., *U.S.A.* **77 G3** 36 32N 85 27W
Dalgān, *Iran* **45 E8** 27 31N 59 19 E
Dalhart, *U.S.A.* **81 G3** 36 4N 102 31W
Dalhousie, *Canada* **71 C6** 48 5N 66 26W
Dalhousie, *India* **42 C6** 32 38N 75 58 E
Dali, *Shaanxi, China* **34 G5** 34 48N 109 58 E
Dali, *Yunnan, China* **32 D5** 25 40N 100 10 E
Dalian, *China* **35 E11** 38 50N 121 40 E
Daliang Shan, *China* **32 D5** 28 0N 102 45 E
Daling He →, *China* **35 D11** 40 55N 121 40 E
Dāliyat el Karmel, *Israel* **47 C4** 32 43N 35 2 E
Dalkeith, *U.K.* **12 F5** 55 54N 3 4W
Dallas, *Oreg., U.S.A.* **82 D2** 44 55N 123 19W
Dallas, *Tex., U.S.A.* **81 J6** 32 47N 96 49W
Dalmā, *U.A.E.* **45 E7** 24 30N 52 20 E
Dalmacija, *Croatia* **20 C7** 43 20N 17 0 E
Dalmas, L., *Canada* **71 B5** 53 30N 71 50W
Dalmatia = Dalmacija, *Croatia* **20 C7** 43 20N 17 0 E
Dalmau, *India* **43 F9** 26 4N 81 2 E
Dalmellington, *U.K.* **12 F4** 55 19N 4 23W
Dalnegorsk, *Russia* **27 E14** 44 32N 135 33 E
Dalnerechensk, *Russia* **27 E14** 45 50N 133 40 E
Daloa, *Ivory C.* **50 G4** 7 0N 6 30W
Dalry, *U.K.* **12 F4** 55 42N 4 43W
Dalrymple, L., *Australia* **62 C4** 20 40S 147 0 E
Dalsland, *Sweden* **9 G14** 58 50N 12 15 E
Daltenganj, *India* **43 H11** 24 0N 84 4 E
Dalton, *Ga., U.S.A.* **77 H3** 34 46N 84 58W
Dalton, *Mass., U.S.A.* **79 D11** 42 28N 73 11W
Dalton, *Nebr., U.S.A.* **80 E3** 41 25N 102 58W
Dalton Iceberg Tongue, *Antarctica* **5 C9** 66 15S 121 30 E
Dalton-in-Furness, *U.K.* **10 C4** 54 10N 3 11W
Dalvík, *Iceland* **8 D4** 65 58N 18 32W
Dalwallinu, *Australia* **61 F2** 30 17S 116 40 E
Daly →, *Australia* **60 B5** 13 35S 130 19 E

Detour, Pt.

Daly City, *U.S.A.* **84 H4** 37 42N 122 28W
Daly L., *Canada* **73 B7** 56 32N 105 39W
Daly River, *Australia* **60 B5** 13 46S 130 42 E
Daly Waters, *Australia* **62 B1** 16 15S 133 24 E
Dam Doi, *Vietnam* **39 H5** 8 50N 105 12 E
Dam Ha, *Vietnam* **38 B6** 21 21N 107 36 E
Daman, *India* **40 J8** 20 25N 72 57 E
Dāmaneh, *Iran* **45 C6** 33 1N 50 29 E
Damanhûr, *Egypt* **51 B12** 31 0N 30 30 E
Damant L., *Canada* **73 A7** 61 45N 105 5W
Damanzhuang, *China* **34 E9** 38 5N 116 35 E
Damar, *Indonesia* **37 F7** 7 7S 128 40 E
Damaraland, *Namibia* **56 C2** 20 0S 15 0 E
Damascus = Dimashq, *Syria* **47 B5** 33 30N 36 18 E
Damāvand, *Iran* **45 C7** 35 47N 52 0 E
Damāvand, Qolleh-ye, *Iran* **45 C7** 35 56N 52 10 E
Damba, *Angola* **52 F3** 6 44S 15 20 E
Dâmboviţa →, *Romania* **17 F14** 44 12N 26 26 E
Dame Marie, *Haiti* **89 C5** 18 36N 74 26W
Dāmghān, *Iran* **45 B7** 36 10N 54 17 E
Damiel, *Spain* **19 C4** 39 4N 3 37W
Damietta = Dumyât, *Egypt* **51 B12** 31 24N 31 48 E
Daming, *China* **34 F8** 36 15N 115 6 E
Damīr Qābū, *Syria* **44 B4** 36 58N 41 51 E
Dammam = Ad Dammām, *Si. Arabia* **45 E6** 26 20N 50 5 E
Damodar →, *India* **43 H12** 23 17N 87 35 E
Damoh, *India* **43 H8** 23 50N 79 28 E
Dampier, *Australia* **60 D2** 20 41S 116 42 E
Dampier, Selat, *Indonesia* **37 E8** 0 40S 131 0 E
Dampier Arch., *Australia* **60 D2** 20 38S 116 32 E
Damrei, Chuor Phnum, *Cambodia* **39 G4** 11 30N 103 0 E
Dan Xian, *China* **38 C7** 19 31N 109 33 E
Dana, *Indonesia* **37 F6** 11 0S 122 52 E
Dana, L., *Canada* **70 B4** 50 53N 77 20W
Dana, Mt., *U.S.A.* **84 H7** 37 54N 119 12W
Danakil Desert, *Ethiopia* **46 E3** 12 45N 41 0 E
Danané, *Ivory C.* **50 G4** 7 16N 8 9W
Danau Poso, *Indonesia* **37 E6** 1 52S 120 35 E
Danbury, *U.S.A.* **79 E11** 41 24N 73 28W
Danby L., *U.S.A.* **83 J6** 34 13N 115 5W
Dand, *Afghan.* **42 D1** 31 28N 65 32 E
Dandeldhura, *Nepal* **43 E9** 29 20N 80 35 E
Dandeli, *India* **40 M9** 15 5N 74 30 E
Dandong, *China* **35 D13** 40 10N 124 20 E
Danfeng, *China* **34 H6** 33 45N 110 25 E
Danger Is. = Pukapuka, *Cook Is.* **65 J11** 10 53S 165 49W
Danger Pt., *S. Africa* **56 E2** 34 40S 19 17 E
Dangla Shan = Tanggula Shan, *China* **32 C4** 32 40N 92 10 E
Dangrek, Phnom, *Thailand* **38 E5** 14 15N 105 0 E
Dangriga, *Belize* **87 D7** 17 0N 88 13W
Dangshan, *China* **34 G9** 34 27N 116 22 E
Daniel, *U.S.A.* **82 E8** 42 52N 110 4W
Daniel's Harbour, *Canada* **71 B8** 50 13N 57 35W
Danielskuil, *S. Africa* **56 D3** 28 11S 23 33 E
Danielson, *U.S.A.* **79 E13** 41 48N 71 53W
Danilov, *Russia* **24 C7** 58 16N 40 13 E
Daning, *China* **34 F6** 36 28N 110 45 E
Danissa, *Kenya* **54 B5** 3 15N 40 58 E
Dank, *Oman* **45 F8** 23 33N 56 16 E
Dankhar Gompa, *India* **40 C11** 32 10N 78 10 E
Danlí, *Honduras* **88 D2** 14 4N 86 35W
Dannemora, *U.S.A.* **79 B11** 44 43N 73 44W
Dannevirke, *N.Z.* **59 J6** 40 12S 176 8 E
Dannhauser, *S. Africa* **57 D5** 28 0S 30 3 E
Dansville, *U.S.A.* **78 D7** 42 34N 77 42W
Danta, *India* **42 G5** 24 11N 72 46 E
Dantan, *India* **43 J12** 21 57N 87 20 E
Dante, *Somali Rep.* **46 E5** 10 25N 51 16 E
Danube = Dunărea →, *Europe* **17 F15** 45 20N 29 40 E
Danvers, *U.S.A.* **79 D14** 42 34N 70 56W
Danville, *Ill., U.S.A.* **76 E2** 40 8N 87 37W
Danville, *Ky., U.S.A.* **76 G3** 37 39N 84 46W
Danville, *Pa., U.S.A.* **79 F8** 40 58N 76 37W
Danville, *Va., U.S.A.* **77 G6** 36 36N 79 23W
Danville, *Vt., U.S.A.* **79 B12** 44 25N 72 9W
Danzig = Gdańsk, *Poland* **17 A10** 54 22N 18 40 E
Dapaong, *Togo* **50 F6** 10 55N 0 16 E
Daqing Shan, *China* **34 D6** 40 40N 111 0 E
Dar Banda, *Africa* **48 F6** 8 0N 23 0 E
Dar el Beida = Casablanca, *Morocco* **50 B4** 33 36N 7 36W
Dar es Salaam, *Tanzania* **54 D4** 6 50S 39 12 E
Dar Mazār, *Iran* **45 D8** 29 14N 57 20 E
Dar'ā, *Syria* **47 C5** 32 36N 36 7 E
Dar'ā □, *Syria* **47 C5** 32 55N 36 10 E
Dārāb, *Iran* **45 D7** 28 50N 54 30 E
Daraban, *Pakistan* **42 D4** 31 44N 70 20 E
Daraina, *Madag.* **57 A8** 13 12S 49 40 E
Daraj, *Libya* **51 B8** 30 10N 10 28 E
Dārān, *Iran* **45 C6** 32 59N 50 24 E
Dārayyā, *Syria* **47 B5** 33 28N 36 15 E
Darband, *Pakistan* **42 B5** 34 20N 72 50 E
Darband, Kūh-e, *Iran* **45 D8** 31 34N 57 8 E
Darbhanga, *India* **43 F11** 26 15N 85 55 E
D'Arcy, *Canada* **72 C4** 50 27N 122 35W
Dardanelle, *Ark., U.S.A.* **81 H8** 35 13N 93 9W
Dardanelle, *Calif., U.S.A.* **84 G7** 38 20N 119 50W
Dardanelles = Çanakkale Boğazı, *Turkey* **21 D12** 40 17N 26 32 E
Dārestān, *Iran* **45 D8** 29 9N 58 42 E
Dârfûr, *Sudan* **51 F10** 13 40N 24 0 E
Dargai, *Pakistan* **42 B4** 34 25N 71 55 E
Dargan Ata, *Turkmenistan* **26 E7** 40 29N 62 10 E
Dargaville, *N.Z.* **59 F4** 35 57S 173 52 E
Darhan, *Mongolia* **32 B5** 49 37N 106 21 E
Darhan Muminggan Lianheqi, *China* **34 D6** 41 40N 110 28 E
Darıca, *Turkey* **21 D13** 40 45N 29 23 E
Darién, G. del, *Colombia* **92 B3** 9 0N 77 0W
Dariganga = Ovoot, *Mongolia* **34 B7** 45 21N 113 45 E
Darjeeling = Darjiling, *India* **43 F13** 27 3N 88 18 E
Darjiling, *India* **43 F13** 27 3N 88 18 E
Darkan, *Australia* **61 F2** 33 20S 116 43 E
Darkhana, *Pakistan* **42 D5** 30 39N 72 11 E
Darkhazīneh, *Iran* **45 D6** 31 54N 48 39 E
Darkot Pass, *Pakistan* **43 A5** 36 45N 73 26 E
Darling Downs, *Australia* **63 D5** 27 30S 150 30 E
Darling Ra., *Australia* **61 F2** 32 30S 116 0 E
Darlington, *U.K.* **10 C6** 54 32N 1 33W
Darlington, *U.S.A.* **77 H6** 34 18N 79 52W
Darlington □, *U.K.* **10 C6** 54 32N 1 33W
Darlington, L., *S. Africa* **56 E4** 33 10S 25 9 E
Darlot, L., *Australia* **61 E3** 27 48S 121 35 E
Darłowo, *Poland* **16 A9** 54 25N 16 25 E
Darmstadt, *Germany* **16 D5** 49 51N 8 39 E
Darnah, *Libya* **51 B10** 32 45N 22 45 E
Darnall, *S. Africa* **57 D5** 29 23S 31 18 E
Darnley, C., *Antarctica* **5 C6** 68 0S 69 0 E
Darnley B., *Canada* **68 B7** 69 30N 123 30W
Darr →, *Australia* **62 C3** 23 39S 143 50 E
Darra Pezu, *Pakistan* **42 C4** 32 19N 70 44 E
Darrequeira, *Argentina* **94 D3** 37 42S 63 10W
Darrington, *U.S.A.* **82 B3** 48 15N 121 36W
Dart →, *U.K.* **11 G4** 50 24N 3 39W
Dart, C., *Antarctica* **5 D14** 73 6S 126 20W
Dartford, *U.K.* **11 F8** 51 26N 0 13 E
Dartmoor, *U.K.* **11 G4** 50 38N 3 57W
Dartmouth, *Canada* **71 D7** 44 40N 63 30W
Dartmouth, *U.K.* **11 G4** 50 21N 3 36W
Dartmouth, L., *Australia* **63 D4** 26 4S 145 18 E
Dartuch, C. = Artrutx, C. de, *Spain* **22 B10** 39 55N 3 49 E
Darvaza, *Turkmenistan* **26 E6** 40 11N 58 24 E
Darvel, Teluk = Lahad Datu, Teluk, *Malaysia* **37 D5** 4 50N 118 20 E
Darwen, *U.K.* **10 D5** 53 42N 2 29W
Darwendale, *Zimbabwe* **57 B5** 17 41S 30 33 E
Darwha, *India* **40 J10** 20 15N 77 45 E
Darwin, *Australia* **60 B5** 12 25S 130 51 E
Darwin, *U.S.A.* **85 J9** 36 15N 117 35W
Darya Khan, *Pakistan* **42 D4** 31 48N 71 6 E
Daryoi Amu = Amudarya →, *Uzbekistan* **26 E6** 43 58N 59 34 E
Dās, *U.A.E.* **45 E7** 25 20N 53 30 E
Dashen, Ras, *Ethiopia* **46 E2** 13 8N 38 26 E
Dashetai, *China* **34 D5** 41 0N 109 5 E
Dashhowuz, *Turkmenistan* **26 E6** 41 49N 59 58 E
Dashköpri, *Turkmenistan* **45 B9** 36 16N 62 8 E
Dasht, *Iran* **45 B8** 37 17N 56 7 E
Dasht →, *Pakistan* **40 G2** 25 10N 61 40 E
Daska, *Pakistan* **42 C6** 32 20N 74 20 E
Dasuya, *India* **42 D6** 31 49N 75 38 E
Datça, *Turkey* **21 F12** 36 46N 27 40 E
Datia, *India* **43 G8** 25 39N 78 27 E
Datong, *China* **34 D7** 40 6N 113 18 E
Dattakhel, *Pakistan* **42 C3** 32 54N 69 46 E
Datu, Tanjung, *Indonesia* **36 D3** 2 5N 109 39 E
Datu Piang, *Phil.* **37 C6** 7 2N 124 30 E
Datuk, Tanjong = Datu, Tanjung, *Indonesia* **36 D3** 2 5N 109 39 E
Daud Khel, *Pakistan* **42 C4** 32 53N 71 34 E
Daudnagar, *India* **43 G11** 25 2N 84 24 E
Daugava →, *Latvia* **9 H21** 57 4N 24 3 E
Daugavpils, *Latvia* **9 J22** 55 53N 26 32 E
Daulpur, *India* **42 F7** 26 45N 77 59 E
Dauphin, *Canada* **73 C8** 51 9N 100 5W
Dauphin, *U.S.A.* **78 F8** 40 22N 76 56W
Dauphin L., *Canada* **73 C9** 51 20N 99 45W
Dauphiné, *France* **18 D6** 45 15N 5 25 E
Dausa, *India* **42 F7** 26 52N 76 20 E
Davangere, *India* **40 M9** 14 25N 75 55 E
Davao, *Phil.* **37 C7** 7 0N 125 40 E
Davao G., *Phil.* **37 C7** 6 30N 125 48 E
Dāvar Panāh, *Iran* **45 E9** 27 25N 62 15 E
Davenport, *Calif., U.S.A.* **84 H4** 37 1N 122 12W
Davenport, *Iowa, U.S.A.* **80 E9** 41 32N 90 35W
Davenport, *Wash., U.S.A.* **82 C4** 47 39N 118 9W
Davenport Ra., *Australia* **62 C1** 20 28S 134 0 E
Daventry, *U.K.* **11 E6** 52 16N 1 10W
David, *Panama* **88 E3** 8 30N 82 30W
David City, *U.S.A.* **80 E6** 41 15N 97 8W
David Gorodok = Davyd Haradok, *Belarus* **17 B14** 52 4N 27 8 E
Davidson, *Canada* **73 C7** 51 16N 105 59W
Davis, *U.S.A.* **84 G5** 38 33N 121 44W
Davis Dam, *U.S.A.* **85 K12** 35 11N 114 34W
Davis Inlet, *Canada* **71 A7** 55 50N 60 59W
Davis Mts., *U.S.A.* **81 K2** 30 50N 103 55W
Davis Sea, *Antarctica* **5 C7** 66 0S 92 0 E
Davis Str., *N. Amer.* **69 B14** 65 0N 58 0W
Davos, *Switz.* **18 C8** 46 48N 9 49 E
Davy L., *Canada* **73 B7** 58 53N 108 18W
Davyd Haradok, *Belarus* **17 B14** 52 4N 27 8 E
Dawei, *Burma* **38 E2** 14 2N 98 12 E
Dawes Ra., *Australia* **62 C5** 24 40S 150 40 E
Dawlish, *U.K.* **11 G4** 50 35N 3 28W
Dawna Ra., *Burma* **38 D2** 16 30N 98 30 E
Dawros Hd., *Ireland* **13 B3** 54 50N 8 33W
Dawson, *Canada* **68 B6** 64 10N 139 30W
Dawson, *U.S.A.* **77 K3** 31 46N 84 27W
Dawson, I., *Chile* **96 G2** 53 50S 70 50W
Dawson B., *Canada* **73 C8** 52 53N 100 49W
Dawson Creek, *Canada* **72 B4** 55 45N 120 15W
Dawson Inlet, *Canada* **73 A10** 61 50N 93 25W
Dawson Ra., *Australia* **62 C4** 24 30S 149 48 E
Dax, *France* **18 E3** 43 44N 1 3W
Daxian, *China* **32 C5** 31 15N 107 23 E
Daxindian, *China* **35 F11** 37 30N 120 50 E
Daxinggou, *China* **35 C15** 43 25N 129 40 E
Daxue Shan, *China* **32 C5** 30 30N 101 30 E
Dayr az Zawr, *Syria* **44 C4** 35 20N 40 5 E
Daysland, *Canada* **72 C6** 52 50N 112 20W
Dayton, *Nev., U.S.A.* **84 F7** 39 14N 119 36W
Dayton, *Ohio, U.S.A.* **76 F3** 39 45N 84 12W
Dayton, *Pa., U.S.A.* **78 F5** 40 53N 79 15W
Dayton, *Tenn., U.S.A.* **77 H3** 35 30N 85 1W
Dayton, *Wash., U.S.A.* **82 C4** 46 19N 117 59W
Dayton, *Wyo., U.S.A.* **82 D10** 44 53N 107 16W
Daytona Beach, *U.S.A.* **77 L5** 29 13N 81 1W
Dayville, *U.S.A.* **82 D4** 44 28N 119 32W
De Aar, *S. Africa* **56 E3** 30 39S 24 0 E
De Funiak Springs, *U.S.A.* **77 K2** 30 43N 86 7W
De Grey →, *Australia* **60 D2** 20 12S 119 13 E
De Haan, *Belgium* **15 C3** 51 16N 3 2 E
De Kalb, *U.S.A.* **80 E10** 41 56N 88 46W
De Land, *U.S.A.* **77 L5** 29 2N 81 18W
De Leon, *U.S.A.* **81 J5** 32 7N 98 32W
De Panne, *Belgium* **15 C2** 51 6N 2 34 E
De Pere, *U.S.A.* **76 C1** 44 27N 88 4W
De Queen, *U.S.A.* **81 H7** 34 2N 94 21W
De Quincy, *U.S.A.* **81 K8** 30 27N 93 26W
De Ridder, *U.S.A.* **81 K8** 30 51N 93 17W
De Smet, *U.S.A.* **80 C6** 44 23N 97 33W
De Soto, *U.S.A.* **80 F9** 38 8N 90 34W
De Tour Village, *U.S.A.* **76 C4** 46 0N 83 56W
De Witt, *U.S.A.* **81 H9** 34 18N 91 20W
Dead Sea, *Asia* **47 D4** 31 30N 35 30 E
Deadwood, *U.S.A.* **80 C3** 44 23N 103 44W
Deadwood L., *Canada* **72 B3** 59 10N 128 30W
Deal, *U.K.* **11 F9** 51 13N 1 25 E
Deal I., *Australia* **62 F4** 39 30S 147 20 E
Dealesville, *S. Africa* **56 D4** 28 41S 25 44 E
Dean →, *Canada* **72 C3** 52 49N 126 58W
Dean, Forest of, *U.K.* **11 F5** 51 45N 2 33W
Dean Chan., *Canada* **72 C3** 52 30N 127 15W
Deán Funes, *Argentina* **94 C3** 30 20S 64 20W
Dease →, *Canada* **72 B3** 59 56N 128 32W
Dease L., *Canada* **72 B2** 58 40N 130 5W
Dease Lake, *Canada* **72 B2** 58 25N 130 6W
Death Valley, *U.S.A.* **85 J10** 36 15N 116 50W
Death Valley Junction, *U.S.A.* **85 J10** 36 20N 116 25W
Death Valley National Park, *U.S.A.* **85 J10** 36 45N 117 15W
Debar, *Macedonia* **21 D9** 41 31N 20 30 E
Debden, *Canada* **73 C7** 53 30N 106 50W
Dębica, *Poland* **17 C11** 50 2N 21 25 E
Debolt, *Canada* **72 B5** 55 12N 118 1W
Deborah East, L., *Australia* **61 F2** 30 45S 119 0 E
Deborah West, L., *Australia* **61 F2** 30 45S 118 50 E
Debre Markos, *Ethiopia* **46 E2** 10 20N 37 40 E
Debre Tabor, *Ethiopia* **46 E2** 11 50N 38 26 E
Debre Zeyit, *Ethiopia* **46 F2** 11 48N 38 30 E
Debrecen, *Hungary* **17 E11** 47 33N 21 42 E
Decatur, *Ala., U.S.A.* **77 H2** 34 36N 86 59W
Decatur, *Ga., U.S.A.* **77 J3** 33 47N 84 18W
Decatur, *Ill., U.S.A.* **80 F10** 39 51N 88 57W
Decatur, *Ind., U.S.A.* **76 E3** 40 50N 84 56W
Decatur, *Tex., U.S.A.* **81 J6** 33 14N 97 35W
Deccan, *India* **40 L11** 18 0N 79 0 E
Deception Bay, *Australia* **63 D5** 27 10S 153 5 E
Deception L., *Canada* **73 B8** 56 33N 104 13W
Dechhu, *India* **42 F5** 26 46N 72 20 E
Děčín, *Czech Rep.* **16 C8** 50 47N 14 12 E
Deckerville, *U.S.A.* **78 C2** 43 32N 82 44W
Decorah, *U.S.A.* **80 D9** 43 18N 91 48W
Dedéagach = Alexandroúpolis, *Greece* **21 D11** 40 50N 25 54 E
Dedham, *U.S.A.* **79 D13** 42 15N 71 10W
Dedza, *Malawi* **55 E3** 14 20S 34 20 E
Dee →, *Aberds., U.K.* **12 D6** 57 9N 2 5W
Dee →, *Dumf. & Gall., U.K.* **12 G4** 54 51N 4 3W
Dee →, *Wales, U.K.* **10 D4** 53 22N 3 17W
Deep B., *Canada* **72 A5** 61 15N 116 35W
Deepwater, *Australia* **63 D5** 29 25S 151 51 E
Deer →, *Canada* **73 B10** 58 23N 94 13W
Deer L., *Canada* **73 C10** 52 40N 94 20W
Deer Lake, *Nfld., Canada* **71 C8** 49 11N 57 27W
Deer Lake, *Ont., Canada* **73 C10** 52 36N 94 20W
Deer Lodge, *U.S.A.* **82 C7** 46 24N 112 44W
Deer Park, *U.S.A.* **82 C5** 47 57N 117 28W
Deer River, *U.S.A.* **80 B8** 47 20N 93 48W
Deeragun, *Australia* **62 B4** 19 16S 146 33 E
Deerdepoort, *S. Africa* **56 C4** 24 37S 26 27 E
Deferiet, *U.S.A.* **79 B9** 44 2N 75 41W
Defiance, *U.S.A.* **76 E3** 41 17N 84 22W
Degana, *India* **42 F6** 26 50N 74 20 E
Dégelis, *Canada* **71 C6** 47 30N 68 35W
Deggendorf, *Germany* **16 D7** 48 50N 12 57 E
Degh →, *Pakistan* **42 D5** 31 3N 73 21 E
Deh Bīd, *Iran* **45 D7** 30 39N 53 11 E
Deh-e Shīr, *Iran* **45 D7** 31 29N 53 45 E
Dehaj, *Iran* **45 D7** 30 42N 54 53 E
Dehak, *Iran* **45 E9** 27 11N 62 37 E
Dehdez, *Iran* **45 D6** 31 43N 50 17 E
Dehej, *India* **42 J5** 21 44N 72 40 E
Dehestān, *Iran* **45 D7** 28 30N 55 35 E
Dehgolān, *Iran* **44 C5** 35 17N 47 25 E
Dehibat, *Tunisia* **51 B8** 32 0N 10 47 E
Dehlorān, *Iran* **44 C5** 32 41N 47 16 E
Dehnow-e Kūhestān, *Iran* **45 E8** 27 58N 58 32 E
Dehra Dun, *India* **42 D8** 30 20N 78 4 E
Dehri, *India* **43 G11** 24 50N 84 15 E
Dehui, *China* **35 B13** 44 30N 125 40 E
Deinze, *Belgium* **15 D3** 50 59N 3 32 E
Dej, *Romania* **17 E12** 47 10N 23 52 E
Deka →, *Zimbabwe* **56 B4** 18 4S 26 42 E
Dekese, *Dem. Rep. of the Congo* **52 E4** 3 24S 21 24 E
Del Mar, *U.S.A.* **85 N9** 32 58N 117 16W
Del Norte, *U.S.A.* **83 H10** 37 41N 106 21W
Del Rio, *U.S.A.* **81 L4** 29 22N 100 54W
Delambre I., *Australia* **60 D2** 20 26S 117 5 E
Delano, *U.S.A.* **85 K7** 35 46N 119 15W
Delano Peak, *U.S.A.* **83 G7** 38 22N 112 22W
Delareyville, *S. Africa* **56 D4** 26 41S 25 26 E
Delaronde L., *Canada* **73 C7** 54 3N 107 3W
Delavan, *U.S.A.* **80 D10** 42 38N 88 39W
Delaware, *U.S.A.* **76 E4** 40 18N 83 4W
Delaware □, *U.S.A.* **76 F8** 39 0N 75 20W
Delaware →, *U.S.A.* **79 G9** 39 15N 75 20W
Delaware B., *U.S.A.* **76 F8** 39 0N 75 10W
Delay →, *Canada* **71 A5** 56 56N 71 28W
Delevan, *U.S.A.* **78 D6** 42 29N 78 29W
Delft, *Neths.* **15 B4** 52 1N 4 22 E
Delfzijl, *Neths.* **15 A6** 53 20N 6 55 E
Delgado, C., *Mozam.* **55 E5** 10 45S 40 40 E
Delgerhet, *Mongolia* **34 B6** 45 50N 110 30 E
Delgo, *Sudan* **51 D12** 20 6N 30 40 E
Delhi, *Canada* **78 D4** 42 51N 80 30W
Delhi, *India* **42 E7** 28 38N 77 17 E
Delhi, *La., U.S.A.* **81 J9** 32 28N 91 30W
Delhi, *N.Y., U.S.A.* **79 D10** 42 17N 74 55W
Delia, *Canada* **72 C6** 51 38N 112 23W
Delice, *Turkey* **25 G5** 39 54N 34 2 E
Delicias, *Mexico* **86 B3** 28 10N 105 30W
Delījān, *Iran* **45 C6** 33 59N 50 40 E
Déline, *Canada* **68 B7** 65 10N 123 30W
Delisle, *Canada* **73 C7** 51 55N 107 8W
Dell City, *U.S.A.* **83 L11** 31 56N 105 12W
Dell Rapids, *U.S.A.* **80 D6** 43 50N 96 43W
Delmar, *U.S.A.* **79 D11** 42 37N 73 47W
Delmenhorst, *Germany* **16 B5** 53 3N 8 37 E
Delonga, Ostrova, *Russia* **27 B15** 76 40N 149 20 E
Deloraine, *Australia* **62 G4** 41 30S 146 40 E
Deloraine, *Canada* **73 D8** 49 15N 100 29W
Delphi, *U.S.A.* **76 E2** 40 36N 86 41W
Delphos, *U.S.A.* **76 E3** 40 51N 84 21W
Delportshoop, *S. Africa* **56 D3** 28 22S 24 20 E
Delray Beach, *U.S.A.* **77 M5** 26 28N 80 4W
Delta, *Colo., U.S.A.* **83 G9** 38 44N 108 4W
Delta, *Utah, U.S.A.* **82 G7** 39 21N 112 35W
Delta Junction, *U.S.A.* **68 B5** 64 2N 145 44W
Deltona, *U.S.A.* **77 L5** 28 54N 81 16W
Delungra, *Australia* **63 D5** 29 39S 150 51 E
Delvada, *India* **42 J4** 20 46N 71 2 E
Delvinë, *Albania* **21 E9** 39 59N 20 6 E
Demak, *Indonesia* **37 G14** 6 53S 110 38 E
Demanda, Sierra de la, *Spain* **19 A4** 42 15N 3 0W
Demavand = Damāvand, *Iran* **45 C7** 35 47N 52 0 E
Dembia, *Dem. Rep. of the Congo* **54 B2** 3 33N 25 48 E
Dembidolo, *Ethiopia* **46 F1** 8 34N 34 50 E
Demchok, *India* **43 C8** 32 42N 79 29 E
Demer →, *Belgium* **15 D4** 50 57N 4 42 E
Deming, *N. Mex., U.S.A.* **83 K10** 32 16N 107 46W
Deming, *Wash., U.S.A.* **84 B4** 48 50N 122 13W
Demini →, *Brazil* **92 D6** 0 46S 62 56W
Demirci, *Turkey* **21 E13** 39 2N 28 38 E
Demirköy, *Turkey* **21 D12** 41 49N 27 45 E
Demopolis, *U.S.A.* **77 J2** 32 31N 87 50W
Dempo, *Indonesia* **36 E2** 4 2S 103 15 E
Den Burg, *Neths.* **15 A4** 53 3N 4 47 E
Den Chai, *Thailand* **38 D3** 17 59N 100 4 E
Den Haag = 's-Gravenhage, *Neths.* **15 B4** 52 7N 4 17 E
Den Helder, *Neths.* **15 B4** 52 57N 4 45 E
Den Oever, *Neths.* **15 B5** 52 56N 5 2 E
Denair, *U.S.A.* **84 H6** 37 32N 120 48W
Denau, *Uzbekistan* **26 F7** 38 16N 67 54 E
Denbigh, *Canada* **78 A7** 45 8N 77 15W
Denbigh, *U.K.* **10 D4** 53 12N 3 25W
Denbighshire □, *U.K.* **10 D4** 53 8N 3 22W
Dendang, *Indonesia* **36 E3** 3 7S 107 56 E
Dendermonde, *Belgium* **15 C4** 51 2N 4 5 E
Dengfeng, *China* **34 G7** 34 25N 113 2 E
Dengkou, *China* **34 D4** 40 18N 106 55 E
Denham, *Australia* **61 E1** 25 56S 113 31 E
Denham Ra., *Australia* **62 C4** 21 55S 147 46 E
Denham Sd., *Australia* **61 E1** 25 45S 113 15 E
Denholm, *Canada* **73 C7** 52 39N 108 1W
Denia, *Spain* **19 C6** 38 49N 0 8 E
Denial B., *Australia* **63 E1** 32 14S 133 32 E
Denison, *Iowa, U.S.A.* **80 E7** 42 1N 95 21W
Denison, *Tex., U.S.A.* **81 J6** 33 45N 96 33W
Denison Plains, *Australia* **60 C4** 18 35S 128 0 E
Denizli, *Turkey* **25 G4** 37 42N 29 2 E
Denman Glacier, *Antarctica* **5 C7** 66 45S 99 25 E
Denmark, *Australia* **61 F2** 34 59S 117 25 E
Denmark ■, *Europe* **9 J13** 55 45N 10 0 E
Denmark Str., *Atl. Oc.* **4 C6** 66 0N 30 0W
Dennison, *U.S.A.* **78 F3** 40 24N 81 19W
Denny, *U.K.* **12 E5** 56 1N 3 55W
Denpasar, *Indonesia* **36 F5** 8 45S 115 14 E
Denton, *Mont., U.S.A.* **82 C9** 47 19N 109 57W
Denton, *Tex., U.S.A.* **81 J6** 33 13N 97 8W
D'Entrecasteaux, Pt., *Australia* **61 F2** 34 50S 115 57 E
Denver, *Colo., U.S.A.* **80 F2** 39 44N 104 59W
Denver, *Pa., U.S.A.* **79 F8** 40 14N 76 8W
Denver City, *U.S.A.* **81 J3** 32 58N 102 50W
Deoband, *India* **42 E7** 29 42N 77 43 E
Deogarh, *India* **42 G5** 25 32N 73 54 E
Deoghar, *India* **43 G12** 24 30N 86 42 E
Deolali, *India* **40 K8** 19 58N 73 50 E
Deoli = Devli, *India* **42 G6** 25 50N 75 20 E
Deora, *India* **42 F4** 26 22N 70 55 E
Deori, *India* **43 H8** 23 24N 79 1 E
Deoria, *India* **43 F10** 26 31N 83 48 E
Deosai Mts., *Pakistan* **43 B6** 35 40N 75 0 E
Deosri, *India* **43 F14** 26 46N 90 29 E
Depalpur, *India* **42 H6** 22 51N 75 33 E
Deping, *China* **35 F9** 37 25N 116 58 E
Deposit, *U.S.A.* **79 D9** 42 4N 75 25W
Depuch I., *Australia* **60 D2** 20 37S 117 44 E
Deputatskiy, *Russia* **27 C14** 69 18N 139 54 E
Dera Ghazi Khan, *Pakistan* **42 D4** 30 5N 70 43 E
Dera Ismail Khan, *Pakistan* **42 D4** 31 50N 70 50 E
Derabugti, *Pakistan* **42 E3** 29 2N 69 9 E
Derawar Fort, *Pakistan* **42 E4** 28 46N 71 20 E
Derbent, *Russia* **25 F8** 42 5N 48 15 E
Derby, *Australia* **60 C3** 17 18S 123 38 E
Derby, *U.K.* **10 E6** 52 56N 1 28W
Derby, *Conn., U.S.A.* **79 E11** 41 19N 73 5W
Derby, *Kans., U.S.A.* **81 G6** 37 33N 97 16W
Derby, *N.Y., U.S.A.* **78 D6** 42 41N 78 58W
Derby City □, *U.K.* **10 E6** 52 56N 1 28W
Derby Line, *U.S.A.* **79 B12** 45 0N 72 6W
Derbyshire □, *U.K.* **10 D6** 53 11N 1 38W
Derg →, *U.K.* **13 B4** 54 44N 7 26W
Derg, L., *Ireland* **13 D3** 53 0N 8 20W
Dergaon, *India* **41 F19** 26 45N 94 0 E
Dermott, *U.S.A.* **81 J9** 33 32N 91 26W
Derry = Londonderry, *U.K.* **13 B4** 55 0N 7 20W
Derry = Londonderry □, *U.K.* **13 B4** 55 0N 7 20W
Derry, *N.H., U.S.A.* **79 D13** 42 53N 71 19W
Derry, *Pa., U.S.A.* **78 F5** 40 20N 79 18W
Derryveagh Mts., *Ireland* **13 B3** 54 56N 8 11W
Derwent →, *Cumb., U.K.* **10 C4** 54 39N 3 33W
Derwent →, *Derby, U.K.* **10 E6** 52 57N 1 28W
Derwent →, *N. Yorks., U.K.* **10 D7** 53 45N 0 58W
Derwent Water, *U.K.* **10 C4** 54 35N 3 9W
Des Moines, *Iowa, U.S.A.* **80 E8** 41 35N 93 37W
Des Moines, *N. Mex., U.S.A.* **81 G3** 36 46N 103 50W
Des Moines →, *U.S.A.* **80 E9** 40 23N 91 25W
Desaguadero →, *Argentina* **94 C2** 34 30S 66 46W
Desaguadero →, *Bolivia* **92 G5** 16 35S 69 5W
Descanso, Pta., *Mexico* **85 N9** 32 21N 117 3W
Deschaillons, *Canada* **71 C5** 46 32N 72 7W
Deschambault L., *Canada* **73 C8** 54 50N 103 30W
Deschutes →, *U.S.A.* **82 D3** 45 38N 120 55W
Dese, *Ethiopia* **46 E2** 11 5N 39 40 E
Deseado →, *Argentina* **96 F3** 47 45S 65 54W
Desert Center, *U.S.A.* **85 M11** 33 43N 115 24W
Desert Hot Springs, *U.S.A.* **85 M10** 33 58N 116 30W
Deshnok, *India* **42 F5** 27 48N 73 21 E
Desna →, *Ukraine* **17 C16** 50 33N 30 32 E
Desolación, I., *Chile* **96 G2** 53 0S 74 0W
Despeñaperros, Paso, *Spain* **19 C4** 38 24N 3 30W
Dessau, *Germany* **16 C7** 51 51N 12 14 E
Dessye = Dese, *Ethiopia* **46 E2** 11 5N 39 40 E
Desuri, *India* **42 G5** 25 18N 73 35 E
Det Udom, *Thailand* **38 E5** 14 54N 105 5 E
Dete, *Zimbabwe* **56 B4** 18 38S 26 50 E
Detmold, *Germany* **16 C5** 51 56N 8 52 E
Detour, Pt., *U.S.A.* **76 C2** 45 40N 86 40W

Edenton

Downpatrick Hd., Ireland .. 13 B2 54 20N 9 21W
Downsville, U.S.A. 79 D10 42 5N 74 50W
Downton, Mt., Canada 72 C4 52 42N 124 52W
Dowsārī, Iran .... 45 D8 28 25N 57 59 E
Doyle, U.S.A. 84 E6 40 2N 120 6W
Doylestown, U.S.A. 79 F9 40 21N 75 10W
Dozois, Rés., Canada 70 C4 47 30N 77 5W
Dra Khel, Pakistan .... 42 F2 27 58N 66 45 E
Drachten, Neths. .... 15 A6 53 7N 6 5 E
Drăgăşani, Romania ...... 17 F13 44 39N 24 17 E
Dragichyn, Belarus .... 17 B13 52 15N 25 8 E
Dragoman, Prokhod,
Bulgaria .... 21 C10 42 58N 22 53 E
Draguignan, France ...... 18 E7 43 32N 6 27 E
Drain, U.S.A. 82 E2 43 40N 123 19W
Drake, U.S.A. 80 B4 47 55N 100 23W
Drake Passage, S. Ocean .. 5 B17 58 0S 68 0W
Drakensberg, S. Africa .... 57 D4 31 0S 28 0 E
Dráma, Greece .... 21 D11 41 9N 24 10 E
Drammen, Norway .... 9 G14 59 42N 10 12 E
Drangajökull, Iceland 8 C2 66 9N 22 15W
Dras, India .... 43 B6 34 25N 75 48 E
Drau = Drava →, Croatia . 21 B8 45 33N 18 55 E
Drava →, Croatia .... 21 B8 45 33N 18 55 E
Drayton Valley, Canada ... 72 C6 53 12N 114 58W
Drenthe □, Neths. .... 15 B6 52 52N 6 40 E
Drepanum, C., Cyprus .... 23 E11 34 54N 32 19 E
Dresden, Canada 78 D2 42 35N 82 11W
Dresden, Germany .... 16 C7 51 3N 13 44 E
Dreux, France .... 18 B4 48 44N 1 23 E
Driffield, U.K. 10 C7 54 0N 0 26W
Driftwood, U.S.A. 78 E6 41 20N 78 8W
Driggs, U.S.A. 82 E8 43 44N 111 6W
Drin →, Albania .... 21 C8 42 1N 19 38 E
Drina →, Bos.-H. .... 21 B8 44 53N 19 21 E
Drøbak, Norway .... 9 G14 59 39N 10 39 E
Drobeta-Turnu Severin,
Romania .... 17 F12 44 39N 22 41 E
Drochia, Moldova .... 17 D14 48 2N 27 48 E
Drogheda, Ireland 13 C5 53 43N 6 22W
Drogichin = Dragichyn,
Belarus .... 17 B13 52 15N 25 8 E
Drogobych = Drohobych,
Ukraine .... 17 D12 49 20N 23 30 E
Drohobych, Ukraine ...... 17 D12 49 20N 23 30 E
Droichead Atha =
Drogheda, Ireland 13 C5 53 43N 6 22W
Droichead Nua, Ireland ... 13 C5 53 11N 6 48W
Droitwich, U.K. 11 E5 52 16N 2 8W
Dromore, U.K. 13 B4 54 31N 7 28W
Dromore West, Ireland 13 B3 54 15N 8 52W
Dronfield, U.K. 10 D6 53 19N 1 27W
Dronten, Neths. .... 15 B5 52 32N 5 43 E
Drumbo, Canada 78 C4 43 16N 80 35W
Drumheller, Canada 72 C6 51 25N 112 40W
Drummond, U.S.A. 82 C7 46 40N 113 9W
Drummond I., U.S.A. 76 C4 46 1N 83 39W
Drummond Pt., Australia .. 63 E2 34 9S 135 16 E
Drummond Ra., Australia . 62 C4 23 45S 147 10 E
Drummondville, Canada .. 70 C5 45 55N 72 25W
Drumright, U.S.A. 81 H6 35 59N 96 36W
Druskininkai, Lithuania ... 9 J20 54 3N 23 58 E
Drut →, Belarus .... 17 B16 53 8N 30 5 E
Druzhina, Russia .... 27 C15 68 14N 145 18 E
Dry Tortugas, U.S.A. 88 B3 24 38N 82 55W
Dryden, Canada 73 D10 49 47N 92 50W
Dryden, U.S.A. 79 D8 42 30N 76 18W
Drygalski I., Antarctica ... 5 C7 66 0S 92 0 E
Drysdale →, Australia .... 60 B4 13 59S 126 51 E
Drysdale I., Australia .... 62 A2 11 41S 136 0 E
Du Bois, U.S.A. 78 E6 41 8N 78 46W
Du Gué →, Canada 70 A5 57 21N 70 45W
Du Quoin, U.S.A. 80 G10 38 1N 89 14W
Duanesburg, U.S.A. 79 D10 42 45N 74 11W
Duaringa, Australia ...... 62 C4 23 42S 149 42 E
Ḍubā, Si. Arabia .... 44 E2 27 10N 35 40 E
Dubai = Dubayy, U.A.E. ... 46 B6 25 18N 55 20 E
Dubăsari, Moldova .... 17 E15 47 15N 29 10 E
Dubăsari Vdkhr., Moldova . 17 E15 47 30N 29 0 E
Dubawnt →, Canada 73 A8 64 33N 100 6W
Dubawnt, L., Canada 73 A8 63 4N 101 42W
Dubayy, U.A.E. .... 46 B6 25 18N 55 20 E
Dubele, Dem. Rep. of
the Congo .... 54 B2 2 56N 29 35 E
Dublin, Ireland 13 C5 53 21N 6 15W
Dublin, Ga., U.S.A. 77 J4 32 32N 82 54W
Dublin, Tex., U.S.A. 81 J5 32 5N 98 21W
Dublin □, Ireland 13 C5 53 24N 6 20W
Dubno, Ukraine .... 17 C13 50 25N 25 45 E
Dubois, U.S.A. 82 D7 44 10N 112 14W
Dubossary = Dubăsari,
Moldova .... 17 E15 47 15N 29 10 E
Dubossary Vdkhr. =
Dubăsari Vdkhr.,
Moldova .... 17 E15 47 30N 29 0 E
Dubovka, Russia .... 25 E7 49 5N 44 50 E
Dubrajpur, India .... 43 H12 23 48N 87 25 E
Dubréka, Guinea 50 G3 9 46N 13 31W
Dubrovitsa = Dubrovytsya,
Ukraine .... 17 C14 51 31N 26 35 E
Dubrovnik, Croatia .... 21 C8 42 39N 18 6 E
Dubrovytsya, Ukraine .... 17 C14 51 31N 26 35 E
Dubuque, U.S.A. 80 D9 42 30N 90 41W
Duchesne, U.S.A. 82 F8 40 10N 110 24W
Duchess, Australia .... 62 C2 21 20S 139 50 E
Ducie I., Pac. Oc. 65 K15 24 40S 124 48W
Duck →, U.S.A. 77 G2 36 2N 87 52W
Duck Cr. →, Australia .... 60 D2 22 37S 116 53 E
Duck Lake, Canada 73 C7 52 50N 106 16W
Duck Mountain Prov. Park,
Canada 73 C8 51 45N 101 0W
Duckwall, Mt., U.S.A. 84 H6 37 58N 120 7W
Dudhi, India .... 41 G13 24 15N 83 10 E
Dudinka, Russia .... 27 C9 69 30N 86 13 E
Dudley, U.K. 11 E5 52 31N 2 5W
Dudwa, India .... 43 E9 28 30N 80 41 E
Duero = Douro →, Europe 19 B1 41 8N 8 40W
Dufftown, U.K. 12 D5 57 27N 3 8W
Dūghī Kalā, Afghan. ...... 40 C3 32 20N 62 50 E
Dugi Otok, Croatia .... 16 G8 44 0N 15 3 E
Duifken Pt., Australia .... 62 A3 12 33S 141 38 E
Duisburg, Germany ...... 16 C4 51 26N 6 45 E
Duiwelskloof, S. Africa ... 57 C5 23 42S 30 10 E
Dūkdamīn, Iran .... 45 C8 35 59N 57 43 E
Dukelský Průsmyk,
Slovak Rep. .... 17 D11 49 25N 21 42 E
Dukhān, Qatar .... 45 E6 25 25N 50 50 E
Duki, Pakistan .... 40 D6 30 14N 68 25 E
Duku, Nigeria .... 51 F8 10 43N 10 43 E
Dulce, U.S.A. 83 H10 36 56N 107 0W
Dulce →, Argentina 94 C3 30 32S 62 33W
Dulce, G., Costa Rica 88 E3 8 40N 83 20W
Dulf, Iraq .... 44 C5 35 7N 45 51 E
Dulit, Banjaran, Malaysia . 36 D4 3 15N 114 30 E
Duliu, China .... 34 E9 39 2N 116 55 E
Dullewala, Pakistan ...... 42 D4 31 50N 71 25 E
Dullstroom, S. Africa ..... 57 D5 25 27S 30 7 E
Dulq Maghār, Syria ...... 44 B3 36 22N 38 39 E
Duluth, U.S.A. 80 B8 46 47N 92 6W
Dum Dum, India .... 43 H13 22 39N 88 33 E
Dum Duma, India .... 41 F19 27 40N 95 40 E
Dūmā, Syria .... 47 B5 33 34N 36 24 E
Dumaguete, Phil. .... 37 C6 9 17N 123 15 E
Dumai, Indonesia .... 36 D2 1 35N 101 28 E
Dumaran, Phil. .... 37 B5 10 33N 119 50 E
Dumas, Ark., U.S.A. 81 J9 33 53N 91 29W
Dumas, Tex., U.S.A. 81 H4 35 52N 101 58W
Ḍumayr, Syria .... 47 B5 33 39N 36 42 E
Dumbarton, U.K. 12 F4 55 57N 4 33W
Dumbleyung, Australia ... 61 F2 33 17S 117 42 E
Dumfries, U.K. 12 F5 55 4N 3 37W
Dumfries & Galloway □,
U.K. 12 F5 55 9N 3 58W
Dumka, India .... 43 G12 24 12N 87 15 E
Dumoine →, Canada 70 C4 46 13N 77 51W
Dumoine, L., Canada 70 C4 46 55N 77 55W
Dumraon, India .... 43 G11 25 33N 84 8 E
Dumyât, Egypt .... 51 B12 31 24N 31 48 E
Dún Dealgan = Dundalk,
Ireland 13 B5 54 1N 6 24W
Dun Laoghaire, Ireland ... 13 C5 53 17N 6 8W
Duna = Dunărea →, Europe 17 F15 45 20N 29 40 E
Dunagiri, India .... 43 D8 30 31N 79 52 E
Dunaj = Dunărea →,
Europe .... 17 F15 45 20N 29 40 E
Dunakeszi, Hungary ...... 17 E10 47 37N 19 8 E
Dunărea →, Europe ...... 17 F15 45 20N 29 40 E
Dunaújváros, Hungary .... 17 E10 46 58N 18 57 E
Dunav = Dunărea →,
Europe .... 17 F15 45 20N 29 40 E
Dunay, Russia .... 30 C6 42 52N 132 22 E
Dunback, N.Z. .... 59 L3 45 23S 170 36 E
Dunbar, U.K. 12 E6 56 0N 2 31W
Dunblane, U.K. 12 E5 56 11N 3 58W
Duncan, Canada 72 D4 48 45N 123 40W
Duncan, Ariz., U.S.A. 83 K9 32 43N 109 6W
Duncan, Okla., U.S.A. 81 H6 34 30N 97 57W
Duncan, L., Canada 70 B4 53 29N 77 58W
Duncan L., Canada 72 A6 62 51N 113 58W
Duncan Town, Bahamas .. 88 B4 22 15N 75 45W
Duncannon, U.S.A. 78 F7 40 23N 77 2W
Duncansby Head, U.K. 12 C5 58 38N 3 1W
Duncansville, U.S.A. 78 F6 40 25N 78 26W
Dundalk, Canada 78 B4 44 10N 80 24W
Dundalk, Ireland 13 B5 54 1N 6 24W
Dundalk, U.S.A. 76 F7 39 16N 76 32W
Dundalk Bay, Ireland 13 C5 53 55N 6 15W
Dundas, Canada 78 C5 43 17N 79 59W
Dundas, L., Australia ..... 61 F3 32 35S 121 50 E
Dundas I., Canada 72 C2 54 30N 130 50W
Dundas Str., Australia .... 60 B5 11 15S 131 35 E
Dundee, S. Africa .... 57 D5 28 11S 30 15 E
Dundee, U.K. 12 E6 56 28N 2 59W
Dundee, U.S.A. 78 D8 42 32N 76 59W
Dundee City □, U.K. 12 E6 56 30N 2 58W
Dundgovĭ □, Mongolia .... 34 B4 45 10N 106 0 E
Dundrum, U.K. 13 B6 54 16N 5 52W
Dundrum B., U.K. 13 B6 54 13N 5 47W
Dunedin, N.Z. .... 59 L3 45 50S 170 33 E
Dunedin, U.S.A. 77 L4 28 1N 82 47W
Dunfermline, U.K. 12 E5 56 5N 3 27W
Dungannon, Canada 78 C3 43 51N 81 36W
Dungannon, U.K. 13 B5 54 31N 6 46W
Dungarpur, India .... 42 H5 23 52N 73 45 E
Dungarvan, Ireland 13 D4 52 5N 7 37W
Dungarvan Harbour, Ireland 13 D4 52 4N 7 35W
Dungeness, U.K. .... 11 G8 50 54N 0 59 E
Dungo, L. do, Angola ..... 56 B2 17 15S 19 0 E
Dungu, Dem. Rep. of
the Congo .... 54 B2 3 40N 28 32 E
Dungun, Malaysia .... 39 K4 4 45N 103 25 E
Dunhua, China .... 35 C15 43 20N 128 14 E
Dunhuang, China .... 32 B4 40 8N 94 36 E
Dunk I., Australia .... 62 B4 17 59S 146 29 E
Dunkeld, Australia .... 63 E4 33 25S 149 29 E
Dunkeld, U.K. 12 E5 56 34N 3 35W
Dunkerque, France ...... 18 A5 51 2N 2 20 E
Dunkery Beacon, U.K. 11 F4 51 9N 3 36W
Dunkirk = Dunkerque,
France .... 18 A5 51 2N 2 20 E
Dunkirk, U.S.A. 78 D5 42 29N 79 20W
Dúnleary = Dun Laoghaire,
Ireland 13 C5 53 17N 6 8W
Dunleer, Ireland 13 C5 53 50N 6 24W
Dunmanus B., Ireland 13 E2 51 31N 9 50W
Dunmanway, Ireland 13 E2 51 43N 9 6W
Dunmara, Australia ...... 62 B1 16 42S 133 25 E
Dunmore, U.S.A. 79 E9 41 25N 75 38W
Dunmore Hd., Ireland 13 D1 52 10N 10 35W
Dunmore Town, Bahamas . 88 A4 25 30N 76 39W
Dunn, U.S.A. 77 H6 35 19N 78 37W
Dunnellon, U.S.A. 77 L4 29 3N 82 28W
Dunnet Hd., U.K. 12 C5 58 40N 3 21W
Dunning, U.S.A. 80 E4 41 50N 100 6W
Dunnville, Canada 78 D5 42 54N 79 36W
Dunoon, U.K. 12 F4 55 57N 4 56W
Dunphy, U.S.A. 82 F5 40 42N 116 31W
Duns, U.K. 12 F6 55 47N 2 20W
Dunseith, U.S.A. 80 A4 48 50N 100 3W
Dunsmuir, U.S.A. 82 F2 41 13N 122 16W
Dunstable, U.K. 11 F7 51 53N 0 32W
Dunstan Mts., N.Z. ...... 59 L2 44 53S 169 35 E
Dunster, Canada 72 C5 53 8N 119 50W
Dunvegan L., Canada 73 A7 60 8N 107 10W
Duolun, China .... 34 C9 42 12N 116 28 E
Duong Dong, Vietnam .... 39 G4 10 13N 103 58 E
Dupree, U.S.A. 80 C4 45 4N 101 35W
Dupuyer, U.S.A. 82 B7 48 13N 112 30W
Duque de Caxias, Brazil ... 95 A7 22 45S 43 19W
Durack →, Australia ..... 60 C4 15 33S 127 52 E
Durack Ra., Australia ..... 60 C4 16 50S 127 40 E
Durance →, France ...... 18 E6 43 55N 4 45 E
Durand, U.S.A. 80 C9 44 38N 91 58W
Durango, Mexico 86 C4 24 3N 104 39W
Durango, U.S.A. 83 H10 37 16N 107 53W
Durango □, Mexico 86 C4 25 0N 105 0W
Durant, Miss., U.S.A. 81 J10 33 4N 89 51W
Durant, Okla., U.S.A. 81 J6 33 59N 96 25W
Durazno, Uruguay 94 C4 33 25S 56 31W
Durazzo = Durrës, Albania 21 D8 41 19N 19 28 E
Durban, S. Africa .... 57 D5 29 49S 31 1 E
Durbuy, Belgium .... 15 D5 50 21N 5 28 E
Düren, Germany .... 16 C4 50 48N 6 29 E
Durg, India .... 41 J12 21 15N 81 22 E
Durgapur, India .... 43 H12 23 30N 87 20 E
Durham, Canada 78 B4 44 10N 80 49W
Durham, U.K. 10 C6 54 47N 1 34W
Durham, Calif., U.S.A. 84 F5 39 39N 121 48W
Durham, N.C., U.S.A. 77 H6 35 59N 78 54W
Durham, N.H., U.S.A. 79 C14 43 8N 70 56W
Durham □, U.K. 10 C6 54 42N 1 45W
Ḍurmā, Si. Arabia .... 44 E5 24 37N 46 8 E
Durmitor,
Montenegro, Yug. ...... 21 C8 43 10N 19 0 E
Durness, U.K. 12 C4 58 34N 4 45W
Durrës, Albania .... 21 D8 41 19N 19 28 E
Durrow, Ireland 13 D4 52 51N 7 24W
Dursey I., Ireland 13 E1 51 36N 10 12W
Dursunbey, Turkey ...... 21 E13 39 35N 28 37 E
Duru, Dem. Rep. of
the Congo .... 54 B2 4 14N 28 50 E
Durūz, Jabal ad, Jordan ... 47 C5 32 35N 36 40 E
D'Urville, Tanjung,
Indonesia .... 37 E9 1 28S 137 54 E
D'Urville I., N.Z. .... 59 J4 40 50S 173 55 E
Duryea, U.S.A. 79 E9 41 20N 75 45W
Dushak, Turkmenistan .... 26 F7 37 13N 60 1 E
Dushanbe, Tajikistan ..... 26 F7 38 33N 68 48 E
Dushore, U.S.A. 79 E8 41 31N 76 24W
Dusky Sd., N.Z. .... 59 L1 45 47S 166 30 E
Dussejour, C., Australia ... 60 B4 14 45S 128 13 E
Düsseldorf, Germany ..... 16 C4 51 14N 6 47 E
Dutch Harbor, U.S.A. 68 C3 53 53N 166 32W
Dutlwe, Botswana .... 56 C3 23 58S 23 46 E
Dutton, Canada 78 D3 42 39N 81 30W
Dutton →, Australia ..... 62 C3 20 44S 143 10 E
Duwayhin, Khawr, U.A.E. . 45 E6 24 20N 51 25 E
Duyun, China .... 32 D5 26 18N 107 29 E
Duzdab = Zāhedān, Iran ... 45 D9 29 30N 60 50 E
Dvina, Severnaya →,
Russia .... 24 B7 64 32N 40 30 E
Dvinsk = Daugavpils, Latvia 9 J22 55 53N 26 32 E
Dvinskaya Guba, Russia .. 24 B6 65 0N 39 0 E
Dwarka, India .... 42 H3 22 18N 69 8 E
Dwellingup, Australia .... 61 F2 32 43S 116 4 E
Dwight, Canada 78 A5 45 20N 79 1W
Dwight, U.S.A. 76 E1 41 5N 88 26W
Dyatlovo = Dzyatlava,
Belarus .... 17 B13 53 28N 25 28 E
Dyce, U.K. 12 D6 57 13N 2 12W
Dyer, C., Canada 69 B13 66 40N 61 0W
Dyer Bay, Canada 78 A3 45 10N 81 20W
Dyer Plateau, Antarctica .. 5 D17 70 45S 65 30W
Dyersburg, U.S.A. 81 G10 36 3N 89 23W
Dyfi →, U.K. 11 E3 52 32N 4 3W
Dymer, Ukraine .... 17 C16 50 47N 30 18 E
Dysart, Australia .... 62 C4 22 32S 148 23 E
Dzamin Üüd = Borhoyn Tal,
Mongolia .... 34 C6 43 50N 111 58 E
Dzerzhinsk, Russia ...... 24 C7 56 14N 43 30 E
Dzhalinda, Russia .... 27 D13 53 26N 124 0 E
Dzhambul = Taraz,
Kazakstan .... 26 E8 42 54N 71 22 E
Dzhankoy, Ukraine ...... 25 E5 45 40N 34 20 E
Dzhezkazgan =
Zhezqazghan, Kazakstan 26 E7 47 44N 67 40 E
Dzhizak = Jizzakh,
Uzbekistan .... 26 E7 40 6N 67 50 E
Dzhugdzur, Khrebet, Russia 27 D14 57 30N 138 0 E
Dzhungarskiye Vorota =
Dzungarian Gates, Asia . 32 B3 45 0N 82 0 E
Działdowo, Poland .... 17 B11 53 15N 20 15 E
Dzibilchaltun, Mexico 87 C7 21 5N 89 36W
Dzierżoniów, Poland ..... 17 C9 50 45N 16 39 E
Dzilam de Bravo, Mexico .. 87 C7 21 24N 88 53W
Dzungaria = Junggar Pendi,
China .... 32 B3 44 30N 86 0 E
Dzungarian Gates, Asia ... 32 B3 45 0N 82 0 E
Dzuumod, Mongolia ...... 32 B5 47 45N 106 58 E
Dzyarzhynsk, Belarus ..... 17 B14 53 40N 27 1 E
Dzyatlava, Belarus .... 17 B13 53 28N 25 28 E

E

Eabamet L., Canada 70 B2 51 30N 87 46W
Eads, U.S.A. 80 F3 38 29N 102 47W
Eagar, U.S.A. 83 J9 34 6N 109 17W
Eagle, Alaska, U.S.A. 68 B5 64 47N 141 12W
Eagle, Colo., U.S.A. 82 G10 39 39N 106 50W
Eagle →, Canada 71 B8 53 36N 57 26W
Eagle Butte, U.S.A. 80 C4 45 0N 101 10W
Eagle Grove, U.S.A. 80 D8 42 40N 93 54W
Eagle L., Canada 73 D10 49 42N 93 13W
Eagle L., Calif., U.S.A. ... 82 F3 40 39N 120 45W
Eagle L., Maine, U.S.A. ... 77 B11 46 20N 69 22W
Eagle Lake, Canada 78 A6 45 8N 78 29W
Eagle Lake, Maine, U.S.A. . 77 B11 47 3N 68 36W
Eagle Lake, Tex., U.S.A. .. 81 L6 29 35N 96 20W
Eagle Mountain, U.S.A. ... 85 M11 33 49N 115 27W
Eagle Nest, U.S.A. 83 H11 36 33N 105 16W
Eagle Pass, U.S.A. 81 L4 28 43N 100 30W
Eagle Pk., U.S.A. 84 G7 38 10N 119 25W
Eagle Pt., Australia ...... 60 C3 16 11S 124 23 E
Eagle River, Mich., U.S.A. . 76 B1 47 24N 88 18W
Eagle River, Wis., U.S.A. .. 80 C10 45 55N 89 15W
Eaglehawk, Australia ..... 63 F3 36 44S 144 15 E
Eagles Mere, U.S.A. 79 E8 41 25N 76 33W
Ealing □, U.K. 11 F7 51 31N 0 20W
Ear Falls, Canada 73 C10 50 38N 93 13W
Earle, U.S.A. 81 H9 35 16N 90 28W
Earlimart, U.S.A. 85 K7 35 53N 119 16W
Earn →, U.K. 12 E5 56 21N 3 18W
Earn, L., U.K. 12 E4 56 23N 4 13W
Earnslaw, Mt., N.Z. ...... 59 L2 44 32S 168 27 E
Earth, U.S.A. 81 H3 34 14N 102 24W
Easley, U.S.A. 77 H4 34 50N 82 36W
East Anglia, U.K. .... 10 E9 52 30N 1 0 E
East Angus, Canada 71 C5 45 30N 71 40W
East Aurora, U.S.A. 78 D6 42 46N 78 37W
East Ayrshire □, U.K. 12 F4 55 26N 4 11W
East Bengal, Bangla. ..... 41 H17 24 0N 90 0 E
East Beskids = Vychodné
Beskydy, Europe .... 17 D11 49 20N 22 0 E
East Brady, U.S.A. 78 F5 40 59N 79 36W
East C., N.Z. .... 59 G7 37 42S 178 35 E
East Chicago, U.S.A. 76 E2 41 38N 87 27W
East China Sea, Asia ..... 33 D7 30 0N 126 0 E
East Coulee, Canada 72 C6 51 23N 112 27W
East Dereham, U.K. ...... 11 E8 52 41N 0 57 E
East Dunbartonshire □,
U.K. 12 F4 55 57N 4 13W
East Falkland, Falk. Is. 96 G5 51 30S 58 30W
East Grand Forks, U.S.A. .. 80 B6 47 56N 97 1W
East Greenwich, U.S.A. ... 79 E13 41 40N 71 27W
East Grinstead, U.K. 11 F8 51 7N 0 0W
East Hartford, U.S.A. 79 E12 41 46N 72 39W
East Helena, U.S.A. 82 C8 46 35N 111 56W
East Indies, Asia .... 28 K15 0 0 120 0 E
East Kilbride, U.K. 12 F4 55 47N 4 11W
East Lansing, U.S.A. 76 D3 42 44N 84 29W
East Liverpool, U.S.A. 78 F4 40 37N 80 35W
East London, S. Africa .... 57 E4 33 0S 27 55 E
East Lothian □, U.K. 12 F6 55 58N 2 44W
East Main = Eastmain,
Canada 70 B4 52 10N 78 30W
East Northport, U.S.A. 79 F11 40 53N 73 20W
East Orange, U.S.A. 79 F10 40 46N 74 13W
East Pacific Ridge, Pac. Oc. 65 J17 15 0S 110 0W
East Palestine, U.S.A. 78 F4 40 50N 80 33W
East Pine, Canada 72 B4 55 48N 120 12W
East Point, U.S.A. 77 J3 33 41N 84 27W
East Providence, U.S.A. .. 79 E13 41 49N 71 23W
East Pt., Canada 71 C7 46 27N 61 58W
East Renfrewshire □, U.K. . 12 F4 55 46N 4 21W
East Retford = Retford, U.K. 10 D7 53 19N 0 56W
East Riding of Yorkshire □,
U.K. 10 D7 53 55N 0 30W
East Rochester, U.S.A. ... 78 C7 43 7N 77 29W
East St. Louis, U.S.A. 80 F9 38 37N 90 9W
East Schelde =
Oosterschelde →, Neths. 15 C4 51 33N 4 0 E
East Sea = Japan, Sea of,
Asia .... 30 E7 40 0N 135 0 E
East Siberian Sea, Russia . 27 B17 73 0N 160 0 E
East Stroudsburg, U.S.A. . 79 E9 41 1N 75 11W
East Sussex □, U.K. ..... 11 G8 50 56N 0 19 E
East Tawas, U.S.A. 76 C4 44 17N 83 29W
East Timor ■, Asia ...... 37 F7 8 50S 126 0 E
East Toorale, Australia ... 63 E4 30 27S 145 28 E
East Walker →, U.S.A. ... 84 G7 38 52N 119 10W
East Windsor, U.S.A. 79 F10 40 17N 74 34W
Eastbourne, N.Z. .... 59 J5 41 19S 174 55 E
Eastbourne, U.K. .... 11 G8 50 46N 0 18 E
Eastend, Canada 73 D7 49 32N 108 50W
Easter I. = Pascua, I. de,
Pac. Oc. 65 K17 27 0S 109 0W
Eastern □, Kenya .... 54 C4 0 0 38 30 E
Eastern Cape □, S. Africa . 56 E4 32 0S 26 0 E
Eastern Cr. →, Australia .. 62 C3 20 40S 141 35 E
Eastern Ghats, India ..... 40 N11 14 0N 78 50 E
Eastern Group = Lau
Group, Fiji 59 C9 17 0S 178 30W
Eastern Group, Australia .. 61 F3 33 30S 124 30 E
Eastern Transvaal =
Mpumalanga □, S. Africa 57 B5 26 0S 30 0 E
Easterville, Canada 73 C9 53 8N 99 49W
Easthampton, U.S.A. 79 D12 42 16N 72 40W
Eastlake, U.S.A. 78 E3 41 40N 81 26W
Eastland, U.S.A. 81 J5 32 24N 98 49W
Eastleigh, U.K. 11 G6 50 58N 1 21W
Eastmain, Canada 70 B4 52 10N 78 30W
Eastmain →, Canada 70 B4 52 27N 78 26W
Eastman, Canada 79 A12 45 18N 72 19W
Eastman, U.S.A. 77 J4 32 12N 83 11W
Easton, Md., U.S.A. 76 F7 38 47N 76 5W
Easton, Pa., U.S.A. 79 F9 40 41N 75 13W
Easton, Wash., U.S.A. 84 C5 47 14N 121 11W
Eastpointe, U.S.A. 78 D2 42 27N 82 56W
Eastport, U.S.A. 77 C12 44 56N 67 0W
Eastsound, U.S.A. 84 B4 48 42N 122 55W
Eaton, U.S.A. 80 E2 40 32N 104 42W
Eatonia, Canada 73 C7 51 13N 109 25W
Eatonton, U.S.A. 77 J4 33 20N 83 23W
Eatontown, U.S.A. 79 F10 40 19N 74 4W
Eatonville, U.S.A. 84 D4 46 52N 122 16W
Eau Claire, U.S.A. 80 C9 44 49N 91 30W
Eau Claire, L. à l', Canada . 70 A5 56 10N 74 25W
Ebbw Vale, U.K. 11 F4 51 46N 3 12W
Ebeltoft, Denmark .... 9 H14 56 12N 10 41 E
Ebensburg, U.S.A. 78 F6 40 29N 78 44W
Eberswalde-Finow,
Germany .... 16 B7 52 50N 13 49 E
Ebetsu, Japan .... 30 C10 43 7N 141 34 E
Ebolowa, Cameroon ...... 52 D2 2 55N 11 10 E
Ebro →, Spain .... 19 B6 40 43N 0 54 E
Eceabat, Turkey .... 21 D12 40 11N 26 21 E
Ech Cheliff, Algeria ...... 50 A6 36 10N 1 20 E
Echigo-Sammyaku, Japan 31 F9 36 50N 139 50 E
Echizen-Misaki, Japan ... 31 G7 35 59N 135 57 E
Echo Bay, N.W.T., Canada 68 B8 66 5N 117 55W
Echo Bay, Ont., Canada .. 70 C3 46 29N 84 4W
Echoing →, Canada 70 B1 55 51N 92 5W
Echternach, Lux. .... 15 E6 49 49N 6 25 E
Ecija, Spain 19 D3 37 30N 5 10W
Eclipse Is., Australia ..... 60 B4 13 54S 126 19 E
Eclipse Sd., Canada 69 A11 72 38N 79 0W
Ecuador ■, S. Amer. 92 D3 2 0S 78 0W
Ed Damazin, Sudan ...... 51 F12 11 46N 34 21 E
Ed Debba, Sudan .... 51 E12 18 0N 30 51 E
Ed Dueim, Sudan .... 51 F12 14 0N 32 10 E
Edam, Canada 73 C7 53 11N 108 46W
Edam, Neths. .... 15 B5 52 31N 5 3 E
Eday, U.K. 12 B6 59 11N 2 47W
Eddrachillis B., U.K. 12 C3 58 17N 5 14W
Eddystone Pt., Australia .. 62 G4 40 59S 148 20 E
Ede, Neths. .... 15 B5 52 4N 5 40 E
Edehon L., Canada 73 A9 60 25N 97 15W
Eden, N.C., U.S.A. 77 G6 36 29N 79 53W
Eden, N.Y., U.S.A. 78 D6 42 39N 78 55W
Eden, Tex., U.S.A. 81 K5 31 13N 99 51W
Eden →, U.K. 10 C4 54 57N 3 1W
Edenburg, S. Africa ...... 56 D4 29 43S 25 58 E
Edendale, S. Africa ...... 57 D5 29 39S 30 18 E
Edenderry, Ireland 13 C4 53 21N 7 4W
Edenton, U.S.A. 77 G7 36 4N 76 39W

Edenville

Edenville, S. Africa 57 D4 27 37S 27 34 E
Eder →, Germany 16 C5 51 12N 9 28 E
Edgar, U.S.A. 80 E6 40 22N 97 58W
Edgartown, U.S.A. 79 E14 41 23N 70 31W
Edge Hill, U.K. 11 E6 52 8N 1 26W
Edgefield, U.S.A. 77 J5 33 47N 81 56W
Edgeley, U.S.A. 80 B5 46 22N 98 43W
Edgemont, U.S.A. 80 D3 43 18N 103 50W
Edgeøya, Svalbard 4 B9 77 45N 22 30 E
Édhessa, Greece 21 D10 40 48N 22 5 E
Edievale, N.Z. 59 L2 45 49S 169 22 E
Edina, U.S.A. 80 E8 40 10N 92 11W
Edinboro, U.S.A. 78 E4 41 52N 80 8W
Edinburg, U.S.A. 81 M5 26 18N 98 10W
Edinburgh, U.K. 12 F5 55 57N 3 13W
Edinburgh, City of □, U.K. 12 F5 55 57N 3 17W
Edineţ, Moldova 17 D14 48 9N 27 18 E
Edirne, Turkey 21 D12 41 40N 26 34 E
Edison, U.S.A. 84 B4 48 33N 122 27W
Edmeston, U.S.A. 79 D9 42 42N 75 15W
Edmond, U.S.A. 81 H6 35 39N 97 29W
Edmonds, U.S.A. 84 C4 47 49N 122 23W
Edmonton, Australia 62 B4 17 2S 145 46 E
Edmonton, Canada 72 C6 53 30N 113 30W
Edmund L., Canada 70 B1 54 45N 93 17W
Edmundston, Canada 71 C6 47 23N 68 20W
Edna, U.S.A. 81 L6 28 59N 96 39W
Edremit, Turkey 21 E12 39 34N 27 0 E
Edremit Körfezi, Turkey 21 E12 39 30N 26 45 E
Edson, Canada 72 C5 53 35N 116 28W
Eduardo Castex, Argentina 94 D3 35 50S 64 18W
Edward, L., Africa 54 C2 0 25S 29 40 E
Edward River, Australia 62 A3 14 59S 141 26 E
Edward VII Land, Antarctica 5 E13 80 0S 150 0W
Edwards, Calif., U.S.A. 85 L9 34 55N 117 51W
Edwards, N.Y., U.S.A. 79 B9 44 20N 75 15W
Edwards Air Force Base, U.S.A. 85 L9 34 50N 117 40W
Edwards Plateau, U.S.A. 81 K4 30 45N 101 20W
Edwardsville, U.S.A. 79 E9 41 15N 75 56W
Edzo, Canada 72 A5 62 49N 116 4W
Eeklo, Belgium 15 C3 51 11N 3 33 E
Effingham, U.S.A. 76 F1 39 7N 88 33W
Égadi, Ísole, Italy 20 F5 37 55N 12 16 E
Egan Range, U.S.A. 82 G6 39 35N 114 55W
Eganville, Canada 78 A7 45 32N 77 5W
Eger = Cheb, Czech Rep. 16 C7 50 9N 12 28 E
Eger, Hungary 17 E11 47 53N 20 27 E
Egersund, Norway 9 G12 58 26N 6 1 E
Egg L., Canada 73 B7 55 5N 105 30W
Éghezée, Belgium 15 D4 50 35N 4 55 E
Egmont, Canada 72 D4 49 45N 123 56W
Egmont, C., N.Z. 59 H4 39 16S 173 45 E
Egmont, Mt. = Taranaki, Mt., N.Z. 59 H5 39 17S 174 5 E
Egra, India 43 J12 21 54N 87 32 E
Eğridir, Turkey 25 G5 37 52N 30 51 E
Eğridir Gölü, Turkey 25 G5 37 53N 30 50 E
Egvekinot, Russia 27 C19 66 19N 179 50W
Egypt ■, Africa 51 C12 28 0N 31 0 E
Ehime □, Japan 31 H6 33 30N 132 40 E
Ehrenberg, U.S.A. 85 M12 33 36N 114 31W
Eibar, Spain 19 A4 43 11N 2 28W
Eidsvold, Australia 63 D5 25 25S 151 12 E
Eidsvoll, Norway 9 F14 60 19N 11 14 E
Eifel, Germany 16 C4 50 15N 6 50 E
Eiffel Flats, Zimbabwe 55 F3 18 20S 30 0 E
Eigg, U.K. 12 E2 56 54N 6 10W
Eighty Mile Beach, Australia 60 C3 19 30S 120 40 E
Eil, Somali Rep. 46 F4 8 0N 49 50 E
Eil, L., U.K. 12 E3 56 51N 5 16W
Einasleigh, Australia 62 B3 18 32S 144 5 E
Einasleigh →, Australia 62 B3 17 30S 142 17 E
Eindhoven, Neths. 15 C5 51 26N 5 28 E
Eire = Ireland ■, Europe 13 C4 53 50N 7 52W
Eiríksjökull, Iceland 8 D3 64 46N 20 24W
Eirunepé, Brazil 92 E5 6 35S 69 53W
Eiseb →, Namibia 56 C2 20 33S 20 59 E
Eisenach, Germany 16 C6 50 58N 10 19 E
Eisenerz, Austria 16 E8 47 32N 14 54 E
Eivissa, Spain 22 C7 38 54N 1 26 E
Ejeda, Madag. 57 C7 24 20S 44 31 E
Ejutla, Mexico 87 D5 16 34N 96 44W
Ekalaka, U.S.A. 80 C2 45 53N 104 33W
Eketahuna, N.Z. 59 J5 40 38S 175 43 E
Ekibastuz, Kazakstan 26 D8 51 50N 75 10 E
Ekoli, Dem. Rep. of the Congo 54 C1 0 23S 24 13 E
Eksjö, Sweden 9 H16 57 40N 14 58 E
Ekuma →, Namibia 56 B2 18 40S 16 2 E
Ekwan →, Canada 70 B3 53 12N 82 15W
Ekwan Pt., Canada 70 B3 53 16N 82 7W
El Aaiún, W. Sahara 50 C3 27 9N 13 12W
El Abanico, Chile 94 D1 37 20S 71 31W
El 'Agrûd, Egypt 47 E3 30 14N 34 24 E
El Alamein, Egypt 51 B11 30 48N 28 58 E
El 'Aqaba, W. →, Egypt 47 E2 30 7N 33 54 E
El Arīḥā, West Bank 47 D4 31 52N 35 27 E
El 'Arîsh, Egypt 47 D2 31 8N 33 50 E
El 'Arîsh, W. →, Egypt 47 D2 31 8N 33 47 E
El Asnam = Ech Cheliff, Algeria 50 A6 36 10N 1 20 E
El Bayadh, Algeria 50 B6 33 40N 1 1 E
El Bluff, Nic. 88 D3 11 59N 83 40W
El Brûk, W. →, Egypt 47 E2 30 15N 33 50 E
El Cajon, U.S.A. 85 N10 32 48N 116 58W
El Campo, U.S.A. 81 L6 29 12N 96 16W
El Centro, U.S.A. 85 N11 32 48N 115 34W
El Cerro, Bolivia 92 G6 17 30S 61 40W
El Compadre, Mexico 85 N10 32 20N 116 14W
El Cuy, Argentina 96 D3 39 55S 68 25W
El Cuyo, Mexico 87 C7 21 30N 87 40W
El Daheir, Egypt 47 D3 31 13N 34 10 E
El Dátil, Mexico 86 B2 30 7N 112 15W
El Dere, Somali Rep. 46 G4 3 50N 47 8 E
El Descanso, Mexico 85 N10 32 12N 116 58W
El Desemboque, Mexico 86 A2 30 30N 112 57W
El Diviso, Colombia 92 C3 1 22N 78 14W
El Djouf, Mauritania 50 D4 20 0N 9 0W
El Dorado, Ark., U.S.A. 81 J8 33 12N 92 40W
El Dorado, Kans., U.S.A. 81 G6 37 49N 96 52W
El Dorado, Venezuela 92 B6 6 55N 61 37W
El Escorial, Spain 19 B3 40 35N 4 7W
El Faiyûm, Egypt 51 C12 29 19N 30 50 E
El Fâsher, Sudan 51 F11 13 33N 25 26 E
El Ferrol = Ferrol, Spain 19 A1 43 29N 8 15W
El Fuerte, Mexico 86 B3 26 30N 108 40W
El Gal, Somali Rep. 46 E5 10 58N 50 20 E
El Geneina = Al Junaynah, Sudan 51 F10 13 27N 22 45 E
El Gîza, Egypt 51 C12 30 0N 31 10 E
El Goléa, Algeria 50 B6 30 30N 2 50 E
El Iskandarîya, Egypt 51 B11 31 13N 29 58 E
El Istiwa'iya, Sudan 51 G11 5 0N 28 0 E
El Jadida, Morocco 50 B4 33 11N 8 17W
El Jardal, Honduras 88 D2 14 54N 88 50W
El Kabrît, G., Egypt 47 F2 29 42N 33 16 E
El Khârga, Egypt 51 C12 25 30N 30 33 E
El Khartûm, Sudan 51 E12 15 31N 32 35 E
El Kuntilla, Egypt 47 E3 30 1N 34 45 E
El Maestrazgo, Spain 19 B5 40 30N 0 25W
El Mahalla el Kubra, Egypt 51 B12 31 0N 31 0 E
El Mansûra, Egypt 51 B12 31 0N 31 19 E
El Medano, Canary Is. 22 F3 28 3N 16 32W
El Milagro, Argentina 94 C2 30 59S 65 59W
El Minyâ, Egypt 51 C12 28 7N 30 33 E
El Monte, U.S.A. 85 L8 34 4N 118 1W
El Obeid, Sudan 51 F12 13 8N 30 10 E
El Odaiya, Sudan 51 F11 12 8N 28 12 E
El Oro, Mexico 87 D4 19 48N 100 8W
El Oued, Algeria 50 B7 33 20N 6 58 E
El Palmito, Presa, Mexico 86 B3 25 40N 105 30W
El Paso, U.S.A. 83 L10 31 45N 106 29W
El Paso Robles, U.S.A. 84 K6 35 38N 120 41W
El Portal, U.S.A. 84 H7 37 41N 119 47W
El Porvenir, Mexico 86 A3 31 15N 105 51W
El Prat de Llobregat, Spain 19 B7 41 18N 2 3 E
El Progreso, Honduras 88 C2 15 26N 87 51W
El Pueblito, Mexico 86 B3 29 3N 105 4W
El Pueblo, Canary Is. 22 F2 28 36N 17 47W
El Puerto de Santa María, Spain 19 D2 36 36N 6 13W
El Qâhira, Egypt 51 B12 30 1N 31 14 E
El Qantara, Egypt 47 E1 30 51N 32 20 E
El Quseima, Egypt 47 E3 30 40N 34 15 E
El Real, Panama 92 B3 8 0N 77 40W
El Reno, U.S.A. 81 H6 35 32N 97 57W
El Rio, U.S.A. 85 L7 34 14N 119 10W
El Roque, Pta., Canary Is. 22 F4 28 10N 15 25W
El Rosarito, Mexico 86 B2 28 38N 114 4W
El Saheira, W. →, Egypt 47 E2 30 5N 33 25 E
El Salto, Mexico 86 C3 23 47N 105 22W
El Salvador ■, Cent. Amer. 88 D2 13 50N 89 0W
El Sauce, Nic. 88 D2 13 0N 86 40W
El Sueco, Mexico 86 B3 29 54N 106 24W
El Suweis, Egypt 51 C12 29 58N 32 31 E
El Tamarâni, W. →, Egypt 47 E3 30 7N 34 43 E
El Thamad, Egypt 47 F3 29 40N 34 28 E
El Tigre, Venezuela 92 B6 8 44N 64 15W
El Tîh, Gebal, Egypt 47 F2 29 40N 33 50 E
El Tîna, Khalîg, Egypt 47 D1 31 10N 32 40 E
El Tofo, Chile 94 B1 29 22S 71 18W
El Tránsito, Chile 94 B1 28 52S 70 17W
El Tûr, Egypt 44 D2 28 14N 33 36 E
El Turbio, Argentina 96 G2 51 45S 72 5W
El Uqsur, Egypt 51 C12 25 41N 32 38 E
El Venado, Mexico 86 C4 22 56N 101 10W
El Vergel, Mexico 86 B3 26 28N 106 22W
El Vigía, Venezuela 92 B4 8 38N 71 39W
El Wabeira, Egypt 47 F2 29 34N 33 6 E
El Wak, Kenya 54 B5 2 49N 40 56 E
El Wuz, Sudan 51 E12 15 5N 30 7 E
Elat, Israel 47 F3 29 30N 34 56 E
Elâzığ, Turkey 25 G6 38 37N 39 14 E
Elba, Italy 20 C4 42 46N 10 17 E
Elba, U.S.A. 77 K2 31 25N 86 4W
Elbasan, Albania 21 D9 41 9N 20 9 E
Elbe, U.S.A. 84 D4 46 45N 122 10W
Elbe →, Europe 16 B5 53 50N 9 0 E
Elbert, Mt., U.S.A. 83 G10 39 7N 106 27W
Elberton, U.S.A. 77 H4 34 7N 82 52W
Elbeuf, France 18 B4 49 17N 1 2 E
Elbidtan, Turkey 44 B3 38 13N 37 12 E
Elbing = Elbląg, Poland 17 A10 54 10N 19 25 E
Elbląg, Poland 17 A10 54 10N 19 25 E
Elbow, Canada 73 C7 51 7N 106 35W
Elbrus, Asia 25 F7 43 21N 42 30 E
Elburz Mts. = Alborz, Reshteh-ye Kūhhā-ye, Iran 45 C7 36 0N 52 0 E
Elche, Spain 19 C5 38 15N 0 42W
Elcho I., Australia 62 A2 11 55S 135 45 E
Elda, Spain 19 C5 38 29N 0 47W
Elde →, Germany 16 B6 53 7N 11 15 E
Eldon, Mo., U.S.A. 80 F8 38 21N 92 35W
Eldon, Wash., U.S.A. 84 C3 47 33N 123 3W
Eldora, U.S.A. 80 D8 42 22N 93 5W
Eldorado, Argentina 95 B5 26 28S 54 43W
Eldorado, Canada 78 B7 44 35N 77 31W
Eldorado, Mexico 86 C3 24 20N 107 22W
Eldorado, Ill., U.S.A. 76 G1 37 49N 88 26W
Eldorado, Tex., U.S.A. 81 K4 30 52N 100 36W
Eldorado Springs, U.S.A. 81 G8 37 52N 94 1W
Eldoret, Kenya 54 B4 0 30N 35 17 E
Eldred, U.S.A. 78 E6 41 58N 78 23W
Elea, C., Cyprus 23 D13 35 19N 34 4 E
Eleanora, Pk., Australia 61 F3 32 57S 121 9 E
Elefantes →, Mozam. 57 C5 24 10S 32 40 E
Elektrostal, Russia 24 C6 55 41N 38 32 E
Elephant Butte Reservoir, U.S.A. 83 K10 33 9N 107 11W
Elephant I., Antarctica 5 C18 61 0S 55 0W
Eleuthera, Bahamas 88 B4 25 0N 76 20W
Elgin, Canada 79 B8 44 36N 76 13W
Elgin, U.K. 12 D5 57 39N 3 19W
Elgin, Ill., U.S.A. 76 D1 42 2N 88 17W
Elgin, N. Dak., U.S.A. 80 B4 46 24N 101 51W
Elgin, Oreg., U.S.A. 82 D5 45 34N 117 55W
Elgin, Tex., U.S.A. 81 K6 30 21N 97 22W
Elgon, Mt., Africa 54 B3 1 10N 34 30 E
Eliase, Indonesia 37 F8 8 21S 130 48 E
Elim, Namibia 56 B2 17 48S 15 31 E
Elim, S. Africa 56 E2 34 35S 19 45 E
Elista, Russia 25 E7 46 16N 44 14 E
Elizabeth, N.J., U.S.A. 79 F10 40 39N 74 13W
Elizabeth, N.J., U.S.A. 79 F10 40 40N 74 13W
Elizabeth City, U.S.A. 77 G7 36 18N 76 14W
Elizabethton, U.S.A. 77 G4 36 21N 82 13W
Elizabethtown, Ky., U.S.A. 76 G3 37 42N 85 52W
Elizabethtown, N.Y., U.S.A. 79 B11 44 13N 73 36W
Elizabethtown, Pa., U.S.A. 79 F8 40 9N 76 36W
Ełk, Poland 17 B12 53 50N 22 21 E
Elk →, Canada 72 C5 49 11N 115 14W
Elk →, U.S.A. 77 H2 34 46N 87 16W
Elk City, U.S.A. 81 H5 35 25N 99 25W
Elk Creek, U.S.A. 84 F4 39 36N 122 32W
Elk Grove, U.S.A. 84 G5 38 25N 121 22W
Elk Island Nat. Park, Canada 72 C6 53 35N 112 59W
Elk Lake, Canada 70 C3 47 40N 80 25W
Elk Point, Canada 73 C6 53 54N 110 55W
Elk River, Idaho, U.S.A. 82 C5 46 47N 116 11W
Elk River, Minn., U.S.A. 80 C8 45 18N 93 35W
Elkedra →, Australia 62 C2 21 8S 136 22 E
Elkhart, Ind., U.S.A. 76 E3 41 41N 85 58W
Elkhart, Kans., U.S.A. 81 G4 37 0N 101 54W
Elkhorn, Canada 73 D8 49 59N 101 14W
Elkhorn →, U.S.A. 80 E6 41 8N 96 19W
Elkhovo, Bulgaria 21 C12 42 10N 26 35 E
Elkin, U.S.A. 77 G5 36 15N 80 51W
Elkins, U.S.A. 76 F6 38 55N 79 51W
Elkland, U.S.A. 78 E7 41 59N 77 19W
Elko, Canada 72 D5 49 20N 115 10W
Elko, U.S.A. 82 F6 40 50N 115 46W
Elkton, U.S.A. 78 C1 43 49N 83 11W
Ell, L., Australia 61 E4 29 13S 127 46 E
Ellef Ringnes I., Canada 4 B2 78 30N 102 2W
Ellen, Mt., U.S.A. 79 B12 44 9N 72 56W
Ellenburg, U.S.A. 79 B11 44 54N 73 48W
Ellendale, U.S.A. 80 B5 46 0N 98 32W
Ellensburg, U.S.A. 82 C3 46 59N 120 34W
Ellenville, U.S.A. 79 E10 41 43N 74 24W
Ellesmere, L., N.Z. 59 M4 43 47S 172 28 E
Ellesmere I., Canada 4 B4 79 30N 80 0W
Ellesmere Port, U.K. 10 D5 53 17N 2 54W
Ellice Is. = Tuvalu ■, Pac. Oc. 64 H9 8 0S 178 0 E
Ellicottville, U.S.A. 78 D6 42 17N 78 40W
Elliot, Australia 62 B1 17 33S 133 32 E
Elliot, S. Africa 57 E4 31 22S 27 48 E
Elliot Lake, Canada 70 C3 46 25N 82 35W
Elliotdale = Xhora, S. Africa 57 E4 31 55S 28 38 E
Ellis, U.S.A. 80 F5 38 56N 99 34W
Elliston, Australia 63 E1 33 39S 134 53 E
Ellisville, U.S.A. 81 K10 31 36N 89 12W
Ellon, U.K. 12 D6 57 22N 2 4W
Ellore = Eluru, India 41 L12 16 48N 81 8 E
Ellsworth, Kans., U.S.A. 80 F5 38 44N 98 14W
Ellsworth, Maine, U.S.A. 77 C11 44 33N 68 25W
Ellsworth Land, Antarctica 5 D16 76 0S 89 0W
Ellsworth Mts., Antarctica 5 D16 78 30S 85 0W
Ellwood City, U.S.A. 78 F4 40 52N 80 17W
Elma, Canada 73 D9 49 52N 95 55W
Elma, U.S.A. 84 D3 47 0N 123 25W
Elmalı, Turkey 25 G4 36 44N 29 56 E
Elmhurst, U.S.A. 76 E2 41 53N 87 56W
Elmira, Canada 78 C4 43 36N 80 33W
Elmira, U.S.A. 78 D8 42 6N 76 48W
Elmira Heights, U.S.A. 78 D8 42 8N 76 50W
Elmore, U.S.A. 85 M11 33 7N 115 49W
Elmshorn, Germany 16 B5 53 43N 9 40 E
Elmvale, Canada 78 B5 44 35N 79 52W
Elora, Canada 78 C4 43 41N 80 26W
Eloúnda, Greece 23 D7 35 16N 25 42 E
Eloy, U.S.A. 83 K8 32 45N 111 33W
Elrose, Canada 73 C7 51 12N 108 0W
Elsie, U.S.A. 84 E3 45 52N 123 36W
Elsinore = Helsingør, Denmark 9 H15 56 2N 12 35 E
Eltham, N.Z. 59 H5 39 26S 174 19 E
Eluru, India 41 L12 16 48N 81 8 E
Elvas, Portugal 19 C2 38 50N 7 10W
Elverum, Norway 9 F14 60 53N 11 34 E
Elvire →, Australia 60 C4 17 51S 128 11 E
Elvire, Mt., Australia 61 E2 29 22S 119 36 E
Elwell, L., U.S.A. 82 B8 48 22N 111 17W
Elwood, Ind., U.S.A. 76 E3 40 17N 85 50W
Elwood, Nebr., U.S.A. 80 E5 40 36N 99 52W
Elx = Elche, Spain 19 C5 38 15N 0 42W
Ely, U.K. 11 E8 52 24N 0 16 E
Ely, Minn., U.S.A. 80 B9 47 55N 91 51W
Ely, Nev., U.S.A. 82 G6 39 15N 114 54W
Elyria, U.S.A. 78 E2 41 22N 82 7W
Emāmrūd, Iran 45 B7 36 30N 55 0 E
Emba, Kazakstan 26 E6 48 50N 58 8 E
Emba →, Kazakstan 25 E9 46 55N 53 28 E
Embarcación, Argentina 94 A3 23 10S 64 0W
Embarras Portage, Canada 73 B6 58 27N 111 28W
Embetsu, Japan 30 B10 44 44N 141 47 E
Embi = Emba, Kazakstan 26 E6 48 50N 58 8 E
Embi = Emba →, Kazakstan 25 E9 46 55N 53 28 E
Embóna, Greece 23 C9 36 13N 27 51 E
Embrun, France 18 D7 44 34N 6 30 E
Embu, Kenya 54 C4 0 32S 37 38 E
Emden, Germany 16 B4 53 21N 7 12 E
Emerald, Australia 62 C4 23 32S 148 10 E
Emerson, Canada 73 D9 49 0N 97 10W
Emet, Turkey 21 E13 39 20N 29 15 E
Emi Koussi, Chad 51 E9 19 45N 18 55 E
Eminabad, Pakistan 42 C6 32 2N 74 8 E
Emine, Nos, Bulgaria 21 C12 42 40N 27 56 E
Emlenton, U.S.A. 78 E5 41 11N 79 43W
Emmaus, S. Africa 56 D4 29 2S 25 15 E
Emmaus, U.S.A. 79 F9 40 32N 75 30W
Emmeloord, Neths. 15 B5 52 44N 5 46 E
Emmen, Neths. 15 B6 52 48N 6 57 E
Emmet, Australia 62 C3 24 45S 144 30 E
Emmetsburg, U.S.A. 80 D7 43 7N 94 41W
Emmett, Idaho, U.S.A. 82 E5 43 52N 116 30W
Emmett, Mich., U.S.A. 78 D2 42 59N 82 46W
Emmonak, U.S.A. 68 B3 62 46N 164 30W
Emo, Canada 73 D10 48 38N 93 50W
Empalme, Mexico 86 B2 28 1N 110 49W
Empangeni, S. Africa 57 D5 28 50S 31 52 E
Empedrado, Argentina 94 B4 28 0S 58 46W
Emperor Seamount Chain, Pac. Oc. 64 D9 40 0N 170 0 E
Emporia, Kans., U.S.A. 80 F6 38 25N 96 11W
Emporia, Va., U.S.A. 77 G7 36 42N 77 32W
Emporium, U.S.A. 78 E6 41 31N 78 14W
Empress, Canada 73 C7 50 57N 110 0W
Empty Quarter = Rub' al Khālī, Si. Arabia 46 D4 18 0N 48 0 E
Ems →, Germany 16 B4 53 20N 7 12 E
Emsdale, Canada 78 A5 45 32N 79 19W
Emu, China 35 C15 43 40N 128 6 E
Emu Park, Australia 62 C5 23 13S 150 50 E
'En 'Avrona, Israel 47 F4 29 43N 35 0 E
En Nahud, Sudan 51 F11 12 45N 28 25 E
Ena, Japan 31 G8 35 25N 137 25 E
Enana, Namibia 56 B2 17 30S 16 23 E
Enard B., U.K. 12 C3 58 5N 5 20W
Enare = Inarijärvi, Finland 8 B22 69 0N 28 0 E
Enarotali, Indonesia 37 E9 3 55S 136 21 E
Encampment, U.S.A. 82 F10 41 12N 106 47W
Encantadas, Serra, Brazil 95 C5 30 40S 53 0W
Encarnación, Paraguay 95 B4 27 15S 55 50W
Encarnación de Diaz, Mexico 86 C4 21 30N 102 13W
Encinitas, U.S.A. 85 M9 33 3N 117 17W
Encino, U.S.A. 83 J11 34 39N 105 28W
Endako, Canada 72 C3 54 6N 125 2W
Ende, Indonesia 37 F6 8 45S 121 40 E
Endeavour Str., Australia 62 A3 10 45S 142 0 E
Enderbury I., Kiribati 64 H10 3 8S 171 5W
Enderby, Canada 72 C5 50 35N 119 10W
Enderby I., Australia 60 D2 20 35S 116 30 E
Enderby Land, Antarctica 5 C5 66 0S 53 0 E
Enderlin, U.S.A. 80 B6 46 38N 97 36W
Endicott, U.S.A. 79 D8 42 6N 76 4W
Endwell, U.S.A. 79 D8 42 6N 76 2W
Endyalgout I., Australia 60 B5 11 40S 132 35 E
Eneabba, Australia 61 E2 29 49S 115 16 E
Enewetak Atoll, Marshall Is. 64 F8 11 30N 162 15 E
Enez, Turkey 21 D12 40 45N 26 5 E
Enfield, Canada 71 D7 44 56N 63 32W
Enfield, Conn., U.S.A. 79 E12 41 58N 72 36W
Enfield, N.H., U.S.A. 79 C12 43 39N 72 9W
Engadin, Switz. 18 C9 46 45N 10 10 E
Engaño, C., Dom. Rep. 89 C6 18 30N 68 20W
Engaño, C., Phil. 37 A6 18 35N 122 23 E
Engaru, Japan 30 B11 44 3N 143 31 E
Engcobo, S. Africa 57 E4 31 37S 28 0 E
Engels, Russia 25 D8 51 28N 46 6 E
Engemann L., Canada 73 B7 58 0N 106 55W
Enggano, Indonesia 36 F2 5 20S 102 40 E
England, U.S.A. 81 H9 34 33N 91 58W
England □, U.K. 10 D7 53 0N 2 0W
Englee, Canada 71 B8 50 45N 56 5W
Englehart, Canada 70 C4 47 49N 79 52W
Englewood, U.S.A. 80 F2 39 39N 104 59W
English →, Canada 73 C10 50 35N 93 30W
English Bazar = Ingraj Bazar, India 43 G13 24 58N 88 10 E
English Channel, Europe 11 G6 50 0N 2 0W
English River, Canada 70 C1 49 14N 91 0W
Enid, U.S.A. 81 G6 36 24N 97 53W
Enkhuizen, Neths. 15 B5 52 42N 5 17 E
Enna, Italy 20 F6 37 34N 14 16 E
Ennadai, Canada 73 A8 61 8N 100 53W
Ennadai L., Canada 73 A8 61 0N 101 0W
Ennedi, Chad 51 E10 17 15N 22 0 E
Enngonia, Australia 63 D4 29 21S 145 50 E
Ennis, Ireland 13 D3 52 51N 8 59W
Ennis, Mont., U.S.A. 82 D8 45 21N 111 44W
Ennis, Tex., U.S.A. 81 J6 32 20N 96 38W
Enniscorthy, Ireland 13 D5 52 30N 6 34W
Enniskillen, U.K. 13 B4 54 21N 7 39W
Ennistimon, Ireland 13 D2 52 57N 9 17W
Enns →, Austria 16 D8 48 14N 14 32 E
Enontekiö, Finland 8 B20 68 23N 23 37 E
Enosburg Falls, U.S.A. 79 B12 44 55N 72 48W
Enriquillo, L., Dom. Rep. 89 C5 18 20N 72 5W
Enschede, Neths. 15 B6 52 13N 6 53 E
Ensenada, Argentina 94 C4 34 55S 57 55W
Ensenada, Mexico 86 A1 31 50N 116 50W
Ensenada de los Muertos, Mexico 86 C2 23 59N 109 50W
Ensiola, Pta. de n', Spain 22 B9 39 7N 2 55 E
Entebbe, Uganda 54 B3 0 4N 32 28 E
Enterprise, Canada 72 A5 60 47N 115 45W
Enterprise, Ala., U.S.A. 77 K3 31 19N 85 51W
Enterprise, Oreg., U.S.A. 82 D5 45 25N 117 17W
Entre Ríos, Bolivia 94 A3 21 30S 64 25W
Entre Ríos □, Argentina 94 C4 30 30S 58 30W
Entroncamento, Portugal 19 C1 39 28N 8 28W
Enugu, Nigeria 50 G7 6 30N 7 30 E
Enumclaw, U.S.A. 84 C5 47 12N 121 59W
Eólie, Ís., Italy 20 E6 38 30N 14 57 E
Epe, Neths. 15 B5 52 21N 5 59 E
Épernay, France 18 B5 49 3N 3 56 E
Ephesus, Turkey 21 F12 37 55N 27 22 E
Ephraim, U.S.A. 82 G8 39 22N 111 35W
Ephrata, Pa., U.S.A. 79 F8 40 11N 76 11W
Ephrata, Wash., U.S.A. 82 C4 47 19N 119 33W
Épinal, France 18 B7 48 10N 6 27 E
Episkopi, Cyprus 23 E11 34 40N 32 54 E
Episkopí, Greece 23 D6 35 20N 24 20 E
Episkopi Bay, Cyprus 23 E11 34 35N 32 50 E
Epsom, U.K. 11 F7 51 19N 0 16W
Epukiro, Namibia 56 C2 21 40S 19 9 E
Equatorial Guinea ■, Africa 52 D1 2 0N 8 0 E
Er Rachidia, Morocco 50 B5 31 58N 4 20W
Er Rahad, Sudan 51 F12 12 45N 30 32 E
Er Rif, Morocco 50 A5 35 1N 4 1W
Erāwadī Myit = Irrawaddy →, Burma 41 M19 15 50N 95 6 E
Erāwadī Myitwanya = Irrawaddy, Mouths of the, Burma 41 M19 15 30N 95 0 E
Erbil = Arbīl, Iraq 44 B5 36 15N 44 5 E
Erçek, Turkey 44 B4 38 39N 43 36 E
Erciyaş Dağı, Turkey 25 G6 38 30N 35 30 E
Érd, Hungary 17 E10 47 22N 18 56 E
Erdao Jiang →, China 35 C14 43 0N 127 0 E
Erdek, Turkey 21 D12 40 23N 27 47 E
Erdene = Ulaan-Uul, Mongolia 34 B6 44 13N 111 10 E
Erdenetsogt, Mongolia 34 C4 42 55N 106 5 E
Erebus, Mt., Antarctica 5 D11 77 35S 167 0 E
Erechim, Brazil 95 B5 27 35S 52 15W
Ereğli, Konya, Turkey 25 G5 37 31N 34 4 E
Ereğli, Zonguldak, Turkey 25 F5 41 15N 31 24 E
Erenhot, China 34 C7 43 48N 112 2 E
Eresma →, Spain 19 B3 41 26N 4 45W
Erfenisdam, S. Africa 56 D4 28 30S 26 50 E
Erfurt, Germany 16 C6 50 58N 11 2 E
Erg Iguidi, Africa 50 C4 27 0N 7 0 E
Ergani, Turkey 44 B3 38 17N 39 49 E
Ergel, Mongolia 34 C5 43 8N 109 5 E
Ergeni Vozvyshennost, Russia 25 E7 47 0N 44 0 E
Ērgli, Latvia 9 H21 56 54N 25 38 E
Eriboll, L., U.K. 12 C4 58 30N 4 42W
Érice, Italy 20 E5 38 2N 12 35 E
Erie, U.S.A. 78 D4 42 8N 80 5W

Feng Xian

Feng Xian, Shaanxi, China 34 H4 33 54N 106 40 E
Fengcheng, China 35 D13 40 28N 124 5 E
Fengfeng, China 34 F8 36 28N 114 8 E
Fengning, China 34 D9 41 10N 116 33 E
Fengqiu, China 34 G8 35 2N 114 25 E
Fengrun, China 35 E10 39 48N 118 8 E
Fengtai, China 34 E9 39 50N 116 18 E
Fengxiang, China 34 G4 34 29N 107 25 E
Fengyang, China 35 H9 32 51N 117 29 E
Fengzhen, China 34 D7 40 25N 113 2 E
Fenoarivo, Fianarantsoa, Madag. 57 C8 21 43S 46 24 E
Fenoarivo, Fianarantsoa, Madag. 57 C8 20 52S 46 53 E
Fenoarivo Afovoany, Madag. 57 B8 18 26S 46 34 E
Fenoarivo Atsinanana, Madag. 57 B8 17 22S 49 25 E
Fens, The, U.K. 10 E7 52 38N 0 2W
Fenton, U.S.A. 76 D4 42 48N 83 42W
Fenxi, China 34 F6 36 40N 111 31 E
Fenyang, China 34 F6 37 18N 111 48 E
Feodosiya, Ukraine 25 E6 45 2N 35 16 E
Ferdows, Iran 45 C8 33 58N 58 2 E
Ferfer, Somali Rep. 46 F4 5 4N 45 9 E
Fergana = Farghona, Uzbekistan 26 E8 40 23N 71 19 E
Fergus, Canada 78 C4 43 43N 80 24W
Fergus Falls, U.S.A. 80 B6 46 17N 96 4W
Ferkéssédougou, Ivory C. 50 G4 9 35N 5 6W
Ferland, Canada 70 B2 50 19N 88 27W
Fermanagh □, U.K. 13 B4 54 21N 7 40W
Fermo, Italy 20 C5 43 9N 13 43 E
Fermont, Canada 71 B6 52 47N 67 5W
Fermoy, Ireland 13 D3 52 9N 8 16W
Fernández, Argentina 94 B3 27 55S 63 50W
Fernandina Beach, U.S.A. 77 K5 30 40N 81 27W
Fernando de Noronha, Brazil 93 D12 4 0S 33 10W
Fernando Póo = Bioko, Eq. Guin. 52 D1 3 30N 8 40 E
Ferndale, U.S.A. 84 B4 48 51N 122 36W
Fernie, Canada 72 D5 49 30N 115 5W
Fernlees, Australia 62 C4 23 51S 148 7 E
Fernley, U.S.A. 82 G4 39 36N 119 15W
Ferozepore = Firozpur, India 42 D6 30 55N 74 40 E
Ferrara, Italy 20 B4 44 50N 11 35 E
Ferreñafe, Peru 92 E3 6 42S 79 50W
Ferrerías, Spain 22 B11 39 59N 4 1 E
Ferret, C., France 18 D3 44 38N 1 15W
Ferriday, U.S.A. 81 K9 31 38N 91 33W
Ferrol, Spain 19 A1 43 29N 8 15W
Ferron, U.S.A. 83 G8 39 5N 111 8W
Ferrutx, C., Spain 22 B10 39 47N 3 21 E
Ferryland, Canada 71 C9 47 2N 52 53W
Fertile, U.S.A. 80 B6 47 32N 96 17W
Fès, Morocco 50 B5 34 0N 5 0W
Fessenden, U.S.A. 80 B5 47 39N 99 38W
Festus, U.S.A. 80 F9 38 13N 90 24W
Feteşti, Romania 17 F14 44 22N 27 51 E
Fethiye, Turkey 25 G4 36 36N 29 6 E
Fetlar, U.K. 12 A8 60 36N 0 52W
Feuilles →, Canada 69 C12 58 47N 70 4W
Fez = Fès, Morocco 50 B5 34 0N 5 0W
Fezzan, Libya 51 C8 27 0N 13 0 E
Fiambalá, Argentina 94 B2 27 45S 67 37W
Fianarantsoa, Madag. 57 C8 21 26S 47 5 E
Fianarantsoa □, Madag. 57 B8 19 30S 47 0 E
Ficksburg, S. Africa 57 D4 28 51S 27 53 E
Field →, Australia 62 C2 23 48S 138 0 E
Field I., Australia 60 B5 12 5S 132 23 E
Fier, Albania 21 D8 40 43N 19 33 E
Fife □, U.K. 12 E5 56 16N 3 1W
Fife Ness, U.K. 12 E6 56 17N 2 35W
Fifth Cataract, Sudan 51 E12 18 22N 33 50 E
Figeac, France 18 D5 44 37N 2 2 E
Figtree, Zimbabwe 55 G2 20 22S 28 20 E
Figueira da Foz, Portugal 19 B1 40 7N 8 54W
Figueres, Spain 19 A7 42 18N 2 58 E
Figuig, Morocco 50 B5 32 5N 1 11W
Fihaonana, Madag. 57 B8 18 36S 47 12 E
Fiherenana, Madag. 57 B8 18 29S 48 24 E
Fiherenana →, Madag. 57 C7 23 19S 43 37 E
Fiji ■, Pac. Oc. 59 C8 17 20S 179 0 E
Filabusi, Zimbabwe 57 C4 20 34S 29 20 E
Filey, U.K. 10 C7 54 12N 0 18W
Filey B., U.K. 10 C7 54 12N 0 15W
Filfla, Malta 23 D1 35 47N 14 24 E
Filiatrá, Greece 21 F9 37 9N 21 35 E
Filingué, Niger 50 F6 14 21N 3 22 E
Filipstad, Sweden 9 G16 59 43N 14 9 E
Fillmore, Calif., U.S.A. 85 L8 34 24N 118 55W
Fillmore, Utah, U.S.A. 83 G7 38 58N 112 20W
Finch, Canada 79 A9 45 11N 75 7W
Findhorn →, U.K. 12 D5 57 38N 3 38W
Findlay, U.S.A. 76 E4 41 2N 83 39W
Finger L., Canada 70 B1 53 33N 93 30W
Finger Lakes, U.S.A. 79 D8 42 40N 76 30W
Fingoè, Mozam. 55 E3 14 55S 31 50 E
Finisterre, C. = Fisterra, C., Spain 19 A1 42 50N 9 19W
Finke, Australia 62 D1 25 34S 134 35 E
Finland ■, Europe 8 E22 63 0N 27 0 E
Finland, G. of, Europe 9 G21 60 0N 26 0 E
Finlay →, Canada 72 B3 57 0N 125 10W
Finley, U.S.A. 80 B6 47 31N 97 50W
Finn →, Ireland 13 B4 54 51N 7 28W
Finnigan, Mt., Australia 62 B4 15 49S 145 17 E
Finniss, C., Australia 63 E1 33 8S 134 51 E
Finnmark, Norway 8 B20 69 37N 23 57 E
Finnsnes, Norway 8 B18 69 14N 18 0 E
Finspång, Sweden 9 G16 58 43N 15 47 E
Fiora →, Italy 20 C4 42 20N 11 34 E
Fiq, Syria 47 C4 32 46N 35 41 E
Firat = Furāt, Nahr al →, Asia 44 D5 31 0N 47 25 E
Firebag →, Canada 73 B6 57 45N 111 21W
Firebaugh, U.S.A. 84 J6 36 52N 120 27W
Firedrake L., Canada 73 A8 61 25N 104 30W
Firenze, Italy 20 C4 43 46N 11 15 E
Firk →, Iraq 44 D5 30 59N 44 34 E
Firozabad, India 43 F8 27 10N 78 25 E
Firozpur, India 42 D6 30 55N 74 40 E
Firozpur-Jhirka, India 42 F7 27 48N 76 57 E
Fīrūzābād, Iran 45 D7 28 52N 52 35 E
Fīrūzkūh, Iran 45 C7 35 50N 52 50 E
Firvale, Canada 72 C3 52 27N 126 13W
Fish →, Namibia 56 D2 28 7S 17 10 E
Fish →, S. Africa 56 E3 31 30S 20 16 E
Fish River Canyon, Namibia 56 D2 27 40S 17 35 E
Fisher, Australia 61 F5 30 30S 131 0 E
Fisher B., Canada 73 C9 51 35N 97 13W
Fishers I., U.S.A. 79 E13 41 15N 72 0W
Fishguard, U.K. 11 E3 52 0N 4 58W
Fishing L., Canada 73 C9 52 10N 95 24W
Fishkill, U.S.A. 79 E11 41 32N 73 53W
Fisterra, C., Spain 19 A1 42 50N 9 19W
Fitchburg, U.S.A. 79 D13 42 35N 71 48W
Fitz Roy, Argentina 96 F3 47 0S 67 0W
Fitzgerald, Canada 72 B6 59 51N 111 36W
Fitzgerald, U.S.A. 77 K4 31 43N 83 15W
Fitzmaurice →, Australia 60 B5 14 45S 130 5 E
Fitzroy →, Queens., Australia 62 C5 23 32S 150 52 E
Fitzroy →, W. Austral., Australia 60 C3 17 31S 123 35 E
Fitzroy, Mte., Argentina 96 F2 49 17S 73 5W
Fitzroy Crossing, Australia 60 C4 18 9S 125 38 E
Fitzwilliam I., Canada 78 A3 45 30N 81 45W
Fiume = Rijeka, Croatia 16 F8 45 20N 14 21 E
Five Points, U.S.A. 84 J6 36 26N 120 6W
Fizi, Dem. Rep. of the Congo 54 C2 4 17S 28 55 E
Flagstaff, U.S.A. 83 J8 35 12N 111 39W
Flagstaff L., U.S.A. 77 C10 45 12N 70 18W
Flaherty I., Canada 70 A4 56 15N 79 15W
Flåm, Norway 9 F12 60 50N 7 7 E
Flambeau →, U.S.A. 80 C9 45 18N 91 14W
Flamborough Hd., U.K. 10 C7 54 7N 0 5W
Flaming Gorge Reservoir, U.S.A. 82 F9 41 10N 109 25W
Flamingo, Teluk, Indonesia 37 F9 5 30S 138 0 E
Flanders = Flandre, Europe 18 A5 50 50N 2 30 E
Flandre, Europe 18 A5 50 50N 2 30 E
Flandre Occidentale = West-Vlaanderen □, Belgium 15 D2 51 0N 3 0 E
Flandre Orientale = Oost-Vlaanderen □, Belgium 15 C3 51 5N 3 50 E
Flandreau, U.S.A. 80 C6 44 3N 96 36W
Flanigan, U.S.A. 84 E7 40 10N 119 53W
Flannan Is., U.K. 12 C1 58 9N 7 52W
Flåsjön, Sweden 8 D16 64 5N 15 40 E
Flat →, Canada 72 A3 61 33N 125 18W
Flathead L., U.S.A. 82 C7 47 51N 114 8W
Flattery, C., Australia 62 A4 14 58S 145 21 E
Flattery, C., U.S.A. 84 B2 48 23N 124 29W
Flatwoods, U.S.A. 76 F4 38 31N 82 43W
Fleetwood, U.K. 10 D4 53 55N 3 1W
Fleetwood, U.S.A. 79 F9 40 27N 75 49W
Flekkefjord, Norway 9 G12 58 18N 6 39 E
Flemington, U.S.A. 78 E7 41 7N 77 28W
Flensburg, Germany 16 A5 54 47N 9 27 E
Flers, France 18 B3 48 47N 0 33W
Flesherton, Canada 78 B4 44 16N 80 33W
Flesko, Tanjung, Indonesia 37 D6 0 29N 124 30 E
Fleurieu Pen., Australia 63 F2 35 40S 138 5 E
Flevoland □, Neths. 15 B5 52 30N 5 30 E
Flin Flon, Canada 73 C8 54 46N 101 53W
Flinders →, Australia 62 B3 17 36S 140 36 E
Flinders B., Australia 61 F2 34 19S 115 19 E
Flinders Group, Australia 62 A3 14 11S 144 15 E
Flinders I., S. Austral., Australia 63 E1 33 44S 134 41 E
Flinders I., Tas., Australia 62 G4 40 0S 148 0 E
Flinders Reefs, Australia 62 B4 17 37S 148 31 E
Flint, U.K. 10 D4 53 15N 3 8W
Flint, U.S.A. 76 D4 43 1N 83 41W
Flint →, U.S.A. 77 K3 30 57N 84 34W
Flint I., Kiribati 65 J12 11 26S 151 48W
Flintshire □, U.K. 10 D4 53 17N 3 17W
Flodden, U.K. 10 B5 55 37N 2 8W
Floodwood, U.S.A. 80 B8 46 55N 92 55W
Flora, U.S.A. 76 F1 38 40N 88 29W
Florala, U.S.A. 77 K2 31 0N 86 20W
Florence = Firenze, Italy 20 C4 43 46N 11 15 E
Florence, Ala., U.S.A. 77 H2 34 48N 87 41W
Florence, Ariz., U.S.A. 83 K8 33 2N 111 23W
Florence, Colo., U.S.A. 80 F2 38 23N 105 8W
Florence, Oreg., U.S.A. 82 E1 43 58N 124 7W
Florence, S.C., U.S.A. 77 H6 34 12N 79 46W
Florence, L., Australia 63 D2 28 53S 138 9 E
Florencia, Colombia 92 C3 1 36N 75 36W
Florennes, Belgium 15 D4 50 15N 4 35 E
Florenville, Belgium 15 E5 49 40N 5 19 E
Flores, Guatemala 88 C2 16 59N 89 50W
Flores, Indonesia 37 F6 8 35S 121 0 E
Flores I., Canada 72 D3 49 20N 126 10W
Flores Sea, Indonesia 37 F6 6 30S 120 0 E
Floreşti, Moldova 17 E15 47 53N 28 17 E
Floresville, U.S.A. 81 L5 29 8N 98 10W
Floriano, Brazil 93 E10 6 50S 43 0W
Florianópolis, Brazil 95 B6 27 30S 48 30W
Florida, Cuba 88 B4 21 32N 78 14W
Florida, Uruguay 95 C4 34 7S 56 10W
Florida □, U.S.A. 77 L5 28 0N 82 0W
Florida, Straits of, U.S.A. 88 B4 25 0N 80 0W
Florida B., U.S.A. 88 B3 25 0N 80 45W
Florida Keys, U.S.A. 77 N5 24 40N 81 0W
Flórina, Greece 21 D9 40 48N 21 26 E
Florø, Norway 9 F11 61 35N 5 1 E
Flower Station, Canada 79 A8 45 10N 76 41W
Flowerpot I., Canada 78 A3 45 18N 81 38W
Floydada, U.S.A. 81 J4 33 59N 101 20W
Fluk, Indonesia 37 E7 1 42S 127 44 E
Flushing = Vlissingen, Neths. 15 C3 51 26N 3 34 E
Flying Fish, C., Antarctica 5 D15 72 6S 102 29W
Foam Lake, Canada 73 C8 51 40N 103 32W
Foça, Turkey 21 E12 38 39N 26 46 E
Focşani, Romania 17 F14 45 41N 27 15 E
Fóggia, Italy 20 D6 41 27N 15 34 E
Fogo, Canada 71 C9 49 43N 54 17W
Fogo I., Canada 71 C9 49 40N 54 5W
Föhr, Germany 16 A5 54 43N 8 30 E
Foix, France 18 E4 42 58N 1 38 E
Folda, Nord-Trøndelag, Norway 8 D14 64 32N 10 30 E
Folda, Nordland, Norway 8 C16 67 38N 14 50 E
Foley, Botswana 56 C4 21 34S 27 21 E
Foley, U.S.A. 77 K2 30 24N 87 41W
Foleyet, Canada 70 C3 48 15N 82 25W
Folgefonni, Norway 9 F12 60 3N 6 23 E
Foligno, Italy 20 C5 42 57N 12 42 E
Folkestone, U.K. 11 F9 51 5N 1 12 E
Folkston, U.S.A. 77 K5 30 50N 82 0W
Follansbee, U.S.A. 78 F4 40 19N 80 35W
Folsom L., U.S.A. 84 G5 38 42N 121 9W
Fond-du-Lac, Canada 73 B7 59 19N 107 12W
Fond du Lac, U.S.A. 80 D10 43 47N 88 27W
Fond-du-Lac →, Canada 73 B7 59 17N 106 0W
Fonda, U.S.A. 79 D10 42 57N 74 22W
Fondi, Italy 20 D5 41 21N 13 25 E
Fongafale, Tuvalu 64 H9 8 31S 179 13 E
Fonsagrada = A Fonsagrada, Spain 19 A2 43 8N 7 4W
Fonseca, G. de, Cent. Amer. 88 D2 13 10N 87 40W
Fontainebleau, France 18 B5 48 24N 2 40 E
Fontana, U.S.A. 85 L9 34 6N 117 26W
Fontas →, Canada 72 B4 58 14N 121 48W
Fonte Boa, Brazil 92 D5 2 33S 66 0W
Fontenay-le-Comte, France 18 C3 46 28N 0 48W
Fontenelle Reservoir, U.S.A. 82 E8 42 1N 110 3W
Fontur, Iceland 8 C6 66 23N 14 32W
Foochow = Fuzhou, China 33 D6 26 5N 119 16 E
Foping, China 34 H5 33 41N 108 0 E
Forbesganj, India 43 F12 26 17N 87 18 E
Ford City, Calif., U.S.A. 85 K7 35 9N 119 27W
Ford City, Pa., U.S.A. 78 F5 40 46N 79 32W
Førde, Norway 9 F11 61 27N 5 53 E
Ford's Bridge, Australia 63 D4 29 41S 145 29 E
Fordyce, U.S.A. 81 J8 33 49N 92 25W
Forel, Mt., Greenland 4 C6 66 52N 36 55W
Foremost, Canada 72 D6 49 26N 111 34W
Forest, Canada 78 C3 43 6N 82 0W
Forest, U.S.A. 81 J10 32 22N 89 29W
Forest City, Iowa, U.S.A. 80 D8 43 16N 93 39W
Forest City, N.C., U.S.A. 77 H5 35 20N 81 52W
Forest City, Pa., U.S.A. 79 E9 41 39N 75 28W
Forest Grove, U.S.A. 84 E3 45 31N 123 7W
Forestburg, Canada 72 C6 52 35N 112 1W
Foresthill, U.S.A. 84 F6 39 1N 120 49W
Forestier Pen., Australia 62 G4 43 0S 148 0 E
Forestville, Canada 71 C6 48 48N 69 2W
Forestville, Calif., U.S.A. 84 G4 38 28N 122 54W
Forestville, N.Y., U.S.A. 78 D5 42 28N 79 10W
Forfar, U.K. 12 E6 56 39N 2 53W
Forks, U.S.A. 84 C2 47 57N 124 23W
Forksville, U.S.A. 79 E8 41 29N 76 35W
Forlì, Italy 20 B5 44 13N 12 3 E
Forman, U.S.A. 80 B6 46 7N 97 38W
Formby Pt., U.K. 10 D4 53 33N 3 6W
Formentera, Spain 22 C7 38 43N 1 27 E
Formentor, C. de, Spain 22 B10 39 58N 3 13 E
Former Yugoslav Republic of Macedonia = Macedonia ■, Europe 21 D9 41 53N 21 40 E
Fórmia, Italy 20 D5 41 15N 13 37 E
Formosa = Taiwan ■, Asia 33 D7 23 30N 121 0 E
Formosa, Argentina 94 B4 26 15S 58 10W
Formosa, Brazil 93 G9 15 32S 47 20W
Formosa □, Argentina 94 B4 25 0S 60 0W
Formosa, Serra, Brazil 93 F8 12 0S 55 0W
Formosa Bay, Kenya 54 C5 2 40S 40 20 E
Fornells, Spain 22 A11 40 3N 4 7 E
Føroyar, Atl. Oc. 8 F9 62 0N 7 0W
Forres, U.K. 12 D5 57 37N 3 37W
Forrest, Australia 61 F4 30 51S 128 6 E
Forrest, Mt., Australia 61 D4 24 48S 127 45 E
Forrest City, U.S.A. 81 H9 35 1N 90 47W
Forsayth, Australia 62 B3 18 33S 143 34 E
Forssa, Finland 9 F20 60 49N 23 38 E
Forst, Germany 16 C8 51 45N 14 37 E
Forsyth, U.S.A. 82 C10 46 16N 106 41W
Fort Abbas, Pakistan 42 E5 29 12N 72 52 E
Fort Albany, Canada 70 B3 52 15N 81 35W
Fort Ann, U.S.A. 79 C11 43 25N 73 30W
Fort Assiniboine, Canada 72 C6 54 20N 114 45W
Fort Augustus, U.K. 12 D4 57 9N 4 42W
Fort Beaufort, S. Africa 56 E4 32 46S 26 40 E
Fort Benton, U.S.A. 82 C8 47 49N 110 40W
Fort Bragg, U.S.A. 82 G2 39 26N 123 48W
Fort Bridger, U.S.A. 82 F8 41 19N 110 23W
Fort Chipewyan, Canada 73 B6 58 42N 111 8W
Fort Collins, U.S.A. 80 E2 40 35N 105 5W
Fort-Coulonge, Canada 70 C4 45 50N 76 45W
Fort Covington, U.S.A. 79 B10 44 59N 74 29W
Fort Davis, U.S.A. 81 K3 30 35N 103 54W
Fort-de-France, Martinique 89 D7 14 36N 61 2W
Fort Defiance, U.S.A. 83 J9 35 45N 109 5W
Fort Dodge, U.S.A. 80 D7 42 30N 94 11W
Fort Edward, U.S.A. 79 C11 43 16N 73 35W
Fort Erie, Canada 78 D6 42 54N 78 56W
Fort Fairfield, U.S.A. 77 B12 46 46N 67 50W
Fort Frances, Canada 73 D10 48 36N 93 24W
Fort Garland, U.S.A. 83 H11 37 26N 105 26W
Fort George = Chisasibi, Canada 70 B4 53 50N 79 0W
Fort Good-Hope, Canada 68 B7 66 14N 128 40W
Fort Hancock, U.S.A. 83 L11 31 18N 105 51W
Fort Hertz = Putao, Burma 41 F20 27 28N 97 30 E
Fort Hope, Canada 70 B2 51 30N 88 0W
Fort Irwin, U.S.A. 85 K10 35 16N 116 34W
Fort Kent, U.S.A. 77 B11 47 15N 68 36W
Fort Klamath, U.S.A. 82 E3 42 42N 122 0W
Fort Laramie, U.S.A. 80 D2 42 13N 104 31W
Fort Lauderdale, U.S.A. 77 M5 26 7N 80 8W
Fort Liard, Canada 72 A4 60 14N 123 30W
Fort Liberté, Haiti 89 C5 19 42N 71 51W
Fort Lupton, U.S.A. 80 E2 40 5N 104 49W
Fort Mackay, Canada 72 B6 57 12N 111 41W
Fort Macleod, Canada 72 D6 49 45N 113 30W
Fort McMurray, Canada 72 B6 56 44N 111 7W
Fort McPherson, Canada 68 B6 67 30N 134 55W
Fort Madison, U.S.A. 80 E9 40 38N 91 27W
Fort Meade, U.S.A. 77 M5 27 45N 81 48W
Fort Morgan, U.S.A. 80 E3 40 15N 103 48W
Fort Myers, U.S.A. 77 M5 26 39N 81 52W
Fort Nelson, Canada 72 B4 58 50N 122 44W
Fort Nelson →, Canada 72 B4 59 32N 124 0W
Fort Norman = Tulita, Canada 68 B7 64 57N 125 30W
Fort Payne, U.S.A. 77 H3 34 26N 85 43W
Fort Peck, U.S.A. 82 B10 48 1N 106 27W
Fort Peck Dam, U.S.A. 82 C10 48 0N 106 26W
Fort Peck L., U.S.A. 82 C10 48 0N 106 26W
Fort Pierce, U.S.A. 77 M5 27 27N 80 20W
Fort Pierre, U.S.A. 80 C4 44 21N 100 22W
Fort Plain, U.S.A. 79 D10 42 56N 74 37W
Fort Portal, Uganda 54 B3 0 40N 30 20 E
Fort Providence, Canada 72 A5 61 3N 117 40W
Fort Qu'Appelle, Canada 73 C8 50 45N 103 50W
Fort Resolution, Canada 72 A6 61 10N 113 40W
Fort Rixon, Zimbabwe 55 G2 20 2S 29 17 E
Fort Ross, U.S.A. 84 G3 38 32N 123 13W
Fort Rupert = Waskaganish, Canada 70 B4 51 30N 78 40W
Fort St. James, Canada 72 C4 54 30N 124 10W
Fort St. John, Canada 72 B4 56 15N 120 50W
Fort Saskatchewan, Canada 72 C6 53 40N 113 15W
Fort Scott, U.S.A. 81 G7 37 50N 94 42W
Fort Severn, Canada 70 A2 56 0N 87 40W
Fort Shevchenko, Kazakstan 25 F9 44 35N 50 23 E
Fort Simpson, Canada 72 A4 61 45N 121 15W
Fort Smith, Canada 72 B6 60 0N 111 51W
Fort Smith, U.S.A. 81 H7 35 23N 94 25W
Fort Stockton, U.S.A. 81 K3 30 53N 102 53W
Fort Sumner, U.S.A. 81 H2 34 28N 104 15W
Fort Thompson, U.S.A. 80 C5 44 3N 99 26W
Fort Valley, U.S.A. 77 J4 32 33N 83 53W
Fort Vermilion, Canada 72 B5 58 24N 116 0W
Fort Walton Beach, U.S.A. 77 K2 30 25N 86 36W
Fort Wayne, U.S.A. 76 E3 41 4N 85 9W
Fort William, U.K. 12 E3 56 49N 5 7W
Fort Worth, U.S.A. 81 J6 32 45N 97 18W
Fort Yates, U.S.A. 80 B4 46 5N 100 38W
Fort Yukon, U.S.A. 68 B5 66 34N 145 16W
Fortaleza, Brazil 93 D11 3 45S 38 35W
Forteau, Canada 71 B8 51 28N 56 58W
Fortescue →, Australia 60 D2 21 0S 116 4 E
Forth →, U.K. 12 E5 56 9N 3 50W
Forth, Firth of, U.K. 12 E6 56 5N 2 55W
Fortrose, U.K. 12 D4 57 35N 4 9W
Fortuna, Calif., U.S.A. 82 F1 40 36N 124 9W
Fortuna, N. Dak., U.S.A. 80 A3 48 55N 103 47W
Fortune, Canada 71 C8 47 4N 55 50W
Fortune B., Canada 71 C8 47 30N 55 22W
Forūr, Iran 45 E7 26 17N 54 32 E
Foshan, China 33 D6 23 4N 113 5 E
Fosna, Norway 8 E14 63 50N 10 20 E
Fosnavåg, Norway 9 E11 62 22N 5 38 E
Fossano, Italy 18 D7 44 33N 7 43 E
Fossil, U.S.A. 82 D3 45 0N 120 9W
Foster, Canada 79 A12 45 17N 72 30W
Foster →, Canada 73 B7 55 47N 105 49W
Fosters Ra., Australia 62 C1 21 35S 133 48 E
Fostoria, U.S.A. 76 E4 41 10N 83 25W
Fotadrevo, Madag. 57 C8 24 3S 45 1 E
Fougères, France 18 B3 48 21N 1 14W
Foul Pt., Sri Lanka 40 Q12 8 35N 81 18 E
Foula, U.K. 12 A6 60 10N 2 5W
Foulness I., U.K. 11 F8 51 36N 0 55 E
Foulpointe, Madag. 57 B8 17 41S 49 31 E
Foulweather, C., U.S.A. 74 B2 44 50N 124 5W
Foumban, Cameroon 52 C2 5 45N 10 50 E
Fountain, U.S.A. 80 F2 38 41N 104 42W
Fountain Springs, U.S.A. 85 K8 35 54N 118 51W
Fouriesburg, S. Africa 56 D4 28 38S 28 14 E
Foúrnoi, Greece 21 F12 37 36N 26 32 E
Fourth Cataract, Sudan 51 E12 18 47N 32 3 E
Fouta Djalon, Guinea 50 F3 11 20N 12 10W
Foux, Cap-à-, Haiti 89 C5 19 43N 73 27W
Foveaux Str., N.Z. 59 M2 46 42S 168 10 E
Fowey, U.K. 11 G3 50 20N 4 39W
Fowler, Calif., U.S.A. 84 J7 36 38N 119 41W
Fowler, Colo., U.S.A. 80 F3 38 8N 104 2W
Fowlers B., Australia 61 F5 31 59S 132 34 E
Fowman, Iran 45 B6 37 13N 49 19 E
Fox →, Canada 73 B10 56 3N 93 18W
Fox Creek, Canada 72 C5 54 24N 116 48W
Fox Lake, Canada 72 B6 58 28N 114 31W
Fox Valley, Canada 73 C7 50 30N 109 25W
Foxboro, U.S.A. 79 D13 42 4N 71 16W
Foxe Basin, Canada 69 B12 66 0N 77 0W
Foxe Chan., Canada 69 B11 65 0N 80 0W
Foxe Pen., Canada 69 B12 65 0N 76 0W
Foxton, N.Z. 59 J5 40 29S 175 18 E
Foyle, Lough, U.K. 13 A4 55 7N 7 4W
Foynes, Ireland 13 D2 52 37N 9 7W
Foz do Cunene, Angola 56 B1 17 15S 11 48 E
Foz do Iguaçu, Brazil 95 B5 25 30S 54 30W
Frackville, U.S.A. 79 F8 40 47N 76 14W
Fraile Muerto, Uruguay 95 C5 32 31S 54 32W
Framingham, U.S.A. 79 D13 42 17N 71 25W
Franca, Brazil 93 H9 20 33S 47 30W
Francavilla Fontana, Italy 21 D7 40 32N 17 35 E
France ■, Europe 18 C5 47 0N 3 0 E
Frances →, Canada 72 A3 60 16N 129 10W
Frances L., Canada 72 A3 61 23N 129 30W
Franceville, Gabon 52 E2 1 40S 13 32 E
Franche-Comté, France 18 C6 46 50N 5 55 E
Francis Case, L., U.S.A. 80 D5 43 4N 98 34W
Francisco Beltrão, Brazil 95 B5 26 5S 53 4W
Francisco I. Madero, Coahuila, Mexico 86 B4 25 48N 103 18W
Francisco I. Madero, Durango, Mexico 86 C4 24 32N 104 22W
Francistown, Botswana 57 C4 21 7S 27 33 E
François, Canada 71 C8 47 35N 56 45W
François L., Canada 72 C3 54 0N 125 30W
Franeker, Neths. 15 A5 53 12N 5 33 E
Frankford, Canada 78 B7 44 12N 77 36W
Frankfort, S. Africa 57 D4 27 17S 28 30 E
Frankfort, Ind., U.S.A. 76 E2 40 17N 86 31W
Frankfort, Kans., U.S.A. 80 F6 39 42N 96 25W
Frankfort, Ky., U.S.A. 76 F3 38 12N 84 52W
Frankfort, N.Y., U.S.A. 79 C9 43 2N 75 4W
Frankfurt, Brandenburg, Germany 16 B8 52 20N 14 32 E
Frankfurt, Hessen, Germany 16 C5 50 7N 8 41 E
Fränkische Alb, Germany 16 D6 49 10N 11 23 E
Frankland →, Australia 61 G2 35 0S 116 48 E
Franklin, Ky., U.S.A. 77 G2 36 43N 86 35W
Franklin, La., U.S.A. 81 L9 29 48N 91 30W
Franklin, Mass., U.S.A. 79 D13 42 5N 71 24W
Franklin, N.H., U.S.A. 79 C13 43 27N 71 39W
Franklin, Nebr., U.S.A. 80 E5 40 6N 98 57W
Franklin, Pa., U.S.A. 78 E5 41 24N 79 50W
Franklin, Va., U.S.A. 77 G7 36 41N 76 56W
Franklin, W. Va., U.S.A. 76 F6 38 39N 79 20W
Franklin B., Canada 68 B7 69 45N 126 0W
Franklin D. Roosevelt L., U.S.A. 82 B4 48 18N 118 9W
Franklin I., Antarctica 5 D11 76 10S 168 30 E
Franklin L., U.S.A. 82 F6 40 25N 115 22W
Franklin Mts., Canada 68 B7 65 0N 125 0W
Franklin Str., Canada 68 A10 72 0N 96 0W

Gaula

Franklinton, U.S.A. **81 K9** 30 51N 90 9W
Franklinville, U.S.A. **78 D6** 42 20N 78 27W
Franks Pk., U.S.A. **82 E9** 43 58N 109 18W
Fransfontein, Namibia **56 C2** 20 12S 15 1 E
Frantsa Iosifa, Zemlya, Russia **26 A6** 82 0N 55 0 E
Franz, Canada **70 C3** 48 25N 84 30W
Franz Josef Land = Frantsa Iosifa, Zemlya, Russia **26 A6** 82 0N 55 0 E
Fraser, U.S.A. **78 D2** 42 32N 82 57W
Fraser →, B.C., Canada **72 D4** 49 7N 123 11W
Fraser →, Nfld., Canada **71 A7** 56 39N 62 10W
Fraser, Mt., Australia **61 E2** 25 35S 118 20 E
Fraser I., Australia **63 D5** 25 15S 153 10 E
Fraser Lake, Canada **72 C4** 54 0N 124 50W
Fraserburg, S. Africa **56 E3** 31 55S 21 30 E
Fraserburgh, U.K. **12 D6** 57 42N 2 1W
Fraserdale, Canada **70 C3** 49 55N 81 37W
Fray Bentos, Uruguay **94 C4** 33 10S 58 15W
Fredericia, Denmark **9 J13** 55 34N 9 45 E
Frederick, Md., U.S.A. **76 F7** 39 25N 77 25W
Frederick, Okla., U.S.A. **81 H5** 34 23N 99 1W
Frederick, S. Dak., U.S.A. **80 C5** 45 50N 98 31W
Fredericksburg, Pa., U.S.A. **79 F8** 40 27N 76 26W
Fredericksburg, Tex., U.S.A. **81 K5** 30 16N 98 52W
Fredericksburg, Va., U.S.A. **76 F7** 38 18N 77 28W
Fredericktown, Mo., U.S.A. **81 G9** 37 34N 90 18W
Fredericktown, Ohio, U.S.A. **78 F2** 40 29N 82 33W
Frederico I. Madero, Presa, Mexico **86 B3** 28 7N 105 40W
Frederico Westphalen, Brazil **95 B5** 27 22S 53 24W
Fredericton, Canada **71 C6** 45 57N 66 40W
Fredericton Junction, Canada **71 C6** 45 41N 66 40W
Frederikshåb = Paamiut, Greenland **4 C5** 62 0N 49 43W
Frederikshavn, Denmark **9 H14** 57 28N 10 31 E
Frederiksted, U.S. Virgin Is. **89 C7** 17 43N 64 53W
Fredonia, Ariz., U.S.A. **83 H7** 36 57N 112 32W
Fredonia, Kans., U.S.A. **81 G7** 37 32N 95 49W
Fredonia, N.Y., U.S.A. **78 D5** 42 26N 79 20W
Fredrikstad, Norway **9 G14** 59 13N 10 57 E
Free State □, S. Africa **56 D4** 28 30S 27 0 E
Freehold, U.S.A. **79 F10** 40 16N 74 17W
Freel Peak, U.S.A. **84 G7** 38 52N 119 54W
Freeland, U.S.A. **79 E9** 41 1N 75 54W
Freels, C., Canada **71 C9** 49 15N 53 30W
Freeman, Calif., U.S.A. **85 K9** 35 35N 117 53W
Freeman, S. Dak., U.S.A. **80 D6** 43 21N 97 26W
Freeport, Bahamas **88 A4** 26 30N 78 47W
Freeport, Ill., U.S.A. **80 D10** 42 17N 89 36W
Freeport, N.Y., U.S.A. **79 F11** 40 39N 73 35W
Freeport, Ohio, U.S.A. **78 F3** 40 12N 81 15W
Freeport, Pa., U.S.A. **78 F5** 40 41N 79 41W
Freeport, Tex., U.S.A. **81 L7** 28 57N 95 21W
Freetown, S. Leone **50 G3** 8 30N 13 17W
Frégate, L., Canada **70 B5** 53 15N 74 45W
Fregenal de la Sierra, Spain **19 C2** 38 10N 6 39W
Freibourg = Fribourg, Switz. **18 C7** 46 49N 7 9 E
Freiburg, Germany **16 E4** 47 59N 7 51 E
Freire, Chile **96 D2** 38 54S 72 38W
Freirina, Chile **94 B1** 28 30S 71 10W
Freising, Germany **16 D6** 48 24N 11 45 E
Freistadt, Austria **16 D8** 48 30N 14 30 E
Fréjus, France **18 E7** 43 25N 6 44 E
Fremantle, Australia **61 F2** 32 7S 115 47 E
Fremont, Calif., U.S.A. **84 H4** 37 32N 121 57W
Fremont, Mich., U.S.A. **76 D3** 43 28N 85 57W
Fremont, Nebr., U.S.A. **80 E6** 41 26N 96 30W
Fremont, Ohio, U.S.A. **76 E4** 41 21N 83 7W
Fremont →, U.S.A. **83 G8** 38 24N 110 42W
French Camp, U.S.A. **84 H5** 37 53N 121 16W
French Creek →, U.S.A. **78 E5** 41 24N 79 50W
French Guiana ■, S. Amer. **93 C8** 4 0N 53 0W
French Polynesia ■, Pac. Oc. **65 K13** 20 0S 145 0W
Frenchman Cr. →, N. Amer. **82 B10** 48 31N 107 10W
Frenchman Cr. →, U.S.A. **80 E4** 40 14N 100 50W
Fresco →, Brazil **93 E8** 7 15S 51 30W
Freshfield, C., Antarctica **5 C10** 68 25S 151 10 E
Fresnillo, Mexico **86 C4** 23 10N 103 0W
Fresno, U.S.A. **84 J7** 36 44N 119 47W
Fresno Reservoir, U.S.A. **82 B9** 48 36N 109 57W
Frew →, Australia **62 C2** 20 0S 135 38 E
Frewsburg, U.S.A. **78 D5** 42 3N 79 10W
Freycinet Pen., Australia **62 G4** 42 10S 148 25 E
Fria, C., Namibia **56 B1** 18 0S 12 0 E
Friant, U.S.A. **84 J7** 36 59N 119 43W
Frías, Argentina **94 B2** 28 40S 65 5W
Fribourg, Switz. **18 C7** 46 49N 7 9 E
Friday Harbor, U.S.A. **84 B3** 48 32N 123 1W
Friedens, U.S.A. **78 F6** 40 3N 78 59W
Friedrichshafen, Germany **16 E5** 47 39N 9 30 E
Friendly Is. = Tonga ■, Pac. Oc. **59 D11** 19 50S 174 30W
Friendship, U.S.A. **78 D6** 42 12N 78 8W
Friesland □, Neths. **15 A5** 53 5N 5 50 E
Frio →, U.S.A. **81 L5** 28 26N 98 11W
Frio, C., Brazil **90 F6** 22 50S 41 50W
Friona, U.S.A. **81 H3** 34 38N 102 43W
Fritch, U.S.A. **81 H4** 35 38N 101 36W
Frobisher B., Canada **69 B13** 62 30N 66 0W
Frobisher Bay = Iqaluit, Canada **69 B13** 63 44N 68 31W
Frobisher L., Canada **73 B7** 56 20N 108 15W
Frohavet, Norway **8 E13** 64 0N 9 30 E
Frome, U.K. **11 F5** 51 14N 2 19W
Frome →, U.K. **11 G5** 50 41N 2 6W
Front Range, U.S.A. **74 C5** 40 25N 105 45W
Front Royal, U.S.A. **76 F6** 38 55N 78 12W
Frontera, Canary Is. **22 G2** 27 47N 17 59W
Frontera, Mexico **87 D6** 18 30N 92 40W
Fronteras, Mexico **86 A3** 30 56N 109 31W
Frosinone, Italy **20 D5** 41 38N 13 19 E
Frostburg, U.S.A. **76 F6** 39 39N 78 56W
Frostisen, Norway **8 B17** 68 14N 17 10 E
Frøya, Norway **8 E13** 63 43N 8 40 E
Frunze = Bishkek, Kyrgyzstan **26 E8** 42 54N 74 46 E
Frutal, Brazil **93 H9** 20 0S 49 0W
Frýdek-Místek, Czech Rep. **17 D10** 49 40N 18 20 E
Fryeburg, U.S.A. **79 B14** 44 1N 70 59W
Fu Xian = Wafangdian, China **35 E11** 39 38N 121 58 E
Fu Xian, China **34 G5** 36 0N 109 20 E
Fucheng, China **34 F9** 37 50N 116 10 E
Fuchou = Fuzhou, China **33 D6** 26 5N 119 16 E
Fuchū, Japan **31 G6** 34 34N 133 14 E
Fuencaliente, Canary Is. **22 F2** 28 28N 17 50W
Fuencaliente, Pta., Canary Is. **22 F2** 28 27N 17 51W
Fuengirola, Spain **19 D3** 36 32N 4 41W
Fuentes de Oñoro, Spain **19 B2** 40 33N 6 52W
Fuerte →, Mexico **86 B3** 25 50N 109 25W
Fuerte Olimpo, Paraguay **94 A4** 21 0S 57 51W
Fuerteventura, Canary Is. **22 F6** 28 30N 14 0W
Fufeng, China **34 G5** 34 22N 108 0 E
Fugou, China **34 G8** 34 3N 114 25 E
Fugu, China **34 E6** 39 2N 111 3 E
Fuhai, China **32 B3** 47 2N 87 25 E
Fuḩaymī, Iraq **44 C4** 34 16N 42 10 E
Fuji, Japan **31 G9** 35 9N 138 39 E
Fuji-San, Japan **31 G9** 35 22N 138 44 E
Fuji-Yoshida, Japan **31 G9** 35 30N 138 46 E
Fujian □, China **33 D6** 26 0N 118 0 E
Fujinomiya, Japan **31 G9** 35 10N 138 40 E
Fujisawa, Japan **31 G9** 35 22N 139 29 E
Fujiyama, Mt. = Fuji-San, Japan **31 G9** 35 22N 138 44 E
Fukien = Fujian □, China **33 D6** 26 0N 118 0 E
Fukuchiyama, Japan **31 G7** 35 19N 135 9 E
Fukue-Shima, Japan **31 H4** 32 40N 128 45 E
Fukui, Japan **31 F8** 36 5N 136 10 E
Fukui □, Japan **31 G8** 36 0N 136 12 E
Fukuoka, Japan **31 H5** 33 39N 130 21 E
Fukuoka □, Japan **31 H5** 33 30N 131 0 E
Fukushima, Japan **30 F10** 37 44N 140 28 E
Fukushima □, Japan **30 F10** 37 30N 140 15 E
Fukuyama, Japan **31 G6** 34 35N 133 20 E
Fulda, Germany **16 C5** 50 32N 9 40 E
Fulda →, Germany **16 C5** 51 25N 9 39 E
Fulford Harbour, Canada **84 B3** 48 47N 123 27W
Fullerton, Calif., U.S.A. **85 M9** 33 53N 117 56W
Fullerton, Nebr., U.S.A. **80 E6** 41 22N 97 58W
Fulongquan, China **35 B13** 44 20N 124 42 E
Fulton, Mo., U.S.A. **80 F9** 38 52N 91 57W
Fulton, N.Y., U.S.A. **79 C8** 43 19N 76 25W
Funabashi, Japan **31 G10** 35 45N 140 0 E
Funafuti = Fongafale, Tuvalu **64 H9** 8 31S 179 13 E
Funchal, Madeira **22 D3** 32 38N 16 54W
Fundación, Colombia **92 A4** 10 31N 74 11W
Fundão, Portugal **19 B2** 40 8N 7 30W
Fundy, B. of, Canada **71 D6** 45 0N 66 0W
Funhalouro, Mozam. **57 C5** 23 3S 34 25 E
Funing, Hebei, China **35 E10** 39 53N 119 12 E
Funing, Jiangsu, China **35 H10** 33 45N 119 50 E
Funiu Shan, China **34 H7** 33 30N 112 20 E
Funtua, Nigeria **50 F7** 11 30N 7 18 E
Fuping, Hebei, China **34 E8** 38 48N 114 12 E
Fuping, Shaanxi, China **34 G5** 34 42N 109 10 E
Furano, Japan **30 C11** 43 21N 142 23 E
Furāt, Nahr al →, Asia **44 D5** 31 0N 47 25 E
Fūrg, Iran **45 D7** 28 18N 55 13 E
Furnás, Spain **22 B8** 39 3N 1 32 E
Furnas, Représa de, Brazil **95 A6** 20 50S 45 30W
Furneaux Group, Australia **62 G4** 40 10S 147 50 E
Furqlus, Syria **47 A6** 34 36N 37 8 E
Fürstenwalde, Germany **16 B8** 52 22N 14 3 E
Fürth, Germany **16 D6** 49 28N 10 59 E
Furukawa, Japan **30 E10** 38 34N 140 58 E
Fury and Hecla Str., Canada **69 B11** 69 56N 84 0W
Fusagasuga, Colombia **92 C4** 4 21N 74 22W
Fushan, Shandong, China **35 F11** 37 30N 121 15 E
Fushan, Shanxi, China **34 G6** 35 58N 111 51 E
Fushun, China **35 D12** 41 50N 123 56 E
Fusong, China **35 C14** 42 20N 127 15 E
Futuna, Wall. & F. Is. **59 B8** 14 25S 178 20W
Fuxin, China **35 C11** 42 5N 121 48 E
Fuyang, China **34 H8** 33 0N 115 48 E
Fuyang He →, China **34 E9** 38 12N 117 0 E
Fuyu, China **35 B13** 45 12N 124 43 E
Fuzhou, China **33 D6** 26 5N 119 16 E
Fylde, U.K. **10 D5** 53 50N 2 58W
Fyn, Denmark **9 J14** 55 20N 10 30 E
Fyne, L., U.K. **12 F3** 55 59N 5 23W

G

Gabela, Angola **52 G2** 11 0S 14 24 E
Gabès, Tunisia **51 B8** 33 53N 10 2 E
Gabès, G. de, Tunisia **51 B8** 34 0N 10 30 E
Gabon ■, Africa **52 E2** 0 10S 10 0 E
Gaborone, Botswana **56 C4** 24 45S 25 57 E
Gabriels, U.S.A. **79 B10** 44 26N 74 12W
Gābrīk, Iran **45 E8** 25 44N 58 28 E
Gabrovo, Bulgaria **21 C11** 42 52N 25 19 E
Gāch Sār, Iran **45 B6** 36 7N 51 19 E
Gachsārān, Iran **45 D6** 30 15N 50 45 E
Gadag, India **40 M9** 15 30N 75 45 E
Gadap, Pakistan **42 G2** 25 5N 67 28 E
Gadarwara, India **43 H8** 22 50N 78 50 E
Gadhada, India **42 J4** 22 0N 71 35 E
Gadra, Pakistan **42 G4** 25 40N 70 38 E
Gadsden, U.S.A. **77 H3** 34 1N 86 1W
Gadwal, India **40 L10** 16 10N 77 50 E
Gaffney, U.S.A. **77 H5** 35 5N 81 39W
Gafsa, Tunisia **50 B7** 34 24N 8 43 E
Gagaria, India **42 G4** 25 43N 70 46 E
Gagnoa, Ivory C. **50 G4** 6 56N 5 16W
Gagnon, Canada **71 B6** 51 50N 68 5W
Gagnon, L., Canada **73 A6** 62 3N 110 27W
Gahini, Rwanda **54 C3** 1 50S 30 30 E
Gahmar, India **43 G10** 25 27N 83 49 E
Gai Xian = Gaizhou, China **35 D12** 40 22N 122 20 E
Gaïdhouronísi, Greece **23 E7** 34 53N 25 41 E
Gail, U.S.A. **81 J4** 32 46N 101 27W
Gaillimh = Galway, Ireland **13 C2** 53 17N 9 3W
Gaines, U.S.A. **78 E7** 41 46N 77 35W
Gainesville, Fla., U.S.A. **77 L4** 29 40N 82 20W
Gainesville, Ga., U.S.A. **77 H4** 34 18N 83 50W
Gainesville, Mo., U.S.A. **81 G8** 36 36N 92 26W
Gainesville, Tex., U.S.A. **81 J6** 33 38N 97 8W
Gainsborough, U.K. **10 D7** 53 24N 0 46W
Gairloch, L., U.K. **12 D3** 57 43N 5 45W
Gaizhou, China **35 D12** 40 22N 122 20 E
Gaj →, Pakistan **42 F2** 26 26N 67 21 E
Gakuch, Pakistan **43 A5** 36 7N 73 45 E
Galán, Cerro, Argentina **94 B2** 25 55S 66 52W
Galana →, Kenya **54 C5** 3 9S 40 8 E
Galápagos, Pac. Oc. **90 D1** 0 0 91 0W
Galashiels, U.K. **12 F6** 55 37N 2 49W
Galaţi, Romania **17 F15** 45 27N 28 2 E
Galatina, Italy **21 D8** 40 10N 18 10 E
Galax, U.S.A. **77 G5** 36 40N 80 56W
Galcaio, Somali Rep. **46 F4** 6 30N 47 30 E
Galdhøpiggen, Norway **9 F12** 61 38N 8 18 E
Galeana, Chihuahua, Mexico **86 A3** 30 7N 107 38W
Galeana, Nuevo León, Mexico **86 A3** 24 50N 100 4W
Galela, Indonesia **37 D7** 1 50N 127 49 E
Galena, U.S.A. **68 B4** 64 44N 156 56W
Galera Pt., Trin. & Tob. **89 D7** 10 49N 60 54W
Galesburg, U.S.A. **80 E9** 40 57N 90 22W
Galeton, U.S.A. **78 E7** 41 44N 77 39W
Galich, Russia **24 C7** 58 22N 42 24 E
Galicia □, Spain **19 A2** 42 43N 7 45W
Galilee = Hagalil, Israel **47 C4** 32 53N 35 18 E
Galilee, L., Australia **62 C4** 22 20S 145 50 E
Galilee, Sea of = Yam Kinneret, Israel **47 C4** 32 45N 35 35 E
Galinoporni, Cyprus **23 D13** 35 31N 34 18 E
Galion, U.S.A. **78 F2** 40 44N 82 47W
Galiuro Mts., U.S.A. **83 K8** 32 30N 110 20W
Galiwinku, Australia **62 A2** 12 2S 135 34 E
Gallan Hd., U.K. **12 C1** 58 15N 7 2W
Gallatin, U.S.A. **77 G2** 36 24N 86 27W
Galle, Sri Lanka **40 R12** 6 5N 80 10 E
Gállego →, Spain **19 B5** 41 39N 0 51W
Gallegos →, Argentina **96 G3** 51 35S 69 0W
Galley Hd., Ireland **13 E3** 51 32N 8 55W
Gallinas, Pta., Colombia **92 A4** 12 28N 71 40W
Gallipoli = Gelibolu, Turkey **21 D12** 40 28N 26 43 E
Gallipoli, Italy **21 D8** 40 3N 17 58 E
Gallipolis, U.S.A. **76 F4** 38 49N 82 12W
Gällivare, Sweden **8 C19** 67 9N 20 40 E
Galloo I., U.S.A. **79 C8** 43 55N 76 25W
Galloway, U.K. **12 F4** 55 1N 4 29W
Galloway, Mull of, U.K. **12 G4** 54 39N 4 52W
Gallup, U.S.A. **83 J9** 35 32N 108 45W
Galoya, Sri Lanka **40 Q12** 8 10N 80 55 E
Galt, U.S.A. **84 G5** 38 15N 121 18W
Galty Mts., Ireland **13 D3** 52 22N 8 10W
Galtymore, Ireland **13 D3** 52 21N 8 11W
Galva, U.S.A. **80 E9** 41 10N 90 3W
Galveston, U.S.A. **81 L7** 29 18N 94 48W
Galveston B., U.S.A. **81 L7** 29 36N 94 50W
Gálvez, Argentina **94 C3** 32 0S 61 14W
Galway, Ireland **13 C2** 53 17N 9 3W
Galway □, Ireland **13 C2** 53 22N 9 1W
Galway B., Ireland **13 C2** 53 13N 9 10W
Gam →, Vietnam **38 B5** 21 55N 105 12 E
Gamagōri, Japan **31 G8** 34 50N 137 14 E
Gambat, Pakistan **42 F3** 27 17N 68 26 E
Gambhir →, India **42 F6** 26 58N 77 27 E
Gambia ■, W. Afr. **50 F2** 13 25N 16 0W
Gambia →, W. Afr. **50 F2** 13 28N 16 34W
Gambier, U.S.A. **78 F2** 40 22N 82 23W
Gambier, C., Australia **60 B5** 11 56S 130 57 E
Gambo, Canada **71 C9** 48 47N 54 13W
Gamboli, Pakistan **42 E3** 29 53N 68 24 E
Gamboma, Congo **52 E3** 1 55S 15 52 E
Gamka →, S. Africa **56 E3** 33 18S 21 39 E
Gamkab →, Namibia **56 D2** 28 4S 17 54 E
Gamlakarleby = Kokkola, Finland **8 E20** 63 50N 23 8 E
Gammon →, Canada **73 C9** 51 24N 95 44W
Gamtoos →, S. Africa **56 E4** 33 58S 25 1 E
Gan Jiang →, China **33 D6** 29 15N 116 0 E
Ganado, U.S.A. **83 J9** 35 43N 109 33W
Gananoque, Canada **79 B8** 44 20N 76 10W
Ganāveh, Iran **45 D6** 29 35N 50 35 E
Gäncä, Azerbaijan **25 F8** 40 45N 46 20 E
Gancheng, China **38 C7** 18 51N 108 37 E
Gand = Gent, Belgium **15 C3** 51 2N 3 42 E
Ganda, Angola **53 G2** 13 3S 14 35 E
Gandajika, Dem. Rep. of the Congo **52 F4** 6 45S 23 57 E
Gandak →, India **43 G11** 25 39N 85 13 E
Gandava, Pakistan **42 E2** 28 32N 67 32 E
Gander, Canada **71 C9** 48 58N 54 35W
Gander L., Canada **71 C9** 48 58N 54 35W
Ganderowe Falls, Zimbabwe **55 F2** 17 20S 29 10 E
Gandhi Sagar, India **42 G6** 24 40N 75 40 E
Gandhinagar, India **42 H5** 23 15N 72 45 E
Gandía, Spain **19 C5** 38 58N 0 9W
Gando, Pta., Canary Is. **22 G4** 27 55N 15 22W
Ganedidalem = Gani, Indonesia **37 E7** 0 48S 128 14 E
Ganga →, India **43 H14** 23 20N 90 30 E
Ganga Sagar, India **43 J13** 21 38N 88 5 E
Gangan →, India **43 E8** 28 38N 78 58 E
Ganganagar, India **42 E5** 29 56N 73 56 E
Gangapur, India **42 F7** 26 32N 76 49 E
Gangaw, Burma **41 H19** 22 5N 94 5 E
Gangdisê Shan, China **41 D12** 31 20N 81 0 E
Ganges = Ganga →, India **43 H14** 23 20N 90 30 E
Ganges, Canada **72 D4** 48 51N 123 31W
Ganges, Mouths of the, India **43 J14** 21 30N 90 0 E
Gangoh, India **42 E7** 29 46N 77 18 E
Gangroti, India **43 D8** 30 50N 79 10 E
Gangtok, India **41 F16** 27 20N 88 37 E
Gangu, China **34 G3** 34 40N 105 15 E
Gangyao, China **35 B14** 44 12N 126 37 E
Gani, Indonesia **37 E7** 0 48S 128 14 E
Ganj, India **43 F8** 27 45N 78 57 E
Gannett Peak, U.S.A. **82 E9** 43 11N 109 39W
Ganquan, China **34 F5** 36 20N 109 20 E
Gansu □, China **34 G3** 36 0N 104 0 E
Ganta, Liberia **50 G4** 7 15N 8 59W
Gantheaume B., Australia **61 E1** 27 40S 114 10 E
Gantsevichi = Hantsavichy, Belarus **17 B14** 52 49N 26 30 E
Ganyem = Genyem, Indonesia **37 E10** 2 46S 140 12 E
Ganyu, China **35 G10** 34 50N 119 8 E
Ganzhou, China **33 D6** 25 51N 114 56 E
Gao, Mali **50 E5** 16 15N 0 5W
Gaomi, China **35 F10** 36 20N 119 42 E
Gaoping, China **34 G7** 35 45N 112 55 E
Gaotang, China **34 F9** 36 50N 116 15 E
Gaoua, Burkina Faso **50 F5** 10 20N 3 8W
Gaoual, Guinea **50 F3** 11 45N 13 25W
Gaoxiong = Kaohsiung, Taiwan **33 D7** 22 35N 120 16 E
Gaoyang, China **34 E8** 38 40N 115 45 E
Gaoyou Hu, China **35 H10** 32 45N 119 20 E
Gaoyuan, China **35 F9** 37 8N 117 58 E
Gap, France **18 D7** 44 33N 6 5 E
Gapat →, India **43 G10** 24 30N 82 28 E
Gapuwiyak, Australia **62 A2** 12 25S 135 43 E
Gar, China **32 C2** 32 10N 79 58 E
Garabogazköl Aylagy, Turkmenistan **25 F9** 41 0N 53 30 E
Garachico, Canary Is. **22 F3** 28 22N 16 46W
Garachiné, Panama **88 E4** 8 0N 78 12W
Garafia, Canary Is. **22 F2** 28 48N 17 57W
Garah, Australia **63 D4** 29 5S 149 38 E
Garajonay, Canary Is. **22 F2** 28 7N 17 14W
Garanhuns, Brazil **93 E11** 8 50S 36 30W
Garautha, India **43 G8** 25 34N 79 18 E
Garba Tula, Kenya **54 B4** 0 30N 38 32 E
Garberville, U.S.A. **82 F2** 40 6N 123 48W
Garbiyang, India **43 D9** 30 8N 80 54 E
Garda, L. di, Italy **20 B4** 45 40N 10 41 E
Garde L., Canada **73 A7** 62 50N 106 13W
Garden City, Ga., U.S.A. **77 J5** 32 6N 81 9W
Garden City, Kans., U.S.A. **81 G4** 37 58N 100 53W
Garden City, Tex., U.S.A. **81 K4** 31 52N 101 29W
Garden Grove, U.S.A. **85 M9** 33 47N 117 55W
Gardēz, Afghan. **42 C3** 33 37N 69 9 E
Gardiner, Maine, U.S.A. **77 C11** 44 14N 69 47W
Gardiner, Mont., U.S.A. **82 D8** 45 2N 110 22W
Gardiners I., U.S.A. **79 E12** 41 6N 72 6W
Gardner, U.S.A. **79 D13** 42 34N 71 59W
Gardner Canal, Canada **72 C3** 53 27N 128 8W
Gardnerville, U.S.A. **84 G7** 38 56N 119 45W
Gardo, Somali Rep. **46 F4** 9 30N 49 6 E
Garey, U.S.A. **85 L6** 34 53N 120 19W
Garfield, U.S.A. **82 C5** 47 1N 117 9W
Garforth, U.K. **10 D6** 53 47N 1 24W
Gargano, Mte., Italy **20 D6** 41 43N 15 43 E
Garibaldi Prov. Park, Canada **72 D4** 49 50N 122 40W
Gariep, L., S. Africa **56 E4** 30 40S 25 40 E
Garies, S. Africa **56 E2** 30 32S 17 59 E
Garigliano →, Italy **20 D5** 41 13N 13 45 E
Garissa, Kenya **54 C4** 0 25S 39 40 E
Garland, Tex., U.S.A. **81 J6** 32 55N 96 38W
Garland, Utah, U.S.A. **82 F7** 41 47N 112 10W
Garm, Tajikistan **26 F8** 39 0N 70 20 E
Garmāb, Iran **45 C8** 35 25N 56 45 E
Garmisch-Partenkirchen, Germany **16 E6** 47 30N 11 6 E
Garmo, Qullai = Kommunizma, Pik, Tajikistan **26 F8** 39 0N 72 2 E
Garmsār, Iran **45 C7** 35 20N 52 25 E
Garner, U.S.A. **80 D8** 43 6N 93 36W
Garnett, U.S.A. **80 F7** 38 17N 95 14W
Garo Hills, India **43 G14** 25 30N 90 30 E
Garoe, Somali Rep. **46 F4** 8 25N 48 33 E
Garonne →, France **18 D3** 45 2N 0 36W
Garot, India **42 G6** 24 19N 75 41 E
Garoua, Cameroon **51 G8** 9 19N 13 21 E
Garrauli, India **43 G8** 25 5N 79 22 E
Garrison, Mont., U.S.A. **82 C7** 46 31N 112 49W
Garrison, N. Dak., U.S.A. **80 B4** 47 40N 101 25W
Garrison Res. = Sakakawea, L., U.S.A. **80 B4** 47 30N 101 25W
Garron Pt., U.K. **13 A6** 55 3N 5 59W
Garry →, U.K. **12 E5** 56 44N 3 47W
Garry, L., Canada **68 B9** 65 58N 100 18W
Garsen, Kenya **54 C5** 2 20S 40 5 E
Garson L., Canada **73 B6** 56 19N 110 2W
Garu, India **43 H11** 23 40N 84 14 E
Garub, Namibia **56 D2** 26 37S 16 0 E
Garut, Indonesia **37 G12** 7 14S 107 53 E
Garvie Mts., N.Z. **59 L2** 45 30S 168 50 E
Garwa = Garoua, Cameroon **51 G8** 9 19N 13 21 E
Garwa, India **43 G10** 24 11N 83 47 E
Gary, U.S.A. **76 E2** 41 36N 87 20W
Garzê, China **32 C5** 31 38N 100 1 E
Garzón, Colombia **92 C3** 2 10N 75 40W
Gas-San, Japan **30 E10** 38 32N 140 1 E
Gasan Kuli = Esenguly, Turkmenistan **26 F6** 37 37N 53 59 E
Gascogne, France **18 E4** 43 45N 0 20 E
Gascogne, G. de, Europe **18 D2** 44 0N 2 0W
Gascony = Gascogne, France **18 E4** 43 45N 0 20 E
Gascoyne →, Australia **61 D1** 24 52S 113 37 E
Gascoyne Junction, Australia **61 E2** 25 2S 115 17 E
Gashaka, Nigeria **51 G8** 7 20N 11 29 E
Gasherbrum, Pakistan **43 B7** 35 40N 76 40 E
Gashua, Nigeria **51 F8** 12 54N 11 0 E
Gaspé, Canada **71 C7** 48 52N 64 30W
Gaspé, C. de, Canada **71 C7** 48 48N 64 7W
Gaspé, Pén. de, Canada **71 C6** 48 45N 65 40W
Gaspésie, Parc de Conservation de la, Canada **71 C6** 48 55N 65 50W
Gasteiz = Vitoria-Gasteiz, Spain **19 A4** 42 50N 2 41W
Gastonia, U.S.A. **77 H5** 35 16N 81 11W
Gastre, Argentina **96 E3** 42 20S 69 15W
Gata, C., Cyprus **23 E12** 34 34N 33 2 E
Gata, C. de, Spain **19 D4** 36 41N 2 13W
Gata, Sierra de, Spain **19 B2** 40 20N 6 45W
Gataga →, Canada **72 B3** 58 35N 126 59W
Gatehouse of Fleet, U.K. **12 G4** 54 53N 4 12W
Gates, U.S.A. **78 C7** 43 9N 77 42W
Gateshead, U.K. **10 C6** 54 57N 1 35W
Gatesville, U.S.A. **81 K6** 31 26N 97 45W
Gaths, Zimbabwe **55 G3** 20 2S 30 32 E
Gatico, Chile **94 A1** 22 29S 70 20W
Gatineau, Canada **79 A9** 45 29N 75 38W
Gatineau →, Canada **70 C4** 45 27N 75 42W
Gatineau, Parc Nat. de la, Canada **70 C4** 45 40N 76 0W
Gatton, Australia **63 D5** 27 32S 152 17 E
Gatun, L., Panama **88 E4** 9 7N 79 56W
Gatyana, S. Africa **57 E4** 32 16S 28 31 E
Gau, Fiji **59 D8** 18 2S 179 18 E
Gauer L., Canada **73 B9** 57 0N 97 50W
Gauhati, India **41 F17** 26 10N 91 45 E
Gauja →, Latvia **9 H21** 57 10N 24 16 E
Gaula →, Norway **8 E14** 63 21N 10 14 E

Greymouth

Gomal Pass, Pakistan 42 D3 31 56N 69 20 E
Gomati →, India 43 G10 25 32N 83 11 E
Gombari, Dem. Rep. of the Congo 54 B2 2 45N 29 3 E
Gombe, Nigeria 51 F8 10 19N 11 2 E
Gombe →, Tanzania 54 C3 4 38S 31 40 E
Gomel = Homyel, Belarus 17 B16 52 28N 31 0 E
Gomera, Canary Is. 22 F2 28 7N 17 14W
Gómez Palacio, Mexico 86 B4 25 40N 104 0W
Gomīshān, Iran 45 B7 37 4N 54 6 E
Gomogomo, Indonesia 37 F8 6 39S 134 43 E
Gomoh, India 41 H15 23 52N 86 10 E
Gompa = Ganta, Liberia 50 G4 7 15N 8 59W
Gonābād, Iran 45 C8 34 15N 58 45 E
Gonaïves, Haiti 89 C5 19 20N 72 42W
Gonâve, G. de la, Haiti 89 C5 19 29N 72 42W
Gonâve, I. de la, Haiti 89 C5 18 45N 73 0W
Gonbad-e Kāvūs, Iran 45 B7 37 20N 55 25 E
Gonda, India 43 F9 27 9N 81 58 E
Gondal, India 42 J4 21 58N 70 52 E
Gonder, Ethiopia 46 E2 12 39N 37 30 E
Gondia, India 40 J12 21 23N 80 10 E
Gondola, Mozam. 55 F3 19 10S 33 37 E
Gönen, Turkey 21 D12 40 6N 27 39 E
Gonghe, China 32 C5 36 18N 100 32 E
Gongolgon, Australia 63 E4 30 21S 146 54 E
Gongzhuling, China 35 C13 43 30N 124 40 E
Gonzales, Calif., U.S.A. 84 J5 36 30N 121 26W
Gonzales, Tex., U.S.A. 81 L6 29 30N 97 27W
González Chaves, Argentina 94 D3 38 2S 60 5W
Good Hope, C. of, S. Africa 56 E2 34 24S 18 30 E
Gooderham, Canada 78 B6 44 54N 78 21W
Goodhouse, S. Africa 56 D2 28 57S 18 13 E
Gooding, U.S.A. 82 E6 42 56N 114 43W
Goodland, U.S.A. 80 F4 39 21N 101 43W
Goodlow, Canada 72 B4 56 20N 120 8W
Goodooga, Australia 63 D4 29 3S 147 28 E
Goodsprings, U.S.A. 85 K11 35 49N 115 27W
Goole, U.K. 10 D7 53 42N 0 53W
Goomalling, Australia 61 F2 31 15S 116 49 E
Goomeri, Australia 63 D5 26 12S 152 6 E
Goonda, Mozam. 55 F3 19 48S 33 57 E
Goondiwindi, Australia 63 D5 28 30S 150 21 E
Goongarrie, L., Australia 61 F3 30 3S 121 9 E
Goonyella, Australia 62 C4 21 47S 147 58 E
Goose →, Canada 71 B7 53 20N 60 35W
Goose Creek, U.S.A. 77 J5 32 59N 80 2W
Goose L., U.S.A. 82 F3 41 56N 120 26W
Gop, India 40 H6 22 5N 69 50 E
Gopalganj, India 43 F11 26 28N 84 30 E
Göppingen, Germany 16 D5 48 42N 9 39 E
Gorakhpur, India 43 F10 26 47N 83 23 E
Goražde, Bos.-H. 21 C8 43 38N 18 58 E
Gorda, U.S.A. 84 K5 35 53N 121 26W
Gorda, Pta., Canary Is. 22 F2 28 45N 18 0W
Gorda, Pta., Nic. 88 D3 14 20N 83 10W
Gordan B., Australia 60 B5 11 35S 130 10 E
Gordon, U.S.A. 80 D3 42 48N 102 12W
Gordon →, Australia 62 G4 42 27S 145 30 E
Gordon L., Alta., Canada 73 B6 56 30N 110 25W
Gordon L., N.W.T., Canada 72 A6 63 5N 113 11W
Gordonvale, Australia 62 B4 17 5S 145 50 E
Gore, Ethiopia 46 F2 8 12N 35 32 E
Gore, N.Z. 59 M2 46 5S 168 58 E
Gore Bay, Canada 70 C3 45 57N 82 28W
Gorey, Ireland 13 D5 52 41N 6 18W
Gorg, Iran 45 D8 29 29N 59 43 E
Gorgān, Iran 45 B7 36 50N 54 29 E
Gorgona, I., Colombia 92 C3 3 0N 78 10W
Gorham, U.S.A. 79 B13 44 23N 71 10W
Goriganga →, India 43 E9 29 45N 80 23 E
Gorinchem, Neths. 15 C4 51 50N 4 59 E
Goris, Armenia 25 G8 39 31N 46 22 E
Gorízia, Italy 20 B5 45 56N 13 37 E
Gorki = Nizhniy Novgorod, Russia 24 C7 56 20N 44 0 E
Gorkiy = Nizhniy Novgorod, Russia 24 C7 56 20N 44 0 E
Gorkovskoye Vdkhr., Russia 24 C7 57 2N 43 4 E
Görlitz, Germany 16 C8 51 9N 14 58 E
Gorlovka = Horlivka, Ukraine 25 E6 48 19N 38 5 E
Gorman, U.S.A. 85 L8 34 47N 118 51W
Gorna Dzhumayo = Blagoevgrad, Bulgaria 21 C10 42 2N 23 5 E
Gorna Oryakhovitsa, Bulgaria 21 C11 43 7N 25 40 E
Gorno-Altay □, Russia 26 D9 51 0N 86 0 E
Gorno-Altaysk, Russia 26 D9 51 50N 86 5 E
Gornyatski, Russia 24 A11 67 32N 64 3 E
Gornyy, Russia 30 B6 44 57N 133 59 E
Gorodenka = Horodenka, Ukraine 17 D13 48 41N 25 29 E
Gorodok = Horodok, Ukraine 17 D12 49 46N 23 32 E
Gorokhov = Horokhiv, Ukraine 17 C13 50 30N 24 45 E
Goromonzi, Zimbabwe 55 F3 17 52S 31 22 E
Gorong, Kepulauan, Indonesia 37 E8 3 59S 131 25 E
Gorongose →, Mozam. 57 C5 20 30S 34 40 E
Gorongoza, Mozam. 55 F3 18 44S 34 2 E
Gorongoza, Sa. da, Mozam. 55 F3 18 27S 34 2 E
Gorontalo, Indonesia 37 D6 0 35N 123 5 E
Gort, Ireland 13 C3 53 3N 8 49W
Gortis, Greece 23 D6 35 4N 24 58 E
Gorzów Wielkopolski, Poland 16 B8 52 43N 15 15 E
Goshen, Calif., U.S.A. 84 J7 36 21N 119 25W
Goshen, Ind., U.S.A. 76 E3 41 35N 85 50W
Goshen, N.Y., U.S.A. 79 E10 41 24N 74 20W
Goshogawara, Japan 30 D10 40 48N 140 27 E
Goslar, Germany 16 C6 51 54N 10 25 E
Gospič, Croatia 16 F8 44 35N 15 23 E
Gosport, U.K. 11 G6 50 48N 1 9W
Gosse →, Australia 62 B1 19 32S 134 37 E
Göta älv →, Sweden 9 H14 57 42N 11 54 E
Göta kanal, Sweden 9 G16 58 30N 15 58 E
Götaland, Sweden 9 G15 57 30N 14 30 E
Göteborg, Sweden 9 H14 57 43N 11 59 E
Gotha, Germany 16 C6 50 56N 10 42 E
Gothenburg = Göteborg, Sweden 9 H14 57 43N 11 59 E
Gothenburg, U.S.A. 80 E4 40 56N 100 10W
Gotland, Sweden 9 H18 57 30N 18 33 E
Gotō-Rettō, Japan 31 H4 32 55N 129 5 E
Gotska Sandön, Sweden 9 G18 58 24N 19 15 E
Gōtsu, Japan 31 G6 35 0N 132 14 E
Gott Pk., Canada 72 C4 50 18N 122 16W
Göttingen, Germany 16 C5 51 31N 9 55 E
Gottwaldov = Zlín, Czech Rep. 17 D9 49 14N 17 40 E
Goubangzi, China 35 D11 41 20N 121 52 E
Gouda, Neths. 15 B4 52 1N 4 42 E
Goúdhoura, Ákra, Greece 23 E8 34 59N 26 6 E
Gough I., Atl. Oc. 2 G9 40 10S 9 45W
Gouin, Rés., Canada 70 C5 48 35N 74 40W
Goulburn Is., Australia 62 A1 11 40S 133 20 E
Goulimine, Morocco 50 C3 28 56N 10 0W
Gourits →, S. Africa 56 E3 34 21S 21 52 E
Goúrnais, Greece 23 D7 35 19N 25 16 E
Gouverneur, U.S.A. 79 B9 44 20N 75 28W
Gouviá, Greece 23 A3 39 39N 19 50 E
Governador Valadares, Brazil 93 G10 18 15S 41 57W
Governor's Harbour, Bahamas 88 A4 25 10N 76 14W
Govindgarh, India 43 G9 24 23N 81 18 E
Gowan Ra., Australia 62 D4 25 0S 145 0 E
Gowanda, U.S.A. 78 D6 42 28N 78 56W
Gower, U.K. 11 F3 51 35N 4 10W
Gowna, L., Ireland 13 C4 53 51N 7 34W
Goya, Argentina 94 B4 29 10S 59 10W
Goyder Lagoon, Australia 63 D2 27 3S 138 58 E
Goyllarisquisga, Peru 92 F3 10 31S 76 24W
Goz Beïda, Chad 51 F10 12 10N 21 20 E
Gozo, Malta 23 C1 36 3N 14 13 E
Graaff-Reinet, S. Africa 56 E3 32 13S 24 32 E
Gračac, Croatia 16 F8 44 18N 15 57 E
Gracias a Dios, C., Honduras 88 D3 15 0N 83 10W
Graciosa, I., Canary Is. 22 E6 29 15N 13 32W
Grado, Spain 19 A2 43 23N 6 4W
Grady, U.S.A. 81 H3 34 49N 103 19W
Grafham Water, U.K. 11 E7 52 19N 0 18W
Grafton, Australia 63 D5 29 38S 152 58 E
Grafton, N. Dak., U.S.A. 80 A6 48 25N 97 25W
Grafton, W. Va., U.S.A. 76 F5 39 21N 80 2W
Graham, Canada 70 C1 49 20N 90 30W
Graham, U.S.A. 81 J5 33 6N 98 35W
Graham, Mt., U.S.A. 83 K9 32 42N 109 52W
Graham Bell, Ostrov = Greem-Bell, Ostrov, Russia 26 A7 81 0N 62 0 E
Graham I., Canada 72 C2 53 40N 132 30W
Graham Land, Antarctica 5 C17 65 0S 64 0W
Grahamstown, S. Africa 56 E4 33 19S 26 31 E
Grahamsville, U.S.A. 79 E10 41 51N 74 33W
Grain Coast, W. Afr. 50 H3 4 20N 10 0W
Grajaú, Brazil 93 E9 5 50S 46 4W
Grajaú →, Brazil 93 D10 3 41S 44 48W
Grampian, U.S.A. 78 F6 40 58N 78 37W
Grampian Highlands = Grampian Mts., U.K. 12 E5 56 50N 4 0W
Grampian Mts., U.K. 12 E5 56 50N 4 0W
Gran Canaria, Canary Is. 22 G4 27 55N 15 35W
Gran Chaco, S. Amer. 94 B3 25 0S 61 0W
Gran Paradiso, Italy 18 D7 45 33N 7 17 E
Gran Sasso d'Itália, Italy 20 C5 42 27N 13 42 E
Granada, Nic. 88 D2 11 58N 86 0W
Granada, Spain 19 D4 37 10N 3 35W
Granada, U.S.A. 81 F3 38 4N 102 19W
Granadilla de Abona, Canary Is. 22 F3 28 7N 16 33W
Granard, Ireland 13 C4 53 47N 7 30W
Granbury, U.S.A. 81 J6 32 27N 97 47W
Granby, Canada 79 A12 45 25N 72 45W
Granby, U.S.A. 82 F11 40 5N 105 56W
Grand →, Canada 78 D5 42 51N 79 34W
Grand →, Mo., U.S.A. 80 F8 39 23N 93 7W
Grand →, S. Dak., U.S.A. 80 C4 45 40N 100 45W
Grand Bahama, Bahamas 88 A4 26 40N 78 30W
Grand Bank, Canada 71 C8 47 6N 55 48W
Grand Bassam, Ivory C. 50 G5 5 10N 3 49W
Grand-Bourg, Guadeloupe 89 C7 15 53N 61 19W
Grand Canal = Yun Ho →, China 35 E9 39 10N 117 10 E
Grand Canyon, U.S.A. 83 H7 36 3N 112 9W
Grand Canyon National Park, U.S.A. 83 H7 36 15N 112 30W
Grand Cayman, Cayman Is. 88 C3 19 20N 81 20W
Grand Centre, Canada 73 C6 54 25N 110 13W
Grand Coulee, U.S.A. 82 C4 47 57N 119 0W
Grand Coulee Dam, U.S.A. 82 C4 47 57N 118 59W
Grand Erg Occidental, Algeria 50 B6 30 20N 1 0 E
Grand Erg Oriental, Algeria 50 B7 30 0N 6 30 E
Grand Falls, Canada 71 C6 47 3N 67 44W
Grand Falls-Windsor, Canada 71 C8 48 56N 55 40W
Grand Forks, Canada 72 D5 49 0N 118 30W
Grand Forks, U.S.A. 80 B6 47 55N 97 3W
Grand Gorge, U.S.A. 79 D10 42 21N 74 29W
Grand Haven, U.S.A. 76 D2 43 4N 86 13W
Grand I., Mich., U.S.A. 76 B2 46 31N 86 40W
Grand I., N.Y., U.S.A. 78 D6 43 0N 78 58W
Grand Island, U.S.A. 80 E5 40 55N 98 21W
Grand Isle, La., U.S.A. 81 L9 29 14N 90 0W
Grand Isle, Vt., U.S.A. 79 B11 44 43N 73 18W
Grand Junction, U.S.A. 83 G9 39 4N 108 33W
Grand L., N.B., Canada 71 C6 45 57N 66 7W
Grand L., Nfld., Canada 71 C8 49 0N 57 30W
Grand L., Nfld., Canada 71 B7 53 40N 60 30W
Grand L., U.S.A. 81 L8 29 55N 92 47W
Grand Lake, U.S.A. 82 F11 40 15N 105 49W
Grand Manan I., Canada 71 D6 44 45N 66 52W
Grand Marais, Canada 80 B9 47 45N 90 25W
Grand Marais, U.S.A. 76 B3 46 40N 85 59W
Grand-Mère, Canada 70 C5 46 36N 72 40W
Grand Portage, U.S.A. 80 B10 47 58N 89 41W
Grand Prairie, U.S.A. 81 J6 32 47N 97 0W
Grand Rapids, Canada 73 C9 53 12N 99 19W
Grand Rapids, Mich., U.S.A. 76 D2 42 58N 85 40W
Grand Rapids, Minn., U.S.A. 80 B8 47 14N 93 31W
Grand St-Bernard, Col du, Europe 18 D7 45 50N 7 10 E
Grand Teton, U.S.A. 82 E8 43 54N 111 50W
Grand Teton National Park, U.S.A. 82 D8 43 50N 110 50W
Grand Union Canal, U.K. 11 E7 52 7N 0 53W
Grand View, Canada 73 C8 51 10N 100 42W
Grande →, Jujuy, Argentina 94 A2 24 20S 65 2W
Grande →, Mendoza, Argentina 94 D2 36 52S 69 45W
Grande →, Bolivia 92 G6 15 51S 64 39W
Grande →, Bahia, Brazil 93 F10 11 30S 44 30W
Grande →, Minas Gerais, Brazil 93 H8 20 6S 51 4W
Grande, B., Argentina 96 G3 50 30S 68 20W
Grande, Rio →, U.S.A. 81 N6 25 58N 97 9W
Grande Baleine, R. de la →, Canada 70 A4 55 16N 77 47W
Grande Cache, Canada 72 C5 53 53N 119 8W
Grande-Entrée, Canada 71 C7 47 30N 61 40W
Grande Prairie, Canada 72 B5 55 10N 118 50W
Grande-Rivière, Canada 71 C7 48 26N 64 30W
Grande-Vallée, Canada 71 C6 49 14N 65 8W
Grandfalls, U.S.A. 81 K3 31 20N 102 51W
Grandview, U.S.A. 82 C4 46 15N 119 54W
Graneros, Chile 94 C1 34 5S 70 45W
Grangemouth, U.K. 12 E5 56 1N 3 42W
Granger, U.S.A. 82 F9 41 35N 109 58W
Grangeville, U.S.A. 82 D5 45 56N 116 7W
Granisle, Canada 72 C3 54 53N 126 13W
Granite City, U.S.A. 80 F9 38 42N 90 9W
Granite Falls, U.S.A. 80 C7 44 49N 95 33W
Granite L., Canada 71 C8 48 8N 57 5W
Granite Mt., U.S.A. 85 M10 33 5N 116 28W
Granite Pk., U.S.A. 82 D9 45 10N 109 48W
Graniteville, U.S.A. 79 B12 44 8N 72 29W
Granity, N.Z. 59 J3 41 39S 171 51 E
Granja, Brazil 93 D10 3 7S 40 50W
Granollers, Spain 19 B7 41 39N 2 18 E
Grant, U.S.A. 80 E4 40 53N 101 42W
Grant, Mt., U.S.A. 82 G4 38 34N 118 48W
Grant City, U.S.A. 80 E7 40 29N 94 25W
Grant I., Australia 60 B5 11 10S 132 52 E
Grant Range, U.S.A. 83 G6 38 30N 115 25W
Grantham, U.K. 10 E7 52 55N 0 38W
Grantown-on-Spey, U.K. 12 D5 57 20N 3 36W
Grants, U.S.A. 83 J10 35 9N 107 52W
Grants Pass, U.S.A. 82 E2 42 26N 123 19W
Grantsville, U.S.A. 82 F7 40 36N 112 28W
Granville, France 18 B3 48 50N 1 35W
Granville, N. Dak., U.S.A. 80 A4 48 16N 100 47W
Granville, N.Y., U.S.A. 79 C11 43 24N 73 16W
Granville, Ohio, U.S.A. 78 F2 40 4N 82 31W
Granville L., Canada 73 B8 56 18N 100 30W
Graskop, S. Africa 57 C5 24 56S 30 49 E
Grass →, Canada 73 B9 56 3N 96 33W
Grass Range, U.S.A. 82 C9 47 0N 109 0W
Grass River Prov. Park, Canada 73 C8 54 40N 100 50W
Grass Valley, Calif., U.S.A. 84 F6 39 13N 121 4W
Grass Valley, Oreg., U.S.A. 82 D3 45 22N 120 47W
Grasse, France 18 E7 43 38N 6 56 E
Grassflat, U.S.A. 78 F6 41 0N 78 6W
Grasslands Nat. Park, Canada 73 D7 49 11N 107 38W
Grassy, Australia 62 G3 40 3S 144 5 E
Graulhet, France 18 E4 43 45N 1 59 E
Gravelbourg, Canada 73 D7 49 50N 106 35W
's-Gravenhage, Neths. 15 B4 52 7N 4 17 E
Gravenhurst, Canada 78 B5 44 52N 79 20W
Gravesend, Australia 63 D5 29 35S 150 20 E
Gravesend, U.K. 11 F8 51 26N 0 22 E
Gravois, Pointe-à-, Haiti 89 C5 18 15N 73 56W
Grayling, U.S.A. 76 C3 44 40N 84 43W
Grays Harbor, U.S.A. 82 C1 46 59N 124 1W
Grays L., U.S.A. 82 E8 43 4N 111 26W
Grays River, U.S.A. 84 D3 46 21N 123 37W
Graz, Austria 16 E8 47 4N 15 27 E
Greasy L., Canada 72 A4 62 55N 122 12W
Great Abaco I., Bahamas 88 A4 26 25N 77 10W
Great Artesian Basin, Australia 62 C3 23 0S 144 0 E
Great Australian Bight, Australia 61 F5 33 30S 130 0 E
Great Bahama Bank, Bahamas 88 B4 23 15N 78 0W
Great Barrier I., N.Z. 59 G5 36 11S 175 25 E
Great Barrier Reef, Australia 62 B4 18 0S 146 50 E
Great Barrington, U.S.A. 79 D11 42 12N 73 22W
Great Basin, U.S.A. 82 G5 40 0N 117 0W
Great Basin Nat. Park, U.S.A. 82 G6 38 55N 114 14W
Great Bear →, Canada 68 B7 65 0N 124 0W
Great Bear L., Canada 68 B7 65 30N 120 0W
Great Belt = Store Bælt, Denmark 9 J14 55 20N 11 0 E
Great Bend, Kans., U.S.A. 80 F5 38 22N 98 46W
Great Bend, Pa., U.S.A. 79 E9 41 58N 75 45W
Great Blasket I., Ireland 13 D1 52 6N 10 32W
Great Britain, Europe 6 E5 54 0N 2 15W
Great Codroy, Canada 71 C8 47 51N 59 16W
Great Dividing Ra., Australia 62 C4 23 0S 146 0 E
Great Driffield = Driffield, U.K. 10 C7 54 0N 0 26W
Great Exuma I., Bahamas 88 B4 23 30N 75 50W
Great Falls, U.S.A. 82 C8 47 30N 111 17W
Great Fish = Groot Vis →, S. Africa 56 E4 33 28S 27 5 E
Great Guana Cay, Bahamas 88 B4 24 0N 76 20W
Great Inagua I., Bahamas 89 B5 21 0N 73 20W
Great Indian Desert = Thar Desert, India 42 F5 28 0N 72 0 E
Great Karoo, S. Africa 56 E3 31 55S 21 0 E
Great Lake, Australia 62 G4 41 50S 146 40 E
Great Lakes, N. Amer. 66 E11 46 0N 84 0W
Great Malvern, U.K. 11 E5 52 7N 2 18W
Great Miami →, U.S.A. 76 F3 39 20N 84 40W
Great Ormes Head, U.K. 10 D4 53 20N 3 52W
Great Ouse →, U.K. 10 E8 52 48N 0 21 E
Great Palm I., Australia 62 B4 18 45S 146 40 E
Great Plains, N. Amer. 74 A6 47 0N 105 0W
Great Ruaha →, Tanzania 54 D4 7 56S 37 52 E
Great Sacandaga Res., U.S.A. 79 C10 43 6N 74 16W
Great Saint Bernard Pass = Grand St-Bernard, Col du, Europe 18 D7 45 50N 7 10 E
Great Salt L., U.S.A. 82 F7 41 15N 112 40W
Great Salt Lake Desert, U.S.A. 82 F7 40 50N 113 30W
Great Salt Plains L., U.S.A. 81 G5 36 45N 98 8W
Great Sandy Desert, Australia 60 D3 21 0S 124 0 E
Great Sangi = Sangihe, Pulau, Indonesia 37 D7 3 35N 125 30 E
Great Skellig, Ireland 13 E1 51 47N 10 33W
Great Slave L., Canada 72 A5 61 23N 115 38W
Great Smoky Mts. Nat. Park, U.S.A. 77 H4 35 40N 83 40W
Great Snow Mt., Canada 72 B4 57 26N 124 0W
Great Stour = Stour →, U.K. 11 F9 51 18N 1 22 E
Great Victoria Desert, Australia 61 E4 29 30S 126 30 E
Great Wall, China 34 E5 38 30N 109 30 E
Great Whernside, U.K. 10 C6 54 10N 1 58W
Great Yarmouth, U.K. 11 E9 52 37N 1 44 E
Greater Antilles, W. Indies 89 C5 17 40N 74 0W
Greater London □, U.K. 11 F7 51 31N 0 6W
Greater Manchester □, U.K. 10 D5 53 30N 2 15W
Greater Sunda Is., Indonesia 36 F4 7 0S 112 0 E
Greco, C., Cyprus 23 E13 34 57N 34 5 E
Gredos, Sierra de, Spain 19 B3 40 20N 5 0W
Greece, U.S.A. 78 C7 43 13N 77 41W
Greece ■, Europe 21 E9 40 0N 23 0 E
Greeley, Colo., U.S.A. 80 E2 40 25N 104 42W
Greeley, Nebr., U.S.A. 80 E5 41 33N 98 32W
Greem-Bell, Ostrov, Russia 26 A7 81 0N 62 0 E
Green, U.S.A. 82 E2 43 9N 123 22W
Green →, Ky., U.S.A. 76 G2 37 54N 87 30W
Green →, Utah, U.S.A. 83 G9 38 11N 109 53W
Green B., U.S.A. 76 C2 45 0N 87 30W
Green Bay, U.S.A. 76 C2 44 31N 88 0W
Green Cove Springs, U.S.A. 77 L5 29 59N 81 42W
Green Lake, Canada 73 C7 54 17N 107 47W
Green Mts., U.S.A. 79 C12 43 45N 72 45W
Green River, Utah, U.S.A. 83 G8 38 59N 110 10W
Green River, Wyo., U.S.A. 82 F9 41 32N 109 28W
Green Valley, U.S.A. 83 L8 31 52N 110 56W
Greenbank, U.S.A. 84 B4 48 6N 122 34W
Greenbush, Mich., U.S.A. 78 B1 44 35N 83 19W
Greenbush, Minn., U.S.A. 80 A6 48 42N 96 11W
Greencastle, U.S.A. 76 F2 39 38N 86 52W
Greene, U.S.A. 79 D9 42 20N 75 46W
Greenfield, Calif., U.S.A. 84 J5 36 19N 121 15W
Greenfield, Calif., U.S.A. 85 K8 35 15N 119 0W
Greenfield, Ind., U.S.A. 76 F3 39 47N 85 46W
Greenfield, Iowa, U.S.A. 80 E7 41 18N 94 28W
Greenfield, Mass., U.S.A. 79 D12 42 35N 72 36W
Greenfield, Mo., U.S.A. 81 G8 37 25N 93 51W
Greenfield Park, Canada 79 A11 45 29N 73 29W
Greenland ■, N. Amer. 4 C5 66 0N 45 0W
Greenland Sea, Arctic 4 B7 73 0N 10 0W
Greenock, U.K. 12 F4 55 57N 4 46W
Greenore, Ireland 13 B5 54 2N 6 8W
Greenore Pt., Ireland 13 D5 52 14N 6 19W
Greenough, Australia 61 E1 28 58S 114 43 E
Greenough →, Australia 61 E1 28 51S 114 38 E
Greenough Pt., Canada 78 B3 44 58N 81 26W
Greenport, U.S.A. 79 E12 41 6N 72 22W
Greensboro, Ga., U.S.A. 77 J4 33 35N 83 11W
Greensboro, N.C., U.S.A. 77 G6 36 4N 79 48W
Greensboro, Vt., U.S.A. 79 B12 44 36N 72 18W
Greensburg, Ind., U.S.A. 76 F3 39 20N 85 29W
Greensburg, Kans., U.S.A. 81 G5 37 36N 99 18W
Greensburg, Pa., U.S.A. 78 F5 40 18N 79 33W
Greenstone Pt., U.K. 12 D3 57 55N 5 37W
Greenvale, Australia 62 B4 18 59S 145 7 E
Greenville, Ala., U.S.A. 77 K2 31 50N 86 38W
Greenville, Calif., U.S.A. 84 E6 40 8N 120 57W
Greenville, Maine, U.S.A. 77 C11 45 28N 69 35W
Greenville, Mich., U.S.A. 76 D3 43 11N 85 15W
Greenville, Miss., U.S.A. 81 J9 33 24N 91 4W
Greenville, Mo., U.S.A. 81 G9 37 8N 90 27W
Greenville, N.C., U.S.A. 77 H7 35 37N 77 23W
Greenville, N.H., U.S.A. 79 D13 42 46N 71 49W
Greenville, N.Y., U.S.A. 79 D10 42 25N 74 1W
Greenville, Ohio, U.S.A. 76 E3 40 6N 84 38W
Greenville, Pa., U.S.A. 78 E4 41 24N 80 23W
Greenville, S.C., U.S.A. 77 H4 34 51N 82 24W
Greenville, Tenn., U.S.A. 77 G4 36 13N 82 51W
Greenville, Tex., U.S.A. 81 J6 33 8N 96 7W
Greenwater Lake Prov. Park, Canada 73 C8 52 32N 103 30W
Greenwich, Conn., U.S.A. 79 E11 41 2N 73 38W
Greenwich, N.Y., U.S.A. 79 C11 43 5N 73 30W
Greenwich, Ohio, U.S.A. 78 E2 41 2N 82 31W
Greenwich □, U.K. 11 F8 51 29N 0 1 E
Greenwood, Canada 72 D5 49 10N 118 40W
Greenwood, Ark., U.S.A. 81 H7 35 13N 94 16W
Greenwood, Ind., U.S.A. 76 F2 39 37N 86 7W
Greenwood, Miss., U.S.A. 81 J9 33 31N 90 11W
Greenwood, S.C., U.S.A. 77 H4 34 12N 82 10W
Greenwood, Mt., Australia 60 B5 13 48S 130 4 E
Gregory, U.S.A. 80 D5 43 14N 99 20W
Gregory →, Australia 62 B2 17 53S 139 17 E
Gregory, L., S. Austral., Australia 63 D2 28 55S 139 0 E
Gregory, L., W. Austral., Australia 61 E2 25 38S 119 58 E
Gregory Downs, Australia 62 B2 18 35S 138 45 E
Gregory L., Australia 60 D4 20 0S 127 40 E
Gregory Ra., Queens., Australia 62 B3 19 30S 143 40 E
Gregory Ra., W. Austral., Australia 60 D3 21 20S 121 12 E
Greifswald, Germany 16 A7 54 5N 13 23 E
Greiz, Germany 16 C7 50 39N 12 10 E
Gremikha, Russia 24 A6 67 59N 39 47 E
Grenå, Denmark 9 H14 56 25N 10 53 E
Grenada, U.S.A. 81 J10 33 47N 89 49W
Grenada ■, W. Indies 89 D7 12 10N 61 40W
Grenadier I., U.S.A. 79 B8 44 3N 76 22W
Grenadines, St. Vincent 89 D7 12 40N 61 20W
Grenen, Denmark 9 H14 57 44N 10 40 E
Grenfell, Canada 73 C8 50 30N 102 56W
Grenoble, France 18 D6 45 12N 5 42 E
Grenville, C., Australia 62 A3 12 0S 143 13 E
Grenville Chan., Canada 72 C3 53 40N 129 46W
Gresham, U.S.A. 84 E4 45 30N 122 26W
Gresik, Indonesia 37 G15 7 13S 112 38 E
Gretna, U.K. 12 F5 55 0N 3 3W
Grevenmacher, Lux. 15 E6 49 41N 6 26 E
Grey →, Canada 71 C8 47 34N 57 6W
Grey →, N.Z. 59 K3 42 27S 171 12 E
Grey, C., Australia 62 A2 13 0S 136 35 E
Grey Ra., Australia 63 D3 27 0S 143 30 E
Greybull, U.S.A. 82 D9 44 30N 108 3W
Greymouth, N.Z. 59 K3 42 29S 171 13 E

Greystones

Greystones, *Ireland* **13 C5** 53 9N 6 5W
Greytown, *N.Z.* **59 J5** 41 5S 175 29 E
Greytown, *S. Africa* **57 D5** 29 1S 30 36 E
Gribbell I., *Canada* **72 C3** 53 23N 129 0W
Gridley, *U.S.A.* **84 F5** 39 22N 121 42W
Griekwastad, *S. Africa* **56 D3** 28 49S 23 15 E
Griffin, *U.S.A.* **77 J3** 33 15N 84 16W
Griffith, *Canada* **78 A7** 45 15N 77 10W
Griffith I., *Canada* **78 B4** 44 50N 80 55W
Grimaylov = Hrymayliv, *Ukraine* **17 D14** 49 20N 26 5 E
Grimes, *U.S.A.* **84 F5** 39 4N 121 54W
Grimsay, *U.K.* **12 D1** 57 29N 7 14W
Grimsby, *Canada* **78 C5** 43 12N 79 34W
Grimsby, *U.K.* **10 D7** 53 34N 0 5W
Grímsey, *Iceland* **8 C5** 66 33N 17 58W
Grimshaw, *Canada* **72 B5** 56 10N 117 40W
Grimstad, *Norway* **9 G13** 58 20N 8 35 E
Grindstone I., *Canada* **79 B8** 44 43N 76 14W
Grinnell, *U.S.A.* **80 E8** 41 45N 92 43W
Gris-Nez, C., *France* **18 A4** 50 52N 1 35 E
Groais I., *Canada* **71 B8** 50 55N 55 35W
Groblersdal, *S. Africa* **57 D4** 25 15S 29 25 E
Grodno = Hrodna, *Belarus* **17 B12** 53 42N 23 52 E
Grodzyanka = Hrodzyanka, *Belarus* **17 B15** 53 31N 28 42 E
Groesbeck, *U.S.A.* **81 K6** 30 48N 96 31W
Grójec, *Poland* **17 C11** 51 50N 20 58 E
Grong, *Norway* **8 D15** 64 25N 12 8 E
Groningen, *Neths.* **15 A6** 53 15N 6 35 E
Groningen □, *Neths.* **15 A6** 53 16N 6 40 E
Groom, *U.S.A.* **81 H4** 35 12N 101 6W
Groot →, *S. Africa* **56 E3** 33 45S 24 36 E
Groot Berg →, *S. Africa* **56 E2** 32 47S 18 8 E
Groot-Brakrivier, *S. Africa* **56 E3** 34 2S 22 18 E
Groot Karasberge, *Namibia* **56 D2** 27 20S 18 40 E
Groot-Kei →, *S. Africa* **57 E4** 32 41S 28 22 E
Groot Vis →, *S. Africa* **56 E4** 33 28S 27 5 E
Grootdrink, *S. Africa* **56 D3** 28 33S 21 42 E
Groote Eylandt, *Australia* **62 A2** 14 0S 136 40 E
Grootfontein, *Namibia* **56 B2** 19 31S 18 6 E
Grootlaagte →, *Africa* **56 C3** 20 55S 21 27 E
Grootvloer →, *S. Africa* **56 E3** 30 0S 20 40 E
Gros C., *Canada* **72 A6** 61 59N 113 32W
Gros Morne Nat. Park, *Canada* **71 C8** 49 40N 57 50W
Grossa, Pta., *Spain* **22 B8** 39 6N 1 36 E
Grosser Arber, *Germany* **16 D7** 49 6N 13 8 E
Grosseto, *Italy* **20 C4** 42 46N 11 8 E
Grossglockner, *Austria* **16 E7** 47 5N 12 40 E
Groswater B., *Canada* **71 B8** 54 20N 57 40W
Groton, *Conn., U.S.A.* **79 E12** 41 21N 72 5W
Groton, *N.Y., U.S.A.* **79 D8** 42 36N 76 22W
Groton, *S. Dak., U.S.A.* **80 C5** 45 27N 98 6W
Grouard Mission, *Canada* **72 B5** 55 33N 116 9W
Groundhog →, *Canada* **70 C3** 48 45N 82 58W
Grouw, *Neths.* **15 A5** 53 5N 5 51 E
Grove City, *U.S.A.* **78 E4** 41 10N 80 5W
Grove Hill, *U.S.A.* **77 K2** 31 42N 87 47W
Groveland, *U.S.A.* **84 H6** 37 50N 120 14W
Grover City, *U.S.A.* **85 K6** 35 7N 120 37W
Groves, *U.S.A.* **81 L8** 29 57N 93 54W
Groveton, *U.S.A.* **79 B13** 44 36N 71 31W
Groznyy, *Russia* **25 F8** 43 20N 45 45 E
Grudziądz, *Poland* **17 B10** 53 30N 18 47 E
Gruinard B., *U.K.* **12 D3** 57 56N 5 35W
Grundy Center, *U.S.A.* **80 D8** 42 22N 92 47W
Gruver, *U.S.A.* **81 G4** 36 16N 101 24W
Gryazi, *Russia* **24 D6** 52 30N 39 58 E
Gryazovets, *Russia* **24 C7** 58 50N 40 10 E
Gua, *India* **41 H14** 22 18N 85 20 E
Gua Musang, *Malaysia* **39 K3** 4 53N 101 58 E
Guacanayabo, G. de, *Cuba* **88 B4** 20 40N 77 20W
Guachípas →, *Argentina* **94 B2** 25 40S 65 30W
Guadalajara, *Mexico* **86 C4** 20 40N 103 20W
Guadalajara, *Spain* **19 B4** 40 37N 3 12W
Guadalcanal, *Solomon Is.* **64 H8** 9 32S 160 12 E
Guadales, *Argentina* **94 C2** 34 30S 67 55W
Guadalete →, *Spain* **19 D2** 36 35N 6 13W
Guadalquivir →, *Spain* **19 D2** 36 47N 6 22W
Guadalupe = Guadeloupe ■, *W. Indies* **89 C7** 16 20N 61 40W
Guadalupe, *Mexico* **85 N10** 32 4N 116 32W
Guadalupe, *U.S.A.* **85 L6** 34 59N 120 33W
Guadalupe →, *Mexico* **85 N10** 32 6N 116 51W
Guadalupe →, *U.S.A.* **81 L6** 28 27N 96 47W
Guadalupe, Sierra de, *Spain* **19 C3** 39 28N 5 30W
Guadalupe Bravos, *Mexico* **86 A3** 31 20N 106 10W
Guadalupe I., *Pac. Oc.* **66 G8** 29 0N 118 50W
Guadalupe Mts. Nat. Park, *U.S.A.* **81 K2** 32 0N 104 30W
Guadalupe Peak, *U.S.A.* **81 K2** 31 50N 104 52W
Guadalupe y Calvo, *Mexico* **86 B3** 26 6N 106 58W
Guadarrama, Sierra de, *Spain* **19 B4** 41 0N 4 0W
Guadeloupe ■, *W. Indies* **89 C7** 16 20N 61 40W
Guadeloupe Passage, *W. Indies* **89 C7** 16 50N 62 15W
Guadiana →, *Portugal* **19 D2** 37 14N 7 22W
Guadix, *Spain* **19 D4** 37 18N 3 11W
Guafo, Boca del, *Chile* **96 E2** 43 35S 74 0W
Guainía →, *Colombia* **92 C5** 2 1N 67 7W
Guaíra, *Brazil* **95 A5** 24 5S 54 10W
Guaíra □, *Paraguay* **94 B4** 25 45S 56 30W
Guaitecas, Is., *Chile* **96 E2** 44 0S 74 30W
Guajará-Mirim, *Brazil* **92 F5** 10 50S 65 20W
Guajira, Pen. de la, *Colombia* **92 A4** 12 0N 72 0W
Gualán, *Guatemala* **88 C2** 15 8N 89 22W
Gualeguay, *Argentina* **94 C4** 33 10S 59 14W
Gualeguaychú, *Argentina* **94 C4** 33 3S 59 31W
Gualequay →, *Argentina* **94 C4** 33 19S 59 39W
Guam ■, *Pac. Oc.* **64 F6** 13 27N 144 45 E
Guaminí, *Argentina* **94 D3** 37 1S 62 28W
Guamúchil, *Mexico* **86 B3** 25 25N 108 3W
Guanabacoa, *Cuba* **88 B3** 23 8N 82 18W
Guanacaste, Cordillera del, *Costa Rica* **88 D2** 10 40N 85 4W
Guanaceví, *Mexico* **86 B3** 25 40N 106 0W
Guanahani = San Salvador I., *Bahamas* **89 B5** 24 0N 74 40W
Guanajay, *Cuba* **88 B3** 22 56N 82 42W
Guanajuato, *Mexico* **86 C4** 21 0N 101 20W
Guanajuato □, *Mexico* **86 C4** 20 40N 101 20W
Guandacol, *Argentina* **94 B2** 29 30S 68 40W
Guane, *Cuba* **88 B3** 22 10N 84 7W
Guangdong □, *China* **33 D6** 23 0N 113 0 E
Guangling, *China* **34 E8** 39 47N 114 22 E
Guangrao, *China* **35 F10** 37 5N 118 25 E
Guangwu, *China* **34 F3** 37 48N 105 57 E
Guangxi Zhuangzu Zizhiqu □, *China* **33 D5** 24 0N 109 0 E
Guangzhou, *China* **33 D6** 23 5N 113 10 E
Guanipa →, *Venezuela* **92 B6** 9 56N 62 26W
Guannan, *China* **35 G10** 34 8N 119 21 E
Guantánamo, *Cuba* **89 B4** 20 10N 75 14W
Guantao, *China* **34 F8** 36 42N 115 25 E
Guanyun, *China* **35 G10** 34 20N 119 18 E
Guápiles, *Costa Rica* **88 D3** 10 10N 83 46W
Guaporé, *Brazil* **95 B5** 28 51S 51 54W
Guaporé →, *Brazil* **92 F5** 11 55S 65 4W
Guaqui, *Bolivia* **92 G5** 16 41S 68 54W
Guarapari, *Brazil* **95 A7** 20 40S 40 30W
Guarapuava, *Brazil* **95 B5** 25 20S 51 30W
Guaratinguetá, *Brazil* **95 A6** 22 49S 45 9W
Guaratuba, *Brazil* **95 B6** 25 53S 48 38W
Guarda, *Portugal* **19 B2** 40 32N 7 20W
Guardafui, C. = Asir, Ras, *Somali Rep.* **46 E5** 11 55N 51 10 E
Guárico □, *Venezuela* **92 B5** 8 40N 66 35W
Guarujá, *Brazil* **95 A6** 24 2S 46 25W
Guarus, *Brazil* **95 A7** 21 44S 41 20W
Guasave, *Mexico* **86 B3** 25 34N 108 27W
Guasdualito, *Venezuela* **92 B4** 7 15N 70 44W
Guatemala, *Guatemala* **88 D1** 14 40N 90 22W
Guatemala ■, *Cent. Amer.* **88 C1** 15 40N 90 30W
Guaviare →, *Colombia* **92 C5** 4 3N 67 44W
Guaxupé, *Brazil* **95 A6** 21 10S 47 5W
Guayama, *Puerto Rico* **89 C6** 17 59N 66 7W
Guayaquil, *Ecuador* **92 D3** 2 15S 79 52W
Guayaquil, G. de, *Ecuador* **92 D2** 3 10S 81 0W
Guaymas, *Mexico* **86 B2** 27 59N 110 54W
Guba, *Dem. Rep. of the Congo* **55 E2** 10 38S 26 27 E
Gubkin, *Russia* **25 D6** 51 17N 37 32 E
Gudbrandsdalen, *Norway* **9 F14** 61 33N 10 10 E
Guddu Barrage, *Pakistan* **40 E6** 28 30N 69 50 E
Gudur, *India* **40 M11** 14 12N 79 55 E
Guecho = Getxo, *Spain* **19 A4** 43 21N 2 59W
Guelph, *Canada* **78 C4** 43 35N 80 20W
Guéret, *France* **18 C4** 46 11N 1 51 E
Guerneville, *U.S.A.* **84 G4** 38 30N 123 0W
Guernica = Gernika-Lumo, *Spain* **19 A4** 43 19N 2 40W
Guernsey, *U.K.* **11 H5** 49 26N 2 35W
Guernsey, *U.S.A.* **80 D2** 42 19N 104 45W
Guerrero □, *Mexico* **87 D5** 17 30N 100 0W
Gügher, *Iran* **45 D8** 29 28N 56 27 E
Guhakolak, Tanjung, *Indonesia* **37 G11** 6 50S 105 14 E
Guia, *Canary Is.* **22 F4** 28 8N 15 38W
Guia de Isora, *Canary Is.* **22 F3** 28 12N 16 46W
Guia Lopes da Laguna, *Brazil* **95 A4** 21 26S 56 7W
Guiana, *S. Amer.* **90 C4** 5 10N 60 40W
Guidónia-Montecélio, *Italy* **20 C5** 42 1N 12 45 E
Guijá, *Mozam.* **57 C5** 24 27S 33 0 E
Guildford, *U.K.* **11 F7** 51 14N 0 34W
Guilford, *U.S.A.* **79 E12** 41 17N 72 41W
Guilin, *China* **33 D6** 25 18N 110 15 E
Guillaume-Delisle L., *Canada* **70 A4** 56 15N 76 17W
Güimar, *Canary Is.* **22 F3** 28 18N 16 24W
Guimarães, *Portugal* **19 B1** 41 28N 8 24W
Guimaras □, *Phil.* **37 B6** 10 35N 122 37 E
Guinda, *U.S.A.* **84 G4** 38 50N 122 12W
Guinea, *Africa* **48 F4** 8 0N 8 0 E
Guinea ■, *W. Afr.* **50 F3** 10 20N 11 30W
Guinea, Gulf of, *Atl. Oc.* **49 F4** 3 0N 2 30 E
Guinea-Bissau ■, *Africa* **50 F3** 12 0N 15 0W
Güines, *Cuba* **88 B3** 22 50N 82 0W
Guingamp, *France* **18 B2** 48 34N 3 10W
Güiria, *Venezuela* **92 A6** 10 32N 62 18W
Guiuan, *Phil.* **37 B7** 11 5N 125 55 E
Guiyang, *China* **32 D5** 26 32N 106 40 E
Guizhou □, *China* **32 D5** 27 0N 107 0 E
Gujar Khan, *Pakistan* **42 C5** 33 16N 73 19 E
Gujarat □, *India* **42 H4** 23 20N 71 0 E
Gujranwala, *Pakistan* **42 C6** 32 10N 74 12 E
Gujrat, *Pakistan* **42 C6** 32 40N 74 2 E
Gulbarga, *India* **40 L10** 17 20N 76 50 E
Gulbene, *Latvia* **9 H22** 57 8N 26 52 E
Gulf, The, *Asia* **45 E6** 27 0N 50 0 E
Gulfport, *U.S.A.* **81 K10** 30 22N 89 6W
Gulistan, *Pakistan* **42 D2** 30 30N 66 35 E
Gull Lake, *Canada* **73 C7** 50 10N 108 29W
Güllük, *Turkey* **21 F12** 37 14N 27 35 E
Gulmarg, *India* **43 B6** 34 3N 74 25 E
Gulshad, *Kazakstan* **26 E8** 46 45N 74 25 E
Gulu, *Uganda* **54 B3** 2 48N 32 17 E
Gulwe, *Tanzania* **54 D4** 6 30S 36 25 E
Gumal →, *Pakistan* **42 D4** 31 40N 71 50 E
Gumbaz, *Pakistan* **42 D3** 30 2N 69 0 E
Gumel, *Nigeria* **50 F7** 12 39N 9 22 E
Gumla, *India* **43 H11** 23 3N 84 33 E
Gumlu, *Australia* **62 B4** 19 53S 147 41 E
Gumma □, *Japan* **31 F9** 36 30N 138 20 E
Gumzai, *Indonesia* **37 F8** 5 28S 134 42 E
Guna, *India* **42 G7** 24 40N 77 19 E
Gunisao →, *Canada* **73 C9** 53 56N 97 53W
Gunisao L., *Canada* **73 C9** 53 33N 96 15W
Gunjyal, *Pakistan* **42 C4** 32 20N 71 55 E
Gunnbjørn Fjeld, *Greenland* **4 C6** 68 55N 29 47W
Gunnewin, *Australia* **63 D4** 25 59S 148 33 E
Gunnison, *Colo., U.S.A.* **83 G10** 38 33N 106 56W
Gunnison, *Utah, U.S.A.* **82 G8** 39 9N 111 49W
Gunnison →, *U.S.A.* **83 G9** 39 4N 108 35W
Gunpowder, *Australia* **62 B2** 19 42S 139 22 E
Guntakal, *India* **40 M10** 15 11N 77 27 E
Guntersville, *U.S.A.* **77 H2** 34 21N 86 18W
Guntong, *Malaysia* **39 K3** 4 36N 101 3 E
Guntur, *India* **41 L12** 16 23N 80 30 E
Gunungapi, *Indonesia* **37 F7** 6 45S 126 30 E
Gunungsitoli, *Indonesia* **36 D1** 1 15N 97 30 E
Gunza, *Angola* **52 G2** 10 50S 13 50 E
Guo He →, *China* **35 H9** 32 59N 117 10 E
Guoyang, *China* **34 H9** 33 32N 116 12 E
Gupis, *Pakistan* **43 A5** 36 15N 73 20 E
Gurdaspur, *India* **42 C6** 32 5N 75 31 E
Gurdon, *U.S.A.* **81 J8** 33 55N 93 9W
Gurgaon, *India* **42 E7** 28 27N 77 1 E
Gurgueia →, *Brazil* **93 E10** 6 50S 43 24W
Gurha, *India* **42 G4** 25 12N 71 39 E
Guri, Embalse de, *Venezuela* **92 B6** 7 50N 62 52W
Gurkha, *Nepal* **43 E11** 28 5N 84 40 E
Gurley, *Australia* **63 D4** 29 45S 149 48 E
Gurnet Point, *U.S.A.* **79 D14** 42 1N 70 34W
Guruê, *Mozam.* **55 F4** 15 25S 36 58 E
Gurun, *Malaysia* **39 K3** 5 49N 100 27 E
Gürün, *Turkey* **25 G6** 38 43N 37 15 E
Gurupá, *Brazil* **93 D8** 1 25S 51 35W
Gurupá, I. Grande de, *Brazil* **93 D8** 1 25S 51 45W
Gurupi, *Brazil* **93 F9** 11 43S 49 4W
Gurupi →, *Brazil* **93 D9** 1 13S 46 6W
Guruwe, *Zimbabwe* **57 B5** 16 40S 30 42 E
Guryev = Atyraū, *Kazakstan* **25 E9** 47 5N 52 0 E
Gusau, *Nigeria* **50 F7** 12 12N 6 40 E
Gusev, *Russia* **9 J20** 54 35N 22 10 E
Gushan, *China* **35 E12** 39 50N 123 35 E
Gushgy, *Turkmenistan* **26 F7** 35 20N 62 18 E
Gusinoozersk, *Russia* **27 D11** 51 16N 106 27 E
Gustavus, *U.S.A.* **72 B1** 58 25N 135 44W
Gustine, *U.S.A.* **84 H6** 37 16N 121 0W
Güstrow, *Germany* **16 B7** 53 47N 12 10 E
Gütersloh, *Germany* **16 C5** 51 54N 8 24 E
Gutha, *Australia* **61 E2** 28 58S 115 55 E
Guthalungra, *Australia* **62 B4** 19 52S 147 50 E
Guthrie, *Okla., U.S.A.* **81 H6** 35 53N 97 25W
Guthrie, *Tex., U.S.A.* **81 J4** 33 37N 100 19W
Guttenberg, *U.S.A.* **80 D9** 42 47N 91 6W
Gutu, *Zimbabwe* **57 B5** 19 41S 31 9 E
Guyana ■, *S. Amer.* **92 C7** 5 0N 59 0W
Guyane française = French Guiana ■, *S. Amer.* **93 C8** 4 0N 53 0W
Guyang, *China* **34 D6** 41 0N 110 5 E
Guyenne, *France* **18 D4** 44 30N 0 40 E
Guymon, *U.S.A.* **81 G4** 36 41N 101 29W
Guyra, *Australia* **63 E5** 30 15S 151 40 E
Guyuan, *Hebei, China* **34 D8** 41 37N 115 40 E
Guyuan, *Ningxia Huizu, China* **34 G4** 36 0N 106 20 E
Guzhen, *China* **35 H9** 33 22N 117 18 E
Guzmán, L. de, *Mexico* **86 A3** 31 25N 107 25W
Gvardeysk, *Russia* **9 J19** 54 39N 21 5 E
Gwa, *Burma* **41 L19** 17 36N 94 34 E
Gwaai, *Zimbabwe* **55 F2** 19 15S 27 45 E
Gwādar, *Pakistan* **40 G3** 25 10N 62 18 E
Gwalior, *India* **42 F8** 26 12N 78 10 E
Gwanda, *Zimbabwe* **55 G2** 20 55S 29 0 E
Gwane, *Dem. Rep. of the Congo* **54 B2** 4 45N 25 48 E
Gweebarra B., *Ireland* **13 B3** 54 51N 8 23W
Gweedore, *Ireland* **13 A3** 55 3N 8 13W
Gweru, *Zimbabwe* **55 F2** 19 28S 29 45 E
Gwinn, *U.S.A.* **76 B2** 46 19N 87 27W
Gwydir →, *Australia* **63 D4** 29 27S 149 48 E
Gwynedd □, *U.K.* **10 E3** 52 52N 4 10W
Gyandzha = Gäncä, *Azerbaijan* **25 F8** 40 45N 46 20 E
Gyaring Hu, *China* **32 C4** 34 50N 97 40 E
Gydanskiy Poluostrov, *Russia* **26 C8** 70 0N 78 0 E
Gympie, *Australia* **63 D5** 26 11S 152 38 E
Gyöngyös, *Hungary* **17 E10** 47 48N 19 56 E
Győr, *Hungary* **17 E9** 47 41N 17 40 E
Gypsum Pt., *Canada* **72 A6** 61 53N 114 35W
Gypsumville, *Canada* **73 C9** 51 45N 98 40W
Gyula, *Hungary* **17 E11** 46 38N 21 17 E
Gyumri, *Armenia* **25 F7** 40 47N 43 50 E
Gyzylarbat, *Turkmenistan* **26 F6** 39 4N 56 23 E
Gyzyletrek, *Turkmenistan* **45 B7** 37 36N 54 46 E

H

Ha 'Arava →, *Israel* **47 E4** 30 50N 35 20 E
Ha Coi, *Vietnam* **38 B6** 21 26N 107 46 E
Ha Dong, *Vietnam* **38 B5** 20 58N 105 46 E
Ha Giang, *Vietnam* **38 A5** 22 50N 104 59 E
Ha Tien, *Vietnam* **39 G5** 10 23N 104 29 E
Ha Tinh, *Vietnam* **38 C5** 18 20N 105 54 E
Ha Trung, *Vietnam* **38 C5** 19 58N 105 50 E
Haaksbergen, *Neths.* **15 B6** 52 9N 6 45 E
Haapsalu, *Estonia* **9 G20** 58 56N 23 30 E
Haarlem, *Neths.* **15 B4** 52 23N 4 39 E
Haast →, *N.Z.* **59 K2** 43 50S 169 2 E
Haast Bluff, *Australia* **60 D5** 23 22S 132 0 E
Hab →, *Pakistan* **42 G3** 24 53N 66 41 E
Hab Nadi Chauki, *Pakistan* **42 G2** 25 0N 66 50 E
Habaswein, *Kenya* **54 B4** 1 2N 39 30 E
Habay, *Canada* **72 B5** 58 50N 118 44W
Ḥabbānīyah, *Iraq* **44 C4** 33 17N 43 29 E
Haboro, *Japan* **30 B10** 44 22N 141 42 E
Ḥabshān, *U.A.E.* **45 F7** 23 50N 53 37 E
Hachijō-Jima, *Japan* **31 H9** 33 5N 139 45 E
Hachinohe, *Japan* **30 D10** 40 30N 141 29 E
Hachiōji, *Japan* **31 G9** 35 40N 139 20 E
Hachŏn, *N. Korea* **35 D15** 41 29N 129 2 E
Hackensack, *U.S.A.* **79 F10** 40 53N 74 3W
Hackettstown, *U.S.A.* **79 F10** 40 51N 74 50W
Hadali, *Pakistan* **42 C5** 32 16N 72 11 E
Hadarba, Ras, *Sudan* **51 D13** 22 4N 36 51 E
Hadarom □, *Israel* **47 E4** 31 0N 35 0 E
Hadd, Ra's al, *Oman* **46 C6** 22 35N 59 50 E
Hadejia, *Nigeria* **50 F7** 12 30N 10 5 E
Hadera, *Israel* **47 C3** 32 27N 34 55 E
Hadera, N. →, *Israel* **47 C3** 32 28N 34 52 E
Haderslev, *Denmark* **9 J13** 55 15N 9 30 E
Hadhramaut = Ḥaḍramawt, *Yemen* **46 D4** 15 30N 49 30 E
Hadibu, *Yemen* **46 E5** 12 39N 54 2 E
Hadong, *S. Korea* **35 G14** 35 5N 127 44 E
Ḥaḍramawt, *Yemen* **46 D4** 15 30N 49 30 E
Ḥadrānīyah, *Iraq* **44 C4** 35 38N 43 14 E
Hadrian's Wall, *U.K.* **10 B5** 55 0N 2 30W
Haeju, *N. Korea* **35 E13** 38 3N 125 45 E
Haenam, *S. Korea* **35 G14** 34 34N 126 35 E
Haenertsburg, *S. Africa* **57 C4** 24 0S 29 50 E
Haerhpin = Harbin, *China* **35 B14** 45 48N 126 40 E
Hafar al Bāṭin, *Si. Arabia* **44 D5** 28 32N 45 52 E
Ḥafirat al 'Aydā, *Si. Arabia* **44 E3** 26 26N 39 12 E
Ḥafit, *Oman* **45 F7** 23 59N 55 49 E
Hafizabad, *Pakistan* **42 C5** 32 5N 73 40 E
Haflong, *India* **41 G18** 25 10N 93 5 E
Hafnarfjörður, *Iceland* **8 D3** 64 4N 21 57W
Haft Gel, *Iran* **45 D6** 31 30N 49 32 E
Hafun, Ras, *Somali Rep.* **46 E5** 10 29N 51 30 E
Hagalil, *Israel* **47 C4** 32 53N 35 18 E
Hagen, *Germany* **16 C4** 51 21N 7 27 E
Hagerman, *U.S.A.* **81 J2** 33 7N 104 20W
Hagerstown, *U.S.A.* **76 F7** 39 39N 77 43W
Hagersville, *Canada* **78 D4** 42 58N 80 3W
Hagfors, *Sweden* **9 F15** 60 3N 13 45 E
Hagi, *Japan* **31 G5** 34 30N 131 22 E
Hagolan, *Syria* **47 C4** 33 0N 35 45 E
Hagondange, *France* **18 B7** 49 16N 6 11 E
Hags Hd., *Ireland* **13 D2** 52 57N 9 28W
Hague, C. de la, *France* **18 B3** 49 44N 1 56W
Hague, The = 's-Gravenhage, *Neths.* **15 B4** 52 7N 4 17 E
Haguenau, *France* **18 B7** 48 49N 7 47 E
Hai Duong, *Vietnam* **38 B6** 20 56N 106 19 E
Haicheng, *China* **35 D12** 40 50N 122 45 E
Haidar Khel, *Afghan.* **42 C3** 33 58N 68 38 E
Haidargarh, *India* **43 F9** 26 37N 81 22 E
Haifa = Ḥefa, *Israel* **47 C4** 32 46N 35 0 E
Haikou, *China* **33 D6** 20 1N 110 16 E
Ḥā'il, *Si. Arabia* **44 E4** 27 28N 41 45 E
Hailar, *China* **33 B6** 49 10N 119 38 E
Hailey, *U.S.A.* **82 E6** 43 31N 114 19W
Haileybury, *Canada* **70 C4** 47 30N 79 38W
Hailin, *China* **35 B15** 44 37N 129 30 E
Hailong, *China* **35 C13** 42 32N 125 40 E
Hailuoto, *Finland* **8 D21** 65 3N 24 45 E
Hainan □, *China* **33 E5** 19 0N 109 30 E
Hainaut □, *Belgium* **15 D4** 50 30N 4 0 E
Haines, *Alaska, U.S.A.* **72 B1** 59 14N 135 26W
Haines, *Oreg., U.S.A.* **82 D5** 44 55N 117 56W
Haines City, *U.S.A.* **77 L5** 28 7N 81 38W
Haines Junction, *Canada* **72 A1** 60 45N 137 30W
Haiphong, *Vietnam* **32 D5** 20 47N 106 41 E
Haiti ■, *W. Indies* **89 C5** 19 0N 72 30W
Haiya, *Sudan* **51 E13** 18 20N 36 21 E
Haiyang, *China* **35 F11** 36 47N 121 9 E
Haiyuan, *China* **34 F3** 36 35N 105 52 E
Haizhou, *China* **35 G10** 34 37N 119 7 E
Haizhou Wan, *China* **35 G10** 34 50N 119 20 E
Hajdúböszörmény, *Hungary* **17 E11** 47 40N 21 30 E
Hajipur, *India* **43 G11** 25 45N 85 13 E
Ḥājjī Muḥsin, *Iraq* **44 C5** 32 35N 45 29 E
Ḥājjīābād, *Iran* **45 D7** 28 19N 55 55 E
Ḥājjīābād-e Zarrīn, *Iran* **45 C7** 33 9N 54 51 E
Hajnówka, *Poland* **17 B12** 52 47N 23 35 E
Hakansson, Mts., *Dem. Rep. of the Congo* **55 D2** 8 40S 25 45 E
Hakkâri, *Turkey* **44 B4** 37 34N 43 44 E
Hakken-Zan, *Japan* **31 G7** 34 10N 135 54 E
Hakodate, *Japan* **30 D10** 41 45N 140 44 E
Hakos, *Namibia* **56 C2** 23 13S 16 21 E
Haku-San, *Japan* **31 F8** 36 9N 136 46 E
Hakui, *Japan* **31 F8** 36 53N 136 47 E
Hala, *Pakistan* **40 G6** 25 43N 68 20 E
Ḥalab, *Syria* **44 B3** 36 10N 37 15 E
Ḥalabjah, *Iraq* **44 C5** 35 10N 45 58 E
Halaib, *Sudan* **51 D13** 22 12N 36 30 E
Hālat 'Ammār, *Si. Arabia* **44 D3** 29 10N 36 4 E
Halbā, *Lebanon* **47 A5** 34 34N 36 6 E
Halberstadt, *Germany* **16 C6** 51 54N 11 3 E
Halcombe, *N.Z.* **59 J5** 40 8S 175 30 E
Halcon, *Phil.* **37 B6** 13 0N 121 30 E
Halden, *Norway* **9 G14** 59 9N 11 23 E
Haldia, *India* **41 H16** 22 5N 88 3 E
Haldwani, *India* **43 E8** 29 31N 79 30 E
Hale →, *Australia* **62 C2** 24 56S 135 53 E
Halesowen, *U.K.* **11 E5** 52 27N 2 3W
Haleyville, *U.S.A.* **77 H2** 34 14N 87 37W
Halfmoon Bay, *N.Z.* **59 M2** 46 50S 168 5 E
Halfway →, *Canada* **72 B4** 56 12N 121 32W
Halia, *India* **43 G10** 24 50N 82 19 E
Haliburton, *Canada* **78 A6** 45 3N 78 30W
Halifax, *Australia* **62 B4** 18 32S 146 22 E
Halifax, *Canada* **71 D7** 44 38N 63 35W
Halifax, *U.K.* **10 D6** 53 43N 1 52W
Halifax, *U.S.A.* **78 F8** 40 25N 76 55W
Halifax B., *Australia* **62 B4** 18 50S 147 0 E
Halifax I., *Namibia* **56 D2** 26 38S 15 4 E
Halīl →, *Iran* **45 E8** 27 40N 58 30 E
Halkirk, *U.K.* **12 C5** 58 30N 3 29W
Hall Beach = Sanirajak, *Canada* **69 B11** 68 46N 81 12W
Hall Pen., *Canada* **69 B13** 63 30N 66 0W
Hall Pt., *Australia* **60 C3** 15 40S 124 23 E
Halland, *Sweden* **9 H15** 57 8N 12 47 E
Halle, *Belgium* **15 D4** 50 44N 4 13 E
Halle, *Germany* **16 C6** 51 30N 11 56 E
Hällefors, *Sweden* **9 G16** 59 47N 14 31 E
Hallettsville, *U.S.A.* **81 L6** 29 27N 96 57W
Hallim, *S. Korea* **35 H14** 33 24N 126 15 E
Hallingdalselvi →, *Norway* **9 F13** 60 23N 9 35 E
Hallock, *U.S.A.* **80 A6** 48 47N 96 57W
Halls Creek, *Australia* **60 C4** 18 16S 127 38 E
Hallsberg, *Sweden* **9 G16** 59 5N 15 7 E
Hallstead, *U.S.A.* **79 E9** 41 58N 75 45W
Halmahera, *Indonesia* **37 D7** 0 40N 128 0 E
Halmstad, *Sweden* **9 H15** 56 41N 12 52 E
Hälsingborg = Helsingborg, *Sweden* **9 H15** 56 3N 12 42 E
Hälsingland, *Sweden* **9 F16** 61 40N 16 5 E
Halstead, *U.K.* **11 F8** 51 57N 0 40 E
Halti, *Finland* **8 B19** 69 17N 21 18 E
Halton □, *U.K.* **10 D5** 53 22N 2 45W
Haltwhistle, *U.K.* **10 C5** 54 58N 2 26W
Ḥalul, *Qatar* **45 E7** 25 40N 52 40 E
Halvad, *India* **42 H4** 23 1N 71 11 E
Ḥalvān, *Iran* **45 C8** 33 57N 56 15 E
Ham Tan, *Vietnam* **39 G6** 10 40N 107 45 E
Ham Yen, *Vietnam* **38 A5** 22 4N 105 3 E
Hamab, *Namibia* **56 D2** 28 7S 19 16 E
Hamada, *Japan* **31 G6** 34 56N 132 4 E
Hamadān, *Iran* **45 C6** 34 52N 48 32 E
Hamadān □, *Iran* **45 C6** 35 0N 49 0 E
Ḥamāh, *Syria* **44 C3** 35 5N 36 40 E
Hamamatsu, *Japan* **31 G8** 34 45N 137 45 E
Hamar, *Norway* **9 F14** 60 48N 11 7 E
Hamâta, Gebel, *Egypt* **44 E2** 24 17N 35 0 E
Hambantota, *Sri Lanka* **40 R12** 6 10N 81 10 E
Hamber Prov. Park, *Canada* **72 C5** 52 20N 118 0W
Hamburg, *Germany* **16 B5** 53 33N 9 59 E
Hamburg, *Ark., U.S.A.* **81 J9** 33 14N 91 48W
Hamburg, *N.Y., U.S.A.* **78 D6** 42 43N 78 50W
Hamburg, *Pa., U.S.A.* **79 F9** 40 33N 75 59W
Ḥamḍ, W. al →, *Si. Arabia* **44 E3** 24 55N 36 20 E
Hamden, *U.S.A.* **79 E12** 41 23N 72 54W

Herbertsdale

Häme, Finland 9 F20 61 38N 25 10 E
Hämeenlinna, Finland 9 F21 61 0N 24 28 E
Hamelin Pool, Australia 61 E1 26 22S 114 20 E
Hameln, Germany 16 B5 52 6N 9 21 E
Hamerkaz □, Israel 47 C3 32 15N 34 55 E
Hamersley Ra., Australia 60 D2 22 0S 117 45 E
Hamhung, N. Korea 35 E14 39 54N 127 30 E
Hami, China 32 B4 42 55N 93 25 E
Hamilton, Canada 78 C5 43 15N 79 50W
Hamilton, N.Z. 59 G5 37 47S 175 19 E
Hamilton, U.K. 12 F4 55 46N 4 2W
Hamilton, Ala., U.S.A. 77 H1 34 9N 87 59W
Hamilton, Mont., U.S.A. 82 C6 46 15N 114 10W
Hamilton, N.Y., U.S.A. 79 D9 42 50N 75 33W
Hamilton, Ohio, U.S.A. 76 F3 39 24N 84 34W
Hamilton, Tex., U.S.A. 81 K5 31 42N 98 7W
Hamilton →, Australia 62 C2 23 30S 139 47 E
Hamilton City, U.S.A. 84 F4 39 45N 122 1W
Hamilton Inlet, Canada 71 B8 54 0N 57 30W
Hamilton Mt., U.S.A. 79 C10 43 25N 74 22W
Hamina, Finland 9 F22 60 34N 27 12 E
Hamirpur, H.P., India 42 D7 31 41N 76 31 E
Hamirpur, Ut. P., India 43 G9 25 57N 80 9 E
Hamlet, U.S.A. 77 H6 34 53N 79 42W
Hamlin = Hameln, Germany 16 B5 52 6N 9 21 E
Hamlin, N.Y., U.S.A. 78 C7 43 17N 77 55W
Hamlin, Tex., U.S.A. 81 J4 32 53N 100 8W
Hamm, Germany 16 C4 51 40N 7 50 E
Ḥammār, Hawr al, Iraq 44 D5 30 50N 47 10 E
Hammerfest, Norway 8 A20 70 39N 23 41 E
Hammond, Ind., U.S.A. 76 E2 41 38N 87 30W
Hammond, La., U.S.A. 81 K9 30 30N 90 28W
Hammond, N.Y., U.S.A. 79 B9 44 27N 75 42W
Hammondsport, U.S.A. 78 D7 42 25N 77 13W
Hammonton, U.S.A. 76 F8 39 39N 74 48W
Hampden, N.Z. 59 L3 45 18S 170 50 E
Hampshire □, U.K. 11 F6 51 7N 1 23W
Hampshire Downs, U.K. 11 F6 51 15N 1 10W
Hampton, N.B., Canada 71 C6 45 32N 65 51W
Hampton, Ont., Canada 78 C6 43 58N 78 45W
Hampton, Ark., U.S.A. 81 J8 33 32N 92 28W
Hampton, Iowa, U.S.A. 80 D8 42 45N 93 13W
Hampton, N.H., U.S.A. 79 D14 42 57N 70 50W
Hampton, S.C., U.S.A. 77 J5 32 52N 81 7W
Hampton, Va., U.S.A. 76 G7 37 2N 76 21W
Hampton Bays, U.S.A. 79 F12 40 53N 72 30W
Hampton Tableland, Australia 61 F4 32 0S 127 0 E
Hamyang, S. Korea 35 G14 35 32N 127 42 E
Han Pijesak, Bos.-H. 21 B8 44 5N 18 57 E
Hanak, Si. Arabia 44 E3 25 32N 37 0 E
Hanamaki, Japan 30 E10 39 23N 141 7 E
Hanang, Tanzania 54 C4 4 30S 35 25 E
Hanau, Germany 16 C5 50 7N 8 56 E
Hanbogd = Ihbulag, Mongolia 34 C4 43 11N 107 10 E
Hancheng, China 34 G6 35 31N 110 25 E
Hancock, Mich., U.S.A. 80 B10 47 8N 88 35W
Hancock, N.Y., U.S.A. 79 E9 41 57N 75 17W
Handa, Japan 31 G8 34 53N 136 55 E
Handan, China 34 F8 36 35N 114 28 E
Handeni, Tanzania 54 D4 5 25S 38 2 E
Handwara, India 43 B6 34 21N 74 20 E
Hanegev, Israel 47 E4 30 50N 35 0 E
Hanford, U.S.A. 84 J7 36 20N 119 39W
Hang Chat, Thailand 38 C2 18 20N 99 21 E
Hang Dong, Thailand 38 C2 18 41N 98 55 E
Hangang →, S. Korea 35 F14 37 50N 126 30 E
Hangayn Nuruu, Mongolia 32 B4 47 30N 99 0 E
Hangchou = Hangzhou, China 33 C7 30 18N 120 11 E
Hanggin Houqi, China 34 D4 40 58N 107 4 E
Hanggin Qi, China 34 E5 39 52N 108 50 E
Hangu, China 35 E9 39 18N 117 53 E
Hangzhou, China 33 C7 30 18N 120 11 E
Hangzhou Wan, China 33 C7 30 15N 120 45 E
Hanhongor, Mongolia 34 C3 43 55N 104 28 E
Ḥanīdh, Si. Arabia 45 E6 26 35N 48 38 E
Ḥanish, Yemen 46 E3 13 45N 42 46 E
Hankinson, U.S.A. 80 B6 46 4N 96 54W
Hanko, Finland 9 G20 59 50N 22 57 E
Hanksville, U.S.A. 83 G8 38 22N 110 43W
Hanle, India 43 C8 32 42N 79 4 E
Hanmer Springs, N.Z. 59 K4 42 32S 172 50 E
Hann →, Australia 60 C4 17 26S 126 17 E
Hann, Mt., Australia 60 C4 15 45S 126 0 E
Hanna, Canada 72 C6 51 40N 111 54W
Hanna, U.S.A. 82 F10 41 52N 106 34W
Hannah B., Canada 70 B4 51 40N 80 0W
Hannibal, Mo., U.S.A. 80 F9 39 42N 91 22W
Hannibal, N.Y., U.S.A. 79 C8 43 19N 76 35W
Hannover, Germany 16 B5 52 22N 9 46 E
Hanoi, Vietnam 32 D5 21 5N 105 55 E
Hanover = Hannover, Germany 16 B5 52 22N 9 46 E
Hanover, Canada 78 B3 44 9N 81 2W
Hanover, S. Africa 56 E3 31 4S 24 29 E
Hanover, N.H., U.S.A. 79 C12 43 42N 72 17W
Hanover, Ohio, U.S.A. 78 F2 40 4N 82 16W
Hanover, Pa., U.S.A. 76 F7 39 48N 76 59W
Hanover, I., Chile 96 G2 51 0S 74 50W
Hansdiha, India 43 G12 24 36N 87 5 E
Hansi, India 42 E6 29 10N 75 57 E
Hantsavichy, Belarus 17 B14 52 49N 26 30 E
Hanumangarh, India 42 E6 29 35N 74 19 E
Hanzhong, China 34 H4 33 10N 107 1 E
Hanzhuang, China 35 G9 34 33N 117 23 E
Haora, India 43 H13 22 37N 88 20 E
Haparanda, Sweden 8 D21 65 52N 24 8 E
Happy, U.S.A. 81 H4 34 45N 101 52W
Happy Camp, U.S.A. 82 F2 41 48N 123 23W
Happy Valley-Goose Bay, Canada 71 B7 53 15N 60 20W
Hapsu, N. Korea 35 D15 41 13N 128 51 E
Hapur, India 42 E7 28 45N 77 45 E
Ḥaql, Si. Arabia 47 F3 29 10N 34 58 E
Har, Indonesia 37 F8 5 16S 133 14 E
Har-Ayrag, Mongolia 34 B5 45 47N 109 16 E
Har Hu, China 32 C4 38 20N 97 38 E
Har Us Nuur, Mongolia 32 B4 48 0N 92 0 E
Har Yehuda, Israel 47 D3 31 35N 34 57 E
Ḥaraḍ, Si. Arabia 46 C4 24 22N 49 0 E
Haranomachi, Japan 30 F10 37 38N 140 58 E
Harare, Zimbabwe 55 F3 17 43S 31 2 E
Harbin, China 35 B14 45 48N 126 40 E
Harbor Beach, U.S.A. 78 C2 43 51N 82 39W
Harbour Breton, Canada 71 C8 47 29N 55 50W
Harbour Deep, Canada 71 B8 50 25N 56 32W
Harda, India 42 H7 22 27N 77 5 E
Hardangerfjorden, Norway 9 F12 60 5N 6 0 E
Hardangervidda, Norway 9 F12 60 7N 7 20 E
Hardap Dam, Namibia 56 C2 24 32S 17 50 E
Hardenberg, Neths. 15 B6 52 34N 6 37 E
Harderwijk, Neths. 15 B5 52 21N 5 38 E
Hardey →, Australia 60 D2 22 45S 116 8 E
Hardin, U.S.A. 82 D10 45 44N 107 37W
Harding, S. Africa 57 E4 30 35S 29 55 E
Harding Ra., Australia 60 C3 16 17S 124 55 E
Hardisty, Canada 72 C6 52 40N 111 18W
Hardoi, India 43 F9 27 26N 80 6 E
Hardwar = Haridwar, India 42 E8 29 58N 78 9 E
Hardwick, U.S.A. 79 B12 44 30N 72 22W
Hardy, Pen., Chile 96 H3 55 30S 68 20W
Hare B., Canada 71 B8 51 15N 55 45W
Hareid, Norway 9 E12 62 22N 6 1 E
Harer, Ethiopia 46 F3 9 20N 42 8 E
Hargeisa, Somali Rep. 46 F3 9 30N 44 2 E
Hari →, Indonesia 36 E2 1 16S 104 5 E
Haria, Canary Is. 22 E6 29 8N 13 32W
Haridwar, India 42 E8 29 58N 78 9 E
Harim, Jabal al, Oman 45 E8 25 58N 56 14 E
Haringhata →, Bangla. 41 J16 22 0N 89 58 E
Harīrūd →, Asia 40 A2 37 24N 60 38 E
Härjedalen, Sweden 9 E15 62 22N 13 5 E
Harlan, Iowa, U.S.A. 80 E7 41 39N 95 19W
Harlan, Ky., U.S.A. 77 G4 36 51N 83 19W
Harlech, U.K. 10 E3 52 52N 4 6W
Harlem, U.S.A. 82 B9 48 32N 108 47W
Harlingen, Neths. 15 A5 53 11N 5 25 E
Harlingen, U.S.A. 81 M6 26 12N 97 42W
Harlow, U.K. 11 F8 51 46N 0 8 E
Harlowton, U.S.A. 82 C9 46 26N 109 50W
Harnai, Pakistan 42 D2 30 6N 67 56 E
Harney Basin, U.S.A. 82 E4 43 30N 119 0W
Harney L., U.S.A. 82 E4 43 14N 119 8W
Harney Peak, U.S.A. 80 D3 43 52N 103 32W
Härnösand, Sweden 9 E17 62 38N 17 55 E
Haroldswick, U.K. 12 A8 60 48N 0 50W
Harp L., Canada 71 A7 55 5N 61 50W
Harper, Liberia 50 H4 4 25N 7 43W
Harrai, India 43 H8 22 37N 79 13 E
Harrand, Pakistan 42 E4 29 28N 70 3 E
Harricana →, Canada 70 B4 50 56N 79 32W
Harriman, U.S.A. 77 H3 35 56N 84 33W
Harrington Harbour, Canada 71 B8 50 31N 59 30W
Harris, U.K. 12 D2 57 50N 6 55W
Harris, Sd. of, U.K. 12 D1 57 44N 7 6W
Harris L., Australia 63 E2 31 10S 135 10 E
Harris Pt., Canada 78 C2 43 6N 82 9W
Harrisburg, Ill., U.S.A. 81 G10 37 44N 88 32W
Harrisburg, Nebr., U.S.A. 80 E3 41 33N 103 44W
Harrisburg, Pa., U.S.A. 78 F8 40 16N 76 53W
Harrismith, S. Africa 57 D4 28 15S 29 8 E
Harrison, Ark., U.S.A. 81 G8 36 14N 93 7W
Harrison, Maine, U.S.A. 79 B14 44 7N 70 39W
Harrison, Nebr., U.S.A. 80 D3 42 41N 103 53W
Harrison, C., Canada 71 B8 54 55N 57 55W
Harrison L., Canada 72 D4 49 33N 121 50W
Harrisonburg, U.S.A. 76 F6 38 27N 78 52W
Harrisonville, U.S.A. 80 F7 38 39N 94 21W
Harriston, Canada 78 C4 43 57N 80 53W
Harrisville, Mich., U.S.A. 78 B1 44 39N 83 17W
Harrisville, N.Y., U.S.A. 79 B9 44 9N 75 19W
Harrisville, Pa., U.S.A. 78 E5 41 8N 80 0W
Harrodsburg, U.S.A. 76 G3 37 46N 84 51W
Harrogate, U.K. 10 C6 54 0N 1 33W
Harrow □, U.K. 11 F7 51 35N 0 21W
Harrowsmith, Canada 79 B8 44 24N 76 40W
Harry S. Truman Reservoir, U.S.A. 80 F7 38 16N 93 24W
Harsīn, Iran 44 C5 34 18N 47 33 E
Harstad, Norway 8 B17 68 48N 16 30 E
Harsud, India 42 H7 22 6N 76 44 E
Hart, U.S.A. 76 D2 43 42N 86 22W
Hartbees →, S. Africa 56 D3 28 45S 20 32 E
Hartford, Conn., U.S.A. 79 E12 41 46N 72 41W
Hartford, Ky., U.S.A. 76 G2 37 27N 86 55W
Hartford, S. Dak., U.S.A. 80 D6 43 38N 96 57W
Hartford, Wis., U.S.A. 80 D10 43 19N 88 22W
Hartford City, U.S.A. 76 E3 40 27N 85 22W
Hartland, Canada 71 C6 46 20N 67 32W
Hartland Pt., U.K. 11 F3 51 1N 4 32W
Hartlepool, U.K. 10 C6 54 42N 1 13W
Hartlepool □, U.K. 10 C6 54 42N 1 17W
Hartley Bay, Canada 72 C3 53 25N 129 15W
Hartmannberge, Namibia 56 B1 17 0S 13 0 E
Hartney, Canada 73 D8 49 30N 100 35W
Harts →, S. Africa 56 D3 28 24S 24 17 E
Hartselle, U.S.A. 77 H2 34 27N 86 56W
Hartshorne, U.S.A. 81 H7 34 51N 95 34W
Hartstown, U.S.A. 78 E4 41 33N 80 23W
Hartsville, U.S.A. 77 H5 34 23N 80 4W
Hartswater, S. Africa 56 D3 27 34S 24 43 E
Hartwell, U.S.A. 77 H4 34 21N 82 56W
Harunabad, Pakistan 42 E5 29 35N 73 8 E
Harvand, Iran 45 D7 28 25N 53 43 E
Harvey, Australia 61 F2 33 5S 115 54 E
Harvey, Ill., U.S.A. 76 E2 41 36N 87 50W
Harvey, N. Dak., U.S.A. 80 B5 47 47N 99 56W
Harwich, U.K. 11 F9 51 56N 1 17 E
Haryana □, India 42 E7 29 0N 76 10 E
Haryn →, Belarus 17 B14 52 7N 27 17 E
Harz, Germany 16 C6 51 38N 10 44 E
Hasa □, Si. Arabia 45 E6 25 50N 49 0 E
Ḥasanābād, Iran 45 C7 32 8N 52 44 E
Hasdo →, India 43 J10 21 44N 82 44 E
Hashimoto, Japan 31 G7 34 19N 135 37 E
Hashtjerd, Iran 45 C6 35 52N 50 40 E
Haskell, U.S.A. 81 J5 33 10N 99 44W
Haslemere, U.K. 11 F7 51 5N 0 43W
Hasselt, Belgium 15 D5 50 56N 5 21 E
Hassi Messaoud, Algeria 50 B7 31 51N 6 1 E
Hässleholm, Sweden 9 H15 56 10N 13 46 E
Hastings, N.Z. 59 H6 39 39S 176 52 E
Hastings, U.K. 11 G8 50 51N 0 35 E
Hastings, Mich., U.S.A. 76 D3 42 39N 85 17W
Hastings, Minn., U.S.A. 80 C8 44 44N 92 51W
Hastings, Nebr., U.S.A. 80 E5 40 35N 98 23W
Hat Yai, Thailand 39 J3 7 1N 100 27 E
Hatanbulag = Ergel, Mongolia 34 C5 43 8N 109 5 E
Hatay = Antalya, Turkey 25 G5 36 52N 30 45 E
Hatch, U.S.A. 83 K10 32 40N 107 9W
Hatchet L., Canada 73 B8 58 36N 103 40W
Hateruma-Shima, Japan 31 M1 24 3N 123 47 E
Hatgal, Mongolia 32 A5 50 26N 100 9 E
Hathras, India 42 F8 27 36N 78 6 E
Hatia, Bangla. 41 H17 22 30N 91 5 E
Hato Mayor, Dom. Rep. 89 C6 18 46N 69 15W
Hatta, India 43 G8 24 7N 79 36 E
Hatteras, C., U.S.A. 77 H8 35 14N 75 32W
Hattiesburg, U.S.A. 81 K10 31 20N 89 17W
Hatvan, Hungary 17 E10 47 40N 19 45 E
Hau Bon = Cheo Reo, Vietnam 36 B3 13 25N 108 28 E
Hau Duc, Vietnam 38 E7 15 20N 108 13 E
Haugesund, Norway 9 G11 59 23N 5 13 E
Haukipudas, Finland 8 D21 65 12N 25 20 E
Haultain →, Canada 73 B7 55 51N 106 46W
Hauraki G., N.Z. 59 G5 36 35S 175 5 E
Haut Atlas, Morocco 50 B4 32 30N 5 0W
Haut-Zaïre = Orientale □, Dem. Rep. of the Congo 54 B2 2 20N 26 0 E
Hautes Fagnes = Hohe Venn, Belgium 15 D6 50 30N 6 5 E
Hauts Plateaux, Algeria 48 C4 35 0N 1 0 E
Havana = La Habana, Cuba 88 B3 23 8N 82 22W
Havana, U.S.A. 80 E9 40 18N 90 4W
Havant, U.K. 11 G7 50 51N 0 58W
Havasu, L., U.S.A. 85 L12 34 18N 114 28W
Havel →, Germany 16 B7 52 50N 12 3 E
Havelian, Pakistan 42 B5 34 2N 73 10 E
Havelock, Canada 78 B7 44 26N 77 53W
Havelock, N.Z. 59 J4 41 17S 173 48 E
Havelock, U.S.A. 77 H7 34 53N 76 54W
Haverfordwest, U.K. 11 F3 51 48N 4 58W
Haverhill, U.S.A. 79 D13 42 47N 71 5W
Haverstraw, U.S.A. 79 E11 41 12N 73 58W
Havirga, Mongolia 34 B7 45 41N 113 5 E
Havířov, Czech Rep. 17 D10 49 46N 18 20 E
Havlíčkův Brod, Czech Rep. 16 D8 49 36N 15 33 E
Havre, U.S.A. 82 B9 48 33N 109 41W
Havre-Aubert, Canada 71 C7 47 12N 61 56W
Havre-St.-Pierre, Canada 71 B7 50 18N 63 33W
Haw →, U.S.A. 77 H6 35 36N 79 3W
Hawaii □, U.S.A. 74 H16 19 30N 156 30W
Hawaii I., Pac. Oc. 74 J17 20 0N 155 0W
Hawaiian Is., Pac. Oc. 74 H17 20 30N 156 0W
Hawaiian Ridge, Pac. Oc. 65 E11 24 0N 165 0W
Hawarden, U.S.A. 80 D6 43 0N 96 29W
Hawea, L., N.Z. 59 L2 44 28S 169 19 E
Hawera, N.Z. 59 H5 39 35S 174 19 E
Hawick, U.K. 12 F6 55 26N 2 47W
Hawk Junction, Canada 70 C3 48 5N 84 38W
Hawke B., N.Z. 59 H6 39 25S 177 20 E
Hawkesbury, Canada 70 C5 45 37N 74 37W
Hawkesbury I., Canada 72 C3 53 37N 129 3W
Hawkesbury Pt., Australia 62 A1 11 55S 134 5 E
Hawkinsville, U.S.A. 77 J4 32 17N 83 28W
Hawley, Minn., U.S.A. 80 B6 46 53N 96 19W
Hawley, Pa., U.S.A. 79 E9 41 28N 75 11W
Ḥawrān, W. →, Iraq 44 C4 33 58N 42 34 E
Hawsh Müssá, Lebanon 47 B4 33 45N 35 55 E
Hawthorne, U.S.A. 82 G4 38 32N 118 38W
Hay →, Australia 62 C2 24 50S 138 0 E
Hay →, Canada 72 A5 60 50N 116 26W
Hay, C., Australia 60 B4 14 5S 129 29 E
Hay I., Canada 78 B4 44 53N 80 58W
Hay L., Canada 72 B5 58 50N 118 50W
Hay-on-Wye, U.K. 11 E4 52 5N 3 8W
Hay River, Canada 72 A5 60 51N 115 44W
Hay Springs, U.S.A. 80 D3 42 41N 102 41W
Haya = Tehoru, Indonesia 37 E7 3 23S 129 30 E
Hayachine-San, Japan 30 E10 39 34N 141 29 E
Hayden, U.S.A. 82 F10 40 30N 107 16W
Haydon, Australia 62 B3 18 0S 141 30 E
Hayes, U.S.A. 80 C4 44 23N 101 1W
Hayes →, Canada 70 A1 57 3N 92 12W
Hayes Creek, Australia 60 B5 13 43S 131 22 E
Hayle, U.K. 11 G2 50 11N 5 26W
Hayling I., U.K. 11 G7 50 48N 0 59W
Hayrabolu, Turkey 21 D12 41 12N 27 5 E
Hays, Canada 72 C6 50 6N 111 48W
Hays, U.S.A. 80 F5 38 53N 99 20W
Haysyn, Ukraine 17 D15 48 57N 29 25 E
Hayvoron, Ukraine 17 D15 48 22N 29 52 E
Hayward, Calif., U.S.A. 84 H4 37 40N 122 5W
Hayward, Wis., U.S.A. 80 B9 46 1N 91 29W
Haywards Heath, U.K. 11 G7 51 0N 0 5W
Hazafon □, Israel 47 C4 32 40N 35 20 E
Hazārān, Kūh-e, Iran 45 D8 29 35N 57 20 E
Hazard, U.S.A. 76 G4 37 15N 83 12W
Hazaribag, India 43 H11 23 58N 85 26 E
Hazaribag Road, India 43 G11 24 12N 85 57 E
Hazelton, Canada 72 B3 55 20N 127 42W
Hazelton, U.S.A. 80 B4 46 29N 100 17W
Hazen, U.S.A. 80 B4 47 18N 101 38W
Hazlehurst, Ga., U.S.A. 77 K4 31 52N 82 36W
Hazlehurst, Miss., U.S.A. 81 K9 31 52N 90 24W
Hazlet, U.S.A. 79 F10 40 25N 74 12W
Hazleton, U.S.A. 79 F9 40 57N 75 59W
Hazlett, L., Australia 60 D4 21 30S 128 48 E
Hazro, Turkey 44 B4 38 15N 40 47 E
Head of Bight, Australia 61 F5 31 30S 131 25 E
Headlands, Zimbabwe 55 F3 18 15S 32 2 E
Healdsburg, U.S.A. 84 G4 38 37N 122 52W
Healdton, U.S.A. 81 H6 34 14N 97 29W
Heany Junction, Zimbabwe 57 C4 20 6S 28 54 E
Heard I., Ind. Oc. 3 G13 53 0S 74 0 E
Hearne, U.S.A. 81 K6 30 53N 96 36W
Hearst, Canada 70 C3 49 40N 83 41W
Heart →, U.S.A. 80 B4 46 46N 100 50W
Heart's Content, Canada 71 C9 47 54N 53 27W
Heath Pt., Canada 71 C7 49 8N 61 40W
Heavener, U.S.A. 81 H7 34 53N 94 36W
Hebbronville, U.S.A. 81 M5 27 18N 98 41W
Hebei □, China 34 E9 39 0N 116 0 E
Hebel, Australia 63 D4 28 58S 147 47 E
Heber, U.S.A. 85 N11 32 44N 115 32W
Heber City, U.S.A. 82 F8 40 31N 111 25W
Heber Springs, U.S.A. 81 H9 35 30N 92 2W
Hebert, Canada 73 C7 50 30N 107 10W
Hebgen L., U.S.A. 82 D8 44 52N 111 20W
Hebi, China 34 G8 35 57N 114 7 E
Hebrides, U.K. 6 D4 57 30N 7 0W
Hebrides, Sea of the, U.K. 12 D2 57 5N 7 0W
Hebron = Al Khalīl, West Bank 47 D4 31 32N 35 6 E
Hebron, Canada 69 C13 58 5N 62 30W
Hebron, N. Dak., U.S.A. 80 B3 46 54N 102 3W
Hebron, Nebr., U.S.A. 80 E6 40 10N 97 35W
Hecate Str., Canada 72 C2 53 10N 130 30W
Heceta I., U.S.A. 72 B2 55 46N 133 40W
Hechi, China 32 D5 24 40N 108 2 E
Hechuan, China 32 C5 30 2N 106 12 E
Hecla, U.S.A. 80 C5 45 53N 98 9W
Hecla I., Canada 73 C9 51 10N 96 43W
Hede, Sweden 9 E15 62 23N 13 30 E
Hedemora, Sweden 9 F16 60 18N 15 58 E
Heerde, Neths. 15 B6 52 24N 6 2 E
Heerenveen, Neths. 15 B5 52 57N 5 55 E
Heerhugowaard, Neths. 15 B4 52 40N 4 51 E
Heerlen, Neths. 18 A6 50 55N 5 58 E
Ḥefa, Israel 47 C4 32 46N 35 0 E
Ḥefa □, Israel 47 C4 32 40N 35 0 E
Hefei, China 33 C6 31 52N 117 18 E
Hegang, China 33 B8 47 20N 130 19 E
Heichengzhen, China 34 F4 36 24N 106 3 E
Heidelberg, Germany 16 D5 49 24N 8 42 E
Heidelberg, S. Africa 56 E3 34 6S 20 59 E
Heilbron, S. Africa 57 D4 27 16S 27 59 E
Heilbronn, Germany 16 D5 49 9N 9 13 E
Heilongjiang □, China 33 B7 48 0N 126 0 E
Heilunkiang = Heilongjiang □, China 33 B7 48 0N 126 0 E
Heimaey, Iceland 8 E3 63 26N 20 17W
Heinola, Finland 9 F22 61 13N 26 2 E
Heinze Kyun, Burma 38 E1 14 25N 97 45 E
Heishan, China 35 D12 41 40N 122 5 E
Heishui, China 35 C10 42 8N 119 30 E
Hejaz = Ḥijāz □, Si. Arabia 46 C2 24 0N 40 0 E
Hejian, China 34 E9 38 25N 116 5 E
Hejin, China 34 G6 35 35N 110 42 E
Hekımhan, Turkey 44 B3 38 50N 37 55 E
Hekla, Iceland 8 E4 63 56N 19 35W
Hekou, China 32 D5 22 30N 103 59 E
Helan Shan, China 34 E3 38 30N 105 55 E
Helen Atoll, Pac. Oc. 37 D8 2 40N 132 0 E
Helena, Ark., U.S.A. 81 H9 34 32N 90 36W
Helena, Mont., U.S.A. 82 C7 46 36N 112 2W
Helendale, U.S.A. 85 L9 34 44N 117 19W
Helensburgh, U.K. 12 E4 56 1N 4 43W
Helensville, N.Z. 59 G5 36 41S 174 29 E
Helenvale, Australia 62 B4 15 43S 145 14 E
Helgeland, Norway 8 C15 66 7N 13 29 E
Helgoland, Germany 16 A4 54 10N 7 53 E
Heligoland = Helgoland, Germany 16 A4 54 10N 7 53 E
Heligoland B. = Deutsche Bucht, Germany 16 A5 54 15N 8 0 E
Hella, Iceland 8 E3 63 50N 20 24W
Hellertown, U.S.A. 79 F9 40 35N 75 21W
Hellespont = Çanakkale Boğazı, Turkey 21 D12 40 17N 26 32 E
Hellevoetsluis, Neths. 15 C4 51 50N 4 8 E
Hellín, Spain 19 C5 38 31N 1 40W
Helmand □, Afghan. 40 D4 31 20N 64 0 E
Helmand →, Afghan. 40 D2 31 12N 61 34 E
Helmeringhausen, Namibia 56 D2 25 54S 16 57 E
Helmond, Neths. 15 C5 51 29N 5 41 E
Helmsdale, U.K. 12 C5 58 7N 3 39W
Helmsdale →, U.K. 12 C5 58 7N 3 40W
Helong, China 35 C15 42 40N 129 0 E
Helper, U.S.A. 82 G8 39 41N 110 51W
Helsingborg, Sweden 9 H15 56 3N 12 42 E
Helsingfors = Helsinki, Finland 9 F21 60 15N 25 3 E
Helsingør, Denmark 9 H15 56 2N 12 35 E
Helsinki, Finland 9 F21 60 15N 25 3 E
Helston, U.K. 11 G2 50 6N 5 17W
Helvellyn, U.K. 10 C4 54 32N 3 1W
Helwân, Egypt 51 C12 29 50N 31 20 E
Hemel Hempstead, U.K. 11 F7 51 44N 0 28W
Hemet, U.S.A. 85 M10 33 45N 116 58W
Hemingford, U.S.A. 80 D3 42 19N 103 4W
Hemmingford, Canada 79 A11 45 3N 73 35W
Hempstead, U.S.A. 81 K6 30 6N 96 5W
Hemse, Sweden 9 H18 57 15N 18 22 E
Henan □, China 34 H8 34 0N 114 0 E
Henares →, Spain 19 B4 40 24N 3 30W
Henashi-Misaki, Japan 30 D9 40 37N 139 51 E
Henderson, Argentina 94 D3 36 18S 61 43W
Henderson, Ky., U.S.A. 76 G2 37 50N 87 35W
Henderson, N.C., U.S.A. 77 G6 36 20N 78 25W
Henderson, Nev., U.S.A. 85 J12 36 2N 114 59W
Henderson, Tenn., U.S.A. 77 H1 35 26N 88 38W
Henderson, Tex., U.S.A. 81 J7 32 9N 94 48W
Hendersonville, N.C., U.S.A. 77 H4 35 19N 82 28W
Hendersonville, Tenn., U.S.A. 77 G2 36 18N 86 37W
Hendījān, Iran 45 D6 30 14N 49 43 E
Hendorābī, Iran 45 E7 26 40N 53 37 E
Hengcheng, China 34 E4 38 18N 106 28 E
Hengdaohezi, China 35 B15 44 52N 129 0 E
Hengelo, Neths. 15 B6 52 16N 6 48 E
Hengshan, China 34 F5 37 58N 109 5 E
Hengshui, China 34 F8 37 41N 115 40 E
Hengyang, China 33 D6 26 59N 112 22 E
Henlopen, C., U.S.A. 76 F8 38 48N 75 6W
Hennenman, S. Africa 56 D4 27 59S 27 1 E
Hennessey, U.S.A. 81 G6 36 6N 97 54W
Henrietta, U.S.A. 81 J5 33 49N 98 12W
Henrietta, Ostrov = Genriyetty, Ostrov, Russia 27 B16 77 6N 156 30 E
Henrietta Maria, C., Canada 70 A3 55 9N 82 20W
Henry, U.S.A. 80 E10 41 7N 89 22W
Henryetta, U.S.A. 81 H7 35 27N 95 59W
Henryville, Canada 79 A11 45 8N 73 11W
Hensall, Canada 78 C3 43 26N 81 30W
Hentiesbaai, Namibia 56 C1 22 8S 14 18 E
Hentiyn Nuruu, Mongolia 33 B5 48 30N 108 30 E
Henzada, Burma 41 L19 17 38N 95 26 E
Heppner, U.S.A. 82 D4 45 21N 119 33W
Hepworth, Canada 78 B3 44 37N 81 9W
Hequ, China 34 E6 39 20N 111 15 E
Héraðsflói, Iceland 8 D6 65 42N 14 12W
Héraðsvötn →, Iceland 8 D4 65 45N 19 25W
Herald Cays, Australia 62 B4 16 58S 149 9 E
Herāt, Afghan. 40 B3 34 20N 62 7 E
Herāt □, Afghan. 40 B3 35 0N 62 0 E
Herbert →, Australia 62 B4 18 31S 146 17 E
Herberton, Australia 62 B4 17 20S 145 30 E
Herbertsdale, S. Africa 56 E3 34 1S 21 46 E

Herceg-Novi

Herceg-Novi, Montenegro, Yug. 21 C8 42 30N 18 33 E
Herchmer, Canada 73 B10 57 22N 94 10W
Herðubreið, Iceland 8 D5 65 11N 16 21W
Hereford, U.K. 11 E5 52 4N 2 43W
Hereford, U.S.A. 81 H3 34 49N 102 24W
Herefordshire □, U.K. 11 E5 52 8N 2 40W
Herentals, Belgium 15 C4 51 12N 4 51 E
Herford, Germany 16 B5 52 7N 8 39 E
Herington, U.S.A. 80 F6 38 40N 96 57W
Herkimer, U.S.A. 79 D10 43 0N 74 59W
Herlong, U.S.A. 84 E6 40 8N 120 8W
Herm, U.K. 11 H5 49 30N 2 28W
Hermann, U.S.A. 80 F9 38 42N 91 27W
Hermannsburg, Australia 60 D5 23 57S 132 45 E
Hermanus, S. Africa 56 E2 34 27S 19 12 E
Hermiston, U.S.A. 82 D4 45 51N 119 17W
Hermite, I., Chile 96 H3 55 50S 68 0W
Hermon, U.S.A. 79 B9 44 28N 75 14W
Hermon, Mt. = Shaykh, J. ash, Lebanon 47 B4 33 25N 35 50 E
Hermosillo, Mexico 86 B2 29 10N 111 0W
Hernád →, Hungary 17 D11 47 56N 21 8 E
Hernandarias, Paraguay 95 B5 25 20S 54 40W
Hernandez, U.S.A. 84 J6 36 24N 120 46W
Hernando, Argentina 94 C3 32 28S 63 40W
Hernando, U.S.A. 81 H10 34 50N 90 0W
Herndon, U.S.A. 78 F8 40 43N 76 51W
Herne, Germany 15 C7 51 32N 7 14 E
Herne Bay, U.K. 11 F9 51 21N 1 8 E
Herning, Denmark 9 H13 56 8N 8 58 E
Heroica = Caborca, Mexico 86 A2 30 40N 112 10W
Heroica Nogales = Nogales, Mexico 86 A2 31 20N 110 56W
Heron Bay, Canada 70 C2 48 40N 86 25W
Herradura, Pta. de la, Canary Is. 22 F5 28 26N 14 8W
Herreid, U.S.A. 80 C4 45 50N 100 4W
Herrin, U.S.A. 81 G10 37 48N 89 2W
Herriot, Canada 73 B8 56 22N 101 16W
Hershey, U.S.A. 79 F8 40 17N 76 39W
Hersonissos, Greece 23 D7 35 18N 25 22 E
Herstal, Belgium 15 D5 50 40N 5 38 E
Hertford, U.K. 11 F7 51 48N 0 4W
Hertfordshire □, U.K. 11 F7 51 51N 0 5W
's-Hertogenbosch, Neths. 15 C5 51 42N 5 17 E
Hertzogville, S. Africa 56 D4 28 9S 25 30 E
Hervey B., Australia 62 C5 25 0S 152 52 E
Herzliyya, Israel 47 C3 32 10N 34 50 E
Ḥeşār, Fārs, Iran 45 D6 29 52N 50 16 E
Ḥeşār, Markazī, Iran 45 C6 35 50N 49 12 E
Heshui, China 34 G5 35 48N 108 0 E
Heshun, China 34 F7 37 22N 113 32 E
Hesperia, U.S.A. 85 L9 34 25N 117 18W
Hesse = Hessen □, Germany 16 C5 50 30N 9 0 E
Hessen □, Germany 16 C5 50 30N 9 0 E
Hetch Hetchy Aqueduct, U.S.A. 84 H5 37 29N 122 19W
Hettinger, U.S.A. 80 C3 46 0N 102 42W
Heuvelton, U.S.A. 79 B9 44 37N 75 25W
Hewitt, U.S.A. 81 K6 31 27N 97 11W
Hexham, U.K. 10 C5 54 58N 2 4W
Hexigten Qi, China 35 C9 43 18N 117 30 E
Heydarābād, Iran 45 D7 30 33N 55 38 E
Heysham, U.K. 10 C5 54 3N 2 53W
Heze, China 34 G8 35 14N 115 20 E
Hi Vista, U.S.A. 85 L9 34 45N 117 46W
Hialeah, U.S.A. 77 N5 25 50N 80 17W
Hiawatha, U.S.A. 80 F7 39 51N 95 32W
Hibbing, U.S.A. 80 B8 47 25N 92 56W
Hibbs B., Australia 62 G4 42 35S 145 15 E
Hibernia Reef, Australia 60 B3 12 0S 123 23 E
Hickman, U.S.A. 81 G10 36 34N 89 11W
Hickory, U.S.A. 77 H5 35 44N 81 21W
Hicks L., Canada 73 A9 61 25N 100 0W
Hicksville, U.S.A. 79 F11 40 46N 73 32W
Hida-Gawa →, Japan 31 G8 35 26N 137 3 E
Hida-Sammyaku, Japan 31 F8 36 30N 137 40 E
Hidaka-Sammyaku, Japan 30 C11 42 35N 142 45 E
Hidalgo, Mexico 87 C5 24 15N 99 26W
Hidalgo □, Mexico 87 C5 20 30N 99 10W
Hidalgo, Presa M., Mexico 86 B3 26 30N 108 35W
Hidalgo, Pta. del, Canary Is. 22 F3 28 33N 16 19W
Hidalgo del Parral, Mexico 86 B3 26 58N 105 40W
Hierro, Canary Is. 22 G1 27 44N 18 0W
Higashiajima-San, Japan 30 F10 37 40N 140 10 E
Higashiōsaka, Japan 31 G7 34 40N 135 37 E
Higgins, U.S.A. 81 G4 36 7N 100 2W
Higgins Corner, U.S.A. 84 F5 39 2N 121 5W
High Atlas = Haut Atlas, Morocco 50 B4 32 30N 5 0W
High Bridge, U.S.A. 79 F10 40 40N 74 54W
High Level, Canada 72 B5 58 31N 117 8W
High Point, U.S.A. 77 H6 35 57N 80 0W
High Prairie, Canada 72 B5 55 30N 116 30W
High River, Canada 72 C6 50 30N 113 50W
High Tatra = Tatry, Slovak Rep. 17 D11 49 20N 20 0 E
High Veld, Africa 48 J6 27 0S 27 0 E
High Wycombe, U.K. 11 F7 51 37N 0 45W
Highland □, U.K. 12 D4 57 17N 4 21W
Highland Park, U.S.A. 76 D2 42 11N 87 48W
Highmore, U.S.A. 80 C5 44 31N 99 27W
Highrock L., Man., Canada 73 B8 55 45N 100 30W
Highrock L., Sask., Canada 73 B7 57 5N 105 32W
Higüey, Dom. Rep. 89 C6 18 37N 68 42W
Hiiumaa, Estonia 9 G20 58 50N 22 45 E
Ḥijāz □, Si. Arabia 46 C2 24 0N 40 0 E
Hijo = Tagum, Phil. 37 C7 7 33N 125 53 E
Hikari, Japan 31 H5 33 58N 131 58 E
Hiko, U.S.A. 84 H11 37 32N 115 14W
Hikone, Japan 31 G8 35 15N 136 10 E
Hikurangi, N.Z. 59 F5 35 36S 174 17 E
Hikurangi, Mt., N.Z. 59 H6 37 55S 178 4 E
Hildesheim, Germany 16 B5 52 9N 9 56 E
Hill →, Australia 61 F2 30 23S 115 3 E
Hill City, Idaho, U.S.A. 82 E6 43 18N 115 3W
Hill City, Kans., U.S.A. 80 F5 39 22N 99 51W
Hill City, S. Dak., U.S.A. 80 D3 43 56N 103 35W
Hill Island L., Canada 73 A7 60 30N 109 50W
Hillcrest Center, U.S.A. 85 K8 35 23N 118 57W
Hillegom, Neths. 15 B4 52 18N 4 35 E
Hillerød, Denmark 9 J15 55 56N 12 19 E
Hillsboro, Kans., U.S.A. 80 F6 38 21N 97 12W
Hillsboro, N. Dak., U.S.A. 80 B6 47 26N 97 3W
Hillsboro, N.H., U.S.A. 79 C13 43 7N 71 54W
Hillsboro, Ohio, U.S.A. 76 F4 39 12N 83 37W
Hillsboro, Oreg., U.S.A. 84 E4 45 31N 122 59W
Hillsboro, Tex., U.S.A. 81 J6 32 1N 97 8W
Hillsborough, Grenada 89 D7 12 28N 61 28W
Hillsdale, Mich., U.S.A. 76 E3 41 56N 84 38W
Hillsdale, N.Y., U.S.A. 79 D11 42 11N 73 30W
Hillsport, Canada 70 C2 49 27N 85 34W
Hilo, U.S.A. 74 J17 19 44N 155 5W
Hilton, U.S.A. 78 C7 43 17N 77 48W
Hilton Head Island, U.S.A. 77 J5 32 13N 80 45W
Hilversum, Neths. 15 B5 52 14N 5 10 E
Himachal Pradesh □, India 42 D7 31 30N 77 0 E
Himalaya, Asia 43 E11 29 0N 84 0 E
Himatnagar, India 40 H8 23 37N 72 57 E
Himeji, Japan 31 G7 34 50N 134 40 E
Himi, Japan 31 F8 36 50N 136 55 E
Ḥimş, Syria 47 A5 34 40N 36 45 E
Ḥimş □, Syria 47 A6 34 30N 37 0 E
Hinche, Haiti 89 C5 19 9N 72 1W
Hinchinbrook I., Australia 62 B4 18 20S 146 15 E
Hinckley, U.K. 11 E6 52 33N 1 22W
Hinckley, U.S.A. 80 B8 46 1N 92 56W
Hindaun, India 42 F7 26 44N 77 5 E
Hindu Bagh, Pakistan 42 D2 30 56N 67 50 E
Hindu Kush, Asia 40 B7 36 0N 71 0 E
Hindubagh, Pakistan 40 D5 30 56N 67 57 E
Hindupur, India 40 N10 13 49N 77 32 E
Hines Creek, Canada 72 B5 56 20N 118 40W
Hinesville, U.S.A. 77 K5 31 51N 81 36W
Hinganghat, India 40 J11 20 30N 78 52 E
Hingham, U.S.A. 82 B8 48 33N 110 25W
Hingir, India 43 J10 21 57N 83 41 E
Hingoli, India 40 K10 19 41N 77 15 E
Hinna = Imi, Ethiopia 46 F3 6 28N 42 10 E
Hinnøya, Norway 8 B16 68 35N 15 50 E
Hinojosa del Duque, Spain 19 C3 38 30N 5 9W
Hinsdale, U.S.A. 79 D12 42 47N 72 29W
Hinton, Canada 72 C5 53 26N 117 34W
Hinton, U.S.A. 76 G5 37 40N 80 54W
Hirado, Japan 31 H4 33 22N 129 33 E
Hirakud Dam, India 41 J13 21 32N 83 45 E
Hiran →, India 43 H8 23 6N 79 21 E
Hirapur, India 43 G8 24 22N 79 13 E
Hiratsuka, Japan 31 G9 35 19N 139 21 E
Hiroo, Japan 30 C11 42 17N 143 19 E
Hirosaki, Japan 30 D10 40 34N 140 28 E
Hiroshima, Japan 31 G6 34 24N 132 30 E
Hiroshima □, Japan 31 G6 34 50N 133 0 E
Hisar, India 42 E6 29 12N 75 45 E
Hisb →, Iraq 44 D5 31 45N 44 17 E
Ḥismá, Si. Arabia 44 D3 28 30N 36 0 E
Hispaniola, W. Indies 89 C5 19 0N 71 0W
Hīt, Iraq 44 C4 33 38N 42 49 E
Hita, Japan 31 H5 33 20N 130 58 E
Hitachi, Japan 31 F10 36 36N 140 39 E
Hitchin, U.K. 11 F7 51 58N 0 16W
Hitoyoshi, Japan 31 H5 32 13N 130 45 E
Hitra, Norway 8 E13 63 30N 8 45 E
Hixon, Canada 72 C4 53 25N 122 35W
Hiyyon, N. →, Israel 47 E4 30 25N 35 10 E
Hjalmar L., Canada 73 A7 61 33N 109 25W
Hjälmaren, Sweden 9 G16 59 18N 15 40 E
Hjørring, Denmark 9 H13 57 29N 9 59 E
Hkakabo Razi, Burma 41 E20 28 25N 97 23 E
Hlobane, S. Africa 57 D5 27 42S 31 0 E
Hluhluwe, S. Africa 57 D5 28 1S 32 15 E
Hlyboka, Ukraine 17 D13 48 5N 25 56 E
Ho Chi Minh City = Thanh Pho Ho Chi Minh, Vietnam 39 G6 10 58N 106 40 E
Ho Thuong, Vietnam 38 C5 19 32N 105 48 E
Hoa Binh, Vietnam 38 B5 20 50N 105 20 E
Hoa Da, Vietnam 39 G7 11 16N 108 40 E
Hoa Hiep, Vietnam 39 G5 11 34N 105 51 E
Hoai Nhon, Vietnam 38 E7 14 28N 109 1 E
Hoang Lien Son, Vietnam 38 A4 22 0N 104 0 E
Hoanib →, Namibia 56 B2 19 27S 12 46 E
Hoare B., Canada 69 B13 65 17N 62 30W
Hoarusib →, Namibia 56 B2 19 3S 12 36 E
Hobart, Australia 62 G4 42 50S 147 21 E
Hobart, U.S.A. 81 H5 35 1N 99 6W
Hobbs, U.S.A. 81 J3 32 42N 103 8W
Hobbs Coast, Antarctica 5 D14 74 50S 131 0W
Hobe Sound, U.S.A. 77 M5 27 4N 80 8W
Hoboken, U.S.A. 79 F10 40 45N 74 4W
Hobro, Denmark 9 H13 56 39N 9 46 E
Hoburgen, Sweden 9 H18 56 55N 18 7 E
Hochfeld, Namibia 56 C2 21 28S 17 58 E
Hodaka-Dake, Japan 31 F8 36 17N 137 39 E
Hodgeville, Canada 73 C7 50 7N 106 58W
Hodgson, Canada 73 C9 51 13N 97 36W
Hódmezővásárhely, Hungary 17 E11 46 28N 20 22 E
Hodna, Chott el, Algeria 50 A6 35 26N 4 43 E
Hodonín, Czech Rep. 17 D9 48 50N 17 10 E
Hoeamdong, N. Korea 35 C16 42 30N 130 16 E
Hoek van Holland, Neths. 15 C4 52 0N 4 7 E
Hoengsŏng, S. Korea 35 F14 37 29N 127 59 E
Hoeryong, N. Korea 35 C15 42 30N 129 45 E
Hoeyang, N. Korea 35 E14 38 43N 127 36 E
Hof, Germany 16 C6 50 19N 11 55 E
Hofmeyr, S. Africa 56 E4 31 39S 25 50 E
Höfn, Iceland 8 D6 64 15N 15 13W
Hofors, Sweden 9 F17 60 31N 16 15 E
Hofsjökull, Iceland 8 D4 64 49N 18 48W
Hōfu, Japan 31 G5 34 3N 131 34 E
Hogan Group, Australia 63 F4 39 13S 147 1 E
Hogarth, Mt., Australia 62 C2 21 48S 136 58 E
Hoggar = Ahaggar, Algeria 50 D7 23 0N 6 30 E
Hogsty Reef, Bahamas 89 B5 21 41N 73 48W
Hoh →, U.S.A. 84 C2 47 45N 124 29W
Hohe Venn, Belgium 15 D6 50 30N 6 5 E
Hohenwald, U.S.A. 77 H2 35 33N 87 33W
Hoher Rhön = Rhön, Germany 16 C5 50 24N 9 58 E
Hohhot, China 34 D6 40 52N 111 40 E
Hóhlakas, Greece 23 D9 35 57N 27 53 E
Hoi An, Vietnam 38 E7 15 30N 108 19 E
Hoi Xuan, Vietnam 38 B5 20 25N 105 9 E
Hoisington, U.S.A. 80 F5 38 31N 98 47W
Hōjō, Japan 31 H6 33 58N 132 46 E
Hokianga Harbour, N.Z. 59 F4 35 31S 173 22 E
Hokitika, N.Z. 59 K3 42 42S 171 0 E
Hokkaidō □, Japan 30 C11 43 30N 143 0 E
Holbrook, U.S.A. 83 J8 34 54N 110 10W
Holden, U.S.A. 82 G7 39 6N 112 16W
Holdenville, U.S.A. 81 H6 35 5N 96 24W
Holdrege, U.S.A. 80 E5 40 26N 99 23W
Holguín, Cuba 88 B4 20 50N 76 20W
Hollams Bird I., Namibia 56 C1 24 40S 14 30 E
Holland, Mich., U.S.A. 76 D2 42 47N 86 7W
Holland, N.Y., U.S.A. 78 D6 42 38N 78 32W
Hollandale, U.S.A. 81 J9 33 10N 90 51W
Hollandia = Jayapura, Indonesia 37 E10 2 28S 140 38 E
Holley, U.S.A. 78 C6 43 14N 78 2W
Hollidaysburg, U.S.A. 78 F6 40 26N 78 24W
Hollis, U.S.A. 81 H5 34 41N 99 55W
Hollister, Calif., U.S.A. 84 J5 36 51N 121 24W
Hollister, Idaho, U.S.A. 82 E6 42 21N 114 35W
Holly Hill, U.S.A. 77 L5 29 16N 81 3W
Holly Springs, U.S.A. 81 H10 34 46N 89 27W
Hollywood, U.S.A. 77 N5 26 1N 80 9W
Holman, Canada 68 A8 70 44N 117 44W
Hólmavík, Iceland 8 D3 65 42N 21 40W
Holmen, U.S.A. 80 D9 43 58N 91 15W
Holmes Reefs, Australia 62 B4 16 27S 148 0 E
Holmsund, Sweden 8 E19 63 41N 20 20 E
Holroyd →, Australia 62 A3 14 10S 141 36 E
Holstebro, Denmark 9 H13 56 22N 8 37 E
Holsworthy, U.K. 11 G3 50 48N 4 22W
Holton, Canada 71 B8 54 31N 57 12W
Holton, U.S.A. 80 F7 39 28N 95 44W
Holtville, U.S.A. 85 N11 32 49N 115 23W
Holwerd, Neths. 15 A5 53 22N 5 54 E
Holy I., Angl., U.K. 10 D3 53 17N 4 37W
Holy I., Northumb., U.K. 10 B6 55 40N 1 47W
Holyhead, U.K. 10 D3 53 18N 4 38W
Holyoke, Colo., U.S.A. 80 E3 40 35N 102 18W
Holyoke, Mass., U.S.A. 79 D12 42 12N 72 37W
Holyrood, Canada 71 C9 47 27N 53 8W
Homa Bay, Kenya 54 C3 0 36S 34 30 E
Homalin, Burma 41 G19 24 55N 95 0 E
Homand, Iran 45 C8 32 28N 59 37 E
Homathko →, Canada 72 C4 51 0N 124 56W
Hombori, Mali 50 E5 15 20N 1 38W
Home B., Canada 69 B13 68 40N 67 10W
Home Hill, Australia 62 B4 19 43S 147 25 E
Homedale, U.S.A. 82 E5 43 37N 116 56W
Homer, Alaska, U.S.A. 68 C4 59 39N 151 33W
Homer, La., U.S.A. 81 J8 32 48N 93 4W
Homer City, U.S.A. 78 F5 40 32N 79 10W
Homestead, Australia 62 C4 20 20S 145 40 E
Homestead, U.S.A. 77 N5 25 28N 80 29W
Homewood, U.S.A. 84 F6 39 4N 120 8W
Homoine, Mozam. 57 C6 23 55S 35 8 E
Homs = Ḥimş, Syria 47 A5 34 40N 36 45 E
Homyel, Belarus 17 B16 52 28N 31 0 E
Hon Chong, Vietnam 39 G5 10 25N 104 30 E
Hon Me, Vietnam 38 C5 19 23N 105 56 E
Honan = Henan □, China 34 H8 34 0N 114 0 E
Honbetsu, Japan 30 C11 43 7N 143 37 E
Honcut, U.S.A. 84 F5 39 20N 121 32W
Hondeklipbaai, S. Africa 56 E2 30 19S 17 17 E
Hondo, Japan 31 H5 32 27N 130 12 E
Hondo, U.S.A. 81 L5 29 21N 99 9W
Hondo →, Belize 87 D7 18 25N 88 21W
Honduras ■, Cent. Amer. 88 D2 14 40N 86 30W
Honduras, G. de, Caribbean 88 C2 16 50N 87 0W
Hønefoss, Norway 9 F14 60 10N 10 18 E
Honesdale, U.S.A. 79 E9 41 34N 75 16W
Honey L., U.S.A. 84 E6 40 15N 120 19W
Honfleur, France 18 B4 49 25N 0 13 E
Hong →, Vietnam 32 D5 22 0N 104 0 E
Hong Gai, Vietnam 38 B6 20 57N 107 5 E
Hong He →, China 34 H8 32 25N 115 35 E
Hong Kong □, China 33 D6 22 11N 114 14 E
Hongch'ŏn, S. Korea 35 F14 37 44N 127 53 E
Hongjiang, China 33 D5 27 7N 109 59 E
Hongliu He →, China 34 F5 38 0N 109 50 E
Hongor, Mongolia 34 B7 45 45N 112 50 E
Hongsa, Laos 38 C3 19 43N 101 20 E
Hongshui He →, China 33 D5 23 48N 109 30 E
Hongsŏng, S. Korea 35 F14 36 37N 126 38 E
Hongtong, China 34 F6 36 16N 111 40 E
Honguedo, Détroit d', Canada 71 C7 49 15N 64 0W
Hongwon, N. Korea 35 E14 40 0N 127 56 E
Hongze Hu, China 35 H10 33 15N 118 35 E
Honiara, Solomon Is. 64 H7 9 27S 159 57 E
Honiton, U.K. 11 G4 50 47N 3 11W
Honjō, Japan 30 E10 39 23N 140 3 E
Honningsvåg, Norway 8 A21 70 59N 25 59 E
Honolulu, U.S.A. 74 H16 21 19N 157 52W
Honshū, Japan 33 C8 36 0N 138 0 E
Hood, Mt., U.S.A. 82 D3 45 23N 121 42W
Hood, Pt., Australia 61 F2 34 23S 119 34 E
Hood River, U.S.A. 82 D3 45 43N 121 31W
Hoodsport, U.S.A. 84 C3 47 24N 123 9W
Hoogeveen, Neths. 15 B6 52 44N 6 28 E
Hoogezand-Sappemeer, Neths. 15 A6 53 9N 6 45 E
Hooghly = Hugli →, India 43 J13 21 56N 88 4 E
Hooghly-Chinsura = Chunchura, India 43 H13 22 53N 88 27 E
Hook Hd., Ireland 13 D5 52 7N 6 56W
Hook I., Australia 62 C4 20 4S 149 0 E
Hook of Holland = Hoek van Holland, Neths. 15 C4 52 0N 4 7 E
Hooker, U.S.A. 81 G4 36 52N 101 13W
Hooker Creek, Australia 60 C5 18 23S 130 38 E
Hoonah, U.S.A. 72 B1 58 7N 135 27W
Hooper Bay, U.S.A. 68 B3 61 32N 166 6W
Hoopeston, U.S.A. 76 E2 40 28N 87 40W
Hoopstad, S. Africa 56 D4 27 50S 25 55 E
Hoorn, Neths. 15 B5 52 38N 5 4 E
Hoover, U.S.A. 77 J2 33 20N 86 11W
Hoover Dam, U.S.A. 85 K12 36 1N 114 44W
Hooversville, U.S.A. 78 F6 40 9N 78 55W
Hop Bottom, U.S.A. 79 E9 41 42N 75 46W
Hope, Canada 72 D4 49 25N 121 25W
Hope, Ariz., U.S.A. 85 M13 33 43N 113 42W
Hope, Ark., U.S.A. 81 J8 33 40N 93 36W
Hope, L., S. Austral., Australia 63 D2 28 24S 139 18 E
Hope, L., W. Austral., Australia 61 F3 32 35S 120 15 E
Hope I., Canada 78 B4 44 55N 80 11W
Hope Town, Bahamas 88 A4 26 35N 76 57W
Hopedale, Canada 71 A7 55 28N 60 13W
Hopedale, U.S.A. 79 D13 42 8N 71 33W
Hopefield, S. Africa 56 E2 33 3S 18 22 E
Hopei = Hebei □, China 34 E9 39 0N 116 0 E
Hopelchén, Mexico 87 D7 19 46N 89 50W
Hopetoun, Australia 61 F3 33 57S 120 7 E
Hopetown, S. Africa 56 D3 29 34S 24 3 E
Hopevale, Australia 62 B4 15 16S 145 20 E
Hopewell, U.S.A. 76 G7 37 18N 77 17W
Hopkins, L., Australia 60 D4 24 15S 128 35 E
Hopkinsville, U.S.A. 77 G2 36 52N 87 29W
Hopland, U.S.A. 84 G3 38 58N 123 7W
Hoquiam, U.S.A. 84 D3 46 59N 123 53W
Horden Hills, Australia 60 D5 20 15S 130 0 E
Horinger, China 34 D6 40 28N 111 48 E
Horlick Mts., Antarctica 5 E15 84 0S 102 0W
Horlivka, Ukraine 25 E6 48 19N 38 5 E
Hormak, Iran 45 D9 29 58N 60 51 E
Hormoz, Iran 45 E7 27 35N 55 0 E
Hormoz, Jaz.-ye, Iran 45 E8 27 8N 56 28 E
Hormozgān □, Iran 45 E8 27 30N 56 0 E
Hormuz, Kūh-e, Iran 45 E7 27 27N 55 10 E
Hormuz, Str. of, The Gulf 45 E8 26 30N 56 30 E
Horn, Austria 16 D8 48 39N 15 40 E
Horn, Iceland 8 C2 66 28N 22 28W
Horn →, Canada 72 A5 61 30N 118 1W
Horn, Cape = Hornos, C. de, Chile 96 H3 55 50S 67 30W
Horn Head, Ireland 13 A3 55 14N 8 0W
Horn I., Australia 62 A3 10 37S 142 17 E
Horn Mts., Canada 72 A5 62 15N 119 15W
Hornavan, Sweden 8 C17 66 15N 17 30 E
Hornbeck, U.S.A. 81 K8 31 20N 93 24W
Hornbrook, U.S.A. 82 F2 41 55N 122 33W
Horncastle, U.K. 10 D7 53 13N 0 7W
Hornell, U.S.A. 78 D7 42 20N 77 40W
Hornell L., Canada 72 A5 62 20N 119 25W
Hornepayne, Canada 70 C3 49 14N 84 48W
Hornings Mills, Canada 78 B4 44 9N 80 12W
Hornitos, U.S.A. 84 H6 37 30N 120 14W
Hornos, C. de, Chile 96 H3 55 50S 67 30W
Hornsea, U.K. 10 D7 53 55N 0 11W
Horobetsu, Japan 30 C10 42 24N 141 6 E
Horodenka, Ukraine 17 D13 48 41N 25 29 E
Horodok, Khmelnytskyy, Ukraine 17 D14 49 10N 26 34 E
Horodok, Lviv, Ukraine 17 D12 49 46N 23 32 E
Horokhiv, Ukraine 17 C13 50 30N 24 45 E
Horqin Youyi Qianqi, China 35 A12 46 5N 122 3 E
Horqueta, Paraguay 94 A4 23 15S 56 55W
Horse Creek, U.S.A. 80 E3 41 57N 105 10W
Horse Is., Canada 71 B8 50 15N 55 50W
Horsefly L., Canada 72 C4 52 25N 121 0W
Horseheads, U.S.A. 78 D8 42 10N 76 49W
Horsens, Denmark 9 J13 55 52N 9 51 E
Horsham, U.K. 11 F7 51 4N 0 20W
Horten, Norway 9 G14 59 25N 10 32 E
Horton, U.S.A. 80 F7 39 40N 95 32W
Horton →, Canada 68 B7 69 56N 126 52W
Horwood L., Canada 70 C3 48 5N 82 20W
Hose, Gunung-Gunung, Malaysia 36 D4 2 5N 114 6 E
Ḥoseynābād, Khuzestān, Iran 45 C6 32 45N 48 20 E
Ḥoseynābād, Kordestān, Iran 44 C5 35 33N 47 8 E
Hoshangabad, India 42 H7 22 45N 77 45 E
Hoshiarpur, India 42 D6 31 30N 75 58 E
Hospet, India 40 M10 15 15N 76 20 E
Hoste, I., Chile 96 H3 55 0S 69 0W
Hot, Thailand 38 C2 18 8N 98 29 E
Hot Creek Range, U.S.A. 82 G6 38 40N 116 20W
Hot Springs, Ark., U.S.A. 81 H8 34 31N 93 3W
Hot Springs, S. Dak., U.S.A. 80 D3 43 26N 103 29W
Hotagen, Sweden 8 E16 63 50N 14 30 E
Hotan, China 32 C2 37 25N 79 55 E
Hotazel, S. Africa 56 D3 27 17S 22 58 E
Hotchkiss, U.S.A. 83 G10 38 48N 107 43W
Hotham, C., Australia 60 B5 12 2S 131 18 E
Hoting, Sweden 8 D17 64 8N 16 15 E
Hotte, Massif de la, Haiti 89 C5 18 30N 73 45W
Hottentotsbaai, Namibia 56 D1 26 8S 14 59 E
Houei Sai, Laos 38 B3 20 18N 100 26 E
Houffalize, Belgium 15 D5 50 8N 5 48 E
Houghton, Mich., U.S.A. 80 B10 47 7N 88 34W
Houghton, N.Y., U.S.A. 78 D6 42 25N 78 10W
Houghton L., U.S.A. 76 C3 44 21N 84 44W
Houhora Heads, N.Z. 59 F4 34 49S 173 9 E
Houlton, U.S.A. 77 B12 46 8N 67 51W
Houma, U.S.A. 81 L9 29 36N 90 43W
Housatonic →, U.S.A. 79 E11 41 10N 73 7W
Houston, Canada 72 C3 54 25N 126 39W
Houston, Mo., U.S.A. 81 G9 37 22N 91 58W
Houston, Tex., U.S.A. 81 L7 29 46N 95 22W
Hout →, S. Africa 57 C4 23 4S 29 36 E
Houtkraal, S. Africa 56 E3 30 23S 24 5 E
Houtman Abrolhos, Australia 61 E1 28 43S 113 48 E
Hovd, Mongolia 32 B4 48 2N 91 37 E
Hove, U.K. 11 G7 50 50N 0 10W
Hoveyzeh, Iran 45 D6 31 27N 48 4 E
Hövsgöl, Mongolia 34 C5 43 37N 109 39 E
Hövsgöl Nuur, Mongolia 32 A5 51 0N 100 30 E
Howard, Australia 63 D5 25 16S 152 32 E
Howard, Pa., U.S.A. 78 F7 41 1N 77 40W
Howard, S. Dak., U.S.A. 80 C6 44 1N 97 32W
Howe, U.S.A. 82 E7 43 48N 113 0W
Howe I., Canada 79 B8 44 16N 76 17W
Howell, U.S.A. 76 D4 42 36N 83 56W
Howick, Canada 79 A11 45 11N 73 51W
Howick, S. Africa 57 D5 29 28S 30 14 E
Howick Group, Australia 62 A4 14 20S 145 30 E
Howitt, L., Australia 63 D2 27 40S 138 40 E
Howland I., Pac. Oc. 64 G10 0 48N 176 38W
Howrah = Haora, India 43 H13 22 37N 88 20 E
Howth Hd., Ireland 13 C5 53 22N 6 3W
Höxter, Germany 16 C5 51 46N 9 22 E
Hoy, U.K. 12 C5 58 50N 3 15W
Høyanger, Norway 9 F12 61 13N 6 4 E
Hoyerswerda, Germany 16 C8 51 26N 14 14 E
Hoylake, U.K. 10 D4 53 24N 3 10W
Hpa-an = Pa-an, Burma 41 L20 16 51N 97 40 E
Hpungan Pass, Burma 41 F20 27 30N 96 55 E
Hradec Králové, Czech Rep. 16 C8 50 15N 15 50 E
Hrodna, Belarus 17 B12 53 42N 23 52 E
Hrodzyanka, Belarus 17 B15 53 31N 28 42 E
Hron →, Slovak Rep. 17 E10 47 49N 18 45 E
Hrvatska = Croatia ■, Europe 16 F9 45 20N 16 0 E

J

Jūrmala

Jamanxim →, Brazil 93 D7 4 43S 56 18W
Jambi, Indonesia 36 E2 1 38S 103 30 E
Jambi □, Indonesia 36 E2 1 30S 102 30 E
Jambusar, India 42 H5 22 3N 72 51 E
James →, S. Dak., U.S.A. 80 D6 42 52N 97 18W
James →, Va., U.S.A. 76 G7 36 56N 76 27W
James B., Canada 70 B3 54 0N 80 0W
James Ranges, Australia 60 D5 24 10S 132 30 E
James Ross I., Antarctica 5 C18 63 58S 57 50W
Jamesabad, Pakistan 42 G3 25 17N 69 15 E
Jamestown, S. Africa 56 E4 31 6S 26 45 E
Jamestown, N. Dak., U.S.A. 80 B5 46 54N 98 42W
Jamestown, N.Y., U.S.A. 78 D5 42 6N 79 14W
Jamestown, Pa., U.S.A. 78 E4 41 29N 80 27W
Jamīlābād, Iran 45 C6 34 24N 48 28 E
Jamiltepec, Mexico 87 D5 16 17N 97 49W
Jamira →, India 43 J13 21 35N 88 28 E
Jamkhandi, India 40 L9 16 30N 75 15 E
Jammu, India 42 C6 32 43N 74 54 E
Jammu & Kashmir □, India 43 B7 34 25N 77 0 E
Jamnagar, India 42 H4 22 30N 70 6 E
Jamni →, India 43 G8 25 13N 78 35 E
Jampur, Pakistan 42 E4 29 39N 70 40 E
Jamrud, Pakistan 42 C4 33 59N 71 24 E
Jämsä, Finland 9 F21 61 53N 25 10 E
Jamshedpur, India 43 H12 22 44N 86 12 E
Jamtara, India 43 H12 23 59N 86 49 E
Jämtland, Sweden 8 E15 63 31N 14 0 E
Jan L., Canada 73 C8 54 56N 102 55W
Jan Mayen, Arctic 4 B7 71 0N 9 0W
Janakkala, Finland 9 F21 60 54N 24 36 E
Janaúba, Brazil 93 G10 15 48S 43 19W
Jand, Pakistan 42 C5 33 30N 72 6 E
Jandaq, Iran 45 C7 34 3N 54 22 E
Jandia, Canary Is. 22 F5 28 6N 14 21W
Jandia, Pta. de, Canary Is. 22 F5 28 3N 14 31W
Jandola, Pakistan 42 C4 32 20N 70 9 E
Jandowae, Australia 63 D5 26 45S 151 7 E
Janesville, U.S.A. 80 D10 42 41N 89 1W
Jangamo, Mozam. 57 C6 24 6S 35 21 E
Janghai, India 43 G10 25 33N 82 19 E
Janīn, West Bank 47 C4 32 28N 35 18 E
Janjgir, India 43 J10 22 1N 82 34 E
Janjina, Madag. 57 C8 20 30S 45 50 E
Janos, Mexico 86 A3 30 45N 108 10W
Januária, Brazil 93 G10 15 25S 44 25W
Janubio, Canary Is. 22 F6 28 56N 13 50W
Jaora, India 42 H6 23 40N 75 10 E
Japan ■, Asia 31 G8 36 0N 136 0 E
Japan, Sea of, Asia 30 E7 40 0N 135 0 E
Japan Trench, Pac. Oc. 28 F18 32 0N 142 0 E
Japen = Yapen, Indonesia 37 E9 1 50S 136 0 E
Japla, India 43 G11 24 33N 84 1 E
Japurá →, Brazil 92 D5 3 8S 65 46W
Jaquarão, Brazil 95 C5 32 34S 53 23W
Jaqué, Panama 88 E4 7 27N 78 8W
Jarābulus, Syria 44 B3 36 49N 38 1 E
Jarama →, Spain 19 B4 40 24N 3 32W
Jaranwala, Pakistan 42 D5 31 15N 73 26 E
Jarash, Jordan 47 C4 32 17N 35 54 E
Jardim, Brazil 94 A4 21 28S 56 2W
Jardines de la Reina, Arch. de los, Cuba 88 B4 20 50N 78 50W
Jargalang, China 35 C12 43 5N 122 55 E
Jargalant = Hovd, Mongolia 32 B4 48 2N 91 37 E
Jari →, Brazil 93 D8 1 9S 51 54W
Jarīr, W. al →, Si. Arabia 44 E4 25 38N 42 30 E
Jarosław, Poland 17 C12 50 2N 22 42 E
Jarrahdale, Australia 61 F2 32 24S 116 5 E
Jarrahi →, Iran 45 D6 30 49N 48 48 E
Jarres, Plaine des, Laos 38 C4 19 27N 103 10 E
Jartai, China 34 E3 39 45N 105 48 E
Jarud Qi, China 35 B11 44 28N 120 50 E
Järvenpää, Finland 9 F21 60 29N 25 5 E
Jarvis, Canada 78 D4 42 53N 80 6W
Jarvis I., Pac. Oc. 65 H12 0 15S 160 5W
Jarwa, India 43 F10 27 38N 82 30 E
Jasdan, India 42 H4 22 2N 71 12 E
Jashpurnagar, India 43 H11 22 54N 84 9 E
Jasidih, India 43 G12 24 31N 86 39 E
Jāsimīyah, Iraq 44 C5 33 45N 44 41 E
Jasin, Malaysia 39 L4 2 20N 102 26 E
Jāsk, Iran 45 E8 25 38N 57 45 E
Jasło, Poland 17 D11 49 45N 21 30 E
Jaso, India 43 G9 24 30N 80 29 E
Jasper, Alta., Canada 72 C5 52 55N 118 5W
Jasper, Ont., Canada 79 B9 44 52N 75 57W
Jasper, Ala., U.S.A. 77 J2 33 50N 87 17W
Jasper, Fla., U.S.A. 77 K4 30 31N 82 57W
Jasper, Ind., U.S.A. 76 F2 38 24N 86 56W
Jasper, Tex., U.S.A. 81 K8 30 56N 94 1W
Jasper Nat. Park, Canada 72 C5 52 50N 118 8W
Jasrasar, India 42 F5 27 43N 73 49 E
Jászberény, Hungary 17 E10 47 30N 19 55 E
Jataí, Brazil 93 G8 17 58S 51 48W
Jati, Pakistan 42 G3 24 20N 68 19 E
Jatibarang, Indonesia 37 G13 6 28S 108 18 E
Jatinegara, Indonesia 37 G12 6 13S 106 52 E
Játiva = Xátiva, Spain 19 C5 38 59N 0 32W
Jaú, Brazil 95 A6 22 10S 48 30W
Jauja, Peru 92 F3 11 45S 75 15W
Jaunpur, India 43 G10 25 46N 82 44 E
Java = Jawa, Indonesia 36 F3 7 0S 110 0 E
Java Barat □, Indonesia 37 G12 7 0S 107 0 E
Java Sea, Indonesia 36 E3 4 35S 107 15 E
Java Tengah □, Indonesia 37 G14 7 0S 110 0 E
Java Timur □, Indonesia 37 G15 8 0S 113 0 E
Java Trench, Ind. Oc. 36 F3 9 0S 105 0 E
Javhlant = Ulyasutay, Mongolia 32 B4 47 56N 97 28 E
Jawa, Indonesia 36 F3 7 0S 110 0 E
Jawad, India 42 G6 24 36N 74 51 E
Jay Peak, U.S.A. 79 B12 44 55N 72 32W
Jaya, Puncak, Indonesia 37 E9 3 57S 137 17 E
Jayanti, India 41 F16 26 45N 89 40 E
Jayapura, Indonesia 37 E10 2 28S 140 38 E
Jayawijaya, Pegunungan, Indonesia 37 E9 5 0S 139 0 E
Jaynagar, India 41 F15 26 43N 86 9 E
Jayrūd, Syria 44 C3 33 49N 36 44 E
Jayton, U.S.A. 81 J4 33 15N 100 34W
Jāz Mūrīān, Hāmūn-e, Iran 45 E8 27 20N 58 55 E
Jazīreh-ye Shīf, Iran 45 D6 29 4N 50 54 E
Jazminal, Mexico 86 C4 24 56N 101 25W
Jazzīn, Lebanon 47 B4 33 31N 35 35 E
Jean, U.S.A. 85 K11 35 47N 115 20W
Jean Marie River, Canada 72 A4 61 32N 120 38W
Jean Rabel, Haiti 89 C5 19 50N 73 5W
Jeanerette, U.S.A. 81 L9 29 55N 91 40W
Jeanette, Ostrov = Zhannetty, Ostrov, Russia 27 B16 76 43N 158 0 E
Jeannette, U.S.A. 78 F5 40 20N 79 36W
Jebāl Bārez, Kūh-e, Iran 45 D8 28 30N 58 20 E
Jebel, Bahr el →, Sudan 51 G12 9 30N 30 25 E
Jedburgh, U.K. 12 F6 55 29N 2 33W
Jedda = Jiddah, Si. Arabia 46 C2 21 29N 39 10 E
Jeddore L., Canada 71 C8 48 3N 55 55W
Jędrzejów, Poland 17 C11 50 35N 20 15 E
Jefferson, Iowa, U.S.A. 80 D7 42 1N 94 23W
Jefferson, Ohio, U.S.A. 78 E4 41 44N 80 46W
Jefferson, Tex., U.S.A. 81 J7 32 46N 94 21W
Jefferson, Mt., Nev., U.S.A. 82 G5 38 51N 117 0W
Jefferson, Mt., Oreg., U.S.A. 82 D3 44 41N 121 48W
Jefferson City, Mo., U.S.A. 80 F8 38 34N 92 10W
Jefferson City, Tenn., U.S.A. 77 G4 36 7N 83 30W
Jeffersontown, U.S.A. 76 F3 38 12N 85 35W
Jeffersonville, U.S.A. 76 F3 38 17N 85 44W
Jeffrey City, U.S.A. 82 E10 42 30N 107 49W
Jega, Nigeria 50 F6 12 15N 4 23 E
Jēkabpils, Latvia 9 H21 56 29N 25 57 E
Jekyll I., U.S.A. 77 K5 31 4N 81 25W
Jelenia Góra, Poland 16 C8 50 50N 15 45 E
Jelgava, Latvia 9 H20 56 41N 23 49 E
Jemaja, Indonesia 39 L5 3 5N 105 45 E
Jemaluang, Malaysia 39 L4 2 16N 103 52 E
Jember, Indonesia 37 H15 8 11S 113 41 E
Jembongan, Malaysia 36 C5 6 45N 117 20 E
Jena, Germany 16 C6 50 54N 11 35 E
Jena, U.S.A. 81 K8 31 41N 92 8W
Jenkins, U.S.A. 76 G4 37 10N 82 38W
Jenner, U.S.A. 84 G3 38 27N 123 7W
Jennings, U.S.A. 81 K8 30 13N 92 40W
Jepara, Indonesia 37 G14 7 40S 109 14 E
Jequié, Brazil 93 F10 13 51S 40 5W
Jequitinhonha, Brazil 93 G10 16 30S 41 0W
Jequitinhonha →, Brazil 93 G11 15 51S 38 53W
Jerantut, Malaysia 39 L4 3 56N 102 22 E
Jérémie, Haiti 89 C5 18 40N 74 10W
Jerez, Punta, Mexico 87 C5 22 58N 97 40W
Jerez de García Salinas, Mexico 86 C4 22 39N 103 0W
Jerez de la Frontera, Spain 19 D2 36 41N 6 7W
Jerez de los Caballeros, Spain 19 C2 38 20N 6 45W
Jericho = El Arīḥā, West Bank 47 D4 31 52N 35 27 E
Jericho, Australia 62 C4 23 38S 146 6 E
Jerid, Chott = Djerid, Chott, Tunisia 50 B7 33 42N 8 30 E
Jermyn, U.S.A. 79 E9 41 31N 75 31W
Jerome, U.S.A. 82 E6 42 44N 114 31W
Jerramungup, Australia 61 F2 33 55S 118 55 E
Jersey, U.K. 11 H5 49 11N 2 7W
Jersey City, U.S.A. 79 F10 40 44N 74 4W
Jersey Shore, U.S.A. 78 E7 41 12N 77 15W
Jerseyville, U.S.A. 80 F9 39 7N 90 20W
Jerusalem, Israel 47 D4 31 47N 35 10 E
Jervis Inlet, Canada 72 C4 50 0N 123 57W
Jesi = Iesi, Italy 20 C5 43 31N 13 14 E
Jesselton = Kota Kinabalu, Malaysia 36 C5 6 0N 116 4 E
Jessore, Bangla. 41 H16 23 10N 89 10 E
Jesup, U.S.A. 77 K5 31 36N 81 53W
Jesús Carranza, Mexico 87 D5 17 28N 95 1W
Jesús María, Argentina 94 C3 30 59S 64 5W
Jetmore, U.S.A. 81 F5 38 4N 99 54W
Jetpur, India 42 J4 21 45N 70 10 E
Jevnaker, Norway 9 F14 60 15N 10 26 E
Jewett, U.S.A. 78 F3 40 22N 81 2W
Jewett City, U.S.A. 79 E13 41 36N 72 0W
Jeyḥūnābād, Iran 45 C6 34 58N 48 59 E
Jeypore, India 41 K13 18 50N 82 38 E
Jha Jha, India 43 G12 24 46N 86 22 E
Jhaarkand = Jharkhand □, India 43 H11 24 0N 85 50 E
Jhabua, India 42 H6 22 46N 74 36 E
Jhajjar, India 42 E7 28 37N 76 42 E
Jhal, Pakistan 42 E2 28 17N 67 27 E
Jhal Jhao, Pakistan 40 F4 26 20N 65 35 E
Jhalawar, India 42 G7 24 40N 76 10 E
Jhalida, India 43 H11 23 22N 85 58 E
Jhalrapatan, India 42 G7 24 33N 76 10 E
Jhang Maghiana, Pakistan 42 D5 31 15N 72 22 E
Jhansi, India 43 G8 25 30N 78 36 E
Jhargram, India 43 H12 22 27N 86 59 E
Jharia, India 43 H12 23 45N 86 26 E
Jharkhand □, India 43 H11 24 0N 85 50 E
Jharsuguda, India 41 J14 21 56N 84 5 E
Jhelum, Pakistan 42 C5 33 0N 73 45 E
Jhelum →, Pakistan 42 D5 31 20N 72 10 E
Jhilmilli, India 43 H10 23 24N 82 51 E
Jhudo, Pakistan 42 G3 24 58N 69 18 E
Jhunjhunu, India 42 E6 28 10N 75 30 E
Ji-Paraná, Brazil 92 F6 10 52S 62 57W
Ji Xian, Hebei, China 34 F8 37 35N 115 30 E
Ji Xian, Henan, China 34 G8 35 22N 114 5 E
Ji Xian, Shanxi, China 34 F6 36 7N 110 40 E
Jia Xian, Henan, China 34 H7 33 59N 113 12 E
Jia Xian, Shaanxi, China 34 E6 38 12N 110 28 E
Jiamusi, China 33 B8 46 40N 130 26 E
Ji'an, Jiangxi, China 33 D6 27 6N 114 59 E
Ji'an, Jilin, China 35 D14 41 5N 126 10 E
Jianchang, China 35 D11 40 55N 120 35 E
Jianchangying, China 35 D10 40 10N 118 50 E
Jiangcheng, China 32 D5 22 36N 101 52 E
Jiangmen, China 33 D6 22 32N 113 0 E
Jiangsu □, China 35 H11 33 0N 120 0 E
Jiangxi □, China 33 D6 27 30N 116 0 E
Jiao Xian = Jiaozhou, China 35 F11 36 18N 120 1 E
Jiaohe, Hebei, China 34 E9 38 2N 116 20 E
Jiaohe, Jilin, China 35 C14 43 40N 127 22 E
Jiaozhou, China 35 F11 36 18N 120 1 E
Jiaozhou Wan, China 35 F11 36 5N 120 10 E
Jiaozuo, China 34 G7 35 16N 113 12 E
Jiawang, China 35 G9 34 28N 117 26 E
Jiaxiang, China 34 G9 35 25N 116 20 E
Jiaxing, China 33 C7 30 49N 120 45 E
Jiayi = Chiai, Taiwan 33 D7 23 29N 120 25 E
Jibuti = Djibouti ■, Africa 46 E3 12 0N 43 0 E
Jicarón, I., Panama 88 E3 7 10N 81 50W
Jiddah, Si. Arabia 46 C2 21 29N 39 10 E
Jido, India 41 E19 29 2N 94 58 E
Jieshou, China 34 H8 33 18N 115 22 E
Jiexiu, China 34 F6 37 2N 111 55 E
Jiggalong, Australia 60 D3 23 21S 120 47 E
Jigni, India 43 G8 25 45N 79 25 E
Jihlava, Czech Rep. 16 D8 49 28N 15 35 E
Jihlava →, Czech Rep. 17 D9 48 55N 16 36 E
Jijiga, Ethiopia 46 F3 9 20N 42 50 E
Jilin, China 35 C14 43 44N 126 30 E
Jilin □, China 35 C14 44 0N 127 0 E
Jilong = Chilung, Taiwan 33 D7 25 3N 121 45 E
Jim Thorpe, U.S.A. 79 F9 40 52N 75 44W
Jima, Ethiopia 46 F2 7 40N 36 47 E
Jiménez, Mexico 86 B4 27 10N 104 54W
Jimo, China 35 F11 36 23N 120 30 E
Jin Xian = Jinzhou, China 34 E8 38 2N 115 2 E
Jin Xian, China 35 E11 38 55N 121 42 E
Jinan, China 34 F9 36 38N 117 1 E
Jincheng, China 34 G7 35 29N 112 50 E
Jind, India 42 E7 29 19N 76 22 E
Jindřichův Hradec, Czech Rep. 16 D8 49 10N 15 2 E
Jing He →, China 34 G5 34 27N 109 4 E
Jingbian, China 34 F5 37 20N 108 30 E
Jingchuan, China 34 G4 35 20N 107 20 E
Jingdezhen, China 33 D6 29 20N 117 11 E
Jinggu, China 32 D5 23 35N 100 41 E
Jinghai, China 34 E9 38 55N 116 55 E
Jingle, China 34 E6 38 20N 111 55 E
Jingning, China 34 G3 35 30N 105 43 E
Jingpo Hu, China 35 C15 43 55N 128 55 E
Jingtai, China 34 F3 37 10N 104 6 E
Jingxing, China 34 E8 38 2N 114 8 E
Jingyang, China 34 G5 34 30N 108 50 E
Jingyu, China 35 C14 42 25N 126 45 E
Jingyuan, China 34 F3 36 30N 104 40 E
Jingziguan, China 34 H6 33 15N 111 0 E
Jinhua, China 33 D6 29 8N 119 38 E
Jining, Nei Monggol Zizhiqu, China 34 D7 41 5N 113 0 E
Jining, Shandong, China 34 G9 35 22N 116 34 E
Jinja, Uganda 54 B3 0 25N 33 12 E
Jinjang, Malaysia 39 L3 3 13N 101 39 E
Jinji, China 34 F4 37 58N 106 8 E
Jinnah Barrage, Pakistan 40 C7 32 58N 71 33 E
Jinotega, Nic. 88 D2 13 6N 85 59W
Jinotepe, Nic. 88 D2 11 50N 86 10W
Jinsha Jiang →, China 32 D5 28 50N 104 36 E
Jinxi, China 35 D11 40 52N 120 50 E
Jinxiang, China 34 G9 35 5N 116 22 E
Jinzhou, Hebei, China 34 E8 38 2N 115 2 E
Jinzhou, Liaoning, China 35 D11 41 5N 121 3 E
Jiparaná →, Brazil 92 E6 8 3S 62 52W
Jipijapa, Ecuador 92 D2 1 0S 80 40W
Jiquilpan, Mexico 86 D4 19 57N 102 42W
Jishan, China 34 G6 35 34N 110 58 E
Jisr ash Shughūr, Syria 44 C3 35 49N 36 18 E
Jitarning, Australia 61 F2 32 48S 117 57 E
Jitra, Malaysia 39 J3 6 16N 100 25 E
Jiu →, Romania 17 F12 43 47N 23 48 E
Jiudengkou, China 34 E4 39 56N 106 40 E
Jiujiang, China 33 D6 29 42N 115 58 E
Jiutai, China 35 B13 44 10N 125 50 E
Jiuxincheng, China 34 E8 39 17N 115 59 E
Jixi, China 35 B16 45 20N 130 50 E
Jiyang, China 35 F9 37 0N 117 12 E
Jiyuan, China 34 G7 35 7N 112 57 E
Jīzān, Si. Arabia 46 D3 17 0N 42 20 E
Jize, China 34 F8 36 54N 114 56 E
Jizl, Wādī al, Si. Arabia 44 E3 25 39N 38 25 E
Jizō-Zaki, Japan 31 G6 35 34N 133 20 E
Jizzakh, Uzbekistan 26 E7 40 6N 67 50 E
Joaçaba, Brazil 95 B5 27 5S 51 31W
João Pessoa, Brazil 93 E12 7 10S 34 52W
Joaquín V. González, Argentina 94 B3 25 10S 64 0W
Jobat, India 42 H6 22 25N 74 34 E
Jodhpur, India 42 F5 26 23N 73 8 E
Jodiya, India 42 H4 22 42N 70 18 E
Joensuu, Finland 24 B4 62 37N 29 49 E
Jōetsu, Japan 31 F9 37 12N 138 10 E
Jofane, Mozam. 57 C5 21 15S 34 18 E
Jogbani, India 43 F12 26 25N 87 15 E
Jõgeva, Estonia 9 G22 58 45N 26 24 E
Jogjakarta = Yogyakarta, Indonesia 36 F4 7 49S 110 22 E
Johannesburg, S. Africa 57 D4 26 10S 28 2 E
Johannesburg, U.S.A. 85 K9 35 22N 117 38W
Johilla →, India 43 H9 23 37N 81 14 E
John Day, U.S.A. 82 D4 44 25N 118 57W
John Day →, U.S.A. 82 D3 45 44N 120 39W
John D'Or Prairie, Canada 72 B5 58 30N 115 8W
John H. Kerr Reservoir, U.S.A. 77 G6 36 36N 78 18W
John o' Groats, U.K. 12 C5 58 38N 3 4W
Johnnie, U.S.A. 85 J10 36 25N 116 5W
John's Ra., Australia 62 C1 21 55S 133 23 E
Johnson, Kans., U.S.A. 81 G4 37 34N 101 45W
Johnson, Vt., U.S.A. 79 B12 44 38N 72 41W
Johnson City, N.Y., U.S.A. 79 D9 42 7N 75 58W
Johnson City, Tenn., U.S.A. 77 G4 36 19N 82 21W
Johnson City, Tex., U.S.A. 81 K5 30 17N 98 25W
Johnsonburg, U.S.A. 78 E6 41 29N 78 41W
Johnsondale, U.S.A. 85 K8 35 58N 118 32W
Johnson's Crossing, Canada 72 A2 60 29N 133 18W
Johnston, L., Australia 61 F3 32 25S 120 30 E
Johnston Falls = Mambilima Falls, Zambia 55 E2 10 31S 28 45 E
Johnston I., Pac. Oc. 65 F11 17 10N 169 8W
Johnstone Str., Canada 72 C3 50 28N 126 0W
Johnstown, N.Y., U.S.A. 79 C10 43 0N 74 22W
Johnstown, Ohio, U.S.A. 78 F2 40 9N 82 41W
Johnstown, Pa., U.S.A. 78 F6 40 20N 78 55W
Johor Baharu, Malaysia 39 M4 1 28N 103 46 E
Jõhvi, Estonia 9 G22 59 22N 27 27 E
Joinville, Brazil 95 B6 26 15S 48 55W
Joinville I., Antarctica 5 C18 65 0S 55 30W
Jojutla, Mexico 87 D5 18 37N 99 11W
Jokkmokk, Sweden 8 C18 66 35N 19 50 E
Jökulsá á Bru →, Iceland 8 D6 65 40N 14 16W
Jökulsá á Fjöllum →, Iceland 8 C5 66 10N 16 30W
Jolfā, Āzarbājān-e Sharqī, Iran 44 B5 38 57N 45 38 E
Jolfā, Eşfahan, Iran 45 C6 32 58N 51 37 E
Joliet, U.S.A. 76 E1 41 32N 88 5W
Joliette, Canada 70 C5 46 3N 73 24W
Jolo, Phil. 37 C6 6 0N 121 0 E
Jolon, U.S.A. 84 K5 35 58N 121 9W
Jombang, Indonesia 37 G15 7 33S 112 14 E
Jonava, Lithuania 9 J21 55 8N 24 12 E
Jones Sound, Canada 4 B3 76 0N 85 0W
Jonesboro, Ark., U.S.A. 81 H9 35 50N 90 42W
Jonesboro, La., U.S.A. 81 J8 32 15N 92 43W
Joniškis, Lithuania 9 H20 56 13N 23 35 E
Jönköping, Sweden 9 H16 57 45N 14 8 E
Jonquière, Canada 71 C5 48 27N 71 14W
Joplin, U.S.A. 81 G7 37 6N 94 31W
Jora, India 42 F6 26 20N 77 49 E
Jordan, Mont., U.S.A. 82 C10 47 19N 106 55W
Jordan, N.Y., U.S.A. 79 C8 43 4N 76 29W
Jordan ■, Asia 47 E5 31 0N 36 0 E
Jordan →, Asia 47 D4 31 48N 35 32 E
Jordan Valley, U.S.A. 82 E5 42 59N 117 3W
Jorhat, India 41 F19 26 45N 94 12 E
Jörn, Sweden 8 D19 65 4N 20 1 E
Jorong, Indonesia 36 E4 3 58S 114 56 E
Jørpeland, Norway 9 G11 59 3N 6 1 E
Jorquera →, Chile 94 B2 28 3S 69 58W
Jos, Nigeria 50 G7 9 53N 8 51 E
José Batlle y Ordóñez, Uruguay 95 C4 33 20S 55 10W
Joseph, L., Nfld., Canada 71 B6 52 45N 65 18W
Joseph, L., Ont., Canada 78 A5 45 10N 79 44W
Joseph Bonaparte G., Australia 60 B4 14 35S 128 50 E
Joshinath, India 43 D8 30 34N 79 34 E
Joshua Tree, U.S.A. 85 L10 34 8N 116 19W
Joshua Tree National Park, U.S.A. 85 M10 33 55N 116 0W
Jostedalsbreen, Norway 9 F12 61 40N 6 59 E
Jotunheimen, Norway 9 F13 61 35N 8 25 E
Joubertberge, Namibia 56 B1 18 30S 14 0 E
Jourdanton, U.S.A. 81 L5 28 55N 98 33W
Jovellanos, Cuba 88 B3 22 40N 81 10W
Ju Xian, China 35 F10 36 35N 118 20 E
Juan Aldama, Mexico 86 C4 24 20N 103 23W
Juan Bautista Alberdi, Argentina 94 C3 34 26S 61 48W
Juan de Fuca Str., Canada 84 B3 48 15N 124 0W
Juan de Nova, Ind. Oc. 57 B7 17 3S 43 45 E
Juan Fernández, Arch. de, Pac. Oc. 90 G2 33 50S 80 0W
Juan José Castelli, Argentina 94 B3 25 27S 60 57W
Juan L. Lacaze, Uruguay 94 C4 34 26S 57 25W
Juankoski, Finland 8 E23 63 3N 28 19 E
Juárez, Argentina 94 D4 37 40S 59 43W
Juárez, Mexico 85 N11 32 20N 115 57W
Juárez, Sierra de, Mexico 86 A1 32 0N 116 0W
Juàzeiro, Brazil 93 E10 9 30S 40 30W
Juàzeiro do Norte, Brazil 93 E11 7 10S 39 18W
Juba, Sudan 51 H12 4 50N 31 35 E
Jubayl, Lebanon 47 A4 34 5N 35 39 E
Jubbah, Si. Arabia 44 D4 28 2N 40 56 E
Jubbal, India 42 D7 31 5N 77 40 E
Jubbulpore = Jabalpur, India 43 H8 23 9N 79 58 E
Jubilee L., Australia 61 E4 29 0S 126 50 E
Juby, C., Morocco 50 C3 28 0N 12 59W
Júcar = Xúquer →, Spain 19 C5 39 5N 0 10W
Júcaro, Cuba 88 B4 21 37N 78 51W
Juchitán, Mexico 87 D5 16 27N 95 5W
Judaea = Har Yehuda, Israel 47 D3 31 35N 34 57 E
Judith →, U.S.A. 82 C9 47 44N 109 39W
Judith, Pt., U.S.A. 79 E13 41 22N 71 29W
Judith Gap, U.S.A. 82 C9 46 41N 109 45W
Jugoslavia = Yugoslavia ■, Europe 21 B9 43 20N 20 0 E
Juigalpa, Nic. 88 D2 12 6N 85 26W
Juiz de Fora, Brazil 95 A7 21 43S 43 19W
Jujuy □, Argentina 94 A2 23 20S 65 40W
Julesburg, U.S.A. 80 E3 40 59N 102 16W
Juli, Peru 92 G5 16 10S 69 25W
Julia Cr. →, Australia 62 C3 20 0S 141 11 E
Julia Creek, Australia 62 C3 20 39S 141 44 E
Juliaca, Peru 92 G4 15 25S 70 10W
Julian, U.S.A. 85 M10 33 4N 116 38W
Julian L., Canada 70 B4 54 25N 77 57W
Julianatop, Surinam 93 C7 3 40N 56 30W
Julianehåb = Qaqortoq, Greenland 69 B6 60 43N 46 0W
Julimes, Mexico 86 B3 28 25N 105 27W
Jullundur, India 42 D6 31 20N 75 40 E
Julu, China 34 F8 37 15N 115 2 E
Jumbo, Zimbabwe 55 F3 17 30S 30 58 E
Jumbo Pk., U.S.A. 85 J12 36 12N 114 11W
Jumentos Cays, Bahamas 88 B4 23 0N 75 40W
Jumilla, Spain 19 C5 38 28N 1 19W
Jumla, Nepal 43 E10 29 15N 82 13 E
Jumna = Yamuna →, India 43 G9 25 30N 81 53 E
Junagadh, India 42 J4 21 30N 70 30 E
Junction, Tex., U.S.A. 81 K5 30 29N 99 46W
Junction, Utah, U.S.A. 83 G7 38 14N 112 13W
Junction B., Australia 62 A1 11 52S 133 55 E
Junction City, Kans., U.S.A. 80 F6 39 2N 96 50W
Junction City, Oreg., U.S.A. 82 D2 44 13N 123 12W
Junction Pt., Australia 62 A1 11 45S 133 50 E
Jundah, Australia 62 C3 24 46S 143 2 E
Jundiaí, Brazil 95 A6 24 30S 47 0W
Juneau, U.S.A. 72 B2 58 18N 134 25W
Jungfrau, Switz. 18 C7 46 32N 7 58 E
Junggar Pendi, China 32 B3 44 30N 86 0 E
Jungshahi, Pakistan 42 G2 24 52N 67 44 E
Juniata →, U.S.A. 78 F7 40 30N 77 40W
Junín, Argentina 94 C3 34 33S 60 57W
Junín de los Andes, Argentina 96 D2 39 45S 71 0W
Jūnīyah, Lebanon 47 B4 33 59N 35 38 E
Juntas, Chile 94 B2 28 24S 69 58W
Juntura, U.S.A. 82 E4 43 45N 118 5W
Jur, Nahr el →, Sudan 51 G11 8 45N 29 15 E
Jura = Jura, Mts. du, Europe 18 C7 46 40N 6 5 E
Jura = Schwäbische Alb, Germany 16 D5 48 20N 9 30 E
Jura, U.K. 12 F3 56 0N 5 50W
Jura, Mts. du, Europe 18 C7 46 40N 6 5 E
Jura, Sd. of, U.K. 12 F3 55 57N 5 45W
Jurbarkas, Lithuania 9 J20 55 4N 22 46 E
Jurien, Australia 61 F2 30 18S 115 2 E
Jūrmala, Latvia 9 H20 56 58N 23 34 E

Juruá

Juruá →, Brazil 92 D5 2 37S 65 44W
Juruena, Brazil 92 F7 13 0S 58 10W
Juruena →, Brazil 92 E7 7 20S 58 3W
Juruti, Brazil 93 D7 2 9S 56 4W
Justo Daract, Argentina 94 C2 33 52S 65 12W
Jutaí →, Brazil 92 D5 2 43S 66 57W
Juticalpa, Honduras 88 D2 14 40N 86 12W
Jutland = Jylland, Denmark 9 H13 56 25N 9 30 E
Juventud, I. de la, Cuba 88 B3 21 40N 82 40W
Jüy Zar, Iran 44 C5 33 50N 46 18 E
Juye, China 34 G9 35 22N 116 5 E
Jwaneng, Botswana 53 J4 24 45S 24 50 E
Jylland, Denmark 9 H13 56 25N 9 30 E
Jyväskylä, Finland 9 E21 62 14N 25 50 E

K

K2, Pakistan 43 B7 35 58N 76 32 E
Kaap Plateau, S. Africa 56 D3 28 30S 24 0 E
Kaapkruis, Namibia 56 C1 21 55S 13 57 E
Kaapstad = Cape Town, S. Africa 56 E2 33 55S 18 22 E
Kabaena, Indonesia 37 F6 5 15S 122 0 E
Kabala, S. Leone 50 G3 9 38N 11 37W
Kabale, Uganda 54 C3 1 15S 30 0 E
Kabalo, Dem. Rep. of the Congo 54 D2 6 0S 27 0 E
Kabambare, Dem. Rep. of the Congo 54 C2 4 41S 27 39 E
Kabango, Dem. Rep. of the Congo 55 D2 8 35S 28 30 E
Kabanjahe, Indonesia 36 D1 3 6N 98 30 E
Kabardino-Balkar Republic = Kabardino-Balkaria □, Russia 25 F7 43 30N 43 30 E
Kabardino-Balkaria □, Russia 25 F7 43 30N 43 30 E
Kabarega Falls = Murchison Falls, Uganda 54 B3 2 15N 31 30 E
Kabasalan, Phil. 37 C6 7 47N 122 44 E
Kabetogama, U.S.A. 80 A8 48 28N 92 59W
Kabin Buri, Thailand 38 F3 13 57N 101 43 E
Kabinakagami L., Canada 70 C3 48 54N 84 25W
Kabinda, Dem. Rep. of the Congo 52 F4 6 19S 24 20 E
Kabompo, Zambia 55 E1 13 36S 24 14 E
Kabompo →, Zambia 53 G4 14 10S 23 11 E
Kabondo, Dem. Rep. of the Congo 55 D2 8 58S 25 40 E
Kabongo, Dem. Rep. of the Congo 54 D2 7 22S 25 33 E
Kabūd Gonbad, Iran 45 B8 37 5N 59 45 E
Kābul, Afghan. 42 B3 34 28N 69 11 E
Kābul □, Afghan. 40 B6 34 30N 69 0 E
Kābul →, Pakistan 42 C5 33 55N 72 14 E
Kabunga, Dem. Rep. of the Congo 54 C2 1 38S 28 3 E
Kaburuang, Indonesia 37 D7 3 50N 126 30 E
Kabwe, Zambia 55 E2 14 30S 28 29 E
Kachchh, Gulf of, India 42 H3 22 50N 69 15 E
Kachchh, Rann of, India 42 H4 24 0N 70 0 E
Kachchhidhana, India 43 J8 21 44N 78 46 E
Kachebera, Zambia 55 E3 13 50S 32 50 E
Kachikau, Botswana 56 B3 18 8S 24 26 E
Kachin □, Burma 41 G20 26 0N 97 30 E
Kachira, L., Uganda 54 C3 0 40S 31 7 E
Kachiry, Kazakstan 26 D8 53 10N 75 50 E
Kachnara, India 42 H6 23 50N 75 6 E
Kachot, Cambodia 39 G4 11 30N 103 3 E
Kaçkar, Turkey 25 F7 40 45N 41 10 E
Kadan Kyun, Burma 38 F2 12 30N 98 20 E
Kadanai →, Afghan. 42 D1 31 22N 65 45 E
Kadi, India 42 H5 23 18N 72 23 E
Kadipur, India 43 F10 26 10N 82 23 E
Kadirli, Turkey 44 B3 37 23N 36 5 E
Kadiyevka = Stakhanov, Ukraine 25 E6 48 35N 38 40 E
Kadoka, U.S.A. 80 D4 43 50N 101 31W
Kadoma, Zimbabwe 55 F2 18 20S 29 52 E
Kâdugli, Sudan 51 F11 11 0N 29 45 E
Kaduna, Nigeria 50 F7 10 30N 7 21 E
Kaédi, Mauritania 50 E3 16 9N 13 28W
Kaeng Khoï, Thailand 38 E3 14 35N 101 0 E
Kaesŏng, N. Korea 35 F14 37 58N 126 35 E
Kāf, Si. Arabia 44 D3 31 25N 37 29 E
Kafan = Kapan, Armenia 25 G8 39 18N 46 27 E
Kafanchan, Nigeria 50 G7 9 40N 8 20 E
Kafinda, Zambia 55 E3 12 32S 30 20 E
Kafirévs, Ákra, Greece 21 E11 38 9N 24 38 E
Kafue, Zambia 55 F2 15 46S 28 9 E
Kafue →, Zambia 53 H5 15 30S 29 0 E
Kafue Flats, Zambia 55 F2 15 40S 27 25 E
Kafue Nat. Park, Zambia 55 F2 15 0S 25 30 E
Kafulwe, Zambia 55 D2 9 0S 29 1 E
Kaga, Afghan. 42 B4 34 14N 70 10 E
Kaga Bandoro, C.A.R. 52 C3 7 0N 19 10 E
Kagan, Uzbekistan 26 F7 39 43N 64 33 E
Kagawa □, Japan 31 G7 34 15N 134 0 E
Kagera = Ziwa Maghariba □, Tanzania 54 C3 2 0S 31 30 E
Kagera →, Uganda 54 C3 0 57S 31 47 E
Kağızman, Turkey 44 B4 40 5N 43 10 E
Kagoshima, Japan 31 J5 31 35N 130 33 E
Kagoshima □, Japan 31 J5 31 30N 130 30 E
Kagul = Cahul, Moldova 17 F15 45 50N 28 15 E
Kahak, Iran 45 B6 36 6N 49 46 E
Kahama, Tanzania 54 C3 4 8S 32 30 E
Kahan, Pakistan 42 E3 29 18N 68 54 E
Kahang, Malaysia 39 L4 2 12N 103 32 E
Kahayan →, Indonesia 36 E4 3 40S 114 0 E
Kahe, Tanzania 54 C4 3 30S 37 25 E
Kahnūj, Iran 45 E8 27 55N 57 40 E
Kahoka, U.S.A. 80 E9 40 25N 91 44W
Kahoolawe, U.S.A. 74 H16 20 33N 156 37W
Kahramanmaraş, Turkey 25 G6 37 37N 36 53 E
Kahuta, Pakistan 42 C5 33 35N 73 24 E
Kai, Kepulauan, Indonesia 37 F8 5 55S 132 45 E
Kai Besar, Indonesia 37 F8 5 35S 133 0 E
Kai Is. = Kai, Kepulauan, Indonesia 37 F8 5 55S 132 45 E
Kai Kecil, Indonesia 37 F8 5 45S 132 40 E
Kaiapoi, N.Z. 59 K4 43 24S 172 40 E
Kaieteur Falls, Guyana 92 B7 5 1N 59 10W
Kaifeng, China 34 G8 34 48N 114 21 E
Kaikohe, N.Z. 59 F4 35 25S 173 49 E
Kaikoura, N.Z. 59 K4 42 25S 173 43 E
Kaikoura Ra., N.Z. 59 J4 41 59S 173 41 E
Kailu, China 35 C11 43 38N 121 18 E
Kailua Kona, U.S.A. 74 J17 19 39N 155 59W
Kaimana, Indonesia 37 E8 3 39S 133 45 E
Kaimanawa Mts., N.Z. 59 H5 39 15S 175 56 E
Kaimganj, India 43 F8 27 33N 79 24 E
Kaimur Hills, India 43 G10 24 30N 82 0 E
Kainab →, Namibia 56 D2 28 32S 19 34 E
Kainji Res., Nigeria 50 F6 10 1N 4 40 E
Kainuu, Finland 8 D23 64 30N 29 7 E
Kaipara Harbour, N.Z. 59 G5 36 25S 174 14 E
Kaipokok B., Canada 71 B8 54 54N 59 47W
Kaira, India 42 H5 22 45N 72 50 E
Kairana, India 42 E7 29 24N 77 15 E
Kaironi, Indonesia 37 E8 0 47S 133 40 E
Kairouan, Tunisia 51 A8 35 45N 10 5 E
Kaiserslautern, Germany 16 D4 49 26N 7 45 E
Kaitaia, N.Z. 59 F4 35 8S 173 17 E
Kaitangata, N.Z. 59 M2 46 17S 169 51 E
Kaithal, India 42 E7 29 48N 76 26 E
Kaitu →, Pakistan 42 C4 33 10N 70 30 E
Kaiyuan, China 35 C13 42 28N 124 1 E
Kajaani, Finland 8 D22 64 17N 27 46 E
Kajabbi, Australia 62 C3 20 0S 140 1 E
Kajana = Kajaani, Finland 8 D22 64 17N 27 46 E
Kajang, Malaysia 39 L3 2 59N 101 48 E
Kajiado, Kenya 54 C4 1 53S 36 48 E
Kajo Kaji, Sudan 51 H12 3 58N 31 40 E
Kakabeka Falls, Canada 70 C2 48 24N 89 37W
Kakadu Nat. Park, Australia 60 B5 12 30S 132 5 E
Kakamas, S. Africa 56 D3 28 45S 20 33 E
Kakamega, Kenya 54 B3 0 20N 34 46 E
Kakanui Mts., N.Z. 59 L3 45 10S 170 30 E
Kakdwip, India 43 J13 21 53N 88 11 E
Kake, Japan 31 G6 34 36N 132 19 E
Kake, U.S.A. 72 B2 56 59N 133 57W
Kakegawa, Japan 31 G9 34 45N 138 1 E
Kakeroma-Jima, Japan 31 K4 28 8N 129 14 E
Kakhovka, Ukraine 25 E5 46 45N 33 30 E
Kakhovske Vdskh., Ukraine 25 E5 47 5N 34 0 E
Kakinada, India 41 L13 16 57N 82 11 E
Kakisa →, Canada 72 A5 61 3N 118 10W
Kakisa L., Canada 72 A5 60 56N 117 43W
Kakogawa, Japan 31 G7 34 46N 134 51 E
Kakwa →, Canada 72 C5 54 37N 118 28W
Kāl Güsheh, Iran 45 D8 30 59N 58 12 E
Kal Safīd, Iran 44 C5 34 52N 47 23 E
Kalaallit Nunaat = Greenland ■, N. Amer. 4 C5 66 0N 45 0W
Kalabagh, Pakistan 42 C4 33 0N 71 28 E
Kalabahi, Indonesia 37 F6 8 13S 124 31 E
Kalach, Russia 25 D7 50 22N 41 0 E
Kaladan →, Burma 41 J18 20 20N 93 5 E
Kaladar, Canada 78 B7 44 37N 77 5W
Kalahari, Africa 56 C3 24 0S 21 30 E
Kalahari Gemsbok Nat. Park, S. Africa 56 D3 25 30S 20 30 E
Kalajoki, Finland 8 D20 64 12N 24 10 E
Kālak, Iran 45 E8 25 29N 59 22 E
Kalakamati, Botswana 57 C4 20 40S 27 25 E
Kalakan, Russia 27 D12 55 15N 116 45 E
K'alak'unlun Shank'ou = Karakoram Pass, Pakistan 43 B7 35 33N 77 50 E
Kalam, Pakistan 43 B5 35 34N 72 30 E
Kalama, Dem. Rep. of the Congo 54 C2 2 52S 28 35 E
Kalama, U.S.A. 84 E4 46 1N 122 51W
Kalámai, Greece 21 F10 37 3N 22 10 E
Kalamata = Kalámai, Greece 21 F10 37 3N 22 10 E
Kalamazoo, U.S.A. 76 D3 42 17N 85 35W
Kalamazoo →, U.S.A. 76 D2 42 40N 86 10W
Kalambo Falls, Tanzania 55 D3 8 37S 31 35 E
Kalan, Turkey 44 B3 39 7N 39 32 E
Kalannie, Australia 61 F2 30 22S 117 5 E
Kalāntarī, Iran 45 C7 32 10N 54 8 E
Kalao, Indonesia 37 F6 7 21S 121 0 E
Kalaotoa, Indonesia 37 F6 7 20S 121 50 E
Kalasin, Thailand 38 D4 16 26N 103 30 E
Kalat, Pakistan 40 E5 29 8N 66 31 E
Kalāteh, Iran 45 B7 36 33N 55 41 E
Kalāteh-ye Ganj, Iran 45 E8 27 31N 57 55 E
Kalbarri, Australia 61 E1 27 40S 114 10 E
Kalce, Slovenia 16 F8 45 54N 14 13 E
Kale, Turkey 21 F13 37 27N 28 49 E
Kalegauk Kyun, Burma 41 M20 15 33N 97 35 E
Kalehe, Dem. Rep. of the Congo 54 C2 2 6S 28 50 E
Kalema, Tanzania 54 C3 1 12S 31 55 E
Kalemie, Dem. Rep. of the Congo 54 D2 5 55S 29 9 E
Kalewa, Burma 41 H19 23 10N 94 15 E
Kaleybar, Iran 44 B5 38 47N 47 2 E
Kalgan = Zhangjiakou, China 34 D8 40 48N 114 55 E
Kalgoorlie-Boulder, Australia 61 F3 30 40S 121 22 E
Kali →, India 43 F8 27 6N 79 55 E
Kali Sindh →, India 42 G6 25 32N 76 17 E
Kaliakra, Nos, Bulgaria 21 C13 43 21N 28 30 E
Kalianda, Indonesia 36 F3 5 50S 105 45 E
Kalibo, Phil. 37 B6 11 43N 122 22 E
Kalima, Dem. Rep. of the Congo 54 C2 2 33S 26 32 E
Kalimantan □, Indonesia 36 E4 0 0 114 0 E
Kalimantan Barat □, Indonesia 36 E4 0 0 110 30 E
Kalimantan Selatan □, Indonesia 36 E5 2 30S 115 30 E
Kalimantan Tengah □, Indonesia 36 E4 2 0S 113 30 E
Kalimantan Timur □, Indonesia 36 D5 1 30N 116 30 E
Kálimnos, Greece 21 F12 37 0N 27 0 E
Kalimpong, India 43 F13 27 4N 88 35 E
Kalinin = Tver, Russia 24 C6 56 55N 35 55 E
Kaliningrad, Russia 9 J19 54 42N 20 32 E
Kalinkavichy, Belarus 17 B15 52 12N 29 20 E
Kalinkovichi = Kalinkavichy, Belarus 17 B15 52 12N 29 20 E
Kaliro, Uganda 54 B3 0 56N 33 30 E
Kalispell, U.S.A. 82 B6 48 12N 114 19W
Kalisz, Poland 17 C10 51 45N 18 8 E
Kaliua, Tanzania 54 D3 5 5S 31 48 E
Kalix, Sweden 8 D20 65 53N 23 12 E
Kalix →, Sweden 8 D20 65 50N 23 11 E
Kalka, India 42 D7 30 46N 76 57 E
Kalkarindji, Australia 60 C5 17 30S 130 47 E
Kalkaska, U.S.A. 76 C3 44 44N 85 11W
Kalkfeld, Namibia 56 C2 20 57S 16 14 E
Kalkfontein, Botswana 56 C3 22 4S 20 57 E
Kalkrand, Namibia 56 C2 24 1S 17 35 E
Kallavesi, Finland 8 E22 62 58N 27 30 E
Kallsjön, Sweden 8 E15 63 38N 13 0 E
Kalmar, Sweden 9 H17 56 40N 16 20 E
Kalmyk Republic = Kalmykia □, Russia 25 E8 46 5N 46 1 E
Kalmykia □, Russia 25 E8 46 5N 46 1 E
Kalmykovo, Kazakstan 25 E9 49 0N 51 47 E
Kalna, India 43 H13 23 13N 88 25 E
Kalnai, India 43 H10 22 46N 83 30 E
Kalocsa, Hungary 17 E10 46 32N 19 0 E
Kalokhorio, Cyprus 23 E12 34 51N 33 2 E
Kaloko, Dem. Rep. of the Congo 54 D2 6 47S 25 48 E
Kalol, Gujarat, India 42 H5 22 37N 73 31 E
Kalol, Gujarat, India 42 H5 23 15N 72 33 E
Kalomo, Zambia 55 F2 17 0S 26 30 E
Kalpi, India 43 F8 26 8N 79 47 E
Kalu, Pakistan 42 G2 25 5N 67 39 E
Kaluga, Russia 24 D6 54 35N 36 10 E
Kalulushi, Zambia 55 E2 12 50S 28 3 E
Kalundborg, Denmark 9 J14 55 41N 11 5 E
Kalush, Ukraine 17 D13 49 3N 24 23 E
Kalutara, Sri Lanka 40 R12 6 35N 80 0 E
Kalya, Russia 24 B10 60 15N 59 59 E
Kama, Dem. Rep. of the Congo 54 C2 3 30S 27 5 E
Kama →, Russia 24 C9 55 45N 52 0 E
Kamachumu, Tanzania 54 C3 1 37S 31 37 E
Kamaishi, Japan 30 E10 39 16N 141 53 E
Kamalia, Pakistan 42 D5 30 44N 72 42 E
Kaman, India 42 F6 27 39N 77 16 E
Kamanjab, Namibia 56 B2 19 35S 14 51 E
Kamapanda, Zambia 55 E1 12 5S 24 0 E
Kamaran, Yemen 46 D3 15 21N 42 35 E
Kamativi, Zimbabwe 56 B4 18 20S 27 6 E
Kambalda, Australia 61 F3 31 10S 121 37 E
Kambar, Pakistan 42 F3 27 37N 68 1 E
Kambarka, Russia 24 C9 56 15N 54 11 E
Kambolé, Zambia 55 D3 8 47S 30 48 E
Kambos, Cyprus 23 D11 35 2N 32 44 E
Kambove, Dem. Rep. of the Congo 55 E2 10 51S 26 33 E
Kamchatka, Poluostrov, Russia 27 D16 57 0N 160 0 E
Kamchatka Pen. = Kamchatka, Poluostrov, Russia 27 D16 57 0N 160 0 E
Kamchiya →, Bulgaria 21 C12 43 4N 27 44 E
Kamen, Russia 26 D9 53 50N 81 30 E
Kamen-Rybolov, Russia 30 B6 44 46N 132 2 E
Kamenjak, Rt, Croatia 16 F7 44 47N 13 55 E
Kamenka, Russia 24 A7 65 58N 44 0 E
Kamenka Bugskaya = Kamyanka-Buzka, Ukraine 17 C13 50 8N 24 16 E
Kamensk Uralskiy, Russia 26 D7 56 25N 62 2 E
Kamenskoye, Russia 27 C17 62 45N 165 30 E
Kameoka, Japan 31 G7 35 0N 135 35 E
Kamiah, U.S.A. 82 C5 46 14N 116 2W
Kamieskroon, S. Africa 56 E2 30 9S 17 56 E
Kamilukuak, L., Canada 73 A8 62 22N 101 40W
Kamin-Kashyrskyy, Ukraine 17 C13 51 39N 24 56 E
Kamina, Dem. Rep. of the Congo 55 D2 8 45S 25 0 E
Kaminak L., Canada 73 A10 62 10N 95 0W
Kaministiquia, Canada 70 C1 48 32N 89 35W
Kaminoyama, Japan 30 E10 38 9N 140 17 E
Kamiros, Greece 23 C9 36 20N 27 56 E
Kamituga, Dem. Rep. of the Congo 54 C2 3 2S 28 10 E
Kamla →, India 43 G12 25 35N 86 36 E
Kamloops, Canada 72 C4 50 40N 120 20W
Kamo, Japan 30 F9 37 39N 139 3 E
Kamoke, Pakistan 42 C6 32 4N 74 4 E
Kampala, Uganda 54 B3 0 20N 32 30 E
Kampang Chhnang, Cambodia 39 F5 12 20N 104 35 E
Kampar, Malaysia 39 K3 4 18N 101 9 E
Kampar →, Indonesia 36 D2 0 30N 103 8 E
Kampen, Neths. 15 B5 52 33N 5 53 E
Kampene, Dem. Rep. of the Congo 52 E5 3 36S 26 40 E
Kamphaeng Phet, Thailand 38 D2 16 28N 99 30 E
Kampolombo, L., Zambia 55 E2 11 37S 29 42 E
Kampong Saom, Cambodia 39 G4 10 38N 103 30 E
Kampong Saom, Chaak, Cambodia 39 G4 10 50N 103 32 E
Kampong To, Thailand 39 J3 6 3N 101 13 E
Kampot, Cambodia 39 G5 10 36N 104 10 E
Kampuchea = Cambodia ■, Asia 38 F5 12 15N 105 0 E
Kampung Air Putih, Malaysia 39 K4 4 15N 103 10 E
Kampung Jerangau, Malaysia 39 K4 4 50N 103 10 E
Kampung Raja, Malaysia 39 K4 5 45N 102 35 E
Kampungbaru = Tolitoli, Indonesia 37 D6 1 5N 120 50 E
Kamrau, Teluk, Indonesia 37 E8 3 30S 133 36 E
Kamsack, Canada 73 C8 51 34N 101 54W
Kamskoye Vdkhr., Russia 24 C10 58 41N 56 7 E
Kamuchawie L., Canada 73 B8 56 18N 101 59W
Kamui-Misaki, Japan 30 C10 43 20N 140 21 E
Kamyanets-Podilskyy, Ukraine 17 D14 48 45N 26 40 E
Kamyanka-Buzka, Ukraine 17 C13 50 8N 24 16 E
Kāmyārān, Iran 44 C5 34 47N 46 56 E
Kamyshin, Russia 25 D8 50 10N 45 24 E
Kanaaupscow, Canada 70 B4 54 2N 76 30W
Kanaaupscow →, Canada 69 C12 53 39N 77 9W
Kanab, U.S.A. 83 H7 37 3N 112 32W
Kanab →, U.S.A. 83 H7 36 24N 112 38W
Kanagi, Japan 30 D10 40 54N 140 27 E
Kanairiktok →, Canada 71 A7 55 2N 60 18W
Kananga, Dem. Rep. of the Congo 52 F4 5 55S 22 18 E
Kanash, Russia 24 C8 55 30N 47 32 E
Kanaskat, U.S.A. 84 C5 47 19N 121 54W
Kanastraíon, Ákra = Palioúrion, Ákra, Greece 21 E10 39 57N 23 45 E
Kanawha →, U.S.A. 76 F4 38 50N 82 9W
Kanazawa, Japan 31 F8 36 30N 136 38 E
Kanchanaburi, Thailand 38 E2 14 2N 99 31 E
Kanchenjunga, Nepal 43 F13 27 50N 88 10 E
Kanchipuram, India 40 N11 12 52N 79 45 E
Kandaghat, India 42 D7 30 59N 77 7 E
Kandahar = Qandahār, Afghan. 40 D4 31 32N 65 30 E
Kandalaksha, Russia 24 A5 67 9N 32 30 E
Kandalakshskiy Zaliv, Russia 24 A6 66 0N 35 0 E
Kandangan, Indonesia 36 E5 2 50S 115 20 E
Kandanghaur, Indonesia 37 G13 6 21S 108 6 E
Kandanos, Greece 23 D5 35 19N 23 44 E
Kandavu, Fiji 59 D8 19 0S 178 15 E
Kandhkot, Pakistan 42 E3 28 16N 69 8 E
Kandhla, India 42 E7 29 18N 77 19 E
Kandi, Benin 50 F6 11 7N 2 55 E
Kandi, India 43 H13 23 58N 88 5 E
Kandiaro, Pakistan 42 F3 27 4N 68 13 E
Kandla, India 42 H4 23 0N 70 10 E
Kandreho, Madag. 57 B8 17 29S 46 6 E
Kandy, Sri Lanka 40 R12 7 18N 80 43 E
Kane, U.S.A. 78 E6 41 40N 78 49W
Kane Basin, Greenland 4 B4 79 1N 70 0W
Kaneohe, U.S.A. 74 H16 21 25N 157 48W
Kang, Botswana 56 C3 23 41S 22 50 E
Kangān, Fārs, Iran 45 E7 27 50N 52 3 E
Kangān, Hormozgān, Iran 45 E8 25 48N 57 28 E
Kangar, Malaysia 39 J3 6 27N 100 12 E
Kangaroo Mts., Australia 62 C3 23 29S 141 51 E
Kangasala, Finland 9 F21 61 28N 24 4 E
Kangāvar, Iran 45 C6 34 40N 48 0 E
Kangdong, N. Korea 35 E14 39 9N 126 5 E
Kangean, Kepulauan, Indonesia 36 F5 6 55S 115 23 E
Kangean Is. = Kangean, Kepulauan, Indonesia 36 F5 6 55S 115 23 E
Kanggye, N. Korea 35 D14 41 0N 126 35 E
Kanggyŏng, S. Korea 35 F14 36 10N 127 0 E
Kanghwa, S. Korea 35 F14 37 45N 126 30 E
Kangikajik, Greenland 4 B6 70 7N 22 0W
Kangiqsliniq = Rankin Inlet, Canada 68 B10 62 30N 93 0W
Kangiqsualujjuaq, Canada 69 C13 58 30N 65 59W
Kangiqsujuaq, Canada 69 B12 61 30N 72 0W
Kangiqtugaapik = Clyde River, Canada 69 A13 70 30N 68 30W
Kangirsuk, Canada 69 B13 60 0N 70 0W
Kangnŭng, S. Korea 35 F15 37 45N 128 54 E
Kangping, China 35 C12 42 43N 123 18 E
Kangra, India 42 C7 32 6N 76 16 E
Kangto, India 41 F18 27 50N 92 35 E
Kanhar →, India 43 G10 24 28N 83 8 E
Kaniama, Dem. Rep. of the Congo 54 D1 7 30S 24 12 E
Kaniapiskau = Caniapiscau →, Canada 71 A6 56 40N 69 30W
Kaniapiskau, Res. = Caniapiscau, Rés. de, Canada 71 B6 54 10N 69 55W
Kanin, Poluostrov, Russia 24 A8 68 0N 45 0 E
Kanin Nos, Mys, Russia 24 A7 68 39N 43 32 E
Kanin Pen. = Kanin, Poluostrov, Russia 24 A8 68 0N 45 0 E
Kanjut Sar, Pakistan 43 A6 36 7N 75 25 E
Kankaanpää, Finland 9 F20 61 44N 22 50 E
Kankakee, U.S.A. 76 E2 41 7N 87 52W
Kankakee →, U.S.A. 76 E1 41 23N 88 15W
Kankan, Guinea 50 F4 10 23N 9 15W
Kankendy = Xankändi, Azerbaijan 25 G8 39 52N 46 49 E
Kanker, India 41 J12 20 10N 81 40 E
Kankroli, India 42 G5 25 4N 73 53 E
Kannapolis, U.S.A. 77 H5 35 30N 80 37W
Kannauj, India 43 F8 27 3N 79 56 E
Kannod, India 40 H10 22 45N 76 40 E
Kano, Nigeria 50 F7 12 2N 8 30 E
Kan'onji, Japan 31 G6 34 7N 133 39 E
Kanowit, Malaysia 36 D4 2 14N 112 20 E
Kanoya, Japan 31 J5 31 25N 130 50 E
Kanpetlet, Burma 41 J18 21 10N 93 59 E
Kanpur, India 43 F9 26 28N 80 20 E
Kansas □, U.S.A. 80 F6 38 30N 99 0W
Kansas →, U.S.A. 80 F7 39 7N 94 37W
Kansas City, Kans., U.S.A. 80 F7 39 7N 94 38W
Kansas City, Mo., U.S.A. 80 F7 39 6N 94 35W
Kansenia, Dem. Rep. of the Congo 55 E2 10 20S 26 0 E
Kansk, Russia 27 D10 56 20N 95 37 E
Kansŏng, S. Korea 35 E15 38 24N 128 30 E
Kansu = Gansu □, China 34 G3 36 0N 104 0 E
Kantaphor, India 42 H7 22 35N 76 34 E
Kantharalak, Thailand 38 E5 14 39N 104 39 E
Kantli →, India 42 E6 28 20N 75 30 E
Kantō □, Japan 31 F9 36 15N 139 30 E
Kantō-Sanchi, Japan 31 G9 35 59N 138 50 E
Kanturk, Ireland 13 D3 52 11N 8 54W
Kanuma, Japan 31 F9 36 34N 139 42 E
Kanus, Namibia 56 D2 27 50S 18 39 E
Kanye, Botswana 56 C4 24 55S 25 28 E
Kanzenze, Dem. Rep. of the Congo 55 E2 10 30S 25 12 E
Kanzi, Ras, Tanzania 54 D4 7 1S 39 33 E
Kaohsiung, Taiwan 33 D7 22 35N 120 16 E
Kaokoveld, Namibia 56 B1 19 15S 14 30 E
Kaolack, Senegal 50 F2 14 5N 16 8W
Kaoshan, China 35 B13 44 38N 124 50 E
Kapaa, U.S.A. 74 G15 22 5N 159 19W
Kapadvanj, India 42 H5 23 5N 73 0 E
Kapan, Armenia 25 G8 39 18N 46 27 E
Kapanga, Dem. Rep. of the Congo 52 F4 8 30S 22 40 E
Kapchagai = Qapshaghay, Kazakstan 26 E8 43 51N 77 14 E
Kapela = Velika Kapela, Croatia 16 F8 45 10N 15 5 E
Kapema, Dem. Rep. of the Congo 55 E2 10 45S 28 22 E
Kapfenberg, Austria 16 E8 47 26N 15 18 E
Kapiri Mposhi, Zambia 55 E2 13 59S 28 43 E
Kapiskau →, Canada 70 B3 52 47N 81 55W
Kapit, Malaysia 36 D4 2 0N 112 55 E
Kapiti I., N.Z. 59 J5 40 50S 174 56 E
Kaplan, U.S.A. 81 K8 30 0N 92 17W
Kapoe, Thailand 39 H2 9 34N 98 32 E
Kapoeta, Sudan 51 H12 4 50N 33 35 E

Korshunovo

Korshunovo, Russia 27 D12 58 37N 110 10 E
Korsør, Denmark 9 J14 55 20N 11 9 E
Kortrijk, Belgium 15 D3 50 50N 3 17 E
Korwai, India 42 G8 24 7N 78 5 E
Koryakskoye Nagorye, Russia 27 C18 61 0N 171 0 E
Koryŏng, S. Korea 35 G15 35 44N 128 15 E
Kos, Greece 21 F12 36 50N 27 15 E
Koschagyl, Kazakstan 25 E9 46 40N 54 0 E
Kościan, Poland 17 B9 52 5N 16 40 E
Kosciusko, U.S.A. 81 J10 33 4N 89 35W
Kosha, Sudan 51 D12 20 50N 30 30 E
K'oshih = Kashi, China 32 C2 39 30N 76 2 E
Koshiki-Rettō, Japan 31 J4 31 45N 129 49 E
Kosi, India 42 F7 27 48N 77 29 E
Kosi →, India 43 E8 28 41N 78 57 E
Košice, Slovak Rep. 17 D11 48 42N 21 15 E
Koskhinoú, Greece 23 C10 36 23N 28 13 E
Koslan, Russia 24 B8 63 34N 49 14 E
Kosŏng, N. Korea 35 E15 38 40N 128 22 E
Kosovo □, Yugoslavia 21 C9 42 30N 21 0 E
Kosovska Mitrovica, Kosovo, Yug. 21 C9 42 54N 20 52 E
Kossou, L. de, Ivory C. 50 G4 6 59N 5 31W
Koster, S. Africa 56 D4 25 52S 26 54 E
Kôstî, Sudan 51 F12 13 8N 32 43 E
Kostopil, Ukraine 17 C14 50 51N 26 22 E
Kostroma, Russia 24 C7 57 50N 40 58 E
Kostrzyn, Poland 16 B8 52 35N 14 39 E
Koszalin, Poland 16 A9 54 11N 16 8 E
Kot Addu, Pakistan 42 D4 30 30N 71 0 E
Kot Kapura, India 42 D6 30 35N 74 50 E
Kot Moman, Pakistan 42 C5 32 13N 73 0 E
Kot Sultan, Pakistan 42 D4 30 46N 70 56 E
Kota, India 42 G6 25 14N 75 49 E
Kota Baharu, Malaysia 39 J4 6 7N 102 14 E
Kota Barrage, India 42 G6 25 6N 75 51 E
Kota Belud, Malaysia 36 C5 6 21N 116 26 E
Kota Kinabalu, Malaysia 36 C5 6 0N 116 4 E
Kota Kubu Baharu, Malaysia 39 L3 3 34N 101 39 E
Kota Tinggi, Malaysia 39 M4 1 44N 103 53 E
Kotaagung, Indonesia 36 F2 5 38S 104 29 E
Kotabaru, Indonesia 36 E5 3 20S 116 20 E
Kotabumi, Indonesia 36 E2 4 49S 104 54 E
Kotamobagu, Indonesia 37 D6 0 57N 124 31 E
Kotcho L., Canada 72 B4 59 7N 121 12W
Kotdwara, India 43 E8 29 45N 78 32 E
Kotelnich, Russia 24 C8 58 22N 48 24 E
Kotelnikovo, Russia 25 E7 47 38N 43 8 E
Kotelnyy, Ostrov, Russia 27 B14 75 10N 139 0 E
Kothari →, India 42 G6 25 20N 75 4 E
Kothi, Mad. P., India 43 H10 23 21N 82 3 E
Kothi, Mad. P., India 43 G9 24 45N 80 40 E
Kotiro, Pakistan 42 F2 26 17N 67 13 E
Kotka, Finland 9 F22 60 28N 26 58 E
Kotlas, Russia 24 B8 61 17N 46 43 E
Kotli, Pakistan 42 C5 33 30N 73 55 E
Kotma, India 43 H9 23 12N 81 58 E
Kotmul, Pakistan 43 B6 35 32N 75 10 E
Kotor, Montenegro, Yug. 21 C8 42 25N 18 47 E
Kotovsk, Ukraine 17 E15 47 45N 29 35 E
Kotputli, India 42 F7 27 43N 76 12 E
Kotri, Pakistan 42 G3 25 22N 68 22 E
Kotturu, India 40 M10 14 45N 76 10 E
Kotuy →, Russia 27 B11 71 54N 102 6 E
Kotzebue, U.S.A. 68 B3 66 53N 162 39W
Koudougou, Burkina Faso 50 F5 12 10N 2 20W
Koufonísi, Greece 23 E8 34 56N 26 8 E
Kougaberge, S. Africa 56 E3 33 48S 23 50 E
Kouilou →, Congo 52 E2 4 10S 12 5 E
Koula Moutou, Gabon 52 E2 1 15S 12 25 E
Koulen = Kulen, Cambodia 38 F5 13 50N 104 40 E
Kouloúra, Greece 23 A3 39 42N 19 54 E
Koúm-bournoú, Ákra, Greece 23 C10 36 15N 28 11 E
Koumala, Australia 62 C4 21 38S 149 15 E
Koumra, Chad 51 G9 8 50N 17 35 E
Kounradskiy, Kazakstan 26 E8 46 59N 75 0 E
Kountze, U.S.A. 81 K7 30 22N 94 19W
Kouris →, Cyprus 23 E11 34 38N 32 54 E
Kourou, Fr. Guiana 93 B8 5 9N 52 39W
Kousseri, Cameroon 51 F8 12 0N 14 55 E
Kouvola, Finland 9 F22 60 52N 26 43 E
Kovdor, Russia 24 A5 67 34N 30 24 E
Kovel, Ukraine 17 C13 51 11N 24 38 E
Kovrov, Russia 24 C7 56 25N 41 25 E
Kowanyama, Australia 62 B3 15 29S 141 44 E
Kowŏn, N. Korea 35 E14 39 26N 127 14 E
Köyceğiz, Turkey 21 F13 36 57N 28 40 E
Koza, Japan 31 L3 26 19N 127 46 E
Kozan, Turkey 44 B2 37 26N 35 50 E
Kozáni, Greece 21 D9 40 19N 21 47 E
Kozhikode = Calicut, India 40 P9 11 15N 75 43 E
Kozhva, Russia 24 A10 65 10N 57 0 E
Kozyatyn, Ukraine 17 D15 49 45N 28 50 E
Kra, Isthmus of = Kra, Kho Khot, Thailand 39 G2 10 15N 99 30 E
Kra, Kho Khot, Thailand 39 G2 10 15N 99 30 E
Kra Buri, Thailand 39 G2 10 22N 98 46 E
Kraai →, S. Africa 56 E4 30 40S 26 45 E
Krabi, Thailand 39 H2 8 4N 98 55 E
Kracheh, Cambodia 38 F6 12 32N 106 10 E
Kragan, Indonesia 37 G14 6 43S 111 38 E
Kragerø, Norway 9 G13 58 52N 9 25 E
Kragujevac, Serbia, Yug. 21 B9 44 2N 20 56 E
Krajina, Bos.-H. 20 B7 44 45N 16 35 E
Krakatau = Rakata, Pulau, Indonesia 36 F3 6 10S 105 20 E
Krakatoa = Rakata, Pulau, Indonesia 36 F3 6 10S 105 20 E
Krakor, Cambodia 38 F5 12 32N 104 12 E
Kraków, Poland 17 C10 50 4N 19 57 E
Kralanh, Cambodia 38 F4 13 35N 103 25 E
Kraljevo, Serbia, Yug. 21 C9 43 44N 20 41 E
Kramatorsk, Ukraine 25 E6 48 50N 37 30 E
Kramfors, Sweden 9 E17 62 55N 17 48 E
Kranj, Slovenia 16 E8 46 16N 14 22 E
Krankskop, S. Africa 57 D5 28 0S 30 47 E
Krasavino, Russia 24 B8 60 58N 46 29 E
Kraskino, Russia 27 E14 42 44N 130 48 E
Kraśnik, Poland 17 C12 50 55N 22 15 E
Krasnoarmeysk, Russia 26 D5 51 0N 45 42 E
Krasnodar, Russia 25 E6 45 5N 39 0 E
Krasnokamsk, Russia 24 C10 58 4N 55 48 E
Krasnoperekopsk, Ukraine 25 E5 46 0N 33 54 E
Krasnorechenskiy, Russia 30 B7 44 41N 135 14 E
Krasnoselkup, Russia 26 C9 65 20N 82 10 E
Krasnoturinsk, Russia 24 C11 59 46N 60 12 E
Krasnoufimsk, Russia 24 C10 56 36N 57 38 E
Krasnouralsk, Russia 24 C11 58 21N 60 3 E
Krasnovishersk, Russia 24 B10 60 23N 57 3 E
Krasnovodsk = Türkmenbashi, Turkmenistan 25 G9 40 5N 53 5 E
Krasnoyarsk, Russia 27 D10 56 8N 93 0 E
Krasnyy Kut, Russia 25 D8 50 50N 47 0 E
Krasnýy Luch, Ukraine 25 E6 48 13N 39 0 E
Krasnyy Yar, Russia 25 E8 46 43N 48 23 E
Kratie = Kracheh, Cambodia 38 F6 12 32N 106 10 E
Krau, Indonesia 37 E10 3 19S 140 5 E
Kravanh, Chuor Phnum, Cambodia 39 G4 12 0N 103 32 E
Krefeld, Germany 16 C4 51 20N 6 33 E
Kremen, Croatia 16 F8 44 28N 15 53 E
Kremenchug = Kremenchuk, Ukraine 25 E5 49 5N 33 25 E
Kremenchuk, Ukraine 25 E5 49 5N 33 25 E
Kremenchuksk Vdskh., Ukraine 25 E5 49 20N 32 30 E
Kremenets, Ukraine 17 C13 50 8N 25 43 E
Kremmling, U.S.A. 82 F10 40 4N 106 24W
Krems, Austria 16 D8 48 25N 15 36 E
Kretinga, Lithuania 9 J19 55 53N 21 15 E
Kribi, Cameroon 52 D1 2 57N 9 56 E
Krichev = Krychaw, Belarus 17 B16 53 40N 31 41 E
Kriós, Ákra, Greece 23 D5 35 13N 23 34 E
Krishna →, India 41 M12 15 57N 80 59 E
Krishnanagar, India 43 H13 23 24N 88 33 E
Kristiansand, Norway 9 G13 58 8N 8 1 E
Kristianstad, Sweden 9 H16 56 2N 14 9 E
Kristiansund, Norway 8 E12 63 7N 7 45 E
Kristiinankaupunki, Finland 9 E19 62 16N 21 21 E
Kristinehamn, Sweden 9 G16 59 18N 14 7 E
Kristinestad = Kristiinankaupunki, Finland 9 E19 62 16N 21 21 E
Kríti, Greece 23 D7 35 15N 25 0 E
Kritsá, Greece 23 D7 35 10N 25 41 E
Krivoy Rog = Kryvyy Rih, Ukraine 25 E5 47 51N 33 20 E
Krk, Croatia 16 F8 45 8N 14 40 E
Krokodil →, Mozam. 57 D5 25 14S 32 18 E
Krong Kaoh Kong, Cambodia 36 B2 11 35N 103 0 E
Kronprins Olav Kyst, Antarctica 5 C5 69 0S 42 0 E
Kronshtadt, Russia 24 B4 59 57N 29 51 E
Kroonstad, S. Africa 56 D4 27 43S 27 19 E
Kropotkin, Russia 25 E7 45 28N 40 28 E
Krosno, Poland 17 D11 49 42N 21 46 E
Krotoszyn, Poland 17 C9 51 42N 17 23 E
Kroussón, Greece 23 D6 35 13N 24 59 E
Kruger Nat. Park, S. Africa 57 C5 23 30S 31 40 E
Krugersdorp, S. Africa 57 D4 26 5S 27 46 E
Kruisfontein, S. Africa 56 E3 33 59S 24 43 E
Krung Thep = Bangkok, Thailand 38 F3 13 45N 100 35 E
Krupki, Belarus 17 A15 54 19N 29 8 E
Kruševac, Serbia, Yug. 21 C9 43 35N 21 28 E
Krychaw, Belarus 17 B16 53 40N 31 41 E
Krymskiy Poluostrov = Krymskyy Pivostriv, Ukraine 25 F5 45 0N 34 0 E
Krymskyy Pivostriv, Ukraine 25 F5 45 0N 34 0 E
Kryvyy Rih, Ukraine 25 E5 47 51N 33 20 E
Ksar el Kebir, Morocco 50 B4 35 0N 6 0W
Ksar es Souk = Er Rachidia, Morocco 50 B5 31 58N 4 20W
Kuala Belait, Malaysia 36 D4 4 35N 114 11 E
Kuala Berang, Malaysia 39 K4 5 5N 103 1 E
Kuala Dungun = Dungun, Malaysia 39 K4 4 45N 103 25 E
Kuala Kangsar, Malaysia 39 K3 4 46N 100 56 E
Kuala Kelawang, Malaysia 39 L4 2 56N 102 5 E
Kuala Kerai, Malaysia 39 K4 5 30N 102 12 E
Kuala Lipis, Malaysia 39 K4 4 10N 102 3 E
Kuala Lumpur, Malaysia 39 L3 3 9N 101 41 E
Kuala Nerang, Malaysia 39 J3 6 16N 100 37 E
Kuala Pilah, Malaysia 39 L4 2 45N 102 15 E
Kuala Rompin, Malaysia 39 L4 2 49N 103 29 E
Kuala Selangor, Malaysia 39 L3 3 20N 101 15 E
Kuala Sepetang, Malaysia 39 K3 4 49N 100 28 E
Kuala Terengganu, Malaysia 39 K4 5 20N 103 8 E
Kualajelai, Indonesia 36 E4 2 58S 110 46 E
Kualakapuas, Indonesia 36 E4 2 55S 114 20 E
Kualakurun, Indonesia 36 E4 1 10S 113 50 E
Kualapembuang, Indonesia 36 E4 3 14S 112 38 E
Kualasimpang, Indonesia 36 D1 4 17N 98 3 E
Kuancheng, China 35 D10 40 37N 118 30 E
Kuandang, Indonesia 37 D6 0 56N 123 1 E
Kuandian, China 35 D13 40 45N 124 45 E
Kuangchou = Guangzhou, China 33 D6 23 5N 113 10 E
Kuantan, Malaysia 39 L4 3 49N 103 20 E
Kuba = Quba, Azerbaijan 25 F8 41 21N 48 32 E
Kuban →, Russia 25 E6 45 20N 37 30 E
Kubokawa, Japan 31 H6 33 12N 133 8 E
Kucha Gompa, India 43 B7 34 25N 76 56 E
Kuchaman, India 42 F6 27 13N 74 47 E
Kuchinda, India 43 J11 21 44N 84 21 E
Kuching, Malaysia 36 D4 1 33N 110 25 E
Kuchino-eruba-Jima, Japan 31 J5 30 28N 130 12 E
Kuchino-Shima, Japan 31 K4 29 57N 129 55 E
Kuchinotsu, Japan 31 H5 32 36N 130 11 E
Kucing = Kuching, Malaysia 36 D4 1 33N 110 25 E
Kud →, Pakistan 42 F2 26 5N 66 20 E
Kuda, India 40 H7 23 10N 71 15 E
Kudat, Malaysia 36 C5 6 55N 116 55 E
Kudus, Indonesia 37 G14 6 48S 110 51 E
Kudymkar, Russia 24 C9 59 1N 54 39 E
Kueiyang = Guiyang, China 32 D5 26 32N 106 40 E
Kufra Oasis = Al Kufrah, Libya 51 D10 24 17N 23 15 E
Kufstein, Austria 16 E7 47 35N 12 11 E
Kugluktuk, Canada 68 B8 67 50N 115 5W
Kugong I., Canada 70 A4 56 18N 79 50W
Kūhak, Iran 40 F3 27 12N 63 10 E
Kuhan, Pakistan 42 E2 28 19N 67 14 E
Kūhbonān, Iran 45 D8 31 23N 56 19 E
Kūhestak, Iran 45 E8 26 47N 57 2 E
Kuhin, Iran 45 B6 36 22N 49 40 E
Kūhīrī, Iran 45 E9 26 55N 61 2 E
Kūhpāyeh, Eşfahan, Iran 45 C7 32 44N 52 20 E
Kūhpāyeh, Kermān, Iran 45 D8 30 35N 57 15 E
Kūhrān, Kūh-e, Iran 45 E8 26 46N 58 12 E
Kui Buri, Thailand 39 F2 12 3N 99 52 E
Kuiseb →, Namibia 56 B2 22 59S 14 31 E
Kuito, Angola 53 G3 12 22S 16 55 E
Kuiu I., U.S.A. 72 B2 57 45N 134 10W
Kujang, N. Korea 35 E14 39 57N 126 1 E
Kuji, Japan 30 D10 40 11N 141 46 E
Kujū-San, Japan 31 H5 33 5N 131 15 E
Kukës, Albania 21 C9 42 5N 20 27 E
Kukup, Malaysia 39 M4 1 20N 103 27 E
Kula, Turkey 21 E13 38 32N 28 40 E
Kulachi, Pakistan 42 D4 31 56N 70 27 E
Kulai, Malaysia 39 M4 1 44N 103 35 E
Kulal, Mt., Kenya 54 B4 2 42N 36 57 E
Kulasekarappattinam, India 40 Q11 8 20N 78 5 E
Kuldīga, Latvia 9 H19 56 58N 21 59 E
Kuldja = Yining, China 26 E9 43 58N 81 10 E
Kulen, Cambodia 38 F5 13 50N 104 40 E
Kulgam, India 43 C6 33 36N 75 2 E
Kulgera, Australia 62 D1 25 50S 133 18 E
Kulim, Malaysia 39 K3 5 22N 100 34 E
Kulin, Australia 61 F2 32 40S 118 2 E
Kŭlob, Tajikistan 26 F7 37 55N 69 50 E
Kulsary, Kazakstan 25 E9 46 59N 54 1 E
Kulti, India 43 H12 23 43N 86 50 E
Kulu, India 42 D7 31 58N 77 6 E
Kulumbura, Australia 60 B4 13 55S 126 35 E
Kulunda, Russia 26 D8 52 35N 78 57 E
Kulungar, Afghan. 42 C3 34 0N 69 2 E
Kūlvand, Iran 45 D7 31 21N 54 35 E
Kulyab = Kŭlob, Tajikistan 26 F7 37 55N 69 50 E
Kuma →, Russia 25 F8 44 55N 47 0 E
Kumagaya, Japan 31 F9 36 9N 139 22 E
Kumai, Indonesia 36 E4 2 44S 111 43 E
Kumamba, Kepulauan, Indonesia 37 E9 1 36S 138 45 E
Kumamoto, Japan 31 H5 32 45N 130 45 E
Kumamoto □, Japan 31 H5 32 55N 130 55 E
Kumanovo, Macedonia 21 C9 42 9N 21 42 E
Kumara, N.Z. 59 K3 42 37S 171 12 E
Kumarina, Australia 61 D2 24 41S 119 32 E
Kumasi, Ghana 50 G5 6 41N 1 38W
Kumayri = Gyumri, Armenia 25 F7 40 47N 43 50 E
Kumba, Cameroon 52 D1 4 36N 9 24 E
Kumbakonam, India 40 P11 10 58N 79 25 E
Kumbarilla, Australia 63 D5 27 15S 150 55 E
Kumbhraj, India 42 G7 24 22N 77 3 E
Kumbia, Australia 63 D5 26 41S 151 39 E
Kŭmch'ŏn, N. Korea 35 E14 38 10N 126 29 E
Kumdok, India 43 C8 33 32N 78 10 E
Kume-Shima, Japan 31 L3 26 20N 126 47 E
Kumertau, Russia 24 D10 52 45N 55 57 E
Kumharsain, India 42 D7 31 19N 77 27 E
Kŭmhwa, S. Korea 35 E14 38 17N 127 28 E
Kumi, Uganda 54 B3 1 30N 33 58 E
Kumla, Sweden 9 G16 59 8N 15 10 E
Kumo, Nigeria 51 F8 10 1N 11 12 E
Kumon Bum, Burma 41 F20 26 30N 97 15 E
Kunashir, Ostrov, Russia 27 E15 44 0N 146 0 E
Kunda, Estonia 9 G22 59 30N 26 34 E
Kunda, India 43 G9 25 43N 81 31 E
Kundar →, Pakistan 42 D3 31 56N 69 19 E
Kundian, Pakistan 42 C4 32 27N 71 28 E
Kundla, India 42 J4 21 21N 71 25 E
Kunga →, Bangla. 43 J13 21 46N 89 30 E
Kunghit I., Canada 72 C2 52 6N 131 3W
Kungrad = Qŭnghirot, Uzbekistan 26 E6 43 6N 58 54 E
Kungsbacka, Sweden 9 H15 57 30N 12 5 E
Kungur, Russia 24 C10 57 25N 56 57 E
Kunhar →, Pakistan 43 B5 34 20N 73 30 E
Kuningan, Indonesia 37 G13 6 59S 108 29 E
Kunlong, Burma 41 H21 23 20N 98 50 E
Kunlun Shan, Asia 32 C3 36 0N 86 30 E
Kunming, China 32 D5 25 1N 102 41 E
Kunsan, S. Korea 35 G14 35 59N 126 45 E
Kununurra, Australia 60 C4 15 40S 128 50 E
Kunwari →, India 43 F8 26 26N 79 11 E
Kunya-Urgench = Köneürgench, Turkmenistan 26 E6 42 19N 59 10 E
Kuopio, Finland 8 E22 62 53N 27 35 E
Kupa →, Croatia 16 F9 45 28N 16 24 E
Kupang, Indonesia 37 F6 10 19S 123 39 E
Kupreanof I., U.S.A. 72 B2 56 50N 133 30W
Kupyansk-Uzlovoi, Ukraine 25 E6 49 40N 37 43 E
Kuqa, China 32 B3 41 35N 82 30 E
Kür →, Azerbaijan 25 G8 39 29N 49 15 E
Kür Dili, Azerbaijan 45 B6 39 3N 49 13 E
Kura = Kür →, Azerbaijan 25 G8 39 29N 49 15 E
Kuranda, Australia 62 B4 16 48S 145 35 E
Kuranga, India 42 H3 22 4N 69 10 E
Kurashiki, Japan 31 G6 34 40N 133 50 E
Kurayoshi, Japan 31 G6 35 26N 133 50 E
Kŭrdzhali, Bulgaria 21 D11 41 38N 25 21 E
Kure, Japan 31 G6 34 14N 132 32 E
Kuressaare, Estonia 9 G20 58 15N 22 30 E
Kurgan, Russia 26 D7 55 26N 65 18 E
Kuri, India 42 F4 26 37N 70 43 E
Kuria Maria Is. = Khurīyā Murīyā, Jazā'ir, Oman 46 D6 17 30N 55 58 E
Kuridala, Australia 62 C3 21 16S 140 29 E
Kurigram, Bangla. 41 G16 25 49N 89 39 E
Kurikka, Finland 9 E20 62 36N 22 24 E
Kuril Is. = Kurilskiye Ostrova, Russia 27 E15 45 0N 150 0 E
Kuril Trench, Pac. Oc. 28 E19 44 0N 153 0 E
Kurilsk, Russia 27 E15 45 14N 147 53 E
Kurilskiye Ostrova, Russia 27 E15 45 0N 150 0 E
Kurino, Japan 31 J5 31 57N 130 43 E
Kurinskaya Kosa = Kür Dili, Azerbaijan 45 B6 39 3N 49 13 E
Kurnool, India 40 M11 15 45N 78 0 E
Kuro-Shima, Kagoshima, Japan 31 J4 30 50N 129 57 E
Kuro-Shima, Okinawa, Japan 31 M2 24 14N 124 1 E
Kurow, N.Z. 59 L3 44 44S 170 29 E
Kurram →, Pakistan 42 C4 32 36N 71 20 E
Kurri Kurri, Australia 63 E5 32 50S 151 28 E
Kurrimine, Australia 62 B4 17 47S 146 6 E
Kurshskiy Zaliv, Russia 9 J19 55 9N 21 6 E
Kursk, Russia 24 D6 51 42N 36 11 E
Kuruçay, Turkey 44 B3 39 39N 38 29 E
Kuruktag, China 32 B3 41 0N 89 0 E
Kuruman, S. Africa 56 D3 27 28S 23 28 E
Kuruman →, S. Africa 56 D3 26 56S 20 39 E
Kurume, Japan 31 H5 33 15N 130 30 E
Kurunegala, Sri Lanka 40 R12 7 30N 80 23 E
Kurya, Russia 24 B10 61 42N 57 9 E
Kus Gölü, Turkey 21 D12 40 10N 27 55 E
Kuşadası, Turkey 21 F12 37 52N 27 15 E
Kusatsu, Japan 31 F9 36 37N 138 36 E
Kusawa L., Canada 72 A1 60 20N 136 13W
Kushalgarh, India 42 H6 23 10N 74 27 E
Kushikino, Japan 31 J5 31 44N 130 16 E
Kushima, Japan 31 J5 31 29N 131 14 E
Kushimoto, Japan 31 H7 33 28N 135 47 E
Kushiro, Japan 30 C12 43 0N 144 25 E
Kushiro-Gawa →, Japan 30 C12 42 59N 144 23 E
Kūshk, Iran 45 D8 28 46N 56 51 E
Kushka = Gushgy, Turkmenistan 26 F7 35 20N 62 18 E
Kūshkī, Iran 44 C5 33 31N 47 13 E
Kushol, India 43 C7 33 40N 76 36 E
Kushtia, Bangla. 41 H16 23 55N 89 5 E
Kushva, Russia 24 C10 58 18N 59 45 E
Kuskokwim B., U.S.A. 68 C3 59 45N 162 25W
Kusmi, India 43 H10 23 17N 83 55 E
Kussharo-Ko, Japan 30 C12 43 38N 144 21 E
Kustanay = Qostanay, Kazakstan 26 D7 53 10N 63 35 E
Kut, Ko, Thailand 39 G4 11 40N 102 35 E
Kütahya, Turkey 25 G5 39 30N 30 2 E
Kutaisi, Georgia 25 F7 42 19N 42 40 E
Kutaraja = Banda Aceh, Indonesia 36 C1 5 35N 95 20 E
Kutch, Gulf of = Kachchh, Gulf of, India 42 H3 22 50N 69 15 E
Kutch, Rann of = Kachchh, Rann of, India 42 H4 24 0N 70 0 E
Kutiyana, India 42 J4 21 36N 70 2 E
Kutno, Poland 17 B10 52 15N 19 23 E
Kutse, Botswana 56 C3 21 7S 22 16 E
Kutu, Dem. Rep. of the Congo 52 E3 2 40S 18 11 E
Kutum, Sudan 51 F10 14 10N 24 40 E
Kuujjuaq, Canada 69 C13 58 6N 68 15W
Kuujjuarapik, Canada 70 A4 55 20N 77 35W
Kuŭp-tong, N. Korea 35 D14 40 45N 126 1 E
Kuusamo, Finland 8 D23 65 57N 29 8 E
Kuusankoski, Finland 9 F22 60 55N 26 38 E
Kuwait = Al Kuwayt, Kuwait 46 B4 29 30N 48 0 E
Kuwait ■, Asia 46 B4 29 30N 47 30 E
Kuwana, Japan 31 G8 35 5N 136 43 E
Kuwana →, India 43 F10 26 25N 83 15 E
Kuybyshev = Samara, Russia 24 D9 53 8N 50 6 E
Kuybyshev, Russia 26 D8 55 27N 78 19 E
Kuybyshevskoye Vdkhr., Russia 24 C8 55 2N 49 30 E
Kuye He →, China 34 E6 38 23N 110 46 E
Küyeh, Iran 44 B5 38 45N 47 57 E
Kūysanjaq, Iraq 44 B5 36 5N 44 38 E
Kuyto, Ozero, Russia 24 B5 65 6N 31 20 E
Kuyumba, Russia 27 C10 60 58N 96 59 E
Kuzey Anadolu Dağları, Turkey 25 F6 41 30N 35 0 E
Kuznetsk, Russia 24 D8 53 12N 46 40 E
Kuzomen, Russia 24 A6 66 22N 36 50 E
Kvænangen, Norway 8 A19 70 5N 21 15 E
Kvaløy, Norway 8 B18 69 40N 18 30 E
Kvarner, Croatia 16 F8 44 50N 14 10 E
Kvarnerič, Croatia 16 F8 44 43N 14 37 E
Kwa-Nobuhle, S. Africa 53 L5 33 50S 25 22 E
Kwabhaca, S. Africa 57 E4 30 51S 29 0 E
Kwakhanai, Botswana 56 C3 21 39S 21 16 E
Kwakoegron, Surinam 93 B7 5 12N 55 25W
Kwale, Kenya 54 C4 4 15S 39 31 E
KwaMashu, S. Africa 57 D5 29 45S 30 58 E
Kwando →, Africa 56 B3 18 27S 23 32 E
Kwangdaeri, N. Korea 35 D14 40 31N 127 32 E
Kwangju, S. Korea 35 G14 35 9N 126 54 E
Kwango →, Dem. Rep. of the Congo 52 E3 3 14S 17 22 E
Kwangsi-Chuang = Guangxi Zhuangzu Zizhiqu □, China 33 D5 24 0N 109 0 E
Kwangtung = Guangdong □, China 33 D6 23 0N 113 0 E
Kwataboahegan →, Canada 70 B3 51 9N 80 50W
Kwatisore, Indonesia 37 E8 3 18S 134 50 E
KwaZulu Natal □, S. Africa 57 D5 29 0S 30 0 E
Kweichow = Guizhou □, China 32 D5 27 0N 107 0 E
Kwekwe, Zimbabwe 55 F2 18 58S 29 48 E
Kwidzyn, Poland 17 B10 53 44N 18 55 E
Kwinana New Town, Australia 61 F2 32 15S 115 47 E
Kwoka, Indonesia 37 E8 0 31S 132 27 E
Kyabra Cr. →, Australia 63 D3 25 36S 142 55 E
Kyaikto, Burma 38 D1 17 20N 97 3 E
Kyakhta, Russia 27 D11 50 30N 106 25 E
Kyancutta, Australia 63 E2 33 8S 135 33 E
Kyaukpadaung, Burma 41 J19 20 52N 95 8 E
Kyaukpyu, Burma 41 K18 19 28N 93 30 E
Kyaukse, Burma 41 J20 21 36N 96 10 E
Kyburz, U.S.A. 84 G6 38 47N 120 18W
Kyelang, India 42 C7 32 35N 77 2 E
Kyenjojo, Uganda 54 B3 0 40N 30 37 E
Kyle, Canada 73 C7 50 50N 108 2W
Kyle Dam, Zimbabwe 55 G3 20 15S 31 0 E
Kyle of Lochalsh, U.K. 12 D3 57 17N 5 44W
Kymijoki →, Finland 9 F22 60 30N 26 55 E
Kynuna, Australia 62 C3 21 37S 141 55 E
Kyō-ga-Saki, Japan 31 G7 35 45N 135 15 E
Kyoga, L., Uganda 54 B3 1 35N 33 0 E
Kyogle, Australia 63 D5 28 40S 153 0 E
Kyongju, S. Korea 35 G15 35 51N 129 14 E
Kyongpyaw, Burma 41 L19 17 12N 95 10 E
Kyŏngsŏng, N. Korea 35 D15 41 35N 129 36 E
Kyōto, Japan 31 G7 35 0N 135 45 E
Kyōto □, Japan 31 G7 35 15N 135 45 E
Kyparissovouno, Cyprus 23 D12 35 19N 33 10 E
Kyperounda, Cyprus 23 E11 34 56N 32 58 E
Kyrenia, Cyprus 23 D12 35 20N 33 20 E
Kyrgyzstan ■, Asia 26 E8 42 0N 75 0 E
Kyrönjoki →, Finland 8 E19 63 14N 21 45 E
Kystatyam, Russia 27 C13 67 20N 123 10 E
Kythréa, Cyprus 23 D12 35 15N 33 29 E

Lapseki

Kyunhla, *Burma* **41 H19** 23 25N 95 15 E
Kyuquot Sound, *Canada* **72 D3** 50 2N 127 22W
Kyūshū, *Japan* **31 H5** 33 0N 131 0 E
Kyūshū □, *Japan* **31 H5** 33 0N 131 0 E
Kyūshū-Sanchi, *Japan* **31 H5** 32 35N 131 17 E
Kyustendil, *Bulgaria* **21 C10** 42 16N 22 41 E
Kyusyur, *Russia* **27 B13** 70 19N 127 30 E
Kyyiv, *Ukraine* **17 C16** 50 30N 30 28 E
Kyyivske Vdskh., *Ukraine* **17 C16** 51 0N 30 25 E
Kyzyl, *Russia* **27 D10** 51 50N 94 30 E
Kyzyl Kum, *Uzbekistan* **26 E7** 42 30N 65 0 E
Kyzyl-Kyya, *Kyrgyzstan* **26 E8** 40 16N 72 8 E
Kzyl-Orda = Qyzylorda, *Kazakstan* **26 E7** 44 48N 65 28 E

L

La Alcarria, *Spain* **19 B4** 40 31N 2 45W
La Asunción, *Venezuela* **92 A6** 11 2N 63 53W
La Baie, *Canada* **71 C5** 48 19N 70 53W
La Banda, *Argentina* **94 B3** 27 45S 64 10W
La Barca, *Mexico* **86 C4** 20 20N 102 40W
La Barge, *U.S.A.* **82 E8** 42 16N 110 12W
La Belle, *U.S.A.* **77 M5** 26 46N 81 26W
La Biche →, *Canada* **72 B4** 59 57N 123 50W
La Biche, L., *Canada* **72 C6** 54 50N 112 5W
La Bomba, *Mexico* **86 A1** 31 53N 115 2W
La Calera, *Chile* **94 C1** 32 50S 71 10W
La Canal = Sa Canal, *Spain* **22 C7** 38 51N 1 23 E
La Carlota, *Argentina* **94 C3** 33 30S 63 20W
La Ceiba, *Honduras* **88 C2** 15 40N 86 50W
La Chaux-de-Fonds, *Switz.* **18 C7** 47 7N 6 50 E
La Chorrera, *Panama* **88 E4** 8 53N 79 47W
La Cocha, *Argentina* **94 B2** 27 50S 65 40W
La Concepción, *Panama* **88 E3** 8 31N 82 37W
La Concordia, *Mexico* **87 D6** 16 8N 92 38W
La Coruña = A Coruña, *Spain* **19 A1** 43 20N 8 25W
La Crescent, *U.S.A.* **80 D9** 43 50N 91 18W
La Crete, *Canada* **72 B5** 58 11N 116 24W
La Crosse, *Kans., U.S.A.* **80 F5** 38 32N 99 18W
La Crosse, *Wis., U.S.A.* **80 D9** 43 48N 91 15W
La Cruz, *Costa Rica* **88 D2** 11 4N 85 39W
La Cruz, *Mexico* **86 C3** 23 55N 106 54W
La Désirade, *Guadeloupe* **89 C7** 16 18N 61 3W
La Escondida, *Mexico* **86 C5** 24 6N 99 55W
La Esmeralda, *Paraguay* **94 A3** 22 16S 62 33W
La Esperanza, *Cuba* **88 B3** 22 46N 83 44W
La Esperanza, *Honduras* **88 D2** 14 15N 88 10W
La Estrada = A Estrada, *Spain* **19 A1** 42 43N 8 27W
La Fayette, *U.S.A.* **77 H3** 34 42N 85 17W
La Fé, *Cuba* **88 B3** 22 2N 84 15W
La Follette, *U.S.A.* **77 G3** 36 23N 84 7W
La Grande, *U.S.A.* **82 D4** 45 20N 118 5W
La Grande →, *Canada* **70 B5** 53 50N 79 0W
La Grande Deux, Rés., *Canada* **70 B4** 53 40N 76 55W
La Grande Quatre, Rés., *Canada* **70 B5** 54 0N 73 15W
La Grande Trois, Rés., *Canada* **70 B4** 53 40N 75 10W
La Grange, *Calif., U.S.A.* **84 H6** 37 42N 120 27W
La Grange, *Ga., U.S.A.* **77 J3** 33 2N 85 2W
La Grange, *Ky., U.S.A.* **76 F3** 38 25N 85 23W
La Grange, *Tex., U.S.A.* **81 L6** 29 54N 96 52W
La Guaira, *Venezuela* **92 A5** 10 36N 66 56W
La Habana, *Cuba* **88 B3** 23 8N 82 22W
La Independencia, *Mexico* **87 D6** 16 31N 91 47W
La Isabela, *Dom. Rep.* **89 C5** 19 58N 71 2W
La Junta, *U.S.A.* **81 F3** 37 59N 103 33W
La Laguna, *Canary Is.* **22 F3** 28 28N 16 18W
La Libertad, *Guatemala* **88 C1** 16 47N 90 7W
La Libertad, *Mexico* **86 B2** 29 55N 112 41W
La Ligua, *Chile* **94 C1** 32 30S 71 16W
La Línea de la Concepción, *Spain* **19 D3** 36 15N 5 23W
La Loche, *Canada* **73 B7** 56 29N 109 26W
La Louvière, *Belgium* **15 D4** 50 27N 4 10 E
La Malbaie, *Canada* **71 C5** 47 40N 70 10W
La Mancha, *Spain* **19 C4** 39 10N 2 54W
La Martre, L., *Canada* **72 A5** 63 15N 117 55W
La Mesa, *U.S.A.* **85 N9** 32 46N 117 3W
La Misión, *Mexico* **86 A1** 32 5N 116 50W
La Moure, *U.S.A.* **80 B5** 46 21N 98 18W
La Negra, *Chile* **94 A1** 23 46S 70 18W
La Oliva, *Canary Is.* **22 F6** 28 36N 13 57W
La Orotava, *Canary Is.* **22 F3** 28 22N 16 31W
La Oroya, *Peru* **92 F3** 11 32S 75 54W
La Palma, *Canary Is.* **22 F2** 28 40N 17 50W
La Palma, *Panama* **88 E4** 8 15N 78 0W
La Palma del Condado, *Spain* **19 D2** 37 21N 6 38W
La Paloma, *Chile* **94 C1** 30 35S 71 0W
La Pampa □, *Argentina* **94 D2** 36 50S 66 0W
La Paragua, *Venezuela* **92 B6** 6 50N 63 20W
La Paz, *Entre Ríos, Argentina* **94 C4** 30 50S 59 45W
La Paz, *San Luis, Argentina* **94 C2** 33 30S 67 20W
La Paz, *Bolivia* **92 G5** 16 20S 68 10W
La Paz, *Honduras* **88 D2** 14 20N 87 47W
La Paz, *Mexico* **86 C2** 24 10N 110 20W
La Paz Centro, *Nic.* **88 D2** 12 20N 86 41W
La Pedrera, *Colombia* **92 D5** 1 18S 69 43W
La Pérade, *Canada* **71 C5** 46 35N 72 12W
La Perouse Str., *Asia* **30 B11** 45 40N 142 0 E
La Pesca, *Mexico* **87 C5** 23 46N 97 47W
La Piedad, *Mexico* **86 C4** 20 20N 102 1W
La Pine, *U.S.A.* **82 E3** 43 40N 121 30W
La Plata, *Argentina* **94 D4** 35 0S 57 55W
La Pocatière, *Canada* **71 C5** 47 22N 70 2W
La Porte, *Ind., U.S.A.* **76 E2** 41 36N 86 43W
La Porte, *Tex., U.S.A.* **81 L7** 29 39N 95 1W
La Purísima, *Mexico* **86 B2** 26 10N 112 4W
La Push, *U.S.A.* **84 C2** 47 55N 124 38W
La Quiaca, *Argentina* **94 A2** 22 5S 65 35W
La Restinga, *Canary Is.* **22 G2** 27 38N 17 59W
La Rioja, *Argentina* **94 B2** 29 20S 67 0W
La Rioja □, *Argentina* **94 B2** 29 30S 67 0W
La Rioja □, *Spain* **19 A4** 42 20N 2 20W
La Robla, *Spain* **19 A3** 42 50N 5 41W
La Roche-en-Ardenne, *Belgium* **15 D5** 50 11N 5 35 E
La Roche-sur-Yon, *France* **18 C3** 46 40N 1 25W
La Rochelle, *France* **18 C3** 46 10N 1 9W
La Roda, *Spain* **19 C4** 39 13N 2 15W
La Romana, *Dom. Rep.* **89 C6** 18 27N 68 57W
La Ronge, *Canada* **73 B7** 55 5N 105 20W
La Rumorosa, *Mexico* **85 N10** 32 33N 116 4W
La Sabina = Sa Savina, *Spain* **22 C7** 38 44N 1 25 E
La Salle, *U.S.A.* **80 E10** 41 20N 89 6W
La Santa, *Canary Is.* **22 E6** 29 5N 13 40W
La Sarre, *Canada* **70 C4** 48 45N 79 15W
La Scie, *Canada* **71 C8** 49 57N 55 36W
La Selva Beach, *U.S.A.* **84 J5** 36 56N 121 51W
La Serena, *Chile* **94 B1** 29 55S 71 10W
La Seu d'Urgell, *Spain* **19 A6** 42 22N 1 23 E
La Seyne-sur-Mer, *France* **18 E6** 43 7N 5 52 E
La Soufrière, *St. Vincent* **89 D7** 13 20N 61 11W
La Spézia, *Italy* **18 D8** 44 7N 9 50 E
La Tagua, *Colombia* **92 C4** 0 3N 74 40W
La Tortuga, *Venezuela* **89 D6** 11 0N 65 22W
La Tuque, *Canada* **70 C5** 47 30N 72 50W
La Unión, *Chile* **96 E2** 40 10S 73 0W
La Unión, *El Salv.* **88 D2** 13 20N 87 50W
La Unión, *Mexico* **86 D4** 17 58N 101 49W
La Urbana, *Venezuela* **92 B5** 7 8N 66 56W
La Vall d'Uixó, *Spain* **19 C5** 39 49N 0 15W
La Vega, *Dom. Rep.* **89 C5** 19 20N 70 30W
La Vela de Coro, *Venezuela* **92 A5** 11 27N 69 34W
La Venta, *Mexico* **87 D6** 18 8N 94 3W
La Ventura, *Mexico* **86 C4** 24 38N 100 54W
Labasa, *Fiji* **59 C8** 16 30S 179 10 E
Labe = Elbe →, *Europe* **16 B5** 53 50N 9 0 E
Labé, *Guinea* **50 F3** 11 24N 12 16W
Laberge, L., *Canada* **72 A1** 61 11N 135 12W
Labinsk, *Russia* **25 F7** 44 40N 40 48 E
Labis, *Malaysia* **39 L4** 2 22N 103 2 E
Laboulaye, *Argentina* **94 C3** 34 10S 63 30W
Labrador, *Canada* **71 B7** 53 20N 61 0W
Labrador City, *Canada* **71 B6** 52 57N 66 55W
Labrador Sea, *Atl. Oc.* **69 C14** 57 0N 54 0W
Lábrea, *Brazil* **92 E6** 7 15S 64 51W
Labuan, *Malaysia* **36 C5** 5 20N 115 14 E
Labuan, Pulau, *Malaysia* **36 C5** 5 21N 115 13 E
Labuha, *Indonesia* **37 E7** 0 30S 127 30 E
Labuhan, *Indonesia* **37 G11** 6 22S 105 50 E
Labuhanbajo, *Indonesia* **37 F6** 8 28S 119 54 E
Labuk, Telok, *Malaysia* **36 C5** 6 10N 117 50 E
Labyrinth, L., *Australia* **63 E2** 30 40S 135 11 E
Labytnangi, *Russia* **26 C7** 66 39N 66 21 E
Lac Bouchette, *Canada* **71 C5** 48 16N 72 11W
Lac Édouard, *Canada* **70 C5** 47 40N 72 16W
Lac La Biche, *Canada* **72 C6** 54 45N 111 58W
Lac la Martre = Wha Ti, *Canada* **68 B8** 63 8N 117 16W
Lac La Ronge Prov. Park, *Canada* **73 B7** 55 9N 104 41W
Lac-Mégantic, *Canada* **71 C5** 45 35N 70 53W
Lac Thien, *Vietnam* **38 F7** 12 25N 108 11 E
Lacanau, *France* **18 D3** 44 58N 1 5W
Lacantúm →, *Mexico* **87 D6** 16 36N 90 40W
Laccadive Is. = Lakshadweep Is., *India* **29 H11** 10 0N 72 30 E
Lacepede Is., *Australia* **60 C3** 16 55S 122 0 E
Lacerdónia, *Mozam.* **55 F4** 18 3S 35 35 E
Lacey, *U.S.A.* **84 C4** 47 7N 122 49W
Lachhmangarh, *India* **42 F6** 27 50N 75 4 E
Lachi, *Pakistan* **42 C4** 33 25N 71 20 E
Lachine, *Canada* **79 A11** 45 30N 73 40W
Lachute, *Canada* **70 C5** 45 39N 74 21W
Lackawanna, *U.S.A.* **78 D6** 42 50N 78 50W
Lackawaxen, *U.S.A.* **79 E10** 41 29N 74 59W
Lacolle, *Canada* **79 A11** 45 5N 73 22W
Lacombe, *Canada* **72 C6** 52 30N 113 44W
Lacona, *U.S.A.* **79 C8** 43 39N 76 10W
Laconia, *U.S.A.* **79 C13** 43 32N 71 28W
Ladakh Ra., *India* **43 C8** 34 0N 78 0 E
Ladismith, *S. Africa* **56 E3** 33 28S 21 15 E
Lādīz, *Iran* **45 D9** 28 55N 61 15 E
Ladnun, *India* **42 F6** 27 38N 74 25 E
Ladoga, L. = Ladozhskoye Ozero, *Russia* **24 B5** 61 15N 30 30 E
Ladozhskoye Ozero, *Russia* **24 B5** 61 15N 30 30 E
Lady Elliott I., *Australia* **62 C5** 24 7S 152 42 E
Lady Grey, *S. Africa* **56 E4** 30 43S 27 13 E
Ladybrand, *S. Africa* **56 D4** 29 9S 27 29 E
Ladysmith, *Canada* **72 D4** 49 0N 123 49W
Ladysmith, *S. Africa* **57 D4** 28 32S 29 46 E
Ladysmith, *U.S.A.* **80 C9** 45 28N 91 12W
Lae, *Papua N. G.* **64 H6** 6 40S 147 2 E
Laem Ngop, *Thailand* **39 F4** 12 10N 102 26 E
Laem Pho, *Thailand* **39 J3** 6 55N 101 19 E
Læsø, *Denmark* **9 H14** 57 15N 11 5 E
Lafayette, *Colo., U.S.A.* **80 F2** 39 58N 105 12W
Lafayette, *Ind., U.S.A.* **76 E2** 40 25N 86 54W
Lafayette, *La., U.S.A.* **81 K9** 30 14N 92 1W
Lafayette, *Tenn., U.S.A.* **77 G2** 36 31N 86 2W
Laferte →, *Canada* **72 A5** 61 53N 117 44W
Lafia, *Nigeria* **50 G7** 8 30N 8 34 E
Lafleche, *Canada* **73 D7** 49 45N 106 40W
Lagan →, *U.K.* **13 B6** 54 36N 5 55W
Lagarfljót →, *Iceland* **8 D6** 65 40N 14 18W
Lågen →, *Oppland, Norway* **9 F14** 61 8N 10 25 E
Lågen →, *Vestfold, Norway* **9 G14** 59 3N 10 3 E
Laghouat, *Algeria* **50 B6** 33 50N 2 59 E
Lagoa Vermelha, *Brazil* **95 B5** 28 13S 51 32W
Lagonoy G., *Phil.* **37 B6** 13 35N 123 50 E
Lagos, *Nigeria* **50 G6** 6 25N 3 27 E
Lagos, *Portugal* **19 D1** 37 5N 8 41W
Lagos de Moreno, *Mexico* **86 C4** 21 21N 101 55W
Lagrange, *Australia* **60 C3** 18 45S 121 43 E
Lagrange B., *Australia* **60 C3** 18 38S 121 42 E
Laguna, *Brazil* **95 B6** 28 30S 48 50W
Laguna, *U.S.A.* **83 J10** 35 2N 107 25W
Laguna Beach, *U.S.A.* **85 M9** 33 33N 117 47W
Laguna Limpia, *Argentina* **94 B4** 26 32S 59 45W
Lagunas, *Chile* **94 A2** 21 0S 69 45W
Lagunas, *Peru* **92 E3** 5 10S 75 35W
Lahad Datu, *Malaysia* **37 C5** 5 0N 118 20 E
Lahad Datu, Teluk, *Malaysia* **37 D5** 4 50N 118 20 E
Lahan Sai, *Thailand* **38 E4** 14 25N 102 52 E
Lahanam, *Laos* **38 D5** 16 16N 105 16 E
Lahar, *India* **43 F8** 26 12N 78 57 E
Laharpur, *India* **43 F9** 27 43N 80 56 E
Lahat, *Indonesia* **36 E2** 3 45S 103 30 E
Lahewa, *Indonesia* **36 D1** 1 22N 97 12 E
Lāhījān, *Iran* **45 B6** 37 10N 50 6 E
Lahn →, *Germany* **16 C4** 50 19N 7 37 E
Laholm, *Sweden* **9 H15** 56 30N 13 2 E
Lahore, *Pakistan* **42 D6** 31 32N 74 22 E
Lahri, *Pakistan* **42 E3** 29 11N 68 13 E
Lahti, *Finland* **9 F21** 60 58N 25 40 E
Lahtis = Lahti, *Finland* **9 F21** 60 58N 25 40 E
Laï, *Chad* **51 G9** 9 25N 16 18 E
Lai Chau, *Vietnam* **38 A4** 22 5N 103 3 E
Laila = Laylá, *Si. Arabia* **46 C4** 22 10N 46 40 E
Laingsburg, *S. Africa* **56 E3** 33 9S 20 52 E
Lainio älv →, *Sweden* **8 C20** 67 35N 22 40 E
Lairg, *U.K.* **12 C4** 58 2N 4 24W
Laishui, *China* **34 E8** 39 23N 115 45 E
Laiwu, *China* **35 F9** 36 15N 117 40 E
Laixi, *China* **35 F11** 36 50N 120 31 E
Laiyang, *China* **35 F11** 36 59N 120 45 E
Laiyuan, *China* **34 E8** 39 20N 114 40 E
Laizhou, *China* **35 F10** 37 8N 119 57 E
Laizhou Wan, *China* **35 F10** 37 30N 119 30 E
Laja →, *Mexico* **86 C4** 20 55N 100 46W
Lajes, *Brazil* **95 B5** 27 48S 50 20W
Lak Sao, *Laos* **38 C5** 18 11N 104 59 E
Lakaband, *Pakistan* **42 D3** 31 2N 69 15 E
Lake Alpine, *U.S.A.* **84 G7** 38 29N 120 0W
Lake Andes, *U.S.A.* **80 D5** 43 9N 98 32W
Lake Arthur, *U.S.A.* **81 K8** 30 5N 92 41W
Lake Charles, *U.S.A.* **81 K8** 30 14N 93 13W
Lake City, *Colo., U.S.A.* **83 G10** 38 2N 107 19W
Lake City, *Fla., U.S.A.* **77 K4** 30 11N 82 38W
Lake City, *Mich., U.S.A.* **76 C3** 44 20N 85 13W
Lake City, *Minn., U.S.A.* **80 C8** 44 27N 92 16W
Lake City, *Pa., U.S.A.* **78 D4** 42 1N 80 21W
Lake City, *S.C., U.S.A.* **77 J6** 33 52N 79 45W
Lake Cowichan, *Canada* **72 D4** 48 49N 124 3W
Lake District, *U.K.* **10 C4** 54 35N 3 20 E
Lake Elsinore, *U.S.A.* **85 M9** 33 38N 117 20W
Lake George, *U.S.A.* **79 C11** 43 26N 73 43W
Lake Grace, *Australia* **61 F2** 33 7S 118 28 E
Lake Harbour = Kimmirut, *Canada* **69 B13** 62 50N 69 50W
Lake Havasu City, *U.S.A.* **85 L12** 34 27N 114 22W
Lake Hughes, *U.S.A.* **85 L8** 34 41N 118 26W
Lake Isabella, *U.S.A.* **85 K8** 35 38N 118 28W
Lake Jackson, *U.S.A.* **81 L7** 29 3N 95 27W
Lake Junction, *U.S.A.* **82 D8** 44 35N 110 28W
Lake King, *Australia* **61 F2** 33 5S 119 45 E
Lake Lenore, *Canada* **73 C8** 52 24N 104 59W
Lake Louise, *Canada* **72 C5** 51 30N 116 10W
Lake Mead National Recreation Area, *U.S.A.* **85 K12** 36 15N 114 30W
Lake Mills, *U.S.A.* **80 D8** 43 25N 93 32W
Lake Placid, *U.S.A.* **79 B11** 44 17N 73 59W
Lake Pleasant, *U.S.A.* **79 C10** 43 28N 74 25W
Lake Providence, *U.S.A.* **81 J9** 32 48N 91 10W
Lake St. Peter, *Canada* **78 A6** 45 18N 78 2W
Lake Superior Prov. Park, *Canada* **70 C3** 47 45N 84 45W
Lake Village, *U.S.A.* **81 J9** 33 20N 91 17W
Lake Wales, *U.S.A.* **77 M5** 27 54N 81 35W
Lake Worth, *U.S.A.* **77 M5** 26 37N 80 3W
Lakeba, *Fiji* **59 D9** 18 13S 178 47W
Lakefield, *Canada* **78 B6** 44 25N 78 16W
Lakehurst, *U.S.A.* **79 F10** 40 1N 74 19W
Lakeland, *Australia* **62 B3** 15 49S 144 57 E
Lakeland, *U.S.A.* **77 M5** 28 3N 81 57W
Lakeport, *Calif., U.S.A.* **84 F4** 39 3N 122 55W
Lakeport, *Mich., U.S.A.* **78 C2** 43 7N 82 30W
Lakeside, *Ariz., U.S.A.* **83 J9** 34 9N 109 58W
Lakeside, *Calif., U.S.A.* **85 N10** 32 52N 116 55W
Lakeside, *Nebr., U.S.A.* **80 D3** 42 3N 102 26W
Lakeside, *Ohio, U.S.A.* **78 E2** 41 32N 82 46W
Lakeview, *U.S.A.* **82 E3** 42 11N 120 21W
Lakeville, *U.S.A.* **80 C8** 44 39N 93 14W
Lakewood, *Colo., U.S.A.* **80 F2** 39 44N 105 5W
Lakewood, *N.J., U.S.A.* **79 F10** 40 6N 74 13W
Lakewood, *N.Y., U.S.A.* **78 D5** 42 6N 79 19W
Lakewood, *Ohio, U.S.A.* **78 E3** 41 29N 81 48W
Lakewood, *Wash., U.S.A.* **84 C4** 47 11N 122 32W
Lakha, *India* **42 F4** 26 9N 70 54 E
Lakhaniá, *Greece* **23 D9** 35 58N 27 54 E
Lakhimpur, *India* **43 F9** 27 57N 80 46 E
Lakhnadon, *India* **43 H8** 22 36N 79 36 E
Lakhonpheng, *Laos* **38 E5** 15 54N 105 34 E
Lakhpat, *India* **42 H3** 23 48N 68 47 E
Lakin, *U.S.A.* **81 G4** 37 57N 101 15W
Lakitusaki →, *Canada* **70 B3** 54 21N 82 25W
Lakki, *Pakistan* **42 C4** 32 36N 70 55 E
Lákkoi, *Greece* **23 D5** 35 24N 23 57 E
Lakonikós Kólpos, *Greece* **21 F10** 36 40N 22 40 E
Lakor, *Indonesia* **37 F7** 8 15S 128 17 E
Lakota, *Ivory C.* **50 G4** 5 50N 5 30W
Lakota, *U.S.A.* **80 A5** 48 2N 98 21W
Laksar, *India* **42 E8** 29 46N 78 3 E
Laksefjorden, *Norway* **8 A22** 70 45N 26 50 E
Lakselv, *Norway* **8 A21** 70 2N 25 0 E
Lakshadweep Is., *India* **29 H11** 10 0N 72 30 E
Lakshmanpur, *India* **43 H10** 22 58N 83 3 E
Lakshmikantapur, *India* **43 H13** 22 5N 88 20 E
Lala Ghat, *India* **41 G18** 24 30N 92 40 E
Lala Musa, *Pakistan* **42 C5** 32 40N 73 57 E
Lalago, *Tanzania* **54 C3** 3 28S 33 58 E
Lalapanzi, *Zimbabwe* **55 F3** 19 20S 30 15 E
L'Albufera, *Spain* **19 C5** 39 20N 0 27W
Lalganj, *India* **43 G11** 25 52N 85 13 E
Lalgola, *India* **43 G13** 24 25N 88 15 E
Lālī, *Iran* **45 C6** 32 21N 49 6 E
Lalibela, *Ethiopia* **46 E2** 12 2N 39 2 E
Lalin, *China* **35 B14** 45 12N 127 0 E
Lalín, *Spain* **19 A1** 42 40N 8 5W
Lalin He →, *China* **35 B13** 45 32N 125 40 E
Lalitpur, *India* **43 G8** 24 42N 78 28 E
Lalkua, *India* **43 E8** 29 5N 79 31 E
Lalsot, *India* **42 F7** 26 34N 76 20 E
Lam, *Vietnam* **38 B6** 21 21N 106 31 E
Lam Pao Res., *Thailand* **38 D4** 16 50N 103 15 E
Lamaing, *Burma* **41 M20** 15 25N 97 53 E
Lamar, *Colo., U.S.A.* **80 F3** 38 5N 102 37W
Lamar, *Mo., U.S.A.* **81 G7** 37 30N 94 16W
Lamas, *Peru* **92 E3** 6 28S 76 31W
Lambaréné, *Gabon* **52 E2** 0 41S 10 12 E
Lambay I., *Ireland* **13 C5** 53 29N 6 1W
Lambert Glacier, *Antarctica* **5 D6** 71 0S 70 0 E
Lambert's Bay, *S. Africa* **56 E2** 32 5S 18 17 E
Lambeth, *Canada* **78 D3** 42 54N 81 18W
Lambomakondro, *Madag.* **57 C7** 22 41S 44 44 E
Lame Deer, *U.S.A.* **82 D10** 45 37N 106 40W
Lamego, *Portugal* **19 B2** 41 5N 7 52W
Lamèque, *Canada* **71 C7** 47 45N 64 38W
Lamesa, *U.S.A.* **81 J4** 32 44N 101 58W
Lamía, *Greece* **21 E10** 38 55N 22 26 E
Lammermuir Hills, *U.K.* **12 F6** 55 50N 2 40W
Lamoille →, *U.S.A.* **79 B11** 44 38N 73 13W
Lamon B., *Phil.* **37 B6** 14 30N 122 20 E
Lamont, *Canada* **72 C6** 53 46N 112 50W
Lamont, *Calif., U.S.A.* **85 K8** 35 15N 118 55W
Lamont, *Wyo., U.S.A.* **82 E10** 42 13N 107 29W
Lampa, *Peru* **92 G4** 15 22S 70 22W
Lampang, *Thailand* **38 C2** 18 16N 99 32 E
Lampasas, *U.S.A.* **81 K5** 31 4N 98 11W
Lampazos de Naranjo, *Mexico* **86 B4** 27 2N 100 32W
Lampedusa, *Medit. S.* **20 G5** 35 36N 12 40 E
Lampeter, *U.K.* **11 E3** 52 7N 4 4W
Lampione, *Medit. S.* **20 G5** 35 33N 12 20 E
Lampman, *Canada* **73 D8** 49 25N 102 50W
Lampung □, *Indonesia* **36 F2** 5 30S 104 30 E
Lamta, *India* **43 H9** 22 8N 80 7 E
Lamu, *Kenya* **54 C5** 2 16S 40 55 E
Lamy, *U.S.A.* **83 J11** 35 29N 105 53W
Lan Xian, *China* **34 E6** 38 15N 111 35 E
Lanak La, *India* **43 B8** 34 27N 79 32 E
Lanak'o Shank'ou = Lanak La, *India* **43 B8** 34 27N 79 32 E
Lanark, *Canada* **79 A8** 45 1N 76 22W
Lanark, *U.K.* **12 F5** 55 40N 3 47W
Lanbi Kyun, *Burma* **39 G2** 10 50N 98 20 E
Lancang Jiang →, *China* **32 D5** 21 40N 101 10 E
Lancashire □, *U.K.* **10 D5** 53 50N 2 48W
Lancaster, *Canada* **79 A10** 45 10N 74 30W
Lancaster, *U.K.* **10 C5** 54 3N 2 48W
Lancaster, *Calif., U.S.A.* **85 L8** 34 42N 118 8W
Lancaster, *Ky., U.S.A.* **76 G3** 37 37N 84 35W
Lancaster, *N.H., U.S.A.* **79 B13** 44 29N 71 34W
Lancaster, *N.Y., U.S.A.* **78 D6** 42 54N 78 40W
Lancaster, *Ohio, U.S.A.* **76 F4** 39 43N 82 36W
Lancaster, *Pa., U.S.A.* **79 F8** 40 2N 76 19W
Lancaster, *S.C., U.S.A.* **77 H5** 34 43N 80 46W
Lancaster, *Wis., U.S.A.* **80 D9** 42 51N 90 43W
Lancaster Sd., *Canada* **69 A11** 74 13N 84 0W
Lancelin, *Australia* **61 F2** 31 0S 115 18 E
Lanchow = Lanzhou, *China* **34 F2** 36 1N 103 52 E
Lanciano, *Italy* **20 C6** 42 14N 14 23 E
Lancun, *China* **35 F11** 36 25N 120 10 E
Landeck, *Austria* **16 E6** 47 9N 10 34 E
Lander, *U.S.A.* **82 E9** 42 50N 108 44W
Lander →, *Australia* **60 D5** 22 0S 132 0 E
Landes, *France* **18 D3** 44 0N 1 0W
Landi Kotal, *Pakistan* **42 B4** 34 7N 71 6 E
Landisburg, *U.S.A.* **78 F7** 40 21N 77 19W
Land's End, *U.K.* **11 G2** 50 4N 5 44W
Landsborough Cr. →, *Australia* **62 C3** 22 28S 144 35 E
Landshut, *Germany* **16 D7** 48 34N 12 8 E
Landskrona, *Sweden* **9 J15** 55 53N 12 50 E
Lanesboro, *U.S.A.* **79 E9** 41 57N 75 34W
Lanett, *U.S.A.* **77 J3** 32 52N 85 12W
Lang Qua, *Vietnam* **38 A5** 22 16N 104 27 E
Lang Shan, *China* **34 D4** 41 0N 106 30 E
Lang Son, *Vietnam* **38 B6** 21 52N 106 42 E
Lang Suan, *Thailand* **39 H2** 9 57N 99 4 E
La'nga Co, *China* **41 D12** 30 45N 81 15 E
Langar, *Iran* **45 C9** 35 23N 60 25 E
Langara I., *Canada* **72 C2** 54 14N 133 1W
Langdon, *U.S.A.* **80 A5** 48 45N 98 22W
Langeberg, *S. Africa* **56 E3** 33 55S 21 0 E
Langeberge, *S. Africa* **56 D3** 28 15S 22 33 E
Langeland, *Denmark* **9 J14** 54 56N 10 48 E
Langenburg, *Canada* **73 C8** 50 51N 101 43W
Langholm, *U.K.* **12 F5** 55 9N 3 0W
Langjökull, *Iceland* **8 D3** 64 39N 20 12W
Langkawi, Pulau, *Malaysia* **39 J2** 6 25N 99 45 E
Langklip, *S. Africa* **56 D3** 28 12S 20 20 E
Langkon, *Malaysia* **36 C5** 6 30N 116 40 E
Langlade, *St- P. & M.* **71 C8** 46 50N 56 20W
Langley, *Canada* **84 A4** 49 7N 122 39W
Langøya, *Norway* **8 B16** 68 45N 14 50 E
Langreo, *Spain* **19 A3** 43 18N 5 40W
Langres, *France* **18 C6** 47 52N 5 20 E
Langres, Plateau de, *France* **18 C6** 47 45N 5 3 E
Langsa, *Indonesia* **36 D1** 4 30N 97 57 E
Langtry, *U.S.A.* **81 L4** 29 49N 101 34W
Langu, *Thailand* **39 J2** 6 53N 99 47 E
Languedoc, *France* **18 E5** 43 58N 3 55 E
Langxiangzhen, *China* **34 E9** 39 43N 116 8 E
Lanigan, *Canada* **73 C7** 51 51N 105 2W
Lankao, *China* **34 G8** 34 48N 114 50 E
Länkäran, *Azerbaijan* **25 G8** 38 48N 48 52 E
Lannion, *France* **18 B2** 48 46N 3 29W
L'Annonciation, *Canada* **70 C5** 46 25N 74 55W
Lansdale, *U.S.A.* **79 F9** 40 14N 75 17W
Lansdowne, *Canada* **79 B8** 44 24N 76 1W
Lansdowne, *India* **43 E8** 29 50N 78 41 E
Lansdowne House, *Canada* **70 B2** 52 14N 87 53W
L'Anse, *U.S.A.* **76 B1** 46 45N 88 27W
L'Anse au Loup, *Canada* **71 B8** 51 32N 56 50W
L'Anse aux Meadows, *Canada* **71 B8** 51 36N 55 32W
Lansford, *U.S.A.* **79 F9** 40 50N 75 53W
Lansing, *U.S.A.* **76 D3** 42 44N 84 33W
Lanta Yai, Ko, *Thailand* **39 J2** 7 35N 99 3 E
Lantian, *China* **34 G5** 34 11N 109 20 E
Lanus, *Argentina* **94 C4** 34 44S 58 27W
Lanusei, *Italy* **20 E3** 39 52N 9 34 E
Lanzarote, *Canary Is.* **22 F6** 29 0N 13 40W
Lanzhou, *China* **34 F2** 36 1N 103 52 E
Lao Bao, *Laos* **38 D6** 16 35N 106 30 E
Lao Cai, *Vietnam* **38 A4** 22 30N 103 57 E
Laoag, *Phil.* **37 A6** 18 7N 120 34 E
Laoang, *Phil.* **37 B7** 12 32N 125 8 E
Laoha He →, *China* **35 C11** 43 25N 120 35 E
Laois □, *Ireland* **13 D4** 52 57N 7 36W
Laon, *France* **18 B5** 49 33N 3 35 E
Laona, *U.S.A.* **76 C1** 45 34N 88 40W
Laos ■, *Asia* **38 D5** 17 45N 105 0 E
Lapa, *Brazil* **95 B6** 25 46S 49 44W
Lapeer, *U.S.A.* **76 D4** 43 3N 83 19W
Lapithos, *Cyprus* **23 D12** 35 21N 33 11 E
Lapland = Lappland, *Europe* **8 B21** 68 7N 24 0 E
Laporte, *U.S.A.* **79 E8** 41 25N 76 30W
Lappeenranta, *Finland* **9 F23** 61 3N 28 12 E
Lappland, *Europe* **8 B21** 68 7N 24 0 E
Laprida, *Argentina* **94 D3** 37 34S 60 45W
Lapseki, *Turkey* **21 D12** 40 20N 26 41 E

Laptev Sea

Laptev Sea, *Russia* **27 B13** 76 0N 125 0 E
Lapua, *Finland* **8 E20** 62 58N 23 0 E
L'Áquila, *Italy* **20 C5** 42 22N 13 22 E
Lār, Āzarbājān-e Sharqī,
Iran **44 B5** 38 30N 47 52 E
Lār, *Fārs, Iran* **45 E7** 27 40N 54 14 E
Laramie, *U.S.A.* **80 E2** 41 19N 105 35W
Laramie →, *U.S.A.* **82 F11** 42 13N 104 33W
Laramie Mts., *U.S.A.* **80 E2** 42 0N 105 30W
Laranjeiras do Sul, *Brazil* **95 B5** 25 23S 52 23W
Larantuka, *Indonesia* **37 F6** 8 21S 122 55 E
Larat, *Indonesia* **37 F8** 7 0S 132 0 E
Larde, *Mozam.* **55 F4** 16 28S 39 43 E
Larder Lake, *Canada* **70 C4** 48 5N 79 40W
Lardhos, Ákra = Líndhos,
Ákra, *Greece* **23 C10** 36 4N 28 10 E
Lardhos, Órmos, *Greece* **23 C10** 36 4N 28 2 E
Laredo, *U.S.A.* **81 M5** 27 30N 99 30W
Laredo Sd., *Canada* **72 C3** 52 30N 128 53W
Largo, *U.S.A.* **77 M4** 27 55N 82 47W
Largs, *U.K.* **12 F4** 55 47N 4 52W
Lariang, *Indonesia* **37 E5** 1 26S 119 17 E
Larimore, *U.S.A.* **80 B6** 47 54N 97 38W
Lārīn, *Iran* **45 C7** 35 55N 52 19 E
Lárisa, *Greece* **21 E10** 39 36N 22 27 E
Larkana, *Pakistan* **42 F3** 27 32N 68 18 E
Larnaca, *Cyprus* **23 E12** 34 55N 33 38 E
Larnaca Bay, *Cyprus* **23 E12** 34 53N 33 45 E
Larne, *U.K.* **13 B6** 54 51N 5 51W
Larned, *U.S.A.* **80 F5** 38 11N 99 6W
Larose, *U.S.A.* **81 L9** 29 34N 90 23W
Larrimah, *Australia* **60 C5** 15 35S 133 12 E
Larsen Ice Shelf, *Antarctica* **5 C17** 67 0S 62 0W
Larvik, *Norway* **9 G14** 59 4N 10 2 E
Las Animas, *U.S.A.* **80 F3** 38 4N 103 13W
Las Anod, *Somali Rep.* **46 F4** 8 26N 47 19 E
Las Aves, Is., *W. Indies* **89 C7** 15 45N 63 55W
Las Brenãs, *Argentina* **94 B3** 27 5S 61 7W
Las Cejas, *Argentina* **96 B4** 26 53S 64 44W
Las Chimeneas, *Mexico* **85 N10** 32 8N 116 5W
Las Cruces, *U.S.A.* **83 K10** 32 19N 106 47W
Las Flores, *Argentina* **94 D4** 36 10S 59 7W
Las Heras, *Argentina* **94 C2** 32 51S 68 49W
Las Lajas, *Argentina* **96 D2** 38 30S 70 25W
Las Lomitas, *Argentina* **94 A3** 24 43S 60 35W
Las Palmas, *Argentina* **94 B4** 27 8S 58 45W
Las Palmas, *Canary Is.* **22 F4** 28 7N 15 26W
Las Palmas →, *Mexico* **85 N10** 32 26N 116 54W
Las Piedras, *Uruguay* **95 C4** 34 44S 56 14W
Las Pipinas, *Argentina* **94 D4** 35 30S 57 19W
Las Plumas, *Argentina* **96 E3** 43 40S 67 15W
Las Rosas, *Argentina* **94 C3** 32 30S 61 35W
Las Tablas, *Panama* **88 E3** 7 49N 80 14W
Las Termas, *Argentina* **94 B3** 27 29S 64 52W
Las Toscas, *Argentina* **94 B4** 28 21S 59 18W
Las Truchas, *Mexico* **86 D4** 17 57N 102 13W
Las Varillas, *Argentina* **94 C3** 31 50S 62 50W
Las Vegas, *N. Mex., U.S.A.* **83 J11** 35 36N 105 13W
Las Vegas, *Nev., U.S.A.* **85 J11** 36 10N 115 9W
Lascano, *Uruguay* **95 C5** 33 35S 54 12W
Lash-e Joveyn, *Afghan.* **40 D2** 31 45N 61 30 E
Lashburn, *Canada* **73 C7** 53 10N 109 40W
Lashio, *Burma* **41 H20** 22 56N 97 45 E
Lashkar, *India* **42 F8** 26 10N 78 10 E
Lasíthi, *Greece* **23 D7** 35 11N 25 31 E
Lasíthi □, *Greece* **23 D7** 35 5N 25 50 E
Lāsjerd, *Iran* **45 C7** 35 24N 53 4 E
Lassen Pk., *U.S.A.* **82 F3** 40 29N 121 31W
Lassen Volcanic National
Park, *U.S.A.* **82 F3** 40 30N 121 20W
Last Mountain L., *Canada* **73 C7** 51 5N 105 14W
Lastchance Cr. →, *U.S.A.* **84 E5** 40 2N 121 15W
Lastoursville, *Gabon* **52 E2** 0 55S 12 38 E
Lastovo, *Croatia* **20 C7** 42 46N 16 55 E
Lat Yao, *Thailand* **38 E2** 15 45N 99 48 E
Latacunga, *Ecuador* **92 D3** 0 50S 78 35W
Latakia = Al Lādhiqīyah,
Syria **44 C2** 35 30N 35 45 E
Latchford, *Canada* **70 C4** 47 20N 79 50W
Latehar, *India* **43 H11** 23 45N 84 30 E
Latham, *Australia* **61 E2** 29 44S 116 20 E
Lathi, *India* **42 F4** 27 43N 71 23 E
Lathrop Wells, *U.S.A.* **85 J10** 36 39N 116 24W
Latina, *Italy* **20 D5** 41 28N 12 52 E
Latium = Lazio □, *Italy* **20 C5** 42 10N 12 30 E
Laton, *U.S.A.* **84 J7** 36 26N 119 41W
Latouche Treville, C.,
Australia **60 C3** 18 27S 121 49 E
Latrobe, *Australia* **62 G4** 41 14S 146 30 E
Latrobe, *U.S.A.* **78 F5** 40 19N 79 23W
Latvia ■, *Europe* **9 H20** 56 50N 24 0 E
Lau Group, *Fiji* **59 C9** 17 0S 178 30W
Lauchhammer, *Germany* **16 C7** 51 29N 13 47 E
Laughlin, *U.S.A.* **83 J6** 35 8N 114 35W
Laukaa, *Finland* **9 E21** 62 24N 25 56 E
Launceston, *Australia* **62 G4** 41 24S 147 8 E
Launceston, *U.K.* **11 G3** 50 38N 4 22W
Laune →, *Ireland* **13 D2** 52 7N 9 47W
Launglon Bok, *Burma* **38 F1** 13 50N 97 54 E
Laura, *Australia* **62 B3** 15 32S 144 32 E
Laurel, *Miss., U.S.A.* **81 K10** 31 41N 89 8W
Laurel, *Mont., U.S.A.* **82 D9** 45 40N 108 46W
Laurencekirk, *U.K.* **12 E6** 56 50N 2 28W
Laurens, *U.S.A.* **77 H4** 34 30N 82 1W
Laurentian Plateau, *Canada* **71 B6** 52 0N 70 0W
Lauria, *Italy* **20 E6** 40 2N 15 50 E
Laurie L., *Canada* **73 B8** 56 35N 101 57W
Laurinburg, *U.S.A.* **77 H6** 34 47N 79 28W
Laurium, *U.S.A.* **76 B1** 47 14N 88 27W
Lausanne, *Switz.* **18 C7** 46 32N 6 38 E
Laut, *Indonesia* **39 K6** 4 45N 108 0 E
Laut, Pulau, *Indonesia* **36 E5** 3 40S 116 10 E
Laut Kecil, Kepulauan,
Indonesia **36 E5** 4 45S 115 40 E
Lautoka, *Fiji* **59 C7** 17 37S 177 27 E
Lavagh More, *Ireland* **13 B3** 54 46N 8 6W
Laval, *France* **18 B3** 48 4N 0 48W
Lavalle, *Argentina* **94 B2** 28 15S 65 15W
Lavant Station, *Canada* **79 A8** 45 3N 76 42W
Lāvar Meydān, *Iran* **45 D7** 30 20N 54 30 E
Laverton, *Australia* **61 E3** 28 44S 122 29 E
Lavras, *Brazil* **95 A7** 21 20S 45 0W
Lávrion, *Greece* **21 F11** 37 40N 24 4 E
Lávris, *Greece* **23 D6** 35 25N 24 40 E
Lavumisa, *Swaziland* **57 D5** 27 20S 31 55 E
Lawas, *Malaysia* **36 D5** 4 55N 115 25 E
Lawele, *Indonesia* **37 F6** 5 13S 122 57 E
Lawng Pit, *Burma* **41 G20** 25 30N 97 25 E
Lawqah, *Si. Arabia* **44 D4** 29 49N 42 45 E
Lawrence, *N.Z.* **59 L2** 45 55S 169 41 E
Lawrence, *Kans., U.S.A.* **80 F7** 38 58N 95 14W
Lawrence, *Mass., U.S.A.* **79 D13** 42 43N 71 10W
Lawrenceburg, *Ind., U.S.A.* **76 F3** 39 6N 84 52W
Lawrenceburg, *Tenn.,*
U.S.A. **77 H2** 35 14N 87 20W
Lawrenceville, *Ga., U.S.A.* **77 J4** 33 57N 83 59W
Lawrenceville, *Pa., U.S.A.* **78 E7** 41 59N 77 8W
Laws, *U.S.A.* **84 H8** 37 24N 118 20W
Lawton, *U.S.A.* **81 H5** 34 37N 98 25W
Lawu, *Indonesia* **37 G14** 7 40S 111 13 E
Laxford, L., *U.K.* **12 C3** 58 24N 5 6W
Laylá, *Si. Arabia* **46 C4** 22 10N 46 40 E
Laylān, *Iraq* **44 C5** 35 18N 44 31 E
Layton, *U.S.A.* **82 F7** 41 4N 111 58W
Laytonville, *U.S.A.* **82 G2** 39 41N 123 29W
Lazarivo, *Madag.* **57 C8** 23 54S 44 59 E
Lazio □, *Italy* **20 C5** 42 10N 12 30 E
Lazo, *Russia* **30 C6** 43 25N 133 55 E
Le Creusot, *France* **18 C6** 46 48N 4 24 E
Le François, *Martinique* **89 D7** 14 38N 60 57W
Le Havre, *France* **18 B4** 49 30N 0 5 E
Le Mans, *France* **18 C4** 48 0N 0 10 E
Le Mars, *U.S.A.* **80 D6** 42 47N 96 10W
Le Mont-St-Michel, *France* **18 B3** 48 40N 1 30W
Le Moule, *Guadeloupe* **89 C7** 16 20N 61 22W
Le Puy-en-Velay, *France* **18 D5** 45 3N 3 52 E
Le Sueur, *U.S.A.* **80 C8** 44 28N 93 55W
Le Thuy, *Vietnam* **38 D6** 17 14N 106 49 E
Le Touquet-Paris-Plage,
France **18 A4** 50 30N 1 36 E
Le Tréport, *France* **18 A4** 50 3N 1 20 E
Le Verdon-sur-Mer, *France* **18 D3** 45 33N 1 4W
Lea →, *U.K.* **11 F8** 51 31N 0 1 E
Leach, *Cambodia* **39 F4** 12 21N 103 46 E
Lead, *U.S.A.* **80 C3** 44 21N 103 46W
Leader, *Canada* **73 C7** 50 50N 109 30W
Leadville, *U.S.A.* **83 G10** 39 15N 106 18W
Leaf →, *U.S.A.* **81 K10** 30 59N 88 44W
Leaf Rapids, *Canada* **73 B9** 56 30N 99 59W
Leamington, *Canada* **78 D2** 42 3N 82 36W
Leamington, *U.S.A.* **82 G7** 39 32N 112 17W
Leamington Spa = Royal
Leamington Spa, *U.K.* **11 E6** 52 18N 1 31W
Leandro Norte Alem,
Argentina **95 B4** 27 34S 55 15W
Leane, L., *Ireland* **13 D2** 52 2N 9 32W
Learmonth, *Australia* **60 D1** 22 13S 114 10 E
Leask, *Canada* **73 C7** 53 5N 106 45W
Leatherhead, *U.K.* **11 F7** 51 18N 0 20W
Leavenworth, *Kans., U.S.A.* **80 F7** 39 19N 94 55W
Leavenworth, *Wash., U.S.A.* **82 C3** 47 36N 120 40W
Lebak, *Phil.* **37 C6** 6 32N 124 5 E
Lebam, *U.S.A.* **84 D3** 46 34N 123 33W
Lebanon, *Ind., U.S.A.* **76 E2** 40 3N 86 28W
Lebanon, *Kans., U.S.A.* **80 F5** 39 49N 98 33W
Lebanon, *Ky., U.S.A.* **76 G3** 37 34N 85 15W
Lebanon, *Mo., U.S.A.* **81 G8** 37 41N 92 40W
Lebanon, *N.H., U.S.A.* **79 C12** 43 39N 72 15W
Lebanon, *Oreg., U.S.A.* **82 D2** 44 32N 122 55W
Lebanon, *Pa., U.S.A.* **79 F8** 40 20N 76 26W
Lebanon, *Tenn., U.S.A.* **77 G2** 36 12N 86 18W
Lebanon ■, *Asia* **47 B5** 34 0N 36 0 E
Lebec, *U.S.A.* **85 L8** 34 50N 118 52W
Lebel-sur-Quévillon,
Canada **70 C4** 49 3N 76 59W
Lebomboberge, *S. Africa* **57 C5** 24 30S 32 0 E
Lębork, *Poland* **17 A9** 54 33N 17 46 E
Lebrija, *Spain* **19 D2** 36 53N 6 5W
Lebu, *Chile* **94 D1** 37 40S 73 47W
Lecce, *Italy* **21 D8** 40 23N 18 11 E
Lecco, *Italy* **18 D8** 45 51N 9 23 E
Lech →, *Germany* **16 D6** 48 43N 10 56 E
Lechtenes Mills, *U.S.A.* **78 B6** 41 5N 78 17W
Łęczyca, *Poland* **17 B10** 52 5N 19 15 E
Ledong, *China* **38 C7** 18 41N 109 5 E
Leduc, *Canada* **72 C6** 53 15N 113 30W
Lee, *U.S.A.* **79 D11** 42 19N 73 15W
Lee →, *Ireland* **13 E3** 51 53N 8 56W
Lee Vining, *U.S.A.* **84 H7** 37 58N 119 7W
Leech L., *U.S.A.* **80 B7** 47 10N 94 24W
Leechburg, *U.S.A.* **78 F5** 40 37N 79 36W
Leeds, *U.K.* **10 D6** 53 48N 1 33W
Leeds, *U.S.A.* **77 J2** 33 33N 86 33W
Leek, *Neths.* **15 A6** 53 10N 6 24 E
Leek, *U.K.* **10 D5** 53 7N 2 1W
Leeman, *Australia* **61 E1** 29 57S 114 58 E
Leeper, *U.S.A.* **78 E5** 41 22N 79 18W
Leer, *Germany* **16 B4** 53 13N 7 26 E
Leesburg, *U.S.A.* **77 L5** 28 49N 81 53W
Leesville, *U.S.A.* **81 K8** 31 9N 93 16W
Leetonia, *U.S.A.* **78 F4** 40 53N 80 45W
Leeu Gamka, *S. Africa* **56 E3** 32 47S 21 59 E
Leeuwarden, *Neths.* **15 A5** 53 15N 5 48 E
Leeuwin, C., *Australia* **61 F2** 34 20S 115 9 E
Leeward Is., *Atl. Oc.* **89 C7** 16 30N 63 30W
Lefka, *Cyprus* **23 D11** 35 6N 32 51 E
Lefkoniko, *Cyprus* **23 D12** 35 18N 33 44 E
Lefroy, *Canada* **78 B5** 44 16N 79 34W
Lefroy, L., *Australia* **61 F3** 31 21S 121 40 E
Leganés, *Spain* **19 B4** 40 19N 3 45W
Legazpi, *Phil.* **37 B6** 13 10N 123 45 E
Legendre I., *Australia* **60 D2** 20 22S 116 55 E
Leghorn = Livorno, *Italy* **20 C4** 43 33N 10 19 E
Legionowo, *Poland* **17 B11** 52 25N 20 50 E
Legnago, *Italy* **20 B4** 45 11N 11 18 E
Legnica, *Poland* **16 C9** 51 12N 16 10 E
Leh, *India* **43 B7** 34 9N 77 35 E
Lehigh Acres, *U.S.A.* **77 M5** 26 36N 81 39W
Lehighton, *U.S.A.* **79 F9** 40 50N 75 43W
Lehututu, *Botswana* **56 C3** 23 54S 21 55 E
Leiah, *Pakistan* **42 D4** 30 58N 70 58 E
Leicester, *U.K.* **11 E6** 52 38N 1 8W
Leicester City □, *U.K.* **11 E6** 52 38N 1 8W
Leicestershire □, *U.K.* **11 E6** 52 41N 1 17W
Leichhardt →, *Australia* **62 B2** 17 35S 139 48 E
Leichhardt Ra., *Australia* **62 C4** 20 46S 147 40 E
Leiden, *Neths.* **15 B4** 52 9N 4 30 E
Leie →, *Belgium* **15 C3** 51 2N 3 45 E
Leine →, *Germany* **16 B5** 52 43N 9 36 E
Leinster, *Australia* **61 E3** 27 51S 120 36 E
Leinster □, *Ireland* **13 C4** 53 3N 7 8W
Leinster, Mt., *Ireland* **13 D5** 52 37N 6 46W
Leipzig, *Germany* **16 C7** 51 18N 12 22 E
Leiria, *Portugal* **19 C1** 39 46N 8 53W
Leirvik, *Norway* **9 G11** 59 47N 5 28 E
Leisler, Mt., *Australia* **60 D4** 23 23S 129 20 E
Leith, *U.K.* **12 F5** 55 59N 3 11W
Leith Hill, *U.K.* **11 F7** 51 11N 0 22W
Leitrim, *Ireland* **13 B3** 54 0N 8 5W
Leitrim □, *Ireland* **13 B4** 54 8N 8 0W
Leizhou Bandao, *China* **33 D6** 21 0N 110 0 E
Lek →, *Neths.* **15 C4** 51 54N 4 35 E
Leka, *Norway* **8 D14** 65 5N 11 35 E
Lékva Óros, *Greece* **23 D6** 35 18N 24 3 E
Leland, *Mich., U.S.A.* **76 C3** 45 1N 85 45W
Leland, *Miss., U.S.A.* **81 J9** 33 24N 90 54W
Leleque, *Argentina* **96 E2** 42 28S 71 0W
Lelystad, *Neths.* **15 B5** 52 30N 5 25 E
Léman, L., *Europe* **18 C7** 46 26N 6 30 E
Lemera, *Dem. Rep. of*
the Congo **54 C2** 3 0S 28 55 E
Lemhi Ra., *U.S.A.* **82 D7** 44 30N 113 30W
Lemmer, *Neths.* **15 B5** 52 51N 5 43 E
Lemmon, *U.S.A.* **80 C3** 45 57N 102 10W
Lemon Grove, *U.S.A.* **85 N9** 32 45N 117 2W
Lemoore, *U.S.A.* **84 J7** 36 18N 119 46W
Lemvig, *Denmark* **9 H13** 56 33N 8 20 E
Lena →, *Russia* **27 B13** 72 52N 126 40 E
Léndas, *Greece* **23 E6** 34 56N 24 56 E
Lendeh, *Iran* **45 D6** 30 58N 50 25 E
Lenggong, *Malaysia* **39 K3** 5 6N 100 58 E
Lengua de Vaca, Pta., *Chile* **94 C1** 30 14S 71 38W
Leninabad = Khŭjand,
Tajikistan **26 E7** 40 17N 69 37 E
Leninakan = Gyumri,
Armenia **25 F7** 40 47N 43 50 E
Leningrad = Sankt-
Peterburg, *Russia* **24 C5** 59 55N 30 20 E
Leninogorsk, *Kazakstan* **26 D9** 50 20N 83 30 E
Leninsk, *Russia* **25 E8** 48 40N 45 15 E
Leninsk-Kuznetskiy, *Russia* **26 D9** 54 44N 86 10 E
Lenkoran = Länkäran,
Azerbaijan **25 G8** 38 48N 48 52 E
Lenmalu, *Indonesia* **37 E8** 1 45S 130 15 E
Lennox, *U.S.A.* **80 D6** 43 21N 96 53W
Lennoxville, *Canada* **79 A13** 45 22N 71 51W
Lenoir, *U.S.A.* **77 H5** 35 55N 81 32W
Lenoir City, *U.S.A.* **77 H3** 35 48N 84 16W
Lenore L., *Canada* **73 C8** 52 30N 104 59W
Lenox, *U.S.A.* **79 D11** 42 22N 73 17W
Lens, *France* **18 A5** 50 26N 2 50 E
Lensk, *Russia* **27 C12** 60 48N 114 55 E
Lentini, *Italy* **20 F6** 37 17N 15 0 E
Lenwood, *U.S.A.* **85 L9** 34 53N 117 7W
Lenya, *Burma* **36 B1** 11 33N 98 57 E
Leoben, *Austria* **16 E8** 47 22N 15 5 E
Leodhas = Lewis, *U.K.* **12 C2** 58 9N 6 40W
Leola, *U.S.A.* **80 C5** 45 43N 98 56W
Leominster, *U.K.* **11 E5** 52 14N 2 43W
Leominster, *U.S.A.* **79 D13** 42 32N 71 46W
León, *Mexico* **86 C4** 21 7N 101 40W
León, *Nic.* **88 D2** 12 20N 86 51W
León, *Spain* **19 A3** 42 38N 5 34W
Leon, *U.S.A.* **80 E8** 40 44N 93 45W
Leon →, *U.S.A.* **81 K6** 31 14N 97 28W
León, Montes de, *Spain* **19 A2** 42 30N 6 18W
Leonardtown, *U.S.A.* **76 F7** 38 17N 76 38W
Leonardville, *Namibia* **56 C2** 23 29S 18 49 E
Leonora, *Australia* **61 E3** 28 49S 121 19 E
Leopoldina, *Brazil* **95 A7** 21 28S 42 40W
Leopoldsburg, *Belgium* **15 C5** 51 7N 5 13 E
Leoti, *U.S.A.* **80 F4** 38 29N 101 21W
Leova, *Moldova* **17 E15** 46 28N 28 15 E
Leoville, *Canada* **73 C7** 53 39N 107 33W
Lepel = Lyepyel, *Belarus* **24 D4** 54 50N 28 40 E
Lépo, L. do, *Angola* **56 B2** 17 0S 19 0 E
Leppävirta, *Finland* **9 E22** 62 29N 27 46 E
Lerdo, *Mexico* **86 B4** 25 32N 103 32W
Leribe, *Lesotho* **57 D4** 28 51S 28 3 E
Lérida = Lleida, *Spain* **19 B6** 41 37N 0 39 E
Lerwick, *U.K.* **12 A7** 60 9N 1 9W
Les Cayes, *Haiti* **89 C5** 18 15N 73 46W
Les Sables-d'Olonne,
France **18 C3** 46 30N 1 45W
Lesbos = Lésvos, *Greece* **21 E12** 39 10N 26 20 E
Leshan, *China* **32 D5** 29 33N 103 41 E
Leshukonskoye, *Russia* **24 B8** 64 54N 45 46 E
Leskov I., *Antarctica* **5 B1** 56 0S 28 0W
Leskovac, *Serbia, Yug.* **21 C9** 43 0N 21 58 E
Lesopilnoye, *Russia* **30 A7** 46 44N 134 20 E
Lesotho ■, *Africa* **57 D4** 29 40S 28 0 E
Lesozavodsk, *Russia* **27 E14** 45 30N 133 29 E
Lesse →, *Belgium* **15 D4** 50 15N 4 54 E
Lesser Antilles, *W. Indies* **89 D7** 15 0N 61 0W
Lesser Slave L., *Canada* **72 B5** 55 30N 115 25W
Lesser Sunda Is., *Indonesia* **37 F6** 7 0S 120 0 E
Lessines, *Belgium* **15 D3** 50 42N 3 50 E
Lester, *U.S.A.* **84 C5** 47 12N 121 29W
Lestock, *Canada* **73 C8** 51 19N 103 59W
Lesuer I., *Australia* **60 B4** 13 50S 127 17 E
Lésvos, *Greece* **21 E12** 39 10N 26 20 E
Leszno, *Poland* **17 C9** 51 50N 16 30 E
Letaba, *S. Africa* **57 C5** 23 59S 31 50 E
Letchworth, *U.K.* **11 F7** 51 59N 0 13W
Lethbridge, *Canada* **72 D6** 49 45N 112 45W
Lethem, *Guyana* **92 C7** 3 20N 59 50W
Leti, Kepulauan, *Indonesia* **37 F7** 8 10S 128 0 E
Leti Is. = Leti, Kepulauan,
Indonesia **37 F7** 8 10S 128 0 E
Letiahau →, *Botswana* **56 C3** 21 16S 24 0 E
Leticia, *Colombia* **92 D5** 4 9S 70 0W
Leting, *China* **35 E10** 39 23N 118 55 E
Letjiesbos, *S. Africa* **56 E3** 32 34S 22 16 E
Letlhakane, *Botswana* **56 C4** 21 27S 25 30 E
Letlhakeng, *Botswana* **56 C3** 24 0S 24 59 E
Letong, *Indonesia* **36 D3** 2 58N 105 42 E
Letpadan, *Burma* **41 L19** 17 45N 95 45 E
Letpan, *Burma* **41 K19** 19 28N 94 10 E
Letsôk-aw Kyun, *Burma* **39 G2** 11 30N 98 25 E
Letterkenny, *Ireland* **13 B4** 54 57N 7 45W
Leucadia, *U.S.A.* **85 M9** 33 4N 117 18W
Leuser, G., *Indonesia* **36 D1** 3 46N 97 12 E
Leuven, *Belgium* **15 D4** 50 52N 4 42 E
Leuze-en-Hainaut, *Belgium* **15 D3** 50 36N 3 37 E
Levádhia, *Greece* **21 E10** 38 27N 22 54 E
Levanger, *Norway* **8 E14** 63 45N 11 19 E
Levelland, *U.S.A.* **81 J3** 33 35N 102 23W
Leven, *U.K.* **12 E6** 56 12N 3 0W
Leven, L., *U.K.* **12 E5** 56 12N 3 22W
Leven, Toraka, *Madag.* **57 A8** 12 30S 47 45 E
Leveque C., *Australia* **60 C3** 16 20S 123 0 E
Levice, *Slovak Rep.* **17 D10** 48 13N 18 35 E
Levin, *N.Z.* **59 J5** 40 37S 175 18 E
Lévis, *Canada* **71 C5** 46 48N 71 9W
Levis, L., *Canada* **72 A5** 62 37N 117 58W
Levittown, *N.Y., U.S.A.* **79 F11** 40 44N 73 31W
Levittown, *Pa., U.S.A.* **79 F10** 40 9N 74 51W
Levkás, *Greece* **21 E9** 38 40N 20 43 E
Levkímmi, *Greece* **23 B4** 39 25N 20 3 E
Levkímmi, Ákra, *Greece* **23 B4** 39 29N 20 4 E
Levkôsia = Nicosia, *Cyprus* **23 D12** 35 10N 33 25 E
Levskigrad = Karlovo,
Bulgaria **21 C11** 42 38N 24 47 E
Levuka, *Fiji* **59 C8** 17 34S 179 0 E
Lewes, *U.K.* **11 G8** 50 52N 0 1 E
Lewes, *U.S.A.* **76 F8** 38 46N 75 9W
Lewis, *U.K.* **12 C2** 58 9N 6 40W
Lewis →, *U.S.A.* **84 E4** 45 51N 122 48W
Lewis, Butt of, *U.K.* **12 C2** 58 31N 6 16W
Lewis Ra., *Australia* **60 D4** 20 3S 128 50 E
Lewis Range, *U.S.A.* **82 C7** 48 5N 113 5W
Lewis Run, *U.S.A.* **78 E6** 41 52N 78 40W
Lewisburg, *Pa., U.S.A.* **78 F8** 40 58N 76 54W
Lewisburg, *Tenn., U.S.A.* **77 H2** 35 27N 86 48W
Lewisburg, *W. Va., U.S.A.* **76 G5** 37 48N 80 27W
Lewisporte, *Canada* **71 C8** 49 15N 55 3W
Lewiston, *Idaho, U.S.A.* **82 C5** 46 25N 117 1W
Lewiston, *Maine, U.S.A.* **77 C11** 44 6N 70 13W
Lewiston, *N.Y., U.S.A.* **78 C5** 43 11N 79 3W
Lewistown, *Mont., U.S.A.* **82 C9** 47 4N 109 26W
Lewistown, *Pa., U.S.A.* **78 F7** 40 36N 77 34W
Lexington, *Ill., U.S.A.* **80 E10** 40 39N 88 47W
Lexington, *Ky., U.S.A.* **76 F3** 38 3N 84 30W
Lexington, *Mich., U.S.A.* **78 C2** 43 16N 82 32W
Lexington, *Mo., U.S.A.* **80 F8** 39 11N 93 52W
Lexington, *N.C., U.S.A.* **77 H5** 35 49N 80 15W
Lexington, *N.Y., U.S.A.* **79 D10** 42 15N 74 22W
Lexington, *Nebr., U.S.A.* **80 E5** 40 47N 99 45W
Lexington, *Ohio, U.S.A.* **78 F2** 40 41N 82 35W
Lexington, *Tenn., U.S.A.* **77 H1** 35 39N 88 24W
Lexington, *Va., U.S.A.* **76 G6** 37 47N 79 27W
Lexington Park, *U.S.A.* **76 F7** 38 16N 76 27W
Leyburn, *U.K.* **10 C6** 54 19N 1 48W
Leyland, *U.K.* **10 D5** 53 42N 2 43W
Leyte □, *Phil.* **37 B6** 11 0N 125 0 E
Lezhë, *Albania* **21 D8** 41 47N 19 39 E
Lhasa, *China* **32 D4** 29 25N 90 58 E
Lhazê, *China* **32 D3** 29 5N 87 38 E
Lhokkruet, *Indonesia* **36 D1** 4 55N 95 24 E
Lhokseumawe, *Indonesia* **36 C1** 5 10N 97 10 E
L'Hospitalet de Llobregat,
Spain **19 B7** 41 21N 2 6 E
Li, *Thailand* **38 D2** 17 48N 98 57 E
Li Xian, *Gansu, China* **34 G3** 34 10N 105 5 E
Li Xian, *Hebei, China* **34 E8** 38 30N 115 35 E
Lianga, *Phil.* **37 C7** 8 38N 126 6 E
Liangcheng,
Nei Monggol Zizhiqu,
China **34 D7** 40 28N 112 25 E
Liangcheng, *Shandong,*
China **35 G10** 35 32N 119 37 E
Liangdang, *China* **34 H4** 33 56N 106 18 E
Liangpran, *Indonesia* **36 D4** 1 4N 114 23 E
Lianshanguan, *China* **35 D12** 40 53N 123 43 E
Lianshui, *China* **35 H10** 33 42N 119 20 E
Lianyungang, *China* **35 G10** 34 40N 119 11 E
Liao He →, *China* **35 D11** 41 0N 121 50 E
Liaocheng, *China* **34 F8** 36 28N 115 58 E
Liaodong Bandao, *China* **35 E12** 40 0N 122 30 E
Liaodong Wan, *China* **35 D11** 40 20N 121 10 E
Liaoning □, *China* **35 D12** 41 40N 122 30 E
Liaoyang, *China* **35 D12** 41 15N 122 58 E
Liaoyuan, *China* **35 C13** 42 58N 125 2 E
Liaozhong, *China* **35 D12** 41 23N 122 50 E
Liard →, *Canada* **72 A4** 61 51N 121 18W
Liard River, *Canada* **72 B3** 59 25N 126 5W
Liari, *Pakistan* **42 G2** 25 37N 66 30 E
Libau = Liepāja, *Latvia* **9 H19** 56 30N 21 0 E
Libby, *U.S.A.* **82 B6** 48 23N 115 33W
Libenge, *Dem. Rep. of*
the Congo **52 D3** 3 40N 18 55 E
Liberal, *U.S.A.* **81 G4** 37 3N 100 55W
Liberec, *Czech Rep.* **16 C8** 50 47N 15 7 E
Liberia, *Costa Rica* **88 D2** 10 40N 85 30W
Liberia ■, *W. Afr.* **50 G4** 6 30N 9 30W
Liberty, *Mo., U.S.A.* **80 F7** 39 15N 94 25W
Liberty, *N.Y., U.S.A.* **79 E10** 41 48N 74 45W
Liberty, *Pa., U.S.A.* **78 E7** 41 34N 77 6W
Liberty, *Tex., U.S.A.* **81 K7** 30 3N 94 48W
Lîbîya, Sahrâ', *Africa* **51 C10** 25 0N 25 0 E
Libobo, Tanjung, *Indonesia* **37 E7** 0 54S 128 28 E
Libode, *S. Africa* **57 E4** 31 33S 29 2 E
Libourne, *France* **18 D3** 44 55N 0 14W
Libramont, *Belgium* **15 E5** 49 55N 5 23 E
Libreville, *Gabon* **52 D1** 0 25N 9 26 E
Libya ■, *N. Afr.* **51 C9** 27 0N 17 0 E
Libyan Desert = Lîbîya,
Sahrâ', *Africa* **51 C10** 25 0N 25 0 E
Licantén, *Chile* **94 D1** 35 55S 72 0W
Licata, *Italy* **20 F5** 37 6N 13 56 E
Licheng, *China* **34 F7** 36 28N 113 20 E
Lichfield, *U.K.* **11 E6** 52 41N 1 49W
Lichinga, *Mozam.* **55 E4** 13 13S 35 11 E
Lichtenburg, *S. Africa* **56 D4** 26 8S 26 8 E
Licking →, *U.S.A.* **76 F3** 39 6N 84 30W
Lida, *Belarus* **9 K21** 53 53N 25 15 E
Lidköping, *Sweden* **9 G15** 58 31N 13 7 E
Liebig, Mt., *Australia* **60 D5** 23 18S 131 22 E
Liechtenstein ■, *Europe* **18 C8** 47 8N 9 35 E
Liège, *Belgium* **15 D5** 50 38N 5 35 E
Liège □, *Belgium* **15 D5** 50 32N 5 35 E
Liegnitz = Legnica, *Poland* **16 C9** 51 12N 16 10 E
Lienart, *Dem. Rep. of*
the Congo **54 B2** 3 3N 25 31 E
Lienyünchiangshih =
Lianyungang, *China* **35 G10** 34 40N 119 11 E
Lienz, *Austria* **16 E7** 46 50N 12 46 E
Liepāja, *Latvia* **9 H19** 56 30N 21 0 E
Lier, *Belgium* **15 C4** 51 7N 4 34 E
Lièvre →, *Canada* **70 C4** 45 31N 75 26W
Liffey →, *Ireland* **13 C5** 53 21N 6 13W
Lifford, *Ireland* **13 B4** 54 51N 7 29W
Lifudzin, *Russia* **30 B7** 44 21N 134 58 E
Lightning Ridge, *Australia* **63 D4** 29 22S 148 0 E
Lignonier, *U.S.A.* **78 F5** 40 15N 79 14W
Liguria □, *Italy* **18 D8** 44 30N 8 50 E
Ligurian Sea, *Medit. S.* **20 C3** 43 20N 9 0 E

Lookout, C.

Lihou Reefs and Cays, *Australia* **62 B5** 17 25S 151 40 E
Lihue, *U.S.A.* **74 H15** 21 59N 159 23W
Lijiang, *China* **32 D5** 26 55N 100 20 E
Likasi, *Dem. Rep. of the Congo* **55 E2** 10 55S 26 48 E
Likoma I., *Malawi* **55 E3** 12 3S 34 45 E
Likumburu, *Tanzania* **55 D4** 9 43S 35 8 E
Lille, *France* **18 A5** 50 38N 3 3 E
Lille Bælt, *Denmark* **9 J13** 55 20N 9 45 E
Lillehammer, *Norway* **9 F14** 61 8N 10 30 E
Lillesand, *Norway* **9 G13** 58 15N 8 23 E
Lillian Pt., *Australia* **61 E4** 27 40S 126 6 E
Lillooet, *Canada* **72 C4** 50 44N 121 57W
Lillooet →, *Canada* **72 D4** 49 15N 121 57W
Lilongwe, *Malawi* **55 E3** 14 0S 33 48 E
Liloy, *Phil.* **37 C6** 8 4N 122 39 E
Lim →, *Bos.-H.* **21 C8** 43 45N 19 15 E
Lima, *Indonesia* **37 E7** 3 39S 127 58 E
Lima, *Peru* **92 F3** 12 0S 77 0W
Lima, *Mont., U.S.A.* **82 D7** 44 38N 112 36W
Lima, *Ohio, U.S.A.* **76 E3** 40 44N 84 6W
Lima →, *Portugal* **19 B1** 41 41N 8 50W
Liman, *Indonesia* **37 G14** 7 48S 111 45 E
Limassol, *Cyprus* **23 E12** 34 42N 33 1 E
Limavady, *U.K.* **13 A5** 55 3N 6 56W
Limay →, *Argentina* **96 D3** 39 0S 68 0W
Limay Mahuida, *Argentina* **94 D2** 37 10S 66 45W
Limbang, *Brunei* **36 D5** 4 42N 115 6 E
Limbaži, *Latvia* **9 H21** 57 31N 24 42 E
Limbdi, *India* **42 H4** 22 34N 71 51 E
Limbe, *Cameroon* **52 D1** 4 1N 9 10 E
Limburg, *Germany* **16 C5** 50 22N 8 4 E
Limburg □, *Belgium* **15 C5** 51 2N 5 25 E
Limburg □, *Neths.* **15 C5** 51 20N 5 55 E
Limeira, *Brazil* **95 A6** 22 35S 47 28W
Limerick, *Ireland* **13 D3** 52 40N 8 37W
Limerick, *U.S.A.* **79 C14** 43 41N 70 48W
Limerick □, *Ireland* **13 D3** 52 30N 8 50W
Limestone, *U.S.A.* **78 D6** 42 2N 78 38W
Limestone →, *Canada* **73 B10** 56 31N 94 7W
Limfjorden, *Denmark* **9 H13** 56 55N 9 0 E
Limia = Lima →, *Portugal* **19 B1** 41 41N 8 50W
Limingen, *Norway* **8 D15** 64 48N 13 35 E
Limmen Bight, *Australia* **62 A2** 14 40S 135 35 E
Limmen Bight →, *Australia* **62 B2** 15 7S 135 44 E
Límnos, *Greece* **21 E11** 39 50N 25 5 E
Limoges, *Canada* **79 A9** 45 20N 75 16W
Limoges, *France* **18 D4** 45 50N 1 15 E
Limón, *Costa Rica* **88 E3** 10 0N 83 2W
Limon, *U.S.A.* **80 F3** 39 16N 103 41W
Limousin, *France* **18 D4** 45 30N 1 30 E
Limoux, *France* **18 E5** 43 4N 2 12 E
Limpopo →, *Africa* **57 D5** 25 5S 33 30 E
Limuru, *Kenya* **54 C4** 1 2S 36 35 E
Lin Xian, *China* **34 F6** 37 57N 110 58 E
Linares, *Chile* **94 D1** 35 50S 71 40W
Linares, *Mexico* **87 C5** 24 50N 99 40W
Linares, *Spain* **19 C4** 38 10N 3 40W
Lincheng, *China* **34 F8** 37 25N 114 30 E
Lincoln, *Argentina* **94 C3** 34 55S 61 30W
Lincoln, *N.Z.* **59 K4** 43 38S 172 30 E
Lincoln, *U.K.* **10 D7** 53 14N 0 32W
Lincoln, *Calif., U.S.A.* **84 G5** 38 54N 121 17W
Lincoln, *Ill., U.S.A.* **80 E10** 40 9N 89 22W
Lincoln, *Kans., U.S.A.* **80 F5** 39 3N 98 9W
Lincoln, *Maine, U.S.A.* **77 C11** 45 22N 68 30W
Lincoln, *N.H., U.S.A.* **79 B13** 44 3N 71 40W
Lincoln, *N. Mex., U.S.A.* **83 K11** 33 30N 105 23W
Lincoln, *Nebr., U.S.A.* **80 E6** 40 49N 96 41W
Lincoln City, *U.S.A.* **82 D1** 44 57N 124 1W
Lincoln Hav = Lincoln Sea, *Arctic* **4 A5** 84 0N 55 0W
Lincoln Sea, *Arctic* **4 A5** 84 0N 55 0W
Lincolnshire □, *U.K.* **10 D7** 53 14N 0 32W
Lincolnshire Wolds, *U.K.* **10 D7** 53 26N 0 13W
Lincolnton, *U.S.A.* **77 H5** 35 29N 81 16W
Lind, *U.S.A.* **82 C4** 46 58N 118 37W
Linda, *U.S.A.* **84 F5** 39 8N 121 34W
Linden, *Guyana* **92 B7** 6 0N 58 10W
Linden, *Ala., U.S.A.* **77 J2** 32 18N 87 48W
Linden, *Calif., U.S.A.* **84 G5** 38 1N 121 5W
Linden, *Tex., U.S.A.* **81 J7** 33 1N 94 22W
Lindenhurst, *U.S.A.* **79 F11** 40 41N 73 23W
Lindesnes, *Norway* **9 H12** 57 58N 7 3 E
Líndhos, *Greece* **23 C10** 36 6N 28 4 E
Líndhos, Ákra, *Greece* **23 C10** 36 4N 28 10 E
Lindi, *Tanzania* **55 D4** 9 58S 39 38 E
Lindi □, *Tanzania* **55 D4** 9 40S 38 30 E
Lindi →, *Dem. Rep. of the Congo* **54 B2** 0 33N 25 5 E
Lindsay, *Canada* **78 B6** 44 22N 78 43W
Lindsay, *Calif., U.S.A.* **84 J7** 36 12N 119 5W
Lindsay, *Okla., U.S.A.* **81 H6** 34 50N 97 38W
Lindsborg, *U.S.A.* **80 F6** 38 35N 97 40W
Linesville, *U.S.A.* **78 E4** 41 39N 80 26W
Linfen, *China* **34 F6** 36 3N 111 30 E
Ling Xian, *China* **34 F9** 37 22N 116 30 E
Lingao, *China* **38 C7** 19 56N 109 42 E
Lingayen, *Phil.* **37 A6** 16 1N 120 14 E
Lingayen G., *Phil.* **37 A6** 16 10N 120 15 E
Lingbi, *China* **35 H9** 33 33N 117 33 E
Lingchuan, *China* **34 G7** 35 45N 113 12 E
Lingen, *Germany* **16 B4** 52 31N 7 19 E
Lingga, *Indonesia* **36 E2** 0 12S 104 37 E
Lingga, Kepulauan, *Indonesia* **36 E2** 0 10S 104 30 E
Lingga Arch. = Lingga, Kepulauan, *Indonesia* **36 E2** 0 10S 104 30 E
Lingle, *U.S.A.* **80 D2** 42 8N 104 21W
Lingqiu, *China* **34 E8** 39 28N 114 22 E
Lingshi, *China* **34 F6** 36 48N 111 48 E
Lingshou, *China* **34 E8** 38 20N 114 20 E
Lingshui, *China* **38 C8** 18 27N 110 0 E
Lingtai, *China* **34 G4** 35 0N 107 40 E
Linguère, *Senegal* **50 E2** 15 25N 15 5W
Lingwu, *China* **34 E4** 38 6N 106 20 E
Lingyuan, *China* **35 D10** 41 10N 119 15 E
Linhai, *China* **33 D7** 28 50N 121 8 E
Linhares, *Brazil* **93 G10** 19 25S 40 4W
Linhe, *China* **34 D4** 40 48N 107 20 E
Linjiang, *China* **35 D14** 41 50N 127 0 E
Linköping, *Sweden* **9 G16** 58 28N 15 36 E
Linkou, *China* **35 B16** 45 15N 130 18 E
Linnhe, L., *U.K.* **12 E3** 56 36N 5 25W
Linosa, *Medit. S.* **20 G5** 35 51N 12 50 E
Linqi, *China* **34 G7** 35 45N 113 52 E
Linqing, *China* **34 F8** 36 50N 115 42 E
Linqu, *China* **35 F10** 36 25N 118 30 E
Linru, *China* **34 G7** 34 11N 112 52 E
Lins, *Brazil* **95 A6** 21 40S 49 44W
Linta →, *Madag.* **57 D7** 25 2S 44 5 E
Linton, *Ind., U.S.A.* **76 F2** 39 2N 87 10W
Linton, *N. Dak., U.S.A.* **80 B4** 46 16N 100 14W
Lintong, *China* **34 G5** 34 20N 109 10 E
Linwood, *Canada* **78 C4** 43 35N 80 43W
Linxi, *China* **35 C10** 43 36N 118 2 E
Linxia, *China* **32 C5** 35 36N 103 10 E
Linyanti →, *Africa* **56 B4** 17 50S 25 5 E
Linyi, *China* **35 G10** 35 5N 118 21 E
Linz, *Austria* **16 D8** 48 18N 14 18 E
Linzhenzhen, *China* **34 F5** 36 30N 109 59 E
Linzi, *China* **35 F10** 36 50N 118 20 E
Lion, G. du, *France* **18 E6** 43 10N 4 0 E
Lionárisso, *Cyprus* **23 D13** 35 28N 34 8 E
Lions, G. of = Lion, G. du, *France* **18 E6** 43 10N 4 0 E
Lion's Den, *Zimbabwe* **55 F3** 17 15S 30 5 E
Lion's Head, *Canada* **78 B3** 44 58N 81 15W
Lipa, *Phil.* **37 B6** 13 57N 121 10 E
Lipali, *Mozam.* **55 F4** 15 50S 35 50 E
Lípari, *Italy* **20 E6** 38 26N 14 58 E
Lípari, Is. = Eólie, Ís., *Italy* **20 E6** 38 30N 14 57 E
Lipcani, *Moldova* **17 D14** 48 14N 26 48 E
Lipetsk, *Russia* **24 D6** 52 37N 39 35 E
Lipkany = Lipcani, *Moldova* **17 D14** 48 14N 26 48 E
Lipovcy Manzovka, *Russia* **30 B6** 44 12N 132 26 E
Lipovets, *Ukraine* **17 D15** 49 12N 29 1 E
Lippe →, *Germany* **16 C4** 51 39N 6 36 E
Lipscomb, *U.S.A.* **81 G4** 36 14N 100 16W
Lira, *Uganda* **54 B3** 2 17N 32 57 E
Liria = Lliria, *Spain* **19 C5** 39 37N 0 35W
Lisala, *Dem. Rep. of the Congo* **52 D4** 2 12N 21 38 E
Lisboa, *Portugal* **19 C1** 38 42N 9 10W
Lisbon = Lisboa, *Portugal* **19 C1** 38 42N 9 10W
Lisbon, *N. Dak., U.S.A.* **80 B6** 46 27N 97 41W
Lisbon, *N.H., U.S.A.* **79 B13** 44 13N 71 55W
Lisbon, *Ohio, U.S.A.* **78 F4** 40 46N 80 46W
Lisbon Falls, *U.S.A.* **77 D10** 44 0N 70 4W
Lisburn, *U.K.* **13 B5** 54 31N 6 3W
Liscannor B., *Ireland* **13 D2** 52 55N 9 24W
Lishi, *China* **34 F6** 37 31N 111 8 E
Lishu, *China* **35 C13** 43 20N 124 18 E
Lisianski I., *Pac. Oc.* **64 E10** 26 2N 174 0W
Lisichansk = Lysychansk, *Ukraine* **25 E6** 48 55N 38 30 E
Lisieux, *France* **18 B4** 49 10N 0 12 E
Liski, *Russia* **25 D6** 51 3N 39 30 E
Lismore, *Australia* **63 D5** 28 44S 153 21 E
Lismore, *Ireland* **13 D4** 52 8N 7 55W
Lista, *Norway* **9 G12** 58 7N 6 39 E
Lister, Mt., *Antarctica* **5 D11** 78 0S 162 0 E
Liston, *Australia* **63 D5** 28 39S 152 6 E
Listowel, *Canada* **78 C4** 43 44N 80 58W
Listowel, *Ireland* **13 D2** 52 27N 9 29W
Litani →, *Lebanon* **47 B4** 33 20N 35 15 E
Litchfield, *Calif., U.S.A.* **84 E6** 40 24N 120 23W
Litchfield, *Conn., U.S.A.* **79 E11** 41 45N 73 11W
Litchfield, *Ill., U.S.A.* **80 F10** 39 11N 89 39W
Litchfield, *Minn., U.S.A.* **80 C7** 45 8N 94 32W
Líthinon, Ákra, *Greece* **23 E6** 34 55N 24 44 E
Lithuania ■, *Europe* **9 J20** 55 30N 24 0 E
Lititz, *U.S.A.* **79 F8** 40 9N 76 18W
Litoměřice, *Czech Rep.* **16 C8** 50 33N 14 10 E
Little Abaco I., *Bahamas* **88 A4** 26 50N 77 30W
Little Barrier I., *N.Z.* **59 G5** 36 12S 175 8 E
Little Belt Mts., *U.S.A.* **82 C8** 46 40N 110 45W
Little Blue →, *U.S.A.* **80 F6** 39 42N 96 41W
Little Buffalo →, *Canada* **72 A6** 61 0N 113 46W
Little Cayman, *Cayman Is.* **88 C3** 19 41N 80 3W
Little Churchill →, *Canada* **73 B9** 57 30N 95 22W
Little Colorado →, *U.S.A.* **83 H8** 36 12N 111 48W
Little Current, *Canada* **70 C3** 45 55N 82 0W
Little Current →, *Canada* **70 B3** 50 57N 84 36W
Little Falls, *Minn., U.S.A.* **80 C7** 45 59N 94 22W
Little Falls, *N.Y., U.S.A.* **79 C10** 43 3N 74 51W
Little Fork →, *U.S.A.* **80 A8** 48 31N 93 35W
Little Grand Rapids, *Canada* **73 C9** 52 0N 95 29W
Little Humboldt →, *U.S.A.* **82 F5** 41 1N 117 43W
Little Inagua I., *Bahamas* **89 B5** 21 40N 73 50W
Little Karoo, *S. Africa* **56 E3** 33 45S 21 0 E
Little Lake, *U.S.A.* **85 K9** 35 56N 117 55W
Little Laut Is. = Laut Kecil, Kepulauan, *Indonesia* **36 E5** 4 45S 115 40 E
Little Mecatina = Petit-Mécatina →, *Canada* **71 B8** 50 40N 59 30W
Little Minch, *U.K.* **12 D2** 57 35N 6 45W
Little Missouri →, *U.S.A.* **80 B3** 47 36N 102 25W
Little Ouse →, *U.K.* **11 E9** 52 22N 1 12 E
Little Rann, *India* **42 H4** 23 25N 71 25 E
Little Red →, *U.S.A.* **81 H9** 35 11N 91 27W
Little River, *N.Z.* **59 K4** 43 45S 172 49 E
Little Rock, *U.S.A.* **81 H8** 34 45N 92 17W
Little Ruaha →, *Tanzania* **54 D4** 7 57S 37 53 E
Little Sable Pt., *U.S.A.* **76 D2** 43 38N 86 33W
Little Sioux →, *U.S.A.* **80 E6** 41 48N 96 4W
Little Smoky →, *Canada* **72 C5** 54 44N 117 11W
Little Snake →, *U.S.A.* **82 F9** 40 27N 108 26W
Little Valley, *U.S.A.* **78 D6** 42 15N 78 48W
Little Wabash →, *U.S.A.* **76 G1** 37 55N 88 5W
Little White →, *U.S.A.* **80 D4** 43 40N 100 40W
Littlefield, *U.S.A.* **81 J3** 33 55N 102 20W
Littlehampton, *U.K.* **11 G7** 50 49N 0 32W
Littleton, *U.S.A.* **79 B13** 44 18N 71 46W
Liu He →, *China* **35 D11** 40 55N 121 35 E
Liuba, *China* **34 H4** 33 38N 106 55 E
Liugou, *China* **35 D10** 40 57N 118 15 E
Liuhe, *China* **35 C13** 42 17N 125 43 E
Liukang Tenggaja = Sabalana, Kepulauan, *Indonesia* **37 F5** 6 45S 118 50 E
Liuli, *Tanzania* **55 E3** 11 3S 34 38 E
Liuwa Plain, *Zambia* **53 G4** 14 20S 22 30 E
Liuzhou, *China* **33 D5** 24 22N 109 22 E
Liuzhuang, *China* **35 H11** 33 12N 120 18 E
Livadhia, *Cyprus* **23 E12** 34 57N 33 38 E
Live Oak, *Calif., U.S.A.* **84 F5** 39 17N 121 40W
Live Oak, *Fla., U.S.A.* **77 K4** 30 18N 82 59W
Liveras, *Cyprus* **23 D11** 35 23N 32 57 E
Livermore, *U.S.A.* **84 H5** 37 41N 121 47W
Livermore, Mt., *U.S.A.* **81 K2** 30 38N 104 11W
Livermore Falls, *U.S.A.* **77 C11** 44 29N 70 11W
Liverpool, *Canada* **71 D7** 44 5N 64 41W
Liverpool, *U.K.* **10 D4** 53 25N 3 0W
Liverpool, *U.S.A.* **79 C8** 43 6N 76 13W
Liverpool Bay, *U.K.* **10 D4** 53 30N 3 20W
Livingston, *Guatemala* **88 C2** 15 50N 88 50W
Livingston, *U.K.* **12 F5** 55 54N 3 30W
Livingston, *Ala., U.S.A.* **77 J1** 32 35N 88 11W
Livingston, *Calif., U.S.A.* **84 H6** 37 23N 120 43W
Livingston, *Mont., U.S.A.* **82 D8** 45 40N 110 34W
Livingston, *S.C., U.S.A.* **77 J5** 33 32N 80 53W
Livingston, *Tenn., U.S.A.* **77 G3** 36 23N 85 19W
Livingston, *Tex., U.S.A.* **81 K7** 30 43N 94 56W
Livingston, L., *U.S.A.* **81 K7** 30 50N 95 10W
Livingston Manor, *U.S.A.* **79 E10** 41 54N 74 50W
Livingstone, *Zambia* **55 F2** 17 46S 25 52 E
Livingstone Mts., *Tanzania* **55 D3** 9 40S 34 20 E
Livingstonia, *Malawi* **55 E3** 10 38S 34 5 E
Livny, *Russia* **24 D6** 52 30N 37 30 E
Livonia, *Mich., U.S.A.* **76 D4** 42 23N 83 23W
Livonia, *N.Y., U.S.A.* **78 D7** 42 49N 77 40W
Livorno, *Italy* **20 C4** 43 33N 10 19 E
Livramento, *Brazil* **95 C4** 30 55S 55 30W
Liwale, *Tanzania* **55 D4** 9 48S 37 58 E
Lizard I., *Australia* **62 A4** 14 42S 145 30 E
Lizard Pt., *U.K.* **11 H2** 49 57N 5 13W
Ljubljana, *Slovenia* **16 E8** 46 4N 14 33 E
Ljungan →, *Sweden* **9 E17** 62 18N 17 23 E
Ljungby, *Sweden* **9 H15** 56 49N 13 55 E
Ljusdal, *Sweden* **9 F17** 61 46N 16 3 E
Ljusnan →, *Sweden* **9 F17** 61 12N 17 8 E
Ljusne, *Sweden* **9 F17** 61 13N 17 7 E
Llancanelo, Salina, *Argentina* **94 D2** 35 40S 69 8W
Llandeilo, *U.K.* **11 F4** 51 53N 3 59W
Llandovery, *U.K.* **11 F4** 51 59N 3 48W
Llandrindod Wells, *U.K.* **11 E4** 52 14N 3 22W
Llandudno, *U.K.* **10 D4** 53 19N 3 50W
Llanelli, *U.K.* **11 F3** 51 41N 4 10W
Llanes, *Spain* **19 A3** 43 25N 4 50W
Llangollen, *U.K.* **10 E4** 52 58N 3 11W
Llanidloes, *U.K.* **11 E4** 52 27N 3 31W
Llano, *U.S.A.* **81 K5** 30 45N 98 41W
Llano →, *U.S.A.* **81 K5** 30 39N 98 26W
Llano Estacado, *U.S.A.* **81 J3** 33 30N 103 0W
Llanos, *S. Amer.* **92 C4** 5 0N 71 35W
Llanquihue, L., *Chile* **96 E1** 41 10S 72 50W
Llanwrtyd Wells, *U.K.* **11 E4** 52 7N 3 38W
Llebeig, C. des, *Spain* **22 B9** 39 33N 2 18 E
Lleida, *Spain* **19 B6** 41 37N 0 39 E
Llentrisca, C., *Spain* **22 C7** 38 52N 1 15 E
Llera, *Mexico* **87 C5** 23 19N 99 1W
Lleyn Peninsula, *U.K.* **10 E3** 52 51N 4 36W
Llico, *Chile* **94 C1** 34 46S 72 5W
Lliria, *Spain* **19 C5** 39 37N 0 35W
Llobregat →, *Spain* **19 B7** 41 19N 2 9 E
Lloret de Mar, *Spain* **19 B7** 41 41N 2 53 E
Lloyd B., *Australia* **62 A3** 12 45S 143 27 E
Lloyd L., *Canada* **73 B7** 57 22N 108 57W
Lloydminster, *Canada* **73 C7** 53 17N 110 0W
Llucmajor, *Spain* **22 B9** 39 29N 2 53 E
Llullaillaco, Volcán, *S. Amer.* **94 A2** 24 43S 68 30W
Lo →, *Vietnam* **38 B5** 21 18N 105 25 E
Loa, *U.S.A.* **83 G8** 38 24N 111 39W
Loa →, *Chile* **94 A1** 21 26S 70 41W
Loaita I., *S. China Sea* **36 B4** 10 41N 114 25 E
Loange →, *Dem. Rep. of the Congo* **52 E4** 4 17S 20 2 E
Lobatse, *Botswana* **56 D4** 25 12S 25 40 E
Lobería, *Argentina* **94 D4** 38 10S 58 40W
Lobito, *Angola* **53 G2** 12 18S 13 35 E
Lobos, *Argentina* **94 D4** 35 10S 59 0W
Lobos, I., *Mexico* **86 B2** 27 15N 110 30W
Lobos, I. de, *Canary Is.* **22 F6** 28 45N 13 50W
Loc Binh, *Vietnam* **38 B6** 21 46N 106 54 E
Loc Ninh, *Vietnam* **39 G6** 11 50N 106 34 E
Locarno, *Switz.* **18 C8** 46 10N 8 47 E
Loch Baghasdail = Lochboisdale, *U.K.* **12 D1** 57 9N 7 20W
Loch Garman = Wexford, *Ireland* **13 D5** 52 20N 6 28W
Loch Nam Madadh = Lochmaddy, *U.K.* **12 D1** 57 36N 7 10W
Lochaber, *U.K.* **12 E3** 56 59N 5 1W
Locharbriggs, *U.K.* **12 F5** 55 7N 3 35W
Lochboisdale, *U.K.* **12 D1** 57 9N 7 20W
Loche, L. La, *Canada* **73 B7** 56 30N 109 30W
Lochem, *Neths.* **15 B6** 52 9N 6 26 E
Loches, *France* **18 C4** 47 7N 1 0 E
Lochgilphead, *U.K.* **12 E3** 56 2N 5 26W
Lochinver, *U.K.* **12 C3** 58 9N 5 14W
Lochmaddy, *U.K.* **12 D1** 57 36N 7 10W
Lochnagar, *Australia* **62 C4** 23 33S 145 38 E
Lochnagar, *U.K.* **12 E5** 56 57N 3 15W
Lochy, L., *U.K.* **12 E4** 57 0N 4 53W
Lock, *Australia* **63 E2** 33 34S 135 46 E
Lock Haven, *U.S.A.* **78 E7** 41 8N 77 28W
Lockeford, *U.S.A.* **84 G5** 38 10N 121 9W
Lockeport, *Canada* **71 D6** 43 47N 65 4W
Lockerbie, *U.K.* **12 F5** 55 7N 3 21W
Lockhart, *U.S.A.* **81 L6** 29 53N 97 40W
Lockhart, L., *Australia* **61 F2** 33 15S 119 3 E
Lockhart River, *Australia* **62 A3** 12 58S 143 30 E
Lockney, *U.S.A.* **81 H4** 34 7N 101 27W
Lockport, *U.S.A.* **78 C6** 43 10N 78 42W
Lod, *Israel* **47 D3** 31 57N 34 54 E
Lodeinoye Pole, *Russia* **24 B5** 60 44N 33 33 E
Lodge Bay, *Canada* **71 B8** 52 14N 55 51W
Lodge Grass, *U.S.A.* **82 D10** 45 19N 107 22W
Lodgepole Cr. →, *U.S.A.* **80 E2** 41 20N 104 30W
Lodhran, *Pakistan* **42 E4** 29 32N 71 30 E
Lodi, *Italy* **18 D8** 45 19N 9 30 E
Lodi, *Calif., U.S.A.* **84 G5** 38 8N 121 16W
Lodi, *Ohio, U.S.A.* **78 E3** 41 2N 82 0W
Lodja, *Dem. Rep. of the Congo* **54 C1** 3 30S 23 23 E
Lodwar, *Kenya* **54 B4** 3 10N 35 40 E
Łódź, *Poland* **17 C10** 51 45N 19 27 E
Loei, *Thailand* **38 D3** 17 29N 101 35 E
Loengo, *Dem. Rep. of the Congo* **54 C2** 4 48S 26 30 E
Loeriesfontein, *S. Africa* **56 E2** 31 0S 19 26 E
Lofoten, *Norway* **8 B15** 68 30N 14 0 E
Logan, *Iowa, U.S.A.* **80 E7** 41 39N 95 47W
Logan, *Ohio, U.S.A.* **76 F4** 39 32N 82 25W
Logan, *Utah, U.S.A.* **82 F8** 41 44N 111 50W
Logan, *W. Va., U.S.A.* **76 G5** 37 51N 81 59W
Logan, Mt., *Canada* **68 B5** 60 31N 140 22W
Logandale, *U.S.A.* **85 J12** 36 36N 114 29W
Logansport, *Ind., U.S.A.* **76 E2** 40 45N 86 22W
Logansport, *La., U.S.A.* **81 K8** 31 58N 94 0W
Logone →, *Chad* **51 F9** 12 6N 15 2 E
Logroño, *Spain* **19 A4** 42 28N 2 27W
Lohardaga, *India* **43 H11** 23 27N 84 45 E
Loharia, *India* **42 H6** 23 45N 74 14 E
Loharu, *India* **42 E6** 28 27N 75 49 E
Lohja, *Finland* **9 F21** 60 12N 24 5 E
Lohri Wah →, *Pakistan* **42 F2** 27 27N 67 37 E
Loi-kaw, *Burma* **41 K20** 19 40N 97 17 E
Loimaa, *Finland* **9 F20** 60 50N 23 5 E
Loir →, *France* **18 C3** 47 33N 0 32W
Loire →, *France* **18 C2** 47 16N 2 10W
Loja, *Ecuador* **92 D3** 3 59S 79 16W
Loja, *Spain* **19 D3** 37 10N 4 10W
Loji = Kawasi, *Indonesia* **37 E7** 1 38S 127 28 E
Lokandu, *Dem. Rep. of the Congo* **54 C2** 2 30S 25 45 E
Lokeren, *Belgium* **15 C3** 51 6N 3 59 E
Lokgwabe, *Botswana* **56 C3** 24 10S 21 50 E
Lokichokio, *Kenya* **54 B3** 4 19N 34 13 E
Lokitaung, *Kenya* **54 B4** 4 12N 35 48 E
Lokkan tekojärvi, *Finland* **8 C22** 67 55N 27 35 E
Lokoja, *Nigeria* **50 G7** 7 47N 6 45 E
Lola, Mt., *U.S.A.* **84 F6** 39 26N 120 22W
Loliondo, *Tanzania* **54 C4** 2 2S 35 39 E
Lolland, *Denmark* **9 J14** 54 45N 11 30 E
Lolo, *U.S.A.* **82 C6** 46 45N 114 5W
Lom, *Bulgaria* **21 C10** 43 48N 23 12 E
Lom Kao, *Thailand* **38 D3** 16 53N 101 14 E
Lom Sak, *Thailand* **38 D3** 16 47N 101 15 E
Loma, *U.S.A.* **82 C8** 47 56N 110 30W
Loma Linda, *U.S.A.* **85 L9** 34 3N 117 16W
Lomami →, *Dem. Rep. of the Congo* **54 B1** 0 46N 24 16 E
Lomas de Zamóra, *Argentina* **94 C4** 34 45S 58 25W
Lombadina, *Australia* **60 C3** 16 31S 122 54 E
Lombárdia □, *Italy* **18 D8** 45 40N 9 30 E
Lombardy = Lombárdia □, *Italy* **18 D8** 45 40N 9 30 E
Lomblen, *Indonesia* **37 F6** 8 30S 123 32 E
Lombok, *Indonesia* **36 F5** 8 45S 116 30 E
Lomé, *Togo* **50 G6** 6 9N 1 20 E
Lomela, *Dem. Rep. of the Congo* **52 E4** 2 19S 23 15 E
Lomela →, *Dem. Rep. of the Congo* **52 E4** 0 15S 20 40 E
Lommel, *Belgium* **15 C5** 51 14N 5 19 E
Lomond, *Canada* **72 C6** 50 24N 112 36W
Lomond, L., *U.K.* **12 E4** 56 8N 4 38W
Lomphat, *Cambodia* **38 F6** 13 30N 106 59 E
Lompobatang, *Indonesia* **37 F5** 5 24S 119 56 E
Lompoc, *U.S.A.* **85 L6** 34 38N 120 28W
Łomża, *Poland* **17 B12** 53 10N 22 2 E
Loncoche, *Chile* **96 D2** 39 20S 72 50W
Londa, *India* **40 M9** 15 30N 74 30 E
Londiani, *Kenya* **54 C4** 0 10S 35 33 E
London, *Canada* **78 D3** 42 59N 81 15W
London, *U.K.* **11 F7** 51 30N 0 3W
London, *Ky., U.S.A.* **76 G3** 37 8N 84 5W
London, *Ohio, U.S.A.* **76 F4** 39 53N 83 27W
London, Greater □, *U.K.* **11 F7** 51 36N 0 5W
Londonderry, *U.K.* **13 B4** 55 0N 7 20W
Londonderry □, *U.K.* **13 B4** 55 0N 7 20W
Londonderry, C., *Australia* **60 B4** 13 45S 126 55 E
Londonderry, I., *Chile* **96 H2** 55 0S 71 0W
Londres, *Argentina* **96 B3** 27 43S 67 7W
Londrina, *Brazil* **95 A5** 23 18S 51 10W
Lone Pine, *U.S.A.* **84 J8** 36 36N 118 4W
Lonely Mine, *Zimbabwe* **57 B4** 19 30S 28 49 E
Long B., *U.S.A.* **77 J6** 33 35N 78 45W
Long Beach, *Calif., U.S.A.* **85 M8** 33 47N 118 11W
Long Beach, *N.Y., U.S.A.* **79 F11** 40 35N 73 39W
Long Beach, *Wash., U.S.A.* **84 D2** 46 21N 124 3W
Long Branch, *U.S.A.* **79 F11** 40 18N 74 0W
Long Creek, *U.S.A.* **82 D4** 44 43N 119 6W
Long Eaton, *U.K.* **10 E6** 52 53N 1 15W
Long I., *Australia* **62 C4** 22 8S 149 53 E
Long I., *Bahamas* **89 B4** 23 20N 75 10W
Long I., *Canada* **70 B4** 54 50N 79 20W
Long I., *Ireland* **13 E2** 51 30N 9 34W
Long I., *U.S.A.* **79 F11** 40 45N 73 30W
Long Island Sd., *U.S.A.* **79 E12** 41 10N 73 0W
Long L., *Canada* **70 C2** 49 30N 86 50W
Long Lake, *U.S.A.* **79 C10** 43 58N 74 25W
Long Point B., *Canada* **78 D4** 42 40N 80 10W
Long Prairie →, *U.S.A.* **80 C7** 46 20N 94 36W
Long Pt., *Canada* **78 D4** 42 35N 80 2W
Long Range Mts., *Canada* **71 C8** 49 30N 57 30W
Long Reef, *Australia* **60 B4** 14 1S 125 48 E
Long Spruce, *Canada* **73 B10** 56 24N 94 21W
Long Str. = Longa, Proliv, *Russia* **4 C16** 70 0N 175 0 E
Long Thanh, *Vietnam* **39 G6** 10 47N 106 57 E
Long Xian, *China* **34 G4** 34 55N 106 55 E
Long Xuyen, *Vietnam* **39 G5** 10 19N 105 28 E
Longa, Proliv, *Russia* **4 C16** 70 0N 175 0 E
Longbenton, *U.K.* **10 B6** 55 1N 1 31W
Longboat Key, *U.S.A.* **77 M4** 27 23N 82 39W
Longde, *China* **34 G4** 35 30N 106 20 E
Longford, *Australia* **62 G4** 41 32S 147 3 E
Longford, *Ireland* **13 C4** 53 43N 7 49W
Longford □, *Ireland* **13 C4** 53 42N 7 45W
Longhua, *China* **35 D9** 41 18N 117 45 E
Longido, *Tanzania* **54 C4** 2 43S 36 42 E
Longiram, *Indonesia* **36 E5** 0 5S 115 45 E
Longkou, *China* **35 F11** 37 40N 120 18 E
Longlac, *Canada* **70 C2** 49 45N 86 25W
Longmeadow, *U.S.A.* **79 D12** 42 3N 72 34W
Longmont, *U.S.A.* **80 E2** 40 10N 105 6W
Longnawan, *Indonesia* **36 D4** 1 51N 114 55 E
Longreach, *Australia* **62 C3** 23 28S 144 14 E
Longueuil, *Canada* **79 A11** 45 32N 73 28W
Longview, *Tex., U.S.A.* **81 J7** 32 30N 94 44W
Longview, *Wash., U.S.A.* **84 D4** 46 8N 122 57W
Longxi, *China* **34 G3** 34 53N 104 40 E
Lonoke, *U.S.A.* **81 H9** 34 47N 91 54W
Lonquimay, *Chile* **96 D2** 38 26S 71 14W
Lons-le-Saunier, *France* **18 C6** 46 40N 5 31 E
Looe, *U.K.* **11 G3** 50 22N 4 28W
Lookout, C., *Canada* **70 A3** 55 18N 83 56W
Lookout, C., *U.S.A.* **77 H7** 34 35N 76 32W

Loolmalasin

Mallorytown

McCusker →, Canada 73 B7 55 32N 108 39W
McDame, Canada 72 B3 59 44N 128 59W
McDermitt, U.S.A. 82 F5 41 59N 117 43W
McDonald, U.S.A. 78 F4 40 22N 80 14W
Macdonald, L., Australia 60 D4 23 30S 129 0 E
McDonald Is., Ind. Oc. 3 G13 53 0S 73 0 E
MacDonnell Ranges, Australia 60 D5 23 40S 133 0 E
MacDowell L., Canada 70 B1 52 15N 92 45W
Macduff, U.K. 12 D6 57 40N 2 31W
Macedonia = Makedhonía □, Greece 21 D10 40 39N 22 0 E
Macedonia, U.S.A. 78 E3 41 19N 81 31W
Macedonia ■, Europe 21 D9 41 53N 21 40 E
Maceió, Brazil 93 E11 9 40S 35 41W
Macerata, Italy 20 C5 43 18N 13 27 E
McFarland, U.S.A. 85 K7 35 41N 119 14W
McFarlane →, Canada 73 B7 59 12N 107 58W
McGehee, U.S.A. 81 J9 33 38N 91 24W
McGill, U.S.A. 82 G6 39 23N 114 47W
Macgillycuddy's Reeks, Ireland 13 E2 51 58N 9 45W
McGraw, U.S.A. 79 D8 42 36N 76 8W
McGregor, U.S.A. 80 D9 43 1N 91 11W
McGregor Ra., Australia 63 D3 27 0S 142 45 E
Mach, Pakistan 40 E5 29 50N 67 20 E
Māch Kowr, Iran 45 E9 25 48N 61 28 E
Machado = Jiparaná →, Brazil 92 E6 8 3S 62 52W
Machagai, Argentina 94 B3 26 56S 60 2W
Machakos, Kenya 54 C4 1 30S 37 15 E
Machala, Ecuador 92 D3 3 20S 79 57W
Machanga, Mozam. 57 C6 20 59S 35 0 E
Machattie, L., Australia 62 C2 24 50S 139 48 E
Machava, Mozam. 57 D5 25 54S 32 28 E
Machece, Mozam. 55 F4 19 15S 35 32 E
Macheke, Zimbabwe 57 B5 18 5S 31 51 E
Machhu →, India 42 H4 23 6N 70 46 E
Machias, Maine, U.S.A. 77 C12 44 43N 67 28W
Machias, N.Y., U.S.A. 78 D6 42 25N 78 30W
Machichi →, Canada 73 B10 57 3N 92 6W
Machico, Madeira 22 D3 32 43N 16 44W
Machilipatnam, India 41 L12 16 12N 81 8 E
Machiques, Venezuela 92 A4 10 4N 72 34W
Machupicchu, Peru 92 F4 13 8S 72 30W
Machynlleth, U.K. 11 E4 52 35N 3 50W
Macia, Mozam. 57 D5 25 2S 33 8 E
McIlwraith Ra., Australia 62 A3 13 50S 143 20 E
McInnes L., Canada 73 C10 52 13N 93 45W
McIntosh, U.S.A. 80 C4 45 55N 101 21W
McIntosh L., Canada 73 B8 55 45N 105 0W
Macintosh Ra., Australia 61 E4 27 39S 125 32 E
Macintyre →, Australia 63 D5 28 37S 150 47 E
Mackay, Australia 62 C4 21 8S 149 11 E
Mackay, U.S.A. 82 E7 43 55N 113 37W
MacKay →, Canada 72 B6 57 10N 111 38W
Mackay, L., Australia 60 D4 22 30S 129 0 E
McKay Ra., Australia 60 D3 23 0S 122 30 E
McKeesport, U.S.A. 78 F5 40 21N 79 52W
McKellar, Canada 78 A5 45 30N 79 55W
McKenna, U.S.A. 84 D4 46 56N 122 33W
Mackenzie, Canada 72 B4 55 20N 123 5W
McKenzie, U.S.A. 77 G1 36 8N 88 31W
Mackenzie →, Australia 62 C4 23 38S 149 46 E
Mackenzie →, Canada 68 B6 69 10N 134 20W
McKenzie →, U.S.A. 82 D2 44 7N 123 6W
Mackenzie Bay, Canada 4 B1 69 0N 137 30W
Mackenzie City = Linden, Guyana 92 B7 6 0N 58 10W
Mackenzie Mts., Canada 68 B6 64 0N 130 0W
Mackinaw City, U.S.A. 76 C3 45 47N 84 44W
McKinlay, Australia 62 C3 21 16S 141 18 E
McKinlay →, Australia 62 C3 20 50S 141 28 E
McKinley, Mt., U.S.A. 68 B4 63 4N 151 0W
McKinley Sea, Arctic 4 A7 82 0N 0 0W
McKinney, U.S.A. 81 J6 33 12N 96 37W
Mackinnon Road, Kenya 54 C4 3 40S 39 1 E
McKittrick, U.S.A. 85 K7 35 18N 119 37W
Macklin, Canada 73 C7 52 20N 109 56W
McLaughlin, U.S.A. 80 C4 45 49N 100 49W
Maclean, Australia 63 D5 29 26S 153 16 E
McLean, U.S.A. 81 H4 35 14N 100 36W
McLeansboro, U.S.A. 80 F10 38 6N 88 32W
Maclear, S. Africa 57 E4 31 2S 28 23 E
McLennan, Canada 72 B5 55 42N 116 50W
McLeod →, Canada 72 C5 54 9N 115 44W
MacLeod, B., Canada 73 A7 62 53N 110 0W
McLeod, L., Australia 61 D1 24 9S 113 47 E
MacLeod Lake, Canada 72 C4 54 58N 123 0W
McLoughlin, Mt., U.S.A. 82 E2 42 27N 122 19W
McMechen, U.S.A. 78 G4 39 57N 80 44W
McMinnville, Oreg., U.S.A. 82 D2 45 13N 123 12W
McMinnville, Tenn., U.S.A. 77 H3 35 41N 85 46W
McMurdo Sd., Antarctica 5 D11 77 0S 170 0 E
McMurray = Fort McMurray, Canada 72 B6 56 44N 111 7W
McMurray, U.S.A. 84 B4 48 19N 122 14W
Macodoene, Mozam. 57 C6 23 32S 35 5 E
Macomb, U.S.A. 80 E9 40 27N 90 40W
Mâcon, France 18 C6 46 19N 4 50 E
Macon, Ga., U.S.A. 77 J4 32 51N 83 38W
Macon, Miss., U.S.A. 77 J1 33 7N 88 34W
Macon, Mo., U.S.A. 80 F8 39 44N 92 28W
Macossa, Mozam. 55 F3 17 55S 33 56 E
Macoun L., Canada 73 B8 56 32N 103 40W
Macovane, Mozam. 57 C6 21 30S 35 2 E
McPherson, U.S.A. 80 F6 38 22N 97 40W
McPherson Pk., U.S.A. 85 L7 34 53N 119 53W
McPherson Ra., Australia 63 D5 28 15S 153 15 E
Macquarie →, Australia 63 E4 30 5S 147 30 E
Macquarie Harbour, Australia 62 G4 42 15S 145 23 E
Macquarie Is., Pac. Oc. 64 N7 54 36S 158 55 E
MacRobertson Land, Antarctica 5 D6 71 0S 64 0 E
Macroom, Ireland 13 E3 51 54N 8 57W
MacTier, Canada 78 A5 45 9N 79 46W
Macubela, Mozam. 55 F4 16 53S 37 49 E
Macuiza, Mozam. 55 F3 18 7S 34 29 E
Macusani, Peru 92 F4 14 4S 70 29W
Macuse, Mozam. 55 F4 17 45S 37 10 E
Macuspana, Mexico 87 D6 17 46N 92 36W
Macusse, Angola 56 B3 17 48S 20 23 E
Madadeni, S. Africa 57 D5 27 43S 30 3 E
Madagascar ■, Africa 57 C8 20 0S 47 0 E
Madā'in Sālih, Si. Arabia 44 E3 26 46N 37 57 E
Madama, Niger 51 D8 22 0N 13 40 E
Madame I., Canada 71 C7 45 30N 60 58W
Madaripur, Bangla. 41 H17 23 19N 90 15 E
Madauk, Burma 41 L20 17 56N 96 52 E
Madawaska, Canada 78 A7 45 30N 78 0W
Madawaska →, Canada 78 A8 45 27N 76 21W
Madaya, Burma 41 H20 22 12N 96 10 E
Maddalena, Italy 20 D3 41 16N 9 23 E
Madeira, Atl. Oc. 22 D3 32 50N 17 0W
Madeira →, Brazil 92 D7 3 22S 58 45W
Madeleine, Îs. de la, Canada 71 C7 47 30N 61 40W
Madera, Mexico 86 B3 29 12N 108 7W
Madera, Calif., U.S.A. 84 J6 36 57N 120 3W
Madera, Pa., U.S.A. 78 F6 40 49N 78 26W
Madha, India 40 L9 18 0N 75 30 E
Madhavpur, India 42 J3 21 15N 69 58 E
Madhepura, India 43 F12 26 11N 86 23 E
Madhubani, India 43 F12 26 21N 86 7 E
Madhupur, India 43 G12 24 16N 86 39 E
Madhya Pradesh □, India 42 J8 22 50N 78 0 E
Madidi →, Bolivia 92 F5 12 32S 66 52W
Madikeri, India 40 N9 12 30N 75 45 E
Madill, U.S.A. 81 H6 34 6N 96 46W
Madimba, Dem. Rep. of the Congo 52 E3 4 58S 15 5 E
Ma'din, Syria 44 C3 35 45N 39 36 E
Madingou, Congo 52 E2 4 10S 13 33 E
Madirovalo, Madag. 57 B8 16 26S 46 32 E
Madison, Calif., U.S.A. 84 G5 38 41N 121 59W
Madison, Fla., U.S.A. 77 K4 30 28N 83 25W
Madison, Ind., U.S.A. 76 F3 38 44N 85 23W
Madison, Nebr., U.S.A. 80 E6 41 50N 97 27W
Madison, Ohio, U.S.A. 78 E3 41 46N 81 3W
Madison, S. Dak., U.S.A. 80 D6 44 0N 97 7W
Madison, Wis., U.S.A. 80 D10 43 4N 89 24W
Madison →, U.S.A. 82 D8 45 56N 111 31W
Madison Heights, U.S.A. 76 G6 37 25N 79 8W
Madisonville, Ky., U.S.A. 76 G2 37 20N 87 30W
Madisonville, Tex., U.S.A. 81 K7 30 57N 95 55W
Madista, Botswana 56 C4 21 15S 25 6 E
Madiun, Indonesia 36 F4 7 38S 111 32 E
Madoc, Canada 78 B7 44 30N 77 28W
Madona, Latvia 9 H22 56 53N 26 5 E
Madrakah, Ra's al, Oman 46 D6 19 0N 57 50 E
Madras = Chennai, India 40 N12 13 8N 80 19 E
Madras = Tamil Nadu □, India 40 P10 11 0N 77 0 E
Madras, U.S.A. 82 D3 44 38N 121 8W
Madre, Laguna, U.S.A. 81 M6 27 0N 97 30W
Madre, Sierra, Phil. 37 A6 17 0N 122 0 E
Madre de Dios →, Bolivia 92 F5 10 59S 66 8W
Madre de Dios, I., Chile 96 G1 50 20S 75 10W
Madre del Sur, Sierra, Mexico 87 D5 17 30N 100 0W
Madre Occidental, Sierra, Mexico 86 B3 27 0N 107 0W
Madre Oriental, Sierra, Mexico 86 C5 25 0N 100 0W
Madri, India 42 G5 24 16N 73 32 E
Madrid, Spain 19 B4 40 25N 3 45W
Madrid, U.S.A. 79 B9 44 45N 75 8W
Madura, Australia 61 F4 31 55S 127 0 E
Madura, Indonesia 37 G15 7 30S 114 0 E
Madura, Selat, Indonesia 37 G15 7 30S 113 20 E
Madurai, India 40 Q11 9 55N 78 10 E
Madurantakam, India 40 N11 12 30N 79 50 E
Mae Chan, Thailand 38 B2 20 9N 99 52 E
Mae Hong Son, Thailand 38 C2 19 16N 97 56 E
Mae Khlong →, Thailand 38 F3 13 24N 100 0 E
Mae Phrik, Thailand 38 D2 17 27N 99 7 E
Mae Ramat, Thailand 38 D2 16 58N 98 31 E
Mae Rim, Thailand 38 C2 18 54N 98 57 E
Mae Sot, Thailand 38 D2 16 43N 98 34 E
Mae Suai, Thailand 38 C2 19 39N 99 33 E
Mae Tha, Thailand 38 C2 18 28N 99 8 E
Maebashi, Japan 31 F9 36 24N 139 4 E
Maesteg, U.K. 11 F4 51 36N 3 40W
Maestra, Sierra, Cuba 88 B4 20 15N 77 0W
Maevatanana, Madag. 57 B8 16 56S 46 49 E
Mafeking = Mafikeng, S. Africa 56 D4 25 50S 25 38 E
Mafeking, Canada 73 C8 52 40N 101 10W
Mafeteng, Lesotho 56 D4 29 51S 27 15 E
Mafia I., Tanzania 54 D4 7 45S 39 50 E
Mafikeng, S. Africa 56 D4 25 50S 25 38 E
Mafra, Brazil 95 B6 26 10S 49 55W
Mafra, Portugal 19 C1 38 55N 9 20W
Mafungabusi Plateau, Zimbabwe 55 F2 18 30S 29 8 E
Magadan, Russia 27 D16 59 38N 150 50 E
Magadi, Kenya 54 C4 1 54S 36 19 E
Magadi, L., Kenya 54 C4 1 54S 36 19 E
Magaliesburg, S. Africa 57 D4 26 0S 27 32 E
Magallanes, Estrecho de, Chile 96 G2 52 30S 75 0W
Magangué, Colombia 92 B4 9 14N 74 45W
Magdalen Is. = Madeleine, Îs. de la, Canada 71 C7 47 30N 61 40W
Magdalena, Argentina 94 D4 35 5S 57 30W
Magdalena, Bolivia 92 F6 13 13S 63 57W
Magdalena, Mexico 86 A2 30 50N 112 0W
Magdalena, U.S.A. 83 J10 34 7N 107 15W
Magdalena →, Colombia 92 A4 11 6N 74 51W
Magdalena →, Mexico 86 A2 30 40N 112 25W
Magdalena, B., Mexico 86 C2 24 30N 112 10W
Magdalena, Llano de la, Mexico 86 C2 25 0N 111 30W
Magdeburg, Germany 16 B6 52 7N 11 38 E
Magdelaine Cays, Australia 62 B5 16 33S 150 18 E
Magee, U.S.A. 81 K10 31 52N 89 44W
Magelang, Indonesia 36 F4 7 29S 110 13 E
Magellan's Str. = Magallanes, Estrecho de, Chile 96 G2 52 30S 75 0W
Magenta, L., Australia 61 F2 33 30S 119 2 E
Magerøya, Norway 8 A21 71 3N 25 40 E
Maggiore, Lago, Italy 18 D8 45 57N 8 39 E
Maghâgha, Egypt 51 C12 28 38N 30 50 E
Magherafelt, U.K. 13 B5 54 45N 6 37W
Maghreb, N. Afr. 50 B5 32 0N 4 0W
Magistralnyy, Russia 27 D11 56 16N 107 36 E
Magnetic Pole (North) = North Magnetic Pole, Canada 4 B2 77 58N 102 8W
Magnetic Pole (South) = South Magnetic Pole, Antarctica 5 C9 64 8S 138 8 E
Magnitogorsk, Russia 24 D10 53 27N 59 4 E
Magnolia, Ark., U.S.A. 81 J8 33 16N 93 14W
Magnolia, Miss., U.S.A. 81 K9 31 9N 90 28W
Magog, Canada 79 A12 45 18N 72 9W
Magoro, Uganda 54 B3 1 45N 34 12 E
Magosa = Famagusta, Cyprus 23 D12 35 8N 33 55 E
Magouládhes, Greece 23 A3 39 45N 19 42 E
Magoye, Zambia 55 F2 16 1S 27 30 E
Magozal, Mexico 87 C5 21 34N 97 59W
Magpie, L., Canada 71 B7 51 0N 64 41W
Magrath, Canada 72 D6 49 25N 112 50W
Maguarinho, C., Brazil 93 D9 0 15S 48 30W
Magude, Mozam. 57 D5 25 2S 32 40 E
Mağusa = Famagusta, Cyprus 23 D12 35 8N 33 55 E
Maguse L., Canada 73 A9 61 40N 95 10W
Maguse Pt., Canada 73 A10 61 20N 93 50W
Magvana, India 42 H3 23 13N 69 22 E
Magwe, Burma 41 J19 20 10N 95 0 E
Maha Sarakham, Thailand 38 D4 16 12N 103 16 E
Mahābād, Iran 44 B5 36 50N 45 45 E
Mahabharat Lekh, Nepal 43 E10 28 30N 82 0 E
Mahabo, Madag. 57 C7 20 23S 44 40 E
Mahadeo Hills, India 43 H8 22 20N 78 30 E
Mahaffey, U.S.A. 78 F6 40 53N 78 44W
Mahagi, Dem. Rep. of the Congo 54 B3 2 20N 31 0 E
Mahajamba →, Madag. 57 B8 15 33S 47 8 E
Mahajamba, Helodranon' i, Madag. 57 B8 15 24S 47 5 E
Mahajan, India 42 E5 28 48N 73 56 E
Mahajanga, Madag. 57 B8 15 40S 46 25 E
Mahajanga □, Madag. 57 B8 17 0S 47 0 E
Mahajilo →, Madag. 57 B8 19 42S 45 22 E
Mahakam →, Indonesia 36 E5 0 35S 117 17 E
Mahalapye, Botswana 56 C4 23 1S 26 51 E
Maḩallāt, Iran 45 C6 33 55N 50 30 E
Māhān, Iran 45 D8 30 5N 57 18 E
Mahan →, India 43 H10 23 30N 82 50 E
Mahanadi →, India 41 J15 20 20N 86 25 E
Mahananda →, India 43 G12 25 12N 87 52 E
Mahanoro, Madag. 57 B8 19 54S 48 48 E
Mahanoy City, U.S.A. 79 F8 40 49N 76 9W
Maharashtra □, India 40 J9 20 30N 75 30 E
Mahari Mts., Tanzania 54 D3 6 20S 30 0 E
Mahasham, W. →, Egypt 47 E3 30 15N 34 10 E
Mahasoa, Madag. 57 C8 22 12S 46 6 E
Mahasolo, Madag. 57 B8 19 7S 46 22 E
Mahattat ash Shīdīyah, Jordan 47 F4 29 55N 35 55 E
Mahattat 'Unayzah, Jordan 47 E4 30 30N 35 47 E
Mahavavy →, Madag. 57 B8 15 57S 45 54 E
Mahaxay, Laos 38 D5 17 22N 105 12 E
Mahbubnagar, India 40 L10 16 45N 77 59 E
Maḩḑah, Oman 45 E7 24 24N 55 59 E
Mahdia, Tunisia 51 A8 35 28N 11 0 E
Mahe, India 43 C8 33 10N 78 32 E
Mahendragarh, India 42 E7 28 17N 76 14 E
Mahenge, Tanzania 55 D4 8 45S 36 41 E
Maheno, N.Z. 59 L3 45 10S 170 50 E
Mahesana, India 42 H5 23 39N 72 26 E
Maheshwar, India 42 H6 22 11N 75 35 E
Mahgawan, India 43 F8 26 29N 78 37 E
Mahi →, India 42 H5 22 15N 72 55 E
Mahia Pen., N.Z. 59 H6 39 9S 177 55 E
Mahilyow, Belarus 17 B16 53 55N 30 18 E
Mahmud Kot, Pakistan 42 D4 30 16N 71 0 E
Mahnomen, U.S.A. 80 B7 47 19N 95 58W
Mahoba, India 43 G8 25 15N 79 55 E
Mahón = Maó, Spain 22 B11 39 53N 4 16 E
Mahone Bay, Canada 71 D7 44 30N 64 20W
Mahopac, U.S.A. 79 E11 41 22N 73 45W
Mahuva, India 42 J4 21 5N 71 48 E
Mai-Ndombe, L., Dem. Rep. of the Congo 52 E3 2 0S 18 20 E
Mai-Sai, Thailand 38 B2 20 20N 99 55 E
Maicurú →, Brazil 93 D8 2 14S 54 17W
Maidan Khula, Afghan. 42 C3 33 36N 69 50 E
Maidenhead, U.K. 11 F7 51 31N 0 42W
Maidstone, Canada 73 C7 53 5N 109 20W
Maidstone, U.K. 11 F8 51 16N 0 32 E
Maiduguri, Nigeria 51 F8 12 0N 13 20 E
Maihar, India 43 G9 24 16N 80 45 E
Maijdi, Bangla. 41 H17 22 48N 91 10 E
Maikala Ra., India 41 J12 22 0N 81 0 E
Mailani, India 43 E9 28 17N 80 21 E
Mailsi, Pakistan 42 E5 29 48N 72 15 E
Main →, Germany 16 C5 50 0N 8 18 E
Main →, U.K. 13 B5 54 48N 6 18W
Maine, France 18 C3 48 20N 0 15W
Maine □, U.S.A. 77 C11 45 20N 69 0W
Maine →, Ireland 13 D2 52 9N 9 45W
Maingkwan, Burma 41 F20 26 15N 96 37 E
Mainit, L., Phil. 37 C7 9 31N 125 30 E
Mainland, Orkney, U.K. 12 C5 58 59N 3 8W
Mainland, Shet., U.K. 12 A7 60 15N 1 22W
Mainoru, Australia 62 A1 14 0S 134 6 E
Mainpuri, India 43 F8 27 18N 79 4 E
Maintirano, Madag. 57 B7 18 3S 44 1 E
Mainz, Germany 16 C5 50 1N 8 14 E
Maipú, Argentina 94 D4 36 52S 57 50W
Maiquetía, Venezuela 92 A5 10 36N 66 57W
Mairabari, India 41 F18 26 30N 92 22 E
Maisí, Cuba 89 B5 20 17N 74 9W
Maisí, Pta. de, Cuba 89 B5 20 10N 74 10W
Maitland, N.S.W., Australia 63 E5 32 33S 151 36 E
Maitland, S. Austral., Australia 63 E2 34 23S 137 40 E
Maitland →, Canada 78 C3 43 45N 81 43W
Maiz, Is. del, Nic. 88 D3 12 15N 83 4W
Maizuru, Japan 31 G7 35 25N 135 22 E
Majalengka, Indonesia 37 G13 6 50S 108 13 E
Majene, Indonesia 37 E5 3 38S 118 57 E
Majorca = Mallorca, Spain 22 B10 39 30N 3 0 E
Makaha, Zimbabwe 57 B5 17 20S 32 39 E
Makalamabedi, Botswana 56 C3 20 19S 23 51 E
Makale, Indonesia 37 E5 3 6S 119 51 E
Makamba, Burundi 54 C2 4 8S 29 49 E
Makarikari = Makgadikgadi Salt Pans, Botswana 56 C4 20 40S 25 45 E
Makarovo, Russia 27 D11 57 40N 107 45 E
Makasar = Ujung Pandang, Indonesia 37 F5 5 10S 119 20 E
Makasar, Selat, Indonesia 37 E5 1 0S 118 20 E
Makasar, Str. of = Makasar, Selat, Indonesia 37 E5 1 0S 118 20 E
Makat, Kazakstan 25 E9 47 39N 53 19 E
Makedhonía □, Greece 21 D10 40 39N 22 0 E
Makedonija = Macedonia ■, Europe 21 D9 41 53N 21 40 E
Makeyevka = Makiyivka, Ukraine 25 E6 48 0N 38 0 E
Makgadikgadi Salt Pans, Botswana 56 C4 20 40S 25 45 E
Makhachkala, Russia 25 F8 43 0N 47 30 E
Makhmūr, Iraq 44 C4 35 46N 43 35 E
Makian, Indonesia 37 D7 0 20N 127 20 E
Makindu, Kenya 54 C4 2 18S 37 50 E
Makinsk, Kazakstan 26 D8 52 37N 70 26 E
Makiyivka, Ukraine 25 E6 48 0N 38 0 E
Makkah, Si. Arabia 46 C2 21 30N 39 54 E
Makkovik, Canada 71 A8 55 10N 59 10W
Makó, Hungary 17 E11 46 14N 20 33 E
Makokou, Gabon 52 D2 0 40N 12 50 E
Makongo, Dem. Rep. of the Congo 54 B2 3 25N 26 17 E
Makoro, Dem. Rep. of the Congo 54 B2 3 10N 29 59 E
Makrai, India 40 H10 22 2N 77 0 E
Makran Coast Range, Pakistan 40 G4 25 40N 64 0 E
Makrana, India 42 F6 27 2N 74 46 E
Mákriyialos, Greece 23 D7 35 2N 25 59 E
Mākū, Iran 44 B5 39 15N 44 31 E
Makunda, Botswana 56 C3 22 30S 20 7 E
Makurazaki, Japan 31 J5 31 15N 130 20 E
Makurdi, Nigeria 50 G7 7 43N 8 35 E
Makūyeh, Iran 45 D7 28 7N 53 9 E
Makwassie, S. Africa 56 D4 27 17S 26 0 E
Makwiro, Zimbabwe 57 B5 17 58S 30 25 E
Mal B., Ireland 13 D2 52 50N 9 30W
Mala, Pta., Panama 88 E3 7 28N 80 2W
Malabar Coast, India 40 P9 11 0N 75 0 E
Malabo = Rey Malabo, Eq. Guin. 52 D1 3 45N 8 50 E
Malacca, Str. of, Indonesia 39 L3 3 0N 101 0 E
Malad City, U.S.A. 82 E7 42 12N 112 15W
Maladzyechna, Belarus 17 A14 54 20N 26 50 E
Málaga, Spain 19 D3 36 43N 4 23W
Malagarasi, Tanzania 54 D3 5 5S 30 50 E
Malagarasi →, Tanzania 54 D2 5 12S 29 47 E
Malagasy Rep. = Madagascar ■, Africa 57 C8 20 0S 47 0 E
Malahide, Ireland 13 C5 53 26N 6 9W
Malaimbandy, Madag. 57 C8 20 20S 45 36 E
Malakâl, Sudan 51 G12 9 33N 31 40 E
Malakand, Pakistan 42 B4 34 40N 71 55 E
Malakwal, Pakistan 42 C5 32 34N 73 13 E
Malamala, Indonesia 37 E6 3 21S 120 55 E
Malanda, Australia 62 B4 17 22S 145 35 E
Malang, Indonesia 36 F4 7 59S 112 45 E
Malangen, Norway 8 B18 69 24N 18 37 E
Malanje, Angola 52 F3 9 36S 16 17 E
Mälaren, Sweden 9 G17 59 30N 17 10 E
Malargüe, Argentina 94 D2 35 32S 69 30W
Malartic, Canada 70 C4 48 9N 78 9W
Malaryta, Belarus 17 C13 51 50N 24 3 E
Malatya, Turkey 25 G6 38 25N 38 20 E
Malawi ■, Africa 55 E3 11 55S 34 0 E
Malawi, L. = Nyasa, L., Africa 55 E3 12 30S 34 30 E
Malay Pen., Asia 39 J3 7 25N 100 0 E
Malaya Vishera, Russia 24 C5 58 55N 32 25 E
Malaybalay, Phil. 37 C7 8 5N 125 7 E
Malāyer, Iran 45 C6 34 19N 48 51 E
Malaysia ■, Asia 39 K4 5 0N 110 0 E
Malazgirt, Turkey 25 G7 39 10N 42 33 E
Malbon, Australia 62 C3 21 5S 140 17 E
Malbooma, Australia 63 E1 30 41S 134 11 E
Malbork, Poland 17 B10 54 3N 19 1 E
Malcolm, Australia 61 E3 28 51S 121 25 E
Malcolm, Pt., Australia 61 F3 33 48S 123 45 E
Maldah, India 43 G13 25 2N 88 9 E
Maldegem, Belgium 15 C3 51 14N 3 26 E
Malden, Mass., U.S.A. 79 D13 42 26N 71 4W
Malden, Mo., U.S.A. 81 G10 36 34N 89 57W
Malden I., Kiribati 65 H12 4 3S 155 1W
Maldives ■, Ind. Oc. 29 J11 5 0N 73 0 E
Maldonado, Uruguay 95 C5 34 59S 55 0W
Maldonado, Punta, Mexico 87 D5 16 19N 98 35W
Malé, Maldives 29 J11 4 0N 73 28 E
Malé Karpaty, Slovak Rep. 17 D9 48 30N 17 20 E
Maléa, Ákra, Greece 21 F10 36 28N 23 7 E
Malegaon, India 40 J9 20 30N 74 38 E
Malei, Mozam. 55 F4 17 12S 36 58 E
Malek Kandī, Iran 44 B5 37 9N 46 6 E
Malela, Dem. Rep. of the Congo 54 C2 4 22S 26 8 E
Malema, Mozam. 55 E4 14 57S 37 20 E
Máleme, Greece 23 D5 35 31N 23 49 E
Maleny, Australia 63 D5 26 45S 152 52 E
Malerkotla, India 42 D6 30 32N 75 58 E
Máles, Greece 23 D7 35 6N 25 35 E
Malgomaj, Sweden 8 D17 64 40N 16 30 E
Malha, Sudan 51 E11 15 8N 25 10 E
Malhargarh, India 42 G6 24 17N 74 59 E
Malheur →, U.S.A. 82 D5 44 4N 116 59W
Malheur L., U.S.A. 82 E4 43 20N 118 48W
Mali ■, Africa 50 E5 17 0N 3 0W
Mali →, Burma 41 G20 25 40N 97 40 E
Mali Kyun, Burma 38 F2 13 0N 98 20 E
Malibu, U.S.A. 85 L8 34 2N 118 41W
Maliku, Indonesia 37 E6 0 39S 123 16 E
Malili, Indonesia 37 E6 2 42S 121 6 E
Malimba, Mts., Dem. Rep. of the Congo 54 D2 7 30S 29 30 E
Malin Hd., Ireland 13 A4 55 23N 7 23W
Malin Pen., Ireland 13 A4 55 20N 7 17W
Malindi, Kenya 54 C5 3 12S 40 5 E
Malines = Mechelen, Belgium 15 C4 51 2N 4 29 E
Malino, Indonesia 37 D6 1 0N 121 0 E
Malinyi, Tanzania 55 D4 8 56S 36 0 E
Malita, Phil. 37 C7 6 19N 125 39 E
Maliwun, Burma 36 B1 10 17N 98 40 E
Maliya, India 42 H4 23 5N 70 46 E
Malkara, Turkey 21 D12 40 53N 26 53 E
Mallaig, U.K. 12 D3 57 0N 5 50W
Mallawan, India 43 F9 27 4N 80 12 E
Mallawi, Egypt 51 C12 27 44N 30 44 E
Mállia, Greece 23 D7 35 17N 25 32 E
Mallión, Kólpos, Greece 23 D7 35 19N 25 27 E
Mallorca, Spain 22 B10 39 30N 3 0 E
Mallorytown, Canada 79 B9 44 29N 75 53W

Mallow

Mallow, Ireland 13 D3 52 8N 8 39W
Malmberget, Sweden 8 C19 67 11N 20 40 E
Malmédy, Belgium 15 D6 50 25N 6 2 E
Malmesbury, S. Africa 56 E2 33 28S 18 41 E
Malmö, Sweden 9 J15 55 36N 12 59 E
Malolos, Phil. 37 B6 14 50N 120 49 E
Malombe L., Malawi 55 E4 14 40S 35 15 E
Malone, U.S.A. 79 B10 44 51N 74 18W
Måløy, Norway 9 F11 61 57N 5 6 E
Malpaso, Canary Is. 22 G1 27 43N 18 3W
Malpelo, I. de, Colombia 92 C2 4 3N 81 35W
Malpur, India 42 H5 23 21N 73 27 E
Malpura, India 42 F6 26 17N 75 23 E
Malta, Idaho, U.S.A. 82 E7 42 18N 113 22W
Malta, Mont., U.S.A. 82 B10 48 21N 107 52W
Malta ■, Europe 23 D2 35 50N 14 30 E
Maltahöhe, Namibia 56 C2 24 55S 17 0 E
Malton, Canada 78 C5 43 42N 79 38W
Malton, U.K. 10 C7 54 8N 0 49W
Maluku, Indonesia 37 E7 1 0S 127 0 E
Maluku □, Indonesia 37 E7 3 0S 128 0 E
Maluku Sea = Molucca Sea, Indonesia 37 E6 0 0 125 0 E
Malvan, India 40 L8 16 2N 73 30 E
Malvern, U.S.A. 81 H8 34 22N 92 49W
Malvern Hills, U.K. 11 E5 52 0N 2 19W
Malvinas, Is. = Falkland Is. □, Atl. Oc. 96 G5 51 30S 59 0W
Malya, Tanzania 54 C3 3 5S 33 38 E
Malyn, Ukraine 17 C15 50 46N 29 3 E
Malyy Lyakhovskiy, Ostrov, Russia 27 B15 74 7N 140 36 E
Mama, Russia 27 D12 58 18N 112 54 E
Mamanguape, Brazil 93 E11 6 50S 35 4W
Mamarr Mitlā, Egypt 47 E1 30 2N 32 54 E
Mamasa, Indonesia 37 E5 2 55S 119 20 E
Mambasa, Dem. Rep. of the Congo 54 B2 1 22N 29 3 E
Mamberamo →, Indonesia 37 E9 2 0S 137 50 E
Mambilima Falls, Zambia 55 E2 10 31S 28 45 E
Mambirima, Dem. Rep. of the Congo 55 E2 11 25S 27 33 E
Mambo, Tanzania 54 C4 4 52S 38 22 E
Mambrui, Kenya 54 C5 3 5S 40 5 E
Mamburao, Phil. 37 B6 13 13N 120 39 E
Mameigwess L., Canada 70 B2 52 35N 87 50W
Mammoth, U.S.A. 83 K8 32 43N 110 39W
Mammoth Cave National Park, U.S.A. 76 G3 37 8N 86 13W
Mamoré →, Bolivia 92 F5 10 23S 65 53W
Mamou, Guinea 50 F3 10 15N 12 0W
Mampikony, Madag. 57 B8 16 6S 47 38 E
Mamuju, Indonesia 37 E5 2 41S 118 50 E
Mamuno, Botswana 56 C3 22 16S 20 1 E
Man, Ivory C. 50 G4 7 30N 7 40W
Man, I. of, U.K. 10 C3 54 15N 4 30W
Man-Bazar, India 43 H12 23 4N 86 39 E
Man Na, Burma 41 H20 23 27N 97 19 E
Mana →, Fr. Guiana 93 B8 5 45N 53 55W
Manaar, G. of = Mannar, G. of, Asia 40 Q11 8 30N 79 0 E
Manacapuru, Brazil 92 D6 3 16S 60 37W
Manacor, Spain 22 B10 39 34N 3 13 E
Manado, Indonesia 37 D6 1 29N 124 51 E
Managua, Nic. 88 D2 12 6N 86 20W
Managua, L. de, Nic. 88 D2 12 20N 86 30W
Manakara, Madag. 57 C8 22 8S 48 1 E
Manali, India 42 C7 32 16N 77 10 E
Manama = Al Manāmah, Bahrain 46 B5 26 10N 50 30 E
Manambao →, Madag. 57 B7 17 35S 44 0 E
Manambato, Madag. 57 A8 13 43S 49 7 E
Manambolo →, Madag. 57 B7 19 18S 44 22 E
Manambolosy, Madag. 57 B8 16 2S 49 40 E
Mananara, Madag. 57 B8 16 10S 49 46 E
Mananara →, Madag. 57 C8 23 21S 47 42 E
Mananjary, Madag. 57 C8 21 13S 48 20 E
Manantenina, Madag. 57 C8 24 17S 47 19 E
Manaos = Manaus, Brazil 92 D7 3 0S 60 0W
Manapire →, Venezuela 92 B5 7 42N 66 7W
Manapouri, N.Z. 59 L1 45 34S 167 39 E
Manapouri, L., N.Z. 59 L1 45 32S 167 32 E
Manār, Jabal, Yemen 46 E3 14 2N 44 17 E
Manaravolo, Madag. 57 C8 23 59S 45 39 E
Manas, China 32 B3 44 17N 85 56 E
Manas →, India 41 F17 26 12N 90 40 E
Manaslu, Nepal 43 E11 28 33N 84 33 E
Manasquan, U.S.A. 79 F10 40 8N 74 3W
Manassa, U.S.A. 83 H11 37 11N 105 56W
Manaung, Burma 41 K18 18 45N 93 40 E
Manaus, Brazil 92 D7 3 0S 60 0W
Manawan L., Canada 73 B8 55 24N 103 14W
Manbij, Syria 44 B3 36 31N 37 57 E
Manchegorsk, Russia 26 C4 67 54N 32 58 E
Manchester, U.K. 10 D5 53 29N 2 12W
Manchester, Calif., U.S.A. 84 G3 38 58N 123 41W
Manchester, Conn., U.S.A. 79 E12 41 47N 72 31W
Manchester, Ga., U.S.A. 77 J3 32 51N 84 37W
Manchester, Iowa, U.S.A. 80 D9 42 29N 91 27W
Manchester, Ky., U.S.A. 76 G4 37 9N 83 46W
Manchester, N.H., U.S.A. 79 D13 42 59N 71 28W
Manchester, N.Y., U.S.A. 78 D7 42 56N 77 16W
Manchester, Pa., U.S.A. 79 F8 40 4N 76 43W
Manchester, Tenn., U.S.A. 77 H2 35 29N 86 5W
Manchester, Vt., U.S.A. 79 C11 43 10N 73 5W
Manchester L., Canada 73 A7 61 28N 107 29W
Manchhar L., Pakistan 42 F2 26 25N 67 39 E
Manchuria = Dongbei, China 35 D13 45 0N 125 0 E
Manchurian Plain, China 28 E16 47 0N 124 0 E
Mand →, India 43 J10 21 42N 83 15 E
Mand →, Iran 45 D7 28 20N 52 30 E
Manda, Ludewe, Tanzania 55 E3 10 30S 34 40 E
Manda, Mbeya, Tanzania 54 D3 7 58S 32 29 E
Manda, Mbeya, Tanzania 55 D3 8 30S 32 49 E
Mandabé, Madag. 57 C7 21 0S 44 55 E
Mandaguari, Brazil 95 A5 23 32S 51 42W
Mandah = Töhöm, Mongolia 34 B5 44 27N 108 2 E
Mandal, Norway 9 G12 58 2N 7 25 E
Mandala, Puncak, Indonesia 37 E10 4 44S 140 20 E
Mandalay, Burma 41 J20 22 0N 96 4 E
Mandale = Mandalay, Burma 41 J20 22 0N 96 4 E
Mandalgarh, India 42 G6 25 12N 75 6 E
Mandalgovi, Mongolia 34 B4 45 45N 106 10 E
Mandalī, Iraq 44 C5 33 43N 45 28 E
Mandan, U.S.A. 80 B4 46 50N 100 54W
Mandar, Teluk, Indonesia 37 E5 3 35S 119 15 E
Mandaue, Phil. 37 B6 10 20N 123 56 E
Mandera, Kenya 54 B5 3 55N 41 53 E
Mandi, India 42 D7 31 39N 76 58 E
Mandi Dabwali, India 42 E6 29 58N 74 42 E
Mandimba, Mozam. 55 E4 14 20S 35 40 E
Mandioli, Indonesia 37 E7 0 40S 127 20 E
Mandla, India 43 H9 22 39N 80 30 E
Mandorah, Australia 60 B5 12 32S 130 42 E
Mandoto, Madag. 57 B8 19 34S 46 17 E
Mandra, Pakistan 42 C5 33 23N 73 12 E
Mandrare →, Madag. 57 D8 25 10S 46 30 E
Mandritsara, Madag. 57 B8 15 50S 48 49 E
Mandronarivo, Madag. 57 C8 21 7S 45 38 E
Mandsaur, India 42 G6 24 3N 75 8 E
Mandurah, Australia 61 F2 32 36S 115 48 E
Mandvi, India 42 H3 22 51N 69 22 E
Mandya, India 40 N10 12 30N 77 0 E
Mandzai, Pakistan 42 D2 30 55N 67 6 E
Maneh, Iran 45 B8 37 39N 57 7 E
Manera, Madag. 57 C7 22 55S 44 20 E
Maneroo Cr. →, Australia 62 C3 23 21S 143 53 E
Manfalût, Egypt 51 C12 27 20N 30 52 E
Manfredónia, Italy 20 D6 41 38N 15 55 E
Mangabeiras, Chapada das, Brazil 93 F9 10 0S 46 30W
Mangalia, Romania 17 G15 43 50N 28 35 E
Mangalore, India 40 N9 12 55N 74 47 E
Mangan, India 43 F13 27 31N 88 32 E
Mangaung, S. Africa 53 K5 29 10S 26 25 E
Mangawan, India 43 G9 24 41N 81 33 E
Mangaweka, N.Z. 59 H5 39 48S 175 47 E
Manggar, Indonesia 36 E3 2 50S 108 10 E
Manggawitu, Indonesia 37 E8 4 8S 133 32 E
Mangindrano, Madag. 57 A8 14 17S 48 58 E
Mangkalihat, Tanjung, Indonesia 37 D5 1 2N 118 59 E
Mangla, Pakistan 42 C5 33 7N 73 39 E
Mangla Dam, Pakistan 43 C5 33 9N 73 44 E
Manglaur, India 42 E7 29 44N 77 49 E
Mangnai, China 32 C4 37 52N 91 43 E
Mango, Togo 50 F6 10 20N 0 30 E
Mangoche, Malawi 55 E4 14 25S 35 16 E
Mangoky →, Madag. 57 C7 21 29S 43 41 E
Mangole, Indonesia 37 E6 1 50S 125 55 E
Mangombe, Dem. Rep. of the Congo 54 C2 1 20S 26 48 E
Mangonui, N.Z. 59 F4 35 1S 173 32 E
Mangoro →, Madag. 57 B8 20 0S 48 45 E
Mangrol, Mad. P., India 42 J4 21 7N 70 7 E
Mangrol, Raj., India 42 G6 25 20N 76 31 E
Mangueira, L. da, Brazil 95 C5 33 0S 52 50W
Mangum, U.S.A. 81 H5 34 53N 99 30W
Mangyshlak Poluostrov, Kazakstan 26 E6 44 30N 52 30 E
Manhattan, U.S.A. 80 F6 39 11N 96 35W
Manhiça, Mozam. 57 D5 25 23S 32 49 E
Mania →, Madag. 57 B8 19 42S 45 22 E
Manica, Mozam. 57 B5 18 58S 32 59 E
Manica □, Mozam. 57 B5 19 10S 33 45 E
Manicaland □, Zimbabwe 55 F3 19 0S 32 30 E
Manicoré, Brazil 92 E6 5 48S 61 16W
Manicouagan →, Canada 71 C6 49 30N 68 30W
Manicouagan, Rés., Canada 71 B6 51 5N 68 40W
Maniema □, Dem. Rep. of the Congo 54 C2 3 0S 26 0 E
Manīfah, Si. Arabia 45 E6 27 44N 49 0 E
Manifold, C., Australia 62 C5 22 41S 150 50 E
Manigotagan, Canada 73 C9 51 6N 96 18W
Manigotagan →, Canada 73 C9 51 7N 96 20W
Manihari, India 43 G12 25 21N 87 38 E
Manihiki, Cook Is. 65 J11 10 24S 161 1W
Manika, Plateau de la, Dem. Rep. of the Congo 55 E2 10 0S 25 5 E
Manikpur, India 43 G9 25 4N 81 7 E
Manila, Phil. 37 B6 14 40N 121 3 E
Manila, U.S.A. 82 F9 40 59N 109 43W
Manila B., Phil. 37 B6 14 40N 120 35 E
Maningrida, Australia 62 A1 12 3S 134 13 E
Manipur □, India 41 G19 25 0N 94 0 E
Manipur →, Burma 41 H19 23 45N 94 20 E
Manisa, Turkey 21 E12 38 38N 27 30 E
Manistee, U.S.A. 76 C2 44 15N 86 19W
Manistee →, U.S.A. 76 C2 44 15N 86 21W
Manistique, U.S.A. 76 C2 45 57N 86 15W
Manito L., Canada 73 C7 52 43N 109 43W
Manitoba □, Canada 73 B9 55 30N 97 0W
Manitoba, L., Canada 73 C9 51 0N 98 45W
Manitou, Canada 73 D9 49 15N 98 32W
Manitou, L., Canada 71 B6 50 55N 65 17W
Manitou Is., U.S.A. 76 C3 45 8N 86 0W
Manitou Springs, U.S.A. 80 F2 38 52N 104 55W
Manitoulin I., Canada 70 C3 45 40N 82 30W
Manitouwadge, Canada 70 C2 49 8N 85 48W
Manitowoc, U.S.A. 76 C2 44 5N 87 40W
Manizales, Colombia 92 B3 5 5N 75 32W
Manja, Madag. 57 C7 21 26S 44 20 E
Manjacaze, Mozam. 57 C5 24 45S 34 0 E
Manjakandriana, Madag. 57 B8 18 55S 47 47 E
Manjhand, Pakistan 42 G3 25 50N 68 10 E
Manjil, Iran 45 B6 36 46N 49 30 E
Manjimup, Australia 61 F2 34 15S 116 6 E
Manjra →, India 40 K10 18 49N 77 52 E
Mankato, Kans., U.S.A. 80 F5 39 47N 98 13W
Mankato, Minn., U.S.A. 80 C8 44 10N 94 0W
Mankayane, Swaziland 57 D5 26 40S 31 4 E
Mankera, Pakistan 42 D4 31 23N 71 26 E
Mankota, Canada 73 D7 49 25N 107 5W
Manlay = Üydzin, Mongolia 34 B4 44 9N 107 0 E
Manmad, India 40 J9 20 18N 74 28 E
Mann Ranges, Australia 61 E5 26 6S 130 5 E
Manna, Indonesia 36 E2 4 25S 102 55 E
Mannar, Sri Lanka 40 Q11 9 1N 79 54 E
Mannar, G. of, Asia 40 Q11 8 30N 79 0 E
Mannar I., Sri Lanka 40 Q11 9 5N 79 45 E
Mannheim, Germany 16 D5 49 29N 8 29 E
Manning, Canada 72 B5 56 53N 117 39W
Manning, Oreg., U.S.A. 84 E3 45 45N 123 13W
Manning, S.C., U.S.A. 77 J5 33 42N 80 13W
Manning Prov. Park, Canada 72 D4 49 5N 120 45W
Manoharpur, India 43 H11 22 23N 85 12 E
Manokwari, Indonesia 37 E8 0 54S 134 0 E
Manombo, Madag. 57 C7 22 57S 43 28 E
Manono, Dem. Rep. of the Congo 54 D2 7 15S 27 25 E
Manosque, France 18 E6 43 49N 5 47 E
Manotick, Canada 79 A9 45 13N 75 41W
Manouane →, Canada 71 C5 49 30N 71 10W
Manouane, L., Canada 71 B5 50 45N 70 45W
Manp'o, N. Korea 35 D14 41 6N 126 24 E
Manpojin = Manp'o, N. Korea 35 D14 41 6N 126 24 E
Manpur, Mad. P., India 42 H6 22 26N 75 37 E
Manpur, Mad. P., India 43 H10 23 17N 83 35 E
Manresa, Spain 19 B6 41 48N 1 50 E
Mansa, Gujarat, India 42 H5 23 27N 72 45 E
Mansa, Punjab, India 42 E6 30 0N 75 27 E
Mansa, Zambia 55 E2 11 13S 28 55 E
Mansehra, Pakistan 42 B5 34 20N 73 15 E
Mansel I., Canada 69 B11 62 0N 80 0W
Mansfield, U.K. 10 D6 53 9N 1 11W
Mansfield, La., U.S.A. 81 J8 32 2N 93 43W
Mansfield, Mass., U.S.A. 79 D13 42 2N 71 13W
Mansfield, Ohio, U.S.A. 78 F2 40 45N 82 31W
Mansfield, Pa., U.S.A. 78 E7 41 48N 77 5W
Mansfield, Mt., U.S.A. 79 B12 44 33N 72 49W
Manson Creek, Canada 72 B4 55 37N 124 32W
Manta, Ecuador 92 D2 1 0S 80 40W
Mantalingajan, Mt., Phil. 36 C5 8 55N 117 45 E
Mantare, Tanzania 54 C3 2 42S 33 13 E
Manteca, U.S.A. 84 H5 37 48N 121 13W
Manteo, U.S.A. 77 H8 35 55N 75 40W
Mantes-la-Jolie, France 18 B4 48 58N 1 41 E
Manthani, India 40 K11 18 40N 79 35 E
Manti, U.S.A. 82 G8 39 16N 111 38W
Mantiqueira, Serra da, Brazil 95 A7 22 0S 44 0W
Manton, U.S.A. 76 C3 44 25N 85 24W
Mántova, Italy 20 B4 45 9N 10 48 E
Mänttä, Finland 9 E21 62 0N 24 40 E
Mantua = Mántova, Italy 20 B4 45 9N 10 48 E
Manu, Peru 92 F4 12 10S 70 51W
Manu →, Peru 92 F4 12 16S 70 55W
Manua Is., Amer. Samoa 59 B14 14 13S 169 35W
Manuel Alves →, Brazil 93 F9 11 19S 48 28W
Manui, Indonesia 37 E6 3 35S 123 5 E
Manukau, N.Z. 59 G5 40 43S 175 13 E
Manuripi →, Bolivia 92 F5 11 6S 67 36W
Many, U.S.A. 81 K8 31 34N 93 29W
Manyara, L., Tanzania 54 C4 3 40S 35 50 E
Manych-Gudilo, Ozero, Russia 25 E7 46 24N 42 38 E
Manyonga →, Tanzania 54 C3 4 10S 34 15 E
Manyoni, Tanzania 54 D3 5 45S 34 55 E
Manzai, Pakistan 42 C4 32 12N 70 15 E
Manzanares, Spain 19 C4 39 2N 3 22W
Manzanillo, Cuba 88 B4 20 20N 77 31W
Manzanillo, Mexico 86 D4 19 0N 104 20W
Manzanillo, Pta., Panama 88 E4 9 30N 79 40W
Manzano Mts., U.S.A. 83 J10 34 40N 106 20W
Manzarīyeh, Iran 45 C6 34 53N 50 50 E
Manzhouli, China 33 B6 49 35N 117 25 E
Manzini, Swaziland 57 D5 26 30S 31 25 E
Mao, Chad 51 F9 14 4N 15 19 E
Maó, Spain 22 B11 39 53N 4 16 E
Maoke, Pegunungan, Indonesia 37 E9 3 40S 137 30 E
Maolin, China 35 C12 43 58N 123 30 E
Maoming, China 33 D6 21 50N 110 54 E
Maoxing, China 35 B13 45 28N 124 40 E
Mapam Yumco, China 32 C3 30 45N 81 28 E
Mapastepec, Mexico 87 D6 15 26N 92 54W
Mapia, Kepulauan, Indonesia 37 D8 0 50N 134 20 E
Mapimí, Mexico 86 B4 25 50N 103 50W
Mapimí, Bolsón de, Mexico 86 B4 27 30N 104 15W
Mapinga, Tanzania 54 D4 6 40S 39 12 E
Mapinhane, Mozam. 57 C6 22 20S 35 0 E
Maple Creek, Canada 73 D7 49 55N 109 29W
Maple Valley, U.S.A. 84 C4 47 25N 122 3W
Mapleton, U.S.A. 82 D2 44 2N 123 52W
Mapuera →, Brazil 92 D7 1 5S 57 2W
Mapulanguene, Mozam. 57 C5 24 29S 32 6 E
Maputo, Mozam. 57 D5 25 58S 32 32 E
Maputo □, Mozam. 57 D5 26 0S 32 25 E
Maputo, B. de, Mozam. 57 D5 25 50S 32 45 E
Maqiaohe, China 35 B16 44 40N 130 30 E
Maqnā, Si. Arabia 44 D2 28 25N 34 50 E
Maquela do Zombo, Angola 52 F3 6 0S 15 15 E
Maquinchao, Argentina 96 E3 41 15S 68 50W
Maquoketa, U.S.A. 80 D9 42 4N 90 40W
Mar, Serra do, Brazil 95 B6 25 30S 49 0W
Mar Chiquita, L., Argentina 94 C3 30 40S 62 50W
Mar del Plata, Argentina 94 D4 38 0S 57 30W
Mar Menor, Spain 19 D5 37 40N 0 45W
Mara, Tanzania 54 C3 1 30S 34 32 E
Mara □, Tanzania 54 C3 1 45S 34 20 E
Maraã, Brazil 92 D5 1 52S 65 25W
Marabá, Brazil 93 E9 5 20S 49 5W
Maracá, I. de, Brazil 93 C8 2 10N 50 30W
Maracaibo, Venezuela 92 A4 10 40N 71 37W
Maracaibo, L. de, Venezuela 92 B4 9 40N 71 30W
Maracaju, Brazil 95 A4 21 38S 55 9W
Maracay, Venezuela 92 A5 10 15N 67 28W
Maradi, Niger 50 F7 13 29N 7 20 E
Marāgheh, Iran 44 B5 37 30N 46 12 E
Marāh, Si. Arabia 44 E5 25 0N 45 35 E
Marajó, I. de, Brazil 93 D9 1 0S 49 30W
Marākand, Iran 44 B5 38 51N 45 16 E
Maralal, Kenya 54 B4 1 0N 36 38 E
Maralinga, Australia 61 F5 30 13S 131 32 E
Maran, Malaysia 39 L4 3 35N 102 45 E
Marana, U.S.A. 83 K8 32 27N 111 13W
Maranboy, Australia 60 B5 14 40S 132 39 E
Marand, Iran 44 B5 38 30N 45 45 E
Marang, Malaysia 39 K4 5 12N 103 13 E
Maranguape, Brazil 93 D11 3 55S 38 50W
Maranhão = São Luís, Brazil 93 D10 2 39S 44 15W
Maranhão □, Brazil 93 E9 5 0S 46 0W
Maranoa →, Australia 63 D4 27 50S 148 37 E
Marañón →, Peru 92 D4 4 30S 73 35W
Marão, Mozam. 57 C5 24 18S 34 2 E
Maraş = Kahramanmaraş, Turkey 25 G6 37 37N 36 53 E
Marathasa □, Cyprus 23 E11 34 59N 32 51 E
Marathon, Australia 62 C3 20 51S 143 32 E
Marathon, Canada 70 C2 48 44N 86 23W
Marathon, N.Y., U.S.A. 79 D8 42 27N 76 2W
Marathon, Tex., U.S.A. 81 K3 30 12N 103 15W
Marathóvouno, Cyprus 23 D12 35 13N 33 37 E
Maratua, Indonesia 37 D5 2 10N 118 35 E
Maravatío, Mexico 86 D4 19 51N 100 25W
Marāwih, U.A.E. 45 E7 24 18N 53 18 E
Marbella, Spain 19 D3 36 30N 4 57W
Marble Bar, Australia 60 D2 21 9S 119 44 E
Marble Falls, U.S.A. 81 K5 30 35N 98 16W
Marblehead, U.S.A. 79 D14 42 30N 70 51W
Marburg, Germany 16 C5 50 47N 8 46 E
March, U.K. 11 E8 52 33N 0 5 E
Marche, France 18 C4 46 5N 1 20 E
Marche-en-Famenne, Belgium 15 D5 50 14N 5 19 E
Marchena, Spain 19 D3 37 18N 5 23W
Marco, U.S.A. 77 N5 25 58N 81 44W
Marcos Juárez, Argentina 94 C3 32 42S 62 5W
Marcus I. = Minami-Tori-Shima, Pac. Oc. 64 E7 24 20N 153 58 E
Marcus Necker Ridge, Pac. Oc. 64 F9 20 0N 175 0 E
Marcy, Mt., U.S.A. 79 B11 44 7N 73 56W
Mardan, Pakistan 42 B5 34 20N 72 0 E
Mardin, Turkey 25 G7 37 20N 40 43 E
Maree, L., U.K. 12 D3 57 40N 5 26W
Mareeba, Australia 62 B4 16 59S 145 28 E
Mareetsane, S. Africa 56 D4 26 9S 25 25 E
Marek = Stanke Dimitrov, Bulgaria 21 C10 42 17N 23 9 E
Marengo, U.S.A. 80 E8 41 48N 92 4W
Marenyi, Kenya 54 C4 4 22S 39 8 E
Marerano, Madag. 57 C7 21 23S 44 52 E
Marfa, U.S.A. 81 K2 30 19N 104 1W
Marfa Pt., Malta 23 D1 35 59N 14 19 E
Margaret →, Australia 60 C4 18 9S 125 41 E
Margaret Bay, Canada 72 C3 51 20N 127 35W
Margaret L., Canada 72 B5 58 56N 115 25W
Margaret River, Australia 61 F2 33 57S 115 4 E
Margarita, I. de, Venezuela 92 A6 11 0N 64 0W
Margaritovo, Russia 30 C7 43 25N 134 45 E
Margate, S. Africa 57 E5 30 50S 30 20 E
Margate, U.K. 11 F9 51 23N 1 23 E
Mārgow, Dasht-e, Afghan. 40 D3 30 40N 62 30 E
Marguerite, Canada 72 C4 52 30N 122 25W
Mari El □, Russia 24 C8 56 30N 48 0 E
Mari Indus, Pakistan 42 C4 32 57N 71 34 E
Mari Republic = Mari El □, Russia 24 C8 56 30N 48 0 E
María Elena, Chile 94 A2 22 18S 69 40W
María Grande, Argentina 94 C4 31 45S 59 55W
Maria I., N. Terr., Australia 62 A2 14 52S 135 45 E
Maria I., Tas., Australia 62 G4 42 35S 148 0 E
Maria van Diemen, C., N.Z. 59 F4 34 29S 172 40 E
Mariakani, Kenya 54 C4 3 50S 39 27 E
Marian, Australia 62 C4 21 9S 148 57 E
Marian L., Canada 72 A5 63 0N 116 15W
Mariana Trench, Pac. Oc. 28 H18 13 0N 145 0 E
Marianao, Cuba 88 B3 23 8N 82 24W
Marianna, Ark., U.S.A. 81 H9 34 46N 90 46W
Marianna, Fla., U.S.A. 77 K3 30 46N 85 14W
Marias →, U.S.A. 82 C8 47 56N 110 30W
Mariato, Punta, Panama 88 E3 7 12N 80 52W
Maribor, Slovenia 16 E8 46 36N 15 40 E
Marico →, Africa 56 C4 23 35S 26 57 E
Maricopa, Ariz., U.S.A. 83 K7 33 4N 112 3W
Maricopa, Calif., U.S.A. 85 K7 35 4N 119 24W
Marié →, Brazil 92 D5 0 27S 66 26W
Marie Byrd Land, Antarctica 5 D14 79 30S 125 0W
Marie-Galante, Guadeloupe 89 C7 15 56N 61 16W
Mariecourt = Kangiqsujuaq, Canada 69 B12 61 30N 72 0W
Mariembourg, Belgium 15 D4 50 6N 4 31 E
Mariental, Namibia 56 C2 24 36S 18 0 E
Marienville, U.S.A. 78 E5 41 28N 79 8W
Mariestad, Sweden 9 G15 58 43N 13 50 E
Marietta, Ga., U.S.A. 77 J3 33 57N 84 33W
Marietta, Ohio, U.S.A. 76 F5 39 25N 81 27W
Marieville, Canada 79 A11 45 26N 73 10W
Mariinsk, Russia 26 D9 56 10N 87 20 E
Marijampolė, Lithuania 9 J20 54 33N 23 19 E
Marília, Brazil 95 A6 22 13S 50 0W
Marín, Spain 19 A1 42 23N 8 42W
Marina, U.S.A. 84 J5 36 41N 121 48W
Marinduque, Phil. 37 B6 13 25N 122 0 E
Marine City, U.S.A. 78 D2 42 43N 82 30W
Marinette, U.S.A. 76 C2 45 6N 87 38W
Maringá, Brazil 95 A5 23 26S 52 2W
Marion, Ala., U.S.A. 77 J2 32 38N 87 19W
Marion, Ill., U.S.A. 81 G10 37 44N 88 56W
Marion, Ind., U.S.A. 76 E3 40 32N 85 40W
Marion, Iowa, U.S.A. 80 D9 42 2N 91 36W
Marion, Kans., U.S.A. 80 F6 38 21N 97 1W
Marion, N.C., U.S.A. 77 H5 35 41N 82 1W
Marion, Ohio, U.S.A. 76 E4 40 35N 83 8W
Marion, S.C., U.S.A. 77 H6 34 11N 79 24W
Marion, Va., U.S.A. 77 G5 36 50N 81 31W
Marion, L., U.S.A. 77 J5 33 28N 80 10W
Mariposa, U.S.A. 84 H7 37 29N 119 58W
Mariscal Estigarribia, Paraguay 94 A3 22 3S 60 40W
Maritime Alps = Maritimes, Alpes, Europe 18 D7 44 10N 7 10 E
Maritimes, Alpes, Europe 18 D7 44 10N 7 10 E
Maritsa = Évros →, Greece 21 D12 41 40N 26 34 E
Maritsá, Greece 23 C10 36 22N 28 8 E
Mariupol, Ukraine 25 E6 47 5N 37 31 E
Marīvān, Iran 44 C5 35 30N 46 25 E
Marj 'Uyūn, Lebanon 47 B4 33 20N 35 35 E
Markazī □, Iran 45 C6 35 0N 49 30 E
Markdale, Canada 78 B4 44 19N 80 39W
Marked Tree, U.S.A. 81 H9 35 32N 90 25W
Market Drayton, U.K. 10 E5 52 54N 2 29W
Market Harborough, U.K. 11 E7 52 29N 0 55W
Market Rasen, U.K. 10 D7 53 24N 0 20W
Markham, Canada 78 C5 43 52N 79 16W
Markham, Mt., Antarctica 5 E11 83 0S 164 0 E
Markleeville, U.S.A. 84 G7 38 42N 119 47W
Markovo, Russia 27 C17 64 40N 170 24 E
Marks, Russia 24 D8 51 45N 46 50 E
Marksville, U.S.A. 81 K8 31 8N 92 4W
Marla, Australia 63 D1 27 19S 133 33 E
Marlbank, Canada 78 B7 44 26N 77 6W
Marlboro, Mass., U.S.A. 79 D13 42 19N 71 33W
Marlboro, N.Y., U.S.A. 79 E11 41 36N 73 59W
Marlborough, Australia 62 C4 22 46S 149 52 E
Marlborough, U.K. 11 F6 51 25N 1 43W
Marlborough Downs, U.K. 11 F6 51 27N 1 53W

Medvezhi, Ostrava

Marlin, U.S.A. 81 K6 31 18N 96 54W
Marlow, U.S.A. 81 H6 34 39N 97 58W
Marmagao, India 40 M8 15 25N 73 56 E
Marmara, Turkey 21 D12 40 35N 27 34 E
Marmara, Sea of = Marmara Denizi, Turkey 21 D13 40 45N 28 15 E
Marmara Denizi, Turkey 21 D13 40 45N 28 15 E
Marmaris, Turkey 21 F13 36 50N 28 14 E
Marmion, Mt., Australia 61 E2 29 16S 119 50 E
Marmion L., Canada 70 C1 48 55N 91 20W
Marmolada, Mte., Italy 20 A4 46 26N 11 51 E
Marmora, Canada 78 B7 44 28N 77 41W
Marne →, France 18 B5 48 48N 2 24 E
Maroala, Madag. 57 B8 15 23S 47 59 E
Maroantsetra, Madag. 57 B8 15 26S 49 44 E
Maroelaboom, Namibia 56 B2 19 15S 18 53 E
Marofandilia, Madag. 57 C7 20 7S 44 34 E
Marolambo, Madag. 57 C8 20 2S 48 7 E
Maromandia, Madag. 57 A8 14 13S 48 5 E
Marondera, Zimbabwe 55 F3 18 5S 31 42 E
Maroni →, Fr. Guiana 93 B8 5 30N 54 0W
Maroochydore, Australia 63 D5 26 29S 153 5 E
Marosakoa, Madag. 57 B8 15 26S 46 38 E
Maroseranana, Madag. 57 B8 18 32S 48 51 E
Marotandrano, Madag. 57 B8 16 10S 48 50 E
Marotaolano, Madag. 57 A8 12 47S 49 15 E
Maroua, Cameroon 51 F8 10 40N 14 20 E
Marovato, Madag. 57 B8 15 48S 48 5 E
Marovoay, Madag. 57 B8 16 6S 46 39 E
Marquard, S. Africa 56 D4 28 40S 27 28 E
Marquesas Is. = Marquises, Is., Pac. Oc. 65 H14 9 30S 140 0W
Marquette, U.S.A. 76 B2 46 33N 87 24W
Marquises, Is., Pac. Oc. 65 H14 9 30S 140 0W
Marra, Djebel, Sudan 51 F10 13 10N 24 22 E
Marracuene, Mozam. 57 D5 25 45S 32 35 E
Marrakech, Morocco 50 B4 31 9N 8 0W
Marrawah, Australia 62 G3 40 55S 144 42 E
Marree, Australia 63 D2 29 39S 138 1 E
Marrero, U.S.A. 81 L9 29 54N 90 6W
Marrimane, Mozam. 57 C5 22 58S 33 34 E
Marromeu, Mozam. 57 B6 18 15S 36 25 E
Marrubane, Mozam. 55 F4 18 0S 37 0 E
Marrupa, Mozam. 55 E4 13 8S 37 30 E
Mars Hill, U.S.A. 77 B12 46 31N 67 52W
Marsá Matrûh, Egypt 51 B11 31 19N 27 9 E
Marsabit, Kenya 54 B4 2 18N 38 0 E
Marsala, Italy 20 F5 37 48N 12 26 E
Marsalforn, Malta 23 C1 36 4N 14 15 E
Marseille, France 18 E6 43 18N 5 23 E
Marseilles = Marseille, France 18 E6 43 18N 5 23 E
Marsh I., U.S.A. 81 L9 29 34N 91 53W
Marshall, Ark., U.S.A. 81 H8 35 55N 92 38W
Marshall, Mich., U.S.A. 76 D3 42 16N 84 58W
Marshall, Minn., U.S.A. 80 C7 44 25N 95 45W
Marshall, Mo., U.S.A. 80 F8 39 7N 93 12W
Marshall, Tex., U.S.A. 81 J7 32 33N 94 23W
Marshall →, Australia 62 C2 22 59S 136 59 E
Marshall Is. ■, Pac. Oc. 64 G9 9 0N 171 0 E
Marshalltown, U.S.A. 80 D8 42 3N 92 55W
Marshbrook, Zimbabwe 57 B5 18 33S 31 9 E
Marshfield, Mo., U.S.A. 81 G8 37 15N 92 54W
Marshfield, Vt., U.S.A. 79 B12 44 20N 72 20W
Marshfield, Wis., U.S.A. 80 C9 44 40N 90 10W
Marshūn, Iran 45 B6 36 19N 49 23 E
Märsta, Sweden 9 G17 59 37N 17 52 E
Mart, U.S.A. 81 K6 31 33N 96 50W
Martaban, Burma 41 L20 16 30N 97 35 E
Martaban, G. of, Burma 41 L20 16 5N 96 30 E
Martapura, Kalimantan, Indonesia 36 E4 3 22S 114 47 E
Martapura, Sumatera, Indonesia 36 E2 4 19S 104 22 E
Martelange, Belgium 15 E5 49 49N 5 43 E
Martha's Vineyard, U.S.A. 79 E14 41 25N 70 38W
Martigny, Switz. 18 C7 46 6N 7 3 E
Martigues, France 18 E6 43 24N 5 4 E
Martin, Slovak Rep. 17 D10 49 6N 18 58 E
Martin, S. Dak., U.S.A. 80 D4 43 11N 101 44W
Martin, Tenn., U.S.A. 81 G10 36 21N 88 51W
Martin, L., U.S.A. 77 J3 32 41N 85 55W
Martina Franca, Italy 20 D7 40 42N 17 20 E
Martinborough, N.Z. 59 J5 41 14S 175 29 E
Martinez, Calif., U.S.A. 84 G4 38 1N 122 8W
Martinez, Ga., U.S.A. 77 J4 33 31N 82 4W
Martinique ■, W. Indies 89 D7 14 40N 61 0W
Martinique Passage, W. Indies 89 C7 15 15N 61 0W
Martinópolis, Brazil 95 A5 22 11S 51 12W
Martins Ferry, U.S.A. 78 F4 40 6N 80 44W
Martinsburg, Pa., U.S.A. 78 F6 40 19N 78 20W
Martinsburg, W. Va., U.S.A. 76 F7 39 27N 77 58W
Martinsville, Ind., U.S.A. 76 F2 39 26N 86 25W
Martinsville, Va., U.S.A. 77 G6 36 41N 79 52W
Marton, N.Z. 59 J5 40 4S 175 23 E
Martos, Spain 19 D4 37 44N 3 58W
Marudi, Malaysia 36 D4 4 11N 114 19 E
Maruf, Afghan. 40 D5 31 30N 67 6 E
Marugame, Japan 31 G6 34 15N 133 40 E
Marunga, Angola 56 B3 17 28S 20 2 E
Marungu, Mts., Dem. Rep. of the Congo 54 D3 7 30S 30 0 E
Marv Dasht, Iran 45 D7 29 50N 52 40 E
Marvast, Iran 45 D7 30 30N 54 15 E
Marvel Loch, Australia 61 F2 31 28S 119 29 E
Marwar, India 42 G5 25 43N 73 45 E
Mary, Turkmenistan 26 F7 37 40N 61 50 E
Maryborough = Port Laoise, Ireland 13 C4 53 2N 7 18W
Maryborough, Australia 63 D5 25 31S 152 37 E
Maryfield, Canada 73 D8 49 50N 101 35W
Maryland □, U.S.A. 76 F7 39 0N 76 30W
Maryland Junction, Zimbabwe 55 F3 17 45S 30 31 E
Maryport, U.K. 10 C4 54 44N 3 28W
Mary's Harbour, Canada 71 B8 52 18N 55 51W
Marystown, Canada 71 C8 47 10N 55 10W
Marysville, Canada 72 D5 49 35N 116 0W
Marysville, Calif., U.S.A. 84 F5 39 9N 121 35W
Marysville, Kans., U.S.A. 80 F6 39 51N 96 39W
Marysville, Mich., U.S.A. 78 D2 42 54N 82 29W
Marysville, Ohio, U.S.A. 76 E4 40 14N 83 22W
Marysville, Wash., U.S.A. 84 B4 48 3N 122 11W
Maryville, Mo., U.S.A. 80 E7 40 21N 94 52W
Maryville, Tenn., U.S.A. 77 H4 35 46N 83 58W
Marzūq, Libya 51 C8 25 53N 13 57 E
Masahunga, Tanzania 54 C3 2 6S 33 18 E
Masai Steppe, Tanzania 54 C4 4 30S 36 30 E
Masaka, Uganda 54 C3 0 21S 31 45 E
Masalembo, Kepulauan, Indonesia 36 F4 5 35S 114 30 E
Masalima, Kepulauan, Indonesia 36 F5 5 4S 117 5 E
Masamba, Indonesia 37 E6 2 30S 120 15 E
Masan, S. Korea 35 G15 35 11N 128 32 E
Masandam, Ra's, Oman 46 B6 26 30N 56 30 E
Masasi, Tanzania 55 E4 10 45S 38 52 E
Masaya, Nic. 88 D2 12 0N 86 7W
Masbate, Phil. 37 B6 12 21N 123 36 E
Mascara, Algeria 50 A6 35 26N 0 6 E
Mascota, Mexico 86 C4 20 30N 104 50W
Masela, Indonesia 37 F7 8 9S 129 51 E
Maseru, Lesotho 56 D4 29 18S 27 30 E
Mashaba, Zimbabwe 55 G3 20 2S 30 29 E
Mashābih, Si. Arabia 44 E3 25 35N 36 30 E
Masherbrum, Pakistan 43 B7 35 38N 76 18 E
Mashhad, Iran 45 B8 36 20N 59 35 E
Mashīz, Iran 45 D8 29 56N 56 37 E
Māshkel, Hāmūn-i-, Pakistan 40 E3 28 20N 62 56 E
Mashki Chāh, Pakistan 40 E3 29 5N 62 30 E
Mashonaland, Zimbabwe 53 H6 16 30S 31 0 E
Mashonaland Central □, Zimbabwe 57 B5 17 30S 31 0 E
Mashonaland East □, Zimbabwe 57 B5 18 0S 32 0 E
Mashonaland West □, Zimbabwe 57 B4 17 30S 29 30 E
Mashrakh, India 43 F11 26 7N 84 48 E
Masindi, Uganda 54 B3 1 40N 31 43 E
Masindi Port, Uganda 54 B3 1 43N 32 2 E
Maşīrah, Oman 46 C6 21 0N 58 50 E
Maşīrah, Khalīj, Oman 46 C6 20 10N 58 10 E
Masisi, Dem. Rep. of the Congo 54 C2 1 23S 28 49 E
Masjed Soleyman, Iran 45 D6 31 55N 49 18 E
Mask, L., Ireland 13 C2 53 36N 9 22W
Maskin, Oman 45 F8 23 30N 56 50 E
Masoala, Tanjon' i, Madag. 57 B9 15 59S 50 13 E
Masoarivo, Madag. 57 B7 19 3S 44 19 E
Masohi = Amahai, Indonesia 37 E7 3 20S 128 55 E
Masomeloka, Madag. 57 C8 20 17S 48 37 E
Mason, Nev., U.S.A. 84 G7 38 56N 119 8W
Mason, Tex., U.S.A. 81 K5 30 45N 99 14W
Mason City, U.S.A. 80 D8 43 9N 93 12W
Maspalomas, Canary Is. 22 G4 27 46N 15 35W
Maspalomas, Pta., Canary Is. 22 G4 27 43N 15 36W
Masqat, Oman 46 C6 23 37N 58 36 E
Massa, Italy 18 D9 44 1N 10 9 E
Massachusetts □, U.S.A. 79 D13 42 30N 72 0W
Massachusetts B., U.S.A. 79 D14 42 20N 70 50W
Massakory, Chad 51 F9 13 0N 15 49 E
Massanella, Spain 22 B9 39 48N 2 51 E
Massangena, Mozam. 57 C5 21 34S 33 0 E
Massango, Angola 52 F3 8 2S 16 21 E
Massawa = Mitsiwa, Eritrea 46 D2 15 35N 39 25 E
Massena, U.S.A. 79 B10 44 56N 74 54W
Massénya, Chad 51 F9 11 21N 16 9 E
Masset, Canada 72 C2 54 2N 132 10W
Massif Central, France 18 D5 44 55N 3 0 E
Massillon, U.S.A. 78 F3 40 48N 81 32W
Massinga, Mozam. 57 C6 23 15S 35 22 E
Massingir, Mozam. 57 C5 23 51S 32 4 E
Masson, Canada 79 A9 45 32N 75 25W
Masson I., Antarctica 5 C7 66 10S 93 20 E
Mastanli = Momchilgrad, Bulgaria 21 D11 41 33N 25 23 E
Masterton, N.Z. 59 J5 40 56S 175 39 E
Mastic, U.S.A. 79 F12 40 47N 72 54W
Mastuj, Pakistan 43 A5 36 20N 72 36 E
Mastung, Pakistan 40 E5 29 50N 66 56 E
Masty, Belarus 17 B13 53 27N 24 38 E
Masuda, Japan 31 G5 34 40N 131 51 E
Masvingo, Zimbabwe 55 G3 20 8S 30 49 E
Masvingo □, Zimbabwe 55 G3 21 0S 31 30 E
Maşyāf, Syria 44 C3 35 4N 36 20 E
Matabeleland, Zimbabwe 53 H5 18 0S 27 0 E
Matabeleland North □, Zimbabwe 55 F2 19 0S 28 0 E
Matabeleland South □, Zimbabwe 55 G2 21 0S 29 0 E
Matachewan, Canada 70 C3 47 56N 80 39W
Matadi, Dem. Rep. of the Congo 52 F2 5 52S 13 31 E
Matagalpa, Nic. 88 D2 13 0N 85 58W
Matagami, Canada 70 C4 49 45N 77 34W
Matagami, L., Canada 70 C4 49 50N 77 40W
Matagorda B., U.S.A. 81 L6 28 40N 96 0W
Matagorda I., U.S.A. 81 L6 28 15N 96 30W
Matak, Indonesia 39 L6 3 18N 106 16 E
Mátala, Greece 23 E6 34 59N 24 45 E
Matam, Senegal 50 E3 15 34N 13 17W
Matamoros, Campeche, Mexico 87 D6 18 50N 90 50W
Matamoros, Coahuila, Mexico 86 B4 25 33N 103 15W
Matamoros, Tamaulipas, Mexico 87 B5 25 50N 97 30W
Ma'ṭan as Sarra, Libya 51 D10 21 45N 22 0 E
Matandu →, Tanzania 55 D3 8 45S 34 19 E
Matane, Canada 71 C6 48 50N 67 33W
Matanomadh, India 42 H3 23 33N 68 57 E
Matanzas, Cuba 88 B3 23 0N 81 40W
Matapa, Botswana 56 C3 23 11S 24 39 E
Matapan, C. = Taínaron, Ákra, Greece 21 F10 36 22N 22 27 E
Matapédia, Canada 71 C6 48 0N 66 59W
Matara, Sri Lanka 40 S12 5 58N 80 30 E
Mataram, Indonesia 36 F5 8 41S 116 10 E
Matarani, Peru 92 G4 17 0S 72 10W
Mataranka, Australia 60 B5 14 55S 133 4 E
Matarma, Râs, Egypt 47 E1 30 27N 32 44 E
Mataró, Spain 19 B7 41 32N 2 29 E
Matatiele, S. Africa 57 E4 30 20S 28 49 E
Mataura, N.Z. 59 M2 46 11S 168 51 E
Matehuala, Mexico 86 C4 23 40N 100 40W
Mateke Hills, Zimbabwe 55 G3 21 48S 31 0 E
Matera, Italy 20 D7 40 40N 16 36 E
Matetsi, Zimbabwe 55 F2 18 12S 26 0 E
Mathis, U.S.A. 81 L6 28 6N 97 50W
Mathráki, Greece 23 A3 39 48N 19 31 E
Mathura, India 42 F7 27 30N 77 40 E
Mati, Phil. 37 C7 6 55N 126 15 E
Matiali, India 43 F13 26 56N 88 49 E
Matías Romero, Mexico 87 D5 16 53N 95 2W
Matibane, Mozam. 55 E5 14 49S 40 45 E
Matima, Botswana 56 C3 20 15S 24 26 E
Matiri Ra., N.Z. 59 J4 41 38S 172 20 E
Matjiesfontein, S. Africa 56 E3 33 14S 20 35 E
Matla →, India 43 J13 21 40N 88 40 E
Matlamanyane, Botswana 56 B4 19 33S 25 57 E
Matli, Pakistan 42 G3 25 2N 68 39 E
Matlock, U.K. 10 D6 53 9N 1 33W
Mato Grosso □, Brazil 93 F8 14 0S 55 0W
Mato Grosso, Planalto do, Brazil 93 G8 15 0S 55 0W
Mato Grosso do Sul □, Brazil 93 G8 18 0S 55 0W
Matochkin Shar, Russia 26 B6 73 10N 56 40 E
Matopo Hills, Zimbabwe 55 G2 20 36S 28 20 E
Matopos, Zimbabwe 55 G2 20 20S 28 29 E
Matosinhos, Portugal 19 B1 41 11N 8 42W
Matroosberg, S. Africa 56 E2 33 23S 19 40 E
Maṭruḥ, Oman 46 C6 23 37N 58 30 E
Matsue, Japan 31 G6 35 25N 133 10 E
Matsumae, Japan 30 D10 41 26N 140 7 E
Matsumoto, Japan 31 F9 36 15N 138 0 E
Matsusaka, Japan 31 G8 34 34N 136 32 E
Matsuura, Japan 31 H4 33 20N 129 49 E
Matsuyama, Japan 31 H6 33 45N 132 45 E
Mattagami →, Canada 70 B3 50 43N 81 29W
Mattancheri, India 40 Q10 9 50N 76 15 E
Mattawa, Canada 70 C4 46 20N 78 45W
Matterhorn, Switz. 18 D7 45 58N 7 39 E
Matthew Town, Bahamas 89 B5 20 57N 73 40W
Matthew's Ridge, Guyana 92 B6 7 37N 60 10W
Mattice, Canada 70 C3 49 40N 83 20W
Mattituck, U.S.A. 79 F12 40 59N 72 32W
Mattō, Japan 31 F8 36 31N 136 34 E
Mattoon, U.S.A. 76 F1 39 29N 88 23W
Matuba, Mozam. 57 C5 24 28S 32 49 E
Matucana, Peru 92 F3 11 55S 76 25W
Matūn = Khowst, Afghan. 42 C3 33 22N 69 58 E
Maturín, Venezuela 92 B6 9 45N 63 11W
Mau, Mad. P., India 43 F8 26 17N 78 41 E
Mau, Ut. P., India 43 G10 25 56N 83 33 E
Mau, Ut. P., India 43 G9 25 17N 81 23 E
Mau Escarpment, Kenya 54 C4 0 40S 36 0 E
Mau Ranipur, India 43 G8 25 16N 79 8 E
Maubeuge, France 18 A6 50 17N 3 57 E
Maud, Pt., Australia 60 D1 23 6S 113 45 E
Maudin Sun, Burma 41 M19 16 0N 94 30 E
Maués, Brazil 92 D7 3 20S 57 45W
Mauganj, India 41 G12 24 50N 81 55 E
Maughold Hd., U.K. 10 C3 54 18N 4 18W
Maui, U.S.A. 74 H16 20 48N 156 20W
Maulamyaing = Moulmein, Burma 41 L20 16 30N 97 40 E
Maule □, Chile 94 D1 36 5S 72 30W
Maumee, U.S.A. 76 E4 41 34N 83 39W
Maumee →, U.S.A. 76 E4 41 42N 83 28W
Maumere, Indonesia 37 F6 8 38S 122 13 E
Maun, Botswana 56 C3 20 0S 23 26 E
Mauna Kea, U.S.A. 74 J17 19 50N 155 28W
Mauna Loa, U.S.A. 74 J17 19 30N 155 35W
Maungmagan Kyunzu, Burma 38 E1 14 0N 97 48 E
Maupin, U.S.A. 82 D3 45 11N 121 5W
Maurepas, L., U.S.A. 81 K9 30 15N 90 30W
Maurice, L., Australia 61 E5 29 30S 131 0 E
Mauricie, Parc Nat. de la, Canada 70 C5 46 45N 73 0W
Mauritania ■, Africa 50 E3 20 50N 10 0W
Mauritius ■, Ind. Oc. 49 J9 20 0S 57 0 E
Mauston, U.S.A. 80 D9 43 48N 90 5W
Mavli, India 42 G5 24 45N 73 55 E
Mavuradonha Mts., Zimbabwe 55 F3 16 30S 31 30 E
Mawa, Dem. Rep. of the Congo 54 B2 2 45N 26 40 E
Mawai, India 43 H9 22 30N 81 4 E
Mawana, India 42 E7 29 6N 77 58 E
Mawand, Pakistan 42 E3 29 33N 68 38 E
Mawk Mai, Burma 41 J20 20 14N 97 37 E
Mawlaik, Burma 41 H19 23 40N 94 26 E
Mawlamyine = Moulmein, Burma 41 L20 16 30N 97 40 E
Mawqaq, Si. Arabia 44 E4 27 25N 41 8 E
Mawson Coast, Antarctica 5 C6 68 30S 63 0 E
Max, U.S.A. 80 B4 47 49N 101 18W
Maxcanú, Mexico 87 C6 20 40N 92 0W
Maxesibeni, S. Africa 57 E4 30 49S 29 23 E
Maxhamish L., Canada 72 B4 59 50N 123 17W
Maxixe, Mozam. 57 C6 23 54S 35 17 E
Maxville, Canada 79 A10 45 17N 74 51W
Maxwell, U.S.A. 84 F4 39 17N 122 11W
Maxwelton, Australia 62 C3 20 43S 142 41 E
May, C., U.S.A. 76 F8 38 56N 74 58W
May Pen, Jamaica 88 C4 17 58N 77 15W
Maya →, Russia 27 D14 60 28N 134 28 E
Maya Mts., Belize 87 D7 16 30N 89 0W
Mayaguana, Bahamas 89 B5 22 30N 72 44W
Mayagüez, Puerto Rico 89 C6 18 12N 67 9W
Mayāmey, Iran 45 B7 36 24N 55 42 E
Mayanup, Australia 61 F2 33 57S 116 27 E
Mayapan, Mexico 87 C7 20 30N 89 25W
Mayarí, Cuba 89 B4 20 40N 75 41W
Maybell, U.S.A. 82 F9 40 31N 108 5W
Maybole, U.K. 12 F4 55 21N 4 42W
Maydān, Iraq 44 C5 34 55N 45 37 E
Maydena, Australia 62 G4 42 45S 146 30 E
Mayenne →, France 18 C3 47 30N 0 32W
Mayer, U.S.A. 83 J7 34 24N 112 14W
Mayerthorpe, Canada 72 C5 53 57N 115 8W
Mayfield, Ky., U.S.A. 77 G1 36 44N 88 38W
Mayfield, N.Y., U.S.A. 79 C10 43 6N 74 16W
Mayhill, U.S.A. 83 K11 32 53N 105 29W
Maykop, Russia 25 F7 44 35N 40 10 E
Maymyo, Burma 38 A1 22 2N 96 28 E
Maynard, Mass., U.S.A. 79 D13 42 26N 71 27W
Maynard, Wash., U.S.A. 84 C4 47 59N 122 55W
Maynard Hills, Australia 61 E2 28 28S 119 49 E
Mayne →, Australia 62 C3 23 40S 141 55 E
Maynooth, Ireland 13 C5 53 23N 6 34W
Mayo, Canada 68 B6 63 38N 135 57W
Mayo □, Ireland 13 C2 53 53N 9 3W
Mayon Volcano, Phil. 37 B6 13 15N 123 41 E
Mayor I., N.Z. 59 G6 37 16S 176 17 E
Mayotte, Ind. Oc. 53 G9 12 50S 45 10 E
Maysville, U.S.A. 76 F4 38 39N 83 46W
Mayu, Indonesia 37 D7 1 30N 126 30 E
Mayville, N. Dak., U.S.A. 80 B6 47 30N 97 20W
Mayville, N.Y., U.S.A. 78 D5 42 15N 79 30W
Mayya, Russia 27 C14 61 44N 130 18 E
Mazabuka, Zambia 55 F2 15 52S 27 44 E
Mazagán = El Jadida, Morocco 50 B4 33 11N 8 17W
Mazagão, Brazil 93 D8 0 7S 51 16W
Mazán, Peru 92 D4 3 30S 73 0W
Māzandarān □, Iran 45 B7 36 30N 52 0 E
Mazapil, Mexico 86 C4 24 38N 101 34W
Mazara del Vallo, Italy 20 F5 37 39N 12 35 E
Mazarrón, Spain 19 D5 37 38N 1 19W
Mazaruni →, Guyana 92 B7 6 25N 58 35W
Mazatán, Mexico 86 B2 29 0N 110 8W
Mazatenango, Guatemala 88 D1 14 35N 91 30W
Mazatlán, Mexico 86 C3 23 13N 106 25W
Mažeikiai, Lithuania 9 H20 56 20N 22 20 E
Māzhān, Iran 45 C8 32 30N 59 0 E
Mazīnān, Iran 45 B8 36 19N 56 56 E
Mazoe, Mozam. 55 F3 16 42S 33 7 E
Mazoe →, Mozam. 55 F3 16 20S 33 30 E
Mazowe, Zimbabwe 55 F3 17 28S 30 58 E
Mazurian Lakes = Mazurski, Pojezierze, Poland 17 B11 53 50N 21 0 E
Mazurski, Pojezierze, Poland 17 B11 53 50N 21 0 E
Mazyr, Belarus 17 B15 51 59N 29 15 E
Mbabane, Swaziland 57 D5 26 18S 31 6 E
Mbaïki, C.A.R. 52 D3 3 53N 18 1 E
Mbala, Zambia 55 D3 8 46S 31 24 E
Mbalabala, Zimbabwe 57 C4 20 27S 29 3 E
Mbale, Uganda 54 B3 1 8N 34 12 E
Mbalmayo, Cameroon 52 D2 3 33N 11 33 E
Mbamba Bay, Tanzania 55 E3 11 13S 34 49 E
Mbandaka, Dem. Rep. of the Congo 52 D3 0 1N 18 18 E
Mbanza Congo, Angola 52 F2 6 18S 14 16 E
Mbanza Ngungu, Dem. Rep. of the Congo 52 F2 5 12S 14 53 E
Mbarara, Uganda 54 C3 0 35S 30 40 E
Mbashe →, S. Africa 57 E4 32 15S 28 54 E
Mbenkuru →, Tanzania 55 D4 9 25S 39 50 E
Mberengwa, Zimbabwe 55 G2 20 29S 29 57 E
Mberengwa, Mt., Zimbabwe 55 G2 20 37S 29 55 E
Mbesuma, Zambia 55 E3 10 0S 32 2 E
Mbeya, Tanzania 55 D3 8 54S 33 29 E
Mbeya □, Tanzania 54 D3 8 15S 33 30 E
Mbinga, Tanzania 55 E4 10 50S 35 0 E
Mbini □, Eq. Guin. 52 D2 1 30N 10 0 E
Mbour, Senegal 50 F2 14 22N 16 54W
Mbuji-Mayi, Dem. Rep. of the Congo 54 D1 6 9S 23 40 E
Mbulu, Tanzania 54 C4 3 45S 35 30 E
Mburucuyá, Argentina 94 B4 28 1S 58 14W
Mchinja, Tanzania 55 D4 9 44S 39 45 E
Mchinji, Malawi 55 E3 13 47S 32 58 E
Mdantsane, S. Africa 53 L5 32 56S 27 46 E
Mead, L., U.S.A. 85 J12 36 1N 114 44W
Meade, U.S.A. 81 G4 37 17N 100 20W
Meadow Lake, Canada 73 C7 54 10N 108 26W
Meadow Lake Prov. Park, Canada 73 C7 54 27N 109 0W
Meadow Valley Wash →, U.S.A. 85 J12 36 40N 114 34W
Meadville, U.S.A. 78 E4 41 39N 80 9W
Meaford, Canada 78 B4 44 36N 80 35W
Mealy Mts., Canada 71 B8 53 10N 58 0W
Meander River, Canada 72 B5 59 2N 117 42W
Meares, C., U.S.A. 82 D2 45 37N 124 0W
Mearim →, Brazil 93 D10 3 4S 44 35W
Meath □, Ireland 13 C5 53 40N 6 57W
Meath Park, Canada 73 C7 53 27N 105 22W
Meaux, France 18 B5 48 58N 2 50 E
Mebechi-Gawa →, Japan 30 D10 40 31N 141 31 E
Mecanhelas, Mozam. 55 F4 15 12S 35 54 E
Mecca = Makkah, Si. Arabia 46 C2 21 30N 39 54 E
Mecca, U.S.A. 85 M10 33 34N 116 5W
Mechanicsburg, U.S.A. 78 F8 40 13N 77 1W
Mechanicville, U.S.A. 79 D11 42 54N 73 41W
Mechelen, Belgium 15 C4 51 2N 4 29 E
Mecheria, Algeria 50 B5 33 35N 0 18W
Mecklenburg, Germany 16 B6 53 33N 11 40 E
Mecklenburger Bucht, Germany 16 A6 54 20N 11 40 E
Meconta, Mozam. 55 E4 14 59S 39 50 E
Medan, Indonesia 36 D1 3 40N 98 38 E
Medanosa, Pta., Argentina 96 F3 48 8S 66 0W
Médéa, Algeria 50 A6 36 12N 2 50 E
Medellín, Colombia 92 B3 6 15N 75 35W
Medelpad, Sweden 9 E17 62 33N 16 30 E
Medemblik, Neths. 15 B5 52 46N 5 8 E
Medford, Mass., U.S.A. 79 D13 42 25N 71 7W
Medford, Oreg., U.S.A. 82 E2 42 19N 122 52W
Medford, Wis., U.S.A. 80 C9 45 9N 90 20W
Medgidia, Romania 17 F15 44 15N 28 19 E
Media Agua, Argentina 94 C2 31 58S 68 25W
Media Luna, Argentina 94 C2 34 45S 66 44W
Medianeira, Brazil 95 B5 25 17S 54 5W
Mediaş, Romania 17 E13 46 9N 24 22 E
Medicine Bow, U.S.A. 82 F10 41 54N 106 12W
Medicine Bow Pk., U.S.A. 82 F10 41 21N 106 19W
Medicine Bow Ra., U.S.A. 82 F10 41 10N 106 25W
Medicine Hat, Canada 73 D6 50 0N 110 45W
Medicine Lake, U.S.A. 80 A2 48 30N 104 30W
Medicine Lodge, U.S.A. 81 G5 37 17N 98 35W
Medina = Al Madīnah, Si. Arabia 46 C2 24 35N 39 52 E
Medina, N. Dak., U.S.A. 80 B5 46 54N 99 18W
Medina, N.Y., U.S.A. 78 C6 43 13N 78 23W
Medina, Ohio, U.S.A. 78 E3 41 8N 81 52W
Medina →, U.S.A. 81 L5 29 16N 98 29W
Medina del Campo, Spain 19 B3 41 18N 4 55W
Medina L., U.S.A. 81 L5 29 32N 98 56W
Medina Sidonia, Spain 19 D3 36 28N 5 57W
Medinipur, India 43 H12 22 25N 87 21 E
Mediterranean Sea, Europe 49 C5 35 0N 15 0 E
Médoc, France 18 D3 45 10N 0 50W
Medveditsa →, Russia 25 E7 49 35N 42 41 E
Medvezhi, Ostrava, Russia 27 B17 71 0N 161 0 E

Medvezhyegorsk

Medvezhyegorsk, *Russia* **24 B5** 63 0N 34 25 E
Medway □, *U.K.* **11 F8** 51 25N 0 32 E
Medway →, *U.K.* **11 F8** 51 27N 0 46 E
Meekatharra, *Australia* **61 E2** 26 32S 118 29 E
Meeker, *U.S.A.* **82 F10** 40 2N 107 55W
Meelpaeg Res., *Canada* **71 C8** 48 15N 56 33W
Meerut, *India* **42 E7** 29 1N 77 42 E
Meeteetse, *U.S.A.* **82 D9** 44 9N 108 52W
Mega, *Ethiopia* **46 G2** 3 57N 38 19 E
Mégara, *Greece* **21 F10** 37 58N 23 22 E
Megasini, *India* **43 J12** 21 38N 86 21 E
Meghalaya □, *India* **41 G17** 25 50N 91 0 E
Mégiscane, L., *Canada* **70 C4** 48 35N 75 55W
Meharry, Mt., *Australia* **60 D2** 22 59S 118 35 E
Mehlville, *U.S.A.* **80 F9** 38 30N 90 19W
Mehndawal, *India* **43 F10** 26 58N 83 5 E
Mehr Jān, *Iran* **45 C7** 33 50N 55 6 E
Mehrābād, *Iran* **44 B5** 36 53N 47 55 E
Mehrān, *Iran* **44 C5** 33 7N 46 10 E
Mehrīz, *Iran* **45 D7** 31 35N 54 28 E
Mei Xian, *China* **34 G4** 34 18N 107 55 E
Meiktila, *Burma* **41 J19** 20 53N 95 54 E
Meissen, *Germany* **16 C7** 51 9N 13 29 E
Meizhou, *China* **33 D6** 24 16N 116 6 E
Meja, *India* **43 G10** 25 9N 82 7 E
Mejillones, *Chile* **94 A1** 23 10S 70 30W
Mekele, *Ethiopia* **46 E2** 13 33N 39 30 E
Mekhtar, *Pakistan* **40 D6** 30 30N 69 15 E
Meknès, *Morocco* **50 B4** 33 57N 5 33W
Mekong →, *Asia* **39 H6** 9 30N 106 15 E
Mekongga, *Indonesia* **37 E6** 3 39S 121 15 E
Mekvari = Kür →, *Azerbaijan* **25 G8** 39 29N 49 15 E
Melagiri Hills, *India* **40 N10** 12 20N 77 30 E
Melaka, *Malaysia* **39 L4** 2 15N 102 15 E
Melalap, *Malaysia* **36 C5** 5 10N 116 5 E
Mélambes, *Greece* **23 D6** 35 8N 24 40 E
Melanesia, *Pac. Oc.* **64 H7** 4 0S 155 0 E
Melbourne, *U.S.A.* **77 L5** 28 5N 80 37W
Melchor Múzquiz, *Mexico* **86 B4** 27 50N 101 30W
Melchor Ocampo, *Mexico* **86 C4** 24 52N 101 40W
Mélèzes →, *Canada* **70 A5** 57 40N 69 29W
Melfort, *Canada* **73 C8** 52 50N 104 37W
Melfort, *Zimbabwe* **55 F3** 18 0S 31 25 E
Melhus, *Norway* **8 E14** 63 17N 10 18 E
Melilla, *N. Afr.* **19 E4** 35 21N 2 57W
Melipilla, *Chile* **94 C1** 33 42S 71 15W
Mélissa, Ákra, *Greece* **23 D6** 35 6N 24 33 E
Melita, *Canada* **73 D8** 49 15N 101 0W
Melitopol, *Ukraine* **25 E6** 46 50N 35 22 E
Melk, *Austria* **16 D8** 48 13N 15 20 E
Mellansel, *Sweden* **8 E18** 63 25N 18 17 E
Mellen, *U.S.A.* **80 B9** 46 20N 90 40W
Mellerud, *Sweden* **9 G15** 58 41N 12 28 E
Mellette, *U.S.A.* **80 C5** 45 9N 98 30W
Mellieha, *Malta* **23 D1** 35 57N 14 21 E
Melo, *Uruguay* **95 C5** 32 20S 54 10W
Melolo, *Indonesia* **37 F6** 9 53S 120 40 E
Melouprey, *Cambodia* **38 F5** 13 48N 105 16 E
Melrose, *U.K.* **12 F6** 55 36N 2 43W
Melrose, *Minn., U.S.A.* **80 C7** 45 40N 94 49W
Melrose, *N. Mex., U.S.A.* **81 H3** 34 26N 103 38W
Melstone, *U.S.A.* **82 C10** 46 36N 107 52W
Melton Mowbray, *U.K.* **10 E7** 52 47N 0 54W
Melun, *France* **18 B5** 48 32N 2 39 E
Melville, *Canada* **73 C8** 50 55N 102 50W
Melville, C., *Australia* **62 A3** 14 11S 144 30 E
Melville, L., *Canada* **71 B8** 53 30N 60 0W
Melville B., *Australia* **62 A2** 12 0S 136 45 E
Melville I., *Australia* **60 B5** 11 30S 131 0 E
Melville I., *Canada* **4 B2** 75 30N 112 0W
Melville Pen., *Canada* **69 B11** 68 0N 84 0W
Memba, *Mozam.* **55 E5** 14 11S 40 30 E
Memboro, *Indonesia* **37 F5** 9 30S 119 30 E
Memel = Klaipėda, *Lithuania* **9 J19** 55 43N 21 10 E
Memel, *S. Africa* **57 D4** 27 38S 29 36 E
Memmingen, *Germany* **16 E6** 47 58N 10 10 E
Mempawah, *Indonesia* **36 D3** 0 30N 109 5 E
Memphis, *Mich., U.S.A.* **78 D2** 42 54N 82 46W
Memphis, *Tenn., U.S.A.* **81 H10** 35 8N 90 3W
Memphis, *Tex., U.S.A.* **81 H4** 34 44N 100 33W
Memphremagog, L., *U.S.A.* **79 B12** 45 0N 72 12W
Mena, *U.S.A.* **81 H7** 34 35N 94 15W
Menai Strait, *U.K.* **10 D3** 53 11N 4 13W
Ménaka, *Mali* **50 E6** 15 59N 2 18 E
Menan = Chao Phraya →, *Thailand* **38 F3** 13 32N 100 36 E
Menarandra →, *Madag.* **57 D7** 25 17S 44 30 E
Menard, *U.S.A.* **81 K5** 30 55N 99 47W
Mendawai →, *Indonesia* **36 E4** 3 30S 113 0 E
Mende, *France* **18 D5** 44 31N 3 30 E
Mendez, *Mexico* **87 B5** 25 7N 98 34W
Mendhar, *India* **43 C6** 33 35N 74 10 E
Mendip Hills, *U.K.* **11 F5** 51 17N 2 40W
Mendocino, *U.S.A.* **82 G2** 39 19N 123 48W
Mendocino, C., *U.S.A.* **82 F1** 40 26N 124 25W
Mendota, *Calif., U.S.A.* **84 J6** 36 45N 120 23W
Mendota, *Ill., U.S.A.* **80 E10** 41 33N 89 7W
Mendoza, *Argentina* **94 C2** 32 50S 68 52W
Mendoza □, *Argentina* **94 C2** 33 0S 69 0W
Mene Grande, *Venezuela* **92 B4** 9 49N 70 56W
Menemen, *Turkey* **21 E12** 38 34N 27 3 E
Menen, *Belgium* **15 D3** 50 47N 3 7 E
Menggala, *Indonesia* **36 E3** 4 30S 105 15 E
Mengjin, *China* **34 G7** 34 55N 112 45 E
Mengyin, *China* **35 G9** 35 40N 117 58 E
Mengzi, *China* **32 D5** 23 20N 103 22 E
Menihek, *Canada* **71 B6** 54 28N 56 36W
Menihek L., *Canada* **71 B6** 54 0N 67 0W
Menin = Menen, *Belgium* **15 D3** 50 47N 3 7 E
Menlo Park, *U.S.A.* **84 H4** 37 27N 122 12W
Menominee, *U.S.A.* **76 C2** 45 6N 87 37W
Menominee →, *U.S.A.* **76 C2** 45 6N 87 36W
Menomonie, *U.S.A.* **80 C9** 44 53N 91 55W
Menongue, *Angola* **53 G3** 14 48S 17 52 E
Menorca, *Spain* **22 B11** 40 0N 4 0 E
Mentakab, *Malaysia* **39 L4** 3 29N 102 21 E
Mentawai, Kepulauan, *Indonesia* **36 E1** 2 0S 99 0 E
Menton, *France* **18 E7** 43 50N 7 29 E
Mentor, *U.S.A.* **78 E3** 41 40N 81 21W
Menzelinsk, *Russia* **24 C9** 55 47N 53 11 E
Menzies, *Australia* **61 E3** 29 40S 121 2 E
Meob B., *Namibia* **56 B2** 24 25S 14 34 E
Me'ona, *Israel* **47 B4** 33 1N 35 15 E
Meoqui, *Mexico* **86 B3** 28 17N 105 29W
Mepaco, *Mozam.* **55 F3** 15 57S 30 48 E
Meppel, *Neths.* **15 B6** 52 42N 6 12 E
Merabéllou, Kólpos, *Greece* **23 D7** 35 10N 25 50 E
Merak, *Indonesia* **37 F12** 6 10N 106 26 E
Meramangye, L., *Australia* **61 E5** 28 25S 132 13 E
Meran = Merano, *Italy* **20 A4** 46 40N 11 9 E
Merano, *Italy* **20 A4** 46 40N 11 9 E
Merauke, *Indonesia* **37 F10** 8 29S 140 24 E
Merca, *Somali Rep.* **46 G3** 1 48N 44 50 E
Merced, *U.S.A.* **84 H6** 37 18N 120 29W
Merced →, *U.S.A.* **84 H6** 37 21N 120 59W
Merced Pk., *U.S.A.* **84 H7** 37 36N 119 24W
Mercedes, *Buenos Aires, Argentina* **94 C4** 34 40S 59 30W
Mercedes, *Corrientes, Argentina* **94 B4** 29 10S 58 5W
Mercedes, *San Luis, Argentina* **94 C2** 33 40S 65 21W
Mercedes, *Uruguay* **94 C4** 33 12S 58 0W
Mercedes, *U.S.A.* **81 M6** 26 9N 97 55W
Merceditas, *Chile* **94 B1** 28 20S 70 35W
Mercer, *N.Z.* **59 G5** 37 16S 175 5 E
Mercer, *U.S.A.* **78 E4** 41 14N 80 15W
Mercer Island, *U.S.A.* **84 C4** 47 35N 122 15W
Mercury, *U.S.A.* **85 J11** 36 40N 115 58W
Mercy C., *Canada* **69 B13** 65 0N 63 30W
Mere, *U.K.* **11 F5** 51 6N 2 16W
Meredith, C., *Falk. Is.* **96 G4** 52 15S 60 40W
Meredith, L., *U.S.A.* **81 H4** 35 43N 101 33W
Mergui, *Burma* **38 F2** 12 26N 98 34 E
Mergui Arch. = Myeik Kyunzu, *Burma* **39 G1** 11 30N 97 30 E
Mérida, *Mexico* **87 C7** 20 58N 89 37W
Mérida, *Spain* **19 C2** 38 55N 6 25W
Mérida, *Venezuela* **92 B4** 8 24N 71 8W
Mérida, Cord. de, *Venezuela* **92 B4** 9 0N 71 0W
Meriden, *U.K.* **11 E6** 52 26N 1 38W
Meriden, *U.S.A.* **79 E12** 41 32N 72 48W
Meridian, *Calif., U.S.A.* **84 F5** 39 9N 121 55W
Meridian, *Idaho, U.S.A.* **82 E5** 43 37N 116 24W
Meridian, *Miss., U.S.A.* **77 J1** 32 22N 88 42W
Merinda, *Australia* **62 C4** 20 2S 148 11 E
Merir, *Pac. Oc.* **37 D8** 4 10N 132 30 E
Merirumã, *Brazil* **93 C8** 1 15N 54 50W
Merkel, *U.S.A.* **81 J5** 32 28N 100 1W
Mermaid Reef, *Australia* **60 C2** 17 6S 119 36 E
Merredin, *Australia* **61 F2** 31 28S 118 18 E
Merrick, *U.K.* **12 F4** 55 8N 4 28W
Merrickville, *Canada* **79 B9** 44 55N 75 50W
Merrill, *Oreg., U.S.A.* **82 E3** 42 1N 121 36W
Merrill, *Wis., U.S.A.* **80 C10** 45 11N 89 41W
Merrimack →, *U.S.A.* **79 D14** 42 49N 70 49W
Merriman, *U.S.A.* **80 D4** 42 55N 101 42W
Merritt, *Canada* **72 C4** 50 10N 120 45W
Merritt Island, *U.S.A.* **77 L5** 28 21N 80 42W
Merry I., *Canada* **70 A4** 55 29N 77 31W
Merryville, *U.S.A.* **81 K8** 30 45N 93 33W
Mersch, *Lux.* **15 E6** 49 44N 6 7 E
Mersea I., *U.K.* **11 F8** 51 47N 0 58 E
Merseburg, *Germany* **16 C6** 51 22N 11 59 E
Mersey →, *U.K.* **10 D4** 53 25N 3 1W
Merseyside □, *U.K.* **10 D4** 53 31N 3 2W
Mersin, *Turkey* **25 G5** 36 51N 34 36 E
Mersing, *Malaysia* **39 L4** 2 25N 103 50 E
Merta, *India* **42 F6** 26 39N 74 4 E
Merta Road, *India* **42 F5** 26 43N 73 55 E
Merthyr Tydfil, *U.K.* **11 F4** 51 45N 3 22W
Merthyr Tydfil □, *U.K.* **11 F4** 51 46N 3 21W
Mértola, *Portugal* **19 D2** 37 40N 7 40W
Mertzon, *U.S.A.* **81 K4** 31 16N 100 49W
Meru, *Kenya* **54 B4** 0 3N 37 40 E
Meru, *Tanzania* **54 C4** 3 15S 36 46 E
Mesa, *U.S.A.* **83 K8** 33 25N 111 50W
Mesa Verde National Park, *U.S.A.* **83 H9** 37 11N 108 29W
Mesanagrós, *Greece* **23 C9** 36 1N 27 49 E
Mesaoría □, *Cyprus* **23 D12** 35 12N 33 14 E
Mesarás, Kólpos, *Greece* **23 D6** 35 6N 24 47 E
Mesgouez, L., *Canada* **70 B5** 51 20N 75 0W
Meshed = Mashhad, *Iran* **45 B8** 36 20N 59 35 E
Meshoppen, *U.S.A.* **79 E8** 41 36N 76 3W
Mesilinka →, *Canada* **72 B4** 56 6N 124 30W
Mesilla, *U.S.A.* **83 K10** 32 16N 106 48W
Mesolóngion, *Greece* **21 E9** 38 21N 21 28 E
Mesopotamia = Al Jazirah, *Iraq* **44 C5** 33 30N 44 0 E
Mesopotamia, *U.S.A.* **78 E4** 41 27N 80 57W
Mesquite, *U.S.A.* **83 H6** 36 47N 114 6W
Messaad, *Algeria* **50 B6** 34 8N 3 30 E
Messalo →, *Mozam.* **55 E4** 12 25S 39 15 E
Messina, *Italy* **20 E6** 38 11N 15 34 E
Messina, *S. Africa* **57 C5** 22 20S 30 5 E
Messina, Str. di, *Italy* **20 F6** 38 15N 15 35 E
Messíni, *Greece* **21 F10** 37 4N 22 1 E
Messiniakós Kólpos, *Greece* **21 F10** 36 45N 22 5 E
Messonghi, *Greece* **23 B3** 39 29N 19 56 E
Mesta →, *Bulgaria* **21 D11** 40 54N 24 49 E
Meta →, *S. Amer.* **92 B5** 6 12N 67 28W
Meta Incognita Peninsula, *Canada* **69 B13** 62 40N 68 0W
Metabetchouan, *Canada* **71 C5** 48 26N 71 52W
Metairie, *U.S.A.* **81 L9** 29 58N 90 10W
Metaline Falls, *U.S.A.* **82 B5** 48 52N 117 22W
Metán, *Argentina* **94 B3** 25 30S 65 0W
Metangula, *Mozam.* **55 E3** 12 40S 34 50 E
Metengobalame, *Mozam.* **55 E3** 14 49S 34 30 E
Methven, *N.Z.* **59 K3** 43 38S 171 40 E
Metil, *Mozam.* **55 F4** 16 24S 39 0 E
Metlakatla, *U.S.A.* **68 C6** 55 8N 131 35W
Metropolis, *U.S.A.* **81 G10** 37 9N 88 44W
Metu, *Ethiopia* **46 F2** 8 18N 35 35 E
Metz, *France* **18 B7** 49 8N 6 10 E
Meulaboh, *Indonesia* **36 D1** 4 11N 96 3 E
Meureudu, *Indonesia* **36 C1** 5 19N 96 10 E
Meuse →, *Europe* **18 A6** 50 45N 5 41 E
Mexia, *U.S.A.* **81 K6** 31 41N 96 29W
Mexiana, I., *Brazil* **93 D9** 0 0 49 30W
Mexicali, *Mexico* **85 N11** 32 40N 115 30W
Mexican Plateau, *Mexico* **66 G9** 25 0N 104 0W
Mexican Water, *U.S.A.* **83 H9** 36 57N 109 32W
México, *Mexico* **87 D5** 19 20N 99 10W
Mexico, *Maine, U.S.A.* **79 B14** 44 34N 70 33W
Mexico, *Mo., U.S.A.* **80 F9** 39 10N 91 53W
Mexico, *N.Y., U.S.A.* **79 C8** 43 28N 76 18W
México □, *Mexico* **87 D5** 19 20N 99 10W
Mexico ■, *Cent. Amer.* **86 C4** 25 0N 105 0W
Mexico, G. of, *Cent. Amer.* **87 C7** 25 0N 90 0W
Mexico B., *U.S.A.* **79 C8** 43 35N 76 20W
Meydān-e Naftūn, *Iran* **45 D6** 31 56N 49 18 E
Meydani, Ra's-e, *Iran* **45 E8** 25 24N 59 6 E
Meymaneh, *Afghan.* **40 B4** 35 53N 64 38 E
Mezen, *Russia* **24 A7** 65 50N 44 20 E
Mezen →, *Russia* **24 A7** 65 44N 44 22 E
Mézenc, Mt., *France* **18 D6** 44 54N 4 11 E
Mezhdurechenskiy, *Russia* **26 D7** 59 36N 65 56 E
Mezőkövesd, *Hungary* **17 E11** 47 49N 20 35 E
Mezőtúr, *Hungary* **17 E11** 47 1N 20 41 E
Mezquital, *Mexico* **86 C4** 23 29N 104 23W
Mfolozi →, *S. Africa* **57 D5** 28 25S 32 26 E
Mgeta, *Tanzania* **55 D4** 8 22S 36 6 E
Mhlaba Hills, *Zimbabwe* **55 F3** 18 30S 30 30 E
Mhow, *India* **42 H6** 22 33N 75 50 E
Miahuatlán, *Mexico* **87 D5** 16 21N 96 36W
Miami, *Fla., U.S.A.* **77 N5** 25 47N 80 11W
Miami, *Okla., U.S.A.* **81 G7** 36 53N 94 53W
Miami, *Tex., U.S.A.* **81 H4** 35 42N 100 38W
Miami Beach, *U.S.A.* **77 N5** 25 47N 80 8W
Mian Xian, *China* **34 H4** 33 10N 106 32 E
Mianchi, *China* **34 G6** 34 48N 111 48 E
Miāndarreh, *Iran* **45 C7** 35 37N 53 39 E
Miāndowāb, *Iran* **44 B5** 37 0N 46 5 E
Miandrivazo, *Madag.* **57 B8** 19 31S 45 29 E
Miāneh, *Iran* **44 B5** 37 30N 47 40 E
Mianwali, *Pakistan* **42 C4** 32 38N 71 28 E
Miarinarivo, *Antananarivo, Madag.* **57 B8** 18 57S 46 55 E
Miarinarivo, *Toamasina, Madag.* **57 B8** 16 38S 48 15 E
Miariravaratra, *Madag.* **57 C8** 20 13S 47 31 E
Miass, *Russia* **24 D11** 54 59N 60 6 E
Mica, *S. Africa* **57 C5** 24 10S 30 48 E
Michalovce, *Slovak Rep.* **17 D11** 48 47N 21 58 E
Michigan □, *U.S.A.* **76 C3** 44 0N 85 0W
Michigan, L., *U.S.A.* **76 D2** 44 0N 87 0W
Michigan City, *U.S.A.* **76 E2** 41 43N 86 54W
Michipicoten I., *Canada* **70 C2** 47 40N 85 40W
Michoacan □, *Mexico* **86 D4** 19 0N 102 0W
Michurin, *Bulgaria* **21 C12** 42 9N 27 51 E
Michurinsk, *Russia* **24 D7** 52 58N 40 27 E
Mico, Pta., *Nic.* **88 D3** 12 0N 83 30W
Micronesia, *Pac. Oc.* **64 G7** 11 0N 160 0 E
Micronesia, Federated States of ■, *Pac. Oc.* **64 G7** 9 0N 150 0 E
Midai, *Indonesia* **39 L6** 3 0N 107 47 E
Midale, *Canada* **73 D8** 49 25N 103 20W
Middelburg, *Neths.* **15 C3** 51 30N 3 36 E
Middelburg, *Eastern Cape, S. Africa* **56 E4** 31 30S 25 0 E
Middelburg, *Mpumalanga, S. Africa* **57 D4** 25 49S 29 28 E
Middelpos, *S. Africa* **56 E3** 31 55S 20 13 E
Middelwit, *S. Africa* **56 C4** 24 51S 27 3 E
Middle Alkali L., *U.S.A.* **82 F3** 41 27N 120 5W
Middle Bass I., *U.S.A.* **78 E2** 41 41N 82 49W
Middle East, *Asia* **28 F7** 38 0N 40 0 E
Middle Fork Feather →, *U.S.A.* **84 F5** 38 33N 121 30W
Middle I., *Australia* **61 F3** 34 6S 123 11 E
Middle Loup →, *U.S.A.* **80 E5** 41 17N 98 24W
Middle Sackville, *Canada* **71 D7** 44 47N 63 42W
Middleboro, *U.S.A.* **79 E14** 41 54N 70 55W
Middleburg, *Fla., U.S.A.* **77 K5** 30 4N 81 52W
Middleburg, *N.Y., U.S.A.* **79 D10** 42 36N 74 20W
Middleburg, *Pa., U.S.A.* **78 F7** 40 47N 77 3W
Middlebury, *U.S.A.* **79 B11** 44 1N 73 10W
Middlemount, *Australia* **62 C4** 22 50S 148 40 E
Middleport, *N.Y., U.S.A.* **78 C6** 43 13N 78 29W
Middleport, *Ohio, U.S.A.* **76 F4** 39 0N 82 3W
Middlesboro, *U.S.A.* **77 G4** 36 36N 83 43W
Middlesbrough, *U.K.* **10 C6** 54 35N 1 13W
Middlesbrough □, *U.K.* **10 C6** 54 28N 1 13W
Middlesex, *Belize* **88 C2** 17 2N 88 31W
Middlesex, *N.J., U.S.A.* **79 F10** 40 36N 74 30W
Middlesex, *N.Y., U.S.A.* **78 D7** 42 42N 77 16W
Middleton, *Australia* **62 C3** 22 22S 141 32 E
Middleton, *Canada* **71 D6** 44 57N 65 4W
Middleton Cr. →, *Australia* **62 C3** 22 35S 141 51 E
Middletown, *U.K.* **13 B5** 54 17N 6 51W
Middletown, *Calif., U.S.A.* **84 G4** 38 45N 122 37W
Middletown, *Conn., U.S.A.* **79 E12** 41 34N 72 39W
Middletown, *N.Y., U.S.A.* **79 E10** 41 27N 74 25W
Middletown, *Ohio, U.S.A.* **76 F3** 39 31N 84 24W
Middletown, *Pa., U.S.A.* **79 F8** 40 12N 76 44W
Midhurst, *U.K.* **11 G7** 50 59N 0 44W
Midi, Canal du →, *France* **18 E4** 43 45N 1 21 E
Midland, *Canada* **78 B5** 44 45N 79 50W
Midland, *Calif., U.S.A.* **85 M12** 33 52N 114 48W
Midland, *Mich., U.S.A.* **76 D3** 43 37N 84 14W
Midland, *Pa., U.S.A.* **78 F4** 40 39N 80 27W
Midland, *Tex., U.S.A.* **81 K3** 32 0N 102 3W
Midlands □, *Zimbabwe* **55 F2** 19 40S 29 0 E
Midleton, *Ireland* **13 E3** 51 55N 8 10W
Midlothian, *U.S.A.* **81 J6** 32 30N 97 0W
Midlothian □, *U.K.* **12 F5** 55 51N 3 5W
Midongy, Tangorombohitr' i, *Madag.* **57 C8** 23 30S 47 0 E
Midongy Atsimo, *Madag.* **57 C8** 23 35S 47 1 E
Midway Is., *Pac. Oc.* **64 E10** 28 13N 177 22W
Midway Wells, *U.S.A.* **85 N11** 32 41N 115 7W
Midwest, *U.S.A.* **82 E10** 43 25N 106 16W
Midwest City, *U.S.A.* **81 H6** 35 27N 97 24W
Midyat, *Turkey* **44 B4** 37 25N 41 23 E
Midžor, *Bulgaria* **21 C10** 43 24N 22 40 E
Mie □, *Japan* **31 G8** 34 30N 136 10 E
Międzychód, *Poland* **16 B8** 52 35N 15 53 E
Międzyrzec Podlaski, *Poland* **17 C12** 51 58N 22 45 E
Mielec, *Poland* **17 C11** 50 15N 21 25 E
Mienga, *Angola* **56 B2** 17 12S 19 48 E
Miercurea-Ciuc, *Romania* **17 E13** 46 21N 25 48 E
Mieres, *Spain* **19 A3** 43 18N 5 48W
Mifflintown, *U.S.A.* **78 F7** 40 34N 77 24W
Mifraz Hefa, *Israel* **47 C4** 32 52N 35 0 E
Miguel Alemán, Presa, *Mexico* **87 D5** 18 15N 96 40W
Mihara, *Japan* **31 G6** 34 24N 133 5 E
Mikese, *Tanzania* **54 D4** 6 48S 37 55 E
Mikhaylovgrad = Montana, *Bulgaria* **21 C10** 43 27N 23 16 E
Mikhaylovka, *Russia* **25 D7** 50 3N 43 5 E
Mikkeli, *Finland* **9 F22** 61 43N 27 15 E
Mikkwa →, *Canada* **72 B6** 58 25N 114 46W
Míkonos, *Greece* **21 F11** 37 30N 25 25 E
Mikumi, *Tanzania* **54 D4** 7 26S 37 0 E
Mikun, *Russia* **24 B9** 62 20N 50 0 E
Milaca, *U.S.A.* **80 C8** 45 45N 93 39W
Milagro, *Ecuador* **92 D3** 2 11S 79 36W
Milan = Milano, *Italy* **18 D8** 45 28N 9 12 E
Milan, *Mo., U.S.A.* **80 E8** 40 12N 93 7W
Milan, *Tenn., U.S.A.* **77 H1** 35 55N 88 46W
Milange, *Mozam.* **55 F4** 16 3S 35 45 E
Milano, *Italy* **18 D8** 45 28N 9 12 E
Milanoa, *Madag.* **57 A8** 13 35S 49 47 E
Milâs, *Turkey* **21 F12** 37 20N 27 50 E
Mílatos, *Greece* **23 D7** 35 18N 25 34 E
Milazzo, *Italy* **20 E6** 38 13N 15 15 E
Milbank, *U.S.A.* **80 C6** 45 13N 96 38W
Milbanke Sd., *Canada* **72 C3** 52 15N 128 35W
Milden, *Canada* **73 C7** 51 29N 107 32W
Mildenhall, *U.K.* **11 E8** 52 21N 0 32 E
Mildmay, *Canada* **78 B3** 44 3N 81 7W
Miles, *Australia* **63 D5** 26 40S 150 9 E
Miles City, *U.S.A.* **80 B2** 46 25N 105 51W
Milestone, *Canada* **73 D8** 49 59N 104 31W
Miletus, *Turkey* **21 F12** 37 30N 27 18 E
Milford, *Calif., U.S.A.* **84 E6** 40 10N 120 22W
Milford, *Conn., U.S.A.* **79 E11** 41 14N 73 3W
Milford, *Del., U.S.A.* **76 F8** 38 55N 75 26W
Milford, *Mass., U.S.A.* **79 D13** 42 8N 71 31W
Milford, *N.H., U.S.A.* **79 D13** 42 50N 71 39W
Milford, *Pa., U.S.A.* **79 E10** 41 19N 74 48W
Milford, *Utah, U.S.A.* **83 G7** 38 24N 113 1W
Milford Haven, *U.K.* **11 F2** 51 42N 5 7W
Milford Sd., *N.Z.* **59 L1** 44 41S 167 47 E
Milh, Bahr al, *Iraq* **44 C4** 32 40N 43 35 E
Milikapiti, *Australia* **60 B5** 11 26S 130 40 E
Miling, *Australia* **61 F2** 30 30S 116 17 E
Milk →, *U.S.A.* **82 B10** 48 4N 106 19W
Milk River, *Canada* **72 D6** 49 10N 112 5W
Mill I., *Antarctica* **5 C8** 66 0S 101 30 E
Mill Valley, *U.S.A.* **84 H4** 37 54N 122 32W
Millau, *France* **18 D5** 44 8N 3 4 E
Millbridge, *Canada* **78 B7** 44 41N 77 36W
Millbrook, *Canada* **78 B6** 44 10N 78 29W
Millbrook, *U.S.A.* **79 E11** 41 47N 73 42W
Mille Lacs, L. des, *Canada* **70 C1** 48 45N 90 35W
Mille Lacs L., *U.S.A.* **80 B8** 46 15N 93 39W
Milledgeville, *U.S.A.* **77 J4** 33 5N 83 14W
Millen, *U.S.A.* **77 J5** 32 48N 81 57W
Millennium I. = Caroline I., *Kiribati* **65 H12** 9 15S 150 3W
Miller, *U.S.A.* **80 C5** 44 31N 98 59W
Millersburg, *Ohio, U.S.A.* **78 F3** 40 33N 81 55W
Millersburg, *Pa., U.S.A.* **78 F8** 40 32N 76 58W
Millerton, *U.S.A.* **79 E11** 41 57N 73 31W
Millerton L., *U.S.A.* **84 J7** 37 1N 119 41W
Millheim, *U.S.A.* **78 F7** 40 54N 77 29W
Millington, *U.S.A.* **81 H10** 35 20N 89 53W
Millinocket, *U.S.A.* **77 C11** 45 39N 68 43W
Millmerran, *Australia* **63 D5** 27 53S 151 16 E
Millom, *U.K.* **10 C4** 54 13N 3 16W
Mills L., *Canada* **72 A5** 61 30N 118 20W
Millsboro, *U.S.A.* **78 G5** 40 0N 80 0W
Milltown Malbay, *Ireland* **13 D2** 52 52N 9 24W
Millville, *N.J., U.S.A.* **76 F8** 39 24N 75 2W
Millville, *Pa., U.S.A.* **79 E8** 41 7N 76 32W
Millwood L., *U.S.A.* **81 J8** 33 42N 93 58W
Milne →, *Australia* **62 C2** 21 10S 137 33 E
Milo, *U.S.A.* **77 C11** 45 15N 68 59W
Milos, *Greece* **21 F11** 36 44N 24 25 E
Milparinka, *Australia* **63 D3** 29 46S 141 57 E
Milton, *N.S., Canada* **71 D7** 44 4N 64 45W
Milton, *Ont., Canada* **78 C5** 43 31N 79 53W
Milton, *N.Z.* **59 M2** 46 7S 169 59 E
Milton, *Calif., U.S.A.* **84 G6** 38 3N 120 51W
Milton, *Fla., U.S.A.* **77 K2** 30 38N 87 3W
Milton, *Pa., U.S.A.* **78 F8** 41 1N 76 51W
Milton, *Vt., U.S.A.* **79 B11** 44 38N 73 7W
Milton-Freewater, *U.S.A.* **82 D4** 45 56N 118 23W
Milton Keynes, *U.K.* **11 E7** 52 1N 0 44W
Milton Keynes □, *U.K.* **11 E7** 52 1N 0 44W
Milverton, *Canada* **78 C4** 43 34N 80 55W
Milwaukee, *U.S.A.* **76 D2** 43 2N 87 55W
Milwaukee Deep, *Atl. Oc.* **89 C6** 19 50N 68 0W
Milwaukie, *U.S.A.* **84 E4** 45 27N 122 38W
Min Jiang →, *Fujian, China* **33 D6** 26 0N 119 35 E
Min Jiang →, *Sichuan, China* **32 D5** 28 45N 104 40 E
Min Xian, *China* **34 G3** 34 25N 104 5 E
Mina Pirquitas, *Argentina* **94 A2** 22 40S 66 30W
Mīnā Su'ud, *Si. Arabia* **45 D6** 28 45N 48 28 E
Mīnā'al Aḥmadī, *Kuwait* **45 D6** 29 5N 48 10 E
Minago →, *Canada* **73 C9** 54 33N 98 59W
Minaki, *Canada* **73 D10** 49 59N 94 40W
Minamata, *Japan* **31 H5** 32 10N 130 30 E
Minami-Tori-Shima, *Pac. Oc.* **64 E7** 24 20N 153 58 E
Minas, *Uruguay* **95 C4** 34 20S 55 10W
Minas, Sierra de las, *Guatemala* **88 C2** 15 9N 89 31W
Minas Basin, *Canada* **71 C7** 45 20N 64 12W
Minas Gerais □, *Brazil* **93 G9** 18 50S 46 0W
Minatitlán, *Mexico* **87 D6** 17 59N 94 31W
Minbu, *Burma* **41 J19** 20 10N 94 52 E
Minchinabad, *Pakistan* **42 D5** 30 10N 73 34 E
Mindanao, *Phil.* **37 C6** 8 0N 125 0 E
Mindanao Sea = Bohol Sea, *Phil.* **37 C6** 9 0N 124 0 E
Mindanao Trench, *Pac. Oc.* **37 B7** 12 0N 126 6 E
Minden, *Canada* **78 B6** 44 55N 78 43W
Minden, *Germany* **16 B5** 52 17N 8 55 E
Minden, *La., U.S.A.* **81 J8** 32 37N 93 17W
Minden, *Nev., U.S.A.* **84 G7** 38 57N 119 46W
Mindiptana, *Indonesia* **37 F10** 5 55S 140 22 E
Mindoro, *Phil.* **37 B6** 13 0N 121 0 E
Mindoro Str., *Phil.* **37 B6** 12 30N 120 30 E
Mine, *Japan* **31 G5** 34 12N 131 7 E
Minehead, *U.K.* **11 F4** 51 12N 3 29W
Mineola, *N.Y., U.S.A.* **79 F11** 40 45N 73 39W
Mineola, *Tex., U.S.A.* **81 J7** 32 40N 95 29W
Mineral King, *U.S.A.* **84 J8** 36 27N 118 36W
Mineral Wells, *U.S.A.* **81 J5** 32 48N 98 7W
Minersville, *U.S.A.* **79 F8** 40 41N 76 16W
Minerva, *U.S.A.* **78 F3** 40 44N 81 6W
Minetto, *U.S.A.* **79 C8** 43 24N 76 28W

Montgomery

Mingäçevir Su Anbarı, Azerbaijan 25 F8 40 57N 46 50 E
Mingan, Canada 71 B7 50 20N 64 0W
Mingechaurskoye Vdkhr. = Mingäçevir Su Anbarı, Azerbaijan 25 F8 40 57N 46 50 E
Mingela, Australia 62 B4 19 52S 146 38 E
Mingenew, Australia 61 E2 29 12S 115 21 E
Mingera Cr. →, Australia 62 C2 20 38S 137 45 E
Mingin, Burma 41 H19 22 50N 94 30 E
Mingo Junction, U.S.A. 78 F4 40 19N 80 37W
Mingteke Daban = Mintaka Pass, Pakistan 43 A6 37 0N 74 58 E
Mingyuegue, China 35 C15 43 2N 128 50 E
Minho = Miño →, Spain 19 A2 41 52N 8 40W
Minho, Portugal 19 B1 41 25N 8 20W
Minidoka, U.S.A. 82 E7 42 45N 113 29W
Minigwal, L., Australia 61 E3 29 31S 123 14 E
Minilya →, Australia 61 D1 23 45S 114 0 E
Minilya Roadhouse, Australia 61 D1 23 55S 114 0 E
Minipi L., Canada 71 B7 52 25N 60 45W
Mink L., Canada 72 A5 61 54N 117 40W
Minna, Nigeria 50 G7 9 37N 6 30 E
Minneapolis, Kans., U.S.A. 80 F6 39 8N 97 42W
Minneapolis, Minn., U.S.A. 80 C8 44 59N 93 16W
Minnedosa, Canada 73 C9 50 14N 99 50W
Minnesota □, U.S.A. 80 B8 46 0N 94 15W
Minnesota →, U.S.A. 80 C8 44 54N 93 9W
Minnewaukan, U.S.A. 80 A5 48 4N 99 15W
Minnipa, Australia 63 E2 32 51S 135 9 E
Minnitaki L., Canada 70 C1 49 57N 92 10W
Mino, Japan 31 G8 35 32N 136 55 E
Miño →, Spain 19 A2 41 52N 8 40W
Minorca = Menorca, Spain 22 B11 40 0N 4 0 E
Minot, U.S.A. 80 A4 48 14N 101 18W
Minqin, China 34 E2 38 38N 103 20 E
Minsk, Belarus 17 B14 53 52N 27 30 E
Mińsk Mazowiecki, Poland 17 B11 52 10N 21 33 E
Mintabie, Australia 63 D1 27 15S 133 7 E
Mintaka Pass, Pakistan 43 A6 37 0N 74 58 E
Minto, Canada 71 C6 46 5N 66 5W
Minto, L., Canada 70 A5 57 13N 75 0W
Minton, Canada 73 D8 49 10N 104 35W
Minturn, U.S.A. 82 G10 39 35N 106 26W
Minusinsk, Russia 27 D10 53 43N 91 20 E
Minutang, India 41 E20 28 15N 96 30 E
Miquelon, Canada 70 C4 49 25N 76 27W
Miquelon, St- P. & M. 71 C8 47 8N 56 22W
Mīr Kūh, Iran 45 E8 26 22N 58 55 E
Mīr Shahdād, Iran 45 E8 26 15N 58 29 E
Mira, Italy 20 B5 45 26N 12 8 E
Mira por vos Cay, Bahamas 89 B5 22 9N 74 30W
Miraj, India 40 L9 16 50N 74 45 E
Miram Shah, Pakistan 42 C4 33 0N 70 2 E
Miramar, Argentina 94 D4 38 15S 57 50W
Miramar, Mozam. 57 C6 23 50S 35 35 E
Miramichi, Canada 71 C6 47 2N 65 28W
Miramichi B., Canada 71 C7 47 15N 65 0W
Miranda, Brazil 93 H7 20 10S 56 15W
Miranda →, Brazil 92 G7 19 25S 57 20W
Miranda de Ebro, Spain 19 A4 42 41N 2 57W
Miranda do Douro, Portugal 19 B2 41 30N 6 16W
Mirandópolis, Brazil 95 A5 21 9S 51 6W
Mirango, Malawi 55 E3 13 32S 34 58 E
Mirassol, Brazil 95 A6 20 46S 49 28W
Mirbāţ, Oman 46 D5 17 0N 54 45 E
Miri, Malaysia 36 D4 4 23N 113 59 E
Miriam Vale, Australia 62 C5 24 20S 151 33 E
Mirim, L., S. Amer. 95 C5 32 45S 52 50W
Mirnyy, Russia 27 C12 62 33N 113 53 E
Mirokhan, Pakistan 42 F3 27 46N 68 6 E
Mirond L., Canada 73 B8 55 6N 102 47W
Mirpur, Pakistan 43 C5 33 32N 73 56 E
Mirpur Batoro, Pakistan 42 G3 24 44N 68 16 E
Mirpur Bibiwari, Pakistan 42 E2 28 33N 67 44 E
Mirpur Khas, Pakistan 42 G3 25 30N 69 0 E
Mirpur Sakro, Pakistan 42 G2 24 33N 67 41 E
Mirtağ, Turkey 44 B4 38 23N 41 56 E
Miryang, S. Korea 35 G15 35 31N 128 44 E
Mirzapur, India 43 G10 25 10N 82 34 E
Mirzapur-cum-Vindhyachal = Mirzapur, India 43 G10 25 10N 82 34 E
Misantla, Mexico 87 D5 19 56N 96 50W
Misawa, Japan 30 D10 40 41N 141 24 E
Miscou I., Canada 71 C7 47 57N 64 31W
Mish'āb, Ra's al, Si. Arabia 45 D6 28 15N 48 43 E
Mishan, China 33 B8 45 37N 131 48 E
Mishawaka, U.S.A. 76 E2 41 40N 86 11W
Mishima, Japan 31 G9 35 10N 138 52 E
Misión, Mexico 85 N10 32 6N 116 53W
Misiones □, Argentina 95 B5 27 0S 55 0W
Misiones □, Paraguay 94 B4 27 0S 56 0W
Miskah, Si. Arabia 44 E4 24 49N 42 56 E
Miskitos, Cayos, Nic. 88 D3 14 26N 82 50W
Miskolc, Hungary 17 D11 48 7N 20 50 E
Misoke, Dem. Rep. of the Congo 54 C2 0 42S 28 2 E
Misool, Indonesia 37 E8 1 52S 130 10 E
Mişrātah, Libya 51 B9 32 24N 15 3 E
Missanabie, Canada 70 C3 48 20N 84 6W
Missinaibi →, Canada 70 B3 50 43N 81 29W
Missinaibi L., Canada 70 C3 48 23N 83 40W
Mission, Canada 72 D4 49 10N 122 15W
Mission, S. Dak., U.S.A. 80 D4 43 18N 100 39W
Mission, Tex., U.S.A. 81 M5 26 13N 98 20W
Mission Beach, Australia 62 B4 17 53S 146 6 E
Mission Viejo, U.S.A. 85 M9 33 36N 117 40W
Missisa L., Canada 70 B2 52 20N 85 7W
Missisicabi →, Canada 70 B4 51 14N 79 31W
Mississagi →, Canada 70 C3 46 15N 83 9W
Mississauga, Canada 78 C5 43 32N 79 35W
Mississippi □, U.S.A. 81 J10 33 0N 90 0W
Mississippi →, U.S.A. 81 L10 29 9N 89 15W
Mississippi L., Canada 79 A8 45 5N 76 10W
Mississippi River Delta, U.S.A. 81 L9 29 10N 89 15W
Mississippi Sd., U.S.A. 81 K10 30 20N 89 0W
Missoula, U.S.A. 82 C7 46 52N 114 1W
Missouri □, U.S.A. 80 F8 38 25N 92 30W
Missouri →, U.S.A. 80 F9 38 49N 90 7W
Missouri City, U.S.A. 81 L7 29 37N 95 32W
Missouri Valley, U.S.A. 80 E7 41 34N 95 53W
Mist, U.S.A. 84 E3 45 59N 123 15W
Mistassibi →, Canada 71 B5 48 53N 72 13W
Mistassini, Canada 71 C5 48 53N 72 12W
Mistassini →, Canada 71 C5 48 42N 72 20W
Mistassini, L., Canada 70 B5 51 0N 73 30W
Mistastin L., Canada 71 A7 55 57N 63 20W
Mistinibi, L., Canada 71 A7 55 56N 64 17W
Misty L., Canada 73 B8 58 53N 101 40W
Misurata = Mişrātah, Libya 51 B9 32 24N 15 3 E
Mitchell, Australia 63 D4 26 29S 147 58 E
Mitchell, Canada 78 C3 43 28N 81 12W
Mitchell, Nebr., U.S.A. 80 E3 41 57N 103 49W
Mitchell, Oreg., U.S.A. 82 D3 44 34N 120 9W
Mitchell, S. Dak., U.S.A. 80 D6 43 43N 98 2W
Mitchell →, Australia 62 B3 15 12S 141 35 E
Mitchell, Mt., U.S.A. 77 H4 35 46N 82 16W
Mitchell Ranges, Australia 62 A2 12 49S 135 36 E
Mitchelstown, Ireland 13 D3 52 15N 8 16W
Mitha Tiwana, Pakistan 42 C5 32 13N 72 6 E
Mithi, Pakistan 42 G3 24 44N 69 48 E
Mithrao, Pakistan 42 F3 27 28N 69 40 E
Mitilíni, Greece 21 E12 39 6N 26 35 E
Mito, Japan 31 F10 36 20N 140 30 E
Mitrovica = Kosovska Mitrovica, Kosovo, Yug. 21 C9 42 54N 20 52 E
Mitsinjo, Madag. 57 B8 16 1S 45 52 E
Mitsiwa, Eritrea 46 D2 15 35N 39 25 E
Mitsukaidō, Japan 31 F9 36 1N 139 59 E
Mittimatalik = Pond Inlet, Canada 69 A12 72 40N 77 0W
Mitú, Colombia 92 C4 1 15N 70 13W
Mitumba, Tanzania 54 D3 7 8S 31 2 E
Mitumba, Mts., Dem. Rep. of the Congo 54 D2 7 0S 27 30 E
Mitwaba, Dem. Rep. of the Congo 55 D2 8 2S 27 17 E
Mityana, Uganda 54 B3 0 23N 32 2 E
Mixteco →, Mexico 87 D5 18 11N 98 30W
Miyagi □, Japan 30 E10 38 15N 140 45 E
Miyāh, W. el →, Syria 44 C3 34 44N 39 57 E
Miyake-Jima, Japan 31 G9 34 5N 139 30 E
Miyako, Japan 30 E10 39 40N 141 59 E
Miyako-Jima, Japan 31 M2 24 45N 125 20 E
Miyako-Rettō, Japan 31 M2 24 24N 125 0 E
Miyakonojō, Japan 31 J5 31 40N 131 5 E
Miyani, India 42 J3 21 50N 69 26 E
Miyanoura-Dake, Japan 31 J5 30 20N 130 31 E
Miyazaki, Japan 31 J5 31 56N 131 30 E
Miyazaki □, Japan 31 H5 32 30N 131 30 E
Miyazu, Japan 31 G7 35 35N 135 10 E
Miyet, Bahr el = Dead Sea, Asia 47 D4 31 30N 35 30 E
Miyoshi, Japan 31 G6 34 48N 132 51 E
Miyun, China 34 D9 40 28N 116 50 E
Miyun Shuiku, China 35 D9 40 30N 117 0 E
Mizdah, Libya 51 B8 31 30N 13 0 E
Mizen Hd., Cork, Ireland 13 E2 51 27N 9 50W
Mizen Hd., Wick., Ireland 13 D5 52 51N 6 4W
Mizhi, China 34 F6 37 47N 110 12 E
Mizoram □, India 41 H18 23 30N 92 40 E
Mizpe Ramon, Israel 47 E3 30 34N 34 49 E
Mizusawa, Japan 30 E10 39 8N 141 8 E
Mjölby, Sweden 9 G16 58 20N 15 10 E
Mjøsa, Norway 9 F14 60 40N 11 0 E
Mkata, Tanzania 54 D4 5 45S 38 20 E
Mkokotoni, Tanzania 54 D4 5 55S 39 15 E
Mkomazi, Tanzania 54 C4 4 40S 38 7 E
Mkomazi →, S. Africa 57 E5 30 12S 30 50 E
Mkulwe, Tanzania 55 D3 8 37S 32 20 E
Mkumbi, Ras, Tanzania 54 D4 7 38S 39 55 E
Mkushi, Zambia 55 E2 14 25S 29 15 E
Mkushi River, Zambia 55 E2 13 32S 29 45 E
Mkuze, S. Africa 57 D5 27 10S 32 0 E
Mladá Boleslav, Czech Rep. 16 C8 50 27N 14 53 E
Mlala Hills, Tanzania 54 D3 6 50S 31 40 E
Mlange = Mulanje, Malawi 55 F4 16 2S 35 33 E
Mlanje, Pic, Malawi 53 H7 15 57S 35 38 E
Mława, Poland 17 B11 53 9N 20 25 E
Mljet, Croatia 20 C7 42 43N 17 30 E
Mmabatho, S. Africa 56 D4 25 49S 25 30 E
Mo i Rana, Norway 8 C16 66 20N 14 7 E
Moa, Cuba 89 B4 20 40N 74 56W
Moa, Indonesia 37 F7 8 0S 128 0 E
Moab, U.S.A. 83 G9 38 35N 109 33W
Moala, Fiji 59 D8 18 36S 179 53 E
Moama, Australia 63 F3 36 7S 144 46 E
Moamba, Mozam. 57 D5 25 36S 32 15 E
Moapa, U.S.A. 85 J12 36 40N 114 37W
Moate, Ireland 13 C4 53 24N 7 44W
Moba, Dem. Rep. of the Congo 54 D2 7 0S 29 48 E
Mobārakābād, Iran 45 D7 28 24N 53 20 E
Mobaye, C.A.R. 52 D4 4 25N 21 5 E
Mobayi, Dem. Rep. of the Congo 52 D4 4 15N 21 8 E
Moberley Lake, Canada 72 B4 55 50N 121 44W
Moberly, U.S.A. 80 F8 39 25N 92 26W
Mobile, U.S.A. 77 K1 30 41N 88 3W
Mobile B., U.S.A. 77 K2 30 30N 88 0W
Mobridge, U.S.A. 80 C4 45 32N 100 26W
Mobutu Sese Seko, L. = Albert, L., Africa 54 B3 1 30N 31 0 E
Moc Chau, Vietnam 38 B5 20 50N 104 38 E
Moc Hoa, Vietnam 39 G5 10 46N 105 56 E
Mocabe Kasari, Dem. Rep. of the Congo 55 D2 9 58S 26 12 E
Moçambique, Mozam. 55 F5 15 3S 40 42 E
Moçâmedes = Namibe, Angola 53 H2 15 7S 12 11 E
Mocanaqua, U.S.A. 79 E8 41 9N 76 8W
Mochudi, Botswana 56 C4 24 27S 26 7 E
Mocimboa da Praia, Mozam. 55 E5 11 25S 40 20 E
Moclips, U.S.A. 84 C2 47 14N 124 13W
Mocoa, Colombia 92 C3 1 7N 76 35W
Mococa, Brazil 95 A6 21 28S 47 0W
Mocorito, Mexico 86 B3 25 30N 107 53W
Moctezuma, Mexico 86 B3 29 50N 109 0W
Moctezuma →, Mexico 87 C5 21 59N 98 34W
Mocuba, Mozam. 55 F4 16 54S 36 57 E
Mocúzari, Presa, Mexico 86 B3 27 10N 109 10W
Modane, France 18 D7 45 12N 6 40 E
Modasa, India 42 H5 23 30N 73 21 E
Modder →, S. Africa 56 D3 29 2S 24 37 E
Modderrivier, S. Africa 56 D3 29 2S 24 38 E
Módena, Italy 20 B4 44 40N 10 55 E
Modena, U.S.A. 83 H7 37 48N 113 56W
Modesto, U.S.A. 84 H6 37 39N 121 0W
Módica, Italy 20 F6 36 52N 14 46 E
Moebase, Mozam. 55 F4 17 3S 38 41 E
Moengo, Surinam 93 B8 5 45N 54 20W
Moffat, U.K. 12 F5 55 21N 3 27W
Moga, India 42 D6 30 48N 75 8 E
Mogadishu = Muqdisho, Somali Rep. 46 G4 2 2N 45 25 E
Mogador = Essaouira, Morocco 50 B4 31 32N 9 42W
Mogalakwena →, S. Africa 57 C4 22 38S 28 40 E
Mogami-Gawa →, Japan 30 E10 38 45N 140 0 E
Mogán, Canary Is. 22 G4 27 53N 15 43W
Mogaung, Burma 41 G20 25 20N 97 0 E
Mogi das Cruzes, Brazil 95 A6 23 31S 46 11W
Mogi-Guaçu →, Brazil 95 A6 20 53S 48 10W
Mogi-Mirim, Brazil 95 A6 22 29S 47 0W
Mogilev = Mahilyow, Belarus 17 B16 53 55N 30 18 E
Mogilev-Podolskiy = Mohyliv-Podilskyy, Ukraine 17 D14 48 26N 27 48 E
Mogincual, Mozam. 55 F5 15 35S 40 25 E
Mogocha, Russia 27 D12 53 40N 119 50 E
Mogok, Burma 41 H20 23 0N 96 40 E
Mogollon Rim, U.S.A. 83 J8 34 10N 110 50W
Mogumber, Australia 61 F2 31 2S 116 3 E
Mohács, Hungary 17 F10 45 58N 18 41 E
Mohales Hoek, Lesotho 56 E4 30 7S 27 26 E
Mohall, U.S.A. 80 A4 48 46N 101 31W
Moḥammadābād, Iran 45 B8 37 52N 59 5 E
Mohammedia, Morocco 50 B4 33 44N 7 21W
Mohana →, India 43 G11 24 43N 85 0 E
Mohanlalganj, India 43 F9 26 41N 80 58 E
Mohave, L., U.S.A. 85 K12 35 12N 114 34W
Mohawk →, U.S.A. 79 D11 42 47N 73 41W
Mohenjodaro, Pakistan 42 F3 27 19N 68 7 E
Mohicanville Reservoir, U.S.A. 78 F3 40 45N 82 0W
Mohoro, Tanzania 54 D4 8 6S 39 8 E
Mohyliv-Podilskyy, Ukraine 17 D14 48 26N 27 48 E
Moidart, L., U.K. 12 E3 56 47N 5 52W
Moira →, Canada 78 B7 44 21N 77 24W
Moíres, Greece 23 D6 35 4N 24 56 E
Moisaküla, Estonia 9 G21 58 3N 25 12 E
Moisie, Canada 71 B6 50 12N 66 1W
Moisie →, Canada 71 B6 50 14N 66 5W
Mojave, U.S.A. 85 K8 35 3N 118 10W
Mojave Desert, U.S.A. 85 L10 35 0N 116 30W
Mojo, Bolivia 94 A2 21 48S 65 33W
Mojokerto, Indonesia 37 G15 7 28S 112 26 E
Mokai, N.Z. 59 H5 38 32S 175 56 E
Mokambo, Dem. Rep. of the Congo 55 E2 12 25S 28 20 E
Mokameh, India 43 G11 25 24N 85 55 E
Mokau, N.Z. 59 H5 38 42S 174 39 E
Mokelumne →, U.S.A. 84 G5 38 13N 121 28W
Mokelumne Hill, U.S.A. 84 G6 38 18N 120 43W
Mokhós, Greece 23 D7 35 16N 25 27 E
Mokhotlong, Lesotho 57 D4 29 22S 29 2 E
Mokokchung, India 41 F19 26 15N 94 30 E
Mokolo →, S. Africa 57 C4 23 14S 27 43 E
Mokp'o, S. Korea 35 G14 34 50N 126 25 E
Mokra Gora, Yugoslavia 21 C9 42 50N 20 30 E
Mol, Belgium 15 C5 51 11N 5 5 E
Molchanovo, Russia 26 D9 57 40N 83 50 E
Mold, U.K. 10 D4 53 9N 3 8W
Moldavia = Moldova ■, Europe 17 E15 47 0N 28 0 E
Molde, Norway 8 E12 62 45N 7 9 E
Moldova ■, Europe 17 E15 47 0N 28 0 E
Moldoveanu, Vf., Romania 17 F13 45 36N 24 45 E
Mole →, U.K. 11 F7 51 24N 0 21W
Mole Creek, Australia 62 G4 41 34S 146 24 E
Molepolole, Botswana 56 C4 24 28S 25 28 E
Molfetta, Italy 20 D7 41 12N 16 36 E
Moline, U.S.A. 80 E9 41 30N 90 31W
Molinos, Argentina 94 B2 25 28S 66 15W
Moliro, Dem. Rep. of the Congo 54 D3 8 12S 30 30 E
Mollendo, Peru 92 G4 17 0S 72 0W
Mollerin, L., Australia 61 F2 30 30S 117 35 E
Molodechno = Maladzyechna, Belarus 17 A14 54 20N 26 50 E
Molokai, U.S.A. 74 H16 21 8N 157 0W
Molopo →, Africa 56 D3 27 30S 20 13 E
Molotov = Perm, Russia 24 C10 58 0N 56 10 E
Molson L., Canada 73 C9 54 22N 96 40W
Molteno, S. Africa 56 E4 31 22S 26 22 E
Molu, Indonesia 37 F8 6 45S 131 40 E
Molucca Sea, Indonesia 37 E6 0 0 125 0 E
Moluccas = Maluku, Indonesia 37 E7 1 0S 127 0 E
Moma, Dem. Rep. of the Congo 54 C1 1 35S 23 52 E
Moma, Mozam. 55 F4 16 47S 39 4 E
Mombasa, Kenya 54 C4 4 2S 39 43 E
Mombetsu, Japan 30 B11 44 21N 143 22 E
Momchilgrad, Bulgaria 21 D11 41 33N 25 23 E
Momi, Dem. Rep. of the Congo 54 C2 1 42S 27 0 E
Mompós, Colombia 92 B4 9 14N 74 26W
Møn, Denmark 9 J15 54 57N 12 20 E
Mon □, Burma 41 L20 16 0N 97 30 E
Mona, Canal de la, W. Indies 89 C6 18 30N 67 45W
Mona, Isla, Puerto Rico 89 C6 18 5N 67 54W
Mona, Pta., Costa Rica 88 E3 9 37N 82 36W
Monaca, U.S.A. 78 F4 40 41N 80 17W
Monaco ■, Europe 18 E7 43 46N 7 23 E
Monadhliath Mts., U.K. 12 D4 57 10N 4 4W
Monadnock, Mt., U.S.A. 79 D12 42 52N 72 7W
Monaghan, Ireland 13 B5 54 15N 6 57W
Monaghan □, Ireland 13 B5 54 11N 6 56W
Monahans, U.S.A. 81 K3 31 36N 102 54W
Monapo, Mozam. 55 E5 14 56S 40 19 E
Monar, L., U.K. 12 D3 57 26N 5 8W
Monarch Mt., Canada 72 C3 51 55N 125 57W
Monashee Mts., Canada 72 C5 51 0N 118 43W
Monasterevin, Ireland 13 C4 53 8N 7 4W
Monastir = Bitola, Macedonia 21 D9 41 1N 21 20 E
Moncayo, Sierra del, Spain 19 B5 41 48N 1 50W
Monchegorsk, Russia 24 A5 67 54N 32 58 E
Mönchengladbach, Germany 16 C4 51 11N 6 27 E
Monchique, Portugal 19 D1 37 19N 8 38W
Moncks Corner, U.S.A. 77 J5 33 12N 80 1W
Monclova, Mexico 86 B4 26 50N 101 30W
Moncton, Canada 71 C7 46 7N 64 51W
Mondego →, Portugal 19 B1 40 9N 8 52W
Mondeodo, Indonesia 37 E6 3 34S 122 9 E
Mondovì, Italy 18 D7 44 23N 7 49 E
Mondrain I., Australia 61 F3 34 9S 122 14 E
Monessen, U.S.A. 78 F5 40 9N 79 54W
Monett, U.S.A. 81 G8 36 55N 93 55W
Moneymore, U.K. 13 B5 54 41N 6 40W
Monforte de Lemos, Spain 19 A2 42 31N 7 33W
Mong Hsu, Burma 41 J21 21 54N 98 30 E
Mong Kung, Burma 41 J20 21 35N 97 35 E
Mong Nai, Burma 41 J20 20 32N 97 46 E
Mong Pawk, Burma 41 H21 22 4N 99 16 E
Mong Ton, Burma 41 J21 20 17N 98 45 E
Mong Wa, Burma 41 J22 21 26N 100 27 E
Mong Yai, Burma 41 H21 22 21N 98 3 E
Mongalla, Sudan 51 G12 5 8N 31 42 E
Mongers, L., Australia 61 E2 29 25S 117 5 E
Monghyr = Munger, India 43 G12 25 23N 86 30 E
Mongibello = Etna, Italy 20 F6 37 50N 14 55 E
Mongo, Chad 51 F9 12 14N 18 43 E
Mongolia ■, Asia 27 E10 47 0N 103 0 E
Mongu, Zambia 53 H4 15 16S 23 12 E
Mônguâ, Angola 56 B2 16 43S 15 20 E
Monifieth, U.K. 12 E6 56 30N 2 48W
Monkey Bay, Malawi 55 E4 14 7S 35 1 E
Monkey Mia, Australia 61 E1 25 48S 113 43 E
Monkey River, Belize 87 D7 16 22N 88 29W
Monkoto, Dem. Rep. of the Congo 52 E4 1 38S 20 35 E
Monkton, Canada 78 C3 43 35N 81 5W
Monmouth, U.K. 11 F5 51 48N 2 42W
Monmouth, Ill., U.S.A. 80 E9 40 55N 90 39W
Monmouth, Oreg., U.S.A. 82 D2 44 51N 123 14W
Monmouthshire □, U.K. 11 F5 51 48N 2 54W
Mono L., U.S.A. 84 H7 38 1N 119 1W
Monolith, U.S.A. 85 K8 35 7N 118 22W
Monólithos, Greece 23 C9 36 7N 27 45 E
Monongahela, U.S.A. 78 F5 40 12N 79 56W
Monópoli, Italy 20 D7 40 57N 17 18 E
Monroe, Ga., U.S.A. 77 J4 33 47N 83 43W
Monroe, La., U.S.A. 81 J8 32 30N 92 7W
Monroe, Mich., U.S.A. 76 E4 41 55N 83 24W
Monroe, N.C., U.S.A. 77 H5 34 59N 80 33W
Monroe, N.Y., U.S.A. 79 E10 41 20N 74 11W
Monroe, Utah, U.S.A. 83 G7 38 38N 112 7W
Monroe, Wash., U.S.A. 84 C5 47 51N 121 58W
Monroe, Wis., U.S.A. 80 D10 42 36N 89 38W
Monroe City, U.S.A. 80 F9 39 39N 91 44W
Monroeton, U.S.A. 79 E8 41 43N 76 29W
Monroeville, Ala., U.S.A. 77 K2 31 31N 87 20W
Monroeville, Pa., U.S.A. 78 F5 40 26N 79 45W
Monrovia, Liberia 50 G3 6 18N 10 47W
Mons, Belgium 15 D3 50 27N 3 58 E
Monse, Indonesia 37 E6 4 7S 123 15 E
Mont-de-Marsan, France 18 E3 43 54N 0 31W
Mont-Joli, Canada 71 C6 48 37N 68 10W
Mont-Laurier, Canada 70 C4 46 35N 75 30W
Mont-Louis, Canada 71 C6 49 15N 65 44W
Mont-St-Michel, Le = Le Mont-St-Michel, France 18 B3 48 40N 1 30W
Mont Tremblant, Parc Recr. du, Canada 70 C5 46 30N 74 30W
Montagu, S. Africa 56 E3 33 45S 20 8 E
Montagu I., Antarctica 5 B1 58 25S 26 20W
Montague, Canada 71 C7 46 10N 62 39W
Montague, I., Mexico 86 A2 31 40N 114 56W
Montague Ra., Australia 61 E2 27 15S 119 30 E
Montague Sd., Australia 60 B4 14 28S 125 20 E
Montalbán, Spain 19 B5 40 50N 0 45W
Montalvo, U.S.A. 85 L7 34 15N 119 12W
Montana, Bulgaria 21 C10 43 27N 23 16 E
Montaña, Peru 92 E4 6 0S 73 0W
Montana □, U.S.A. 82 C9 47 0N 110 0W
Montaña Clara, I., Canary Is. 22 E6 29 17N 13 33W
Montargis, France 18 C5 47 59N 2 43 E
Montauban, France 18 D4 44 2N 1 21 E
Montauk, U.S.A. 79 E13 41 3N 71 57W
Montauk Pt., U.S.A. 79 E13 41 4N 71 52W
Montbéliard, France 18 C7 47 31N 6 48 E
Montceau-les-Mines, France 18 C6 46 40N 4 23 E
Montclair, U.S.A. 79 F10 40 49N 74 13W
Monte Albán, Mexico 87 D5 17 2N 96 45W
Monte Alegre, Brazil 93 D8 2 0S 54 0W
Monte Azul, Brazil 93 G10 15 9S 42 53W
Monte Bello Is., Australia 60 D2 20 30S 115 45 E
Monte-Carlo, Monaco 18 E7 43 46N 7 23 E
Monte Caseros, Argentina 94 C4 30 10S 57 50W
Monte Comán, Argentina 94 C2 34 40S 67 53W
Monte Cristi, Dom. Rep. 89 C5 19 52N 71 39W
Monte Lindo →, Paraguay 94 A4 23 56S 57 12W
Monte Patria, Chile 94 C1 30 42S 70 58W
Monte Quemado, Argentina 94 B3 25 53S 62 41W
Monte Rio, U.S.A. 84 G4 38 28N 123 0W
Monte Santu, C. di, Italy 20 D3 40 5N 9 44 E
Monte Vista, U.S.A. 83 H10 37 35N 106 9W
Monteagudo, Argentina 95 B5 27 14S 54 8W
Montebello, Canada 70 C5 45 40N 74 55W
Montecito, U.S.A. 85 L7 34 26N 119 40W
Montecristo, Italy 20 C4 42 20N 10 19 E
Montego Bay, Jamaica 88 C4 18 30N 78 0W
Montélimar, France 18 D6 44 33N 4 45 E
Montello, U.S.A. 80 D10 43 48N 89 20W
Montemorelos, Mexico 87 B5 25 11N 99 42W
Montenegro, Brazil 95 B5 29 39S 51 29W
Montenegro □, Yugoslavia 21 C8 42 40N 19 20 E
Montepuez, Mozam. 55 E4 13 8S 38 59 E
Montepuez →, Mozam. 55 E5 12 32S 40 27 E
Monterey, U.S.A. 84 J5 36 37N 121 55W
Monterey B., U.S.A. 84 J5 36 45N 122 0W
Montería, Colombia 92 B3 8 46N 75 53W
Monteros, Argentina 94 B2 27 11S 65 30W
Monterrey, Mexico 86 B4 25 40N 100 30W
Montes Claros, Brazil 93 G10 16 30S 43 50W
Montesano, U.S.A. 84 D3 46 59N 123 36W
Montesilvano, Italy 20 C6 42 29N 14 8 E
Montevideo, Uruguay 95 C4 34 50S 56 11W
Montevideo, U.S.A. 80 C7 44 57N 95 43W
Montezuma, U.S.A. 80 E8 41 35N 92 32W
Montgomery = Sahiwal, Pakistan 42 D5 30 45N 73 8 E
Montgomery, U.K. 11 E4 52 34N 3 8W

Montgomery

Montgomery, Ala., U.S.A. 77 J2 32 23N 86 19W
Montgomery, Pa., U.S.A. 78 E8 41 10N 76 53W
Montgomery, W. Va., U.S.A. 76 F5 38 11N 81 19W
Montgomery City, U.S.A. 80 F9 38 59N 91 30W
Monticello, Ark., U.S.A. 81 J9 33 38N 91 47W
Monticello, Fla., U.S.A. 77 K4 30 33N 83 52W
Monticello, Ind., U.S.A. 76 E2 40 45N 86 46W
Monticello, Iowa, U.S.A. 80 D9 42 15N 91 12W
Monticello, Ky., U.S.A. 77 G3 36 50N 84 51W
Monticello, Minn., U.S.A. 80 C8 45 18N 93 48W
Monticello, Miss., U.S.A. 81 K9 31 33N 90 7W
Monticello, N.Y., U.S.A. 79 E10 41 39N 74 42W
Monticello, Utah, U.S.A. 83 H9 37 52N 109 21W
Montijo, Portugal 19 C1 38 41N 8 54W
Montilla, Spain 19 D3 37 36N 4 40W
Montluçon, France 18 C5 46 22N 2 36 E
Montmagny, Canada 71 C5 46 58N 70 34W
Montmartre, Canada 73 C8 50 14N 103 27W
Montmorillon, France 18 C4 46 26N 0 50 E
Monto, Australia 62 C5 24 52S 151 6 E
Montoro, Spain 19 C3 38 1N 4 27W
Montour Falls, U.S.A. 78 D8 42 21N 76 51W
Montoursville, U.S.A. 78 E8 41 15N 76 55W
Montpelier, Idaho, U.S.A. 82 E8 42 19N 111 18W
Montpelier, Vt., U.S.A. 79 B12 44 16N 72 35W
Montpellier, France 18 E5 43 37N 3 52 E
Montréal, Canada 79 A11 45 31N 73 34W
Montreal →, Canada 70 C3 47 14N 84 39W
Montreal L., Canada 73 C7 54 20N 105 45W
Montreal Lake, Canada 73 C7 54 3N 105 46W
Montreux, Switz. 18 C7 46 26N 6 55 E
Montrose, U.K. 12 E6 56 44N 2 27W
Montrose, Colo., U.S.A. 83 G10 38 29N 107 53W
Montrose, Pa., U.S.A. 79 E9 41 50N 75 53W
Monts, Pte. des, Canada 71 C6 49 20N 67 12W
Montserrat ■, W. Indies 89 C7 16 40N 62 10W
Montuiri, Spain 22 B9 39 34N 2 59 E
Monywa, Burma 41 H19 22 7N 95 11 E
Monza, Italy 18 D8 45 35N 9 16 E
Monze, Zambia 55 F2 16 17S 27 29 E
Monze, C., Pakistan 42 G2 24 47N 66 37 E
Monzón, Spain 19 B6 41 52N 0 10 E
Mooers, U.S.A. 79 B11 44 58N 73 35W
Mooi →, S. Africa 57 D5 28 45S 30 34 E
Mooi River, S. Africa 57 D4 29 13S 29 50 E
Moonah →, Australia 62 C2 22 3S 138 33 E
Moonda, L., Australia 62 D3 25 52S 140 25 E
Moonie, Australia 63 D5 27 46S 150 20 E
Moonie →, Australia 63 D4 29 19S 148 43 E
Moora, Australia 61 F2 30 37S 115 58 E
Moorcroft, U.S.A. 80 C2 44 16N 104 57W
Moore →, Australia 61 F2 31 22S 115 30 E
Moore, L., Australia 61 E2 29 50S 117 35 E
Moore Park, Australia 62 C5 24 43S 152 17 E
Moore Reefs, Australia 62 B4 16 0S 149 5 E
Moorefield, U.S.A. 76 F6 39 5N 78 59W
Moores Res., U.S.A. 79 B13 44 45N 71 50W
Moorfoot Hills, U.K. 12 F5 55 44N 3 8W
Moorhead, U.S.A. 80 B6 46 53N 96 45W
Moorpark, U.S.A. 85 L8 34 17N 118 53W
Moorreesburg, S. Africa 56 E2 33 6S 18 38 E
Moose →, Canada 70 B3 51 20N 80 25W
Moose →, U.S.A. 79 C9 43 38N 75 24W
Moose Creek, Canada 79 A10 45 15N 74 58W
Moose Factory, Canada 70 B3 51 16N 80 32W
Moose Jaw, Canada 73 C7 50 24N 105 30W
Moose Jaw →, Canada 73 C7 50 34N 105 18W
Moose Lake, Canada 73 C8 53 43N 100 20W
Moose Lake, U.S.A. 80 B8 46 27N 92 46W
Moose Mountain Prov. Park, Canada 73 D8 49 48N 102 25W
Moosehead L., U.S.A. 77 C11 45 38N 69 40W
Mooselookmeguntic L., U.S.A. 77 C10 44 55N 70 49W
Moosilauke, Mt., U.S.A. 79 B13 44 3N 71 40W
Moosomin, Canada 73 C8 50 9N 101 40W
Moosonee, Canada 70 B3 51 17N 80 39W
Moosup, U.S.A. 79 E13 41 43N 71 53W
Mopane, S. Africa 57 C4 22 37S 29 52 E
Mopeia Velha, Mozam. 55 F4 17 30S 35 40 E
Mopipi, Botswana 56 C3 21 6S 24 55 E
Mopoi, C.A.R. 54 A2 5 6N 26 54 E
Mopti, Mali 50 F5 14 30N 4 0W
Moqor, Afghan. 42 C2 32 50N 67 42 E
Moquegua, Peru 92 G4 17 15S 70 46W
Mora, Sweden 9 F16 61 2N 14 38 E
Mora, Minn., U.S.A. 80 C8 45 53N 93 18W
Mora, N. Mex., U.S.A. 83 J11 35 58N 105 20W
Mora →, U.S.A. 81 H2 35 35N 104 25W
Moradabad, India 43 E8 28 50N 78 50 E
Morafenobe, Madag. 57 B7 17 50S 44 53 E
Moramanga, Madag. 57 B8 18 56S 48 12 E
Moran, Kans., U.S.A. 81 G7 37 55N 95 10W
Moran, Wyo., U.S.A. 82 E8 43 53N 110 37W
Moranbah, Australia 62 C4 22 1S 148 6 E
Morant Cays, Jamaica 88 C4 17 22N 76 0W
Morant Pt., Jamaica 88 C4 17 55N 76 12W
Morar, India 42 F8 26 14N 78 14 E
Morar, L., U.K. 12 E3 56 57N 5 40W
Moratuwa, Sri Lanka 40 R11 6 45N 79 55 E
Morava →, Serbia, Yug. 21 B9 44 36N 21 4 E
Morava →, Slovak Rep. 17 D9 48 10N 16 59 E
Moravia, U.S.A. 79 D8 42 43N 76 25W
Moravian Hts. = Českomoravská Vrchovina, Czech Rep. 16 D8 49 30N 15 40 E
Morawa, Australia 61 E2 29 13S 116 0 E
Morawhanna, Guyana 92 B7 8 30N 59 40W
Moray □, U.K. 12 D5 57 31N 3 18W
Moray Firth, U.K. 12 D5 57 40N 3 52W
Morbi, India 42 H4 22 50N 70 42 E
Morden, Canada 73 D9 49 15N 98 10W
Mordovian Republic = Mordvinia □, Russia 24 D7 54 20N 44 30 E
Mordvinia □, Russia 24 D7 54 20N 44 30 E
Morea, Greece 6 H10 37 45N 22 10 E
Moreau →, U.S.A. 80 C4 45 18N 100 43W
Morecambe, U.K. 10 C5 54 5N 2 52W
Morecambe B., U.K. 10 C5 54 7N 3 0W
Moree, Australia 63 D4 29 28S 149 54 E
Morehead, U.S.A. 76 F4 38 11N 83 26W
Morehead City, U.S.A. 77 H7 34 43N 76 43W
Morel →, India 42 F7 26 13N 76 36 E
Morelia, Mexico 86 D4 19 42N 101 7W
Morella, Australia 62 C3 23 0S 143 52 E
Morella, Spain 19 B5 40 35N 0 5W
Morelos, Mexico 86 B3 26 42N 107 40W
Morelos □, Mexico 87 D5 18 40N 99 10W
Morena, India 42 F8 26 30N 78 4 E
Morena, Sierra, Spain 19 C3 38 20N 4 0W
Moreno Valley, U.S.A. 85 M10 33 56N 117 15W
Moresby I., Canada 72 C2 52 30N 131 40W
Moreton I., Australia 63 D5 27 10S 153 25 E
Morey, Spain 22 B10 39 44N 3 20 E
Morgan, U.S.A. 82 F8 41 2N 111 41W
Morgan City, U.S.A. 81 L9 29 42N 91 12W
Morgan Hill, U.S.A. 84 H5 37 8N 121 39W
Morganfield, U.S.A. 76 G2 37 41N 87 55W
Morganton, U.S.A. 77 H5 35 45N 81 41W
Morgantown, U.S.A. 76 F6 39 38N 79 57W
Morgenzon, S. Africa 57 D4 26 45S 29 36 E
Morghak, Iran 45 D8 29 7N 57 54 E
Morhar →, India 43 G11 25 29N 85 11 E
Moriarty, U.S.A. 83 J10 34 59N 106 3W
Morice L., Canada 72 C3 53 50N 127 40W
Morinville, Canada 72 C6 53 49N 113 41W
Morioka, Japan 30 E10 39 45N 141 8 E
Moris, Mexico 86 B3 28 8N 108 32W
Morlaix, France 18 B2 48 36N 3 52W
Mornington, I., Chile 96 F1 49 50S 75 30W
Mornington I., Australia 62 B2 16 30S 139 30 E
Moro, Pakistan 42 F2 26 40N 68 0 E
Moro →, Pakistan 42 E2 29 42N 67 22 E
Moro G., Phil. 37 C6 6 30N 123 0 E
Morocco ■, N. Afr. 50 B4 32 0N 5 50W
Morogoro, Tanzania 54 D4 6 50S 37 40 E
Morogoro □, Tanzania 54 D4 8 0S 37 0 E
Moroleón, Mexico 86 C4 20 8N 101 32W
Morombe, Madag. 57 C7 21 45S 43 22 E
Moron, Argentina 94 C4 34 39S 58 37W
Morón, Cuba 88 B4 22 8N 78 39W
Morón de la Frontera, Spain 19 D3 37 6N 5 28W
Morona →, Peru 92 D3 4 40S 77 10W
Morondava, Madag. 57 C7 20 17S 44 17 E
Morongo Valley, U.S.A. 85 L10 34 3N 116 37W
Moroni, Comoros Is. 49 H8 11 40S 43 16 E
Moroni, U.S.A. 82 G8 39 32N 111 35W
Morotai, Indonesia 37 D7 2 10N 128 30 E
Moroto, Uganda 54 B3 2 28N 34 42 E
Moroto Summit, Kenya 54 B3 2 30N 34 43 E
Morpeth, U.K. 10 B6 55 10N 1 41W
Morphou, Cyprus 23 D11 35 12N 32 59 E
Morphou Bay, Cyprus 23 D11 35 15N 32 50 E
Morrilton, U.S.A. 81 H8 35 9N 92 44W
Morrinhos, Brazil 93 G9 17 45S 49 10W
Morrinsville, N.Z. 59 G5 37 40S 175 32 E
Morris, Canada 73 D9 49 25N 97 22W
Morris, Ill., U.S.A. 80 E10 41 22N 88 26W
Morris, Minn., U.S.A. 80 C7 45 35N 95 55W
Morris, N.Y., U.S.A. 79 D9 42 33N 75 15W
Morris, Pa., U.S.A. 78 E7 41 35N 77 17W
Morris, Mt., Australia 61 E5 26 9S 131 4 E
Morrisburg, Canada 79 B9 44 55N 75 7W
Morristown, Ariz., U.S.A. 83 K7 33 51N 112 37W
Morristown, N.J., U.S.A. 79 F10 40 48N 74 29W
Morristown, N.Y., U.S.A. 79 B9 44 35N 75 39W
Morristown, Tenn., U.S.A. 77 G4 36 13N 83 18W
Morrisville, N.Y., U.S.A. 79 D9 42 53N 75 35W
Morrisville, Pa., U.S.A. 79 F10 40 13N 74 47W
Morrisville, Vt., U.S.A. 79 B12 44 34N 72 36W
Morro, Pta., Chile 94 B1 27 6S 71 0W
Morro Bay, U.S.A. 84 K6 35 22N 120 51W
Morro del Jable, Canary Is. 22 F5 28 3N 14 23W
Morro Jable, Pta. de, Canary Is. 22 F5 28 2N 14 20W
Morrosquillo, G. de, Colombia 88 E4 9 35N 75 40W
Morrumbene, Mozam. 57 C6 23 31S 35 16 E
Morshansk, Russia 24 D7 53 28N 41 50 E
Morteros, Argentina 94 C3 30 50S 62 0W
Mortlach, Canada 73 C7 50 27N 106 4W
Morton, Tex., U.S.A. 81 J3 33 44N 102 46W
Morton, Wash., U.S.A. 84 D4 46 34N 122 17W
Morvan, France 18 C6 47 5N 4 3 E
Morven, Australia 63 D4 26 22S 147 5 E
Morvern, U.K. 12 E3 56 38N 5 44W
Morzhovets, Ostrov, Russia 24 A7 66 44N 42 35 E
Moscos Is., Burma 38 E1 14 0N 97 30 E
Moscow = Moskva, Russia 24 C6 55 45N 37 35 E
Moscow, Idaho, U.S.A. 82 C5 46 44N 117 0W
Moscow, Pa., U.S.A. 79 E9 41 20N 75 31W
Mosel →, Europe 18 A7 50 22N 7 36 E
Moselle = Mosel →, Europe 18 A7 50 22N 7 36 E
Moses Lake, U.S.A. 82 C4 47 8N 119 17W
Mosgiel, N.Z. 59 L3 45 53S 170 21 E
Moshaweng →, S. Africa 56 D3 26 35S 22 50 E
Moshi, Tanzania 54 C4 3 22S 37 18 E
Moshupa, Botswana 56 C4 24 46S 25 29 E
Mosjøen, Norway 8 D15 65 51N 13 12 E
Moskenesøya, Norway 8 C15 67 58N 13 0 E
Moskenstraumen, Norway 8 C15 67 47N 12 45 E
Moskva, Russia 24 C6 55 45N 37 35 E
Mosomane, Botswana 56 C4 24 2S 26 19 E
Mosonmagyaróvár, Hungary 17 E9 47 52N 17 18 E
Mosquera, Colombia 92 C3 2 35N 78 24W
Mosquero, U.S.A. 81 H3 35 47N 103 58W
Mosquitia, Honduras 88 C3 15 20N 84 10W
Mosquito Coast = Mosquitia, Honduras 88 C3 15 20N 84 10W
Mosquito Creek L., U.S.A. 78 E4 41 18N 80 46W
Mosquito L., Canada 73 A8 62 35N 103 20W
Mosquitos, G. de los, Panama 88 E3 9 15N 81 10W
Moss, Norway 9 G14 59 27N 10 40 E
Mossbank, Canada 73 D7 49 56N 105 56W
Mossburn, N.Z. 59 L2 45 41S 168 15 E
Mosselbaai, S. Africa 56 E3 34 11S 22 8 E
Mossendjo, Congo 52 E2 2 55S 12 42 E
Mossman, Australia 62 B4 16 21S 145 15 E
Mossoró, Brazil 93 E11 5 10S 37 15W
Mossuril, Mozam. 55 E5 14 58S 40 42 E
Most, Czech Rep. 16 C7 50 31N 13 38 E
Mosta, Malta 23 D1 35 54N 14 24 E
Mostaganem, Algeria 50 A6 35 54N 0 5 E
Mostar, Bos.-H. 21 C7 43 22N 17 50 E
Mostardas, Brazil 95 C5 31 2S 50 51W
Mostiska = Mostyska, Ukraine 17 D12 49 48N 23 4 E
Mosty = Masty, Belarus 17 B13 53 27N 24 38 E
Mostyska, Ukraine 17 D12 49 48N 23 4 E
Mosul = Al Mawşil, Iraq 44 B4 36 15N 43 5 E
Mosŭlpo, S. Korea 35 H14 33 20N 126 17 E
Motagua →, Guatemala 88 C2 15 44N 88 14W
Motala, Sweden 9 G16 58 32N 15 1 E
Motaze, Mozam. 57 C5 24 48S 32 52 E
Moth, India 43 G8 25 43N 78 57 E
Motherwell, U.K. 12 F5 55 47N 3 58W
Motihari, India 43 F11 26 30N 84 55 E
Motozintla de Mendoza, Mexico 87 D6 15 21N 92 14W
Motril, Spain 19 D4 36 31N 3 37W
Mott, U.S.A. 80 B3 46 23N 102 20W
Motueka, N.Z. 59 J4 41 7S 173 1 E
Motueka →, N.Z. 59 J4 41 5S 173 1 E
Motul, Mexico 87 C7 21 0N 89 20W
Mouchalagane →, Canada 71 B6 50 56N 68 41W
Moúdhros, Greece 21 E11 39 50N 25 18 E
Mouila, Gabon 52 E2 1 50S 11 0 E
Moulianá, Greece 23 D7 35 10N 25 59 E
Moulins, France 18 C5 46 35N 3 19 E
Moulmein, Burma 41 L20 16 30N 97 40 E
Moulouya, O. →, Morocco 50 B5 35 5N 2 25W
Moultrie, U.S.A. 77 K4 31 11N 83 47W
Moultrie, L., U.S.A. 77 J5 33 20N 80 5W
Mound City, Mo., U.S.A. 80 E7 40 7N 95 14W
Mound City, S. Dak., U.S.A. 80 C4 45 44N 100 4W
Moundou, Chad 51 G9 8 40N 16 10 E
Moundsville, U.S.A. 78 G4 39 55N 80 44W
Moung, Cambodia 38 F4 12 46N 103 27 E
Mount Airy, U.S.A. 77 G5 36 31N 80 37W
Mount Albert, Canada 78 B5 44 8N 79 19W
Mount Barker, Australia 61 F2 34 38S 117 40 E
Mount Brydges, Canada 78 D3 42 54N 81 29W
Mount Burr, Australia 63 F3 37 34S 140 26 E
Mount Carmel, Ill., U.S.A. 76 F2 38 25N 87 46W
Mount Carmel, Pa., U.S.A. 79 F8 40 47N 76 24W
Mount Charleston, U.S.A. 85 J11 36 16N 115 37W
Mount Clemens, U.S.A. 78 D2 42 35N 82 53W
Mount Coolon, Australia 62 C4 21 25S 147 25 E
Mount Darwin, Zimbabwe 55 F3 16 47S 31 38 E
Mount Desert I., U.S.A. 77 C11 44 21N 68 20W
Mount Dora, U.S.A. 77 L5 28 48N 81 38W
Mount Edziza Prov. Park, Canada 72 B2 57 30N 130 45W
Mount Fletcher, S. Africa 57 E4 30 40S 28 30 E
Mount Forest, Canada 78 C4 43 59N 80 43W
Mount Garnet, Australia 62 B4 17 37S 145 6 E
Mount Holly, U.S.A. 79 G10 39 59N 74 47W
Mount Holly Springs, U.S.A. 78 F7 40 7N 77 12W
Mount Hope, Australia 63 E2 34 7S 135 23 E
Mount Isa, Australia 62 C2 20 42S 139 26 E
Mount Jewett, U.S.A. 78 E6 41 44N 78 39W
Mount Kisco, U.S.A. 79 E11 41 12N 73 44W
Mount Laguna, U.S.A. 85 N10 32 52N 116 25W
Mount Larcom, Australia 62 C5 23 48S 150 59 E
Mount Magnet, Australia 61 E2 28 2S 117 47 E
Mount Maunganui, N.Z. 59 G6 37 40S 176 14 E
Mount Molloy, Australia 62 B4 16 42S 145 20 E
Mount Morgan, Australia 62 C5 23 40S 150 25 E
Mount Morris, U.S.A. 78 D7 42 44N 77 52W
Mount Pearl, Canada 71 C9 47 31N 52 47W
Mount Penn, U.S.A. 79 F9 40 20N 75 54W
Mount Perry, Australia 63 D5 25 13S 151 42 E
Mount Pleasant, Iowa, U.S.A. 80 E9 40 58N 91 33W
Mount Pleasant, Mich., U.S.A. 76 D3 43 36N 84 46W
Mount Pleasant, Pa., U.S.A. 78 F5 40 9N 79 33W
Mount Pleasant, S.C., U.S.A. 77 J6 32 47N 79 52W
Mount Pleasant, Tenn., U.S.A. 77 H2 35 32N 87 12W
Mount Pleasant, Tex., U.S.A. 81 J7 33 9N 94 58W
Mount Pleasant, Utah, U.S.A. 82 G8 39 33N 111 27W
Mount Pocono, U.S.A. 79 E9 41 7N 75 22W
Mount Rainier Nat. Park, U.S.A. 84 D5 46 55N 121 50W
Mount Revelstoke Nat. Park, Canada 72 C5 51 5N 118 30W
Mount Robson Prov. Park, Canada 72 C5 53 0N 119 0W
Mount Selinda, Zimbabwe 57 C5 20 24S 32 43 E
Mount Shasta, U.S.A. 82 F2 41 19N 122 19W
Mount Signal, U.S.A. 85 N11 32 39N 115 37W
Mount Sterling, Ill., U.S.A. 80 F9 39 59N 90 45W
Mount Sterling, Ky., U.S.A. 76 F4 38 4N 83 56W
Mount Surprise, Australia 62 B3 18 10S 144 17 E
Mount Union, U.S.A. 78 F7 40 23N 77 53W
Mount Upton, U.S.A. 79 D9 42 26N 75 23W
Mount Vernon, Ill., U.S.A. 76 F1 38 19N 88 55W
Mount Vernon, Ind., U.S.A. 80 F10 38 17N 88 57W
Mount Vernon, N.Y., U.S.A. 79 F11 40 55N 73 50W
Mount Vernon, Ohio, U.S.A. 78 F2 40 23N 82 29W
Mount Vernon, Wash., U.S.A. 84 B4 48 25N 122 20W
Mountain Ash, U.K. 11 F4 51 40N 3 23W
Mountain Center, U.S.A. 85 M10 33 42N 116 44W
Mountain City, Nev., U.S.A. 82 F6 41 50N 115 58W
Mountain City, Tenn., U.S.A. 77 G5 36 29N 81 48W
Mountain Dale, U.S.A. 79 E10 41 41N 74 32W
Mountain Grove, U.S.A. 81 G8 37 8N 92 16W
Mountain Home, Ark., U.S.A. 81 G8 36 20N 92 23W
Mountain Home, Idaho, U.S.A. 82 E6 43 8N 115 41W
Mountain Iron, U.S.A. 80 B8 47 32N 92 37W
Mountain Pass, U.S.A. 85 K11 35 29N 115 35W
Mountain View, Ark., U.S.A. 81 H8 35 52N 92 7W
Mountain View, Calif., U.S.A. 84 H4 37 23N 122 5W
Mountain View, Hawaii, U.S.A. 74 J17 19 33N 155 7W
Mountainair, U.S.A. 83 J10 34 31N 106 15W
Mountlake Terrace, U.S.A. 84 C4 47 47N 122 19W
Mountmellick, Ireland 13 C4 53 7N 7 20W
Mountrath, Ireland 13 D4 53 0N 7 28W
Moura, Australia 62 C4 24 35S 149 58 E
Moura, Brazil 92 D6 1 32S 61 38W
Moura, Portugal 19 C2 38 7N 7 30W
Mourdi, Dépression du, Chad 51 E10 18 10N 23 0 E
Mourilyan, Australia 62 B4 17 35S 146 3 E
Mourne →, U.K. 13 B4 54 52N 7 26W
Mourne Mts., U.K. 13 B5 54 10N 6 0W
Mourniai, Greece 23 D6 35 29N 24 1 E
Mournies = Mourniai, Greece 23 D6 35 29N 24 1 E
Mouscron, Belgium 15 D3 50 45N 3 12 E
Moussoro, Chad 51 F9 13 41N 16 35 E
Moutong, Indonesia 37 D6 0 28N 121 13 E
Movas, Mexico 86 B3 28 10N 109 25W
Moville, Ireland 13 A4 55 11N 7 3W
Mowandjum, Australia 60 C3 17 22S 123 40 E
Moy →, Ireland 13 B2 54 8N 9 8W
Moyale, Kenya 54 B4 3 30N 39 0 E
Moyen Atlas, Morocco 50 B4 33 0N 5 0W
Moyne, L. le, Canada 71 A6 56 45N 68 47W
Moyo, Indonesia 36 F5 8 10S 117 40 E
Moyobamba, Peru 92 E3 6 0S 77 0W
Moyyero →, Russia 27 C11 68 44N 103 42 E
Moyynty, Kazakstan 26 E8 47 10N 73 18 E
Mozambique = Moçambique, Mozam. 55 F5 15 3S 40 42 E
Mozambique ■, Africa 55 F4 19 0S 35 0 E
Mozambique Chan., Africa 57 B7 17 30S 42 30 E
Mozdok, Russia 25 F7 43 45N 44 48 E
Mozdūrān, Iran 45 B9 36 9N 60 35 E
Mozhnābād, Iran 45 C9 34 7N 60 6 E
Mozyr = Mazyr, Belarus 17 B15 51 59N 29 15 E
Mpanda, Tanzania 54 D3 6 23S 31 1 E
Mphoengs, Zimbabwe 57 C4 21 10S 27 51 E
Mpika, Zambia 55 E3 11 51S 31 25 E
Mpulungu, Zambia 55 D3 8 51S 31 5 E
Mpumalanga, S. Africa 57 D5 29 50S 30 33 E
Mpumalanga □, S. Africa 57 B5 26 0S 30 0 E
Mpwapwa, Tanzania 54 D4 6 23S 36 30 E
Mqanduli, S. Africa 57 E4 31 49S 28 45 E
Msambansovu, Zimbabwe 55 F3 15 50S 30 3 E
M'sila →, Algeria 50 A6 35 30N 4 29 E
Msoro, Zambia 55 E3 13 35S 31 50 E
Mstislavl = Mstsislaw, Belarus 17 A16 54 0N 31 50 E
Mstsislaw, Belarus 17 A16 54 0N 31 50 E
Mtama, Tanzania 55 E4 10 17S 39 21 E
Mtamvuna →, S. Africa 57 E5 31 6S 30 12 E
Mtilikwe →, Zimbabwe 55 G3 21 9S 31 30 E
Mtubatuba, S. Africa 57 D5 28 30S 32 8 E
Mtwalume, S. Africa 57 E5 30 30S 30 38 E
Mtwara-Mikindani, Tanzania 55 E5 10 20S 40 20 E
Mu Gia, Deo, Vietnam 38 D5 17 40N 105 47 E
Mu Us Shamo, China 34 E5 39 0N 109 0 E
Muang Chiang Rai = Chiang Rai, Thailand 38 C2 19 52N 99 50 E
Muang Khong, Laos 38 E5 14 7N 105 51 E
Muang Lamphun, Thailand 38 C2 18 40N 99 2 E
Muang Pak Beng, Laos 38 C3 19 54N 101 8 E
Muar, Malaysia 39 L4 2 3N 102 34 E
Muarabungo, Indonesia 36 E2 1 28S 102 52 E
Muaraenim, Indonesia 36 E2 3 40S 103 50 E
Muarajuloi, Indonesia 36 E4 0 12S 114 3 E
Muarakaman, Indonesia 36 E5 0 2S 116 45 E
Muaratebo, Indonesia 36 E2 1 30S 102 26 E
Muaratembesi, Indonesia 36 E2 1 42S 103 8 E
Muaratewe, Indonesia 36 E4 0 58S 114 52 E
Mubarakpur, India 43 F10 26 6N 83 18 E
Mubarraz = Al Mubarraz, Si. Arabia 45 E6 25 30N 49 40 E
Mubende, Uganda 54 B3 0 33N 31 22 E
Mubi, Nigeria 51 F8 10 18N 13 16 E
Mubur, Pulau, Indonesia 39 L6 3 20N 106 12 E
Mucajaí →, Brazil 92 C6 2 25N 60 52W
Muchachos, Roque de los, Canary Is. 22 F2 28 44N 17 52W
Muchinga Mts., Zambia 55 E3 11 30S 31 30 E
Muck, U.K. 12 E2 56 50N 6 15W
Muckadilla, Australia 63 D4 26 35S 148 23 E
Mucuri, Brazil 93 G11 18 0S 39 36W
Mucusso, Angola 56 B3 18 1S 21 25 E
Muda, Canary Is. 22 F6 28 34N 13 57W
Mudanjiang, China 35 B15 44 38N 129 30 E
Mudanya, Turkey 21 D13 40 25N 28 50 E
Muddy Cr. →, U.S.A. 83 H8 38 24N 110 42W
Mudjatik →, Canada 73 B7 56 1N 107 36W
Muecate, Mozam. 55 E4 14 55S 39 40 E
Mueda, Mozam. 55 E4 11 36S 39 28 E
Mueller Ra., Australia 60 C4 18 18S 126 46 E
Muende, Mozam. 55 E3 14 28S 33 0 E
Muerto, Mar, Mexico 87 D6 16 10N 94 10W
Mufulira, Zambia 55 E2 12 32S 28 15 E
Mufumbiro Range, Africa 54 C2 1 25S 29 30 E
Mughal Sarai, India 43 G10 25 18N 83 7 E
Mughayrā', Si. Arabia 44 D3 29 17N 37 41 E
Mugi, Japan 31 H7 33 40N 134 25 E
Mugila, Mts., Dem. Rep. of the Congo 54 D2 7 0S 28 50 E
Muğla, Turkey 21 F13 37 15N 28 22 E
Mugu, Nepal 43 E10 29 45N 82 30 E
Muhammad, Ras, Egypt 44 E2 27 44N 34 16 E
Muhammad Qol, Sudan 51 D13 20 53N 37 9 E
Muhammadabad, India 43 F10 26 4N 83 25 E
Muhesi →, Tanzania 54 D4 7 0S 35 20 E
Mühlhausen, Germany 16 C6 51 12N 10 27 E
Mühlig Hofmann fjell, Antarctica 5 D3 72 30S 5 0 E
Muhos, Finland 8 D22 64 47N 25 59 E
Muhu, Estonia 9 G20 58 36N 23 11 E
Muhutwe, Tanzania 54 C3 1 35S 31 45 E
Muine Bheag, Ireland 13 D5 52 42N 6 58W
Muir, L., Australia 61 F2 34 30S 116 40 E
Mujnak = Muynak, Uzbekistan 26 E6 43 44N 59 10 E
Mukacheve, Ukraine 17 D12 48 27N 22 45 E
Mukachevo = Mukacheve, Ukraine 17 D12 48 27N 22 45 E
Mukah, Malaysia 36 D4 2 55N 112 5 E
Mukandwara, India 42 G6 24 49N 75 59 E
Mukdahan, Thailand 38 D5 16 32N 104 43 E
Mukden = Shenyang, China 35 D12 41 48N 123 27 E
Mukerian, India 42 D6 31 57N 75 37 E
Mukhtuya = Lensk, Russia 27 C12 60 48N 114 55 E
Mukinbudin, Australia 61 F2 30 55S 118 5 E
Mukishi, Dem. Rep. of the Congo 55 D1 8 30S 24 44 E
Mukomuko, Indonesia 36 E2 2 30S 101 10 E
Mukomwenze, Dem. Rep. of the Congo 54 D2 6 49S 27 15 E

Nampō-Shotō

Nampō-Shotō, Japan 31 J10 32 0N 140 0 E
Nampula, Mozam. 55 F4 15 6S 39 15 E
Namrole, Indonesia 37 E7 3 46S 126 46 E
Namse Shankou, China 41 E13 30 0N 82 25 E
Namsen →, Norway 8 D14 64 28N 11 37 E
Namsos, Norway 8 D14 64 29N 11 30 E
Namtsy, Russia 27 C13 62 43N 129 37 E
Namtu, Burma 41 H20 23 5N 97 28 E
Namtumbo, Tanzania 55 E4 10 30S 36 4 E
Namu, Canada 72 C3 51 52N 127 50W
Namur, Belgium 15 D4 50 27N 4 52 E
Namur □, Belgium 15 D4 50 17N 5 0 E
Namutoni, Namibia 56 B2 18 49S 16 55 E
Namwala, Zambia 55 F2 15 44S 26 30 E
Namwŏn, S. Korea 35 G14 35 23N 127 23 E
Nan, Thailand 38 C3 18 48N 100 46 E
Nan →, Thailand 38 E3 15 42N 100 9 E
Nan-ch'ang = Nanchang, China 33 D6 28 42N 115 55 E
Nanaimo, Canada 72 D4 49 10N 124 0W
Nanam, N. Korea 35 D15 41 44N 129 40 E
Nanango, Australia 63 D5 26 40S 152 0 E
Nanao, Japan 31 F8 37 0N 137 0 E
Nanchang, China 33 D6 28 42N 115 55 E
Nanching = Nanjing, China 33 C6 32 2N 118 47 E
Nanchong, China 32 C5 30 43N 106 2 E
Nancy, France 18 B7 48 42N 6 12 E
Nanda Devi, India 43 D8 30 23N 79 59 E
Nanda Kot, India 43 D9 30 17N 80 5 E
Nandan, Japan 31 G7 34 10N 134 42 E
Nanded, India 40 K10 19 10N 77 20 E
Nandewar Ra., Australia 63 E5 30 15S 150 35 E
Nandi, Fiji 59 C7 17 42S 177 20 E
Nandigram, India 43 H12 22 1N 87 58 E
Nandurbar, India 40 J9 21 20N 74 15 E
Nandyal, India 40 M11 15 30N 78 30 E
Nanga-Eboko, Cameroon 52 D2 4 41N 12 22 E
Nanga Parbat, Pakistan 43 B6 35 10N 74 35 E
Nangade, Mozam. 55 E4 11 5S 39 36 E
Nangapinoh, Indonesia 36 E4 0 20S 111 44 E
Nangarhār □, Afghan. 40 B7 34 20N 70 0 E
Nangatayap, Indonesia 36 E4 1 32S 110 34 E
Nangeya Mts., Uganda 54 B3 3 30N 33 30 E
Nangong, China 34 F8 37 23N 115 22 E
Nanhuang, China 35 F11 36 58N 121 48 E
Nanjeko, Zambia 55 F1 15 31S 23 30 E
Nanjing, China 33 C6 32 2N 118 47 E
Nanjirinji, Tanzania 55 D4 9 41S 39 5 E
Nankana Sahib, Pakistan 42 D5 31 27N 73 38 E
Nanking = Nanjing, China 33 C6 32 2N 118 47 E
Nankoku, Japan 31 H6 33 39N 133 44 E
Nanning, China 32 D5 22 48N 108 20 E
Nannup, Australia 61 F2 33 59S 115 48 E
Nanpara, India 43 F9 27 52N 81 33 E
Nanpi, China 34 E9 38 2N 116 45 E
Nanping, China 33 D6 26 38N 118 10 E
Nanripe, Mozam. 55 E4 13 52S 38 52 E
Nansei-Shotō = Ryūkyū-rettō, Japan 31 M3 26 0N 126 0 E
Nansen Sd., Canada 4 A3 81 0N 91 0W
Nanshan I., S. China Sea 36 B5 10 45N 115 49 E
Nansio, Tanzania 54 C3 2 3S 33 4 E
Nantes, France 18 C3 47 12N 1 33W
Nanticoke, U.S.A. 79 E8 41 12N 76 0W
Nanton, Canada 72 C6 50 21N 113 46W
Nantong, China 33 C7 32 1N 120 52 E
Nantucket I., U.S.A. 76 E10 41 16N 70 5W
Nantwich, U.K. 10 D5 53 4N 2 31W
Nanty Glo, U.S.A. 78 F6 40 28N 78 50W
Nanuque, Brazil 93 G10 17 50S 40 21W
Nanusa, Kepulauan, Indonesia 37 D7 4 45N 127 1 E
Nanutarra Roadhouse, Australia 60 D2 22 32S 115 30 E
Nanyang, China 34 H7 33 11N 112 30 E
Nanyuki, Kenya 54 B4 0 2N 37 4 E
Nao, C. de la, Spain 19 C6 38 44N 0 14 E
Naococane, L., Canada 71 B5 52 50N 70 45W
Napa, U.S.A. 84 G4 38 18N 122 17W
Napa →, U.S.A. 84 G4 38 10N 122 19W
Napanee, Canada 78 B8 44 15N 77 0W
Napanoch, U.S.A. 79 E10 41 44N 74 22W
Nape, Laos 38 C5 18 18N 105 6 E
Nape Pass = Keo Neua, Deo, Vietnam 38 C5 18 23N 105 10 E
Napier, N.Z. 59 H6 39 30S 176 56 E
Napier Broome B., Australia 60 B4 14 2S 126 37 E
Napier Pen., Australia 62 A2 12 4S 135 43 E
Napierville, Canada 79 A11 45 11N 73 25W
Naples = Nápoli, Italy 20 D6 40 50N 14 15 E
Naples, U.S.A. 77 M5 26 8N 81 48W
Napo →, Peru 92 D4 3 20S 72 40W
Napoleon, N. Dak., U.S.A. 80 B5 46 30N 99 46W
Napoleon, Ohio, U.S.A. 76 E3 41 23N 84 8W
Nápoli, Italy 20 D6 40 50N 14 15 E
Napopo, Dem. Rep. of the Congo 54 B2 4 15N 28 0 E
Naqb, Ra's an, Jordan 47 F4 30 0N 35 29 E
Naqqāsh, Iran 45 C6 35 40N 49 6 E
Nara, Japan 31 G7 34 40N 135 49 E
Nara, Mali 50 E4 15 10N 7 20W
Nara □, Japan 31 G8 34 30N 136 0 E
Nara Canal, Pakistan 42 G3 24 30N 69 20 E
Nara Visa, U.S.A. 81 H3 35 37N 103 6W
Naraini, India 43 G9 25 11N 80 29 E
Narasapur, India 41 L12 16 26N 81 40 E
Narathiwat, Thailand 39 J3 6 30N 101 48 E
Narayanganj, Bangla. 41 H17 23 40N 90 33 E
Narayanpet, India 40 L10 16 45N 77 30 E
Narbonne, France 18 E5 43 11N 3 0 E
Nardīn, Iran 45 B7 37 3N 55 59 E
Nardò, Italy 21 D8 40 11N 18 2 E
Narembeen, Australia 61 F2 32 7S 118 24 E
Narendranagar, India 42 D8 30 10N 78 18 E
Nares Str., Arctic 66 A13 80 0N 70 0W
Naretha, Australia 61 F3 31 0S 124 45 E
Narew →, Poland 17 B11 52 26N 20 41 E
Nari →, Pakistan 42 F2 28 0N 67 40 E
Narin, Afghan. 40 A6 36 5N 69 0 E
Narindra, Helodranon' i, Madag. 57 A8 14 55S 47 30 E
Narita, Japan 31 G10 35 47N 140 19 E
Narmada →, India 42 J5 21 38N 72 36 E
Narmland, Sweden 9 F15 60 0N 13 30 E
Narnaul, India 42 E7 28 5N 76 11 E
Narodnaya, Russia 24 A10 65 5N 59 58 E
Narok, Kenya 54 C4 1 55S 35 52 E
Narowal, Pakistan 42 C6 32 6N 74 52 E
Narrabri, Australia 63 E4 30 19S 149 46 E
Narran →, Australia 63 D4 28 37S 148 12 E
Narrogin, Australia 61 F2 32 58S 117 14 E
Narrow Hills Prov. Park, Canada 73 C8 54 0N 104 37W
Narsimhapur, India 43 H8 22 54N 79 14 E
Narsinghgarh, India 42 H7 23 45N 76 40 E
Naruto, Japan 31 G7 34 11N 134 37 E
Narva, Estonia 24 C4 59 23N 28 12 E
Narva →, Russia 9 G22 59 27N 28 2 E
Narva Bay, Estonia 9 G19 59 35N 27 35 E
Narvik, Norway 8 B17 68 28N 17 26 E
Narwana, India 42 E7 29 39N 76 6 E
Naryan-Mar, Russia 24 A9 67 42N 53 12 E
Narym, Russia 26 D9 59 0N 81 30 E
Naryn, Kyrgyzstan 26 E8 41 26N 75 58 E
Nasa, Norway 8 C16 66 29N 15 23 E
Naseby, N.Z. 59 L3 45 1S 170 10 E
Naselle, U.S.A. 84 D3 46 22N 123 49W
Naser, Buheirat en, Egypt 51 D12 23 0N 32 30 E
Nashua, Mont., U.S.A. 82 B10 48 8N 106 22W
Nashua, N.H., U.S.A. 79 D13 42 45N 71 28W
Nashville, Ark., U.S.A. 81 J8 33 57N 93 51W
Nashville, Ga., U.S.A. 77 K4 31 12N 83 15W
Nashville, Tenn., U.S.A. 77 G2 36 10N 86 47W
Nasik, India 40 K8 19 58N 73 50 E
Nasirabad, India 42 F6 26 15N 74 45 E
Nasirabad, Pakistan 42 E3 28 23N 68 24 E
Naskaupi →, Canada 71 B7 53 47N 60 51W
Naṣrābād, Iran 45 C6 34 8N 51 26 E
Naṣriān-e Pā'īn, Iran 44 C5 32 52N 46 52 E
Nass →, Canada 72 C3 55 0N 129 40W
Nassau, Bahamas 88 A4 25 5N 77 20W
Nassau, U.S.A. 79 D11 42 31N 73 37W
Nassau, B., Chile 96 H3 55 20S 68 0W
Nasser, L. = Naser, Buheirat en, Egypt 51 D12 23 0N 32 30 E
Nasser City = Kôm Ombo, Egypt 51 D12 24 25N 32 52 E
Nässjö, Sweden 9 H16 57 39N 14 42 E
Nastapoka →, Canada 70 A4 56 55N 76 33W
Nastapoka, Is., Canada 70 A4 56 55N 76 50W
Nata, Botswana 56 C4 20 12S 26 12 E
Nata →, Botswana 56 C4 20 14S 26 10 E
Natal, Brazil 93 E11 5 47S 35 13W
Natal, Indonesia 36 D1 0 35N 99 7 E
Natal, S. Africa 53 K6 28 30S 30 30 E
Naṭanz, Iran 45 C6 33 30N 51 55 E
Natashquan, Canada 71 B7 50 14N 61 46W
Natashquan →, Canada 71 B7 50 7N 61 50W
Natchez, U.S.A. 81 K9 31 34N 91 24W
Natchitoches, U.S.A. 81 K8 31 46N 93 5W
Nathdwara, India 42 G5 24 55N 73 50 E
Nati, Pta., Spain 22 A10 40 3N 3 50 E
Nation →, Canada 72 B4 55 30N 123 32W
National City, U.S.A. 85 N9 32 41N 117 6W
Natitingou, Benin 50 F6 10 20N 1 26 E
Natividad, I., Mexico 86 B1 27 50N 115 10W
Natkyizin, Burma 38 E1 14 57N 97 59 E
Natron, L., Tanzania 54 C4 2 20S 36 0 E
Natrona Heights, U.S.A. 78 F5 40 37N 79 44W
Natukanaoka Pan, Namibia 56 B2 18 40S 15 45 E
Natuna Besar, Kepulauan, Indonesia 39 L7 4 0N 108 15 E
Natuna Is. = Natuna Besar, Kepulauan, Indonesia 39 L7 4 0N 108 15 E
Natuna Selatan, Kepulauan, Indonesia 39 L7 2 45N 109 0 E
Natural Bridge, U.S.A. 79 B9 44 5N 75 30W
Naturaliste, C., Australia 62 G4 40 50S 148 15 E
Nau Qala, Afghan. 42 B3 34 5N 68 5 E
Naugatuck, U.S.A. 79 E11 41 30N 73 3W
Naujaat = Repulse Bay, Canada 69 B11 66 30N 86 30W
Naumburg, Germany 16 C6 51 9N 11 47 E
Nā'ūr at Tunayb, Jordan 47 D4 31 48N 35 57 E
Nauru ■, Pac. Oc. 64 H8 1 0S 166 0 E
Naushahra = Nowshera, Pakistan 40 C8 34 0N 72 0 E
Naushahro, Pakistan 42 F3 26 50N 68 7 E
Naushon I., U.S.A. 79 E14 41 29N 70 45W
Nauta, Peru 92 D4 4 31S 73 35W
Nautanwa, India 41 F13 27 20N 83 25 E
Nautla, Mexico 87 C5 20 20N 96 50W
Nava, Mexico 86 B4 28 25N 100 46W
Navadwip, India 43 H13 23 34N 88 20 E
Navahrudak, Belarus 17 B13 53 40N 25 50 E
Navajo Reservoir, U.S.A. 83 H10 36 48N 107 36W
Navalmoral de la Mata, Spain 19 C3 39 52N 5 33W
Navan = An Uaimh, Ireland 13 C5 53 39N 6 41W
Navarino, I., Chile 96 H3 55 0S 67 40W
Navarra □, Spain 19 A5 42 40N 1 40W
Navarre, U.S.A. 78 F3 40 43N 81 31W
Navarro →, U.S.A. 84 F3 39 11N 123 45W
Navasota, U.S.A. 81 K6 30 23N 96 5W
Navassa I., W. Indies 89 C5 18 30N 75 0W
Naver →, U.K. 12 C4 58 32N 4 14W
Navibandar, India 42 J3 21 26N 69 48 E
Navidad, Chile 94 C1 33 57S 71 50W
Naviraí, Brazil 95 A5 23 8S 54 13W
Navlakhi, India 42 H4 22 58N 70 28 E
Năvodari, Romania 17 F15 44 19N 28 36 E
Navoi = Nawoiy, Uzbekistan 26 E7 40 9N 65 22 E
Navojoa, Mexico 86 B3 27 0N 109 30W
Navolato, Mexico 86 C3 24 47N 107 42W
Návpaktos, Greece 21 E9 38 24N 21 50 E
Návplion, Greece 21 F10 37 33N 22 50 E
Navsari, India 40 J8 20 57N 72 59 E
Nawa Kot, Pakistan 42 E4 28 21N 71 24 E
Nawab Khan, Pakistan 42 D3 30 17N 69 12 E
Nawabganj, Ut. P., India 43 F9 26 56N 81 14 E
Nawabganj, Ut. P., India 43 E8 28 32N 79 40 E
Nawabshah, Pakistan 42 F3 26 15N 68 25 E
Nawada, India 43 G11 24 50N 85 33 E
Nawakot, Nepal 43 F11 27 55N 85 10 E
Nawalgarh, India 42 F6 27 50N 75 15 E
Nawanshahr, India 43 C6 32 33N 74 48 E
Nawar, Dasht-i-, Afghan. 42 C3 33 52N 68 0 E
Nawoiy, Uzbekistan 26 E7 40 9N 65 22 E
Naxçıvan, Azerbaijan 25 G8 39 12N 45 15 E
Naxçıvan □, Azerbaijan 25 G8 39 25N 45 26 E
Náxos, Greece 21 F11 37 8N 25 25 E
Nay, Mui, Vietnam 36 B3 12 55N 109 23 E
Nāy Band, Būshehr, Iran 45 E7 27 20N 52 40 E
Nāy Band, Khorāsān, Iran 45 C8 32 20N 57 34 E
Nayakhan, Russia 27 C16 61 56N 159 0 E
Nayarit □, Mexico 86 C4 22 0N 105 0W
Nayoro, Japan 30 B11 44 21N 142 28 E
Nayyāl, W. →, Si. Arabia 44 D3 28 35N 39 4 E
Nazaré, Brazil 93 F11 13 2S 39 0W
Nazareth = Naẓerat, Israel 47 C4 32 42N 35 17 E
Nazareth, U.S.A. 79 F9 40 44N 75 19W
Nazas, Mexico 86 B4 25 10N 104 6W
Nazas →, Mexico 86 B4 25 35N 103 25W
Nazca, Peru 92 F4 14 50S 74 57W
Naze, The, U.K. 11 F9 51 53N 1 18 E
Naẓerat, Israel 47 C4 32 42N 35 17 E
Nāzīk, Iran 44 B5 39 1N 45 4 E
Nazilli, Turkey 21 F13 37 55N 28 15 E
Nazko, Canada 72 C4 53 1N 123 37W
Nazko →, Canada 72 C4 53 7N 123 34W
Nazret, Ethiopia 46 F2 8 32N 39 22 E
Nazwá, Oman 46 C6 22 56N 57 32 E
Nchanga, Zambia 55 E2 12 30S 27 49 E
Ncheu, Malawi 55 E3 14 50S 34 47 E
Ndala, Tanzania 54 C3 4 45S 33 15 E
Ndalatando, Angola 52 F2 9 12S 14 48 E
Ndareda, Tanzania 54 C4 4 12S 35 30 E
Ndélé, C.A.R. 52 C4 8 25N 20 36 E
Ndjamena, Chad 51 F8 12 10N 14 59 E
Ndola, Zambia 55 E2 13 0S 28 34 E
Ndoto Mts., Kenya 54 B4 2 0N 37 0 E
Nduguti, Tanzania 54 C3 4 18S 34 41 E
Neagh, Lough, U.K. 13 B5 54 37N 6 25W
Neah Bay, U.S.A. 84 B2 48 22N 124 37W
Neale, L., Australia 60 D5 24 15S 130 0 E
Neápolis, Greece 23 D7 35 15N 25 37 E
Near Is., U.S.A. 68 C1 52 30N 174 0 E
Neath, U.K. 11 F4 51 39N 3 48W
Neath Port Talbot □, U.K. 11 F4 51 42N 3 45W
Nebine Cr. →, Australia 63 D4 29 27S 146 56 E
Nebitdag, Turkmenistan 25 G9 39 30N 54 22 E
Nebo, Australia 62 C4 21 42S 148 42 E
Nebraska □, U.S.A. 80 E5 41 30N 99 30W
Nebraska City, U.S.A. 80 E7 40 41N 95 52W
Nébrodi, Monti, Italy 20 F6 37 54N 14 35 E
Necedah, U.S.A. 80 C9 44 2N 90 4W
Nechako →, Canada 72 C4 53 30N 122 44W
Neches →, U.S.A. 81 L8 29 58N 93 51W
Neckar →, Germany 16 D5 49 27N 8 29 E
Necochea, Argentina 94 D4 38 30S 58 50W
Needles, Canada 72 D5 49 53N 118 7W
Needles, U.S.A. 85 L12 34 51N 114 37W
Needles, The, U.K. 11 G6 50 39N 1 35W
Ñeembucú □, Paraguay 94 B4 27 0S 58 0W
Neemuch = Nimach, India 42 G6 24 30N 74 56 E
Neenah, U.S.A. 76 C1 44 11N 88 28W
Neepawa, Canada 73 C9 50 15N 99 30W
Neftçala, Azerbaijan 25 G8 39 19N 49 12 E
Neftekumsk, Russia 25 F7 44 46N 44 50 E
Nefyn, U.K. 10 E3 52 56N 4 31W
Negapatam = Nagappattinam, India 40 P11 10 46N 79 51 E
Negaunee, U.S.A. 76 B2 46 30N 87 36W
Negele, Ethiopia 46 F2 5 20N 39 36 E
Negev Desert = Hanegev, Israel 47 E4 30 50N 35 0 E
Negombo, Sri Lanka 40 R11 7 12N 79 50 E
Negotin, Serbia, Yug. 21 B10 44 16N 22 37 E
Negra, Pta., Peru 92 E2 6 6S 81 10W
Negrais, C. = Maudin Sun, Burma 41 M19 16 0N 94 30 E
Negril, Jamaica 88 C4 18 22N 78 20W
Negro →, Argentina 96 E4 41 2S 62 47W
Negro →, Brazil 92 D7 3 0S 60 0W
Negro →, Uruguay 95 C4 33 24S 58 22W
Negros, Phil. 37 C6 9 30N 122 40 E
Neguac, Canada 71 C6 47 15N 65 5W
Nehalem →, U.S.A. 84 E3 45 40N 123 56W
Nehāvand, Iran 45 C6 35 56N 49 31 E
Nehbandān, Iran 45 D9 31 35N 60 5 E
Nei Monggol Zizhiqu □, China 34 D7 42 0N 112 0 E
Neijiang, China 32 D5 29 35N 104 55 E
Neillsville, U.S.A. 80 C9 44 34N 90 36W
Neilton, U.S.A. 82 C2 47 25N 123 53W
Neiqiu, China 34 F8 37 15N 114 30 E
Neiva, Colombia 92 C3 2 56N 75 18W
Neixiang, China 34 H6 33 10N 111 52 E
Nejanilini L., Canada 73 B9 59 33N 97 48W
Nejd = Najd, Si. Arabia 46 B3 26 30N 42 0 E
Nekā, Iran 45 B7 36 39N 53 19 E
Nekemte, Ethiopia 46 F2 9 4N 36 30 E
Neksø, Denmark 9 J16 55 4N 15 8 E
Nelia, Australia 62 C3 20 39S 142 12 E
Neligh, U.S.A. 80 D5 42 8N 98 2W
Nelkan, Russia 27 D14 57 40N 136 4 E
Nellore, India 40 M11 14 27N 79 59 E
Nelson, Canada 72 D5 49 30N 117 20W
Nelson, N.Z. 59 J4 41 18S 173 16 E
Nelson, U.K. 10 D5 53 50N 2 13W
Nelson, Ariz., U.S.A. 83 J7 35 31N 113 19W
Nelson, Nev., U.S.A. 85 K12 35 42N 114 50W
Nelson →, Canada 73 C9 54 33N 98 2W
Nelson, Estrecho, Chile 96 G2 51 30S 75 0W
Nelson Forks, Canada 72 B4 59 30N 124 0W
Nelson House, Canada 73 B9 55 47N 98 51W
Nelson L., Canada 73 B8 55 48N 100 7W
Nelspoort, S. Africa 56 E3 32 7S 23 0 E
Nelspruit, S. Africa 57 D5 25 29S 30 59 E
Néma, Mauritania 50 E4 16 40N 7 15W
Neman, Russia 9 J20 55 2N 22 2 E
Neman →, Lithuania 9 J19 55 25N 21 10 E
Nemeiben L., Canada 73 B7 55 20N 105 20W
Némiscau, Canada 70 B4 51 18N 76 54W
Némiscau, L., Canada 70 B4 51 25N 76 40W
Nemunas = Neman →, Lithuania 9 J19 55 25N 21 10 E
Nemuro, Japan 30 C12 43 20N 145 35 E
Nemuro-Kaikyō, Japan 30 C12 43 30N 145 30 E
Nen Jiang →, China 35 B13 45 28N 124 30 E
Nenagh, Ireland 13 D3 52 52N 8 11W
Nenasi, Malaysia 39 L4 3 9N 103 23 E
Nene →, U.K. 11 E8 52 49N 0 11 E
Nenjiang, China 33 B7 49 10N 125 10 E
Neno, Malawi 55 F3 15 25S 34 40 E
Neodesha, U.S.A. 81 G7 37 25N 95 41W
Neosho, U.S.A. 81 G7 36 52N 94 22W
Neosho →, U.S.A. 81 H7 36 48N 95 18W
Nepal ■, Asia 43 F11 28 0N 84 30 E
Nepalganj, Nepal 43 E9 28 5N 81 40 E
Nepalganj Road, India 43 E9 28 1N 81 41 E
Nephi, U.S.A. 82 G8 39 43N 111 50W
Nephin, Ireland 13 B2 54 1N 9 22W
Neptune, U.S.A. 79 F10 40 13N 74 2W
Nerang, Australia 63 D5 27 58S 153 20 E
Nerchinsk, Russia 27 D12 52 0N 116 39 E
Néret, L., Canada 71 B5 54 45N 70 44W
Neretva →, Croatia 21 C7 43 1N 17 27 E
Neringa, Lithuania 9 J19 55 20N 21 5 E
Neryungri, Russia 27 D13 57 38N 124 28 E
Nescopeck, U.S.A. 79 E8 41 3N 76 12W
Ness, L., U.K. 12 D4 57 15N 4 32W
Ness City, U.S.A. 80 F5 38 27N 99 54W
Nesterov, Poland 17 C12 50 4N 23 58 E
Nesvizh = Nyasvizh, Belarus 17 B14 53 14N 26 38 E
Netanya, Israel 47 C3 32 20N 34 51 E
Netarhat, India 43 H11 23 29N 84 16 E
Nete →, Belgium 15 C4 51 7N 4 14 E
Netherdale, Australia 62 C4 21 10S 148 33 E
Netherlands ■, Europe 15 C5 52 0N 5 30 E
Netherlands Antilles ■, W. Indies 92 A5 12 15N 69 0W
Netrang, India 42 J5 21 39N 73 21 E
Nettilling L., Canada 69 B12 66 30N 71 0W
Netzahualcoyotl, Presa, Mexico 87 D6 17 10N 93 30W
Neubrandenburg, Germany 16 B7 53 33N 13 15 E
Neuchâtel, Switz. 18 C7 47 0N 6 55 E
Neuchâtel, Lac de, Switz. 18 C7 46 53N 6 50 E
Neufchâteau, Belgium 15 E5 49 50N 5 25 E
Neumünster, Germany 16 A5 54 4N 9 58 E
Neunkirchen, Germany 16 D4 49 20N 7 9 E
Neuquén, Argentina 96 D3 38 55S 68 0W
Neuquén □, Argentina 94 D2 38 0S 69 50W
Neuruppin, Germany 16 B7 52 55N 12 48 E
Neuse →, U.S.A. 77 H7 35 6N 76 29W
Neusiedler See, Austria 17 E9 47 50N 16 47 E
Neustrelitz, Germany 16 B7 53 21N 13 4 E
Neva →, Russia 24 C5 59 50N 30 30 E
Nevada, Iowa, U.S.A. 80 D8 42 1N 93 27W
Nevada, Mo., U.S.A. 81 G7 37 51N 94 22W
Nevada □, U.S.A. 82 G5 39 0N 117 0W
Nevada City, U.S.A. 84 F6 39 16N 121 1W
Nevado, Cerro, Argentina 94 D2 35 30S 68 32W
Nevel, Russia 24 C4 56 0N 29 55 E
Nevers, France 18 C5 47 0N 3 9 E
Neville, Canada 73 D7 49 58N 107 39W
Nevinnomyssk, Russia 25 F7 44 40N 42 0 E
Nevis, St. Kitts & Nevis 89 C7 17 0N 62 30W
Nevşehir, Turkey 44 B2 38 33N 34 40 E
Nevyansk, Russia 24 C11 57 30N 60 13 E
New →, U.S.A. 76 F5 38 10N 81 12W
New Aiyansh, Canada 72 B3 55 12N 129 4W
New Albany, Ind., U.S.A. 76 F3 38 18N 85 49W
New Albany, Miss., U.S.A. 81 H10 34 29N 89 0W
New Albany, Pa., U.S.A. 79 E8 41 36N 76 27W
New Amsterdam, Guyana 92 B7 6 15N 57 36W
New Angledool, Australia 63 D4 29 5S 147 55 E
New Baltimore, U.S.A. 78 D2 42 41N 82 44W
New Bedford, U.S.A. 79 E14 41 38N 70 56W
New Berlin, N.Y., U.S.A. 79 D9 42 37N 75 20W
New Berlin, Pa., U.S.A. 78 F8 40 50N 76 57W
New Bern, U.S.A. 77 H7 35 7N 77 3W
New Bethlehem, U.S.A. 78 F5 41 0N 79 20W
New Bloomfield, U.S.A. 78 F7 40 25N 77 11W
New Boston, U.S.A. 81 J7 33 28N 94 25W
New Braunfels, U.S.A. 81 L5 29 42N 98 8W
New Brighton, N.Z. 59 K4 43 29S 172 43 E
New Brighton, U.S.A. 78 F4 40 42N 80 19W
New Britain, Papua N. G. 64 H7 5 50S 150 20 E
New Britain, U.S.A. 79 E12 41 40N 72 47W
New Brunswick, U.S.A. 79 F10 40 30N 74 27W
New Brunswick □, Canada 71 C6 46 50N 66 30W
New Caledonia ■, Pac. Oc. 64 K8 21 0S 165 0 E
New Castile = Castilla-La Mancha □, Spain 19 C4 39 30N 3 30W
New Castle, Ind., U.S.A. 76 F3 39 55N 85 22W
New Castle, Pa., U.S.A. 78 F4 41 0N 80 21W
New City, U.S.A. 79 E11 41 9N 73 59W
New Concord, U.S.A. 78 G3 39 59N 81 54W
New Cumberland, U.S.A. 78 F4 40 30N 80 36W
New Cuyama, U.S.A. 85 L7 34 57N 119 38W
New Delhi, India 42 E7 28 37N 77 13 E
New Denver, Canada 72 D5 50 0N 117 25W
New Don Pedro Reservoir, U.S.A. 84 H6 37 43N 120 24W
New England, U.S.A. 80 B3 46 32N 102 52W
New England Ra., Australia 63 E5 30 20S 151 45 E
New Forest, U.K. 11 G6 50 53N 1 34W
New Galloway, U.K. 12 F4 55 5N 4 9W
New Glasgow, Canada 71 C7 45 35N 62 36W
New Guinea, Oceania 28 K17 4 0S 136 0 E
New Hamburg, Canada 78 C4 43 23N 80 42W
New Hampshire □, U.S.A. 79 C13 44 0N 71 30W
New Hampton, U.S.A. 80 D8 43 3N 92 19W
New Hanover, S. Africa 57 D5 29 22S 30 31 E
New Hartford, U.S.A. 79 C9 43 4N 75 18W
New Haven, Conn., U.S.A. 79 E12 41 18N 72 55W
New Haven, Mich., U.S.A. 78 D2 42 44N 82 48W
New Hazelton, Canada 72 B3 55 20N 127 30W
New Hebrides = Vanuatu ■, Pac. Oc. 64 J8 15 0S 168 0 E
New Holland, U.S.A. 79 F8 40 6N 76 5W
New Iberia, U.S.A. 81 K9 30 1N 91 49W
New Ireland, Papua N. G. 64 H7 3 20S 151 50 E
New Jersey □, U.S.A. 76 E8 40 0N 74 30W
New Kensington, U.S.A. 78 F5 40 34N 79 46W
New Lexington, U.S.A. 76 F4 39 43N 82 13W
New Liskeard, Canada 70 C4 47 31N 79 41W
New London, Conn., U.S.A. 79 E12 41 22N 72 6W
New London, Ohio, U.S.A. 78 E2 41 5N 82 24W
New London, Wis., U.S.A. 80 C10 44 23N 88 45W
New Madrid, U.S.A. 81 G10 36 36N 89 32W
New Martinsville, U.S.A. 76 F5 39 39N 80 52W
New Meadows, U.S.A. 82 D5 44 58N 116 18W
New Melones L., U.S.A. 84 H6 37 57N 120 31W
New Mexico □, U.S.A. 83 J10 34 30N 106 0W
New Milford, Conn., U.S.A. 79 E11 41 35N 73 25W
New Milford, Pa., U.S.A. 79 E9 41 52N 75 44W
New Norcia, Australia 61 F2 30 57S 116 13 E
New Norfolk, Australia 62 G4 42 46S 147 2 E
New Orleans, U.S.A. 81 L9 29 58N 90 4W

North East Lincolnshire

New Philadelphia, *U.S.A.* **78 F3** 40 30N 81 27W
New Plymouth, *N.Z.* **59 H5** 39 4S 174 5 E
New Plymouth, *U.S.A.* **82 E5** 43 58N 116 49W
New Port Richey, *U.S.A.* **77 L4** 28 16N 82 43W
New Providence, *Bahamas* **88 A4** 25 25N 78 35W
New Quay, *U.K.* **11 E3** 52 13N 4 21W
New Radnor, *U.K.* **11 E4** 52 15N 3 9W
New Richmond, *Canada* **71 C6** 48 15N 65 45W
New Richmond, *U.S.A.* **80 C8** 45 7N 92 32W
New Roads, *U.S.A.* **81 K9** 30 42N 91 26W
New Rochelle, *U.S.A.* **79 F11** 40 55N 73 47W
New Rockford, *U.S.A.* **80 B5** 47 41N 99 8W
New Romney, *U.K.* **11 G8** 50 59N 0 57 E
New Ross, *Ireland* **13 D5** 52 23N 6 57W
New Salem, *U.S.A.* **80 B4** 46 51N 101 25W
New Scone, *U.K.* **12 E5** 56 25N 3 24W
New Siberian I. = Novaya Sibir, Ostrov, *Russia* **27 B16** 75 10N 150 0 E
New Siberian Is. = Novosibirskiye Ostrova, *Russia* **27 B15** 75 0N 142 0 E
New Smyrna Beach, *U.S.A.* **77 L5** 29 1N 80 56W
New Town, *U.S.A.* **80 B3** 47 59N 102 30W
New Tredegar, *U.K.* **11 F4** 51 44N 3 16W
New Ulm, *U.S.A.* **80 C7** 44 19N 94 28W
New Waterford, *Canada* **71 C7** 46 13N 60 4W
New Westminster, *Canada* **84 A4** 49 13N 122 55W
New York, *U.S.A.* **79 F11** 40 45N 74 0W
New York □, *U.S.A.* **79 D9** 43 0N 75 0W
New York Mts., *U.S.A.* **83 J6** 35 0N 115 20W
New Zealand ■, *Oceania* **59 J6** 40 0S 176 0 E
Newaj →, *India* **42 G7** 24 24N 76 49 E
Newala, *Tanzania* **55 E4** 10 58S 39 18 E
Newark, *Del., U.S.A.* **76 F8** 39 41N 75 46W
Newark, *N.J., U.S.A.* **79 F10** 40 44N 74 10W
Newark, *N.Y., U.S.A.* **78 C7** 43 3N 77 6W
Newark, *Ohio, U.S.A.* **78 F2** 40 3N 82 24W
Newark-on-Trent, *U.K.* **10 D7** 53 5N 0 48W
Newark Valley, *U.S.A.* **79 D8** 42 14N 76 11W
Newberg, *U.S.A.* **82 D2** 45 18N 122 58W
Newberry, *Mich., U.S.A.* **76 B3** 46 21N 85 30W
Newberry, *S.C., U.S.A.* **77 H5** 34 17N 81 37W
Newberry Springs, *U.S.A.* **85 L10** 34 50N 116 41W
Newboro L., *Canada* **79 B8** 44 38N 76 20W
Newbridge = Droichead Nua, *Ireland* **13 C5** 53 11N 6 48W
Newburgh, *Canada* **78 B8** 44 19N 76 52W
Newburgh, *U.S.A.* **79 E10** 41 30N 74 1W
Newbury, *U.K.* **11 F6** 51 24N 1 20W
Newbury, *N.H., U.S.A.* **79 B12** 43 19N 72 3W
Newbury, *Vt., U.S.A.* **79 B12** 44 5N 72 4W
Newburyport, *U.S.A.* **77 D10** 42 49N 70 53W
Newcastle, *N.B., Canada* **71 C6** 47 1N 65 38W
Newcastle, *Ont., Canada* **70 D4** 43 55N 78 35W
Newcastle, *S. Africa* **57 D4** 27 45S 29 58 E
Newcastle, *U.K.* **13 B6** 54 13N 5 54W
Newcastle, *Calif., U.S.A.* **84 G5** 38 53N 121 8W
Newcastle, *Wyo., U.S.A.* **80 D2** 43 50N 104 11W
Newcastle Emlyn, *U.K.* **11 E3** 52 2N 4 28W
Newcastle Ra., *Australia* **60 C5** 15 45S 130 15 E
Newcastle-under-Lyme, *U.K.* **10 D5** 53 1N 2 14W
Newcastle-upon-Tyne, *U.K.* **10 C6** 54 58N 1 36W
Newcastle Waters, *Australia* **62 B1** 17 30S 133 28 E
Newcastle West, *Ireland* **13 D2** 52 27N 9 3W
Newcomb, *U.S.A.* **79 C10** 43 58N 74 10W
Newcomerstown, *U.S.A.* **78 F3** 40 16N 81 36W
Newdegate, *Australia* **61 F2** 33 6S 119 0 E
Newell, *Australia* **62 B4** 16 20S 145 16 E
Newell, *U.S.A.* **80 C3** 44 43N 103 25W
Newfane, *U.S.A.* **78 C6** 43 17N 78 43W
Newfield, *U.S.A.* **79 D8** 42 18N 76 33W
Newfound L., *U.S.A.* **79 C13** 43 40N 71 47W
Newfoundland, *Canada* **66 E14** 49 0N 55 0W
Newfoundland, *U.S.A.* **79 E9** 41 18N 75 19W
Newfoundland □, *Canada* **71 B8** 53 0N 58 0W
Newhall, *U.S.A.* **85 L8** 34 23N 118 32W
Newhaven, *U.K.* **11 G8** 50 47N 0 3 E
Newkirk, *U.S.A.* **81 G6** 36 53N 97 3W
Newlyn, *U.K.* **11 G2** 50 6N 5 34W
Newman, *Australia* **60 D2** 23 18S 119 45 E
Newman, *U.S.A.* **84 H5** 37 19N 121 1W
Newmarket, *Canada* **78 B5** 44 3N 79 28W
Newmarket, *Ireland* **13 D2** 52 13N 9 0W
Newmarket, *U.K.* **11 E8** 52 15N 0 25 E
Newmarket, *U.S.A.* **79 C14** 43 4N 70 56W
Newnan, *U.S.A.* **77 J3** 33 23N 84 48W
Newport, *Ireland* **13 C2** 53 53N 9 33W
Newport, *I. of W., U.K.* **11 G6** 50 42N 1 17W
Newport, *Newp., U.K.* **11 F5** 51 35N 3 0W
Newport, *Ark., U.S.A.* **81 H9** 35 37N 91 16W
Newport, *Ky., U.S.A.* **76 F3** 39 5N 84 30W
Newport, *N.H., U.S.A.* **79 C12** 43 22N 72 10W
Newport, *N.Y., U.S.A.* **79 C9** 43 11N 75 1W
Newport, *Oreg., U.S.A.* **82 D1** 44 39N 124 3W
Newport, *Pa., U.S.A.* **78 F7** 40 29N 77 8W
Newport, *R.I., U.S.A.* **79 E13** 41 29N 71 19W
Newport, *Tenn., U.S.A.* **77 H4** 35 58N 83 11W
Newport, *Vt., U.S.A.* **79 B12** 44 56N 72 13W
Newport, *Wash., U.S.A.* **82 B5** 48 11N 117 3W
Newport □, *U.K.* **11 F4** 51 33N 3 1W
Newport Beach, *U.S.A.* **85 M9** 33 37N 117 56W
Newport News, *U.S.A.* **76 G7** 36 59N 76 25W
Newport Pagnell, *U.K.* **11 E7** 52 5N 0 43W
Newquay, *U.K.* **11 G2** 50 25N 5 6W
Newry, *U.K.* **13 B5** 54 11N 6 21W
Newton, *Ill., U.S.A.* **80 F10** 38 59N 88 10W
Newton, *Iowa, U.S.A.* **80 E8** 41 42N 93 3W
Newton, *Kans., U.S.A.* **81 F6** 38 3N 97 21W
Newton, *Mass., U.S.A.* **79 D13** 42 21N 71 12W
Newton, *Miss., U.S.A.* **81 J10** 32 19N 89 10W
Newton, *N.C., U.S.A.* **77 H5** 35 40N 81 13W
Newton, *N.J., U.S.A.* **79 E10** 41 3N 74 45W
Newton, *Tex., U.S.A.* **81 K8** 30 51N 93 46W
Newton Abbot, *U.K.* **11 G4** 50 32N 3 37W
Newton Aycliffe, *U.K.* **10 C6** 54 37N 1 34W
Newton Falls, *U.S.A.* **78 E4** 41 11N 80 59W
Newton Stewart, *U.K.* **12 G4** 54 57N 4 30W
Newtonmore, *U.K.* **12 D4** 57 4N 4 8W
Newtown, *U.K.* **11 E4** 52 31N 3 19W
Newtownabbey, *U.K.* **13 B6** 54 40N 5 56W
Newtownards, *U.K.* **13 B6** 54 36N 5 42W
Newtownbarry = Bunclody, *Ireland* **13 D5** 52 39N 6 40W
Newtownstewart, *U.K.* **13 B4** 54 43N 7 23W
Newville, *U.S.A.* **78 F7** 40 10N 77 24W
Neya, *Russia* **24 C7** 58 21N 43 49 E
Neyrīz, *Iran* **45 D7** 29 15N 54 19 E
Neyshābūr, *Iran* **45 B8** 36 10N 58 50 E
Nezhin = Nizhyn, *Ukraine* **25 D5** 51 5N 31 55 E
Nezperce, *U.S.A.* **82 C5** 46 14N 116 14W
Ngabang, *Indonesia* **36 D3** 0 23N 109 55 E
Ngabordamlu, Tanjung, *Indonesia* **37 F8** 6 56S 134 11 E
N'Gage, *Angola* **52 F3** 7 46S 15 16 E
Ngami Depression, *Botswana* **56 C3** 20 30S 22 46 E
Ngamo, *Zimbabwe* **55 F2** 19 3S 27 32 E
Nganglong Kangri, *China* **41 C12** 33 0N 81 0 E
Ngao, *Thailand* **38 C2** 18 46N 99 59 E
Ngaoundéré, *Cameroon* **52 C2** 7 15N 13 35 E
Ngapara, *N.Z.* **59 L3** 44 57S 170 46 E
Ngara, *Tanzania* **54 C3** 2 29S 30 40 E
Ngawi, *Indonesia* **37 G14** 7 24S 111 26 E
Nghia Lo, *Vietnam* **38 B5** 21 33N 104 28 E
Ngoma, *Malawi* **55 E3** 13 8S 33 45 E
Ngomahura, *Zimbabwe* **55 G3** 20 26S 30 43 E
Ngomba, *Tanzania* **55 D3** 8 20S 32 53 E
Ngoring Hu, *China* **32 C4** 34 55N 97 5 E
Ngorongoro, *Tanzania* **54 C4** 3 11S 35 32 E
Ngozi, *Burundi* **54 C2** 2 54S 29 50 E
Ngudu, *Tanzania* **54 C3** 2 58S 33 25 E
Nguigmi, *Niger* **51 F8** 14 20N 13 20 E
Nguiu, *Australia* **60 B5** 11 46S 130 38 E
Ngukurr, *Australia* **62 A1** 14 44S 134 44 E
Ngulu Atoll, *Pac. Oc.* **37 C9** 8 0N 137 30 E
Ngunga, *Tanzania* **54 C3** 3 37S 33 37 E
Nguru, *Nigeria* **51 F8** 12 56N 10 29 E
Nguru Mts., *Tanzania* **54 D4** 6 0S 37 30 E
Nguyen Binh, *Vietnam* **38 A5** 22 39N 105 56 E
Nha Trang, *Vietnam* **39 F7** 12 16N 109 10 E
Nhacoongo, *Mozam.* **57 C6** 24 18S 35 14 E
Nhamaabué, *Mozam.* **55 F4** 17 25S 35 5 E
Nhamundá →, *Brazil* **93 D7** 2 12S 56 41W
Nhangulaze, L., *Mozam.* **57 C5** 24 0S 34 30 E
Nho Quan, *Vietnam* **38 B5** 20 18N 105 45 E
Nhulunbuy, *Australia* **62 A2** 12 10S 137 20 E
Nia-nia, *Dem. Rep. of the Congo* **54 B2** 1 30N 27 40 E
Niagara Falls, *Canada* **78 C5** 43 7N 79 5W
Niagara Falls, *U.S.A.* **78 C6** 43 5N 79 4W
Niagara-on-the-Lake, *Canada* **78 C5** 43 15N 79 4W
Niah, *Malaysia* **36 D4** 3 58N 113 46 E
Niamey, *Niger* **50 F6** 13 27N 2 6 E
Niangara, *Dem. Rep. of the Congo* **54 B2** 3 42N 27 50 E
Niantic, *U.S.A.* **79 E12** 41 20N 72 11W
Nias, *Indonesia* **36 D1** 1 0N 97 30 E
Niassa □, *Mozam.* **55 E4** 13 30S 36 0 E
Nibāk, *Si. Arabia* **45 E7** 24 25N 50 50 E
Nicaragua ■, *Cent. Amer.* **88 D2** 11 40N 85 30W
Nicaragua, L. de, *Nic.* **88 D2** 12 0N 85 30W
Nicastro, *Italy* **20 E7** 38 59N 16 19 E
Nice, *France* **18 E7** 43 42N 7 14 E
Niceville, *U.S.A.* **77 K2** 30 31N 86 30W
Nichicun, L., *Canada* **71 B5** 53 5N 71 0W
Nichinan, *Japan* **31 J5** 31 38N 131 23 E
Nicholás, Canal, *W. Indies* **88 B3** 23 30N 80 5W
Nicholasville, *U.S.A.* **76 G3** 37 53N 84 34W
Nichols, *U.S.A.* **79 D8** 42 1N 76 22W
Nicholson, *Australia* **60 C4** 18 2S 128 54 E
Nicholson, *U.S.A.* **79 E9** 41 37N 75 47W
Nicholson →, *Australia* **62 B2** 17 31S 139 36 E
Nicholson L., *Canada* **73 A8** 62 40N 102 40W
Nicholson Ra., *Australia* **61 E2** 27 15S 116 45 E
Nicholville, *U.S.A.* **79 B10** 44 41N 74 39W
Nicobar Is., *Ind. Oc.* **29 J13** 9 0N 93 0 E
Nicola, *Canada* **72 C4** 50 12N 120 40W
Nicolls Town, *Bahamas* **88 A4** 25 8N 78 0W
Nicosia, *Cyprus* **23 D12** 35 10N 33 25 E
Nicoya, *Costa Rica* **88 D2** 10 9N 85 27W
Nicoya, G. de, *Costa Rica* **88 E3** 10 0N 85 0W
Nicoya, Pen. de, *Costa Rica* **88 E2** 9 45N 85 40W
Nidd →, *U.K.* **10 D6** 53 59N 1 23W
Niedersachsen □, *Germany* **16 B5** 52 50N 9 0 E
Niekerkshoop, *S. Africa* **56 D3** 29 19S 22 51 E
Niemba, *Dem. Rep. of the Congo* **54 D2** 5 58S 28 24 E
Niemen = Neman →, *Lithuania* **9 J19** 55 25N 21 10 E
Nienburg, *Germany* **16 B5** 52 39N 9 13 E
Nieu Bethesda, *S. Africa* **56 E3** 31 51S 24 34 E
Nieuw Amsterdam, *Surinam* **93 B7** 5 53N 55 5W
Nieuw Nickerie, *Surinam* **93 B7** 6 0N 56 59W
Nieuwoudtville, *S. Africa* **56 E2** 31 23S 19 7 E
Nieuwpoort, *Belgium* **15 C2** 51 8N 2 45 E
Nieves, Pico de las, *Canary Is.* **22 G4** 27 57N 15 35W
Niğde, *Turkey* **25 G5** 37 58N 34 40 E
Nigel, *S. Africa* **57 D4** 26 27S 28 25 E
Niger ■, *W. Afr.* **50 E7** 17 30N 10 0 E
Niger →, *W. Afr.* **50 G7** 5 33N 6 33 E
Nigeria ■, *W. Afr.* **50 G7** 8 30N 8 0 E
Nighasin, *India* **43 E9** 28 14N 80 52 E
Nightcaps, *N.Z.* **59 L2** 45 57S 168 2 E
Nii-Jima, *Japan* **31 G9** 34 20N 139 15 E
Niigata, *Japan* **30 F9** 37 58N 139 0 E
Niigata □, *Japan* **31 F9** 37 15N 138 45 E
Niihama, *Japan* **31 H6** 33 55N 133 16 E
Niihau, *U.S.A.* **74 H14** 21 54N 160 9W
Niimi, *Japan* **31 G6** 34 59N 133 28 E
Niitsu, *Japan* **30 F9** 37 48N 139 7 E
Nijil, *Jordan* **47 E4** 30 32N 35 33 E
Nijkerk, *Neths.* **15 B5** 52 13N 5 30 E
Nijmegen, *Neths.* **15 C5** 51 50N 5 52 E
Nijverdal, *Neths.* **15 B6** 52 22N 6 28 E
Nīk Pey, *Iran* **45 B6** 36 50N 48 10 E
Nikiniki, *Indonesia* **37 F6** 9 49S 124 30 E
Nikkō, *Japan* **31 F9** 36 45N 139 35 E
Nikolayev = Mykolayiv, *Ukraine* **25 E5** 46 58N 32 0 E
Nikolayevsk, *Russia* **25 E8** 50 0N 45 35 E
Nikolayevsk-na-Amur, *Russia* **27 D15** 53 8N 140 44 E
Nikolskoye, *Russia* **27 D17** 55 12N 166 0 E
Nikopol, *Ukraine* **25 E5** 47 35N 34 25 E
Nīkshahr, *Iran* **45 E9** 26 15N 60 10 E
Nikšić, *Montenegro, Yug.* **21 C8** 42 50N 18 57 E
Nîl, Nahr en →, *Africa* **51 B12** 30 10N 31 6 E
Nîl el Abyad →, *Sudan* **51 E12** 15 38N 32 31 E
Nîl el Azraq →, *Sudan* **51 E12** 15 38N 32 31 E
Nila, *Indonesia* **37 F7** 6 44S 129 31 E
Niland, *U.S.A.* **85 M11** 33 14N 115 31W
Nile = Nîl, Nahr en →, *Africa* **51 B12** 30 10N 31 6 E
Niles, *Mich., U.S.A.* **76 E2** 41 50N 86 15W
Niles, *Ohio, U.S.A.* **78 E4** 41 11N 80 46W
Nim Ka Thana, *India* **42 F6** 27 44N 75 48 E
Nimach, *India* **42 G6** 24 30N 74 56 E
Nimbahera, *India* **42 G6** 24 37N 74 45 E
Nîmes, *France* **18 E6** 43 50N 4 23 E
Nimfaíon, Ákra = Pínnes, Ákra, *Greece* **21 D11** 40 5N 24 20 E
Nīnawá, *Iraq* **44 B4** 36 25N 43 10 E
Nindigully, *Australia* **63 D4** 28 21S 148 50 E
Nineveh = Nīnawá, *Iraq* **44 B4** 36 25N 43 10 E
Ning Xian, *China* **34 G4** 35 30N 107 58 E
Ning'an, *China* **35 B15** 44 22N 129 20 E
Ningbo, *China* **33 D7** 29 51N 121 28 E
Ningcheng, *China* **35 D10** 41 32N 119 53 E
Ningjin, *China* **34 F8** 37 35N 114 57 E
Ningjing Shan, *China* **32 D4** 30 0N 98 20 E
Ningling, *China* **34 G8** 34 25N 115 22 E
Ningpo = Ningbo, *China* **33 D7** 29 51N 121 28 E
Ningqiang, *China* **34 H4** 32 47N 106 15 E
Ningshan, *China* **34 H5** 33 21N 108 21 E
Ningsia Hui A.R. = Ningxia Huizu Zizhiqu □, *China* **34 F4** 38 0N 106 0 E
Ningwu, *China* **34 E7** 39 0N 112 18 E
Ningxia Huizu Zizhiqu □, *China* **34 F4** 38 0N 106 0 E
Ningyang, *China* **34 G9** 35 47N 116 45 E
Ninh Binh, *Vietnam* **38 B5** 20 15N 105 55 E
Ninh Giang, *Vietnam* **38 B6** 20 44N 106 24 E
Ninh Hoa, *Vietnam* **38 F7** 12 30N 109 7 E
Ninh Ma, *Vietnam* **38 F7** 12 48N 109 21 E
Ninove, *Belgium* **15 D4** 50 51N 4 2 E
Nioaque, *Brazil* **95 A4** 21 5S 55 50W
Niobrara, *U.S.A.* **80 D6** 42 45N 98 2W
Niobrara →, *U.S.A.* **80 D6** 42 46N 98 3W
Nioro du Sahel, *Mali* **50 E4** 15 15N 9 30W
Niort, *France* **18 C3** 46 19N 0 29W
Nipawin, *Canada* **73 C8** 53 20N 104 0W
Nipigon, *Canada* **70 C2** 49 0N 88 17W
Nipigon, L., *Canada* **70 C2** 49 50N 88 30W
Nipishish L., *Canada* **71 B7** 54 12N 60 45W
Nipissing, L., *Canada* **70 C4** 46 20N 80 0W
Nipomo, *U.S.A.* **85 K6** 35 3N 120 29W
Nipton, *U.S.A.* **85 K11** 35 28N 115 16W
Niquelândia, *Brazil* **93 F9** 14 33S 48 23W
Nīr, *Iran* **44 B5** 38 2N 47 59 E
Nirasaki, *Japan* **31 G9** 35 42N 138 27 E
Nirmal, *India* **40 K11** 19 3N 78 20 E
Nirmali, *India* **43 F12** 26 20N 86 35 E
Niš, *Serbia, Yug.* **21 C9** 43 19N 21 58 E
Nişāb, *Si. Arabia* **44 D5** 29 11N 44 43 E
Nişāb, *Yemen* **46 E4** 14 25N 46 29 E
Nishinomiya, *Japan* **31 G7** 34 45N 135 20 E
Nishino'omote, *Japan* **31 J5** 30 43N 130 59 E
Nishiwaki, *Japan* **31 G7** 34 59N 134 58 E
Niskibi →, *Canada* **70 A2** 56 29N 88 9W
Nisqually →, *U.S.A.* **84 C4** 47 6N 122 42W
Nissáki, *Greece* **23 A3** 39 43N 19 52 E
Nissum Bredning, *Denmark* **9 H13** 56 40N 8 20 E
Nistru = Dnister →, *Europe* **17 E16** 46 18N 30 17 E
Nisutlin →, *Canada* **72 A2** 60 14N 132 34W
Nitchequon, *Canada* **71 B5** 53 10N 70 58W
Niterói, *Brazil* **95 A7** 22 52S 43 0W
Nith →, *Canada* **78 C4** 43 12N 80 23W
Nith →, *U.K.* **12 F5** 55 14N 3 33W
Nitra, *Slovak Rep.* **17 D10** 48 19N 18 4 E
Nitra →, *Slovak Rep.* **17 E10** 47 46N 18 10 E
Niuafo'ou, *Tonga* **59 B11** 15 30S 175 58W
Niue, *Cook Is.* **65 J11** 19 2S 169 54W
Niut, *Indonesia* **36 D4** 0 55N 110 6 E
Niuzhuang, *China* **35 D12** 40 58N 122 28 E
Nivala, *Finland* **8 E21** 63 56N 24 57 E
Nivelles, *Belgium* **15 D4** 50 35N 4 20 E
Nivernais, *France* **18 C5** 47 15N 3 30 E
Niwas, *India* **43 H9** 23 3N 80 26 E
Nixon, *U.S.A.* **81 L6** 29 16N 97 46W
Nizamabad, *India* **40 K11** 18 45N 78 7 E
Nizamghat, *India* **41 E19** 28 20N 95 45 E
Nizhne Kolymsk, *Russia* **27 C17** 68 34N 160 55 E
Nizhnekamsk, *Russia* **24 C9** 55 38N 51 49 E
Nizhneudinsk, *Russia* **27 D10** 54 54N 99 3 E
Nizhnevartovsk, *Russia* **26 C8** 60 56N 76 38 E
Nizhniy Novgorod, *Russia* **24 C7** 56 20N 44 0 E
Nizhniy Tagil, *Russia* **24 C10** 57 55N 59 57 E
Nizhyn, *Ukraine* **25 D5** 51 5N 31 55 E
Nizip, *Turkey* **44 B3** 37 5N 37 50 E
Nízké Tatry, *Slovak Rep.* **17 D10** 48 55N 19 30 E
Njakwa, *Malawi* **55 E3** 11 1S 33 56 E
Njanji, *Zambia* **55 E3** 14 25S 31 46 E
Njinjo, *Tanzania* **55 D4** 8 48S 38 54 E
Njombe, *Tanzania* **55 D3** 9 20S 34 50 E
Njombe →, *Tanzania* **54 D4** 6 56S 35 6 E
Nkana, *Zambia* **55 E2** 12 50S 28 8 E
Nkandla, *S. Africa* **57 D5** 28 37S 31 5 E
Nkayi, *Zimbabwe* **55 F2** 19 41S 29 20 E
Nkhotakota, *Malawi* **55 E3** 12 56S 34 15 E
Nkongsamba, *Cameroon* **52 D1** 4 55N 9 55 E
Nkurenkuru, *Namibia* **56 B2** 17 42S 18 32 E
Nmai →, *Burma* **41 G20** 25 30N 97 25 E
Noakhali = Maijdi, *Bangla.* **41 H17** 22 48N 91 10 E
Nobel, *Canada* **78 A4** 45 25N 80 6W
Nobeoka, *Japan* **31 H5** 32 36N 131 41 E
Noblesville, *U.S.A.* **76 E3** 40 3N 86 1W
Nocera Inferiore, *Italy* **20 D6** 40 44N 14 38 E
Nocona, *U.S.A.* **81 J6** 33 47N 97 44W
Noda, *Japan* **31 G9** 35 56N 139 52 E
Nogales, *Mexico* **86 A2** 31 20N 110 56W
Nogales, *U.S.A.* **83 L8** 31 20N 110 56W
Nōgata, *Japan* **31 H5** 33 48N 130 44 E
Noggerup, *Australia* **61 F2** 33 32S 116 5 E
Noginsk, *Russia* **27 C10** 64 30N 90 50 E
Nogoa →, *Australia* **62 C4** 23 40S 147 55 E
Nogoyá, *Argentina* **94 C4** 32 24S 59 48W
Nohar, *India* **42 E6** 29 11N 74 49 E
Nohta, *India* **43 H8** 23 40N 79 34 E
Noires, Mts., *France* **18 B2** 48 7N 3 28W
Noirmoutier, Î. de, *France* **18 C2** 46 58N 2 10W
Nojane, *Botswana* **56 C3** 23 15S 20 14 E
Nojima-Zaki, *Japan* **31 G9** 34 54N 139 53 E
Nok Kundi, *Pakistan* **40 E3** 28 50N 62 45 E
Nokaneng, *Botswana* **56 B3** 19 40S 22 17 E
Nokia, *Finland* **9 F20** 61 30N 23 30 E
Nokomis, *Canada* **73 C8** 51 35N 105 0W
Nokomis L., *Canada* **73 B8** 57 0N 103 0W
Nola, *C.A.R.* **52 D3** 3 35N 16 4 E
Noma Omuramba →, *Namibia* **56 B3** 18 52S 20 53 E
Nombre de Dios, *Panama* **88 E4** 9 34N 79 28W
Nome, *U.S.A.* **68 B3** 64 30N 165 25W
Nomo-Zaki, *Japan* **31 H4** 32 35N 129 44 E
Nonacho L., *Canada* **73 A7** 61 42N 109 40W
Nonda, *Australia* **62 C3** 20 40S 142 28 E
Nong Chang, *Thailand* **38 E2** 15 23N 99 51 E
Nong Het, *Laos* **38 C4** 19 29N 103 59 E
Nong Khai, *Thailand* **38 D4** 17 50N 102 46 E
Nong'an, *China* **35 B13** 44 25N 125 5 E
Nongoma, *S. Africa* **57 D5** 27 58S 31 35 E
Nonoava, *Mexico* **86 B3** 27 28N 106 44W
Nonoava →, *Mexico* **86 B3** 27 29N 106 45W
Nonthaburi, *Thailand* **38 F3** 13 51N 100 34 E
Noonamah, *Australia* **60 B5** 12 40S 131 4 E
Noord Brabant □, *Neths.* **15 C5** 51 40N 5 0 E
Noord Holland □, *Neths.* **15 B4** 52 30N 4 45 E
Noordbeveland, *Neths.* **15 C3** 51 35N 3 50 E
Noordoostpolder, *Neths.* **15 B5** 52 45N 5 45 E
Noordwijk, *Neths.* **15 B4** 52 14N 4 26 E
Nootka I., *Canada* **72 D3** 49 32N 126 42W
Nopiming Prov. Park, *Canada* **73 C9** 50 30N 95 37W
Noralee, *Canada* **72 C3** 53 59N 126 26W
Noranda = Rouyn-Noranda, *Canada* **70 C4** 48 20N 79 0W
Norco, *U.S.A.* **85 M9** 33 56N 117 33W
Nord-Kivu □, *Dem. Rep. of the Congo* **54 C2** 1 0S 29 0 E
Nord-Ostsee-Kanal, *Germany* **16 A5** 54 12N 9 32 E
Nordaustlandet, *Svalbard* **4 B9** 79 14N 23 0 E
Nordegg, *Canada* **72 C5** 52 29N 116 5W
Norderney, *Germany* **16 B4** 53 42N 7 9 E
Norderstedt, *Germany* **16 B5** 53 42N 10 1 E
Nordfjord, *Norway* **9 F11** 61 55N 5 30 E
Nordfriesische Inseln, *Germany* **16 A5** 54 40N 8 20 E
Nordhausen, *Germany* **16 C6** 51 30N 10 47 E
Norðoyar, *Færoe Is.* **8 E9** 62 17N 6 35W
Nordkapp, *Norway* **8 A21** 71 10N 25 50 E
Nordkapp, *Svalbard* **4 A9** 80 31N 20 0 E
Nordkinn = Kinnarodden, *Norway* **6 A11** 71 8N 27 40 E
Nordkinn-halvøya, *Norway* **8 A22** 70 55N 27 40 E
Nordrhein-Westfalen □, *Germany* **16 C4** 51 45N 7 30 E
Nordvik, *Russia* **27 B12** 74 2N 111 32 E
Nore →, *Ireland* **13 D4** 52 25N 6 58W
Norfolk, *Nebr., U.S.A.* **80 D6** 42 2N 97 25W
Norfolk, *Va., U.S.A.* **76 G7** 36 51N 76 17W
Norfolk □, *U.K.* **11 E8** 52 39N 0 54 E
Norfolk I., *Pac. Oc.* **64 K8** 28 58S 168 3 E
Norfork L., *U.S.A.* **81 G8** 36 15N 92 14W
Norilsk, *Russia* **27 C9** 69 20N 88 6 E
Norma, Mt., *Australia* **62 C3** 20 55S 140 42 E
Normal, *U.S.A.* **80 E10** 40 31N 88 59W
Norman, *U.S.A.* **81 H6** 35 13N 97 26W
Norman →, *Australia* **62 B3** 19 18S 141 51 E
Norman Wells, *Canada* **68 B7** 65 17N 126 51W
Normanby →, *Australia* **62 A3** 14 23S 144 10 E
Normandie, *France* **18 B4** 48 45N 0 10 E
Normandin, *Canada* **70 C5** 48 49N 72 31W
Normandy = Normandie, *France* **18 B4** 48 45N 0 10 E
Normanhurst, Mt., *Australia* **61 E3** 25 4S 122 30 E
Normanton, *Australia* **62 B3** 17 40S 141 10 E
Normétal, *Canada* **70 C4** 49 0N 79 22W
Norquay, *Canada* **73 C8** 51 53N 102 5W
Norquinco, *Argentina* **96 E2** 41 51S 70 55W
Norrbotten □, *Sweden* **8 C19** 66 30N 22 30 E
Norris Point, *Canada* **71 C8** 49 31N 57 53W
Norristown, *U.S.A.* **79 F9** 40 7N 75 21W
Norrköping, *Sweden* **9 G17** 58 37N 16 11 E
Norrland, *Sweden* **9 E16** 62 15N 15 45 E
Norrtälje, *Sweden* **9 G18** 59 46N 18 42 E
Norseman, *Australia* **61 F3** 32 8S 121 43 E
Norsk, *Russia* **27 D14** 52 30N 130 5 E
Norte, Pta. del, *Canary Is.* **22 G2** 27 51N 17 57W
Norte, Serra do, *Brazil* **92 F7** 11 20S 59 0W
North, C., *Canada* **71 C7** 47 2N 60 20W
North Adams, *U.S.A.* **79 D11** 42 42N 73 7W
North Arm, *Canada* **72 A5** 62 0N 114 30W
North Augusta, *U.S.A.* **77 J5** 33 30N 81 59W
North Ayrshire □, *U.K.* **12 F4** 55 45N 4 44W
North Bass I., *U.S.A.* **78 E2** 41 43N 82 49W
North Battleford, *Canada* **73 C7** 52 50N 108 17W
North Bay, *Canada* **70 C4** 46 20N 79 30W
North Belcher Is., *Canada* **70 A4** 56 50N 79 50W
North Bend, *Oreg., U.S.A.* **82 E1** 43 24N 124 14W
North Bend, *Pa., U.S.A.* **78 E7** 41 20N 77 42W
North Bend, *Wash., U.S.A.* **84 C5** 47 30N 121 47W
North Bennington, *U.S.A.* **79 D11** 42 56N 73 15W
North Berwick, *U.K.* **12 E6** 56 4N 2 42W
North Berwick, *U.S.A.* **79 C14** 43 18N 70 44W
North C., *Canada* **71 C7** 47 5N 64 0W
North C., *N.Z.* **59 F4** 34 23S 173 4 E
North Canadian →, *U.S.A.* **81 H7** 35 16N 95 31W
North Canton, *U.S.A.* **78 F3** 40 53N 81 24W
North Cape = Nordkapp, *Norway* **8 A21** 71 10N 25 50 E
North Cape = Nordkapp, *Svalbard* **4 A9** 80 31N 20 0 E
North Caribou L., *Canada* **70 B1** 52 50N 90 40W
North Carolina □, *U.S.A.* **77 H6** 35 30N 80 0W
North Cascades National Park, *U.S.A.* **82 B3** 48 45N 121 10W
North Channel, *Canada* **70 C3** 46 0N 83 0W
North Channel, *U.K.* **12 F3** 55 13N 5 52W
North Charleston, *U.S.A.* **77 J6** 32 53N 79 58W
North Chicago, *U.S.A.* **76 D2** 42 19N 87 51W
North Creek, *U.S.A.* **79 C11** 43 41N 73 59W
North Dakota □, *U.S.A.* **80 B5** 47 30N 100 15W
North Downs, *U.K.* **11 F8** 51 19N 0 21 E
North East, *U.S.A.* **78 D5** 42 13N 79 50W
North East Frontier Agency = Arunachal Pradesh □, *India* **41 F19** 28 0N 95 0 E
North East Lincolnshire □, *U.K.* **10 D7** 53 34N 0 2W

North Eastern

North Eastern □, *Kenya* **54 B5** 1 30N 40 0 E
North Esk →, *U.K.* **12 E6** 56 46N 2 24W
North European Plain, *Europe* **6 E10** 55 0N 25 0 E
North Foreland, *U.K.* **11 F9** 51 22N 1 28 E
North Fork, *U.S.A.* **84 H7** 37 14N 119 21W
North Fork American →, *U.S.A.* **84 G5** 38 57N 120 59W
North Fork Feather →, *U.S.A.* **84 F5** 38 33N 121 30W
North Fork Grand →, *U.S.A.* **80 C3** 45 47N 102 16W
North Fork Red →, *U.S.A.* **81 H5** 34 24N 99 14W
North Frisian Is. = Nordfriesische Inseln, *Germany* **16 A5** 54 40N 8 20 E
North Gower, *Canada* **79 A9** 45 8N 75 43W
North Hd., *Australia* **61 F1** 30 14S 114 59 E
North Henik L., *Canada* **73 A9** 61 45N 97 40W
North Highlands, *U.S.A.* **84 G5** 38 40N 121 23W
North Horr, *Kenya* **54 B4** 3 20N 37 8 E
North I., *Kenya* **54 B4** 4 5N 36 5 E
North I., *N.Z.* **59 H5** 38 0S 175 0 E
North Kingsville, *U.S.A.* **78 E4** 41 54N 80 42W
North Knife →, *Canada* **73 B10** 58 53N 94 45W
North Koel →, *India* **43 G10** 24 45N 83 50 E
North Korea ■, *Asia* **35 E14** 40 0N 127 0 E
North Lakhimpur, *India* **41 F19** 27 14N 94 7 E
North Lanarkshire □, *U.K.* **12 F5** 55 52N 3 56W
North Las Vegas, *U.S.A.* **85 J11** 36 12N 115 7W
North Lincolnshire □, *U.K.* **10 D7** 53 36N 0 30W
North Little Rock, *U.S.A.* **81 H8** 34 45N 92 16W
North Loup →, *U.S.A.* **80 E5** 41 17N 98 24W
North Magnetic Pole, *Canada* **4 B2** 77 58N 102 8W
North Minch, *U.K.* **12 C3** 58 5N 5 55W
North Moose L., *Canada* **73 C8** 54 11N 100 6W
North Myrtle Beach, *U.S.A.* **77 J6** 33 48N 78 42W
North Nahanni →, *Canada* **72 A4** 62 15N 123 20W
North Olmsted, *U.S.A.* **78 E3** 41 25N 81 56W
North Ossetia □, *Russia* **25 F7** 43 30N 44 30 E
North Pagai, I. = Pagai Utara, Pulau, *Indonesia* **36 E2** 2 35S 100 0 E
North Palisade, *U.S.A.* **84 H8** 37 6N 118 31W
North Platte, *U.S.A.* **80 E4** 41 8N 100 46W
North Platte →, *U.S.A.* **80 E4** 41 7N 100 42W
North Pole, *Arctic* **4 A** 90 0N 0 0W
North Portal, *Canada* **73 D8** 49 0N 102 33W
North Powder, *U.S.A.* **82 D5** 45 2N 117 55W
North Pt., *U.S.A.* **78 A1** 45 2N 83 16W
North Rhine Westphalia = Nordrhein-Westfalen □, *Germany* **16 C4** 51 45N 7 30 E
North River, *Canada* **71 B8** 53 49N 57 6W
North Ronaldsay, *U.K.* **12 B6** 59 22N 2 26W
North Saskatchewan →, *Canada* **73 C7** 53 15N 105 5W
North Sea, *Europe* **6 D6** 56 0N 4 0 E
North Seal →, *Canada* **73 B9** 58 50N 98 7W
North Somerset □, *U.K.* **11 F5** 51 24N 2 45W
North Sporades = Vóriai Sporádhes, *Greece* **21 E10** 39 15N 23 30 E
North Sydney, *Canada* **71 C7** 46 12N 60 15W
North Syracuse, *U.S.A.* **79 C8** 43 8N 76 7W
North Taranaki Bight, *N.Z.* **59 H5** 38 50S 174 15 E
North Thompson →, *Canada* **72 C4** 50 40N 120 20W
North Tonawanda, *U.S.A.* **78 C6** 43 2N 78 53W
North Troy, *U.S.A.* **79 B12** 45 0N 72 24W
North Truchas Pk., *U.S.A.* **83 J11** 36 0N 105 30W
North Twin I., *Canada* **70 B4** 53 20N 80 0W
North Tyne →, *U.K.* **10 B5** 55 0N 2 8W
North Uist, *U.K.* **12 D1** 57 40N 7 15W
North Vancouver, *Canada* **72 D4** 49 19N 123 4W
North Vernon, *U.S.A.* **76 F3** 39 0N 85 38W
North Wabasca L., *Canada* **72 B6** 56 0N 113 55W
North Walsham, *U.K.* **10 E9** 52 50N 1 22 E
North-West □, *S. Africa* **56 D4** 27 0S 25 0 E
North West C., *Australia* **60 D1** 21 45S 114 9 E
North West Christmas I. Ridge, *Pac. Oc.* **65 G11** 6 30N 165 0W
North West Frontier □, *Pakistan* **42 C4** 34 0N 72 0 E
North West Highlands, *U.K.* **12 D4** 57 33N 4 58W
North West River, *Canada* **71 B7** 53 30N 60 10W
North Western □, *Zambia* **55 E2** 13 30S 25 30 E
North Wildwood, *U.S.A.* **76 F8** 39 0N 74 48W
North York Moors, *U.K.* **10 C7** 54 23N 0 53W
North Yorkshire □, *U.K.* **10 C6** 54 15N 1 25W
Northallerton, *U.K.* **10 C6** 54 20N 1 26W
Northam, *Australia* **61 F2** 31 35S 116 42 E
Northam, *S. Africa* **56 C4** 24 56S 27 18 E
Northampton, *Australia* **61 E1** 28 27S 114 33 E
Northampton, *U.K.* **11 E7** 52 15N 0 53W
Northampton, *Mass., U.S.A.* **79 D12** 42 19N 72 38W
Northampton, *Pa., U.S.A.* **79 F9** 40 41N 75 30W
Northamptonshire □, *U.K.* **11 E7** 52 16N 0 55W
Northbridge, *U.S.A.* **79 D13** 42 9N 71 39W
Northcliffe, *Australia* **61 F2** 34 39S 116 7 E
Northeast Providence Chan., *W. Indies* **88 A4** 26 0N 76 0W
Northern □, *Malawi* **55 E3** 11 0S 34 0 E
Northern □, *Zambia* **55 E3** 10 30S 31 0 E
Northern Areas □, *Pakistan* **43 A5** 36 0N 73 0 E
Northern Cape □, *S. Africa* **56 D3** 30 0S 20 0 E
Northern Circars, *India* **41 L13** 17 30N 82 30 E
Northern Indian L., *Canada* **73 B9** 57 20N 97 20W
Northern Ireland □, *U.K.* **13 B5** 54 45N 7 0W
Northern Light L., *Canada* **70 C1** 48 15N 90 39W
Northern Marianas ■, *Pac. Oc.* **64 F6** 17 0N 145 0 E
Northern Province □, *S. Africa* **57 C4** 24 0S 29 0 E
Northern Territory □, *Australia* **60 D5** 20 0S 133 0 E
Northfield, *Minn., U.S.A.* **80 C8** 44 27N 93 9W
Northfield, *Vt., U.S.A.* **79 B12** 44 9N 72 40W
Northland □, *N.Z.* **59 F4** 35 30S 173 30 E
Northome, *U.S.A.* **80 B7** 47 52N 94 17W
Northport, *Ala., U.S.A.* **77 J2** 33 14N 87 35W
Northport, *Wash., U.S.A.* **82 B5** 48 55N 117 48W
Northumberland □, *U.K.* **10 B6** 55 12N 2 0W
Northumberland Is., *Australia* **62 C4** 21 30S 149 50 E
Northumberland Str., *Canada* **71 C7** 46 20N 64 0W
Northville, *U.S.A.* **79 C10** 43 13N 74 11W
Northwest Providence Channel, *W. Indies* **88 A4** 26 0N 78 0W
Northwest Territories □, *Canada* **68 B9** 63 0N 118 0W
Northwood, *Iowa, U.S.A.* **80 D8** 43 27N 93 13W
Northwood, *N. Dak., U.S.A.* **80 B6** 47 44N 97 34W
Norton, *U.S.A.* **80 F5** 39 50N 99 53W
Norton, *Zimbabwe* **55 F3** 17 52S 30 40 E
Norton Sd., *U.S.A.* **68 B3** 63 50N 164 0W
Norwalk, *Calif., U.S.A.* **85 M8** 33 54N 118 5W
Norwalk, *Conn., U.S.A.* **79 E11** 41 7N 73 22W
Norwalk, *Iowa, U.S.A.* **80 E8** 41 29N 93 41W
Norwalk, *Ohio, U.S.A.* **78 E2** 41 15N 82 37W
Norway, *Maine, U.S.A.* **77 C10** 44 13N 70 32W
Norway, *Mich., U.S.A.* **76 C2** 45 47N 87 55W
Norway ■, *Europe* **8 E14** 63 0N 11 0 E
Norway House, *Canada* **73 C9** 53 59N 97 50W
Norwegian Sea, *Atl. Oc.* **4 C8** 66 0N 1 0 E
Norwich, *Canada* **78 D4** 42 59N 80 36W
Norwich, *U.K.* **11 E9** 52 38N 1 18 E
Norwich, *Conn., U.S.A.* **79 E12** 41 31N 72 5W
Norwich, *N.Y., U.S.A.* **79 D9** 42 32N 75 32W
Norwood, *Canada* **78 B7** 44 23N 77 59W
Norwood, *U.S.A.* **79 B10** 44 45N 75 0W
Noshiro, *Japan* **30 D10** 40 12N 140 0 E
Noşratābād, *Iran* **45 D8** 29 55N 60 0 E
Noss Hd., *U.K.* **12 C5** 58 28N 3 3W
Nossob →, *S. Africa* **56 D3** 26 55S 20 45 E
Nosy Barren, *Madag.* **53 H8** 18 25S 43 40 E
Nosy Be, *Madag.* **53 G9** 13 25S 48 15 E
Nosy Boraha, *Madag.* **57 B8** 16 50S 49 55 E
Nosy Lava, *Madag.* **57 A8** 14 33S 47 36 E
Nosy Varika, *Madag.* **57 C8** 20 35S 48 32 E
Noteć →, *Poland* **16 B8** 52 44N 15 26 E
Notikewin →, *Canada* **72 B5** 57 2N 117 38W
Notodden, *Norway* **9 G13** 59 35N 9 17 E
Notre Dame B., *Canada* **71 C8** 49 45N 55 30W
Notre Dame de Koartac = Quaqtaq, *Canada* **69 B13** 60 55N 69 40W
Notre-Dame-des-Bois, *Canada* **79 A13** 45 24N 71 4W
Notre Dame d'Ivugivic = Ivujivik, *Canada* **69 B12** 62 24N 77 55W
Notre-Dame-du-Nord, *Canada* **70 C4** 47 36N 79 30W
Nottawasaga B., *Canada* **78 B4** 44 35N 80 15W
Nottaway →, *Canada* **70 B4** 51 22N 78 55W
Nottingham, *U.K.* **10 E6** 52 58N 1 10W
Nottingham, City of □, *U.K.* **10 E6** 52 58N 1 10W
Nottingham I., *Canada* **69 B12** 63 20N 77 55W
Nottinghamshire □, *U.K.* **10 D6** 53 10N 1 3W
Nottoway →, *U.S.A.* **76 G7** 36 33N 76 55W
Notwane →, *Botswana* **56 C4** 23 35S 26 58 E
Nouâdhibou, *Mauritania* **50 D2** 20 54N 17 0W
Nouâdhibou, Ras, *Mauritania* **50 D2** 20 50N 17 0W
Nouakchott, *Mauritania* **50 E2** 18 9N 15 58W
Nouméa, *N. Cal.* **64 K8** 22 17S 166 30 E
Noupoort, *S. Africa* **56 E3** 31 10S 24 57 E
Nouveau Comptoir = Wemindji, *Canada* **70 B4** 53 0N 78 49W
Nouvelle-Amsterdam, I., *Ind. Oc.* **3 F13** 38 30S 77 30 E
Nouvelle-Calédonie = New Caledonia ■, *Pac. Oc.* **64 K8** 21 0S 165 0 E
Nova Casa Nova, *Brazil* **93 E10** 9 25S 41 5W
Nova Esperança, *Brazil* **95 A5** 23 8S 52 24W
Nova Friburgo, *Brazil* **95 A7** 22 16S 42 30W
Nova Gaia = Cambundi-Catembo, *Angola* **52 G3** 10 10S 17 35 E
Nova Iguaçu, *Brazil* **95 A7** 22 45S 43 28W
Nova Iorque, *Brazil* **93 E10** 7 0S 44 5W
Nova Lima, *Brazil* **95 A7** 19 59S 43 51W
Nova Lisboa = Huambo, *Angola* **53 G3** 12 42S 15 54 E
Nova Lusitânia, *Mozam.* **55 F3** 19 50S 34 34 E
Nova Mambone, *Mozam.* **57 C6** 21 0S 35 3 E
Nova Scotia □, *Canada* **71 C7** 45 10N 63 0W
Nova Sofala, *Mozam.* **57 C5** 20 7S 34 42 E
Nova Venécia, *Brazil* **93 G10** 18 45S 40 24W
Nova Zagora, *Bulgaria* **21 C11** 42 32N 26 1 E
Novar, *Canada* **78 A5** 45 27N 79 15W
Novara, *Italy* **18 D8** 45 28N 8 38 E
Novato, *U.S.A.* **84 G4** 38 6N 122 35W
Novaya Ladoga, *Russia* **24 B5** 60 7N 32 16 E
Novaya Lyalya, *Russia* **24 C11** 59 4N 60 45 E
Novaya Sibir, Ostrov, *Russia* **27 B16** 75 10N 150 0 E
Novaya Zemlya, *Russia* **26 B6** 75 0N 56 0 E
Nové Zámky, *Slovak Rep.* **17 D10** 48 2N 18 8 E
Novgorod, *Russia* **24 C5** 58 30N 31 25 E
Novgorod-Severskiy = Novhorod-Siverskyy, *Ukraine* **24 D5** 52 2N 33 10 E
Novhorod-Siverskyy, *Ukraine* **24 D5** 52 2N 33 10 E
Novi Lígure, *Italy* **18 D8** 44 46N 8 47 E
Novi Pazar, *Serbia, Yug.* **21 C9** 43 12N 20 28 E
Novi Sad, *Serbia, Yug.* **21 B8** 45 18N 19 52 E
Nôvo Hamburgo, *Brazil* **95 B5** 29 37S 51 7W
Novo Mesto, *Slovenia* **20 B6** 45 47N 15 12 E
Novo Remanso, *Brazil* **93 E10** 9 41S 42 4W
Novoataysk, *Russia* **26 D9** 53 30N 84 0 E
Novocherkassk, *Russia* **25 E7** 47 27N 40 15 E
Novogrudok = Navahrudak, *Belarus* **17 B13** 53 40N 25 50 E
Novohrad-Volynskyy, *Ukraine* **17 C14** 50 34N 27 35 E
Novokachalinsk, *Russia* **30 B6** 45 5N 132 0 E
Novokazalinsk = Zhangaqazaly, *Kazakstan* **26 E7** 45 48N 62 6 E
Novokuybyshevsk, *Russia* **24 D8** 53 7N 49 58 E
Novokuznetsk, *Russia* **26 D9** 53 45N 87 10 E
Novomoskovsk, *Russia* **24 D6** 54 5N 38 15 E
Novorossiysk, *Russia* **25 F6** 44 43N 37 46 E
Novorybnoye, *Russia* **27 B11** 72 50N 105 50 E
Novoselytsya, *Ukraine* **17 D14** 48 14N 26 15 E
Novoshakhtinsk, *Russia* **25 E6** 47 46N 39 58 E
Novosibirsk, *Russia* **26 D9** 55 0N 83 5 E
Novosibirskiye Ostrova, *Russia* **27 B15** 75 0N 142 0 E
Novotroitsk, *Russia* **24 D10** 51 10N 58 15 E
Novouzensk, *Russia* **25 D8** 50 32N 48 17 E
Novovolynsk, *Ukraine* **17 C13** 50 45N 24 4 E
Novska, *Croatia* **20 B7** 45 19N 17 0 E
Novvy Urengoy, *Russia* **26 C8** 65 48N 76 52 E
Novyy Bor, *Russia* **24 A9** 66 43N 52 19 E
Novyy Port, *Russia* **26 C8** 67 40N 72 30 E
Now Shahr, *Iran* **45 B6** 36 40N 51 30 E
Nowa Sól, *Poland* **16 C8** 51 48N 15 44 E
Nowata, *U.S.A.* **81 G7** 36 42N 95 38W
Nowbarān, *Iran* **45 C6** 35 8N 49 42 E
Nowghāb, *Iran* **45 C8** 33 53N 59 4 E
Nowgong, *Assam, India* **41 F18** 26 20N 92 50 E
Nowgong, *Mad. P., India* **43 G8** 25 4N 79 27 E
Nowshera, *Pakistan* **40 C8** 34 0N 72 0 E
Nowy Sącz, *Poland* **17 D11** 49 40N 20 41 E
Nowy Targ, *Poland* **17 D11** 49 29N 20 2 E
Nowy Tomyśl, *Poland* **16 B9** 52 19N 16 10 E
Noxen, *U.S.A.* **79 E8** 41 25N 76 4W
Noxon, *U.S.A.* **82 C6** 48 0N 115 43W
Noyabr'sk, *Russia* **26 C8** 64 34N 76 21 E
Noyon, *France* **18 B5** 49 34N 2 59 E
Noyon, *Mongolia* **34 C2** 43 2N 102 4 E
Nqutu, *S. Africa* **57 D5** 28 13S 30 32 E
Nsanje, *Malawi* **55 F4** 16 55S 35 12 E
Nsomba, *Zambia* **55 E2** 10 45S 29 51 E
Nu Jiang →, *China* **32 D4** 29 58N 97 25 E
Nu Shan, *China* **32 D4** 26 0N 99 20 E
Nubia, *Africa* **48 D7** 21 0N 32 0 E
Nubian Desert = Nûbîya, Es Sahrâ en, *Sudan* **51 D12** 21 30N 33 30 E
Nûbîya, Es Sahrâ en, *Sudan* **51 D12** 21 30N 33 30 E
Nuboai, *Indonesia* **37 E9** 2 10S 136 30 E
Nubra →, *India* **43 B7** 34 35N 77 35 E
Nueces →, *U.S.A.* **81 M6** 27 51N 97 30W
Nueltin L., *Canada* **73 A9** 60 30N 99 30W
Nueva Asunción □, *Paraguay* **94 A3** 21 0S 61 0W
Nueva Gerona, *Cuba* **88 B3** 21 53N 82 49W
Nueva Palmira, *Uruguay* **94 C4** 33 52S 58 20W
Nueva Rosita, *Mexico* **86 B4** 28 0N 101 11W
Nueva San Salvador, *El Salv.* **88 D2** 13 40N 89 18W
Nuéve de Julio, *Argentina* **94 D3** 35 30S 61 0W
Nuevitas, *Cuba* **88 B4** 21 30N 77 20W
Nuevo, G., *Argentina* **96 E4** 43 0S 64 30W
Nuevo Casas Grandes, *Mexico* **86 A3** 30 22N 108 0W
Nuevo Guerrero, *Mexico* **87 B5** 26 34N 99 15W
Nuevo Laredo, *Mexico* **87 B5** 27 30N 99 30W
Nuevo León □, *Mexico* **86 C5** 25 0N 100 0W
Nuevo Rocafuerte, *Ecuador* **92 D3** 0 55S 75 27W
Nugget Pt., *N.Z.* **59 M2** 46 27S 169 50 E
Nuhaka, *N.Z.* **59 H6** 39 3S 177 45 E
Nukey Bluff, *Australia* **63 E2** 32 26S 135 29 E
Nukhuyb, *Iraq* **44 C4** 32 4N 42 3 E
Nuku'alofa, *Tonga* **59 E12** 21 10S 174 0W
Nukus, *Uzbekistan* **26 E6** 42 27N 59 41 E
Nullagine, *Australia* **60 D3** 21 53S 120 7 E
Nullagine →, *Australia* **60 D3** 21 20S 120 20 E
Nullarbor, *Australia* **61 F5** 31 28S 130 55 E
Nullarbor Plain, *Australia* **61 F4** 31 10S 129 0 E
Numalla, L., *Australia* **63 D3** 28 43S 144 20 E
Numan, *Nigeria* **51 G8** 9 29N 12 3 E
Numata, *Japan* **31 F9** 36 45N 139 4 E
Numazu, *Japan* **31 G9** 35 7N 138 51 E
Numbulwar, *Australia* **62 A2** 14 15S 135 45 E
Numfoor, *Indonesia* **37 E8** 1 0S 134 50 E
Nunaksaluk I., *Canada* **71 A7** 55 49N 60 20W
Nunap Isua, *Greenland* **69 C15** 59 48N 43 55W
Nunavut □, *Canada* **69 B11** 66 0N 85 0W
Nunda, *U.S.A.* **78 D7** 42 35N 77 56W
Nungarin, *Australia* **61 F2** 31 12S 118 6 E
Nungo, *Mozam.* **55 E4** 13 23S 37 43 E
Nungwe, *Tanzania* **54 C3** 2 48S 32 2 E
Nunivak I., *U.S.A.* **68 B3** 60 10N 166 30W
Nunkun, *India* **43 C7** 33 57N 76 2 E
Nùoro, *Italy* **20 D3** 40 20N 9 20 E
Nūrābād, *Iran* **45 E8** 27 47N 57 12 E
Nuremberg = Nürnberg, *Germany* **16 D6** 49 27N 11 3 E
Nuri, *Mexico* **86 B3** 28 2N 109 22W
Nurmes, *Finland* **8 E23** 63 33N 29 10 E
Nürnberg, *Germany* **16 D6** 49 27N 11 3 E
Nurpur, *Pakistan* **42 D4** 31 53N 71 54 E
Nurran, L. = Terewah, L., *Australia* **63 D4** 29 52S 147 35 E
Nurrari Lakes, *Australia* **61 E5** 29 1S 130 5 E
Nusa Barung, *Indonesia* **37 H15** 8 30S 113 30 E
Nusa Kambangan, *Indonesia* **37 G13** 7 40S 108 10 E
Nusa Tenggara Barat □, *Indonesia* **36 F5** 8 50S 117 30 E
Nusa Tenggara Timur □, *Indonesia* **37 F6** 9 30S 122 0 E
Nusaybin, *Turkey* **25 G7** 37 3N 41 10 E
Nushki, *Pakistan* **42 E2** 29 35N 66 0 E
Nuuk, *Greenland* **69 B14** 64 10N 51 35W
Nuwakot, *Nepal* **43 E10** 28 10N 83 55 E
Nuweiba', *Egypt* **44 D2** 28 59N 34 39 E
Nuwerus, *S. Africa* **56 E2** 31 8S 18 24 E
Nuweveldberge, *S. Africa* **56 E3** 32 10S 21 45 E
Nuyts, C., *Australia* **61 F5** 32 2S 132 21 E
Nuyts, Pt., *Australia* **61 G2** 35 4S 116 38 E
Nuyts Arch., *Australia* **63 E1** 32 35S 133 20 E
Nxau-Nxau, *Botswana* **56 B3** 18 57S 21 4 E
Nyabing, *Australia* **61 F2** 33 33S 118 9 E
Nyack, *U.S.A.* **79 E11** 41 5N 73 55W
Nyagan, *Russia* **26 C7** 62 30N 65 38 E
Nyahanga, *Tanzania* **54 C3** 2 20S 33 37 E
Nyahua, *Tanzania* **54 D3** 5 25S 33 23 E
Nyahururu, *Kenya* **54 B4** 0 2N 36 27 E
Nyainqentanglha Shan, *China* **32 D4** 30 0N 90 0 E
Nyakanazi, *Tanzania* **54 C3** 3 2S 31 10 E
Nyâlâ, *Sudan* **51 F10** 12 2N 24 58 E
Nyamandhlovu, *Zimbabwe* **55 F2** 19 55S 28 16 E
Nyambiti, *Tanzania* **54 C3** 2 48S 33 27 E
Nyamwaga, *Tanzania* **54 C3** 1 27S 34 33 E
Nyandekwa, *Tanzania* **54 C3** 3 57S 32 32 E
Nyandoma, *Russia* **24 B7** 61 40N 40 12 E
Nyangana, *Namibia* **56 B3** 18 0S 20 40 E
Nyanguge, *Tanzania* **54 C3** 2 30S 33 12 E
Nyanza, *Rwanda* **54 C2** 2 20S 29 42 E
Nyanza □, *Kenya* **54 C3** 0 10S 34 15 E
Nyanza-Lac, *Burundi* **54 C2** 4 21S 29 36 E
Nyasa, L., *Africa* **55 E3** 12 30S 34 30 E
Nyasvizh, *Belarus* **17 B14** 53 14N 26 38 E
Nyazepetrovsk, *Russia* **24 C10** 56 3N 59 36 E
Nyazura, *Zimbabwe* **55 F3** 18 40S 32 16 E
Nyazwidzi →, *Zimbabwe* **55 G3** 20 0S 31 17 E
Nybro, *Sweden* **9 H16** 56 44N 15 55 E
Nyda, *Russia* **26 C8** 66 40N 72 58 E
Nyeri, *Kenya* **54 C4** 0 23S 36 56 E
Nyíregyháza, *Hungary* **17 E11** 47 58N 21 47 E
Nykøbing, *Storstrøm, Denmark* **9 J14** 54 56N 11 52 E
Nykøbing, *Vestsjælland, Denmark* **9 J14** 55 55N 11 40 E
Nykøbing, *Viborg, Denmark* **9 H13** 56 48N 8 51 E
Nyköping, *Sweden* **9 G17** 58 45N 17 1 E
Nylstroom, *S. Africa* **57 C4** 24 42S 28 22 E
Nynäshamn, *Sweden* **9 G17** 58 54N 17 57 E
Nyoma Rap, *India* **43 C8** 33 10N 78 40 E
Nyoman = Neman →, *Lithuania* **9 J19** 55 25N 21 10 E
Nysa, *Poland* **17 C9** 50 30N 17 22 E
Nysa →, *Europe* **16 B8** 52 4N 14 46 E
Nyssa, *U.S.A.* **82 E5** 43 53N 117 0W
Nyunzu, *Dem. Rep. of the Congo* **54 D2** 5 57S 27 58 E
Nyurba, *Russia* **27 C12** 63 17N 118 28 E
Nzega, *Tanzania* **54 C3** 4 10S 33 12 E
Nzérékoré, *Guinea* **50 G4** 7 49N 8 48W
Nzeto, *Angola* **52 F2** 7 10S 12 52 E
Nzilo, Chutes de, *Dem. Rep. of the Congo* **55 E2** 10 18S 25 27 E
Nzubuka, *Tanzania* **54 C3** 4 45S 32 50 E

O

Ō-Shima, *Japan* **31 G9** 34 44N 139 24 E
Oa, Mull of, *U.K.* **12 F2** 55 35N 6 20W
Oacoma, *U.S.A.* **80 D5** 43 48N 99 24W
Oahe, L., *U.S.A.* **80 C4** 44 27N 100 24W
Oahe Dam, *U.S.A.* **80 C4** 44 27N 100 24W
Oahu, *U.S.A.* **74 H16** 21 28N 157 58W
Oak Harbor, *U.S.A.* **84 B4** 48 18N 122 39W
Oak Hill, *U.S.A.* **76 G5** 37 59N 81 9W
Oak Ridge, *U.S.A.* **77 G3** 36 1N 84 16W
Oak View, *U.S.A.* **85 L7** 34 24N 119 18W
Oakan-Dake, *Japan* **30 C12** 43 27N 144 10 E
Oakdale, *Calif., U.S.A.* **84 H6** 37 46N 120 51W
Oakdale, *La., U.S.A.* **81 K8** 30 49N 92 40W
Oakes, *U.S.A.* **80 B5** 46 8N 98 6W
Oakesdale, *U.S.A.* **82 C5** 47 8N 117 15W
Oakey, *Australia* **63 D5** 27 25S 151 43 E
Oakfield, *U.S.A.* **78 C6** 43 4N 78 16W
Oakham, *U.K.* **11 E7** 52 40N 0 43W
Oakhurst, *U.S.A.* **84 H7** 37 19N 119 40W
Oakland, *U.S.A.* **84 H4** 37 49N 122 16W
Oakley, *Idaho, U.S.A.* **82 E7** 42 15N 113 53W
Oakley, *Kans., U.S.A.* **80 F4** 39 8N 100 51W
Oakover →, *Australia* **60 D3** 21 0S 120 40 E
Oakridge, *U.S.A.* **82 E2** 43 45N 122 28W
Oakville, *Canada* **78 C5** 43 27N 79 41W
Oakville, *U.S.A.* **84 D3** 46 51N 123 14W
Oamaru, *N.Z.* **59 L3** 45 5S 170 59 E
Oasis, *Calif., U.S.A.* **85 M10** 33 28N 116 6W
Oasis, *Nev., U.S.A.* **84 H9** 37 29N 117 55W
Oates Land, *Antarctica* **5 C11** 69 0S 160 0 E
Oatlands, *Australia* **62 G4** 42 17S 147 21 E
Oatman, *U.S.A.* **85 K12** 35 1N 114 19W
Oaxaca, *Mexico* **87 D5** 17 2N 96 40W
Oaxaca □, *Mexico* **87 D5** 17 0N 97 0W
Ob →, *Russia* **26 C7** 66 45N 69 30 E
Oba, *Canada* **70 C3** 49 4N 84 7W
Obama, *Japan* **31 G7** 35 30N 135 45 E
Oban, *U.K.* **12 E3** 56 25N 5 29W
Obbia, *Somali Rep.* **46 F4** 5 25N 48 30 E
Obera, *Argentina* **95 B4** 27 21S 55 2W
Oberhausen, *Germany* **16 C4** 51 28N 6 51 E
Oberlin, *Kans., U.S.A.* **80 F4** 39 49N 100 32W
Oberlin, *La., U.S.A.* **81 K8** 30 37N 92 46W
Oberlin, *Ohio, U.S.A.* **78 E2** 41 18N 82 13W
Obi, Kepulauan, *Indonesia* **37 E7** 1 23S 127 45 E
Obi Is. = Obi, Kepulauan, *Indonesia* **37 E7** 1 23S 127 45 E
Óbidos, *Brazil* **93 D7** 1 50S 55 30W
Obihiro, *Japan* **30 C11** 42 56N 143 12 E
Obilatu, *Indonesia* **37 E7** 1 25S 127 20 E
Obluchye, *Russia* **27 E14** 49 1N 131 4 E
Obo, *C.A.R.* **54 A2** 5 20N 26 32 E
Oboa, Mt., *Uganda* **54 B3** 1 45N 34 45 E
Oboyan, *Russia* **26 D4** 51 15N 36 21 E
Obozerskaya = Obozerskiy, *Russia* **24 B7** 63 34N 40 21 E
Obozerskiy, *Russia* **24 B7** 63 34N 40 21 E
Observatory Inlet, *Canada* **72 B3** 55 10N 129 54W
Obshchi Syrt, *Russia* **6 E16** 52 0N 53 0 E
Obskaya Guba, *Russia* **26 C8** 69 0N 73 0 E
Obuasi, *Ghana* **50 G5** 6 17N 1 40W
Ocala, *U.S.A.* **77 L4** 29 11N 82 8W
Ocampo, *Chihuahua, Mexico* **86 B3** 28 9N 108 24W
Ocampo, *Tamaulipas, Mexico* **87 C5** 22 50N 99 20W
Ocaña, *Spain* **19 C4** 39 55N 3 30W
Oconomowoc, *U.S.A.* **80 D10** 43 7N 88 30W
Occidental, Cordillera, *Colombia* **92 C3** 5 0N 76 0W
Ocean City, *Md., U.S.A.* **76 F8** 38 20N 75 5W
Ocean City, *N.J., U.S.A.* **76 F8** 39 17N 74 35W
Ocean City, *Wash., U.S.A.* **84 C2** 47 4N 124 10W
Ocean Falls, *Canada* **72 C3** 52 18N 127 48W
Ocean I. = Banaba, *Kiribati* **64 H8** 0 45S 169 50 E
Ocean Park, *U.S.A.* **84 D2** 46 30N 124 3W
Oceano, *U.S.A.* **85 K6** 35 6N 120 37W
Oceanport, *U.S.A.* **79 F10** 40 19N 74 3W
Oceanside, *U.S.A.* **85 M9** 33 12N 117 23W
Ochil Hills, *U.K.* **12 E5** 56 14N 3 40W
Ocilla, *U.S.A.* **77 K4** 31 36N 83 15W
Ocmulgee →, *U.S.A.* **77 K4** 31 58N 82 33W
Ocnița, *Moldova* **17 D14** 48 25N 27 30 E
Oconee →, *U.S.A.* **77 K4** 31 58N 82 33W
Oconto, *U.S.A.* **76 C2** 44 53N 87 52W
Oconto Falls, *U.S.A.* **76 C1** 44 52N 88 9W
Ocosingo, *Mexico* **87 D6** 17 10N 92 15W
Ocotal, *Nic.* **88 D2** 13 41N 86 31W
Ocotlán, *Mexico* **86 C4** 20 21N 102 42W
Ocotlán de Morelos, *Mexico* **87 D5** 16 48N 96 40W
Ōda, *Japan* **31 G6** 35 11N 132 30 E
Ódáðahraun, *Iceland* **8 D5** 65 5N 17 0W
Odate, *Japan* **30 D10** 40 16N 140 34 E
Odawara, *Japan* **31 G9** 35 20N 139 6 E

Orūmīyeh, Daryācheh-ye

Odda, *Norway* **9 F12** 60 3N 6 35 E
Odei →, *Canada* **73 B9** 56 6N 96 54W
Ödemiş, *Turkey* **21 E13** 38 15N 28 0 E
Odendaalsrus, *S. Africa* **56 D4** 27 48S 26 45 E
Odense, *Denmark* **9 J14** 55 22N 10 23 E
Oder →, *Europe* **16 B8** 53 33N 14 38 E
Odesa, *Ukraine* **25 E5** 46 30N 30 45 E
Odessa = Odesa, *Ukraine* **25 E5** 46 30N 30 45 E
Odessa, *Canada* **79 B8** 44 17N 76 43W
Odessa, *Tex., U.S.A.* **81 K3** 31 52N 102 23W
Odessa, *Wash., U.S.A.* **82 C4** 47 20N 118 41W
Odiakwe, *Botswana* **56 C4** 20 12S 25 17 E
Odienné, *Ivory C.* **50 G4** 9 30N 7 34W
Odintsovo, *Russia* **24 C6** 55 39N 37 15 E
O'Donnell, *U.S.A.* **81 J4** 32 58N 101 50W
Odorheiu Secuiesc, *Romania* **17 E13** 46 21N 25 21 E
Odra = Oder →, *Europe* **16 B8** 53 33N 14 38 E
Odzi, *Zimbabwe* **57 B5** 19 0S 32 20 E
Odzi →, *Zimbabwe* **57 B5** 19 45S 32 23 E
Oeiras, *Brazil* **93 E10** 7 0S 42 8W
Oelrichs, *U.S.A.* **80 D3** 43 11N 103 14W
Oelwein, *U.S.A.* **80 D9** 42 41N 91 55W
Oenpelli, *Australia* **60 B5** 12 20S 133 4 E
Ofanto →, *Italy* **20 D7** 41 22N 16 13 E
Offa, *Nigeria* **50 G6** 8 13N 4 42 E
Offaly □, *Ireland* **13 C4** 53 15N 7 30W
Offenbach, *Germany* **16 C5** 50 6N 8 44 E
Offenburg, *Germany* **16 D4** 48 28N 7 56 E
Ofotfjorden, *Norway* **8 B17** 68 27N 17 0 E
Ōfunato, *Japan* **30 E10** 39 4N 141 43 E
Oga, *Japan* **30 E9** 39 55N 139 50 E
Oga-Hantō, *Japan* **30 E9** 39 58N 139 47 E
Ogaden, *Ethiopia* **46 F3** 7 30N 45 30 E
Ōgaki, *Japan* **31 G8** 35 21N 136 37 E
Ogallala, *U.S.A.* **80 E4** 41 8N 101 43W
Ogasawara Gunto, *Pac. Oc.* **28 G18** 27 0N 142 0 E
Ogbomosho, *Nigeria* **50 G6** 8 1N 4 11 E
Ogden, *U.S.A.* **82 F7** 41 13N 111 58W
Ogdensburg, *U.S.A.* **79 B9** 44 42N 75 30W
Ogeechee →, *U.S.A.* **77 K5** 31 50N 81 3W
Ogilby, *U.S.A.* **85 N12** 32 49N 114 50W
Oglio →, *Italy* **20 B4** 45 2N 10 39 E
Ogmore, *Australia* **62 C4** 22 37S 149 35 E
Ogoki, *Canada* **70 B2** 51 38N 85 58W
Ogoki →, *Canada* **70 B2** 51 38N 85 57W
Ogoki L., *Canada* **70 B2** 50 50N 87 10W
Ogoki Res., *Canada* **70 B2** 50 45N 88 15W
Ogooué →, *Gabon* **52 E1** 1 0S 9 0 E
Ogowe = Ogooué →, *Gabon* **52 E1** 1 0S 9 0 E
Ogre, *Latvia* **9 H21** 56 49N 24 36 E
Ogurchinskiy, Ostrov, *Turkmenistan* **45 B7** 38 55N 53 2 E
Ohai, *N.Z.* **59 L2** 45 55S 168 0 E
Ohakune, *N.Z.* **59 H5** 39 24S 175 24 E
Ohata, *Japan* **30 D10** 41 24N 141 10 E
Ohau, L., *N.Z.* **59 L2** 44 15S 169 53 E
Ohio □, *U.S.A.* **78 F2** 40 15N 82 45W
Ohio →, *U.S.A.* **76 G1** 36 59N 89 8W
Ohře →, *Czech Rep.* **16 C8** 50 30N 14 10 E
Ohrid, *Macedonia* **21 D9** 41 8N 20 52 E
Ohridsko Jezero, *Macedonia* **21 D9** 41 8N 20 52 E
Ohrigstad, *S. Africa* **57 C5** 24 39S 30 36 E
Oiapoque, *Brazil* **93** 3 50N 51 50W
Oikou, *China* **35 E9** 38 35N 117 42 E
Oil City, *U.S.A.* **78 E5** 41 26N 79 42W
Oil Springs, *Canada* **78 D2** 42 47N 82 7W
Oildale, *U.S.A.* **85 K7** 35 25N 119 1W
Oise →, *France* **18 B5** 49 0N 2 4 E
Ōita, *Japan* **31 H5** 33 14N 131 36 E
Ōita □, *Japan* **31 H5** 33 15N 131 30 E
Oiticica, *Brazil* **93 E10** 5 3S 41 5W
Ojacaliente, *Mexico* **86 C4** 22 34N 102 15W
Ojai, *U.S.A.* **85 L7** 34 27N 119 15W
Ojinaga, *Mexico* **86 B4** 29 34N 104 25W
Ojiya, *Japan* **31 F9** 37 18N 138 48 E
Ojos del Salado, Cerro, *Argentina* **94 B2** 27 0S 68 40W
Oka →, *Russia* **24 C7** 56 20N 43 59 E
Okaba, *Indonesia* **37 F9** 8 6S 139 42 E
Okahandja, *Namibia* **56 C2** 22 0S 16 59 E
Okanagan L., *Canada* **72 D5** 50 0N 119 30W
Okanogan, *U.S.A.* **82 B4** 48 22N 119 35W
Okanogan →, *U.S.A.* **82 B4** 48 6N 119 44W
Okaputa, *Namibia* **56 C2** 20 5S 17 0 E
Okara, *Pakistan* **42 D5** 30 50N 73 31 E
Okaukuejo, *Namibia* **56 B2** 19 10S 16 0 E
Okavango Swamps, *Botswana* **56 B3** 18 45S 22 45 E
Okaya, *Japan* **31 F9** 36 5N 138 10 E
Okayama, *Japan* **31 G6** 34 40N 133 54 E
Okayama □, *Japan* **31 G6** 35 0N 133 50 E
Okazaki, *Japan* **31 G8** 34 57N 137 10 E
Okeechobee, *U.S.A.* **77 M5** 27 15N 80 50W
Okeechobee, L., *U.S.A.* **77 M5** 27 0N 80 50W
Okefenokee Swamp, *U.S.A.* **77 K4** 30 40N 82 20W
Okehampton, *U.K.* **11 G4** 50 44N 4 0W
Okha, *India* **42 H3** 22 27N 69 4 E
Okha, *Russia* **27 D15** 53 40N 143 0 E
Okhotsk, *Russia* **27 D15** 59 20N 143 10 E
Okhotsk, Sea of, *Asia* **27 D15** 55 0N 145 0 E
Okhotskiy Perevoz, *Russia* **27 C14** 61 52N 135 35 E
Okhtyrka, *Ukraine* **25 D5** 50 25N 35 0 E
Oki-Shotō, *Japan* **31 F6** 36 5N 133 15 E
Okiep, *S. Africa* **56 D2** 29 39S 17 53 E
Okinawa □, *Japan* **31 L4** 26 40N 128 0 E
Okinawa-Guntō, *Japan* **31 L4** 26 40N 128 0 E
Okinawa-Jima, *Japan* **31 L4** 26 32N 128 0 E
Okino-erabu-Shima, *Japan* **31 L4** 27 21N 128 33 E
Oklahoma □, *U.S.A.* **81 H6** 35 20N 97 30W
Oklahoma City, *U.S.A.* **81 H6** 35 30N 97 30W
Okmulgee, *U.S.A.* **81 H7** 35 37N 95 58W
Oknitsa = Ocniţa, *Moldova* **17 D14** 48 25N 27 30 E
Okolo, *Uganda* **54 B3** 2 37N 31 8 E
Okolona, *U.S.A.* **81 J10** 34 0N 88 45W
Okombahe, *Namibia* **56 C2** 21 23S 15 22 E
Okotoks, *Canada* **72 C6** 50 43N 113 58W
Oksibil, *Indonesia* **37 E10** 4 59S 140 35 E
Oksovskiy, *Russia* **24 B6** 62 33N 39 57 E
Oktabrsk = Oktyabrsk, *Kazakstan* **25 E10** 49 28N 57 25 E
Oktyabrsk, *Kazakstan* **25 E10** 49 28N 57 25 E
Oktyabrskiy = Aktsyabrski, *Belarus* **17 B15** 52 38N 28 53 E
Oktyabrskiy, *Russia* **24 D9** 54 28N 53 28 E
Oktyabrskoy Revolyutsii, Ostrov, *Russia* **27 B10** 79 30N 97 0 E
Okuru, *N.Z.* **59 K2** 43 55S 168 55 E
Okushiri-Tō, *Japan* **30 C9** 42 15N 139 30 E
Okwa →, *Botswana* **56 C3** 22 30S 23 0 E
Ola, *U.S.A.* **81 H8** 35 2N 93 13W
Ólafsfjörður, *Iceland* **8 C4** 66 4N 18 39W
Ólafsvík, *Iceland* **8 D2** 64 53N 23 43W
Olancha, *U.S.A.* **85 J8** 36 17N 118 1W
Olancha Pk., *U.S.A.* **85 J8** 36 15N 118 7W
Olanchito, *Honduras* **88 C2** 15 30N 86 30W
Öland, *Sweden* **9 H17** 56 45N 16 38 E
Olascoaga, *Argentina* **94 D3** 35 15S 60 39W
Olathe, *U.S.A.* **80 F7** 38 53N 94 49W
Olavarría, *Argentina* **94 D3** 36 55S 60 20W
Oława, *Poland* **17 C9** 50 57N 17 20 E
Ólbia, *Italy* **20 D3** 40 55N 9 31 E
Olcott, *U.S.A.* **78 C6** 43 20N 78 42W
Old Bahama Chan. = Bahama, Canal Viejo de, *W. Indies* **88 B4** 22 10N 77 30W
Old Baldy Pk. = San Antonio, Mt., *U.S.A.* **85 L9** 34 17N 117 38W
Old Castile = Castilla y Leon □, *Spain* **19 B3** 42 0N 5 0W
Old Crow, *Canada* **68 B6** 67 30N 139 55W
Old Dale, *U.S.A.* **85 L11** 34 8N 115 47W
Old Forge, *N.Y., U.S.A.* **79 C10** 43 43N 74 58W
Old Forge, *Pa., U.S.A.* **79 E9** 41 22N 75 45W
Old Perlican, *Canada* **71 C9** 48 5N 53 1W
Old Shinyanga, *Tanzania* **54 C3** 3 33S 33 27 E
Old Speck Mt., *U.S.A.* **79 B14** 44 34N 70 57W
Old Town, *U.S.A.* **77 C11** 44 56N 68 39W
Old Washington, *U.S.A.* **78 F3** 40 2N 81 27W
Old Wives L., *Canada* **73 C7** 50 5N 106 0W
Oldbury, *U.K.* **11 F5** 51 38N 2 33W
Oldcastle, *Ireland* **13 C4** 53 46N 7 10W
Oldeani, *Tanzania* **54 C4** 3 22S 35 35 E
Oldenburg, *Germany* **16 B5** 53 9N 8 13 E
Oldenzaal, *Neths.* **15 B6** 52 19N 6 53 E
Oldham, *U.K.* **10 D5** 53 33N 2 7W
Oldman →, *Canada* **72 D6** 49 57N 111 42W
Oldmeldrum, *U.K.* **12 D6** 57 20N 2 19W
Olds, *Canada* **72 C6** 51 50N 114 10W
Oldziyt, *Mongolia* **34 B5** 44 40N 109 1 E
Olean, *U.S.A.* **78 D6** 42 5N 78 26W
Olekma →, *Russia* **27 C13** 60 22N 120 42 E
Olekminsk, *Russia* **27 C13** 60 25N 120 30 E
Oleksandriya, *Ukraine* **17 C14** 50 37N 26 19 E
Olema, *U.S.A.* **84 G4** 38 3N 122 47W
Olenegorsk, *Russia* **24 A5** 68 9N 33 18 E
Olenek, *Russia* **27 C12** 68 28N 112 18 E
Olenek →, *Russia* **27 B13** 73 0N 120 10 E
Oléron, Î. d', *France* **18 D3** 45 55N 1 15W
Oleśnica, *Poland* **17 C9** 51 13N 17 22 E
Olevsk, *Ukraine* **17 C14** 51 12N 27 39 E
Olga, *Russia* **27 E14** 43 50N 135 14 E
Olga, L., *Canada* **70 C4** 49 47N 77 15W
Olga, Mt., *Australia* **61 E5** 25 20S 130 50 E
Olhão, *Portugal* **19 D2** 37 3N 7 48W
Olifants →, *Africa* **57 C5** 23 57S 31 58 E
Olifants →, *Namibia* **56 C2** 25 30S 19 30 E
Olifantshoek, *S. Africa* **56 D3** 27 57S 22 42 E
Ólimbos, Óros, *Greece* **21 D10** 40 6N 22 23 E
Olímpia, *Brazil* **95 A6** 20 44S 48 54W
Olinda, *Brazil* **93 E12** 8 1S 34 51W
Oliva, *Argentina* **94 C3** 32 0S 63 38W
Olivehurst, *U.S.A.* **84 F5** 39 6N 121 34W
Olivenza, *Spain* **19 C2** 38 41N 7 9W
Oliver, *Canada* **72 D5** 49 13N 119 37W
Oliver L., *Canada* **73 B8** 56 56N 103 22W
Ollagüe, *Chile* **94 A2** 21 15S 68 10W
Olney, *Ill., U.S.A.* **76 F1** 38 44N 88 5W
Olney, *Tex., U.S.A.* **81 J5** 33 22N 98 45W
Olomane →, *Canada* **71 B7** 50 14N 60 37W
Olomouc, *Czech Rep.* **17 D9** 49 38N 17 12 E
Olonets, *Russia* **24 B5** 61 0N 32 54 E
Olongapo, *Phil.* **37 B6** 14 50N 120 18 E
Olot, *Spain* **19 A7** 42 11N 2 30 E
Olovyannaya, *Russia* **27 D12** 50 58N 115 35 E
Oloy →, *Russia* **27 C16** 66 29N 159 29 E
Olsztyn, *Poland* **17 B11** 53 48N 20 29 E
Olt →, *Romania* **17 G13** 43 43N 24 51 E
Olteniţa, *Romania* **17 F14** 44 7N 26 42 E
Olton, *U.S.A.* **81 H3** 34 11N 102 8W
Olymbos, *Cyprus* **23 D12** 35 21N 33 45 E
Olympia, *Greece* **21 F9** 37 39N 21 39 E
Olympia, *U.S.A.* **84 D4** 47 3N 122 53W
Olympic Dam, *Australia* **63 E2** 30 30S 136 55 E
Olympic Mts., *U.S.A.* **84 C3** 47 55N 123 45W
Olympic Nat. Park, *U.S.A.* **84 C3** 47 48N 123 30W
Olympus, *Cyprus* **23 E11** 34 56N 32 52 E
Olympus, Mt. = Ólimbos, Óros, *Greece* **21 D10** 40 6N 22 23 E
Olympus, Mt. = Uludağ, *Turkey* **21 D13** 40 4N 29 13 E
Olympus, Mt., *U.S.A.* **84 C3** 47 48N 123 43W
Olyphant, *U.S.A.* **79 E9** 41 27N 75 36W
Om →, *Russia* **26 D8** 54 59N 73 22 E
Om Koi, *Thailand* **38 D2** 17 48N 98 22 E
Ōma, *Japan* **30 D10** 41 45N 141 5 E
Ōmachi, *Japan* **31 F8** 36 30N 137 50 E
Omae-Zaki, *Japan* **31 G9** 34 36N 138 14 E
Ōmagari, *Japan* **30 E10** 39 27N 140 29 E
Omagh, *U.K.* **13 B4** 54 36N 7 19W
Omagh □, *U.K.* **13 B4** 54 35N 7 15W
Omaha, *U.S.A.* **80 E7** 41 17N 95 58W
Omak, *U.S.A.* **82 B4** 48 25N 119 31W
Omalos, *Greece* **23 D5** 35 19N 23 55 E
Oman ■, *Asia* **46 C6** 23 0N 58 0 E
Oman, G. of, *Asia* **45 E8** 24 30N 58 30 E
Omaruru, *Namibia* **56 C2** 21 26S 16 0 E
Omaruru →, *Namibia* **56 C1** 22 7S 14 15 E
Omate, *Peru* **92 G4** 16 45S 71 0W
Ombai, Selat, *Indonesia* **37 F6** 8 30S 124 50 E
Omboué, *Gabon* **52 E1** 1 35S 9 15 E
Ombrone →, *Italy* **20 C4** 42 42N 11 5 E
Omdurmân, *Sudan* **51 E12** 15 40N 32 28 E
Omemee, *Canada* **78 B6** 44 18N 78 33W
Omeonga, *Dem. Rep. of the Congo* **54 C1** 3 40S 24 22 E
Ometepe, I. de, *Nic.* **88 D2** 11 32N 85 35W
Ometepec, *Mexico* **87 D5** 16 39N 98 23W
Ominato, *Japan* **30 D10** 41 17N 141 10 E
Omineca →, *Canada* **72 B4** 56 3N 124 16W
Omitara, *Namibia* **56 C2** 22 16S 18 2 E
Ōmiya, *Japan* **31 G9** 35 54N 139 38 E
Ommen, *Neths.* **15 B6** 52 31N 6 26 E
Ömnögovĭ □, *Mongolia* **34 C3** 43 15N 104 0 E
Omo →, *Ethiopia* **46 F2** 6 25N 36 10 E
Omodhos, *Cyprus* **23 E11** 34 51N 32 48 E
Omolon →, *Russia* **27 C16** 68 42N 158 36 E
Omono-Gawa →, *Japan* **30 E10** 39 46N 140 3 E
Omsk, *Russia* **26 D8** 55 0N 73 12 E
Omsukchan, *Russia* **27 C16** 62 32N 155 48 E
Ōmu, *Japan* **30 B11** 44 34N 142 58 E
Omul, Vf., *Romania* **17 F13** 45 27N 25 29 E
Ōmura, *Japan* **31 H4** 32 56N 129 57 E
Omuramba Omatako →, *Namibia* **56 B2** 17 45S 20 25 E
Omuramba Ovambo →, *Namibia* **56 B2** 18 45S 16 59 E
Ōmuta, *Japan* **31 H5** 33 5N 130 26 E
Onaga, *U.S.A.* **80 F6** 39 29N 96 10W
Onalaska, *U.S.A.* **80 D9** 43 53N 91 14W
Onancock, *U.S.A.* **76 G8** 37 43N 75 45W
Onang, *Indonesia* **37 E5** 3 2S 118 49 E
Onaping L., *Canada* **70 C3** 47 3N 81 30W
Onavas, *Mexico* **86 B3** 28 28N 109 30W
Onawa, *U.S.A.* **80 D6** 42 2N 96 6W
Oncócua, *Angola* **56 B1** 16 30S 13 25 E
Onda, *Spain* **19 C5** 39 55N 0 17W
Ondaejin, *N. Korea* **35 D15** 41 34N 129 40 E
Ondangwa, *Namibia* **56 B2** 17 57S 16 4 E
Ondjiva, *Angola* **56 B2** 16 48S 15 50 E
Öndörshil, *Mongolia* **34 B5** 45 13N 108 5 E
Öndverðarnes, *Iceland* **8 D1** 64 52N 24 0W
One Tree, *Australia* **63 E3** 34 11S 144 43 E
Onega, *Russia* **24 B6** 64 0N 38 10 E
Onega →, *Russia* **24 B6** 63 58N 38 2 E
Onega, G. of = Onezhskaya Guba, *Russia* **24 B6** 64 24N 36 38 E
Onega, L. = Onezhskoye Ozero, *Russia* **24 B6** 61 44N 35 22 E
Oneida, *U.S.A.* **79 C9** 43 6N 75 39W
Oneida L., *U.S.A.* **79 C9** 43 12N 75 54W
O'Neill, *U.S.A.* **80 D5** 42 27N 98 39W
Onekotan, Ostrov, *Russia* **27 E16** 49 25N 154 45 E
Onema, *Dem. Rep. of the Congo* **54 C1** 4 35S 24 30 E
Oneonta, *U.S.A.* **79 D9** 42 27N 75 4W
Oneşti, *Romania* **17 E14** 46 17N 26 47 E
Onezhskaya Guba, *Russia* **24 B6** 64 24N 36 38 E
Onezhskoye Ozero, *Russia* **24 B6** 61 44N 35 22 E
Ongarue, *N.Z.* **59 H5** 38 42S 175 19 E
Ongers →, *S. Africa* **56 E3** 31 4S 23 13 E
Ongerup, *Australia* **61 F2** 33 58S 118 28 E
Ongjin, *N. Korea* **35 F13** 37 56N 125 21 E
Ongkharak, *Thailand* **38 E3** 14 8N 101 1 E
Ongniud Qi, *China* **35 C10** 43 0N 118 38 E
Ongoka, *Dem. Rep. of the Congo* **54 C2** 1 20S 26 0 E
Ongole, *India* **40 M12** 15 33N 80 2 E
Ongon = Havirga, *Mongolia* **34 B7** 45 41N 113 5 E
Onida, *U.S.A.* **80 C4** 44 42N 100 4W
Onilahy →, *Madag.* **57 C7** 23 34S 43 45 E
Onitsha, *Nigeria* **50 G7** 6 6N 6 42 E
Onoda, *Japan* **31 G5** 33 59N 131 11 E
Onpyŏng-ni, *S. Korea* **35 H14** 33 25N 126 55 E
Onslow, *Australia* **60 D2** 21 40S 115 12 E
Onslow B., *U.S.A.* **77 H7** 34 20N 77 15W
Ontake-San, *Japan* **31 G8** 35 53N 137 29 E
Ontario, *Calif., U.S.A.* **85 L9** 34 4N 117 39W
Ontario, *Oreg., U.S.A.* **82 D5** 44 2N 116 58W
Ontario □, *Canada* **70 B2** 48 0N 83 0W
Ontario, L., *N. Amer.* **78 C7** 43 20N 78 0W
Ontonagon, *U.S.A.* **80 B10** 46 52N 89 19W
Onyx, *U.S.A.* **85 K8** 35 41N 118 14W
Oodnadatta, *Australia* **63 D2** 27 33S 135 30 E
Ooldea, *Australia* **61 F5** 30 27S 131 50 E
Oombulgurri, *Australia* **60 C4** 15 15S 127 45 E
Oorindi, *Australia* **62 C3** 20 40S 141 1 E
Oost-Vlaanderen □, *Belgium* **15 C3** 51 5N 3 50 E
Oostende, *Belgium* **15 C2** 51 15N 2 54 E
Oosterhout, *Neths.* **15 C4** 51 39N 4 47 E
Oosterschelde →, *Neths.* **15 C4** 51 33N 4 0 E
Oosterwolde, *Neths.* **15 B6** 53 0N 6 17 E
Ootacamund = Udagamandalam, *India* **40 P10** 11 30N 76 44 E
Ootsa L., *Canada* **72 C3** 53 50N 126 2W
Opala, *Dem. Rep. of the Congo* **54 C1** 0 40S 24 20 E
Opanake, *Sri Lanka* **40 R12** 6 35N 80 40 E
Opasatika, *Canada* **70 C3** 49 30N 82 50W
Opasquia Prov. Park, *Canada* **70 B1** 53 33N 93 5W
Opava, *Czech Rep.* **17 D9** 49 57N 17 58 E
Opelika, *U.S.A.* **77 J3** 32 39N 85 23W
Opelousas, *U.S.A.* **81 K8** 30 32N 92 5W
Opémisca, L., *Canada* **70 C5** 49 56N 74 52W
Opheim, *U.S.A.* **82 B10** 48 51N 106 24W
Ophthalmia Ra., *Australia* **60 D2** 23 15S 119 30 E
Opinaca →, *Canada* **70 B4** 52 15N 78 2W
Opinaca, Rés., *Canada* **70 B4** 52 39N 76 20W
Opinnagau →, *Canada* **70 B3** 54 12N 82 25W
Opiscoteo, L., *Canada* **71 B6** 53 10N 68 10W
Opole, *Poland* **17 C9** 50 42N 17 58 E
Oponono L., *Namibia* **56 B2** 18 8S 15 45 E
Oporto = Porto, *Portugal* **19 B1** 41 8N 8 40W
Opotiki, *N.Z.* **59 H6** 38 1S 177 19 E
Opp, *U.S.A.* **77 K2** 31 17N 86 16W
Oppdal, *Norway* **9 E13** 62 35N 9 41 E
Opportunity, *U.S.A.* **82 C5** 47 39N 117 15W
Opua, *N.Z.* **59 F5** 35 19S 174 9 E
Opunake, *N.Z.* **59 H4** 39 26S 173 52 E
Opuwo, *Namibia* **56 B1** 18 3S 13 45 E
Ora, *Cyprus* **23 E12** 34 51N 33 12 E
Oracle, *U.S.A.* **83 K8** 32 37N 110 46W
Oradea, *Romania* **17 E11** 47 2N 21 58 E
Öræfajökull, *Iceland* **8 D5** 64 2N 16 39W
Orai, *India* **43 G8** 25 58N 79 30 E
Oral = Zhayyq →, *Kazakstan* **25 E9** 47 0N 51 48 E
Oral, *Kazakstan* **25 D9** 51 20N 51 20 E
Oran, *Algeria* **50 A5** 35 45N 0 39W
Orange, *France* **18 D6** 44 8N 4 47 E
Orange, *Calif., U.S.A.* **85 M9** 33 47N 117 51W
Orange, *Mass., U.S.A.* **79 D12** 42 35N 72 19W
Orange, *Tex., U.S.A.* **81 K8** 30 6N 93 44W
Orange, *Va., U.S.A.* **76 F6** 38 15N 78 7W
Orange →, *S. Africa* **56 D2** 28 41S 16 28 E
Orange, C., *Brazil* **93 C8** 4 20N 51 30W
Orange Cove, *U.S.A.* **84 J7** 36 38N 119 19W
Orange Free State = Free State □, *S. Africa* **56 D4** 28 30S 27 0 E
Orange Grove, *U.S.A.* **81 M6** 27 58N 97 56W
Orange Walk, *Belize* **87 D7** 18 6N 88 33W
Orangeburg, *U.S.A.* **77 J5** 33 30N 80 52W
Orangeville, *Canada* **78 C4** 43 55N 80 5W
Oranienburg, *Germany* **16 B7** 52 45N 13 14 E
Oranje = Orange →, *S. Africa* **56 D2** 28 41S 16 28 E
Oranje Vrystaat = Free State □, *S. Africa* **56 D4** 28 30S 27 0 E
Oranjemund, *Namibia* **56 D2** 28 38S 16 29 E
Oranjerivier, *S. Africa* **56 D3** 29 40S 24 12 E
Orapa, *Botswana* **53 J5** 21 15S 25 30 E
Oras, *Phil.* **37 B7** 12 9N 125 28 E
Orașul Stalin = Brașov, *Romania* **17 F13** 45 38N 25 35 E
Orbetello, *Italy* **20 C4** 42 27N 11 13 E
Orbisonia, *U.S.A.* **78 F7** 40 15N 77 54W
Orcas I., *U.S.A.* **84 B4** 48 42N 122 56W
Orchard City, *U.S.A.* **83 G10** 38 50N 107 58W
Orchila, I., *Venezuela* **89 D6** 11 48N 66 10W
Orcutt, *U.S.A.* **85 L6** 34 52N 120 27W
Ord, *U.S.A.* **80 E5** 41 36N 98 56W
Ord →, *Australia* **60 C4** 15 33S 128 15 E
Ord, Mt., *Australia* **60 C4** 17 20S 125 34 E
Orderville, *U.S.A.* **83 H7** 37 17N 112 38W
Ordos = Mu Us Shamo, *China* **34 E5** 39 0N 109 0 E
Ordu, *Turkey* **25 F6** 40 55N 37 53 E
Ordway, *U.S.A.* **80 F3** 38 13N 103 46W
Ordzhonikidze = Vladikavkaz, *Russia* **25 F7** 43 0N 44 35 E
Ore, *Dem. Rep. of the Congo* **54 B2** 3 17N 29 30 E
Ore Mts. = Erzgebirge, *Germany* **16 C7** 50 27N 12 55 E
Örebro, *Sweden* **9 G16** 59 20N 15 18 E
Oregon, *U.S.A.* **80 D10** 42 1N 89 20W
Oregon □, *U.S.A.* **82 E3** 44 0N 121 0W
Oregon City, *U.S.A.* **84 E4** 45 21N 122 36W
Orekhovo-Zuyevo, *Russia* **24 C6** 55 50N 38 55 E
Orel, *Russia* **24 D6** 52 57N 36 3 E
Orem, *U.S.A.* **82 F8** 40 19N 111 42W
Ören, *Turkey* **21 F12** 37 3N 27 57 E
Orenburg, *Russia* **24 D10** 51 45N 55 6 E
Orense = Ourense, *Spain* **19 A2** 42 19N 7 55W
Orepuki, *N.Z.* **59 M1** 46 19S 167 46 E
Orestiás, *Greece* **21 D12** 41 30N 26 33 E
Orestos Pereyra, *Mexico* **86 B3** 26 31N 105 40W
Orford Ness, *U.K.* **11 E9** 52 5N 1 35 E
Organos, Pta. de los, *Canary Is.* **22 F2** 28 12N 17 17W
Orgaz, *Spain* **19 C4** 39 39N 3 53W
Orgeyev = Orhei, *Moldova* **17 E15** 47 24N 28 50 E
Orhaneli, *Turkey* **21 E13** 39 54N 28 59 E
Orhangazi, *Turkey* **21 D13** 40 29N 29 18 E
Orhei, *Moldova* **17 E15** 47 24N 28 50 E
Orhon Gol →, *Mongolia* **32 A5** 50 21N 106 0 E
Oriental, Cordillera, *Colombia* **92 B4** 6 0N 73 0W
Orientale □, *Dem. Rep. of the Congo* **54 B2** 2 20N 26 0 E
Oriente, *Argentina* **94 D3** 38 44S 60 37W
Orihuela, *Spain* **19 C5** 38 7N 0 55W
Orillia, *Canada* **78 B5** 44 40N 79 24W
Orinoco →, *Venezuela* **92 B6** 9 15N 61 30W
Orion, *Canada* **73 D6** 49 27N 110 49W
Oriskany, *U.S.A.* **79 C9** 43 10N 75 20W
Orissa □, *India* **41 K14** 20 0N 84 0 E
Orissaare, *Estonia* **9 G20** 58 34N 23 5 E
Oristano, *Italy* **20 E3** 39 54N 8 36 E
Oristano, G. di, *Italy* **20 E3** 39 50N 8 29 E
Orizaba, *Mexico* **87 D5** 18 51N 97 6W
Orkanger, *Norway* **8 E13** 63 18N 9 52 E
Orkla →, *Norway* **8 E13** 63 18N 9 51 E
Orkney, *S. Africa* **56 D4** 26 58S 26 40 E
Orkney □, *U.K.* **12 B5** 59 2N 3 13W
Orkney Is., *U.K.* **12 B6** 59 0N 3 0W
Orland, *U.S.A.* **84 F4** 39 45N 122 12W
Orlando, *U.S.A.* **77 L5** 28 33N 81 23W
Orléanais, *France* **18 C5** 48 0N 2 0 E
Orléans, *France* **18 C4** 47 54N 1 52 E
Orleans, *U.S.A.* **79 B12** 44 49N 72 12W
Orléans, I. d', *Canada* **71 C5** 46 54N 70 58W
Ormara, *Pakistan* **40 G4** 25 16N 64 33 E
Ormoc, *Phil.* **37 B6** 11 0N 124 37 E
Ormond, *N.Z.* **59 H6** 38 33S 177 56 E
Ormond Beach, *U.S.A.* **77 L5** 29 17N 81 3W
Ormskirk, *U.K.* **10 D5** 53 35N 2 54W
Ormstown, *Canada* **79 A11** 45 8N 74 0W
Örnsköldsvik, *Sweden* **8 E18** 63 17N 18 40 E
Oro, *N. Korea* **35 D14** 40 1N 127 27 E
Oro →, *Mexico* **86 B3** 25 35N 105 2W
Oro Grande, *U.S.A.* **85 L9** 34 36N 117 20W
Oro Valley, *U.S.A.* **83 K8** 32 26N 110 58W
Orocué, *Colombia* **92 C4** 4 48N 71 20W
Orofino, *U.S.A.* **82 C5** 46 29N 116 15W
Orol Dengizi = Aral Sea, *Asia* **26 E7** 44 30N 60 0 E
Oromocto, *Canada* **71 C6** 45 54N 66 29W
Orono, *Canada* **78 C6** 43 59N 78 37W
Orono, *U.S.A.* **77 C11** 44 53N 68 40W
Oronsay, *U.K.* **12 E2** 56 1N 6 15W
Oroqen Zizhiqi, *China* **33 A7** 50 34N 123 43 E
Oroquieta, *Phil.* **37 C6** 8 32N 123 44 E
Orosháza, *Hungary* **17 E11** 46 32N 20 42 E
Orotukan, *Russia* **27 C16** 62 16N 151 42 E
Oroville, *Calif., U.S.A.* **84 F5** 39 31N 121 33W
Oroville, *Wash., U.S.A.* **82 B4** 48 56N 119 26W
Oroville, L., *U.S.A.* **84 F5** 39 33N 121 29W
Orrville, *U.S.A.* **78 F3** 40 50N 81 46W
Orsha, *Belarus* **24 D5** 54 30N 30 25 E
Orsk, *Russia* **26 D6** 51 12N 58 34 E
Orşova, *Romania* **17 F12** 44 41N 22 25 E
Ortaca, *Turkey* **21 F13** 36 49N 28 45 E
Ortegal, C., *Spain* **19 A2** 43 43N 7 52W
Orthez, *France* **18 E3** 43 29N 0 48W
Ortigueira, *Spain* **19 A2** 43 40N 7 50W
Orting, *U.S.A.* **84 C4** 47 6N 122 12W
Ortles, *Italy* **18 C9** 46 31N 10 33 E
Ortón →, *Bolivia* **92 F5** 10 50S 67 0W
Ortonville, *U.S.A.* **80 C6** 45 19N 96 27W
Orūmīyeh, *Iran* **44 B5** 37 40N 45 0 E
Orūmīyeh, Daryācheh-ye, *Iran* **44 B5** 37 50N 45 30 E

Pench'i

Pandegelang, *Indonesia* .. **37 G12** 6 25S 106 5 E
Pandhana, *India* .... **42 J7** 21 42N 76 13 E
Pandharpur, *India* .... **40 L9** 17 41N 75 20 E
Pando, *Uruguay* **95 C4** 34 44S 56 0W
Pando, L. = Hope, L.,
Australia .... **63 D2** 28 24S 139 18 E
Pandokrátor, *Greece* ...... **23 A3** 39 45N 19 50 E
Pandora, *Costa Rica* **88 E3** 9 43N 83 3W
Panevėžys, *Lithuania* ..... **9 J21** 55 42N 24 25 E
Panfilov, *Kazakstan* .... **26 E8** 44 10N 80 0 E
Pang-Long, *Burma* .... **41 H21** 23 11N 98 45 E
Pang-Yang, *Burma* .... **41 H21** 22 7N 98 48 E
Panga, *Dem. Rep. of*
the Congo .... **54 B2** 1 52N 26 18 E
Pangalanes, Canal des =
Ampangalana,
Lakandranon', *Madag.* .. **57 C8** 22 48S 47 50 E
Pangani, *Tanzania* .... **54 D4** 5 25S 38 58 E
Pangani →, *Tanzania* ..... **54 D4** 5 26S 38 58 E
Pangfou = Bengbu, *China* . **35 H9** 32 58N 117 20 E
Pangil, *Dem. Rep. of*
the Congo .... **54 C2** 3 10S 26 35 E
Pangkah, Tanjung,
Indonesia .... **37 G15** 6 51S 112 33 E
Pangkajene, *Indonesia* .... **37 E5** 4 46S 119 34 E
Pangkalanbrandan,
Indonesia .... **36 D1** 4 1N 98 20 E
Pangkalanbuun, *Indonesia* **36 E4** 2 41S 111 37 E
Pangkalpinang, *Indonesia* . **36 E3** 2 0S 106 0 E
Pangnirtung, *Canada* **69 B13** 66 8N 65 54W
Pangong Tso, *India* .... **42 B8** 34 40N 78 40 E
Panguitch, *U.S.A.* **83 H7** 37 50N 112 26W
Pangutaran Group, *Phil.* ... **37 C6** 6 18N 120 34 E
Panhandle, *U.S.A.* **81 H4** 35 21N 101 23W
Pani Mines, *India* .... **42 H5** 22 29N 73 50 E
Pania-Mutombo, *Dem. Rep.*
of the Congo .... **54 D1** 5 11S 23 51 E
Panikota I., *India* .... **42 J4** 20 46N 71 21 E
Panipat, *India* .... **42 E7** 29 25N 77 2 E
Panjal Range, *India* .... **42 C7** 32 30N 76 50 E
Panjang, Hon, *Vietnam* .... **39 H4** 9 20N 103 28 E
Panjgur, *Pakistan* .... **40 F4** 27 0N 64 5 E
Panjim = Panaji, *India* ..... **40 M8** 15 25N 73 50 E
Panjin, *China* .... **35 D12** 41 3N 122 2 E
Panjinad Barrage, *Pakistan* **40 E7** 29 22N 71 15 E
Panjnad →, *Pakistan* ..... **42 E4** 28 57N 70 30 E
Panjwai, *Afghan.* .... **42 D1** 31 26N 65 27 E
Panmunjŏm, *N. Korea* ..... **35 F14** 37 59N 126 38 E
Panna, *India* .... **43 G9** 24 40N 80 15 E
Panna Hills, *India* .... **43 G9** 24 40N 81 15 E
Pannawonica, *Australia* ... **60 D2** 21 39S 116 19 E
Pannirtuuq = Pangnirtung,
Canada **69 B13** 66 8N 65 54W
Pano Akil, *Pakistan* .... **42 F3** 27 51N 69 7 E
Pano Lefkara, *Cyprus* ..... **23 E12** 34 53N 33 20 E
Pano Panayia, *Cyprus* ..... **23 E11** 34 55N 32 38 E
Panorama, *Brazil* **95 A5** 21 21S 51 51W
Pánormon, *Greece* .... **23 D6** 35 25N 24 41 E
Pansemal, *India* .... **42 J6** 21 39N 74 42 E
Panshan = Panjin, *China* .. **35 D12** 41 3N 122 2 E
Panshi, *China* .... **35 C14** 42 58N 126 5 E
Pantanal, *Brazil* **92 H7** 17 30S 57 40W
Pantar, *Indonesia* .... **37 F6** 8 28S 124 10 E
Pante Macassar, *E. Timor* .. **37 F6** 9 30S 123 58 E
Pante Makasar = Pante
Macassar, *E. Timor* ..... **37 F6** 9 30S 123 58 E
Pantelleria, *Italy* .... **20 F4** 36 50N 11 57 E
Pánuco, *Mexico* **87 C5** 22 0N 98 15W
Paola, *Malta* .... **23 D2** 35 52N 14 30 E
Paola, *U.S.A.* **80 F7** 38 35N 94 53W
Paonia, *U.S.A.* **83 G10** 38 52N 107 36W
Paoting = Baoding, *China* . **34 E8** 38 50N 115 28 E
Paot'ou = Baotou, *China* .. **34 D6** 40 32N 110 2 E
Paoua, *C.A.R.* .... **52 C3** 7 9N 16 20 E
Pápa, *Hungary* .... **17 E9** 47 22N 17 30 E
Papa Stour, *U.K.* **12 A7** 60 20N 1 42W
Papa Westray, *U.K.* **12 B6** 59 20N 2 55W
Papagayo →, *Mexico* **87 D5** 16 36N 99 43W
Papagayo, G. de, *Costa Rica* **88 D2** 10 30N 85 50W
Papakura, *N.Z.* .... **59 G5** 37 4S 174 59 E
Papantla, *Mexico* **87 C5** 20 30N 97 30W
Papar, *Malaysia* .... **36 C5** 5 45N 116 0 E
Papeete, *Tahiti* **65 J13** 17 32S 149 34W
Paphos, *Cyprus* .... **23 E11** 34 46N 32 25 E
Papien Chiang = Da →,
Vietnam .... **38 B5** 21 15N 105 20 E
Papigochic →, *Mexico* **86 B3** 29 9N 109 40W
Paposo, *Chile* **94 B1** 25 0S 70 30W
Papoutsa, *Cyprus* .... **23 E12** 34 54N 33 4 E
Papua New Guinea ■,
Oceania .... **64 H6** 8 0S 145 0 E
Papudo, *Chile* **94 C1** 32 29S 71 27W
Papun, *Burma* .... **41 K20** 18 2N 97 30 E
Papunya, *Australia* .... **60 D5** 23 15S 131 54 E
Pará = Belém, *Brazil* **93 D9** 1 20S 48 30W
Pará □, *Brazil* **93 D8** 3 20S 52 0W
Paraburdoo, *Australia* .... **60 D2** 23 14S 117 32 E
Paracatu, *Brazil* **93 G9** 17 10S 46 50W
Paracel Is., *S. China Sea* .. **36 A4** 15 50N 112 0 E
Parachinar, *Pakistan* ...... **42 C4** 33 55N 70 5 E
Paradhísi, *Greece* .... **23 C10** 36 18N 28 7 E
Paradip, *India* .... **41 J15** 20 15N 86 35 E
Paradise, *Calif., U.S.A.* **84 F5** 39 46N 121 37W
Paradise, *Nev., U.S.A.* **85 J11** 36 9N 115 10W
Paradise →, *Canada* **71 B8** 53 27N 57 19W
Paradise Hill, *Canada* **73 C7** 53 32N 109 28W
Paradise River, *Canada* ... **71 B8** 53 27N 57 17W
Paradise Valley, *U.S.A.* **82 F5** 41 30N 117 32W
Parado, *Indonesia* .... **37 F5** 8 42S 118 30 E
Paragould, *U.S.A.* **81 G9** 36 3N 90 29W
Paragua →, *Venezuela* **92 B6** 6 55N 62 55W
Paraguaçu →, *Brazil* **93 F11** 12 45S 38 54W
Paraguaçu Paulista, *Brazil* . **95 A5** 22 22S 50 35W
Paraguaná, Pen. de,
Venezuela **92 A5** 12 0N 70 0W
Paraguarí, *Paraguay* **94 B4** 25 36S 57 0W
Paraguarí □, *Paraguay* **94 B4** 26 0S 57 10W
Paraguay ■, *S. Amer.* **94 A4** 23 0S 57 0W
Paraguay →, *Paraguay* ... **94 B4** 27 18S 58 38W
Paraíba = João Pessoa,
Brazil **93 E12** 7 10S 34 52W
Paraíba □, *Brazil* **93 E11** 7 0S 36 0W
Paraíba do Sul →, *Brazil* .. **95 A7** 21 37S 41 3W
Parainen, *Finland* .... **9 F20** 60 18N 22 18 E
Paraiso, *Mexico* **87 D6** 18 24N 93 14W
Parak, *Iran* .... **45 E7** 27 38N 52 25 E
Parakou, *Benin* .... **50 G6** 9 25N 2 40 E
Paralimni, *Cyprus* .... **23 D12** 35 2N 33 58 E
Paramaribo, *Surinam* **93 B7** 5 50N 55 10W
Paramushir, Ostrov, *Russia* **27 D16** 50 24N 156 0 E
Paran →, *Israel* .... **47 E4** 30 20N 35 10 E
Paraná, *Argentina* **94 C3** 31 45S 60 30W
Paranã, *Brazil* **93 F9** 12 30S 47 48W
Paraná □, *Brazil* **95 A5** 24 30S 51 0W
Paraná →, *Argentina* **94 C4** 33 43S 59 15W
Paranaguá, *Brazil* **95 B6** 25 30S 48 30W
Paranaíba, *Brazil* **93 G8** 19 40S 51 11W
Paranaíba →, *Brazil* **93 H8** 20 6S 51 4W
Paranapanema →, *Brazil* . **95 A5** 22 40S 53 9W
Paranapiacaba, Serra do,
Brazil **95 A6** 24 31S 48 35W
Paranavaí, *Brazil* **95 A5** 23 4S 52 56W
Parang, *Maguindanao, Phil.* **37 C6** 7 23N 124 16 E
Parang, *Sulu, Phil.* .... **37 C6** 5 55N 120 54 E
Parângul Mare, Vf.,
Romania .... **17 F12** 45 20N 23 37 E
Paraparaumu, *N.Z.* .... **59 J5** 40 57S 175 3 E
Parbati →, *Mad. P., India* . **42 G7** 25 50N 76 30 E
Parbati →, *Raj., India* .... **42 F7** 26 54N 77 53 E
Parbhani, *India* .... **40 K10** 19 8N 76 52 E
Parchim, *Germany* .... **16 B6** 53 26N 11 52 E
Pardes Hanna-Karkur, *Israel* **47 C3** 32 28N 34 57 E
Pardo →, *Bahia, Brazil* **93 G11** 15 40S 39 0W
Pardo →, *Mato Grosso,*
Brazil **95 A5** 21 46S 52 9W
Pardubice, *Czech Rep.* .... **16 C8** 50 3N 15 45 E
Pare, *Indonesia* .... **37 G15** 7 43S 112 12 E
Pare Mts., *Tanzania* ...... **54 C4** 4 0S 37 45 E
Parecis, Serra dos, *Brazil* .. **92 F7** 13 0S 60 0W
Paren, *Russia* .... **27 C17** 62 30N 163 15 E
Parent, *Canada* **70 C5** 47 55N 74 35W
Parent, L., *Canada* **70 C4** 48 31N 77 1W
Parepare, *Indonesia* ...... **37 E5** 4 0S 119 40 E
Párga, *Greece* .... **21 E9** 39 15N 20 29 E
Pargo, Pta. do, *Madeira* ... **22 D2** 32 49N 17 17W
Pariaguán, *Venezuela* **92 B6** 8 51N 64 34W
Paricutín, Cerro, *Mexico* ... **86 D4** 19 28N 102 15W
Parigi, *Indonesia* .... **37 E6** 0 50S 120 5 E
Parika, *Guyana* **92 B7** 6 50N 58 20W
Parima, Serra, *Brazil* **92 C6** 2 30N 64 0W
Parinari, *Peru* **92 D4** 4 35S 74 25W
Pariñas, Pta., *S. Amer.* **90 D2** 4 30S 82 0W
Parintins, *Brazil* **93 D7** 2 40S 56 50W
Pariparit Kyun, *Burma* .... **41 M18** 14 55N 93 45 E
Paris, *Canada* **78 C4** 43 12N 80 25W
Paris, *France* .... **18 B5** 48 50N 2 20 E
Paris, *Idaho, U.S.A.* **82 E8** 42 14N 111 24W
Paris, *Ky., U.S.A.* **76 F3** 38 13N 84 15W
Paris, *Tenn., U.S.A.* **77 G1** 36 18N 88 19W
Paris, *Tex., U.S.A.* **81 J7** 33 40N 95 33W
Parish, *U.S.A.* **79 C8** 43 25N 76 8W
Parishville, *U.S.A.* **79 B10** 44 38N 74 49W
Park, *U.S.A.* **84 B4** 48 45N 122 18W
Park City, *U.S.A.* **81 G6** 37 48N 97 20W
Park Falls, *U.S.A.* **80 C9** 45 56N 90 27W
Park Head, *Canada* **78 B3** 44 36N 81 9W
Park Hills, *U.S.A.* **81 G9** 37 53N 90 28W
Park Range, *U.S.A.* **82 G10** 40 0N 106 30W
Park Rapids, *U.S.A.* **80 B7** 46 55N 95 4W
Park River, *U.S.A.* **80 A6** 48 24N 97 45W
Park Rynie, *S. Africa* ..... **57 E5** 30 25S 30 45 E
Parkā Bandar, *Iran* .... **45 E8** 25 55N 59 35 E
Parkano, *Finland* .... **9 E20** 62 1N 23 0 E
Parker, *Ariz., U.S.A.* **85 L12** 34 9N 114 17W
Parker, *Pa., U.S.A.* **78 E5** 41 5N 79 41W
Parker Dam, *U.S.A.* **85 L12** 34 18N 114 8W
Parkersburg, *U.S.A.* **76 F5** 39 16N 81 34W
Parkfield, *U.S.A.* **84 K6** 35 54N 120 26W
Parkhill, *Canada* **78 C3** 43 15N 81 38W
Parkland, *U.S.A.* **84 C4** 47 9N 122 26W
Parkston, *U.S.A.* **80 D6** 43 24N 97 59W
Parksville, *Canada* **72 D4** 49 20N 124 21W
Parla, *Spain* **19 B4** 40 14N 3 46W
Parma, *Italy* .... **18 D9** 44 48N 10 20 E
Parma, *Idaho, U.S.A.* **82 E5** 43 47N 116 57W
Parma, *Ohio, U.S.A.* **78 E3** 41 23N 81 43W
Parnaguá, *Brazil* **93 F10** 10 10S 44 38W
Parnaíba, *Brazil* **93 D10** 2 54S 41 47W
Parnaíba →, *Brazil* **93 D10** 3 0S 41 50W
Parnassós, *Greece* .... **21 E10** 38 35N 22 30 E
Pärnu, *Estonia* .... **9 G21** 58 28N 24 33 E
Páros, *Greece* .... **21 F11** 37 5N 25 12 E
Parowan, *U.S.A.* **83 H7** 37 51N 112 50W
Parral, *Chile* **94 D1** 36 10S 71 52W
Parras, *Mexico* **86 B4** 25 30N 102 20W
Parrett →, *U.K.* **11 F4** 51 12N 3 1W
Parris I., *U.S.A.* **77 J5** 32 20N 80 41W
Parrsboro, *Canada* **71 C7** 45 30N 64 25W
Parry I., *Canada* **78 A4** 45 18N 80 10W
Parry Is., *Canada* **4 B2** 77 0N 110 0W
Parry Sound, *Canada* **78 A5** 45 20N 80 0W
Parsnip →, *Canada* **72 B4** 55 10N 123 2W
Parsons, *U.S.A.* **81 G7** 37 20N 95 16W
Parsons Ra., *Australia* .... **62 A2** 13 30S 135 15 E
Partinico, *Italy* .... **20 E5** 38 3N 13 7 E
Partridge I., *Canada* **70 A2** 55 59N 87 37W
Paru →, *Brazil* **93 D8** 1 33S 52 38W
Parvān □, *Afghan.* .... **40 B6** 35 0N 69 0 E
Parvatipuram, *India* ...... **41 K13** 18 50N 83 25 E
Parvatsar, *India* .... **42 F6** 26 52N 74 49 E
Parys, *S. Africa* .... **56 D4** 26 52S 27 29 E
Pas, Pta. des, *Spain* ...... **22 C7** 38 46N 1 26 E
Pasadena, *Canada* **71 C8** 49 1N 57 36W
Pasadena, *Calif., U.S.A.* ... **85 L8** 34 9N 118 9W
Pasadena, *Tex., U.S.A.* **81 L7** 29 43N 95 13W
Pasaje →, *Argentina* **94 B3** 25 39S 63 56W
Pascagoula, *U.S.A.* **81 K10** 30 21N 88 33W
Pascagoula →, *U.S.A.* **81 K10** 30 23N 88 37W
Paşcani, *Romania* .... **17 E14** 47 14N 26 45 E
Pasco, *U.S.A.* **82 C4** 46 14N 119 6W
Pasco, Cerro de, *Peru* **92 F3** 10 45S 76 10W
Pasco I., *Australia* .... **60 D2** 20 57S 115 20 E
Pascoag, *U.S.A.* **79 E13** 41 57N 71 42W
Pascua, I. de, *Pac. Oc.* **65 K17** 27 0S 109 0W
Pasfield L., *Canada* **73 B7** 58 24N 105 20W
Pashmakli = Smolyan,
Bulgaria .... **21 D11** 41 36N 24 38 E
Pasir Mas, *Malaysia* ...... **39 J4** 6 2N 102 8 E
Pasir Putih, *Malaysia* ..... **39 K4** 5 50N 102 24 E
Pasirian, *Indonesia* ...... **37 H15** 8 13S 113 8 E
Pasirkuning, *Indonesia* ... **36 E2** 0 30S 104 33 E
Paskūh, *Iran* .... **45 E9** 27 34N 61 39 E
Pasley, C., *Australia* ...... **61 F3** 33 52S 123 35 E
Pašman, *Croatia* .... **16 G8** 43 58N 15 20 E
Pasni, *Pakistan* .... **40 G3** 25 15N 63 27 E
Paso Cantinela, *Mexico* ... **85 N11** 32 33N 115 47W
Paso de Indios, *Argentina* . **96 E3** 43 55S 69 0W
Paso de los Libres,
Argentina **94 B4** 29 44S 57 10W
Paso de los Toros, *Uruguay* **94 C4** 32 45S 56 30W
Paso Robles, *U.S.A.* **83 J3** 35 38N 120 41W
Paspébiac, *Canada* **71 C6** 48 3N 65 17W
Pasrur, *Pakistan* .... **42 C6** 32 16N 74 43 E
Passage West, *Ireland* **13 E3** 51 52N 8 21W
Passaic, *U.S.A.* **79 F10** 40 51N 74 7W
Passau, *Germany* .... **16 D7** 48 34N 13 28 E
Passero, C., *Italy* .... **20 F6** 36 41N 15 10 E
Passo Fundo, *Brazil* **95 B5** 28 10S 52 20W
Passos, *Brazil* **93 H9** 20 45S 46 37W
Pastavy, *Belarus* .... **9 J22** 55 4N 26 50 E
Pastaza →, *Peru* **92 D3** 4 50S 76 52W
Pasto, *Colombia* **92 C3** 1 13N 77 17W
Pasuruan, *Indonesia* ..... **37 G15** 7 40S 112 44 E
Patagonia, *Argentina* **96 F3** 45 0S 69 0W
Patagonia, *U.S.A.* **83 L8** 31 33N 110 45W
Patambar, *Iran* .... **45 D9** 29 45N 60 17 E
Patan, *Gujarat, India* ..... **40 H8** 23 54N 72 14 E
Patan, *Maharashtra, India* . **42 H5** 23 54N 72 14 E
Patani, *Indonesia* .... **37 D7** 0 20N 128 50 E
Pataudi, *India* .... **42 E7** 28 18N 76 48 E
Patchogue, *U.S.A.* **79 F11** 40 46N 73 1W
Patea, *N.Z.* .... **59 H5** 39 45S 174 30 E
Patensie, *S. Africa* .... **56 E3** 33 46S 24 49 E
Paternò, *Italy* .... **20 F6** 37 34N 14 54 E
Pateros, *U.S.A.* **82 B4** 48 3N 119 54W
Paterson, *U.S.A.* **79 F10** 40 55N 74 11W
Paterson Ra., *Australia* ... **60 D3** 21 45S 122 10 E
Pathankot, *India* .... **42 C6** 32 18N 75 45 E
Pathfinder Reservoir, *U.S.A.* **82 E10** 42 28N 106 51W
Pathiu, *Thailand* .... **39 G2** 10 42N 99 19 E
Pathum Thani, *Thailand* ... **38 E3** 14 1N 100 32 E
Pati, *Indonesia* .... **37 G14** 6 45S 111 1 E
Patía →, *Colombia* **92 C3** 2 13N 78 40W
Patiala, *Punjab, India* ..... **42 D7** 30 23N 76 26 E
Patiala, *Ut. P., India* ...... **43 F8** 27 43N 79 1 E
Patkai Bum, *India* .... **41 F19** 27 0N 95 30 E
Pátmos, *Greece* .... **21 F12** 37 21N 26 36 E
Patna, *India* .... **43 G11** 25 35N 85 12 E
Pato Branco, *Brazil* **95 B5** 26 13S 52 40W
Patonga, *Uganda* .... **54 B3** 2 45N 33 15 E
Patos, *Brazil* **93 E11** 6 55S 37 16W
Patos, L. dos, *Brazil* **95 C5** 31 20S 51 0W
Patos, Río de los →,
Argentina **94 C2** 31 18S 69 25W
Patos de Minas, *Brazil* **93 G9** 18 35S 46 32W
Patquía, *Argentina* **94 C2** 30 2S 66 55W
Pátrai, *Greece* .... **21 E9** 38 14N 21 47 E
Pátraikós Kólpos, *Greece* . **21 E9** 38 17N 21 30 E
Patras = Pátrai, *Greece* ... **21 E9** 38 14N 21 47 E
Patrocínio, *Brazil* **93 G9** 18 57S 47 0W
Patta, *Kenya* .... **54 C5** 2 10S 41 0 E
Pattani, *Thailand* .... **39 J3** 6 48N 101 15 E
Pattaya, *Thailand* .... **36 B2** 12 52N 100 55 E
Patten, *U.S.A.* **77 C11** 46 0N 68 38W
Patterson, *Calif., U.S.A.* ... **84 H5** 37 28N 121 8W
Patterson, *La., U.S.A.* **81 L9** 29 42N 91 18W
Patterson, Mt., *U.S.A.* **84 G7** 38 29N 119 20W
Patti, *Punjab, India* .... **42 D6** 31 17N 74 54 E
Patti, *Ut. P., India* .... **43 G10** 25 55N 82 12 E
Pattoki, *Pakistan* .... **42 D5** 31 5N 73 52 E
Patton, *U.S.A.* **78 F6** 40 38N 78 39W
Patuakhali, *Bangla.* ...... **41 H17** 22 20N 90 25 E
Patuanak, *Canada* **73 B7** 55 55N 107 43W
Patuca →, *Honduras* **88 C3** 15 50N 84 18W
Patuca, Punta, *Honduras* .. **88 C3** 15 49N 84 14W
Pátzcuaro, *Mexico* **86 D4** 19 30N 101 40W
Pau, *France* **18 E3** 43 19N 0 25W
Pauk, *Burma* .... **41 J19** 21 27N 94 30 E
Paul I., *Canada* **71 A7** 56 30N 61 20W
Paul Smiths, *U.S.A.* **79 B10** 44 26N 74 15W
Paulatuk, *Canada* **68 B7** 69 25N 124 0W
Paulis = Isiro, *Dem. Rep. of*
the Congo .... **54 B2** 2 53N 27 40 E
Paulistana, *Brazil* **93 E10** 8 9S 41 9W
Paulo Afonso, *Brazil* **93 E11** 9 21S 38 15W
Paulpietersburg, *S. Africa* . **57 D5** 27 23S 30 50 E
Pauls Valley, *U.S.A.* **81 H6** 34 44N 97 13W
Pauma Valley, *U.S.A.* **85 M10** 33 16N 116 58W
Pauri, *India* .... **43 D8** 30 9N 78 47 E
Pāveh, *Iran* .... **44 C5** 35 3N 46 22 E
Pavia, *Italy* .... **18 D8** 45 7N 9 8 E
Pavilion, *U.S.A.* **78 D6** 42 52N 78 1W
Pāvilosta, *Latvia* .... **9 H19** 56 53N 21 14 E
Pavlodar, *Kazakstan* ...... **26 D8** 52 33N 77 0 E
Pavlograd = Pavlohrad,
Ukraine .... **25 E6** 48 30N 35 52 E
Pavlohrad, *Ukraine* .... **25 E6** 48 30N 35 52 E
Pavlovo, *Russia* .... **24 C7** 55 58N 43 5 E
Pavlovsk, *Russia* .... **25 D7** 50 26N 40 5 E
Pavlovskaya, *Russia* ...... **25 E6** 46 17N 39 47 E
Pawayan, *India* .... **43 E9** 28 4N 80 6 E
Pawhuska, *U.S.A.* **81 G6** 36 40N 96 20W
Pawling, *U.S.A.* **79 E11** 41 34N 73 36W
Pawnee, *U.S.A.* **81 G6** 36 20N 96 48W
Pawnee City, *U.S.A.* **80 E6** 40 7N 96 9W
Pawtucket, *U.S.A.* **79 E13** 41 53N 71 23W
Paximádhia, *Greece* ...... **23 E6** 35 0N 24 35 E
Paxoí, *Greece* .... **21 E9** 39 14N 20 12 E
Paxton, *Ill., U.S.A.* **76 E1** 40 27N 88 6W
Paxton, *Nebr., U.S.A.* **80 E4** 41 7N 101 21W
Payakumbuh, *Indonesia* .. **36 E2** 0 20S 100 35 E
Payette, *U.S.A.* **82 D5** 44 5N 116 56W
Payne Bay = Kangirsuk,
Canada **69 B13** 60 0N 70 0W
Payne L., *Canada* **69 C12** 59 30N 74 30W
Paynes Find, *Australia* .... **61 E2** 29 15S 117 42 E
Paynesville, *U.S.A.* **80 C7** 45 23N 94 43W
Paysandú, *Uruguay* **94 C4** 32 19S 58 8W
Payson, *U.S.A.* **83 J8** 34 14N 111 20W
Paz →, *Guatemala* **88 D1** 13 44N 90 10W
Paz, B. de la, *Mexico* **86 C2** 24 15N 110 25W
Pāzanān, *Iran* .... **45 D6** 30 35N 49 59 E
Pazardzhik, *Bulgaria* ...... **21 C11** 42 12N 24 20 E
Pe Ell, *U.S.A.* **84 D3** 46 34N 123 18W
Peabody, *U.S.A.* **79 D14** 42 31N 70 56W
Peace →, *Canada* **72 B6** 59 0N 111 25W
Peace Point, *Canada* **72 B6** 59 7N 112 27W
Peace River, *Canada* **72 B5** 56 15N 117 18W
Peach Springs, *U.S.A.* **83 J7** 35 32N 113 25W
Peachland, *Canada* **72 D5** 49 47N 119 45W
Peachtree City, *U.S.A.* **77 J3** 33 25N 84 35W
Peak, The = Kinder Scout,
U.K. **10 D6** 53 24N 1 52W
Peak District, *U.K.* **10 D6** 53 10N 1 50W
Peak Hill, *Australia* .... **61 E2** 25 35S 118 43 E
Peak Ra., *Australia* .... **62 C4** 22 50S 148 20 E
Peake Cr. →, *Australia* ... **63 D2** 28 2S 136 7 E
Peale, Mt., *U.S.A.* **83 G9** 38 26N 109 14W
Pearblossom, *U.S.A.* **85 L9** 34 30N 117 55W
Pearl →, *U.S.A.* **81 K10** 30 11N 89 32W
Pearl City, *U.S.A.* **74 H16** 21 24N 157 59W
Pearl Harbor, *U.S.A.* **74 H16** 21 21N 157 57W
Pearl River, *U.S.A.* **79 E10** 41 4N 74 2W
Pearsall, *U.S.A.* **81 L5** 28 54N 99 6W
Peary Land, *Greenland* **4 A6** 82 40N 33 0W
Pease →, *U.S.A.* **81 H5** 34 12N 99 2W
Peawanuck, *Canada* **69 C11** 55 15N 85 12W
Pebane, *Mozam.* .... **55 F4** 17 10S 38 8 E
Pebas, *Peru* **92 D4** 3 10S 71 46W
Pebble Beach, *U.S.A.* **84 J5** 36 34N 121 57W
Peć, *Kosovo, Yug.* .... **21 C9** 42 40N 20 17 E
Pechenga, *Russia* .... **24 A5** 69 29N 31 4 E
Pechenizhyn, *Ukraine* .... **17 D13** 48 30N 24 48 E
Pechiguera, Pta., *Canary Is.* **22 F6** 28 51N 13 53W
Pechora, *Russia* .... **24 A10** 65 10N 57 11 E
Pechora →, *Russia* .... **24 A9** 68 13N 54 15 E
Pechorskaya Guba, *Russia* **24 A9** 68 40N 54 0 E
Pečory, *Russia* .... **9 H22** 57 48N 27 40 E
Pecos, *U.S.A.* **81 K3** 31 26N 103 30W
Pecos →, *U.S.A.* **81 L3** 29 42N 101 22W
Pécs, *Hungary* .... **17 E10** 46 5N 18 15 E
Pedder, L., *Australia* ...... **62 G4** 42 55S 146 10 E
Peddie, *S. Africa* .... **57 E4** 33 14S 27 7 E
Pedernales, *Dom. Rep.* **89 C5** 18 2N 71 44W
Pedieos →, *Cyprus* .... **23 D12** 35 10N 33 54 E
Pedirka, *Australia* .... **63 D2** 26 40S 135 14 E
Pedra Azul, *Brazil* **93 G10** 16 2S 41 17W
Pedreiras, *Brazil* **93 D10** 4 32S 44 40W
Pedro Afonso, *Brazil* **93 E9** 9 0S 48 10W
Pedro Cays, *Jamaica* **88 C4** 17 5N 77 48W
Pedro de Valdivia, *Chile* ... **94 A2** 22 55S 69 38W
Pedro Juan Caballero,
Paraguay **95 A4** 22 30S 55 40W
Pee Dee →, *U.S.A.* **77 J6** 33 22N 79 16W
Peebles, *U.K.* **12 F5** 55 40N 3 11W
Peekskill, *U.S.A.* **79 E11** 41 17N 73 55W
Peel, *U.K.* **10 C3** 54 13N 4 40W
Peel →, *Canada* **68 B6** 67 0N 135 0W
Peel Sound, *Canada* **68 A10** 73 0N 96 0W
Peera Peera Poolanna L.,
Australia .... **63 D2** 26 30S 138 0 E
Peerless Lake, *Canada* **72 B6** 56 37N 114 40W
Peers, *Canada* **72 C5** 53 40N 116 0W
Pegasus Bay, *N.Z.* .... **59 K4** 43 20S 173 10 E
Pegu, *Burma* .... **41 L20** 17 20N 96 29 E
Pegu Yoma, *Burma* .... **41 K20** 19 0N 96 0 E
Pehuajó, *Argentina* **94 D3** 35 45S 62 0W
Pei Xian = Pizhou, *China* .. **34 G9** 34 44N 116 55 E
Peine, *Chile* **94 A2** 23 45S 68 8W
Peine, *Germany* .... **16 B6** 52 19N 10 14 E
Peip'ing = Beijing, *China* .. **34 E9** 39 55N 116 20 E
Peipus, L. = Chudskoye,
Ozero, *Russia* .... **9 G22** 58 13N 27 30 E
Peixe, *Brazil* **93 F9** 12 0S 48 40W
Peixe →, *Brazil* **93 H8** 21 31S 51 58W
Pekalongan, *Indonesia* .... **36 F3** 6 53S 109 40 E
Pekan, *Malaysia* .... **39 L4** 3 30N 103 25 E
Pekanbaru, *Indonesia* ..... **36 D2** 0 30N 101 15 E
Pekin, *U.S.A.* **80 E10** 40 35N 89 40W
Peking = Beijing, *China* ... **34 E9** 39 55N 116 20 E
Pelabuhan Kelang,
Malaysia .... **39 L3** 3 0N 101 23 E
Pelabuhan Ratu, Teluk,
Indonesia .... **37 G12** 7 5S 106 30 E
Pelabuhanratu, *Indonesia* . **37 G12** 7 0S 106 32 E
Pelagie, Is., *Italy* .... **20 G5** 35 39N 12 33 E
Pelaihari, *Indonesia* ...... **36 E4** 3 55S 114 45 E
Peleaga, Vf., *Romania* .... **17 F12** 45 22N 22 55 E
Pelée, Mt., *Martinique* **89 D7** 14 48N 61 10W
Pelee, Pt., *Canada* **70 D3** 41 54N 82 31W
Pelee I., *Canada* **78 E2** 41 47N 82 40W
Pelekech, *Kenya* .... **54 B4** 3 52N 35 8 E
Peleng, *Indonesia* .... **37 E6** 1 20S 123 30 E
Pelican, *U.S.A.* **72 B1** 57 58N 136 14W
Pelican L., *Canada* **73 C8** 52 28N 100 20W
Pelican Narrows, *Canada* .. **73 B8** 55 10N 102 56W
Pelješac, *Croatia* .... **20 C7** 42 55N 17 25 E
Pelkosenniemi, *Finland* ... **8 C22** 67 6N 27 28 E
Pella, *S. Africa* .... **56 D2** 29 1S 19 6 E
Pella, *U.S.A.* **80 E8** 41 25N 92 55W
Pello, *Finland* .... **8 C21** 66 47N 23 59 E
Pelly →, *Canada* **68 B6** 62 47N 137 19W
Pelly Bay, *Canada* **69 B11** 68 38N 89 50W
Peloponnese =
Pelopónnisos □, *Greece* **21 F10** 37 10N 22 0 E
Pelopónnisos □, *Greece* .. **21 F10** 37 10N 22 0 E
Pelorus Sd., *N.Z.* .... **59 J4** 40 59S 173 59 E
Pelotas, *Brazil* **95 C5** 31 42S 52 23W
Pelotas →, *Brazil* **95 B5** 27 28S 51 55W
Pelvoux, Massif du, *France* **18 D7** 44 52N 6 20 E
Pemalang, *Indonesia* ..... **37 G13** 6 53S 109 23 E
Pemanggil, Pulau, *Malaysia* **39 L5** 2 37N 104 21 E
Pematangsiantar, *Indonesia* **36 D1** 2 57N 99 5 E
Pemba, *Mozam.* .... **55 E5** 12 58S 40 30 E
Pemba, *Zambia* .... **55 F2** 16 30S 27 28 E
Pemba Channel, *Tanzania* . **54 D4** 5 0S 39 37 E
Pemba I., *Tanzania* .... **54 D4** 5 0S 39 45 E
Pemberton, *Australia* ..... **61 F2** 34 30S 116 0 E
Pemberton, *Canada* **72 C4** 50 25N 122 50W
Pembina, *U.S.A.* **80 A6** 48 58N 97 15W
Pembroke, *Canada* **70 C4** 45 50N 77 7W
Pembroke, *U.K.* **11 F3** 51 41N 4 55W
Pembrokeshire □, *U.K.* **11 F3** 51 52N 4 56W
Pen-y-Ghent, *U.K.* **10 C5** 54 10N 2 14W
Penang = Pinang, *Malaysia* **39 K3** 5 25N 100 15 E
Penápolis, *Brazil* **95 A6** 21 30S 50 0W
Peñarroya-Pueblonuevo,
Spain **19 C3** 38 19N 5 16W
Penarth, *U.K.* **11 F4** 51 26N 3 11W
Peñas, C. de, *Spain* **19 A3** 43 42N 5 52W
Penas, G. de, *Chile* **96 F2** 47 0S 75 0W
Peñas del Chache,
Canary Is. **22 E6** 29 6N 13 33W
Pench'i = Benxi, *China* .... **35 D12** 41 20N 123 48 E

Pend Oreille

Pend Oreille →, *U.S.A.* ... **82 B5** 49 4N 117 37W
Pend Oreille, L., *U.S.A.* ... **82 C5** 48 10N 116 21W
Pendembu, *S. Leone* ... **50 G3** 9 7N 11 14W
Pender B., *Australia* ... **60 C3** 16 45S 122 42 E
Pendleton, *U.S.A.* ... **82 D4** 45 40N 118 47W
Pendra, *India* ... **43 H9** 22 46N 81 57 E
Penedo, *Brazil* ... **93 F11** 10 15S 36 36W
Penetanguishene, *Canada* ... **78 B5** 44 50N 79 55W
Penfield, *U.S.A.* ... **78 E6** 41 13N 78 35W
Pengalengan, *Indonesia* ... **37 G12** 7 9S 107 30 E
Penge, *Kasai-Or.,*
Dem. Rep. of the Congo **54 D1** 5 30S 24 33 E
Penge, *Sud-Kivu,*
Dem. Rep. of the Congo **54 C2** 4 27S 28 25 E
Penglai, *China* ... **35 F11** 37 48N 120 42 E
Penguin, *Australia* ... **62 G4** 41 8S 146 6 E
Penhalonga, *Zimbabwe* ... **55 F3** 18 52S 32 40 E
Peniche, *Portugal* ... **19 C1** 39 19N 9 22W
Penicuik, *U.K.* ... **12 F5** 55 50N 3 13W
Penida, *Indonesia* ... **36 F5** 8 45S 115 30 E
Peninsular Malaysia □,
Malaysia ... **39 L4** 4 0N 102 0 E
Penitente, Serra do, *Brazil* . **93 E9** 8 45S 46 20W
Penkridge, *U.K.* ... **10 E5** 52 44N 2 6W
Penmarch, Pte. de, *France* **18 C1** 47 48N 4 22W
Penn Hills, *U.S.A.* ... **78 F5** 40 28N 79 52W
Penn Yan, *U.S.A.* ... **78 D7** 42 40N 77 3W
Pennant, *Canada* ... **73 C7** 50 32N 108 14W
Penner →, *India* ... **40 M12** 14 35N 80 10 E
Pennines, *U.K.* ... **10 C5** 54 45N 2 27W
Pennington, *U.S.A.* ... **84 F5** 39 15N 121 47W
Pennsburg, *U.S.A.* ... **79 F9** 40 23N 75 29W
Pennsylvania □, *U.S.A.* ... **76 E7** 40 45N 77 30W
Penny, *Canada* ... **72 C4** 53 51N 121 20W
Penobscot →, *U.S.A.* ... **77 C11** 44 30N 68 48W
Penobscot B., *U.S.A.* ... **77 C11** 44 35N 68 50W
Penong, *Australia* ... **61 F5** 31 56S 133 1 E
Penonomé, *Panama* ... **88 E3** 8 31N 80 21W
Penrith, *U.K.* ... **10 C5** 54 40N 2 45W
Penryn, *U.K.* ... **11 G2** 50 9N 5 7W
Pensacola, *U.S.A.* ... **77 K2** 30 25N 87 13W
Pensacola Mts., *Antarctica* **5 E1** 84 0S 40 0W
Pense, *Canada* ... **73 C8** 50 25N 104 59W
Penticton, *Canada* ... **72 D5** 49 30N 119 38W
Pentland, *Australia* ... **62 C4** 20 32S 145 25 E
Pentland Firth, *U.K.* ... **12 C5** 58 43N 3 10W
Pentland Hills, *U.K.* ... **12 F5** 55 48N 3 25W
Penza, *Russia* ... **24 D8** 53 15N 45 5 E
Penzance, *U.K.* ... **11 G2** 50 7N 5 33W
Penzhino, *Russia* ... **27 C17** 63 30N 167 55 E
Penzhinskaya Guba, *Russia* **27 C17** 61 30N 163 0 E
Peoria, *Ariz., U.S.A.* ... **83 K7** 33 35N 112 14W
Peoria, *Ill., U.S.A.* ... **80 E10** 40 42N 89 36W
Pepacton Reservoir, *U.S.A.* **79 D10** 42 5N 74 58W
Pepani →, *S. Africa* ... **56 D3** 25 49S 22 47 E
Pera Hd., *Australia* ... **62 A3** 12 55S 141 37 E
Perabumulih, *Indonesia* ... **36 E2** 3 27S 104 15 E
Perak →, *Malaysia* ... **39 K3** 4 0N 100 50 E
Pérama, *Kérkira, Greece* ... **23 A3** 39 34N 19 54 E
Pérama, *Kríti, Greece* ... **23 D6** 35 20N 24 40 E
Peräpohjola, *Finland* ... **8 C22** 66 16N 26 10 E
Percé, *Canada* ... **71 C7** 48 31N 64 13W
Perche, Collines du, *France* **18 B4** 48 30N 0 40 E
Percival Lakes, *Australia* .. **60 D4** 21 25S 125 0 E
Percy Is., *Australia* ... **62 C5** 21 39S 150 16 E
Perdido, Mte., *Spain* ... **19 A6** 42 40N 0 5 E
Perdu, Mt. = Perdido, Mte.,
Spain ... **19 A6** 42 40N 0 5 E
Pereira, *Colombia* ... **92 C3** 4 49N 75 43W
Perenjori, *Australia* ... **61 E2** 29 26S 116 16 E
Pereyaslav-Khmelnytskyy,
Ukraine ... **25 D5** 50 3N 31 28 E
Pérez, I., *Mexico* ... **87 C7** 22 24N 89 42W
Pergamino, *Argentina* ... **94 C3** 33 52S 60 30W
Pergau →, *Malaysia* ... **39 K3** 5 23N 102 2 E
Perham, *U.S.A.* ... **80 B7** 46 36N 95 34W
Perhentian, Kepulauan,
Malaysia ... **36 C2** 5 54N 102 42 E
Péribonca →, *Canada* ... **71 C5** 48 45N 72 5W
Péribonca, L., *Canada* ... **71 B5** 50 1N 71 10W
Perico, *Argentina* ... **94 A2** 24 20S 65 5W
Pericos, *Mexico* ... **86 B3** 25 3N 107 42W
Périgueux, *France* ... **18 D4** 45 10N 0 42 E
Perijá, Sierra de, *Colombia* **92 B4** 9 30N 73 3W
Peristerona →, *Cyprus* ... **23 D12** 35 8N 33 5 E
Perito Moreno, *Argentina* ... **96 F2** 46 36S 70 56W
Perkasie, *U.S.A.* ... **79 F9** 40 22N 75 18W
Perlas, Arch. de las,
Panama ... **88 E4** 8 41N 79 7W
Perlas, Punta de, *Nic.* ... **88 D3** 12 30N 83 30W
Perm, *Russia* ... **24 C10** 58 0N 56 10 E
Pernambuco = Recife, *Brazil* **93 E12** 8 0S 35 0W
Pernambuco □, *Brazil* ... **93 E11** 8 0S 37 0W
Pernik, *Bulgaria* ... **21 C10** 42 35N 23 2 E
Peron Is., *Australia* ... **60 B5** 13 9S 130 4 E
Peron Pen., *Australia* ... **61 E1** 26 0S 113 10 E
Perow, *Canada* ... **72 C3** 54 35N 126 10W
Perpendicular Pt., *Australia* **63 E5** 31 37S 152 52 E
Perpignan, *France* ... **18 E5** 42 42N 2 53 E
Perris, *U.S.A.* ... **85 M9** 33 47N 117 14W
Perry, *Fla., U.S.A.* ... **77 K4** 30 7N 83 35W
Perry, *Ga., U.S.A.* ... **77 J4** 32 28N 83 44W
Perry, *Iowa, U.S.A.* ... **80 E7** 41 51N 94 6W
Perry, *Okla., U.S.A.* ... **81 G6** 36 17N 97 14W
Perryton, *U.S.A.* ... **81 G4** 36 24N 100 48W
Perryville, *U.S.A.* ... **81 G10** 37 43N 89 52W
Persepolis, *Iran* ... **45 D7** 29 55N 52 50 E
Pershotravensk, *Ukraine* .. **17 C14** 50 13N 27 40 E
Persia = Iran ■, *Asia* ... **45 C7** 33 0N 53 0 E
Persian Gulf = Gulf, The,
Asia ... **45 E6** 27 0N 50 0 E
Perth, *Australia* ... **61 F2** 31 57S 115 52 E
Perth, *Canada* ... **79 B8** 44 55N 76 15W
Perth, *U.K.* ... **12 E5** 56 24N 3 26W
Perth & Kinross □, *U.K.* ... **12 E5** 56 45N 3 55W
Perth Amboy, *U.S.A.* ... **79 F10** 40 31N 74 16W
Perth-Andover, *Canada* ... **71 C6** 46 44N 67 42W
Peru, *Ind., U.S.A.* ... **76 E2** 40 45N 86 4W
Peru, *N.Y., U.S.A.* ... **79 B11** 44 35N 73 32W
Peru ■, *S. Amer.* ... **92 D4** 4 0S 75 0W
Peru Basin, *Pac. Oc.* ... **65 J18** 20 0S 95 0W
Peru-Chile Trench, *Pac. Oc.* **92 G3** 20 0S 72 0W
Perúgia, *Italy* ... **20 C5** 43 7N 12 23 E
Pervomaysk, *Ukraine* ... **25 E5** 48 10N 30 46 E
Pervouralsk, *Russia* ... **24 C10** 56 59N 59 59 E
Pésaro, *Italy* ... **20 C5** 43 54N 12 55 E
Pescara, *Italy* ... **20 C6** 42 28N 14 13 E
Peshawar, *Pakistan* ... **42 B4** 34 2N 71 37 E
Peshkopi, *Albania* ... **21 D9** 41 41N 20 25 E
Peshtigo, *U.S.A.* ... **76 C2** 45 4N 87 46W
Pesqueira, *Brazil* ... **93 E11** 8 20S 36 42W
Petah Tiqwa, *Israel* ... **47 C3** 32 6N 34 53 E
Petaling Jaya, *Malaysia* ... **39 L3** 3 4N 101 42 E
Petaloudhes, *Greece* ... **23 C10** 36 18N 28 5 E
Petaluma, *U.S.A.* ... **84 G4** 38 14N 122 39W
Pétange, *Lux.* ... **15 E5** 49 33N 5 55 E
Petaro, *Pakistan* ... **42 G3** 25 31N 68 18 E
Petatlán, *Mexico* ... **86 D4** 17 31N 101 16W
Petauke, *Zambia* ... **55 E3** 14 14S 31 20 E
Petawawa, *Canada* ... **70 C4** 45 54N 77 17W
Petén Itzá, L., *Guatemala* .. **88 C2** 16 58N 89 50W
Peter I.s Øy, *Antarctica* ... **5 C16** 69 0S 91 0W
Peter Pond L., *Canada* ... **73 B7** 55 55N 108 44W
Peterbell, *Canada* ... **70 C3** 48 36N 83 21W
Peterborough, *Canada* ... **78 B6** 44 20N 78 20W
Peterborough, *U.K.* ... **11 E7** 52 35N 0 15W
Peterborough, *U.S.A.* ... **79 D13** 42 53N 71 57W
Peterborough □, *U.K.* ... **11 E7** 52 35N 0 15W
Peterculter, *U.K.* ... **12 D6** 57 6N 2 16W
Peterhead, *U.K.* ... **12 D7** 57 31N 1 48W
Peterlee, *U.K.* ... **10 C6** 54 47N 1 20W
Petermann Bjerg,
Greenland ... **66 B17** 73 7N 28 25W
Petermann Ranges,
Australia ... **60 E5** 26 0S 130 30 E
Petersburg, *Alaska, U.S.A.* **68 C6** 56 48N 132 58W
Petersburg, *Pa., U.S.A.* ... **78 F6** 40 34N 78 3W
Petersburg, *Va., U.S.A.* ... **76 G7** 37 14N 77 24W
Petersburg, *W. Va., U.S.A.* **76 F6** 39 1N 79 5W
Petersfield, *U.K.* ... **11 F7** 51 1N 0 56W
Petit Goâve, *Haiti* ... **89 C5** 18 27N 72 51W
Petit Jardin, *Canada* ... **71 C8** 48 28N 59 14W
Petit Lac Manicouagan,
Canada ... **71 B6** 51 25N 67 40W
Petit-Mécatina →, *Canada* **71 B8** 50 40N 59 30W
Petit-Mécatina, I. du,
Canada ... **71 B8** 50 30N 59 25W
Petitcodiac, *Canada* ... **71 C6** 45 57N 65 11W
Petite Baleine →, *Canada* . **70 A4** 56 0N 76 45W
Petite Saguenay, *Canada* .. **71 C5** 48 15N 70 4W
Petitot →, *Canada* ... **72 A4** 60 14N 123 29W
Petitsikapau L., *Canada* ... **71 B6** 54 37N 66 25W
Petlad, *India* ... **42 H5** 22 30N 72 45 E
Peto, *Mexico* ... **87 C7** 20 10N 88 53W
Petone, *N.Z.* ... **59 J5** 41 13S 174 53 E
Petorca, *Chile* ... **94 C1** 32 15S 70 56W
Petoskey, *U.S.A.* ... **76 C3** 45 22N 84 57W
Petra, *Jordan* ... **47 E4** 30 20N 35 22 E
Petra, *Spain* ... **22 B10** 39 37N 3 6 E
Petra, Ostrova, *Russia* ... **4 B13** 76 15N 118 30 E
Petra Velikogo, Zaliv,
Russia ... **30 C6** 42 40N 132 0 E
Petrich, *Bulgaria* ... **21 D10** 41 24N 23 13 E
Petrified Forest National
Park, *U.S.A.* ... **83 J9** 35 0N 109 30W
Petrikov = Pyetrikaw,
Belarus ... **17 B15** 52 11N 28 29 E
Petrograd = Sankt-
Peterburg, *Russia* ... **24 C5** 59 55N 30 20 E
Petrolândia, *Brazil* ... **93 E11** 9 5S 38 20W
Petrolia, *Canada* ... **78 D2** 42 54N 82 9W
Petrolina, *Brazil* ... **93 E10** 9 24S 40 30W
Petropavl, *Kazakstan* ... **26 D7** 54 53N 69 13 E
Petropavlovsk = Petropavl,
Kazakstan ... **26 D7** 54 53N 69 13 E
Petropavlovsk-
Kamchatskiy, *Russia* ... **27 D16** 53 3N 158 43 E
Petrópolis, *Brazil* ... **95 A7** 22 33S 43 9W
Petroşani, *Romania* ... **17 F12** 45 28N 23 20 E
Petrovaradin, *Serbia, Yug.* **21 B8** 45 16N 19 55 E
Petrovsk, *Russia* ... **24 D8** 52 22N 45 19 E
Petrovsk-Zabaykalskiy,
Russia ... **27 D11** 51 20N 108 55 E
Petrozavodsk, *Russia* ... **24 B5** 61 41N 34 20 E
Petrus Steyn, *S. Africa* ... **57 D4** 27 38S 28 8 E
Petrusburg, *S. Africa* ... **56 D4** 29 4S 25 26 E
Peumo, *Chile* ... **94 C1** 34 21S 71 12W
Peureulak, *Indonesia* ... **36 D1** 4 48N 97 45 E
Pevek, *Russia* ... **27 C18** 69 41N 171 19 E
Pforzheim, *Germany* ... **16 D5** 48 52N 8 41 E
Phagwara, *India* ... **40 D9** 31 10N 75 40 E
Phaistós, *Greece* ... **23 D6** 35 2N 24 50 E
Phala, *Botswana* ... **56 C4** 23 45S 26 50 E
Phalera = Phulera, *India* ... **42 F6** 26 52N 75 16 E
Phalodi, *India* ... **42 F5** 27 12N 72 24 E
Phan, *Thailand* ... **38 C2** 19 28N 99 43 E
Phan Rang, *Vietnam* ... **39 G7** 11 34N 109 0 E
Phan Ri = Hoa Da, *Vietnam* **39 G7** 11 16N 108 40 E
Phan Thiet, *Vietnam* ... **39 G7** 11 1N 108 9 E
Phanat Nikhom, *Thailand* ... **38 F3** 13 27N 101 11 E
Phangan, Ko, *Thailand* ... **39 H3** 9 45N 100 0 E
Phangnga, *Thailand* ... **39 H2** 8 28N 98 30 E
Phanom Sarakham,
Thailand ... **38 F3** 13 45N 101 21 E
Phaphund, *India* ... **43 F8** 26 36N 79 28 E
Pharenda, *India* ... **43 F10** 27 5N 83 17 E
Pharr, *U.S.A.* ... **81 M5** 26 12N 98 11W
Phatthalung, *Thailand* ... **39 J3** 7 39N 100 6 E
Phayao, *Thailand* ... **38 C2** 19 11N 99 55 E
Phelps, *U.S.A.* ... **78 D7** 42 58N 77 3W
Phelps L., *Canada* ... **73 B8** 59 15N 103 15W
Phenix City, *U.S.A.* ... **77 J3** 32 28N 85 0W
Phet Buri, *Thailand* ... **38 F2** 13 1N 99 55 E
Phetchabun, *Thailand* ... **38 D3** 16 25N 101 8 E
Phetchabun, Thiu Khao,
Thailand ... **38 E3** 16 0N 101 20 E
Phetchaburi = Phet Buri,
Thailand ... **38 F2** 13 1N 99 55 E
Phi Phi, Ko, *Thailand* ... **39 J2** 7 45N 98 46 E
Phiafay, *Laos* ... **38 E6** 14 48N 106 0 E
Phibun Mangsahan,
Thailand ... **38 E5** 15 14N 105 14 E
Phichai, *Thailand* ... **38 D3** 17 22N 100 10 E
Phichit, *Thailand* ... **38 D3** 16 26N 100 22 E
Philadelphia, *Miss., U.S.A.* **81 J10** 32 46N 89 7W
Philadelphia, *N.Y., U.S.A.* **79 B9** 44 9N 75 43W
Philadelphia, *Pa., U.S.A.* ... **79 G9** 39 57N 75 10W
Philip, *U.S.A.* ... **80 C4** 44 2N 101 40W
Philippeville, *Belgium* ... **15 D4** 50 12N 4 33 E
Philippi, *U.S.A.* ... **76 F5** 39 9N 80 3W
Philippi L., *Australia* ... **62 C2** 24 20S 138 55 E
Philippines ■, *Asia* ... **37 B6** 12 0N 123 0 E
Philippolis, *S. Africa* ... **56 E4** 30 15S 25 16 E
Philippopolis = Plovdiv,
Bulgaria ... **21 C11** 42 8N 24 44 E
Philipsburg, *Canada* ... **79 A11** 45 2N 73 5W
Philipsburg, *Mont., U.S.A.* **82 C7** 46 20N 113 18W
Philipsburg, *Pa., U.S.A.* ... **78 F6** 40 54N 78 13W
Philipstown = Daingean,
Ireland ... **13 C4** 53 18N 7 17W
Philipstown, *S. Africa* ... **56 E3** 30 28S 24 30 E
Phillips, *U.S.A.* ... **80 C9** 45 42N 90 24W
Phillipsburg, *Kans., U.S.A.* **80 F5** 39 45N 99 19W
Phillipsburg, *N.J., U.S.A.* .. **79 F9** 40 42N 75 12W
Philmont, *U.S.A.* ... **79 D11** 42 15N 73 39W
Philomath, *U.S.A.* ... **82 D2** 44 32N 123 22W
Phimai, *Thailand* ... **38 E4** 15 13N 102 30 E
Phitsanulok, *Thailand* ... **38 D3** 16 50N 100 12 E
Phnom Dangrek, *Thailand* **36 B2** 14 20N 104 0 E
Phnom Penh, *Cambodia* ... **39 G5** 11 33N 104 55 E
Phnum Penh = Phnom
Penh, *Cambodia* ... **39 G5** 11 33N 104 55 E
Phoenicia, *U.S.A.* ... **79 D10** 42 5N 74 14W
Phoenix, *Ariz., U.S.A.* ... **83 K7** 33 27N 112 4W
Phoenix, *N.Y., U.S.A.* ... **79 C8** 43 14N 76 18W
Phoenix Is., *Kiribati* ... **64 H10** 3 30S 172 0W
Phoenixville, *U.S.A.* ... **79 F9** 40 8N 75 31W
Phon, *Thailand* ... **38 E4** 15 49N 102 36 E
Phon Tiou, *Laos* ... **38 D5** 17 53N 104 37 E
Phong →, *Thailand* ... **38 D4** 16 23N 102 56 E
Phong Saly, *Laos* ... **38 B4** 21 42N 102 9 E
Phong Tho, *Vietnam* ... **38 A4** 22 32N 103 21 E
Phonhong, *Laos* ... **38 C4** 18 30N 102 25 E
Phonum, *Thailand* ... **39 H2** 8 49N 98 48 E
Phosphate Hill, *Australia* .. **62 C2** 21 53S 139 58 E
Photharam, *Thailand* ... **38 F2** 13 41N 99 51 E
Phra Nakhon Si Ayutthaya,
Thailand ... **38 E3** 14 25N 100 30 E
Phra Thong, Ko, *Thailand* . **39 H2** 9 5N 98 17 E
Phrae, *Thailand* ... **38 C3** 18 7N 100 9 E
Phrom Phiram, *Thailand* ... **38 D3** 17 2N 100 12 E
Phu Dien, *Vietnam* ... **38 C5** 18 58N 105 31 E
Phu Loi, *Laos* ... **38 B4** 20 14N 103 14 E
Phu Ly, *Vietnam* ... **38 B5** 20 35N 105 50 E
Phu Quoc, Dao, *Vietnam* ... **39 G4** 10 20N 104 0 E
Phu Tho, *Vietnam* ... **38 B5** 21 24N 105 13 E
Phuc Yen, *Vietnam* ... **38 B5** 21 16N 105 45 E
Phuket, *Thailand* ... **39 J2** 7 52N 98 22 E
Phuket, Ko, *Thailand* ... **39 J2** 8 0N 98 22 E
Phul, *India* ... **42 D6** 30 19N 75 14 E
Phulad, *India* ... **42 G5** 25 38N 73 49 E
Phulchari, *Bangla.* ... **43 G13** 25 11N 89 37 E
Phulera, *India* ... **42 F6** 26 52N 75 16 E
Phulpur, *India* ... **43 G10** 25 31N 82 49 E
Phun Phin, *Thailand* ... **39 H2** 9 7N 99 12 E
Piacenza, *Italy* ... **18 D8** 45 1N 9 40 E
Pian Cr. →, *Australia* ... **63 E4** 30 2S 148 12 E
Pianosa, *Italy* ... **20 C4** 42 35N 10 5 E
Piapot, *Canada* ... **73 D7** 49 59N 109 8W
Piatra Neamţ, *Romania* ... **17 E14** 46 56N 26 21 E
Piauí □, *Brazil* ... **93 E10** 7 0S 43 0W
Piauí →, *Brazil* ... **93 E10** 6 38S 42 42W
Piave →, *Italy* ... **20 B5** 45 32N 12 44 E
Pibor Post, *Sudan* ... **51 G12** 6 47N 33 3 E
Picardie, *France* ... **18 B5** 49 50N 3 0 E
Picardy = Picardie, *France* . **18 B5** 49 50N 3 0 E
Picayune, *U.S.A.* ... **81 K10** 30 32N 89 41W
Pichhor, *India* ... **43 G8** 25 58N 78 20 E
Pichilemu, *Chile* ... **94 C1** 34 22S 72 0W
Pichor, *India* ... **42 G8** 25 11N 78 11 E
Pickerel L., *Canada* ... **70 C1** 48 40N 91 25W
Pickering, *U.K.* ... **10 C7** 54 15N 0 46W
Pickering, Vale of, *U.K.* ... **10 C7** 54 14N 0 45W
Pickle Lake, *Canada* ... **70 B1** 51 30N 90 12W
Pickwick L., *U.S.A.* ... **77 H1** 35 4N 88 15W
Pico Truncado, *Argentina* ... **96 F3** 46 40S 68 0W
Picos, *Brazil* ... **93 E10** 7 5S 41 28W
Picton, *Canada* ... **78 B7** 44 1N 77 9W
Picton, *N.Z.* ... **59 J5** 41 18S 174 3 E
Pictou, *Canada* ... **71 C7** 45 41N 62 42W
Picture Butte, *Canada* ... **72 D6** 49 55N 112 45W
Picún Leufú, *Argentina* ... **96 D3** 39 30S 69 5W
Pidurutalagala, *Sri Lanka* ... **40 R12** 7 10N 80 50 E
Piedmont = Piemonte □,
Italy ... **18 D7** 45 0N 8 0 E
Piedmont, *Ala., U.S.A.* ... **77 J3** 33 55N 85 37W
Piedmont, *S.C., U.S.A.* ... **75 D10** 34 0N 81 30W
Piedras Negras, *Mexico* ... **86 B4** 28 42N 100 31W
Pieksämäki, *Finland* ... **9 E22** 62 18N 27 10 E
Piemonte □, *Italy* ... **18 D7** 45 0N 8 0 E
Pienaarsrivier, *S. Africa* ... **57 D4** 25 15S 28 18 E
Piercefield, *U.S.A.* ... **79 B10** 44 13N 74 35W
Pierceland, *Canada* ... **73 C7** 54 20N 109 46W
Pierpont, *U.S.A.* ... **78 E4** 41 45N 80 34W
Pierre, *U.S.A.* ... **80 C4** 44 22N 100 21W
Pierre E. Trudeau, Mt. =
Logan, Mt., *Canada* ... **68 B5** 60 31N 140 22W
Piet Retief, *S. Africa* ... **57 D5** 27 1S 30 50 E
Pietarsaari, *Finland* ... **8 E20** 63 40N 22 43 E
Pietermaritzburg, *S. Africa* **57 D5** 29 35S 30 25 E
Pietersburg, *S. Africa* ... **57 C4** 23 54S 29 25 E
Pietrosul, Vf., *Maramureş,*
Romania ... **17 E13** 47 35N 24 43 E
Pietrosul, Vf., *Suceava,*
Romania ... **17 E13** 47 12N 25 18 E
Pigeon L., *Canada* ... **78 B6** 44 27N 78 30W
Piggott, *U.S.A.* ... **81 G9** 36 23N 90 11W
Pigüe, *Argentina* ... **94 D3** 37 36S 62 25W
Pihani, *India* ... **43 F9** 27 36N 80 15 E
Pihlajavesi, *Finland* ... **9 F23** 61 45N 28 45 E
Pijijiapan, *Mexico* ... **87 D6** 15 42N 93 14W
Pikangikum Berens, *Canada* **73 C10** 51 49N 94 0W
Pikes Peak, *U.S.A.* ... **80 F2** 38 50N 105 3W
Piketberg, *S. Africa* ... **56 E2** 32 55S 18 40 E
Pikeville, *U.S.A.* ... **76 G4** 37 29N 82 31W
Pikou, *China* ... **35 E12** 39 18N 122 22 E
Pikwitonei, *Canada* ... **73 B9** 55 35N 97 9W
Piła, *Poland* ... **17 B9** 53 10N 16 48 E
Pilani, *India* ... **42 E6** 28 22N 75 33 E
Pilar, *Paraguay* ... **94 B4** 26 50S 58 20W
Pilaya →, *Bolivia* ... **92 H6** 20 55S 64 4W
Pilbara, *Australia* ... **60 D2** 23 35S 117 25 E
Pilcomayo →, *Paraguay* ... **94 B4** 25 21S 57 42W
Pilgrim's Rest, *S. Africa* ... **57 C5** 24 55S 30 44 E
Pilibhit, *India* ... **43 E8** 28 40N 79 50 E
Pilica →, *Poland* ... **17 C11** 51 52N 21 17 E
Pilkhawa, *India* ... **42 E7** 28 43N 77 42 E
Pilliga, *Australia* ... **63 E4** 30 21S 148 54 E
Pílos, *Greece* ... **21 F9** 36 55N 21 42 E
Pilot Mound, *Canada* ... **73 D9** 49 15N 98 54W
Pilot Point, *U.S.A.* ... **81 J6** 33 24N 96 58W
Pilot Rock, *U.S.A.* ... **82 D4** 45 29N 118 50W
Pilsen = Plzeň, *Czech Rep.* . **16 D7** 49 45N 13 22 E
Pima, *U.S.A.* ... **83 K9** 32 54N 109 50W
Pimenta Bueno, *Brazil* ... **92 F6** 11 35S 61 10W
Pimentel, *Peru* ... **92 E3** 6 45S 79 55W
Pinang, *Malaysia* ... **39 K3** 5 25N 100 15 E
Pinar, C. des, *Spain* ... **22 B10** 39 53N 3 12 E
Pinar del Río, *Cuba* ... **88 B3** 22 26N 83 40W
Pınarhisar, *Turkey* ... **21 D12** 41 37N 27 30 E
Pinatubo, Mt., *Phil.* ... **37 A6** 15 8N 120 21 E
Pincher Creek, *Canada* ... **72 D6** 49 30N 113 57W
Pinchi L., *Canada* ... **72 C4** 54 38N 124 30W
Pinckneyville, *U.S.A.* ... **80 F10** 38 5N 89 23W
Pińczów, *Poland* ... **17 C11** 50 32N 20 32 E
Pindar, *Australia* ... **61 E2** 28 30S 115 47 E
Pindi Gheb, *Pakistan* ... **42 C5** 33 14N 72 21 E
Pindos Óros, *Greece* ... **21 E9** 40 0N 21 0 E
Pindus Mts. = Pindos Óros,
Greece ... **21 E9** 40 0N 21 0 E
Pine →, *B.C., Canada* ... **72 B4** 56 8N 120 43W
Pine →, *Sask., Canada* ... **73 B7** 58 50N 105 38W
Pine, C., *Canada* ... **71 C9** 46 37N 53 32W
Pine Bluff, *U.S.A.* ... **81 H9** 34 13N 92 1W
Pine Bluffs, *U.S.A.* ... **80 E2** 41 11N 104 4W
Pine City, *U.S.A.* ... **80 C8** 45 50N 92 59W
Pine Cr. →, *U.S.A.* ... **78 E7** 41 10N 77 16W
Pine Creek, *Australia* ... **60 B5** 13 50S 131 50 E
Pine Falls, *Canada* ... **73 C9** 50 34N 96 11W
Pine Flat Res., *U.S.A.* ... **84 J7** 36 50N 119 20W
Pine Grove, *U.S.A.* ... **79 F8** 40 33N 76 23W
Pine Pass, *Canada* ... **72 B4** 55 25N 122 42W
Pine Point, *Canada* ... **72 A6** 60 50N 114 28W
Pine Ridge, *U.S.A.* ... **80 D3** 43 2N 102 33W
Pine River, *Canada* ... **73 C8** 51 45N 100 30W
Pine River, *U.S.A.* ... **80 B7** 46 43N 94 24W
Pine Valley, *U.S.A.* ... **85 N10** 32 50N 116 32W
Pinecrest, *U.S.A.* ... **84 G6** 38 12N 120 1W
Pinedale, *Calif., U.S.A.* ... **84 J7** 36 50N 119 48W
Pinedale, *Wyo., U.S.A.* ... **82 E9** 42 52N 109 52W
Pinega →, *Russia* ... **24 B8** 64 30N 44 19 E
Pinehill, *Australia* ... **62 C4** 23 38S 146 57 E
Pinehouse L., *Canada* ... **73 B7** 55 32N 106 35W
Pineimuta →, *Canada* ... **70 B1** 52 8N 88 33W
Pinerolo, *Italy* ... **18 D7** 44 53N 7 21 E
Pinetop, *U.S.A.* ... **83 J9** 34 8N 109 56W
Pinetown, *S. Africa* ... **57 D5** 29 48S 30 54 E
Pineville, *U.S.A.* ... **81 K8** 31 19N 92 26W
Ping →, *Thailand* ... **38 E3** 15 42N 100 9 E
Pingaring, *Australia* ... **61 F2** 32 40S 118 32 E
Pingding, *China* ... **34 F7** 37 47N 113 38 E
Pingdingshan, *China* ... **34 H7** 33 43N 113 27 E
Pingdong, *Taiwan* ... **33 D7** 22 39N 120 30 E
Pingdu, *China* ... **35 F10** 36 42N 119 59 E
Pingelly, *Australia* ... **61 F2** 32 32S 117 5 E
Pingliang, *China* ... **34 G4** 35 35N 106 31 E
Pinglu, *China* ... **34 E7** 39 31N 112 30 E
Pingluo, *China* ... **34 E4** 38 52N 106 30 E
Pingquan, *China* ... **35 D10** 41 1N 118 37 E
Pingrup, *Australia* ... **61 F2** 33 32S 118 29 E
P'ingtung, *Taiwan* ... **33 D7** 22 38N 120 30 E
Pingwu, *China* ... **34 H3** 32 25N 104 30 E
Pingxiang, *China* ... **32 D5** 22 6N 106 46 E
Pingyao, *China* ... **34 F7** 37 12N 112 10 E
Pingyi, *China* ... **35 G9** 35 30N 117 35 E
Pingyin, *China* ... **34 F9** 36 20N 116 25 E
Pingyuan, *China* ... **34 F9** 37 10N 116 22 E
Pinhal, *Brazil* ... **95 A6** 22 10S 46 46W
Pinheiro, *Brazil* ... **93 D9** 2 31S 45 5W
Pinheiro Machado, *Brazil* . **95 C5** 31 34S 53 23W
Pinhel, *Portugal* ... **19 B2** 40 50N 7 1W
Pini, *Indonesia* ... **36 D1** 0 10N 98 40 E
Piniós →, *Greece* ... **21 E10** 39 55N 22 41 E
Pinjarra, *Australia* ... **61 F2** 32 37S 115 52 E
Pink Mountain, *Canada* ... **72 B4** 57 3N 122 52W
Pinnacles, *U.S.A.* ... **84 J5** 36 33N 121 19W
Pinnes, Ákra, *Greece* ... **21 D11** 40 5N 24 20 E
Pinon Hills, *U.S.A.* ... **85 L9** 34 26N 117 39W
Pinos, *Mexico* ... **86 C4** 22 20N 101 40W
Pinos, Mt., *U.S.A.* ... **85 L7** 34 49N 119 8W
Pinos Pt., *U.S.A.* ... **83 H3** 36 38N 121 57W
Pinotepa Nacional, *Mexico* **87 D5** 16 19N 98 3W
Pinrang, *Indonesia* ... **37 E5** 3 46S 119 41 E
Pins, Pte. aux, *Canada* ... **78 D3** 42 15N 81 51W
Pinsk, *Belarus* ... **17 B14** 52 10N 26 1 E
Pintados, *Chile* ... **92 H5** 20 35S 69 40W
Pinyug, *Russia* ... **24 B8** 60 5N 48 0 E
Pioche, *U.S.A.* ... **83 H6** 37 56N 114 27W
Piombino, *Italy* ... **20 C4** 42 55N 10 32 E
Pioner, Ostrov, *Russia* ... **27 B10** 79 50N 92 0 E
Piorini, L., *Brazil* ... **92 D6** 3 15S 62 35W
Piotrków Trybunalski,
Poland ... **17 C10** 51 23N 19 43 E
Pīp, *Iran* ... **45 E9** 26 45N 60 10 E
Pipar, *India* ... **42 F5** 26 25N 73 31 E
Pipar Road, *India* ... **42 F5** 26 27N 73 27 E
Piparia, *Mad. P., India* ... **42 H8** 22 45N 78 23 E
Piparia, *Mad. P., India* ... **42 J7** 21 49N 77 37 E
Pipestone, *U.S.A.* ... **80 D6** 44 0N 96 19W
Pipestone →, *Canada* ... **70 B2** 52 53N 89 23W
Pipestone Cr. →, *Canada* ... **73 D8** 49 38N 100 15W
Piplan, *Pakistan* ... **42 C4** 32 17N 71 21 E
Piploda, *India* ... **42 H6** 23 37N 74 56 E
Pipmuacan, Rés., *Canada* ... **71 C5** 49 45N 70 30W
Pippingarra, *Australia* ... **60 D2** 20 27S 118 42 E
Piqua, *U.S.A.* ... **76 E3** 40 9N 84 15W
Piquiri →, *Brazil* ... **95 A5** 24 3S 54 14W
Pīr Sohrāb, *Iran* ... **45 E9** 25 44N 60 54 E
Piracicaba, *Brazil* ... **95 A6** 22 45S 47 40W
Piracuruca, *Brazil* ... **93 D10** 3 50S 41 50W
Piræus = Piraiévs, *Greece* ... **21 F10** 37 57N 23 42 E
Piraiévs, *Greece* ... **21 F10** 37 57N 23 42 E
Pirajuí, *Brazil* ... **95 A6** 21 59S 49 29W
Piram I., *India* ... **42 J5** 21 36N 72 21 E
Pirané, *Argentina* ... **94 B4** 25 42S 59 6W
Pirapora, *Brazil* ... **93 G10** 17 20S 44 56W
Pirawa, *India* ... **42 G7** 24 10N 76 2 E
Pírgos, *Greece* ... **21 F9** 37 40N 21 27 E
Piribebuy, *Paraguay* ... **94 B4** 25 26S 57 2W
Pirimapun, *Indonesia* ... **37 F9** 6 20S 138 24 E
Pirin Planina, *Bulgaria* ... **21 D10** 41 40N 23 30 E
Pírineos = Pyrénées,
Europe ... **18 E4** 42 45N 0 18 E
Piripiri, *Brazil* ... **93 D10** 4 15S 41 46W

Portsmouth

Pirmasens, Germany ..... 16 D4 49 12N 7 36 E
Pirot, Serbia, Yug. .... 21 C10 43 9N 22 33 E
Piru, Indonesia .... 37 E7 3 4S 128 12 E
Piru, U.S.A. 85 L8 34 25N 118 48W
Pisa, Italy .... 20 C4 43 43N 10 23 E
Pisagua, Chile 92 G4 19 40S 70 15W
Pisco, Peru 92 F3 13 50S 76 12W
Písek, Czech Rep. .... 16 D8 49 19N 14 10 E
Pishan, China .... 32 C2 37 30N 78 33 E
Pishīn, Iran .... 45 E9 26 6N 61 47 E
Pishin, Pakistan .... 42 D2 30 35N 67 0 E
Pishin Lora →, Pakistan .. 42 E1 29 9N 64 5 E
Pising, Indonesia .... 37 F6 5 8S 121 53 E
Pismo Beach, U.S.A. 85 K6 35 9N 120 38W
Pissis, Cerro, Argentina ... 94 B2 27 45S 68 48W
Pissouri, Cyprus .... 23 E11 34 40N 32 42 E
Pistóia, Italy .... 20 C4 43 55N 10 54 E
Pistol B., Canada 73 A10 62 25N 92 37W
Pisuerga →, Spain 19 B3 41 33N 4 52W
Pit →, U.S.A. 82 F2 40 47N 122 6W
Pitcairn I., Pac. Oc. 65 K14 25 5S 130 5W
Pite älv →, Sweden .... 8 D19 65 20N 21 25 E
Piteå, Sweden .... 8 D19 65 20N 21 25 E
Piteşti, Romania .... 17 F13 44 52N 24 54 E
Pithapuram, India .... 41 L13 17 10N 82 15 E
Pithara, Australia .... 61 F2 30 20S 116 35 E
Pithoragarh, India .... 43 E9 29 35N 80 13 E
Pithoro, Pakistan .... 42 G3 25 31N 69 23 E
Pitlochry, U.K. 12 E5 56 42N 3 44W
Pitsilia □, Cyprus .... 23 E12 34 55N 33 0 E
Pitt I., Canada 72 C3 53 30N 129 50W
Pittsburg, Calif., U.S.A. ... 84 G5 38 2N 121 53W
Pittsburg, Kans., U.S.A. ... 81 G7 37 25N 94 42W
Pittsburg, Tex., U.S.A. 81 J7 33 0N 94 59W
Pittsburgh, U.S.A. 78 F5 40 26N 80 1W
Pittsfield, Ill., U.S.A. 80 F9 39 36N 90 49W
Pittsfield, Maine, U.S.A. ... 77 C11 44 47N 69 23W
Pittsfield, Mass., U.S.A. ... 79 D11 42 27N 73 15W
Pittsfield, N.H., U.S.A. 79 C13 43 18N 71 20W
Pittston, U.S.A. 79 E9 41 19N 75 47W
Pittsworth, Australia ..... 63 D5 27 41S 151 37 E
Pituri →, Australia .... 62 C2 22 35S 138 30 E
Piura, Peru 92 E2 5 15S 80 38W
Pixley, U.S.A. 84 K7 35 58N 119 18W
Pizhou, China .... 34 G9 34 44N 116 55 E
Placentia, Canada 71 C9 47 20N 54 0W
Placentia B., Canada 71 C9 47 0N 54 40W
Placerville, U.S.A. 84 G6 38 44N 120 48W
Placetas, Cuba 88 B4 22 15N 79 44W
Plainfield, N.J., U.S.A. 79 F10 40 37N 74 25W
Plainfield, Ohio, U.S.A. 78 F3 40 13N 81 43W
Plainfield, Vt., U.S.A. 79 B12 44 17N 72 26W
Plains, Mont., U.S.A. 82 C6 47 28N 114 53W
Plains, Tex., U.S.A. 81 J3 33 11N 102 50W
Plainview, Nebr., U.S.A. .. 80 D6 42 21N 97 47W
Plainview, Tex., U.S.A. 81 H4 34 11N 101 43W
Plainwell, U.S.A. 76 D3 42 27N 85 38W
Plaistow, U.S.A. 79 D13 42 50N 71 6W
Pláka, Ákra, Greece ...... 23 D8 35 11N 26 19 E
Plana Cays, Bahamas 89 B5 22 38N 73 30W
Planada, U.S.A. 84 H6 37 16N 120 19W
Plano, U.S.A. 81 J6 33 1N 96 42W
Plant City, U.S.A. 77 M4 28 1N 82 7W
Plaquemine, U.S.A. 81 K9 30 17N 91 14W
Plasencia, Spain 19 B2 40 3N 6 8W
Plaster City, U.S.A. 85 N11 32 47N 115 51W
Plaster Rock, Canada 71 C6 46 53N 67 22W
Plastun, Russia .... 30 B8 44 45N 136 19 E
Plata, Río de la, S. Amer. .. 94 C4 34 45S 57 30W
Plátani →, Italy .... 20 F5 37 23N 13 16 E
Plátanos, Greece .... 23 D5 35 28N 23 33 E
Platte, U.S.A. 80 D5 43 23N 98 51W
Platte →, Mo., U.S.A. 80 F7 39 16N 94 50W
Platte →, Nebr., U.S.A. ... 80 E7 41 4N 95 53W
Platteville, U.S.A. 80 D9 42 44N 90 29W
Plattsburgh, U.S.A. 79 B11 44 42N 73 28W
Plattsmouth, U.S.A. 80 E7 41 1N 95 53W
Plauen, Germany .... 16 C7 50 30N 12 8 E
Plavinas, Latvia .... 9 H21 56 35N 25 46 E
Playa Blanca, Canary Is. .. 22 F6 28 55N 13 37W
Playa Blanca Sur, Canary Is. 22 F6 28 51N 13 50W
Playa de las Americas,
Canary Is. 22 F3 28 5N 16 43W
Playa de Mogán, Canary Is. 22 G4 27 48N 15 47W
Playa del Inglés, Canary Is. 22 G4 27 45N 15 33W
Playa Esmerelda, Canary Is. 22 F5 28 8N 14 16W
Playgreen L., Canada 73 C9 54 0N 98 15W
Pleasant Bay, Canada 71 C7 46 51N 60 48W
Pleasant Hill, U.S.A. 84 H4 37 57N 122 4W
Pleasant Mount, U.S.A. 79 E9 41 44N 75 26W
Pleasanton, Calif., U.S.A. .. 84 H5 37 39N 121 52W
Pleasanton, Tex., U.S.A. .. 81 L5 28 58N 98 29W
Pleasantville, N.J., U.S.A. . 76 F8 39 24N 74 32W
Pleasantville, Pa., U.S.A. .. 78 E5 41 35N 79 34W
Plei Ku, Vietnam .... 38 F7 13 57N 108 0 E
Plenty →, Australia ...... 62 C2 23 25S 136 31 E
Plenty, B. of, N.Z. .... 59 G6 37 45S 177 0 E
Plentywood, U.S.A. 80 A2 48 47N 104 34W
Plesetsk, Russia .... 24 B7 62 43N 40 20 E
Plessisville, Canada 71 C5 46 14N 71 47W
Plétipi, L., Canada 71 B5 51 44N 70 6W
Pleven, Bulgaria .... 21 C11 43 26N 24 37 E
Plevlja, Montenegro, Yug. . 21 C8 43 21N 19 21 E
Plevna, Canada 78 B8 44 58N 76 59W
Płock, Poland .... 17 B10 52 32N 19 40 E
Plöckenstein, Germany ... 16 D7 48 46N 13 51 E
Ploieşti, Romania .... 17 F14 44 57N 26 5 E
Plonge, Lac la, Canada 73 B7 55 8N 107 20W
Plovdiv, Bulgaria .... 21 C11 42 8N 24 44 E
Plum, U.S.A. 78 F5 40 29N 79 47W
Plum I., U.S.A. 79 E12 41 11N 72 12W
Plumas, U.S.A. 84 F7 39 45N 120 4W
Plummer, U.S.A. 82 C5 47 20N 116 53W
Plumtree, Zimbabwe ...... 55 G2 20 27S 27 55 E
Plungė, Lithuania .... 9 J19 55 53N 21 59 E
Plymouth, U.K. 11 G3 50 22N 4 10W
Plymouth, Calif., U.S.A. ... 84 G6 38 29N 120 51W
Plymouth, Ind., U.S.A. 76 E2 41 21N 86 19W
Plymouth, Mass., U.S.A. .. 79 E14 41 57N 70 40W
Plymouth, N.C., U.S.A. 77 H7 35 52N 76 43W
Plymouth, N.H., U.S.A. 79 C13 43 46N 71 41W
Plymouth, Pa., U.S.A. 79 E9 41 14N 75 57W
Plymouth, Wis., U.S.A. 76 D2 43 45N 87 59W
Plynlimon = Pumlumon
Fawr, U.K. 11 E4 52 28N 3 46W
Plzeň, Czech Rep. .... 16 D7 49 45N 13 22 E
Po →, Italy .... 20 B5 44 57N 12 4 E
Po Hai = Bo Hai, China .... 35 E10 39 0N 119 0 E
Pobeda, Russia .... 27 C15 65 12N 146 12 E
Pobedy, Pik, Kyrgyzstan .. 26 E8 42 0N 79 58 E
Pocahontas, Ark., U.S.A. .. 81 G9 36 16N 90 58W
Pocahontas, Iowa, U.S.A. . 80 D7 42 44N 94 40W
Pocatello, U.S.A. 82 E7 42 52N 112 27W
Pochutla, Mexico 87 D5 15 50N 96 31W
Pocito Casas, Mexico 86 B2 28 32N 111 6W
Pocomoke City, U.S.A. 76 F8 38 5N 75 34W
Poços de Caldas, Brazil ... 95 A6 21 50S 46 33W
Podgorica,
Montenegro, Yug. ...... 21 C8 42 30N 19 19 E
Podilska Vysochyna,
Ukraine .... 17 D14 49 0N 28 0 E
Podolsk, Russia .... 24 C6 55 25N 37 30 E
Podporozhye, Russia ...... 24 B5 60 55N 34 2 E
Pofadder, S. Africa .... 56 D2 29 10S 19 22 E
Pogranitšnyi, Russia ...... 30 B5 44 25N 131 24 E
Poh, Indonesia .... 37 E6 0 46S 122 51 E
P'ohang, S. Korea .... 35 F15 36 1N 129 23 E
Pohjanmaa, Finland .... 8 E20 62 58N 22 50 E
Pohnpei, Micronesia ...... 64 G7 6 55N 158 10 E
Pohri, India .... 42 G6 25 32N 77 22 E
Poinsett, C., Antarctica .... 5 C8 65 42S 113 18 E
Point Arena, U.S.A. 84 G3 38 55N 123 41W
Point Baker, U.S.A. 72 B2 56 21N 133 37W
Point Edward, Canada 70 D3 43 0N 82 30W
Point Hope, U.S.A. 68 B3 68 21N 166 47W
Point L., Canada 68 B8 65 15N 113 4W
Point Pedro, Sri Lanka .... 40 Q12 9 50N 80 15 E
Point Pleasant, N.J., U.S.A. 79 F10 40 5N 74 4W
Point Pleasant, W. Va.,
U.S.A. 76 F4 38 51N 82 8W
Pointe-à-Pitre, Guadeloupe 89 C7 16 10N 61 30W
Pointe-Claire, Canada 79 A11 45 26N 73 50W
Pointe-Gatineau, Canada .. 79 A9 45 28N 75 42W
Pointe-Noire, Congo ...... 52 E2 4 48S 11 53 E
Poisonbush Ra., Australia . 60 D3 22 30S 121 30 E
Poissonnier Pt., Australia . 60 C2 19 57S 119 10 E
Poitiers, France .... 18 C4 46 35N 0 20 E
Poitou, France 18 C3 46 40N 0 10W
Pojoaque, U.S.A. 83 J11 35 54N 106 1W
Pokaran, India .... 40 F7 27 0N 71 50 E
Pokataroo, Australia ...... 63 D4 29 30S 148 36 E
Pokhara, Nepal .... 43 E10 28 14N 83 58 E
Poko, Dem. Rep. of
the Congo .... 54 B2 3 7N 26 52 E
Pokrovsk = Engels, Russia 25 D8 51 28N 46 6 E
Pokrovsk, Russia .... 27 C13 61 29N 129 0 E
Pola = Pula, Croatia ...... 16 F7 44 54N 13 57 E
Polacca, U.S.A. 83 J8 35 50N 110 23W
Polan, Iran .... 45 E9 25 30N 61 10 E
Poland ■, Europe .... 17 C10 52 0N 20 0 E
Polar Bear Prov. Park,
Canada 70 A2 55 0N 83 45W
Polatsk, Belarus .... 24 C4 55 30N 28 50 E
Polcura, Chile 94 D1 37 17S 71 43W
Polessk, Russia .... 9 J19 54 50N 21 8 E
Polesye = Pripet Marshes,
Europe .... 17 B15 52 10N 28 10 E
Polevskoy, Russia .... 24 C11 56 26N 60 11 E
Pŏlgyo-ri, S. Korea .... 35 G14 34 51N 127 21 E
Police, Poland .... 16 B8 53 33N 14 33 E
Polillo Is., Phil. .... 37 B6 14 56N 122 0 E
Polis, Cyprus .... 23 D11 35 2N 32 26 E
Políyiros, Greece .... 21 D10 40 23N 23 25 E
Polk, U.S.A. 78 E5 41 22N 79 56W
Pollachi, India .... 40 P10 10 35N 77 0 E
Pollença, Spain .... 22 B10 39 54N 3 1 E
Pollença, B. de, Spain ..... 22 B10 39 53N 3 8 E
Polnovat, Russia .... 26 C7 63 50N 65 54 E
Polonne, Ukraine .... 17 C14 50 6N 27 30 E
Polonnoye = Polonne,
Ukraine .... 17 C14 50 6N 27 30 E
Polson, U.S.A. 82 C6 47 41N 114 9W
Poltava, Ukraine .... 25 E5 49 35N 34 35 E
Põltsamaa, Estonia .... 9 G21 58 41N 25 58 E
Polunochnoye, Russia ..... 26 C7 60 52N 60 25 E
Põlva, Estonia .... 9 G22 58 3N 27 3 E
Polyarny, Russia .... 24 A5 69 8N 33 20 E
Polynesia, Pac. Oc. 65 J11 10 0S 162 0W
Polynésie française =
French Polynesia ■,
Pac. Oc. 65 K13 20 0S 145 0W
Pomaro, Mexico 86 D4 18 20N 103 18W
Pombal, Portugal 19 C1 39 55N 8 40W
Pómbia, Greece .... 23 E6 35 0N 24 51 E
Pomene, Mozam. .... 57 C6 22 53S 35 33 E
Pomeroy, Ohio, U.S.A. 76 F4 39 2N 82 2W
Pomeroy, Wash., U.S.A. ... 82 C5 46 28N 117 36W
Pomézia, Italy .... 20 D5 41 40N 12 30 E
Pomona, Australia .... 63 D5 26 22S 152 52 E
Pomona, U.S.A. 85 L9 34 4N 117 45W
Pomorskie, Pojezierze,
Poland .... 17 B9 53 40N 16 37 E
Pomos, Cyprus .... 23 D11 35 9N 32 33 E
Pomos, C., Cyprus .... 23 D11 35 10N 32 33 E
Pompano Beach, U.S.A. ... 77 M5 26 14N 80 8W
Pompeys Pillar, U.S.A. 82 D10 45 59N 107 57W
Pompton Lakes, U.S.A. 79 F10 41 0N 74 17W
Ponape = Pohnpei,
Micronesia .... 64 G7 6 55N 158 10 E
Ponask L., Canada 70 B1 54 0N 92 41W
Ponca, U.S.A. 80 D6 42 34N 96 43W
Ponca City, U.S.A. 81 G6 36 42N 97 5W
Ponce, Puerto Rico 89 C6 18 1N 66 37W
Ponchatoula, U.S.A. 81 K9 30 26N 90 26W
Poncheville, L., Canada 70 B4 50 10N 76 55W
Pond, U.S.A. 85 K7 35 43N 119 20W
Pond Inlet, Canada 69 A12 72 40N 77 0W
Pondicherry, India .... 40 P11 11 59N 79 50 E
Ponds, I. of, Canada 71 B8 53 27N 55 52W
Ponferrada, Spain 19 A2 42 32N 6 35W
Ponnani, India .... 40 P9 10 45N 75 59 E
Ponoka, Canada 72 C6 52 42N 113 40W
Ponorogo, Indonesia ...... 37 G14 7 52S 111 27 E
Ponoy, Russia .... 24 A7 67 0N 41 13 E
Ponoy →, Russia .... 24 A7 66 59N 41 17 E
Ponta do Sol, Madeira 22 D2 32 42N 17 7W
Ponta Grossa, Brazil 95 B5 25 7S 50 10W
Ponta Pora, Brazil 95 A4 22 20S 55 35W
Pontarlier, France .... 18 C7 46 54N 6 20 E
Pontchartrain L., U.S.A. ... 81 K10 30 5N 90 5W
Ponte do Pungué, Mozam. 55 F3 19 30S 34 33 E
Ponte Nova, Brazil 95 A7 20 25S 42 54W
Ponteix, Canada 73 D7 49 46N 107 29W
Pontevedra, Spain 19 A1 42 26N 8 40W
Pontiac, Ill., U.S.A. 80 E10 40 53N 88 38W
Pontiac, Mich., U.S.A. 76 D4 42 38N 83 18W
Pontian Kecil, Malaysia ... 39 M4 1 29N 103 23 E
Pontianak, Indonesia ..... 36 E3 0 3S 109 15 E
Pontine Is. = Ponziane,
Ísole, Italy .... 20 D5 40 55N 12 57 E
Pontine Mts. = Kuzey
Anadolu Dağları, Turkey 25 F6 41 30N 35 0 E
Pontivy, France 18 B2 48 5N 2 58W
Pontoise, France .... 18 B5 49 3N 2 5 E
Ponton →, Canada 72 B5 58 27N 116 11W
Pontypool, Canada 78 B6 44 6N 78 38W
Pontypool, U.K. 11 F4 51 42N 3 2W
Ponziane, Ísole, Italy ...... 20 D5 40 55N 12 57 E
Poochera, Australia .... 63 E1 32 43S 134 51 E
Poole, U.K. 11 G6 50 43N 1 59W
Poole □, U.K. 11 G6 50 43N 1 59W
Poona = Pune, India ...... 40 K8 18 29N 73 57 E
Poopó, L. de, Bolivia 92 G5 18 30S 67 35W
Popayán, Colombia 92 C3 2 27N 76 36W
Poperinge, Belgium ...... 15 D2 50 51N 2 42 E
Poplar, U.S.A. 80 A2 48 7N 105 12W
Poplar →, Canada 73 C9 53 0N 97 19W
Poplar Bluff, U.S.A. 81 G9 36 46N 90 24W
Poplarville, U.S.A. 81 K10 30 51N 89 32W
Popocatépetl, Volcán,
Mexico 87 D5 19 2N 98 38W
Popokabaka, Dem. Rep. of
the Congo .... 52 F3 5 41S 16 40 E
Poprad, Slovak Rep. .... 17 D11 49 3N 20 18 E
Porali →, Pakistan .... 42 G2 25 58N 66 26 E
Porbandar, India .... 40 J6 21 44N 69 43 E
Porcher I., Canada 72 C2 53 50N 130 30W
Porcupine →, Canada 73 B8 59 11N 104 46W
Porcupine →, U.S.A. 68 B5 66 34N 145 19W
Pordenone, Italy .... 20 B5 45 57N 12 39 E
Pori, Finland .... 9 F19 61 29N 21 48 E
Porlamar, Venezuela 92 A6 10 57N 63 51W
Poronaysk, Russia .... 27 E15 49 13N 143 0 E
Poroshiri-Dake, Japan ..... 30 C11 42 41N 142 52 E
Poroto Mts., Tanzania ..... 55 D3 9 0S 33 30 E
Porpoise B., Antarctica .... 5 C9 66 0S 127 0 E
Porreres, Spain .... 22 B10 39 31N 3 2 E
Porsangen, Norway .... 8 A21 70 40N 25 40 E
Porsgrunn, Norway .... 9 G13 59 10N 9 40 E
Port Alberni, Canada 72 D4 49 14N 124 50W
Port Alfred, S. Africa ...... 56 E4 33 36S 26 55 E
Port Alice, Canada 72 C3 50 20N 127 25W
Port Allegany, U.S.A. 78 E6 41 48N 78 17W
Port Allen, U.S.A. 81 K9 30 27N 91 12W
Port Alma, Australia ...... 62 C5 23 38S 150 53 E
Port Angeles, U.S.A. 84 B3 48 7N 123 27W
Port Antonio, Jamaica 88 C4 18 10N 76 30W
Port Aransas, U.S.A. 81 M6 27 50N 97 4W
Port Arthur = Lüshun, China 35 E11 38 45N 121 15 E
Port Arthur, Australia ..... 62 G4 43 7S 147 50 E
Port Arthur, U.S.A. 81 L8 29 54N 93 56W
Port au Choix, Canada 71 B8 50 43N 57 22W
Port au Port B., Canada ... 71 C8 48 40N 58 50W
Port-au-Prince, Haiti 89 C5 18 40N 72 20W
Port Austin, U.S.A. 78 B2 44 3N 83 1W
Port Bell, Uganda .... 54 B3 0 18N 32 35 E
Port Bergé Vaovao, Madag. 57 B8 15 33S 47 40 E
Port Blandford, Canada 71 C9 48 20N 54 10W
Port Bradshaw, Australia .. 62 A2 12 30S 137 20 E
Port Burwell, Canada 78 D4 42 40N 80 48W
Port Canning, India .... 43 H13 22 23N 88 40 E
Port-Cartier, Canada 71 B6 50 2N 66 50W
Port Chalmers, N.Z. .... 59 L3 45 49S 170 30 E
Port Charlotte, U.S.A. 77 M4 26 59N 82 6W
Port Chester, U.S.A. 79 F11 41 0N 73 40W
Port Clements, Canada 72 C2 53 40N 132 10W
Port Clinton, U.S.A. 76 E4 41 31N 82 56W
Port Colborne, Canada 78 D5 42 50N 79 10W
Port Coquitlam, Canada ... 72 D4 49 15N 122 45W
Port Credit, Canada 78 C5 43 33N 79 35W
Port Curtis, Australia ..... 62 C5 23 57S 151 20 E
Port d'Alcúdia, Spain ..... 22 B10 39 50N 3 7 E
Port Dalhousie, Canada 78 C5 43 13N 79 16W
Port Darwin, Australia .... 60 B5 12 24S 130 45 E
Port Darwin, Falk. Is. 96 G5 51 50S 59 0W
Port Davey, Australia ..... 62 G4 43 16S 145 55 E
Port-de-Paix, Haiti 89 C5 19 50N 72 50W
Port de Pollença, Spain ... 22 B10 39 54N 3 4 E
Port de Sóller, Spain ...... 22 B9 39 48N 2 42 E
Port Dickson, Malaysia .... 39 L3 2 30N 101 49 E
Port Douglas, Australia .... 62 B4 16 30S 145 30 E
Port Dover, Canada 78 D4 42 47N 80 12W
Port Edward, Canada 72 C2 54 12N 130 10W
Port Elgin, Canada 78 B3 44 25N 81 25W
Port Elizabeth, S. Africa ... 56 E4 33 58S 25 40 E
Port Ellen, U.K. 12 F2 55 38N 6 11W
Port Erin, U.K. 10 C3 54 5N 4 45W
Port Essington, Australia .. 60 B5 11 15S 132 10 E
Port Etienne = Nouâdhibou,
Mauritania 50 D2 20 54N 17 0W
Port Ewen, U.S.A. 79 E11 41 54N 73 59W
Port Gamble, U.S.A. 84 C4 47 51N 122 35W
Port-Gentil, Gabon .... 52 E1 0 40S 8 50 E
Port Germein, Australia ... 63 E2 33 1S 138 1 E
Port Gibson, U.S.A. 81 K9 31 58N 90 59W
Port Glasgow, U.K. 12 F4 55 56N 4 41W
Port Harcourt, Nigeria .... 50 H7 4 40N 7 10 E
Port Hardy, Canada 72 C3 50 41N 127 30W
Port Harrison = Inukjuak,
Canada 69 C12 58 25N 78 15W
Port Hawkesbury, Canada . 71 C7 45 36N 61 22W
Port Hedland, Australia ... 60 D2 20 25S 118 35 E
Port Henry, U.S.A. 79 B11 44 3N 73 28W
Port Hood, Canada 71 C7 46 0N 61 32W
Port Hope, Canada 78 C6 43 56N 78 20W
Port Hope, U.S.A. 78 C2 43 57N 82 43W
Port Hope Simpson,
Canada 71 B8 52 33N 56 18W
Port Hueneme, U.S.A. 85 L7 34 7N 119 12W
Port Huron, U.S.A. 78 D2 42 58N 82 26W
Port Jefferson, U.S.A. 79 F11 40 57N 73 3W
Port Jervis, U.S.A. 79 E10 41 22N 74 41W
Port Kelang = Pelabuhan
Kelang, Malaysia .... 39 L3 3 0N 101 23 E
Port Kenny, Australia ..... 63 E1 33 10S 134 41 E
Port Lairge = Waterford,
Ireland 13 D4 52 15N 7 8W
Port Laoise, Ireland 13 C4 53 2N 7 18W
Port Lavaca, U.S.A. 81 L6 28 37N 96 38W
Port Leyden, U.S.A. 79 C9 43 35N 75 21W
Port Loko, S. Leone 50 G3 8 48N 12 46W
Port Louis, Mauritius ..... 49 H9 20 10S 57 30 E
Port Lyautey = Kenitra,
Morocco 50 B4 34 15N 6 40W
Port McNeill, Canada 72 C3 50 35N 127 6W
Port Maria, Jamaica 88 C4 18 25N 76 55W
Port Matilda, U.S.A. 78 F6 40 48N 78 3W
Port Mellon, Canada 72 D4 49 32N 123 31W
Port-Menier, Canada 71 C7 49 51N 64 15W
Port Moody, Canada 84 A4 49 17N 122 51W
Port Morant, Jamaica 88 C4 17 54N 76 19W
Port Moresby, Papua N. G. 64 H6 9 24S 147 8 E
Port Musgrave, Australia .. 62 A3 11 55S 141 50 E
Port Neches, U.S.A. 81 L8 30 0N 93 59W
Port Nolloth, S. Africa .... 56 D2 29 17S 16 52 E
Port Nouveau-Québec =
Kangiqsualujjuaq,
Canada 69 C13 58 30N 65 59W
Port of Spain, Trin. & Tob. 89 D7 10 40N 61 31W
Port Orange, U.S.A. 77 L5 29 9N 80 59W
Port Orchard, U.S.A. 84 C4 47 32N 122 38W
Port Orford, U.S.A. 82 E1 42 45N 124 30W
Port Pegasus, N.Z. .... 59 M1 47 12S 167 41 E
Port Perry, Canada 78 B6 44 6N 78 56W
Port Radium = Echo Bay,
Canada 68 B8 66 5N 117 55W
Port Renfrew, Canada 72 D4 48 30N 124 20W
Port Roper, Australia ..... 62 A2 14 45S 135 25 E
Port Rowan, Canada 78 D4 42 40N 80 30W
Port Safaga = Bûr Safâga,
Egypt .... 44 E2 26 43N 33 57 E
Port Said = Bûr Sa'îd, Egypt 51 B12 31 16N 32 18 E
Port St. Joe, U.S.A. 77 L3 29 49N 85 18W
Port St. Johns =
Umzimvubu, S. Africa .. 57 E4 31 38S 29 33 E
Port St. Lucie, U.S.A. 77 M5 27 20N 80 20W
Port Sanilac, U.S.A. 78 C2 43 26N 82 33W
Port Severn, Canada 78 B5 44 48N 79 43W
Port Shepstone, S. Africa . 57 E5 30 44S 30 28 E
Port Simpson, Canada 72 C2 54 30N 130 20W
Port Stanley = Stanley,
Falk. Is. 96 G5 51 40S 59 51W
Port Stanley, Canada 78 D3 42 40N 81 10W
Port Sudan = Bûr Sûdân,
Sudan .... 51 E13 19 32N 37 9 E
Port Sulphur, U.S.A. 81 L10 29 29N 89 42W
Port Talbot, U.K. 11 F4 51 35N 3 47W
Port Townsend, U.S.A. 84 B4 48 7N 122 45W
Port-Vendres, France ..... 18 E5 42 32N 3 8 E
Port Vila, Vanuatu .... 64 J8 17 45S 168 18 E
Port Vladimir, Russia ..... 24 A5 69 25N 33 6 E
Port Washington, U.S.A. .. 76 D2 43 23N 87 53W
Port Weld = Kuala
Sepetang, Malaysia .... 39 K3 4 49N 100 28 E
Porta Orientalis, Romania . 17 F12 45 6N 22 18 E
Portadown, U.K. 13 B5 54 25N 6 27W
Portaferry, U.K. 13 B6 54 23N 5 33W
Portage, Pa., U.S.A. 78 F6 40 23N 78 41W
Portage, Wis., U.S.A. 80 D10 43 33N 89 28W
Portage La Prairie, Canada 73 D9 49 58N 98 18W
Portageville, U.S.A. 81 G10 36 26N 89 42W
Portalegre, Portugal 19 C2 39 19N 7 25W
Portales, U.S.A. 81 H3 34 11N 103 20W
Portarlington, Ireland 13 C4 53 9N 7 14W
Portbou, Spain .... 19 A7 42 25N 3 9 E
Porter L., N.W.T., Canada . 73 A7 61 41N 108 5W
Porter L., Sask., Canada ... 73 B7 56 20N 107 20W
Porterville, S. Africa ..... 56 E2 33 0S 19 0 E
Porterville, U.S.A. 84 J8 36 4N 119 1W
Porthcawl, U.K. 11 F4 51 29N 3 42W
Porthill, U.S.A. 82 B5 48 59N 116 30W
Porthmadog, U.K. 10 E3 52 55N 4 8W
Portile de Fier, Europe .... 17 F12 44 44N 22 30 E
Portimão, Portugal 19 D1 37 8N 8 32W
Portishead, U.K. 11 F5 51 29N 2 46W
Portknockie, U.K. 12 D6 57 42N 2 51W
Portland, Canada 79 B8 44 42N 76 12W
Portland, Conn., U.S.A. ... 79 E12 41 34N 72 38W
Portland, Maine, U.S.A. .. 69 D12 43 39N 70 16W
Portland, Mich., U.S.A. ... 76 D3 42 52N 84 54W
Portland, Oreg., U.S.A. ... 84 E4 45 32N 122 37W
Portland, Pa., U.S.A. 79 F9 40 55N 75 6W
Portland, Tex., U.S.A. 81 M6 27 53N 97 20W
Portland, I. of, U.K. 11 G5 50 33N 2 26W
Portland Bill, U.K. 11 G5 50 31N 2 28W
Portland Canal, U.S.A. 72 B2 55 56N 130 0W
Portmadoc = Porthmadog,
U.K. 10 E3 52 55N 4 8W
Porto, Portugal 19 B1 41 8N 8 40W
Pôrto Alegre, Brazil 95 C5 30 5S 51 10W
Porto Amboim = Gunza,
Angola .... 52 G2 10 50S 13 50 E
Porto Cristo, Spain ...... 22 B10 39 33N 3 20 E
Pôrto de Móz, Brazil 93 D8 1 41S 52 13W
Porto Empédocle, Italy .... 20 F5 37 17N 13 32 E
Pôrto Esperança, Brazil ... 92 G7 19 37S 57 29W
Pôrto Franco, Brazil 93 E9 6 20S 47 24W
Porto Mendes, Brazil 95 A5 24 30S 54 15W
Porto Moniz, Madeira 22 D2 32 52N 17 11W
Pôrto Murtinho, Brazil 92 H7 21 45S 57 55W
Pôrto Nacional, Brazil 93 F9 10 40S 48 30W
Porto-Novo, Benin .... 50 G6 6 23N 2 42 E
Porto Petro, Spain .... 22 B10 39 22N 3 13 E
Porto Santo, I. de, Madeira 50 B2 33 45N 16 25W
Pôrto São José, Brazil 95 A5 22 43S 53 10W
Pôrto Seguro, Brazil 93 G11 16 26S 39 5W
Porto Tórres, Italy .... 20 D3 40 50N 8 24 E
Pôrto União, Brazil 95 B5 26 10S 51 10W
Pôrto Válter, Brazil 92 E4 8 15S 72 40W
Porto-Vecchio, France .... 18 F8 41 35N 9 16 E
Pôrto Velho, Brazil 92 E6 8 46S 63 54W
Portobelo, Panama 88 E4 9 35N 79 42W
Portoferráio, Italy .... 20 C4 42 48N 10 20 E
Portola, U.S.A. 84 F6 39 49N 120 28W
Portoscuso, Italy .... 20 E3 39 12N 8 24 E
Portoviejo, Ecuador 92 D2 1 7S 80 28W
Portpatrick, U.K. 12 G3 54 51N 5 7W
Portree, U.K. 12 D2 57 25N 6 12W
Portrush, U.K. 13 A5 55 12N 6 40W
Portsmouth, Domin. 89 C7 15 34N 61 27W
Portsmouth, U.K. 11 G6 50 48N 1 6W
Portsmouth, N.H., U.S.A. .. 77 D10 43 5N 70 45W
Portsmouth, Ohio, U.S.A. . 76 F4 38 44N 82 57W
Portsmouth, R.I., U.S.A. .. 79 E13 41 36N 71 15W
Portsmouth, Va., U.S.A. ... 76 G7 36 50N 76 18W
Portsmouth □, U.K. 11 G6 50 48N 1 6W

Portsoy

Portsoy, U.K. 12 D6 57 41N 2 41W
Portstewart, U.K. 13 A5 55 11N 6 43W
Porttipahtan tekojärvi, Finland 8 B22 68 5N 26 40 E
Portugal ■, Europe 19 C1 40 0N 8 0W
Portumna, Ireland 13 C3 53 6N 8 14W
Portville, U.S.A. 78 D6 42 3N 78 20W
Porvenir, Chile 96 G2 53 10S 70 16W
Porvoo, Finland 9 F21 60 24N 25 40 E
Posadas, Argentina 95 B4 27 30S 55 50W
Poshan = Boshan, China 35 F9 36 28N 117 49 E
Posht-e-Badam, Iran 45 C7 33 2N 55 23 E
Poso, Indonesia 37 E6 1 20S 120 55 E
Posong, S. Korea 35 G14 34 46N 127 5 E
Posse, Brazil 93 F9 14 4S 46 18W
Possession I., Antarctica 5 D11 72 4S 172 0 E
Possum Kingdom L., U.S.A. 81 J5 32 52N 98 26W
Post, U.S.A. 81 J4 33 12N 101 23W
Post Falls, U.S.A. 82 C5 47 43N 116 57W
Postavy = Pastavy, Belarus 9 J22 55 4N 26 50 E
Poste-de-la-Baleine = Kuujjuarapik, Canada 70 A4 55 20N 77 35W
Postmasburg, S. Africa 56 D3 28 18S 23 5 E
Postojna, Slovenia 16 F8 45 46N 14 12 E
Poston, U.S.A. 85 M12 34 0N 114 24W
Postville, Canada 71 B8 54 54N 59 47W
Potchefstroom, S. Africa 56 D4 26 41S 27 7 E
Poteau, U.S.A. 81 H7 35 3N 94 37W
Poteet, U.S.A. 81 L5 29 2N 98 35W
Potenza, Italy 20 D6 40 38N 15 48 E
Poteriteri, L., N.Z. 59 M1 46 5S 167 10 E
Potgietersrus, S. Africa 57 C4 24 10S 28 55 E
Poti, Georgia 25 F7 42 10N 41 38 E
Potiskum, Nigeria 51 F8 11 39N 11 2 E
Potomac →, U.S.A. 76 G7 38 0N 76 23W
Potosí, Bolivia 92 G5 19 38S 65 50W
Potosi Mt., U.S.A. 85 K11 35 57N 115 29W
Pototan, Phil. 37 B6 10 54N 122 38 E
Potrerillos, Chile 94 B2 26 30S 69 30W
Potsdam, Germany 16 B7 52 25N 13 4 E
Potsdam, U.S.A. 79 B10 44 40N 74 59W
Pottersville, U.S.A. 79 C11 43 43N 73 50W
Pottstown, U.S.A. 79 F9 40 15N 75 39W
Pottsville, U.S.A. 79 F8 40 41N 76 12W
Pottuvil, Sri Lanka 40 R12 6 55N 81 50 E
Pouce Coupé, Canada 72 B4 55 40N 120 10W
Poughkeepsie, U.S.A. 79 E11 41 42N 73 56W
Poulaphouca Res., Ireland 13 C5 53 8N 6 30W
Poulsbo, U.S.A. 84 C4 47 44N 122 39W
Poultney, U.S.A. 79 C11 43 31N 73 14W
Poulton-le-Fylde, U.K. 10 D5 53 51N 2 58W
Pouso Alegre, Brazil 95 A6 22 14S 45 57W
Pouthisat, Cambodia 38 F4 12 34N 103 50 E
Považská Bystrica, Slovak Rep. 17 D10 49 8N 18 27 E
Povenets, Russia 24 B5 62 50N 34 50 E
Poverty B., N.Z. 59 H7 38 43S 178 2 E
Póvoa de Varzim, Portugal 19 B1 41 25N 8 46W
Povungnituk = Puvirnituq, Canada 69 B12 60 2N 77 10W
Powassan, Canada 70 C4 46 5N 79 25W
Poway, U.S.A. 85 N9 32 58N 117 2W
Powder →, U.S.A. 80 B2 46 45N 105 26W
Powder River, U.S.A. 82 E10 43 2N 106 59W
Powell, U.S.A. 82 D9 44 45N 108 46W
Powell, L., U.S.A. 83 H8 36 57N 111 29W
Powell River, Canada 72 D4 49 50N 124 35W
Powers, U.S.A. 76 C2 45 41N 87 32W
Powys □, U.K. 11 E4 52 20N 3 20W
Poyang Hu, China 33 D6 29 5N 116 20 E
Poyarkovo, Russia 27 E13 49 36N 128 41 E
Poza Rica, Mexico 87 C5 20 33N 97 27W
Požarevac, Serbia, Yug. 21 B9 44 35N 21 18 E
Poznań, Poland 17 B9 52 25N 16 55 E
Pozo, U.S.A. 85 K6 35 20N 120 24W
Pozo Almonte, Chile 92 H5 20 10S 69 50W
Pozo Colorado, Paraguay 94 A4 23 30S 58 45W
Pozoblanco, Spain 19 C3 38 23N 4 51W
Pozzuoli, Italy 20 D6 40 49N 14 7 E
Prachin Buri, Thailand 38 E3 14 0N 101 25 E
Prachuap Khiri Khan, Thailand 39 G2 11 49N 99 48 E
Prado, Brazil 93 G11 17 20S 39 13W
Prague = Praha, Czech Rep. 16 C8 50 5N 14 22 E
Praha, Czech Rep. 16 C8 50 5N 14 22 E
Praia, C. Verde Is. 49 E1 14 55N 23 30W
Prainha, Amazonas, Brazil 92 E6 7 10S 60 30W
Prainha, Pará, Brazil 93 D8 1 45S 53 30W
Prairie, Australia 62 C3 20 50S 144 35 E
Prairie City, U.S.A. 82 D4 44 28N 118 43W
Prairie Dog Town Fork →, U.S.A. 81 H5 34 30N 99 23W
Prairie du Chien, U.S.A. 80 D9 43 3N 91 9W
Prairies, L. of the, Canada 73 C8 51 16N 101 32W
Pran Buri, Thailand 38 F2 12 23N 99 55 E
Prapat, Indonesia 36 D1 2 41N 98 58 E
Prasonísi, Ákra, Greece 23 D9 35 42N 27 46 E
Prata, Brazil 93 G9 19 25S 48 54W
Pratabpur, India 43 H10 23 28N 83 15 E
Pratapgarh, Raj., India 42 G6 24 2N 74 40 E
Pratapgarh, Ut. P., India 43 G9 25 56N 81 59 E
Prato, Italy 20 C4 43 53N 11 6 E
Pratt, U.S.A. 81 G5 37 39N 98 44W
Prattville, U.S.A. 77 J2 32 28N 86 29W
Pravia, Spain 19 A2 43 30N 6 12W
Praya, Indonesia 36 F5 8 39S 116 17 E
Precordillera, Argentina 94 C2 30 0S 69 1W
Preeceville, Canada 73 C8 51 57N 102 40W
Preiļi, Latvia 9 H22 56 18N 26 43 E
Premont, U.S.A. 81 M5 27 22N 98 7W
Prentice, U.S.A. 80 C9 45 33N 90 17W
Preobrazheniye, Russia 30 C6 42 54N 133 54 E
Preparis North Channel, Ind. Oc. 41 M18 15 12N 93 40 E
Preparis South Channel, Ind. Oc. 41 M18 14 36N 93 40 E
Přerov, Czech Rep. 17 D9 49 28N 17 27 E
Prescott, Canada 79 B9 44 45N 75 30W
Prescott, Ariz., U.S.A. 83 J7 34 33N 112 28W
Prescott, Ark., U.S.A. 81 J8 33 48N 93 23W
Prescott Valley, U.S.A. 83 J7 34 40N 112 18W
Preservation Inlet, N.Z. 59 M1 46 8S 166 35 E
Presho, U.S.A. 80 D4 43 54N 100 3W
Presidencia de la Plaza, Argentina 94 B4 27 0S 59 50W
Presidencia Roque Saenz Peña, Argentina 94 B3 26 45S 60 30W
Presidente Epitácio, Brazil 93 H8 21 56S 52 6W
Presidente Hayes □, Paraguay 94 A4 24 0S 59 0W
Presidente Prudente, Brazil 95 A5 22 5S 51 25W
Presidio, Mexico 86 B4 29 29N 104 23W
Presidio, U.S.A. 81 L2 29 34N 104 22W
Prešov, Slovak Rep. 17 D11 49 0N 21 15 E
Prespa, L. = Prespansko Jezero, Macedonia 21 D9 40 55N 21 0 E
Prespansko Jezero, Macedonia 21 D9 40 55N 21 0 E
Presque I., U.S.A. 78 D4 42 9N 80 6W
Presque Isle, U.S.A. 77 B12 46 41N 68 1W
Prestatyn, U.K. 10 D4 53 20N 3 24W
Presteigne, U.K. 11 E5 52 17N 3 0W
Preston, Canada 78 C4 43 23N 80 21W
Preston, U.K. 10 D5 53 46N 2 42W
Preston, Idaho, U.S.A. 82 E8 42 6N 111 53W
Preston, Minn., U.S.A. 80 D8 43 40N 92 5W
Preston, C., Australia 60 D2 20 51S 116 12 E
Prestonburg, U.S.A. 76 G4 37 39N 82 46W
Prestwick, U.K. 12 F4 55 29N 4 37W
Pretoria, S. Africa 57 D4 25 44S 28 12 E
Préveza, Greece 21 E9 38 57N 20 47 E
Prey Veng, Cambodia 39 G5 11 35N 105 29 E
Pribilof Is., U.S.A. 68 C2 57 0N 170 0W
Příbram, Czech Rep. 16 D8 49 41N 14 2 E
Price, U.S.A. 82 G8 39 36N 110 49W
Price I., Canada 72 C3 52 23N 128 41W
Prichard, U.S.A. 77 K1 30 44N 88 5W
Priekule, Latvia 9 H19 56 26N 21 35 E
Prienai, Lithuania 9 J20 54 38N 23 57 E
Prieska, S. Africa 56 D3 29 40S 22 42 E
Priest L., U.S.A. 82 B5 48 35N 116 52W
Priest River, U.S.A. 82 B5 48 10N 116 54W
Priest Valley, U.S.A. 84 J6 36 10N 120 39W
Prievidza, Slovak Rep. 17 D10 48 46N 18 36 E
Prikaspiyskaya Nizmennost = Caspian Depression, Eurasia 25 E8 47 0N 48 0 E
Prilep, Macedonia 21 D9 41 21N 21 32 E
Priluki = Pryluky, Ukraine 25 D5 50 30N 32 24 E
Prime Seal I., Australia 62 G4 40 3S 147 43 E
Primrose L., Canada 73 C7 54 55N 109 45W
Prince Albert, Canada 73 C7 53 15N 105 50W
Prince Albert, S. Africa 56 E3 33 12S 22 2 E
Prince Albert Mts., Antarctica 5 D11 76 0S 161 30 E
Prince Albert Nat. Park, Canada 73 C7 54 0N 106 25W
Prince Albert Pen., Canada 68 A8 72 30N 116 0W
Prince Albert Sd., Canada 68 A8 70 25N 115 0W
Prince Alfred, C., Canada 4 B1 74 20N 124 40W
Prince Charles I., Canada 69 B12 67 47N 76 12W
Prince Charles Mts., Antarctica 5 D6 72 0S 67 0 E
Prince Edward I. □, Canada 71 C7 46 20N 63 20W
Prince Edward Is., Ind. Oc. 3 G11 46 35S 38 0 E
Prince Edward Pt., Canada 78 C8 43 56N 76 52W
Prince George, Canada 72 C4 53 55N 122 50W
Prince of Wales, C., U.S.A. 66 C3 65 36N 168 5W
Prince of Wales I., Australia 62 A3 10 40S 142 10 E
Prince of Wales I., Canada 68 A10 73 0N 99 0W
Prince of Wales I., U.S.A. 68 C6 55 47N 132 50W
Prince Patrick I., Canada 4 B2 77 0N 120 0W
Prince Regent Inlet, Canada 4 B3 73 0N 90 0W
Prince Rupert, Canada 72 C2 54 20N 130 20W
Princess Charlotte B., Australia 62 A3 14 25S 144 0 E
Princess May Ranges, Australia 60 C4 15 30S 125 30 E
Princess Royal I., Canada 72 C3 53 0N 128 40W
Princeton, Canada 72 D4 49 27N 120 30W
Princeton, Calif., U.S.A. 84 F4 39 24N 122 1W
Princeton, Ill., U.S.A. 80 E10 41 23N 89 28W
Princeton, Ind., U.S.A. 76 F2 38 21N 87 34W
Princeton, Ky., U.S.A. 76 G2 37 7N 87 53W
Princeton, Mo., U.S.A. 80 E8 40 24N 93 35W
Princeton, N.J., U.S.A. 79 F10 40 21N 74 39W
Princeton, W. Va., U.S.A. 76 G5 37 22N 81 6W
Principe, I. de, Atl. Oc. 48 F4 1 37N 7 27 E
Principe da Beira, Brazil 92 F6 12 20S 64 30W
Prineville, U.S.A. 82 D3 44 18N 120 51W
Prins Harald Kyst, Antarctica 5 D4 70 0S 35 1 E
Prinsesse Astrid Kyst, Antarctica 5 D3 70 45S 12 30 E
Prinsesse Ragnhild Kyst, Antarctica 5 D4 70 15S 27 30 E
Prinzapolca, Nic. 88 D3 13 20N 83 35W
Priozersk, Russia 24 B5 61 2N 30 7 E
Pripet = Prypyat →, Europe 17 C16 51 20N 30 15 E
Pripet Marshes, Europe 17 B15 52 10N 28 10 E
Pripyat Marshes = Pripet Marshes, Europe 17 B15 52 10N 28 10 E
Pripyats = Prypyat →, Europe 17 C16 51 20N 30 15 E
Priština, Kosovo, Yug. 21 C9 42 40N 21 13 E
Privas, France 18 D6 44 45N 4 37 E
Privolzhskaya Vozvyshennost, Russia 25 D8 51 0N 46 0 E
Prizren, Kosovo, Yug. 21 C9 42 13N 20 45 E
Probolinggo, Indonesia 37 G15 7 46S 113 13 E
Proctor, U.S.A. 79 C11 43 40N 73 2W
Proddatur, India 40 M11 14 45N 78 30 E
Prodhromos, Cyprus 23 E11 34 57N 32 50 E
Profítis Ilías, Greece 23 C9 36 17N 27 56 E
Profondeville, Belgium 15 D4 50 23N 4 52 E
Progreso, Coahuila, Mexico 86 B4 27 28N 101 4W
Progreso, Yucatán, Mexico 87 C7 21 20N 89 40W
Prokopyevsk, Russia 26 D9 54 0N 86 45 E
Prokuplje, Serbia, Yug. 21 C9 43 16N 21 36 E
Prome = Pyè, Burma 41 K19 18 49N 95 13 E
Prophet →, Canada 72 B4 58 48N 122 40W
Prophet River, Canada 72 B4 58 6N 122 43W
Propriá, Brazil 93 F11 10 13S 36 51W
Proserpine, Australia 62 C4 20 21S 148 36 E
Prosna →, Poland 17 B9 52 6N 17 44 E
Prospect, U.S.A. 79 C9 43 18N 75 9W
Prosser, U.S.A. 82 C4 46 12N 119 46W
Prostějov, Czech Rep. 17 D9 49 30N 17 9 E
Proston, Australia 63 D5 26 8S 151 32 E
Provence, France 18 E6 43 40N 5 46 E
Providence, Ky., U.S.A. 76 G2 37 24N 87 46W
Providence, R.I., U.S.A. 79 E13 41 49N 71 24W
Providence Bay, Canada 70 C3 45 41N 82 15W
Providence Mts., U.S.A. 85 K11 35 10N 115 15W
Providencia, I. de, Colombia 88 D3 13 25N 81 26W
Provideniya, Russia 27 C19 64 23N 173 18W
Provins, France 18 B5 48 33N 3 15 E
Provo, U.S.A. 82 F8 40 14N 111 39W
Provost, Canada 73 C6 52 25N 110 20W
Prudhoe Bay, U.S.A. 68 A5 70 18N 148 22W
Prudhoe I., Australia 62 C4 21 19S 149 41 E
Prud'homme, Canada 73 C7 52 20N 105 54W
Pruszków, Poland 17 B11 52 9N 20 49 E
Prut →, Romania 17 F15 45 28N 28 10 E
Pruzhany, Belarus 17 B13 52 33N 24 28 E
Prydz B., Antarctica 5 C6 69 0S 74 0 E
Pryluky, Ukraine 25 D5 50 30N 32 24 E
Pryor, U.S.A. 81 G7 36 19N 95 19W
Prypyat →, Europe 17 C16 51 20N 30 15 E
Przemyśl, Poland 17 D12 49 50N 22 45 E
Przhevalsk = Karakol, Kyrgyzstan 26 E8 42 30N 78 20 E
Psará, Greece 21 E11 38 37N 25 38 E
Psira, Greece 23 D7 35 12N 25 52 E
Pskov, Russia 24 C4 57 50N 28 25 E
Ptich = Ptsich →, Belarus 17 B15 52 9N 28 52 E
Ptolemais, Greece 21 D9 40 30N 21 43 E
Ptsich →, Belarus 17 B15 52 9N 28 52 E
Pu Xian, China 34 F6 36 24N 111 6 E
Pua, Thailand 38 C3 19 11N 100 55 E
Puán, Argentina 94 D3 37 30S 62 45W
Puan, S. Korea 35 G14 35 44N 126 44 E
Pucallpa, Peru 92 E4 8 25S 74 30W
Pudasjärvi, Finland 8 D22 65 23N 26 53 E
Pudozh, Russia 24 B6 61 48N 36 32 E
Pudukkottai, India 40 P11 10 28N 78 47 E
Puebla, Mexico 87 D5 19 3N 98 12W
Puebla □, Mexico 87 D5 18 30N 98 0W
Pueblo, U.S.A. 80 F2 38 16N 104 37W
Pueblo Hundido, Chile 94 B1 26 20S 70 5W
Puelches, Argentina 94 D2 38 5S 65 51W
Puelén, Argentina 94 D2 37 32S 67 38W
Puente Alto, Chile 94 C1 33 32S 70 35W
Puente-Genil, Spain 19 D3 37 22N 4 47W
Puerco →, U.S.A. 83 J10 34 22N 107 50W
Puerto, Canary Is. 22 F2 28 5N 17 20W
Puerto Aisén, Chile 96 F2 45 27S 73 0W
Puerto Ángel, Mexico 87 D5 15 40N 96 29W
Puerto Arista, Mexico 87 D6 15 56N 93 48W
Puerto Armuelles, Panama 88 E3 8 20N 82 51W
Puerto Ayacucho, Venezuela 92 B5 5 40N 67 35W
Puerto Barrios, Guatemala 88 C2 15 40N 88 32W
Puerto Bermejo, Argentina 94 B4 26 55S 58 34W
Puerto Bermúdez, Peru 92 F4 10 20S 74 58W
Puerto Bolívar, Ecuador 92 D3 3 19S 79 55W
Puerto Cabello, Venezuela 92 A5 10 28N 68 1W
Puerto Cabezas, Nic. 88 D3 14 0N 83 30W
Puerto Cabo Gracias á Dios, Nic. 88 D3 15 0N 83 10W
Puerto Carreño, Colombia 92 B5 6 12N 67 22W
Puerto Castilla, Honduras 88 C2 16 0N 86 0W
Puerto Chicama, Peru 92 E3 7 45S 79 20W
Puerto Coig, Argentina 96 G3 50 54S 69 15W
Puerto Cortés, Costa Rica 88 E3 8 55N 84 0W
Puerto Cortés, Honduras 88 C2 15 51N 88 0W
Puerto Cumarebo, Venezuela 92 A5 11 29N 69 30W
Puerto de Alcudia = Port d'Alcúdia, Spain 22 B10 39 50N 3 7 E
Puerto de Andraitx, Spain 22 B9 39 32N 2 23 E
Puerto de Cabrera, Spain 22 B9 39 8N 2 56 E
Puerto de Gran Tarajal, Canary Is. 22 F5 28 13N 14 1W
Puerto de la Cruz, Canary Is. 22 F3 28 24N 16 32W
Puerto de Pozo Negro, Canary Is. 22 F6 28 19N 13 55W
Puerto de Sóller = Port de Sóller, Spain 22 B9 39 48N 2 42 E
Puerto del Carmen, Canary Is. 22 F6 28 55N 13 38W
Puerto del Rosario, Canary Is. 22 F6 28 30N 13 52W
Puerto Deseado, Argentina 96 F3 47 55S 66 0W
Puerto Escondido, Mexico 87 D5 15 50N 97 3W
Puerto Heath, Bolivia 92 F5 12 34S 68 39W
Puerto Inírida, Colombia 92 C5 3 53N 67 52W
Puerto Juárez, Mexico 87 C7 21 11N 86 49W
Puerto La Cruz, Venezuela 92 A6 10 13N 64 38W
Puerto Leguízamo, Colombia 92 D4 0 12S 74 46W
Puerto Limón, Colombia 92 C4 3 23N 73 30W
Puerto Lobos, Argentina 96 E3 42 0S 65 3W
Puerto Madryn, Argentina 96 E3 42 48S 65 4W
Puerto Maldonado, Peru 92 F5 12 30S 69 10W
Puerto Manotí, Cuba 88 B4 21 22N 76 50W
Puerto Montt, Chile 96 E2 41 28S 73 0W
Puerto Morazán, Nic. 88 D2 12 51N 87 11W
Puerto Morelos, Mexico 87 C7 20 49N 86 52W
Puerto Natales, Chile 96 G2 51 45S 72 15W
Puerto Padre, Cuba 88 B4 21 13N 76 35W
Puerto Páez, Venezuela 92 B5 6 13N 67 28W
Puerto Peñasco, Mexico 86 A2 31 20N 113 33W
Puerto Pinasco, Paraguay 94 A4 22 36S 57 50W
Puerto Plata, Dom. Rep. 89 C5 19 48N 70 45W
Puerto Pollensa = Port de Pollença, Spain 22 B10 39 54N 3 4 E
Puerto Princesa, Phil. 37 C5 9 46N 118 45 E
Puerto Quepos, Costa Rica 88 E3 9 29N 84 6W
Puerto Rico, Canary Is. 22 G4 27 47N 15 42W
Puerto Rico ■, W. Indies 89 C6 18 15N 66 45W
Puerto Rico Trench, Atl. Oc. 89 C6 19 50N 66 0W
Puerto San Julián, Argentina 96 F3 49 18S 67 43W
Puerto Sastre, Paraguay 94 A4 22 2S 57 55W
Puerto Suárez, Bolivia 92 G7 18 58S 57 52W
Puerto Vallarta, Mexico 86 C3 20 36N 105 15W
Puerto Wilches, Colombia 92 B4 7 21N 73 54W
Puertollano, Spain 19 C3 38 43N 4 7W
Pueyrredón, L., Argentina 96 F2 47 20S 72 0W
Puffin I., Ireland 13 E1 51 50N 10 24W
Pugachev, Russia 24 D8 52 0N 48 49 E
Pugal, India 42 E5 28 30N 72 48 E
Puge, Tanzania 54 C3 4 45S 33 11 E
Puget Sound, U.S.A. 82 C2 47 50N 122 30W
Pugŏdong, N. Korea 35 C16 42 5N 130 0 E
Pugu, Tanzania 54 D4 6 55S 39 4 E
Pūgūnzī, Iran 45 E8 25 49N 59 10 E
Puig Major, Spain 22 B9 39 48N 2 47 E
Puigcerdà, Spain 19 A6 42 24N 1 50 E
Puigpunyent, Spain 22 B9 39 38N 2 32 E
Pujon-chŏsuji, N. Korea 35 D14 40 35N 127 35 E
Pukaki L., N.Z. 59 L3 44 4S 170 1 E
Pukapuka, Cook Is. 65 J11 10 53S 165 49W
Pukaskwa Nat. Park, Canada 70 C2 48 20N 86 0W
Pukatawagan, Canada 73 B8 55 45N 101 20W
Pukchin, N. Korea 35 D13 40 12N 125 45 E
Pukch'ŏng, N. Korea 35 D15 40 14N 128 10 E
Pukekohe, N.Z. 59 G5 37 12S 174 55 E
Pukhrayan, India 43 F8 26 14N 79 51 E
Pula, Croatia 16 F7 44 54N 13 57 E
Pulacayo, Bolivia 92 H5 20 25S 66 41W
Pulandian, China 35 E11 39 25N 121 58 E
Pularumpi, Australia 60 B5 11 24S 130 26 E
Pulaski, N.Y., U.S.A. 79 C8 43 34N 76 8W
Pulaski, Tenn., U.S.A. 77 H2 35 12N 87 2W
Pulaski, Va., U.S.A. 76 G5 37 3N 80 47W
Pulau →, Indonesia 37 F9 5 50S 138 15 E
Puławy, Poland 17 C11 51 23N 21 59 E
Pulga, U.S.A. 84 F5 39 48N 121 29W
Pulicat L., India 40 N12 13 40N 80 15 E
Pullman, U.S.A. 82 C5 46 44N 117 10W
Pulo-Anna, Pac. Oc. 37 D8 4 30N 132 5 E
Pulog, Mt., Phil. 37 A6 16 40N 120 50 E
Pułtusk, Poland 17 B11 52 43N 21 6 E
Pumlumon Fawr, U.K. 11 E4 52 28N 3 46W
Puná, I., Ecuador 92 D2 2 55S 80 5W
Punakha, Bhutan 41 F16 27 42N 89 52 E
Punasar, India 42 F5 27 6N 73 6 E
Punata, Bolivia 92 G5 17 32S 65 50W
Punch, India 43 C6 33 48N 74 4 E
Punch →, Pakistan 42 C5 33 12N 73 40 E
Punda Maria, S. Africa 57 C5 22 40S 31 5 E
Pune, India 40 K8 18 29N 73 57 E
P'ungsan, N. Korea 35 D15 40 50N 128 9 E
Pungue, Ponte de, Mozam. 55 F3 19 0S 34 0 E
Punjab □, India 42 D7 31 0N 76 0 E
Punjab □, Pakistan 42 E6 32 0N 72 30 E
Puno, Peru 92 G4 15 55S 70 3W
Punpun →, India 43 G11 25 31N 85 18 E
Punta Alta, Argentina 96 D4 38 53S 62 4W
Punta Arenas, Chile 96 G2 53 10S 71 0W
Punta de Díaz, Chile 94 B1 28 0S 70 45W
Punta Gorda, Belize 87 D7 16 10N 88 45W
Punta Gorda, U.S.A. 77 M5 26 56N 82 3W
Punta Prieta, Mexico 86 B2 28 58N 114 17W
Punta Prima, Spain 22 B11 39 48N 4 16 E
Puntarenas, Costa Rica 88 E3 10 0N 84 50W
Punto Fijo, Venezuela 92 A4 11 50N 70 13W
Punxsatawney, U.S.A. 78 F6 40 57N 78 59W
Puquio, Peru 92 F4 14 45S 74 10W
Pur →, Russia 26 C8 67 31N 77 55 E
Purace, Vol., Colombia 92 C3 2 21N 76 23W
Puralia = Puruliya, India 43 H12 23 17N 86 24 E
Puranpur, India 43 E9 28 31N 80 9 E
Purbeck, Isle of, U.K. 11 G6 50 39N 1 59W
Purcell, U.S.A. 81 H6 35 1N 97 22W
Purcell Mts., Canada 72 D5 49 55N 116 15W
Puri, India 41 K14 19 50N 85 58 E
Purmerend, Neths. 15 B4 52 32N 4 58 E
Purnia, India 43 G12 25 45N 87 31 E
Pursat = Pouthisat, Cambodia 38 F4 12 34N 103 50 E
Purukcahu, Indonesia 36 E4 0 35S 114 35 E
Puruliya, India 43 H12 23 17N 86 24 E
Purus →, Brazil 92 D6 3 42S 61 28W
Purvis, U.S.A. 81 K10 31 9N 89 25W
Purwa, India 43 F9 26 28N 80 47 E
Purwakarta, Indonesia 37 G12 6 35S 107 29 E
Purwodadi, Indonesia 37 G14 7 7S 110 55 E
Purwokerto, Indonesia 37 G13 7 25S 109 14 E
Puryŏng, N. Korea 35 C15 42 5N 129 43 E
Pusa, India 43 G11 25 59N 85 41 E
Pusan, S. Korea 35 G15 35 5N 129 0 E
Pushkino, Russia 25 D8 51 16N 47 0 E
Putahow L., Canada 73 B8 59 54N 100 40W
Putao, Burma 41 F20 27 28N 97 30 E
Putaruru, N.Z. 59 H5 38 2S 175 50 E
Putignano, Italy 20 D7 40 51N 17 7 E
Puting, Tanjung, Indonesia 36 E4 3 31S 111 46 E
Putnam, U.S.A. 79 E13 41 55N 71 55W
Putorana, Gory, Russia 27 C10 69 0N 95 0 E
Puttalam, Sri Lanka 40 Q11 8 1N 79 55 E
Puttgarden, Germany 16 A6 54 30N 11 10 E
Putumayo →, S. Amer. 92 D5 3 7S 67 58W
Putussibau, Indonesia 36 D4 0 50N 112 56 E
Puvirnituq, Canada 69 B12 60 2N 77 10W
Puy-de-Dôme, France 18 D5 45 46N 2 57 E
Puyallup, U.S.A. 84 C4 47 12N 122 18W
Puyang, China 34 G8 35 40N 115 1 E
Pūzeh Rīg, Iran 45 E8 27 20N 58 40 E
Pwani □, Tanzania 54 D4 7 0S 39 0 E
Pweto, Dem. Rep. of the Congo 55 D2 8 25S 28 51 E
Pwllheli, U.K. 10 E3 52 53N 4 25W
Pya-ozero, Russia 24 A5 66 5N 30 58 E
Pyapon, Burma 41 L19 16 20N 95 40 E
Pyasina →, Russia 27 B9 73 30N 87 0 E
Pyatigorsk, Russia 25 F7 44 2N 43 6 E
Pyè, Burma 41 K19 18 49N 95 13 E
Pyetrikaw, Belarus 17 B15 52 11N 28 29 E
Pyhäjoki, Finland 8 D21 64 28N 24 14 E
Pyinmana, Burma 41 K20 19 45N 96 12 E
Pyla, C., Cyprus 23 E12 34 56N 33 51 E
Pymatuning Reservoir, U.S.A. 78 E4 41 30N 80 28W
Pyŏktong, N. Korea 35 D13 40 50N 125 50 E
Pyŏnggang, N. Korea 35 E14 38 24N 127 17 E
P'yŏngt'aek, S. Korea 35 F14 37 1N 127 4 E
P'yŏngyang, N. Korea 35 E13 39 0N 125 30 E
Pyote, U.S.A. 81 K3 31 32N 103 8W
Pyramid L., U.S.A. 82 G4 40 1N 119 35W
Pyramid Pk., U.S.A. 85 J10 36 25N 116 37W
Pyrénées, Europe 18 E4 42 45N 0 18 E
Pyu, Burma 41 K20 18 30N 96 28 E

Q

Qaanaaq, Greenland 4 B4 77 40N 69 0W
Qachasnek, S. Africa 57 E4 30 6S 28 42 E
Qa'el Jafr, Jordan 47 E5 30 20N 36 25 E
Qa'emābād, Iran 45 D9 31 44N 60 2 E
Qā'emshahr, Iran 45 B7 36 30N 52 53 E
Qagan Nur, China 34 C8 43 30N 114 55 E

Raquette

Qahar Youyi Zhongqi, China 34 D7 41 12N 112 40 E
Qahremānshahr = Bākhtarān, Iran 44 C5 34 23N 47 0 E
Qaidam Pendi, China 32 C4 37 0N 95 0 E
Qajarīyeh, Iran 45 D6 31 1N 48 22 E
Qala, Ras il, Malta 23 C1 36 1N 14 20 E
Qala-i-Jadid = Spīn Búldak, Afghan. 42 D2 31 1N 66 25 E
Qala Viala, Pakistan 42 D2 30 49N 67 17 E
Qala Yangi, Afghan. 42 B2 34 20N 66 30 E
Qal'at al Akhḑar, Si. Arabia 44 E3 28 0N 37 10 E
Qal'at Dīzah, Iraq 44 B5 36 11N 45 7 E
Qal'at Şāliḩ, Iraq 44 D5 31 31N 47 16 E
Qal'at Sukkar, Iraq 44 D5 31 51N 46 5 E
Qamani'tuaq = Baker Lake, Canada 68 B10 64 20N 96 3W
Qamdo, China 32 C4 31 15N 97 6 E
Qamruddin Karez, Pakistan 42 D3 31 45N 68 20 E
Qandahār, Afghan. 40 D4 31 32N 65 30 E
Qandahār □, Afghan. 40 D4 31 0N 65 0 E
Qapān, Iran 45 B7 37 40N 55 47 E
Qapshaghay, Kazakstan 26 E8 43 51N 77 14 E
Qaqortoq, Greenland 69 B6 60 43N 46 0W
Qara Qash →, India 43 B8 35 0N 78 30 E
Qarabutaq, Kazakstan 26 E7 49 59N 60 14 E
Qaraghandy, Kazakstan 26 E8 49 50N 73 10 E
Qārah, Si. Arabia 44 D4 29 55N 40 3 E
Qarataū, Kazakstan 26 E8 43 10N 70 28 E
Qarataū, Kazakstan 26 E7 43 30N 69 30 E
Qareh →, Iran 44 B5 39 25N 47 22 E
Qareh Tekān, Iran 45 B6 36 38N 49 29 E
Qarqan He →, China 32 C3 39 30N 88 30 E
Qarqaraly, Kazakstan 26 E8 49 26N 75 30 E
Qarshi, Uzbekistan 26 F7 38 53N 65 48 E
Qartabā, Lebanon 47 A4 34 4N 35 50 E
Qaryat al Gharab, Iraq 44 D5 31 27N 44 48 E
Qaryat al 'Ulyā, Si. Arabia 44 E5 27 33N 47 42 E
Qasr 'Amra, Jordan 44 D3 31 48N 36 35 E
Qaşr-e Qand, Iran 45 E9 26 15N 60 45 E
Qasr Farâfra, Egypt 51 C11 27 0N 28 1 E
Qatanā, Syria 47 B5 33 26N 36 4 E
Qatar ■, Asia 46 B5 25 30N 51 15 E
Qatlīsh, Iran 45 B8 37 50N 57 19 E
Qattâra, Munkhafed el, Egypt 51 C11 29 30N 27 30 E
Qattâra Depression = Qattâra, Munkhafed el, Egypt 51 C11 29 30N 27 30 E
Qawām al Ḩamzah, Iraq 44 D5 31 43N 44 58 E
Qāyen, Iran 45 C8 33 40N 59 10 E
Qazaqstan = Kazakstan ■, Asia 26 E7 50 0N 70 0 E
Qazimämmäd, Azerbaijan 45 A6 40 3N 49 0 E
Qazvin, Iran 45 B6 36 15N 50 0 E
Qena, Egypt 51 C12 26 10N 32 43 E
Qeqertarsuaq, Greenland 4 C5 69 15N 53 38W
Qeqertarsuaq, Greenland 69 B5 69 45N 53 30W
Qeshlāq, Iran 44 C5 34 55N 46 28 E
Qeshm, Iran 45 E8 26 55N 56 10 E
Qeys, Iran 45 E7 26 32N 53 58 E
Qezel Owzen →, Iran 45 B6 36 45N 49 22 E
Qezi'ot, Israel 47 E3 30 52N 34 26 E
Qi Xian, China 34 G8 34 40N 114 48 E
Qian Gorlos, China 35 B13 45 5N 124 42 E
Qian Xian, China 34 G5 34 31N 108 15 E
Qianyang, China 34 G4 34 40N 107 8 E
Qikiqtarjuaq, Canada 69 B13 67 33N 63 0W
Qila Safed, Pakistan 40 E2 29 0N 61 30 E
Qila Saifullāh, Pakistan 42 D3 30 45N 68 17 E
Qilian Shan, China 32 C4 38 30N 96 0 E
Qin He →, China 34 G7 35 1N 113 22 E
Qin Ling = Qinling Shandi, China 34 H5 33 50N 108 10 E
Qin'an, China 34 G3 34 48N 105 40 E
Qing Xian, China 34 E9 38 35N 116 45 E
Qingcheng, China 35 F9 37 15N 117 40 E
Qingdao, China 35 F11 36 5N 120 20 E
Qingfeng, China 34 G8 35 52N 115 8 E
Qinghai □, China 32 C4 36 0N 98 0 E
Qinghai Hu, China 32 C5 36 40N 100 10 E
Qinghecheng, China 35 D13 41 28N 124 15 E
Qinghemen, China 35 D11 41 48N 121 25 E
Qingjian, China 34 F6 37 8N 110 8 E
Qingjiang = Huaiyin, China 35 H10 33 30N 119 2 E
Qingshui, China 34 G4 34 48N 106 8 E
Qingshuihe, China 34 E6 39 55N 111 35 E
Qingtongxia Shuiku, China 34 F3 37 50N 105 58 E
Qingxu, China 34 F7 37 34N 112 22 E
Qingyang, China 34 F4 36 2N 107 55 E
Qingyuan, China 35 C13 42 10N 124 55 E
Qingyun, China 35 F9 37 45N 117 20 E
Qinhuangdao, China 35 E10 39 56N 119 30 E
Qinling Shandi, China 34 H5 33 50N 108 10 E
Qinshui, China 34 G7 35 40N 112 8 E
Qinyang = Jiyuan, China 34 G7 35 7N 112 57 E
Qinyuan, China 34 F7 36 29N 112 20 E
Qinzhou, China 32 D5 21 58N 108 38 E
Qionghai, China 38 C8 19 15N 110 26 E
Qiongzhou Haixia, China 38 B8 20 10N 110 15 E
Qiqihar, China 27 E13 47 26N 124 0 E
Qiraîya, W. →, Egypt 47 E3 30 27N 34 0 E
Qiryat Ata, Israel 47 C4 32 47N 35 6 E
Qiryat Gat, Israel 47 D3 31 32N 34 46 E
Qiryat Mal'akhi, Israel 47 D3 31 44N 34 44 E
Qiryat Shemona, Israel 47 B4 33 13N 35 35 E
Qiryat Yam, Israel 47 C4 32 51N 35 4 E
Qishan, China 34 G4 34 25N 107 38 E
Qitai, China 32 B3 44 2N 89 35 E
Qixia, China 35 F11 37 17N 120 52 E
Qızılağac Körfäzi, Azerbaijan 45 B6 39 9N 49 0 E
Qojūr, Iran 44 B5 36 12N 47 55 E
Qom, Iran 45 C6 34 40N 51 0 E
Qomolangma Feng = Everest, Mt., Nepal 43 E12 28 5N 86 58 E
Qomsheh, Iran 45 D6 32 0N 51 55 E
Qoraqalpoghistan □, Uzbekistan 26 E6 43 0N 58 0 E
Qostanay, Kazakstan 26 D7 53 10N 63 35 E
Quabbin Reservoir, U.S.A. 79 D12 42 20N 72 20W
Quairading, Australia 61 F2 32 0S 117 21 E
Quakertown, U.S.A. 79 F9 40 26N 75 21W
Qualicum Beach, Canada 72 D4 49 22N 124 26W
Quamby, Australia 62 C3 20 22S 140 17 E
Quan Long = Ca Mau, Vietnam 39 H5 9 7N 105 8 E
Quanah, U.S.A. 81 H5 34 18N 99 44W
Quang Ngai, Vietnam 38 E7 15 13N 108 58 E
Quang Tri, Vietnam 38 D6 16 45N 107 13 E
Quang Yen, Vietnam 38 B6 20 56N 106 52 E
Quantock Hills, U.K. 11 F4 51 8N 3 10W
Quanzhou, China 33 D6 24 55N 118 34 E
Qu'Appelle, Canada 73 C8 50 33N 103 53W
Quaqtaq, Canada 69 B13 60 55N 69 40W
Quaraí, Brazil 94 C4 30 15S 56 20W
Quartu Sant'Élena, Italy 20 E3 39 15N 9 10 E
Quartzsite, U.S.A. 85 M12 33 40N 114 13W
Quatsino Sd., Canada 72 C3 50 25N 127 58W
Quba, Azerbaijan 25 F8 41 21N 48 32 E
Qūchān, Iran 45 B8 37 10N 58 27 E
Québec, Canada 71 C5 46 52N 71 13W
Québec □, Canada 71 C6 48 0N 74 0W
Queen Alexandra Ra., Antarctica 5 E11 85 0S 170 0 E
Queen Charlotte City, Canada 72 C2 53 15N 132 2W
Queen Charlotte Is., Canada 72 C2 53 20N 132 10W
Queen Charlotte Sd., Canada 72 C3 51 0N 128 0W
Queen Charlotte Strait, Canada 72 C3 50 45N 127 10W
Queen Elizabeth Is., Canada 66 B10 76 0N 95 0W
Queen Elizabeth Nat. Park, Uganda 54 C3 0 0 30 0 E
Queen Mary Land, Antarctica 5 D7 70 0S 95 0 E
Queen Maud G., Canada 68 B9 68 15N 102 30W
Queen Maud Land, Antarctica 5 D3 72 30S 12 0 E
Queen Maud Mts., Antarctica 5 E13 86 0S 160 0W
Queens Chan., Australia 60 C4 15 0S 129 30 E
Queensland □, Australia 62 C3 22 0S 142 0 E
Queenstown, Australia 62 G4 42 4S 145 35 E
Queenstown, N.Z. 59 L2 45 1S 168 40 E
Queenstown, S. Africa 56 E4 31 52S 26 52 E
Queets, U.S.A. 84 C2 47 32N 124 20W
Queguay Grande →, Uruguay 94 C4 32 9S 58 9W
Queimadas, Brazil 93 F11 11 0S 39 38W
Quelimane, Mozam. 55 F4 17 53S 36 58 E
Quellón, Chile 96 E2 43 7S 73 37W
Quelpart = Cheju do, S. Korea 35 H14 33 29N 126 34 E
Quemado, N. Mex., U.S.A. 83 J9 34 20N 108 30W
Quemado, Tex., U.S.A. 81 L4 28 58N 100 35W
Quemú-Quemú, Argentina 94 D3 36 3S 63 36W
Quequén, Argentina 94 D4 38 30S 58 30W
Querétaro, Mexico 86 C4 20 36N 100 23W
Querétaro □, Mexico 86 C5 20 30N 100 0W
Queshan, China 34 H8 32 55N 114 2 E
Quesnel, Canada 72 C4 53 0N 122 30W
Quesnel →, Canada 72 C4 52 58N 122 29W
Quesnel L., Canada 72 C4 52 30N 121 20W
Questa, U.S.A. 83 H11 36 42N 105 36W
Quetico Prov. Park, Canada 70 C1 48 30N 91 45W
Quetta, Pakistan 42 D2 30 15N 66 55 E
Quezaltenango, Guatemala 88 D1 14 50N 91 30W
Quezon City, Phil. 37 B6 14 38N 121 0 E
Qufār, Si. Arabia 44 E4 27 26N 41 37 E
Qui Nhon, Vietnam 38 F7 13 40N 109 13 E
Quibaxe, Angola 52 F2 8 24S 14 27 E
Quibdo, Colombia 92 B3 5 42N 76 40W
Quiberon, France 18 C2 47 29N 3 9W
Quiet L., Canada 72 A2 61 5N 133 5W
Quiindy, Paraguay 94 B4 25 58S 57 14W
Quila, Mexico 86 C3 24 23N 107 13W
Quilán, C., Chile 96 E2 43 15S 74 30W
Quilcene, U.S.A. 84 C4 47 49N 122 53W
Quilimarí, Chile 94 C1 32 5S 71 30W
Quilino, Argentina 94 C3 30 14S 64 29W
Quill Lakes, Canada 73 C8 51 55N 104 13W
Quillabamba, Peru 92 F4 12 50S 72 50W
Quillagua, Chile 94 A2 21 40S 69 40W
Quillaicillo, Chile 94 C1 31 17S 71 40W
Quillota, Chile 94 C1 32 54S 71 16W
Quilmes, Argentina 94 C4 34 43S 58 15W
Quilon, India 40 Q10 8 50N 76 38 E
Quilpie, Australia 63 D3 26 35S 144 11 E
Quilpué, Chile 94 C1 33 5S 71 33W
Quilua, Mozam. 55 F4 16 17S 39 54 E
Quimilí, Argentina 94 B3 27 40S 62 30W
Quimper, France 18 B1 48 0N 4 9W
Quimperlé, France 18 C2 47 53N 3 33W
Quinault →, U.S.A. 84 C2 47 21N 124 18W
Quincy, Calif., U.S.A. 84 F6 39 56N 120 57W
Quincy, Fla., U.S.A. 77 K3 30 35N 84 34W
Quincy, Ill., U.S.A. 80 F9 39 56N 91 23W
Quincy, Mass., U.S.A. 79 D14 42 15N 71 0W
Quincy, Wash., U.S.A. 82 C4 47 22N 119 56W
Quines, Argentina 94 C2 32 13S 65 48W
Quinga, Mozam. 55 F5 15 49S 40 15 E
Quinns Rocks, Australia 61 F2 31 40S 115 42 E
Quintana Roo □, Mexico 87 D7 19 0N 88 0W
Quintanar de la Orden, Spain 19 C4 39 36N 3 5W
Quintero, Chile 94 C1 32 45S 71 30W
Quirihue, Chile 94 D1 36 15S 72 35W
Quirinópolis, Brazil 93 G8 18 32S 50 30W
Quissanga, Mozam. 55 E5 12 24S 40 28 E
Quissico, Mozam. 57 C5 24 42S 34 44 E
Quitilipi, Argentina 94 B3 26 50S 60 13W
Quitman, U.S.A. 77 K4 30 47N 83 34W
Quito, Ecuador 92 D3 0 15S 78 35W
Quixadá, Brazil 93 D11 4 55S 39 0W
Quixaxe, Mozam. 55 F5 15 17S 40 4 E
Qulan, Kazakstan 26 E8 42 55N 72 43 E
Qul'ân, Jazâ'ir, Egypt 44 E2 24 22N 35 31 E
Qumbu, S. Africa 57 E4 31 10S 28 48 E
Quneitra, Syria 47 B4 33 7N 35 48 E
Qŭnghirot, Uzbekistan 26 E6 43 6N 58 54 E
Quoin I., Australia 60 B4 14 54S 129 32 E
Quoin Pt., S. Africa 56 E2 34 46S 19 37 E
Qŭqon, Uzbekistan 26 E8 40 30N 70 57 E
Qurnat as Sawdā', Lebanon 47 A5 34 18N 36 6 E
Quşaybā', Si. Arabia 44 E4 26 53N 43 35 E
Qusaybah, Iraq 44 C4 34 24N 40 59 E
Quseir, Egypt 44 E2 26 7N 34 16 E
Qūshchī, Iran 44 B5 37 59N 45 3 E
Quthing, Lesotho 57 E4 30 25S 27 36 E
Qūţīābād, Iran 45 C6 35 47N 48 30 E
Quwo, China 34 G6 35 38N 111 25 E
Quyang, China 34 E8 38 35N 114 40 E
Quynh Nhai, Vietnam 38 B4 21 49N 103 33 E
Quyon, Canada 79 A8 45 31N 76 14W
Quzhou, China 33 D6 28 57N 118 54 E
Quzi, China 34 F4 36 20N 107 20 E
Qyzylorda, Kazakstan 26 E7 44 48N 65 28 E

R

Ra, Ko, Thailand 39 H2 9 13N 98 16 E
Raahe, Finland 8 D21 64 40N 24 28 E
Raalte, Neths. 15 B6 52 23N 6 16 E
Raasay, U.K. 12 D2 57 25N 6 4W
Raasay, Sd. of, U.K. 12 D2 57 30N 6 8W
Raba, Indonesia 37 F5 8 36S 118 55 E
Rába →, Hungary 17 E9 47 38N 17 38 E
Rabai, Kenya 54 C4 3 50S 39 31 E
Rabat, Malta 23 D1 35 53N 14 25 E
Rabat, Morocco 50 B4 34 2N 6 48W
Rabaul, Papua N. G. 64 H7 4 24S 152 18 E
Rābigh, Si. Arabia 46 C2 22 50N 39 5 E
Râbniţa, Moldova 17 E15 47 45N 29 0 E
Rābor, Iran 45 D8 29 17N 56 55 E
Race, C., Canada 71 C9 46 40N 53 5W
Rach Gia, Vietnam 39 G5 10 5N 105 5 E
Rachid, Mauritania 50 E3 18 45N 11 35W
Racibórz, Poland 17 C10 50 7N 18 18 E
Racine, U.S.A. 76 D2 42 41N 87 51W
Rackerby, U.S.A. 84 F5 39 26N 121 22W
Radama, Nosy, Madag. 57 A8 14 0S 47 47 E
Radama, Saikanosy, Madag. 57 A8 14 16S 47 53 E
Rădăuţi, Romania 17 E13 47 50N 25 59 E
Radcliff, U.S.A. 76 G3 37 51N 85 57W
Radekhiv, Ukraine 17 C13 50 25N 24 32 E
Radekhov = Radekhiv, Ukraine 17 C13 50 25N 24 32 E
Radford, U.S.A. 76 G5 37 8N 80 34W
Radhanpur, India 42 H4 23 50N 71 38 E
Radhwa, Jabal, Si. Arabia 44 E3 24 34N 38 18 E
Radisson, Qué., Canada 70 B4 53 47N 77 37W
Radisson, Sask., Canada 73 C7 52 30N 107 20W
Radium Hot Springs, Canada 72 C5 50 35N 116 2W
Radnor Forest, U.K. 11 E4 52 17N 3 10W
Radom, Poland 17 C11 51 23N 21 12 E
Radomsko, Poland 17 C10 51 5N 19 28 E
Radomyshl, Ukraine 17 C15 50 30N 29 12 E
Radstock, C., Australia 63 E1 33 12S 134 20 E
Radviliškis, Lithuania 9 J20 55 49N 23 33 E
Radville, Canada 73 D8 49 30N 104 15W
Rae, Canada 72 A5 62 50N 116 3W
Rae Bareli, India 43 F9 26 18N 81 20 E
Rae Isthmus, Canada 69 B11 66 40N 87 30W
Raeren, Belgium 15 D6 50 41N 6 7 E
Raeside, L., Australia 61 E3 29 20S 122 0 E
Raetihi, N.Z. 59 H5 39 25S 175 17 E
Rafaela, Argentina 94 C3 31 10S 61 30W
Rafah, Gaza Strip 47 D3 31 18N 34 14 E
Rafai, C.A.R. 54 B1 4 59N 23 58 E
Rafḩā, Si. Arabia 44 D4 29 35N 43 35 E
Rafsanjān, Iran 45 D8 30 30N 56 5 E
Raft Pt., Australia 60 C3 16 4S 124 26 E
Râgâ, Sudan 51 G11 8 28N 25 41 E
Ragachow, Belarus 17 B16 53 8N 30 5 E
Ragama, Sri Lanka 40 R11 7 0N 79 50 E
Ragged, Mt., Australia 61 F3 33 27S 123 25 E
Raghunathpalli, India 43 H11 22 14N 84 48 E
Raghunathpur, India 43 H12 23 33N 86 40 E
Raglan, N.Z. 59 G5 37 55S 174 55 E
Ragusa, Italy 20 F6 36 55N 14 44 E
Raha, Indonesia 37 E6 4 55S 123 0 E
Rahaeng = Tak, Thailand 38 D2 16 52N 99 8 E
Rahatgarh, India 43 H8 23 47N 78 22 E
Rahimyar Khan, Pakistan 42 E4 28 30N 70 25 E
Rāhjerd, Iran 45 C6 34 22N 50 22 E
Rahon, India 42 D7 31 3N 76 7 E
Raichur, India 40 L10 16 10N 77 20 E
Raiganj, India 43 G13 25 37N 88 10 E
Raigarh, India 41 J13 21 56N 83 25 E
Raijua, Indonesia 37 F6 10 37S 121 36 E
Raikot, India 42 D6 30 41N 75 42 E
Railton, Australia 62 G4 41 25S 146 28 E
Rainbow Lake, Canada 72 B5 58 30N 119 23W
Rainier, U.S.A. 84 D4 46 53N 122 41W
Rainier, Mt., U.S.A. 84 D5 46 52N 121 46W
Rainy L., Canada 73 D10 48 42N 93 10W
Rainy River, Canada 73 D10 48 43N 94 29W
Raippaluoto, Finland 8 E19 63 13N 21 14 E
Raipur, India 41 J12 21 17N 81 45 E
Raisen, India 42 H8 23 20N 77 48 E
Raisio, Finland 9 F20 60 28N 22 11 E
Raj Nandgaon, India 41 J12 21 5N 81 5 E
Raj Nilgiri, India 43 J12 21 28N 86 46 E
Raja, Ujung, Indonesia 36 D1 3 40N 96 25 E
Raja Ampat, Kepulauan, Indonesia 37 E7 0 30S 130 0 E
Rajahmundry, India 41 L12 17 1N 81 48 E
Rajang →, Malaysia 36 D4 2 30N 112 0 E
Rajanpur, Pakistan 42 E4 29 6N 70 19 E
Rajapalaiyam, India 40 Q10 9 25N 77 35 E
Rajasthan □, India 42 F5 26 45N 73 30 E
Rajasthan Canal, India 42 F5 28 0N 72 0 E
Rajauri, India 43 C6 33 25N 74 21 E
Rajgarh, Mad. P., India 42 G7 24 2N 76 45 E
Rajgarh, Raj., India 42 F7 27 14N 76 38 E
Rajgarh, Raj., India 42 E6 28 40N 75 25 E
Rajgir, India 43 G11 25 2N 85 25 E
Rajkot, India 42 H4 22 15N 70 56 E
Rajmahal Hills, India 43 G12 24 30N 87 30 E
Rajpipla, India 40 J8 21 50N 73 30 E
Rajpur, India 42 H6 22 18N 74 21 E
Rajpura, India 42 D7 30 25N 76 32 E
Rajshahi, Bangla. 41 G16 24 22N 88 39 E
Rajshahi □, Bangla. 43 G13 25 0N 89 0 E
Rajula, India 42 J4 21 3N 71 26 E
Rakaia, N.Z. 59 K4 43 45S 172 1 E
Rakaia →, N.Z. 59 K4 43 36S 172 15 E
Rakan, Ra's, Qatar 45 E6 26 10N 51 20 E
Rakaposhi, Pakistan 43 A6 36 10N 74 25 E
Rakata, Pulau, Indonesia 36 F3 6 10S 105 20 E
Rakhiv, Ukraine 17 D13 48 3N 24 12 E
Rakhni, Pakistan 42 D3 30 4N 69 56 E
Rakhni →, Pakistan 42 E3 29 31N 69 36 E
Rakitnoye, Russia 30 B7 45 36N 134 17 E
Rakops, Botswana 56 C3 21 1S 24 28 E
Rakvere, Estonia 9 G22 59 20N 26 25 E
Raleigh, U.S.A. 77 H6 35 47N 78 39W
Ralls, U.S.A. 81 J4 33 41N 101 24W
Ralston, U.S.A. 78 E8 41 30N 76 57W
Ram →, Canada 72 A4 62 1N 123 41W
Rām Allāh, West Bank 47 D4 31 55N 35 10 E
Rama, Nic. 88 D3 12 9N 84 15W
Ramakona, India 43 J8 21 43N 78 50 E
Raman, Thailand 39 J3 6 29N 101 18 E
Ramanathapuram, India 40 Q11 9 25N 78 55 E
Ramanetaka, B. de, Madag. 57 A8 14 13S 47 52 E
Ramanujganj, India 43 H10 23 48N 83 42 E
Ramat Gan, Israel 47 C3 32 4N 34 48 E
Ramatlhabama, S. Africa 56 D4 25 37S 25 33 E
Ramban, India 43 C6 33 14N 75 12 E
Rambipuji, Indonesia 37 H15 8 12S 113 37 E
Ramechhap, Nepal 43 F12 27 25N 86 10 E
Ramganga →, India 43 F8 27 5N 79 58 E
Ramgarh, Bihar, India 43 H11 23 40N 85 35 E
Ramgarh, Raj., India 42 F6 27 16N 75 14 E
Ramgarh, Raj., India 42 F4 27 30N 70 36 E
Rāmhormoz, Iran 45 D6 31 15N 49 35 E
Ramīān, Iran 45 B7 37 3N 55 16 E
Ramingining, Australia 62 A2 12 19S 135 3 E
Ramla, Israel 47 D3 31 55N 34 52 E
Ramnad = Ramanathapuram, India 40 Q11 9 25N 78 55 E
Ramnagar, Jammu & Kashmir, India 43 C6 32 47N 75 18 E
Ramnagar, Ut. P., India 43 E8 29 24N 79 7 E
Râmnicu Sărat, Romania 17 F14 45 26N 27 3 E
Râmnicu Vâlcea, Romania 17 F13 45 9N 24 21 E
Ramona, U.S.A. 85 M10 33 2N 116 52W
Ramore, Canada 70 C3 48 30N 80 25W
Ramotswa, Botswana 56 C4 24 50S 25 52 E
Rampur, H.P., India 42 D7 31 26N 77 43 E
Rampur, Mad. P., India 42 H5 23 25N 73 53 E
Rampur, Ut. P., India 43 E8 28 50N 79 5 E
Rampur Hat, India 43 G12 24 10N 87 50 E
Rampura, India 42 G6 24 30N 75 27 E
Ramrama Tola, India 43 J8 21 52N 79 55 E
Ramree I., Burma 41 K19 19 0N 94 0 E
Rāmsar, Iran 45 B6 36 53N 50 41 E
Ramsey, U.K. 10 C3 54 20N 4 22W
Ramsey, U.S.A. 79 E10 41 4N 74 9W
Ramsey L., Canada 70 C3 47 13N 82 15W
Ramsgate, U.K. 11 F9 51 20N 1 25 E
Ramtek, India 40 J11 21 20N 79 15 E
Rana Pratap Sagar Dam, India 42 G6 24 58N 75 38 E
Ranaghat, India 43 H13 23 15N 88 35 E
Ranahu, Pakistan 42 G3 25 55N 69 45 E
Ranau, Malaysia 36 C5 6 2N 116 40 E
Rancagua, Chile 94 C1 34 10S 70 50W
Rancheria →, Canada 72 A3 60 13N 129 7W
Ranchester, U.S.A. 82 D10 44 54N 107 10W
Ranchi, India 43 H11 23 19N 85 27 E
Rancho Cucamonga, U.S.A. 85 L9 34 10N 117 30W
Randalstown, U.K. 13 B5 54 45N 6 19W
Randers, Denmark 9 H14 56 29N 10 1 E
Randfontein, S. Africa 57 D4 26 8S 27 45 E
Randle, U.S.A. 84 D5 46 32N 121 57W
Randolph, Mass., U.S.A. 79 D13 42 10N 71 2W
Randolph, N.Y., U.S.A. 78 D6 42 10N 78 59W
Randolph, Utah, U.S.A. 82 F8 41 40N 111 11W
Randolph, Vt., U.S.A. 79 C12 43 55N 72 40W
Randsburg, U.S.A. 85 K9 35 22N 117 39W
Råne älv →, Sweden 8 D20 65 50N 22 20 E
Rangae, Thailand 39 J3 6 19N 101 44 E
Rangaunu B., N.Z. 59 F4 34 51S 173 15 E
Rangeley, U.S.A. 79 B14 44 58N 70 39W
Rangeley L., U.S.A. 79 B14 44 55N 70 43W
Rangely, U.S.A. 82 F9 40 5N 108 48W
Ranger, U.S.A. 81 J5 32 28N 98 41W
Rangia, India 41 F17 26 28N 91 38 E
Rangiora, N.Z. 59 K4 43 19S 172 36 E
Rangitaiki →, N.Z. 59 G6 37 54S 176 49 E
Rangitata →, N.Z. 59 K3 43 45S 171 15 E
Rangkasbitung, Indonesia 37 G12 6 21S 106 15 E
Rangon →, Burma 41 L20 16 28N 96 40 E
Rangoon, Burma 41 L20 16 45N 96 20 E
Rangpur, Bangla. 41 G16 25 42N 89 22 E
Rangsit, Thailand 38 F3 13 59N 100 37 E
Ranibennur, India 40 M9 14 35N 75 30 E
Raniganj, Ut. P., India 43 F9 27 3N 82 13 E
Raniganj, W. Bengal, India 41 H15 23 40N 87 5 E
Ranikhet, India 43 E8 29 39N 79 25 E
Raniwara, India 40 G8 24 50N 72 10 E
Rāniyah, Iraq 44 B5 36 15N 44 53 E
Ranka, India 43 H10 23 59N 83 47 E
Ranken →, Australia 62 C2 20 31S 137 36 E
Rankin, U.S.A. 81 K4 31 13N 101 56W
Rankin Inlet, Canada 68 B10 62 30N 93 0W
Rannoch, L., U.K. 12 E4 56 41N 4 20W
Rannoch Moor, U.K. 12 E4 56 38N 4 48W
Ranobe, Helodranon' i, Madag. 57 C7 23 3S 43 33 E
Ranohira, Madag. 57 C8 22 29S 45 24 E
Ranomafana, Toamasina, Madag. 57 B8 18 57S 48 50 E
Ranomafana, Toliara, Madag. 57 C8 24 34S 47 0 E
Ranomena, Madag. 57 C8 23 25S 47 17 E
Ranong, Thailand 39 H2 9 56N 98 40 E
Ranotsara Nord, Madag. 57 C8 22 48S 46 36 E
Rānsa, Iran 45 C6 33 39N 48 18 E
Ransiki, Indonesia 37 E8 1 30S 134 10 E
Rantabe, Madag. 57 B8 15 42S 49 39 E
Rantauprapat, Indonesia 36 D1 2 15N 99 50 E
Rantemario, Indonesia 37 E5 3 15S 119 57 E
Rantoul, U.S.A. 76 E1 40 19N 88 9W
Raoyang, China 34 E8 38 15N 115 45 E
Rapa, Pac. Oc. 65 K13 27 35S 144 20W
Rapallo, Italy 18 D8 44 21N 9 14 E
Rapar, India 42 H4 23 34N 70 38 E
Rāpch, Iran 45 E8 25 40N 59 15 E
Raper, C., Canada 69 B13 69 44N 67 6W
Rapid City, U.S.A. 80 D3 44 5N 103 14W
Rapid River, U.S.A. 76 C2 45 55N 86 58W
Rapla, Estonia 9 G21 59 1N 24 52 E
Rapti →, India 43 F10 26 18N 83 41 E
Raquette →, U.S.A. 79 B10 45 0N 74 42W

Raquette Lake

Raquette Lake, U.S.A. 79 C10 43 49N 74 40W
Rarotonga, Cook Is. 65 K12 21 30S 160 0W
Ra's al 'Ayn, Syria 44 B4 36 45N 40 12 E
Ra's al Khaymah, U.A.E. 46 B6 25 50N 55 59 E
Rasca, Pta. de la, Canary Is. 22 G3 27 59N 16 41W
Raseiniai, Lithuania 9 J20 55 25N 23 5 E
Rashmi, India 42 G6 25 4N 74 22 E
Rasht, Iran 45 B6 37 20N 49 40 E
Rasi Salai, Thailand 38 E5 15 20N 104 9 E
Rason L., Australia 61 E3 28 45S 124 25 E
Rasra, India 43 G10 25 50N 83 50 E
Rasul, Pakistan 42 C5 32 42N 73 34 E
Rat Buri, Thailand 38 F2 13 30N 99 54 E
Rat Islands, U.S.A. 68 C1 52 0N 178 0 E
Rat L., Canada 73 B9 56 10N 99 40W
Ratangarh, India 42 E6 28 5N 74 35 E
Raṭāwī, Iraq 44 D5 30 38N 47 13 E
Rath, India 43 G8 25 36N 79 37 E
Rath Luirc, Ireland 13 D3 52 21N 8 40W
Rathdrum, Ireland 13 D5 52 56N 6 14W
Rathenow, Germany 16 B7 52 37N 12 19 E
Rathkeale, Ireland 13 D3 52 32N 8 56W
Rathlin I., U.K. 13 A5 55 18N 6 14W
Rathmelton, Ireland 13 A4 55 2N 7 38W
Ratibor = Racibórz, Poland 17 C10 50 7N 18 18 E
Ratlam, India 42 H6 23 20N 75 0 E
Ratnagiri, India 40 L8 16 57N 73 18 E
Ratodero, Pakistan 42 F3 27 48N 68 18 E
Raton, U.S.A. 81 G2 36 54N 104 24W
Rattaphum, Thailand 39 J3 7 8N 100 16 E
Rattray Hd., U.K. 12 D7 57 38N 1 50W
Ratz, Mt., Canada 72 B2 57 23N 132 12W
Raub, Malaysia 39 L3 3 47N 101 52 E
Rauch, Argentina 94 D4 36 45S 59 5W
Raudales de Malpaso, Mexico 87 D6 17 30N 23 30W
Raufarhöfn, Iceland 8 C6 66 27N 15 57W
Raufoss, Norway 9 F14 60 44N 10 37 E
Raukumara Ra., N.Z. 59 H6 38 5S 177 55 E
Rauma, Finland 9 F19 61 10N 21 30 E
Raurkela, India 43 H11 22 14N 84 50 E
Rausu-Dake, Japan 30 B12 44 4N 145 7 E
Rava-Ruska, Poland 17 C12 50 15N 23 42 E
Rava Russkaya = Rava-Ruska, Poland 17 C12 50 15N 23 42 E
Ravalli, U.S.A. 82 C6 47 17N 114 11W
Ravānsar, Iran 44 C5 34 43N 46 40 E
Rāvar, Iran 45 D8 31 20N 56 51 E
Ravena, U.S.A. 79 D11 42 28N 73 49W
Ravenna, Italy 20 B5 44 25N 12 12 E
Ravenna, Nebr., U.S.A. 80 E5 41 1N 98 55W
Ravenna, Ohio, U.S.A. 78 E3 41 9N 81 15W
Ravensburg, Germany 16 E5 47 46N 9 36 E
Ravenshoe, Australia 62 B4 17 37S 145 29 E
Ravensthorpe, Australia 61 F3 33 35S 120 2 E
Ravenswood, Australia 62 C4 20 6S 146 54 E
Ravenswood, U.S.A. 76 F5 38 57N 81 46W
Ravi →, Pakistan 42 D4 30 35N 71 49 E
Rawalpindi, Pakistan 42 C5 33 38N 73 8 E
Rawāndūz, Iraq 44 B5 36 40N 44 30 E
Rawang, Malaysia 39 L3 3 20N 101 35 E
Rawene, N.Z. 59 F4 35 25S 173 32 E
Rawlinna, Australia 61 F4 30 58S 125 28 E
Rawlins, U.S.A. 82 F10 41 47N 107 14W
Rawlinson Ra., Australia 61 D4 24 40S 128 30 E
Rawson, Argentina 96 E3 43 15S 65 5W
Raxaul, India 43 F11 26 59N 84 51 E
Ray, U.S.A. 80 A3 48 21N 103 10W
Ray, C., Canada 71 C8 47 33N 59 15W
Rayadurg, India 40 M10 14 40N 76 50 E
Rayagada, India 41 K13 19 15N 83 20 E
Raychikhinsk, Russia 27 E13 49 46N 129 25 E
Rāyen, Iran 45 D8 29 34N 57 26 E
Rayleigh, U.K. 11 F8 51 36N 0 37 E
Raymond, Canada 72 D6 49 30N 112 35W
Raymond, Calif., U.S.A. 84 H7 37 13N 119 54W
Raymond, N.H., U.S.A. 79 C13 43 2N 71 11W
Raymond, Wash., U.S.A. 84 D3 46 41N 123 44W
Raymondville, U.S.A. 81 M6 26 29N 97 47W
Raymore, Canada 73 C8 51 25N 104 31W
Rayón, Mexico 86 B2 29 43N 110 35W
Rayong, Thailand 38 F3 12 40N 101 20 E
Rayville, U.S.A. 81 J9 32 29N 91 46W
Raz, Pte. du, France 18 C1 48 2N 4 47W
Razan, Iran 45 C6 35 23N 49 2 E
Razdel'naya = Rozdilna, Ukraine 17 E16 46 50N 30 2 E
Razdolnoye, Russia 30 C5 43 30N 131 52 E
Razeh, Iran 45 C6 32 47N 48 9 E
Razgrad, Bulgaria 21 C12 43 33N 26 34 E
Razim, Lacul, Romania 17 F15 44 50N 29 0 E
Razmak, Pakistan 42 C3 32 45N 69 50 E
Ré, Î. de, France 18 C3 46 12N 1 30W
Reading, U.K. 11 F7 51 27N 0 58W
Reading, U.S.A. 79 F9 40 20N 75 56W
Reading □, U.K. 11 F7 51 27N 0 58W
Realicó, Argentina 94 D3 35 0S 64 15W
Ream, Cambodia 39 G4 10 34N 103 39 E
Reata, Mexico 86 B4 26 8N 101 5W
Reay Forest, U.K. 12 C4 58 22N 4 55W
Rebi, Indonesia 37 F8 6 23S 134 7 E
Rebiana, Libya 51 D10 24 12N 22 10 E
Rebun-Tō, Japan 30 B10 45 23N 141 2 E
Recherche, Arch. of the, Australia 61 F3 34 15S 122 50 E
Rechna Doab, Pakistan 42 D5 31 35N 73 30 E
Rechytsa, Belarus 17 B16 52 21N 30 24 E
Recife, Brazil 93 E12 8 0S 35 0W
Recklinghausen, Germany 15 C7 51 37N 7 12 E
Reconquista, Argentina 94 B4 29 10S 59 45W
Recreo, Argentina 94 B2 29 25S 65 10W
Red →, La., U.S.A. 81 K9 31 1N 91 45W
Red →, N. Dak., U.S.A. 68 C10 49 0N 97 15W
Red Bank, U.S.A. 79 F10 40 21N 74 5W
Red Bay, Canada 71 B8 51 44N 56 25W
Red Bluff, U.S.A. 82 F2 40 11N 122 15W
Red Bluff L., U.S.A. 81 K3 31 54N 103 55W
Red Cloud, U.S.A. 80 E5 40 5N 98 32W
Red Creek, U.S.A. 79 C8 43 14N 76 45W
Red Deer, Canada 72 C6 52 20N 113 50W
Red Deer →, Alta., Canada 73 C7 50 58N 110 0W
Red Deer →, Man., Canada 73 C8 52 53N 101 1W
Red Deer L., Canada 73 C8 52 55N 101 20W
Red Hook, U.S.A. 79 E11 41 55N 73 53W
Red Indian L., Canada 71 C8 48 35N 57 0W
Red L., Canada 73 C10 51 3N 93 49W
Red Lake, Canada 73 C10 51 3N 93 49W
Red Lake Falls, U.S.A. 80 B6 47 53N 96 16W
Red Lake Road, Canada 73 C10 49 59N 93 25W
Red Lodge, U.S.A. 82 D9 45 11N 109 15W
Red Mountain, U.S.A. 85 K9 35 37N 117 38W
Red Oak, U.S.A. 80 E7 41 1N 95 14W
Red Rock, Canada 70 C2 48 55N 88 15W
Red Rock, L., U.S.A. 80 E8 41 22N 92 59W
Red Rocks Pt., Australia 61 F4 32 13S 127 32 E
Red Sea, Asia 46 C2 25 0N 36 0 E
Red Slate Mt., U.S.A. 84 H8 37 31N 118 52W
Red Sucker L., Canada 70 B1 54 9N 93 40W
Red Tower Pass = Turnu Roşu, P., Romania 17 F13 45 33N 24 17 E
Red Wing, U.S.A. 80 C8 44 34N 92 31W
Redang, Malaysia 36 C2 5 49N 103 2 E
Redange, Lux. 15 E5 49 46N 5 52 E
Redcar, U.K. 10 C6 54 37N 1 4W
Redcar & Cleveland □, U.K. 10 C7 54 29N 1 0W
Redcliff, Canada 73 C6 50 10N 110 50W
Redcliffe, Australia 63 D5 27 12S 153 0 E
Redcliffe, Mt., Australia 61 E3 28 30S 121 30 E
Reddersburg, S. Africa 56 D4 29 41S 26 10 E
Redding, U.S.A. 82 F2 40 35N 122 24W
Redditch, U.K. 11 E6 52 18N 1 55W
Redfield, U.S.A. 80 C5 44 53N 98 31W
Redford, U.S.A. 79 B11 44 38N 73 48W
Redlands, U.S.A. 85 M9 34 4N 117 11W
Redmond, Oreg., U.S.A. 82 D3 44 17N 121 11W
Redmond, Wash., U.S.A. 84 C4 47 41N 122 7W
Redon, France 18 C2 47 40N 2 6W
Redonda, Antigua 89 C7 16 58N 62 19W
Redondela, Spain 19 A1 42 15N 8 38W
Redondo Beach, U.S.A. 85 M8 33 50N 118 23W
Redruth, U.K. 11 G2 50 14N 5 14W
Redvers, Canada 73 D8 49 35N 101 40W
Redwater, Canada 72 C6 53 55N 113 6W
Redwood, U.S.A. 79 B9 44 18N 75 48W
Redwood City, U.S.A. 84 H4 37 30N 122 15W
Redwood Falls, U.S.A. 80 C7 44 32N 95 7W
Redwood National Park, U.S.A. 82 F1 41 40N 124 5W
Ree, L., Ireland 13 C3 53 35N 8 0W
Reed, L., Canada 73 C8 54 38N 100 30W
Reed City, U.S.A. 76 D3 43 53N 85 31W
Reedley, U.S.A. 84 J7 36 36N 119 27W
Reedsburg, U.S.A. 80 D9 43 32N 90 0W
Reedsport, U.S.A. 82 E1 43 42N 124 6W
Reedsville, U.S.A. 78 F7 40 39N 77 35W
Reefton, N.Z. 59 K3 42 6S 171 51 E
Reese →, U.S.A. 82 F5 40 48N 117 4W
Refugio, U.S.A. 81 L6 28 18N 97 17W
Regensburg, Germany 16 D7 49 1N 12 6 E
Reggâne = Zaouiet Reggâne, Algeria 50 C6 26 32N 0 3 E
Réggio di Calábria, Italy 20 E6 38 6N 15 39 E
Réggio nell'Emília, Italy 20 B4 44 43N 10 36 E
Reghin, Romania 17 E13 46 46N 24 42 E
Regina, Canada 73 C8 50 27N 104 35W
Regina Beach, Canada 73 C8 50 47N 105 0W
Registro, Brazil 95 A6 24 29S 47 49W
Rehar →, India 43 H10 23 55N 82 40 E
Rehli, India 43 H8 23 38N 79 5 E
Rehoboth, Namibia 56 C2 23 15S 17 4 E
Rehovot, Israel 47 D3 31 54N 34 48 E
Reichenbach, Germany 16 C7 50 37N 12 17 E
Reid, Australia 61 F4 30 49S 128 26 E
Reidsville, U.S.A. 77 G6 36 21N 79 40W
Reigate, U.K. 11 F7 51 14N 0 12W
Reims, France 18 B6 49 15N 4 1 E
Reina Adelaida, Arch., Chile 96 G2 52 20S 74 0W
Reindeer →, Canada 73 B8 55 36N 103 11W
Reindeer I., Canada 73 C9 52 30N 98 0W
Reindeer L., Canada 73 B8 57 15N 102 15W
Reinga, C., N.Z. 59 F4 34 25S 172 43 E
Reinosa, Spain 19 A3 43 2N 4 15W
Reitz, S. Africa 57 D4 27 48S 28 29 E
Reivilo, S. Africa 56 D3 27 36S 24 8 E
Reliance, Canada 73 A7 63 0N 109 20W
Rembang, Indonesia 37 G14 6 42S 111 21 E
Remedios, Panama 88 E3 8 15N 81 50W
Remeshk, Iran 45 E8 26 55N 58 50 E
Remich, Lux. 15 E6 49 32N 6 22 E
Remscheid, Germany 15 C7 51 11N 7 12 E
Ren Xian, China 34 F8 37 8N 114 40 E
Rendsburg, Germany 16 A5 54 17N 9 39 E
Renfrew, Canada 79 A8 45 30N 76 40W
Renfrewshire □, U.K. 12 F4 55 49N 4 38W
Rengat, Indonesia 36 E2 0 30S 102 45 E
Rengo, Chile 94 C1 34 24S 70 50W
Reni, Ukraine 17 F15 45 28N 28 15 E
Rennell Sd., Canada 72 C2 53 23N 132 35W
Renner Springs, Australia 62 B1 18 20S 133 47 E
Rennes, France 18 B3 48 7N 1 41W
Rennie L., Canada 73 A7 61 32N 105 35W
Reno, U.S.A. 84 F7 39 31N 119 48W
Reno →, Italy 20 B5 44 38N 12 16 E
Renovo, U.S.A. 78 E7 41 20N 77 45W
Renqiu, China 34 E9 38 43N 116 5 E
Rensselaer, Ind., U.S.A. 76 E2 40 57N 87 9W
Rensselaer, N.Y., U.S.A. 79 D11 42 38N 73 45W
Renteria, Spain 19 A5 43 19N 1 54W
Renton, U.S.A. 84 C4 47 29N 122 12W
Reotipur, India 43 G10 25 33N 83 45 E
Republic, Mo., U.S.A. 81 G8 37 7N 93 29W
Republic, Wash., U.S.A. 82 B4 48 39N 118 44W
Republican →, U.S.A. 80 F6 39 4N 96 48W
Repulse Bay, Canada 69 B11 66 30N 86 30W
Requena, Peru 92 E4 5 5S 73 52W
Requena, Spain 19 C5 39 30N 1 4W
Reşadiye = Datça, Turkey 21 F12 36 46N 27 40 E
Reserve, U.S.A. 83 K9 33 43N 108 45W
Resht = Rasht, Iran 45 B6 37 20N 49 40 E
Resistencia, Argentina 94 B4 27 30S 59 0W
Reşiţa, Romania 17 F11 45 18N 21 53 E
Resolution I., Canada 69 B13 61 30N 65 0W
Resolution I., N.Z. 59 L1 45 40S 166 40 E
Ressano Garcia, Mozam. 57 D5 25 25S 32 0 E
Reston, Canada 73 D8 49 33N 101 6W
Retalhuleu, Guatemala 88 D1 14 33N 91 46W
Retenue, L. de, Dem. Rep. of the Congo 55 E2 11 0S 27 0 E
Retford, U.K. 10 D7 53 19N 0 56W
Réthimnon, Greece 23 D6 35 18N 24 30 E
Réthimnon □, Greece 23 D6 35 23N 24 28 E
Reti, Pakistan 42 E3 28 5N 69 48 E
Réunion ■, Ind. Oc. 49 J9 21 0S 56 0 E
Reus, Spain 19 B6 41 10N 1 5 E
Reutlingen, Germany 16 D5 48 29N 9 12 E
Reval = Tallinn, Estonia 9 G21 59 22N 24 48 E
Revda, Russia 24 C10 56 48N 59 57 E
Revelganj, India 43 G11 25 50N 84 40 E
Revelstoke, Canada 72 C5 51 0N 118 10W
Reventazón, Peru 92 E2 6 10S 80 58W
Revillagigedo, Is. de, Pac. Oc. 86 D2 18 40N 112 0W
Revuè →, Mozam. 55 F3 19 50S 34 0 E
Rewa, India 43 G9 24 33N 81 25 E
Rewari, India 42 E7 28 15N 76 40 E
Rexburg, U.S.A. 82 E8 43 49N 111 47W
Rey, Iran 45 C6 35 35N 51 25 E
Rey, I. del, Panama 88 E4 8 20N 78 30W
Rey Malabo, Eq. Guin. 52 D1 3 45N 8 50 E
Reyðarfjörður, Iceland 8 D6 65 2N 14 13W
Reyes, Pt., U.S.A. 84 H3 38 0N 123 0W
Reykjahlið, Iceland 8 D5 65 40N 16 55W
Reykjanes, Iceland 8 E2 63 48N 22 40W
Reykjavík, Iceland 8 D3 64 10N 21 57W
Reynolds Ra., Australia 60 D5 22 30S 133 0 E
Reynoldsville, U.S.A. 78 E6 41 5N 78 58W
Reynosa, Mexico 87 B5 26 5N 98 18W
Rēzekne, Latvia 9 H22 56 30N 27 17 E
Rezvān, Iran 45 E8 27 34N 56 6 E
Rhayader, U.K. 11 E4 52 18N 3 29W
Rhein →, Europe 15 C6 51 52N 6 2 E
Rhein-Main-Donau-Kanal, Germany 16 D6 49 1N 11 27 E
Rheine, Germany 16 B4 52 17N 7 26 E
Rheinland-Pfalz □, Germany 16 C4 50 0N 7 0 E
Rhin = Rhein →, Europe 15 C6 51 52N 6 2 E
Rhine = Rhein →, Europe 15 C6 51 52N 6 2 E
Rhinebeck, U.S.A. 79 E11 41 56N 73 55W
Rhineland-Palatinate = Rheinland-Pfalz □, Germany 16 C4 50 0N 7 0 E
Rhinelander, U.S.A. 80 C10 45 38N 89 25W
Rhinns Pt., U.K. 12 F2 55 40N 6 29W
Rhino Camp, Uganda 54 B3 3 0N 31 22 E
Rhir, Cap, Morocco 50 B4 30 38N 9 54W
Rhode Island □, U.S.A. 79 E13 41 40N 71 30W
Rhodes = Ródhos, Greece 23 C10 36 15N 28 10 E
Rhodesia = Zimbabwe ■, Africa 55 F3 19 0S 30 0 E
Rhodope Mts. = Rhodopi Planina, Bulgaria 21 D11 41 40N 24 20 E
Rhodopi Planina, Bulgaria 21 D11 41 40N 24 20 E
Rhön, Germany 16 C5 50 24N 9 58 E
Rhondda, U.K. 11 F4 51 39N 3 31W
Rhondda Cynon Taff □, U.K. 11 F4 51 42N 3 27W
Rhône →, France 18 E6 43 28N 4 42 E
Rhum, U.K. 12 E2 57 0N 6 20W
Rhyl, U.K. 10 D4 53 20N 3 29W
Riachão, Brazil 93 E9 7 20S 46 37W
Riasi, India 43 C6 33 10N 74 50 E
Riau □, Indonesia 36 D2 0 0 102 35 E
Riau, Kepulauan, Indonesia 36 D2 0 30N 104 20 E
Riau Arch. = Riau, Kepulauan, Indonesia 36 D2 0 30N 104 20 E
Ribadeo, Spain 19 A2 43 35N 7 5W
Ribas do Rio Pardo, Brazil 93 H8 20 27S 53 46W
Ribble →, U.K. 10 D5 53 52N 2 25W
Ribe, Denmark 9 J13 55 19N 8 44 E
Ribeira Brava, Madeira 22 D2 32 41N 17 4W
Ribeirão Prêto, Brazil 95 A6 21 10S 47 50W
Riberalta, Bolivia 92 F5 11 0S 66 0W
Riccarton, N.Z. 59 K4 43 32S 172 37 E
Rice, U.S.A. 85 L12 34 5N 114 51W
Rice L., Canada 78 B6 44 12N 78 10W
Rice Lake, U.S.A. 80 C9 45 30N 91 44W
Rich, C., Canada 78 B4 44 43N 80 38W
Richards Bay, S. Africa 57 D5 28 48S 32 6 E
Richardson →, Canada 73 B6 58 25N 111 14W
Richardson Lakes, U.S.A. 76 C10 44 46N 70 58W
Richardson Springs, U.S.A. 84 F5 39 51N 121 46W
Riche, C., Australia 61 F2 34 36S 118 47 E
Richey, U.S.A. 80 B2 47 39N 105 4W
Richfield, U.S.A. 83 G8 38 46N 112 5W
Richfield Springs, U.S.A. 79 D10 42 51N 74 59W
Richford, U.S.A. 79 B12 45 0N 72 40W
Richibucto, Canada 71 C7 46 42N 64 54W
Richland, Ga., U.S.A. 77 J3 32 5N 84 40W
Richland, Wash., U.S.A. 82 C4 46 17N 119 18W
Richland Center, U.S.A. 80 D9 43 21N 90 23W
Richlands, U.S.A. 76 G5 37 6N 81 48W
Richmond, Australia 62 C3 20 43S 143 8 E
Richmond, N.Z. 59 J4 41 20S 173 12 E
Richmond, U.K. 10 C6 54 25N 1 43W
Richmond, Calif., U.S.A. 84 H4 37 56N 122 21W
Richmond, Ind., U.S.A. 76 F3 39 50N 84 53W
Richmond, Ky., U.S.A. 76 G3 37 45N 84 18W
Richmond, Mich., U.S.A. 78 D2 42 49N 82 45W
Richmond, Mo., U.S.A. 80 F8 39 17N 93 58W
Richmond, Tex., U.S.A. 81 L7 29 35N 95 46W
Richmond, Utah, U.S.A. 82 F8 41 56N 111 48W
Richmond, Va., U.S.A. 76 G7 37 33N 77 27W
Richmond, Vt., U.S.A. 79 B12 44 24N 72 59W
Richmond Hill, Canada 78 C5 43 52N 79 27W
Richmond Ra., Australia 63 D5 29 0S 152 45 E
Richwood, U.S.A. 76 F5 38 14N 80 32W
Ridder = Leninogorsk, Kazakstan 26 D9 50 20N 83 30 E
Riddlesburg, U.S.A. 78 F6 40 9N 78 15W
Ridgecrest, U.S.A. 85 K9 35 38N 117 40W
Ridgefield, Conn., U.S.A. 79 E11 41 17N 73 30W
Ridgefield, Wash., U.S.A. 84 E4 45 49N 122 45W
Ridgeland, U.S.A. 77 J5 32 29N 80 59W
Ridgetown, Canada 78 D3 42 26N 81 52W
Ridgewood, U.S.A. 79 F10 40 59N 74 7W
Ridgway, U.S.A. 78 E6 41 25N 78 44W
Riding Mountain Nat. Park, Canada 73 C9 50 50N 100 0W
Ridley, Mt., Australia 61 F3 33 12S 122 7 E
Riebeek-Oos, S. Africa 56 E4 33 10S 26 10 E
Ried, Austria 16 D7 48 14N 13 30 E
Riesa, Germany 16 C7 51 17N 13 17 E
Riet →, S. Africa 56 D3 29 0S 23 54 E
Rietbron, S. Africa 56 E3 32 54S 23 10 E
Rietfontein, Namibia 56 C3 21 58S 20 58 E
Rieti, Italy 20 C5 42 24N 12 51 E
Riffe L., U.S.A. 84 D4 46 32N 122 26W
Rifle, U.S.A. 82 G10 39 32N 107 47W
Rift Valley □, Kenya 54 B4 0 20N 36 0 E
Rīga, Latvia 9 H21 56 53N 24 8 E
Riga, G. of, Latvia 9 H20 57 40N 23 45 E
Rīgān, Iran 45 D8 28 37N 58 58 E
Rigas Jūras Līcis = Riga, G. of, Latvia 9 H20 57 40N 23 45 E
Rigaud, Canada 79 A10 45 29N 74 18W
Rigby, U.S.A. 82 E8 43 40N 111 55W
Rīgestān, Afghan. 40 D4 30 15N 65 0 E
Riggins, U.S.A. 82 D5 45 25N 116 19W
Rigolet, Canada 71 B8 54 10N 58 23W
Rihand Dam, India 43 G10 24 9N 83 2 E
Riihimäki, Finland 9 F21 60 45N 24 48 E
Riiser-Larsen-halvøya, Antarctica 5 C4 68 0S 35 0 E
Rijeka, Croatia 16 F8 45 20N 14 21 E
Rijssen, Neths. 15 B6 52 19N 6 31 E
Rikuzentakada, Japan 30 E10 39 0N 141 40 E
Riley, U.S.A. 82 E4 43 32N 119 28W
Rimah, Wadi ar →, Si. Arabia 44 E4 26 5N 41 30 E
Rimbey, Canada 72 C6 52 35N 114 15W
Rimersburg, U.S.A. 78 E5 41 3N 79 30W
Rímini, Italy 20 B5 44 3N 12 33 E
Rimouski, Canada 71 C6 48 27N 68 30W
Rimrock, U.S.A. 84 D5 46 38N 121 10W
Rinca, Indonesia 37 F5 8 45S 119 35 E
Rincón de Romos, Mexico 86 C4 22 14N 102 18W
Rinconada, Argentina 94 A2 22 26S 66 10W
Rind →, India 43 G9 25 53N 80 33 E
Ringas, India 42 F6 27 21N 75 34 E
Ringkøbing, Denmark 9 H13 56 5N 8 15 E
Ringvassøy, Norway 8 B18 69 56N 19 15 E
Ringwood, U.S.A. 79 E10 41 7N 74 15W
Rinjani, Indonesia 36 F5 8 24S 116 28 E
Rio Branco, Brazil 92 E5 9 58S 67 49W
Río Branco, Uruguay 95 C5 32 40S 53 40W
Río Bravo del Norte →, Mexico 87 B5 25 57N 97 9W
Rio Brilhante, Brazil 95 A5 21 48S 54 33W
Rio Claro, Brazil 95 A6 22 19S 47 35W
Rio Claro, Trin. & Tob. 89 D7 10 20N 61 25W
Río Colorado, Argentina 96 D4 39 0S 64 0W
Río Cuarto, Argentina 94 C3 33 10S 64 25W
Rio das Pedras, Mozam. 57 C6 23 8S 35 28 E
Rio de Janeiro, Brazil 95 A7 23 0S 43 12W
Rio de Janeiro □, Brazil 95 A7 22 50S 43 0W
Rio do Sul, Brazil 95 B6 27 13S 49 37W
Río Gallegos, Argentina 96 G3 51 35S 69 15W
Rio Grande = Grande, Rio →, U.S.A. 81 N6 25 58N 97 9W
Río Grande, Argentina 96 G3 53 50S 67 45W
Rio Grande, Brazil 95 C5 32 0S 52 20W
Río Grande, Mexico 86 C4 23 50N 103 2W
Río Grande, Nic. 88 D3 12 54N 83 33W
Rio Grande City, U.S.A. 81 M5 26 23N 98 49W
Río Grande de Santiago →, Mexico 86 C3 21 36N 105 26W
Rio Grande do Norte □, Brazil 93 E11 5 40S 36 0W
Rio Grande do Sul □, Brazil 95 C5 30 0S 53 0W
Río Hato, Panama 88 E3 8 22N 80 10W
Río Lagartos, Mexico 87 C7 21 36N 88 10W
Rio Largo, Brazil 93 E11 9 28S 35 50W
Río Mulatos, Bolivia 92 G5 19 40S 66 50W
Río Muni = Mbini □, Eq. Guin. 52 D2 1 30N 10 0 E
Rio Negro, Brazil 95 B6 26 0S 49 55W
Rio Pardo, Brazil 95 C5 30 0S 52 30W
Rio Rancho, U.S.A. 83 J10 35 14N 106 38W
Río Segundo, Argentina 94 C3 31 40S 63 59W
Río Tercero, Argentina 94 C3 32 15S 64 8W
Rio Verde, Brazil 93 G8 17 50S 51 0W
Río Verde, Mexico 87 C5 21 56N 99 59W
Rio Vista, U.S.A. 84 G5 38 10N 121 42W
Ríobamba, Ecuador 92 D3 1 50S 78 45W
Ríohacha, Colombia 92 A4 11 33N 72 55W
Ríosucio, Colombia 92 B3 7 27N 77 7W
Riou L., Canada 73 B7 59 7N 106 25W
Ripley, Canada 78 B3 44 4N 81 35W
Ripley, Calif., U.S.A. 85 M12 33 32N 114 39W
Ripley, N.Y., U.S.A. 78 D5 42 16N 79 43W
Ripley, Tenn., U.S.A. 81 H10 35 45N 89 32W
Ripley, W. Va., U.S.A. 76 F5 38 49N 81 43W
Ripon, U.K. 10 C6 54 9N 1 31W
Ripon, Calif., U.S.A. 84 H5 37 44N 121 7W
Ripon, Wis., U.S.A. 76 D1 43 51N 88 50W
Rishā', W. ar →, Si. Arabia 44 E5 25 33N 44 5 E
Rishiri-Tō, Japan 30 B10 45 11N 141 15 E
Rishon le Ẓiyyon, Israel 47 D3 31 58N 34 48 E
Rison, U.S.A. 81 J8 33 58N 92 11W
Risør, Norway 9 G13 58 43N 9 13 E
Rita Blanca Cr. →, U.S.A. 81 H3 35 40N 102 29W
Ritter, Mt., U.S.A. 84 H7 37 41N 119 12W
Rittman, U.S.A. 78 F3 40 58N 81 47W
Ritzville, U.S.A. 82 C4 47 8N 118 23W
Riva del Garda, Italy 20 B4 45 53N 10 50 E
Rivadavia, Buenos Aires, Argentina 94 D3 35 29S 62 59W
Rivadavia, Mendoza, Argentina 94 C2 33 13S 68 30W
Rivadavia, Salta, Argentina 94 A3 24 5S 62 54W
Rivadavia, Chile 94 B1 29 57S 70 35W
Rivas, Nic. 88 D2 11 30N 85 50W
River Cess, Liberia 50 G4 5 30N 9 32W
River Jordan, Canada 84 B2 48 26N 124 3W
Rivera, Argentina 94 D3 37 12S 63 14W
Rivera, Uruguay 95 C4 31 0S 55 50W
Riverbank, U.S.A. 84 H6 37 44N 120 56W
Riverdale, U.S.A. 84 J7 36 26N 119 52W
Riverhead, U.S.A. 79 F12 40 55N 72 40W
Riverhurst, Canada 73 C7 50 55N 106 50W
Rivers, Canada 73 C8 50 2N 100 14W
Rivers Inlet, Canada 72 C3 51 42N 127 15W
Riversdale, S. Africa 56 E3 34 7S 21 15 E
Riverside, U.S.A. 85 M9 33 59N 117 22W
Riverton, Canada 73 C9 51 1N 97 0W
Riverton, N.Z. 59 M2 46 21S 168 0 E
Riverton, U.S.A. 82 E9 43 2N 108 23W
Riverton Heights, U.S.A. 84 C4 47 28N 122 17W
Riviera, U.S.A. 85 K12 35 4N 114 35W
Riviera di Levante, Italy 18 D8 44 15N 9 30 E
Riviera di Ponente, Italy 18 D8 44 10N 8 20 E
Rivière-au-Renard, Canada 71 C7 48 59N 64 23W
Rivière-du-Loup, Canada 71 C6 47 50N 69 30W

Rzhev

Rivière-Pentecôte, *Canada* **71 C6** 49 57N 67 1W
Rivière-Pilote, *Martinique* . **89 D7** 14 26N 60 53W
Rivière St. Paul, *Canada* .. **71 B8** 51 28N 57 45W
Rivne, *Ukraine* .... **17 C14** 50 40N 26 10 E
Rivoli, *Italy* .... **18 D7** 45 3N 7 31 E
Riyadh = Ar Riyāḍ,
Si. Arabia .... **46 C4** 24 41N 46 42 E
Rize, *Turkey* .... **25 F7** 41 0N 40 30 E
Rizhao, *China* .... **35 G10** 35 25N 119 30 E
Rizokarpaso, *Cyprus* ...... **23 D13** 35 36N 34 23 E
Rizzuto, C., *Italy* .... **20 E7** 38 53N 17 5 E
Rjukan, *Norway* .... **9 G13** 59 54N 8 33 E
Road Town, *Br. Virgin Is.* .. **89 C7** 18 27N 64 37W
Roan Plateau, *U.S.A.* **82 G9** 39 20N 109 20W
Roanne, *France* .... **18 C6** 46 3N 4 4 E
Roanoke, *Ala., U.S.A.* **77 J3** 33 9N 85 22W
Roanoke, *Va., U.S.A.* **76 G6** 37 16N 79 56W
Roanoke →, *U.S.A.* **77 H7** 35 57N 76 42W
Roanoke I., *U.S.A.* **77 H8** 35 55N 75 40W
Roanoke Rapids, *U.S.A.* ... **77 G7** 36 28N 77 40W
Roatán, *Honduras* **88 C2** 16 18N 86 35W
Robāt Sang, *Iran* .... **45 C8** 35 35N 59 10 E
Robbins I., *Australia* ...... **62 G4** 40 42S 145 0 E
Robe →, *Australia* .... **60 D2** 21 42S 116 15 E
Robert Lee, *U.S.A.* **81 K4** 31 54N 100 29W
Robertsdale, *U.S.A.* **78 F6** 40 11N 78 6W
Robertsganj, *India* .... **43 G10** 24 44N 83 4 E
Robertson, *S. Africa* ...... **56 E2** 33 46S 19 50 E
Robertson I., *Antarctica* ... **5 C18** 65 15S 59 30W
Robertson Ra., *Australia* .. **60 D3** 23 15S 121 0 E
Roberval, *Canada* **71 C5** 48 32N 72 15W
Robeson Chan., *Greenland* . **4 A4** 82 0N 61 30W
Robesonia, *U.S.A.* **79 F8** 40 21N 76 8W
Robinson, *U.S.A.* **76 F2** 39 0N 87 44W
Robinson →, *Australia* .... **62 B2** 16 3S 137 16 E
Robinson Ra., *Australia* ... **61 E2** 25 40S 119 0 E
Roblin, *Canada* **73 C8** 51 14N 101 21W
Roboré, *Bolivia* **92 G7** 18 10S 59 45W
Robson, *Canada* **72 D5** 49 20N 117 41W
Robson, Mt., *Canada* **72 C5** 53 10N 119 10W
Robstown, *U.S.A.* **81 M6** 27 47N 97 40W
Roca, C. da, *Portugal* **19 C1** 38 40N 9 31W
Roca Partida, I., *Mexico* ... **86 D2** 19 1N 112 2W
Rocas, I., *Brazil* **93 D12** 4 0S 34 1W
Rocha, *Uruguay* **95 C5** 34 30S 54 25W
Rochdale, *U.K.* **10 D5** 53 38N 2 9W
Rochefort, *Belgium* .... **15 D5** 50 9N 5 12 E
Rochefort, *France* **18 D3** 45 56N 0 57W
Rochelle, *U.S.A.* **80 E10** 41 56N 89 4W
Rocher River, *Canada* **72 A6** 61 23N 112 44W
Rochester, *U.K.* .... **11 F8** 51 23N 0 31 E
Rochester, *Ind., U.S.A.* **76 E2** 41 4N 86 13W
Rochester, *Minn., U.S.A.* .. **80 C8** 44 1N 92 28W
Rochester, *N.H., U.S.A.* ... **79 C14** 43 18N 70 59W
Rochester, *N.Y., U.S.A.* ... **78 C7** 43 10N 77 37W
Rock →, *Canada* **72 A3** 60 7N 127 7W
Rock Creek, *U.S.A.* **78 E4** 41 40N 80 52W
Rock Falls, *U.S.A.* **80 E10** 41 47N 89 41W
Rock Hill, *U.S.A.* **77 H5** 34 56N 81 1W
Rock Island, *U.S.A.* **80 E9** 41 30N 90 34W
Rock Rapids, *U.S.A.* **80 D6** 43 26N 96 10W
Rock Sound, *Bahamas* **88 B4** 24 54N 76 12W
Rock Springs, *Mont., U.S.A.* **82 C10** 46 49N 106 15W
Rock Springs, *Wyo., U.S.A.* **82 F9** 41 35N 109 14W
Rock Valley, *U.S.A.* **80 D6** 43 12N 96 18W
Rockall, *Atl. Oc.* **6 D3** 57 37N 13 42W
Rockdale, *Tex., U.S.A.* **81 K6** 30 39N 97 0W
Rockdale, *Wash., U.S.A.* ... **84 C5** 47 22N 121 28W
Rockefeller Plateau,
Antarctica **5 E14** 80 0S 140 0W
Rockford, *U.S.A.* **80 D10** 42 16N 89 6W
Rockglen, *Canada* **73 D7** 49 11N 105 57W
Rockhampton, *Australia* ... **62 C5** 23 22S 150 32 E
Rockingham, *Australia* .... **61 F2** 32 15S 115 38 E
Rockingham, *U.S.A.* **77 H6** 34 57N 79 46W
Rockingham B., *Australia* .. **62 B4** 18 5S 146 10 E
Rocklake, *U.S.A.* **80 A5** 48 47N 99 15W
Rockland, *Canada* **79 A9** 45 33N 75 17W
Rockland, *Idaho, U.S.A.* ... **82 E7** 42 34N 112 53W
Rockland, *Maine, U.S.A.* ... **77 C11** 44 6N 69 7W
Rockland, *Mich., U.S.A.* ... **80 B10** 46 44N 89 11W
Rocklin, *U.S.A.* **84 G5** 38 48N 121 14W
Rockmart, *U.S.A.* **77 H3** 34 0N 85 3W
Rockport, *Mass., U.S.A.* ... **79 D14** 42 39N 70 37W
Rockport, *Mo., U.S.A.* **80 E7** 40 25N 95 31W
Rockport, *Tex., U.S.A.* **81 L6** 28 2N 97 3W
Rocksprings, *U.S.A.* **81 K4** 30 1N 100 13W
Rockville, *Conn., U.S.A.* ... **79 E12** 41 52N 72 28W
Rockville, *Md., U.S.A.* **76 F7** 39 5N 77 9W
Rockwall, *U.S.A.* **81 J6** 32 56N 96 28W
Rockwell City, *U.S.A.* **80 D7** 42 24N 94 38W
Rockwood, *Canada* **78 C4** 43 37N 80 8W
Rockwood, *Maine, U.S.A.* .. **77 C11** 45 41N 69 45W
Rockwood, *Tenn., U.S.A.* .. **77 H3** 35 52N 84 41W
Rocky Ford, *U.S.A.* **80 F3** 38 3N 103 43W
Rocky Gully, *Australia* .... **61 F2** 34 30S 116 57 E
Rocky Harbour, *Canada* ... **71 C8** 49 36N 57 55W
Rocky Island L., *Canada* ... **70 C3** 46 55N 83 0W
Rocky Lane, *Canada* **72 B5** 58 31N 116 22W
Rocky Mount, *U.S.A.* **77 H7** 35 57N 77 48W
Rocky Mountain House,
Canada **72 C6** 52 22N 114 55W
Rocky Mountain National
Park, *U.S.A.* **82 F11** 40 25N 105 45W
Rocky Mts., *N. Amer.* **82 G10** 49 0N 115 0W
Rocky Point, *Namibia* ..... **56 B2** 19 3S 12 30 E
Rod, *Pakistan* .... **40 E3** 28 10N 63 5 E
Rødbyhavn, *Denmark* ..... **9 J14** 54 39N 11 22 E
Roddickton, *Canada* **71 B8** 50 51N 56 8W
Rodez, *France* .... **18 D5** 44 21N 2 33 E
Rodhopoú, *Greece* .... **23 D5** 35 34N 23 45 E
Ródhos, *Greece* .... **23 C10** 36 15N 28 10 E
Rodney, *Canada* **78 D3** 42 34N 81 41W
Rodney, C., *N.Z.* .... **59 G5** 36 17S 174 50 E
Rodriguez, *Ind. Oc.* ...... **3 E13** 19 45S 63 20 E
Roe →, *U.K.* **13 A5** 55 6N 6 59W
Roebling, *U.S.A.* **79 F10** 40 7N 74 47W
Roebourne, *Australia* ..... **60 D2** 20 44S 117 9 E
Roebuck B., *Australia* .... **60 C3** 18 5S 122 20 E
Roermond, *Neths.* .... **15 C6** 51 12N 6 0 E
Roes Welcome Sd., *Canada* **69 B11** 65 0N 87 0W
Roeselare, *Belgium* .... **15 D3** 50 57N 3 7 E
Rogachev = Ragachow,
Belarus .... **17 B16** 53 8N 30 5 E
Rogagua, L., *Bolivia* **92 F5** 13 43S 66 50W
Rogatyn, *Ukraine* .... **17 D13** 49 24N 24 36 E
Rogdhia, *Greece* .... **23 D7** 35 22N 25 1 E
Rogers, *U.S.A.* **81 G7** 36 20N 94 7W
Rogers City, *U.S.A.* **76 C4** 45 25N 83 49W
Rogersville, *Canada* **71 C6** 46 44N 65 26W
Roggan →, *Canada* **70 B4** 54 24N 79 25W
Roggan L., *Canada* **70 B4** 54 8N 77 50W
Roggeveldberge, *S. Africa* **56 E3** 32 10S 20 10 E
Rogoaguado, L., *Bolivia* ... **92 F5** 13 0S 65 30W
Rogue →, *U.S.A.* **82 E1** 42 26N 124 26W
Róhda, *Greece* .... **23 A3** 39 48N 19 46 E
Rohnert Park, *U.S.A.* **84 G4** 38 16N 122 40W
Rohri, *Pakistan* .... **42 F3** 27 45N 68 51 E
Rohri Canal, *Pakistan* .... **42 F3** 26 15N 68 27 E
Rohtak, *India* .... **42 E7** 28 55N 76 43 E
Roi Et, *Thailand* .... **38 D4** 16 4N 103 40 E
Roja, *Latvia* .... **9 H20** 57 29N 22 43 E
Rojas, *Argentina* **94 C3** 34 10S 60 45W
Rojo, C., *Mexico* **87 C5** 21 33N 97 20W
Rokan →, *Indonesia* ..... **36 D2** 2 0N 100 50 E
Rokiškis, *Lithuania* .... **9 J21** 55 55N 25 35 E
Rolândia, *Brazil* **95 A5** 23 18S 51 23W
Rolla, *U.S.A.* **81 G9** 37 57N 91 46W
Rolleston, *Australia* ...... **62 C4** 24 28S 148 35 E
Rollingstone, *Australia* ... **62 B4** 19 2S 146 24 E
Roma, *Australia* .... **63 D4** 26 32S 148 49 E
Roma, *Italy* .... **20 D5** 41 54N 12 29 E
Roma, *Sweden* .... **9 H18** 57 32N 18 26 E
Roma, *U.S.A.* **81 M5** 26 25N 99 1W
Romain C., *U.S.A.* **77 J6** 33 0N 79 22W
Romaine, *Canada* **71 B7** 50 13N 60 40W
Romaine →, *Canada* **71 B7** 50 18N 63 47W
Roman, *Romania* .... **17 E14** 46 57N 26 55 E
Romang, *Indonesia* .... **37 F7** 7 30S 127 20 E
Români, *Egypt* .... **47 E1** 30 59N 32 38 E
Romania ■, *Europe* .... **17 F12** 46 0N 25 0 E
Romano, Cayo, *Cuba* **88 B4** 22 0N 77 30W
Romanovka =
Basarabeasca, *Moldova* . **17 E15** 46 21N 28 58 E
Romans-sur-Isère, *France* . **18 D6** 45 3N 5 3 E
Romblon, *Phil.* .... **37 B6** 12 33N 122 17 E
Rome = Roma, *Italy* ...... **20 D5** 41 54N 12 29 E
Rome, *Ga., U.S.A.* **77 H3** 34 15N 85 10W
Rome, *N.Y., U.S.A.* **79 C9** 43 13N 75 27W
Rome, *Pa., U.S.A.* **79 E8** 41 51N 76 21W
Romney, *U.S.A.* **76 F6** 39 21N 78 45W
Romney Marsh, *U.K.* ...... **11 F8** 51 2N 0 54 E
Rømø, *Denmark* .... **9 J13** 55 10N 8 30 E
Romorantin-Lanthenay,
France .... **18 C4** 47 21N 1 45 E
Romsdalen, *Norway* ...... **9 E12** 62 25N 7 52 E
Romsey, *U.K.* **11 G6** 51 0N 1 29W
Ron, *Vietnam* .... **38 D6** 17 53N 106 27 E
Rona, *U.K.* **12 D3** 57 34N 5 59W
Ronan, *U.S.A.* **82 C6** 47 32N 114 6W
Roncador, Cayos,
Caribbean **88 D3** 13 32N 80 4W
Roncador, Serra do, *Brazil* **93 F8** 12 30S 52 30W
Ronda, *Spain* **19 D3** 36 46N 5 12W
Rondane, *Norway* .... **9 F13** 61 57N 9 50 E
Rondônia □, *Brazil* **92 F6** 11 0S 63 0W
Rondonópolis, *Brazil* **93 G8** 16 28S 54 38W
Rong, Koh, *Cambodia* .... **39 G4** 10 45N 103 15 E
Ronge, L. la, *Canada* **73 B7** 55 6N 105 17W
Rønne, *Denmark* .... **9 J16** 55 6N 14 43 E
Ronne Ice Shelf, *Antarctica* **5 D18** 78 0S 60 0W
Ronsard, C., *Australia* .... **61 D1** 24 46S 113 10 E
Ronse, *Belgium* .... **15 D3** 50 45N 3 35 E
Roodepoort, *S. Africa* ..... **57 D4** 26 11S 27 54 E
Roof Butte, *U.S.A.* **83 H9** 36 28N 109 5W
Rooiboklaagte →, *Namibia* **56 C3** 20 50S 21 0 E
Roorkee, *India* .... **42 E7** 29 52N 77 59 E
Roosendaal, *Neths.* ...... **15 C4** 51 32N 4 29 E
Roosevelt, *U.S.A.* **82 F8** 40 18N 109 59W
Roosevelt →, *Brazil* **92 E6** 7 35S 60 20W
Roosevelt, Mt., *Canada* ... **72 B3** 58 26N 125 20W
Roosevelt I., *Antarctica* ... **5 D12** 79 30S 162 0W
Roper →, *Australia* ...... **62 A2** 14 43S 135 27 E
Roper Bar, *Australia* ..... **62 A1** 14 44S 134 44 E
Roque Pérez, *Argentina* ... **94 D4** 35 25S 59 24W
Roquetas de Mar, *Spain* ... **19 D4** 36 46N 2 36W
Roraima □, *Brazil* **92 C6** 2 0N 61 30W
Roraima, Mt., *Venezuela* .. **92 B6** 5 10N 60 40W
Røros, *Norway* .... **9 E14** 62 35N 11 23 E
Rosa, *Zambia* .... **55 D3** 9 33S 31 15 E
Rosa, L., *Bahamas* **89 B5** 21 0N 73 30W
Rosa, Monte, *Europe* ..... **18 D7** 45 57N 7 53 E
Rosalia, *U.S.A.* **82 C5** 47 14N 117 22W
Rosamond, *U.S.A.* **85 L8** 34 52N 118 10W
Rosario, *Argentina* **94 C3** 33 0S 60 40W
Rosário, *Brazil* **93 D10** 3 0S 44 15W
Rosario, *Baja Calif., Mexico* **86 B1** 30 0N 115 50W
Rosario, *Sinaloa, Mexico* .. **86 C3** 23 0N 105 52W
Rosario, *Paraguay* **94 A4** 24 30S 57 35W
Rosario de la Frontera,
Argentina **94 B3** 25 50S 65 0W
Rosario de Lerma,
Argentina **94 A2** 24 59S 65 35W
Rosario del Tala, *Argentina* **94 C4** 32 20S 59 10W
Rosário do Sul, *Brazil* **95 C5** 30 15S 54 55W
Rosarito, *Mexico* **85 N9** 32 18N 117 4W
Roscoe, *U.S.A.* **79 E10** 41 56N 74 55W
Roscommon, *Ireland* **13 C3** 53 38N 8 11W
Roscommon □, *Ireland* ... **13 C3** 53 49N 8 23W
Roscrea, *Ireland* **13 D4** 52 57N 7 49W
Rose →, *Australia* .... **62 A2** 14 16S 135 45 E
Rose Blanche, *Canada* **71 C8** 47 38N 58 45W
Rose Pt., *Canada* **72 C2** 54 11N 131 39W
Rose Valley, *Canada* **73 C8** 52 19N 103 49W
Roseau, *Domin.* **89 C7** 15 20N 61 24W
Roseau, *U.S.A.* **80 A7** 48 51N 95 46W
Rosebery, *Australia* ...... **62 G4** 41 46S 145 33 E
Rosebud, *S. Dak., U.S.A.* .. **80 D4** 43 14N 100 51W
Rosebud, *Tex., U.S.A.* **81 K6** 31 4N 96 59W
Roseburg, *U.S.A.* **82 E2** 43 13N 123 20W
Rosedale, *U.S.A.* **81 J9** 33 51N 91 2W
Roseland, *U.S.A.* **84 G4** 38 25N 122 43W
Rosemary, *Canada* **72 C6** 50 46N 112 5W
Rosenberg, *U.S.A.* **81 L7** 29 34N 95 49W
Rosenheim, *Germany* ..... **16 E7** 47 51N 12 7 E
Roses, G. de, *Spain* ...... **19 A7** 42 10N 3 15 E
Rosetown, *Canada* **73 C7** 51 35N 107 59W
Roseville, *Calif., U.S.A.* ... **84 G5** 38 45N 121 17W
Roseville, *Mich., U.S.A.* ... **78 D2** 42 30N 82 56W
Rosewood, *Australia* ..... **63 D5** 27 38S 152 36 E
Roshkhvār, *Iran* .... **45 C8** 34 58N 59 37 E
Rosignano Marittimo, *Italy* **20 C4** 43 24N 10 28 E
Rosignol, *Guyana* **92 B7** 6 15N 57 30W
Roşiori de Vede, *Romania* . **17 F13** 44 9N 25 0 E
Roskilde, *Denmark* ...... **9 J15** 55 38N 12 3 E
Roslavl, *Russia* .... **24 D5** 53 57N 32 55 E
Rosmead, *S. Africa* ...... **56 E4** 31 29S 25 8 E
Ross, *Australia* .... **62 G4** 42 2S 147 30 E
Ross, *N.Z.* .... **59 K3** 42 53S 170 49 E
Ross I., *Antarctica* .... **5 D11** 77 30S 168 0 E
Ross Ice Shelf, *Antarctica* . **5 E12** 80 0S 180 0 E
Ross L., *U.S.A.* **82 B3** 48 44N 121 4W
Ross-on-Wye, *U.K.* **11 F5** 51 54N 2 34W
Ross River, *Australia* ..... **62 C1** 23 44S 134 30 E
Ross River, *Canada* **72 A2** 62 30N 131 30W
Ross Sea, *Antarctica* ...... **5 D11** 74 0S 178 0 E
Rossall Pt., *U.K.* **10 D4** 53 55N 3 3W
Rossan Pt., *Ireland* **13 B3** 54 42N 8 47W
Rossano, *Italy* .... **20 E7** 39 36N 16 39 E
Rossburn, *Canada* **73 C8** 50 40N 100 49W
Rosseau, *Canada* **78 A5** 45 16N 79 39W
Rosseau L., *Canada* **78 A5** 45 10N 79 35W
Rosses, The, *Ireland* **13 A3** 55 2N 8 20W
Rossignol, L., *Canada* **70 B5** 52 43N 73 40W
Rossignol Res., *Canada* ... **71 D6** 44 12N 65 10W
Rossland, *Canada* **72 D5** 49 6N 117 50W
Rosslare, *Ireland* **13 D5** 52 17N 6 24W
Rosso, *Mauritania* **50 E2** 16 40N 15 45W
Rossosh, *Russia* .... **25 D6** 50 15N 39 28 E
Røssvatnet, *Norway* ..... **8 D16** 65 45N 14 5 E
Røst, *Norway* .... **8 C15** 67 32N 12 0 E
Rosthern, *Canada* **73 C7** 52 40N 106 20W
Rostock, *Germany* .... **16 A7** 54 5N 12 8 E
Rostov, *Don, Russia* ...... **25 E6** 47 15N 39 45 E
Rostov, *Yaroslavl, Russia* . **24 C6** 57 14N 39 25 E
Roswell, *Ga., U.S.A.* **77 H3** 34 2N 84 22W
Roswell, *N. Mex., U.S.A.* .. **81 J2** 33 24N 104 32W
Rotan, *U.S.A.* **81 J4** 32 51N 100 28W
Rother →, *U.K.* .... **11 G8** 50 59N 0 45 E
Rotherham, *U.K.* **10 D6** 53 26N 1 20W
Rothes, *U.K.* **12 D5** 57 32N 3 13W
Rothesay, *Canada* **71 C6** 45 23N 66 0W
Rothesay, *U.K.* **12 F3** 55 50N 5 3W
Roti, *Indonesia* .... **37 F6** 10 50S 123 0 E
Rotondo, Mte., *France* .... **18 E8** 42 14N 9 8 E
Rotoroa, L., *N.Z.* .... **59 J4** 41 55S 172 39 E
Rotorua, *N.Z.* .... **59 H6** 38 9S 176 16 E
Rotorua, L., *N.Z.* .... **59 H6** 38 5S 176 18 E
Rotterdam, *Neths.* .... **15 C4** 51 55N 4 30 E
Rotterdam, *U.S.A.* **79 D10** 42 48N 74 1W
Rottnest I., *Australia* ..... **61 F2** 32 0S 115 27 E
Rottumeroog, *Neths.* ..... **15 A6** 53 33N 6 34 E
Rottweil, *Germany* .... **16 D5** 48 9N 8 37 E
Rotuma, *Fiji* .... **64 J9** 12 25S 177 5 E
Roubaix, *France* .... **18 A5** 50 40N 3 10 E
Rouen, *France* .... **18 B4** 49 27N 1 4 E
Rouleau, *Canada* **73 C8** 50 10N 104 56W
Round Mountain, *U.S.A.* ... **82 G5** 38 43N 117 4W
Round Mt., *Australia* ..... **63 E5** 30 26S 152 16 E
Round Rock, *U.S.A.* **81 K6** 30 31N 97 41W
Roundup, *U.S.A.* **82 C9** 46 27N 108 33W
Rousay, *U.K.* **12 B5** 59 10N 3 2W
Rouses Point, *U.S.A.* **79 B11** 44 59N 73 22W
Rouseville, *U.S.A.* **78 E5** 41 28N 79 42W
Roussillon, *France* .... **18 E5** 42 30N 2 35 E
Rouxville, *S. Africa* ...... **56 E4** 30 25S 26 50 E
Rouyn-Noranda, *Canada* ... **70 C4** 48 20N 79 0W
Rovaniemi, *Finland* ...... **8 C21** 66 29N 25 41 E
Rovereto, *Italy* .... **20 B4** 45 53N 11 3 E
Rovigo, *Italy* .... **20 B4** 45 4N 11 47 E
Rovinj, *Croatia* .... **16 F7** 45 5N 13 40 E
Rovno = Rivne, *Ukraine* ... **17 C14** 50 40N 26 10 E
Rovuma = Ruvuma →,
Tanzania .... **55 E5** 10 29S 40 28 E
Row'ān, *Iran* .... **45 C6** 35 8N 48 51 E
Rowena, *Australia* .... **63 D4** 29 48S 148 55 E
Rowley Shoals, *Australia* .. **60 C2** 17 30S 119 0 E
Roxas, *Phil.* .... **37 B6** 11 36N 122 49 E
Roxboro, *U.S.A.* **77 G6** 36 24N 78 59W
Roxburgh, *N.Z.* .... **59 L2** 45 33S 169 19 E
Roxbury, *U.S.A.* **78 F7** 40 6N 77 39W
Roy, *Mont., U.S.A.* **82 C9** 47 20N 108 58W
Roy, *N. Mex., U.S.A.* **81 H2** 35 57N 104 12W
Roy, *Utah, U.S.A.* **82 F7** 41 10N 112 2W
Royal Canal, *Ireland* **13 C4** 53 30N 7 13W
Royal Leamington Spa,
U.K. **11 E6** 52 18N 1 31W
Royal Tunbridge Wells,
U.K. .... **11 F8** 51 7N 0 16 E
Royan, *France* **18 D3** 45 37N 1 2W
Royston, *U.K.* **11 E7** 52 3N 0 0W
Rozdilna, *Ukraine* .... **17 E16** 46 50N 30 2 E
Rozhyshche, *Ukraine* .... **17 C13** 50 54N 25 15 E
Rtishchevo, *Russia* ...... **24 C7** 52 18N 43 46 E
Ruacaná, *Namibia* .... **56 B1** 17 27S 14 21 E
Ruahine Ra., *N.Z.* .... **59 H6** 39 55S 176 2 E
Ruapehu, *N.Z.* .... **59 H5** 39 17S 175 35 E
Ruapuke I., *N.Z.* .... **59 M2** 46 46S 168 31 E
Ruâq, W. →, *Egypt* ...... **47 F2** 30 0N 33 49 E
Rub' al Khālī, *Si. Arabia* .. **46 D4** 18 0N 48 0 E
Rubeho Mts., *Tanzania* ... **54 D4** 6 50S 36 25 E
Rubh a' Mhail, *U.K.* **12 F2** 55 56N 6 8W
Rubha Hunish, *U.K.* **12 D2** 57 42N 6 20W
Rubha Robhanais = Lewis,
Butt of, *U.K.* **12 C2** 58 31N 6 16W
Rubicon →, *U.S.A.* **84 G5** 38 53N 121 4W
Rubio, *Venezuela* **92 B4** 7 43N 72 22W
Rubtsovsk, *Russia* .... **26 D9** 51 30N 81 10 E
Ruby L., *U.S.A.* **82 F6** 40 10N 115 28W
Ruby Mts., *U.S.A.* **82 F6** 40 30N 115 20W
Rubyvale, *Australia* ...... **62 C4** 23 25S 147 42 E
Rūd Sar, *Iran* .... **45 B6** 37 8N 50 18 E
Rudall →, *Australia* ..... **60 D3** 22 34S 122 13 E
Rudewa, *Tanzania* .... **55 E3** 10 7S 34 40 E
Rudnyy, *Kazakstan* ...... **26 D7** 52 57N 63 7 E
Rudolfa, Ostrov, *Russia* ... **26 A6** 81 45N 58 30 E
Rudyard, *U.S.A.* **76 B3** 46 14N 84 36W
Rufiji →, *Tanzania* ...... **54 D4** 7 50S 39 15 E
Rufino, *Argentina* **94 C3** 34 20S 62 50W
Rufunsa, *Zambia* .... **55 F2** 15 4S 29 34 E
Rugby, *U.K.* **11 E6** 52 23N 1 16W
Rugby, *U.S.A.* **80 A5** 48 22N 100 0W
Rügen, *Germany* .... **16 A7** 54 22N 13 24 E
Ruhengeri, *Rwanda* ...... **54 C2** 1 30S 29 36 E
Ruhnu, *Estonia* .... **9 H20** 57 48N 23 15 E
Ruhr →, *Germany* .... **16 C4** 51 27N 6 43 E
Ruhuhu →, *Tanzania* .... **55 E3** 10 31S 34 34 E
Ruidoso, *U.S.A.* **83 K11** 33 20N 105 41W
Ruivo, Pico, *Madeira* **22 D3** 32 45N 16 56W
Rujm Tal'at al Jamā'ah,
Jordan .... **47 E4** 30 24N 35 30 E
Ruk, *Pakistan* .... **42 F3** 27 50N 68 42 E
Rukhla, *Pakistan* .... **42 C4** 32 27N 71 57 E
Ruki →, *Dem. Rep. of
the Congo* .... **52 E3** 0 5N 18 17 E
Rukwa □, *Tanzania* ...... **54 D3** 7 0S 31 30 E
Rukwa, L., *Tanzania* ..... **54 D3** 8 0S 32 20 E
Rulhieres, C., *Australia* ... **60 B4** 13 56S 127 22 E
Rum = Rhum, *U.K.* **12 E2** 57 0N 6 20W
Rum Cay, *Bahamas* **89 B5** 23 40N 74 58W
Rum Jungle, *Australia* .... **60 B5** 13 0S 130 59 E
Rumāḥ, *Si. Arabia* .... **44 E5** 25 29N 47 10 E
Rumania = Romania ■,
Europe .... **17 F12** 46 0N 25 0 E
Rumaylah, *Iraq* .... **44 D5** 30 47N 47 37 E
Rumbêk, *Sudan* .... **51 G11** 6 54N 29 37 E
Rumford, *U.S.A.* **77 C10** 44 33N 70 33W
Rumia, *Poland* .... **17 A10** 54 37N 18 25 E
Rumoi, *Japan* .... **30 C10** 43 56N 141 39 E
Rumonge, *Burundi* .... **54 C2** 3 59S 29 26 E
Rumson, *U.S.A.* **79 F11** 40 23N 74 0W
Rumuruti, *Kenya* .... **54 B4** 0 17N 36 32 E
Runan, *China* .... **34 H8** 33 0N 114 30 E
Runanga, *N.Z.* .... **59 K3** 42 25S 171 15 E
Runaway, C., *N.Z.* .... **59 G6** 37 32S 177 59 E
Runcorn, *U.K.* **10 D5** 53 21N 2 44W
Rundu, *Namibia* .... **56 B2** 17 52S 19 43 E
Rungwa, *Tanzania* .... **54 D3** 6 55S 33 32 E
Rungwa →, *Tanzania* .... **54 D3** 7 36S 31 50 E
Rungwe, *Tanzania* .... **55 D3** 9 11S 33 32 E
Rungwe, Mt., *Tanzania* ... **52 F6** 9 8S 33 40 E
Runton Ra., *Australia* .... **60 D3** 23 31S 123 6 E
Ruoqiang, *China* .... **32 C3** 38 55N 88 10 E
Rupa, *India* .... **41 F18** 27 15N 92 21 E
Rupar, *India* .... **42 D7** 31 2N 76 38 E
Rupat, *Indonesia* .... **36 D2** 1 45N 101 40 E
Rupen →, *India* .... **42 H4** 23 28N 71 31 E
Rupert, *U.S.A.* **82 E7** 42 37N 113 41W
Rupert →, *Canada* **70 B4** 51 29N 78 45W
Rupert B., *Canada* **70 B4** 51 35N 79 0W
Rupert House =
Waskaganish, *Canada* .. **70 B4** 51 30N 78 40W
Rupsa, *India* .... **43 J12** 21 37N 87 1 E
Rurrenabaque, *Bolivia* **92 F5** 14 30S 67 32W
Rusambo, *Zimbabwe* ..... **55 F3** 16 30S 32 4 E
Rusape, *Zimbabwe* ...... **55 F3** 18 35S 32 8 E
Ruschuk = Ruse, *Bulgaria* . **21 C12** 43 48N 25 59 E
Ruse, *Bulgaria* .... **21 C12** 43 48N 25 59 E
Rush, *Ireland* **13 C5** 53 31N 6 6W
Rushan, *China* .... **35 F11** 36 56N 121 30 E
Rushden, *U.K.* **11 E7** 52 18N 0 35W
Rushmore, Mt., *U.S.A.* **80 D3** 43 53N 103 28W
Rushville, *Ill., U.S.A.* **80 E9** 40 7N 90 34W
Rushville, *Ind., U.S.A.* **76 F3** 39 37N 85 27W
Rushville, *Nebr., U.S.A.* ... **80 D3** 42 43N 102 28W
Russas, *Brazil* **93 D11** 4 55S 37 50W
Russell, *Canada* **73 C8** 50 50N 101 20W
Russell, *Kans., U.S.A.* **80 F5** 38 54N 98 52W
Russell, *N.Y., U.S.A.* **79 B9** 44 27N 75 9W
Russell, *Pa., U.S.A.* **78 E5** 41 56N 79 8W
Russell L., *Man., Canada* .. **73 B8** 56 15N 101 30W
Russell L., *N.W.T., Canada* **72 A5** 63 5N 115 44W
Russellkonda, *India* ..... **41 K14** 19 57N 84 42 E
Russellville, *Ala., U.S.A.* .. **77 H2** 34 30N 87 44W
Russellville, *Ark., U.S.A.* .. **81 H8** 35 17N 93 8W
Russellville, *Ky., U.S.A.* .. **77 G2** 36 51N 86 53W
Russia ■, *Eurasia* .... **27 C11** 62 0N 105 0 E
Russian →, *U.S.A.* **84 G3** 38 27N 123 8W
Russkoye Ustie, *Russia* ... **4 B15** 71 0N 149 0 E
Rustam, *Pakistan* .... **42 B5** 34 25N 72 13 E
Rustam Shahr, *Pakistan* ... **42 F2** 26 58N 66 6 E
Rustavi, *Georgia* .... **25 F8** 41 30N 45 0 E
Rustenburg, *S. Africa* .... **56 D4** 25 41S 27 14 E
Ruston, *U.S.A.* **81 J8** 32 32N 92 38W
Rutana, *Burundi* .... **54 C3** 3 55S 30 0 E
Ruteng, *Indonesia* .... **37 F6** 8 35S 120 30 E
Ruth, *U.S.A.* **78 C2** 43 42N 82 45W
Rutherford, *U.S.A.* **84 G4** 38 26N 122 24W
Rutland, *U.S.A.* **79 C12** 43 37N 72 58W
Rutland □, *U.K.* **11 E7** 52 38N 0 40W
Rutland Water, *U.K.* **11 E7** 52 39N 0 38W
Rutledge →, *Canada* **73 A6** 61 4N 112 0W
Rutledge L., *Canada* **73 A6** 61 33N 110 47W
Rutshuru, *Dem. Rep. of
the Congo* .... **54 C2** 1 13S 29 25 E
Ruvu, *Tanzania* .... **54 D4** 6 49S 38 43 E
Ruvu →, *Tanzania* .... **54 D4** 6 23S 38 52 E
Ruvuma □, *Tanzania* ..... **55 E4** 10 20S 36 0 E
Ruvuma →, *Tanzania* .... **55 E5** 10 29S 40 28 E
Ruwais, *U.A.E.* .... **45 E7** 24 5N 52 50 E
Ruwenzori, *Africa* .... **54 B2** 0 30N 29 55 E
Ruya →, *Zimbabwe* ...... **57 B5** 16 27S 32 5 E
Ruyigi, *Burundi* .... **54 C3** 3 29S 30 15 E
Ružomberok, *Slovak Rep.* . **17 D10** 49 3N 19 17 E
Rwanda ■, *Africa* .... **54 C3** 2 0S 30 0 E
Ryan, L., *U.K.* **12 G3** 55 0N 5 2W
Ryazan, *Russia* .... **24 D6** 54 40N 39 40 E
Ryazhsk, *Russia* .... **24 D7** 53 45N 40 3 E
Rybache = Rybachye,
Kazakstan .... **26 E9** 46 40N 81 20 E
Rybachiy Poluostrov,
Russia .... **24 A5** 69 43N 32 0 E
Rybachye, *Kazakstan* .... **26 E9** 46 40N 81 20 E
Rybinsk, *Russia* .... **24 C6** 58 5N 38 50 E
Rybinskoye Vdkhr., *Russia* **24 C6** 58 30N 38 25 E
Rybnitsa = Râbniţa,
Moldova .... **17 E15** 47 45N 29 0 E
Rycroft, *Canada* **72 B5** 55 45N 118 40W
Ryde, *U.K.* **11 G6** 50 43N 1 9W
Ryderwood, *U.S.A.* **84 D3** 46 23N 123 3W
Rye, *U.K.* .... **11 G8** 50 57N 0 45 E
Rye →, *U.K.* **10 C7** 54 11N 0 44W
Rye Bay, *U.K.* .... **11 G8** 50 52N 0 49 E
Rye Patch Reservoir, *U.S.A.* **82 F4** 40 28N 118 19W
Ryegate, *U.S.A.* **82 C9** 46 18N 109 15W
Ryley, *Canada* **72 C6** 53 17N 112 26W
Ryōtsu, *Japan* .... **30 E9** 38 5N 138 26 E
Rypin, *Poland* .... **17 B10** 53 3N 19 25 E
Ryūgasaki, *Japan* .... **31 G10** 35 54N 140 11 E
Ryūkyū Is. = Ryūkyū-rettō,
Japan .... **31 M3** 26 0N 126 0 E
Ryūkyū-rettō, *Japan* ..... **31 M3** 26 0N 126 0 E
Rzeszów, *Poland* .... **17 C11** 50 0N 21 58 E
Rzhev, *Russia* .... **24 C5** 56 20N 34 20 E

S

Sa, *Thailand* **38 C3** 18 34N 100 45 E
Sa Canal, *Spain* **22 C7** 38 51N 1 23 E
Sa Conillera, *Spain* **22 C7** 38 59N 1 13 E
Sa Dec, *Vietnam* **39 G5** 10 20N 105 46 E
Sa Dragonera, *Spain* **22 B9** 39 35N 2 19 E
Sa Mesquida, *Spain* **22 B11** 39 55N 4 16 E
Sa Savina, *Spain* **22 C7** 38 44N 1 25 E
Sa'ādatābād, *Fārs, Iran* **45 D7** 30 10N 53 5 E
Sa'ādatābād, *Hormozgān, Iran* **45 D7** 28 3N 55 53 E
Sa'ādatābād, *Kermān, Iran* **45 D7** 29 40N 55 51 E
Saale →, *Germany* **16 C6** 51 56N 11 54 E
Saalfeld, *Germany* **16 C6** 50 38N 11 21 E
Saar →, *Europe* **18 B7** 49 41N 6 32 E
Saarbrücken, *Germany* **16 D4** 49 14N 6 59 E
Saaremaa, *Estonia* **9 G20** 58 30N 22 30 E
Saarijärvi, *Finland* **9 E21** 62 43N 25 16 E
Saariselkä, *Finland* **8 B23** 68 16N 28 15 E
Sab 'Ābar, *Syria* **44 C3** 33 46N 37 41 E
Saba, *W. Indies* **89 C7** 17 42N 63 26W
Šabac, *Serbia, Yug.* **21 B8** 44 48N 19 42 E
Sabadell, *Spain* **19 B7** 41 28N 2 7 E
Sabah □, *Malaysia* **36 C5** 6 0N 117 0 E
Sabak Bernam, *Malaysia* **39 L3** 3 46N 100 58 E
Sabalān, Kūhhā-ye, *Iran* **44 B5** 38 15N 47 45 E
Sabalana, Kepulauan, *Indonesia* **37 F5** 6 45S 118 50 E
Sábana de la Mar, *Dom. Rep.* **89 C6** 19 7N 69 24W
Sábanalarga, *Colombia* **92 A4** 10 38N 74 55W
Sabang, *Indonesia* **36 C1** 5 50N 95 15 E
Sabará, *Brazil* **93 G10** 19 55S 43 46W
Sabarmati →, *India* **42 H5** 22 18N 72 22 E
Sabattis, *U.S.A.* **79 B10** 44 6N 74 40W
Sabaria, *Indonesia* **37 E9** 2 5S 138 18 E
Sabhah, *Libya* **51 C8** 27 9N 14 29 E
Sabi →, *India* **42 E7** 28 29N 76 44 E
Sabie, *S. Africa* **57 D5** 25 10S 30 48 E
Sabinal, *Mexico* **86 A3** 30 58N 107 25W
Sabinal, *U.S.A.* **81 L5** 29 19N 99 28W
Sabinas, *Mexico* **86 B4** 27 50N 101 10W
Sabinas →, *Mexico* **86 B4** 27 37N 100 42W
Sabinas Hidalgo, *Mexico* **86 B4** 26 33N 100 10W
Sabine →, *U.S.A.* **81 L8** 29 59N 93 47W
Sabine L., *U.S.A.* **81 L8** 29 53N 93 51W
Sabine Pass, *U.S.A.* **81 L8** 29 44N 93 54W
Sabinsville, *U.S.A.* **78 E7** 41 52N 77 31W
Sabkhet el Bardawîl, *Egypt* **47 D2** 31 10N 33 15 E
Sablayan, *Phil.* **37 B6** 12 50N 120 50 E
Sable, *Canada* **71 A6** 55 30N 68 21W
Sable, C., *Canada* **71 D6** 43 29N 65 38W
Sable, C., *U.S.A.* **75 E10** 25 9N 81 8W
Sable I., *Canada* **71 D8** 44 0N 60 0W
Sabrina Coast, *Antarctica* **5 C9** 68 0S 120 0 E
Sabulubbek, *Indonesia* **36 E1** 1 36S 98 40 E
Sabzevār, *Iran* **45 B8** 36 15N 57 40 E
Sabzvārān, *Iran* **45 D8** 28 45N 57 50 E
Sac City, *U.S.A.* **80 D7** 42 25N 95 0W
Săcele, *Romania* **17 F13** 45 37N 25 41 E
Sachigo →, *Canada* **70 A2** 55 6N 88 58W
Sachigo, L., *Canada* **70 B1** 53 50N 92 12W
Sachsen □, *Germany* **16 C7** 50 55N 13 10 E
Sachsen-Anhalt □, *Germany* **16 C7** 52 0N 12 0 E
Sackets Harbor, *U.S.A.* **79 C8** 43 57N 76 7W
Sackville, *Canada* **71 C7** 45 54N 64 22W
Saco, *Maine, U.S.A.* **77 D10** 43 30N 70 27W
Saco, *Mont., U.S.A.* **82 B10** 48 28N 107 21W
Sacramento, *U.S.A.* **84 G5** 38 35N 121 29W
Sacramento →, *U.S.A.* **84 G5** 38 3N 121 56W
Sacramento Mts., *U.S.A.* **83 K11** 32 30N 105 30W
Sacramento Valley, *U.S.A.* **84 G5** 39 30N 122 0W
Sada-Misaki, *Japan* **31 H6** 33 20N 132 1 E
Sadabad, *India* **42 F8** 27 27N 78 3 E
Sadani, *Tanzania* **54 D4** 5 58S 38 35 E
Sadao, *Thailand* **39 J3** 6 38N 100 26 E
Sadd el Aali, *Egypt* **51 D12** 23 54N 32 54 E
Saddle Mt., *U.S.A.* **84 E3** 45 58N 123 41W
Sadimi, *Dem. Rep. of the Congo* **55 D1** 9 25S 23 32 E
Sado, *Japan* **30 F9** 38 0N 138 25 E
Sadon, *Burma* **41 G20** 25 28N 97 55 E
Sadra, *India* **42 H5** 23 21N 72 43 E
Sadri, *India* **42 G5** 25 11N 73 26 E
Sæby, *Denmark* **9 H14** 57 21N 10 30 E
Saegertown, *U.S.A.* **78 E4** 41 43N 80 9W
Şafājah, *Si. Arabia* **44 E3** 26 25N 39 0 E
Säffle, *Sweden* **9 G15** 59 8N 12 55 E
Safford, *U.S.A.* **83 K9** 32 50N 109 43W
Saffron Walden, *U.K.* **11 E8** 52 1N 0 16 E
Safi, *Morocco* **50 B4** 32 18N 9 20W
Şafīābād, *Iran* **45 B8** 36 45N 57 58 E
Safīd Dasht, *Iran* **45 C6** 33 27N 48 11 E
Safīd Kūh, *Afghan.* **40 B3** 34 45N 63 0 E
Safīd Rūd →, *Iran* **45 B6** 37 23N 50 11 E
Safipur, *India* **43 F9** 26 44N 80 21 E
Safwān, *Iraq* **44 D5** 30 7N 47 43 E
Sag Harbor, *U.S.A.* **79 F12** 41 0N 72 18W
Saga, *Japan* **31 H5** 33 15N 130 16 E
Saga □, *Japan* **31 H5** 33 15N 130 20 E
Sagae, *Japan* **30 E10** 38 22N 140 17 E
Sagamore, *U.S.A.* **78 F5** 40 46N 79 14W
Sagar, *Karnataka, India* **40 M9** 14 14N 75 6 E
Sagar, *Mad. P., India* **43 H8** 23 50N 78 44 E
Sagara, L., *Tanzania* **54 D3** 5 20S 31 0 E
Saginaw, *U.S.A.* **76 D4** 43 26N 83 56W
Saginaw →, *U.S.A.* **76 D4** 43 39N 83 51W
Saginaw B., *U.S.A.* **76 D4** 43 50N 83 40W
Saglouc = Salluit, *Canada* **69 B12** 62 14N 75 38W
Sagŏ-ri, *S. Korea* **35 G14** 35 25N 126 49 E
Sagua la Grande, *Cuba* **88 B3** 22 50N 80 10W
Saguache, *U.S.A.* **83 G10** 38 5N 106 8W
Saguaro Nat. Park, *U.S.A.* **83 K8** 32 12N 110 38W
Saguenay →, *Canada* **71 C5** 48 22N 71 0W
Sagunt, *Spain* **19 C5** 39 42N 0 18W
Sagunto = Sagunt, *Spain* **19 C5** 39 42N 0 18W
Sagwara, *India* **42 H6** 23 41N 74 1 E
Sahagún, *Spain* **19 A3** 42 18N 5 2W
Saḩam al Jawlān, *Syria* **47 C4** 32 45N 35 55 E
Sahamandrevo, *Madag.* **57 C8** 23 15S 45 35 E
Sahand, Kūh-e, *Iran* **44 B5** 37 44N 46 27 E
Sahara, *Africa* **50 D6** 23 0N 5 0 E
Saharan Atlas = Saharien, Atlas, *Algeria* **50 B6** 33 30N 1 0 E
Saharanpur, *India* **42 E7** 29 58N 77 33 E
Saharien, Atlas, *Algeria* **50 B6** 33 30N 1 0 E
Saharsa, *India* **43 G12** 25 53N 86 36 E
Sahasinaka, *Madag.* **57 C8** 21 49S 47 49 E
Sahaswan, *India* **43 E8** 28 5N 78 45 E
Sahel, *Africa* **50 E5** 16 0N 5 0 E
Sahibganj, *India* **43 G12** 25 12N 87 40 E
Sāḩilīyah, *Iraq* **44 C4** 33 43N 42 42 E
Sahiwal, *Pakistan* **42 D5** 30 45N 73 8 E
Şahneh, *Iran* **44 C5** 34 29N 47 41 E
Sahuaripa, *Mexico* **86 B3** 29 0N 109 13W
Sahuarita, *U.S.A.* **83 L8** 31 57N 110 58W
Sahuayo, *Mexico* **86 C4** 20 4N 102 43W
Sai →, *India* **43 G10** 25 39N 82 47 E
Sai Buri, *Thailand* **39 J3** 6 43N 101 45 E
Sa'id Bundas, *Sudan* **51 G10** 8 24N 24 48 E
Sa'īdābād, *Kermān, Iran* **45 D7** 29 30N 55 45 E
Sa'īdābād, *Semnān, Iran* **45 B7** 36 8N 54 11 E
Sa'īdīyeh, *Iran* **45 B6** 36 20N 48 55 E
Saidpur, *Bangla.* **41 G16** 25 48N 89 0 E
Saidpur, *India* **43 G10** 25 33N 83 11 E
Saidu, *Pakistan* **43 B5** 34 43N 72 24 E
Saigon = Thanh Pho Ho Chi Minh, *Vietnam* **39 G6** 10 58N 106 40 E
Saijō, *Japan* **31 H6** 33 55N 133 11 E
Saikanosy Masoala, *Madag.* **57 B9** 15 45S 50 10 E
Saikhoa Ghat, *India* **41 F19** 27 50N 95 40 E
Saiki, *Japan* **31 H5** 32 58N 131 51 E
Sailana, *India* **42 H6** 23 28N 74 55 E
Sailolof, *Indonesia* **37 E8** 1 15S 130 46 E
Saimaa, *Finland* **9 F23** 61 15N 28 15 E
Şa'in Dezh, *Iran* **44 B5** 36 40N 46 25 E
St. Abb's Head, *U.K.* **12 F6** 55 55N 2 8W
St. Alban's, *Canada* **71 C8** 47 51N 55 50W
St. Albans, *U.K.* **11 F7** 51 45N 0 19W
St. Albans, *Vt., U.S.A.* **79 B11** 44 49N 73 5W
St. Albans, *W. Va., U.S.A.* **76 F5** 38 23N 81 50W
St. Alban's Head, *U.K.* **11 G5** 50 34N 2 4W
St. Albert, *Canada* **72 C6** 53 37N 113 32W
St. Andrew's, *Canada* **71 C8** 47 45N 59 15W
St. Andrews, *U.K.* **12 E6** 56 20N 2 47W
St-Anicet, *Canada* **79 A10** 45 8N 74 22W
St. Ann B., *Canada* **71 C7** 46 22N 60 25W
St. Ann's Bay, *Jamaica* **88 C4** 18 26N 77 15W
St. Anthony, *Canada* **71 B8** 51 22N 55 35W
St. Anthony, *U.S.A.* **82 E8** 43 58N 111 41W
St. Antoine, *Canada* **71 C7** 46 22N 64 45W
St-Augustin →, *Canada* **71 B8** 51 16N 58 40W
St-Augustin-Saguenay, *Canada* **71 B8** 51 13N 58 38W
St. Augustine, *U.S.A.* **77 L5** 29 54N 81 19W
St. Austell, *U.K.* **11 G3** 50 20N 4 47W
St. Barbe, *Canada* **71 B8** 51 12N 56 46W
St-Barthélemy, *W. Indies* **89 C7** 17 50N 62 50W
St. Bees Hd., *U.K.* **10 C4** 54 31N 3 38W
St. Bride's, *Canada* **71 C9** 46 56N 54 10W
St. Brides B., *U.K.* **11 F2** 51 49N 5 9W
St-Brieuc, *France* **18 B2** 48 30N 2 46W
St. Catharines, *Canada* **78 C5** 43 10N 79 15W
St. Catherines I., *U.S.A.* **77 K5** 31 40N 81 10W
St. Catherine's Pt., *U.K.* **11 G6** 50 34N 1 18W
St-Chamond, *France* **18 D6** 45 28N 4 31 E
St. Charles, *Ill., U.S.A.* **76 E1** 41 54N 88 19W
St. Charles, *Mo., U.S.A.* **80 F9** 38 47N 90 29W
St. Charles, *Va., U.S.A.* **76 F7** 36 48N 83 4W
St. Christopher-Nevis = St. Kitts & Nevis ■, *W. Indies* **89 C7** 17 20N 62 40W
St. Clair, *Mich., U.S.A.* **78 D2** 42 50N 82 30W
St. Clair, *Pa., U.S.A.* **79 F8** 40 43N 76 12W
St. Clair →, *U.S.A.* **78 D2** 42 38N 82 31W
St. Clair, L., *Canada* **70 D3** 42 30N 82 45W
St. Clair, L., *U.S.A.* **78 D2** 42 27N 82 39W
St. Clairsville, *U.S.A.* **78 F4** 40 5N 80 54W
St. Claude, *Canada* **73 D9** 49 40N 98 20W
St-Clet, *Canada* **79 A10** 45 21N 74 13W
St. Cloud, *Fla., U.S.A.* **77 L5** 28 15N 81 17W
St. Cloud, *Minn., U.S.A.* **80 C7** 45 34N 94 10W
St. Cricq, C., *Australia* **61 E1** 25 17S 113 6 E
St. Croix, *U.S. Virgin Is.* **89 C7** 17 45N 64 45W
St. Croix →, *U.S.A.* **80 C8** 44 45N 92 48W
St. Croix Falls, *U.S.A.* **80 C8** 45 24N 92 38W
St. David's, *Canada* **71 C8** 48 12N 58 52W
St. David's, *U.K.* **11 F2** 51 53N 5 16W
St. David's Head, *U.K.* **11 F2** 51 54N 5 19W
St-Denis, *France* **18 B5** 48 56N 2 22 E
St-Dizier, *France* **18 B6** 48 38N 4 56 E
St. Elias, Mt., *U.S.A.* **68 B5** 60 18N 140 56W
St. Elias Mts., *Canada* **72 A1** 60 33N 139 28W
St. Elias Mts., *U.S.A.* **68 C6** 60 0N 138 0W
St-Étienne, *France* **18 D6** 45 27N 4 22 E
St. Eugène, *Canada* **79 A10** 45 30N 74 28W
St. Eustatius, *W. Indies* **89 C7** 17 20N 63 0W
St-Félicien, *Canada* **70 C5** 48 40N 72 25W
St-Flour, *France* **18 D5** 45 2N 3 6 E
St. Francis, *U.S.A.* **80 F4** 39 47N 101 48W
St. Francis →, *U.S.A.* **81 H9** 34 38N 90 36W
St. Francis, C., *S. Africa* **56 E3** 34 14S 24 49 E
St. Francisville, *U.S.A.* **81 K9** 30 47N 91 23W
St-François, L., *Canada* **79 A10** 45 10N 74 22W
St-Gabriel, *Canada* **70 C5** 46 17N 73 24W
St. Gallen = Sankt Gallen, *Switz.* **18 C8** 47 26N 9 22 E
St-Gaudens, *France* **18 E4** 43 6N 0 44 E
St. George, *Australia* **63 D4** 28 1S 148 30 E
St. George, *Canada* **71 C6** 45 11N 66 50W
St. George, *S.C., U.S.A.* **77 J5** 33 11N 80 35W
St. George, *Utah, U.S.A.* **83 H7** 37 6N 113 35W
St. George, C., *Canada* **71 C8** 48 30N 59 16W
St. George, C., *U.S.A.* **77 L3** 29 40N 85 5W
St. George Ra., *Australia* **60 C4** 18 40S 125 0 E
St. George's, *Canada* **71 C8** 48 26N 58 31W
St-Georges, *Canada* **71 C5** 46 8N 70 40W
St. George's, *Grenada* **89 D7** 12 5N 61 43W
St. George's B., *Canada* **71 C8** 48 24N 58 53W
St. Georges Basin, *N.S.W., Australia* **63 F5** 35 7S 150 36 E
St. Georges Basin, *W. Austral., Australia* **60 C4** 15 23S 125 2 E
St. George's Channel, *Europe* **13 E6** 52 0N 6 0W
St. Gotthard P. = San Gottardo, P. del, *Switz.* **18 C8** 46 33N 8 33 E
St. Helena, *U.S.A.* **82 G2** 38 30N 122 28W
St. Helena ■, *Atl. Oc.* **48 H3** 15 55S 5 44W
St. Helena, Mt., *U.S.A.* **84 G4** 38 40N 122 36W
St. Helena B., *S. Africa* **56 E2** 32 40S 18 10 E
St. Helens, *Australia* **62 G4** 41 20S 148 15 E
St. Helens, *U.K.* **10 D5** 53 27N 2 44W
St. Helens, *U.S.A.* **84 E4** 45 52N 122 48W
St. Helens, Mt., *U.S.A.* **84 D4** 46 12N 122 12W
St. Helier, *U.K.* **11 H5** 49 10N 2 7W
St-Hubert, *Belgium* **15 D5** 50 2N 5 23 E
St-Hyacinthe, *Canada* **70 C5** 45 40N 72 58W
St. Ignace, *U.S.A.* **76 C3** 45 52N 84 44W
St. Ignace I., *Canada* **70 C2** 48 45N 88 0W
St. Ignatius, *U.S.A.* **82 C6** 47 19N 114 6W
St. Ives, *U.K.* **11 G2** 50 12N 5 30W
St. James, *U.S.A.* **80 D7** 43 59N 94 38W
St-Jean →, *Canada* **71 B7** 50 17N 64 20W
St-Jean, L., *Canada* **71 C5** 48 40N 72 0W
St-Jean-Port-Joli, *Canada* **71 C5** 47 15N 70 13W
St-Jean-sur-Richelieu, *Canada* **79 A11** 45 20N 73 20W
St-Jérôme, *Canada* **70 C5** 45 47N 74 0W
St. John, *Canada* **71 C6** 45 20N 66 8W
St. John, *U.S.A.* **81 G5** 38 0N 98 46W
St. John →, *U.S.A.* **77 C12** 45 12N 66 5W
St. John, C., *Canada* **71 C8** 50 0N 55 32W
St. John's, *Antigua* **89 C7** 17 6N 61 51W
St. John's, *Canada* **71 C9** 47 35N 52 40W
St. Johns, *Ariz., U.S.A.* **83 J9** 34 30N 109 22W
St. Johns, *Mich., U.S.A.* **76 D3** 43 0N 84 33W
St. Johns →, *U.S.A.* **77 K5** 30 24N 81 24W
St. John's Pt., *Ireland* **13 B3** 54 34N 8 27W
St. Johnsbury, *U.S.A.* **79 B12** 44 25N 72 1W
St. Johnsville, *U.S.A.* **79 D10** 43 0N 74 43W
St. Joseph, *La., U.S.A.* **81 K9** 31 55N 91 14W
St. Joseph, *Mo., U.S.A.* **80 F7** 39 46N 94 50W
St. Joseph →, *U.S.A.* **76 D2** 42 7N 86 29W
St. Joseph, I., *Canada* **70 C3** 46 12N 83 58W
St. Joseph, L., *Canada* **70 B1** 51 10N 90 35W
St-Jovite, *Canada* **70 C5** 46 8N 74 38W
St. Kitts & Nevis ■, *W. Indies* **89 C7** 17 20N 62 40W
St. Laurent, *Canada* **73 C9** 50 25N 97 58W
St. Lawrence, *Australia* **62 C4** 22 16S 149 31 E
St. Lawrence, *Canada* **71 C8** 46 54N 55 23W
St. Lawrence →, *Canada* **71 C6** 49 30N 66 0W
St. Lawrence, Gulf of, *Canada* **71 C7** 48 25N 62 0W
St. Lawrence I., *U.S.A.* **68 B3** 63 30N 170 30W
St. Leonard, *Canada* **71 C6** 47 12N 67 58W
St. Lewis →, *Canada* **71 B8** 52 26N 56 11W
St-Lô, *France* **18 B3** 49 7N 1 5W
St. Louis, *Senegal* **50 E2** 16 8N 16 27W
St. Louis, *U.S.A.* **80 F9** 38 37N 90 12W
St. Louis →, *U.S.A.* **80 B8** 47 15N 92 45W
St. Lucia ■, *W. Indies* **89 D7** 14 0N 60 50W
St. Lucia, L., *S. Africa* **57 D5** 28 5S 32 30 E
St. Lucia Channel, *W. Indies* **89 D7** 14 15N 61 0W
St. Maarten, *W. Indies* **89 C7** 18 0N 63 5W
St. Magnus B., *U.K.* **12 A7** 60 25N 1 35W
St-Malo, *France* **18 B2** 48 39N 2 1W
St-Marc, *Haiti* **89 C5** 19 10N 72 41W
St. Maries, *U.S.A.* **82 C5** 47 19N 116 35W
St-Martin, *W. Indies* **89 C7** 18 0N 63 0W
St. Martin, L., *Canada* **73 C9** 51 40N 98 30W
St. Marys, *Australia* **62 G4** 41 35S 148 11 E
St. Marys, *Canada* **78 C3** 43 20N 81 10W
St. Mary's, *Corn., U.K.* **11 H1** 49 55N 6 18W
St. Mary's, *Orkney, U.K.* **12 C6** 58 54N 2 54W
St. Marys, *Ga., U.S.A.* **77 K5** 30 44N 81 33W
St. Marys, *Pa., U.S.A.* **78 E6** 41 26N 78 34W
St. Mary's, C., *Canada* **71 C9** 46 50N 54 12W
St. Mary's B., *Canada* **71 C9** 46 50N 53 50W
St. Marys Bay, *Canada* **71 D6** 44 25N 66 10W
St-Mathieu, Pte., *France* **18 B1** 48 20N 4 45W
St. Matthew I., *U.S.A.* **68 B2** 60 24N 172 42W
St. Matthews, I. = Zadetkyi Kyun, *Burma* **39 G1** 10 0N 98 25 E
St-Maurice →, *Canada* **70 C5** 46 21N 72 31W
St-Nazaire, *France* **18 C2** 47 17N 2 12W
St. Neots, *U.K.* **11 E7** 52 14N 0 15W
St-Niklaas, *Belgium* **15 C4** 51 10N 4 8 E
St-Omer, *France* **18 A5** 50 45N 2 15 E
St-Pamphile, *Canada* **71 C6** 46 58N 69 48W
St. Pascal, *Canada* **71 C6** 47 32N 69 48W
St. Paul, *Canada* **72 C6** 54 0N 111 17W
St. Paul, *Minn., U.S.A.* **80 C8** 44 57N 93 6W
St. Paul, *Nebr., U.S.A.* **80 E5** 41 13N 98 27W
St-Paul →, *Canada* **71 B8** 51 27N 57 42W
St. Paul, I., *Ind. Oc.* **3 F13** 38 55S 77 34 E
St. Paul I., *Canada* **71 C7** 47 12N 60 9W
St. Peter, *U.S.A.* **80 C8** 44 20N 93 57W
St. Peter Port, *U.K.* **11 H5** 49 26N 2 33W
St. Peters, *N.S., Canada* **71 C7** 45 40N 60 53W
St. Peters, *P.E.I., Canada* **71 C7** 46 25N 62 35W
St. Petersburg = Sankt-Peterburg, *Russia* **24 C5** 59 55N 30 20 E
St. Petersburg, *U.S.A.* **77 M4** 27 46N 82 39W
St-Pie, *Canada* **79 A12** 45 30N 72 54W
St-Pierre, *St- P. & M.* **71 C8** 46 46N 56 12W
St-Pierre, L., *Canada* **70 C5** 46 12N 72 52W
St-Pierre et Miquelon □, *St- P. & M.* **71 C8** 46 55N 56 10W
St. Quentin, *Canada* **71 C6** 47 30N 67 23W
St-Quentin, *France* **18 B5** 49 50N 3 16 E
St. Regis, *U.S.A.* **82 C6** 47 18N 115 6W
St. Sebastien, Tanjon' i, *Madag.* **57 A8** 12 26S 48 44 E
St-Siméon, *Canada* **71 C6** 47 51N 69 54W
St. Simons I., *U.S.A.* **77 K5** 31 12N 81 15W
St. Simons Island, *U.S.A.* **77 K5** 31 9N 81 22W
St. Stephen, *Canada* **71 C6** 45 16N 67 17W
St. Thomas, *Canada* **78 D3** 42 45N 81 10W
St. Thomas I., *U.S. Virgin Is.* **89 C7** 18 20N 64 55W
St-Tite, *Canada* **70 C5** 46 45N 72 34W
St-Tropez, *France* **18 E7** 43 17N 6 38 E
St. Troud = St. Truiden, *Belgium* **15 D5** 50 48N 5 10 E
St. Truiden, *Belgium* **15 D5** 50 48N 5 10 E
St. Vincent & the Grenadines ■, *W. Indies* **89 D7** 13 0N 61 10W
St. Vincent Passage, *W. Indies* **89 D7** 13 30N 61 0W
St-Vith, *Belgium* **15 D6** 50 17N 6 9 E
St. Walburg, *Canada* **73 C7** 53 39N 109 12W
Ste-Agathe-des-Monts, *Canada* **70 C5** 46 3N 74 17W
Ste-Anne, L., *Canada* **71 B6** 50 0N 67 42W
Ste-Anne-des-Monts, *Canada* **71 C6** 49 8N 66 30W
Ste. Genevieve, *U.S.A.* **80 G9** 37 59N 90 2W
Ste-Marguerite →, *Canada* **71 B6** 50 9N 66 36W
Ste-Marie, *Martinique* **89 D7** 14 48N 61 1W
Ste-Marie de la Madeleine, *Canada* **71 C5** 46 26N 71 0W
Ste-Rose, *Guadeloupe* **89 C7** 16 20N 61 45W
Ste. Rose du Lac, *Canada* **73 C9** 51 4N 99 30W
Saintes, *France* **18 D3** 45 45N 0 37W
Saintes, I. des, *Guadeloupe* **89 C7** 15 50N 61 35W
Saintfield, *U.K.* **13 B6** 54 28N 5 49W
Saintonge, *France* **18 D3** 45 40N 0 50W
Saipan, *Pac. Oc.* **64 F6** 15 12N 145 45 E
Sairang, *India* **41 H18** 23 50N 92 45 E
Sairecábur, Cerro, *Bolivia* **94 A2** 22 43S 67 54W
Saitama □, *Japan* **31 F9** 36 25N 139 30 E
Saiyid, *Pakistan* **42 C5** 33 7N 73 2 E
Sajama, *Bolivia* **92 G5** 18 7S 69 0W
Sajószentpéter, *Hungary* **17 D11** 48 12N 20 44 E
Sajum, *India* **43 C8** 33 20N 79 0 E
Sak →, *S. Africa* **56 E3** 30 52S 20 25 E
Sakai, *Japan* **31 G7** 34 30N 135 30 E
Sakaide, *Japan* **31 G6** 34 19N 133 50 E
Sakaiminato, *Japan* **31 G6** 35 38N 133 11 E
Sakākah, *Si. Arabia* **44 D4** 30 0N 40 8 E
Sakakawea, L., *U.S.A.* **80 B4** 47 30N 101 25W
Sakami →, *Canada* **70 B4** 53 40N 76 40W
Sakami, L., *Canada* **70 B4** 53 15N 77 0W
Sakania, *Dem. Rep. of the Congo* **55 E2** 12 43S 28 30 E
Sakaraha, *Madag.* **57 C7** 22 55S 44 32 E
Sakarya, *Turkey* **25 F5** 40 48N 30 25 E
Sakashima-Guntō, *Japan* **31 M2** 24 46N 124 0 E
Sakata, *Japan* **30 E9** 38 55N 139 50 E
Sakchu, *N. Korea* **35 D13** 40 23N 125 2 E
Sakeny →, *Madag.* **57 C8** 20 0S 45 25 E
Sakha □, *Russia* **27 C13** 66 0N 130 0 E
Sakhalin, *Russia* **27 D15** 51 0N 143 0 E
Sakhalinskiy Zaliv, *Russia* **27 D15** 54 0N 141 0 E
Šakiai, *Lithuania* **9 J20** 54 59N 23 2 E
Sakon Nakhon, *Thailand* **38 D5** 17 10N 104 9 E
Sakrand, *Pakistan* **42 F3** 26 10N 68 15 E
Sakri, *India* **43 F12** 26 13N 86 5 E
Sakrivier, *S. Africa* **56 E3** 30 54S 20 28 E
Sakti, *India* **43 H10** 22 2N 82 58 E
Sakuma, *Japan* **31 G8** 35 3N 137 49 E
Sakurai, *Japan* **31 G7** 34 30N 135 51 E
Sala, *Sweden* **9 G17** 59 58N 16 35 E
Sala Consilina, *Italy* **20 D6** 40 23N 15 36 E
Sala-y-Gómez, *Pac. Oc.* **65 K17** 26 28S 105 28W
Salaberry-de-Valleyfield, *Canada* **79 A10** 45 15N 74 8W
Saladas, *Argentina* **94 B4** 28 15S 58 40W
Saladillo, *Argentina* **94 D4** 35 40S 59 55W
Salado →, *Buenos Aires, Argentina* **94 D4** 35 44S 57 22W
Salado →, *La Pampa, Argentina* **96 D3** 37 30S 67 0W
Salado →, *Santa Fe, Argentina* **94 C3** 31 40S 60 41W
Salado →, *Mexico* **81 M5** 26 52N 99 19W
Salaga, *Ghana* **50 G5** 8 31N 0 31W
Şalāh, *Syria* **47 C5** 32 40N 36 45 E
Sálakhos, *Greece* **23 C9** 36 17N 27 57 E
Şalālah, *Oman* **46 D5** 16 56N 53 59 E
Salamanca, *Chile* **94 C1** 31 46S 70 59W
Salamanca, *Spain* **19 B3** 40 58N 5 39W
Salamanca, *U.S.A.* **78 D6** 42 10N 78 43W
Salāmatābād, *Iran* **44 C5** 35 39N 47 50 E
Salamis, *Cyprus* **23 D12** 35 11N 33 54 E
Salamís, *Greece* **21 F10** 37 56N 23 30 E
Salar de Atacama, *Chile* **94 A2** 23 30S 68 25W
Salar de Uyuni, *Bolivia* **92 H5** 20 30S 67 45W
Salatiga, *Indonesia* **37 G14** 7 19S 110 30 E
Salavat, *Russia* **24 D10** 53 21N 55 55 E
Salaverry, *Peru* **92 E3** 8 15S 79 0W
Salawati, *Indonesia* **37 E8** 1 7S 130 52 E
Salaya, *India* **42 H3** 22 19N 69 35 E
Salayar, *Indonesia* **37 F6** 6 7S 120 30 E
Salcombe, *U.K.* **11 G4** 50 14N 3 47W
Saldanha, *S. Africa* **56 E2** 33 0S 17 58 E
Saldanha B., *S. Africa* **56 E2** 33 6S 18 0 E
Saldus, *Latvia* **9 H20** 56 38N 22 30 E
Salé, *Morocco* **50 B4** 34 3N 6 48W
Sale, *U.K.* **10 D5** 53 26N 2 19W
Salekhard, *Russia* **26 C7** 66 30N 66 35 E
Salem, *India* **40 P11** 11 40N 78 11 E
Salem, *Ill., U.S.A.* **76 F1** 38 38N 88 57W
Salem, *Ind., U.S.A.* **76 F2** 38 36N 86 6W
Salem, *Mass., U.S.A.* **79 D14** 42 31N 70 53W
Salem, *Mo., U.S.A.* **81 G9** 37 39N 91 32W
Salem, *N.H., U.S.A.* **79 D13** 42 45N 71 12W
Salem, *N.J., U.S.A.* **76 F8** 39 34N 75 28W
Salem, *N.Y., U.S.A.* **79 C11** 43 10N 73 20W
Salem, *Ohio, U.S.A.* **78 F4** 40 54N 80 52W
Salem, *Oreg., U.S.A.* **82 D2** 44 56N 123 2W
Salem, *S. Dak., U.S.A.* **80 D6** 43 44N 97 23W
Salem, *Va., U.S.A.* **76 G5** 37 18N 80 3W
Salerno, *Italy* **20 D6** 40 41N 14 47 E
Salford, *U.K.* **10 D5** 53 30N 2 18W
Salgótarján, *Hungary* **17 D10** 48 5N 19 47 E
Salgueiro, *Brazil* **93 E11** 8 4S 39 6W
Salibabu, *Indonesia* **37 D7** 3 51N 126 40 E
Salida, *U.S.A.* **74 C5** 38 32N 106 0W
Salihli, *Turkey* **21 E13** 38 28N 28 8 E
Salihorsk, *Belarus* **17 B14** 52 51N 27 27 E
Salima, *Malawi* **53 G6** 13 47S 34 28 E
Salina, *Italy* **20 E6** 38 34N 14 50 E
Salina, *Kans., U.S.A.* **80 F6** 38 50N 97 37W
Salina, *Utah, U.S.A.* **83 G8** 38 58N 111 51W
Salina Cruz, *Mexico* **87 D5** 16 10N 95 10W
Salinas, *Brazil* **93 G10** 16 10S 42 10W
Salinas, *Chile* **94 A2** 23 31S 69 29W
Salinas, *Ecuador* **92 D2** 2 10S 80 58W
Salinas, *U.S.A.* **84 J5** 36 40N 121 39W
Salinas →, *Guatemala* **87 D6** 16 28N 90 31W
Salinas →, *U.S.A.* **84 J5** 36 45N 121 48W
Salinas, B. de, *Nic.* **88 D2** 11 4N 85 45W
Salinas, Pampa de las, *Argentina* **94 C2** 31 58S 66 42W
Salinas Ambargasta, *Argentina* **94 B3** 29 0S 65 0W
Salinas de Hidalgo, *Mexico* **86 C4** 22 30N 101 40W
Salinas Grandes, *Argentina* **94 C3** 30 0S 65 0W
Saline →, *Ark., U.S.A.* **81 J8** 33 10N 92 8W

Seyhan

Sasyk, Ozero, *Ukraine* **17 F15** 45 45N 29 20 E
Sata-Misaki, *Japan* **31 J5** 31 0N 130 40 E
Satadougou, *Mali* **50 F3** 12 25N 11 25W
Satakunta, *Finland* **9 F20** 61 45N 23 0 E
Satara, *India* **40 L8** 17 44N 73 58 E
Satara, *S. Africa* **57 C5** 24 29S 31 47 E
Satbarwa, *India* **43 H11** 23 55N 84 16 E
Satevó, *Mexico* **86 B3** 27 57N 106 7W
Satilla →, *U.S.A.* **77 K5** 30 59N 81 29W
Satka, *Russia* **24 C10** 55 3N 59 1 E
Satmala Hills, *India* **40 J9** 20 15N 74 40 E
Satna, *India* **43 G9** 24 35N 80 50 E
Sátoraljaújhely, *Hungary* **17 D11** 48 25N 21 41 E
Satpura Ra., *India* **40 J10** 21 25N 76 10 E
Satsuna-Shotō, *Japan* **31 K5** 30 0N 130 0 E
Sattahip, *Thailand* **38 F3** 12 41N 100 54 E
Satu Mare, *Romania* **17 E12** 47 46N 22 55 E
Satui, *Indonesia* **36 E5** 3 50S 115 27 E
Satun, *Thailand* **39 J3** 6 43N 100 2 E
Saturnina →, *Brazil* **92 F7** 12 15S 58 10W
Sauce, *Argentina* **94 C4** 30 5S 58 46W
Sauceda, *Mexico* **86 B4** 25 55N 101 18W
Saucillo, *Mexico* **86 B3** 28 1N 105 17W
Sauda, *Norway* **9 G12** 59 40N 6 20 E
Sauðarkrókur, *Iceland* **8 D4** 65 45N 19 40W
Saudi Arabia ■, *Asia* **46 B3** 26 0N 44 0 E
Sauerland, *Germany* **16 C4** 51 12N 7 59 E
Saugeen →, *Canada* **78 B3** 44 30N 81 22W
Saugerties, *U.S.A.* **79 D11** 42 5N 73 57W
Saugus, *U.S.A.* **85 L8** 34 25N 118 32W
Sauk Centre, *U.S.A.* **80 C7** 45 44N 94 57W
Sauk Rapids, *U.S.A.* **80 C7** 45 35N 94 10W
Sault Ste. Marie, *Canada* **70 C3** 46 30N 84 20W
Sault Ste. Marie, *U.S.A.* **69 D11** 46 30N 84 21W
Saumlaki, *Indonesia* **37 F8** 7 55S 131 20 E
Saumur, *France* **18 C3** 47 15N 0 5W
Saunders C., *N.Z.* **59 L3** 45 53S 170 45 E
Saunders I., *Antarctica* **5 B1** 57 48S 26 28W
Saunders Point, *Australia* **61 E4** 27 52S 125 38 E
Saurimo, *Angola* **52 F4** 9 40S 20 12 E
Sausalito, *U.S.A.* **84 H4** 37 51N 122 29W
Savá, *Honduras* **88 C2** 15 32N 86 15W
Sava →, *Serbia, Yug.* **21 B9** 44 50N 20 26 E
Savage, *U.S.A.* **80 B2** 47 27N 104 21W
Savage I. = Niue, *Cook Is.* **65 J11** 19 2S 169 54W
Savage River, *Australia* **62 G4** 41 31S 145 14 E
Savai'i, *Samoa* **59 A12** 13 28S 172 24W
Savalou, *Benin* **50 G6** 7 57N 1 58 E
Savane, *Mozam.* **55 F4** 19 37S 35 8 E
Savanna, *U.S.A.* **80 D9** 42 5N 90 8W
Savanna-la-Mar, *Jamaica* **88 C4** 18 10N 78 10W
Savannah, *Ga., U.S.A.* **77 J5** 32 5N 81 6W
Savannah, *Mo., U.S.A.* **80 F7** 39 56N 94 50W
Savannah, *Tenn., U.S.A.* **77 H1** 35 14N 88 15W
Savannah →, *U.S.A.* **77 J5** 32 2N 80 53W
Savannakhet, *Laos* **38 D5** 16 30N 104 49 E
Savant L., *Canada* **70 B1** 50 16N 90 44W
Savant Lake, *Canada* **70 B1** 50 14N 90 40W
Save →, *Mozam.* **57 C5** 21 16S 34 0 E
Sāveh, *Iran* **45 C6** 35 2N 50 20 E
Savelugu, *Ghana* **50 G5** 9 38N 0 54W
Savo, *Finland* **8 E22** 62 45N 27 30 E
Savoie □, *France* **18 D7** 45 26N 6 25 E
Savona, *Italy* **18 D8** 44 17N 8 30 E
Savona, *U.S.A.* **78 D7** 42 17N 77 13W
Savonlinna, *Finland* **24 B4** 61 52N 28 53 E
Savoy = Savoie □, *France* **18 D7** 45 26N 6 25 E
Savur, *Turkey* **44 B4** 37 34N 40 53 E
Sawahlunto, *Indonesia* **36 E2** 0 40S 100 52 E
Sawai, *Indonesia* **37 E7** 3 0S 129 5 E
Sawai Madhopur, *India* **42 G7** 26 0N 76 25 E
Sawang Daen Din, *Thailand* **38 D4** 17 28N 103 28 E
Sawankhalok, *Thailand* **38 D2** 17 19N 99 50 E
Sawara, *Japan* **31 G10** 35 55N 140 30 E
Sawatch Range, *U.S.A.* **83 G10** 38 30N 106 30W
Sawel Mt., *U.K.* **13 B4** 54 50N 7 2W
Sawi, *Thailand* **39 G2** 10 14N 99 5 E
Sawmills, *Zimbabwe* **55 F2** 19 30S 28 2 E
Sawtooth Range, *U.S.A.* **82 E6** 44 3N 114 58W
Sawu, *Indonesia* **37 F6** 10 35S 121 50 E
Sawu Sea, *Indonesia* **37 F6** 9 30S 121 50 E
Saxby →, *Australia* **62 B3** 18 25S 140 53 E
Saxmundham, *U.K.* **11 E9** 52 13N 1 30 E
Saxony = Sachsen □, *Germany* **16 C7** 50 55N 13 10 E
Saxony, Lower = Niedersachsen □, *Germany* **16 B5** 52 50N 9 0 E
Saxton, *U.S.A.* **78 F6** 40 13N 78 15W
Sayabec, *Canada* **71 C6** 48 35N 67 41W
Sayaboury, *Laos* **38 C3** 19 15N 101 45 E
Sayán, *Peru* **92 F3** 11 8S 77 12W
Sayan, Vostochnyy, *Russia* **27 D10** 54 0N 96 0 E
Sayan, Zapadnyy, *Russia* **27 D10** 52 30N 94 0 E
Saydā, *Lebanon* **47 B4** 33 35N 35 25 E
Sayhandulaan = Oldziyt, *Mongolia* **34 B5** 44 40N 109 1 E
Sayḥūt, *Yemen* **46 D5** 15 12N 51 10 E
Saynshand, *Mongolia* **33 B6** 44 55N 110 11 E
Sayre, *Okla., U.S.A.* **81 H5** 35 18N 99 38W
Sayre, *Pa., U.S.A.* **79 E8** 41 59N 76 32W
Sayreville, *U.S.A.* **79 F10** 40 28N 74 22W
Sayula, *Mexico* **86 D4** 19 50N 103 40W
Sayward, *Canada* **72 C3** 50 21N 125 55W
Sazanit, *Albania* **21 D8** 40 30N 19 20 E
Sázava →, *Czech Rep.* **16 D8** 49 53N 14 24 E
Sazin, *Pakistan* **43 B5** 35 35N 73 30 E
Scafell Pike, *U.K.* **10 C4** 54 27N 3 14W
Scalloway, *U.K.* **12 A7** 60 9N 1 17W
Scalpay, *U.K.* **12 D3** 57 18N 6 0W
Scandia, *Canada* **72 C6** 50 20N 112 0W
Scandicci, *Italy* **20 C4** 43 45N 11 11 E
Scandinavia, *Europe* **8 E16** 64 0N 12 0 E
Scapa Flow, *U.K.* **12 C5** 58 53N 3 3W
Scappoose, *U.S.A.* **84 E4** 45 45N 122 53W
Scarba, *U.K.* **12 E3** 56 11N 5 43W
Scarborough, *Trin. & Tob.* **89 D7** 11 11N 60 42W
Scarborough, *U.K.* **10 C7** 54 17N 0 24W
Scariff I., *Ireland* **13 E1** 51 44N 10 15W
Scarp, *U.K.* **12 C1** 58 1N 7 8W
Scebeli, Wabi →, *Somali Rep.* **46 G3** 2 0N 44 0 E
Schaffhausen, *Switz.* **18 C8** 47 42N 8 39 E
Schagen, *Neths.* **15 B4** 52 49N 4 48 E
Schaghticoke, *U.S.A.* **79 D11** 42 54N 73 35W
Schefferville, *Canada* **71 B6** 54 48N 66 50W
Schelde →, *Belgium* **15 C4** 51 15N 4 16 E
Schell Creek Ra., *U.S.A.* **82 G6** 39 15N 114 30W
Schellsburg, *U.S.A.* **78 F6** 40 3N 78 39W
Schenectady, *U.S.A.* **79 D11** 42 49N 73 57W
Schenevus, *U.S.A.* **79 D10** 42 33N 74 50W
Schiedam, *Neths.* **15 C4** 51 55N 4 25 E
Schiermonnikoog, *Neths.* **15 A6** 53 30N 6 15 E
Schio, *Italy* **20 B4** 45 43N 11 21 E
Schleswig, *Germany* **16 A5** 54 31N 9 34 E
Schleswig-Holstein □, *Germany* **16 A5** 54 30N 9 30 E
Schoharie, *U.S.A.* **79 D10** 42 40N 74 19W
Schoharie →, *U.S.A.* **79 D10** 42 57N 74 18W
Scholls, *U.S.A.* **84 E4** 45 24N 122 56W
Schouten I., *Australia* **62 G4** 42 20S 148 20 E
Schouten Is. = Supiori, *Indonesia* **37 E9** 1 0S 136 0 E
Schouwen, *Neths.* **15 C3** 51 43N 3 45 E
Schreiber, *Canada* **70 C2** 48 45N 87 20W
Schroffenstein, *Namibia* **56 D2** 27 11S 18 42 E
Schroon Lake, *U.S.A.* **79 C11** 43 50N 73 46W
Schuler, *Canada* **73 C6** 50 20N 110 6W
Schumacher, *Canada* **70 C3** 48 30N 81 16W
Schurz, *U.S.A.* **82 G4** 38 57N 118 49W
Schuyler, *U.S.A.* **80 E6** 41 27N 97 4W
Schuylerville, *U.S.A.* **79 C11** 43 6N 73 35W
Schuylkill →, *U.S.A.* **79 G9** 39 53N 75 12W
Schuylkill Haven, *U.S.A.* **79 F8** 40 37N 76 11W
Schwäbische Alb, *Germany* **16 D5** 48 20N 9 30 E
Schwaner, Pegunungan, *Indonesia* **36 E4** 1 0S 112 30 E
Schwarzrand, *Namibia* **56 D2** 25 37S 16 50 E
Schwarzwald, *Germany* **16 D5** 48 30N 8 20 E
Schwedt, *Germany* **16 B8** 53 3N 14 16 E
Schweinfurt, *Germany* **16 C6** 50 3N 10 14 E
Schweizer-Reneke, *S. Africa* **56 D4** 27 11S 25 18 E
Schwenningen = Villingen-Schwenningen, *Germany* **16 D5** 48 3N 8 26 E
Schwerin, *Germany* **16 B6** 53 36N 11 22 E
Schwyz, *Switz.* **18 C8** 47 2N 8 39 E
Sciacca, *Italy* **20 F5** 37 31N 13 3 E
Scilla, *Italy* **20 E6** 38 15N 15 43 E
Scilly, Isles of, *U.K.* **11 H1** 49 56N 6 22W
Scioto →, *U.S.A.* **76 F4** 38 44N 83 1W
Scituate, *U.S.A.* **79 D14** 42 12N 70 44W
Scobey, *U.S.A.* **80 A2** 48 47N 105 25W
Scoresbysund = Ittoqqortoormiit, *Greenland* **4 B6** 70 20N 23 0W
Scotia, *Calif., U.S.A.* **82 F1** 40 29N 124 6W
Scotia, *N.Y., U.S.A.* **79 D11** 42 50N 73 58W
Scotia Sea, *Antarctica* **5 B18** 56 5S 56 0W
Scotland, *Canada* **78 C4** 43 1N 80 22W
Scotland □, *U.K.* **12 E5** 57 0N 4 0W
Scott, C., *Australia* **60 B4** 13 30S 129 49 E
Scott City, *U.S.A.* **80 F4** 38 29N 100 54W
Scott Glacier, *Antarctica* **5 C8** 66 15S 100 5 E
Scott I., *Antarctica* **5 C11** 67 0S 179 0 E
Scott Is., *Canada* **72 C3** 50 48N 128 40W
Scott L., *Canada* **73 B7** 59 55N 106 18W
Scott Reef, *Australia* **60 B3** 14 0S 121 50 E
Scottburgh, *S. Africa* **57 E5** 30 15S 30 47 E
Scottdale, *U.S.A.* **78 F5** 40 6N 79 35W
Scottish Borders □, *U.K.* **12 F6** 55 35N 2 50W
Scottsbluff, *U.S.A.* **80 E3** 41 52N 103 40W
Scottsboro, *U.S.A.* **77 H3** 34 40N 86 2W
Scottsburg, *U.S.A.* **76 F3** 38 41N 85 47W
Scottsdale, *Australia* **62 G4** 41 9S 147 31 E
Scottsdale, *U.S.A.* **83 K7** 33 29N 111 56W
Scottsville, *Ky., U.S.A.* **77 G2** 36 45N 86 11W
Scottsville, *N.Y., U.S.A.* **78 C7** 43 2N 77 47W
Scottville, *U.S.A.* **76 D2** 43 58N 86 17W
Scranton, *U.S.A.* **79 E9** 41 25N 75 40W
Scugog, L., *Canada* **78 B6** 44 10N 78 55W
Scunthorpe, *U.K.* **10 D7** 53 36N 0 39W
Seabrook, L., *Australia* **61 F2** 30 55S 119 40 E
Seaford, *U.K.* **11 G8** 50 47N 0 7 E
Seaford, *U.S.A.* **76 F8** 38 39N 75 37W
Seaforth, *Australia* **62 C4** 20 55S 148 57 E
Seaforth, *Canada* **78 C3** 43 35N 81 25W
Seaforth, L., *U.K.* **12 D2** 57 52N 6 36W
Seagraves, *U.S.A.* **81 J3** 32 57N 102 34W
Seaham, *U.K.* **10 C6** 54 50N 1 20W
Seal →, *Canada* **73 B10** 59 4N 94 48W
Seal L., *Canada* **71 B7** 54 20N 61 30W
Sealy, *U.S.A.* **81 L6** 29 47N 96 9W
Searchlight, *U.S.A.* **85 K12** 35 28N 114 55W
Searcy, *U.S.A.* **81 H9** 35 15N 91 44W
Searles L., *U.S.A.* **85 K9** 35 44N 117 21W
Seascale, *U.K.* **10 C4** 54 24N 3 29W
Seaside, *Calif., U.S.A.* **84 J5** 36 37N 121 50W
Seaside, *Oreg., U.S.A.* **84 E3** 46 0N 123 56W
Seattle, *U.S.A.* **84 C4** 47 36N 122 20W
Seaview Ra., *Australia* **62 B4** 18 40S 145 45 E
Sebago L., *U.S.A.* **79 C14** 43 52N 70 34W
Sebago Lake, *U.S.A.* **79 C14** 43 51N 70 34W
Sebastián Vizcaino, B., *Mexico* **86 B2** 28 0N 114 30W
Sebastopol = Sevastopol, *Ukraine* **25 F5** 44 35N 33 30 E
Sebastopol, *U.S.A.* **84 G4** 38 24N 122 49W
Sebewaing, *U.S.A.* **76 D4** 43 44N 83 27W
Sebha = Sabhah, *Libya* **51 C8** 27 9N 14 29 E
Şebinkarahisar, *Turkey* **25 F6** 40 22N 38 28 E
Sebring, *Fla., U.S.A.* **77 M5** 27 30N 81 27W
Sebring, *Ohio, U.S.A.* **78 F3** 40 55N 81 2W
Sebringville, *Canada* **78 C3** 43 24N 81 4W
Sebta = Ceuta, *N. Afr.* **19 E3** 35 52N 5 18W
Sebuku, *Indonesia* **36 E5** 3 30S 116 25 E
Sebuku, Teluk, *Malaysia* **36 D5** 4 0N 118 10 E
Sechelt, *Canada* **72 D4** 49 25N 123 42W
Sechura, Desierto de, *Peru* **92 E2** 6 0S 80 30W
Secretary I., *N.Z.* **59 L1** 45 15S 166 56 E
Secunderabad, *India* **40 L11** 17 28N 78 30 E
Security-Widefield, *U.S.A.* **80 F2** 38 45N 104 45W
Sedalia, *U.S.A.* **80 F8** 38 42N 93 14W
Sedan, *France* **18 B6** 49 43N 4 57 E
Sedan, *U.S.A.* **81 G6** 37 8N 96 11W
Seddon, *N.Z.* **59 J5** 41 40S 174 7 E
Seddonville, *N.Z.* **59 J4** 41 33S 172 1 E
Sedé Boqér, *Israel* **47 E3** 30 52N 34 47 E
Sedeh, *Fārs, Iran* **45 D7** 30 45N 52 11 E
Sedeh, *Khorāsān, Iran* **45 C8** 33 20N 59 14 E
Sederot, *Israel* **47 D3** 31 32N 34 37 E
Sédhiou, *Senegal* **50 F2** 12 44N 15 30W
Sedley, *Canada* **73 C8** 50 10N 104 0W
Sedona, *U.S.A.* **83 J8** 34 52N 111 46W
Sedova, Pik, *Russia* **26 B6** 73 29N 54 58 E
Sedro Woolley, *U.S.A.* **84 B4** 48 30N 122 14W
Seeheim, *Namibia* **56 D2** 26 50S 17 45 E
Seeis, *Namibia* **56 C2** 22 29S 17 39 E
Seekoei →, *S. Africa* **56 E4** 30 18S 25 1 E
Seeley's Bay, *Canada* **79 B8** 44 29N 76 14W
Seferihisar, *Turkey* **21 E12** 38 10N 26 50 E
Seg-ozero, *Russia* **24 B5** 63 20N 33 46 E
Segamat, *Malaysia* **39 L4** 2 30N 102 50 E
Segesta, *Italy* **20 F5** 37 56N 12 50 E
Seget, *Indonesia* **37 E8** 1 24S 130 58 E
Segezha, *Russia* **24 B5** 63 44N 34 19 E
Ségou, *Mali* **50 F4** 13 30N 6 16W
Segovia = Coco →, *Cent. Amer.* **88 D3** 15 0N 83 8W
Segovia, *Spain* **19 B3** 40 57N 4 10W
Segre →, *Spain* **19 B6** 41 40N 0 43 E
Séguéla, *Ivory C.* **50 G4** 7 55N 6 40W
Seguin, *U.S.A.* **81 L6** 29 34N 97 58W
Segundo →, *Argentina* **94 C3** 30 53S 62 44W
Segura →, *Spain* **19 C5** 38 3N 0 44W
Seh Konj, Kūh-e, *Iran* **45 D8** 30 6N 57 30 E
Seh Qal'eh, *Iran* **45 C8** 33 40N 58 24 E
Sehitwa, *Botswana* **56 C3** 20 30S 22 30 E
Sehore, *India* **42 H7** 23 10N 77 5 E
Sehwan, *Pakistan* **42 F2** 26 28N 67 53 E
Seil, *U.K.* **12 E3** 56 18N 5 38W
Seiland, *Norway* **8 A20** 70 25N 23 15 E
Seiling, *U.S.A.* **81 G5** 36 9N 98 56W
Seinäjoki, *Finland* **9 E20** 62 40N 22 51 E
Seine →, *France* **18 B4** 49 26N 0 26 E
Seistan = Sīstān, *Asia* **45 D9** 30 50N 61 0 E
Seistan, Daryācheh-ye = Sīstān, Daryācheh-ye, *Iran* **45 D9** 31 0N 61 0 E
Sekayu, *Indonesia* **36 E2** 2 51S 103 51 E
Seke, *Tanzania* **54 C3** 3 20S 33 31 E
Sekenke, *Tanzania* **54 C3** 4 18S 34 11 E
Sekondi-Takoradi, *Ghana* **50 H5** 4 58N 1 45W
Sekuma, *Botswana* **56 C3** 24 36S 23 50 E
Selah, *U.S.A.* **82 C3** 46 39N 120 32W
Selama, *Malaysia* **39 K3** 5 12N 100 42 E
Selaru, *Indonesia* **37 F8** 8 9S 131 0 E
Selby, *U.K.* **10 D6** 53 47N 1 5W
Selby, *U.S.A.* **80 C4** 45 31N 100 2W
Selçuk, *Turkey* **21 F12** 37 56N 27 22 E
Selden, *U.S.A.* **80 F4** 39 33N 100 34W
Sele →, *Italy* **20 D6** 40 29N 14 56 E
Selebi-Pikwe, *Botswana* **57 C4** 21 58S 27 48 E
Selemdzha →, *Russia* **27 D13** 51 42N 128 53 E
Selenga = Selenge Mörön →, *Asia* **32 A5** 52 16N 106 16 E
Selenge Mörön →, *Asia* **32 A5** 52 16N 106 16 E
Seletan, Tanjung, *Indonesia* **36 E4** 4 10S 114 40 E
Sélibabi, *Mauritania* **50 E3** 15 10N 12 15W
Seligman, *U.S.A.* **83 J7** 35 20N 112 53W
Selîma, El Wâhât el, *Sudan* **51 D11** 21 22N 29 19 E
Selinda Spillway →, *Botswana* **56 B3** 18 35S 23 10 E
Selinsgrove, *U.S.A.* **78 F8** 40 48N 76 52W
Selkirk, *Canada* **73 C9** 50 10N 96 55W
Selkirk, *U.K.* **12 F6** 55 33N 2 50W
Selkirk I., *Canada* **73 C9** 53 20N 99 6W
Selkirk Mts., *Canada* **68 C8** 51 15N 117 40W
Selliá, *Greece* **23 D6** 35 12N 24 23 E
Sells, *U.S.A.* **83 L8** 31 55N 111 53W
Selma, *Ala., U.S.A.* **77 J2** 32 25N 87 1W
Selma, *Calif., U.S.A.* **84 J7** 36 34N 119 37W
Selma, *N.C., U.S.A.* **77 H6** 35 32N 78 17W
Selmer, *U.S.A.* **77 H1** 35 10N 88 36W
Selowandoma Falls, *Zimbabwe* **55 G3** 21 15S 31 50 E
Selpele, *Indonesia* **37 E8** 0 1S 130 5 E
Selsey Bill, *U.K.* **11 G7** 50 43N 0 47W
Seltso, *Russia* **24 D5** 53 22N 34 4 E
Selu, *Indonesia* **37 F8** 7 32S 130 55 E
Selva, *Argentina* **94 B3** 29 50S 62 0W
Selvas, *Brazil* **92 E5** 6 30S 67 0W
Selwyn L., *Canada* **73 B8** 60 0N 104 30W
Selwyn Mts., *Canada* **68 B6** 63 0N 130 0W
Selwyn Ra., *Australia* **62 C3** 21 10S 140 0 E
Seman →, *Albania* **21 D8** 40 47N 19 30 E
Semarang, *Indonesia* **36 F4** 7 0S 110 26 E
Sembabule, *Uganda* **54 C3** 0 4S 31 25 E
Semeru, *Indonesia* **37 H15** 8 4S 112 55 E
Semey, *Kazakstan* **26 D9** 50 30N 80 10 E
Seminoe Reservoir, *U.S.A.* **82 F10** 42 9N 106 55W
Seminole, *Okla., U.S.A.* **81 H6** 35 14N 96 41W
Seminole, *Tex., U.S.A.* **81 J3** 32 43N 102 39W
Seminole Draw →, *U.S.A.* **81 J3** 32 27N 102 20W
Semipalatinsk = Semey, *Kazakstan* **26 D9** 50 30N 80 10 E
Semirara Is., *Phil.* **37 B6** 12 0N 121 20 E
Semitau, *Indonesia* **36 D4** 0 29N 111 57 E
Semiyarka, *Kazakstan* **26 D8** 50 55N 78 23 E
Semiyarskoye = Semiyarka, *Kazakstan* **26 D8** 50 55N 78 23 E
Semmering P., *Austria* **16 E8** 47 41N 15 45 E
Semnān, *Iran* **45 C7** 35 40N 53 23 E
Semnān □, *Iran* **45 C7** 36 0N 54 0 E
Semporna, *Malaysia* **37 D5** 4 30N 118 33 E
Semuda, *Indonesia* **36 E4** 2 51S 112 58 E
Sen →, *Cambodia* **36 B3** 13 45N 105 12 E
Senā, *Iran* **45 D6** 28 27N 51 36 E
Sena, *Mozam.* **55 F4** 17 25S 35 0 E
Sena Madureira, *Brazil* **92 E5** 9 5S 68 45W
Senador Pompeu, *Brazil* **93 E11** 5 40S 39 20W
Senanga, *Zambia* **53 H4** 16 7S 23 16 E
Senatobia, *U.S.A.* **81 H10** 34 37N 89 58W
Sencelles, *Spain* **22 B9** 39 39N 2 54 E
Sendai, *Kagoshima, Japan* **31 J5** 31 50N 130 20 E
Sendai, *Miyagi, Japan* **30 E10** 38 15N 140 53 E
Sendai-Wan, *Japan* **30 E10** 38 15N 141 0 E
Sendhwa, *India* **42 J6** 21 41N 75 6 E
Seneca, *U.S.A.* **77 H4** 34 41N 82 57W
Seneca Falls, *U.S.A.* **79 D8** 42 55N 76 48W
Seneca L., *U.S.A.* **78 D8** 42 40N 76 54W
Senecaville L., *U.S.A.* **78 G3** 39 55N 81 25W
Senegal ■, *W. Afr.* **50 F3** 14 30N 14 30W
Sénégal →, *W. Afr.* **50 E2** 15 48N 16 32W
Senegambia, *Africa* **48 E2** 12 45N 12 0W
Senekal, *S. Africa* **57 D4** 28 20S 27 36 E
Senga Hill, *Zambia* **55 D3** 9 19S 31 11 E
Senge Khambab = Indus →, *Pakistan* **42 G2** 24 20N 67 47 E
Sengua →, *Zimbabwe* **55 F2** 17 7S 28 5 E
Senhor-do-Bonfim, *Brazil* **93 F10** 10 30S 40 10W
Senigállia, *Italy* **20 C5** 43 43N 13 13 E
Senj, *Croatia* **16 F8** 45 0N 14 58 E
Senja, *Norway* **8 B17** 69 25N 17 30 E
Senkaku-Shotō, *Japan* **31 L1** 25 45N 124 0 E
Senlis, *France* **18 B5** 49 13N 2 35 E
Senmonorom, *Cambodia* **38 F6** 12 27N 107 12 E
Senneterre, *Canada* **70 C4** 48 25N 77 15W
Seno, *Laos* **38 D5** 16 35N 104 50 E
Sens, *France* **18 B5** 48 11N 3 15 E
Senta, *Serbia, Yug.* **21 B9** 45 55N 20 3 E
Sentani, *Indonesia* **37 E10** 2 36S 140 37 E
Sentery, *Dem. Rep. of the Congo* **54 D2** 5 17S 25 42 E
Sentinel, *U.S.A.* **83 K7** 32 52N 113 13W
Seo de Urgel = La Seu d'Urgell, *Spain* **19 A6** 42 22N 1 23 E
Seohara, *India* **43 E8** 29 15N 78 33 E
Seonath →, *India* **43 J10** 21 44N 82 28 E
Seondha, *India* **43 F8** 26 9N 78 48 E
Seoni, *India* **43 H8** 22 5N 79 30 E
Seoni Malwa, *India* **42 H8** 22 27N 77 28 E
Seoul = Sŏul, *S. Korea* **35 F14** 37 31N 126 58 E
Sepīdān, *Iran* **45 D7** 30 20N 52 5 E
Sepo-ri, *N. Korea* **35 E14** 38 57N 127 25 E
Sepone, *Laos* **38 D6** 16 45N 106 13 E
Sept-Îles, *Canada* **71 B6** 50 13N 66 22W
Sequim, *U.S.A.* **84 B3** 48 5N 123 6W
Sequoia National Park, *U.S.A.* **84 J8** 36 30N 118 30W
Seraing, *Belgium* **15 D5** 50 35N 5 32 E
Seraja, *Indonesia* **39 L7** 2 41N 108 35 E
Serakhis →, *Cyprus* **23 D11** 35 13N 32 55 E
Seram, *Indonesia* **37 E7** 3 10S 129 0 E
Seram Sea, *Indonesia* **37 E7** 2 30S 128 30 E
Seranantsara, *Madag.* **57 B8** 18 30S 49 5 E
Serang, *Indonesia* **37 G12** 6 8S 106 10 E
Serasan, *Indonesia* **39 L7** 2 29N 109 4 E
Serbia □, *Yugoslavia* **21 C9** 43 30N 21 0 E
Serdobsk, *Russia* **24 D7** 52 28N 44 10 E
Seremban, *Malaysia* **39 L3** 2 43N 101 53 E
Serengeti Plain, *Tanzania* **54 C4** 2 40S 35 0 E
Serenje, *Zambia* **55 E3** 13 14S 30 15 E
Sereth = Siret →, *Romania* **17 F14** 45 24N 28 1 E
Sergino, *Russia* **26 C7** 62 25N 65 12 E
Sergipe □, *Brazil* **93 F11** 10 30S 37 30W
Sergiyev Posad, *Russia* **24 C6** 56 20N 38 10 E
Seria, *Brunei* **36 D4** 4 37N 114 23 E
Serian, *Malaysia* **36 D4** 1 10N 110 31 E
Seribu, Kepulauan, *Indonesia* **36 F3** 5 36S 106 33 E
Sérifos, *Greece* **21 F11** 37 9N 24 30 E
Sérigny →, *Canada* **71 A6** 56 47N 66 0W
Seringapatam Reef, *Australia* **60 B3** 13 38S 122 5 E
Sermata, *Indonesia* **37 F7** 8 15S 128 50 E
Serov, *Russia* **24 C11** 59 29N 60 35 E
Serowe, *Botswana* **56 C4** 22 25S 26 43 E
Serpentine Lakes, *Australia* **61 E4** 28 30S 129 10 E
Serpukhov, *Russia* **24 D6** 54 55N 37 28 E
Serra do Navio, *Brazil* **93 C8** 0 59N 52 3W
Sérrai, *Greece* **21 D10** 41 5N 23 31 E
Serrezuela, *Argentina* **94 C2** 30 40S 65 20W
Serrinha, *Brazil* **93 F11** 11 39S 39 0W
Sertanópolis, *Brazil* **95 A5** 23 4S 51 2W
Serua, *Indonesia* **37 F8** 6 18S 130 1 E
Serui, *Indonesia* **37 E9** 1 53S 136 10 E
Serule, *Botswana* **56 C4** 21 57S 27 20 E
Sese Is., *Uganda* **54 C3** 0 20S 32 20 E
Sesepe, *Indonesia* **37 E7** 1 30S 127 59 E
Sesfontein, *Namibia* **56 B1** 19 7S 13 39 E
Sesheke, *Zambia* **56 B3** 17 29S 24 13 E
S'Espalmador, *Spain* **22 C7** 38 47N 1 26 E
S'Espardell, *Spain* **22 C7** 38 48N 1 29 E
S'Estanyol, *Spain* **22 B9** 39 22N 2 54 E
Setana, *Japan* **30 C9** 42 26N 139 51 E
Sète, *France* **18 E5** 43 25N 3 42 E
Sete Lagôas, *Brazil* **93 G10** 19 27S 44 16W
Sétif, *Algeria* **50 A7** 36 9N 5 26 E
Seto, *Japan* **31 G8** 35 14N 137 6 E
Setonaikai, *Japan* **31 G6** 34 20N 133 30 E
Settat, *Morocco* **50 B4** 33 0N 7 40W
Setting L., *Canada* **73 C9** 55 0N 98 38W
Settle, *U.K.* **10 C5** 54 5N 2 16W
Settlement Pt., *Bahamas* **77 M6** 26 40N 79 0W
Settlers, *S. Africa* **57 C4** 25 2S 28 30 E
Setúbal, *Portugal* **19 C1** 38 30N 8 58W
Setúbal, B. de, *Portugal* **19 C1** 38 40N 8 56W
Seul, Lac, *Canada* **70 B1** 50 20N 92 30W
Sevan, Ozero = Sevana Lich, *Armenia* **25 F8** 40 30N 45 20 E
Sevana Lich, *Armenia* **25 F8** 40 30N 45 20 E
Sevastopol, *Ukraine* **25 F5** 44 35N 33 30 E
Seven Sisters, *Canada* **72 C3** 54 56N 128 10W
Severn →, *Canada* **70 A2** 56 2N 87 36W
Severn →, *U.K.* **11 F5** 51 35N 2 40W
Severn L., *Canada* **70 B1** 53 54N 90 48W
Severnaya Zemlya, *Russia* **27 B10** 79 0N 100 0 E
Severnyye Uvaly, *Russia* **24 C8** 60 0N 50 0 E
Severo-Kurilsk, *Russia* **27 D16** 50 40N 156 8 E
Severo-Yeniseyskiy, *Russia* **27 C10** 60 22N 93 1 E
Severodvinsk, *Russia* **24 B6** 64 27N 39 58 E
Severomorsk, *Russia* **24 A5** 69 5N 33 27 E
Severouralsk, *Russia* **24 B10** 60 9N 59 57 E
Sevier, *U.S.A.* **83 G7** 38 39N 112 11W
Sevier →, *U.S.A.* **83 G7** 39 4N 113 6W
Sevier Desert, *U.S.A.* **82 G7** 39 40N 112 45W
Sevier L., *U.S.A.* **82 G7** 38 54N 113 9W
Sevilla, *Spain* **19 D2** 37 23N 5 58W
Seville = Sevilla, *Spain* **19 D2** 37 23N 5 58W
Sevlievo, *Bulgaria* **21 C11** 43 2N 25 6 E
Sewani, *India* **42 E6** 28 58N 75 39 E
Seward, *Alaska, U.S.A.* **68 B5** 60 7N 149 27W
Seward, *Nebr., U.S.A.* **80 E6** 40 55N 97 6W
Seward, *Pa., U.S.A.* **78 F5** 40 25N 79 1W
Seward Peninsula, *U.S.A.* **68 B3** 65 30N 166 0W
Sewell, *Chile* **94 C1** 34 10S 70 23W
Sewer, *Indonesia* **37 F8** 5 53S 134 40 E
Sewickley, *U.S.A.* **78 F4** 40 32N 80 12W
Sexsmith, *Canada* **72 B5** 55 21N 118 47W
Seychelles ■, *Ind. Oc.* **29 K9** 5 0S 56 0 E
Seyðisfjörður, *Iceland* **8 D6** 65 16N 13 57W
Seydişehir, *Turkey* **25 G5** 37 25N 31 51 E
Seydvān, *Iran* **44 B5** 38 34N 45 2 E
Seyhan →, *Turkey* **44 B2** 36 43N 34 53 E

Seym →, *Ukraine* **25 D5** 51 27N 32 34 E
Seymour, *S. Africa* **57 E4** 32 33S 26 46 E
Seymour, *Conn., U.S.A.* **79 E11** 41 24N 73 4W
Seymour, *Ind., U.S.A.* **76 F3** 38 58N 85 53W
Seymour, *Tex., U.S.A.* **81 J5** 33 35N 99 16W
Sfântu Gheorghe, *Romania* **17 F13** 45 52N 25 48 E
Sfax, *Tunisia* **51 B8** 34 49N 10 48 E
Shaanxi □, *China* **34 G5** 35 0N 109 0 E
Shaba = Katanga □, *Dem. Rep. of the Congo* **54 D2** 8 0S 25 0 E
Shabogamo L., *Canada* **71 B6** 53 15N 66 30W
Shabunda, *Dem. Rep. of the Congo* **54 C2** 2 40S 27 16 E
Shache, *China* **32 C2** 38 20N 77 10 E
Shackleton Ice Shelf, *Antarctica* **5 C8** 66 0S 100 0 E
Shackleton Inlet, *Antarctica* **5 E11** 83 0S 160 0 E
Shādegān, *Iran* **45 D6** 30 40N 48 38 E
Shadi, *India* **43 C7** 33 24N 77 14 E
Shadrinsk, *Russia* **26 D7** 56 5N 63 32 E
Shadyside, *U.S.A.* **78 G4** 39 58N 80 45W
Shafter, *U.S.A.* **85 K7** 35 30N 119 16W
Shaftesbury, *U.K.* **11 F5** 51 0N 2 11W
Shagram, *Pakistan* **43 A5** 36 24N 72 20 E
Shah Alizai, *Pakistan* **42 E2** 29 25N 66 33 E
Shah Bunder, *Pakistan* **42 G2** 24 13N 67 56 E
Shahabad, *Punjab, India* **42 D7** 30 10N 76 55 E
Shahabad, *Raj., India* **42 G7** 25 15N 77 11 E
Shahabad, *Ut. P., India* **43 F8** 27 36N 79 56 E
Shahadpur, *Pakistan* **42 G3** 25 55N 68 35 E
Shahba, *Syria* **47 C5** 32 52N 36 38 E
Shahdād, *Iran* **45 D8** 30 30N 57 40 E
Shahdād, Namakzār-e, *Iran* **45 D8** 30 20N 58 20 E
Shahdadkot, *Pakistan* **42 F2** 27 50N 67 55 E
Shahdol, *India* **43 H9** 23 19N 81 26 E
Shahe, *China* **34 F8** 37 0N 114 32 E
Shahganj, *India* **43 F10** 26 3N 82 44 E
Shahgarh, *India* **40 F6** 27 15N 69 50 E
Shahjahanpur, *India* **43 F8** 27 54N 79 57 E
Shahpur, *India* **42 H7** 22 12N 77 58 E
Shahpur, *Baluchistan, Pakistan* **42 E3** 28 46N 68 27 E
Shahpur, *Punjab, Pakistan* **42 C5** 32 17N 72 26 E
Shahpur Chakar, *Pakistan* **42 F3** 26 9N 68 39 E
Shahpura, *Mad. P., India* **43 H9** 23 10N 80 45 E
Shahpura, *Raj., India* **42 G6** 25 38N 74 56 E
Shahr-e Bābak, *Iran* **45 D7** 30 7N 55 9 E
Shahr-e Kord, *Iran* **45 C6** 32 15N 50 55 E
Shāhrakht, *Iran* **45 C9** 33 38N 60 16 E
Shahrig, *Pakistan* **42 D2** 30 15N 67 40 E
Shahukou, *China* **34 D7** 40 20N 112 18 E
Shaikhabad, *Afghan.* **42 B3** 34 2N 68 45 E
Shajapur, *India* **42 H7** 23 27N 76 21 E
Shakargarh, *Pakistan* **42 C6** 32 17N 75 10 E
Shakawe, *Botswana* **56 B3** 18 28S 21 49 E
Shaker Heights, *U.S.A.* **78 E3** 41 29N 81 32W
Shakhty, *Russia* **25 E7** 47 40N 40 16 E
Shakhunya, *Russia* **24 C8** 57 40N 46 46 E
Shaki, *Nigeria* **50 G6** 8 41N 3 21 E
Shallow Lake, *Canada* **78 B3** 44 36N 81 5W
Shalqar, *Kazakstan* **26 E6** 47 48N 59 39 E
Shaluli Shan, *China* **32 C4** 30 40N 99 55 E
Shām, *Iran* **45 E8** 26 39N 57 21 E
Shām, Bādiyat ash, *Asia* **44 C3** 32 0N 40 0 E
Shamâl Kordofân □, *Sudan* **48 E6** 15 0N 30 0 E
Shamattawa, *Canada* **70 A1** 55 51N 92 5W
Shamattawa →, *Canada* **70 A2** 55 1N 85 23W
Shamīl, *Iran* **45 E8** 27 30N 56 55 E
Shāmkūh, *Iran* **45 C8** 35 47N 57 50 E
Shamli, *India* **42 E7** 29 32N 77 18 E
Shammar, Jabal, *Si. Arabia* **44 E4** 27 40N 41 0 E
Shamo = Gobi, *Asia* **34 C6** 44 0N 110 0 E
Shamo, L., *Ethiopia* **46 F2** 5 45N 37 30 E
Shamokin, *U.S.A.* **79 F8** 40 47N 76 34W
Shamrock, *U.S.A.* **81 H4** 35 13N 100 15W
Shamva, *Zimbabwe* **55 F3** 17 20S 31 32 E
Shan □, *Burma* **41 J21** 21 30N 98 30 E
Shan Xian, *China* **34 G9** 34 50N 116 5 E
Shanchengzhen, *China* **35 C13** 42 20N 125 20 E
Shāndak, *Iran* **45 D9** 28 28N 60 27 E
Shandon, *U.S.A.* **84 K6** 35 39N 120 23W
Shandong □, *China* **35 G10** 36 0N 118 0 E
Shandong Bandao, *China* **35 F11** 37 0N 121 0 E
Shang Xian = Shangzhou, *China* **34 H5** 33 50N 109 58 E
Shanga, *Nigeria* **50 F6** 11 12N 4 33 E
Shangalowe, *Dem. Rep. of the Congo* **55 E2** 10 50S 26 30 E
Shangani, *Zimbabwe* **57 B4** 19 41S 29 20 E
Shangani →, *Zimbabwe* **55 F2** 18 41S 27 10 E
Shangbancheng, *China* **35 D10** 40 50N 118 1 E
Shangdu, *China* **34 D7** 41 30N 113 30 E
Shanghai, *China* **33 C7** 31 15N 121 26 E
Shanghe, *China* **35 F9** 37 20N 117 10 E
Shangnan, *China* **34 H6** 33 32N 110 50 E
Shangqiu, *China* **34 G8** 34 26N 115 36 E
Shangrao, *China* **33 D6** 28 25N 117 59 E
Shangshui, *China* **34 H8** 33 42N 114 35 E
Shangzhi, *China* **35 B14** 45 22N 127 56 E
Shangzhou, *China* **34 H5** 33 50N 109 58 E
Shanhetun, *China* **35 B14** 44 33N 127 15 E
Shannon, *N.Z.* **59 J5** 40 33S 175 25 E
Shannon →, *Ireland* **13 D2** 52 35N 9 30W
Shannon, Mouth of the, *Ireland* **13 D2** 52 30N 9 55W
Shannon Airport, *Ireland* **13 D3** 52 42N 8 57W
Shansi = Shanxi □, *China* **34 F7** 37 0N 112 0 E
Shantar, Ostrov Bolshoy, *Russia* **27 D14** 55 9N 137 40 E
Shantipur, *India* **43 H13** 23 17N 88 25 E
Shantou, *China* **33 D6** 23 18N 116 40 E
Shantung = Shandong □, *China* **35 G10** 36 0N 118 0 E
Shanxi □, *China* **34 F7** 37 0N 112 0 E
Shanyang, *China* **34 H5** 33 31N 109 55 E
Shanyin, *China* **34 E7** 39 25N 112 56 E
Shaoguan, *China* **33 D6** 24 48N 113 35 E
Shaoxing, *China* **33 D7** 30 0N 120 35 E
Shaoyang, *China* **33 D6** 27 14N 111 25 E
Shap, *U.K.* **10 C5** 54 32N 2 40W
Shapinsay, *U.K.* **12 B6** 59 3N 2 51W
Shaqra', *Si. Arabia* **44 E5** 25 15N 45 16 E
Shaqrā', *Yemen* **46 E4** 13 22N 45 44 E
Sharafkhāneh, *Iran* **44 B5** 38 11N 45 29 E
Sharbot Lake, *Canada* **79 B8** 44 46N 76 41W
Shari, *Japan* **30 C12** 43 55N 144 40 E
Sharjah = Ash Shāriqah, *U.A.E.* **46 B6** 25 23N 55 26 E
Shark B., *Australia* **61 E1** 25 30S 113 32 E
Sharon, *Mass., U.S.A.* **79 D13** 42 7N 71 11W
Sharon, *Pa., U.S.A.* **78 E4** 41 14N 80 31W
Sharon Springs, *Kans., U.S.A.* **80 F4** 38 54N 101 45W
Sharon Springs, *N.Y., U.S.A.* **79 D10** 42 48N 74 37W
Sharp Pt., *Australia* **62 A3** 10 58S 142 43 E
Sharpe L., *Canada* **70 B1** 54 24N 93 40W
Sharpsville, *U.S.A.* **78 E4** 41 15N 80 29W
Sharya, *Russia* **24 C8** 58 22N 45 20 E
Shashemene, *Ethiopia* **46 F2** 7 13N 38 33 E
Shashi, *Botswana* **57 C4** 21 15S 27 27 E
Shashi, *China* **33 C6** 30 25N 112 14 E
Shashi →, *Africa* **55 G2** 21 14S 29 20 E
Shasta, Mt., *U.S.A.* **82 F2** 41 25N 122 12W
Shasta L., *U.S.A.* **82 F2** 40 43N 122 25W
Shatt al Arab = Arab, Shatt al →, *Asia* **45 D6** 30 0N 48 31 E
Shaunavon, *Canada* **73 D7** 49 35N 108 25W
Shaver L., *U.S.A.* **84 H7** 37 9N 119 18W
Shaw →, *Australia* **60 D2** 20 21S 119 17 E
Shaw I., *Australia* **62 C4** 20 30S 149 2 E
Shawanaga, *Canada* **78 A4** 45 31N 80 17W
Shawangunk Mts., *U.S.A.* **79 E10** 41 35N 74 30W
Shawano, *U.S.A.* **76 C1** 44 47N 88 36W
Shawinigan, *Canada* **70 C5** 46 35N 72 50W
Shawnee, *U.S.A.* **81 H6** 35 20N 96 55W
Shay Gap, *Australia* **60 D3** 20 30S 120 10 E
Shaybārā, *Si. Arabia* **44 E3** 25 26N 36 47 E
Shaykh, J. ash, *Lebanon* **47 B4** 33 25N 35 50 E
Shaykh Miskīn, *Syria* **47 C5** 32 49N 36 9 E
Shaykh Sa'īd, *Iraq* **44 C5** 32 34N 46 17 E
Shcherbakov = Rybinsk, *Russia* **24 C6** 58 5N 38 50 E
Shchuchinsk, *Kazakstan* **26 D8** 52 56N 70 12 E
She Xian, *China* **34 F7** 36 30N 113 40 E
Shebele = Scebeli, Wabi →, *Somali Rep.* **46 G3** 2 0N 44 0 E
Sheboygan, *U.S.A.* **76 D2** 43 46N 87 45W
Shediac, *Canada* **71 C7** 46 14N 64 32W
Sheelin, L., *Ireland* **13 C4** 53 48N 7 20W
Sheep Haven, *Ireland* **13 A4** 55 11N 7 52W
Sheerness, *U.K.* **11 F8** 51 26N 0 47 E
Sheet Harbour, *Canada* **71 D7** 44 56N 62 31W
Sheffield, *U.K.* **10 D6** 53 23N 1 28W
Sheffield, *Ala., U.S.A.* **77 H2** 34 46N 87 41W
Sheffield, *Mass., U.S.A.* **79 D11** 42 5N 73 21W
Sheffield, *Pa., U.S.A.* **78 E5** 41 42N 79 3W
Sheikhpura, *India* **43 G11** 25 9N 85 53 E
Shekhupura, *Pakistan* **42 D5** 31 42N 73 58 E
Shelburne, *N.S., Canada* **71 D6** 43 47N 65 20W
Shelburne, *Ont., Canada* **78 B4** 44 4N 80 15W
Shelburne, *U.S.A.* **79 B11** 44 23N 73 14W
Shelburne B., *Australia* **62 A3** 11 50S 142 50 E
Shelburne Falls, *U.S.A.* **79 D12** 42 36N 72 45W
Shelby, *Mich., U.S.A.* **76 D2** 43 37N 86 22W
Shelby, *Miss., U.S.A.* **81 J9** 33 57N 90 46W
Shelby, *Mont., U.S.A.* **82 B8** 48 30N 111 51W
Shelby, *N.C., U.S.A.* **77 H5** 35 17N 81 32W
Shelby, *Ohio, U.S.A.* **78 F2** 40 53N 82 40W
Shelbyville, *Ill., U.S.A.* **80 F10** 39 24N 88 48W
Shelbyville, *Ind., U.S.A.* **76 F3** 39 31N 85 47W
Shelbyville, *Ky., U.S.A.* **76 F3** 38 13N 85 14W
Shelbyville, *Tenn., U.S.A.* **77 H2** 35 29N 86 28W
Sheldon, *U.S.A.* **80 D7** 43 11N 95 51W
Sheldrake, *Canada* **71 B7** 50 20N 64 51W
Shelikhova, Zaliv, *Russia* **27 D16** 59 30N 157 0 E
Shell Lakes, *Australia* **61 E4** 29 20S 127 30 E
Shellbrook, *Canada* **73 C7** 53 13N 106 24W
Shelter I, *U.S.A.* **79 E12** 41 5N 72 21W
Shelton, *Conn., U.S.A.* **79 E11** 41 19N 73 5W
Shelton, *Wash., U.S.A.* **84 C3** 47 13N 123 6W
Shen Xian, *China* **34 F8** 36 15N 115 40 E
Shenandoah, *Iowa, U.S.A.* **80 E7** 40 46N 95 22W
Shenandoah, *Pa., U.S.A.* **79 F8** 40 49N 76 12W
Shenandoah, *Va., U.S.A.* **76 F6** 38 29N 78 37W
Shenandoah →, *U.S.A.* **76 F7** 39 19N 77 44W
Shenandoah National Park, *U.S.A.* **76 F6** 38 35N 78 22W
Shenchi, *China* **34 E7** 39 8N 112 10 E
Shendam, *Nigeria* **50 G7** 8 49N 9 30 E
Shendī, *Sudan* **51 E12** 16 46N 33 22 E
Shengfang, *China* **34 E9** 39 3N 116 42 E
Shenjingzi, *China* **35 B13** 44 40N 124 30 E
Shenmu, *China* **34 E6** 38 50N 110 29 E
Shenqiu, *China* **34 H8** 33 25N 115 5 E
Shensi = Shaanxi □, *China* **34 G5** 35 0N 109 0 E
Shenyang, *China* **35 D12** 41 48N 123 27 E
Sheo, *India* **42 F4** 26 11N 71 15 E
Sheopur Kalan, *India* **40 G10** 25 40N 76 40 E
Shepetivka, *Ukraine* **17 C14** 50 10N 27 10 E
Shepetovka = Shepetivka, *Ukraine* **17 C14** 50 10N 27 10 E
Sheppey, I. of, *U.K.* **11 F8** 51 25N 0 48 E
Shepton Mallet, *U.K.* **11 F5** 51 11N 2 33W
Sheqi, *China* **34 H7** 33 12N 112 57 E
Sher Qila, *Pakistan* **43 A6** 36 7N 74 2 E
Sherborne, *U.K.* **11 G5** 50 57N 2 31W
Sherbro I., *S. Leone* **50 G3** 7 30N 12 40W
Sherbrooke, *N.S., Canada* **71 C7** 45 8N 61 59W
Sherbrooke, *Qué., Canada* **79 A13** 45 28N 71 57W
Sherburne, *U.S.A.* **79 D9** 42 41N 75 30W
Shergarh, *India* **42 F5** 26 20N 72 18 E
Sherghati, *India* **43 G11** 24 34N 84 47 E
Sheridan, *Ark., U.S.A.* **81 H8** 34 19N 92 24W
Sheridan, *Wyo., U.S.A.* **82 D10** 44 48N 106 58W
Sheringham, *U.K.* **10 E9** 52 56N 1 13 E
Sherkin I., *Ireland* **13 E2** 51 28N 9 26W
Sherkot, *India* **43 E8** 29 22N 78 35 E
Sherman, *U.S.A.* **81 J6** 33 40N 96 35W
Sherpur, *India* **43 G10** 25 34N 83 47 E
Sherridon, *Canada* **73 B8** 55 8N 101 5W
Sherwood Forest, *U.K.* **10 D6** 53 6N 1 7W
Sherwood Park, *Canada* **72 C6** 53 31N 113 19W
Sheslay →, *Canada* **72 B2** 58 48N 132 5W
Shethanei L., *Canada* **73 B9** 58 48N 97 50W
Shetland □, *U.K.* **12 A7** 60 30N 1 30W
Shetland Is., *U.K.* **12 A7** 60 30N 1 30W
Shetrunji →, *India* **42 J5** 21 19N 72 7 E
Sheyenne →, *U.S.A.* **80 B6** 47 2N 96 50W
Shibām, *Yemen* **46 D4** 16 0N 48 36 E
Shibata, *Japan* **30 F9** 37 57N 139 20 E
Shibecha, *Japan* **30 C12** 43 17N 144 36 E
Shibetsu, *Japan* **30 B11** 44 10N 142 23 E
Shibogama L., *Canada* **70 B2** 53 35N 88 15W
Shibushi, *Japan* **31 J5** 31 25N 131 8 E
Shickshinny, *U.S.A.* **79 E8** 41 9N 76 9W
Shickshock Mts. = Chic-Chocs, Mts., *Canada* **71 C6** 48 55N 66 0W
Shidao, *China* **35 F12** 36 50N 122 25 E
Shido, *Japan* **31 G7** 34 19N 134 10 E
Shiel, L., *U.K.* **12 E3** 56 48N 5 34W
Shield, C., *Australia* **62 A2** 13 20S 136 20 E
Shīeli, *Kazakstan* **26 E7** 44 20N 66 15 E
Shiga □, *Japan* **31 G8** 35 20N 136 0 E
Shiguaigou, *China* **34 D6** 40 52N 110 15 E
Shihchiachuangi = Shijiazhuang, *China* **34 E8** 38 2N 114 28 E
Shijiazhuang, *China* **34 E8** 38 2N 114 28 E
Shikarpur, *India* **42 E8** 28 17N 78 7 E
Shikarpur, *Pakistan* **42 F3** 27 57N 68 39 E
Shikohabad, *India* **43 F8** 27 6N 78 36 E
Shikoku □, *Japan* **31 H6** 33 30N 133 30 E
Shikoku-Sanchi, *Japan* **31 H6** 33 30N 133 30 E
Shiliguri, *India* **41 F16** 26 45N 88 25 E
Shilka, *Russia* **27 D12** 52 0N 115 55 E
Shilka →, *Russia* **27 D13** 53 20N 121 26 E
Shillelagh, *Ireland* **13 D5** 52 45N 6 32W
Shillington, *U.S.A.* **79 F9** 40 18N 75 58W
Shillong, *India* **41 G17** 25 35N 91 53 E
Shilo, *West Bank* **47 C4** 32 4N 35 18 E
Shilou, *China* **34 F6** 37 0N 110 48 E
Shimabara, *Japan* **31 H5** 32 48N 130 20 E
Shimada, *Japan* **31 G9** 34 49N 138 10 E
Shimane □, *Japan* **31 G6** 35 0N 132 30 E
Shimanovsk, *Russia* **27 D13** 52 15N 127 30 E
Shimizu, *Japan* **31 G9** 35 0N 138 30 E
Shimodate, *Japan* **31 F9** 36 20N 139 55 E
Shimoga, *India* **40 N9** 13 57N 75 32 E
Shimoni, *Kenya* **54 C4** 4 38S 39 20 E
Shimonoseki, *Japan* **31 H5** 33 58N 130 55 E
Shimpuru Rapids, *Angola* **56 B2** 17 45S 19 55 E
Shin, L., *U.K.* **12 C4** 58 5N 4 30W
Shinano-Gawa →, *Japan* **31 F9** 36 50N 138 30 E
Shināş, *Oman* **45 E8** 24 46N 56 28 E
Shīndand, *Afghan.* **40 C3** 33 12N 62 8 E
Shinglehouse, *U.S.A.* **78 E6** 41 58N 78 12W
Shingū, *Japan* **31 H7** 33 40N 135 55 E
Shingwidzi, *S. Africa* **57 C5** 23 5S 31 25 E
Shinjō, *Japan* **30 E10** 38 46N 140 18 E
Shinshār, *Syria* **47 A5** 34 36N 36 43 E
Shinyanga, *Tanzania* **54 C3** 3 45S 33 27 E
Shinyanga □, *Tanzania* **54 C3** 3 50S 34 0 E
Shio-no-Misaki, *Japan* **31 H7** 33 25N 135 45 E
Shiogama, *Japan* **30 E10** 38 19N 141 1 E
Shiojiri, *Japan* **31 F8** 36 6N 137 58 E
Shipchenski Prokhod, *Bulgaria* **21 C11** 42 45N 25 15 E
Shiping, *China* **32 D5** 23 45N 102 23 E
Shippegan, *Canada* **71 C7** 47 45N 64 45W
Shippensburg, *U.S.A.* **78 F7** 40 3N 77 31W
Shippenville, *U.S.A.* **78 E5** 41 15N 79 28W
Shiprock, *U.S.A.* **83 H9** 36 47N 108 41W
Shiqma, N. →, *Israel* **47 D3** 31 37N 34 30 E
Shiquan, *China* **34 H5** 33 5N 108 15 E
Shiquan He = Indus →, *Pakistan* **42 G2** 24 20N 67 47 E
Shīr Kūh, *Iran* **45 D7** 31 39N 54 3 E
Shiragami-Misaki, *Japan* **30 D10** 41 24N 140 12 E
Shirakawa, *Fukushima, Japan* **31 F10** 37 7N 140 13 E
Shirakawa, *Gifu, Japan* **31 F8** 36 17N 136 56 E
Shirane-San, *Gumma, Japan* **31 F9** 36 48N 139 22 E
Shirane-San, *Yamanashi, Japan* **31 G9** 35 42N 138 9 E
Shiraoi, *Japan* **30 C10** 42 33N 141 21 E
Shīrāz, *Iran* **45 D7** 29 42N 52 30 E
Shire →, *Africa* **55 F4** 17 42S 35 19 E
Shiretoko-Misaki, *Japan* **30 B12** 44 21N 145 20 E
Shirinab →, *Pakistan* **42 D2** 30 15N 66 28 E
Shiriya-Zaki, *Japan* **30 D10** 41 25N 141 30 E
Shiroishi, *Japan* **30 F10** 38 0N 140 37 E
Shīrvān, *Iran* **45 B8** 37 30N 57 50 E
Shirwa, L. = Chilwa, L., *Malawi* **55 F4** 15 15S 35 40 E
Shivpuri, *India* **42 G7** 25 26N 77 42 E
Shixian, *China* **35 C15** 43 5N 129 50 E
Shizuishan, *China* **34 E4** 39 15N 106 50 E
Shizuoka, *Japan* **31 G9** 34 57N 138 24 E
Shizuoka □, *Japan* **31 G9** 35 15N 138 40 E
Shklov = Shklow, *Belarus* **17 A16** 54 16N 30 15 E
Shklow, *Belarus* **17 A16** 54 16N 30 15 E
Shkoder = Shkodër, *Albania* **21 C8** 42 4N 19 32 E
Shkodër, *Albania* **21 C8** 42 4N 19 32 E
Shkumbini →, *Albania* **21 D8** 41 2N 19 31 E
Shmidta, Ostrov, *Russia* **27 A10** 81 0N 91 0 E
Shō-Gawa →, *Japan* **31 F8** 36 47N 137 4 E
Shoal L., *Canada* **73 D9** 49 33N 95 1W
Shoal Lake, *Canada* **73 C8** 50 30N 100 35W
Shōdo-Shima, *Japan* **31 G7** 34 30N 134 15 E
Sholapur = Solapur, *India* **40 L9** 17 43N 75 56 E
Shologontsy, *Russia* **27 C12** 66 13N 114 0 E
Shōmrōn, *West Bank* **47 C4** 32 15N 35 13 E
Shoreham by Sea, *U.K.* **11 G7** 50 50N 0 16W
Shori →, *Pakistan* **42 E3** 28 29N 69 44 E
Shorkot Road, *Pakistan* **42 D5** 30 47N 72 15 E
Shoshone, *Calif., U.S.A.* **85 K10** 35 58N 116 16W
Shoshone, *Idaho, U.S.A.* **82 E6** 42 56N 114 25W
Shoshone L., *U.S.A.* **82 D8** 44 22N 110 43W
Shoshone Mts., *U.S.A.* **82 G5** 39 20N 117 25W
Shoshong, *Botswana* **56 C4** 22 56S 26 31 E
Shoshoni, *U.S.A.* **82 E9** 43 14N 108 7W
Shouguang, *China* **35 F10** 37 52N 118 45 E
Shouyang, *China* **34 F7** 37 54N 113 8 E
Show Low, *U.S.A.* **83 J9** 34 15N 110 2W
Shreveport, *U.S.A.* **81 J8** 32 31N 93 45W
Shrewsbury, *U.K.* **11 E5** 52 43N 2 45W
Shri Mohangarh, *India* **42 F4** 27 17N 71 18 E
Shrirampur, *India* **43 H13** 22 44N 88 21 E
Shropshire □, *U.K.* **11 E5** 52 36N 2 45W
Shū, *Kazakstan* **26 E8** 43 36N 73 42 E
Shū →, *Kazakstan* **28 E10** 45 0N 67 44 E
Shuangcheng, *China* **35 B14** 45 20N 126 15 E
Shuanggou, *China* **35 G9** 34 2N 117 30 E
Shuangliao, *China* **35 C12** 43 29N 123 30 E
Shuangshanzi, *China* **35 D10** 40 20N 119 8 E
Shuangyang, *China* **35 C13** 43 28N 125 40 E
Shuangyashan, *China* **33 B8** 46 28N 131 5 E
Shuguri Falls, *Tanzania* **55 D4** 8 33S 37 22 E
Shuiye, *China* **34 F8** 36 7N 114 8 E
Shujalpur, *India* **42 H7** 23 18N 76 46 E
Shukpa Kunzang, *India* **43 B8** 34 22N 78 22 E
Shulan, *China* **35 B14** 44 28N 127 0 E
Shule, *China* **32 C2** 39 25N 76 3 E
Shumagin Is., *U.S.A.* **68 C4** 55 7N 160 30W
Shumen, *Bulgaria* **21 C12** 43 18N 26 55 E
Shumikha, *Russia* **26 D7** 55 10N 63 15 E
Shuo Xian = Shuozhou, *China* **34 E7** 39 20N 112 33 E
Shuozhou, *China* **34 E7** 39 20N 112 33 E
Shūr →, *Fārs, Iran* **45 D7** 28 30N 55 0 E
Shūr →, *Kermān, Iran* **45 D8** 30 52N 57 37 E
Shūr →, *Yazd, Iran* **45 D7** 31 45N 55 15 E
Shūr Āb, *Iran* **45 C6** 34 23N 51 11 E
Shūr Gaz, *Iran* **45 D8** 29 10N 59 20 E
Shūrāb, *Iran* **45 C8** 33 43N 56 29 E
Shūrjestān, *Iran* **45 D7** 31 24N 52 25 E
Shurugwi, *Zimbabwe* **55 F3** 19 40S 30 0 E
Shūsf, *Iran* **45 D9** 31 50N 60 5 E
Shūshtar, *Iran* **45 D6** 32 0N 48 50 E
Shuswap L., *Canada* **72 C5** 50 55N 119 3W
Shuyang, *China* **35 G10** 34 10N 118 42 E
Shūzū, *Iran* **45 D7** 29 52N 54 30 E
Shwebo, *Burma* **41 H19** 22 30N 95 45 E
Shwegu, *Burma* **41 G20** 24 15N 96 26 E
Shweli →, *Burma* **41 H20** 23 45N 96 45 E
Shymkent, *Kazakstan* **26 E7** 42 18N 69 36 E
Shyok, *India* **43 B8** 34 13N 78 12 E
Shyok →, *Pakistan* **43 B6** 35 13N 75 53 E
Si Chon, *Thailand* **39 H2** 9 0N 99 54 E
Si Kiang = Xi Jiang →, *China* **33 D6** 22 5N 113 20 E
Si-ngan = Xi'an, *China* **34 G5** 34 15N 109 0 E
Si Prachan, *Thailand* **38 E3** 14 37N 100 9 E
Si Racha, *Thailand* **38 F3** 13 10N 100 48 E
Si Xian, *China* **35 H9** 33 30N 117 50 E
Siahaf →, *Pakistan* **42 E3** 29 3N 68 57 E
Siahan Range, *Pakistan* **40 F4** 27 30N 64 40 E
Siaksriindrapura, *Indonesia* **36 D2** 0 51N 102 0 E
Sialkot, *Pakistan* **42 C6** 32 32N 74 30 E
Siam = Thailand ■, *Asia* **38 E4** 16 0N 102 0 E
Sian = Xi'an, *China* **34 G5** 34 15N 109 0 E
Siantan, *Indonesia* **36 D3** 3 10N 106 15 E
Sīāreh, *Iran* **45 D9** 28 5N 60 14 E
Siargao I., *Phil.* **37 C7** 9 52N 126 3 E
Siari, *Pakistan* **43 B7** 34 55N 76 40 E
Siasi, *Phil.* **37 C6** 5 34N 120 50 E
Siau, *Indonesia* **37 D7** 2 50N 125 25 E
Šiauliai, *Lithuania* **9 J20** 55 56N 23 15 E
Sibâi, Gebel el, *Egypt* **44 E2** 25 45N 34 10 E
Sibay, *Russia* **24 D10** 52 42N 58 39 E
Sibayi, L., *S. Africa* **57 D5** 27 20S 32 45 E
Šibenik, *Croatia* **20 C6** 43 48N 15 54 E
Siberia, *Russia* **4 D13** 60 0N 100 0 E
Siberut, *Indonesia* **36 E1** 1 30S 99 0 E
Sibi, *Pakistan* **42 E2** 29 30N 67 54 E
Sibil = Oksibil, *Indonesia* **37 E10** 4 59S 140 35 E
Sibiti, *Congo* **52 E2** 3 38S 13 19 E
Sibiu, *Romania* **17 F13** 45 45N 24 9 E
Sibley, *U.S.A.* **80 D7** 43 24N 95 45W
Sibolga, *Indonesia* **36 D1** 1 42N 98 45 E
Sibsagar, *India* **41 F19** 27 0N 94 36 E
Sibu, *Malaysia* **36 D4** 2 18N 111 49 E
Sibuco, *Phil.* **37 C6** 7 20N 122 10 E
Sibuguey B., *Phil.* **37 C6** 7 50N 122 45 E
Sibut, *C.A.R.* **52 C3** 5 46N 19 10 E
Sibutu, *Phil.* **37 D5** 4 45N 119 30 E
Sibutu Passage, *E. Indies* **37 D5** 4 50N 120 0 E
Sibuyan I., *Phil.* **37 B6** 12 25N 122 40 E
Sibuyan Sea, *Phil.* **37 B6** 12 30N 122 20 E
Sicamous, *Canada* **72 C5** 50 49N 119 0W
Siccus →, *Australia* **63 E2** 31 26S 139 30 E
Sichuan □, *China* **32 C5** 30 30N 103 0 E
Sicilia, *Italy* **20 F6** 37 30N 14 30 E
Sicily = Sicilia, *Italy* **20 F6** 37 30N 14 30 E
Sicuani, *Peru* **92 F4** 14 21S 71 10W
Sidári, *Greece* **23 A3** 39 47N 19 41 E
Siddhapur, *India* **42 H5** 23 56N 72 25 E
Siddipet, *India* **40 K11** 18 5N 78 51 E
Sidhauli, *India* **43 F9** 27 17N 80 50 E
Sídheros, Ákra, *Greece* **23 D8** 35 19N 26 19 E
Sidhi, *India* **43 G9** 24 25N 81 53 E
Sidi-bel-Abbès, *Algeria* **50 A5** 35 13N 0 39W
Sidi Ifni, *Morocco* **50 C3** 29 29N 10 12W
Sidlaw Hills, *U.K.* **12 E5** 56 32N 3 2W
Sidley, Mt., *Antarctica* **5 D14** 77 2S 126 2W
Sidmouth, *U.K.* **11 G4** 50 40N 3 15W
Sidmouth, C., *Australia* **62 A3** 13 25S 143 36 E
Sidney, *Canada* **72 D4** 48 39N 123 24W
Sidney, *Mont., U.S.A.* **80 B2** 47 43N 104 9W
Sidney, *N.Y., U.S.A.* **79 D9** 42 19N 75 24W
Sidney, *Nebr., U.S.A.* **80 E3** 41 8N 102 59W
Sidney, *Ohio, U.S.A.* **76 E3** 40 17N 84 9W
Sidney Lanier, L., *U.S.A.* **77 H4** 34 10N 84 4W
Sidoarjo, *Indonesia* **37 G15** 7 27S 112 43 E
Sidon = Saydā, *Lebanon* **47 B4** 33 35N 35 25 E
Sidra, G. of = Surt, Khalīj, *Libya* **51 B9** 31 40N 18 30 E
Siedlce, *Poland* **17 B12** 52 10N 22 20 E
Sieg →, *Germany* **16 C4** 50 46N 7 6 E
Siegen, *Germany* **16 C5** 50 51N 8 0 E
Siem Pang, *Cambodia* **38 E6** 14 7N 106 23 E
Siem Reap = Siemreab, *Cambodia* **38 F4** 13 20N 103 52 E
Siemreab, *Cambodia* **38 F4** 13 20N 103 52 E
Siena, *Italy* **20 C4** 43 19N 11 21 E
Sieradz, *Poland* **17 C10** 51 37N 18 41 E
Sierra Blanca, *U.S.A.* **83 L11** 31 11N 105 22W
Sierra Blanca Peak, *U.S.A.* **83 K11** 33 23N 105 49W
Sierra City, *U.S.A.* **84 F6** 39 34N 120 38W
Sierra Colorada, *Argentina* **96 E3** 40 35S 67 50W
Sierra Gorda, *Chile* **94 A2** 22 50S 69 15W
Sierra Leone ■, *W. Afr.* **50 G3** 9 0N 12 0W
Sierra Madre, *Mexico* **87 D6** 16 0N 93 0W
Sierra Mojada, *Mexico* **86 B4** 27 19N 103 42W
Sierra Nevada, *Spain* **19 D4** 37 3N 3 15W
Sierra Nevada, *U.S.A.* **84 H8** 39 0N 120 30W
Sierra Vista, *U.S.A.* **83 L8** 31 33N 110 18W
Sierraville, *U.S.A.* **84 F6** 39 36N 120 22W
Sífnos, *Greece* **21 F11** 37 0N 24 45 E
Sifton, *Canada* **73 C8** 51 21N 100 8W
Sifton Pass, *Canada* **72 B3** 57 52N 126 15W
Sighetu-Marmaţiei, *Romania* **17 E12** 47 57N 23 52 E

Suphan Dağı

Stanley, *Falk. Is.* **96 G5** 51 40S 59 51W
Stanley, *U.K.* **10 C6** 54 53N 1 41W
Stanley, *Idaho, U.S.A.* **82 D6** 44 13N 114 56W
Stanley, *N. Dak., U.S.A.* **80 A3** 48 19N 102 23W
Stanley, *N.Y., U.S.A.* **78 D7** 42 48N 77 6W
Stanovoy Khrebet, *Russia* **27 D13** 55 0N 130 0 E
Stanovoy Ra. = Stanovoy Khrebet, *Russia* **27 D13** 55 0N 130 0 E
Stansmore Ra., *Australia* **60 D4** 21 23S 128 33 E
Stanthorpe, *Australia* **63 D5** 28 36S 151 59 E
Stanton, *U.S.A.* **81 J4** 32 8N 101 48W
Stanwood, *U.S.A.* **84 B4** 48 15N 122 23W
Staples, *U.S.A.* **80 B7** 46 21N 94 48W
Star City, *Canada* **73 C8** 52 50N 104 20W
Star Lake, *U.S.A.* **79 B9** 44 10N 75 2W
Stara Planina, *Bulgaria* **21 C10** 43 15N 23 0 E
Stara Zagora, *Bulgaria* **21 C11** 42 26N 25 39 E
Starachowice, *Poland* **17 C11** 51 3N 21 2 E
Staraya Russa, *Russia* **24 C5** 57 58N 31 23 E
Starbuck I., *Kiribati* **65 H12** 5 37S 155 55W
Stargard Szczeciński, *Poland* **16 B8** 53 20N 15 0 E
Staritsa, *Russia* **24 C5** 56 33N 34 55 E
Starke, *U.S.A.* **77 L4** 29 57N 82 7W
Starogard Gdański, *Poland* **17 B10** 53 59N 18 30 E
Starokonstantinov = Starokonstyantyniv, *Ukraine* **17 D14** 49 48N 27 10 E
Starokonstyantyniv, *Ukraine* **17 D14** 49 48N 27 10 E
Start Pt., *U.K.* **11 G4** 50 13N 3 39W
Staryy Chartoriysk, *Ukraine* **17 C13** 51 15N 25 54 E
Staryy Oskol, *Russia* **25 D6** 51 19N 37 55 E
State College, *U.S.A.* **78 F7** 40 48N 77 52W
Stateline, *U.S.A.* **84 G7** 38 57N 119 56W
Staten, I. = Estados, I. de Los, *Argentina* **96 G4** 54 40S 64 30W
Staten I., *U.S.A.* **79 F10** 40 35N 74 9W
Statesboro, *U.S.A.* **77 J5** 32 27N 81 47W
Statesville, *U.S.A.* **77 H5** 35 47N 80 53W
Stauffer, *U.S.A.* **85 L7** 34 45N 119 3W
Staunton, *Ill., U.S.A.* **80 F10** 39 1N 89 47W
Staunton, *Va., U.S.A.* **76 F6** 38 9N 79 4W
Stavanger, *Norway* **9 G11** 58 57N 5 40 E
Staveley, *N.Z.* **59 K3** 43 40S 171 32 E
Stavelot, *Belgium* **15 D5** 50 23N 5 55 E
Stavern, *Norway* **9 G14** 59 0N 10 1 E
Stavoren, *Neths.* **15 B5** 52 53N 5 22 E
Stavropol, *Russia* **25 E7** 45 5N 42 0 E
Stavros, *Cyprus* **23 D11** 35 1N 32 38 E
Stavrós, *Greece* **23 D6** 35 12N 24 45 E
Stavrós, Ákra, *Greece* **23 D6** 35 26N 24 58 E
Stawell →, *Australia* **62 C3** 20 20S 142 55 E
Stayner, *Canada* **78 B4** 44 25N 80 5W
Stayton, *U.S.A.* **82 D2** 44 48N 122 48W
Steamboat Springs, *U.S.A.* **82 F10** 40 29N 106 50W
Steele, *U.S.A.* **80 B5** 46 51N 99 55W
Steelton, *U.S.A.* **78 F8** 40 14N 76 50W
Steen River, *Canada* **72 B5** 59 40N 117 12W
Steenkool = Bintuni, *Indonesia* **37 E8** 2 7S 133 32 E
Steens Mt., *U.S.A.* **82 E4** 42 35N 118 40W
Steenwijk, *Neths.* **15 B6** 52 47N 6 7 E
Steep Pt., *Australia* **61 E1** 26 8S 113 8 E
Steep Rock, *Canada* **73 C9** 51 30N 98 48W
Stefanie L. = Chew Bahir, *Ethiopia* **46 G2** 4 40N 36 50 E
Stefansson Bay, *Antarctica* **5 C5** 67 20S 59 8 E
Steiermark □, *Austria* **16 E8** 47 26N 15 0 E
Steilacoom, *U.S.A.* **84 C4** 47 10N 122 36W
Steilrandberge, *Namibia* **56 B1** 17 45S 13 20 E
Steinbach, *Canada* **73 D9** 49 32N 96 40W
Steinhausen, *Namibia* **56 C2** 21 49S 18 20 E
Steinkjer, *Norway* **8 D14** 64 1N 11 31 E
Steinkopf, *S. Africa* **56 D2** 29 18S 17 43 E
Stellarton, *Canada* **71 C7** 45 32N 62 30W
Stellenbosch, *S. Africa* **56 E2** 33 58S 18 50 E
Stendal, *Germany* **16 B6** 52 36N 11 53 E
Steornabhaigh = Stornoway, *U.K.* **12 C2** 58 13N 6 23W
Stepanakert = Xankändi, *Azerbaijan* **25 G8** 39 52N 46 49 E
Stephens I., *Canada* **72 C2** 54 10N 130 45W
Stephens L., *Canada* **73 B9** 56 32N 95 0W
Stephenville, *Canada* **71 C8** 48 31N 58 35W
Stephenville, *U.S.A.* **81 J5** 32 13N 98 12W
Stepnoi = Elista, *Russia* **25 E7** 46 16N 44 14 E
Steppe, *Asia* **28 D9** 50 0N 50 0 E
Sterkstroom, *S. Africa* **56 E4** 31 32S 26 32 E
Sterling, *Colo., U.S.A.* **80 E3** 40 37N 103 13W
Sterling, *Ill., U.S.A.* **80 E10** 41 48N 89 42W
Sterling, *Kans., U.S.A.* **80 F5** 38 13N 98 12W
Sterling City, *U.S.A.* **81 K4** 31 51N 101 0W
Sterling Heights, *U.S.A.* **76 D4** 42 35N 83 0W
Sterling Run, *U.S.A.* **78 E6** 41 25N 78 12W
Sterlitamak, *Russia* **24 D10** 53 40N 56 0 E
Stérnes, *Greece* **23 D6** 35 30N 24 9 E
Stettin = Szczecin, *Poland* **16 B8** 53 27N 14 27 E
Stettiner Haff, *Germany* **16 B8** 53 47N 14 15 E
Stettler, *Canada* **72 C6** 52 19N 112 40W
Steubenville, *U.S.A.* **78 F4** 40 22N 80 37W
Stevenage, *U.K.* **11 F7** 51 55N 0 13W
Stevens Point, *U.S.A.* **80 C10** 44 31N 89 34W
Stevenson, *U.S.A.* **84 E5** 45 42N 121 53W
Stevenson L., *Canada* **73 C9** 53 55N 96 0W
Stevensville, *U.S.A.* **82 C6** 46 30N 114 5W
Stewart, *Canada* **72 B3** 55 56N 129 57W
Stewart, *U.S.A.* **84 F7** 39 5N 119 46W
Stewart →, *Canada* **68 B6** 63 19N 139 26W
Stewart, C., *Australia* **62 A1** 11 57S 134 56 E
Stewart, I., *Chile* **96 G2** 54 50S 71 15W
Stewart I., *N.Z.* **59 M1** 46 58S 167 54 E
Stewarts Point, *U.S.A.* **84 G3** 38 39N 123 24W
Stewartville, *U.S.A.* **80 D8** 43 51N 92 29W
Stewiacke, *Canada* **71 C7** 45 9N 63 22W
Steynsburg, *S. Africa* **56 E4** 31 15S 25 49 E
Steyr, *Austria* **16 D8** 48 3N 14 25 E
Steytlerville, *S. Africa* **56 E3** 33 17S 24 19 E
Stigler, *U.S.A.* **81 H7** 35 15N 95 8W
Stikine →, *Canada* **72 B2** 56 40N 132 30W
Stilfontein, *S. Africa* **56 D4** 26 51S 26 50 E
Stillwater, *N.Z.* **59 K3** 42 27S 171 20 E
Stillwater, *Minn., U.S.A.* **80 C8** 45 3N 92 49W
Stillwater, *N.Y., U.S.A.* **79 D11** 42 55N 73 41W
Stillwater, *Okla., U.S.A.* **81 G6** 36 7N 97 4W
Stillwater Range, *U.S.A.* **82 G4** 39 50N 118 5W
Stillwater Reservoir, *U.S.A.* **79 C9** 43 54N 75 3W
Stilwell, *U.S.A.* **81 H7** 35 49N 94 38W
Štip, *Macedonia* **21 D10** 41 42N 22 10 E
Stirling, *Canada* **78 B7** 44 18N 77 33W
Stirling, *U.K.* **12 E5** 56 8N 3 57W
Stirling □, *U.K.* **12 E4** 56 12N 4 18W
Stirling Ra., *Australia* **61 F2** 34 23S 118 0 E
Stittsville, *Canada* **79 A9** 45 15N 75 55W
Stjernøya, *Norway* **8 A20** 70 20N 22 40 E
Stjørdalshalsen, *Norway* **8 E14** 63 29N 10 51 E
Stockerau, *Austria* **16 D9** 48 24N 16 12 E
Stockholm, *Sweden* **9 G18** 59 20N 18 3 E
Stockport, *U.K.* **10 D5** 53 25N 2 9W
Stocksbridge, *U.K.* **10 D6** 53 29N 1 35W
Stockton, *Calif., U.S.A.* **84 H5** 37 58N 121 17W
Stockton, *Kans., U.S.A.* **80 F5** 39 26N 99 16W
Stockton, *Mo., U.S.A.* **81 G8** 37 42N 93 48W
Stockton-on-Tees, *U.K.* **10 C6** 54 35N 1 19W
Stockton-on-Tees □, *U.K.* **10 C6** 54 35N 1 19W
Stockton Plateau, *U.S.A.* **81 K3** 30 30N 102 30W
Stoeng Treng, *Cambodia* **38 F5** 13 31N 105 58 E
Stoer, Pt. of, *U.K.* **12 C3** 58 16N 5 23W
Stoke-on-Trent, *U.K.* **10 D5** 53 1N 2 11W
Stoke-on-Trent □, *U.K.* **10 D5** 53 1N 2 11W
Stokes Pt., *Australia* **62 G3** 40 10S 143 56 E
Stokes Ra., *Australia* **60 C5** 15 50S 130 50 E
Stokksnes, *Iceland* **8 D6** 64 14N 14 58W
Stokmarknes, *Norway* **8 B16** 68 34N 14 54 E
Stolac, *Bos.-H.* **21 C7** 43 5N 17 59 E
Stolbovoy, Ostrov, *Russia* **27 B14** 74 44N 135 14 E
Stolbtsy = Stowbtsy, *Belarus* **17 B14** 53 30N 26 43 E
Stolin, *Belarus* **17 C14** 51 53N 26 50 E
Stomíon, *Greece* **23 D5** 35 21N 23 32 E
Stone, *U.K.* **10 E5** 52 55N 2 9W
Stoneboro, *U.S.A.* **78 E4** 41 20N 80 7W
Stonehaven, *U.K.* **12 E6** 56 59N 2 12W
Stonehenge, *Australia* **62 C3** 24 22S 143 17 E
Stonehenge, *U.K.* **11 F6** 51 9N 1 45W
Stonewall, *Canada* **73 C9** 50 10N 97 19W
Stony L., *Man., Canada* **73 B9** 58 51N 98 40W
Stony L., *Ont., Canada* **78 B6** 44 30N 78 5W
Stony Point, *U.S.A.* **79 E11** 41 14N 73 59W
Stony Pt., *U.S.A.* **79 C8** 43 50N 76 18W
Stony Rapids, *Canada* **73 B7** 59 16N 105 50W
Stony Tunguska = Tunguska, Podkamennaya →, *Russia* **27 C10** 61 50N 90 13 E
Stonyford, *U.S.A.* **84 F4** 39 23N 122 33W
Stora Lulevatten, *Sweden* **8 C18** 67 10N 19 30 E
Storavan, *Sweden* **8 D18** 65 45N 18 10 E
Stord, *Norway* **9 G11** 59 52N 5 23 E
Store Bælt, *Denmark* **9 J14** 55 20N 11 0 E
Storm B., *Australia* **62 G4** 43 10S 147 30 E
Storm Lake, *U.S.A.* **80 D7** 42 39N 95 13W
Stormberge, *S. Africa* **56 E4** 31 16S 26 17 E
Stormsrivier, *S. Africa* **56 E3** 33 59S 23 52 E
Stornoway, *U.K.* **12 C2** 58 13N 6 23W
Storozhinets = Storozhynets, *Ukraine* **17 D13** 48 14N 25 45 E
Storozhynets, *Ukraine* **17 D13** 48 14N 25 45 E
Storrs, *U.S.A.* **79 E12** 41 49N 72 15W
Storsjön, *Sweden* **8 E16** 63 9N 14 30 E
Storuman, *Sweden* **8 D17** 65 5N 17 10 E
Storuman, sjö, *Sweden* **8 D17** 65 13N 16 50 E
Stouffville, *Canada* **78 C5** 43 58N 79 15W
Stoughton, *Canada* **73 D8** 49 40N 103 0W
Stour →, *Dorset, U.K.* **11 G6** 50 43N 1 47W
Stour →, *Kent, U.K.* **11 F9** 51 18N 1 22 E
Stour →, *Suffolk, U.K.* **11 F9** 51 57N 1 4 E
Stourbridge, *U.K.* **11 E5** 52 28N 2 8W
Stout L., *Canada* **73 C10** 52 0N 94 40W
Stove Pipe Wells Village, *U.S.A.* **85 J9** 36 35N 117 11W
Stow, *U.S.A.* **78 E3** 41 10N 81 27W
Stowbtsy, *Belarus* **17 B14** 53 30N 26 43 E
Stowmarket, *U.K.* **11 E9** 52 12N 1 0 E
Strabane, *U.K.* **13 B4** 54 50N 7 27W
Strahan, *Australia* **62 G4** 42 9S 145 20 E
Stralsund, *Germany* **16 A7** 54 18N 13 4 E
Strand, *S. Africa* **56 E2** 34 9S 18 48 E
Stranda, *Møre og Romsdal, Norway* **9 E12** 62 19N 6 58 E
Stranda, *Nord-Trøndelag, Norway* **8 E14** 63 33N 10 14 E
Strangford L., *U.K.* **13 B6** 54 30N 5 37W
Stranraer, *U.K.* **12 G3** 54 54N 5 1W
Strasbourg, *Canada* **73 C8** 51 4N 104 55W
Strasbourg, *France* **18 B7** 48 35N 7 42 E
Stratford, *Canada* **78 C4** 43 23N 81 0W
Stratford, *N.Z.* **59 H5** 39 20S 174 19 E
Stratford, *Calif., U.S.A.* **84 J7** 36 11N 119 49W
Stratford, *Conn., U.S.A.* **79 E11** 41 12N 73 8W
Stratford, *Tex., U.S.A.* **81 G3** 36 20N 102 4W
Stratford-upon-Avon, *U.K.* **11 E6** 52 12N 1 42W
Strath Spey, *U.K.* **12 D5** 57 9N 3 49W
Strathaven, *U.K.* **12 F4** 55 40N 4 5W
Strathcona Prov. Park, *Canada* **72 D3** 49 38N 125 40W
Strathmore, *Canada* **72 C6** 51 5N 113 18W
Strathmore, *U.K.* **12 E5** 56 37N 3 7W
Strathmore, *U.S.A.* **84 J7** 36 9N 119 4W
Strathnaver, *Canada* **72 C4** 53 20N 122 33W
Strathpeffer, *U.K.* **12 D4** 57 35N 4 32W
Strathroy, *Canada* **78 D3** 42 58N 81 38W
Strathy Pt., *U.K.* **12 C4** 58 36N 4 1W
Strattanville, *U.S.A.* **78 E5** 41 12N 79 19W
Stratton, *U.S.A.* **79 A14** 45 8N 70 26W
Stratton Mt., *U.S.A.* **79 C12** 43 4N 72 55W
Straubing, *Germany* **16 D7** 48 52N 12 34 E
Straumnes, *Iceland* **8 C2** 66 26N 23 8W
Strawberry →, *U.S.A.* **82 F8** 40 10N 110 24W
Streaky B., *Australia* **63 E1** 32 48S 134 13 E
Streaky Bay, *Australia* **63 E1** 32 51S 134 18 E
Streator, *U.S.A.* **80 E10** 41 8N 88 50W
Streetsboro, *U.S.A.* **78 E3** 41 14N 81 21W
Streetsville, *Canada* **78 C5** 43 35N 79 42W
Strelka, *Russia* **27 D10** 58 5N 93 3 E
Streng →, *Cambodia* **38 F4** 13 12N 103 37 E
Streymoy, *Færoe Is.* **8 E9** 62 8N 7 5W
Strezhevoy, *Russia* **26 C8** 60 42N 77 34 E
Strimón →, *Greece* **21 D10** 40 46N 23 51 E
Strimonikós Kólpos, *Greece* **21 D11** 40 33N 24 0 E
Stroma, *U.K.* **12 C5** 58 41N 3 7W
Strómboli, *Italy* **20 E6** 38 47N 15 13 E
Stromeferry, *U.K.* **12 D3** 57 21N 5 33W
Stromness, *U.K.* **12 C5** 58 58N 3 17W
Stromsburg, *U.S.A.* **80 E6** 41 7N 97 36W
Strömstad, *Sweden* **9 G14** 58 56N 11 10 E
Strömsund, *Sweden* **8 E16** 63 51N 15 33 E
Strongsville, *U.S.A.* **78 E3** 41 19N 81 50W
Stronsay, *U.K.* **12 B6** 59 7N 2 35W
Stroud, *U.K.* **11 F5** 51 45N 2 13W
Stroudsburg, *U.S.A.* **79 F9** 40 59N 75 12W
Stroumbi, *Cyprus* **23 E11** 34 53N 32 29 E
Struer, *Denmark* **9 H13** 56 30N 8 35 E
Strumica, *Macedonia* **21 D10** 41 28N 22 41 E
Struthers, *Canada* **70 C2** 48 41N 85 51W
Struthers, *U.S.A.* **78 E4** 41 4N 80 39W
Stryker, *U.S.A.* **82 B6** 48 41N 114 46W
Stryy, *Ukraine* **17 D12** 49 16N 23 48 E
Strzelecki Cr. →, *Australia* **63 D2** 29 37S 139 59 E
Stuart, *Fla., U.S.A.* **77 M5** 27 12N 80 15W
Stuart, *Nebr., U.S.A.* **80 D5** 42 36N 99 8W
Stuart →, *Canada* **72 C4** 54 0N 123 35W
Stuart Bluff Ra., *Australia* **60 D5** 22 50S 131 52 E
Stuart L., *Canada* **72 C4** 54 30N 124 30W
Stuart Ra., *Australia* **63 D1** 29 10S 134 56 E
Stull L., *Canada* **70 B1** 54 24N 92 34W
Stung Treng = Stoeng Treng, *Cambodia* **38 F5** 13 31N 105 58 E
Stupart →, *Canada* **70 A1** 56 0N 93 25W
Sturgeon B., *Canada* **73 C9** 52 0N 97 50W
Sturgeon Bay, *U.S.A.* **76 C2** 44 50N 87 23W
Sturgeon Falls, *Canada* **70 C4** 46 25N 79 57W
Sturgeon L., *Alta., Canada* **72 B5** 55 6N 117 32W
Sturgeon L., *Ont., Canada* **70 C1** 50 0N 90 45W
Sturgeon L., *Ont., Canada* **78 B6** 44 28N 78 43W
Sturgis, *Canada* **73 C8** 51 56N 102 36W
Sturgis, *Mich., U.S.A.* **76 E3** 41 48N 85 25W
Sturgis, *S. Dak., U.S.A.* **80 C3** 44 25N 103 31W
Sturt Cr. →, *Australia* **60 C4** 19 8S 127 50 E
Stutterheim, *S. Africa* **56 E4** 32 33S 27 28 E
Stuttgart, *Germany* **16 D5** 48 48N 9 11 E
Stuttgart, *U.S.A.* **81 H9** 34 30N 91 33W
Stuyvesant, *U.S.A.* **79 D11** 42 23N 73 45W
Stykkishólmur, *Iceland* **8 D2** 65 2N 22 40W
Styria = Steiermark □, *Austria* **16 E8** 47 26N 15 0 E
Su Xian = Suzhou, *China* **34 H9** 33 41N 116 59 E
Suakin, *Sudan* **51 E13** 19 8N 37 20 E
Suan, *N. Korea* **35 E14** 38 42N 126 22 E
Suaqui, *Mexico* **86 B3** 29 12N 109 41W
Suar, *India* **43 E8** 29 2N 79 3 E
Subang, *Indonesia* **37 G12** 6 34S 107 45 E
Subansiri →, *India* **41 F18** 26 48N 93 50 E
Subarnarekha →, *India* **43 H12** 22 34N 87 24 E
Subayhah, *Si. Arabia* **44 D3** 30 2N 38 50 E
Subi, *Indonesia* **39 L7** 2 58N 108 50 E
Subotica, *Serbia, Yug.* **21 A8** 46 6N 19 39 E
Suceava, *Romania* **17 E14** 47 38N 26 16 E
Suchan, *Russia* **30 C6** 43 8N 133 9 E
Suchitoto, *El Salv.* **88 D2** 13 56N 89 0W
Suchou = Suzhou, *China* **33 C7** 31 19N 120 38 E
Süchow = Xuzhou, *China* **35 G9** 34 18N 117 10 E
Suck →, *Ireland* **13 C3** 53 17N 8 3W
Sucre, *Bolivia* **92 G5** 19 0S 65 15W
Sucuriú →, *Brazil* **93 H8** 20 47S 51 38W
Sud, Pte. du, *Canada* **71 C7** 49 3N 62 14W
Sud-Kivu □, *Dem. Rep. of the Congo* **54 C2** 3 30S 28 0 E
Sud-Ouest, Pte. du, *Canada* **71 C7** 49 23N 63 36W
Sudan, *U.S.A.* **81 H3** 34 4N 102 32W
Sudan ■, *Africa* **51 E11** 15 0N 30 0 E
Sudbury, *Canada* **70 C3** 46 30N 81 0W
Sudbury, *U.K.* **11 E8** 52 2N 0 45 E
Sûdd, *Sudan* **51 G12** 8 20N 30 0 E
Sudeten Mts. = Sudety, *Europe* **17 C9** 50 20N 16 45 E
Sudety, *Europe* **17 C9** 50 20N 16 45 E
Suðuroy, *Færoe Is.* **8 F9** 61 32N 6 50W
Sudi, *Tanzania* **55 E4** 10 11S 39 57 E
Sudirman, Pegunungan, *Indonesia* **37 E9** 4 30S 137 0 E
Sueca, *Spain* **19 C5** 39 12N 0 21W
Suemez I., *U.S.A.* **72 B2** 55 15N 133 20W
Suez = El Suweis, *Egypt* **51 C12** 29 58N 32 31 E
Suez, G. of = Suweis, Khalîg el, *Egypt* **51 C12** 28 40N 33 0 E
Suez Canal = Suweis, Qanâ es, *Egypt* **51 B12** 31 0N 32 20 E
Suffield, *Canada* **72 C6** 50 12N 111 10W
Suffolk, *U.S.A.* **76 G7** 36 44N 76 35W
Suffolk □, *U.K.* **11 E9** 52 16N 1 0 E
Sugargrove, *U.S.A.* **78 E5** 41 59N 79 21W
Sugarive →, *India* **43 F12** 26 16N 86 24 E
Suguk = Salluit, *Canada* **69 B12** 62 14N 75 38W
Şuḩār, *Oman* **46 C6** 24 20N 56 40 E
Sühbaatar □, *Mongolia* **34 B8** 45 30N 114 0 E
Suhl, *Germany* **16 C6** 50 36N 10 42 E
Sui, *Pakistan* **42 E3** 28 37N 69 19 E
Sui Xian, *China* **34 G8** 34 25N 115 2 E
Suide, *China* **34 F6** 37 30N 110 12 E
Suifenhe, *China* **35 B16** 44 25N 131 10 E
Suihua, *China* **33 B7** 46 32N 126 55 E
Suining, *China* **35 H9** 33 56N 117 58 E
Suiping, *China* **34 H7** 33 10N 113 59 E
Suir →, *Ireland* **13 D4** 52 16N 7 9W
Suisun City, *U.S.A.* **84 G4** 38 15N 122 2W
Suiyang, *China* **35 B16** 44 30N 130 56 E
Suizhong, *China* **35 D11** 40 21N 120 20 E
Sujangarh, *India* **42 F6** 27 42N 74 31 E
Sukabumi, *Indonesia* **37 G12** 6 56S 106 50 E
Sukadana, *Indonesia* **36 E3** 1 10S 110 0 E
Sukagawa, *Japan* **31 F10** 37 17N 140 23 E
Sukaraja, *Indonesia* **36 E4** 2 28S 110 25 E
Sukarnapura = Jayapura, *Indonesia* **37 E10** 2 28S 140 38 E
Sukch'ŏn, *N. Korea* **35 E13** 39 22N 125 35 E
Sukhona →, *Russia* **24 C6** 61 15N 46 39 E
Sukhothai, *Thailand* **38 D2** 17 1N 99 49 E
Sukhumi = Sokhumi, *Georgia* **25 F7** 43 0N 41 0 E
Sukkur, *Pakistan* **42 F3** 27 42N 68 54 E
Sukkur Barrage, *Pakistan* **42 F3** 27 40N 68 50 E
Sukri →, *India* **42 G4** 25 4N 71 43 E
Sukumo, *Japan* **31 H6** 32 56N 132 44 E
Sukunka →, *Canada* **72 B4** 55 45N 121 15W
Sula, Kepulauan, *Indonesia* **37 E7** 1 45S 125 0 E
Sulaco →, *Honduras* **88 C2** 15 2N 87 44W
Sulaiman Range, *Pakistan* **42 D3** 30 30N 69 50 E
Sūlār, *Iran* **45 D6** 31 53N 51 54 E
Sulawesi Sea = Celebes Sea, *Indonesia* **37 D6** 3 0N 123 0 E
Sulawesi Selatan □, *Indonesia* **37 E6** 2 30S 125 0 E
Sulawesi Utara □, *Indonesia* **37 D6** 1 0N 122 30 E
Sulima, *S. Leone* **50 G3** 6 58N 11 32W
Sulina, *Romania* **17 F15** 45 10N 29 40 E
Sulitjelma, *Norway* **8 C17** 67 9N 16 3 E
Sullana, *Peru* **92 D2** 4 52S 80 39W
Sullivan, *Ill., U.S.A.* **80 F10** 39 36N 88 37W
Sullivan, *Ind., U.S.A.* **76 F2** 39 6N 87 24W
Sullivan, *Mo., U.S.A.* **80 F9** 38 13N 91 10W
Sullivan Bay, *Canada* **72 C3** 50 55N 126 50W
Sullivan I. = Lanbi Kyun, *Burma* **39 G2** 10 50N 98 20 E
Sulphur, *La., U.S.A.* **81 K8** 30 14N 93 23W
Sulphur, *Okla., U.S.A.* **81 H6** 34 31N 96 58W
Sulphur Pt., *Canada* **72 A6** 60 56N 114 48W
Sulphur Springs, *U.S.A.* **81 J7** 33 8N 95 36W
Sultan, *Canada* **70 C3** 47 36N 82 47W
Sultan, *U.S.A.* **84 C5** 47 52N 121 49W
Sultanpur, *Mad. P., India* **42 H8** 23 9N 77 56 E
Sultanpur, *Punjab, India* **42 D6** 31 13N 75 11 E
Sultanpur, *Ut. P., India* **43 F10** 26 18N 82 4 E
Sulu Arch., *Phil.* **37 C6** 6 0N 121 0 E
Sulu Sea, *E. Indies* **37 C6** 8 0N 120 0 E
Suluq, *Libya* **51 B10** 31 44N 20 14 E
Sulzberger Ice Shelf, *Antarctica* **5 D10** 78 0S 150 0 E
Sumalata, *Indonesia* **37 D6** 1 0N 122 31 E
Sumampa, *Argentina* **94 B3** 29 25S 63 29W
Sumatera □, *Indonesia* **36 D2** 0 40N 100 20 E
Sumatera Barat □, *Indonesia* **36 E2** 1 0S 101 0 E
Sumatera Utara □, *Indonesia* **36 D1** 2 30N 98 0 E
Sumatra = Sumatera □, *Indonesia* **36 D2** 0 40N 100 20 E
Sumba, *Indonesia* **37 F5** 9 45S 119 35 E
Sumba, Selat, *Indonesia* **37 F5** 9 0S 118 40 E
Sumbawa, *Indonesia* **36 F5** 8 26S 117 30 E
Sumbawa Besar, *Indonesia* **36 F5** 8 30S 117 26 E
Sumbawanga □, *Tanzania* **52 F6** 8 0S 31 30 E
Sumbe, *Angola* **52 G2** 11 10S 13 48 E
Sumburgh Hd., *U.K.* **12 B7** 59 52N 1 17W
Sumdeo, *India* **43 D8** 31 26N 78 44 E
Sumdo, *India* **43 B8** 35 6N 78 41 E
Sumedang, *Indonesia* **37 G12** 6 52S 107 55 E
Šumen = Shumen, *Bulgaria* **21 C12** 43 18N 26 55 E
Sumenep, *Indonesia* **37 G15** 7 1S 113 52 E
Sumgait = Sumqayıt, *Azerbaijan* **25 F8** 40 34N 49 38 E
Summer L., *U.S.A.* **82 E3** 42 50N 120 45W
Summerland, *Canada* **72 D5** 49 32N 119 41W
Summerside, *Canada* **71 C7** 46 24N 63 47W
Summersville, *U.S.A.* **76 F5** 38 17N 80 51W
Summerville, *Ga., U.S.A.* **77 H3** 34 29N 85 21W
Summerville, *S.C., U.S.A.* **77 J5** 33 1N 80 11W
Summit Lake, *Canada* **72 C4** 54 20N 122 40W
Summit Peak, *U.S.A.* **83 H10** 37 21N 106 42W
Sumner, *Iowa, U.S.A.* **80 D8** 42 51N 92 6W
Sumner, *Wash., U.S.A.* **84 C4** 47 12N 122 14W
Sumoto, *Japan* **31 G7** 34 21N 134 54 E
Šumperk, *Czech Rep.* **17 D9** 49 59N 16 59 E
Sumqayıt, *Azerbaijan* **25 F8** 40 34N 49 38 E
Sumter, *U.S.A.* **77 J5** 33 55N 80 21W
Sumy, *Ukraine* **25 D5** 50 57N 34 50 E
Sun City, *Ariz., U.S.A.* **83 K7** 33 36N 112 17W
Sun City, *Calif., U.S.A.* **85 M9** 33 42N 117 11W
Sun City Center, *U.S.A.* **77 M4** 27 43N 82 18W
Sun Lakes, *U.S.A.* **83 K8** 33 10N 111 52W
Sun Valley, *U.S.A.* **82 E6** 43 42N 114 21W
Sunagawa, *Japan* **30 C10** 43 29N 141 55 E
Sunan, *N. Korea* **35 E13** 39 15N 125 40 E
Sunart, L., *U.K.* **12 E3** 56 42N 5 43W
Sunburst, *U.S.A.* **82 B8** 48 53N 111 55W
Sunbury, *U.S.A.* **79 F8** 40 52N 76 48W
Sunchales, *Argentina* **94 C3** 30 58S 61 35W
Suncho Corral, *Argentina* **94 B3** 27 55S 63 27W
Sunch'ŏn, *S. Korea* **35 G14** 34 52N 127 31 E
Suncook, *U.S.A.* **79 C13** 43 8N 71 27W
Sunda, Selat, *Indonesia* **36 F3** 6 20S 105 30 E
Sunda Is., *Indonesia* **28 K14** 5 0S 105 0 E
Sunda Str. = Sunda, Selat, *Indonesia* **36 F3** 6 20S 105 30 E
Sundance, *Canada* **73 B10** 56 32N 94 4W
Sundance, *U.S.A.* **80 C2** 44 24N 104 23W
Sundar Nagar, *India* **42 D7** 31 32N 76 53 E
Sundarbans, The, *Asia* **41 J16** 22 0N 89 0 E
Sundargarh, *India* **41 H14** 22 4N 84 5 E
Sundays = Sondags →, *S. Africa* **56 E4** 33 44S 25 51 E
Sunderland, *Canada* **78 B5** 44 16N 79 4W
Sunderland, *U.K.* **10 C6** 54 55N 1 23W
Sundre, *Canada* **72 C6** 51 49N 114 38W
Sundsvall, *Sweden* **9 E17** 62 23N 17 17 E
Sung Hei, *Vietnam* **39 G6** 10 20N 106 2 E
Sungai Kolok, *Thailand* **39 J3** 6 2N 101 58 E
Sungai Lembing, *Malaysia* **39 L4** 3 55N 103 3 E
Sungai Petani, *Malaysia* **39 K3** 5 37N 100 30 E
Sungaigerong, *Indonesia* **36 E2** 2 59S 104 52 E
Sungailiat, *Indonesia* **36 E3** 1 51S 106 8 E
Sungaipenuh, *Indonesia* **36 E2** 2 1S 101 20 E
Sungari = Songhua Jiang →, *China* **33 B8** 47 45N 132 30 E
Sunghua Chiang = Songhua Jiang →, *China* **33 B8** 47 45N 132 30 E
Sunland Park, *U.S.A.* **83 L10** 31 50N 106 40W
Sunndalsøra, *Norway* **9 E13** 62 40N 8 33 E
Sunnyside, *U.S.A.* **82 C3** 46 20N 120 0W
Sunnyvale, *U.S.A.* **84 H4** 37 23N 122 2W
Suntar, *Russia* **27 C12** 62 15N 117 30 E
Suomenselkä, *Finland* **8 E21** 62 52N 24 0 E
Suomussalmi, *Finland* **8 D23** 64 54N 29 10 E
Suoyarvi, *Russia* **24 B5** 62 3N 32 20 E
Supai, *U.S.A.* **83 H7** 36 15N 112 41W
Supaul, *India* **43 F12** 26 10N 86 40 E
Superior, *Ariz., U.S.A.* **83 K8** 33 18N 111 6W
Superior, *Mont., U.S.A.* **82 C6** 47 12N 114 53W
Superior, *Nebr., U.S.A.* **80 E5** 40 1N 98 4W
Superior, *Wis., U.S.A.* **80 B8** 46 44N 92 6W
Superior, L., *N. Amer.* **70 C2** 47 0N 87 0W
Suphan Buri, *Thailand* **38 E3** 14 14N 100 10 E
Suphan Dağı, *Turkey* **44 B4** 38 54N 42 48 E

T

Tsuyama

Toledo, Brazil 95 A5 24 44S 53 45W
Toledo, Spain 19 C3 39 50N 4 2W
Toledo, Ohio, U.S.A. 76 E4 41 39N 83 33W
Toledo, Oreg., U.S.A. 82 D2 44 37N 123 56W
Toledo, Wash., U.S.A. 82 C2 46 26N 122 51W
Toledo, Montes de, Spain 19 C3 39 33N 4 20W
Toledo Bend Reservoir, U.S.A. 81 K8 31 11N 93 34W
Tolga, Australia 62 B4 17 15S 145 29 E
Toliara, Madag. 57 C7 23 21S 43 40 E
Toliara □, Madag. 57 C8 21 0S 45 0 E
Tolima, Colombia 92 C3 4 40N 75 19W
Tolitoli, Indonesia 37 D6 1 5N 120 50 E
Tollhouse, U.S.A. 84 H7 37 1N 119 24W
Tolo, Teluk, Indonesia 37 E6 2 20S 122 10 E
Toluca, Mexico 87 D5 19 20N 99 40W
Tom Burke, S. Africa 57 C4 23 5S 28 0 E
Tom Price, Australia 60 D2 22 40S 117 48 E
Tomah, U.S.A. 80 D9 43 59N 90 30W
Tomahawk, U.S.A. 80 C10 45 28N 89 44W
Tomakomai, Japan 30 C10 42 38N 141 36 E
Tomales, U.S.A. 84 G4 38 15N 122 53W
Tomales B., U.S.A. 84 G3 38 15N 123 58W
Tomar, Portugal 19 C1 39 36N 8 25W
Tomaszów Mazowiecki, Poland 17 C10 51 30N 20 2 E
Tomatlán, Mexico 86 D3 19 56N 105 15W
Tombador, Serra do, Brazil 92 F7 12 0S 58 0W
Tombigbee →, U.S.A. 77 K2 31 8N 87 57W
Tombouctou, Mali 50 E5 16 50N 3 0W
Tombstone, U.S.A. 83 L8 31 43N 110 4W
Tombua, Angola 56 B1 15 55S 11 55 E
Tomé, Chile 94 D1 36 36S 72 57W
Tomelloso, Spain 19 C4 39 10N 3 2W
Tomini, Indonesia 37 D6 0 30N 120 30 E
Tomini, Teluk, Indonesia 37 E6 0 10S 121 0 E
Tomintoul, U.K. 12 D5 57 15N 3 23W
Tomkinson Ranges, Australia 61 E4 26 11S 129 5 E
Tommot, Russia 27 D13 59 4N 126 20 E
Tomnop Ta Suos, Cambodia 39 G5 11 20N 104 15 E
Tomo →, Colombia 92 B5 5 20N 67 48W
Toms Place, U.S.A. 84 H8 37 34N 118 41W
Toms River, U.S.A. 79 G10 39 58N 74 12W
Tomsk, Russia 26 D9 56 30N 85 5 E
Tonalá, Mexico 87 D6 16 8N 93 41W
Tonantins, Brazil 92 D5 2 45S 67 45W
Tonasket, U.S.A. 82 B4 48 42N 119 26W
Tonawanda, U.S.A. 78 D6 43 1N 78 53W
Tonbridge, U.K. 11 F8 51 11N 0 17 E
Tondano, Indonesia 37 D6 1 35N 124 54 E
Tondoro, Namibia 56 B2 17 45S 18 50 E
Tone →, Australia 61 F2 34 25S 116 25 E
Tone-Gawa →, Japan 31 F9 35 44N 140 51 E
Tonekābon, Iran 45 B6 36 45N 51 12 E
Tong Xian, China 34 E9 39 55N 116 35 E
Tonga ■, Pac. Oc. 59 D11 19 50S 174 30W
Tonga Trench, Pac. Oc. 64 J10 18 0S 173 0W
Tongaat, S. Africa 57 D5 29 33S 31 9 E
Tongareva, Cook Is. 65 H12 9 0S 158 0W
Tongatapu Group, Tonga 59 E12 21 0S 175 0W
Tongchŏn-ni, N. Korea 35 E14 39 50N 127 25 E
Tongchuan, China 34 G5 35 6N 109 3 E
Tongeren, Belgium 15 D5 50 47N 5 28 E
Tongguan, China 34 G6 34 40N 110 25 E
Tonghua, China 35 D13 41 42N 125 58 E
Tongjosŏn Man, N. Korea 35 E15 39 30N 128 0 E
Tongking, G. of = Tonkin, G. of, Asia 32 E5 20 0N 108 0 E
Tongliao, China 35 C12 43 38N 122 18 E
Tongling, China 33 C6 30 55N 117 48 E
Tongnae, S. Korea 35 G15 35 12N 129 5 E
Tongobory, Madag. 57 C7 23 32S 44 20 E
Tongoy, Chile 94 C1 30 16S 71 31W
Tongres = Tongeren, Belgium 15 D5 50 47N 5 28 E
Tongsa Dzong, Bhutan 41 F17 27 31N 90 31 E
Tongue, U.K. 12 C4 58 29N 4 25W
Tongue →, U.S.A. 80 B2 46 25N 105 52W
Tongwei, China 34 G3 35 0N 105 5 E
Tongxin, China 34 F3 36 59N 105 58 E
Tongyang, N. Korea 35 E14 39 9N 126 53 E
Tongyu, China 35 B12 44 45N 123 4 E
Tonj, Sudan 51 G11 7 20N 28 44 E
Tonk, India 42 F6 26 6N 75 54 E
Tonkawa, U.S.A. 81 G6 36 41N 97 18W
Tonkin = Bac Phan, Vietnam 38 B5 22 0N 105 0 E
Tonkin, G. of, Asia 32 E5 20 0N 108 0 E
Tonle Sap, Cambodia 38 F4 13 0N 104 0 E
Tono, Japan 30 E10 39 19N 141 32 E
Tonopah, U.S.A. 83 G5 38 4N 117 14W
Tonosí, Panama 88 E3 7 20N 80 20W
Tons →, Haryana, India 42 D7 30 30N 77 39 E
Tons →, Ut. P., India 43 F10 26 1N 83 33 E
Tønsberg, Norway 9 G14 59 19N 10 25 E
Toobanna, Australia 62 B4 18 42S 146 9 E
Toodyay, Australia 61 F2 31 34S 116 28 E
Tooele, U.S.A. 82 F7 40 32N 112 18W
Toompine, Australia 63 D3 27 15S 144 19 E
Toora-Khem, Russia 27 D10 52 28N 96 17 E
Toowoomba, Australia 63 D5 27 32S 151 56 E
Top-ozero, Russia 24 A5 65 35N 32 0 E
Top Springs, Australia 60 C5 16 37S 131 51 E
Topaz, U.S.A. 84 G7 38 41N 119 30W
Topeka, U.S.A. 80 F7 39 3N 95 40W
Topley, Canada 72 C3 54 49N 126 18W
Topocalma, Pta., Chile 94 C1 34 10S 72 2W
Topock, U.S.A. 85 L12 34 46N 114 29W
Topol'čany, Slovak Rep. 17 D10 48 35N 18 12 E
Topolobampo, Mexico 86 B3 25 40N 109 4W
Toppenish, U.S.A. 82 C3 46 23N 120 19W
Toraka Vestale, Madag. 57 B7 16 20S 43 58 E
Torata, Peru 92 G4 17 23S 70 1W
Torbalı, Turkey 21 E12 38 10N 27 21 E
Torbat-e Heydārīyeh, Iran 45 C8 35 15N 59 12 E
Torbat-e Jām, Iran 45 C9 35 16N 60 35 E
Torbay, Canada 71 C9 47 40N 52 42W
Torbay □, U.K. 11 G4 50 26N 3 31W
Tordesillas, Spain 19 B3 41 30N 5 0W
Torfaen □, U.K. 11 F4 51 43N 3 3W
Torgau, Germany 16 C7 51 34N 13 0 E
Torhout, Belgium 15 C3 51 5N 3 7 E
Tori-Shima, Japan 31 J10 30 29N 140 19 E
Torin, Mexico 86 B2 27 33N 110 15W
Torino, Italy 18 D7 45 3N 7 40 E
Torit, Sudan 51 H12 4 27N 32 31 E
Torkamān, Iran 44 B5 37 35N 47 23 E
Tormes →, Spain 19 B2 41 18N 6 29W
Tornado Mt., Canada 72 D6 49 55N 114 40W
Torne älv →, Sweden 8 D21 65 50N 24 12 E
Torneå = Tornio, Finland 8 D21 65 50N 24 12 E
Torneträsk, Sweden 8 B18 68 24N 19 15 E
Tornio, Finland 8 D21 65 50N 24 12 E
Tornionjoki →, Finland 8 D21 65 50N 24 12 E
Tornquist, Argentina 94 D3 38 8S 62 15W
Toro, Spain 22 B11 39 59N 4 8 E
Toro, Cerro del, Chile 94 B2 29 10S 69 50W
Toro Pk., U.S.A. 85 M10 33 34N 116 24W
Toroníios Kólpos, Greece 21 D10 40 5N 23 30 E
Toronto, Canada 78 C5 43 39N 79 20W
Toronto, U.S.A. 78 F4 40 28N 80 36W
Toropets, Russia 24 C5 56 30N 31 40 E
Tororo, Uganda 54 B3 0 45N 34 12 E
Toros Dağları, Turkey 25 G5 37 0N 32 30 E
Torpa, India 43 H11 22 57N 85 6 E
Torquay, U.K. 11 G4 50 27N 3 32W
Torrance, U.S.A. 85 M8 33 50N 118 19W
Torre de Moncorvo, Portugal 19 B2 41 12N 7 8W
Torre del Greco, Italy 20 D6 40 47N 14 22 E
Torrejón de Ardoz, Spain 19 B4 40 27N 3 29W
Torrelavega, Spain 19 A3 43 20N 4 5W
Torremolinos, Spain 19 D3 36 38N 4 30W
Torrens Cr. →, Australia 62 C4 22 23S 145 9 E
Torrens Creek, Australia 62 C4 20 48S 145 3 E
Torrent, Spain 19 C5 39 27N 0 28W
Torreón, Mexico 86 B4 25 33N 103 26W
Torres, Brazil 95 B5 29 21S 49 44W
Torres, Mexico 86 B2 28 46N 110 47W
Torres Strait, Australia 64 H6 9 50S 142 20 E
Torres Vedras, Portugal 19 C1 39 5N 9 15W
Torrevieja, Spain 19 D5 37 59N 0 42W
Torrey, U.S.A. 83 G8 38 18N 111 25W
Torridge →, U.K. 11 G3 51 0N 4 13W
Torridon, L., U.K. 12 D3 57 35N 5 50W
Torrington, Conn., U.S.A. 79 E11 41 48N 73 7W
Torrington, Wyo., U.S.A. 80 D2 42 4N 104 11W
Tórshavn, Færoe Is. 8 E9 62 5N 6 56W
Tortola, Br. Virgin Is. 89 C7 18 19N 64 45W
Tortosa, Spain 19 B6 40 49N 0 31 E
Tortosa, C., Spain 19 B6 40 41N 0 52 E
Tortue, I. de la, Haiti 89 B5 20 5N 72 57W
Torūd, Iran 45 C7 35 25N 55 5 E
Toruń, Poland 17 B10 53 2N 18 39 E
Tory I., Ireland 13 A3 55 16N 8 14W
Tosa, Japan 31 H6 33 24N 133 23 E
Tosa-Shimizu, Japan 31 H6 32 52N 132 58 E
Tosa-Wan, Japan 31 H6 33 15N 133 30 E
Toscana □, Italy 20 C4 43 25N 11 0 E
Toshkent, Uzbekistan 26 E7 41 20N 69 10 E
Tostado, Argentina 94 B3 29 15S 61 50W
Tostón, Pta. de, Canary Is. 22 F5 28 42N 14 2W
Tosu, Japan 31 H5 33 22N 130 31 E
Toteng, Botswana 56 C3 20 22S 22 58 E
Totma, Russia 24 C7 60 0N 42 40 E
Totnes, U.K. 11 G4 50 26N 3 42W
Totness, Surinam 93 B7 5 53N 56 19W
Totonicapán, Guatemala 88 D1 14 58N 91 12W
Totten Glacier, Antarctica 5 C8 66 45S 116 10 E
Tottenham, Canada 78 B5 44 1N 79 49W
Tottori, Japan 31 G7 35 30N 134 15 E
Tottori □, Japan 31 G7 35 30N 134 12 E
Toubkal, Djebel, Morocco 50 B4 31 0N 8 0W
Tougan, Burkina Faso 50 F5 13 11N 2 58W
Touggourt, Algeria 50 B7 33 6N 6 4 E
Toul, France 18 B6 48 40N 5 53 E
Toulon, France 18 E6 43 10N 5 55 E
Toulouse, France 18 E4 43 37N 1 27 E
Toummo, Niger 51 D8 22 45N 14 8 E
Toungoo, Burma 41 K20 19 0N 96 30 E
Touraine, France 18 C4 47 20N 0 30 E
Tourane = Da Nang, Vietnam 38 D7 16 4N 108 13 E
Tourcoing, France 18 A5 50 42N 3 10 E
Touriñán, C., Spain 19 A1 43 3N 9 18W
Tournai, Belgium 15 D3 50 35N 3 25 E
Tournon-sur-Rhône, France 18 D6 45 4N 4 50 E
Tours, France 18 C4 47 22N 0 40 E
Toussora, Mt., C.A.R. 52 C4 9 7N 23 14 E
Touws →, S. Africa 56 E3 33 45S 21 11 E
Touwsrivier, S. Africa 56 E3 33 20S 20 2 E
Towada, Japan 30 D10 40 37N 141 13 E
Towada-Ko, Japan 30 D10 40 28N 140 55 E
Towanda, U.S.A. 79 E8 41 46N 76 27W
Towang, India 41 F17 27 37N 91 50 E
Tower, U.S.A. 80 B8 47 48N 92 17W
Towerhill Cr. →, Australia 62 C3 22 28S 144 35 E
Towner, U.S.A. 80 A4 48 21N 100 25W
Townsend, U.S.A. 82 C8 46 19N 111 31W
Townshend I., Australia 62 C5 22 10S 150 31 E
Townsville, Australia 62 B4 19 15S 146 45 E
Towson, U.S.A. 76 F7 39 24N 76 36W
Towuti, Danau, Indonesia 37 E6 2 45S 121 32 E
Toya-Ko, Japan 30 C10 42 35N 140 51 E
Toyama, Japan 31 F8 36 40N 137 15 E
Toyama □, Japan 31 F8 36 45N 137 30 E
Toyama-Wan, Japan 31 F8 37 0N 137 30 E
Toyohashi, Japan 31 G8 34 45N 137 25 E
Toyokawa, Japan 31 G8 34 48N 137 27 E
Toyonaka, Japan 31 G7 34 50N 135 28 E
Toyooka, Japan 31 G7 35 35N 134 48 E
Toyota, Japan 31 G8 35 3N 137 7 E
Tozeur, Tunisia 50 B7 33 56N 8 8 E
Trá Li = Tralee, Ireland 13 D2 52 16N 9 42W
Tra On, Vietnam 39 H5 9 58N 105 55 E
Trabzon, Turkey 25 F6 41 0N 39 45 E
Tracadie, Canada 71 C7 47 30N 64 55W
Tracy, Calif., U.S.A. 84 H5 37 44N 121 26W
Tracy, Minn., U.S.A. 80 C7 44 14N 95 37W
Trafalgar, C., Spain 19 D2 36 10N 6 2W
Trail, Canada 72 D5 49 5N 117 40W
Trainor L., Canada 72 A4 60 24N 120 17W
Trákhonas, Cyprus 23 D12 35 12N 33 21 E
Tralee, Ireland 13 D2 52 16N 9 42W
Tralee B., Ireland 13 D2 52 17N 9 55W
Tramore, Ireland 13 D4 52 10N 7 10W
Tramore B., Ireland 13 D4 52 9N 7 10W
Tran Ninh, Cao Nguyen, Laos 38 C4 19 30N 103 10 E
Tranås, Sweden 9 G16 58 3N 14 59 E
Trancas, Argentina 94 B2 26 11S 65 20W
Trang, Thailand 39 J2 7 33N 99 38 E
Trangahy, Madag. 57 B7 19 7S 44 31 E
Trangan, Indonesia 37 F8 6 40S 134 20 E
Trani, Italy 20 D7 41 17N 16 25 E
Tranoroa, Madag. 57 C8 24 42S 45 4 E
Tranqueras, Uruguay 95 C4 31 13S 55 45W
Transantarctic Mts., Antarctica 5 E12 85 0S 170 0W
Transilvania, Romania 17 E12 46 30N 24 0 E
Transilvanian Alps = Carpaţii Meridionali, Romania 17 F13 45 30N 25 0 E
Transvaal, S. Africa 53 K5 25 0S 29 0 E
Transylvania = Transilvania, Romania 17 E12 46 30N 24 0 E
Trápani, Italy 20 E5 38 1N 12 29 E
Trapper Pk., U.S.A. 82 D6 45 54N 114 18W
Trasimeno, L., Italy 20 C5 43 8N 12 6 E
Trat, Thailand 39 F4 12 14N 102 33 E
Tratani →, Pakistan 42 E3 29 19N 68 20 E
Traun, Austria 16 D8 48 14N 14 15 E
Travemünde, Germany 16 B6 53 57N 10 52 E
Travers, Mt., N.Z. 59 K4 42 1S 172 45 E
Traverse City, U.S.A. 76 C3 44 46N 85 38W
Travis, L., U.S.A. 81 K5 30 24N 97 55W
Travnik, Bos.-H. 21 B7 44 17N 17 39 E
Trébbia →, Italy 18 D8 45 4N 9 41 E
Třebíč, Czech Rep. 16 D8 49 14N 15 55 E
Trebinje, Bos.-H. 21 C8 42 44N 18 22 E
Trebonne, Australia 62 B4 18 37S 146 5 E
Tregaron, U.K. 11 E4 52 14N 3 56W
Tregrosse Is., Australia 62 B5 17 41S 150 43 E
Treherne, Canada 73 D9 49 38N 98 42W
Treinta y Tres, Uruguay 95 C5 33 16S 54 17W
Trelawney, Zimbabwe 57 B5 17 30S 30 30 E
Trelew, Argentina 96 E3 43 10S 65 20W
Trelleborg, Sweden 9 J15 55 20N 13 10 E
Tremadog Bay, U.K. 10 E3 52 51N 4 18W
Tremonton, U.S.A. 82 F7 41 43N 112 10W
Tremp, Spain 19 A6 42 10N 0 52 E
Trenche →, Canada 70 C5 47 46N 72 53W
Trenčín, Slovak Rep. 17 D10 48 52N 18 4 E
Trenggalek, Indonesia 37 H14 8 3S 111 43 E
Trenque Lauquen, Argentina 94 D3 36 5S 62 45W
Trent →, Canada 78 B7 44 6N 77 34W
Trent →, U.K. 10 D7 53 41N 0 42W
Trento, Italy 20 A4 46 4N 11 8 E
Trenton, Canada 78 B7 44 10N 77 34W
Trenton, Mo., U.S.A. 80 E8 40 5N 93 37W
Trenton, N.J., U.S.A. 79 F10 40 14N 74 46W
Trenton, Nebr., U.S.A. 80 E4 40 11N 101 1W
Trepassey, Canada 71 C9 46 43N 53 25W
Tres Arroyos, Argentina 94 D3 38 26S 60 20W
Três Corações, Brazil 95 A6 21 44S 45 15W
Três Lagoas, Brazil 93 H8 20 50S 51 43W
Tres Lomas, Argentina 94 D3 36 27S 62 51W
Tres Marías, Islas, Mexico 86 C3 21 25N 106 28W
Tres Montes, C., Chile 96 F1 46 50S 75 30W
Tres Pinos, U.S.A. 84 J5 36 48N 121 19W
Três Pontas, Brazil 95 A6 21 23S 45 29W
Tres Puentes, Chile 94 B1 27 50S 70 15W
Tres Puntas, C., Argentina 96 F3 47 0S 66 0W
Três Rios, Brazil 95 A7 22 6S 43 15W
Tres Valles, Mexico 87 D5 18 15N 96 8W
Tresco, U.K. 11 H1 49 57N 6 20W
Treviso, Italy 20 B5 45 40N 12 15 E
Triabunna, Australia 62 G4 42 30S 147 55 E
Triánda, Greece 23 C10 36 25N 28 10 E
Triangle, Zimbabwe 57 C5 21 2S 31 28 E
Tribal Areas □, Pakistan 42 C4 33 0N 70 0 E
Tribulation, C., Australia 62 B4 16 5S 145 29 E
Tribune, U.S.A. 80 F4 38 28N 101 45W
Trichinopoly = Tiruchchirappalli, India 40 P11 10 45N 78 45 E
Trichur, India 40 P10 10 30N 76 18 E
Trier, Germany 16 D4 49 45N 6 38 E
Trieste, Italy 20 B5 45 40N 13 46 E
Triglav, Slovenia 16 E7 46 21N 13 50 E
Trikkala, Greece 21 E9 39 34N 21 47 E
Trikomo, Cyprus 23 D12 35 17N 33 52 E
Trikora, Puncak, Indonesia 37 E9 4 15S 138 45 E
Trim, Ireland 13 C5 53 33N 6 48W
Trincomalee, Sri Lanka 40 Q12 8 38N 81 15 E
Trindade, Brazil 93 G9 16 40S 49 30W
Trindade, I., Atl. Oc. 2 F8 20 20S 29 50W
Trinidad, Bolivia 92 F6 14 46S 64 50W
Trinidad, Cuba 88 B4 21 48N 80 0W
Trinidad, Trin. & Tob. 89 D7 10 30N 61 15W
Trinidad, Uruguay 94 C4 33 30S 56 50W
Trinidad, U.S.A. 81 G2 37 10N 104 31W
Trinidad →, Mexico 87 D5 17 49N 95 9W
Trinidad & Tobago ■, W. Indies 89 D7 10 30N 61 20W
Trinity, Canada 71 C9 48 59N 53 55W
Trinity, U.S.A. 81 K7 30 57N 95 22W
Trinity →, Calif., U.S.A. 82 F2 41 11N 123 42W
Trinity →, Tex., U.S.A. 81 L7 29 45N 94 43W
Trinity B., Canada 71 C9 48 20N 53 10W
Trinity Is., U.S.A. 68 C4 56 33N 154 25W
Trinity Range, U.S.A. 82 F4 40 15N 118 45W
Trinkitat, Sudan 51 E13 18 45N 37 51 E
Trinway, U.S.A. 78 F2 40 9N 82 1W
Tripoli = Tarābulus, Lebanon 47 A4 34 31N 35 50 E
Tripoli = Tarābulus, Libya 51 B8 32 49N 13 7 E
Trípolis, Greece 21 F10 37 31N 22 25 E
Tripolitania, N. Afr. 51 B8 31 0N 13 0 E
Tripura □, India 41 H18 24 0N 92 0 E
Tripylos, Cyprus 23 E11 34 59N 32 41 E
Tristan da Cunha, Atl. Oc. 49 K2 37 6S 12 20W
Trisul, India 43 D8 30 19N 79 47 E
Trivandrum, India 40 Q10 8 41N 77 0 E
Trnava, Slovak Rep. 17 D9 48 23N 17 35 E
Trochu, Canada 72 C6 51 50N 113 13W
Trodely I., Canada 70 B4 52 15N 79 26W
Troglav, Croatia 20 C7 43 56N 16 36 E
Troilus, L., Canada 70 B5 50 50N 74 35W
Trois-Pistoles, Canada 71 C6 48 5N 69 10W
Trois-Rivières, Canada 70 C5 46 25N 72 34W
Troitsk, Russia 26 D7 54 10N 61 35 E
Troitsko Pechorsk, Russia 24 B10 62 40N 56 10 E
Trölladyngja, Iceland 8 D5 64 54N 17 16W
Trollhättan, Sweden 9 G15 58 17N 12 20 E
Trollheimen, Norway 8 E13 62 46N 9 1 E
Trombetas →, Brazil 93 D7 1 55S 55 35W
Tromsø, Norway 8 B18 69 40N 18 56 E
Trona, U.S.A. 85 K9 35 46N 117 23W
Tronador, Mte., Argentina 96 E2 41 10S 71 50W
Trøndelag, Norway 8 D14 64 17N 11 50 E
Trondheim, Norway 8 E14 63 36N 10 25 E
Trondheimsfjorden, Norway 8 E14 63 35N 10 30 E
Troodos, Cyprus 23 E11 34 55N 32 52 E
Troon, U.K. 12 F4 55 33N 4 39W
Tropic, U.S.A. 83 H7 37 37N 112 5W
Trostan, U.K. 13 A5 55 3N 6 10W
Trout →, Canada 72 A5 61 19N 119 51W
Trout L., N.W.T., Canada 72 A4 60 40N 121 14W
Trout L., Ont., Canada 73 C10 51 20N 93 15W
Trout Lake, Canada 72 B6 56 30N 114 32W
Trout Lake, U.S.A. 84 E5 46 0N 121 32W
Trout River, Canada 71 C8 49 29N 58 8W
Trout Run, U.S.A. 78 E7 41 23N 77 3W
Trouville-sur-Mer, France 18 B4 49 21N 0 5 E
Trowbridge, U.K. 11 F5 51 18N 2 12W
Troy, Turkey 21 E12 39 57N 26 12 E
Troy, Ala., U.S.A. 77 K3 31 48N 85 58W
Troy, Kans., U.S.A. 80 F7 39 47N 95 5W
Troy, Mo., U.S.A. 80 F9 38 59N 90 59W
Troy, Mont., U.S.A. 82 B6 48 28N 115 53W
Troy, N.Y., U.S.A. 79 D11 42 44N 73 41W
Troy, Ohio, U.S.A. 76 E3 40 2N 84 12W
Troy, Pa., U.S.A. 79 E8 41 47N 76 47W
Troyes, France 18 B6 48 19N 4 3 E
Truchas Peak, U.S.A. 81 H2 35 58N 105 39W
Trucial States = United Arab Emirates ■, Asia 46 C5 23 50N 54 0 E
Truckee, U.S.A. 84 F6 39 20N 120 11W
Trudovoye, Russia 30 C6 43 17N 132 5 E
Trujillo, Honduras 88 C2 16 0N 86 0W
Trujillo, Peru 92 E3 8 6S 79 0W
Trujillo, Spain 19 C3 39 28N 5 55W
Trujillo, U.S.A. 81 H2 35 32N 104 42W
Trujillo, Venezuela 92 B4 9 22N 70 38W
Truk, Micronesia 64 G7 7 25N 151 46 E
Trumann, U.S.A. 81 H9 35 41N 90 31W
Trumansburg, U.S.A. 79 D8 42 33N 76 40W
Trumbull, Mt., U.S.A. 83 H7 36 25N 113 8W
Trung-Phan = Annam, Vietnam 38 E7 16 0N 108 0 E
Truro, Canada 71 C7 45 21N 63 14W
Truro, U.K. 11 G2 50 16N 5 4W
Truskavets, Ukraine 17 D12 49 17N 23 30 E
Trutch, Canada 72 B4 57 44N 122 57W
Truth or Consequences, U.S.A. 83 K10 33 8N 107 15W
Trutnov, Czech Rep. 16 C8 50 37N 15 54 E
Truxton, U.S.A. 79 D8 42 45N 76 2W
Tryonville, U.S.A. 78 E5 41 42N 79 48W
Tsandi, Namibia 56 B1 17 42S 14 50 E
Tsaratanana, Madag. 57 B8 16 47S 47 39 E
Tsaratanana, Mt. de, Madag. 57 A8 14 0S 49 0 E
Tsarevo = Michurin, Bulgaria 21 C12 42 9N 27 51 E
Tsau, Botswana 56 C3 20 8S 22 22 E
Tselinograd = Astana, Kazakstan 26 D8 51 10N 71 30 E
Tses, Namibia 56 D2 25 58S 18 8 E
Tsetserleg, Mongolia 32 B5 47 36N 101 32 E
Tshabong, Botswana 56 D3 26 2S 22 29 E
Tshane, Botswana 56 C3 24 5S 21 54 E
Tshela, Dem. Rep. of the Congo 52 E2 4 57S 13 4 E
Tshesebe, Botswana 57 C4 21 51S 27 32 E
Tshibeke, Dem. Rep. of the Congo 54 C2 2 40S 28 35 E
Tshibinda, Dem. Rep. of the Congo 54 C2 2 23S 28 43 E
Tshikapa, Dem. Rep. of the Congo 52 F4 6 28S 20 48 E
Tshilenge, Dem. Rep. of the Congo 54 D1 6 17S 23 48 E
Tshinsenda, Dem. Rep. of the Congo 55 E2 12 20S 28 0 E
Tshofa, Dem. Rep. of the Congo 54 D2 5 13S 25 16 E
Tshwane, Botswana 56 C3 22 24S 22 1 E
Tsigara, Botswana 56 C4 20 22S 25 54 E
Tsihombe, Madag. 57 D8 25 10S 45 41 E
Tsiigehtchic, Canada 68 B6 67 15N 134 0W
Tsimlyansk Res. = Tsimlyanskoye Vdkhr., Russia 25 E7 48 0N 43 0 E
Tsimlyanskoye Vdkhr., Russia 25 E7 48 0N 43 0 E
Tsinan = Jinan, China 34 F9 36 38N 117 1 E
Tsineng, S. Africa 56 D3 27 5S 23 5 E
Tsinghai = Qinghai □, China 32 C4 36 0N 98 0 E
Tsingtao = Qingdao, China 35 F11 36 5N 120 20 E
Tsinjoarivo, Madag. 57 B8 19 37S 47 40 E
Tsinjomitondraka, Madag. 57 B8 15 40S 47 8 E
Tsiroanomandidy, Madag. 57 B8 18 46S 46 2 E
Tsitondroina, Madag. 57 C8 21 19S 46 0 E
Tsivory, Madag. 57 C8 24 4S 46 5 E
Tskhinvali, Georgia 25 F7 42 14N 44 1 E
Tsna →, Russia 24 D7 54 55N 41 58 E
Tso Moriri, L., India 43 C8 32 50N 78 20 E
Tsobis, Namibia 56 B2 19 27S 17 30 E
Tsodilo Hill, Botswana 56 B3 18 49S 21 43 E
Tsogttsetsiy = Baruunsuu, Mongolia 34 C3 43 43N 105 35 E
Tsolo, S. Africa 57 E4 31 18S 28 37 E
Tsomo, S. Africa 57 E4 32 0S 27 42 E
Tsu, Japan 31 G8 34 45N 136 25 E
Tsu L., Canada 72 A6 60 40N 111 52W
Tsuchiura, Japan 31 F10 36 5N 140 15 E
Tsugaru-Kaikyō, Japan 30 D10 41 35N 141 0 E
Tsumeb, Namibia 56 B2 19 9S 17 44 E
Tsumis, Namibia 56 C2 23 39S 17 29 E
Tsuruga, Japan 31 G8 35 45N 136 2 E
Tsurugi-San, Japan 31 H7 33 51N 134 6 E
Tsuruoka, Japan 30 E9 38 44N 139 50 E
Tsushima, Gifu, Japan 31 G8 35 10N 136 43 E
Tsushima, Nagasaki, Japan 31 G4 34 20N 129 20 E
Tsuyama, Japan 31 G7 35 3N 134 0 E

Tsyelyakhany

Tsyelyakhany, Belarus 17 B13 52 30N 25 46 E
Tual, Indonesia 37 F8 5 38S 132 44 E
Tuam, Ireland 13 C3 53 31N 8 51W
Tuamotu Arch. = Tuamotu Is., Pac. Oc. 65 J13 17 0S 144 0W
Tuamotu Is., Pac. Oc. 65 J13 17 0S 144 0W
Tuamotu Ridge, Pac. Oc. 65 K14 20 0S 138 0W
Tuao, Phil. 37 A6 17 55N 121 22 E
Tuapse, Russia 25 F6 44 5N 39 10 E
Tuatapere, N.Z. 59 M1 46 8S 167 41 E
Tuba City, U.S.A. 83 H8 36 8N 111 14W
Tuban, Indonesia 37 G15 6 54S 112 3 E
Tubani, Botswana 56 C3 24 46S 24 18 E
Tubarão, Brazil 95 B6 28 30S 49 0W
Tūbās, West Bank 47 C4 32 20N 35 22 E
Tubas →, Namibia 56 C2 22 54S 14 35 E
Tübingen, Germany 16 D5 48 31N 9 4 E
Tubruq, Libya 51 B10 32 7N 23 55 E
Tubuai Is., Pac. Oc. 65 K13 25 0S 150 0W
Tuc Trung, Vietnam 39 G6 11 1N 107 12 E
Tucacas, Venezuela 92 A5 10 48N 68 19W
Tuchodi →, Canada 72 B4 58 17N 123 42W
Tuckanarra, Australia 61 E2 27 7S 118 5 E
Tucson, U.S.A. 83 K8 32 13N 110 58W
Tucumán □, Argentina 94 B2 26 48S 66 2W
Tucumcari, U.S.A. 81 H3 35 10N 103 44W
Tucupita, Venezuela 92 B6 9 2N 62 3W
Tucuruí, Brazil 93 D9 3 42S 49 44W
Tucuruí, Reprêsa de, Brazil 93 D9 4 0S 49 30W
Tudela, Spain 19 A5 42 4N 1 39W
Tudmur, Syria 44 C3 34 36N 38 15 E
Tudor, L., Canada 71 A6 55 50N 65 25W
Tugela →, S. Africa 57 D5 29 14S 31 30 E
Tuguegarao, Phil. 37 A6 17 35N 121 42 E
Tugur, Russia 27 D14 53 44N 136 45 E
Tui, Spain 19 A1 42 3N 8 39W
Tuineje, Canary Is. 22 F5 28 19N 14 3W
Tukangbesi, Kepulauan, Indonesia 37 F6 6 0S 124 0 E
Tukarak I., Canada 70 A4 56 15N 78 45W
Tukayyid, Iraq 44 D5 29 47N 45 36 E
Tuktoyaktuk, Canada 68 B6 69 27N 133 2W
Tukums, Latvia 9 H20 56 58N 23 10 E
Tukuyu, Tanzania 55 D3 9 17S 33 35 E
Tula, Hidalgo, Mexico 87 C5 20 5N 99 20W
Tula, Tamaulipas, Mexico 87 C5 23 0N 99 40W
Tula, Russia 24 D6 54 13N 37 38 E
Tulancingo, Mexico 87 C5 20 5N 99 22W
Tulare, U.S.A. 84 J7 36 13N 119 21W
Tulare Lake Bed, U.S.A. 84 K7 36 0N 119 48W
Tularosa, U.S.A. 83 K10 33 5N 106 1W
Tulbagh, S. Africa 56 E2 33 16S 19 6 E
Tulcán, Ecuador 92 C3 0 48N 77 43W
Tulcea, Romania 17 F15 45 13N 28 46 E
Tulchyn, Ukraine 17 D15 48 41N 28 49 E
Tūleh, Iran 45 C7 34 35N 52 33 E
Tulemalu L., Canada 73 A9 62 58N 99 25W
Tuli, Zimbabwe 55 G2 21 58S 29 13 E
Tulia, U.S.A. 81 H4 34 32N 101 46W
Tulita, Canada 68 B7 64 57N 125 30W
Ţūlkarm, West Bank 47 C4 32 19N 35 2 E
Tulla, Ireland 13 D3 52 53N 8 46W
Tullahoma, U.S.A. 77 H2 35 22N 86 13W
Tullamore, Ireland 13 C4 53 16N 7 31W
Tulle, France 18 D4 45 16N 1 46 E
Tullow, Ireland 13 D5 52 49N 6 45W
Tully, Australia 62 B4 17 56S 145 55 E
Tully, U.S.A. 79 D8 42 48N 76 7W
Tulsa, U.S.A. 81 G7 36 10N 95 55W
Tulsequah, Canada 72 B2 58 39N 133 35W
Tulua, Colombia 92 C3 4 6N 76 11W
Tulun, Russia 27 D11 54 32N 100 35 E
Tulungagung, Indonesia 37 H14 8 5S 111 54 E
Tuma →, Nic. 88 D3 13 6N 84 35W
Tumaco, Colombia 92 C3 1 50N 78 45W
Tumatumari, Guyana 92 B7 5 20N 58 55W
Tumba, Sweden 9 G17 59 12N 17 48 E
Tumba, L., Dem. Rep. of the Congo 52 E3 0 50S 18 0 E
Tumbaya, Argentina 94 A2 23 50S 65 26W
Tumbes, Peru 92 D2 3 37S 80 27W
Tumbwe, Dem. Rep. of the Congo 55 E2 11 25S 27 15 E
Tumd Youqi, China 34 D6 40 30N 110 30 E
Tumen, China 35 C15 43 0N 129 50 E
Tumen Jiang →, China 35 C16 42 20N 130 35 E
Tumeremo, Venezuela 92 B6 7 18N 61 30W
Tumkur, India 40 N10 13 18N 77 6 E
Tump, Pakistan 40 F3 26 7N 62 16 E
Tumpat, Malaysia 39 J4 6 11N 102 10 E
Tumu, Ghana 50 F5 10 56N 1 56W
Tumucumaque, Serra, Brazil 93 C8 2 0N 55 0W
Tumwater, U.S.A. 84 C4 47 1N 122 54W
Tuna, India 42 H4 22 59N 70 5 E
Tunas de Zaza, Cuba 88 B4 21 39N 79 34W
Tunbridge Wells = Royal Tunbridge Wells, U.K. 11 F8 51 7N 0 16 E
Tundla, India 42 F8 27 12N 78 17 E
Tunduru, Tanzania 55 E4 11 8S 37 25 E
Tundzha →, Bulgaria 21 C11 41 40N 26 35 E
Tungabhadra →, India 40 M11 15 57N 78 15 E
Tungla, Nic. 88 D3 13 24N 84 21W
Tungsten, Canada 72 A3 61 57N 128 16W
Tunguska, Nizhnyaya →, Russia 27 C9 65 48N 88 4 E
Tunguska, Podkamennaya →, Russia 27 C10 61 50N 90 13 E
Tunica, U.S.A. 81 H9 34 41N 90 23W
Tunis, Tunisia 50 A7 36 50N 10 11 E
Tunisia ■, Africa 50 B6 33 30N 9 10 E
Tunja, Colombia 92 B4 5 33N 73 25W
Tunkhannock, U.S.A. 79 E9 41 32N 75 57W
Tunliu, China 34 F7 36 13N 112 52 E
Tunnsjøen, Norway 8 D15 64 45N 13 25 E
Tunungayualok I., Canada 71 A7 56 0N 61 0W
Tununiursiq = Arctic Bay, Canada 69 A11 73 1N 85 7W
Tunuyán, Argentina 94 C2 33 35S 69 0W
Tunuyán →, Argentina 94 C2 33 33S 67 30W
Tuolumne, U.S.A. 84 H6 37 58N 120 15W
Tuolumne →, U.S.A. 84 H5 37 36N 121 13W
Tūp Āghāj, Iran 44 B5 36 3N 47 50 E
Tupã, Brazil 95 A5 21 57S 50 28W
Tupelo, U.S.A. 77 H1 34 16N 88 43W
Tupinambaranas, Brazil 92 D7 3 0S 58 0W
Tupiza, Bolivia 94 A2 21 30S 65 40W
Tupman, U.S.A. 85 K7 35 18N 119 21W
Tupper, Canada 72 B4 55 32N 120 1W
Tupper Lake, U.S.A. 79 B10 44 14N 74 28W
Tupungato, Cerro, S. Amer. 94 C2 33 15S 69 50W
Tuquan, China 35 B11 45 18N 121 38 E
Túquerres, Colombia 92 C3 1 5N 77 37W
Tura, Russia 27 C11 64 20N 100 17 E
Turabah, Si. Arabia 46 C3 28 20N 43 15 E
Tūrān, Iran 45 C8 35 39N 56 42 E
Turan, Russia 27 D10 51 55N 95 0 E
Ţurayf, Si. Arabia 44 D3 31 41N 38 39 E
Turda, Romania 17 E12 46 34N 23 47 E
Turek, Poland 17 B10 52 3N 18 30 E
Turen, Venezuela 92 B5 9 17N 69 6W
Turfan = Turpan, China 32 B3 43 58N 89 10 E
Turfan Depression = Turpan Hami, China 28 E12 42 40N 89 25 E
Turgeon →, Canada 70 C4 50 0N 78 56W
Tŭrgovishte, Bulgaria 21 C12 43 17N 26 38 E
Turgutlu, Turkey 21 E12 38 30N 27 43 E
Turgwe →, Zimbabwe 57 C5 21 31S 32 15 E
Turia →, Spain 19 C5 39 27N 0 19W
Turiaçu, Brazil 93 D9 1 40S 45 19W
Turiaçu →, Brazil 93 D9 1 36S 45 19W
Turin = Torino, Italy 18 D7 45 3N 7 40 E
Turkana, L., Africa 54 B4 3 30N 36 5 E
Turkestan = Türkistan, Kazakstan 26 E7 43 17N 68 16 E
Turkey ■, Eurasia 25 G6 39 0N 36 0 E
Turkey Creek, Australia 60 C4 17 2S 128 12 E
Türkistan, Kazakstan 26 E7 43 17N 68 16 E
Türkmenbashi, Turkmenistan 25 G9 40 5N 53 5 E
Turkmenistan ■, Asia 26 F6 39 0N 59 0 E
Turks & Caicos Is. ■, W. Indies 89 B5 21 20N 71 20W
Turks Island Passage, W. Indies 89 B5 21 30N 71 30W
Turku, Finland 9 F20 60 30N 22 19 E
Turkwel →, Kenya 54 B4 3 6N 36 6 E
Turlock, U.S.A. 84 H6 37 30N 120 51W
Turnagain →, Canada 72 B3 59 12N 127 35W
Turnagain, C., N.Z. 59 J6 40 28S 176 38 E
Turneffe Is., Belize 87 D7 17 20N 87 50W
Turner, U.S.A. 82 B9 48 51N 108 24W
Turner Pt., Australia 62 A1 11 47S 133 32 E
Turner Valley, Canada 72 C6 50 40N 114 17W
Turners Falls, U.S.A. 79 D12 42 36N 72 33W
Turnhout, Belgium 15 C4 51 19N 4 57 E
Turnor L., Canada 73 B7 56 35N 108 35W
Tŭrnovo = Veliko Tŭrnovo, Bulgaria 21 C11 43 5N 25 41 E
Turnu Măgurele, Romania 17 G13 43 46N 24 56 E
Turnu Roşu, P., Romania 17 F13 45 33N 24 17 E
Turpan, China 32 B3 43 58N 89 10 E
Turpan Hami, China 28 E12 42 40N 89 25 E
Turriff, U.K. 12 D6 57 32N 2 27W
Tursāq, Iraq 44 C5 33 27N 45 47 E
Turtle Head I., Australia 62 A3 10 56S 142 37 E
Turtle L., Canada 73 C7 53 36N 108 38W
Turtle Lake, U.S.A. 80 B4 47 31N 100 53W
Turtleford, Canada 73 C7 53 23N 108 57W
Turukhansk, Russia 27 C9 65 21N 88 5 E
Tuscaloosa, U.S.A. 77 J2 33 12N 87 34W
Tuscany = Toscana □, Italy 20 C4 43 25N 11 0 E
Tuscarawas →, U.S.A. 78 F3 40 24N 81 25W
Tuscarora Mt., U.S.A. 78 F7 40 55N 77 55W
Tuscola, Ill., U.S.A. 76 F1 39 48N 88 17W
Tuscola, Tex., U.S.A. 81 J5 32 12N 99 48W
Tuscumbia, U.S.A. 77 H2 34 44N 87 42W
Tuskegee, U.S.A. 77 J3 32 25N 85 42W
Tustin, U.S.A. 85 M9 33 44N 117 49W
Tuticorin, India 40 Q11 8 50N 78 12 E
Tutóia, Brazil 93 D10 2 45S 42 20W
Tutong, Brunei 36 D4 4 47N 114 40 E
Tutrakan, Bulgaria 21 B12 44 2N 26 40 E
Tuttle Creek L., U.S.A. 80 F6 39 22N 96 40W
Tuttlingen, Germany 16 E5 47 58N 8 48 E
Tutuala, Indonesia 37 F7 8 25S 127 15 E
Tutuila, Amer. Samoa 59 B13 14 19S 170 50W
Tutume, Botswana 53 J5 20 30S 27 5 E
Tututepec, Mexico 87 D5 16 9N 97 38W
Tuva □, Russia 27 D10 51 30N 95 0 E
Tuvalu ■, Pac. Oc. 64 H9 8 0S 178 0 E
Tuxpan, Mexico 87 C5 20 58N 97 23W
Tuxtla Gutiérrez, Mexico 87 D6 16 50N 93 10W
Tuy = Tui, Spain 19 A1 42 3N 8 39W
Tuy An, Vietnam 38 F7 13 17N 109 16 E
Tuy Duc, Vietnam 39 F6 12 15N 107 27 E
Tuy Hoa, Vietnam 38 F7 13 5N 109 10 E
Tuy Phong, Vietnam 39 G7 11 14N 108 43 E
Tuya L., Canada 72 B2 59 7N 130 35W
Tuyen Hoa, Vietnam 38 D6 17 50N 106 10 E
Tuyen Quang, Vietnam 38 B5 21 50N 105 10 E
Tūysarkān, Iran 45 C6 34 33N 48 27 E
Tuz Gölü, Turkey 25 G5 38 42N 33 18 E
Ţūz Khurmātū, Iraq 44 C5 34 56N 44 38 E
Tuzla, Bos.-H. 21 B8 44 34N 18 41 E
Tver, Russia 24 C6 56 55N 35 55 E
Twain, U.S.A. 84 E5 40 1N 121 3W
Twain Harte, U.S.A. 84 G6 38 2N 120 14W
Tweed, Canada 78 B7 44 29N 77 19W
Tweed →, U.K. 12 F6 55 45N 2 0W
Tweed Heads, Australia 63 D5 28 10S 153 31 E
Tweedsmuir Prov. Park, Canada 72 C3 53 0N 126 20W
Twentynine Palms, U.S.A. 85 L10 34 8N 116 3W
Twillingate, Canada 71 C9 49 42N 54 45W
Twin Bridges, U.S.A. 82 D7 45 33N 112 20W
Twin Falls, Canada 71 B7 53 30N 64 32W
Twin Falls, U.S.A. 82 E6 42 34N 114 28W
Twin Valley, U.S.A. 80 B6 47 16N 96 16W
Twinsburg, U.S.A. 78 E3 41 18N 81 26W
Twitchell Reservoir, U.S.A. 85 L6 34 59N 120 19W
Two Harbors, U.S.A. 80 B9 47 2N 91 40W
Two Hills, Canada 72 C6 53 43N 111 52W
Two Rivers, U.S.A. 76 C2 44 9N 87 34W
Two Rocks, Australia 61 F2 31 30S 115 35 E
Tyachiv, Ukraine 17 D12 48 1N 23 35 E
Tychy, Poland 17 C10 50 9N 18 59 E
Tyler, Minn., U.S.A. 80 C6 44 18N 96 8W
Tyler, Tex., U.S.A. 81 J7 32 21N 95 18W
Tynda, Russia 27 D13 55 10N 124 43 E
Tyndall, U.S.A. 80 D6 43 0N 97 50W
Tyne →, U.K. 10 C6 54 59N 1 32W
Tyne & Wear □, U.K. 10 B6 55 6N 1 17W
Tynemouth, U.K. 10 B6 55 1N 1 26W
Tyre = Sūr, Lebanon 47 B4 33 19N 35 16 E
Tyrifjorden, Norway 9 F14 60 2N 10 8 E
Tyrol = Tirol □, Austria 16 E6 47 3N 10 43 E
Tyrone, U.S.A. 78 F6 40 40N 78 14W
Tyrone □, U.K. 13 B4 54 38N 7 11W
Tyrrell L., Canada 73 A7 63 7N 105 27W
Tyrrhenian Sea, Medit. S. 20 E5 40 0N 12 30 E
Tysfjorden, Norway 8 B17 68 7N 16 25 E
Tyulgan, Russia 24 D10 52 22N 56 12 E
Tyumen, Russia 26 D7 57 11N 65 29 E
Tywi →, U.K. 11 F3 51 48N 4 21W
Tywyn, U.K. 11 E3 52 35N 4 5W
Tzaneen, S. Africa 57 C5 23 47S 30 9 E
Tzermiádhes, Greece 23 D7 35 12N 25 29 E
Tzukong = Zigong, China 32 D5 29 15N 104 48 E

U

U Taphao, Thailand 38 F3 12 35N 101 0 E
U.S.A. = United States of America ■, N. Amer. 74 C7 37 0N 96 0W
Uatumã →, Brazil 92 D7 2 26S 57 37W
Uaupés, Brazil 92 D5 0 8S 67 5W
Uaupés →, Brazil 92 C5 0 2N 67 16W
Uaxactún, Guatemala 88 C2 17 25N 89 29W
Ubá, Brazil 95 A7 21 8S 43 0W
Ubaitaba, Brazil 93 F11 14 18S 39 20W
Ubangi = Oubangi →, Dem. Rep. of the Congo 52 E3 0 30S 17 50 E
Ubauro, Pakistan 42 E3 28 15N 69 45 E
Ubayyiḑ, W. al →, Iraq 44 C4 32 34N 43 48 E
Ube, Japan 31 H5 33 56N 131 15 E
Úbeda, Spain 19 C4 38 3N 3 23W
Uberaba, Brazil 93 G9 19 50S 47 55W
Uberlândia, Brazil 93 G9 19 0S 48 20W
Ubolratna Res., Thailand 38 D4 16 45N 102 30 E
Ubombo, S. Africa 57 D5 27 31S 32 4 E
Ubon Ratchathani, Thailand 38 E5 15 15N 104 50 E
Ubondo, Dem. Rep. of the Congo 54 C2 0 55S 25 42 E
Ubort →, Belarus 17 B15 52 6N 28 30 E
Ubundu, Dem. Rep. of the Congo 54 C2 0 22S 25 30 E
Ucayali →, Peru 92 D4 4 30S 73 30W
Uchab, Namibia 56 B2 19 47S 17 42 E
Uchiura-Wan, Japan 30 C10 42 25N 140 40 E
Uchquduq, Uzbekistan 26 E7 41 50N 62 50 E
Uchur →, Russia 27 D14 58 48N 130 35 E
Ucluelet, Canada 72 D3 48 57N 125 32W
Uda →, Russia 27 D14 54 42N 135 14 E
Udagamandalam, India 40 P10 11 30N 76 44 E
Udainagar, India 42 H7 22 33N 76 13 E
Udaipur, India 42 G5 24 36N 73 44 E
Udaipur Garhi, Nepal 43 F12 27 0N 86 35 E
Udala, India 43 J12 21 35N 86 34 E
Uddevalla, Sweden 9 G14 58 21N 11 55 E
Uddjaur, Sweden 8 D17 65 56N 17 49 E
Uden, Neths. 15 C5 51 40N 5 37 E
Udgir, India 40 K10 18 25N 77 5 E
Udhampur, India 43 C6 33 0N 75 5 E
Údine, Italy 20 A5 46 3N 13 14 E
Udmurtia □, Russia 24 C9 57 30N 52 30 E
Udon Thani, Thailand 38 D4 17 29N 102 46 E
Udupi, India 40 N9 13 25N 74 42 E
Udzungwa Range, Tanzania 55 D4 9 30S 35 10 E
Ueda, Japan 31 F9 36 24N 138 16 E
Uedineniya, Os., Russia 4 B12 78 0N 85 0 E
Uele →, Dem. Rep. of the Congo 52 D4 3 45N 24 45 E
Uelen, Russia 27 C19 66 10N 170 0W
Uelzen, Germany 16 B6 52 57N 10 32 E
Ufa, Russia 24 D10 54 45N 55 55 E
Ufa →, Russia 24 D10 54 40N 56 0 E
Ugab →, Namibia 56 C1 20 55S 13 30 E
Ugalla →, Tanzania 54 D3 5 8S 30 42 E
Uganda ■, Africa 54 B3 2 0N 32 0 E
Ugie, S. Africa 57 E4 31 10S 28 13 E
Uglegorsk, Russia 27 E15 49 5N 142 2 E
Ugljan, Croatia 16 F8 44 12N 15 10 E
Uhlenhorst, Namibia 56 C2 23 45S 17 55 E
Uhrichsville, U.S.A. 78 F3 40 24N 81 21W
Uibhist a Deas = South Uist, U.K. 12 D1 57 20N 7 15W
Uibhist a Tuath = North Uist, U.K. 12 D1 57 40N 7 15W
Uig, U.K. 12 D2 57 35N 6 21W
Uíge, Angola 52 F2 7 30S 14 40 E
Uijŏngbu, S. Korea 35 F14 37 48N 127 0 E
Ŭiju, N. Korea 35 D13 40 15N 124 35 E
Uinta Mts., U.S.A. 82 F8 40 45N 110 30W
Uis, Namibia 56 B2 21 8S 14 49 E
Uitenhage, S. Africa 56 E4 33 40S 25 28 E
Uithuizen, Neths. 15 A6 53 24N 6 41 E
Ujh →, India 42 C6 32 10N 75 18 E
Ujhani, India 43 F8 28 0N 79 6 E
Uji-guntō, Japan 31 J4 31 15N 129 25 E
Ujjain, India 42 H6 23 9N 75 43 E
Ujung Pandang, Indonesia 37 F5 5 10S 119 20 E
Uka, Russia 27 D17 57 50N 162 0 E
Ukara I., Tanzania 54 C3 1 50S 33 0 E
Uke-Shima, Japan 31 K4 28 2N 129 14 E
Ukerewe I., Tanzania 54 C3 2 0S 33 0 E
Ukhrul, India 41 G19 25 10N 94 25 E
Ukhta, Russia 24 B9 63 34N 53 41 E
Ukiah, U.S.A. 84 F3 39 9N 123 13W
Ukki Fort, India 43 C7 33 28N 76 54 E
Ukmergė, Lithuania 9 J21 55 15N 24 45 E
Ukraine ■, Europe 25 E5 49 0N 32 0 E
Ukwi, Botswana 56 C3 23 29S 20 30 E
Ulaan-Uul, Mongolia 34 B6 44 13N 111 10 E
Ulaanbaatar, Mongolia 27 E11 47 55N 106 53 E
Ulaangom, Mongolia 32 A4 50 5N 92 10 E
Ulaanjirem, Mongolia 34 B3 45 5N 105 30 E
Ulamba, Dem. Rep. of the Congo 55 D1 9 3S 23 38 E
Ulan Bator = Ulaanbaatar, Mongolia 27 E11 47 55N 106 53 E
Ulan Ude, Russia 27 D11 51 45N 107 40 E
Ulaya, Morogoro, Tanzania 54 D4 7 3S 36 55 E
Ulaya, Tabora, Tanzania 54 C3 4 25S 33 30 E
Ulcinj, Montenegro, Yug. 21 D8 41 58N 19 10 E
Ulco, S. Africa 56 D3 28 21S 24 15 E
Ulefoss, Norway 9 G13 59 17N 9 16 E
Ulhasnagar, India 40 K8 19 15N 73 10 E
Uliastay = Ulyasutay, Mongolia 32 B4 47 56N 97 28 E
Ulithi Atoll, Pac. Oc. 37 B9 10 0N 139 30 E
Ullapool, U.K. 12 D3 57 54N 5 9W
Ullswater, U.K. 10 C5 54 34N 2 52W
Ullŭng-do, S. Korea 31 F5 37 30N 130 30 E
Ulm, Germany 16 D5 48 23N 9 58 E
Ulmarra, Australia 63 D5 29 37S 153 4 E
Ulongué, Mozam. 55 E3 14 37S 34 19 E
Ulricehamn, Sweden 9 H15 57 46N 13 26 E
Ulsan, S. Korea 35 G15 35 20N 129 15 E
Ulsta, U.K. 12 A7 60 30N 1 9W
Ulster □, U.K. 13 B5 54 35N 6 30W
Ulubat Gölü, Turkey 21 D13 40 9N 28 35 E
Uludağ, Turkey 21 D13 40 4N 29 13 E
Uluguru Mts., Tanzania 54 D4 7 15S 37 40 E
Ulungur He →, China 32 B3 47 1N 87 24 E
Uluru = Ayers Rock, Australia 61 E5 25 23S 131 5 E
Uluru Nat. Park, Australia 61 E5 25 15S 131 20 E
Ulutau, Kazakstan 26 E7 48 39N 67 1 E
Ulva, U.K. 12 E2 56 29N 6 13W
Ulverston, U.K. 10 C4 54 13N 3 5W
Ulverstone, Australia 62 G4 41 11S 146 11 E
Ulya, Russia 27 D15 59 10N 142 0 E
Ulyanovsk = Simbirsk, Russia 24 D8 54 20N 48 25 E
Ulyasutay, Mongolia 32 B4 47 56N 97 28 E
Ulysses, U.S.A. 81 G4 37 35N 101 22W
Umala, Bolivia 92 G5 17 25S 68 5W
Uman, Ukraine 17 D16 48 40N 30 12 E
Umaria, India 41 H12 23 35N 80 50 E
Umarkot, Pakistan 40 G6 25 15N 69 40 E
Umarpada, India 42 J5 21 27N 73 30 E
Umatilla, U.S.A. 82 D4 45 55N 119 21W
Umba, Russia 24 A5 66 42N 34 11 E
Umbagog L., U.S.A. 79 B13 44 46N 71 3W
Umbakumba, Australia 62 A2 13 47S 136 50 E
Umbrella Mts., N.Z. 59 L2 45 35S 169 5 E
Ume älv →, Sweden 8 E19 63 45N 20 20 E
Umeå, Sweden 8 E19 63 45N 20 20 E
Umera, Indonesia 37 E7 0 12S 129 37 E
Umfuli →, Zimbabwe 55 F2 17 30S 29 23 E
Umgusa, Zimbabwe 55 F2 19 29S 27 52 E
Umkomaas, S. Africa 57 E5 30 13S 30 48 E
Umlazi, S. Africa 53 L6 29 59S 30 54 E
Umm ad Daraj, J., Jordan 47 C4 32 18N 35 48 E
Umm al Qaywayn, U.A.E. 45 E7 25 30N 55 35 E
Umm al Qittayn, Jordan 47 C5 32 18N 36 40 E
Umm Bāb, Qatar 45 E6 25 12N 50 48 E
Umm el Fahm, Israel 47 C4 32 31N 35 9 E
Umm Keddada, Sudan 51 F11 13 33N 26 35 E
Umm Lajj, Si. Arabia 44 E3 25 0N 37 23 E
Umm Ruwaba, Sudan 51 F12 12 50N 31 20 E
Umnak I., U.S.A. 68 C3 53 15N 168 20W
Umniati →, Zimbabwe 55 F2 16 49S 28 45 E
Umpqua →, U.S.A. 82 E1 43 40N 124 12W
Umreth, India 42 H5 22 41N 73 4 E
Umtata, S. Africa 57 E4 31 36S 28 49 E
Umuarama, Brazil 95 A5 23 45S 53 20W
Umvukwe Ra., Zimbabwe 55 F3 16 45S 30 45 E
Umzimvubu, S. Africa 57 E4 31 38S 29 33 E
Umzingwane →, Zimbabwe 55 G2 22 12S 29 56 E
Umzinto, S. Africa 57 E5 30 15S 30 45 E
Una, India 42 J4 20 46N 71 8 E
Una →, Bos.-H. 16 F9 45 0N 16 20 E
Unadilla, U.S.A. 79 D9 42 20N 75 19W
Unalakleet, U.S.A. 68 B3 63 52N 160 47W
Unalaska, U.S.A. 68 C3 53 53N 166 32W
Unalaska I., U.S.A. 68 C3 53 35N 166 50W
'Unayzah, Si. Arabia 44 E4 26 6N 43 58 E
'Unāzah, J., Asia 44 C3 32 12N 39 18 E
Uncía, Bolivia 92 G5 18 25S 66 40W
Uncompahgre Peak, U.S.A. 83 G10 38 4N 107 28W
Uncompahgre Plateau, U.S.A. 83 G9 38 20N 108 15W
Ungava, Pén. d', Canada 69 C12 60 0N 74 0W
Ungava B., Canada 69 C13 59 30N 67 30W
Ungeny = Ungheni, Moldova 17 E14 47 11N 27 51 E
Unggi, N. Korea 35 C16 42 16N 130 28 E
Ungheni, Moldova 17 E14 47 11N 27 51 E
União da Vitória, Brazil 95 B5 26 13S 51 5W
Unimak I., U.S.A. 68 C3 54 45N 164 0W
Union, Miss., U.S.A. 81 J10 32 34N 89 7W
Union, Mo., U.S.A. 80 F9 38 27N 91 0W
Union, S.C., U.S.A. 77 H5 34 43N 81 37W
Union City, Calif., U.S.A. 84 H4 37 36N 122 1W
Union City, N.J., U.S.A. 79 F10 40 45N 74 2W
Union City, Pa., U.S.A. 78 E5 41 54N 79 51W
Union City, Tenn., U.S.A. 81 G10 36 26N 89 3W
Union Gap, U.S.A. 82 C3 46 33N 120 28W
Union Springs, U.S.A. 77 J3 32 9N 85 43W
Uniondale, S. Africa 56 E3 33 39S 23 7 E
Uniontown, U.S.A. 76 F6 39 54N 79 44W
Unionville, U.S.A. 80 E8 40 29N 93 1W
United Arab Emirates ■, Asia 46 C5 23 50N 54 0 E
United Kingdom ■, Europe 7 E5 53 0N 2 0W
United States of America ■, N. Amer. 74 C7 37 0N 96 0W
Unity, Canada 73 C7 52 30N 109 5W
University Park, U.S.A. 83 K10 32 17N 106 45W
Unjha, India 42 H5 23 46N 72 24 E
Unnao, India 43 F9 26 35N 80 30 E
Unst, U.K. 12 A8 60 44N 0 53W
Unuk →, Canada 72 B2 56 5N 131 3W
Uozu, Japan 31 F8 36 48N 137 24 E
Upata, Venezuela 92 B6 8 1N 62 24W
Upemba, L., Dem. Rep. of the Congo 55 D2 8 30S 26 20 E
Upernavik, Greenland 4 B5 72 49N 56 20W
Upington, S. Africa 56 D3 28 25S 21 15 E
Upleta, India 42 J4 21 46N 70 16 E
Upolu, Samoa 59 A13 13 58S 172 0W
Upper Alkali L., U.S.A. 82 F3 41 47N 120 8W
Upper Arrow L., Canada 72 C5 50 30N 117 50W
Upper Foster L., Canada 73 B7 56 47N 105 20W

Vergara

Upper Hutt, *N.Z.* 59 J5 41 8S 175 5 E
Upper Klamath L., *U.S.A.* 82 E3 42 25N 121 55W
Upper Lake, *U.S.A.* 84 F4 39 10N 122 54W
Upper Musquodoboit, *Canada* 71 C7 45 10N 62 58W
Upper Red L., *U.S.A.* 80 A7 48 8N 94 45W
Upper Sandusky, *U.S.A.* 76 E4 40 50N 83 17W
Upper Volta = Burkina Faso ■, *Africa* 50 F5 12 0N 1 0W
Uppland, *Sweden* 9 F17 59 59N 17 48 E
Uppsala, *Sweden* 9 G17 59 53N 17 38 E
Upshi, *India* 43 C7 33 48N 77 52 E
Upstart, C., *Australia* 62 B4 19 41S 147 45 E
Upton, *U.S.A.* 80 C2 44 6N 104 38W
Ur, *Iraq* 44 D5 30 55N 46 25 E
Urad Qianqi, *China* 34 D5 40 40N 108 30 E
Urakawa, *Japan* 30 C11 42 9N 142 47 E
Ural = Zhayyq →, *Kazakstan* 25 E9 47 0N 51 48 E
Ural Mts. = Uralskie Gory, *Eurasia* 24 C10 60 0N 59 0 E
Uralsk = Oral, *Kazakstan* 25 D9 51 20N 51 20 E
Uralskie Gory, *Eurasia* 24 C10 60 0N 59 0 E
Urambo, *Tanzania* 54 D3 5 4S 32 0 E
Urandangi, *Australia* 62 C2 21 32S 138 14 E
Uranium City, *Canada* 73 B7 59 34N 108 37W
Uraricoera →, *Brazil* 92 C6 3 2N 60 30W
Urawa, *Japan* 31 G9 35 50N 139 40 E
Uray, *Russia* 26 C7 60 5N 65 15 E
'Uray'irah, *Si. Arabia* 45 E6 25 57N 48 53 E
Urbana, *Ill., U.S.A.* 76 E1 40 7N 88 12W
Urbana, *Ohio, U.S.A.* 76 E4 40 7N 83 45W
Urbino, *Italy* 20 C5 43 43N 12 38 E
Urbión, Picos de, *Spain* 19 A4 42 1N 2 52W
Urcos, *Peru* 92 F4 13 40S 71 38W
Urdinarrain, *Argentina* 94 C4 32 37S 58 52W
Urdzhar, *Kazakstan* 26 E9 47 5N 81 38 E
Ure →, *U.K.* 10 C6 54 5N 1 20W
Ures, *Mexico* 86 B2 29 30N 110 30W
Urfa = Sanliurfa, *Turkey* 25 G6 37 12N 38 50 E
Urganch, *Uzbekistan* 26 E7 41 40N 60 41 E
Urgench = Urganch, *Uzbekistan* 26 E7 41 40N 60 41 E
Ürgüp, *Turkey* 44 B2 38 38N 34 56 E
Uri, *India* 43 B6 34 8N 74 2 E
Uribia, *Colombia* 92 A4 11 43N 72 16W
Uriondo, *Bolivia* 94 A3 21 41S 64 41W
Urique, *Mexico* 86 B3 27 13N 107 55W
Urique →, *Mexico* 86 B3 26 29N 107 58W
Urk, *Neths.* 15 B5 52 39N 5 36 E
Urla, *Turkey* 21 E12 38 20N 26 47 E
Urmia = Orūmīyeh, *Iran* 44 B5 37 40N 45 0 E
Urmia, L. = Orūmīyeh, Daryācheh-ye, *Iran* 44 B5 37 50N 45 30 E
Uroševac, *Kosovo, Yug.* 21 C9 42 23N 21 10 E
Uruaçu, *Brazil* 93 F9 14 30S 49 10W
Uruapan, *Mexico* 86 D4 19 30N 102 0W
Urubamba →, *Peru* 92 F4 10 43S 73 48W
Uruçara, *Brazil* 92 D7 2 32S 57 45W
Uruçuí, *Brazil* 93 E10 7 20S 44 28W
Uruguai →, *Brazil* 95 B5 26 0S 53 30W
Uruguaiana, *Brazil* 94 B4 29 50S 57 0W
Uruguay ■, *S. Amer.* 94 C4 32 30S 56 30W
Uruguay →, *S. Amer.* 94 C4 34 12S 58 18W
Urumchi = Ürümqi, *China* 26 E9 43 45N 87 45 E
Ürümqi, *China* 26 E9 43 45N 87 45 E
Urup, Ostrov, *Russia* 27 E16 46 0N 151 0 E
Usa →, *Russia* 24 A10 66 16N 59 49 E
Uşak, *Turkey* 25 G4 38 43N 29 28 E
Usakos, *Namibia* 56 C2 21 54S 15 31 E
Usedom, *Germany* 16 B8 53 55N 14 2 E
Useless Loop, *Australia* 61 E1 26 8S 113 23 E
Ush-Tobe, *Kazakstan* 26 E8 45 16N 78 0 E
Ushakova, Ostrov, *Russia* 4 A12 82 0N 80 0 E
Ushant = Ouessant, Î. d', *France* 18 B1 48 28N 5 6W
Ushashi, *Tanzania* 54 C3 1 59S 33 57 E
Ushibuka, *Japan* 31 H5 32 11N 130 1 E
Ushuaia, *Argentina* 96 G3 54 50S 68 23W
Ushumun, *Russia* 27 D13 52 47N 126 32 E
Usk, *Canada* 72 C3 54 38N 128 26W
Usk →, *U.K.* 11 F5 51 33N 2 58W
Uska, *India* 43 F10 27 12N 83 7 E
Usman, *Russia* 24 D6 52 5N 39 48 E
Usoke, *Tanzania* 54 D3 5 8S 32 24 E
Usolye Sibirskoye, *Russia* 27 D11 52 48N 103 40 E
Uspallata, P. de, *Argentina* 94 C2 32 37S 69 22W
Uspenskiy, *Kazakstan* 26 E8 48 41N 72 43 E
Ussuri →, *Asia* 30 A7 48 27N 135 0 E
Ussuriysk, *Russia* 27 E14 43 48N 131 59 E
Ussurka, *Russia* 30 B6 45 12N 133 31 E
Ust-Aldan = Batamay, *Russia* 27 C13 63 30N 129 15 E
Ust-Amginskoye = Khandyga, *Russia* 27 C14 62 42N 135 35 E
Ust-Bolsheretsk, *Russia* 27 D16 52 50N 156 15 E
Ust-Chaun, *Russia* 27 C18 68 47N 170 30 E
Ust-Ilimpeya = Yukta, *Russia* 27 C11 63 26N 105 42 E
Ust-Ilimsk, *Russia* 27 D11 58 3N 102 39 E
Ust-Ishim, *Russia* 26 D8 57 45N 71 10 E
Ust-Kamchatsk, *Russia* 27 D17 56 10N 162 28 E
Ust-Kamenogorsk = Öskemen, *Kazakstan* 26 E9 50 0N 82 36 E
Ust-Khayryuzovo, *Russia* 27 D16 57 15N 156 45 E
Ust-Kut, *Russia* 27 D11 56 50N 105 42 E
Ust-Kuyga, *Russia* 27 B14 70 1N 135 43 E
Ust-Maya, *Russia* 27 C14 60 30N 134 28 E
Ust-Mil, *Russia* 27 D14 59 40N 133 11 E
Ust-Nera, *Russia* 27 C15 64 35N 143 15 E
Ust-Nyukzha, *Russia* 27 D13 56 34N 121 37 E
Ust-Olenek, *Russia* 27 B12 73 0N 120 5 E
Ust-Omchug, *Russia* 27 C15 61 9N 149 38 E
Ust-Port, *Russia* 26 C9 69 40N 84 26 E
Ust-Tsilma, *Russia* 24 A9 65 28N 52 11 E
Ust Urt = Ustyurt Plateau, *Asia* 26 E6 44 0N 55 0 E
Ust-Usa, *Russia* 24 A10 66 2N 56 57 E
Ust-Vorkuta, *Russia* 24 A11 67 24N 64 0 E
Ústí nad Labem, *Czech Rep.* 16 C8 50 41N 14 3 E
Ústica, *Italy* 20 E5 38 42N 13 11 E
Ustinov = Izhevsk, *Russia* 24 C9 56 51N 53 14 E
Ustyurt Plateau, *Asia* 26 E6 44 0N 55 0 E
Usu, *China* 32 B3 44 27N 84 40 E
Usuki, *Japan* 31 H5 33 8N 131 49 E
Usulután, *El Salv.* 88 D2 13 25N 88 28W
Usumacinta →, *Mexico* 87 D6 17 0N 91 0W
Usumbura = Bujumbura, *Burundi* 54 C2 3 16S 29 18 E
Usure, *Tanzania* 54 C3 4 40S 34 22 E
Usutuo →, *Mozam.* 57 D5 26 48S 32 7 E
Uta, *Indonesia* 37 E9 4 33S 136 0 E
Utah □, *U.S.A.* 82 G8 39 20N 111 30W
Utah L., *U.S.A.* 82 F8 40 10N 111 58W
Utarni, *India* 42 F4 26 5N 71 58 E
Utatlan, *Guatemala* 88 C1 15 2N 91 11W
Ute Creek →, *U.S.A.* 81 H3 35 21N 103 50W
Utena, *Lithuania* 9 J21 55 27N 25 40 E
Utete, *Tanzania* 54 D4 8 0S 38 45 E
Uthai Thani, *Thailand* 38 E3 15 22N 100 3 E
Uthal, *Pakistan* 42 G2 25 44N 66 40 E
Utiariti, *Brazil* 92 F7 13 0S 58 10W
Utica, *N.Y., U.S.A.* 79 C9 43 6N 75 14W
Utica, *Ohio, U.S.A.* 78 F2 40 14N 82 27W
Utikuma L., *Canada* 72 B5 55 50N 115 30W
Utopia, *Australia* 62 C1 22 14S 134 33 E
Utraula, *India* 43 F10 27 19N 82 25 E
Utrecht, *Neths.* 15 B5 52 5N 5 8 E
Utrecht, *S. Africa* 57 D5 27 38S 30 20 E
Utrecht □, *Neths.* 15 B5 52 6N 5 7 E
Utrera, *Spain* 19 D3 37 12N 5 48W
Utsjoki, *Finland* 8 B22 69 51N 26 59 E
Utsunomiya, *Japan* 31 F9 36 30N 139 50 E
Uttar Pradesh □, *India* 43 F9 27 0N 80 0 E
Uttaradit, *Thailand* 38 D3 17 36N 100 5 E
Uttaranchal □, *India* 43 D8 30 0N 79 30 E
Uttoxeter, *U.K.* 10 E6 52 53N 1 52W
Uummannarsuaq = Nunap Isua, *Greenland* 69 C15 59 48N 43 55W
Uusikaarlepyy, *Finland* 8 E20 63 32N 22 31 E
Uusikaupunki, *Finland* 9 F19 60 47N 21 25 E
Uva, *Russia* 24 C9 56 59N 52 13 E
Uvalde, *U.S.A.* 81 L5 29 13N 99 47W
Uvat, *Russia* 26 D7 59 5N 68 50 E
Uvinza, *Tanzania* 54 D3 5 5S 30 24 E
Uvira, *Dem. Rep. of the Congo* 54 C2 3 22S 29 3 E
Uvs Nuur, *Mongolia* 32 A4 50 20N 92 30 E
'Uwairidh, Ḥarrat al, *Si. Arabia* 44 E3 26 50N 38 0 E
Uwajima, *Japan* 31 H6 33 10N 132 35 E
Uweinat, Jebel, *Sudan* 51 D10 21 54N 24 58 E
Uxbridge, *Canada* 78 B5 44 6N 79 7W
Uxin Qi, *China* 34 E5 38 50N 109 5 E
Uxmal, *Mexico* 87 C7 20 22N 89 46W
Üydzin, *Mongolia* 34 B4 44 9N 107 0 E
Uyo, *Nigeria* 50 G7 5 1N 7 53 E
Uyûn Mûsa, *Egypt* 47 F1 29 53N 32 40 E
Uyuni, *Bolivia* 92 H5 20 28S 66 47W
Uzbekistan ■, *Asia* 26 E7 41 30N 65 0 E
Uzen, *Kazakstan* 25 F9 43 29N 52 54 E
Uzen, Mal →, *Kazakstan* 25 E8 49 4N 49 44 E
Uzerche, *France* 18 D4 45 25N 1 34 E
Uzh →, *Ukraine* 17 C16 51 15N 30 12 E
Uzhgorod = Uzhhorod, *Ukraine* 17 D12 48 36N 22 18 E
Uzhhorod, *Ukraine* 17 D12 48 36N 22 18 E
Užice, *Serbia, Yug.* 21 C8 43 55N 19 50 E
Uzunköprü, *Turkey* 21 D12 41 16N 26 43 E

V

Vaal →, *S. Africa* 56 D3 29 4S 23 38 E
Vaal Dam, *S. Africa* 57 D4 27 0S 28 14 E
Vaalwater, *S. Africa* 57 C4 24 15S 28 8 E
Vaasa, *Finland* 8 E19 63 6N 21 38 E
Vác, *Hungary* 17 E10 47 49N 19 10 E
Vacaria, *Brazil* 95 B5 28 31S 50 52W
Vacaville, *U.S.A.* 84 G5 38 21N 121 59W
Vach = Vakh →, *Russia* 26 C8 60 45N 76 45 E
Vache, Î. à, *Haiti* 89 C5 18 2N 73 35W
Vadnagar, *India* 42 H5 23 47N 72 40 E
Vadodara, *India* 42 H5 22 20N 73 10 E
Vadsø, *Norway* 8 A23 70 3N 29 50 E
Vaduz, *Liech.* 18 C8 47 8N 9 31 E
Værøy, *Norway* 8 C15 67 40N 12 40 E
Vágar, *Færoe Is.* 8 E9 62 5N 7 15W
Vågsfjorden, *Norway* 8 B17 68 50N 16 50 E
Váh →, *Slovak Rep.* 17 D9 47 43N 18 7 E
Vahsel B., *Antarctica* 5 D1 75 0S 35 0W
Váï, *Greece* 23 D8 35 15N 26 18 E
Vaigach, *Russia* 26 B6 70 10N 59 0 E
Vail, *U.S.A.* 74 C5 39 40N 106 20W
Vaisali →, *India* 43 F8 26 28N 78 53 E
Vakh →, *Russia* 26 C8 60 45N 76 45 E
Val-d'Or, *Canada* 70 C4 48 7N 77 47W
Val Marie, *Canada* 73 D7 49 15N 107 45W
Valahia, *Romania* 17 F13 44 35N 25 0 E
Valandovo, *Macedonia* 21 D10 41 19N 22 34 E
Valcheta, *Argentina* 96 E3 40 40S 66 8W
Valdayskaya Vozvyshennost, *Russia* 24 C5 57 0N 33 30 E
Valdepeñas, *Spain* 19 C4 38 43N 3 25W
Valdés, Pen., *Argentina* 96 E4 42 30S 63 45W
Valdez, *U.S.A.* 68 B5 61 7N 146 16W
Valdivia, *Chile* 96 D2 39 50S 73 14W
Valdosta, *U.S.A.* 77 K4 30 50N 83 17W
Valdres, *Norway* 9 F13 61 5N 9 5 E
Vale, *U.S.A.* 82 E5 43 59N 117 15W
Vale of Glamorgan □, *U.K.* 11 F4 51 28N 3 25W
Valemount, *Canada* 72 C5 52 50N 119 15W
Valença, *Brazil* 93 F11 13 20S 39 5W
Valença do Piauí, *Brazil* 93 E10 6 20S 41 45W
Valence, *France* 18 D6 44 57N 4 54 E
Valencia, *Spain* 19 C5 39 27N 0 23W
Valencia, *U.S.A.* 83 J10 34 48N 106 43W
Valencia, *Venezuela* 92 A5 10 11N 68 0W
Valencia □, *Spain* 19 C5 39 20N 0 40W
Valencia, G. de, *Spain* 19 C6 39 30N 0 20 E
Valencia de Alcántara, *Spain* 19 C2 39 25N 7 14W
Valencia I., *Ireland* 13 E1 51 54N 10 22W
Valenciennes, *France* 18 A5 50 20N 3 34 E
Valentim, Sa. do, *Brazil* 93 E10 6 0S 43 30W
Valentin, *Russia* 30 C7 43 8N 134 17 E
Valentine, *U.S.A.* 81 K2 30 35N 104 30W
Valera, *Venezuela* 92 B4 9 19N 70 37W
Valga, *Estonia* 9 H22 57 47N 26 2 E
Valier, *U.S.A.* 82 B7 48 18N 112 16W
Valjevo, *Serbia, Yug.* 21 B8 44 18N 19 53 E
Valka, *Latvia* 9 H21 57 42N 25 57 E
Valkeakoski, *Finland* 9 F20 61 16N 24 2 E
Valkenswaard, *Neths.* 15 C5 51 21N 5 29 E
Vall de Uxó = La Vall d'Uixó, *Spain* 19 C5 39 49N 0 15W
Valladolid, *Mexico* 87 C7 20 40N 88 11W
Valladolid, *Spain* 19 B3 41 38N 4 43W
Valldemossa, *Spain* 22 B9 39 43N 2 37 E
Valle de la Pascua, *Venezuela* 92 B5 9 13N 66 0W
Valle de las Palmas, *Mexico* 85 N10 32 20N 116 43W
Valle de Santiago, *Mexico* 86 C4 20 25N 101 15W
Valle de Suchil, *Mexico* 86 C4 23 38N 103 55W
Valle de Zaragoza, *Mexico* 86 B3 27 28N 105 49W
Valle Fértil, Sierra del, *Argentina* 94 C2 30 20S 68 0W
Valle Hermoso, *Mexico* 87 B5 25 35N 97 40W
Valledupar, *Colombia* 92 A4 10 29N 73 15W
Vallehermoso, *Canary Is.* 22 F2 28 10N 17 15W
Vallejo, *U.S.A.* 84 G4 38 7N 122 14W
Vallenar, *Chile* 94 B1 28 30S 70 50W
Valletta, *Malta* 23 D2 35 54N 14 31 E
Valley Center, *U.S.A.* 85 M9 33 13N 117 2W
Valley City, *U.S.A.* 80 B6 46 55N 98 0W
Valley Falls, *Oreg., U.S.A.* 82 E3 42 29N 120 17W
Valley Falls, *R.I., U.S.A.* 79 E13 41 54N 71 24W
Valley Springs, *U.S.A.* 84 G6 38 12N 120 50W
Valley View, *U.S.A.* 79 F8 40 39N 76 33W
Valley Wells, *U.S.A.* 85 K11 35 27N 115 46W
Valleyview, *Canada* 72 B5 55 5N 117 17W
Vallimanca, Arroyo, *Argentina* 94 D4 35 40S 59 10W
Valls, *Spain* 19 B6 41 18N 1 15 E
Valmiera, *Latvia* 9 H21 57 37N 25 29 E
Valognes, *France* 18 B3 49 30N 1 28W
Valona = Vlorë, *Albania* 21 D8 40 32N 19 28 E
Valozhyn, *Belarus* 17 A14 54 3N 26 30 E
Valparaíso, *Chile* 94 C1 33 2S 71 40W
Valparaíso, *Mexico* 86 C4 22 50N 103 32W
Valparaiso, *U.S.A.* 76 E2 41 28N 87 4W
Valparaíso □, *Chile* 94 C1 33 2S 71 40W
Vals →, *S. Africa* 56 D4 27 23S 26 30 E
Vals, Tanjung, *Indonesia* 37 F9 8 26S 137 25 E
Valsad, *India* 40 J8 20 40N 72 58 E
Valverde, *Canary Is.* 22 G2 27 48N 17 55W
Valverde del Camino, *Spain* 19 D2 37 35N 6 47W
Vammala, *Finland* 9 F20 61 20N 22 54 E
Vámos, *Greece* 23 D6 35 24N 24 13 E
Van, *Turkey* 25 G7 38 30N 43 20 E
Van, L. = Van Gölü, *Turkey* 25 G7 38 30N 43 0 E
Van Alstyne, *U.S.A.* 81 J6 33 25N 96 35W
Van Blommestein Meer, *Surinam* 93 C7 4 45N 55 5W
Van Buren, *Canada* 71 C6 47 10N 67 55W
Van Buren, *Ark., U.S.A.* 81 H7 35 26N 94 21W
Van Buren, *Maine, U.S.A.* 77 B11 47 10N 67 58W
Van Buren, *Mo., U.S.A.* 81 G9 37 0N 91 1W
Van Canh, *Vietnam* 38 F7 13 37N 109 0 E
Van Diemen, C., *N. Terr., Australia* 60 B5 11 9S 130 24 E
Van Diemen, C., *Queens., Australia* 62 B2 16 30S 139 46 E
Van Diemen G., *Australia* 60 B5 11 45S 132 0 E
Van Gölü, *Turkey* 25 G7 38 30N 43 0 E
Van Horn, *U.S.A.* 81 K2 31 3N 104 50W
Van Ninh, *Vietnam* 38 F7 12 42N 109 14 E
Van Rees, Pegunungan, *Indonesia* 37 E9 2 35S 138 15 E
Van Wert, *U.S.A.* 76 E3 40 52N 84 35W
Van Yen, *Vietnam* 38 B5 21 4N 104 42 E
Vanadzor, *Armenia* 25 F7 40 48N 44 30 E
Vanavara, *Russia* 27 C11 60 22N 102 16 E
Vancouver, *Canada* 72 D4 49 15N 123 10W
Vancouver, *U.S.A.* 84 E4 45 38N 122 40W
Vancouver, C., *Australia* 61 G2 35 2S 118 11 E
Vancouver I., *Canada* 72 D3 49 50N 126 0W
Vandalia, *Ill., U.S.A.* 80 F10 38 58N 89 6W
Vandalia, *Mo., U.S.A.* 80 F9 39 19N 91 29W
Vandenburg, *U.S.A.* 85 L6 34 35N 120 33W
Vanderbijlpark, *S. Africa* 57 D4 26 42S 27 54 E
Vandergrift, *U.S.A.* 78 F5 40 36N 79 34W
Vanderhoof, *Canada* 72 C4 54 0N 124 0W
Vanderkloof Dam, *S. Africa* 56 E3 30 4S 24 40 E
Vanderlin I., *Australia* 62 B2 15 44S 137 2 E
Vänern, *Sweden* 9 G15 58 47N 13 30 E
Vänersborg, *Sweden* 9 G15 58 26N 12 19 E
Vang Vieng, *Laos* 38 C4 18 58N 102 32 E
Vanga, *Kenya* 54 C4 4 35S 39 12 E
Vangaindrano, *Madag.* 57 C8 23 21S 47 36 E
Vanguard, *Canada* 73 D7 49 55N 107 20W
Vanino, *Russia* 27 E15 48 50N 140 5 E
Vanna, *Norway* 8 A18 70 6N 19 50 E
Vännäs, *Sweden* 8 E18 63 58N 19 48 E
Vannes, *France* 18 C2 47 40N 2 47W
Vanrhynsdorp, *S. Africa* 56 E2 31 36S 18 44 E
Vansbro, *Sweden* 9 F16 60 32N 14 15 E
Vansittart B., *Australia* 60 B4 14 3S 126 17 E
Vantaa, *Finland* 9 F21 60 18N 24 58 E
Vanua Balavu, *Fiji* 59 C9 17 40S 178 57W
Vanua Levu, *Fiji* 59 C8 16 33S 179 15 E
Vanuatu ■, *Pac. Oc.* 64 J8 15 0S 168 0 E
Vanwykvlei, *S. Africa* 56 E3 30 18S 21 49 E
Vanzylsrus, *S. Africa* 56 D3 26 52S 22 4 E
Vapnyarka, *Ukraine* 17 D15 48 32N 28 45 E
Varanasi, *India* 43 G10 25 22N 83 0 E
Varangerfjorden, *Norway* 8 A23 70 3N 29 25 E
Varangerhalvøya, *Norway* 8 A23 70 25N 29 30 E
Varaždin, *Croatia* 16 E9 46 20N 16 20 E
Varberg, *Sweden* 9 H15 57 6N 12 20 E
Vardar = Axiós →, *Greece* 21 D10 40 57N 22 35 E
Varde, *Denmark* 9 J13 55 38N 8 29 E
Vardø, *Norway* 8 A24 70 23N 31 5 E
Varella, Mui, *Vietnam* 38 F7 12 54N 109 26 E
Varèna, *Lithuania* 9 J21 54 12N 24 30 E
Varese, *Italy* 18 D8 45 48N 8 50 E
Varginha, *Brazil* 95 A6 21 33S 45 25W
Varillas, *Chile* 94 A1 24 0S 70 10W
Varkaus, *Finland* 9 E22 62 19N 27 50 E
Varna, *Bulgaria* 21 C12 43 13N 27 56 E
Värnamo, *Sweden* 9 H16 57 10N 14 3 E
Vars, *Canada* 79 A9 45 21N 75 21W
Varysburg, *U.S.A.* 78 D6 42 46N 78 19W
Varzaneh, *Iran* 45 C7 32 25N 52 40 E
Vasa Barris →, *Brazil* 93 F11 11 10S 37 10W
Vascongadas = País Vasco □, *Spain* 19 A4 42 50N 2 45W
Vasht = Khāsh, *Iran* 40 E2 28 15N 61 15 E
Vasilevichi, *Belarus* 17 B15 52 15N 29 50 E
Vasilkov = Vasylkiv, *Ukraine* 17 C16 50 7N 30 15 E
Vaslui, *Romania* 17 E14 46 38N 27 42 E
Vassar, *Canada* 73 D9 49 10N 95 55W
Vassar, *U.S.A.* 76 D4 43 22N 83 35W
Västerås, *Sweden* 9 G17 59 37N 16 38 E
Västerbotten, *Sweden* 8 D18 64 36N 20 4 E
Västerdalälven →, *Sweden* 9 F16 60 30N 14 7 E
Västervik, *Sweden* 9 H17 57 43N 16 33 E
Västmanland, *Sweden* 9 G16 59 45N 16 20 E
Vasto, *Italy* 20 C6 42 8N 14 40 E
Vasylkiv, *Ukraine* 17 C16 50 7N 30 15 E
Vatersay, *U.K.* 12 E1 56 55N 7 32W
Vatican City ■, *Europe* 20 D5 41 54N 12 27 E
Vatili, *Cyprus* 23 D12 35 6N 33 40 E
Vatnajökull, *Iceland* 8 D5 64 30N 16 48W
Vatoa, *Fiji* 59 D9 19 50S 178 13W
Vatólakkos, *Greece* 23 D5 35 27N 23 53 E
Vatoloha, *Madag.* 57 B8 17 52S 47 48 E
Vatomandry, *Madag.* 57 B8 19 20S 48 59 E
Vatra-Dornei, *Romania* 17 E13 47 22N 25 22 E
Vatrak →, *India* 42 H5 23 9N 73 2 E
Vättern, *Sweden* 9 G16 58 25N 14 30 E
Vaughn, *Mont., U.S.A.* 82 C8 47 33N 111 33W
Vaughn, *N. Mex., U.S.A.* 83 J11 34 36N 105 13W
Vaujours L., *Canada* 70 A5 55 27N 74 15W
Vaupés = Uaupés →, *Brazil* 92 C5 0 2N 67 16W
Vaupes □, *Colombia* 92 C4 1 0N 71 0W
Vauxhall, *Canada* 72 C6 50 5N 112 9W
Vav, *India* 42 G4 24 22N 71 31 E
Vavatenina, *Madag.* 57 B8 17 28S 49 12 E
Vava'u, *Tonga* 59 D12 18 36S 174 0W
Vawkavysk, *Belarus* 17 B13 53 9N 24 30 E
Växjö, *Sweden* 9 H16 56 52N 14 50 E
Vaygach, Ostrov, *Russia* 26 C6 70 0N 60 0 E
Váyia, Ákra, *Greece* 23 C10 36 15N 28 11 E
Vechte →, *Neths.* 15 B6 52 34N 6 6 E
Vedea →, *Romania* 17 G13 43 42N 25 41 E
Vedia, *Argentina* 94 C3 34 30S 61 31W
Veendam, *Neths.* 15 A6 53 5N 6 52 E
Veenendaal, *Neths.* 15 B5 52 2N 5 34 E
Vefsna →, *Norway* 8 D15 65 48N 13 10 E
Vega, *Norway* 8 D14 65 40N 11 55 E
Vega, *U.S.A.* 81 H3 35 15N 102 26W
Vegreville, *Canada* 72 C6 53 30N 112 5W
Vejer de la Frontera, *Spain* 19 D3 36 15N 5 59W
Vejle, *Denmark* 9 J13 55 43N 9 30 E
Velas, C., *Costa Rica* 88 D2 10 21N 85 52W
Velasco, Sierra de, *Argentina* 94 B2 29 20S 67 10W
Velddrif, *S. Africa* 56 E2 32 42S 18 11 E
Velebit Planina, *Croatia* 16 F8 44 50N 15 20 E
Veles, *Macedonia* 21 D9 41 46N 21 47 E
Vélez-Málaga, *Spain* 19 D3 36 48N 4 5W
Vélez Rubio, *Spain* 19 D4 37 41N 2 5W
Velhas →, *Brazil* 93 G10 17 13S 44 49W
Velika Kapela, *Croatia* 16 F8 45 10N 15 5 E
Velikaya →, *Russia* 24 C4 57 48N 28 10 E
Velikaya Kema, *Russia* 30 B8 45 30N 137 12 E
Veliki Ustyug, *Russia* 24 B8 60 47N 46 20 E
Velikiye Luki, *Russia* 24 C5 56 25N 30 32 E
Veliko Tŭrnovo, *Bulgaria* 21 C11 43 5N 25 41 E
Velikonda Range, *India* 40 M11 14 45N 79 10 E
Velletri, *Italy* 20 D5 41 41N 12 47 E
Vellore, *India* 40 N11 12 57N 79 10 E
Velsk, *Russia* 24 B7 61 10N 42 5 E
Velva, *U.S.A.* 80 A4 48 4N 100 56W
Venado Tuerto, *Argentina* 94 C3 33 50S 62 0W
Vendée □, *France* 18 C3 46 50N 1 35W
Vendôme, *France* 18 C4 47 47N 1 3 E
Venézia, *Italy* 20 B5 45 27N 12 21 E
Venézia, G. di, *Italy* 20 B5 45 15N 13 0 E
Venezuela ■, *S. Amer.* 92 B5 8 0N 66 0W
Venezuela, G. de, *Venezuela* 92 A4 11 30N 71 0W
Vengurla, *India* 40 M8 15 53N 73 45 E
Venice = Venézia, *Italy* 20 B5 45 27N 12 21 E
Venice, *U.S.A.* 77 M4 27 6N 82 27W
Venkatapuram, *India* 41 K12 18 20N 80 30 E
Venlo, *Neths.* 15 C6 51 22N 6 11 E
Vennesla, *Norway* 9 G12 58 15N 7 59 E
Venray, *Neths.* 15 C6 51 31N 6 0 E
Ventana, Punta de la, *Mexico* 86 C3 24 4N 109 48W
Ventana, Sa. de la, *Argentina* 94 D3 38 0S 62 30W
Ventersburg, *S. Africa* 56 D4 28 7S 27 9 E
Venterstad, *S. Africa* 56 E4 30 47S 25 48 E
Ventnor, *U.K.* 11 G6 50 36N 1 12W
Ventoténe, *Italy* 20 D5 40 47N 13 25 E
Ventoux, Mt., *France* 18 D6 44 10N 5 17 E
Ventspils, *Latvia* 9 H19 57 25N 21 32 E
Ventuarí →, *Venezuela* 92 C5 3 58N 67 2W
Ventucopa, *U.S.A.* 85 L7 34 50N 119 29W
Ventura, *U.S.A.* 85 L7 34 17N 119 18W
Vera, *Argentina* 94 B3 29 30S 60 20W
Vera, *Spain* 19 D5 37 15N 1 51W
Veracruz, *Mexico* 87 D5 19 10N 96 10W
Veracruz □, *Mexico* 87 D5 19 0N 96 15W
Veraval, *India* 42 J4 20 53N 70 27 E
Verbánia, *Italy* 18 D8 45 56N 8 33 E
Vercelli, *Italy* 18 D8 45 19N 8 25 E
Verdalsøra, *Norway* 8 E14 63 48N 11 30 E
Verde →, *Argentina* 96 E3 41 56S 65 5W
Verde →, *Goiás, Brazil* 93 G8 18 1S 50 14W
Verde →, *Mato Grosso do Sul, Brazil* 93 H8 21 25S 52 20W
Verde →, *Chihuahua, Mexico* 86 B3 26 29N 107 58W
Verde →, *Oaxaca, Mexico* 87 D5 15 59N 97 50W
Verde →, *Veracruz, Mexico* 86 C4 21 10N 102 50W
Verde →, *Paraguay* 94 A4 23 9S 57 37W
Verde →, *U.S.A.* 74 D4 33 33N 111 40W
Verde, Cay, *Bahamas* 88 B4 23 0N 75 5W
Verden, *Germany* 16 B5 52 55N 9 14 E
Verdi, *U.S.A.* 84 F7 39 31N 119 59W
Verdun, *France* 18 B6 49 9N 5 24 E
Vereeniging, *S. Africa* 57 D4 26 38S 27 57 E
Verga, C., *Guinea* 50 F3 10 30N 14 10W
Vergara, *Uruguay* 95 C5 32 56S 53 57W

Vergemont Cr.

Vergemont Cr. →, Australia 62 C3 24 16S 143 16 E
Vergennes, U.S.A. 79 B11 44 10N 73 15W
Verín, Spain 19 B2 41 57N 7 27W
Verkhnevilyuysk, Russia 27 C13 63 27N 120 18 E
Verkhniy Baskunchak, Russia 25 E8 48 14N 46 44 E
Verkhoyansk, Russia 27 C14 67 35N 133 25 E
Verkhoyansk Ra. = Verkhoyanskiy Khrebet, Russia 27 C13 66 0N 129 0 E
Verkhoyanskiy Khrebet, Russia 27 C13 66 0N 129 0 E
Vermilion, Canada 73 C6 53 20N 110 50W
Vermilion, U.S.A. 78 E2 41 25N 82 22W
Vermilion →, Alta., Canada 73 C6 53 22N 110 51W
Vermilion →, Qué., Canada 70 C5 47 38N 72 56W
Vermilion, B., U.S.A. 81 L9 29 45N 91 55W
Vermilion Bay, Canada 73 D10 49 51N 93 34W
Vermilion L., U.S.A. 80 B8 47 53N 92 26W
Vermillion, U.S.A. 80 D6 42 47N 96 56W
Vermont □, U.S.A. 79 C12 44 0N 73 0W
Vernal, U.S.A. 82 F9 40 27N 109 32W
Vernalis, U.S.A. 84 H5 37 36N 121 17W
Verner, Canada 70 C3 46 25N 80 8W
Verneukpan, S. Africa 56 E3 30 0S 21 0 E
Vernon, Canada 72 C5 50 20N 119 15W
Vernon, U.S.A. 81 H5 34 9N 99 17W
Vernonia, U.S.A. 84 E3 45 52N 123 11W
Vero Beach, U.S.A. 77 M5 27 38N 80 24W
Véroia, Greece 21 D10 40 34N 22 12 E
Verona, Canada 79 B8 44 29N 76 42W
Verona, Italy 20 B4 45 27N 10 59 E
Verona, U.S.A. 80 D10 42 59N 89 32W
Versailles, France 18 B5 48 48N 2 8 E
Vert, C., Senegal 50 F2 14 45N 17 30W
Verulam, S. Africa 57 D5 29 38S 31 2 E
Verviers, Belgium 15 D5 50 37N 5 52 E
Veselovskoye Vdkhr., Russia 25 E7 46 58N 41 25 E
Vesoul, France 18 C7 47 40N 6 11 E
Vesterålen, Norway 8 B16 68 45N 15 0 E
Vestfjorden, Norway 8 C15 67 55N 14 0 E
Vestmannaeyjar, Iceland 8 E3 63 27N 20 15W
Vestspitsbergen, Svalbard 4 B8 78 40N 17 0 E
Vestvågøy, Norway 8 B15 68 18N 13 50 E
Vesuvio, Italy 20 D6 40 49N 14 26 E
Vesuvius, Mt. = Vesuvio, Italy 20 D6 40 49N 14 26 E
Veszprém, Hungary 17 E9 47 8N 17 57 E
Vetlanda, Sweden 9 H16 57 24N 15 3 E
Vetlugu →, Russia 24 C8 56 36N 46 4 E
Vettore, Mte., Italy 20 C5 42 49N 13 16 E
Veurne, Belgium 15 C2 51 5N 2 40 E
Veys, Iran 45 D6 31 30N 49 0 E
Vezhen, Bulgaria 21 C11 42 50N 24 20 E
Vi Thanh, Vietnam 39 H5 9 42N 105 26 E
Viacha, Bolivia 92 G5 16 39S 68 18W
Viamão, Brazil 95 C5 30 5S 51 0W
Viana, Brazil 93 D10 3 13S 44 55W
Viana do Alentejo, Portugal 19 C2 38 17N 7 59W
Viana do Castelo, Portugal 19 B1 41 42N 8 50W
Vianden, Lux. 15 E6 49 56N 6 12 E
Viangchan = Vientiane, Laos 38 D4 17 58N 102 36 E
Vianópolis, Brazil 93 G9 16 40S 48 35W
Viaréggio, Italy 20 C4 43 52N 10 14 E
Vibo Valéntia, Italy 20 E7 38 40N 16 6 E
Viborg, Denmark 9 H13 56 27N 9 23 E
Vic, Spain 19 B7 41 58N 2 19 E
Vicenza, Italy 20 B4 45 33N 11 33 E
Vich = Vic, Spain 19 B7 41 58N 2 19 E
Vichada →, Colombia 92 C5 4 55N 67 50W
Vichy, France 18 C5 46 9N 3 26 E
Vicksburg, Ariz., U.S.A. 85 M13 33 45N 113 45W
Vicksburg, Miss., U.S.A. 81 J9 32 21N 90 53W
Victor, India 42 J4 21 0N 71 30 E
Victor, U.S.A. 78 D7 42 58N 77 24W
Victoria = Labuan, Malaysia 36 C5 5 20N 115 14 E
Victoria, Argentina 94 C3 32 40S 60 10W
Victoria, Canada 72 D4 48 30N 123 25W
Victoria, Chile 96 D2 38 13S 72 20W
Victoria, Malta 23 C1 36 2N 14 14 E
Victoria, Kans., U.S.A. 80 F5 38 52N 99 9W
Victoria, Tex., U.S.A. 81 L6 28 48N 97 0W
Victoria →, Australia 60 C4 15 10S 129 40 E
Victoria, Grand L., Canada 70 C4 47 31N 77 30W
Victoria, L., Africa 54 C3 1 0S 33 0 E
Victoria, Mt., Burma 41 J18 21 15N 93 55 E
Victoria Beach, Canada 73 C9 50 40N 96 35W
Victoria de Durango = Durango, Mexico 86 C4 24 3N 104 39W
Victoria de las Tunas, Cuba 88 B4 20 58N 76 59W
Victoria Falls, Zimbabwe 55 F2 17 58S 25 52 E
Victoria Harbour, Canada 78 B5 44 45N 79 45W
Victoria I., Canada 68 A8 71 0N 111 0W
Victoria L., Canada 71 C8 48 20N 57 27W
Victoria Ld., Antarctica 5 D11 75 0S 160 0 E
Victoria Nile →, Uganda 54 B3 2 14N 31 26 E
Victoria River, Australia 60 C5 16 25S 131 0 E
Victoria Str., Canada 68 B9 69 30N 100 0W
Victoria West, S. Africa 56 E3 31 25S 23 4 E
Victoriaville, Canada 71 C5 46 4N 71 56W
Victorica, Argentina 94 D2 36 20S 65 30W
Victorville, U.S.A. 85 L9 34 32N 117 18W
Vicuña, Chile 94 C1 30 0S 70 50W
Vicuña Mackenna, Argentina 94 C3 33 53S 64 25W
Vidal, U.S.A. 85 L12 34 7N 114 31W
Vidal Junction, U.S.A. 85 L12 34 11N 114 34W
Vidalia, U.S.A. 77 J4 32 13N 82 25W
Vidho, Greece 23 A3 39 38N 19 55 E
Vidin, Bulgaria 21 C10 43 59N 22 50 E
Vidisha, India 42 H7 23 28N 77 53 E
Vidzy, Belarus 9 J22 55 23N 26 37 E
Viedma, Argentina 96 E4 40 50S 63 0W
Viedma, L., Argentina 96 F2 49 30S 72 30W
Vielsalm, Belgium 15 D5 50 17N 5 54 E
Vieng Pou Kha, Laos 38 B3 20 41N 101 4 E
Vienna = Wien, Austria 16 D9 48 12N 16 22 E
Vienna, Ill., U.S.A. 81 G10 37 25N 88 54W
Vienna, Mo., U.S.A. 80 F9 38 11N 91 57W
Vienne, France 18 D6 45 31N 4 53 E
Vienne →, France 18 C4 47 13N 0 5 E
Vientiane, Laos 38 D4 17 58N 102 36 E
Vientos, Paso de los, Caribbean 89 C5 20 0N 74 0W
Vierzon, France 18 C5 47 13N 2 5 E
Vietnam ■, Asia 38 C6 19 0N 106 0 E
Vigan, Phil. 37 A6 17 35N 120 28 E
Vigévano, Italy 18 D8 45 19N 8 51 E
Vigia, Brazil 93 D9 0 50S 48 5W
Vigía Chico, Mexico 87 D7 19 46N 87 35W
Víglas, Ákra, Greece 23 D9 35 54N 27 51 E
Vigo, Spain 19 A1 42 12N 8 41W
Vihowa, Pakistan 42 D4 31 8N 70 30 E
Vihowa →, Pakistan 42 D4 31 8N 70 41 E
Vijayawada, India 41 L12 16 31N 80 39 E
Vijosë →, Albania 21 D8 40 37N 19 24 E
Vík, Iceland 8 E4 63 25N 19 1W
Vikeke, E. Timor 37 F7 8 52S 126 23 E
Viking, Canada 72 C6 53 7N 111 50W
Vikna, Norway 8 D14 64 55N 10 58 E
Vila da Maganja, Mozam. 55 F4 17 18S 37 30 E
Vila de João Belo = Xai-Xai, Mozam. 57 D5 25 6S 33 31 E
Vila do Bispo, Portugal 19 D1 37 5N 8 53W
Vila Franca de Xira, Portugal 19 C1 38 57N 8 59W
Vila Gamito, Mozam. 55 E3 14 12S 33 0 E
Vila Gomes da Costa, Mozam. 57 C5 24 20S 33 37 E
Vila Machado, Mozam. 55 F3 19 15S 34 14 E
Vila Mouzinho, Mozam. 55 E3 14 48S 34 25 E
Vila Nova de Gaia, Portugal 19 B1 41 8N 8 37W
Vila Real, Portugal 19 B2 41 17N 7 48W
Vila-real de los Infantes, Spain 19 C5 39 55N 0 3W
Vila Real de Santo António, Portugal 19 D2 37 10N 7 28W
Vila Vasco da Gama, Mozam. 55 E3 14 54S 32 14 E
Vila Velha, Brazil 95 A7 20 20S 40 17W
Vilagarcía de Arousa, Spain 19 A1 42 34N 8 46W
Vilaine →, France 18 C2 47 30N 2 27W
Vilanandro, Tanjona, Madag. 57 B7 16 11S 44 27 E
Vilanculos, Mozam. 57 C6 22 1S 35 17 E
Vilanova i la Geltrú, Spain 19 B6 41 13N 1 40 E
Vileyka, Belarus 17 A14 54 30N 26 53 E
Vilhelmina, Sweden 8 D17 64 35N 16 39 E
Vilhena, Brazil 92 F6 12 40S 60 5W
Viliga, Russia 27 C16 61 36N 156 56 E
Viliya →, Lithuania 9 J21 55 8N 24 16 E
Viljandi, Estonia 9 G21 58 28N 25 30 E
Vilkitskogo, Proliv, Russia 27 B11 78 0N 103 0 E
Vilkovo = Vylkove, Ukraine 17 F15 45 28N 29 32 E
Villa Abecia, Bolivia 94 A2 21 0S 68 18W
Villa Ahumada, Mexico 86 A3 30 38N 106 30W
Villa Ana, Argentina 94 B4 28 28S 59 40W
Villa Ángela, Argentina 94 B3 27 34S 60 45W
Villa Bella, Bolivia 92 F5 10 25S 65 22W
Villa Bens = Tarfaya, Morocco 50 C3 27 55N 12 55W
Villa Cañás, Argentina 94 C3 34 0S 61 35W
Villa Cisneros = Dakhla, W. Sahara 50 D2 23 50N 15 53W
Villa Colón, Argentina 94 C2 31 38S 68 20W
Villa Constitución, Argentina 94 C3 33 15S 60 20W
Villa de María, Argentina 94 B3 29 55S 63 43W
Villa Dolores, Argentina 94 C2 31 58S 65 15W
Villa Frontera, Mexico 86 B4 26 56N 101 27W
Villa Guillermina, Argentina 94 B4 28 15S 59 29W
Villa Hayes, Paraguay 94 B4 25 5S 57 20W
Villa Iris, Argentina 94 D3 38 12S 63 12W
Villa Juárez, Mexico 86 B4 27 37N 100 44W
Villa María, Argentina 94 C3 32 20S 63 10W
Villa Mazán, Argentina 94 B2 28 40S 66 30W
Villa Montes, Bolivia 94 A3 21 10S 63 30W
Villa Ocampo, Argentina 94 B4 28 30S 59 20W
Villa Ocampo, Mexico 86 B3 26 29N 105 30W
Villa Ojo de Agua, Argentina 94 B3 29 30S 63 44W
Villa San José, Argentina 94 C4 32 12S 58 15W
Villa San Martín, Argentina 94 B3 28 15S 64 9W
Villa Unión, Mexico 86 C3 23 12N 106 14W
Villacarlos, Spain 22 B11 39 53N 4 17 E
Villacarrillo, Spain 19 C4 38 7N 3 3W
Villach, Austria 16 E7 46 37N 13 51 E
Villafranca de los Caballeros, Spain 22 B10 39 34N 3 25 E
Villagrán, Mexico 87 C5 24 29N 99 29W
Villaguay, Argentina 94 C4 32 0S 59 0W
Villahermosa, Mexico 87 D6 17 59N 92 55W
Villajoyosa, Spain 19 C5 38 30N 0 12W
Villalba, Spain 19 A2 43 26N 7 40W
Villanueva, U.S.A. 81 H2 35 16N 105 22W
Villanueva de la Serena, Spain 19 C3 38 59N 5 50W
Villanueva y Geltrú = Vilanova i la Geltrú, Spain 19 B6 41 13N 1 40 E
Villarreal = Vila-real de los Infantes, Spain 19 C5 39 55N 0 3W
Villarrica, Chile 96 D2 39 15S 72 15W
Villarrica, Paraguay 94 B4 25 40S 56 30W
Villarrobledo, Spain 19 C4 39 18N 2 36W
Villavicencio, Argentina 94 C2 32 28S 69 0W
Villavicencio, Colombia 92 C4 4 9N 73 37W
Villaviciosa, Spain 19 A3 43 32N 5 27W
Villazón, Bolivia 94 A2 22 0S 65 35W
Ville-Marie, Canada 70 C4 47 20N 79 30W
Ville Platte, U.S.A. 81 K8 30 41N 92 17W
Villena, Spain 19 C5 38 39N 0 52W
Villeneuve-d'Ascq, France 18 A5 50 38N 3 9 E
Villeneuve-sur-Lot, France 18 D4 44 24N 0 42 E
Villiers, S. Africa 57 D4 27 2S 28 36 E
Villingen-Schwenningen, Germany 16 D5 48 3N 8 26 E
Vilna, Canada 72 C6 54 7N 111 55W
Vilnius, Lithuania 9 J21 54 38N 25 19 E
Vilvoorde, Belgium 15 D4 50 56N 4 26 E
Vilyuy →, Russia 27 C13 64 24N 126 26 E
Vilyuysk, Russia 27 C13 63 40N 121 35 E
Viña del Mar, Chile 94 C1 33 0S 71 30W
Vinarós, Spain 19 B6 40 30N 0 27 E
Vincennes, U.S.A. 76 F2 38 41N 87 32W
Vincent, U.S.A. 85 L8 34 33N 118 11W
Vinchina, Argentina 94 B2 28 45S 68 15W
Vindelälven →, Sweden 8 E18 63 55N 19 50 E
Vindeln, Sweden 8 D18 64 12N 19 43 E
Vindhya Ra., India 42 H7 22 50N 77 0 E
Vineland, U.S.A. 76 F8 39 29N 75 2W
Vinh, Vietnam 38 C5 18 45N 105 38 E
Vinh Linh, Vietnam 38 D6 17 4N 107 2 E
Vinh Long, Vietnam 39 G5 10 16N 105 57 E
Vinh Yen, Vietnam 38 B5 21 21N 105 35 E
Vinita, U.S.A. 81 G7 36 39N 95 9W
Vinkovci, Croatia 21 B8 45 19N 18 48 E
Vinnitsa = Vinnytsya, Ukraine 17 D15 49 15N 28 30 E
Vinnytsya, Ukraine 17 D15 49 15N 28 30 E
Vinton, Calif., U.S.A. 84 F6 39 48N 120 10W
Vinton, Iowa, U.S.A. 80 D8 42 10N 92 1W
Vinton, La., U.S.A. 81 K8 30 11N 93 35W
Virac, Phil. 37 B6 13 30N 124 20 E
Virachei, Cambodia 38 F6 13 59N 106 49 E
Virago Sd., Canada 72 C2 54 0N 132 30W
Viramgam, India 42 H5 23 5N 72 0 E
Viranşehir, Turkey 44 B3 37 13N 39 45 E
Virawah, Pakistan 42 G4 24 31N 70 46 E
Virden, Canada 73 D8 49 50N 100 56W
Vire, France 18 B3 48 50N 0 53W
Vírgenes, C., Argentina 96 G3 52 19S 68 21W
Virgin →, U.S.A. 83 H6 36 28N 114 21W
Virgin Gorda, Br. Virgin Is. 89 C7 18 30N 64 26W
Virgin Is. (British) ■, W. Indies 89 C7 18 30N 64 30W
Virgin Is. (U.S.) ■, W. Indies 89 C7 18 20N 65 0W
Virginia, S. Africa 56 D4 28 8S 26 55 E
Virginia, U.S.A. 80 B8 47 31N 92 32W
Virginia □, U.S.A. 76 G7 37 30N 78 45W
Virginia Beach, U.S.A. 76 G8 36 51N 75 59W
Virginia City, Mont., U.S.A. 82 D8 45 18N 111 56W
Virginia City, Nev., U.S.A. 84 F7 39 19N 119 39W
Virginia Falls, Canada 72 A3 61 38N 125 42W
Virginiatown, Canada 70 C4 48 9N 79 36W
Viroqua, U.S.A. 80 D9 43 34N 90 53W
Virovitica, Croatia 20 B7 45 51N 17 21 E
Virpur, India 42 J4 21 51N 70 42 E
Virton, Belgium 15 E5 49 35N 5 32 E
Virudunagar, India 40 Q10 9 30N 77 58 E
Vis, Croatia 20 C7 43 4N 16 10 E
Visalia, U.S.A. 84 J7 36 20N 119 18W
Visayan Sea, Phil. 37 B6 11 30N 123 30 E
Visby, Sweden 9 H18 57 37N 18 18 E
Viscount Melville Sd., Canada 4 B2 74 10N 108 0W
Visé, Belgium 15 D5 50 44N 5 41 E
Višegrad, Bos.-H. 21 C8 43 47N 19 17 E
Viseu, Brazil 93 D9 1 10S 46 5W
Viseu, Portugal 19 B2 40 40N 7 55W
Vishakhapatnam, India 41 L13 17 45N 83 20 E
Visnagar, India 42 H5 23 45N 72 32 E
Viso, Mte., Italy 18 D7 44 38N 7 5 E
Visokoi I., Antarctica 5 B1 56 43S 27 15W
Vista, U.S.A. 85 M9 33 12N 117 14W
Vistula = Wisła →, Poland 17 A10 54 22N 18 55 E
Vitebsk = Vitsyebsk, Belarus 24 C5 55 10N 30 15 E
Viterbo, Italy 20 C5 42 25N 12 6 E
Viti Levu, Fiji 59 C7 17 30S 177 30 E
Vitigudino, Spain 19 B2 41 1N 6 26W
Vitim, Russia 27 D12 59 28N 112 35 E
Vitim →, Russia 27 D12 59 26N 112 34 E
Vitória, Brazil 93 H10 20 20S 40 22W
Vitória da Conquista, Brazil 93 F10 14 51S 40 51W
Vitória de São Antão, Brazil 93 E11 8 10S 35 20W
Vitoria-Gasteiz, Spain 19 A4 42 50N 2 41W
Vitsyebsk, Belarus 24 C5 55 10N 30 15 E
Vittória, Italy 20 F6 36 57N 14 32 E
Vittório Véneto, Italy 20 B5 45 59N 12 18 E
Viveiro, Spain 19 A2 43 39N 7 38W
Vivian, U.S.A. 81 J8 32 53N 93 59W
Vizcaíno, Desierto de, Mexico 86 B2 27 40N 113 50W
Vizcaíno, Sierra, Mexico 86 B2 27 30N 114 0W
Vize, Turkey 21 D12 41 34N 27 45 E
Vizianagaram, India 41 K13 18 6N 83 30 E
Vlaardingen, Neths. 15 C4 51 55N 4 21 E
Vladikavkaz, Russia 25 F7 43 0N 44 35 E
Vladimir, Russia 24 C7 56 15N 40 30 E
Vladimir Volynskiy = Volodymyr-Volynskyy, Ukraine 17 C13 50 50N 24 18 E
Vladivostok, Russia 27 E14 43 10N 131 53 E
Vlieland, Neths. 15 A4 53 16N 4 55 E
Vlissingen, Neths. 15 C3 51 26N 3 34 E
Vlorë, Albania 21 D8 40 32N 19 28 E
Vltava →, Czech Rep. 16 D8 50 21N 14 30 E
Vo Dat, Vietnam 39 G6 11 9N 107 31 E
Voe, U.K. 12 A7 60 21N 1 16W
Vogelkop = Doberai, Jazirah, Indonesia 37 E8 1 25S 133 0 E
Vogelsberg, Germany 16 C5 50 31N 9 12 E
Voghera, Italy 18 D8 44 59N 9 1 E
Vohibinany, Madag. 57 B8 18 49S 49 4 E
Vohilava, Madag. 57 C8 21 4S 48 0 E
Vohimarina = Iharana, Madag. 57 A9 13 25S 50 0 E
Vohimena, Tanjon' i, Madag. 57 D8 25 36S 45 8 E
Vohipeno, Madag. 57 C8 22 22S 47 51 E
Voi, Kenya 54 C4 3 25S 38 32 E
Voiron, France 18 D6 45 22N 5 35 E
Voisey B., Canada 71 A7 56 15N 61 50W
Vojmsjön, Sweden 8 D17 64 55N 16 40 E
Vojvodina □, Serbia, Yug. 21 B9 45 20N 20 0 E
Volborg, U.S.A. 80 C2 45 51N 105 41W
Volcano Is. = Kazan-Rettō, Pac. Oc. 64 E6 25 0N 141 0 E
Volda, Norway 9 E12 62 9N 6 5 E
Volga →, Russia 25 E8 46 0N 48 30 E
Volga Hts. = Privolzhskaya Vozvyshennost, Russia 25 D8 51 0N 46 0 E
Volgodonsk, Russia 25 E7 47 33N 42 5 E
Volgograd, Russia 25 E7 48 40N 44 25 E
Volgogradskoye Vdkhr., Russia 25 D8 50 0N 45 20 E
Volkhov →, Russia 24 B5 60 8N 32 20 E
Volkovysk = Vawkavysk, Belarus 17 B13 53 9N 24 30 E
Volksrust, S. Africa 57 D4 27 24S 29 53 E
Volochanka, Russia 27 B10 71 0N 94 28 E
Volodymyr-Volynskyy, Ukraine 17 C13 50 50N 24 18 E
Vologda, Russia 24 C6 59 10N 39 45 E
Vólos, Greece 21 E10 39 24N 22 59 E
Volovets, Ukraine 17 D12 48 43N 23 11 E
Volozhin = Valozhyn, Belarus 17 A14 54 3N 26 30 E
Volsk, Russia 24 D8 52 5N 47 22 E
Volta →, Ghana 48 F4 5 46N 0 41 E
Volta, L., Ghana 50 G6 7 30N 0 0W
Volta Redonda, Brazil 95 A7 22 31S 44 5W
Voltaire, C., Australia 60 B4 14 16S 125 35 E
Volterra, Italy 20 C4 43 24N 10 51 E
Volturno →, Italy 20 D5 41 1N 13 55 E
Volzhskiy, Russia 25 E7 48 56N 44 46 E
Vondrozo, Madag. 57 C8 22 49S 47 20 E
Vopnafjörður, Iceland 8 D6 65 45N 14 50W
Vóriai Sporádhes, Greece 21 E10 39 15N 23 30 E
Vorkuta, Russia 24 A11 67 48N 64 20 E
Vormsi, Estonia 9 G20 59 1N 23 13 E
Voronezh, Russia 25 D6 51 40N 39 10 E
Voroshilovgrad = Luhansk, Ukraine 25 E6 48 38N 39 15 E
Voroshilovsk = Alchevsk, Ukraine 25 E6 48 30N 38 45 E
Võrts Järv, Estonia 9 G22 58 16N 26 3 E
Võru, Estonia 9 H22 57 48N 26 54 E
Vosges, France 18 B7 48 20N 7 10 E
Voss, Norway 9 F12 60 38N 6 26 E
Vostok I., Kiribati 65 J12 10 5S 152 23W
Votkinsk, Russia 24 C9 57 0N 53 55 E
Votkinskoye Vdkhr., Russia 24 C10 57 22N 55 12 E
Votsuri-Shima, Japan 31 M1 25 45N 123 29 E
Vouga →, Portugal 19 B1 40 41N 8 40W
Voúxa, Ákra, Greece 23 D5 35 37N 23 32 E
Vozhe, Ozero, Russia 24 B6 60 45N 39 0 E
Voznesensk, Ukraine 25 E5 47 35N 31 21 E
Voznesenye, Russia 24 B6 61 0N 35 28 E
Vrangelya, Ostrov, Russia 27 B19 71 0N 180 0 E
Vranje, Serbia, Yug. 21 C9 42 34N 21 54 E
Vratsa, Bulgaria 21 C10 43 15N 23 30 E
Vrbas →, Bos.-H. 20 B7 45 8N 17 29 E
Vrede, S. Africa 57 D4 27 24S 29 6 E
Vredefort, S. Africa 56 D4 27 0S 27 22 E
Vredenburg, S. Africa 56 E2 32 56S 18 0 E
Vredendal, S. Africa 56 E2 31 41S 18 35 E
Vrindavan, India 42 F7 27 37N 77 40 E
Vríses, Greece 23 D6 35 23N 24 13 E
Vršac, Serbia, Yug. 21 B9 45 8N 21 20 E
Vryburg, S. Africa 56 D3 26 55S 24 45 E
Vryheid, S. Africa 57 D5 27 45S 30 47 E
Vu Liet, Vietnam 38 C5 18 43N 105 23 E
Vukovar, Croatia 21 B8 45 21N 18 59 E
Vulcan, Canada 72 C6 50 25N 113 15W
Vulcan, Romania 17 F12 45 23N 23 17 E
Vulcaneşti, Moldova 17 F15 45 41N 28 18 E
Vulcano, Italy 20 E6 38 24N 14 58 E
Vulkaneshty = Vulcaneşti, Moldova 17 F15 45 41N 28 18 E
Vunduzi →, Mozam. 55 F3 18 56S 34 1 E
Vung Tau, Vietnam 39 G6 10 21N 107 4 E
Vyatka = Kirov, Russia 24 C8 58 35N 49 40 E
Vyatka →, Russia 24 C9 55 37N 51 28 E
Vyatskiye Polyany, Russia 24 C9 56 14N 51 5 E
Vyazemskiy, Russia 27 E14 47 32N 134 45 E
Vyazma, Russia 24 C5 55 10N 34 15 E
Vyborg, Russia 24 B4 60 43N 28 47 E
Vychegda →, Russia 24 B8 61 18N 46 36 E
Vychodné Beskydy, Europe 17 D11 49 20N 22 0 E
Vyg-ozero, Russia 24 B5 63 47N 34 29 E
Vylkove, Ukraine 17 F15 45 28N 29 32 E
Vynohradiv, Ukraine 17 D12 48 9N 23 2 E
Vyrnwy, L., U.K. 10 E4 52 48N 3 31W
Vyshniy Volochek, Russia 24 C5 57 30N 34 30 E
Vyshzha = imeni 26 Bakinskikh Komissarov, Turkmenistan 45 B7 39 22N 54 10 E
Vyškov, Czech Rep. 17 D9 49 17N 17 0 E
Vytegra, Russia 24 B6 61 0N 36 27 E

W

W.A.C. Bennett Dam, Canada 72 B4 56 2N 122 6W
Waal →, Neths. 15 C5 51 37N 5 0 E
Waalwijk, Neths. 15 C5 51 42N 5 4 E
Wabana, Canada 71 C9 47 40N 53 0W
Wabasca →, Canada 72 B5 58 22N 115 20W
Wabasca-Desmarais, Canada 72 B6 55 57N 113 56W
Wabash, U.S.A. 76 E3 40 48N 85 49W
Wabash →, U.S.A. 76 G1 37 48N 88 2W
Wabigoon L., Canada 73 D10 49 44N 92 44W
Wabowden, Canada 73 C9 54 55N 98 38W
Wabuk Pt., Canada 70 A2 55 20N 85 5W
Wabush, Canada 71 B6 52 55N 66 52W
Waco, U.S.A. 81 K6 31 33N 97 9W
Waconichi, L., Canada 70 B5 50 8N 74 0W
Wad Hamid, Sudan 51 E12 16 30N 32 45 E
Wad Medanî, Sudan 51 F12 14 28N 33 30 E
Wad Thana, Pakistan 42 F2 27 22N 66 23 E
Wadai, Africa 48 E5 12 0N 19 0 E
Wadayama, Japan 31 G7 35 19N 134 52 E
Waddeneilanden, Neths. 15 A5 53 20N 5 10 E
Waddenzee, Neths. 15 A5 53 6N 5 10 E
Waddington, U.S.A. 79 B9 44 52N 75 12W
Waddington, Mt., Canada 72 C3 51 23N 125 15W
Waddy Pt., Australia 63 C5 24 58S 153 21 E
Wadebridge, U.K. 11 G3 50 31N 4 51W
Wadena, Canada 73 C8 51 57N 103 47W
Wadena, U.S.A. 80 B7 46 26N 95 8W
Wadeye, Australia 60 B4 14 28S 129 52 E
Wadhams, Canada 72 C3 51 30N 127 30W
Wādī as Sīr, Jordan 47 D4 31 56N 35 49 E
Wadi Halfa, Sudan 51 D12 21 53N 31 19 E
Wadsworth, Nev., U.S.A. 82 G4 39 38N 119 17W
Wadsworth, Ohio, U.S.A. 78 E3 41 2N 81 44W
Waegwan, S. Korea 35 G15 35 59N 128 23 E
Wafangdian, China 35 E11 39 38N 121 58 E
Wafrah, Si. Arabia 44 D5 28 33N 47 56 E
Wageningen, Neths. 15 C5 51 58N 5 40 E
Wager B., Canada 69 B11 65 26N 88 40W
Waghete, Indonesia 37 E9 4 10S 135 50 E
Wagin, Australia 61 F2 33 17S 117 25 E
Wagner, U.S.A. 80 D5 43 5N 98 18W
Wagon Mound, U.S.A. 81 G2 36 1N 104 42W

West Beskids

Wagoner, *U.S.A.* **81 H7** 35 58N 95 22W
Wah, *Pakistan* **42 C5** 33 45N 72 40 E
Wahai, *Indonesia* **37 E7** 2 48S 129 35 E
Wahiawa, *U.S.A.* **74 H15** 21 30N 158 2W
Wâḥid, *Egypt* **47 E1** 30 48N 32 21 E
Wahnai, *Afghan.* **42 C1** 32 40N 65 50 E
Wahoo, *U.S.A.* **80 E6** 41 13N 96 37W
Wahpeton, *U.S.A.* **80 B6** 46 16N 96 36W
Waiau →, *N.Z.* **59 K4** 42 47S 173 22 E
Waibeem, *Indonesia* **37 E8** 0 30S 132 59 E
Waigeo, *Indonesia* **37 E8** 0 20S 130 40 E
Waihi, *N.Z.* **59 G5** 37 23S 175 52 E
Waihou →, *N.Z.* **59 G5** 37 15S 175 40 E
Waika, *Dem. Rep. of the Congo* **54 C2** 2 22S 25 42 E
Waikabubak, *Indonesia* **37 F5** 9 45S 119 25 E
Waikari, *N.Z.* **59 K4** 42 58S 172 41 E
Waikato →, *N.Z.* **59 G5** 37 23S 174 43 E
Waikopokopu, *N.Z.* **59 H6** 39 3S 177 52 E
Waikouaiti, *N.Z.* **59 L3** 45 36S 170 41 E
Wailuku, *U.S.A.* **74 H16** 20 53N 156 30W
Waimakariri →, *N.Z.* **59 K4** 43 24S 172 42 E
Waimate, *N.Z.* **59 L3** 44 45S 171 3 E
Wainganga →, *India* **40 K11** 18 50N 79 55 E
Waingapu, *Indonesia* **37 F6** 9 35S 120 11 E
Waini →, *Guyana* **92 B7** 8 20N 59 50W
Wainwright, *Canada* **73 C6** 52 50N 110 50W
Waiouru, *N.Z.* **59 H5** 39 28S 175 41 E
Waipara, *N.Z.* **59 K4** 43 3S 172 46 E
Waipawa, *N.Z.* **59 H6** 39 56S 176 38 E
Waipiro, *N.Z.* **59 H7** 38 2S 178 22 E
Waipu, *N.Z.* **59 F5** 35 59S 174 29 E
Waipukurau, *N.Z.* **59 J6** 40 1S 176 33 E
Wairakei, *N.Z.* **59 H6** 38 37S 176 6 E
Wairarapa, L., *N.Z.* **59 J5** 41 14S 175 15 E
Wairoa, *N.Z.* **59 H6** 39 3S 177 25 E
Waitaki →, *N.Z.* **59 L3** 44 56S 171 7 E
Waitara, *N.Z.* **59 H5** 38 59S 174 15 E
Waitsburg, *U.S.A.* **82 C5** 46 16N 118 9W
Waiuku, *N.Z.* **59 G5** 37 15S 174 45 E
Wajima, *Japan* **31 F8** 37 30N 137 0 E
Wajir, *Kenya* **54 B5** 1 42N 40 5 E
Wakasa, *Japan* **31 G7** 35 20N 134 24 E
Wakasa-Wan, *Japan* **31 G7** 35 40N 135 30 E
Wakatipu, L., *N.Z.* **59 L2** 45 5S 168 33 E
Wakaw, *Canada* **73 C7** 52 39N 105 44W
Wakayama, *Japan* **31 G7** 34 15N 135 15 E
Wakayama □, *Japan* **31 H7** 33 50N 135 30 E
Wake Forest, *U.S.A.* **77 H6** 35 59N 78 30W
Wake I., *Pac. Oc.* **64 F8** 19 18N 166 36 E
WaKeeney, *U.S.A.* **80 F5** 39 1N 99 53W
Wakefield, *N.Z.* **59 J4** 41 24S 173 5 E
Wakefield, *U.K.* **10 D6** 53 41N 1 29W
Wakefield, *Mass., U.S.A.* **79 D13** 42 30N 71 4W
Wakefield, *Mich., U.S.A.* **80 B10** 46 29N 89 56W
Wakkanai, *Japan* **30 B10** 45 28N 141 35 E
Wakkerstroom, *S. Africa* **57 D5** 27 24S 30 10 E
Wakre, *Indonesia* **37 E8** 0 19S 131 5 E
Wakuach, L., *Canada* **71 A6** 55 34N 67 32W
Walamba, *Zambia* **55 E2** 13 30S 28 42 E
Wałbrzych, *Poland* **16 C9** 50 45N 16 18 E
Walbury Hill, *U.K.* **11 F6** 51 21N 1 28W
Walcheren, *Neths.* **15 C3** 51 30N 3 35 E
Walcott, *U.S.A.* **82 F10** 41 46N 106 51W
Wałcz, *Poland* **16 B9** 53 17N 16 27 E
Waldburg Ra., *Australia* **61 D2** 24 40S 117 35 E
Walden, *Colo., U.S.A.* **82 F10** 40 44N 106 17W
Walden, *N.Y., U.S.A.* **79 E10** 41 34N 74 11W
Waldport, *U.S.A.* **82 D1** 44 26N 124 4W
Waldron, *U.S.A.* **81 H7** 34 54N 94 5W
Walebing, *Australia* **61 F2** 30 41S 116 13 E
Wales □, *U.K.* **11 E3** 52 19N 4 43W
Walgett, *Australia* **63 E4** 30 0S 148 5 E
Walgreen Coast, *Antarctica* **5 D15** 75 15S 105 0W
Walker, *U.S.A.* **80 B7** 47 6N 94 35W
Walker, L., *Canada* **71 B6** 50 20N 67 11W
Walker L., *Canada* **73 C9** 54 42N 95 57W
Walker L., *U.S.A.* **82 G4** 38 42N 118 43W
Walkerston, *Australia* **62 C4** 21 11S 149 8 E
Walkerton, *Canada* **78 B3** 44 10N 81 10W
Wall, *U.S.A.* **80 D3** 44 0N 102 8W
Walla Walla, *U.S.A.* **82 C4** 46 4N 118 20W
Wallace, *Idaho, U.S.A.* **82 C6** 47 28N 115 56W
Wallace, *N.C., U.S.A.* **77 H7** 34 44N 77 59W
Wallaceburg, *Canada* **78 D2** 42 34N 82 23W
Wallachia = Valahia, *Romania* **17 F13** 44 35N 25 0 E
Wallal, *Australia* **63 D4** 26 32S 146 7 E
Wallam Cr. →, *Australia* **63 D4** 28 40S 147 20 E
Wallambin, L., *Australia* **61 F2** 30 57S 117 35 E
Wallangarra, *Australia* **63 D5** 28 56S 151 58 E
Wallenpaupack, L., *U.S.A.* **79 E9** 41 25N 75 15W
Wallingford, *U.S.A.* **79 E12** 41 27N 72 50W
Wallis & Futuna, Is., *Pac. Oc.* **64 J10** 13 18S 176 10W
Wallowa, *U.S.A.* **82 D5** 45 34N 117 32W
Wallowa Mts., *U.S.A.* **82 D5** 45 20N 117 30W
Walls, *U.K.* **12 A7** 60 14N 1 33W
Wallula, *U.S.A.* **82 C4** 46 5N 118 54W
Wallumbilla, *Australia* **63 D4** 26 33S 149 9 E
Walmsley, L., *Canada* **73 A7** 63 25N 108 36W
Walney, I. of, *U.K.* **10 C4** 54 6N 3 15W
Walnut Creek, *U.S.A.* **84 H4** 37 54N 122 4W
Walnut Ridge, *U.S.A.* **81 G9** 36 4N 90 57W
Walpole, *Australia* **61 F2** 34 58S 116 44 E
Walpole, *U.S.A.* **79 D13** 42 9N 71 15W
Walsall, *U.K.* **11 E6** 52 35N 1 58W
Walsenburg, *U.S.A.* **81 G2** 37 38N 104 47W
Walsh, *U.S.A.* **81 G3** 37 23N 102 17W
Walsh →, *Australia* **62 B3** 16 31S 143 42 E
Walterboro, *U.S.A.* **77 J5** 32 55N 80 40W
Walters, *U.S.A.* **81 H5** 34 22N 98 19W
Waltham, *U.S.A.* **79 D13** 42 23N 71 14W
Waltman, *U.S.A.* **82 E10** 43 4N 107 12W
Walton, *U.S.A.* **79 D9** 42 10N 75 8W
Walton-on-the-Naze, *U.K.* **11 F9** 51 51N 1 17 E
Walvis Bay, *Namibia* **56 C1** 23 0S 14 28 E
Walvisbaai = Walvis Bay, *Namibia* **56 C1** 23 0S 14 28 E
Wamba, *Dem. Rep. of the Congo* **54 B2** 2 10N 27 57 E
Wamba, *Kenya* **54 B4** 0 58N 37 19 E
Wamego, *U.S.A.* **80 F6** 39 12N 96 18W
Wamena, *Indonesia* **37 E9** 4 4S 138 57 E
Wamsutter, *U.S.A.* **82 F9** 41 40N 107 58W
Wamulan, *Indonesia* **37 E7** 3 27S 126 7 E
Wan Xian, *China* **34 E8** 38 47N 115 7 E
Wana, *Pakistan* **42 C3** 32 20N 69 32 E
Wanaaring, *Australia* **63 D3** 29 38S 144 9 E
Wanaka, *N.Z.* **59 L2** 44 42S 169 9 E
Wanaka L., *N.Z.* **59 L2** 44 33S 169 7 E
Wanapitei L., *Canada* **70 C3** 46 45N 80 40W
Wandel Sea = McKinley Sea, *Arctic* **4 A7** 82 0N 0 0W
Wanderer, *Zimbabwe* **55 F3** 19 36S 30 1 E
Wandhari, *Pakistan* **42 F2** 27 42N 66 48 E
Wandoan, *Australia* **63 D4** 26 5S 149 55 E
Wanfu, *China* **35 D12** 40 8N 122 38 E
Wang →, *Thailand* **38 D2** 17 8N 99 2 E
Wang Noi, *Thailand* **38 E3** 14 13N 100 44 E
Wang Saphung, *Thailand* **38 D3** 17 18N 101 46 E
Wang Thong, *Thailand* **38 D3** 16 50N 100 26 E
Wanga, *Dem. Rep. of the Congo* **54 B2** 2 58N 29 12 E
Wangal, *Indonesia* **37 F8** 6 8S 134 9 E
Wanganui, *N.Z.* **59 H5** 39 56S 175 3 E
Wangary, *Australia* **63 E2** 34 35S 135 29 E
Wangdu, *China* **34 E8** 38 40N 115 7 E
Wangerooge, *Germany* **16 B4** 53 47N 7 54 E
Wangi, *Kenya* **54 C5** 1 58S 40 58 E
Wangiwangi, *Indonesia* **37 F6** 5 22S 123 37 E
Wangqing, *China* **35 C15** 43 12N 129 42 E
Wankaner, *India* **42 H4** 22 35N 71 0 E
Wanless, *Canada* **73 C8** 54 11N 101 21W
Wanning, *China* **38 C8** 18 48N 110 22 E
Wanon Niwat, *Thailand* **38 D4** 17 38N 103 46 E
Wanquan, *China* **34 D8** 40 50N 114 40 E
Wanrong, *China* **34 G6** 35 25N 110 50 E
Wantage, *U.K.* **11 F6** 51 35N 1 25W
Wapakoneta, *U.S.A.* **76 E3** 40 34N 84 12W
Wapato, *U.S.A.* **82 C3** 46 27N 120 25W
Wapawekka L., *Canada* **73 C8** 54 55N 104 40W
Wapikopa L., *Canada* **70 B2** 52 56N 87 53W
Wapiti →, *Canada* **72 B5** 55 5N 118 18W
Wappingers Falls, *U.S.A.* **79 E11** 41 36N 73 55W
Wapsipinicon →, *U.S.A.* **80 E9** 41 44N 90 19W
Warangal, *India* **40 L11** 17 58N 79 35 E
Waraseoni, *India* **43 J9** 21 45N 80 2 E
Waratah, *Australia* **62 G4** 41 30S 145 30 E
Warburton, *Australia* **61 E4** 26 8S 126 35 E
Warburton Ra., *Australia* **61 E4** 25 55S 126 28 E
Ward, *N.Z.* **59 J5** 41 49S 174 11 E
Ward →, *Australia* **63 D4** 26 28S 146 6 E
Ward Mt., *U.S.A.* **84 H8** 37 12N 118 54W
Warden, *S. Africa* **57 D4** 27 50S 29 0 E
Wardha, *India* **40 J11** 20 45N 78 39 E
Wardha →, *India* **40 K11** 19 57N 79 11 E
Ware, *Canada* **72 B3** 57 26N 125 41W
Ware, *U.S.A.* **79 D12** 42 16N 72 14W
Waregem, *Belgium* **15 D3** 50 53N 3 27 E
Wareham, *U.S.A.* **79 E14** 41 46N 70 43W
Waremme, *Belgium* **15 D5** 50 43N 5 15 E
Warialda, *Australia* **63 D5** 29 29S 150 33 E
Wariap, *Indonesia* **37 E8** 1 30S 134 5 E
Warin Chamrap, *Thailand* **38 E5** 15 12N 104 53 E
Warkopi, *Indonesia* **37 E8** 1 12S 134 9 E
Warm Springs, *U.S.A.* **83 G5** 38 10N 116 20W
Warman, *Canada* **73 C7** 52 19N 106 30W
Warmbad, *Namibia* **56 D2** 28 25S 18 42 E
Warmbad, *S. Africa* **57 C4** 24 51S 28 19 E
Warminster, *U.K.* **11 F5** 51 12N 2 10W
Warminster, *U.S.A.* **79 F9** 40 12N 75 6W
Warner Mts., *U.S.A.* **82 F3** 41 40N 120 15W
Warner Robins, *U.S.A.* **77 J4** 32 37N 83 36W
Waroona, *Australia* **61 F2** 32 50S 115 58 E
Warrego →, *Australia* **63 E4** 30 24S 145 21 E
Warrego Ra., *Australia* **62 C4** 24 58S 146 0 E
Warren, *Ark., U.S.A.* **81 J8** 33 37N 92 4W
Warren, *Mich., U.S.A.* **76 D4** 42 30N 83 0W
Warren, *Minn., U.S.A.* **80 A6** 48 12N 96 46W
Warren, *Ohio, U.S.A.* **78 E4** 41 14N 80 49W
Warren, *Pa., U.S.A.* **78 E5** 41 51N 79 9W
Warrenpoint, *U.K.* **13 B5** 54 6N 6 15W
Warrensburg, *Mo., U.S.A.* **80 F8** 38 46N 93 44W
Warrensburg, *N.Y., U.S.A.* **79 C11** 43 29N 73 46W
Warrenton, *S. Africa* **56 D3** 28 9S 24 47 E
Warrenton, *U.S.A.* **84 D3** 46 10N 123 56W
Warri, *Nigeria* **50 G7** 5 30N 5 41 E
Warrina, *Australia* **63 D2** 28 12S 135 50 E
Warrington, *U.K.* **10 D5** 53 24N 2 35W
Warrington, *U.S.A.* **77 K2** 30 23N 87 17W
Warrington □, *U.K.* **10 D5** 53 24N 2 35W
Warroad, *U.S.A.* **80 A7** 48 54N 95 19W
Warruwi, *Australia* **62 A1** 11 36S 133 20 E
Warsa, *Indonesia* **37 E9** 0 47S 135 55 E
Warsak Dam, *Pakistan* **42 B4** 34 11N 71 19 E
Warsaw = Warszawa, *Poland* **17 B11** 52 13N 21 0 E
Warsaw, *Ind., U.S.A.* **76 E3** 41 14N 85 51W
Warsaw, *N.Y., U.S.A.* **78 D6** 42 45N 78 8W
Warsaw, *Ohio, U.S.A.* **78 F3** 40 20N 82 0W
Warszawa, *Poland* **17 B11** 52 13N 21 0 E
Warta →, *Poland* **16 B8** 52 35N 14 39 E
Warthe = Warta →, *Poland* **16 B8** 52 35N 14 39 E
Waru, *Indonesia* **37 E8** 3 30S 130 36 E
Warwick, *Australia* **63 D5** 28 10S 152 1 E
Warwick, *U.K.* **11 E6** 52 18N 1 35W
Warwick, *N.Y., U.S.A.* **79 E10** 41 16N 74 22W
Warwick, *R.I., U.S.A.* **79 E13** 41 42N 71 28W
Warwickshire □, *U.K.* **11 E6** 52 14N 1 38W
Wasaga Beach, *Canada* **78 B4** 44 31N 80 1W
Wasagaming, *Canada* **73 C9** 50 39N 99 58W
Wasatch Ra., *U.S.A.* **82 F8** 40 30N 111 15W
Wasbank, *S. Africa* **57 D5** 28 15S 30 9 E
Wasco, *Calif., U.S.A.* **85 K7** 35 36N 119 20W
Wasco, *Oreg., U.S.A.* **82 D3** 45 36N 120 42W
Waseca, *U.S.A.* **80 C8** 44 5N 93 30W
Wasekamio L., *Canada* **73 B7** 56 45N 108 45W
Wash, The, *U.K.* **10 E8** 52 58N 0 20 E
Washago, *Canada* **78 B5** 44 45N 79 20W
Washburn, *N. Dak., U.S.A.* **80 B4** 47 17N 101 2W
Washburn, *Wis., U.S.A.* **80 B9** 46 40N 90 54W
Washim, *India* **40 J10** 20 3N 77 0 E
Washington, *U.K.* **10 C6** 54 55N 1 30W
Washington, *D.C., U.S.A.* **76 F7** 38 54N 77 2W
Washington, *Ga., U.S.A.* **77 J4** 33 44N 82 44W
Washington, *Ind., U.S.A.* **76 F2** 38 40N 87 10W
Washington, *Iowa, U.S.A.* **80 E9** 41 18N 91 42W
Washington, *Mo., U.S.A.* **80 F9** 38 33N 91 1W
Washington, *N.C., U.S.A.* **77 H7** 35 33N 77 3W
Washington, *N.J., U.S.A.* **79 F10** 40 46N 74 59W
Washington, *Pa., U.S.A.* **78 F4** 40 10N 80 15W
Washington, *Utah, U.S.A.* **83 H7** 37 8N 113 31W
Washington □, *U.S.A.* **82 C3** 47 30N 120 30W
Washington, Mt., *U.S.A.* **79 B13** 44 16N 71 18W
Washington Court House, *U.S.A.* **76 F4** 39 32N 83 26W
Washington I., *U.S.A.* **76 C2** 45 23N 86 54W
Washougal, *U.S.A.* **84 E4** 45 35N 122 21W
Wasian, *Indonesia* **37 E8** 1 47S 133 19 E
Wasilla, *U.S.A.* **68 B5** 61 35N 149 26W
Wasior, *Indonesia* **37 E8** 2 43S 134 30 E
Waskaganish, *Canada* **70 B4** 51 30N 78 40W
Waskaiowaka, L., *Canada* **73 B9** 56 33N 96 23W
Waskesiu Lake, *Canada* **73 C7** 53 55N 106 5W
Wasserkuppe, *Germany* **16 C5** 50 29N 9 55 E
Waswanipi, *Canada* **70 C4** 49 40N 76 29W
Waswanipi, L., *Canada* **70 C4** 49 35N 76 40W
Watampone, *Indonesia* **37 E6** 4 29S 120 25 E
Water Park Pt., *Australia* **62 C5** 22 56S 150 47 E
Water Valley, *U.S.A.* **81 H10** 34 10N 89 38W
Waterberge, *S. Africa* **57 C4** 24 10S 28 0 E
Waterbury, *Conn., U.S.A.* **79 E11** 41 33N 73 3W
Waterbury, *Vt., U.S.A.* **79 B12** 44 20N 72 46W
Waterbury L., *Canada* **73 B8** 58 10N 104 22W
Waterdown, *Canada* **78 C5** 43 20N 79 53W
Waterford, *Canada* **78 D4** 42 56N 80 17W
Waterford, *Ireland* **13 D4** 52 15N 7 8W
Waterford, *Calif., U.S.A.* **84 H6** 37 38N 120 46W
Waterford, *Pa., U.S.A.* **78 E5** 41 57N 79 59W
Waterford □, *Ireland* **13 D4** 52 10N 7 40W
Waterford Harbour, *Ireland* **13 D5** 52 8N 6 58W
Waterhen L., *Canada* **73 C9** 52 10N 99 40W
Waterloo, *Belgium* **15 D4** 50 43N 4 25 E
Waterloo, *Ont., Canada* **78 C4** 43 30N 80 32W
Waterloo, *Qué., Canada* **79 A12** 45 22N 72 32W
Waterloo, *Ill., U.S.A.* **80 F9** 38 20N 90 9W
Waterloo, *Iowa, U.S.A.* **80 D8** 42 30N 92 21W
Waterloo, *N.Y., U.S.A.* **78 D8** 42 54N 76 52W
Watersmeet, *U.S.A.* **80 B10** 46 16N 89 11W
Waterton Lakes Nat. Park, *U.S.A.* **82 B7** 48 45N 115 0W
Watertown, *Conn., U.S.A.* **79 E11** 41 36N 73 7W
Watertown, *N.Y., U.S.A.* **79 C9** 43 59N 75 55W
Watertown, *S. Dak., U.S.A.* **80 C6** 44 54N 97 7W
Watertown, *Wis., U.S.A.* **80 D10** 43 12N 88 43W
Waterval-Boven, *S. Africa* **57 D5** 25 40S 30 18 E
Waterville, *Canada* **79 A13** 45 16N 71 54W
Waterville, *Maine, U.S.A.* **77 C11** 44 33N 69 38W
Waterville, *N.Y., U.S.A.* **79 D9** 42 56N 75 23W
Waterville, *Pa., U.S.A.* **78 E7** 41 19N 77 21W
Waterville, *Wash., U.S.A.* **82 C3** 47 39N 120 4W
Watervliet, *U.S.A.* **79 D11** 42 44N 73 42W
Wates, *Indonesia* **37 G14** 7 51S 110 10 E
Watford, *Canada* **78 D3** 42 57N 81 53W
Watford, *U.K.* **11 F7** 51 40N 0 24W
Watford City, *U.S.A.* **80 B3** 47 48N 103 17W
Wathaman →, *Canada* **73 B8** 57 16N 102 59W
Wathaman L., *Canada* **73 B8** 56 58N 103 44W
Watheroo, *Australia* **61 F2** 30 15S 116 0 E
Wating, *China* **34 G4** 35 40N 106 38 E
Watkins Glen, *U.S.A.* **78 D8** 42 23N 76 52W
Watling I. = San Salvador I., *Bahamas* **89 B5** 24 0N 74 40W
Watonga, *U.S.A.* **81 H5** 35 51N 98 25W
Watrous, *Canada* **73 C7** 51 40N 105 25W
Watrous, *U.S.A.* **81 H2** 35 48N 104 59W
Watsa, *Dem. Rep. of the Congo* **54 B2** 3 4N 29 30 E
Watseka, *U.S.A.* **76 E2** 40 47N 87 44W
Watson, *Australia* **61 F5** 30 29S 131 31 E
Watson, *Canada* **73 C8** 52 10N 104 30W
Watson Lake, *Canada* **72 A3** 60 6N 128 49W
Watsontown, *U.S.A.* **78 E8** 41 5N 76 52W
Watsonville, *U.S.A.* **84 J5** 36 55N 121 45W
Wattiwarriganna Cr. →, *Australia* **63 D2** 28 57S 136 10 E
Watuata = Batuata, *Indonesia* **37 F6** 6 12S 122 42 E
Watubela, Kepulauan, *Indonesia* **37 E8** 4 28S 131 35 E
Watubela Is. = Watubela, Kepulauan, *Indonesia* **37 E8** 4 28S 131 35 E
Wau = Wâw, *Sudan* **51 G11** 7 45N 28 1 E
Waubamik, *Canada* **78 A4** 45 27N 80 1W
Waubay, *U.S.A.* **80 C6** 45 20N 97 18W
Wauchope, *Australia* **62 C1** 20 36S 134 15 E
Wauchula, *U.S.A.* **77 M5** 27 33N 81 49W
Waukarlycarly, L., *Australia* **60 D3** 21 18S 121 56 E
Waukegan, *U.S.A.* **76 D2** 42 22N 87 50W
Waukesha, *U.S.A.* **76 D1** 43 1N 88 14W
Waukon, *U.S.A.* **80 D9** 43 16N 91 29W
Waupaca, *U.S.A.* **80 C10** 44 21N 89 5W
Waupun, *U.S.A.* **80 D10** 43 38N 88 44W
Waurika, *U.S.A.* **81 H6** 34 10N 98 0W
Wausau, *U.S.A.* **80 C10** 44 58N 89 38W
Wautoma, *U.S.A.* **80 C10** 44 4N 89 18W
Wauwatosa, *U.S.A.* **76 D2** 43 3N 88 0W
Waveney →, *U.K.* **11 E9** 52 35N 1 39 E
Waverley, *N.Z.* **59 H5** 39 46S 174 37 E
Waverly, *Iowa, U.S.A.* **80 D8** 42 44N 92 29W
Waverly, *N.Y., U.S.A.* **79 E8** 42 1N 76 32W
Wavre, *Belgium* **15 D4** 50 43N 4 38 E
Wâw, *Sudan* **51 G11** 7 45N 28 1 E
Wāw al Kabīr, *Libya* **51 C9** 25 20N 16 43 E
Wawa, *Canada* **70 C3** 47 59N 84 47W
Wawanesa, *Canada* **73 D9** 49 36N 99 40W
Wawona, *U.S.A.* **84 H7** 37 32N 119 39W
Waxahachie, *U.S.A.* **81 J6** 32 24N 96 51W
Way, L., *Australia* **61 E3** 26 45S 120 16 E
Waycross, *U.S.A.* **77 K4** 31 13N 82 21W
Wayland, *U.S.A.* **78 D7** 42 34N 77 35W
Wayne, *Nebr., U.S.A.* **80 D6** 42 14N 97 1W
Wayne, *W. Va., U.S.A.* **76 F4** 38 13N 82 27W
Waynesboro, *Ga., U.S.A.* **77 J4** 33 6N 82 1W
Waynesboro, *Miss., U.S.A.* **77 K1** 31 40N 88 39W
Waynesboro, *Pa., U.S.A.* **76 F7** 39 45N 77 35W
Waynesboro, *Va., U.S.A.* **76 F6** 38 4N 78 53W
Waynesburg, *U.S.A.* **76 F5** 39 54N 80 11W
Waynesville, *U.S.A.* **77 H4** 35 28N 82 58W
Waynoka, *U.S.A.* **81 G5** 36 35N 98 53W
Wazirabad, *Pakistan* **42 C6** 32 30N 74 8 E
We, *Indonesia* **36 C1** 5 51N 95 18 E
Weald, The, *U.K.* **11 F8** 51 4N 0 20 E
Wear →, *U.K.* **10 C6** 54 55N 1 23W
Weatherford, *Okla., U.S.A.* **81 H5** 35 32N 98 43W
Weatherford, *Tex., U.S.A.* **81 J6** 32 46N 97 48W
Weaverville, *U.S.A.* **82 F2** 40 44N 122 56W
Webb City, *U.S.A.* **81 G7** 37 9N 94 28W
Webequie, *Canada* **70 B2** 52 59N 87 21W
Webster, *Mass., U.S.A.* **79 D13** 42 3N 71 53W
Webster, *N.Y., U.S.A.* **78 C7** 43 13N 77 26W
Webster, *S. Dak., U.S.A.* **80 C6** 45 20N 97 31W
Webster City, *U.S.A.* **80 D8** 42 28N 93 49W
Webster Springs, *U.S.A.* **76 F5** 38 29N 80 25W
Weda, *Indonesia* **37 D7** 0 21N 127 50 E
Weda, Teluk, *Indonesia* **37 D7** 0 20N 128 0 E
Weddell I., *Falk. Is.* **96 G4** 51 50S 61 0W
Weddell Sea, *Antarctica* **5 D1** 72 30S 40 0W
Wedgeport, *Canada* **71 D6** 43 44N 65 59W
Wedza, *Zimbabwe* **55 F3** 18 40S 31 33 E
Wee Waa, *Australia* **63 E4** 30 11S 149 26 E
Weed, *U.S.A.* **82 F2** 41 25N 122 23W
Weed Heights, *U.S.A.* **84 G7** 38 59N 119 13W
Weedsport, *U.S.A.* **79 C8** 43 3N 76 35W
Weedville, *U.S.A.* **78 E6** 41 17N 78 30W
Weenen, *S. Africa* **57 D5** 28 48S 30 7 E
Weert, *Neths.* **15 C5** 51 15N 5 43 E
Wei He →, *Hebei, China* **34 F8** 36 10N 115 45 E
Wei He →, *Shaanxi, China* **34 G6** 34 38N 110 15 E
Weichang, *China* **35 D9** 41 58N 117 49 E
Weichuan, *China* **34 G7** 34 20N 113 59 E
Weiden, *Germany* **16 D7** 49 41N 12 10 E
Weifang, *China* **35 F10** 36 44N 119 7 E
Weihai, *China* **35 F12** 37 30N 122 6 E
Weimar, *Germany* **16 C6** 50 58N 11 19 E
Weinan, *China* **34 G5** 34 31N 109 29 E
Weipa, *Australia* **62 A3** 12 40S 141 50 E
Weir →, *Australia* **63 D4** 28 20S 149 50 E
Weir →, *Canada* **73 B10** 56 54N 93 21W
Weir River, *Canada* **73 B10** 56 49N 94 6W
Weirton, *U.S.A.* **78 F4** 40 24N 80 35W
Weiser, *U.S.A.* **82 D5** 44 10N 117 0W
Weishan, *China* **35 G9** 34 47N 117 5 E
Weiyuan, *China* **34 G3** 35 7N 104 10 E
Wejherowo, *Poland* **17 A10** 54 35N 18 12 E
Wekusko L., *Canada* **73 C9** 54 40N 99 50W
Welch, *U.S.A.* **76 G5** 37 26N 81 35W
Welkom, *S. Africa* **56 D4** 28 0S 26 46 E
Welland, *Canada* **78 D5** 43 0N 79 15W
Welland →, *U.K.* **11 E7** 52 51N 0 5W
Wellesley Is., *Australia* **62 B2** 16 42S 139 30 E
Wellingborough, *U.K.* **11 E7** 52 19N 0 41W
Wellington, *Canada* **78 C7** 43 57N 77 20W
Wellington, *N.Z.* **59 J5** 41 19S 174 46 E
Wellington, *S. Africa* **56 E2** 33 38S 19 1 E
Wellington, *Somst., U.K.* **11 G4** 50 58N 3 13W
Wellington, *Telford & Wrekin, U.K.* **11 E5** 52 42N 2 30W
Wellington, *Colo., U.S.A.* **80 E2** 40 42N 105 0W
Wellington, *Kans., U.S.A.* **81 G6** 37 16N 97 24W
Wellington, *Nev., U.S.A.* **84 G7** 38 45N 119 23W
Wellington, *Ohio, U.S.A.* **78 E2** 41 10N 82 13W
Wellington, *Tex., U.S.A.* **81 H4** 34 51N 100 13W
Wellington, I., *Chile* **96 F2** 49 30S 75 0W
Wells, *U.K.* **11 F5** 51 13N 2 39W
Wells, *Maine, U.S.A.* **79 C14** 43 20N 70 35W
Wells, *N.Y., U.S.A.* **79 C10** 43 24N 74 17W
Wells, *Nev., U.S.A.* **82 F6** 41 7N 114 58W
Wells, L., *Australia* **61 E3** 26 44S 123 15 E
Wells, Mt., *Australia* **60 C4** 17 25S 127 8 E
Wells Gray Prov. Park, *Canada* **72 C4** 52 30N 120 15W
Wells-next-the-Sea, *U.K.* **10 E8** 52 57N 0 51 E
Wells River, *U.S.A.* **79 B12** 44 9N 72 4W
Wellsboro, *U.S.A.* **78 E7** 41 45N 77 18W
Wellsburg, *U.S.A.* **78 F4** 40 16N 80 37W
Wellsville, *N.Y., U.S.A.* **78 D7** 42 7N 77 57W
Wellsville, *Ohio, U.S.A.* **78 F4** 40 36N 80 39W
Wellsville, *Utah, U.S.A.* **82 F8** 41 38N 111 56W
Wellton, *U.S.A.* **83 K6** 32 40N 114 8W
Wels, *Austria* **16 D8** 48 9N 14 1 E
Welshpool, *U.K.* **11 E4** 52 39N 3 8W
Welwyn Garden City, *U.K.* **11 F7** 51 48N 0 12W
Wem, *U.K.* **10 E5** 52 52N 2 44W
Wembere →, *Tanzania* **54 C3** 4 10S 34 15 E
Wemindji, *Canada* **70 B4** 53 0N 78 49W
Wen Xian, *China* **34 G7** 34 55N 113 5 E
Wenatchee, *U.S.A.* **82 C3** 47 25N 120 19W
Wenchang, *China* **38 C8** 19 38N 110 42 E
Wenchi, *Ghana* **50 G5** 7 46N 2 8W
Wenchow = Wenzhou, *China* **33 D7** 28 0N 120 38 E
Wenden, *U.S.A.* **85 M13** 33 49N 113 33W
Wendeng, *China* **35 F12** 37 15N 122 5 E
Wendesi, *Indonesia* **37 E8** 2 30S 134 17 E
Wendover, *U.S.A.* **82 F6** 40 44N 114 2W
Wenlock →, *Australia* **62 A3** 12 2S 141 55 E
Wenshan, *China* **32 D5** 23 20N 104 18 E
Wenshang, *China* **34 G9** 35 45N 116 30 E
Wenshui, *China* **34 F7** 37 26N 112 1 E
Wensleydale, *U.K.* **10 C6** 54 17N 2 0W
Wensu, *China* **32 B3** 41 15N 80 10 E
Wensum →, *U.K.* **10 E8** 52 40N 1 15 E
Wentzel L., *Canada* **72 B6** 59 2N 114 28W
Wenut, *Indonesia* **37 E8** 3 11S 133 19 E
Wenxi, *China* **34 G6** 35 20N 111 10 E
Wenxian, *China* **34 H3** 32 43N 104 36 E
Wenzhou, *China* **33 D7** 28 0N 120 38 E
Weott, *U.S.A.* **82 F2** 40 20N 123 55W
Wepener, *S. Africa* **56 D4** 29 42S 27 3 E
Werda, *Botswana* **56 D3** 25 24S 23 15 E
Weri, *Indonesia* **37 E8** 3 10S 132 38 E
Werra →, *Germany* **16 C5** 51 24N 9 39 E
Weser →, *Germany* **16 B5** 53 36N 8 28 E
Wesiri, *Indonesia* **37 F7** 7 30S 126 30 E
Weslemkoon L., *Canada* **78 A7** 45 2N 77 25W
Wesleyville, *Canada* **71 C9** 49 8N 53 36W
Wesleyville, *U.S.A.* **78 D4** 42 9N 80 0W
Wessel, C., *Australia* **62 A2** 10 59S 136 46 E
Wessel Is., *Australia* **62 A2** 11 10S 136 45 E
Wessington Springs, *U.S.A.* **80 C5** 44 5N 98 34W
West, *U.S.A.* **81 K6** 31 48N 97 6W
West →, *U.S.A.* **79 D12** 42 52N 72 33W
West Baines →, *Australia* **60 C4** 15 38S 129 59 E
West Bank □, *Asia* **47 C4** 32 6N 35 13 E
West Bend, *U.S.A.* **76 D1** 43 25N 88 11W
West Bengal □, *India* **43 H13** 23 0N 88 0 E
West Berkshire □, *U.K.* **11 F6** 51 25N 1 17W
West Beskids = Západné Beskydy, *Europe* **17 D10** 49 30N 19 0 E

X

Y

175

Yevpatoriya

Yevpatoriya, Ukraine **25 E5** 45 15N 33 20 E
Yeysk, Russia **25 E6** 46 40N 38 12 E
Yezd = Yazd, Iran **45 D7** 31 55N 54 27 E
Yhati, Paraguay **94 B4** 25 45S 56 35W
Yhú, Paraguay **95 B4** 25 0S 56 0W
Yi →, Uruguay **94 C4** 33 7S 57 8W
Yi 'Allaq, G., Egypt **47 E2** 30 22N 33 32 E
Yi He →, China **35 G10** 34 10N 118 8 E
Yi Xian, Hebei, China **34 E8** 39 20N 115 30 E
Yi Xian, Liaoning, China **35 D11** 41 30N 121 22 E
Yialiás →, Cyprus **23 D12** 35 9N 33 44 E
Yialousa, Cyprus **23 D13** 35 32N 34 10 E
Yianisádhes, Greece **23 D8** 35 20N 26 10 E
Yiannitsa, Greece **21 D10** 40 46N 22 24 E
Yibin, China **32 D5** 28 45N 104 32 E
Yichang, China **33 C6** 30 40N 111 20 E
Yicheng, China **34 G6** 35 42N 111 40 E
Yichuan, China **34 F6** 36 2N 110 10 E
Yichun, China **33 B7** 47 44N 128 52 E
Yidu, China **35 F10** 36 43N 118 28 E
Yijun, China **34 G5** 35 28N 109 8 E
Yıldız Dağları, Turkey **21 D12** 41 48N 27 36 E
Yilehuli Shan, China **33 A7** 51 20N 124 20 E
Yimianpo, China **35 B15** 45 7N 128 2 E
Yinchuan, China **34 E4** 38 30N 106 15 E
Yindarlgooda, L., Australia **61 F3** 30 40S 121 52 E
Ying He →, China **34 H9** 32 30N 116 30 E
Ying Xian, China **34 E7** 39 32N 113 10 E
Yingkou, China **35 D12** 40 37N 122 18 E
Yining, China **26 E9** 43 58N 81 10 E
Yinmabin, Burma **41 H19** 22 10N 94 55 E
Yiofiros →, Greece **23 D7** 35 20N 25 6 E
Yirga Alem, Ethiopia **46 F2** 6 48N 38 22 E
Yirrkala, Australia **62 A2** 12 14S 136 56 E
Yishan, China **32 D5** 24 28N 108 38 E
Yishui, China **35 G10** 35 47N 118 30 E
Yíthion, Greece **21 F10** 36 46N 22 34 E
Yitong, China **35 C13** 43 13N 125 20 E
Yiyang, Henan, China **34 G7** 34 27N 112 10 E
Yiyang, Hunan, China **33 D6** 28 35N 112 18 E
Yli-Kitka, Finland **8 C23** 66 8N 28 30 E
Ylitornio, Finland **8 C20** 66 19N 23 39 E
Ylivieska, Finland **8 D21** 64 4N 24 28 E
Yoakum, U.S.A. **81 L6** 29 17N 97 9W
Yog Pt., Phil. **37 B6** 14 6N 124 12 E
Yogyakarta, Indonesia **36 F4** 7 49S 110 22 E
Yoho Nat. Park, Canada **72 C5** 51 25N 116 30W
Yojoa, L. de, Honduras **88 D2** 14 53N 88 0W
Yŏju, S. Korea **35 F14** 37 20N 127 35 E
Yokadouma, Cameroon **52 D2** 3 26N 14 55 E
Yokkaichi, Japan **31 G8** 34 55N 136 38 E
Yoko, Cameroon **52 C2** 5 32N 12 20 E
Yokohama, Japan **31 G9** 35 27N 139 28 E
Yokosuka, Japan **31 G9** 35 20N 139 40 E
Yokote, Japan **30 E10** 39 20N 140 30 E
Yola, Nigeria **51 G8** 9 10N 12 29 E
Yolaina, Cordillera de, Nic. **88 D3** 11 30N 84 0W
Yoloten, Turkmenistan **45 B9** 37 18N 62 21 E
Yom →, Thailand **36 A2** 15 35N 100 1 E
Yonago, Japan **31 G6** 35 25N 133 19 E
Yonaguni-Jima, Japan **31 M1** 24 27N 123 0 E
Yŏnan, N. Korea **35 F14** 37 55N 126 11 E
Yonezawa, Japan **30 F10** 37 57N 140 4 E
Yong Peng, Malaysia **39 L4** 2 0N 103 3 E
Yong Sata, Thailand **39 J2** 7 8N 99 41 E
Yongamp'o, N. Korea **35 E13** 39 56N 124 23 E
Yongcheng, China **34 H9** 33 55N 116 20 E
Yŏngch'ŏn, S. Korea **35 G15** 35 58N 128 56 E
Yongdeng, China **34 F2** 36 38N 103 25 E
Yŏngdŏk, S. Korea **35 F15** 36 24N 129 22 E
Yŏngdŭngpo, S. Korea **35 F14** 37 31N 126 54 E
Yonghe, China **34 F6** 36 46N 110 38 E
Yŏnghŭng, N. Korea **35 E14** 39 31N 127 18 E
Yongji, China **34 G6** 34 52N 110 28 E
Yŏngju, S. Korea **35 F15** 36 50N 128 40 E
Yongnian, China **34 F8** 36 47N 114 29 E
Yongning, China **34 E4** 38 15N 106 14 E
Yongqing, China **34 E9** 39 25N 116 28 E
Yŏngwŏl, S. Korea **35 F15** 37 11N 128 28 E
Yonibana, S. Leone **50 G3** 8 30N 12 19W
Yonkers, U.S.A. **79 F11** 40 56N 73 54W
Yonne →, France **18 B5** 48 23N 2 58 E
York, Australia **61 F2** 31 52S 116 47 E
York, U.K. **10 D6** 53 58N 1 6W
York, Ala., U.S.A. **81 J10** 32 29N 88 18W
York, Nebr., U.S.A. **80 E6** 40 52N 97 36W
York, Pa., U.S.A. **76 F7** 39 58N 76 44W
York, C., Australia **62 A3** 10 42S 142 31 E
York, City of □, U.K. **10 D6** 53 58N 1 6W
York, Kap, Greenland **4 B4** 75 55N 66 25W
York, Vale of, U.K. **10 C6** 54 15N 1 25W
York Haven, U.S.A. **78 F8** 40 7N 76 46W
York Sd., Australia **60 C4** 15 0S 125 5 E
Yorkshire Wolds, U.K. **10 C7** 54 8N 0 31W
Yorkton, Canada **73 C8** 51 11N 102 28W
Yorkville, U.S.A. **84 G3** 38 52N 123 13W
Yoro, Honduras **88 C2** 15 9N 87 7W
Yoron-Jima, Japan **31 L4** 27 2N 128 26 E
Yos Sudarso, Pulau = Dolak, Pulau, Indonesia **37 F9** 8 0S 138 30 E
Yosemite National Park, U.S.A. **84 H7** 37 45N 119 40W
Yosemite Village, U.S.A. **84 H7** 37 45N 119 35W
Yoshkar Ola, Russia **24 C8** 56 38N 47 55 E
Yŏsu, S. Korea **35 G14** 34 47N 127 45 E
Yotvata, Israel **47 F4** 29 55N 35 2 E
Youbou, Canada **84 B2** 48 53N 124 13W
Youghal, Ireland **13 E4** 51 56N 7 52W
Youghal B., Ireland **13 E4** 51 55N 7 49W
Young, Australia **63 E4** 34 19S 148 18 E
Young, Canada **73 C7** 51 47N 105 45W
Young, Uruguay **94 C4** 32 44S 57 36W
Youngstown, Canada **73 C6** 51 35N 111 10W
Youngstown, N.Y., U.S.A. **78 C5** 43 15N 79 3W
Youngstown, Ohio, U.S.A. **78 E4** 41 6N 80 39W
Youngsville, U.S.A. **78 E5** 41 51N 79 19W
Youngwood, U.S.A. **78 F5** 40 14N 79 34W
Youyu, China **34 D7** 40 10N 112 20 E
Yozgat, Turkey **25 G5** 39 51N 34 47 E
Ypané →, Paraguay **94 A4** 23 29S 57 19W
Ypres = Ieper, Belgium **15 D2** 50 51N 2 53 E
Yreka, U.S.A. **82 F2** 41 44N 122 38W
Ystad, Sweden **9 J15** 55 26N 13 50 E
Ysyk-Köl, Kyrgyzstan **26 E8** 42 25N 77 15 E
Ythan →, U.K. **12 D7** 57 19N 1 59W
Ytyk-Kyuyel, Russia **27 C14** 62 30N 133 45 E
Yu Jiang →, China **33 D6** 23 22N 110 3 E
Yu Xian = Yuzhou, China **34 G7** 34 10N 113 28 E
Yu Xian, Hebei, China **34 E8** 39 50N 114 35 E
Yu Xian, Shanxi, China **34 E7** 38 5N 113 20 E
Yuan Jiang →, China **33 D6** 28 55N 111 50 E
Yuanqu, China **34 G6** 35 18N 111 40 E
Yuanyang, China **34 G7** 35 3N 113 58 E
Yuba →, U.S.A. **84 F5** 39 8N 121 36W
Yuba City, U.S.A. **84 F5** 39 8N 121 37W
Yūbari, Japan **30 C10** 43 4N 141 59 E
Yūbetsu, Japan **30 B11** 44 13N 143 50 E
Yucatán □, Mexico **87 C7** 21 30N 86 30W
Yucatán, Canal de, Caribbean **88 B2** 22 0N 86 30W
Yucatán, Península de, Mexico **66 H11** 19 30N 89 0W
Yucatán Basin, Cent. Amer. **66 H11** 19 0N 86 0W
Yucatan Str. = Yucatán, Canal de, Caribbean **88 B2** 22 0N 86 30W
Yucca, U.S.A. **85 L12** 34 52N 114 9W
Yucca Valley, U.S.A. **85 L10** 34 8N 116 27W
Yucheng, China **34 F9** 36 55N 116 32 E
Yuci, China **34 F7** 37 42N 112 46 E
Yuendumu, Australia **60 D5** 22 16S 131 49 E
Yugoslavia ■, Europe **21 B9** 43 20N 20 0 E
Yukon →, U.S.A. **68 B3** 62 32N 163 54W
Yukon Territory □, Canada **68 B6** 63 0N 135 0W
Yukta, Russia **27 C11** 63 26N 105 42 E
Yukuhashi, Japan **31 H5** 33 44N 130 59 E
Yulara, Australia **61 E5** 25 10S 130 55 E
Yule →, Australia **60 D2** 20 41S 118 17 E
Yuleba, Australia **63 D4** 26 37S 149 24 E
Yülin, Hainan, China **39 C7** 18 10N 109 31 E
Yulin, Shaanxi, China **34 E5** 38 20N 109 30 E
Yuma, Ariz., U.S.A. **85 N12** 32 43N 114 37W
Yuma, Colo., U.S.A. **80 E3** 40 8N 102 43W
Yuma, B. de, Dom. Rep. **89 C6** 18 20N 68 35W
Yumbe, Uganda **54 B3** 3 28N 31 15 E
Yumbi, Dem. Rep. of the Congo **54 C2** 1 12S 26 15 E
Yumen, China **32 C4** 39 50N 97 30 E
Yun Ho →, China **35 E9** 39 10N 117 10 E
Yuna, Australia **61 E2** 28 20S 115 0 E
Yuncheng, Henan, China **34 G8** 35 36N 115 57 E
Yuncheng, Shanxi, China **34 G6** 35 2N 111 0 E
Yungas, Bolivia **92 G5** 17 0S 66 0W
Yungay, Chile **94 D1** 37 10S 72 5W
Yunnan □, China **32 D5** 25 0N 102 0 E
Yunxi, China **34 H6** 33 0N 110 22 E
Yupyongdong, N. Korea **35 D15** 41 49N 128 53 E
Yurga, Russia **26 D9** 55 42N 84 51 E
Yurimaguas, Peru **92 E3** 5 55S 76 7W
Yuscarán, Honduras **88 D2** 13 58N 86 45W
Yushe, China **34 F7** 37 4N 112 58 E
Yushu, Jilin, China **35 B14** 44 43N 126 38 E
Yushu, Qinghai, China **32 C4** 33 5N 96 55 E
Yutai, China **34 G9** 35 0N 116 45 E
Yutian, China **35 E9** 39 53N 117 45 E
Yuxarı Qarabağ = Nagorno-Karabakh, Azerbaijan **25 F8** 39 55N 46 45 E
Yuxi, China **32 D5** 24 30N 102 35 E
Yuzawa, Japan **30 E10** 39 10N 140 30 E
Yuzhno-Sakhalinsk, Russia **27 E15** 46 58N 142 45 E
Yuzhou, China **34 G7** 34 10N 113 28 E
Yvetot, France **18 B4** 49 37N 0 44 E

Z

Zaanstad, Neths. **15 B4** 52 27N 4 50 E
Zāb al Kabīr →, Iraq **44 C4** 36 1N 43 24 E
Zāb aş Şagīr →, Iraq **44 C4** 35 17N 43 29 E
Zabaykalsk, Russia **27 E12** 49 40N 117 25 E
Zābol, Iran **45 D9** 31 0N 61 32 E
Zābolī, Iran **45 E9** 27 10N 61 35 E
Zabrze, Poland **17 C10** 50 18N 18 50 E
Zacapa, Guatemala **88 D2** 14 59N 89 31W
Zacapu, Mexico **86 D4** 19 50N 101 43W
Zacatecas, Mexico **86 C4** 22 49N 102 34W
Zacatecas □, Mexico **86 C4** 23 30N 103 0W
Zacatecoluca, El Salv. **88 D2** 13 29N 88 51W
Zachary, U.S.A. **81 K9** 30 39N 91 9W
Zacoalco, Mexico **86 C4** 20 14N 103 33W
Zacualtipán, Mexico **87 C5** 20 39N 98 36W
Zadar, Croatia **16 F8** 44 8N 15 14 E
Zadetkyi Kyun, Burma **39 G1** 10 0N 98 25 E
Zafarqand, Iran **45 C7** 33 11N 52 29 E
Zafra, Spain **19 C2** 38 26N 6 30W
Żagań, Poland **16 C8** 51 39N 15 22 E
Zagaoua, Chad **51 E10** 15 30N 22 24 E
Zagazig, Egypt **51 B12** 30 40N 31 30 E
Zāgheh, Iran **45 C6** 33 30N 48 42 E
Zagorsk = Sergiyev Posad, Russia **24 C6** 56 20N 38 10 E
Zagreb, Croatia **16 F9** 45 50N 15 58 E
Zāgros, Kūhhā-ye, Iran **45 C6** 33 45N 48 5 E
Zagros Mts. = Zāgros, Kūhhā-ye, Iran **45 C6** 33 45N 48 5 E
Zāhedān, Fārs, Iran **45 D7** 28 46N 53 52 E
Zāhedān, Sīstān va Balūchestān, Iran **45 D9** 29 30N 60 50 E
Zahlah, Lebanon **47 B4** 33 52N 35 50 E
Zaïre = Congo →, Africa **52 F2** 6 4S 12 24 E
Zaječar, Serbia, Yug. **21 C10** 43 53N 22 18 E
Zaka, Zimbabwe **57 C5** 20 20S 31 29 E
Zakamensk, Russia **27 D11** 50 23N 103 17 E
Zakhodnaya Dzvina = Daugava →, Latvia **9 H21** 57 4N 24 3 E
Zākhū, Iraq **44 B4** 37 10N 42 50 E
Zákinthos, Greece **21 F9** 37 47N 20 57 E
Zakopane, Poland **17 D10** 49 18N 19 57 E
Zákros, Greece **23 D8** 35 6N 26 10 E
Zalaegerszeg, Hungary **17 E9** 46 53N 16 47 E
Zalău, Romania **17 E12** 47 12N 23 3 E
Zaleshchiki = Zalishchyky, Ukraine **17 D13** 48 45N 25 45 E
Zalew Wiślany, Poland **17 A10** 54 20N 19 50 E
Zalingei, Sudan **51 F10** 12 51N 23 29 E
Zalishchyky, Ukraine **17 D13** 48 45N 25 45 E
Zama L., Canada **72 B5** 58 45N 119 5W
Zambeke, Dem. Rep. of the Congo **54 B2** 2 8N 25 17 E
Zambeze →, Africa **55 F4** 18 35S 36 20 E
Zambezi = Zambeze →, Africa **55 F4** 18 35S 36 20 E
Zambezi, Zambia **53 G4** 13 30S 23 15 E
Zambezia □, Mozam. **55 F4** 16 15S 37 30 E
Zambia ■, Africa **55 F2** 15 0S 28 0 E
Zamboanga, Phil. **37 C6** 6 59N 122 3 E
Zamora, Mexico **86 D4** 20 0N 102 21W
Zamora, Spain **19 B3** 41 30N 5 45W
Zamość, Poland **17 C12** 50 43N 23 15 E
Zandvoort, Neths. **15 B4** 52 22N 4 32 E
Zanesville, U.S.A. **78 G2** 39 56N 82 1W
Zangābād, Iran **44 B5** 38 26N 46 44 E
Zangue →, Mozam. **55 F4** 17 50S 35 21 E
Zanjān, Iran **45 B6** 36 40N 48 35 E
Zanjān □, Iran **45 B6** 37 20N 49 30 E
Zanjān →, Iran **45 B6** 37 8N 47 47 E
Zante = Zákinthos, Greece **21 F9** 37 47N 20 57 E
Zanthus, Australia **61 F3** 31 2S 123 34 E
Zanzibar, Tanzania **54 D4** 6 12S 39 12 E
Zaouiet El-Kala = Bordj Omar Driss, Algeria **50 C7** 28 10N 6 40 E
Zaouiet Reggâne, Algeria **50 C6** 26 32N 0 3 E
Zaozhuang, China **35 G9** 34 50N 117 35 E
Zap Suyu = Zāb al Kabīr →, Iraq **44 C4** 36 1N 43 24 E
Zapadnaya Dvina = Daugava →, Latvia **9 H21** 57 4N 24 3 E
Západné Beskydy, Europe **17 D10** 49 30N 19 0 E
Zapala, Argentina **96 D2** 39 0S 70 5W
Zapaleri, Cerro, Bolivia **94 A2** 22 49S 67 11W
Zapata, U.S.A. **81 M5** 26 55N 99 16W
Zapolyarnyy, Russia **24 A5** 69 26N 30 51 E
Zaporizhzhya, Ukraine **25 E6** 47 50N 35 10 E
Zaporozhye = Zaporizhzhya, Ukraine **25 E6** 47 50N 35 10 E
Zara, Turkey **44 B3** 39 58N 37 43 E
Zaragoza, Coahuila, Mexico **86 B4** 28 30N 101 0W
Zaragoza, Nuevo León, Mexico **87 C5** 24 0N 99 46W
Zaragoza, Spain **19 B5** 41 39N 0 53W
Zarand, Kermān, Iran **45 D8** 30 46N 56 34 E
Zarand, Markazī, Iran **45 C6** 35 18N 50 25 E
Zaranj, Afghan. **40 D2** 30 55N 61 55 E
Zarasai, Lithuania **9 J22** 55 40N 26 20 E
Zarate, Argentina **94 C4** 34 7S 59 0W
Zard, Kūh-e, Iran **45 C6** 32 22N 50 4 E
Zāreh, Iran **45 C6** 35 7N 49 9 E
Zaria, Nigeria **50 F7** 11 0N 7 40 E
Zarneh, Iran **44 C5** 33 55N 46 10 E
Zarós, Greece **23 D6** 35 8N 24 54 E
Zarqā', Nahr az →, Jordan **47 C4** 32 10N 35 37 E
Zarrīn, Iran **45 C7** 32 46N 54 37 E
Zaruma, Ecuador **92 D3** 3 40S 79 38W
Żary, Poland **16 C8** 51 37N 15 10 E
Zarzis, Tunisia **51 B8** 33 31N 11 2 E
Zaskar →, India **43 B7** 34 13N 77 20 E
Zaskar Mts., India **43 C7** 33 15N 77 30 E
Zastron, S. Africa **56 E4** 30 18S 27 7 E
Zavāreh, Iran **45 C7** 33 29N 52 28 E
Zave, Zimbabwe **57 B5** 17 6S 30 1 E
Zavitinsk, Russia **27 D13** 50 10N 129 20 E
Zavodovski, I., Antarctica **5 B1** 56 0S 27 45W
Zawiercie, Poland **17 C10** 50 30N 19 24 E
Zāwiyat al Baydā = Al Bayḍā, Libya **51 B10** 32 50N 21 44 E
Zāyā, Iraq **44 C5** 33 33N 44 13 E
Zāyandeh →, Iran **45 C7** 32 35N 52 0 E
Zaysan, Kazakstan **26 E9** 47 28N 84 52 E
Zaysan, Oz., Kazakstan **26 E9** 48 0N 83 0 E
Zayü, China **32 D4** 28 48N 97 27 E
Zazafotsy, Madag. **57 C8** 21 11S 46 21 E
Zbarazh, Ukraine **17 D13** 49 43N 25 44 E
Zdolbuniv, Ukraine **17 C14** 50 30N 26 15 E
Zduńska Wola, Poland **17 C10** 51 37N 18 59 E
Zeballos, Canada **72 D3** 49 59N 126 50W
Zebediela, S. Africa **57 C4** 24 20S 29 17 E
Zeebrugge, Belgium **15 C3** 51 19N 3 12 E
Zeehan, Australia **62 G4** 41 52S 145 25 E
Zeeland □, Neths. **15 C3** 51 30N 3 50 E
Zeerust, S. Africa **56 D4** 25 31S 26 4 E
Zefat, Israel **47 C4** 32 58N 35 29 E
Zeil, Mt., Australia **60 D5** 23 30S 132 23 E
Zeila, Somali Rep. **46 E3** 11 21N 43 30 E
Zeist, Neths. **15 B5** 52 5N 5 15 E
Zeitz, Germany **16 C7** 51 2N 12 7 E
Zelenograd, Russia **24 C6** 56 1N 37 12 E
Zelenogradsk, Russia **9 J19** 54 53N 20 29 E
Zelienople, U.S.A. **78 F4** 40 48N 80 8W
Zémio, C.A.R. **54 A2** 5 2N 25 5 E
Zemun, Serbia, Yug. **21 B9** 44 51N 20 25 E
Zenica, Bos.-H. **21 B7** 44 10N 17 57 E
Žepče, Bos.-H. **21 B8** 44 28N 18 2 E
Zevenaar, Neths. **15 C6** 51 56N 6 5 E
Zeya, Russia **27 D13** 53 48N 127 14 E
Zeya →, Russia **27 D13** 51 42N 128 53 E
Zêzere →, Portugal **19 C1** 39 28N 8 20W
Zghartā, Lebanon **47 A4** 34 21N 35 53 E
Zgorzelec, Poland **16 C8** 51 10N 15 0 E
Zhabinka, Belarus **17 B13** 52 13N 24 2 E
Zhailma, Kazakstan **26 D7** 51 37N 61 33 E
Zhambyl = Taraz, Kazakstan **26 E8** 42 54N 71 22 E
Zhangaqazaly, Kazakstan **26 E7** 45 48N 62 6 E
Zhangbei, China **34 D8** 41 10N 114 45 E
Zhangguangcai Ling, China **35 B15** 45 0N 129 0 E
Zhangjiakou, China **34 D8** 40 48N 114 55 E
Zhangwu, China **35 C12** 42 43N 123 52 E
Zhangye, China **32 C5** 38 50N 100 23 E
Zhangzhou, China **33 D6** 24 30N 117 35 E
Zhanhua, China **35 F10** 37 40N 118 8 E
Zhanjiang, China **33 D6** 21 15N 110 20 E
Zhannetty, Ostrov, Russia **27 B16** 76 43N 158 0 E
Zhanyi, China **32 D5** 25 38N 103 48 E
Zhanyu, China **35 B12** 44 30N 122 30 E
Zhao Xian, China **34 F8** 37 43N 114 45 E
Zhaocheng, China **34 F6** 36 22N 111 38 E
Zhaotong, China **32 D5** 27 20N 103 44 E
Zhaoyuan, Heilongjiang, China **35 B13** 45 27N 125 0 E
Zhaoyuan, Shandong, China **35 F11** 37 20N 120 23 E
Zhashkiv, Ukraine **17 D16** 49 15N 30 5 E
Zhashui, China **34 H5** 33 40N 109 8 E
Zhayyq →, Kazakstan **25 E9** 47 0N 51 48 E
Zhdanov = Mariupol, Ukraine **25 E6** 47 5N 37 31 E
Zhecheng, China **34 G8** 34 7N 115 20 E
Zhejiang □, China **33 D7** 29 0N 120 0 E
Zheleznodorozhnyy, Russia **24 B9** 62 35N 50 55 E
Zheleznogorsk-Ilimskiy, Russia **27 D11** 56 34N 104 8 E
Zhen'an, China **34 H5** 33 27N 109 9 E
Zhengding, China **34 E8** 38 8N 114 32 E
Zhengzhou, China **34 G7** 34 45N 113 34 E
Zhenlai, China **35 B12** 45 50N 123 5 E
Zhenping, China **34 H7** 33 10N 112 16 E
Zhenyuan, China **34 G4** 35 35N 107 30 E
Zhetiqara, Kazakstan **26 D7** 52 11N 61 12 E
Zhezqazghan, Kazakstan **26 E7** 47 44N 67 40 E
Zhidan, China **34 F5** 36 48N 108 48 E
Zhigansk, Russia **27 C13** 66 48N 123 27 E
Zhilinda, Russia **27 C12** 70 0N 114 20 E
Zhitomir = Zhytomyr, Ukraine **17 C15** 50 20N 28 40 E
Zhlobin, Belarus **17 B16** 52 55N 30 0 E
Zhmerinka = Zhmerynka, Ukraine **17 D15** 49 2N 28 2 E
Zhmerynka, Ukraine **17 D15** 49 2N 28 2 E
Zhob, Pakistan **42 D3** 31 20N 69 31 E
Zhob →, Pakistan **42 C3** 32 4N 69 50 E
Zhodino = Zhodzina, Belarus **17 A15** 54 5N 28 17 E
Zhodzina, Belarus **17 A15** 54 5N 28 17 E
Zhokhova, Ostrov, Russia **27 B16** 76 4N 152 40 E
Zhongdian, China **32 D4** 27 48N 99 42 E
Zhongning, China **34 F3** 37 29N 105 40 E
Zhongtiao Shan, China **34 G6** 35 0N 111 10 E
Zhongwei, China **34 F3** 37 30N 105 12 E
Zhongyang, China **34 F6** 37 20N 111 11 E
Zhoucun, China **35 F9** 36 47N 117 48 E
Zhouzhi, China **34 G5** 34 10N 108 12 E
Zhuanghe, China **35 E12** 39 40N 123 0 E
Zhucheng, China **35 G10** 36 0N 119 27 E
Zhugqu, China **34 H3** 33 40N 104 30 E
Zhumadian, China **34 H8** 32 59N 114 2 E
Zhuo Xian = Zhuozhou, China **34 E8** 39 28N 115 58 E
Zhuolu, China **34 D8** 40 20N 115 12 E
Zhuozhou, China **34 E8** 39 28N 115 58 E
Zhuozi, China **34 D7** 41 0N 112 25 E
Zhytomyr, Ukraine **17 C15** 50 20N 28 40 E
Ziārān, Iran **45 B6** 36 7N 50 32 E
Ziarat, Pakistan **42 D2** 30 25N 67 49 E
Zibo, China **35 F10** 36 47N 118 3 E
Zichang, China **34 F5** 37 18N 109 40 E
Zielona Góra, Poland **16 C8** 51 57N 15 31 E
Zierikzee, Neths. **15 C3** 51 40N 3 55 E
Zigey, Chad **51 F9** 14 43N 15 50 E
Zigong, China **32 D5** 29 15N 104 48 E
Ziguinchor, Senegal **50 F2** 12 35N 16 20W
Zihuatanejo, Mexico **86 D4** 17 38N 101 33W
Žilina, Slovak Rep. **17 D10** 49 12N 18 42 E
Zillah, Libya **51 C9** 28 30N 17 33 E
Zima, Russia **27 D11** 54 0N 102 5 E
Zimapán, Mexico **87 C5** 20 54N 99 20W
Zimba, Zambia **55 F2** 17 20S 26 11 E
Zimbabwe, Zimbabwe **55 G3** 20 16S 30 54 E
Zimbabwe ■, Africa **55 F3** 19 0S 30 0 E
Zimnicea, Romania **17 G13** 43 40N 25 22 E
Zinder, Niger **50 F7** 13 48N 9 0 E
Zinga, Tanzania **55 D4** 9 16S 38 49 E
Zion National Park, U.S.A. **83 H7** 37 15N 113 5W
Ziros, Greece **23 D8** 35 5N 26 8 E
Zirreh, Gowd-e, Afghan. **40 E3** 29 45N 62 0 E
Zitácuaro, Mexico **86 D4** 19 28N 100 21W
Zitundo, Mozam. **57 D5** 26 48S 32 47 E
Ziwa Magharibi □, Tanzania **54 C3** 2 0S 31 30 E
Ziway, L., Ethiopia **46 F2** 8 0N 38 50 E
Ziyang, China **34 H5** 32 32N 108 31 E
Zlatograd, Bulgaria **21 D11** 41 22N 25 7 E
Zlatoust, Russia **24 C10** 55 10N 59 40 E
Zlín, Czech Rep. **17 D9** 49 14N 17 40 E
Zmeinogorsk, Kazakstan **26 D9** 51 10N 82 13 E
Znojmo, Czech Rep. **16 D9** 48 50N 16 2 E
Zobeyrī, Iran **44 C5** 34 10N 46 40 E
Zobia, Dem. Rep. of the Congo **54 B2** 3 0N 25 59 E
Zoetermeer, Neths. **15 B4** 52 3N 4 30 E
Zolochev = Zolochiv, Ukraine **17 D13** 49 45N 24 51 E
Zolochiv, Ukraine **17 D13** 49 45N 24 51 E
Zomba, Malawi **55 F4** 15 22S 35 19 E
Zongo, Dem. Rep. of the Congo **52 D3** 4 20N 18 35 E
Zonguldak, Turkey **25 F5** 41 28N 31 50 E
Zonqor Pt., Malta **23 D2** 35 51N 14 34 E
Zorritos, Peru **92 D2** 3 43S 80 40W
Zou Xiang, China **34 G9** 35 30N 116 58 E
Zouar, Chad **51 D9** 20 30N 16 32 E
Zouérate = Zouîrât, Mauritania **50 D3** 22 44N 12 21W
Zouîrât, Mauritania **50 D3** 22 44N 12 21W
Zoutkamp, Neths. **15 A6** 53 20N 6 18 E
Zrenjanin, Serbia, Yug. **21 B9** 45 22N 20 23 E
Zufār, Oman **46 D5** 17 40N 54 0 E
Zug, Switz. **18 C8** 47 10N 8 31 E
Zugspitze, Germany **16 E6** 47 25N 10 59 E
Zuid-Holland □, Neths. **15 C4** 52 0N 4 35 E
Zuidbeveland, Neths. **15 C3** 51 30N 3 50 E
Zuidhorn, Neths. **15 A6** 53 15N 6 23 E
Zula, Eritrea **46 D2** 15 17N 39 40 E
Zumbo, Mozam. **55 F3** 15 35S 30 26 E
Zumpango, Mexico **87 D5** 19 48N 99 6W
Zunhua, China **35 D9** 40 18N 117 58 E
Zuni, U.S.A. **83 J9** 35 4N 108 51W
Zunyi, China **32 D5** 27 42N 106 53 E
Zurbātīyah, Iraq **44 C5** 33 9N 46 3 E
Zürich, Switz. **18 C8** 47 22N 8 32 E
Zutphen, Neths. **15 B6** 52 9N 6 12 E
Zuwārah, Libya **51 B8** 32 58N 12 1 E
Zūzan, Iran **45 C8** 34 22N 59 53 E
Zverinogolovskoye, Russia **26 D7** 54 26N 64 50 E
Zvishavane, Zimbabwe **55 G3** 20 17S 30 2 E
Zvolen, Slovak Rep. **17 D10** 48 33N 19 10 E
Zwettl, Austria **16 D8** 48 35N 15 9 E
Zwickau, Germany **16 C7** 50 44N 12 30 E
Zwolle, Neths. **15 B6** 52 31N 6 6 E
Zwolle, U.S.A. **81 K8** 31 38N 93 39W
Żyrardów, Poland **17 B11** 52 3N 20 28 E
Zyryan, Kazakstan **26 E9** 49 43N 84 20 E
Zyryanka, Russia **27 C16** 65 45N 150 51 E
Zyryanovsk = Zyryan, Kazakstan **26 E9** 49 43N 84 20 E
Żywiec, Poland **17 D10** 49 42N 19 10 E
Zyyi, Cyprus **23 E12** 34 43N 33 20 E

World: Regions in the News

FORMER YUGOSLAVIA

YUGOSLAVIA
Population 10,761,000
(Serb 62.6%, Albanian 16.5%,
Montenegrin 5%, Hungarian 3.3%,
Muslim 3.2%)
 Serbia Population: 5,799,800
 (Serb 87.7%, excluding the
 provinces of Kosovo and
 Vojvodina)
 Kosovo Population: 2,084,4000
 (Albanian 81.6%, Serb 9.9%)
 Vojvodena Population: 1,980,800
 (Serb 56.8%, Hungarian 16.9%)
 Montenegro Population: 635,000
 (Montenegrin 61.9%, Muslim
 14.6%, Albanian 7%)

CROATIA
Population: 4,960,000
(Croat 78.1%, Serb 12.2%)

SLOVENIA
Population: 2,055,000
(Slovene 88%, Croat 3%, Serb 2%)

MACEDONIA (F. Y. R. O. M.)
Population: 2,157,000
(Macedonian 64%, Albanian 21.7%,
Turkish 5%, Romanian 3%,
Serb 2%)

BOSNIA-HERZEGOVINA
Population: 4,601,000
(Muslim 49%, Serb 31.2%,
Croat 17.2%)

0   100   200 km

- – · – · International boundaries
- – · · – Republic boundaries
- – – – Province boundaries
- ■ Capital cities
- Dayton Peace Agreement Boundary
- Muslim–Croat Federation
- Bosnian Serb Republic

THREE NEW STATES IN INDIA

- Chhattisgarh: Created 01/11/00
 (formerly part of Madhya Pradesh)
 Population: 17.6 million
 Capital: Raipur
- Uttaranchal: Created 09/11/00
 (formerly part of Uttar Pradesh)
 Population: 7.0 million
 Provisional capital: Dehra Dun
- Jharkhand: Created 15/11/00
 (formerly part of Bihar)
 Population: 26.9 million
 Capital: Ranchi

0   100   200 km

KASHMIR

0   100   200 km

- Aksai Chin – Administered by China, claimed by India
- Shaksam Valley – Administered by China, claimed by India
- Azad Kashmir – Administered by Pakistan, claimed by India
- Northern Areas – Administered by Pakistan, claimed by India
- Siachen Glacier – Administered by India, claimed by Pakistan
- Jammu and Kashmir – Administered by India

THE NEAR EAST

0   25   50 km

- – · – · 1949 Armistice Line
- – – – 1974 Cease–fire Line
- Palestinian control
- Joint Israeli/Palestinian control
- *Efrata* ● Main Jewish settlements in the West Bank and Gaza Strip
- *Halhul* □ Main Palestinian Arab towns in the West Bank and Gaza Strip
- Road corridor linking Gaza and West Bank

ISRAEL
Population: 5,321,000 (inc. East
Jerusalem and Jewish settlers in the
areas under Israeli administration.
Jewish 82%, Arab Muslim 13.8%,
Arab Christian 2.5%, Druze 1.7%)

West Bank
Population: 1,122,900 (Palestinian
Arabs 97% [of whom Arab Muslim
85%, Jewish 7%, Christian 8%])

Gaza Strip
Population: 748,400 (Arab 98%)

JORDAN
Population: 5,558,000 (Arab 99% [of
whom about 50% are Palestinian Arab])

LEBANON
Population: 3,327,000 (Arab 93% [of
whom 83% are Lebanese Arab and
10% Palestinian Arab])

COUNTRIES AND REPUBLICS OF THE CAUCASUS REGION

RUSSIAN REPUBLICS
 North Ossetia (Alania)
 Population: 695,000
 (Ossetian 53%, Russian 29%,
 Chechen 5.2%, Armenian 1.9%)
 Chechenia Population: 1,308,000
 (Chechen and Ingush 70.7%,
 Russian 23.1%, Armenian 1.2%)
 Ingushetia (Split from Chechenia
 in June 1993) Population: 250,000

GEORGIA
Population: 5,777,000
(Georgian 70.1%, Armenian 8.1%,
Russian 6.3%, Azerbaijani 5.7%,
Ossetian 3%, Greek 2%,
Abkhazian 2%)
 Abkhazia Population: 537,500
 (Georgian 45.7%, Abkhazian 17.8%,
 Armenian 14.6%, Russian 14.3%)
 Ajaria Population: 382,000
 (Georgian 82.8%, Russian 7.7%,
 Armenian 4%)

ARMENIA
Population: 3,968,000
(Armenian 93%, Azerbaijani 3%)
 Nagorno-Karabakh
 Population: 192,400 (Armenian
 76.9%, Azerbaijani 21.5%)

AZERBAIJAN
Population: 8,324,000
(Azerbaijani 83%, Russian 6%,
Armenian 6%, Lezgin 2%)
 Naxçivan Population: 300,400

THE CAUCASUS

0   100   200 km

- – · – · International boundaries
- – – – Republic boundaries

Georgia, Armenia and Azerbaijan
achieved independence in 1991.
Abkhazia, Ajaria and South Ossetia
seek independence from Georgia.
Chechenia has been trying to break
away from Russia since 1991, but
Russia has resisted with military force.
Hostility also continues between
Armenia and Azerbaijan over the
enclave of Nagorno-Karabakh.

FORMER YUGOSLAVIA
THE NEAR EAST
THE CAUCASUS
KASHMIR
NEW STATES IN INDIA

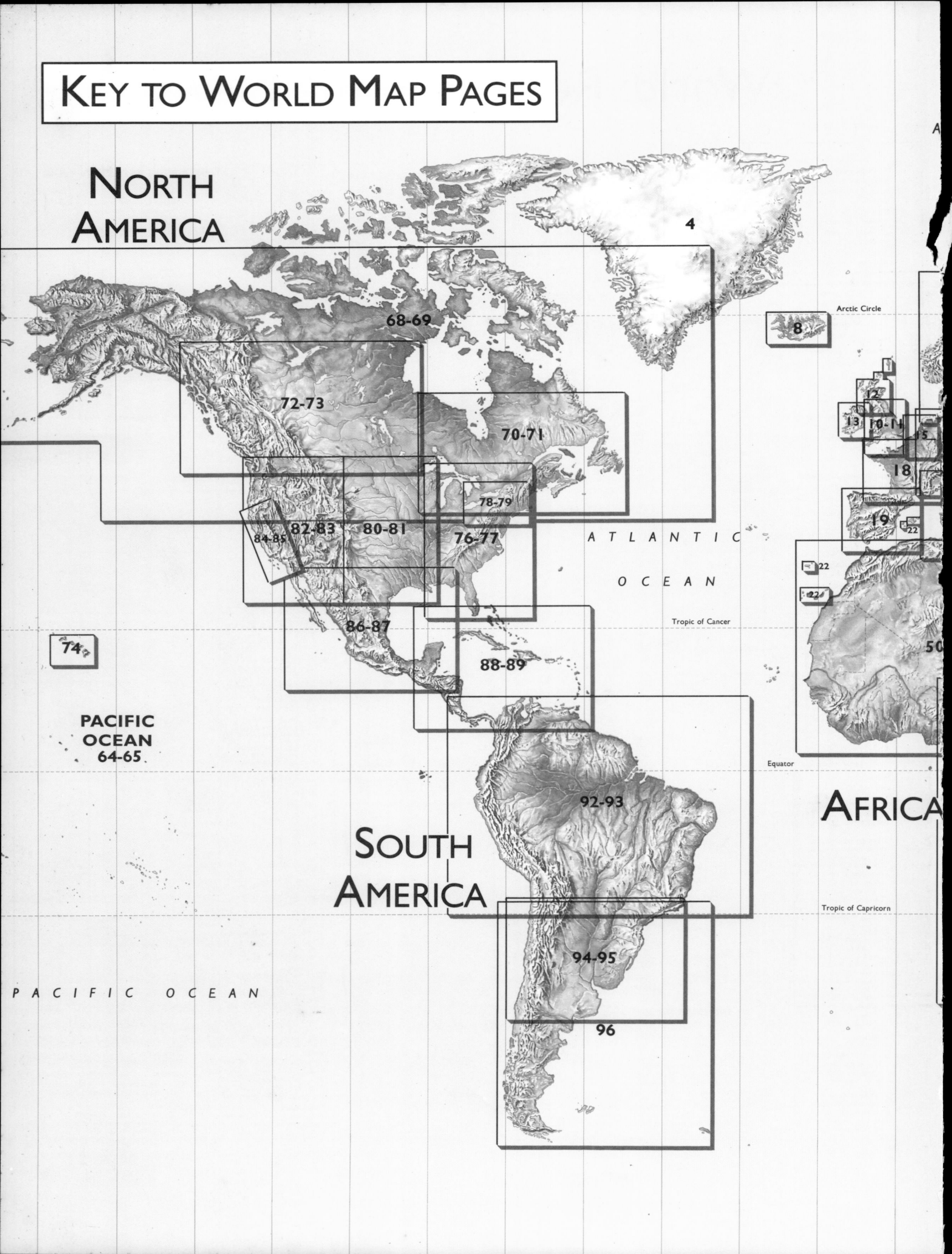

KEY TO WORLD MAP PAGES

NORTH
AMERICA

4

Arctic Circle

8

68-69

72-73

70-71

12

13 **10-11**

15

18

78-79

19

22

76-77

ATLANTIC

22

82-83 **80-81**

84-85

OCEAN

22

86-87

OCEAN

Tropic of Cancer

50

74

88-89

PACIFIC
OCEAN
64-65

Equator

92-93

AFRICA

SOUTH

AMERICA

Tropic of Capricorn

94-95

PACIFIC   OCEAN

96